THE 1966

WORLD
BOOK

REVIEWING EVENTS OF 1965

YEAR
BOOK

An Annual Supplement to
THE WORLD BOOK ENCYCLOPEDIA

FIELD ENTERPRISES EDUCATIONAL CORPORATION, PUBLISHERS

Merchandise Mart Plaza, Chicago, Illinois 60654

CHICAGO · LONDON · ROME · STOCKHOLM · SYDNEY · TORONTO

Photographs identified as *PICTURES OF THE YEAR* were entries in the national photography competition sponsored jointly by the National Press Photographers Association, the University of Missouri School of Journalism, and THE WORLD BOOK ENCYCLOPEDIA SCIENCE SERVICE.

PREFACE

"In Europe, many people think that America is a country resisting change. But this, obviously, is not so. You speak of your 'continuing revolution' in social welfare, in education, in economics. If only the rest of the world could understand the revolutionary nature of America, then the estrangement between your country and people of the developing nations would not continue."

Paul-Henri Spaak, foreign minister of Belgium, was summing up his reactions to the annual meeting of THE YEAR BOOK Board of Editors held last fall in Bermuda. James Reston, Lawrence Cremin, Sylvia Porter, and the other Board Members had just reviewed the many changes that were taking place on the American scene. They were, figuratively speaking, standing apart from current events and looking back on the year. From the perspective of 12 months, a master plan of change began to emerge from the apparent formlessness of the year's events. Only then could the true dimensions of the "continuing American revolution" be seen. And from this master plan, THE YEAR BOOK Editors could lay down the guidelines for this 1966 edition.

The ability to stand off from the events of the day and to see them with the perspective of a year is one of the special values of THE YEAR BOOK. Certainly the *Focus* articles have become valuable commentaries on current affairs because of this perspective. The *Special Reports*, which may reach back six or a dozen years—or more—to draw their conclusions, extend this matter of perspective even further. A prime example in this edition is *Paths to Dialogue* in which theologian Jaroslav Pelikan goes back to before World War I to pick up the beginning of the ecumenical movement, and traces its development through 1965's historic session of Vatican Council II. Occasionally, it may even be necessary to look into the future to get a realistic perspective on where we stand today. In *How Far Will We Go in Space*, Dr. Isaac Asimov looks beyond the heady successes of the year's Gemini flights and evaluates man's limitations—as well as his possibilities—in space.

With this edition, Dr. Asimov assumes a new role in THE YEAR BOOK. He becomes a Contributing Editor and in this capacity will write *Special Reports* on the dynamic world of science. Taking Dr. Asimov's place on the Board of Editors is Harrison S. Brown. Dr. Brown is professor of geochemistry at California Institute of Technology and foreign secretary of the National Academy of Science. As witnessed by his *Focus* article in this volume, Dr. Brown has a firm grasp on the problems—as well as the progress—of science.

The relentless pattern of change, of which Paul-Henri Spaak spoke, has not left THE YEAR BOOK untouched. In the past five years, THE YEAR BOOK has evolved into a new kind of publication; one that goes beyond the recording of facts and attempts to capture the excitement of the year's events and put them in their proper perspective in the current of time. As Executive Editor, Roy M. Fisher has been the guiding hand behind this transformation. On Jan. 1, 1966, he became the Editor of the *Chicago Daily News*, a newspaper published by our parent company, Field Enterprises, Inc. We wish him well on his new assignment, and pledge ourselves to implementing the objectives which have guided THE YEAR BOOK thus far.   A.R.H.

TABLE OF CONTENTS

A Chronology of the Most Important Events of 1965 Will Be Found on Pages 10 to 14. A Preview of 1966 Will Be Found on Pages 625 and 626.

THE YEAR IN FOCUS . . . . page 15

The members of THE YEAR BOOK Board of Editors focus their attention on significant developments of the year.

YEAR BOOK SPECIAL REPORTS . . page 63

Eight special articles and the exclusive YEAR BOOK Trans-Vision® bring special treatment to subjects chosen for their current importance and lasting interest.

EDITORIAL STAFF

THE GOLDEN ANNIVERSARY
of THE WORLD BOOK ENCYCLOPEDIA

In terms of a human life, 50 years represent a considerable span of time. This is true even in the life of a publishing company, such as ours. And yet, as we now find ourselves in our 50th year, we do not *feel* old; in fact, we feel quite young and hearty. Nonetheless, this is an appropriate time to look back on the record of the past and to assess the challenges and responsibilities of the future.

The first edition of THE WORLD BOOK ENCYCLOPEDIA was published on January 24, 1917. Countless changes have taken place in the world since that distant time, and these startling, often even fantastic changes, have been mirrored in the development of THE WORLD BOOK itself. The Encyclopedia has, for example, grown from eight volumes to 20. Now, in our 50th year, it is still undergoing constant revision, still molding its character to meet the expanding demands of the "knowledge explosion."

No one man can be given credit for conceiving the Encyclopedia or bringing it to life, but of the many who worked on the first edition, the name of Editor in Chief Michael Vincent O'Shea stands out. O'Shea dreamed of THE WORLD BOOK as a unique reference work and, until his death in 1932, directed a program of continuing revision and expansion, highlighted by a "new" edition of 13 volumes in 1929.

Four years later, in 1933, THE WORLD BOOK ENCYCLOPEDIA appeared in 19 volumes. It was arranged in the unit-letter system, one of the many ease-of-use features that firmly established the Encyclopedia as the leader in its field. The 1930s also saw the formation of an Editorial Advisory Board, composed of distinguished educators, including Dr. Hollis L. Caswell, now General Chairman of all our Editorial Advisory Boards.

In 1945, THE WORLD BOOK ENCYCLOPEDIA became the property of Field Enterprises, Inc. Two years later, a major revision of the Encyclopedia was published under the guidance of Editor in Chief J. Morris Jones. Throughout the 1940s and 1950s, Mr. Jones pushed the dynamic current revision program, culminating in the 1960 edition of 20 volumes.

Each year, at a cost of more than a million dollars, between 4,000 and 5,000 pages of the Encyclopedia undergo some type of revision to keep the set up-to-date, authoritative, and easy to use. The funds needed for these revisions have been available, not only because of the wide acceptance of our publications, but because of the deep dedication to education of our late publisher, Marshall Field. Mr. Field passed away in 1965, and our sense of personal loss can never be erased. But we pledge ourselves to continue the commitment to education which was so much a part of him.

That commitment is reflected, not only in our program of continually updating the Encyclopedia, but in the existence of our other publications: CHILDCRAFT, The *How* and *Why*® Library, THE WORLD BOOK ENCYCLOPEDIA DICTIONARY, the *Cyclo-teacher*® Learning Aid, THE WORLD BOOK ATLAS, THE WORLD BOOK YEAR BOOK, and THE CHILDCRAFT ANNUAL. It is reflected, too, in our newest publication, SCIENCE YEAR, and in the World Book Encyclopedia Science Service, Inc.

Our attitude toward all our publications is one of "eternal discontent." We constantly try to make them more useful, more vital, more interesting, and more colorful. The challenge we face is clear: as people engaged in the great adventure of education, we must keep abreast of mankind's ever-increasing search for knowledge, and we must present that knowledge to you in a manner that is meaningful and easy to grasp. We assure you that we will always continue this quest.

Bailey K. Howard

OUR 50TH YEAR

CHAIRMAN OF THE BOARD
AND CHIEF EXECUTIVE OFFICER
FIELD ENTERPRISES EDUCATIONAL CORP.

CONTRIBUTORS

Anderson, Joseph P., M.S.S.A., Ph.B.; Exec. Director, National Association of Social Workers.
Social Organizations

Asimov, Isaac, Ph.D.; Associate. Professor of Biochemistry, Boston University School of Medicine.
Special Report

Atkinson, Brooks, A.B.; Journalist; Drama Critic; Pulitzer Prize for Journalism, 1947.
Special Report

Bedingfield, Robert E.; Assistant to the Financial-Business Editor, *The New York Times.*
Industry Articles

Bhote, Keki R., B.E., M.Sc.; Author; Lecturer.
INDIA; PAKISTAN Special Report

Bradley, Van Allen, B.J.; Literary Editor, *Chicago Daily News.*
LITERATURE

Bregman, Jacob I., B.S., M.S., Ph.D.; Director, Chemical Sciences, Illinois Institute of Technology Research Institute.
Special Report

Brown, Kenneth; Journalist.
Europe Articles

Bryan, Leslie A., Ph.D., LL.B.; Dir., Institute of Aviation, University of Illinois.
AVIATION

Burnet, Alastair, B.A.; Editor, *The Economist.*
British Commonwealth Articles

Cain, Charles C., III, A.B.; Automotive Editor, Associated Press.
AUTOMOBILE; RUBBER

Carner, Charles; Public Relations Officer, American Library Association.
AMERICAN LIBRARY ASSOCIATION

Carruth, Hayden, A.B., M.A.; Poet.
LITERATURE (Poetry)

Churchill, Rhona; Feature Writer, *Daily Mail,* London.
GREAT BRITAIN (Close-Up)

Colegrove, Kenneth, Ph.D., Litt. D.; Professor Emeritus, Northwestern University.
CIVIL RIGHTS

Commager, Henry Steele, Ph.B., A.M., Ph.D.; Speranza Lecturer, Columbia University; Author, *The Blue and the Gray.*
DEATHS (Close-Up)

Conley, Clare, B.A.; Managing Editor, *Field & Stream.*
HUNTING AND FISHING

Cook, Robert C.; President, Population Reference Bureau.
POPULATION

Covell, Florence Byerly, B.S.; Home Fashion Coordinator, Famous-Barr Co.
INTERIOR DECORATION

Csida, June Bundy; Former Radio-TV Editor, *Music Business Magazine.*
RADIO; TELEVISION

Dammann, Harle; Foreign Correspondent.
Eastern Europe Articles

Dammann, Tom, B.A.; Foreign Correspondent.
Eastern Europe Articles

Darby, Edwin W., B.S.J.; Financial Editor, *Chicago Sun-Times.*
Business Articles

Dewald, William G., Ph.D.; Associate Professor of Economics, Ohio State University.
Finance Articles

Dumouchel, J. Robert; Director of Community Relations, Land Clearance for Redevelopment Authority of Kansas City, Mo.
CITY PLANNING; HOUSING

Dunaway, James O., B.S.; Eastern Editor, *Track and Field News.*
Sports Articles

Eckler, A. Ross, A.B., A.M., Ph.D.; Director, U.S. Bureau of the Census.
CENSUS

Farr, David M. L., M.A., D.Phil.; Dean of Arts, Carleton University, Ottawa.
CANADA

Feather, Leonard G.; Author, *Encyclopedia of Jazz.*
Music Articles

Feinberg, Harold, B.A., M.A., Ph.D.; Assoc. Prof., University of Ill. School of Medicine. BIOCHEMISTRY; BIOLOGY

Fenner, Frank E., B.S., FPSA, ARPS; WORLD BOOK ENCYCLOPEDIA Photographs Editor.
PHOTOGRAPHY

Freeman, Leslie G., Jr., Ph.D.; Assistant Professor, Department of Anthropology, University of Chicago.
ANTHROPOLOGY; ARCHAEOLOGY

French, Charles E., B.S., A.M., Ph.D.; Professor, Department of Agricultural Economics, Purdue University.
AGRICULTURE

Freudenheim, Milt, A.B.; United Nations Correspondent, *Chicago Daily News.*
UNITED NATIONS

Friesen, Ernest C., A.B., LL.B.; Assistant Deputy Attorney General, Department of Justice. Law Articles

Gassner, John, M.A.; Sterling Professor of Playwriting and Dramatic Literature, Yale University. THEATER

Gayn, Mark, B.A.; Communist Affairs Analyst, *Toronto Star.*
Special Report

Goy, Robert W., B.S., Ph.D.; Senior Scientist, Oregon Regional Primate Research Center.
PSYCHOLOGY

Grevatt, Ren, B.A., M.B.A.; Public Relations Specialist.
RECORDINGS FOR CHILDREN

Griffin, Alice, M.A., Ph.D.; Associate Professor of English, Hunter College.
THEATER, AMATEUR

Haefele, Edwin T.; Senior Staff, Economics Division, The Brookings Institution. Transportation Articles

Harper, Frank B., A.B., B.J.; Agricultural writer.
Agricultural Articles

Havighurst, Robert J., Ph.D.; Prof. of Education, University of Chicago; Author, *Older People.*
OLD AGE

Hechinger, Fred M., B.A., LL.D.; Education Editor, *The New York Times.*
EDUCATION

Holmes, Jay E., B.A.; Deputy Director, Special Operations, Manned Space Flight Center, NASA.
SPACE TRAVEL

Husén, Torsten, M.A., Ph.D.; Prof. of Education, University of Stockholm.
EDUCATION (Close-Up)

Hussey, Hugh H., M.D.; Director of Scientific Activities, American Medical Association.
Medical Articles

Isaacs, Stanley, B.A.; Sports Columnist, *Newsday.*
Sports Articles

Jessup, M.E., A.B.; News Editor, *Civil Engineering.* Engineering Articles

Johnson, Robert I., A.B.; Director, Adler Planetarium.
ASTRONOMY

Jones, Virgil Carrington, B.A.(J); Author.
CIVIL WAR CENTENNIAL

Joseph, Lou, B.A.; Asst. Director, Bureau of Public Information, American Dental Association. DENTISTRY

Kennedy, Rose F. (Mrs. Joseph P.), Hyannis Port, Mass. Special Report

Kertzer, Morris N., M.A., D.H.L.; Rabbi, Larchmont Temple, New York.
JEWS AND JUDAISM

Knight, Arthur, B.A.; Professor, University of So. California Department of Cinema. MOTION PICTURES

Knight, George A. F., M.A., D.B.; Professor of Old Testament, McCormick Theological Seminary.
TRANS-VISION®

Koczy, F. F., Ph.D.; Chairman, Division of Physical Sciences, University of Miami. OCEAN

Koenig, Louis W., M.A., Ph.D.; Professor of Government, New York University. PRESIDENT (Close-Up)

Lach, Alma, Diplome de Cordon Bleu. FOOD

Lenormand, Sergei; Manager, Public Information, Illinois Institute of Technology Research Institute. Science Articles; Special Report

Lewis, Ralph H., A.B., M.A.; Chief, Museum Branch, National Park Service. MUSEUMS

Lief, Donald W., A.B.; Managing Editor, *Nation's Cities*. City Articles

Lisagor, Peter, A.B.; Chief, Washington Bureau, *Chicago Daily News*. Political Party Articles

Logan, Rayford W., A.B., A.M., Ph.D.; Professor of History, Howard University. NEGRO

Lohman, Joseph D., B.A., M.A.; Dean, School of Criminology, University of California. CRIME; PRISON

MacFarland, Douglas C., Ph.D.; Chief, Division of Services to the Blind, Dept. of Health, Education, and Welfare. BLINDNESS

Maki, John M., B.A., M.A., Ph.D.; Professor of Japanese Politics, University of Washington. JAPAN; KOREA

Malia, Thomas M., Ph.B.; Executive Editor, *Telecommunications Reports*. COMMUNICATIONS

Manchester, P. W.; Managing Editor, *Dance News;* New York Dance Critic, *Christian Science Monitor*. DANCING

Marsh, Robert C., A.M., Ed.D.; Music Critic, *Chicago Sun-Times*. MUSIC

Marty, Martin E., B.D., S.T.M., Ph.D.; Associate Editor, *The Christian Century*. PROTESTANT

Mattick, Hans W., B.A., M.A.; Director, Chicago Youth Development Project. JUVENILE DELINQUENCY

Mauldin, William H.; Editorial Cartoonist, *Chicago Sun-Times*; Pulitzer Prize, 1944 and 1958. Cartoons

Maxon, John, M.A., Ph.D.; Director of Fine Arts, The Art Institute of Chicago. PAINTING AND SCULPTURE

McCaul, Eugene B.; Director, Statistical Department, American Transit Association. TRANSIT

McGaffin, William, A.B., B.Sc.; Washington Correspondent, *Chicago Daily News*. U.S. Government Articles

Mencher, Melvin, B.A.; Assoc. Professor, Graduate School of Journalism, Columbia University. PUBLISHING

Miller, Richard, A.B., B.Arch.; Partner, Helge Westermann, Richard Miller, Associates. ARCHITECTURE

Milne, Lorus J., Ph.D.; Professor of Zoology, University of New Hampshire. Special Report

Milne, Margery, Ph.D.; Honorary Fellow in Zoology, University of New Hampshire. Special Report

Morse, Walter F., B.A.; Assistant City Editor, *Chicago Sun-Times*. Biographies

Morton, Elizabeth H., B.A.; Executive Director, Canadian Library Association. CANADIAN LITERATURE

Mullen, Frances A., Ph.D.; Assistant Superintendent, Chicago Public Schools. CHILD WELFARE

Muller, Herbert J., A.B., A.M., Ph.D.; Distinguished Service Professor, University of Indiana. DEMOCRACY

Newman, Andrew L., A.B., M.A.; Deputy Director of Information, U.S. Department of the Interior. Conservation Articles

O'Brien, Lawrence Francis, LL.B.; Postmaster General. POST OFFICE

O'Leary, Theodore M., A.B.; Special Correspondent, *Sports Illustrated* Magazine. PET; Hobby Articles

Patterson, William D., A.B.; Vice President and Associate Publisher, *The Saturday Review*. HOTEL; TRAVEL

Pelikan, Jaroslav, B.D., Ph.D.; Titus Street Professor of Ecclesiastical History, Yale University. Special Report

Perkins, R. Marlin; Director, St. Louis Zoo. ZOOS AND AQUARIUMS

Prastein, S. Matthew, A.B., M.S., Ph.D.; Assistant Professor of Physics, Illinois Institute of Technology. PHYSICS

Pyle, Howard; President, National Safety Council. SAFETY

Ravenholt, Albert; Special Foreign Correspondent, *Chicago Daily News*. Asia Articles

Rogers, Warren; Chief Washington Correspondent, Hearst Newspapers. Military Articles

Rue, Eloise, M.A., B.A. in L.S.; Associate Professor of Library Science, University of Wisconsin, Milwaukee. LITERATURE FOR CHILDREN

Russell, I. Willis, A.B., M.A., Ph.D.; Professor of English, University of Alabama. WORDS AND PHRASES

Schmemann, The Rev. Alexander, S.T.D.; Dean, St. Vladimir's Seminary. EASTERN ORTHODOX

Shearer, Warren W., Ph.D.; Chairman, Department of Economics, Wabash College. Business Articles

Sheen, Fulton J., Ph.D., D.D., LL.D.; National Director, Society for the Propagation of the Faith, New York City. ROMAN CATHOLIC

Skilling, H. Gordon, B.A., M.A., Ph.D.; Professor of Political Science, Univ. of Toronto. COMMUNISM; RUSSIA

Smothers, Frank; Director of Publications, The Council of State Governments. STATE GOVERNMENT

Spencer, William, A.B., A.M., Ph.D.; Director, Institute of Non-Western Studies, The American University. Africa and Middle East Articles

Stalker, John N., B.A., M.A., Ph.D.; Professor of History, University of Hawaii. Asia Articles

Stern, James L., B.S., Ph.D.; Professor of Economics, University of Wisconsin. AUTOMATION; LABOR

Thomas, Benjamin E., M.A., Ph.D.; Professor of Geography, University of California. Africa Articles

Thompson, Carol L., A.B., M.A.; Editor, *Current History* Magazine. U.S. Government Articles

Uphaus, Robert A., B.S., M.S., Ph.D.; Chemist, Argonne National Laboratory. CHEMISTRY

Wallbank, T. Walter, A.B., A.M., Ph.D.; Professor of History, Univ. of So. California. WORLD, HISTORY OF

Webster, Mary C., B.A.; Editor, *Noticias* Magazine. Latin America Articles

White, Ruth M., B.S. in Ed., B.S. in L.S., A.M.; Headquarters Librarian, American Library Assoc. LIBRARY

Zwecker, Peg, B.S.; Fashion and Beauty Editor, *Chicago Daily News*. FASHION

1965 · CHRONOLOGY · 1965

JANUARY

1—**First World Weather Center Opens** at Suitland, Md., World Meteorological Organization unit.

4—**89th Congress of U.S. Opens** its first session in Washington, D.C. President Johnson delivers State of Union Message, outlining his "Great Society" program for nation.

7—**Indonesia Quits United Nations,** President Sukarno declares, ". . . . since Malaysia has become a Security Council member."

12-13—**Japanese Prime Minister in Washington, D.C.** Eisaku Sato is President Johnson's first foreign visitor of 1965.

15—**Burundi Premier Assassinated** in Bujumbura. Pierre Ngendandumwe in office since Jan. 11.

16—**United States and Canada Sign Automobile Pact.** Lifts tariffs on motor vehicle imports.

18—**New U.S. Secretary of Commerce.** John T. Connor succeeds Luther H. Hodges.

20—**United States Inaugurates President.** Lyndon B. Johnson begins his first elected term. Vice-President Hubert H. Humphrey also takes oath of office.

21—**Indonesia Formally Leaves United Nations.** Submits letter of withdrawal, reducing world organization to 114 member nations.

22—**New British Foreign Minister.** Michael Stewart succeeds Patrick Gordon Walker.
Tiros IX Launched into Orbit at Cape Kennedy. Weather satellite to photograph entire earth once every 24 hours.

23-27—**Buddhists Demonstrations in South Vietnam** force out Premier Tran Van Huong.

24—**Sir Winston Churchill Dies** at 90 in London, great British and world statesman.
India Dedicates Sharavati Hydroelectric Project at Jog. Linganamakki and Talakalale dams and Sharavati power station completed.

26-27—**Premier of Iran Dies of Assassin Bullets.** Hassan Ali Mansur is succeeded by Amir Abbas Hoveida.

29-30—**Burundi Cuts Diplomatic Ties** with Communist China. Orders ambassador to leave Bujumbura.

FEBRUARY

1—**U.S. Air Force Chief of Staff Retires.** Gen. Curtis E. LeMay is succeeded by Gen. John P. McConnell, formerly vice-chief of staff.

1-12—**Queen Elizabeth II in Africa.** First reigning British sovereign to visit Ethiopia, spends last 4 days of visit in Sudan.

3—**OSO II Launched** at Cape Kennedy. Orbiting Solar Observatory designed to create artificial eclipses of sun.
105 Cadets Resign, U.S. Air Force Academy reports during investigation of cheating and theft and sale of examination papers there.

7—**United States Bombs North Vietnam** in Dong Hoi area after Viet Cong attacks in South Vietnam.

9—**U.S. Embassy Attacked in Moscow** by Vietnamese, Chinese, and other demonstrators.

13—**New U.S. Attorney General.** Nicholas deB. Katzenbach, formerly acting head of Department of Justice.

13-17—**Violent Anti-U.S. Demonstrations Follow North Vietnam Air Attacks** in capitals of Hungary, Bulgaria, Uganda, Venezuela, Malaysia, and in Medan, Indonesia.

15—**Canada Unfurls Its New Flag.** Red Maple Leaf replaces Red Ensign (with British Union Jack), semiofficial emblem for some 20 years.
Indonesia Seizes U.S. Information Service Library in Djakarta, third since August, 1964.

16—**Pegasus I Launched** at Cape Kennedy. Winged satellite to check meteoroid hazards.
New South Vietnam Regime. Phanh Khac Suu is Chief of State, and Phan Huy Quat is Premier.

17—**Ranger VIII Launched on Way to Moon** at Cape Kennedy.

17-18—**Gambia Proclaims Independence.** African country joins British Commonwealth.

20—**Ranger VIII Hits Moon** in Sea of Tranquillity area after sending back 7,000 photographs.

21—**Negro Nationalist Malcolm X Shot to Death** in New York City as he addresses his Afro-American Unity organization.
New Premier in Turkey. Suat Hayri Ürgüplü succeeds Ismet Inönü.

22—**Pope Paul VI Creates 27 New Cardinals** at first private consistory of his reign.

24—**East German President in Cairo.** Walter Ulbricht's arrival in United Arab Republic cause of breach with West Germany.

25—**Chile Establishes Diplomatic Relations with Bulgaria** after 17-year break.

MARCH

1—**Bechuanaland Holds First Elections.** Seretse Khama appointed Prime Minister.

3—**British Honduras Inaugurates First Prime Minister,** George C. Price, under new internal self-government constitution.

4—**U.S. Information Agency to Close Libraries in Indonesia,** under attack since 1958.

9—**First "Great Society" Bill Signed** by President Johnson, billion dollar aid program for 11-state Appalachia area.

11—**Tunisia Opposes United Arab Republic on German-Israel Issues.** Refuses to join Arab boycott of West Germany.

17—**America's Grand Old Man of Football Dies** at 102. Amos Alonzo Stagg was college coach for 70 years.

18—**French Gold Purchase of $231,500,000 Reduces U.S. Stock** to $14,563,000,000, lowest since Dec. 28, 1935 ($14,508,000,000).

18-19—**Voskhod II Orbits Earth** for 26 hours with Col. Pavel I. Belyayev and Lieut.-Col. Aleksei A. Leonov aboard. Leonov first man to float in space outside spacecraft.

1965 JANUARY 1965

SUN.	MON.	TUE.	WED.	THU.	FRI.	SAT.
					1	2
3	4	5	6	7	8	9
10	11	12	13	14	15	16
17	18	19	20	21	22	23
24 31	25	26	27	28	29	30

1965 FEBRUARY 1965

SUN.	MON.	TUE.	WED.	THU.	FRI.	SAT.
	1	2	3	4	5	6
7	8	9	10	11	12	13
14	15	16	17	18	19	20
21	22	23	24	25	26	27
28						

1965 MARCH 1965

SUN.	MON.	TUE.	WED.	THU.	FRI.	SAT.
	1	2	3	4	5	6
7	8	9	10	11	12	13
14	15	16	17	18	19	20
21	22	23	24	25	26	27
28	29	30	31			

21—Ranger IX Launched to Moon, last in Ranger luna photographing program.

22—Romania Elects New Head, Nicolae Ceausescu, as First Secretary of Workers' (Communist) party.

23—Gemini III Flight. Maj. Virgil I. Grissom and Lieut.-Col. John W. Young circle earth 3 times in 4 hrs. 54 min.
Honduras National Assembly Elects President. Col. Osvaldo Lopez Arellano was junta head.

24—Ranger IX Hits Alphonsus Crater on Moon. Takes pictures in last minutes of flight.

25—Alabama Freedom Marchers in Montgomery. Trekked 54 miles from Selma. White civil rightist Viola Gregg Liuzzo later shot to death on highway near Lowndesboro, Ala.
New Prime Minister in Ceylon. Dudley Senanayake succeeds Sirimavo Bandaranaike, world's first woman prime minister.

31—Canada Adopts Pension Plan. House of Commons approves federal program.

APRIL

1—New U.S. Secretary of the Treasury. Henry H. Fowler succeeds C. Douglas Dillon.

3—First Commercial Atomic Power Reactor Launched at Vandenberg Air Force Base, California. SNAP (Systems for Nuclear Auxiliary Power) 10A reactor put in orbit for year-long test.

4—Coronation in Sikkim. Maharajah Palden Thondup Namgyal and his American-born Maharani, the former Hope Cooke of New York, are crowned Chogyal (King) and Gyalmo (Queen).

6—World's First Commercial Communications Satellite Launched at Cape Kennedy. Early Bird is first link in global commercial communications space network.
British Budget Submitted to House of Commons. Tax levies to reduce home consumption, increase revenue, and curb capital outflow.

7—Unconditional Talks on Vietnam Proposed by President Johnson in Johns Hopkins University speech. Offers billion-dollar Southeast Asia (also North Vietnam) aid program, and asks Russia, other countries, and United Nations to assist.

8—European Economic Community Agrees to Integrate Agencies: executive bodies and ministerial councils of Coal and Steel, Economic, and Atomic Energy communities, Jan. 1, 1966.

9—U.S. National Council on the Arts Inaugurated by President Johnson.
Astrodome Opens in Houston. New Texas stadium world's largest air-conditioned room.

11—$1,307,582,973 Elementary and Secondary Education Act of 1965 Signed by President Johnson, first of such importance in 20 years.

12—New Prime Minister in The Netherlands. Joseph M. L. T. Cals presents new program, ending government crisis begun in February.

14-15—British Prime Minister in United States. Harold Wilson confers with Washington officials. Supports U.S. Vietnam policy.

15—West Germany Completes Israeli Reparations with final payment on $860,000,000 for millions of Jews killed by the Nazis.

19-22—Italian Premier in United States for First Time. Aldo Moro attends Cabinet meeting with President Johnson.

21—United Nations Disarmament Commission Convenes for first time since August, 1960.

23—Russia Launches Communications Satellite. Molniya I transmits television broadcast from Pacific port of Vladivostok to Moscow.

24—Civil War in Dominican Republic. Ruling junta overthrown by rebels demanding return of deposed President Juan D. Bosch.
Indonesia Seizes Remaining Foreign-Owned Enterprises. Decree signed by Sukarno.
Nepal and India Inaugurate Kosi Barrage, part of project to irrigate 2,600,000 acres in Nepal and Bihar, India.

28—U.S. Marines Land in Dominican Republic to protect and evacuate Americans and citizens of some 30 other countries.

29—Council of Europe Admits Malta, its 18th full member nation.
Explorer XXVII Launched at Wallops Island.

30—Basutoland Begins Internal Self-Government after 97 years of British rule.

MAY

1—Life Peerage for Lady Churchill. Baroness Spencer-Churchill of Chartwell will sit in House of Lords as a crossbencher.

2—14,000 U.S. Troops Committed to Dominican Republic, President Johnson says, "to prevent another Communist state in this hemisphere."
Early Bird Relay Links Europe and North America. European Broadcasting Union and U.S., Canadian, and Mexican networks begin regular use of initial commercial satellite.

3—Cambodia Ends Diplomatic Relations with United States, says Chief of State Prince Norodom Sihanouk.

5—Formal Cease-Fire Signed in Dominican Republic, but fighting continues.

9—Lunik V Launched to Moon by Russia.

11—Israel Museum Opens in Jerusalem, includes four separate museums.

12—Lunik V Hits Sea of Clouds Area on Moon, but fails to make "soft landing."
West Germany and Israel Establish Diplomatic Relations. Governments exchange letters.

12-16—Arab States Cut Diplomatic Ties with West Germany, except Libya, Morocco, and Tunisia.

14—John F. Kennedy Shrine at Runnymede Dedicated by Queen Elizabeth II, where historic Magna Carta was signed 750 years ago.
Communist China Explodes Its Second Atomic Bomb, over its western areas.

11

1965		APRIL		1965			1965		MAY		1965			1965		JUNE		1965		
SUN.	MON.	TUE.	WED.	THU.	FRI.	SAT.	SUN.	MON.	TUE.	WED.	THU.	FRI.	SAT.	SUN.	MON.	TUE.	WED.	THU.	FRI.	SAT.
				1	2	3							1			1	2	3	4	5
4	5	6	7	8	9	10	2	3	4	5	6	7	8	6	7	8	9	10	11	12
11	12	13	14	15	16	17	9	10	11	12	13	14	15	13	14	15	16	17	18	19
18	19	20	21	22	23	24	16	17	18	19	20	21	22	20	21	22	23	24	25	26
25	26	27	28	29	30		23 30	24 31	25	26	27	28	29	27	28	29	30			

15—**New Zealand Inaugurates North-South Islands Undersea Cable,** 354 miles across Cook Strait.

18—**U.S. Confirms 8-Satellite Launching** on March 9 by single rocket at Vandenberg Air Force Base, California.

18-28—**Queen Elizabeth II in West Germany.** First reigning British sovereign to visit there since George V visited Wilhelm II in 1913.

23—**Austria Elects President.** Franz Jonas to begin 6-year term in June.

24—**Inter-American Force in Dominican Republic,** an Organization of American States group.

25—**Pegasus II Launched** at Cape Kennedy. Begins measuring meteoroid density.

29—**IMP Launched at Cape Kennedy.** Interplanetary Monitoring Platform third of 7 designed to look for radiation storms in space.

JUNE

3-7—**Gemini IV Orbits Earth 62 Times** during flight of 97 hrs. 58 min. Maj. Edward H. White II maneuvers outside craft on 3d orbit. Maj. James A. McDivitt worked on other projects.

8—**Lunik VI Launched on Moon Flight** by Russia.

11—**Lunik VI Misses Moon** by 100,000 miles.

14—**Military Takes Control in South Vietnam,** led by Maj. Gen. Nguyen Van Thieu.

17-25—**British Commonwealth Prime Ministers Conference** in London establishes Vietnam Peace Mission headed by Prime Minister Harold Wilson.

19—**Ben Bella Deposed in Algeria** by Defense Minister Col. Houari Boumedienne.

South Vietnam Air Vice-Marshal New Premier. Nguyen Cao Ky replaces Phan Huy Quat.

21—**Excise Tax Reduction Bill Signed** by President Johnson. Urges manufacturers and retailers to lower prices.

22—**Japan and South Korea Sign Amity Treaty,** result of 14 years of intermittent negotiations.

English Parliament Septcentenary Ceremony commemorates conference called in 1265.

24—**South Vietnam Ends Diplomatic Relations with France,** charges it aids Vietnam enemies.

25-26—**United Nations Commemorative Session in San Francisco** marks signing of charter in 1945.

28—**Intercontinental Telephone Via Early Bird Satellite.** President Johnson inaugurates commercial service, calls European capitals.

Gyula Kallai New Premier in Hungary, but János Kádár still heads Communist party.

JULY

1—**Rann of Kutch Cease-Fire in Force.** India and Pakistan to withdraw troops immediately.

2—**Tiros X Launched** at Cape Kennedy.

6—**U.S. Presidential Disability and Vice-President Vacancy Resolution Passed** in Senate. Ratification by 38 of 50 states within 7 years to make proposed amendment part of U.S. Constitution.

France Recalls Permanent Representative from EEC. Boycotts European Economic Community Council meetings "for the moment."

10—**Greek Crown Princess Born in Athens** to King Constantine XIII and Queen Anne-Marie.

14—**Adlai E. Stevenson Collapses on London Street and Dies.** U.S. permanent representative to United Nations since 1960.

14-15—**Mariner IV Completes 228-Day Mars Flight.** Returns first of 22 close-up photographs.

15—**King Constantine XIII Dismisses Greek Premier** George Papandreou.

16—**World's Longest Motor Tunnel Opens in Alps.** Two-lane, $7\frac{1}{4}$-mile Mont Blanc passage links Pèlerins (near Chamonix, France) and Entrèves (near Courmayeur, Italy).

Proton I Launched by Russia. Heaviest payload (26,900 pounds) yet, put into orbit by new booster rocket. Also launches 5 Cosmos satellites with one rocket.

18—**Zond III Put into Orbit** by Russia.

20—**Zond III Photographs Hidden Side of Moon.**

23—**Coinage Bill Signed** by President Johnson. Eliminates silver from quarters and dimes. Reduces half dollar silver content from 90 to 40 per cent.

26—**Maldive Islands Proclaim Independence.** Permits Britain to retain Gan Island air base.

27—**Belgium Government Crisis Ends.** Pierre Harmel succeeds Prime Minister Théodore Lefèvre.

17-Nation Disarmament Committee Reconvenes in Geneva, first time since September, 1964.

28—**Arthur J. Goldberg at United Nations.** Succeeds the late Adlai E. Stevenson as U.S. permanent representative there.

British Conservative Party Elects New Leader. Edward Heath succeeds Sir Alec Douglas-Home.

30—**Medicare-Social Security Bill Signed** by President Johnson at Independence, Mo.

Pegasus III Launched to check on meteoroids.

AUGUST

5—**Fighting in Kashmir.** Pakistanis infiltrate India area disguised as civilians.

6—**U.S. Voting Rights Act of 1965 Signed** by President Johnson.

9—**Singapore Secedes from Malaysia Federation.** Prime Minister Lee Kuan Yew says he was forced to sign accord (August 7) by Malaysia.

11-16—**Los Angeles Riot in Negro Watts Area** set off by traffic arrest. Shops burned and looted, whites attacked, and some 30 persons killed.

12—**New U.S. Ambassador to South Vietnam.** Henry Cabot Lodge replaces Gen. Maxwell D. Taylor.

12-14—**Chicago Negroes Riot on West Side.** Accidental killing of Negro pedestrian sparks fights.

14—**South Korea Ratifies Amity Pact with Japan.** Japan to give its former colony (1910-1945) $800,000,000 in grants and loans.

12

1965   JULY   1965

SUN.	MON.	TUE.	WED.	THU.	FRI.	SAT.
					1	2	3
4	5	6	7	8	9	10
11	12	13	14	15	16	17
18	19	20	21	22	23	24
25	26	27	28	29	30	31

1965   AUGUST   1965

SUN.	MON.	TUE.	WED.	THU.	FRI.	SAT.
1	2	3	4	5	6	7
8	9	10	11	12	13	14
15	16	17	18	19	20	21
22	23	24	25	26	27	28
29	30	31				

1965 SEPTEMBER 1965

SUN.	MON.	TUE.	WED.	THU.	FRI.	SAT.
			1	2	3	4
5	6	7	8	9	10	11
12	13	14	15	16	17	18
19	20	21	22	23	24	25
26	27	28	29	30		

16—**Arthur J. Goldberg's First Formal Speech at United Nations.** New U.S. permanent representative says United States accepts fact that majority of UN members not ready to invoke penalties against Russia, France, and 11 other countries who refuse to pay for UN peacekeeping operations.
Zond III Far-Side-of-Moon Photographs Published by Russia, taken July 20.
Congo Republic Ends Diplomatic Ties with Portugal. Brazzaville also ends air and port rights, and bans Portuguese imports.

19—**Malaysia Elects New Head of State.** Sultan Ismail Nasiruddin Shah, Ruler of Trengganu, succeeds Raja of Perlis Sir Putra Ibin Al-Marhum Syed Hassan Jamalullail.
17 Germans Found Guilty of Auschwitz Murders at end of 20-month trial. Former Nazi camp staff members had part in torture and murder of nearly 4,000,000 persons, mostly Jews.

20—**White Seminarian Killed at Hayneville, Ala.** Civil rightists Jonathan M. Daniels and Roman Catholic priest Richard F. Morrisroe (critically wounded) just freed from jail.

21-29—**Gemini V 8-Day Manned Space Flight.** Lieut.-Col. Leroy G. Cooper, Jr., first to make second such flight (May 15-16, 1963), and Lieut.-Comdr. Charles Conrad, Jr., set duration (190 hrs. 56 min.) and distance (3,000,000 ground miles) records.

24—**Pact to End Yemeni Civil War Signed** by United Arab Republic and Saudi Arabia, who supported Republicans and Royalists.

30—**Natural Neutrinos Found for First Time** in South African gold mine. Case Institute of Technology Frederick Reins reports 7 such natural neutrino events since Feb. 23, 1965.

31—**Dominican Act of Reconciliation Signed.** Provides for provisional government and end of civil war.
United Nations Charter Changes in Force. United States last of Security Council permanent members (5) to deposit its ratification (plus 82 of 114 UN members). Increases Security (11 to 15) and Economic and Social (18 to 27) councils' memberships.

SEPTEMBER

2—**Manager Casey Stengel Says Farewell to New York Mets,** ending 56 years in baseball.

3—**Dominican Republic Inaugurates Provisional President,** Héctor García-Godoy.

4—**Albert Schweitzer Dies at 90** in his jungle hospital at Lambaréné, Gabon.

5-6—**Steel Strike Averted.** Workers ratify and union and industry sign 35-month contract.

9—**Department of Housing and Urban Development Created.** Act signed by President Johnson.
France to Leave NATO in 1969. President De Gaulle says his country will no longer accept North Atlantic Treaty Organization defense system.

12-13—**Labor Party Defeated in Norway Elections** after 30 years (except 3 weeks, 1963) in power.

13—**Experimental Nuclear Power Plant Dedicated** in central Idaho. Makes full use of natural uranium, not just U-235.

14—**Vatican Council II Fourth Session Opens** in Rome.

21—**United Nations General Assembly Opens.** Elects Italian Foreign Minister Amintore Fanfani President of its 20th regular session. Admission of Gambia, Maldive Islands, and Singapore brings membership to 117 nations.
New Premier in Iraq. Abdul Rahman al-Bazzar replaces Arif Abdel Razzak, now in exile.

22-23—**Cease-Fire in Kashmir.** India and Pakistan comply with United Nations resolution, but resume fighting almost immediately.

23—**New Premier in Syria,** Yussef Zayen.

24—**United States to Give Canal to Panama.** President Johnson says new treaty underway.

25—**Deposed President Juan D. Bosch Returns to Dominican Republic.** Demands billion dollar indemnity from United States for April revolt.
Greek Parliament Approves Premier. Stephanos C. Stephanopoulos third in post since July 15.

29—**National Foundation on the Arts and Humanities Created.** Act signed by President Johnson.

OCTOBER

1—**Indonesian Revolt Foiled** by loyal military forces, but resistance continues in Java.
Any Cuban Free to Go to United States. Castro widens initial offer of September 28.

3—**New Immigration Act Ends National Origins Quota System,** signed by President Johnson.

4—**Pope Paul VI at United Nations.** First reigning pope to visit Americas addresses General Assembly during 14 hours in New York City.
Supreme Court of United States Opens 1965-1966 Term. Abe Fortas replaces Arthur J. Goldberg as associate justice.
Pakistan Severs Diplomatic Ties with Malaysia for siding with India on Kashmir dispute.
Lunik VII Launched into Space by Russia.

5—**OV I Launched** at Vandenberg Air Force Base, Orbital Vehicle space satellite.

6-14—**Los Angeles Dodgers Win World Series** by beating Minneapolis Twins 4 games out of 7.

8—**Communist Party Headquarters Burned in Djakarta.** Moslem youths shout, "Long Live America."
Lunik VII Hits Sea of Storms on Moon, but fails to make "soft landing."

10—**New York Newspaper Strike Ends.** *Times* and Guild reach final agreement on 25th day.
Conservative Justice Party Wins Turkey Elections. Süleyman Demirel new premier.

12—**$10,000,000 Experimental Seismic Station Dedicated** near Miles City, Mont., for underground nuclear explosions detection.

13—**Moise Tshombe Dismissed as Congo Premier.** Evariste Kimba to replace him.

1965 OCTOBER 1965

SUN.	MON.	TUE.	WED.	THU.	FRI.	SAT.
					1	2
3	4	5	6	7	8	9
10	11	12	13	14	15	16
17	18	19	20	21	22	23
24/31	25	26	27	28	29	30

1965 NOVEMBER 1965

SUN.	MON.	TUE.	WED.	THU.	FRI.	SAT.
	1	2	3	4	5	6
7	8	9	10	11	12	13
14	15	16	17	18	19	20
21	22	23	24	25	26	27
28	29	30				

1965 DECEMBER 1965

SUN.	MON.	TUE.	WED.	THU.	FRI.	SAT.
			1	2	3	4
5	6	7	8	9	10	11
12	13	14	15	16	17	18
19	20	21	22	23	24	25
26	27	28	29	30	31	

$2,000,000 Space Science Laboratory Dedicated at University of Chicago Enrico Fermi Institute of Nuclear Studies.

14—**OGO II Launched** at Vandenberg Air Force Base, Orbiting Geophysical Observatory.

15—**Second Molniga I Communications Satellite Launched** by Russia.

15-18—**Antiwar Demonstrations in Some 40 U.S. Cities.** Iowa State University group, Associated Student Governments, George Washington University reverse teach in, and Detroit Jaycees supports United States policy in Vietnam.

16—**British Commonwealth of Nations Admits Singapore** as its 22nd member.

16-19—**More Violence in Dominican Republic.** Santo Domingo scene of block-to-block fighting.

17—**New York World's Fair Closes.** Total 2-season attendance surpasses 51,000,000.

20—**Ludwig Erhard Re-Elected Chancellor of West Germany** by Bundestag.

20-21—**New Comet Circles Sun** and enters hairpin orbit. Ikeya-Seki, named for Japanese discoverers, has 10- to 20,000,000 mile tail.

21-26—**Organization of African States Conference** in Accra boycotted by 7 French-speaking nations because Ghana President Kwame Nkrumah aids subversives in their countries.

23—**89th Congress of U.S. First Session Ends.** President Johnson acclaims it nation's greatest.

26—**British House of Commons Installs Its First Labour Party Speaker.** Horace King succeeds the late Sir Harry Hylton-Foster.

28—**Pope Paul VI Formally Promulgates Non-Christian Religions Document.** Includes denial of Jews collective guilt in Crucifixion of Jesus.

29—**Saint Louis Completes Gateway Arch.** Inserts 19-ton apex in nation's tallest (630 feet) monument.

31—**U.S. Medal of Honor Men Support Vietnam War.** March at head of New York City parade.

NOVEMBER

2—**New Prime Minister in Afghanistan.** Mohammed Hashim Maiwandwal replaces Mohammed Yousof.
Proton II Launched into Space by Russia.

3—**New U.S. Postmaster General.** Lawrence F. O'Brien succeeds John A. Gronouski, Jr., now U.S. Ambassador to Poland.

6—**Two Congos Resume Diplomatic Relations** after two-year break.
GEOS I Launched into Space. Geodetic explorer satellite to measure earth.

8—**Canada Retains Liberals.** Prime Minister Lester B. Pearson's party wins elections.

9—**Philippines Elects New President.** Nationalist Ferdinand E. Marcos defeats incumbent Liberalist President Diosdado Macapagal.

9-10—**Electric Power Blackout in Northeast U.S., Ontario, and Quebec.** Hits New York City and other areas at evening rush hour, and remains until morning hours.

11—**Rhodesia Proclaims Independence** refused by Britain because of colony's white government.

12—**Venus II Launched into Space** by Russia. To reach planet Venus about Mar. 1, 1966.

16—**Venus III Launched** by Russia toward Venus.

17—**Communist China Barred from United Nations** for 15th time by vote in General Assembly.
France Orders Guinea Ambassador Out of Paris, after Guinea accused French of part in plot against President Sékou Touré.

24—**Britain's Princess Margaret Ends U.S. Visit,** begun on November 4.

25—**Congo Coup d'État.** Army Commander Gen. Joseph D. Mobutu deposes President Joseph Kasavubu, and takes office himself for 5 years.

26—**France 3d Nation in Space Race.** Orbits its first satellite from Sahara test center.

27—**New Kuwait Ruler.** Sheik Sabah as-Salim as-Sabah succeeds brother, Emir Sheik Abdullah as-Salim as-Sabah, who died November 24.

29—**Dahomey Coup d'Etat.** Provisional President Tahiro Congacou replaces deposed President Sourou Migan Apithy.

DECEMBER

1—**Cuban Air Exodus.** First refugees fly to U.S. under new agreement with Castro regime.

4—**Gemini VII Launched on 14-Day Space Flight** with Lieut.-Col. Frank Borman and Comdr. James A. Lovell, Jr., aboard.

7—**Lunik VIII Hits Ocean of Storms on Moon,** but Russians again fail in "soft landing."

8—**Pope Paul VI Ends Historic Vatican II Council,** adjourns its fourth session.

15—**Gemini VII and VI Rendezvous in Space,** man's first such space meeting.
Organization of African Unity Countries Act Against Britain on Rhodesia issue. Tanzania first to break relations with Britain, followed by Guinea, Senegal, and Niger.

16—**Gemini VI Returns to Earth** with Capt. Walter M. Schirra, Jr., and Maj. Thomas P. Stafford.
Pioneer VI Launched at Cape Kennedy.

17—**Great Britain Acts Against Rhodesia.** Imposes oil embargo, in force immediately.

18—**Gemini VII Returns to Earth.** Lieut.-Col. Frank Borman and Comdr. James A. Lovell, Jr., broke all previous space records.
South Korea and Japan Establish Diplomatic Relations, after each ratify Amity Treaty.

19—**Charles De Gaulle Wins Run-Off Election,** and another 7 years as President of France.

21—**Syria Government Resigns,** formed by Premier Yussef Zayen less than 2 months before.

22—**United Nations General Assembly Adjourns** its 20th regular session for 1965.
New Chief of State in Dahomey. Armed Forces head Gen. Christophe Soglo takes control.

24-25—**Vietnam Christmas Truce.** Major hostilities halted for short period.

30—**Philippines Inaugurate President.** Ferdinand E. Marcos begins his first 4-year term.

CONTENTS OF SECTION ONE

THE YEAR BOOK Board of Editors analyzes the significant developments of 1965 and considers their impact upon contemporary affairs. The Related Articles list following each report directs the reader to THE YEAR BOOK's additional coverage of related subjects.

THE YEAR IN FOCUS

Portrait for THE YEAR BOOK by James Hill

Paul-Henri Spaak
ON THE WORLD

There Was an Increasing Tendency to Settle Conflicts by Violence in a Time of Tension and Crisis

It seems that the cruel memories of World War II are slowly but surely fading away. The millions of military and civilian deaths, the burning cities, the concentration camps, the unspeakable physical and moral misery of those long years has ceased to be a reality affecting our day-to-day life. Those horrors have become a memory, always less and less precise, of a receding past which is progressively losing its intensity and weight.

And now the tendency to settle conflicts between nations through recourse to violence has been redeveloping in a world of tension and crisis. The principles of the United Nations Charter have been adhered to less and less. An aggressive and often fanatical nationalism has again become fashionable. Respect for law is being replaced more and more by recourse to force. The visit of Pope Paul VI to the United Nations, and his cry of anguish and warning, was the most moving demonstration in 1965 of the fear this trend brings to responsible men.

Of all the continents, Asia was the most troubled in 1965.

17

"The similarity between the methods of the Chinese and those of the Nazis is remarkable."

There was war in Vietnam, war between India and Pakistan, a puzzling revolution in Indonesia, a perpetually troubled situation in Laos and Cambodia. These events were the most striking current developments in the great conflict of this century: the conflict in which communism opposes the Free World. Red China is now leading that fight.

China has adopted the most dangerous theories and tactics professed and practiced by the Soviet Union immediately after World War II. China refuses to admit the principle of peaceful coexistence. It maintains that wars of "liberation" are legitimate. This policy is typified by China's determination to foster local conflicts wherever it can do so by systematically approving all forms of nationalism and by endorsing all subversive movements, regardless of their social context.

The similarity between the methods of the Chinese and those of the Nazis is remarkable. In Europe before World War II, too few people read Adolf Hitler's *Mein Kampf*, and those who did so did not, for the most part, take the book seriously. Hitler's statements were too extreme. His aims seemed entirely unreasonable. He expressed his innermost thoughts with considerable candor, however, and he nearly succeeded in accomplishing his purpose.

The Chinese theorists are equally sincere. We would be ill-advised to minimize their intent to dominate the world and to promote the triumph of their economic and social concepts. Their tactics are not much different, and certainly not less cynical, than those of Hitler. When one learns that China, with its massive manpower, felt itself threatened because four Indian cavalrymen crossed its ill-defined border, one cannot help thinking of the so-called suffering of the Germans of Sudetenland which, in Hitler's eyes, justified erasing Czechoslovakia from Europe.

Among the various conflicts of 1965, the one in Vietnam was, of course, the gravest. Not only did it require from the United States an ever greater military effort, it also assumed all the aspects of a real war. It furthermore created a dangerous cleavage between the United States and a large segment of world public opinion. Finally, it seriously impaired the development of a policy of pacific coexistence between the United States and the Soviet Union. As recently as

1963, that policy constituted the great hope for peace among the nations of the world.

The situation which the United States faced in Asia in 1965 was very similar to that which it faced in Europe in 1948. In both instances, the question was simply this: Should the United States permit communists, either Russian or Chinese, to subjugate people refusing to accept their creed?

The United States took part in World War II partly to prevent totalitarian nationalism from overcoming the Western World. It succeeded in that aim. This very success now compels America to prevent the triumph of totalitarian communists. The United States succeeded in Europe through the Marshall Plan and the North Atlantic Treaty Organization (NATO). Will it succeed in Asia? Conditions are different and much less favorable there. Poor people, without democratic traditions and often badly governed, do not provide the basis of resistance to communism present in Europe after World War II.

Obviously, the war in Vietnam has a much broader and deeper significance than victory or defeat in one country. If America fails, or if it changes its policy in Vietnam, logically it has to cease showing any interest in Southeast Asia, and possibly in the whole of Asia. An American defeat in Vietnam would imply that no defense against Communist China could be attempted in Thailand, in Laos, in Cambodia, in the Philippines, in Formosa, in Malaysia and, tomorrow, in India.

The problem America faces is a formidable one. Its magnitude is underestimated in most of the world where public opinion—largely influenced by daily news of the war—reacts sentimentally and unfavorably. People who are well-informed try to explain the situation, but they encounter deep trends they find difficult to overcome. The Vietnamese war creates repercussions in Europe, and influences relations between the United States and its allies. Above all, it influences relations between the United States and the Soviet Union.

The relaxation of tensions between these two great powers, so hopeful a short while ago, has not materialized. It must be admitted that the position of the Soviet Union is difficult. As leader of the communist world, closely watched by the Chinese who constantly accuse it of treason, Russia cannot remain indifferent toward the situation in Vietnam. The Soviet Union is compelled, apparently against its desire, to oppose the United States. At times one wonders if China, while inciting the North Vietnamese to refuse to negotiate with the United States, is not primarily interested in preventing more peaceful relations between the Soviet Union and the U.S.

Whatever the facts may be, the conflict goes on and the chances for a reasonable solution are, for the time being, nonexistent. A broadening of the conflict remains a possibility, and the limits of this extension are unpredictable. Never since the end of World War II, has a local conflict seemed to contain such a threat to the peace of the world.

War between India and Pakistan has again aggravated the situation in Asia. The conflict over Kashmir appears quite difficult to solve, and a true peace depends upon its solution. Chinese influence in that part of the world is apparent in the unconditional support given to Pakistan, and in the senseless quarrel China picked with India. Communist China is sparking the fire, and is visibly seeking to poison present relations between India and Pakistan.

Compared to seething Asia, Africa was relatively calm in 1965. In the past few years, the newly independent countries have sought to achieve stability, and several of them have succeeded. It must be admitted, however, that in many cases their economic development remains insufficient, despite the assistance given them. The problem of these underdeveloped countries is perhaps the most important of all those the world faces. Will the rich countries have the wisdom to understand in time, and to make the effort and sacrifice needed to solve it? This is one of the biggest questions of our time.

Three other phenomena taking place in Africa are worth noting. One, which is faced by both Blacks and Arabs, is an attempt by the Chinese communists to extend their sphere of influence to the continent. Although their efforts so far have shown some small results, notably in Congo (Brazzaville) and certain East African countries, they have generally failed to achieve a dominant role in African politics. They have, however, achieved a subtle victory of sorts. Their propaganda has prevented the development of closer, more harmonious relations between Africa and the Western World.

The second phenomena is one which finds the Blacks and the Arabs pitted against one another for domination of the continent. The Blacks, who seem to have gained a new consciousness of their individuality, have, however, successfully resisted Arab intrigues, personified in Egypt's Gamal Abdel Nasser and—until he was deposed—Algeria's Ahmed Ben Bella.

Finally, there is the problem of Rhodesia. It is humanly tragic, and politically very difficult to solve. The small White minority in that country gave clear evidence in 1965 that it was not willing to be governed by a large Black majority. The government of Ian Smith turned down hopes for settlement by pronouncing itself in favor of a policy of adventure. The decision to proclaim the immediate independence of the country from Great Britain appeared unnecessary. It created profound disquiet in Africa, incurred the opposition of many European states, and gave rise to a crisis in the British Commonwealth of Nations.

In North America, Canada and the United States enjoyed great economic prosperity in 1965, but they did not escape political problems. In Canada, the desire of the French-speaking population for autonomy, even independence, posed a problem difficult to solve. It is complicated by the fact that wisdom and reason have often been torn apart by irrational, sentimental reactions. Canadian leaders will require much tact and understanding to solve this problem. Fortunately, there is reason to believe they will succeed.

The United States also was confronted with many problems in 1965. Its position as the most powerful country in the world constantly requires it to assume heavier and more numerous responsibilities.

One is amazed by the speed with which the conditions of American external life have developed. In 1914, only a half century ago,

"America's historical role in this century becomes more and more precise . . ."

the Monroe Doctrine was still the dominant concept of U.S. international policy, and the nation had relatively little interest in the rest of the world. Today the United States is fully engaged in Africa, Asia, Europe, and Latin America. No international problem can now be solved without its assistance. Because of its involvement in world affairs, the U.S. has developed many enemies. Even its friends do not always show their gratitude for the services the United States has rendered, and the sacrifices it has made.

America's historical role in this century becomes more and more precise: it is the main obstacle to the triumph of communism and, consequently, the outstanding defender of the democratic world. Such a tremendous task is not accomplished without certain errors, but it is only fair to judge the achievement as a whole, and it is a positive one.

During World War II, the U.S. crushed nazism, fascism, and aggressive Japanese militarism. After the war, its efforts permitted Europe to heal its wounds and to protect itself against the creeping danger of Russian communism. Today, in Asia, the United States faces the dangers of Chinese communism. Thus, its historical role continues to take shape.

Latin America is unfortunately still confronted by the same problems that have plagued it in the past. In 1965, Cuba was in the throes of a serious economic crisis which the Castro regime seemed unable to surmount. Social unrest continued to provoke incidents and disturbances in Brazil, Peru, and Uruguay. Upheaval in the Dominican Republic held the attention of people throughout the world.

In looking at Latin America, it is difficult to find much evidence of stability. One receives the impression of a continent that is still groping to find itself. Troubled economic and social conditions make it a fertile breeding ground for subversive propaganda.

Europe in 1965 was least troubled of all the continents. The German problem remained unsolved. But, however great its importance, it does not, for the time being at least, seem likely to disturb the peace.

Western Europe, like the United States, has enjoyed a high degree of economic prosperity for many years. It also knows peace. It owes these two blessings to the creation of the Atlantic Alliance and to the European Economic Community (EEC, or Common Market). These two important achievements are threatened today by the policies of French President Charles de Gaulle.

The French president dislikes anything that has been done without his participation. He was out of power for 13 years and had no part in the creation of the Atlantic Alliance. The Common Market was born at a time when he was showing a marked hostility toward it. He seems bent today on destroying the Atlantic Alliance and reducing the Common Market to the status of an economic organization without any extension in the political field.

Such a policy does not stand any chance of succeeding in Europe. It may bring about the destruction, or serious disturbance of what exists, but it cannot build anything solid and endurable.

The manner in which General De Gaulle was re-elected president of France late in 1965 constituted an obvious setback for him. Some maintain that he cannot ignore what has happened, and that he will have to follow a more flexible policy. Others believe that he may react by adopting a more radical line. It may be, in view of this, that 1966 will be a decisive year for Western Europe and the Atlantic Alliance.

In the communist countries of Eastern Europe, important economic reforms have been carried out or are in prospect. The framework of communist society is being maintained, and the means of production are collectively owned. But within this framework, competition and the profit motive are now encouraged as positive elements. We are also witnessing a certain degree of liberalization in the political regimes of these nations, and an undisputed improvement of relations with neighboring countries having different political systems. Peaceful coexistence is gaining ground.

In the Soviet Union, achievements in space research remained important in 1965, but the economic situation created difficult problems. They were due primarily to the inadequacies of the nation's agriculture, and, secondly, to the growing desire of the Russian people for greater material well-being. The Soviet Union's ideological conflict with China, which openly challenges it for the leadership of world communism, is one of the great events in the world today. The possible consequences of this rivalry are immeasurable. China's imperialism is presently largely intellectual, but tomorrow it may assume other forms. It is perhaps even more dangerous for the Soviet Union than the United States, and there are indications that the Soviet Union is clearly aware of this fact.

The war in Southeast Asia unfortunately prevents the Soviet Union from pursuing its policy of rapprochement with the United States at the pace it desires. But in the given circumstances, its policy is moderate. Its attitude in the India-Pakistan conflict was the most recent proof of this. We can be glad that it is no longer the Soviet Union that seeks to aggravate conflicts.

The United Nations is slowly emerging from the crisis in which it found itself as a result of its extremely serious financial situation. This was caused largely by the refusal of the Soviet Union and France to contribute to the expenses for the peace-keeping operations in the Middle East and in Congo (Léopoldville).

The 1965 General Assembly session was able to follow its normal course after a compromise was reached with the Soviet Union and France on their payments. Thanks in no small measure to the good will of the United States, the organization has come back to life. It has even shown signs of vitality. In the India-Pakistan conflict, the Security Council was able for the first time in many years to make a decision which was effectively carried out, and which, at least for the time being, put a stop to the dangerous military operations that had been going on in that area.

Altogether, however, 1965 was a year in which the international situation deteriorated. It was a year in which the Chinese threat became more pointed. The responsibilities of the United States increased. Africa and Latin America groped for stability. In Europe, the economic stability that had been achieved seemed in danger because of De Gaulle's policies.

Related Articles

For a complete report on the year 1965, see Section Two, THE MIRACLE OF THE MOUNTAIN; THE SILENT STRUGGLE; and articles on the various nations in Section Three. In the same section, see also the following:

Portrait for THE YEAR BOOK by James Hill

James B. Reston

ON THE NATION

It Was a Dazzling Year in "the Continuing American Revolution," Yet the People Were Troubled

Americans are funny people. They were born in rebellion but think they are conservative. They condemn "radicals," but in tinkering around to change and improve things, they are actually more radical than the people they condemn. They admire "practical" people who "live modern" and "keep up with the times," and they revolutionize more things than the "revolutionaries" they criticize.

American life is a continuing and unconscious revolution. Americans hate things that do not work. Mentally, they stick to old political concepts and institutions, but change them with their hands. America wants everybody to be happy, healthy, and useful; an idea regarded as wildly "radical" in some parts of the world. America works toward that ideal in every town, factory, school, and legislature until it changes the things that get in its way.

The year 1965 vividly illustrated this point. For many years before that, there had been conflict on a wide range of questions affecting the well-being of the American people. Then somehow in 1965, by some coincidence of time and

"Suddenly, barriers that had long divided the Congress were swept away."

atmosphere, things changed. There was a bumper crop of progressive legislation.

Even before 1965, there had been some agreement on certain basic facts. The schools had not kept pace with the growth of knowledge and population. The hospitals and doctors had not been able to provide for many old people at prices the sick and elderly could afford. And that was not all.

The universities had not been able to finance the teachers, classrooms, and other essential facilities for all the young men and women in America who had the talent to take advantage of a university education. The states had not been able to guarantee the equal voting rights promised in the U. S. Constitution to all adult citizens, regardless of race. The churches had not been able to provide adequate church-school education for the children of their parishioners without financial aid from the federal government, and the Constitution seemed to forbid such aid to church schools.

In 1965, President Lyndon B. Johnson proposed, and the 89th Congress passed, legislation dealing with all these problems. Suddenly, barriers that had long divided the Congress were swept away. Controversial programs that had lost in the past were accepted. 1965 took its place among the historic years of reform on the home front.

One of America's great historians, Arthur M. Schlesinger, Sr., who died in 1965, had long been fascinated by the patterns of American history. There were, he said, periods of innovation and periods of consolidation in the American story, and they seemed to follow a rough order. They were not, he emphasized, periods of reform followed by periods of reaction which repealed the reforms. Rather, he insisted, the movements of social and economic reform occur and progress in stages, much as a ship rises through a system of locks.

First there comes a surge forward, as society and government, feeling ready for needed reforms, move upward to higher levels. Then there follows, not a drop, not a repeal of what is new, but a level period of absorbing and tidying up the new reforms. This is what is meant by "the continuing American revolution," and 1965 was clearly

one of the creative years on history's scroll.

It created, for example, a number of "firsts." For the first time:

• The elderly in America were provided with hospital and nursing care under the federal government's Social Security system.

• The ancient church-state controversy over federal funds to church schools was set aside, and Washington was able to help finance church schools, as well as provide aid to elementary and secondary schools in areas populated largely by poor families.

• Federal scholarships—not just federal loans—were provided for poor but talented students so that they would have an opportunity to get a college education.

• Limited federal rent subsidies—not nearly as generous as the President proposed —were made available to some low-income families qualifying for federal housing.

• A new Department of Housing and Urban Development was established, with Cabinet rank, to deal with the growing problems of urban and suburban housing, community planning, and mass transportation.

• The federal government, through federal registrars, made good the 95-year-old guarantee of Amendment 15 that the right to vote should not be denied or abridged because of race or creed.

• Finally, a law was passed instructing manufacturers of cigarettes to put on each package a warning that states: "Caution— Habitual Smoking Is Injurious to Health."

In addition to these innovations, Congress made generous grants to higher education; provided $1,100,000,000 to relieve the depressed economic area of Appalachia; and added another $1,900,000,000 for the President's "War on Poverty," and $3,250,000,000 for regional development. It repealed many excise taxes; abolished the national immigration quotas system; and repealed the 25 per cent gold cover on commercial bank deposits held by the Federal Reserve Banks.

There were a number of reasons for this extraordinary record of surmounting old legislative barriers. The first was political. In the presidential election of 1964, the balance of power was upset in favor of the Democratic party, which has been the party of innovation and change since the adminis-

"... President Johnson completed much of the unfinished business of the Roosevelt era ..."

tration of President Woodrow Wilson. President Johnson won the election by the largest margin of votes in history. In the course of this landslide, he carried his party to a two-to-one majority in the House of Representatives and a three-to-one majority in the Senate. The Democrats were also in control of most state and city governments.

The second reason for the legislative breakthrough was personal. President Johnson was not the first former United States Senator to win the presidency—Warren G. Harding had in 1920, Harry S. Truman in 1948; and John F. Kennedy in 1960—but Johnson was the first commanding congressional leader to take over the White House. He had been a prominent Representative from Texas. Later, as Majority Leader of the Senate, he had acquired the reputation of being one of the most astute political craftsmen of this century.

It was not only that President Johnson understood the psychology of Congress and the intricacies of parliamentary maneuver; he also knew the leaders of Congress intimately. He had spent over 30 years on Capitol Hill with them. He knew what things they needed to get elected in their districts, and he exploited all this experience by a persistent, determined, and resourceful personal leadership of his legislative program, in alliance with his friend, the Republican Minority Leader, Senator Everett McKinley Dirksen of Illinois.

A third consideration was at least equally, and perhaps even more, important in the enactment of the administration's legislative program. The nation was unusually prosperous and thus had the resources for new social programs. President Johnson continually pointed out that it was intolerable to have so much poverty, so many slums, and such inadequate schools and hospitals in the midst of such unprecedented wealth.

Senator Dirksen constantly quoted Victor Hugo as saying that no army could withstand the "power of an idea whose time has come." This clarifies the point. The time had come when the majority of American people were ready to do something about unequal voting laws, inadequate hospitals, and all the rest of the deprivations.

As a result, the record of the first half of the 89th Congress was being compared to

Woodrow Wilson's first term, during which the Federal Reserve System and the Federal Trade Commission were established, and the Clayton Anti-Trust Act was passed. Comparisons were being made, too, with the first two terms of Franklin D. Roosevelt's New Deal, during which the Securities Exchange Act was passed, the Federal Deposit Insurance Corporation was created, the Social Security system was established, the right of unions to bargain collectively was strengthened, a minimum-wage law was passed, and an effort was made to restore the farmer's purchasing power by controlling his production and guaranteeing his prices.

In some ways, President Johnson completed much of the unfinished business of the Roosevelt era in 1965, but the trend of reform in American political life had started well before that. President Theodore Roosevelt dramatized it with his Republican administration early in the century. Wilson followed it with his New Freedom from 1912 to 1920. Then, after a period of consolidation under the Republicans, President Roosevelt picked it up again and was followed by his disciple, Lyndon B. Johnson.

"It has been the function of the liberal tradition in American politics," the political scientist, Richard Hofstadter, has written, "at first to broaden the numbers of those who could benefit from the great American bonanza, and then to humanize its workings and help heal its casualties."

There were some striking differences, however, between the New Deal of Franklin Roosevelt and the Great Society of Lyndon Johnson. The New Deal came into being in a period of economic depression, when the people were not only willing to accept reforms, but were demanding them. The Johnson legislative program was carried out in a period of unmatched prosperity, dwindling unemployment, and social stability.

If the New Deal was experimentation and improvisation on a grand scale, the Great Society was a forehanded attempt to solve economic and social problems before they became critical. Thus, 1965 was a time of "preventive reform." It involved not only the problem of persuading a prosperous people to anticipate trouble, but also ex-

"These officials and Congressmen are not distant creatures arguing about trivialities..."

perimentation with new economic theories.

The prosperity of 1965 was assisted by economic policies that were hardly less revolutionary than the reforms they made possible. This illustrates "the continuing American revolution" in the field of ideas. The British economist and philosopher, John Maynard Keynes, had taught over a generation ago that increased government spending and reduced excise and income taxes could stimulate consumers to buy more, and producers to produce more, thus expanding the economy and creating prosperity for an ever increasing percentage of the people. This doctrine was fought for years in the Congress and in some branches of the executive, but gradually the experiment was made, and in 1965, its results won wide public approval.

The significance of this is clear enough. Just as reforms of one generation are sustained in the next, even when the conservative party comes to power, so, too, the experimental ideas of one administration tend to be accepted if they work. A conservative banker made the point at the end of the year: "After the record of the new economics in the last few years, no Republican Secretary of the Treasury in the future is likely to go back to the old system."

It would be wrong, however, even to think of the 1965 record on the home front as the work solely of one party or a politically astute President. The Congress put its stamp on that legislative program, and, as E. W. Kenworthy of *The New York Times* wrote, "it was not a rubber stamp." The Congress scaled down the rent subsidies requested by the President, for example, and made them available only to low-income families eligible for public housing. It modified the so-called "Medicare" bill in a number of ways—particularly in forcing through a Republican proposal for a voluntary supplementary insurance program to partially cover doctor bills and some other health costs for persons over 65 years old.

The impact of all these exertions in Washington illustrates just how much the federal government influences the lives of the American people. These officials and Congressmen are not distant creatures arguing about

trivialities remote from the individual lives of men, women, and children. They make the laws that tax your income; draft your sons into the armed forces; reduce or raise the prices of goods you buy, provide aid to schools, hospitals, roads; and all the rest.

Some legislation proposed by the President, of course, did not pass the Congress. Among these was a measure to repeal Section 14B of the Taft-Hartley Act, which permits the states to enact "right to work" laws banning the union shop. This was postponed for consideration in the second session of the 89th Congress in 1966. Another failure was the administration's "home rule" bill to extend self-government to residents of the District of Columbia. But these were minor misses as compared to the major legislation that became law.

In fact, so much was passed by the end of the year that the question in Washington was: what will be left to do next year and the year after that before the start of the 1968 presidential election?

The answer is that a great deal of "consolidation" remains to be done, and by the time that is finished, new problems of a rising and shifting population will demand new innovations. That is the way "the continuing revolution" works.

The Democratic Majority Leader in the Senate emphasized that in 1966 the "main concern of the Senate will be the perfection, the elaboration, and the refinement of the basic legislation which has been put on the statute books during the past three or four years." The pendulum will not swing back from reform to reaction; it will stay roughly at the point of consolidation until these reforms are digested.

What was particularly striking about 1965 was the contrast between the record of movement and progress in the field of domestic affairs and the record of disappointment, stalemate, and even retrogression in the field of foreign affairs.

These disappointments abroad sharply affected the life of the American people. At the start of the year, the United States had about 60,000 men in Vietnam acting as "advisers" and "assistants" in the war between North and South Vietnam. By the

"... a vast effort ... would have to be undertaken if order was to be restored in the world."

end of the year, the entire picture had changed. The United States had an expeditionary force of about 200,000 men engaged in the front line of an open war against North Vietnamese regular army regiments and Viet Cong guerrillas. It had three aircraft carriers operating in the South China Sea, from where American bombers attacked North Vietnam around the clock. The draft of young men had gone up from about 8,000 to over 40,000 a month. All this was the subject of debate, controversy, and even division throughout the nation.

Elsewhere, the hopes of the administration for the development of effective defensive alliances in the Western Hemisphere, the Atlantic, and the Pacific had failed to materialize. By year's end, it was widely realized that a vast effort of reconstruction would have to be undertaken if order was to be restored in the world.

Fortunately, so much had been accomplished on the home front, so many new programs had been started, and so much had to be digested and refined, that the President was able to begin this work of reconstruction in meetings with Prime Minister Harold Wilson of Great Britain, Chancellor Ludwig Erhard of Germany, President Ayub Khan of Pakistan, and later, Prime Minister Lal Bahadur Shastri of India.

Therefore, 1966 promised to be a year of concentration on foreign affairs and consolidation in domestic affairs. At home, the ship of state had risen in the locks to new heights, revealing new horizons for a nation now approaching 200,000,000 people. But abroad, the outlook was bleak, and despite the successes at home, the spirit of the people was troubled.

Related Articles

For a complete report on the year 1965 in national affairs, see also Section One, PAUL-HENRI SPAAK ON THE WORLD; SYLVIA PORTER ON THE ECONOMY; LAWRENCE A. CREMIN ON EDUCATION; and the following articles in Section Three:

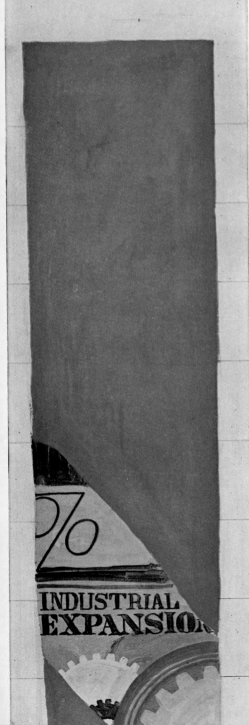

Sylvia Porter
ON THE ECONOMY

*Surging Prosperity Has Given Us
Time to Meet Our Most Serious
International Economic Challenge*

Portrait for THE YEAR BOOK by James Hill

As 1966 began, the United States economy entered its 59th month of strong, broad upturn to the highest peak in world history. No domestic economic event of this modern era transcends in importance this single achievement. Only once before in our history—during the 80-month boom spanning World War II—has an economic upswing lasted so long, and the unhealthily feverish, artificial, inflationary upsurge of 1938–1945 does not belong in the same class as the solid, balanced expansion of 1961–1965.

We continued to shatter virtually every record for business prosperity. We turned out well above $670,000,000,000 in goods and services, thus increasing our gross national product (GNP) by one-third since the expansion began in 1961. Industrial production, weekly earnings, personal income, and after-tax corporate profits hit new peaks.

Stock prices slipped badly in the spring, but subsequently climbed to the highest levels ever. Unemployment among married men—the breadwinners—sank to a near minimum of around 2 per cent. In many fields, employers faced

"The very 'monotony' of our advance was ... a grave danger to our ... good health."

shortages of semiskilled and skilled workers. Only joblessness among unskilled teen-agers, unskilled Negroes, and unskilled older workers held the overall unemployment rate above 4 per cent.

The pace of price increases quickened as 1965 rolled on, and with spending surging upward for the Vietnam war and adding heat to our already heated economy, inflation was a nagging threat at year's end. In December, the Federal Reserve Board raised the basic interest rate of the country—the discount rate—from 4 per cent to $4\frac{1}{2}$ per cent, the highest level since 1930, to slow down borrowing and thus reduce inflationary pressures on the economy.

The very "monotony" of our advance was, in fact, beginning to pose a grave danger to our economy's continuing good health. Millions of Americans—particularly youngsters—think that sustained business upturn is not "news," and that we have found the secret to perpetual prosperity. Confidence in our economy's strength is a good thing; euphoria about it definitely is not. Such an attitude could encourage excesses in spending and borrowing that would bring the upturn to an end. Sustained upturn *is* news. We have *not* found the secret to perpetual prosperity. But we have learned more about how to control the severity of business cycles. Using this knowledge, we have made the maintenance of business expansion a key national goal.

President Lyndon B. Johnson has tilted lances with businessmen and bankers several times—most notably over price and interest rate increases—but the era of "partnership for prosperity" inaugurated when he entered the White House in November, 1963, continued through 1965. Most businessmen trust Mr. Johnson as a man who understands the key role profits play in a prosperous economy and as a man "you can do business with."

Mr. Johnson, in turn, considers policies to maintain the prosperity of business so vital that when a government official was asked whether he foresaw the danger of a recession, he answered, "a recession under Johnson? 'It' wouldn't dare!"

We continue, of course, to face profound problems. To mention only a few, we must find ways to sustain the economic upturn we have achieved, while averting inflationary wage-price increases. We must expand our trade with the European Common Market, despite President Charles de Gaulle's sabotaging activities. We must develop our trade with the Soviet bloc. We must channel funds from the federal government to the states and cities so that they can finance the staggering volume of essential projects under their jurisdiction without loading us with additional backbreaking local taxes. We must slash unemployment among teen-age, older unskilled, and Negro workers. We must get the maximum production benefits from automation and, at the same time, protect workers whose jobs are shot out from under them by technical advances. We must translate Congress' blueprints for a "Great Society" into reality and still not permit federal government spending to become a dangerous inflationary force.

Nonetheless, when 1965 ended, we were so affluent that families were spending an average of 48¢ of every $1 of income on luxuries, rather than on the traditional basic necessities of food, shelter, clothing, and fuel. We were clearly on our way toward turning upside down a necessities-dominated spending pattern which has held throughout the ages of man.

Prosperity is always a "plus," and in 1965 it was particularly so, because it bought us time in which to get our international financial accounts into a semblance of balance and to prevent our foreign creditors from staging a disastrous run on our gold reserves. Had we not been so prosperous, we could by now have lost the battle to defend the dollar. This is our biggest single international economic challenge of the mid-1960s.

"Never again will the United States be able to ignore its balance of payments in formulating domestic policies. There is no once-and-for-all solution either to the problem of maintaining balance in our internal economic expansion, or to the problem of maintaining balance in our external payments." This is the language of bafflegab

"...1965 marked a historic turning point in the Free World's monetary system."

at its worst. But when the chairman of our powerful Federal Reserve Board, William McChesney Martin, Jr., said these words before an academic audience, he flashed a clear warning that the United States no longer will continue to flood the West with dollars in order to finance the growth of the Free World's trade. He also signaled that 1965 marked a historic turning point in the Free World's monetary system.

We have now, for the first time in the post-World War II period, taken stern, urgent actions to close the gap between what we spend abroad and what we earn abroad; that is, to slash the deficit in our balance of payments. We are curbing the outpouring of dollars that in the past two decades has helped the prosperity of nations everywhere.

We have now put the Free World's central bankers on notice that they must seek some source other than the U.S. dollar to provide the increase in money essential for the continuing expansion of world trade. The meaning of this decision to all of us is this: even a moderate slow-down in the growth of trade among Western nations because of a shortage of funds to finance the trade would be deeply deflationary. It could set off a devastating chain reaction in terms of jobs, paychecks, and profits everywhere.

We are now moving toward the first great overhaul of the West's monetary system since that system was created at Bretton Woods, N.H., in 1944. By drying up the red ink in our balance of payments, we are offering a preview of the credit pinch that could occur in the Free World's nations if their supplies of dollars stop climbing so fast. We have dramatized the need to supplement the role the U.S. dollar has played. We have thus established the background against which full-scale negotiations can be held on reform of the international monetary system. In 1965, monetary system reform actually moved from the stage of discussion to negotiation. In the rarefied sphere of international finance, the very fact that the West's top financial powers began bargaining at the highest policy-making level represented major progress.

To understand what is going on today and how much it means, you must turn back to the 1930s. At that time, manipulation of currencies by countries trying to gain a trade advantage for themselves was commonplace. Each nation's attitude was to get the most for itself, and let the devil take the hindmost. Speculation in currencies was intense, and insiders who knew the right people in a nation's government made fortunes overnight by selling one currency and buying another. There was no assurance from month to month what a currency would be worth. There was no machinery for cooperation on stabilization of currencies. As a result, nations had no confidence that the paper money they accepted in payment for goods or services would have a stable value. Because of this, the world's trade marts were in chaos, and disastrous economic depression pervaded the Western world.

On top of this came global war and even greater financial chaos. By 1944, not a currency in the world outside the U.S. dollar had a reliable value. World War II's Lend-Lease arrangements had obscured all normal trade deals and, of course, we were not trading with our enemies.

Then came the conference of Bretton Woods in July, 1944. At this conference, delegates from 44 nations created an International Monetary Fund (IMF). Its purpose was to stabilize currencies so that countries could trade with each other and have faith in the value of the currencies they were using in payment. Moreover, the delegates created an International Bank for Reconstruction and Development—also known as the World Bank—to make postwar loans to member countries for their reconstruction and development. They also made provisions for the settlement of debts among governments and central banks in gold, in such key currencies as the U.S. dollar and the British pound, and in funds borrowed by the nations from the International Monetary Fund.

There was little precedent for an international monetary system of this order. At the start, skeptics dismissed the Bretton Woods institutions as fantastically idealistic and impractical. But in the 21 years since Bretton Woods, the fantastically idealistic and impractical has become the thoroughly

"...a network of reciprocal...arrangements has been developed...to avert financial crises..."

realistic. The system created out of chaos has worked superbly well in stabilizing currencies, as well as in supporting a huge growth in international trade.

In the IMF, 103 nations have pooled their currencies and some gold to give the institution reserves to lend back to nations when their paper monies get in trouble. The IMF's reserves are now above $21,000,000,000, compared to $7,600,000,000 in 1948. And again and again in the postwar era, the IMF has used its reserves to protect currencies under attack. The World Bank has been a remarkably successful financial institution, and its loans have been of tremendous importance in developing and rebuilding economies everywhere.

Since 1962, a network of reciprocal currency arrangements has been developed, and the network has been used repeatedly by the West's central bankers to avert financial crises that could have undermined or even wrecked the economies of the entire Free World. The most recent illustration of such central bank cooperation occurred in September, 1965, when the U.S. and nine other nations—with President De Gaulle's France notably missing—made "new arrangements" to aid Britain's pound and to crush speculators against the pound sterling.

Meanwhile, the Western nations' dependence on reserves of gold, U.S. dollars, and British pounds to settle their debts with each other has been justified. The total of world trade has skyrocketed from $53,300,000,000 in 1948 to a current annual rate of about $170,000,000,000. This is a key reason why jobs and paychecks have grown so much in the West, and why Europe and the U.S. have been so prosperous.

But—and this is a crucial point—it is the U.S. that has been lubricating the monetary machinery with floods of dollars. True, we run a huge surplus in our merchandise trade with other lands, and year after year we export far more goods and services abroad than we import. But our annual spending overseas for other purposes—for military defense, economic aid, tourism, private business investments, and bank loans—has more than wiped out our annual merchandise export surplus and has splattered our balance of payments with red ink. For 15 out of the past 16 years, we have run a deficit in our balance of payments, and this deficit has added more than $35,000,000,000 to foreign holdings of gold and dollars.

As a result of the U.S. deficit, our foreign creditors have accumulated enormous dollar claims against the United States which they can convert into our gold at any time they wish. They have drawn heavily on our gold reserves in recent years. From a high of $24,800,000,000 in 1949, our total gold reserve has sunk to under $14,000,000,000. In view of our unbroken string of balance of payments deficits, cynical central bankers began years ago to circulate "sick, sick, sick" jokes about the U.S. dollar at their annual IMF meetings. (Sample: "The U.S. is the world's poorest developed nation" with the "world's fifth strongest currency.")

In the late 1950s, when President Dwight D. Eisenhower was in the White House, it became apparent that the U.S. could not go on indefinitely priming the world's monetary pumps with dollars. But the measures we took to curtail the outpouring were only half-hearted. Then in late 1964 and 1965, time ran out on us. The deficit in our balance of payments skyrocketed to a crisis annual rate of more than $6,000,000,000; the worst ever. Simultaneously, President De Gaulle stepped-up his drive to downgrade the U.S. dollar and upgrade the French franc with a widely publicized announcement that he was exchanging almost all of France's accumulated dollars for gold. He also proposed that the world abandon the postwar monetary system and return to the long-discredited system of settling international financial accounts only in gold.

President Johnson finally opened a heavy counterattack, on Feb. 10, 1965. At the heart of the attack was a program calling for "voluntary" cooperation by U.S. bankers to slash bank loans in Europe, and by U.S. businessmen to limit direct investments in developed countries, to bring home profits earned overseas, to borrow funds abroad to finance their foreign operations, and to expand their merchandise exports. In the months that followed, the "voluntary" program worked magnificently.

"...what is at stake is nothing less than the ...future prosperity of the West."

Our balance of payments deficit shrank. There were no "sick, sick, sick" jokes about the U.S. dollar at the meeting of the IMF governors in September, 1965. But the progress was not enough to wipe out the red ink. Tighter—although still "voluntary" —guidelines for business investments abroad were announced at year's end. Yet, despite the fact that we still ran a deficit, our determination to meet the balance of payments challenge had become unmistakable.

To demonstrate to the world that we would continue to stand ready to supply gold to qualified foreign holders of U.S. dollars on their demand, Congress eliminated an obsolete requirement that deposits at our Federal Reserve Banks be backed by 25 per cent in gold. This "freed" $4,700,000,000 of the precious yellow metal for sale to our overseas creditors.

Against this background, Secretary of the Treasury Henry H. Fowler called for an IMF conference to bolster the Bretton Woods system. The deputy finance ministers of the so-called "Group of Ten"—Belgium, Canada, France, Italy, Japan, The Netherlands, Sweden, the United Kingdom, the U.S., and West Germany, plus Switzerland as an observer—began formal negotiations to find areas of agreement on various proposals for reform. The negotiations are to be broadened so that they will include representatives of less developed countries.

The bargaining will be tough, prolonged, and often frustrating. It is far too early to speculate on the precise details of the outcome. There are, however, certain fundamental points that can be outlined now. The basic Bretton Woods system will be retained. Gold and the U.S. dollar will continue as key reserves. Ways will be devised to supplement these reserves, possibly through the creation of a new currency reserve unit, backed by various major currencies and acceptable in payment of international debts.

It could take as long as three to five years before a workable supplement is built on top of the superb system we have. International monetary reform surely will assume an increasingly dominant position in the economic sphere as this decade rolls on. This is as it should be, for what is at stake is nothing less than the future of the dollar, the future of world trade, and the future prosperity of the West.

Related Articles

For a complete report on the 1965 year in economics, see Section One, PAUL-HENRI SPAAK ON THE WORLD, JAMES B. RESTON ON THE NATION, and the following articles in Section Three:

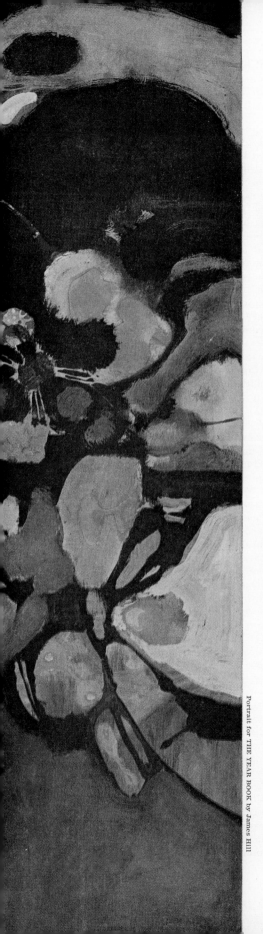

Portrait for THE YEAR BOOK by James Hill

Harrison S. Brown
ON SCIENCE

*Science Faces a Crisis in Handling
The Flow of Data It Generates;
Can It Meet the Challenge?*

More than 300 years ago, a small group of men met at the Bull-Head Tavern in London every Thursday afternoon to discuss science. Although they ate good food and enjoyed each other's company, they met primarily because they found the world of science fascinating. The group, which at various times included such diverse personalities as Sir Christopher Wren, Samuel Pepys, Robert Boyle, and Benjamin Franklin, was part of the world's oldest and most famous scientific society: the Royal Society of London. In 1665, the Society published the first issue of *Philosophical Transactions*, today the oldest surviving scientific journal.

During the three centuries which separate us from these modest beginnings, the number of scientific societies has multiplied several thousandfold. Whereas the founders of the Royal Society could meet in a small room in the Bull-Head Tavern, the most recent meeting of the International Union of Biochemistry drew nearly 7,000 persons from all parts of the world and monopolized two of New York City's largest hotels. Over the same 300-year period, the number

of scientists, technical journals, and individual scientific papers have all doubled about every 15 years. Clearly, this rapid rate of increase cannot continue forever—if for no other reason, the numbers of scientists cannot become greater than the population itself! Nevertheless, it seems likely that such a rate of increase in the field of science will persist for some time to come.

In mid-1965, the first volume (A-C) of the 11th edition of *American Men of Science* (The Physical and Biological Sciences) was published. To be included in the publication, a scientist must be one "whose achievement, by reason of experience and training, is at least equivalent to that associated with the doctorate degree and who continues activity in such work." The entire set of six volumes will, when completed in 1967, contain 130,000 brief biographies of individual scientists. Comparing this with the 98,000 entries in the 10th edition, which was published five years ago, we see that the population of scientists in the United States has increased by 35 per cent in only five years. Presently, one out of every 1,500 persons in the United States is an active scientist.

During the century that followed the birth of the Royal Society and its proceedings, the number of scientific journals increased very slowly. By 1750, the number had reached 10. But shortly thereafter growth began to increase more rapidly. By 1830, there were some 300 periodic, scientific publications.

It soon became evident that no scientist could possibly read, or even scan, all that was being printed. A new invention was needed—and it soon appeared: a journal consisting of abstracts of articles which had appeared in the conventional scientific journals. Since that time, abstract journals have multiplied as rapidly as have the regular journals. The number grew from one in 1830 to 300 in 1950. And now, no scientist can even scan all the journals of abstracts.

Research is becoming increasingly difficult to follow, even for the specialist. Each year, scientific and technical work in the United States alone is described in some 300,000 articles which are published in some 6,000 scientific and technical journals. When we look beyond our national boundaries to the world scientific community, we are confronted by a total of 35,000 journals which publish nearly 2,000,000 articles each year, written by some 750,000 scientists in as many as 50 languages. In the face of such chaotic conditions, an individual scientist cannot hope to keep track of more than an infinitesimal fraction of the flood of data.

With increasing frequency, one hears such questions as: Can we produce meaningful abstracts of abstracts? How short can an abstract be and still give the reader a useful impression of the content of the original article? Can new tools such as the computer be used to help us cope with these problems?

These are important questions, but unfortunately the size of the problem is growing more rapidly than are the efforts aimed at its solution. Clearly, we have reached a crisis in the handling of information.

We can obtain some concept of the ultimate magnitude of the communications problem by attempting to forecast how large the world scientific effort will eventually become. What will the world population of scientists be 50 years from now? How many new facts will they uncover?

Science abroad has been growing as rapidly as in the United States, even in countries that have become industrialized in comparatively recent times. We have seen the Soviet Union emerge as a major scientific and technological power. Since World War II, Japan has moved from being a nation of technical imitators to one of technical innovators. Indicative of this change in 1965 was the awarding of a Nobel prize in physics to Japanese physicist Sin-itiro Tomonaga, for his work in quantum electrodynamics.

In virtually all parts of the world, science and technology are being looked upon as vital to the development of local resources and the improvement of living conditions. To these ends, Brazil has established a National Research Council; The Philippines has set up a National Science Development Board; India has established a Council for Scientific and Industrial Research; Nigeria has formed a Ministry of National Resources and Research. It is clear that science must help feed, clothe, and house the world's burgeoning population.

"'Publish or perish' has become an axiom affecting the destinies of many scientists."

It seems likely that the scientific endeavor will continue to grow as rapidly during the next half century as it has during the past 300 years. As man has moved from the world of nature into the artificial world of industrial-urban civilization, his problems —along with his pleasures—have multiplied. He has become dependent upon the smooth functioning of this new culture for his survival. Yet he is constantly presented with problems of increasing magnitude. As the problems multiply, and solutions become more urgent, our need for scientists and technically trained people will increase.

Yet the proportion of scientists in the population obviously cannot rise forever. There are other important jobs to be done. Only a small percentage of the population is temperamentally and intellectually fit for scientific careers. Nevertheless, studies indicate that the proportion of scientists in the U.S. population might grow eventually from the one scientist per 1,500 persons we find today to something like one scientist per 200 persons.

When we couple these considerations with the likelihood that the population of the United States will about double in the next 50 years, it is quite possible that between now and then, the U.S. population of scientists will increase another tenfold. Little Johnny, born today and destined to be a scientist, would by then be in his scientific prime. He would have some 1,300,000 U.S. scientific colleagues to deal with, and would be confronted, if present trends continue, by some 60,000 U.S. scientific and technical journals containing some 3,000,000 articles annually.

Looking at Johnny's position in the world scientific community 50 years hence, the picture, based on present trends, is an even gloomier one. For during this period, the proportion of scientists in the world population might grow even more rapidly than in the United States.

Fifty years from now Johnny may well have some 8,000,000 scientists with whom he can try to communicate, and there will likely be some 350,000 scientific and technical journals from which to make selections for his own working library. Such fantastic figures serve to emphasize that world science is indeed in the middle of a crisis with respect to the handling of the facts which it generates, and that future procedures for handling scientific information must differ drastically from present ones.

The present procedures for communicating research results have 300 years of tradition behind them and therefore cannot be changed overnight. The scientist, when he finishes a piece of research, takes pride in reporting his results to his colleagues at a scientific meeting. In addition, he feels honor-bound to present his results in the form of a journal article that describes in detail what he did, why he did it, and what his findings were. His standing in the academic community, his ability to obtain funds for his research, and his job opportunities depend in substantial measure upon the quantity and quality of his publications. Unfortunately, the quantity is often considered more important than the quality. "Publish or perish" has become an axiom affecting the destinies of many scientists.

The mechanics of producing a scientific journal are ponderous, and, as a general rule, months—in some cases years—are required for an article which has been submitted to appear in print. A few technical journals, notably *Science* and *Physical Review Letters* in the United States, and *Nature* in England, specialize in rapid publication of brief notes concerning important new research. However, the fraction of ongoing science which eventually appears in such publications is very small.

And in the interest of saving space, some technical journals now edit articles so severely that experimental procedures are given but cursory treatment, and the bulk of space is devoted to abbreviated descriptions of results. It is now predicted that details of experiments, which a scientist must know if he is to attempt to repeat another's experiment, will one day not be published, but instead will be filed in one or more central depositories, perhaps on microfilm or microcards.

Scientific meetings, like journals and societies, are also fragmenting. Most scientists admit that the days of the gigantic

37

"Attempts are being made to utilize ...
modern computers to aid the scientist ..."

generalized scientific conference are numbered. Such meetings have become too large and unwieldy, and the efficiency of communication has decreased. As a result, there has been an increasing tendency for scientists to sponsor national and international meetings on highly specialized topics, thus keeping the meetings fairly small.

The thought of abolishing the existing system of journals and meetings, or even of appreciably modifying it, is extremely distasteful to most scientists. Nevertheless, changes are taking place, some of them subtle, some dramatic.

In fields of science that are particularly active, fellow scientists often exchange "preprints" or copies of manuscripts which have been submitted for publication. Modern inexpensive copying techniques have made it possible for scientists to distribute their findings in this way on a massive scale. Under such circumstances, the ultimate journal article serves the primary purpose of providing a permanent record—and, of course, ensuring some degree of personal security for the author.

These "Invisible Colleges," as such groups have been called, have begun to be organized on a more formal scale. A few years ago, under the sponsorship of the National Institutes of Health, a group was formed which called itself Information Exchange Group No. 1, composed of scientists working in the highly specialized field of "electron transfer and oxidative phosphorylation." The group was formed to improve the exchanges of information in this particular field, which happens to be an active one. It secured the cooperation of every identifiable scientist in the world working in the field. During the first four years of the program, 90 per cent of the important papers published on these and related topics reached the participants three to 12 months before the same papers appeared in the journals.

Attempts are being made to utilize the vast memories and high speeds of modern computers to aid the scientist in locating previously published research. For instance, the National Science Foundation and the American Chemical Society in 1965 initiated a two-year program that will provide

quick access to information on the more than a million chemical compounds now known. The Food and Drug Administration is installing a Central Retrieval Index which will magnetically store three vital index files. The first will provide information on a given product or chemical compound. Using this file, a staff member can ask the computer to print the names of all products which contain a certain compound. A second index will give known biological characteristics of compounds. A third will describe chemical structures.

A working model-size prototype information system has been established at Massachusetts Institute of Technology (M.I.T.) to provide scientists in the Boston-Cambridge, Mass., area with a quick means for searching the literature of 21 physics journals. Remote consoles give rapid access to a time-sharing computer facility which returns information on the source of papers dealing with specific topics and other data, such as the names of authors and their institutional affiliations, citations to the literature, and the location of abstracts. At present, the library of available information exceeds 40,000 articles.

The Institute for Scientific Information in Philadelphia, Pa., has established a commercial scientific information service, the *Science Citation Index*. This computer service provides the titles, authors, and locations of all papers that relate to a particular paper.

Although it is generally recognized that these experiments are useful, and indeed may point the way to a partial solution of the problem, a great deal remains to be done before the situation can accurately be termed "under control."

Unfortunately, there is presently little international coordination of activities aimed at finding solutions to this pressing problem. The United Nations Educational, Scientific, and Cultural Organization (UNESCO) has expressed interest, but is doing very little. The International Council of Scientific Unions is also concerned and has discussed with UNESCO the possibility of establishing a world-wide program of coordinated activities. Thus far, Western Europe's Organization for Economic Cooperation and Development (OECD) has

"... if present trends continue, the current crisis ... will become a catastrophe."

established the most viable of the international programs concerned with scientific information, but its success will probably be restricted by its limited enrollment.

Certainly, if present trends continue, the current crisis in the handling of scientific and technological information will become a catastrophe. Yet, the technical competence for dealing with this problem already exists. Given a concerted international cooperative effort, the situation might be distinctly different 50 years from now. We can imagine that it might be something like this:

Visualize a World Center for Scientific and Technical Information, perhaps composed of a number of subcenters connected by wires and computers. All major laboratories throughout the world would be linked directly to these centers and would be able to obtain answers to complicated questions in a few seconds, or at the most, minutes. Small laboratories would be tied to the large ones and would be able to obtain information almost as quickly.

Technical journals as we now know them may well be important primarily as permanent records of work already reported. Following the completion of an experiment, a scientist would write a description of his experiment together with his results. This preliminary paper would be sent to a central international clearing house, which would examine it to ensure a minimum standard of quality, and then distribute copies to all individuals working in that particular specialized field. The title of the paper, together with other pertinent facts, would be placed on tape and thus would be accessible to researchers in other fields.

The experimental details would be stored in the archives, and thus would be easily and quickly accessible. The results would be submitted to a journal for publication. Once the paper and an abstract were published, the preliminary description would be removed from the tape, and the final paper, together with its abstract, would be introduced into the system instead.

Simultaneously, a group of trained evaluators would abstract data from the published paper for inclusion in special indices giving numerical data, chemical structures, biological effects, and other facts of interest to various specialists.

But enough of wishful daydreaming. Exciting as these prospects are, we are still a considerable distance from solving this tremendous problem. If such a system is actually brought into existence, it will stand out as one of the great experiments in international cooperation. If not, science may well be drowned in a sea of fact. Little did the curious and imaginative men who used to meet in the Bull-Head Tavern in London three hundred years ago realize what they were starting!

Related Articles

For a complete report on the 1965 year in science and in technology, see Section One, JOHN H. GLENN, JR. ON SPACE; Section Two, HOW FAR WILL WE GO IN SPACE?; and the following articles in Section Three:

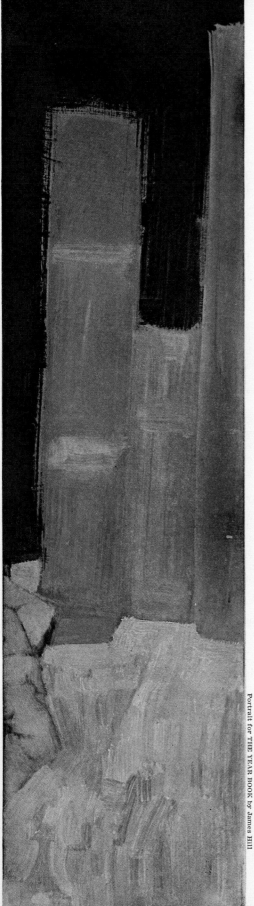

Portrait for THE YEAR BOOK by James Hill

Lawrence A. Cremin
ON EDUCATION

Education Has Truly Become "the First Work of These Times," but Many People Are Disturbed by What Is Happening

"**I**f we are learning anything from our experience," President Lyndon B. Johnson said in the summer of 1964, "we are learning that it is time to go to work, and the first work of these times and the first work of our society is education." True to his words, President Johnson made education the first work of the 89th Congress. And in 10 months, from January to October of 1965, that Congress legislated an educational revolution.

True, certain aspects of the revolution had been set in motion earlier by such legislation as the Civil Rights Act of 1964, which required an end to racial discrimination in all enterprises aided by federal funds. Another factor in the revolution had been the Economic Opportunity Act of 1964, which established a variety of programs, ranging from Project Head Start for preschool children to the Job Corps for youths interested in improving their vocational skills. But the essence of the revolution was embodied in two laws that promised to change American schools and colleges more rapidly and radically than they had changed

41

"... the act ... turns out to be infinitely more than a collection of separate programs."

at any previous time throughout the entire history of the United States.

The first was the Elementary and Secondary Education Act of 1965. Looked at superficially, the various parts of the law appear to be the usual federal-aid-to-education package of the past 50 years. Each section seems to provide special money for some special phase of the school program that is of special interest to some special group lobbying in Washington, D.C.

Thus, there is assistance to school districts with large numbers of poor people (Title I). There is assistance for the purchase of teaching materials (Title II), and support for special supplementary services (Title III), both of which would reach students in private as well as public schools. There is assistance for the development of new teaching techniques and programs (Title IV), and assistance for the strengthening of state departments of education (Title V).

The act promises something to everyone. It attempts to alleviate poverty; it manages to enrich denominational, as well as public, school curricula; and it ends up aiding researchers in the universities, as well as schoolmen on the firing line of education.

When one examines the act closely, however, it turns out to be infinitely more than a collection of separate programs. Indeed, the various provisions, considered in their relationship to one another, really add up to the massive program of federal aid for general educational improvement that citizens and educators have been demanding for a generation.

Consider the sections as follows: Title IV provides money for vastly expanding the program of curriculum research and innovation that has been going on for more than a decade (see THE YEAR BOOK, 1964, pp. 37–41). Titles I, II, and III provide federal funds with which local school districts can bring the fruits of this curriculum research and innovation to their students. The *choice* of programs and materials is, however, left to state and local authorities. (Title I allocates funds on the basis of the number of poor families in a given district, but every state and almost every school district qualify for some aid.)

Title V, recognizing that the coordination and supervision of local education

programs are still state functions under the American system, provides the money with which this coordination and supervision can be dramatically strengthened where the will to do so prevails.

The second of the two laws responsible for the revolution in education was the Higher Education Act of 1965. Here, too, the various titles seem at first glance to provide for nothing more than a random collection of politically attractive programs. But on closer analysis, the programs fit together to form an intriguing whole. Ultimately, the purpose of the act is to hasten the popularization of higher education that has been going forward in the United States since World War II.

To achieve this goal, the act provides in Title IV financial aid for growing numbers of young people to gain access to two-year and four-year colleges. It assists colleges and universities in improving the instruction they offer these young people by providing library materials (Title II), and laboratory and teaching equipment (Title VI), and by encouraging pooling of academic resources (Title III). It also ensures that the colleges and universities will devote part of their resources to an attack on certain pressing social problems in the important realms of housing, transportation, health, and employment (Title I).

This last provision is perhaps the most interesting. It extends to the cities and suburbs the same relationship with the urban colleges that rural areas have enjoyed with the agricultural colleges for more than a century. The scholarship programs and the National Teacher Corps received the widest publicity when the Higher Education Act was debated in October, 1965, but it is the community service programs that may ultimately have the most profound influence.

There is no denying that the attention the agricultural colleges gave to the economic and social problems of rural America in the late 19th and early 20th centuries was crucial in improving the quality of rural life and in making the United States the

"The whole question of who should control the schools came very much to the fore..."

greatest food-producing nation in the world. If urban colleges attack the economic and social problems of present-day American cities with the same vigor, imagination, and resolve, they may become the leading agencies for enriching the urban-industrial civilization of our time.

By definition, living through a revolution is unsettling, and there is no denying that many people—both within and without the ranks of education—were deeply disturbed by these new federal programs. True, both bills passed both houses of Congress by substantial majorities, but that should not obscure the fact that there was vigorous opposition in both instances.

The sharpest debate, of course, came in response to Titles II and III of the Elementary and Secondary Education Act, with their provisions for assistance to students in denominational as well as public schools. Interestingly enough, the National Education Association of the United States, which had long opposed *any* aid to parochial schools, endorsed the programs. The National Catholic Welfare Conference, which had led in earlier opposition to all efforts to confine federal aid to public institutions also gave its endorsement. And support came, too, from the National Council of the Churches of Christ in the United States of America, a leading federation of Protestant churches.

Jewish organizations, however, divided sharply. While Orthodox Jews tended to advocate the programs, Conservative and Reformed Jews vigorously opposed them. They argued that the programs would violate the constitutional requirement of separation of church and state by extending aid to denominational schools. Similarly, the American Civil Liberties Union warned that the participation of religious agencies in supplementary education centers was certain to dilute the principle of public control of publicly supported education.

The concern of these and other organizations did not disappear merely because the bill became law. It is probable that there will be judicial tests of the constitutionality of the act in the near future. Even if it turns out that there is no constitutional dif-

ficulty, there remains the problem of developing effective means of exercising public supervision over the new programs and the agencies that will conduct them.

The whole question of who should control the schools came very much to the fore in 1965. Profound changes were taking place in the structure and leadership of American education. In March, for instance, a group of scholars established a National Academy of Education, which, though independent of government sponsorship, followed the traditions of the National Academy of Sciences and the Royal Society of Great Britain and the French Academy.

The academy was limited to 50 members chosen for the excellence of their published writings on education. Its purpose was to serve as "a forum for conversation, debate, and mutual instruction; a rostrum for the communication of accurate information and informed opinion; a stimulus for fruitful research; and a source of counsel for such public and private agencies as require and request it." As Paul Woodring noted in the *Saturday Review*, however, the unspoken virtue of the new academy was that it provided a model of excellence and leadership in education—the model of the scholar-scientist standing beside the administrator-politician in the formulation of educational policy.

In July, 1965, President Johnson called a White House Conference on Education, under the chairmanship of John Gardner, then president of the Carnegie Corporation of New York. A great deal was written about the conference, ranging from *Time*'s judgment that the participants had explored fresh and significant policy problems, to the *New York Herald Tribune*'s verdict that the whole affair had been little more than a "prayer meeting." The most astute analysis of the significance of the conference came from Fred M. Hechinger of *The New York Times*. "The most striking fact of the White House Conference on Education," he wrote, "was the changing of the guard of educational leadership. The representatives of educational organizations who used to sym-

"'The federal government has neither the wish nor the power to dictate education.'"

bolize the Establishment seemed displaced by men and women who represent themselves and their own ideas."

In October, it was announced that James B. Conant's 1964 proposal for an "Interstate Commission for Planning a Nationwide Educational Policy" had been acted upon. Meeting in Kansas City, Mo., a group of political and educational leaders representing the 50 states resolved to set up an Educational Commission of the States, which would conduct studies, gather information, and make recommendations to its members. Interestingly enough, the chairman of the meeting was Terry Sanford, a former governor of North Carolina and a leading exponent of interstate cooperation in education, who had presided over those sessions of the White House Conference that had explored federal-state relationships.

What became increasingly clear as the year 1965 progressed was that a new educational leadership was coming into power, and that this new leadership was attacking the problems of American education through new political structures and with vastly increased funds. No one could predict what specific solutions would emerge. But change was obviously accelerating, and political conflicts were sharpening.

One serious crisis developed in October, when the then Commissioner Francis Keppel, acting under the Civil Rights Act of 1964, ordered $30,000,000 of federal funds withheld from the schools of Chicago, Ill., after protests that Superintendent Benjamin Willis had failed to act with sufficient vigor against *de facto* racial segregation. The money was released four days later after Mayor Richard J. Daley personally intervened with federal authorities. But the issue itself did not die. Several weeks later, Superintendent Bernard E. Donovan of New York City voiced the fear of many of his fellow superintendents when he asked publicly whether "the schools would be run locally or from Washington."

Commissioner Keppel expressed "sympathy" with the superintendents over some of the administrative problems occasioned by federal programs, but he insisted that the fear of federal control was not well-founded.

President Johnson himself said flatly: "I want to make clear once and for all . . . that the federal government—as long as I am President—intends to be a partner and not a boss in meeting our responsibilities to all the people. The federal government has neither the wish nor the power to dictate education."

It was this concept of federal-state *partnership* that seemed to provide a viable solution to the crisis. Yet no one really believed that a billion dollars could be funneled from Washington into the nation's schools without some measure of federal control. The problem was really one of making that control as responsive as possible to widely differing state and local needs.

One special phase of the conflict about control was the sharp controversy over a "national assessment" of education. This issue burst into the headlines after the White House Conference. Professor John Goodlad of the University of California defined a national assessment for the conference participants as follows: We are accustomed to tests that tell us how well nine-year-old Johnny reads as compared with nine-year-old Billy, or with all other nine-year-olds in the United States. But what we do not have is a quite different series of tests that indicate how a school system in Colorado, for example, measures up in its reading instruction to a school system in Idaho, or how well nine-year-olds in 1965 read as compared with nine-year-olds in 1955. Questions of this type, Goodlad continued, shift the spotlight "from the much-tested individual to the educational effort of 26,000 heterogeneous school districts, 50 states, and the nation as a whole."

Supporters of a national assessment insisted that it would give Americans a way to measure what the schools were accomplishing, and what remained to be done. "How could anyone reasonably object to obtaining additional information on the condition and progress of American education?" asked president John H. Fischer of Columbia's Teachers College.

Opponents replied with expressions of fear that national testing would lead to national conformity and a stifling of local initiative and imagination. "We have more tests than we can use now," charged Harold Taylor, former president of Sarah Lawrence College. "We test for the wrong things. The experience of the Middle East, Far East, and Europe indicates that standardized testing paralyzes thinking. Let us abolish testing and concentrate on teaching."

Arguments over federal aid to the colleges and universities were also very much in the headlines during 1965. In the realm of research, critics were perfectly ready to grant that federally supported university projects since World War II had contributed mightily to American advances in pure and applied science. But they were raising insistent questions about the difficulties that had resulted from this development.

Gerald Piel, publisher of *Scientific American*, charged, in an address to the American Philosophical Society in April, that federal research contracts were dangerously undermining the nation's major universities, turning many professors into "mercenaries of science and scholarship."

Several months later, a congressional subcommittee headed by Representative Henry S. Reuss (D., Wis.) pointed out that 54 universities out of some 2,000 institutions of higher learning receive 60 per cent of the federal funds. Likewise, imbalances occur among the various academic disciplines, with the natural sciences receiving the lion's share of the assistance, and the social sciences and the humanities much less.

Moreover, the subcommittee went on to say, federal research programs had "harmed university education in the sciences by excessively diverting scientific manpower from teaching, and by overemphasizing research to the detriment of teaching." As one scientist commented bitterly in testimony before the subcommittee, "There is no Nobel prize for teaching."

The whole problem of teaching, of course, was at the heart of a good deal of the student unrest that plagued the colleges and universities throughout the year. From Berkeley, Calif., to New Haven, Conn., there were insistent demands that more attention be given to the quality of undergraduate teaching, and that first-rate teachers be rewarded as generously as was the case with first-rate researchers.

Once again, there was no escaping the impact of federal policy. Federal research funds had already drawn some of the best professors from teaching. And now, federal scholarship funds for students promised to aggravate the situation by increasing the pressure of enrollments on facilities that were already sorely taxed. No one was ready to argue that every able American youngster should not have access to a college education. But no one really knew how to make that education truly available without incurring enormous costs on the one hand, or occasioning frightening mechanization on the other.

The problem itself was not new in 1965. What was new was the readiness of college and university authorities to face it seriously and attack it boldly. It was a readiness that had come none too soon for a society truly committed to making education "the first work of these times."

Related Articles

For a complete report on the 1965 year in education, see Section One, RED SMITH ON SPORTS; Section Two, THE NEW NEW ENGLAND; and the following articles in Section Three:

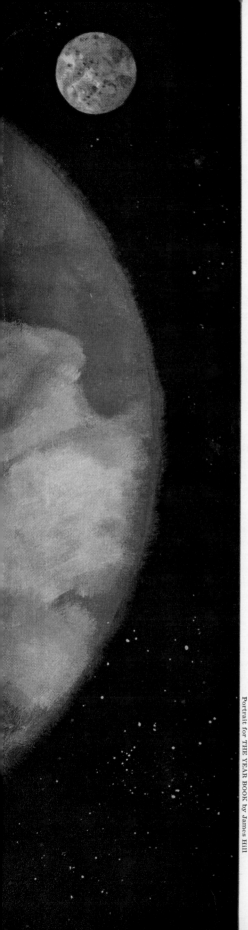

John H. Glenn, Jr.
ON SPACE

*To Ensure the Continued Success of
Our Space Program, We Must Soon Decide
What Our Future Goals Should Be*

A few months ago, my wife, Annie, and I had the opportunity to measure firsthand the effect of the United States' commitment in space exploration upon Western Europeans. At the request of the President of the United States, we visited six European countries. The warmth and magnitude of our reception established beyond any doubt that those peoples are just as deeply interested in space exploration as are Americans and Russians. We saw also that European aerospace scientists are becoming increasingly active. And, perhaps most significantly, we saw a growing —and sometimes almost prayerful—hope that the goals of space science will never be converted into instruments of catastrophic destruction.

Wherever we talked to students, scientists, or political leaders, we encountered the same knowledgeable curiosity that is so evident in America. The people of Europe closely follow our manned flights on radio, television, in the press, and in scientific journals. They are well aware of the contributions to general scientific knowledge made by our

Portrait for THE YEAR BOOK by James Hill

" . . . 1965 was a vigorous and dramatic year in space for the United States."

unmanned flights, such as the highly successful Ranger moon probes and Mariner IV's historic mission to Mars.

We were much impressed, too, by the growing international character of space investigation. In the beginning, space was chiefly the province of the United States and Russia. But France launched a satellite of her own in 1965, and the National Aeronautics and Space Administration (NASA) is cooperating with two European space programs. They are the European Space Research Organization (ESRO) and the European Launch Development Organization (ELDO). In addition, a number of European countries participate in the Free World's global tracking network.

This expansion of space investigation into the historic heartland of Western civilization indicates a certain maturity in man's quest to discover what lies beyond the confines of this planet. It also illustrates that people everywhere are coming to realize that they have a stake in exploring the only limitless physical frontier which mankind has ever attempted to penetrate.

In 20 European cities, audiences expressed to us the unanimous hope that space will not develop into still another frontier for human conflict. In Rome, Pope Paul VI told us that this was a subject of great personal concern to him and a matter to which he addressed his prayers. A leader of one of Europe's largest nations expressed his fear that existing control machinery in this atomic Space Age might not be adequate to ensure peace when many nations acquire the technical capabilities of the United States and Russia.

Both the apprehensions and enthusiasms, as reflected in the mirror of Europe, were indications that 1965 was a vigorous and dramatic year in space for the United States.

After approximately two years of planning, building, and testing, the United States finally set a brisk pace in manned space accomplishment that will be maintained for the next several years. Our Gemini program gave us experience in manned flights of long duration, in maneuvering, in rendezvous techniques, and in extra vehicular activity. It also produced more elaborate scientific experiments than had previously been possible. There was more room than ever before aboard the Gemini vehicles for experiments designed to test the effect of weightlessness on blood cells and the calcium content of human bones. We also had an opportunity to conduct an increasing number of experiments in the environment outside the spacecraft. There was much more time in orbit in which to perform these tests. Nothing so far discovered indicates any serious reasons why man cannot continue to function in space for extended periods as a highly qualified scientific observer, researcher, or experimenter.

New and delicate instrumented satellites and unmanned probes also operated remarkably well in the rigorous environment of space. Researchers are now extending their capabilities and potential contributions to science and society.

The value of the entire U.S. space program becomes increasingly apparent as more and more scientific experiments are carried out. To date, of course, much of the emphasis has been on solving the engineering problems of placing manned and unmanned spacecraft in space. Now that such flights are becoming more regular and more reliable, emphasis is shifting to research and exploration, which is the principal reason for the whole effort. Proof of this is the fact that in 1965 NASA selected its first group of Scientist-Astronauts. The emphasis on scientific research should reassure those who pray that the United States will employ its space capability for peaceful purposes.

The variety of progress in space exploration should be a source of national pride. Recall that in 1965, the United States orbited Tiros IX and X, meteorological satellites placed in a polar orbit that send back pictures of the whole earth; the Orbiting Solar Observatory (OSO II); Pegasus I, a meteoroid detection satellite; and Rangers VIII and IX, the probes which sent back thousands of excellent photographs of the moon. There was also the dazzlingly successful Mars probe of Mariner IV, which relayed to earth the first close-up look at another planet. The manned Gemini series, of course, helped greatly to perfect the skills

"The rate of progress in the space program is still difficult to conceive."

necessary to complete the nation's round trip to the moon via Project Apollo.

Much of the information gleaned from these programs is already being used to practical advantage. The Tiros satellites are an excellent example. Meteorologists around the world are using information obtained from them. Through an automatic picture transmission system, any nation can obtain local cloud-cover pictures, as Tiros IX and X orbit overhead, for an expenditure of only about $30,000 in equipment. The pictures provide forecasters everywhere with an immediate snapshot of the weather pattern affecting their own nation or region, and help them make more accurate short-term predictions regarding weather patterns.

During the five and one-half years since the first Tiros was launched, more than 2,200 storm bulletins have been issued by the weather bureaus of some 50 countries as a result of satellite observations. No one could even begin to estimate how many lives have been saved, or property damage avoided, through the use of this information.

The rate of progress in the space program is still difficult to conceive. Who could possibly have foreseen the benefits that would accrue from the Tiros series when our space program started in 1958? At that time, our first satellite was a small cylinder weighing only 30.8 pounds. Today we have under construction, and are testing, the Saturn V moon rocket which will be capable of placing 240,000 pounds in orbit around the earth. This same rocket has the capacity to place 90,000 pounds—roughly four times the weight of a transcontinental bus—in orbit around the moon. Saturn V is as tall as a 36-story skyscraper. It will launch our first manned lunar expedition.

I well remember the planning we did during Alan Shepard's suborbital Mercury-Redstone flight in 1961 (see THE YEAR BOOK, 1962, page 42). The total flight time of slightly over 15 minutes involved a weightless period of approximately five minutes. Al's activities during his weightless time were precisely blocked out in terms of *seconds* per task—10 seconds for certain control movements, 15 seconds for certain instrument observations. In 1965, by contrast, during the

eight-day mission of Gordo Cooper and Pete Conrad, there were some difficulties with an electrical system requiring that certain checks be made. By then it seemed quite natural to hear Chris Kraft in Mission Control at Houston, Tex. discuss the mission planning like this: "Well, I think we will run that check on Tuesday. If we don't get it in then, we'll try again on Friday." Instead of working with options in terms of seconds, we are now working in terms of days.

The international aspects of the space program have increased enormously since they were first spelled out in the Space Act of 1958. During that time, NASA has participated in the launching of 14 scientific satellites for various countries capable of building their own scientific payloads but not yet capable of putting them into space. All told, we have agreements with 59 countries. We have encouraged other countries to build payloads in this cooperative launch program because such work complements our own knowledge of space.

International cooperation in space has been extended into the field of education. To date, some 140 international research associates have visited NASA centers. One hundred and thirteen international graduate fellows have studied in U.S. universities. Two hundred and twenty-five foreign technical trainees have attended NASA centers. In addition to formal exchanges, NASA and its centers are hosts to numerous foreign visitors. By late 1965, there had been over 12,500 such visitors to the United States.

Cooperation with the Russians continues to be a question about which people are curious. An agreement was reached with the Soviet Union for extensive cooperative effort in 1962. Thus far, however, only three comparatively minor results have been achieved: (1) a one-way communications demonstration using our Echo II satellite; (2) exchanges of magnetic field data in anticipation of an agreed exchange of satellite data; and, (3) an exchange of conventional weather data over a special communications channel set up between Washington and Moscow on a shared-cost basis.

The increasing international interest in space that my wife and I witnessed in

"Our dilemma results partly from the splendid
. . . talent . . . which we now possess."

Europe has been reflected in the United Nations (UN). A declaration of legal principles aimed at guiding space activity was unanimously adopted in the General Assembly. In the International Telecommunications Union, a United Nations agency, agreements were reached on the assignment of radio frequencies for space research and communications.

In another United Nations agency, the World Meteorological Organization, a start was made in the evaluation and planning of requirements for a world weather system (including satellite systems) which promises important benefits.

It is clear that the United States effort in space research and exploration has helped to further international cooperation. The Russian program, however, has remained almost totally secret. Thus, when we attempt to assess Soviet intentions in space, we are forced to assume the worst. Doubtless this is why in 1965 the Department of Defense decided that the Air Force should conduct programs to ensure that the United States does not lag in developing military uses of space.

Experiments in the Manned Orbiting Laboratory (MOL) program remain classified, but there are obvious military advantages to be gained by just the manned surveillance of earth and near-earth space and in communications. MOL is just what its name implies; a laboratory from which experiments can be conducted that will better define future military space needs. It is regrettable that such a step has become necessary, but the United States has had little choice. Not many people realize that astronauts have never orbited over Russia, while the higher latitude and launch inclinations of Soviet manned satellites have permitted their cosmonauts to orbit repeatedly over all 50 of our states.

The problem of how we can best utilize new information obtained from the space program has received considerable attention. In the past, we had the luxury of a generation to assimilate information obtained from scientific breakthroughs and plow it back into the proper educational and industrial channels. But with the current surge of technical data cascading upon us, proper utilization of space research has become increasingly difficult.

To help solve this problem, several systems for utilizing new information have been set up by NASA and are being run on a trial basis at a number of universities. One in particular, at Indiana University, catalogs, cross references, and computerizes such information and makes it immediately available to interested parties in education, business, and industry. This is merely a forerunner of the future, for we have just begun to comprehend the importance of rapid organization and dissemination of new knowledge. Much more must be done.

The long-range future of our space program is important to all of us, but it is difficult to predict what direction it will take. We are still at the beginning of our major explorations, and their basic purpose is to probe the unknown. We must soon decide, however, what direction our space effort should take—beyond existing programs—in the years immediately ahead. The more people who participate in important national decisions, such as how far we should go in space, the better these decisions will be. Abraham Lincoln once said: "If we could first know where we are, and whither we are trending, we could better judge what to do and how to do it."

Our dilemma results partly from the splendid resources in talent, laboratories, and other facilities which we now possess. We have a large technical organization with demonstrated capability. Yet its future, once the Apollo program is completed, is not clearly defined. We face another difficulty that is rarely brought home to the public. In a world of accelerating technology, the talent of some of our best designers and innovators is not fully utilized after their brainchildren enter the long phase of manufacturing, testing, and baptism in space. This is now partly true of some of the key men who were conceptual planners in the Gemini and Apollo programs. Hence, a fundamental decision facing the nation is how soon and to what purposes we should commit this valuable and experienced man-

50

"Who is to say that man's destiny is entirely confined to the surface of this planet?"

power resource that we have now developed.

We could list pages of possible future space activities. They might include space stations of various sizes and differing functions to explore near-earth space, or manned missions to Mars or Venus. Many studies—some completed, some in process of completion—have been undertaken to show where we can most productively direct our efforts, and where such efforts might take us. The difficulty lies in the long lead time necessary to conduct major projects effectively, and no one can state in advance precisely what additional questions will be raised by programs now underway. One of the characteristics of any good scientific experiment is that it raises as many questions as it answers.

Hence, planning for future activities is exceedingly complex, and when we plan, we are talking about committing a good portion of our national technical capability to a particular program. The effect of any such commitment on the business community must certainly be considered, for almost 94 per cent of the present space budget is spent with private industry.

We need full public discussion and eventual concurrence on our major space goals of the future. The problem is that these areas are highly technical. It is difficult for everyone to understand, or to fully appreciate, their importance. My personal hope is that the awareness and interest of the public will be maintained, so that the new,

long-term decisions which we must reach will arise from a consensus of Americans.

In many respects, America faced a situation in 1965 comparable to our commitment to Project Apollo in 1961. Our situation may not be too unlike that which faced us, when, as an embryo nation, we wrestled with the difficult concepts and problems in exploring our western frontier. At that time, even so wise and dedicated a man as Daniel Webster expressed serious reservations about the exploration and development of the land beyond the Mississippi.

"What do we want with this vast worthless area?" Webster asked, "this region of savages and wild beasts, of shifting sands and whirlpools of dust, of cactus and prairie dogs? Of what use could we ever hope to put these great deserts or those great mountain ranges, impenetrable and covered to their base with eternal snow? Mr. President, I will never vote one cent from the public treasury to place the Pacific Coast one inch nearer Boston than it now is."

At a time when the entire earth is faced with a decrease in natural resources and an inexorable increase in population, we are not able to afford Daniel Webster's somewhat myopic view of the future. We have sent our scouts out. Who is to say that man's destiny is entirely confined to the surface of this planet?

Related Articles

For a complete report on the 1965 year in space see also Section Two, How Far Can We Go in Space? See also Section One, Harrison S. Brown on Science, and the following articles in Section Three:

Portrait for THE YEAR BOOK by James Hill

Alistair Cooke
ON THE ARTS

People Were Learning That an Artist
Needs a Patron, and the Lady in the
White House Seemed a Genuine One

We never fail in this annual chronicle to remind the reader that in any of the arts it is just about impossible to chart progress, change, or innovation by the calendar. Bright boys will recall that New York City was shaken to its backbone by the Armory Show of 1913, and they will rightly argue that American painting has never been the same since.

But the now legendary importance of the year 1913 was not what it did to the painter, but what it did to the public. The Armory Show brought together in America for the first time the whole kit and caboodle of European moderns and American experimentalists. Most of the artists were, you might say, painters' painters; but they had made their mark in the art world years—even decades—before 1913. They were content, as most pioneers in the arts have to be, to be respected by their fellows at the bench and derided by the public at large.

Never did the public have such an opportunity for derision as at the Armory Show. One huge Bronx cheer, and a chorus of genteel echoes rose from Coney Island to River-

53

dale. The publicity that ensued rumbled through the newspapers and magazines of Philadelphia, Chicago, and San Francisco. But the mockers had the uneasy feeling, which jeering mobs often do, that they were on the defensive against something vital. Today it is almost too obvious to point out that Matisse, Rousseau, and Picasso, and William Glackens, John Marin, and Albert Ryder did have something new to say, something more durable than the roar of ridicule that met them in the New World.

Events as shattering and as neatly dated as the Armory Show happen very rarely in the arts. But that one is a useful reminder of the perils of dismissing as trash what most people instinctively *feel* is trash. Unhappily, this high-minded critical principle ("Be sure to take a long time to decide that new work is no good") is one on which quacks and charlatans flourish. Because someone told them that the first performance of Igor Stravinsky's *The Rite of Spring* caused riots in the streets of Paris, all atonalists think that if their own novelties are hooted, that fact makes them Stravinsky. Because the abstractionists (who began their first tentative daubs way back in that Armory Show) produced Jackson Pollock and Willem de Kooning, a thousand hackers come to believe that to learn to draw would be an encumbrance to the free-flowing motion of their immortal souls, and that the great thing is to drop gouts of paint on a canvas from a great height.

Despite our frequent warnings about the sin of denouncing new work just because it is new—and difficult—I am going to take the risk of saying that 1965 saw the positive, and to some of us very welcome, exhaustion of several fashions that have for too long been masquerading as historic advances in the art of painting. Almost everything that can be said in abstract painting seems to have been said, at least for the time being. I throw in the cautionary phrase, "at least for the time being," only because I remember, for instance, that the symphony as a form of musical expression was thought to be dead after Beethoven; but great symphonies have been written in our time by Jan Sibelius, Gustav Mahler, and others.

While we still go on hearing much about Pop art and Op art, I think both of them have passed their dizzy peak in the auction rooms where rich people risk coronaries in order to be chic. There is in New York a man who owns a collection of Pop art (corpses made of clay greet you at the door, and there is a canvas dominating the living room that you would swear was an actual monster *photograph* of a can of Heinz vegetable-beef soup) which was appraised in 1962 for just under $500,000. Today it is worth, if anything, a few thousand dollars. The reader would be wise to take heed of this example. Americans have a deep tendency to believe that what is *in* is good, and what is good is *very* expensive.

The whole field of painting in the United States is so confused by stock exchange values, and by the highly ingenious search for what might start a fashion, that it is almost impossible to write a sober survey of what has been creatively important in any given year. Let us just summarize: there is a disenchantment with abstract painting. There is a return, reported by the art schools, to the elements of drawing, especially of the marvelous, liquid complexity of the human figure. This is very cheerful news. For what has been so depressing about the myriad abstractionists of the last few years has been their shocking incompetence as painters—quite aside from the trickier question: Is It Art?

Last year, we dealt with the revolt against the pretense that the Pop and Op movements should be considered as Art. The mortality rate of Op art seems to be guaranteed by the fatal fact that the *initial* shock, or pleasure, is all there is to it: tomorrow it is amusing; the next day, it induces vertigo; the day after that, it is a bore.

The revived school of Mondrian has passed painlessly into cute, daytime dresses, which de-sex their owner by redefining a female body as an easel for the casual distribution of rectangles. A more amusing and harmless revival has been that of *Art Nouveau*, not as easel painting, but as a popular style of commercial art. Full-page advertisements for underwear and perfume appeared in the slick magazines and in the New York Sunday papers of 1965 that could have come straight from *The New York*

Times of 50 or 60 years ago. "Straight" is perhaps inaccurate. Like most revivals, this one was studied; it was more artful and self-conscious than the original. The commercial art schools have developed an odd mania for training whole classes in the decorative style of the turn of the century. The most interesting point about this trend is what started it: Cecil Beaton's set and costume designs for the movie, *My Fair Lady*.

In other days, the popular styles in the arts were encouraged by a rich patron, or enforced by a dictator. Today, a single movie can start the revival of a style that was killed off forever, we thought, by World War I. It would never have been thought of again—nor probably would the Burne-Joneses and the Dante Gabriel Rossettis have begun to fetch high prices again—if the Messrs. Loewe and Lerner had not sat down one day and decided to make a musical of George Bernard Shaw's *Pygmalion*.

Shaw himself, by the way, is said to be in a headlong decline as a well-read writer. For the time being, his ghost must comfort itself with the thought that he is guaranteed a little vicarious immortality through the loving efforts of Jack Warner and Cecil Beaton to celebrate the Edwardian costumes, the Lalique glass, the William Morris wallpapers, the "toned" oak, and the shoulder-high wainscoting of the rooms in which he lived.

A mere return to the traditions of another age is, of course, a useless method of revitalizing any art. But I have a feeling, from the work of some of the new realists, that the time is coming when rebellion for its own sake will be *passé*. I am hopeful that the best of the far-out boys will soon begin to look around the world they live in, rediscover its visual fascination in honestly new terms, and simply forget about shocking the bourgeoisie. This has been the maniacal obsession of everybody from the San Francisco Ginsbergniks and the makers of "underground" movies to the four-letter night club comics and the practitioners on the Cage piano.

In the theater, once again the end-of-year cry was: "The worst season in memory." What this means is that, in the first half of the season anyway, there was the familiar absence of either serious plays or sure-fire hits, on *Broadway*. I stress Broadway because the lamentation has no meaning once you leave what used to be called the "hardened artery" of the commercial theater.

We moaned for years about the lack of any decent alternative to the overpriced show window of Broadway, and by now we have come to take for granted the scores of little theaters in old schoolrooms, bars, stables, basement flats, and abandoned warehouses. In the last week of December, 1965, before the off-Broadway season had really got going, the hungry culture-vulture could stay a mile away from Broadway and yet see plays by Webster, Wycherley, and Robinson Jeffers. He could view a new and superior version by Arthur Miller of his "View from the Bridge"; a repertory of Gilbert and Sullivan; and readings from Shaw and Robert Frost. He could see two needling satires on racial prejudice by an unknown Negro playwright, Douglas Turner Ward; a fine first play about Brooklyn in the 1890s, by one William Alfred; and promising work by newcomers Arkady Leokum and James Broom Lynne. It would be a remarkable Broadway season which offered more. And the off-Broadway season was, at this writing, barely half over.

These comments, of course, merely reflect the theatrical situation in New York. I do not believe that elsewhere there are sufficiently powerful forces at work to enhance the theatrical situation greatly, except in one or two cities such as Minneapolis, where the Minnesota Theater Company performs to packed houses at the Tyrone Guthrie Theater, or in university towns where determined talents can maintain, for a while at least, the pretense that good theater, and/or repertory cinema is a civic necessity.

Most cities these days are oppressed by swelling populations. The cost to the theater resulting from this fact is reflected in the prohibitive prices of real estate. Added to this are the high cost of labor, and the exacting conditions labor is able to demand. Together, these factors make it ruinous for any producer, whether an old-fashioned banker or a new-style Cultural Center, to undertake the staging of work whose only prospective claim on the public's glands is

"... 'in-flight entertainment' has the possibilities of an airborne Cooper Union..."

that it is classic, or serious, or perhaps even possesses qualities of imagination.

The producer dare not be such an impractical idealist. He must promise something that is pretty certain to pay its way, even if it does not make a million dollars. Like the television producer who may yearn to do good work, he is an artist who must also be a successful merchant. In brutal truth, these two requirements do not necessarily have anything in common.

Let us sorrowfully admit that Broadway —which means also the commercial theater in Boston, Chicago, Philadelphia, and San Francisco—is beyond the scope of the ordinary playwright. To be staked to an appearance there, his work, like that of Alan Jay Lerner or Richard Rodgers, must promise some of the properties of a gold mine. Shakespeare would have failed to qualify; as would Ibsen, Chekov, Strindberg, Webster, Congreve, Wycherley, and Sheridan, to name but a few. That is, perhaps, why we must see their work where it belongs; off-Broadway.

The movies in 1965 did not, so far as I could see, produce any startling new talents, outside the well-known Italians, French, and British of the New Wave. If there was a characteristic of 1965, it was the moviemakers' discovery of homosexuality, loneliness, and the world of dreams. The resources of these three interesting fields are, if the 1965 film crop is anything to go on, disappointingly limited.

In 1965, the box office also discovered James Bond, and Sean Connery thereby became, in a single bound, the Number One motion picture favorite of the world. This eminence was not difficult to credit if you had the opportunity, as I did, to watch the long lines of people standing—waiting to see "Goldfinger"—in the sun in Beirut and New Delhi, in the mist in San Francisco and Istanbul, and in Tokyo and London.

The happiest trend that I could discover in 1965 was that which found all sorts of moguls, from the President of the United States to airline executives, learning for the first time that an artist needs a patron.

One of the most promising outlets for music, movies, lectures, and discussions of public affairs was the one bearing the hilarious name of "in-flight entertainment." This trend began with the projection of movies in airplanes on a single central screen—as in the old earthbound Sunday evening Methodist lantern lectures—then progressed to separate screens mounted up near the hatracks. Thereafter, the airlines installed receiving sets for almost as many channels of music and chatter as there are languages available at the elbow of listeners to debates in the United Nations.

Clearly, "in-flight entertainment" has the possibilities of an airborne Cooper Union for the culturally deprived. Clearly, it is a cultural bonanza for the harried, hurrying and successful businessman who is so busy crisscrossing the country to secure the good contract that he often has little time for the good life. The airlines now seek to repair this fault, and since they have a captive, not to say helpless, audience, their opportunities for enlightenment are many.

I myself, who am as harried and deprived as the man next to me in the window seat, have, in six transcontinental flights, seen two bad movies and a good one, heard a knowing lecture on the history of jazz piano and another on the oboe. I have listened to the piano concertos of Mozart and enjoyed the nine symphonies of Beethoven over a stereo system that gave one the illusion of having died and gone to paradise.

The passage by Congress in September of legislation providing for a National Foundation for the Arts and Humanities is an excellent gesture. The act will provide funds to create national opera and ballet companies and a national film institute. It provides for the commissioning of new works of music by American composers and the support of local symphony orchestras. But whether it will become a movement and then a force in the arts is a question yet unanswered. The type of *entrepreneur* that seems to have gained access to the ear of the White House in the last two administrations does not suggest that President Lyndon B. Johnson, any more than President John F. Kennedy, is going to burgeon

"... we saw a program ... that I am afraid ... escaped ... most of the ratings."

into Lorenzo de Medici, or even George IV. And there is no doubt that a patron by any other name is essential to any great public achievement in the arts. This is true whether the matter at hand is a series of concerts, a commission for a set of murals, the creation of a new town, or the preservation of an old street.

These things never get done by accident, or by petition on the part of a few aesthetic and public-minded men. It is not the mayor of New York City who plants trees on Park Avenue; it is the money of Mrs. Albert J. Lasker. Neither the city fathers nor the tenants of the old stretch of Park Avenue from 59th Street to Grand Central Station knew nor cared that they had there an incomparable example of American Romanesque, and a piece of Americana of unrepeatable character. The street was consequently violated and demolished by astute realtors, who wasted no time in creating a garish memorial to the steel-and-glass curtain, fluorescent picture-window school of modern architecture.

At the end of 1965, we saw a program on television done with such charming diffidence that I am afraid it escaped many of the critics and most of the ratings. It was directed with great skill and tact by the Canadian Harry Rasky. Its star was Mrs. Lyndon B. Johnson, touring Washington, D.C., and indicating, in many a quiet plea,

the good sense of caring for places and things that, uncared-for, are replaced by junk. It stirred us with the reminder that we have in the White House a genuine patron of the arts; a tireless and democratic variation of the grand tradition of the indulgent monarch.

This was demonstrated by the passage of the beautiful bill with the dreadful name —the Highway Beautification act. The final bill, it is true, was a hypocritical parody of the original. Instead of having all their federal funds withdrawn if they permit billboards within the prescribed limits, delinquent states will now receive the wrist-slap of a 10 per cent reduction in their federal bounty. Nonetheless, without the pressure of Mrs. Johnson, we should have had no bill at all.

Moreover, since the passage of the bill, she has gone around the country, sometimes scolding, more often pleading, giving heart to the garden clubs, and the city-proud, and the hand-wringing architects, and the tree-loving citizens. She has even cajoled politicians ready to lie down and be buried by the billboard lobby, one of the most ruthless and greedy groups in the history of the breed.

Such is the very human clay of our President that if Mrs. Johnson wants a beautiful America hard enough, by golly he may just insist that she get it!

Related Articles

For a complete report on the 1965 year in the arts, see the following articles in Section Three:

Red Smith

ON SPORTS

*The Yankees Crumbled, Boxing Was Sick,
And Some People Wondered About the
Role of Athletics in Education*

On the calendar of history, A.D. 476 is circled to mark the fall of the Roman Empire. It was 1931 when Great Britain realized its sun was setting, and the British Empire became the British Commonwealth of Nations. Now 1965 has become a date forever memorable. It was the year the Yankee Empire crumbled.

Emperor Augustus "found Rome brick and left it marble." The British Empire reached its fullest flower while Dizzy Disraeli held Victoria's hand. The architect of baseball's mightiest kingdom was Babe Ruth, a fat man with a big stick.

After Ruth's arrival in New York, the Yankees won 29 pennants and 20 world championships. They opened their 1965 campaign with a record of having ruled the American League for 15 of the last 18 summers. Yet in their first full season under the ownership of the Columbia Broadcasting System, they ended with the team in the second division, a slum area they had carefully avoided for 40 years. Even worse, in the estimation of their proprietors, was the fact that their Nielsen rating plummeted.

59

"Was Koufax the greatest pitcher of all time? The answer is maybe."

The Yankee leaders blamed the debacle on injuries to key players like Mickey Mantle and Roger Maris. But the leaders were deluding themselves in the autumn as they had in the spring.

In a cliff-hanging finish in 1964, the Yankees had won the pennant by a single game. When they lost the World Series to the St. Louis Cardinals, they hired the St. Louis manager, Johnny Keane, to do unto their 1965 opposition as he had done unto them. But despite their 1964 ordeals, not a single, regular position on the team was open to newcomers when spring training started. This was not because every position was manned by a perfect ballplayer. It was because the Yankee management could not find one man in the whole minor league organization it considered good enough to make the team.

This had rarely, if ever, been true in the Yankee administration of general managers Ed Barrow and George Weiss. But Ed Barrow was dead, and Weiss was eased out in 1960. Weiss' last team, a pennant winner, won four more championships after he departed. In 1965, the machine he had constructed was wearing out.

Not everybody regarded the Yankees' collapse as a catastrophe. Finishing his first season as manager of the Houston Astros, a team in its accustomed position near the bottom of the National League, Luman Harris compared the performance of his nine with that of the Bronx demigods and was not displeased.

"When I took this job," he said, "I asked Paul Richards (general manager) and Roy Hofheinz (president), 'What do you want me to do?' They said, 'Build us a team like the Yankees.' So now I got a team like the Yankees, and I want a raise." Instead of more money, Luman got fired, and Richards did, too.

As the Yankees sank, the Minnesota Twins soared. This was a muscular team transplanted to the northern prairies from Washington, D.C. It was managed by Sabath Anthony Mele, who grew up as a pretty good street fighter in Astoria, Long Island.

When his authority was challenged by Zoilo Versalles during spring training, Sam Mele stopped trying to win a popularity award in his dugout and slapped a fine on the shortstop. Versalles later became the most valuable player in the league, and the Twins won the pennant.

Then their troubles started. When they met the Los Angeles Dodgers in the World Series, they encountered a left-handed pitcher named Sandy Koufax. The Twins beat Koufax once, but Koufax beat them twice. After Koufax and the Dodgers won the seventh and deciding game, only two questions remained unanswered:

When would Mele's fifth child be born? (It had been expected hourly since the start of the Series, and eventually arrived a day or so afterward.)

Was Koufax the greatest pitcher of all time? The answer is maybe. Certainly he is the best of his time.

Boxing in 1965 created more commotion than either baseball or professional football, and the publicity was not especially savory. When the year opened, the man recognized by the public as heavyweight champion of the world was a brash composer of dreadful couplets, christened Cassius Clay. In 1964, Sonny Liston, then proprietor of the title, had surrendered the championship to Clay. The new titleholder subsequently espoused the Muslim religion and changed his name to Muhammad Ali.

Because the Liston-Clay contract included a provision which, in effect, promised Liston a return bout, the World Boxing Association (WBA) unfrocked Clay as champion. The WBA is an amorphous amalgam of state athletic commissions which disapproves of return-bout contracts. The boxing public does not exactly disapprove of the WBA. It laughs at it. Thus the public laughed when the WBA declared that the real champion was a tall, inoffensive guitar player named Ernie Terrell.

Nobody had been pleased with the conclusion of the first Clay-Liston match. When a rematch was arranged for Boston, the district attorney was so displeased that he chased the fight out of town. It was held in May, in a high school hockey rink in Lewiston, Me. As the indelicate expression goes, "It smelled on ice."

This time Liston took a punch in the first round, fell down, stared thoughtfully at the timekeeper until the count had passed 10, and then got up. In spite of considerable confusion, he was declared knocked out, and Clay remained the champion.

Witnesses cried "Fake!" while politicians howled for laws to ban boxing. No such laws were passed, except for a milk-toast proscription in Connecticut, but a bill to create a federal boxing commission was widely supported. The bill may be enacted into law, but it won't cure boxing's ills. It does not create a federal authority to supersede the inept state commissions. It only sets up a national agency to duplicate and compound the maladministration which already exists in the various states.

Clay made his second defense of the title in November. His opponent this time was Floyd Patterson, who had won the championship in 1956, lost it in 1959, won it back in 1960, and lost it again in 1962. Even for Las Vegas, Nev., where remarkable things happen, the Clay-Patterson fight was a sorry travesty. The referee stopped it in the 12th round. Floyd Patterson had been defenseless since the sixth, but Clay's punches had not rendered him helpless. His trouble was a chronic ailment of the lumbar region of the back, which he had kept secret for 10 years. He had also kept the condition secret from the Nevada boxing authorities, their medical examiner, and the fans who had paid from $6, to watch on closed-circuit television, to $100 for a ringside seat.

Patterson did not do the fans a favor, but he was brave. His back popped out of plumb in the fourth round; he fell down in the sixth, then got up and was still on his feet when the referee couldn't take any more.

Clay, as ever, proclaimed himself the greatest fighter in human history. The record neither supported nor contradicted him. He had boxed three times on the championship level. Once his opponent quit in the corner; once his opponent quit in the ring; and once his opponent was a cripple.

These were the matters the sports public talked about in 1965. Fans talked also about a pain in the neck of Gary Player, a South African health faddist who was golfer of the year; about attractive Arthur Ashe, the first male American Negro to attain international prominence in tennis, and about Milwaukee's courtroom battle to keep its baseball team from moving to Atlanta.

When the major leagues, suddenly and without warning, selected a man named William Eckert, retired lieutenant general of the air force, to succeed retiring baseball commissioner Ford Frick, fans asked: "Who he? The Unknown Soldier?"

There was, however, precious little concern about a problem that bothered a few people and had been bothering some people for years. This was, and is, the question of the proper place of competitive athletics in the educational system.

As far back as 1929, an investigative body known as the Carnegie Foundation reported that the traditional ideal of "a sound mind in a sound body" had got out of joint. Many colleges seemed less interested in sound minds than in bodies that could block hard, tackle sharply, win football games, attract gate receipts, and help pay off a debt on the stadium.

The Carnegie Report made headlines, but had little visible effect in educational circles. On the contrary, colleges polished up on their techniques of recruiting athletes. Twenty-four years after the Carnegie Report, when Jimmy Brown finished high school in Manhasset, Long Island, at least 45 centers of learning competed for the privilege of preparing him to play fullback for the Cleveland Browns.

In 1952, a special committee on athletic policy reported to the American Council on Education that "serious violations not only of sound educational policies but also of good moral conduct are not uncommon." Boiled down, the committee's recommendations were: treat athletes as people, accepting no students who do not qualify for college; pay athletes nothing under the table that other students cannot get over the table; limit each sport to its proper season, with no bowl games or other post-season events.

What happened? Well, two years after the committee deplored "institutional hypocrisy," Michigan State played in the Rose Bowl. Two years after that, Michigan State was back again in Pasadena. And on Jan. 1, 1966, 14 years after the committee called for the elimination of bowl games, Michigan State's unbeaten, untied champions of the Big Ten played in the Rose Bowl for a third time, fighting for culture and the glory of the Pasadena Chamber of Commerce.

Michigan State is singled out here because the chairman of the committee that urged a firm ban on post-season football was John A. Hannah, then and now president of Michigan State. And it was Dr. Hannah's committee that said the responsibility for a sane athletic policy rested with the college president. Maybe it doesn't, though. Maybe it rests somewhere in the state house.

The American Council on Education is not a police force. Its committee recommended that the National Collegiate Athletic Association (NCAA) act as the agency to enforce compliance with the rules. This brought the following response from H. C. Willett, then president of the NCAA:

"The recently adopted athletic policy of the American Council on Education offers little that has not already been the accepted policy of the NCAA."

Since then, the NCAA has been notably active in two fields: First, in the programming and sale of college football to commercial television sponsors; and second, in the sanctioning of bowl games. These have included such cultural exercises as the Sun Bowl, the Gator Bowl, the Tobacco Bowl, the Senior Bowl, the Blue-Gray game, the Gotham Bowl, and the Liberty Bowl. The NCAA has not objected to independent promoters matching undergraduates in athletic contests for personal profit, provided the colleges get most of the swag.

In short, much lip service has been paid to the notion that "competitive athletics are an integral part of any well-rounded educational system," and mighty little has been done about the "institutional hypocrisy" that makes victory on the field an end in itself. Indeed, with the soaring prosperity of professional football, more boys than ever are entering college, not for education, but to attract offers from the Chicago Bears. More than ever before, college stadia are becoming farms for the pro teams. And if educators are disturbed about this, they seldom show it.

Somewhere near the middle stands the college coach. Generally speaking, he is truly enthusiastic about athletics and sincerely interested in young men. He is genuinely gratified when the quarterback earns a degree and goes on to a useful life. But at the same time, he makes a living from amateur sport. He knows that if his teams do not win, his children will eat sparingly.

Hence, he subscribes to practices he secretly deems repugnant. These include the "letter of intent," which is in effect a contract binding a high school graduate to the college that recruits him first. There is the athletic scholarship "subject to review," which means that if a boy doesn't make the team, financial aid can be cut off after any year. Another practice is "red-shirting," or holding an athlete out of competition one season and delaying his progress toward a degree to keep him eligible in his fifth undergraduate year.

Almost inevitably, coaching creates cynics. 'Joe," a famous coach at one great university, was asked by a friend, "Do you have much trouble getting good boys past the dean of admissions?"

Joe scratched his head, frowned, and hesitated. "Well," he said at last, "not if they can run real fast."

Related Articles

For a complete report on the 1965 year in sports, see the following articles in Section Three:

CONTENTS OF SECTION TWO

YEAR BOOK SPECIAL REPORTS

A YEAR BOOK SPECIAL REPORT

LEAVES FROM OUR LIVES

BY ROSE F. KENNEDY

A framed copy of the inaugural address of the 35th President of the United States hangs above a mantel in the home of Mr. and Mrs. Joseph P. Kennedy. The document, bearing a small oval portrait of its author, is signed simply, "To Mother and Dad, from John F. Kennedy." This address, which rings with language fully appropriate to these days, contains this challenge to all Americans: "Ask not what your country can do for you; ask what you can do for your country."

In this article, the mother of John F. Kennedy recounts how she and her husband sought to instill in their children a respect for, and a striving toward, excellence. And she suggests a course to all who would respond to the late President's challenge.

The English writer, Evelyn Waugh, has said one should begin one's memoirs when one is no longer much interested in the future. I do not quite agree. Perhaps, at 75, one should not be too concerned about the future. Yet, I find myself vitally interested in it. I am concerned about what lies ahead for our nation and what our young people are going to do with their lives to serve God, their neighbor, and their country more effectively in the years to come.

I have long been interested in these matters, and hope that the Kennedy family has helped to influence public service for the better; both on the higher levels, where comparatively few serve, and on those rungs beneath, where many thousands serve. The work of these people, as my son Jack, the late President, said, is collectively as necessary as that of the President himself.

It is quieter in my home in Palm Beach, Fla., and at Hyannis Port, Mass., too, than it used to be when the children filled the air with their laughter, their games of charades, their tennis and golf matches, and their debates. It is quieter, of course, than it was later on, when Jack was in residence with his family; not solely as my son, but also as the nation's 35th President. This is a good time for me, I believe, to reminisce—to do so with a great deal of joy, tinged with a little sadness.

The life of politics and government service came naturally to me and my children, who, it might be said, heard political lullabies as babies. Politics was in the very air they breathed. It was served to them at mealtime, so to speak. Nothing could have been more natural for our family. The children's father was United States ambassador to Great Britain from 1937 to 1940, when they were between the ages of six and 23. Their grandfather Kennedy had been an important ward leader in Boston, and had served in both houses of the state legislature. Grandfather Fitzgerald had been in the Congress from 1894 to 1900, and

The opening illustration depicts Rose Kennedy with her grandchildren at her Hyannis Port home. At right, the late President is seated beneath a shadowy portrait of his grandfather, John F. Fitzgerald, and photographs of Boston's old city hall and the White House.

Illustrations by Paul Davis

later had had the opportunity to serve three terms as Boston's mayor.

When Jack was elected to Congress in 1946—his first political office—he represented the same district my father had 50 years earlier, Boston's old 11th Congressional District. It is also an interesting coincidence that the most important action my father performed on the national level was his key role in persuading President Grover Cleveland to veto a highly restrictive immigration bill. One of Jack's last projects was the preparation of his book, *A Nation of Immigrants*. The subject was of great importance both to my father and to my son.

One of my earliest memories has politics for a background. When I was five, my father (Bostonians called him "Honey Fitz" or "Johnny Fitz") took my younger sister Agnes and me to Washington. He introduced us to President William McKinley, who gave us carnations and said that Agnes was the prettiest girl that he had ever seen in the White House. Years later, when I told Jack this story, he asked: "Why didn't he say it to you, Mother?" I had to admit my sister Agnes was the beauty of the family.

I was the first child born to John F. and Mary Fitzgerald. My father was one of nine boys. Perhaps because he had always been surrounded by brothers, he was delighted when I came into the world. He talked to me incessantly, all the time I was growing up. He told me a lot about the history of the Irish people, about their trials and their persecutions. He talked particularly about Boston and the Port of Boston and how it was nearer to Europe than New York and, therefore, he hoped, would have a greater future than New York. He took me to South America, and later tried to encourage the teaching of Spanish in the Boston public schools. He also took my sister and me to Europe, and all the time he was comparing the cities there with the cities at home and the countries there with the United States. Among other observations, he correctly predicted that Germany would become involved in a major war.

At the end of our trip in Europe, my sister and I stayed for a year at a convent in Aachen, Germany. The reason we went to a German convent was that the French convents were closed. There was a crisis between the Roman Catholic church and the French government over the question of government help to Catholic schools. The schools and the convents had been closed, and the nuns had been expatriated to other countries. There were French nuns in the convent where we went, but it was German. I had an opportunity to study German, and this was fortunate because I love music very much, and, if one knows German, one can better understand German operas and symphonies.

Awakening Important Interests

Naturally, when my children came along, I tried to awaken the same interests in them that were so significant in my life. I took them to the historical shrines in and near Boston. They visited Plymouth Rock, Bunker Hill, and other notable places. Jack went there while he was still in short pants. When the children grew older, they went to Europe, just as I had, and saw many of the landmarks of Western history and culture. Joe Junior, Jack, and Kathleen went to Russia when they were in their teens. That was in the 1930s when most people never thought of going to Russia. Later, by the time Jack went to Washington as a congressman, he had been studying the Soviet Union for many years.

I tried to keep the atmosphere in which the children were reared healthy and purposeful. At mealtime, I made an effort to interest them in something worthwhile. When they were very little, I set two tables for supper. The older ones ate at about 6:30; the younger ones an hour earlier. With the older children, we would usually talk about the news, and we had a bulletin board with important news items posted on it. As the children grew more mature, we discussed politics and government constantly. When Joe Junior and Jack went to Choate Academy, *The New York Times* was sent to them regularly, and to the girls in the convents, too. We wanted the children to be interested in the news and receptive to Mr. Kennedy's stories about Washington. When the children came to Palm Beach in the spring, I talked to them a good deal about Easter; why the feast of Easter was at a different time each year, why Lent lasted 40 days, and why we observed the custom of fasting and abstinence. Children of other religions seemed to find the conversations stimulating, too, when they were our guests at dinner.

In 1934, President Franklin D. Roosevelt appointed my husband to the newly formed Securities and Exchange Commission, and he was elected chairman. Later, he became chairman of the U.S. Maritime Commission, which was charged with administering shipping laws. Naturally, there was much talk at home about the merits and demerits of President Roosevelt's New Deal, as Mr. Kennedy saw them. But whatever conversations took place, my husband did not force his views on any of his sons.

The Virtue of Unity

I recall an incident involving Joe Junior that illustrates this, and makes a point that I have always thought interesting. When Joe Junior returned from his visit to Russia, he talked much to his father and all of us about his trip. He said that he thought there might be some merit in the Soviet ideology. His father staunchly defended the capitalistic system. Jack, who was two years younger than Joe, listened intently. He came to me one day and said he thought that Joe Junior "understood the situation better than Dad." I told Mr. Kennedy about this, half jokingly, and he replied, "I don't care what they think about my opinions. I can get along. As long as they stick together, they will be all right." He considered it a great asset for brothers to remain united.

My husband had a theory about child rearing that I believe added much to our sons' success. I dare say that it would have aided them in any field, but especially in public life where poise, a strong sense of purpose, and courage are needed.

Mr. Kennedy believed that the boys should be given responsibilities as soon as they were ready to accept them. Frequently he turned occasions at which he was to be honored into opportunities to enhance the growth of his sons. He did not eclipse his sons, as I have seen other fathers do. He did everything he could to foster their development.

An example of this occurred in 1939 when Jack was a junior at Harvard. His main interest then was in the growing tensions that would shortly flame into World War II. Indeed, this was the main interest of the Kennedy family at that time, because my husband was then serving his third year as ambassador to Great Britain.

Jack got permission to take a semester's leave from Harvard to visit the trouble spots of Europe. He stayed at the embassies in Paris, Moscow, and Warsaw, and interviewed diplomats, newspapermen, and the man in the street. He learned how deeply everybody dreaded the idea of another world war, what their relations were to the Hitler menace, and what they were doing to cope with the issue. Jack's father asked him to send him a detailed report of the political situation wherever he was, and that he did. In September, 1939, a few days after war had been declared, a Nazi U-boat sank the English passenger liner, *Athenia*, in the Atlantic. The survivors, some of them Americans, were taken to Glasgow, Scotland. My husband was deeply troubled by this tragedy, but instead of assigning someone from the embassy staff, he sent young Jack to Glasgow to interview the American survivors, listen to their stories, and assure them that they would be given all possible assistance.

When Jack returned to Harvard, he wrote his senior thesis on what he had learned at firsthand in Europe. He later turned it into a book that became the best seller, *Why England Slept*, which entailed precise and meticulous reporting on conditions in England under Stanley Baldwin as Prime Minister, as well as Neville Chamberlain.

There were similar experiences with the other children. Joe Junior (who was to die in the air over the English Channel while on a mission to destroy German missile sites in 1944) traveled in Spain during that country's civil war. He did so because he wanted to learn about the political ideologies of the two opponents in the momentous struggle which many saw as the prelude to World War II.

Building Self-Confidence

When Bobby (U.S. Senator Robert F. Kennedy) first went to Europe, my husband learned that the late Lord Beaverbrook, whom he knew well, would be on the same boat. He instructed his son to introduce himself to the English publishing tycoon and talk with him.

When the moment arrived for someone to be chosen as manager of Jack's campaign for the U.S. Senate in 1952, Mr. Kennedy did not volunteer to serve himself, nor did he advise Jack to choose a veteran of Massachusetts politics. He urged the candidate to select his brother, Bobby, who was then only 27 years old. The results of the campaign, in which Jack won the Senate seat from Henry Cabot Lodge, show how astutely and successfully Bobby met the challenge.

Experiences like these added to the self-confidence of the children in meeting people and increased their knowledge of world events. There

Joseph P. Kennedy, as United States ambassador to Great Britain, gives a reception at the embassy in London for his son, Harvard undergraduate John F. Kennedy. The year: 1938.

were similar incidents with Teddy (U.S. Senator Edward M. Kennedy) and with my daughters that contributed to their development.

When my husband was asked to speak at the dedication of a gymnasium he had donated to Manhattanville College of the Sacred Heart in memory of our daughter Kathleen, it was Teddy, then a law student at the University of Virginia, who made the speech, not Mr. Kennedy. Kathleen (Jack's pet name for his vivacious sister was "Kick") had died in a plane crash in France in 1948. Teddy spoke quite movingly of what a lovely, wonderful person Kathleen had been, and what a help and inspiration she had been to the family.

Mr. Kennedy gave the children many opportunities, and they responded willingly and without complaint. They tried to do what they were asked. I would like to add that it is sometimes difficult for parents of a large family to remain enthusiastic about children's interests year after year. It was monotonous for me, for instance, to tell bedtime stories for 20 years, but I did so. My husband, for his part, sustained his interest concerning the younger children as keenly as he had for the older ones, in education, and in travel, as well as in politics.

We always required our children to maintain their integrity. We were Catholics, of course, and many of the families in Boston were not of our faith. But I tried to impress the children with the importance of observing the commandments of God and of the church, and of hearing Mass on Sundays before they started off on a cruise or a picnic. Also, we tried to impress upon them that they did not need to drink or smoke just because others did. They realized, even when they were young, that they sometimes had to act independently to fulfill their obligations.

I was deeply gratified when my son Jack, realizing the importance of the day, attended Mass on the morning of his inauguration as President in order to ask God's blessing in his new and important post.

The Desire to Compete

My husband's financial resources were of great assistance, of course, to the growing political aspirations of our sons. Yet, many men of lesser means have attained political eminence. To reach the top, I believe they shared with us the desire to compete—and not to settle for second place. "Don't go for the vice-presidency," I remember my husband telling Jack one night in the library of our home in Palm Beach, "It's just as easy—or difficult—to go for the top."

Mr. Kennedy had his own way of inculcating this. When the children were small, he went to their football games to spur them on. When they raced their sailboats, he often drove near them in his motorboat. When they got home, if they hadn't done well in the race, he wanted to know why. He would make observations, discuss them in detail—the size of the sails, the preparations for the start of the race, and so forth—and become quite annoyed if the Kennedy boys had been careless.

As I look back in time from this present vantage point, I can say that these are some of the qualities we hoped to encourage in our children. But there was something more. As I have already indicated, we wanted them to have a strong sense of religious faith. Coupled with it, we wanted them to have an awareness of an obligation to do something for one's fellow man. I was always deeply impressed by the following quotation from John Cardinal Newman: "God has created me to do Him some definite service. He has committed some work to me which He has not committed to another. I have my mission. I have a part in a great work; I am a link in a chain, a bond of connection between persons. He has not created me for naught. I shall do good, I shall do His work."

Albert Einstein expressed this feeling beautifully and accurately in *The World As I See It:* " ... a hundred times every day I remind myself that my inner and outer life depend on the labors of other men, living and dead, and that I must exert myself in order to give in the same measure as I have received . . ."

Opportunities and Obligations

Because I have always believed in these principles, I used to tell my children that they had been given unusual opportunities, and, hence, must assume unusual obligations. They must not waste their time, talent, and wealth, nor devote these gifts to their own self-aggrandizement, but to some notable work or noble achievement.

My children made this belief their own. My daughter, Eunice, who is married to R. Sargent Shriver, Jr., director of the Peace Corps and the Office of Economic Opportunity, engaged in social work in Chicago for the House of the Good Shepherd. She and her husband were foster parents for four years to three delinquent girls placed in their care by the Juvenile Court of the city. Eunice has also served as secretary of the National Conference on Prevention and Control of Juvenile Delinquency, among other posts. Jean and Patricia have worked with her in the family program to aid the mentally retarded. My sons chose politics, which can be one of the most direct ways of fulfilling such aims.

But before I proceed to the matter of politics and how it has changed during my lifetime, I would like to make two additional points. The first is that I am aware that the Kennedys do not have a monopoly on the desire to serve. They share this feeling with many people in public life. A truly notable example was the late Secretary-General of the United Nations, Dag Hammarskjöld. His writings have meant much to me lately. In his diary, *Markings*, published after his death, he wrote: "You have not done enough, you have never done enough, so long as it is still possible that you have something of value to contribute. This is the answer when you are groaning under what you consider a burden and an uncertainty prolonged *ad infinitum.*"

The second point is that public careers have many tangible satisfactions. Not the least of these is the challenge of having to deal with situations that change even while one is trying to resolve them, the excitement of knowing important and interesting people who are making history all over the world, and the promise of having the tremendous power to influence for good.

The life of politics and government service has changed greatly since my father was mayor of Boston. In those days, politics, especially at the lower levels, was conducted almost entirely on the basis of intense personal loyalties. A man was frequently named to an important job, not because of his qualifications, but because he was a friend of a friend of a local boss. The lesser political leaders spent their time courting immigrant groups, listening to their stories at wakes and weddings, and helping them to find a job or a place to live. The most important city officials based their power on similar webs of personal friendship. Hence, charm and an engaging personality were essential to political success. An important part of my father's job as mayor, for example, was his attendance at hundreds of banquets and balls. Those who knew him still remember that he loved to close many such occasions with a tenor rendition of "Sweet Adeline," his political theme song.

While such characteristics are still important in politics, they are no longer among the indispensable keys to the city hall. Politics has changed greatly over the years, and most authorities agree that its sharpest turn in recent times was called by John F. Kennedy and his aides.

A New Type of Politician

John Kennedy brought into politics, and relied heavily upon, youthful men of his own generation. Like himself, they were originally political amateurs outside the regular party apparatus. But they were university-trained specialists in a variety of fields: political science, economics, public opinion, communications, history. Equally important, they had the modern feeling for efficiency. They were detached students of public affairs; they paid endless attention to detail, and used the most up-to-date techniques available. Their energy and efficiency were truly remarkable. A good example of this was the search that was carried on for Cabinet officers and other top administrative people in the 10 weeks between the election of 1960 and the inauguration.

Jack's brother-in-law, Sargent Shriver, was put in charge of finding candidates for the top posts. For the position of director of the Bureau of the Budget, inquiries were made as far away as Pakistan because one of the candidates for the job had worked there as a U.S. economic adviser. Before Mr. Dean Rusk was selected as Secretary of State, his articles, speeches, and memoranda were collected by Mr. Shriver and brought to the President-elect's home in the Georgetown section of Washington, D.C., where he read them all.

When Sargent Shriver suggested Robert McNamara as Secretary of Defense, inquiries went to bankers, industrialists, labor leaders, and educators, as one would expect. But in addition, information was collected from his friends, from friends of his wife, and even from Mr. McNamara's caddy.

"There are two things about this Cabinet," presidential aide Theodore C. Sorenson was to say later on. "First, these men are all making sacrifices to come to Washington. They are coming because they feel the same way as John Kennedy, that the country needs to move again.

The victorious clan appears at the armory in Hyannis Port to greet the nation on the morning following the election. From left, Robert, Rose, Jacqueline, the President-elect, and Edward.

*Senators Robert and Edward Kennedy sail Nantucket Sound on
a moody autumn day in a sloop that belonged to their brother, John.*

Second, they are all innovators in one way or another. Though they
may be cautious and careful, they are not afraid to try new things."
    This was the kind of leader Jack was. These were the qualities he
sought to develop in himself; the qualities he required in his aides, and

encouraged in others. As his wife, Jacqueline, once very aptly said of him, "He was an idealist without illusions."

For every man elected to a high government post or named by the President to serve in a top position, there are thousands selected to work in less glamorous but vitally important roles. This need for a large number of qualified people creates great opportunities for many to fulfill themselves in exciting careers and serve their country while doing so. And the work of those in career service is, as I said at the outset of this article, as important, collectively, as that of the President of the United States himself.

I know that President John F. Kennedy felt this way, and I know that his enthusiasm, his respect for people and ideas, and his actions in office had a strong effect on the United States Civil Service. There is much public evidence to corroborate this, including his first State of the Union message, in which he wrote, "Let the public service be a proud and lively career. And let every man and woman who works in any area of our national government, in any branch, at any level, be able to say with pride and honor in future years: 'I served the United States government in that hour of the nation's need.' "

It has been brought to my attention that these words "set the tone and the stage for a new relationship between the federal career service and the presidency." So wrote John W. Macy, Jr., chairman of the U.S. Civil Service, after the tragedy of Nov. 22, 1963.

In his article, "A Legacy of Progress: John F. Kennedy and the Federal Civil Service," Mr. Macy referred to the President's State of the Union message and noted that "members of the career service were unaccustomed to such uncommon recognition between the federal career service and the presidency." He went on to describe how the new relationship between the government service and the presidency worked.

"The President frequently cited the dependence of the nation on federal career men and women. He often addressed messages of inspiration and challenge to government employees. He sought to establish ethical and professional goals at even higher levels of service. He took every opportunity to praise federal workers as individuals and as groups when achievement warranted public recognition.

"He frequently called the attention of young people to the challenge in public service and urged them to consider careers in government. He liked to recall for student groups Bismarck's remark that one-third of the students of German universities broke down from overwork, another third from dissipation, and that the other third ruled Germany —and he would ask, 'Which third is here?' "

Incentives to Public Service

To enable the government to attract the kinds of capable young people needed to make it perform best, his administration helped to pass the Salary Reform Act of 1962. This act introduced the principle that government salaries must be reasonably comparable to salaries received for similar work in private industry. Also, among his other activities that indicated his prime concern with the public service was his directive aimed at making careers in the public service as open to women as to men, wherever possible.

There was a good reason for the President to have devoted so much of his time to the federal civil service. It is not only the organization charged with carrying out the goals of any administration, it is also the largest single employer in the United States. It employs more than 2,500,000 people in more different occupations than the 12 largest corporations in the country. And, interestingly, only one-tenth of this vast force works in Washington. The rest are employed in every state in the Union, and throughout the world.

Contrary to what I suspect is a commonly held belief, the government service is *not* composed of hordes of men wearing green eyeshades and women seated at old-fashioned typewriters. Its fastest growing element is its professional, technical, and scientific personnel. In fact, the government employs more people in the physical sciences (38,100) than in general clerical positions (24,600) and more than five times as many in engineering (128,000, according to the latest survey).

Since 1960, the number of people in the physical sciences has risen 29 per cent, the number of engineers 26 per cent, while the number of typists has not increased at all. Between 1954 and 1962, professional personnel rose 40 per cent. During this period, all other types of occupations rose 17 per cent.

Jobs for Young People

As Mr. Macy has said, "The federal work force is predominantly a group of skilled specialists and trained professionals working in a wide variety of fields." This being the case, what kinds of positions are available in career government work for ambitious young people?

Your government needs astronomers to carry on the study of the sun and the planets, biochemists to help unravel the mysteries of cancer and heredity, and computer experts to track the satellites. It needs dieticians, editors, economists, foresters, foreign service personnel, and so on down the line. Indeed, in some fields, such as civil engineering and the use of computers, the government is the largest employer in the world.

Finally, it should be noted that there are similar positions available to properly qualified young people in the state and local government. Indeed, there are three times as many state and city civil servants as there are federal workers.

I have taken the opportunity here of setting down my feelings on a number of themes that are interesting and important to me. It has been indicated to me through the letters I receive from time to time that the public is interested in these matters, too. I found the role my father played in my life a decisive one and so I discussed it here. Next, I was interested in putting down my thoughts on the values that my husband and I stressed with our children. This brought me to a consideration of ways in which politics has changed from my father's time to that of the present generation. Finally, I sought to broaden the view thus presented to indicate paths of public service open to young Americans.

Perhaps I can find no more fitting way to close this article than with an aphorism that was a favorite of the late President. It is one that he often addressed to young audiences, and it sums up much that I have written here. Borrowing an ancient Greek quotation, the President used to say that true happiness can perhaps be best defined as, "the exercise of vital powers along lines of excellence in a life affording them scope."

See also, Section Three, KENNEDY, JOHN F.

A YEAR BOOK SPECIAL REPORT

By Jaroslav Pelikan

Paths to Dialogue

Protestant and Orthodox Observers, *left*, sit beside the statue of
Saint Peter as Roman Catholic prelates meet at Vatican Council II.

After Centuries of Conflict, Christians Are Moving
Toward Reunion. In This Article, a Noted Theologian
Describes the "Great New Fact" About Christianity.

T he most sacred shrine in Christendom is the Church of the Holy Sepulchre in Jerusalem, located at the place where, according to tradition, Jesus was buried. It is a shocking experience for a Christian tourist to visit this shrine. Christians of many backgrounds—Copts, Armenians, Roman Catholics, and Greek Orthodox, among others— all worship here simultaneously every Sunday, but each group has its own service and even its own music. All Christians affirm that the cross of Jesus Christ is the basis of their faith, and yet they cannot pray together at the place where His crucified body was laid to rest.

This separation is not, of course, confined to the Holy Land, but is one of the most obvious and universal facts of life throughout the Christian world. During the past 50 years, Christians of many countries and many denominations have been working to remedy it. What Christians have in common is vastly more important than what separates them, but they have been more successful in showing what divides them than in confessing what unites them. The ecumenical movement is the effort to set the balance straight.

Rediscovery, reconciliation, and reunion among Christians have hit the front pages, locally and internationally. After centuries of Cold War among Christians, Roman Catholics and Protestants have found

Illustrations by Franklin McMahon

Under the twin domes of the Church of the Holy Sepulchre, *upper left*, the babel of rival sects tells of ancient divisions within the Christian Church.

United Press Int.

An ecumenical gesture from Pope Paul VI was his
meeting with leaders of other faiths in the Church of the
Holy Family in New York City after his historic speech to the
United Nations General Assembly in October, 1965.

each other again. Whether in its local congregations or at its national
conventions, every Christian denomination is facing the necessity of
basically rethinking the question of its relation to other churches. This
"great new fact" of modern Christian history has permanently changed
the map of Christendom, and more changes are occurring with each
week's news.

A Roman Catholic cardinal delivered the commencement address
at the 1965 graduation exercises of a Protestant theological seminary.
A Protestant theologian (this one) has become a weekly columnist
for a chain of Roman Catholic newspapers having a circulation of
about 500,000 copies per issue. Local churches throughout the United
States regularly invite clergymen of other denominations to occupy
their pulpits. Joint services for Thanksgiving Day and joint sunrise
services on Easter Sunday are almost universal.

Christian students from various denominational backgrounds band
together on college campuses for discussion, common witness, and
social action. At Selma, Ala., and at all the Selmas, not only "black
and white together," as the freedom song goes, but ministers, rabbis,
priests, and nuns march together for freedom and racial justice. Roman
Catholic bishops in the United States have now been authorized by

The author:
Jaroslav Pelikan,
Titus Street
Professor of
Ecclesiastical
History at Yale
University, has
written widely on
many religious
topics. He is a
member of the
Commission on
Faith and Order of
the World Council
of Churches and
President of the
American Society of
Church History.

World Council of Churches

A leader of the ecumenical movement is the Rev. Dr. Willem A. Visser't Hooft, General Secretary of the World Council of Churches.

United Press Int.

The late Pope John XXIII called for an ecumenical meeting soon after coming to the papacy and opened Vatican Council II in 1962.

the Vatican to permit the celebration of Mass at mixed marriages of Roman Catholics and Protestants and to allow the non-Catholic partner's minister to bless the newlyweds in their home after the Roman Catholic ceremony.

The ecumenical movement began, significantly, with the uneasiness of students in the Western World, and of converts in Africa and the Far East, over the divided state of the Church. In the case of the converts, denominational conflicts that may have seemed justifiable in Europe or the Americas were utterly remote to Christians who had just made the change from Hinduism or fetishism. It was difficult for a Bushman to understand that he was a Norwegian Lutheran or a Southern Baptist. It was even more difficult to persuade a pagan to become a Christian if he was obliged at the same time to choose from among some 300 denominations of Christianity. Thus, Christian division was an offense to the non-Christian world. In 1910, at Edinburgh, Scotland, a World Missionary Conference was held to deal with this offense. From it came, in 1921, the International Missionary Council, in which representatives of many churches worked together for the growth of the Christian mission throughout the world.

While reports of restiveness about denominational competition in the mission field and in the younger churches were coming in, Christian students in the West were expressing similar criticism. In an age when patterns of thought were determined by systems of value and belief other than those derived from the Bible and the Christian tradition, students began to recognize, far earlier than did their elders, that Christians were, relatively speaking, a shrinking minority in a world that was becoming increasingly indifferent to the pretensions of organized religion. The students knew, therefore, that the odds for the survival of Christianity at the vital centers of decision were very poor, and that they were made even worse by divisions among the churches. And so it was from the mission field and from student Christian movements that the earliest clamor came for some attempt to achieve Christian understanding in a divided world.

One concrete form that this understanding was to take was service to the needy. During World War I, Christians on both sides of the conflict did not merely content themselves with claiming divine sanction for their war efforts, as though God were fighting for either the Allies or the Central Powers. They came to see that with the end of the war, millions of Europeans, most of them Christian, would need the kind of aid that could come only from voluntary agencies. For a significant number of these Christians, the war, moreover, provoked a serious re-examination of the social structures and systems that spawn war. Christians learned that the Church could not be content to "save souls," while allowing a society to go its own way toward destruction.

The practical outcome of this recognition was the Universal Christian Conference on Life and Work, which met at Stockholm, Sweden, in 1925 and again at Oxford, England, in 1937. Nathan Söderblom, Archbishop of the Church of Sweden (Lutheran), had issued a call for this kind of a conference to be convened as early as June, 1917.

Seeking to find some Christian answers to the problems of social, political, and economic life, the Conference on Life and Work also proved that Christians could neither find such answers nor expect them to be heeded if they refused to do anything about their own divisions. It furthermore became apparent that if these same Christians wanted to work effectively to alleviate suffering, famine, and disease, their hands had to be united. Christian charity is no place for cut-throat competition. The churches simply had to find ways to cooperate, despite their religious and doctrinal differences.

Those differences would not, however, simply go away. Some of the agitators for Christian understanding have given the impression that all the differences of dogma and theology are due to the stubbornness of a few theologians, and that, with a little good will, all the problems would yield to a consensus. But it is an insult to the seriousness of religious commitment to make these differences seem so trivial. Men have bled and died for their beliefs. Even if those beliefs were mistaken, they deserve to be treated with respect. The Conference on Life and Work had, therefore, to be supplemented by a Conference on Faith and Order; that is, on Christian doctrine and on the proper form of the Church and of its ministry. The Conference on Faith and Order met at Lausanne, Switzerland, in 1927, and at Edinburgh in 1937.

National Council of Churches

The Rev. Dr. Eugene Carson Blake is a former president of the National Council of the Churches of Christ in the U.S.A.

These and other meetings between representatives of various churches disclosed another unifying force that had been at work for several decades. The debates over the critical study of the Bible during the half century before World War I had divided theologians of several major communions into "liberal" and "conservative." As a result, there were, in many ways, deeper differences *within* the denominations than between them. Although these differences sometimes went so far as to produce new splits, more often they served to show that the older conflicts between churches had lost their relevance. It appeared to many, for example, that a surrender of belief in the literal infallibility of the words of the Bible made it pointless to argue whether sprinkling or immersion is the proper form of baptism.

In a positive way, too, the development of Christian thought had opened the door to better understanding between the churches. Partly through a deeper study of the Bible and partly through a growing awareness everywhere that human life is social rather than merely individual, Protestant theology rediscovered the doctrine of the Church, embodied in the Christian belief that God's gift to man in Jesus Christ creates a common bond between all those who name the name of Christ. Sometimes Protestants had spoken as though the distinctive doctrine of Protestantism was its emphasis on the freedom of the individual over and against the authority of the Church. By the end of the 19th century, however, it had become evident to most Protestant churchmen that there is no Christianity apart from the Church. It followed from this that Christians could not afford to treat the unity of the Church as an afterthought. They must find ways both of express-

National Council of Churches

Episcopal Bishop James A. Pike is coauthor of the Blake-Pike proposal for Christian unity.

ing the unity that already existed, and of advancing toward a unity that was both broader and deeper in scope.

Out of all these developments grew the conviction that it is the will of God for the churches to come closer together. The several ecumenical organizations—International Missionary Council, Faith and Order, Life and Work—were concerned with avoiding the ironic spectacle of overlapping and competition among groups whose purpose was to eliminate overlapping and competition. The year 1941 was set for the formation of a World Council of Churches, but because of World War

Michael Taylor

The Archbishop of Canterbury, Dr. Arthur M. Ramsey, presided at an Anglican meeting in May, 1965, that considered union with English Methodism.

II, it was impossible to establish the council until Aug. 23, 1948.

From its headquarters in Geneva, Switzerland, the World Council has helped to coordinate the work of its member churches, especially in the area of service and aid, and to inspire their discussions and negotiations toward closer unity. It is not itself a church, but an agency of about 200 churches. Through its Division of Studies, as well as through Faith and Order, it is also a source of theological insight and research. There are about 900 local and state councils of churches in the United States, together with the National Council of the Churches of Christ in the United States of America, which was formed in December, 1950, to carry out many of the tasks that had previously been undertaken by the churches themselves.

Yet, cooperation between existing denominations, which is the function of such councils, is not enough of a goal for the ecumenical movement. Separation must be replaced by true unity and organic reunion. During the past half century, there have been more than 40 reunions of bodies previously separated, or mergers of bodies that had never been united before. In 1925, for example, Canadian Methodists, nearly all the Congregationalists, and 71 per cent of Canadian Presbyterians formed the United Church of Canada. In 1947, the Church of South India was formed, uniting Methodist, Presbyterian, Congregationalist, Dutch Reformed, and Anglican groups into a new body which is now negotiating with still other churches in India. In 1961, after many years of discussion, the Congregational Christian Churches of the United States and the Evangelical and Reformed Church (both of them already mergers of previously separated groups) established the United Church of Christ. The United Church of Christ, in turn, has been engaged since 1962 in conversations with Episcopalian, Presbyterian, Methodist, Disciples of Christ, and Evangelical United Brethren churches. A continuing agency, the Consultation on Church Union, has been established.

These are only a few of the more dramatic illustrations of the ecumenical ferment throughout the Protestant world. But of the nearly 1,000,000,000 Christians in the world, only about one quarter are Protestant. Most of the rest are Roman Catholic or Eastern Orthodox. It seems somewhat foolish, therefore, to use the word "ecumenical" in the sense of "pan-Protestant." The most important new fact of the ecumenical endeavor during the past several years is that it has become fully ecumenical. Ever since the meeting at Lausanne in 1927, representatives of the Eastern Orthodox traditions have been taking an influential and respected role in ecumenical discussions. At the third assembly of the World Council in New Delhi, India, in 1961, the Eastern Orthodox churches of Russia, Bulgaria, Romania, and Poland became members. Most of the Eastern Orthodox churches in

Behind the diversity of the varied robes worn by the presidents of the World Council of Churches, shown here at the New Delhi assembly in 1961, is a unifying purpose of strengthening the Church in the world. The leaders, *left to right*, are Sir Francis Ibiam, Dr. Martin Niemoeller, Archbishop Iakovos, Dr. Arthur Ramsey, Dr. David Moses, and Charles Parlin.

World Council of Churches

the United States have become increasingly active in state and local councils and in the National Council.

But even Protestantism and Eastern Orthodoxy together represent numerically less than half of Christendom. The largest organization in the Christian world is the Roman Catholic church, in whose vocabu-

Entering the First Methodist Church of Evanston, Ill., for the second meeting of the World Council of Churches in 1954 are, *left to right,* **Dr. Harold A. Bosley, then minister of the church; Bishop G. Bromley Oxnam; Archbishop Athenagoras I; Dr. Marc Boegner; Bishop Eivind Berggrav; Bishop George K. A. Bell; and Bishop C. K. Jacob.**

lary the word "ecumenical" has become standard, especially since the work of the late Pope John XXIII. He created a Secretariat for Promoting Christian Unity and convoked an ecumenical council, Vatican Council II, whose closing sessions were held in the autumn of 1965. Stirred by Pope John's conciliatory spirit and charitable example, Roman Catholics have simultaneously come to look with increasing favor on the ecumenical strivings of other Christians, and have launched an ecumenical movement of their own. As in the case of the ecumenical movement among Protestants, Roman Catholic ecumenism is the culmination of a long development that must be understood, at least in its essentials, if we are to interpret the present situation properly.

Ever since the Reformation of the 16th century, the defenders of Roman Catholicism have been insisting that their cause is just, and that the Reformation and the Reformers were unfaithful to Christian truth. It was said that Martin Luther had been possessed by a demon. Rumor had it that he committed suicide. And no one could deny that he had married a runaway nun. Therefore, each time someone within Roman Catholicism called for renewal and reform, he could be tarred with the brush of Protestantism and consequently dismissed. But like the leaven in the lump, the Christian imperative for the renewal of the Church continued to work.

It was, first of all, an imperative for reform in the structure and life of the Roman Catholic church itself. But it was also a call for some real changes in the relation of the church to society—and in the relation of the church to other Christians. For in spite of the monolithic claim of Roman Catholicism to be *the* Church, it simply could not be denied that there were genuine Christians who were not members of the Roman Catholic church.

The ecumenical movement within non-Roman Catholic Christendom helped to bring all this into focus. Although there was no official Roman Catholic participation in the early conferences, there was increasing interest in them. As early as the Edinburgh World Missionary Conference of 1910, the Roman Catholic bishop of Cremona declared, in a letter to the conference, that there was a unity among Christians "great enough to warrant continuing further discussion tending to promote the union of all believers in Christ." Recently, Augustin Cardinal Bea, president of the Secretariat for Promoting Christian Unity, asserted: "We Catholics must recognize with sincere gratitude that it was our separated brethren, Orthodox, Anglican, and Protestant, who gave the first impulse to the modern unitive movement, and that we have learned much from them, and can learn still more."

Augustin Cardinal Bea, a member of the so-called "liberal" wing of the Roman Catholic Church, is an advocate of church reform.

The name "separated brethren" has now become the usual Roman Catholic term for other Christians, replacing "schismatic," "heretic," and other more vitriolic designations. A noteworthy factor in this change of attitude was the experience of European Christians under Nazi tyranny. In his writings against Roman Catholicism, Luther had called the pope Antichrist, and the Roman Catholics of his day had returned the compliment. With the advent of Adolf Hitler, their descendants learned what an Antichrist is really like. In the process, they found each other.

Groups of Protestants and Roman Catholics met to share in a common life of prayer and Bible study, and to consider the Christian strategy under persecution. In the concentration camps, they learned to share a common death as well. What had been learned in the time of troubles could not be easily forgotten when Hitler and his regime were dead. Even in a time of civil peace, it was unthinkable to return to the same old kind of religious war.

Not only the old ways of religious warfare, but even some of the old ways of religious thought and worship were proving just how obsolete they were. It seemed intolerable to many Roman Catholics that the central act of the church's worship should be conducted in a lan-

Roman Catholic women are taught to interpret Christian teachings through Hindu dances in India, *left*. Pope Paul VI, *right*, pushes through crowds on Via Dolorosa in Jerusalem during his visit to the Holy Land in 1964. While there, he met with Athenagoras I.

United Press Int.

guage that no one has spoken in ordinary society for centuries. The church speaks about so central a doctrine as the sacraments in language conditioned by the centuries-old theology of St. Thomas Aquinas, with the help of the philosophy of Aristotle. This language is quite unintelligible to millions of 20th century men.

Having resisted the findings of Galileo and having established the Spanish Inquisition, the church needed to rethink its relation to modern thought and to the modern state. Meanwhile, the church had been neglecting the very resources of its own tradition, especially the Bible, from which could come the power of authentic renewal.

Nobody of these problems could be said to be unique to the 20th century. Certainly none of them is unique to Roman Catholicism. What is unique is that on both sides of the great divide between Roman Catholicism and other churches thoughtful leaders have tackled these problems and have learned that they will have to solve them together. When Pope John XXIII announced an ecumenical council in 1961, he meant a council that would include Roman Catholics from all over the world, not, as some overly enthusiastic Protestants concluded, a council to discuss reunion with other Christians. Nevertheless, the council has transformed relations between Roman Catholics and other Christians so radically that it will be decades before we can gauge its influence. As one of the Protestant observers at the council put it, "Our presence here . . . is a miracle." Throughout the discussions and

The thrust of ecumenism cuts across boundaries of race, color, and nationality. During a European tour in 1964, the Rev. Martin Luther King conferred with Pope Paul VI, *upper left*. The next year, in a basement of the Baptist church in Selma, Ala., an Episcopalian minister addressed a mixed group during the desegregation fight. Youths, *lower right*, from 15 countries and denominations met in Wisconsin to discuss a Christian response to world problems.

deliberations of the council, delegated observers from various non-Roman Catholic communions watched and listened and prayed, and their presence helped to make the council ecumenical in fact and in spirit, as well as in name.

The decisions of the council also were ecumenical both in fact and in spirit. It reformed the liturgy of the church and opened the way for the replacement of Latin with the language of the people in large parts of the Mass. It came to terms with the contemporary world and adopted a statement on religious liberty that will make a vital difference in the relation of the church to modern society. To other Christians, both Orthodox and Protestant, it extended a fraternal hand, asking not that the prodigals return and do penance for their sins, but that Christians of all traditions work together in a spirit of mutual forgiveness for the achievement of that unity which is the will of God for the Christian Church.

Reviewing the inner life of the Roman Catholic church, the council recognized that being a layman is not a spectator sport in the church; the laymen *are* the church, priests by virtue of their baptism and therefore equipped to carry the message and mission of the church to the world. To the bishops, too, it restored many of their ancient rights that had been surrendered or usurped in an age of overcentralization, and it reasserted the principle of "collegiality" among

Against reddened skies of Old Jerusalem, doves settle peacefully on the ancient wall that divides the Holy City.

bishops. There is scarcely a single aspect of the work and thought of the church that was passed over in the deliberations of Vatican Council II. And most of its actions will certainly have a lasting affect on the whole of the Christian world.

The unspoken assumption behind many of these actions—in fact, as we noted earlier, behind much of the ecumenical movement as a whole—is the shock of the recognition that the percentage of Christians in the world is smaller this year than it was last year, and that next year it will be still smaller. When Christianity became the official religion of the Roman Empire in the 4th century, it embarked on a program of expansion that has carried it from the confines of the Mediterranean world to virtually every race and nation of mankind. Everywhere, it has come as the religion of the dominant group in the human race: European, white, Caucasian, culturally advanced, and Christian were all synonymous terms. The day of Christian-European dominance is over. The sooner Christians of every tradition recognize this fact and accept it, the better it will be for them and for the Christian cause throughout the world.

From this fact, it follows almost inexorably that the divisions which Christians could afford when they were the ruling caste have now become a luxury in which no one can indulge. If the Christian alternative to communism, materialism, and all the other ideologies competing for human loyalty is to be heard and considered, there ought to be a way of presenting that alternative that is neither sectarian nor partisan, but "catholic," that is, universal, in its appeal to all segments of human society.

To put this imperative in another way, Christians of all groups are looking for ways of continuing to emphasize their own historic values, while at the same time learning to affirm values and beliefs which other Christian groups have historically claimed as their own. The Church is what it is because of the Bible, and the Bible is what it is because of the Church. There is no need to choose between the Bible and the Church in the question of Christian authority, but Christians must learn that they cannot have the authority of either without the authority of the other. So it is with preaching and the sacraments, faith and works, freedom and authority, and many of the other antitheses that traditionally create controversy.

It is interesting, moreover, that as Christians huddle together in their new minority status, they do not wish to close their minds to the rest of the human race or even to other religions. On the contrary, one by-product of the new ecumenical spirit is a new openness to the great living religions of mankind. Such openness is not, as it has often been, the result of indifference to the deeper issues, or of ignorance about the fundamental differences. It is, rather, the result of the recognition that all those who believe that there is more to human existence than absurdity, have a stake in the preservation of the values that are an essential part of the human spirit.

A special place belongs to the new relationship between Christians and Jews. Christians have learned—through Biblical study, but even more through the nightmare of anti-Semitism—that, as Christians, they have a special affinity for the people of Abraham, Isaac, and Jacob, the ancestors and brethren of Jesus of Nazareth. Therefore, both the Vatican Council and the World Council of Churches have given particular attention to the place of the people of Israel in the plan of salvation.

As the churches have been unable to face each other without a new awareness of the place of the people of Israel, so it was perhaps inevitable that they turn their gaze also to the Holy Land, whose highways and cities have witnessed the great events that unite Christians in a common faith, as well as the scandals and atrocities that divide them. The same Palestine where sacred shrines exemplify Christian competition every Sunday has been the scene of striking demonstrations of Christian unity. When a new YMCA building was dedicated at Nazareth on April 7, 1965, it brought together Christians of many denominations, including Protestant, Orthodox, and Roman Catholic, with representatives of the Jewish faith in attendance as well. And on Jan. 5, 1964, Pope Paul VI and the primate of Eastern Orthodoxy, Athenagoras I, Patriarch of Constantinople (Istanbul), met in the first encounter between patriarch and pope since the 15th century—and their meeting was in Jerusalem. They prayed together on the Mount of Olives, where on the night of His betrayal, Christ had prayed: "I . . . pray for those who believe in Me . . . that they may all be one, even as Thou, Father, art in Me, and I in Thee, that they also may be in us, so that the world may believe that Thou hast sent Me."

There, on the mountain consecrated forever by Christian memory, these two disciples of Christ united in a prayer that symbolized the beginning of the answer to His prayer. The outcome of their prayer, and of the entire ecumenical movement, still cannot be predicted. It takes more than good will, more even than prayer, to heal the wounds of centuries. But if healing there is to be, it cannot come without good will and prayer. The rest is up to God. On this all Christians agree as they pray, separately and yet together: "Thy will be done on earth as it is in heaven . . . and forgive us our trespasses, as we forgive those who trespass against us."

See also, Section Three, Roman Catholic; Jews And Judaism; Protestant.

The ecumenical movement, about which Jaroslav Pelikan writes in this article, is an important chapter of man's religious history. But it is only one chapter. To understand the sweep and scope of earlier chapters of our religious heritage, see the Trans-Vision® on opposite page.

THE SACRED LAND

Sid Latham, Photo Researchers

O. L. Goldman, FPG

Dr. Charles Glauboch, Photo Researchers

Man is today making rapid and dramatic advances in the conquest of space, disease, poverty, and ignorance. He can look to the future with confidence and excitement. Yet, in so doing, he must not lose touch with his roots, or with the rich heritage embodied in his ideals, institutions, and character. Religion is an essential part of human heritage, and hundreds of millions of people—Christians, Jews, and Moslems alike—look to Palestine as the sacred land, the home of their faith. It is a unique land, one of many contrasts, as depicted on the left by the Jordanian camel corps, the modern city of Tel Aviv-Yafo, and ancient Nazareth. It was in Palestine that Judaism came into being. There Christianity was born. Islam, which had its origin in Arabia, found a home there, too, and became one of the world's great monotheistic faiths.

There was a time from the late Middle Ages and after it was absorbed into the Ottoman Empire in 1517, when Palestine was a land almost without a history, largely a wilderness populated by peasants and Bedouins. Finally, in the 19th century, groups of Jews came back into the area, and the Zionist movement gained momentum. Following World War I, the British ruled the land under a mandate from the League of Nations. Then came Hitlerism, and more Jews poured into Palestine. Bitter feeling developed between them and the Arabs living there. Fighting broke out and continued sporadically until after the formation, in 1948, of two separate states: Israel and the Hashemite Kingdom of Jordan. The Jews have built a flourishing, modern country, and the growth of both Israel and Jordan has been truly spectacular.

To study the development of the Holy Land from ancient times to the present, turn to the last map in this unit and lay down each of the following ones successively. To compare the modern Holy Land with previous periods, lift out the gatefold page and place it over the map to be studied.

Cover: A panorama of religious history spreads before the viewer as he gazes from the Mount of Olives toward Jerusalem. In the foreground is the Garden of Gethsemane, with the Church of St. Mary Magdalene at the right. Beyond looms the Dome of the Rock, or Mosque of Omar. The new Israeli area of Jerusalem is in the background.

COVER PHOTO: Ray Manley, Shostal

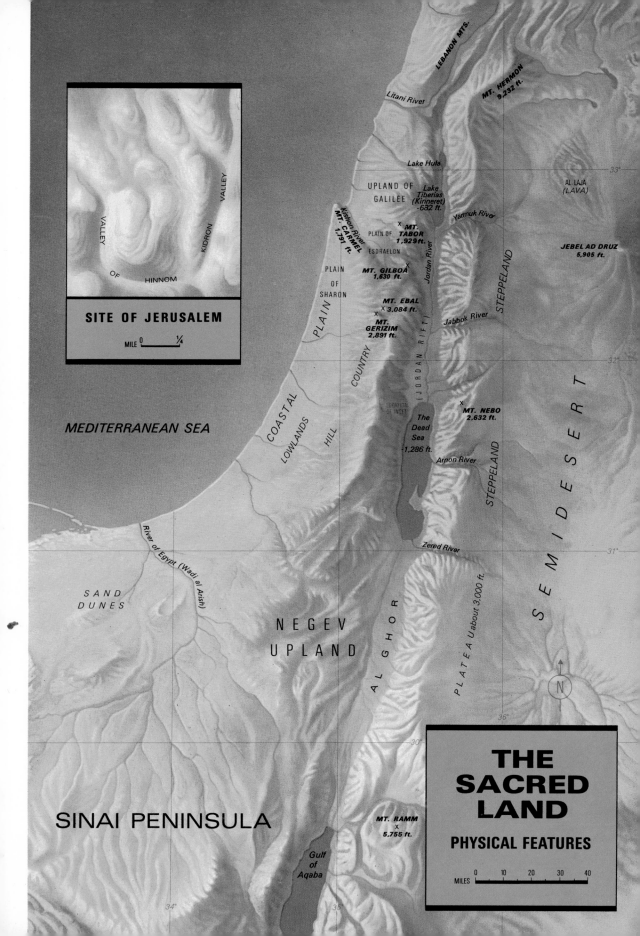

VALLEY

KIDRON VALLEY

VALLEY OF HINNOM

SITE OF JERUSALEM

MILE 0 ¼

LEBANON MTS.

Litani River

MT. HERMON
9,232 ft.

Lake Hula

33°

UPLAND OF GALILEE

Lake Tiberias
(Kinneret)
-632 ft.

AL LAJA
(LAVA)

Yarmuk River

Kishon River
MT. CARMEL
1,791 ft.

PLAIN OF
TABOR
1,929 ft.

X MT.

Jordan River

JEBEL AD DRUZ
5,905 ft.

ESDRAELON

PLAIN
OF
SHARON

MT. GILBOA
1,630 ft.

X

STEPPELAND

MT. EBAL
X 3,084 ft.

MT.
GERIZIM
2,891 ft.

Jabbok River

PLAIN

COUNTRY

HILL

(JORDAN RIFT)

32°

LOCATION
OF INSET

The
Dead
Sea
-1,286 ft.

X MT. NEBO
2,632 ft.

COASTAL

LOWLANDS

MEDITERRANEAN SEA

Arnon River

STEPPELAND

S E M I D E S E R T

River of Egypt (Wadi al Arish)

Zered River

31°

SAND
DUNES

N E G E V

U P L A N D

A L   G H O R

P L A T E A U about 3,000 ft.

36°

N

30°

SINAI PENINSULA

**THE
SACRED
LAND**

PHYSICAL FEATURES

MT. RAMM
X
5,755 ft.

Gulf
of
Aqaba

0   10   20   30   40
MILES

34°

35°

Crusaders stormed into the Holy Land and captured Jerusalem, as shown in this medieval miniature.

A.D. 70 to A.D. 1291. After the fall of Jerusalem, Galilee became a center of Jewish learning. The great rabbinical works such as the Talmud were written there and in Babylonia. Caesarea became the seat of Christian learning and leadership.

By the fifth century, European Christians began to visit the Holy Land as pilgrims. Then, in A.D. 611, the Persians swept over Palestine and in A.D. 615 massacred most of the Christian population. In A.D. 634, an Arab army, representing the new religion of Islam, swarmed in from the desert. Jerusalem became the third city of Islam, after Mecca and Medina. The caliph Omar erected the Dome of the Rock, since known as the Mosque of Omar, on the site of Solomon's Temple.

In 1096, the crusades began, and Christians from Europe invaded the Holy Land. They captured Jerusalem in 1099, and thereafter we speak of the "Latin Kingdom of Jerusalem," though the Franks, as the Moslems called the Europeans, held power with difficulty. By 1187, Moslem invaders had regained much of the Holy Land. European power completely ended in 1291, with the expulsion of the last Franks.

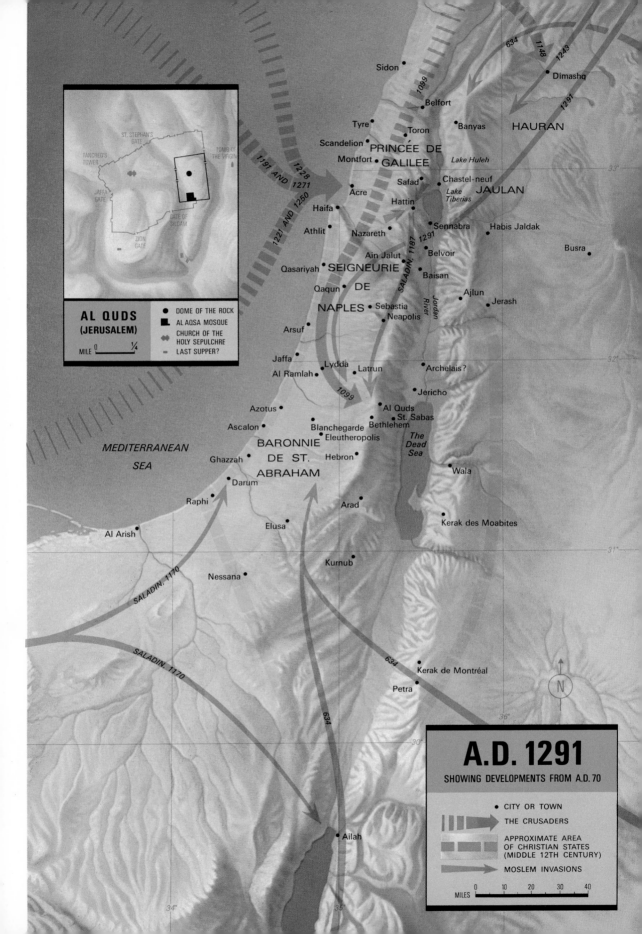

AL QUDS
(JERUSALEM)

MILE 0 ¼

ST. STEPHAN'S
GATE

TANCRED'S
TOWER

TOMB OF
THE VIRGIN

JAFFA
GATE

GATE OF
SILOAM

ZION
GATE

● DOME OF THE ROCK
■ AL AQSA MOSQUE
✥ CHURCH OF THE
HOLY SEPULCHRE
▬ LAST SUPPER?

Sidon

Belfort

Tyre
Toron
Banyas
HAURAN

Scandelion
PRINCÉE DE
Montfort
GALILEE
Lake Huleh

Safad
Chastel-neuf
JAULAN
Acre
Lake
Tiberias

Haifa
Hattin

Athlit
Sennabra
Habis Jaldak

Nazareth
Belvoir
Busra

Ain Jalut

Qasariyah
SEIGNEURIE
Baisan

Qaqun
DE
Ajlun
Jerash

NAPLES
Sebastia
Jordan River

Neapolis

Arsuf

Jaffa
Lydda
Al Ramlah
Latrun
Archelais?

Jericho

Azotus
Al Quds
St. Sabas

Ascalon
Blanchegarde
Bethlehem
Eleutheropolis
The
Dead
BARONNIE
Hebron
Sea
Ghazzah
DE ST.
ABRAHAM
Wala
Darum

Raphi
Arad

Al Arish
Kerak des Moabites

Elusa

Kurnub

Nessana

Kerak de Montréal

Petra

MEDITERRANEAN
SEA

SALADIN, 1170

SALADIN, 1170

Ailah

634
1148
1243
Dimashq
1099
1291
1191 AND 1271
1228
1221 AND 1250
SALADIN 1187
1291
1099
634
634

N

A.D. 1291

SHOWING DEVELOPMENTS FROM A.D. 70

● CITY OR TOWN

▮▮▮ THE CRUSADERS

APPROXIMATE AREA
OF CHRISTIAN STATES
(MIDDLE 12TH CENTURY)

➜ MOSLEM INVASIONS

MILES 0 10 20 30 40

In this early mosaic, Andrew and Simon Peter, left, answer the call of Jesus to join Him in His ministry.

64 B.C. to 4 B.C. Under Roman rule, Herod the Great was placed in charge of the Jews. The people hated him because he violated their religion and despised the significance of their customs. Nonetheless, his passion for building made Jerusalem a beautiful city. Among other projects, he started a program for rebuilding the Temple, and brought water from the southern hills into Jerusalem along an open aqueduct.

Among the most striking documents we have from this general era are the Dead Sea Scrolls, uncovered in the mid-1940's at the northwest end of the Dead Sea. As a result of their discovery, we now possess a number of valuable biblical manuscripts and countless fragments of biblical books. We also possess scrolls dealing with the faith and life of a community which many believe was related to the Jewish religious sect known as the Essenes whose settlement at Qumran has been excavated.

As Herod's reign drew to a close, he ruled more and more by terror and assassination. It was he, according to the Gospel of Matthew, who ordered the "massacre of the innocents," aimed at destroying the infant Jesus. He himself died in 4 B.C.

4 B.C. to A.D. 70. Jesus, by the modern calendar born in about 4 B.C., grew up in Nazareth in Galilee. Much of His ministry was conducted in the hill country east and west of the Sea of Galilee. We know He visited Phoenicia, and He was in Caesarea Philippi. He also passed through Samaria, was active in the area around Jericho, and was crucified in Jerusalem.

The Christian religion, in fact, began in Jerusalem and from there spread in all directions across the world. From the bustling port of Caesarea, Paul set forth on his missionary journeys that carried him to Asia Minor, and into Europe. Later, under arrest in Caesarea, Paul was taken to Rome where some Christians had preceded him.

Meanwhile in Palestine, friction grew between the Jews and the Romans. Some Jews bitterly resented Roman domination, and rebelled. The Romans retaliated, and in A.D. 70, Jerusalem fell after a terrible siege. The Temple Herod had rebuilt was destroyed, and trophies from it were carried to Rome. But the fall of Jerusalem was fatal to neither Judaism nor Christianity. The Jews remained loyal to their faith, and Christianity spread to the ends of the earth.

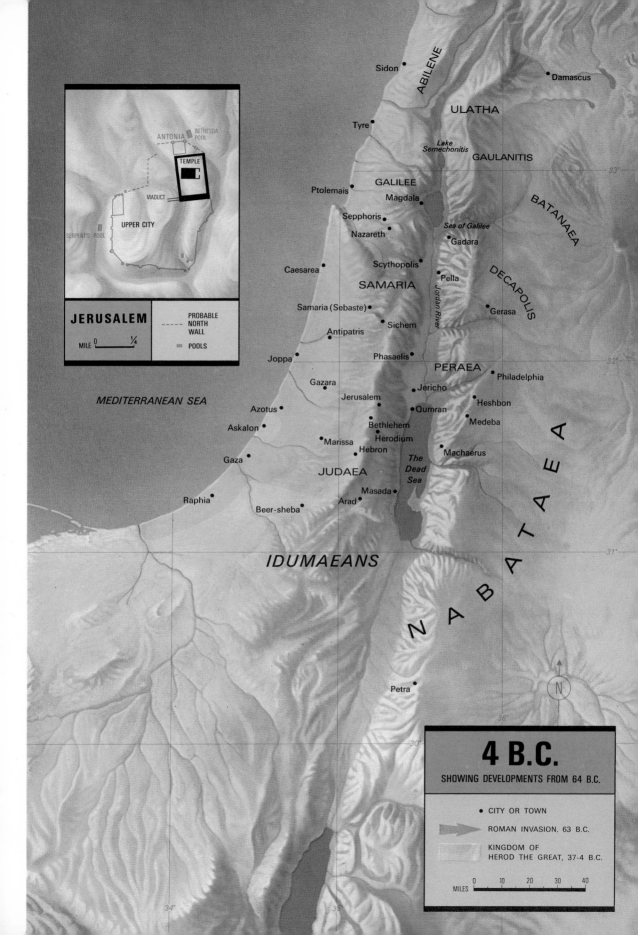

Sidon

Damascus

ABILENE

ULATHA

Tyre

Lake
Semechonitis

GAULANITIS

GALILEE

Ptolemais

Magdala

BATANAEA

Sepphoris

Sea of Galilee

Nazareth

Gadara

Caesarea

Scythopolis

DECAPOLIS

SAMARIA

Pella

Samaria (Sebaste)

Gerasa

Sichem

Antipatris

Jordan River

Joppa

Phasaelis

PERAEA

Philadelphia

Gazara

Jericho

MEDITERRANEAN SEA

Jerusalem

Heshbon

Azotus

Qumran

Medeba

Askalon

Bethlehem

Marissa

Herodium

Hebron

Machaerus

Gaza

The
Dead
Sea

JUDAEA

Raphia

Masada

Arad

Beer-sheba

IDUMAEANS

NABATAEA

Petra

N

JERUSALEM

ANTONIA

BETHESDA
POOL

TEMPLE

VIADUCT

SERPENT'S POOL

UPPER CITY

MILE 0   ¼

PROBABLE
NORTH
WALL

POOLS

33°

32°

37°

30°

36°

34°   35°

4 B.C.

SHOWING DEVELOPMENTS FROM 64 B.C.

● CITY OR TOWN

ROMAN INVASION, 63 B.C.

KINGDOM OF
HEROD THE GREAT, 37-4 B.C.

MILES 0   10   20   30   40

The prophet Isaiah, portrayed by the medieval painter Ugolino, said that God looked for loyalty to Himself and for just social relations among men.

1000 B.C. to 587 B.C. David's son, Solomon, maintained the empire his father had created and raised its prosperity to levels it had never before known. He extended the city of Jerusalem and also built the famous Temple dedicated to the Lord. His fleet, anchored at Ezion-geber, traded with distant lands. But when Solomon died, probably in 922 B.C., his son Rehoboam was not accepted by all of the people.

Thus the kingdom split in two; that in the north became known as Israel and that in the south as Judah. The divided kingdom lasted 200 years. In the 8th century, four great prophets emerged: Amos, Hosea, Isaiah, and Micah. They told the people of both kingdoms that God looked for loyalty to Himself and for just social relations between man and man. In 722-721 B.C., Sargon II, King of Assyria, captured Samaria, the capital of Israel, and the northern kingdom came to an end.

In 598 B.C. and again in 587 B.C., Jerusalem was besieged by Nebuchadnezzar II, King of Babylonia, and its citizens were carried into exile. The city was left desolate, and the royal line of David ended.

The agony of Job is vividly depicted in this statue by sculptor Ivan Mestrovic. Despite the intense suffering Job underwent, he never lost faith in God.

587 B.C. to 64 B.C. In 539 B.C., Cyrus, King of Persia, concluded a triumphant campaign of conquest finally overcoming Babylon. This enlightened monarch decreed that all "displaced persons" in his dominions could go home. By 537 B.C., a brave and idealistic band of Jews, as they were now known, arrived at the ruins of Jerusalem.

But the city itself remained open to siege by the unfriendly people who surrounded it until, in the following century, Nehemiah built a strong wall around it. Ezra expounded the Mosaic Law, and "Wisdom" writers were active. Around 330 B.C., Judah was absorbed into the Hellenistic Empire of Alexander the Great, and Greek culture became a strong influence in Jewish life.

Thereafter, Palestine became territory disputed between the Ptolemies of Egypt and the Seleucid kings of Antioch. Judas Maccabaeus, in 168 B.C., and after him his brothers, fought the Seleucids, recovering the independence of Judah in 141 B.C. The descendants of the Maccabees, the Hasmonaean kings, then ruled the area. The last year of independence for Judah was 64 B.C. Thereafter, Rome gained control.

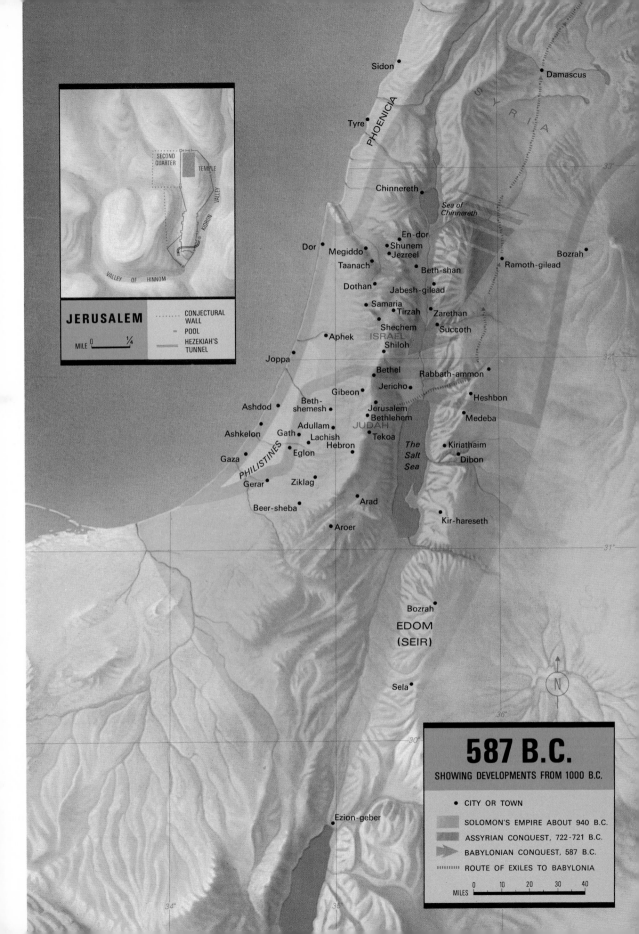

JERUSALEM

MILE 0 .... 1/4

- - - - - CONJECTURAL WALL
═══ POOL
▬▬▬ HEZEKIAH'S TUNNEL

SECOND QUARTER
TEMPLE
KIDRON VALLEY
VALLEY OF HINNOM

Sidon
Damascus
Tyre
PHOENICIA
SYRIA

Chinnereth
Sea of Chinnereth

Dor
Megiddo
Taanach
En-dor
Shunem
Jezreel
Beth-shan
Bozrah
Ramoth-gilead

Dothan
Jabesh-gilead
Samaria
Tirzah
Zarethan
Shechem
Succoth
Aphek
ISRAEL
Shiloh

Joppa
Bethel
Jericho
Rabbath-ammon
Gibeon
Heshbon
Ashdod
Beth-shemesh
Jerusalem
Bethlehem
Medeba
Ashkelon
Gath
Adullam
JUDAH
Lachish
Tekoa
Kiriathaim
Hebron
The Salt Sea
Dibon
Gaza
Eglon
PHILISTINES
Gerar
Ziklag
Beer-sheba
Arad
Kir-hareseth
Aroer

Bozrah

EDOM (SEIR)

Sela

N

Ezion-geber

587 B.C.

SHOWING DEVELOPMENTS FROM 1000 B.C.

- • CITY OR TOWN
- SOLOMON'S EMPIRE ABOUT 940 B.C.
- ASSYRIAN CONQUEST, 722-721 B.C.
- ➤ BABYLONIAN CONQUEST, 587 B.C.
- ·········· ROUTE OF EXILES TO BABYLONIA

0 10 20 30 40
MILES

Baal, a Canaanite deity who was the god of growth, was denounced by the Old Testament prophets. They believed their God to be the Creator of all things.

Rembrandt's painting of Moses breaking the tablets of the Ten Commandments. Later, after his people repented their sins, Moses received a new copy of the tablets.

Before 1500 B.C. The Holy Land lies between the two worlds of the East and the West. It is part of a fertile crescent that stretches from Egypt along the coast of Palestine and then swings down the Tigris-Euphrates Valley. Archaeologists have uncovered traces of human civilization there going back many thousands of years.

Around 1900-1500 B.C., the patriarch Abraham, father of the people who were later to become known as the Israelites, arrived in this, their Promised Land, from Mesopotamia. Thus began what is often called the Age of the Patriarchs. Abraham himself met with Melchizedek, King of Salem, later known as Jerusalem, and the king, though a pagan priest, blessed Abraham. Abraham and his descendants led their flocks about parts of Palestine, or Canaan as it was then called, for several generations.

They came to know the religious ideas of the native Canaanites. These people worshiped several gods, including Astarte, Baal, and El. It was largely in protest against this worship that the religion of the Israelites later developed. As the patriarchal period came to a close, these wandering people were forced by drought to migrate to Egypt.

1500 B.C. to 1000 B.C. One of the most important events of biblical history was the exodus of the Israelites from Egypt. It probably took place around 1280 B.C. During the wandering of the Israelites in the wilderness, Moses, their leader, brought the people the Ten Commandments from Mt. Sinai, the identification of which is today uncertain. Here the Israelites became the covenant people of God.

During this period, the city-states of Philistia and the kingdoms of Ammon and Moab were established. Joshua led the invasion of Canaan and captured, among others, the cities of Ai and Jericho. Eventually, he conquered most of the areas later known as Galilee, Judah, and Samaria. After Joshua's death, individual local leaders, called judges, conquered additional areas and fought back nomadic intruders.

The scattered tribes were finally organized loosely under a monarchy. Saul was their ruler, but he did not prove acceptable to all. It remained for David to unite them. He captured Jebus, or Jerusalem, and made it his capital around 1000 B.C.

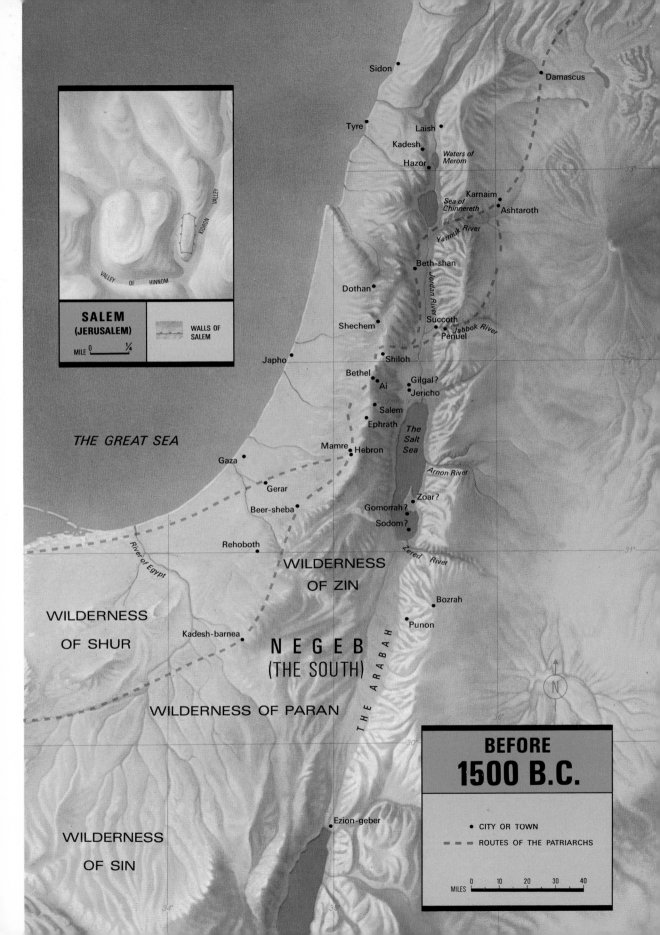

SALEM
(JERUSALEM)

MILE 0 ¼

WALLS OF
SALEM

VALLEY OF HINNOM

KIDRON VALLEY

Sidon

Damascus

Tyre

Laish

Kadesh

Hazor

Waters of Merom

Karnaim

Sea of Chinnereth

Ashtaroth

Yarmuk River

Beth-shan

Jordan River

Dothan

Succoth

Jabbok River

Shechem

Penuel

Japho

Shiloh

Bethel

Ai

Gilgal?

Jericho

Salem

Ephrath

The Salt Sea

Mamre

Hebron

Arnon River

THE GREAT SEA

Gaza

Zoar?

Gerar

Gomorrah?

Beer-sheba

Sodom?

Rehoboth

Zered River

WILDERNESS
OF ZIN

Bozrah

WILDERNESS

Punon

OF SHUR

Kadesh-barnea

N E G E B
(THE SOUTH)

THE ARABAH

River of Egypt

WILDERNESS OF PARAN

N

BEFORE

1500 B.C.

Ezion-geber

WILDERNESS

● CITY OR TOWN

OF SIN

━ ━ ROUTES OF THE PATRIARCHS

MILES 0 10 20 30 40

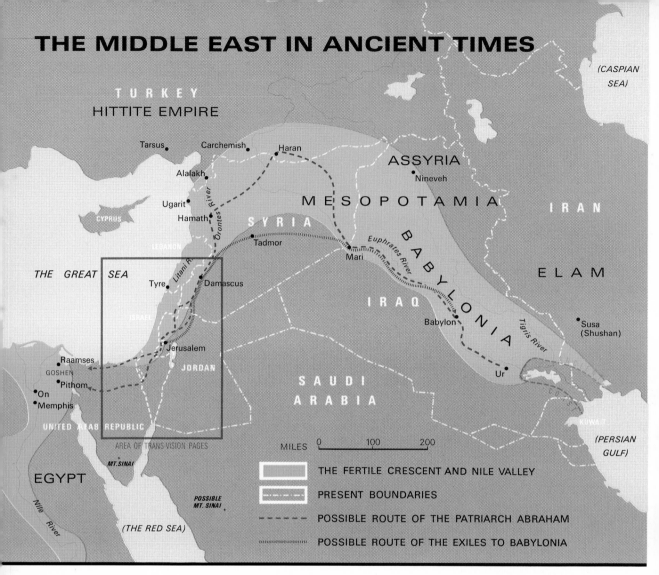

THE MIDDLE EAST IN ANCIENT TIMES

(CASPIAN SEA)

TURKEY
HITTITE EMPIRE

Tarsus
Carchemish
Haran
ASSYRIA
Nineveh

Alalakh

Ugarit
MESOPOTAMIA
IRAN

Hamath
SYRIA
BABYLONIA

CYPRUS

Tadmor

Euphrates River

Mari

ELAM

THE GREAT SEA

Tyre
Damascus
IRAQ

Babylon
Susa (Shushan)

ISRAEL

Tigris River

Jerusalem
JORDAN

Raamses
Ur

GOSHEN

Pithom

On
SAUDI ARABIA
KUWAIT

Memphis

UNITED ARAB REPUBLIC
(PERSIAN GULF)

AREA OF TRANS-VISION PAGES

MILES 0 — 100 — 200

EGYPT

MT. SINAI

Nile River

POSSIBLE MT. SINAI

(THE RED SEA)

THE FERTILE CRESCENT AND NILE VALLEY

PRESENT BOUNDARIES

POSSIBLE ROUTE OF THE PATRIARCH ABRAHAM

POSSIBLE ROUTE OF THE EXILES TO BABYLONIA

Prepared by the editors of THE WORLD BOOK YEAR BOOK.

CONSULTANT

George A. F. Knight, Professor of Old Testament, McCormick Theological Seminary.

ART WORK

Antonio Petrucelli, and the art staff of THE WORLD BOOK YEAR BOOK.

CRITICAL REVIEWERS

E. B. Espenshade, Jr., Chairman, Department of Geography, Northwestern University;
Floyd V. Filson, Dean and Professor of New Testament, McCormick Theological Seminary;
Samuel Sandmel, Professor of Bible and Hellenistic Literature, Hebrew Union College;
Samuel Terrien, Professor of Old Testament, Union Theological Seminary.

PRINTED IN U.S.A. BY THE TRANS-VISION® DIVISION, MILPRINT INCORPORATED.

A YEAR BOOK
SPECIAL REPORT
IN TWO PARTS

CHINA

INDIA

Two principal nations on the continent of Asia are seeking to catch up with the 20th century. The means each uses, and the philosophy it follows, will influence the course of world history. Some historians, in fact, believe that the question of who will control Asia is the most important concern of modern times. In the following two articles, THE WORLD BOOK YEAR BOOK reports on the efforts of China and India to solve one of their most serious problems: feeding their teeming masses. This they must do before they can achieve the ambitious industrial goals that will bring them into the mainstream of 20th-century life.

INSIDE RURAL CHINA

THE MIRACLE OF THE MOUNTAIN

BY MARK GAYN

Chou Min-shan's village, they say only half in jest, is far from anywhere. To reach it, one first takes a milk-run train from Taiyuan, the capital of Shansi province. The train rumbles south through the night, halting at every whistle stop to unload or pick up crowds of sleepy and silent peasants, soldiers, and local officials. The sun just begins to peek over the hills when one arrives at the county seat of Chin Wo. From here, after a brief nap and breakfast at a primitive inn for visiting VIP's, one pursues his journey for another two hours in an aged Russian-built automobile driven by a man who seems to be on first-name terms with every pothole in the dirt road.

I knew the Chinese countryside during the 1930's and the 1940's, and, seeing it now, after such a long time, a strange feeling comes over me. It is as if I have never been away. Everything has remained un-

The author:

Mark Gayn, who was born in China, is a distinguished correspondent and head of the Asia bureau of The Toronto Star. He is one of the few Western writers to view today's China firsthand.

YEAR BOOK photos by Marc Ribaud, Magnum

Older Chinese find their way of life put aside, although the new regime gives lip service to the traditions of filial piety.

changed. There are the same villages with mud huts and crumbling walls that blend with the landscape. There are the same children and mongrels in the dusty streets; the same families pushing the heavy millstones. Many of the carts I pass on the road have rubber tires, but as often as not they are being drawn by human beings. And in the fields I see teams of four or five men, women, and children pulling plows. The air is filled with loess dust, and it bleaches the greenery, the faces of the peasants, and their invariable blue clothing.

After we climb what must be the hundredth hill, we suddenly come upon Chou's village. Though it is famous across the land, it is little more than a couple of dusty roads joined at right angles like a huge "L." The mud homes are strung along the sides of the "L," and Chou's office, a modest gray-brick building with an inner yard, stands where the roads converge.

I am led into a small room with a gray-white sheet hanging over the doorway to help keep out the dust and the flies. A boy brings a basin of hot water with a small towel floating in it, and I mop my face. The room is bare but for a crude table, a few chairs, and a large portrait of Mao Tse-tung, leader of the Chinese Communist party. Next to the portrait is a neatly brushed slogan, "Enhance the revolutionary tradition and strive for greater successes." There are sounds of commotion outside, and Chou strides in briskly. He gives me a happy, boyish smile, grasps my hand in both of his, and begins to pump my arm.

Chou's village of Nan Liu is at the same time a "production brigade," and it is one of the 25 such brigades that make up the *Nan Fan* (southern Fan) commune. (All that seems to be remembered of Fan is that he was a farmer who died a long, long time ago.)

As in the case of the million or so other villages of China, Nan Liu is a fragment of Mao's revolution in the countryside. Fifteen years ago,

the communist leaders still talked of giving the land to those who tilled it. But both reason and dogma militated against unproductive small holdings. Thus, in the fall of 1958, after trying out various types of co-operatives, Peking ordered the creation of communes. These took over nearly all the land, most of the dray animals, and what little mechanized equipment there was. Peking then proclaimed the arrival of socialism in the countryside.

But the revolution did more than merely change the ownership of the land. The country's 74,000 communes today are political, economic, and psychological tools of infinite complexity. In a typical village such as Nan Liu, the state and the Communist party join hands in directing people's minds, lives, and production efforts. From here, they govern, provide medical care, teach, exact taxes, indoctrinate, give military training, and instruct in the use of birth control devices. But Peking is 350 long miles to the northeast, far beyond the mountains, and the villagers have learned to pay heed to the whims and orders of the men closer by—the provincial bosses in Taiyuan, which is 200 miles to the north, or to the legion of officials in the county and the commune. In this multilayered hierarchy, Chou is a key figure. It is through him, as head of the production brigade, that the state and the party get the peasants to work hard, produce more, and think right.

All this emerges as hours pass, and Chou continues his recital. Chou was only 22 years old when he was elected chairman of the brigade back in 1958. He still does not look much older. His slim body, his vigorous gestures, his eagerness, and sincerity are those of a young scout-master. Now and then, he impatiently sweeps up his long black hair when it falls on his forehead.

But it soon becomes apparent that this is Chou's public image. Behind it, one discerns the shadow of the inner man. After 10 hours with him, I begin to feel that this slight youth is very much a man, with an astute mind, a measure of ruthlessness, and a great deal of ambition. Chou is the new Organization Man, one of perhaps a few million through whom the party is seeking to change the countryside.

Chou was 11 years old when a band of guerrillas walked up the hill to Nan Liu and set up a communist regime. He attended the local school, joined the communist youth organization, and in 1956 became a full-fledged communist. The party was clearly pleased with the eager youngster. Two years later, when Peking ordered the creation of village communes as part of its "Great Leap Forward," a meeting was called in Nan Liu to discuss—and approve—Peking's order. Someone stood up and proposed that the village become a production brigade in the new commune and that the peasants study Mao Tse-tung's works, for in these they would find the answers to all their problems. ·

I ask who this someone was. Chou hesitates, and the three or four men in the room shout with delight, "Chou, Chou; it was Chou!" Then they turn to him and say, "*Ni tai chien shu*" ("You're too modest"). Chou blushes and says, "Chairman Mao always tells us that we must guard against arrogance."

$\overline{m}$
$\overline{F}$
$\overline{F}''$
$\overline{F}'$
$\overline{m}_o(\overline{F})$
$\overline{m}(\overline{F}\,\overline{F}'')$
$=\overline{m}_o(\overline{F})$

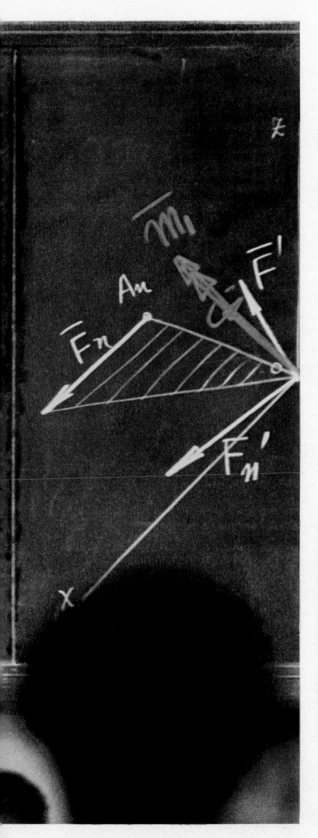

Massive programs to reduce illiteracy and strengthen educational standards consume more than 12 per cent of China's state budget. About four of every 10 persons in rural China can now read, according to official sources. After graduation, students from the Peking Technological School, left, may be assigned menial jobs in the communes, where they are expected to teach other workers and also to learn respect for manual labor.

Universal primary school education is still beyond China's reach, but four out of five children of primary age are said now to attend school. Secondary schools, such as the one in Nanking, below, give high priority to scientific training.

Thirty villages were put into the commune, and among them they organized 25 production brigades. Chou was elected chairman of the brigade in Nan Liu. He has held this post since then, and, as the brigade progressed, his fame spread. In 1960, he was named an "Advanced Worker" for the province. A year later, he became a "Model Worker." In 1964, after the omnipotent *Jen Min Jih Pao* (People's Daily) in Peking twice ran full-page articles on his good works, Chou was named a member of the National People's Congress (parliament) and met Mao Tse-tung. Pilgrims by the thousands began to flock from all corners of China to see how, with the help of Mao's teachings, this youth converted a village that once needed government grain to survive into one that grew enough to feed its people, and still sell a surplus to the state.

As we sit and talk, donkeys bray beyond the wall, and the cook is noisily scrubbing the oversized cast-iron pot set into a clay stove in the yard. Now and then, youngsters bring tea or whisper into Chou's ear. Like him, they look clean, efficient, and ragged. The Chinese countryside wears cotton, and cotton textiles are tightly rationed. The annual ration in Nan Liu is four yards, just about enough for one blue suit. Chou's suit is faded and frayed, and there is a neat patch on the seat of his trousers. His cotton sandals are also in poor repair. But, somehow, I begin to feel that to Chou this is a badge of honor—a visible vow of poverty that he has taken with countless other zealots, and a vow that is expected of the Organization Man.

The sounds of the village at work come to us, and Chou tells me of the revolution in the countryside. It is a story of privation, harsh elements, backbreaking effort, and the infinite variety of methods the party has used to bend the villagers to its will.

"Up to 1958," Chou recalls, "life was very difficult here. Our fields produced little. All we had was 57 head of cattle. Of these, only 40 could be used for work in the fields. Our population kept growing, and we didn't have enough to eat. The government had to give us 70,000 catties of grain (one catty equals 1.33 pounds) to keep us alive.

"From our study of Chairman Mao's works we learned that while China is a great country, it's also a backward one. This is both good and bad. A white sheet of paper can be used for beautiful writing and painting. Thus, we decided to take part in the national revolution by carrying out reform here.

"But we had two problems to start with. Our land was poor and our livestock was meager. These were two mountains on the brigade's shoulders. So our committee studied Chairman Mao's story of Yu Kung and his mountain.* In discussing it, we realized that China has already removed the mountains of imperialism, capitalism, and feudalism. We certainly could remove our own two mountains.

*Yu Kung was an old man who, on discovering a mountain obstructing the entrance to his house, decided to dig it away. When the people called him a fool, Yu Kung said, "If I don't remove this mountain, my sons will. If they won't, *their* sons will." And eventually the mountain was removed.

"We didn't know, however, where to begin. So again we studied Chairman Mao's works, and we found our answer. In moving mountains, he said, people turn to God. But who's God? God is the people themselves. So we decided to call on all our people—we had 680 of them then—to move our mountains. We held a general meeting and we said, 'We must work for three to five years to convert our mountains into fertile fields.' "

At this point, I find myself wondering whether there is any connection between Chou's figurative reference to mountains and the very real mountain I already know is next to Nan Liu. Chou quickly helps me out by explaining just what did take place in Nan Liu.

"In the winter of 1958," he recalls, "we marched to the mountain outside our village. The whole area at the time was swarming with wolves. They had attacked nine persons in the preceding five years. Nonetheless, we moved into their caves, and the beasts disappeared. The mountain was badly eroded by rain. We terraced it, and shaped it so that the rain water would stay in the fields, instead of running off. The earth was frozen three feet deep, but we worked on."

As Chou tells his story, his voice rises, and his gestures become more dramatic. The work, he says, went on for six winters, through 1963. The snow fell; the cold was fierce. But Chou was always there to urge the men and women on. He would say to them, "When our people fought the reactionaries, they paid no heed to rain, storm, and snow. Why should we act differently in this revolution?" Or he would cry, "The weather is cold, but our hearts are warm. The earth is hard, but our will is harder."

Chou was the organizer, the driver, the cheerleader, the slogan-maker, the spinner of tales. From a communist song, he borrowed a phrase which he told me had become a village saying: "There are many lovely and precious things, but the loveliest and the most precious are our government and Chairman Mao." Or, borrowing from another song, he would say, "Our parents took good care of us, but no one is doing as much for us as the party and Chairman Mao." In the end, he made many peasants feel that Chairman Mao had no greater preoccupations than the affairs of Nan Liu, and that the villagers simply had to do well or they would be betraying Mao's confidence.

In his unceasing efforts, Chou was aided by the other 25 communists in the village that by now had some 800 people. One of the 25 was a 68-year-old man, to whom revolution brought literacy. Now he was able to read newspapers, study Chairman Mao's essays, and even write a poem which he delivered at the drop of a hat:

> At night I study Chairman Mao's works
> And keep them in the recesses of my heart.
> My debt to Chairman Mao is so great
> I shall never be able to repay it.

Nan Liu suffered repeated calamities. Despite the careful terracing, heavy rains periodically washed away parts of the mountain, so that it

China's 74,000 communes differ in size and affluence. This one near Peking is one of the best. Its 55,000 persons live in 110 villages and farm 22,000 acres. Average income is about $11 per month. Building at right is the machine shop. Commune boasts a total of 64 tractors.

had to be reterraced. There were devastating droughts. The worst began in 1959 and lasted through the spring and early summer of 1960. When no rain came by May 13—the traditional rain deadline in China's country lore—the old men shook their heads and called it a disaster. The villagers were summoned to a meeting, and Chou recalled Chairman Mao's statement on "learning from the experience of the elders." An oldster was consulted. He said there might be water in a patch of grassland a mile or two away. (Why the older peasants remained silent until that point was not explained.) Teams of peasants dug for three days and nights, and 30 feet down they found enough water for drinking and irrigation. One of the communists in the brigade won some renown by carrying four buckets of water suspended from his shoulder pole, instead of the usual two buckets. "The slogan we adopted," Chou now recalls, "was that each man must sow 1,000 seeds of corn, and then make sure they were irrigated." The rains broke the drought on the 257th day, in July. Despite the drought, the brigade, under Chou's leadership, was able to produce a surplus of grain.

There was also a memorable insect invasion that threatened to destroy the cotton crop. To meet this danger, the village sent its 250 youngsters into the fields. They stayed there for seven days and nights, examining each leaf of each plant. They did not return until they had liquidated 70,000 bugs.

In the face of all such trials, Chou says, there has been a steady improvement in the yield of the reluctant earth. The production of wheat per *mou* (one-sixth of an acre) has gone up 60 per cent. The output of

124

cotton has risen 24 per cent. The livestock—cows, oxen, donkeys—has multiplied almost fourfold to 210 head. ("This," Chou notes, "has given us more manure for fertilizer and more animals for field work.")

The income of the peasants has also risen, Chou tells me. In a year, an average adult toiled 300 workdays, for each of which he was paid the equivalent in cash or grain of 60 cents in American money. (Having visited other communes in China, I suspect that Chou exaggerates. The annual income of each working adult in Nan Liu is probably much closer to $100 a year than to $180.) This compares with the $250 to $300 earned by the average factory worker, who, however, has no pork or cabbage of his own to help enrich his daily menu.

With all the added money in their pockets, Chou contends, the peasants have gone on a shopping spree. Over a period of "a few years," they have bought 75 bicycles and 83 sets of farm tools (hoes, rakes, and such) for private use. The brigade's funds have also gone up, enabling it to buy a small power plant to operate the two new milling machines, eight small rubber-tired carriages for moving anything from potatoes to an ailing grandmother, and, inevitably, loudspeakers. In Nan Liu, as in most villages of China, loudspeakers are as much a part of the landscape as the dust. A person standing in a field a mile or two from the village can still be reached by the sound of a militant song, news broadcasts, Chairman Mao's sayings read by a schoolgirl, or Chou's exhortations.

After lunch, while Chou is talking to the latest busload of Chinese visitors, I leave his office and wander across the road to the village store. The sun is beating down on the dry earth, and the thick dust lies unstirred except when a cart, drawn by three mules, goes by with a heavy load. The cart stops, and three men jump off to pass the time of day with the few villagers in sight. Nearby, despite the heat, a group of young men in trousers and undershirts are tossing a ball.

The store is small, dark, and relatively well-stocked. It has rationed

Tools for commune peasants are made in the tool and die shop, which also serves as a classroom in which peasants are exposed to industrial work.

cotton socks, face cream for the village lovelies, and the red tin dragon images that parents put around the necks of newborn sons to bring them good luck. The store offers rationed cooking oil and two sewing machines, the latter selling at $65 each. (Chou says 30 of these were sold in the preceding two years.) Two girls are pricing a length of flowered cotton. The material for a jacket and trousers would cost them the equivalent of 15 workdays, and they look undecided.

As I come out, I see two youngsters writing on a blackboard by the roadside. What they are writing is a news item announcing that another four planes of the American aggressors have been shot down by the patriotic forces in Laos (regarded in China as an important battleground). Next to the blackboard, two squatting men, looking wholly unconcerned, are reading three-day-old copies of the provincial newspaper. For the first time, I notice that an outside wall of Chou's office is covered with a large mural. It shows young people with eager faces following an older peasant. The inscription says, "Learn from the older peasants." In this village, run by such a young man, there is a touch of irony in the mural.

And then I suddenly realize that although the village looks much as it must have 30 years, or perhaps even a century, ago, it has really changed to a remarkable degree. The peasants still know no condition but poverty. They still live in mud huts and still use primitive tools. The older ones among them, at least, still worship their ancestors. But the bonds that once held the family together are under a powerful strain, and the old virtues and values are being replaced.

Filial piety is still strong, but the young are taught that devotion to the state, the party, and to Chairman Mao is an even greater virtue. Go-betweens still help to arrange marriages, but, more frequently, the youths find their own mates. This is definitely the era of the young, who are impatient to wreck and to rebuild, rather than of the aged, who want to hold on to the accustomed ways. The old social structure, topped by the landlord, the usurer, and the old headman, is gone. Instead, there has come the new breed of communist Organization Men, young, able, and hard-driving. They have seemingly taken monastic vows, use Chairman Mao's works the way the old-time revivalists used the Bible to inspire and to silence all doubt, and they are dedicated to carrying out Peking's policies.

Chou's mission is twofold—to increase production and to change men's souls. His prime tools are political. The party's Central Committee in Peking organizes vast campaigns that sweep across the land like wildfire. In no time at all, they reach Nan Liu. When, for instance, Peking ordered a campaign of support for "the democratic people of Vietnam," Chou had the villagers march through the dust carrying red banners and posters. There was fiery anti-American oratory, and children put on a dance in which they chased a frightened President Lyndon B. Johnson.

Politics in Nan Liu is a serious matter. It is pursued by the Communist party branch, by the communist youth organization, by something called the Poor and Lower-Middle Class Peasants' Association, by the production brigade's propaganda section, and by the women's federation. When the peasants take a break in the fields, they may have to listen to a party agitator, or to a reading of excerpts from Chairman Mao's works. When they return home, they may be visited by a party worker or summoned to a lecture or a public meeting. Chou recalls a recent meeting at which a peasant, taking his cue from one of Chairman Mao's essays, recited his own poem:

> *We're now in Nan Liu village*
> *But our eyes are on the Tien An Men.** *
> *We toil in the fields,*
> *But our minds think of all the world.*

A meeting that starts with poetry may easily turn to condemning the laggards or to exposing internal enemies. I have visited communes elsewhere in China in which as many as 6 per cent of all the adults were described as being hostile to the system. Nan Liu is fortunate. It has only two former landlords whom Chou describes as enemies, and they are being given huge, daily, soul-saving doses of indoctrination.

As with all other villages and towns in the land, Nan Liu also has its militia detachment. It includes nearly all of the able-bodied men and women in the village. With their rifles or Tommy guns, they drill after work in the fields, lying in ambush behind a hillock, or storming the unseen imperialist foe. The task of the militia, Chou explains, is to resist aggression from without and to be vigilant against enemies at home.

Not far from Chou's office stands the village school. Here, the youngsters begin their indoctrination at an early age. At five, they break into a merry song such as this:

> *There is in Peking a golden mountain,*
> *And on it there is a golden sun,*
> *And that sun is Chairman Mao.*

At the age of seven, their dancing instructor is likely to put them through the motions of bayoneting the "American bandit aggressors in Vietnam." The little books they read usually carry colored pictures of soldiers and airplanes, or boys with guns. They extol revolutionary gore and heroes. In nonpolitical subjects, schooling is severely practical. Indeed, under a new reform, the pupils may be spending half their time in the next few years in the classroom and the other half in the fields or cow barns. This is expected to make them better workers and better citizens. Some people grumble that this would also make the children "half-students." Chou scoffs at such criticism.

The sun is beginning to set, and deep shadows fall on Nan Liu when Chou suggests that we see his mountain. We drive up the dirt road that has sunk so deep into the soft loess that one is sometimes below the level of the fields. The road is lined with young trees, and Chou says, "Someday we shall cut these down and build new homes with the

---

*Peking's Gate of Heavenly Calm, from which Mao Tse-tung customarily reviews parades on national holidays.

Despite its effort to catch up with the 20th century, China still has large areas little changed from former times. These Yunnan province women are hoeing in a rice paddy.

A peasant family is permitted a small vegetable garden, perhaps 30 x 50 feet in size, which provides much of its food and profit. The government abolished these plots in the late 1950's, causing a food crisis in the country. Later they were returned. This family plot is in a commune near Shanghai.

Loess soil of north China is fertile, but quickly erodes in wind and rain. Terraces, therefore, are essential, even in wheat fields such as these in Shensi province.

lumber." Not far from the top of the mountain, we turn off the road and suddenly I see the miracle that Chou and the villagers have performed. What had been a bare, rain-scarred mountain, similar to those I view across the valley, has now become a 420-acre field—a succession of terraces of grain and cotton. The wind runs through the field of wheat, ruffles the top-heavy stalks, and keeps on descending until it raises a whirlpool of dust in the village below. Each terrace is perhaps 60 feet wide, and is slanted inward toward the face of the mountain to retain the moisture. The back wall of each terrace is freshly trimmed.

I have seen such terraces from Korea to Indonesia. But this is still an impressive sight, and one suddenly realizes why Peking honors this young man and why pilgrims come to see what he has done. Yet, one is also startled by the primitiveness of this tiny fragment of the new China. Just below me, on a terrace chosen for cotton planting, perhaps a score of men, women, and children are at work, with only two horses to help them. The seeder, the harrow, all the tools are crude and ancient. Some are being dragged by the villagers. Chou's village may be the hope of Peking, but it must also be Peking's despair, for, despite the miracle it has accomplished, this village is still barely emerging from the dark ages of land tilling.

We come down the mountain, and I see some of the small plots— each about 30 x 50 feet—the peasants can call their own. Here, they raise the vegetables needed to supplement whatever grain is allotted to them by the brigade for their "workdays." Here, too, they grow the feed for their animals and fowl. No peasant can own a cow or a mule; these animals belong to the brigade. But he can have two or three pigs to sell to the commune or for his own table (a luxury few can afford).

During the late 1950's, communist zealots abolished the private plots, and the result was suffering. The government in Peking soon ended that practice, as it also ended occasional efforts to house all the peasants in barracks.

Discontent, however, persists. Many peasants still remember the acre or two they received soon after the communist takeover, only to have them confiscated, first for the so-called "co-ops" and then for the communes. Still more peasants object to having commune officers from another village decide what is to be done with the grain and cotton grown in Nan Liu, and how much each peasant is to get as his share. Whether the field is his or not, the peasant feels that the harvest he helped to grow belongs to him, and he wants to see it and feel it and have a say in its division. This is a source of sharp friction between the peasant on one hand and Peking (and Chou) on the other hand. The villagers, finally, feel the new party overseers are sometimes getting too much of their grain for too little work. They also resent the young upstarts who tell the older men what to do, and how to do it. The discontent presents no threat to Peking, but it is there.

Toronto Star photo by Mark Gayn

Chou Min-shan is typical of the new Organization Man in Red China. He is young, energetic, and dedicated to the communist program.

The people of Nan Liu live in acute poverty, but they are not starving. Even in the cruelest years from 1959 to 1962, there was enough food to sustain life, and it was divided equitably. By contrast, the old villagers remember that in a famine in the 1920's, ten people died of hunger in Nan Liu.

The fuller rice bowl is not the only symbol of advance, however. The usurers are gone, and the officials, such as Chou, are honest. The school gives a modicum of learning, and illiteracy among the older people is rapidly declining. The public health system has virtually ended epidemics. I see no children with trachoma or running sores, and no oldsters begging for a few coppers. But Nan Liu is still desperately short of fertilizer, and it woefully lacks modern equipment. (The entire commune, with its 30 villages, owns only four tractors.)

There are still no trained agronomists attached to Chou's brigade, and only now and then will one visit Nan Liu to offer hasty counsel. An observer looks at this famous village and realizes that progress in the Chinese countryside is spotty and heartbreakingly slow. It must be counted not in years, nor even in decades, but in generations. Chou's grandsons will be living in the 21st century when Nan Liu may still be approaching the 20th century. The meaning of Nan Liu for China is plain. No modern industry can be built atop a backward countryside without creating harsh problems for tomorrow. China's atomic plants and new industries to the contrary, the country's advance must continue to be held back by its Nan Liu's.

We drive down to the village and leave the car. On the dusty road, we meet peasants returning from work or going on their errands. No one smiles at Chou. No one greets him. Can it be that the villagers who appreciate the miracle on the mountain have no love for this very hard, young miracle man?

See also Section Three, ASIA; CHINA.

INSIDE RURAL INDIA

THE SILENT STRUGGLE

BY KEKI R. BHOTE

Among the 550,000 villages of India, two of the most typical are known as Alande and Utroli. These dusty hamlets nestle in the foothills of the Western Ghats in the county of Bhor, more than 100 miles by road southeast of Bombay. Here, in the dim past, was the proud home of Sivaji, the "Mountain Rat King," who led his rugged Mahratta warriors down from their mountain hideouts to turn back the ancient Mogul hordes.

The glories of Sivaji still raise a flicker of pride in the people of Alande and Utroli. But until recently little else—surely nothing subsequent to Sivaji's 17th century accomplishments—stirred the villagers from their usual lethargy and their blind repetitions that for hundreds of years made yesterday like today, and today like tomorrow. Only a few years ago, the two villages were just a collection of mud huts plastered with cow dung. They had no roads, no wells, no schools, no self-government.

Lalita Mhasavade, a village level worker in India's Community Development program, teaches a group of women in Utroli how to read and write.

The author:

Keki R. Bhote, who is now a citizen of the United States, is a foreign correspondent for Jame-Jamshed, a leading newspaper in Bombay, and is a widely known lecturer and author. He has made four world tours, interviewing leaders in Asia and Europe.

YEAR BOOK photos by Baldev, Pix

Under a pipal tree in the village of Alande, lower right, G. B. Bandal presides at a meeting of the village council.

The villagers—trampled for centuries by local maharajas, victimized by the excesses of the caste system, immobilized by a rigid family structure—slumbered on in medieval oblivion. Indeed, when independence dawned on India in 1947, Alande and Utroli were scarcely aware that the sun had begun to rise.

Since then, however, a new spirit has swept these villages. Under the guidance of the national government in New Delhi, Alande and Utroli are attempting to catch up with the 20th century. If this is a race for survival against the Red giant to the North of India—and perhaps it is—then China is the hare and India, plodding, flexible, undogmatic, is the tortoise. The outcome of this race will be felt around the world.

India is the second most populous nation on earth. Of its 490,000,000 people (about one out of every seven persons in the world), more than 360,000,000 live in farming villages much like Alande and Utroli. Seven of every 10 workers are engaged in agriculture, and account for about half the national income. Even so, India today cannot feed itself because its crop yields per acre are among the lowest in the world. Because of his primitive methods, the Indian farmer grows only one-fourth as much rice per acre as a Japanese farmer; one-fifth as much cotton as an Egyptian.

India's leaders, heirs to the nonviolent traditions of Mohandas K. Gandhi, believe that progress in their country will be permanent only if it reaches the grass roots of their society, the farmer.

India failed in its first attempt after independence to increase agricultural production. The Grow More Food Campaign, as that initial program was called, was little more than a national campaign of exhortation. A few placards appeared in a few villages. There were some programs to demonstrate modern farming techniques. But the farmers did not respond. By 1951, the program was called off.

After India's first general elections in 1952, the government decided

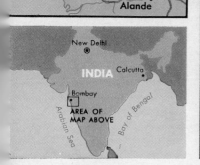

on a new course. It was based on the belief that, given the proper initial help and encouragement, India's villagers had sufficient individual initiative to become the main architects of their own progress. This is the essence of India's new village Community Development program. Community Development, in some form, now reaches most villages.

Because so much of the future of Asia is at stake in this program, I recently revisited my homeland for a firsthand look at how it was proceeding. Even by jet, India is a long way from the United States. When I got behind the wheel of my jeep in Bombay and headed into the hills of the Mountain Rat King, it seemed that the distance surely must be measured not only in miles, but in years as well. I wondered if I might not be received something like a Connecticut Yankee in King Arthur's Court.

It was my hope that I could slip casually into the village, meet the key people, mingle with the villagers, and slip away again. I wanted to escape government handouts, official receptions, and the usual red carpet treatment for visitors from abroad. I wanted a realistic view of village progress, without the rose-tinted glasses of the Ministry of Community Development. My scheme was working out well until my good friend and colleague, photographer Baldev, unslung his camera. People everywhere like to have their pictures taken, and rural Indian villagers are no exception. Baldev became the Pied Piper of Alande and Utroli, and a crowd of delighted children followed him throughout our visit. Notwithstanding, we saw rural India as few outsiders could have hoped to see it.

To understand the Community Development program, one must know a little about its general plan of organization and administration. The basic unit is the block, an area roughly equivalent to a U.S. county. Each block contains about 100 villages and is administered by the Block Development Officer (BDO).

Under the BDO is a team of specialists in agriculture, public health, village industries, and women's programs. The key man on the BDO's staff—indeed the cornerstone of the entire Community Development program—is the village level worker (VLW, or *gram sevak*). Each VLW serves an average of about 10 villages. The VLW is selected from among the villagers and is then trained for two years at one of four national Community Development training centers. He maintains day-to-day contact with the villagers, calling in the specialists when necessary. He must win the confidence and respect of the people. He, along with a *gram sevika* (a woman village level worker), who concentrates on the welfare of the women and children, is the instrument for change.

The male VLW for Alande and Utroli is V. L. Shrotri, a lean, shy man about 30 years old. When I set out to find Shrotri, I soon learned that he shied away from publicity and would slip into crowds whenever I got near him. After considerable persistence, however, I caught up with him as he was standing in a field with two bullocks in the background, discussing rice cultivation with three farmers.

To outward appearances, Shrotri seemed incapable of shouldering

S. K. Dey, minister for Community Development, was graduated from the University of Chicago. Dey left industry to work for the government.

C. S. Subramaniam holds the important post of minister for food and agriculture in the Shastri cabinet. He was born in the same south Indian town, Coimbatore, as was the author.

his responsibilities. A thin man, with bushy black hair and a scar on one cheek, he was a *Matric fail*, a polite term for a high school drop-out. He had had only four months of training for his job, instead of the prescribed two years. *Karma* (the wheel of destiny) had not smiled upon him. With a salary of just $22 a month, he had to support a wife and four children. He traveled on a bicycle between three villages assigned to him, except when he could hitch a ride on a jeep. These hardships seemed to leave him with little ambition to move to a higher position.

Despite his personal problems, Shrotri has helped to change the face of Alande and Utroli. Since he took over his job in 1962, the villages' approach road, once just a cow path, has become a *pucca* (firm road) that can handle jeeps, or even the Chryslers of visiting dignitaries. The road is the villagers' window to the outside world. They built it after they had voted in their own village council to volunteer their own labor. The community well, the council building, and the schoolhouse were built in the same way. The villagers have also erected poles for electricity. Ironically, the poles stand naked today, pointed reminders to visiting government officials to hurry up with electricity from neighboring Phatgar Dam. The school, which once contained only four grades, now has seven. Instead of almost total adult illiteracy, Alande and Utroli now have 225 enthusiastic literates out of an adult population of about 3,000. They are graduates of adult classes started by Shrotri and his female VLW.

But it is in agriculture that these villages are writing their best chapter. With Shrotri's help, the farmers are learning the benefits of fertilizers, hybrid seed, and water conservation. They can now obtain supplies and farm implements at their tiny service cooperative. The

Demonstration plots show how greatly rice yield can be increased by the use of hybrid seed and chemical fertilizer. Plot in foreground was planted in the traditional manner.

Village Level Worker V. L. Shrotri explains to farmers the superior yields obtained from hybrid rice seed containing both Indian and Japanese strains. Pure Indian seed will not stand up to chemical fertilizers and heavy irrigation.

co-op also furnishes them with credit at 8 per cent interest, a lot less than the 40 per cent formerly charged by the moneylenders. These changes have brought a 50 per cent increase in rice yield in Alande and Utroli. Food shortages plague India's big cities, but until the drought of 1965, there was no longer a food problem here.

How has the seemingly mediocre Shrotri managed this change? His success can be partly explained by the sheer need for his services. But much credit is due Shrotri himself. He is of the soil. His approach is low-key; his tools are patience and persuasion. Gradually, Shrotri convinced the skeptics that he knew how to grow more rice per acre than they did. Then the program took hold.

I first met Lalita Mhasavade, Shrotri's female counterpart, in Alande's wooden community building. Lalita's dark complexion set off the flashing whiteness of her teeth and sparkling eyes. Her white sari swayed gently as she led a dozen young girls in a primitive Indian ballet. As I watched the dancers' expressive hands and bodies, and saw the lights in their eyes, I knew that this dance—as most primitive Indian ballets—was intended to convey a message. And the message, I soon learned, was intended for me: "The village has a water shortage and the govern-

Two Peace Corpsmen were assigned to Bhor county. Here, Corpsman Phil Vroman visits a poultry farm he set up in Utroli village.

137

A student recites her lesson in a private school run by the wife of a well-to-do Bhor farmer. Students work in her home with materials sent by the United Nations Children's Fund. Their tuition is only 63 cents a month.

Girls picking peas in a field after their lessons in the classroom learn to perform tasks that are necessary to everyday village life. Their training is based on Gandhi's belief that schooling should not be solely theoretical.

ment must do something about it." Lalita's dance came through loud and clear, but she had made one miscalculation. She thought I was a a visiting government official, and she had devised her dance to nudge me into doing something about the water shortage.

I could scarcely have had a better introduction to Lalita, the dynamic, outgoing girl who is the gram sevika for the villages of Alande and Utroli. No shy, retiring drop-out was this girl. She had graduated from high school, spent two years taking the full Community Development training course, and was now infusing the women of the six villages for which she has responsibility with enthusiasm and faith in the Community Development program.

As I talked with Lalita, other women crowded about us, eager to tell their own story about special village projects. What a contrast this was to my memory of Indian village women, who habitually drew their saris across their face to avoid the gaze of a male stranger! The loss of shyness, Lalita explained, was perhaps the women's first important step toward the 20th century.

"They have come out of their homes to become educated, to form societies, and even to become members of the village council," Lalita said. "They run their own preschool activities for children and they attend tailoring classes and handicraft sessions. The women weave cloth and make paper dolls that they soon will begin to sell in city markets."

Lalita thinks her greatest success has been in setting up a rural radio forum in an area where there is only one radio to a village. The women who attend the forum listen to broadcasts together and then discuss the topics among themselves. They also meet with officials of All India Radio to plan future programs on subjects close to their own needs.

A usurious local moneylender, a breed that is disappearing, studies his books. The government instituted co-ops to end their power. Some villagers are in debt to moneylenders all their lives.

One of the most talked about subjects at these meetings is birth control. The city of Buffalo, N.Y., is a long way from Alande and Utroli, but urban Buffalo and rural India are linked by a most important recent development. It is the invention only five years ago by Dr. Jack Lippes of Buffalo of a simple, inexpensive, and reliable birth control device, called the Lippes Loop. The loop is an inexpensive twist of plastic which a physician can easily insert into a woman's uterus. It will remain in place for years but can be removed anytime. Since India's population has a net increase of 12,000,000 people a year, Indian leaders are speaking of the loop as the medical miracle of the century. (In a sense, it is a miracle, since doctors are not yet sure just how it prevents conception.)

In Alande and Utroli, I talked about the loop with Usha Deshpande, a trim, white-saried field-worker of the public health department. She is responsible for covering 40 of the surrounding villages under the auspices of Community Development.

"Until the Lippes Loop," Usha confessed, "our efforts at birth control got nowhere. In my territory, 154 women have now been fitted with the loop. Alande has none yet, and Utroli has only four. But these figures are misleading. When our doctor came here for the first time, most of the women were busy with the harvest. For the doctor's next

World Diet

*Calories Per Person
Per Day*

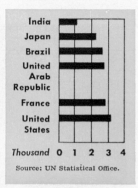

	Thousand	0	1	2	3	4

India
Japan
Brazil
United Arab Republic
France
United States

Source: UN Statistical Office.

Symbolic of India's poverty is this woman cooking chapatties, a flat, unleavened bread, which she and her family will eat with a vegetable stew as their big meal of the day.

visit, we already have signed up 50 women in Utroli and 155 in all of Bhor county, though still none in Alande."

One problem will remain, however. Indian women have no religious taboos against birth control, but they will not practice it until they have had two sons. As a father of five girls told me somewhat ruefully: "I have yet to begin."

In addition to implementing birth control, India's Community Development program is designed to attack another great problem of community life: the caste system. K. N. Kadam, Community Development's social welfare officer for Bhor county, is a veteran of many conflicts between caste Hindus and the untouchables, of whom there are more than 60,000,000 in India.

"We have a three-point program for the so-called untouchables in Bhor," he explained. "We grant them economic subsidies for wells, houses, farm implements, and seeds, as well as interest-free loans up to $100 without security. As has been the practice throughout India since 1955, we give them free scholarships to schools in the towns and cities. Surprisingly, about 100,000 untouchables throughout the country have taken advantage of this opportunity. It is in our social uplift program that we try hardest and succeed least. Untouchables and caste Hindus, you see, have nothing in common culturally. In social matters, we cannot force the pace."

Usha Deshpande, a public health worker in the Community Development program, holds the Lippes Loop as she explains aspects of birth control to women of Alande and Utroli. She is paving the way for the doctor's visit.

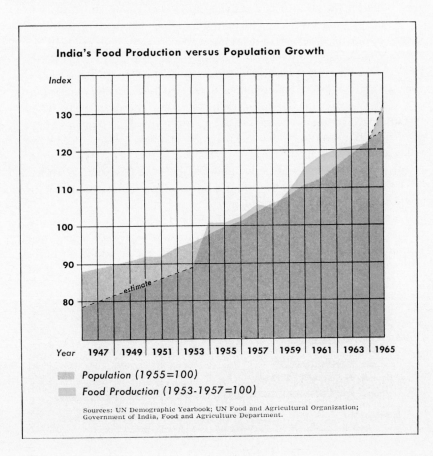

India's Food Production versus Population Growth

Index

130
120
110
100
90
80

estimate

Year 1947 1949 1951 1953 1955 1957 1959 1961 1963 1965

Population (1955=100)

Food Production (1953-1957=100)

Sources: UN Demographic Yearbook; UN Food and Agricultural Organization; Government of India, Food and Agriculture Department.

Despite the drought of 1965, India appears, in the long run, to be winning the grim struggle between a soaring population and hunger. Between 1947 and 1965, population increased from 345,000,000 to 490,000,000, but food output was at last keeping pace.

141

I asked if caste Hindus and untouchables ever exchange visits. "Yes," he said, "on formal occasions, such as meetings, fairs, and marriages." Then he added: "Also at vote-getting time." The power that grows out of the ballot box may yet prove to be the most potent weapon the untouchables have in their struggle for first-class citizenship.

The most notable political achievement of the villagers of Alande and Utroli is *panchayati raj* (village self-government). In Alande, G. B. Bandal, president of the village council, explained its origin. "In 1959," he said, "Jawaharlal Nehru, India's late Prime Minister, became convinced that village India would lie in the sleep of centuries unless real political power was put in its hands. And so panchayati raj was born. Under this system, we villagers run our own local affairs, elect our own representatives, and spend funds allocated to us as we see fit."

Panchayati raj is a three-tiered democratic system. At the village level is the *gram panchayat* (village council), elected by members of the village. Above this, at the block, or county, level, is the *panchayat samiti*, consisting largely of village council presidents. At the district level is the *zila parishad*, composed of panchayat samiti presidents and members who represent the district in the national parliament and the state legislature. The only government employees in this political structure are the village level workers, the block development officers, and their superior at the district level, the Special Development Officer.

Bandal took me to a village council meeting. He made a rambling speech about the shortage of drinking water, grew indignant about the shortage of monies received from the panchayat samiti, threw the Kashmir crisis in for good measure, and then opened the meeting for discussion. I watched the council members in their turbans, sitting expressionless as they listened to Bandal. One by one, they got up to speak. They began slowly, but soon warmed to the point they wished to make. There were no tidy solutions to the shortages Bandal had spoken of, but the villagers were talking in democratic fashion. Their remarks made me recall an old saying of Chester Bowles, U.S. ambassador to India: "The Indian villager may be illiterate but because of the richness of his traditions, he is far from uneducated."

To broaden my sampling of rural India, I traveled across the subcontinent on planes that were seldom on time, on railways so crowded I sometimes had to enter the coaches through the windows, in autos that frequently broke down, in jouncing jeeps, and on a pair of tired

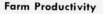

Farm Productivity

Productivity of Farm Labor Measured by Number of Pounds of Grain Produced by Each Farmworker Annually

Source: UN Food and Agricultural Organization. Figures are latest available for each country.

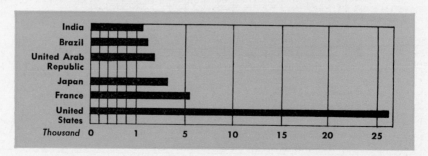

"May you drink of the water of 10 wells!" This was an old Indian saying which meant, "May you be a well-traveled man." That saying indicates how scarce wells were two decades ago. Now every village has water, as does Utroli.

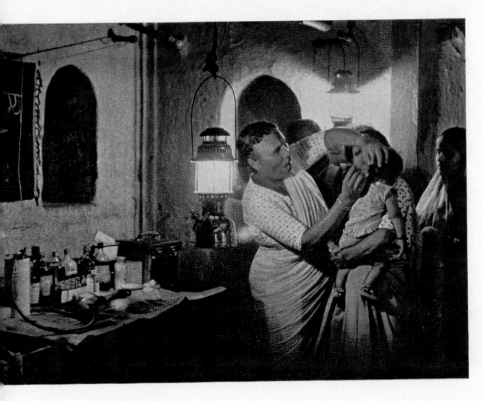

The dai (midwife), is the nearest thing to a doctor in much of rural India. Many are being given modern training by the World Health Organization. Here, the dai examines a child in Utroli.

feet. The heat was oppressive; the monsoons played cat and mouse with schedules; the flies usually beat me to the food in the villages; and the village water was undrinkable. But despite these inconveniences, it was an exhilarating experience.

I traveled to the villages of Tudyalur in south India and Butana in north India. I interviewed cabinet ministers in the government of Prime Minister Lal Bahadur Shastri, as well as university professors, economists, and U.S. aid officials. Most revealing of all was a visit to the Nilokheri National Community Development Training Center, where I interviewed block development, agricultural extension, and social education officers. Their experience, insight, and criticism based on intimate contact with several hundred villages gave me a broader base for some final conclusions on the present state of India's silent struggle. It is these conclusions—tentative, incomplete, and perhaps fallible—which I shall attempt to summarize.

India is so big, so complex, so exciting, and so frustrating that an observer might justifiably draw almost any conclusion he wants from what he sees. He can, for example, draw dire conclusions from the food crisis that developed late in 1965. The monsoon, which customarily drenches the country during the summer, failed to materialize. Rainfall was from 30 to 40 percent below normal. This fact, plus hoarding, confronted India with its worst food shortage since the country won its independence in 1947. An observer can point to the prolonged debates within the government over the use of fertilizers, a delay that has left Indian fields gasping for growth-producing chemicals. He can look at these things and conclude that bungling India will never move ahead.

The government's plan to upgrade rural India entails, in part, bringing water, electricity, and fertilizer to the farms. Here, laborers and modern cranes work to build Nagarjuna Sagar Dam in the state of Andhra Pradesh.

Or, conversely, he can go out on the farms as I did and see how India is beginning to evaluate programs and policies in terms of results. The government now recognizes that water, fertilizer, and electricity are three essentials that it must provide to the villager if he is going to play his part in the nation's development. It has begun to construct dams and irrigation canals. In Madras state, 85 per cent of the farms have been supplied with water and electricity, but this is admittedly the exception. Nonetheless, if India can step-up its output of livestock, poultry, and fish, and increase its storage facilities and marketing outlets, it should be able to feed itself by 1972.

Coupled with the nation's drive to increase its food production, is the program to reduce its soaring birth rate. The goal is to reduce births from 20,000,000 to 13,000,000 per year. The Lippes Loop is the breakthrough that India has been waiting for. The government hopes to give away 5,000,000 loops each year.

Community Development is an educational enterprise in the broad sense, but in the actual matter of schooling, criticism centers about the educational standards. The educational system is still patterned after the British model, geared to turning out a nation of clerks. It does not provide the basic farm education visualized by Gandhi. The present-day village teacher, moreover, lacks the community respect enjoyed by the *guru* (religious teacher) of old. Ceaseless squabbles continue among the proponents of regional languages versus the proponents of Hindi, and those who would retain English as the national language. This foments national disunity, and lowers educational standards.

The tyranny of the caste system, as mentioned previously, still reigns

A symbol of progress in a highly technical field is the atomic power plant in suburban Trombay, which supplies electric power for much of urban Bombay. But the principal fuel throughout India is still dried cakes of cow dung.

in most villages, but there are signs of progress. The story of the two wells is typical. In one village, the caste Hindus refused to share water from a newly constructed well with the untouchables. The latter were forced to dig a well of their own, but the caste Hindus lent their bullocks and moral support. Shocking? Of course. But 10 years ago, the untouchables would not have dared to think of digging a well of their own, nor would the caste Hindus have aided them. The untouchables would have had to beg for water. The evils of the caste system will disappear only as more and more untouchables get off the land to seek the anonymity of the big cities, or as their improved educational and economic status wins the respect of the skeptical caste Hindu, with the nudging of the ballot box.

The political system of grass-roots democracy appears to be developing. The criticism most often voiced against it is that the members of the village councils are conscious of their rights, but not of their responsibilities. Yet, as recently as 1959, they were conscious of neither.

It was hoped that the development of farm cooperatives would help to teach individualistic farmers to work together for mutual benefit, but progress has not been encouraging. This is because the management of the cooperatives is still largely in the hands of the government, and because laws sharply limit their size.

In the government apparatus, the village level worker—the pivot of Community Development—is frequently underqualified and overworked. His boss, the block development officer, often retains the revenue official's patronizing attitude. There appears to be less change in the lower and middle echelons of government than in the people the government is attempting to change. Even worse, many middle level government functionaries display an abject servility to higher authority that muzzles the dialogue of progress. But change is occurring at last in village India, and the most important change is in the villager himself. S. K. Dey, minister for Community Development, told me: "Fifty years ago in the village where I grew up, the sight of a government official would cause the villagers to flee. Today they come into my office; they argue; they demand; they are not afraid."

The Indian peasant—for centuries asleep, mute, fatalistic—has awakened. The distant government which he once viewed as an overpowering tax collector is now his partner. It is this change that is the most promising part of India's development. Throughout hundreds of thousands of its villages, the silent struggle to become a part of the 20th century goes on, unknown to the outside world, unknown even to a large number of India's city dwellers. Few countries have started with less, or attempted more. Despite all the problems and frustrations, the nation's Community Development program is the greatest group dynamic laboratory in the world. In the words of the British historian Arnold J. Toynbee, if it proves successful, "next to the American revolution, India's Community Development will be mankind's greatest achievement."

See also Section Three, ASIA; INDIA.

How Far Will We Go In Space?

BY ISAAC ASIMOV

From the Facts and Capabilities Now at Hand, a Noted Science Writer Projects the Future Accomplishments and Limits of Space Exploration

In 1965, man for the first time "walked in space." Moreover, he remained in orbit longer than he ever had before.

In 1965, we could look at our television screens and watch (live!) close-up pictures of the moon sent back to us by Ranger IX.

In 1965, after a journey of 134,000,000 miles, Mariner IV flew past Mars, and from a distance of 6,000 miles sent back 22 photographs of the planet's surface.

Yet 10 years before that, not a single object had been placed in orbit about the earth. The Space

YEAR BOOK photo by
Ted Polumbaum

The author:
Isaac Asimov is
associate professor
of biochemistry
at Boston University
School of Medicine.
He has written
many articles and
books on science,
among them *The
New Intelligent
Man's Guide to
Science.* Dr. Asimov
has been a member
of THE YEAR BOOK
board of editors, and
with this edition,
he becomes a
contributing editor.

Age had not begun and very few people, except scientists and science-fiction writers, even dreamed it was about to begin.

What lies ahead of us now? If mankind can advance so far in space in less than 10 years, where will he go in the next 10 years? In 20? In a century? Is there anything we *cannot* do in space by 2100, for instance?

It is difficult to predict the future. Yet, our success in 1965 was so heady that we should, for the sake of our own perspective, look at the practical limits of our explorations into space. We should do this hard-headedly, basing our judgment on facts at hand, capabilities we have, and solutions we can reasonably predict.

We can begin by asking where we stand on the matter of unmanned exploration of space. There, the greatest barrier was overcome in 1959, when, for the first time, a rocket was hurled upward by man at a speed of more than seven miles a second. At such speed, a rocket is not confined by gravity to an orbit about the earth. It "escapes," and goes into orbit about the sun. The faster a rocket is hurled, the larger is its orbit about the sun. If it is made to slow down, it will drop closer to the sun. By carefully adjusting a rocket's speed in a mid-flight maneuver, we can place spacecraft close to Venus or Mars, even though these planets at their closest are many millions of miles from us. Mariner II executed a passage within 22,000 miles of Venus in 1962, and Mariner IV passed even closer to Mars in 1965.

It would not take much more refinement to plot the course of an unmanned probe to Jupiter, Saturn, and beyond. This is something that could be done now if our space scientists were not committed to other tasks of greater importance.

It is not enough, however, simply to send a piece of metal toward Jupiter. If a planetary probe is to be useful, the ship must send back signals. The signals tell us its position and provide us with other vital information. From how far out in space can we reasonably expect to be able to receive such messages?

Already space scientists have sent radar waves to Jupiter and have detected the reflection. The distance of such a round trip to Jupiter is about 800,000,000 miles. This is quite an advance over the time, a mere 20 years ago, when it was a great feat to bounce radar waves off the moon—a round-trip distance of less than 500,000 miles. It seems possible that within 10 years or so, our techniques will have developed to the point where we could produce a radar beam that could bounce

The opening illustration depicts a spaceship as it nears the vicinity of a neighboring planet. Inside the roomy cabin, the astronauts, unencumbered by heavy space suits and helmets, tend the banks of flashing lights and switches that control the interplanetary vehicle. Throat mikes and earplug receivers provide the necessary communications. The ruby glass in the ports protects the crewmen from damaging glare as they scan the surface of the planet. Once the spacecraft has completed its mission, a metal screen will slide up to protect the window area of the ship from the impact of meteoroids.

Illustrations by Arthur Lidov

off a body 4,000,000,000 miles away—the distance to Pluto, which is the most remote planet in our solar system.

We will soon be in a position, then, to explore the entire solar system with unmanned probes. By the year 2000, we might well have launched one or more probes to every one of the planets in the solar system. The results of these probes will not, however, all be known by then, for trips to the outer reaches of the solar system take a great deal of time. Mariner IV took more than eight months to reach the vicinity of Mars. If it were traveling to Pluto, many years would be required for the flight.

BEYOND THE SOLAR SYSTEM

Can we explore beyond the solar system? After all, if we propel a rocket at a speed of more than 26 miles a second (escape velocity from the sun at our distance from it), it will no longer remain in orbit about the sun. It will leave the solar system forever. If we aim it correctly, it will eventually approach Proxima Centauri, the nearest star next to the sun, or any other object toward which we might send it. Unfortunately, even the nearest star is almost 7,000 times as far away as Pluto. The flight of an unmanned probe to Proxima Centauri might take many centuries. Nor does it seem that we will be able to develop communication beams of sufficient power to track a probe all the way to the stars. Certainly we will not in the next century or so. In 1965, there was some speculation by the Russians concerning radio signals that might be reaching us from intelligent beings on the planets of stars other than our sun. The Russians had to admit, though, that such signals would have to be sent out by "super-civilizations," intelligent beings with technical know-how vastly exceeding ours.

We must conclude, then, that although we will soon have the ability to explore the entire solar system by instrumented satellites, we will by the year 2000 already have gone about as far as we can in that direction. We do not have the ability to explore far beyond the solar system. We may not have that ability for many centuries, if ever.

And what about manned flight? A lunar probe taking pictures of the moon does not compare in excitement with a man landing on the moon. And will reaching the moon be the end? Can we expect human beings to land someday on the surface of Mars or Jupiter? Where can we draw the line and say: "Here man is not likely to go in the next century and a half?"

Man can explore space in four stages: in journeys that last days, or months, or years, or centuries. The first stage, a trip of a few days, will take him to the moon. We hope to have a man on the moon by 1970. Is there anything to stop us from achieving this goal, with the exception of mechanical failures?

There are two hazards that are being thoroughly studied. First, an astronaut would be exposed to weightlessness for as long as a week. Is this dangerous? Well, during 1965 men were kept weightless for extended periods while in orbit and fulfilled their missions well. That seems to take care of that. Secondly, astronauts will be exposed to

THE INNER SOLAR SYSTEM

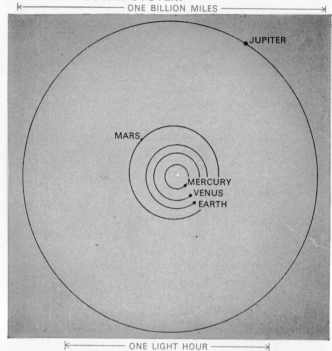

|← ——————— ONE BILLION MILES ——————— →|

JUPITER

MARS

MERCURY
VENUS
EARTH

|← ——————— ONE LIGHT HOUR ——————— →|

Distances to the inner planets of the solar system, *above,* enable them to be reached in a matter of months. But voyages to the outer planets, *below,* would take many years.

THE OUTER SOLAR SYSTEM

BILLIONS OF MILES 0   1   2   3   4

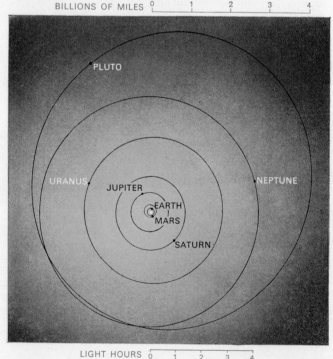

PLUTO

URANUS JUPITER

EARTH
MARS

NEPTUNE

SATURN

LIGHT HOURS 0   1   2   3   4

radiation in the Van Allen belt about the earth and to bursts of high energy particles from the sun, as well as to cosmic rays from beyond the solar system. Can they be protected from this? Dozens of satellites have been sent out by the United States and Russia to study the nature and effects of radiation. Nothing has been reported so far that would make a lunar flight impossible.

The only obstacle, then, that is keeping us from a flight to the moon right now is the need to work out the engineering details necessary to be reasonably certain that we will not only send an astronaut there, but also bring him back alive. Once we reach the moon, there seems to be nothing to prevent us from ferrying machines and supplies there to build a permanent base. The moon, it is true, has no water or atmosphere. It gets unbearably hot during the day and unbearably cold at night. It is subjected to a never-ending rain of tiny meteors and dangerous radiation. An underground cavern could be gouged out, however, and sealed. With material obtained from the surrounding rock and from the earth, conditions could be made quite comfortable and almost identical, except for the low gravity, to those in an air-conditioned enclosure on earth.

By 1980 or 1985, such a base may exist. From an astronomical observatory on the moon men could see the universe much more clearly than on earth. (If the moon is ever highly colonized, it may also be used as a launching site for spaceships.)

The second stage of space exploration—trips of a few months—will place the inner solar system within our grasp. This includes the planets Mars, Venus, and Mercury. Of these, Mars is the least forbidding. Despite its extremely thin and arid atmosphere, Mars just possibly may have simple life-forms on its surface. The main difficulty in reaching Mars involves the length of the journey. Before men can reach Mars, they must spend six months or more in space. Can they remain in isolation that long? Can they carry sufficient supplies? Can they endure weightlessness that long?

Let's consider these problems. Isolation need not have serious effects. Four or five centuries ago, men made voyages that lasted several months across wide oceans under conditions almost as dangerous for them as a flight to Mars would be today. They were even more isolated then than a space traveler would be now. They were truly cut off from home, whereas an astronaut would be in radio communication with the earth at all times—with the encouragement of all humanity constantly in his ear.

The problem of supplies is one for which solutions are being found. First of all, it will not be necessary to pack aboard a spacecraft to Mars the several tons of water and oxygen each man would need during the trip. Instead, the spaceship would carry a miniature chemical plant which would distill and purify waste water and process carbon

The future may see the moon being used as a launching site for spaceships heading out into the solar system. Because of the weak gravitational pull of the moon, only a single booster will be needed for escape into space. Once in flight, the propulsion unit will be dropped away and the retractable wings extended.
The pointed nose of the spacecraft is designed to counteract the effect of radiant heat transfer which becomes dominant at very high re-entry velocities. The sleek, shape of the craft will provide maximum maneuverability when it enters a planetary atmosphere.

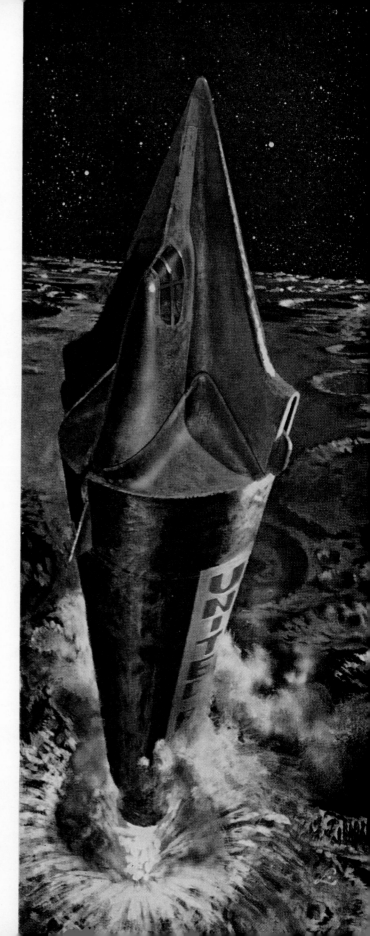

dioxide to recover oxygen for breathing. It is not contemplated, how-ever, that food would be produced aboard ship. Food would be brought along in freeze-dried packages. Unless this were done, the weight would be excessive for take-off.

What about weightlessness? It would seem that a man in a state of weightlessness for six months or more would suffer some physical harm. If, however, a specially designed spaceship, or part of it could be spun slowly, a centrifugal effect would be produced within it that would push the astronaut out toward the walls. This would have the same effect upon him as a gravitational field. It would take no energy to keep the ship spinning once it was put into such motion, and the effect might well be to keep the astronaut healthy and comfortable.

If these problems are solved, astronauts may land on Mars by 1985, and there may be a permanent station there by 1995. Stations might also be established on the two tiny Martian moons, Deimos and Phobos, which have no atmosphere and virtually no gravity.

THE DANGER OF RADIATION

Nothing has been mentioned here about the danger of radiation on a trip to Mars. The principal danger would come from high-energy particles emitted at unpredictable intervals from flares on the sun. Although spaceships to Mars would be moving away from the stronger radiation of the sun, radiation shields would have to be provided to protect the astronauts during periods of intense solar activity. Mars itself has no detectable radiation belts to worry about once the space-ship nears the planet.

Trips to Venus and Mercury would take no longer than the trip to Mars, but those to Mercury would take considerably more energy because of the orbital mechanics involved. Neither Venus nor Mercury is expected to have any radiation belts to speak of. Both are, however, in the direction of the sun whose radiation increases dangerously as it is approached. If the radiation danger can be overcome, and, in all probability it will be, Venus and Mercury can be reached before 2000.

Establishing permanent bases there is another matter. The surface temperature of Venus, as measured by Mariner II, is about $800°$ F. This is the temperature all over the planet's cloud-shrouded surface, both day and night, so it must be at least that hot under the surface. There would be no escaping the heat by burrowing underground. Un-

The planets nearest earth—Mars, Venus, and Mercury—will be the first visited by man. Here an advanced re-entry vehicle approaches the surface of Venus, its cloud cover shining in the sun. The spaceship is about the size of today's jetliners. Out in interplanetary space, its propulsion system might be an advanced ion engine that would be capable of continuous acceleration. As the ship approaches Venus, it would switch to a system producing greater thrust. Radar signals recently bounced off the planet suggest that Venus has mountainous surfaces beneath the cloud cover. But unless data from unmanned probes indicate temperatures much lower than the 800° F. now envisioned, man will probably be content to study the hot planet from a safe distance, perhaps occasionally ducking under the clouds for a somewhat closer look.

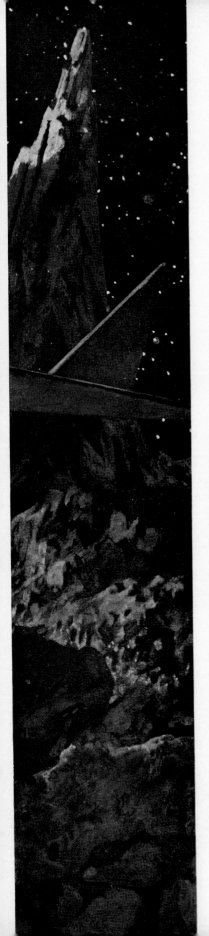

manned probes could reach Venus's surface, and a manned expedition might make a temporary flight beneath the clouds, but it seems unlikely that a permanent base will be established on Venus in the foreseeable future.

Mercury is a better prospect. Until very recently it was thought that Mercury presented only one side to the sun, so that one side was always unbearably hot, while the other was almost at absolute zero, or —459.69° F. If so, we could land on the cold side. It is simple to establish an artificially heated base, whatever the cold. Now, however, we know that Mercury rotates, so that each part of its surface has a day

Improved observation of the sun might be accomplished by placing an unmanned solar observatory on the asteroid Icarus. This small planet—probably between three and eight miles in diameter—has an elongated orbit which takes it from midway to the orbit of Jupiter to within 19,000,000 miles of the sun. The implanting of the solar station would have to be accomplished in a fairly short time while Icarus is nearest the earth and relatively cool. Weightless conditions would necessitate the manned vehicle being lashed to the asteroid. An excavation would be made in its moonlike surface, probably by means of a controlled explosion. Assisted by astronauts attached to the parent ship by booms, the observation station would be lowered into the crater and covered with debris. Then the spaceship would depart, leaving the capsule buried safely underground, with only its sensing devices projecting through the surface. As Icarus neared the neighborhood of the sun, the observatory's sensing devices would take measurements of the sun's magnetic field and its particle fluxes.

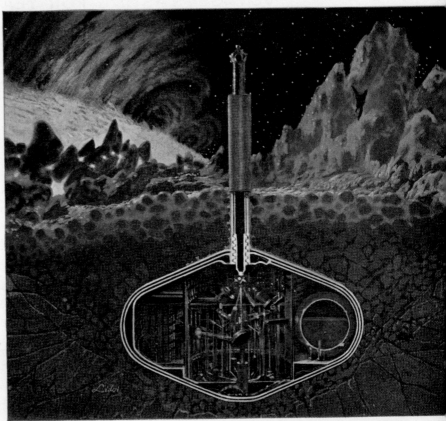

and a night about 59 days long. This means that any expedition landing on Mercury would have to do so at a point far enough into the night shadow for the surface to have cooled down. An underground base would then have to be dug before the landing point had circled into sunlight again.

Mercury approaches to within 28,000,000 miles of the sun. Can men ever expect to approach even closer? One possibility exists. There is a tiny asteroid named Icarus, which at times passes within a few million miles of the earth. It has a very flattened orbit. At one end, it reaches halfway to the orbit of Jupiter, but at the other it falls in toward the sun, speeding about it at a distance of only 19,000,000 miles. If an expedition could reach Icarus while it was passing near the earth and implant the proper instruments there hastily, marvelous observations could be made of the neighborhood of the sun, the charged particles it emits, and the magnetic field it produces.

Any closer approach to the sun by man than Icarus would seem unlikely. Spaceships, manned or unmanned, could be made to skim about the sun at closer distances, but the heat and radiation would very probably be fatal not only to men, but even to instruments, unless they were particularly well-protected. It seems doubtful, therefore, that in the next century and a half, men will succeed in approaching the sun more closely than does Icarus.

VOYAGES LASTING FOR YEARS

The third stage of space exploration—that which will involve voyages lasting years—will carry us to the vast outer solar system. This can be done in graduated steps. Between the orbits of Mars and Jupiter circle thousands of asteroids. A few of them are a hundred miles or more in diameter. Ceres, the largest, is 480 miles in diameter. Once we get to Mars, we will be able to reach the asteroids without too much additional trouble. Perhaps as early as 2000, man will have landed on Ceres. Step by step, other asteroids may be reached. One of the most interesting is Hidalgo. It has a very elongated orbit. At one end, it approaches to within 24,000,000 miles of the orbit of Mars. At the other end, it recedes as far from the sun as does Saturn. Hidalgo's orbit is quite tilted as compared to the orbits of the various planets, so it comes nowhere near Jupiter and Saturn. Still, if an expedition could land on Hidalgo when it was near Mars, men could remain in space for years, studying conditions in the outer solar system at their leisure, knowing that they would eventually return to the neighborhood of the orbit of Mars.

Astronauts could tackle the outer planets one by one, establishing themselves firmly on one, then progressing to the next one. To make these trips, however, even under the best of conditions, astronauts would have to spend many years in space, if spaceships are equipped with chemical rockets of the kind used today. Unless a new kind of rocket is developed, it may well be that man will never pass beyond the asteroids.

The use of nuclear rockets is a possibility. Rockets might be driven by a series of atomic explosions or by exhaust gases expelled by the heat of a nuclear reactor. In either case, rocket ships could be kept under acceleration for longer periods, and would attain higher speeds.

Then, too, there is an ion rocket now being developed by scientists. Ordinary rockets achieve their thrust by hurling large quantities of heated gases backward. This brute force is necessary to lift the spacecraft above the atmosphere and push it into an orbit around the earth. Once in orbit, however, and surrounded by a vacuum, a ship might make use of electrically charged atoms (ions) instead. These can be hurled backward by the action of an electric field. The thrust of the ions is very weak, so the rocket's speed increases very slowly. The ion engine is, however, much more efficient in the long run than an ordinary rocket. Acceleration can be continued for indefinite periods, and speeds approaching that of light itself (186,282 miles per second) could, in theory, be attained. By 2000, when men will have reached Ceres, both nuclear rockets and ion rockets may be in operation. If so, it may be with these that the outer solar system will be explored.

HOW FAR IN A CENTURY?

A generation later, say by 2025, we may well have landed on one or another of Jupiter's satellites. A century from now, a landing may have been made within Saturn's satellite system, with plans in the making for reaching the satellites of Uranus and Neptune. By 2100, perhaps, man will stand on Pluto, at the very limits of the solar system.

Notice that I mention the satellites of Jupiter, Saturn, Uranus, and Neptune. What about those planets themselves? These four planets are giants. Conditions there are far removed from those on the earth. They are frigidly cold and have deep, thick, poisonous atmospheres that have incredible storms, and winds of unimaginable violence. Pressures at the bottom of these atmospheres must be thousands of times greater than ours. Nor are we certain as to the kind of solid surfaces they have.

If astronauts ever did reach the solid surface of the outer giants, they would be subject to gravitational pulls much stronger than those we experience on earth. These pulls would largely immobilize the astronauts, and make the problem of getting off the planet almost insuperable. The difficulties in sending manned expeditions to the surface of the giant planets are so great that for a long time space scientists will be satisfied to send unmanned probes spiraling toward Jupiter, Saturn, Uranus, and Neptune. Manned exploration of these planets will not take place in any forseeable time, but small Pluto can be landed upon.

The fourth stage of space exploration—voyages lasting centuries—will take us to the planets of the nearer stars. As was said previously, the nearest star is almost 7,000 times as far away as Pluto. Why bother?

Well, nowhere in our solar system is there another planet on which man could live comfortably. He would have to huddle underground or beneath domes. Nowhere else in the system, outside the earth, can there be anything more than very primitive life-forms. Out there among the stars, however, there are sure to be other earthlike planets, which may very likely bear life. Some of them might even bear intelligent life. Unfortunately, we cannot detect them until spaceships can get fairly close to the stars that these planets circle.

But can other solar systems be reached?

Certainly the task of reaching even the nearest ones is many times as difficult as that of reaching even the farthest planet of the solar system. A major problem in making such a trip would be to ensure protection against the lethal, high energy particles that would collide with a spaceship, endangering its passengers and instruments. No solution to this problem is yet known. Moreover, even the most advanced rockets we can imagine cannot go faster than the speed of light, and, at the speed of light, a round trip to the nearest star will take nearly nine years. Round trips to more distant stars would take hundreds or thousands of years.

Even by 2100, when mankind may well be in occupation of Pluto, it seems doubtful that any serious attempt would have been made to send out an expedition to the stars. Does that mean, though, that men will *never* reach the stars? "Never" is a pessimistic word. Scientists have speculated on several means of reaching the stars. The first necessity,

of course, is the ability to reach speeds approaching that of light. These may be reached by means of ion rockets or some other technological developments not yet visualized.

Einstein's theory of relativity explains that all internal motions slow down in objects moving at great speeds away from the earth. The faster the speed, the slower the internal motions. All clocks on board a spaceship would slow down. So would every other motion that might be used to measure time. This is the same as saying that time itself would slow down. All atomic motions within human beings would slow down, too. Astronauts would metabolize more slowly, live more slowly, age more slowly.

Such slowed-down individuals would be unable to detect this change. To themselves, they would seem to be living normally. Still, while life seemed to pass in the usual way, they would reach a star in what might seem to them to be about five years. Time on earth would, however, have continued in the ordinary fashion and when the astronauts returned, while they might think only 10 years had passed, they might find that on earth a century had gone by.

If it turns out speeds near that of light are not practical, it may be possible, nonetheless, to live long enough to reach the stars. To achieve this, astronauts could be frozen and put into a kind of suspended animation for decades or generations until their destination was in view. We cannot say as yet, however, whether such suspended animation by low temperature hibernation will ever be possible.

There is a third way out. In place of the small ships used for exploration and colonization of our solar system, a huge ship might be built for voyages to the planets of the stars. Actually it would be a small "planet" itself. On such a "starship," there might be hundreds, or thousands of men; plus room for agriculture and for herds of animals. Whole generations of men and women might be born, grow old, and die while the starship traveled from one star to another.

Would men be willing to spend their lives and the lives of their children and grandchildren on a journey through space? It seems hard to believe that earthmen would choose to do this. Perhaps, though, we will not need earthmen. Once our solar system is colonized, there will be men and women who may never have seen earth; who may have been born on Mars. They will not know earth's blue skies and spacious fields. Their underground home on Mars will not be too different from that on a starship, and the change from one to the other may be quite

Voyages beyond our solar system might take centuries, and thus would require vehicles that could sustain space colonies. The day-to-day activities of this Ferris wheel-type spaceship would take place in the outer ring. The ship would accommodate some 100 passengers, providing each with 5,000 cubic feet of living space. The large wheel, about 300 feet in diameter, would rotate at about four revolutions per minute, producing gravitational effects similar to those on earth. Once put in rotation, the wheel would keep on rotating. The right end of the central shaft is the front of the spaceship, and it would contain the navigational center and a celestial observatory. The four spokes would serve as passageways to the living chambers. The propulsion system, probably of a nuclear type, is located at the rear of the ship.

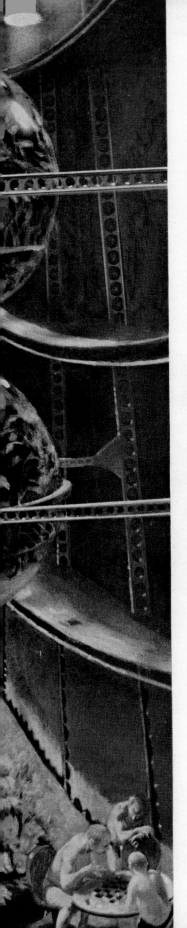

One section of an interstellar spaceship might be devoted to *hydroponics*, the growing of plants in a chemical solution instead of soil. The food produced in such a system would only be supplemental, but the fresh fruits and vegetables would provide the space families with a welcome change from a diet of prepared foods. Some plants needing a humid atmosphere would probably be grown in closed pods. By taking up carbon dioxide and giving off oxygen in photosynthesis, the garden would also contribute to the purification of the spaceship's air. This hydroponic section would require an ample supply of light and water, and thus it could also be used to provide a parklike area for the space travelers. Diversions of all types would be needed to relieve the tedium of a lifetime spent in space. And as on earth, young men would probably seek the company of young women, old men would play chess, and little boys would have trouble keeping their swimsuits up.

possible for them. The stars may not be explored by earthmen at all, but by colonists from Mars and other worlds.

What would these colonists be like? One can't help wondering. They will undoubtedly be accustomed to the lower gravity of the moon and Mars and will also be accustomed to maneuvering under gravity-free conditions. They may be more slightly built than earthmen because of having less gravity to contend with, but they could well be of greater mental stability, since only the most stable would have endured the transplantation from Earth to a life under the difficult conditions of worlds not really fit for human beings. Frightened neither by the confinement of a spaceship nor by the limitless reaches of space, they may be humanity's true answer to the Space Age.

When expeditions are sent to the stars, we need not expect to see them come back. Even a successful expedition to any but the very nearest stars, cannot possibly return to earth in the same century, as we count time. Nor will it be possible to communicate with any human colonies that may be established on the planets of other stars. Even if we develop the ability to transmit communication beams intense enough to reach other stars, it will take dozens of years, even centuries, for such beams to reach the colony. It will take an equal amount of time for the colony to answer.

Let us summarize then. A reasonable guess is that by 2100, mankind will have explored our entire solar system and will have landed on the surface of any planet, satellite, or asteroid he wishes, except for Jupiter, Saturn, Uranus, Neptune, and Venus. He will have studied the sun from close range, but not more closely than from a distance of 19,000,000 miles. Mankind will *not* have made any attempt to reach or colonize planets outside our solar system.

After 2100, a long pause may be enforced on mankind. He will probably have gone as far as he can go without developing technical abilities far beyond what he will possess even then. Those space feats which mankind will not have accomplished by 2100 (a landing on the giant planets, a very close approach to the sun, a voyage to the stars) may not actually be impossible, but they are so difficult that mankind may not even attempt them for many centuries after 2100.

See also Section One, Focus on Space; Section Three, Astronauts; Astronomy, Space Travel.

Polluted America

BY BROOKS ATKINSON

*A Pulitzer Prize-Winning Critic and Lifelong
Naturalist Looks at the Land He Loves and
Issues a Stern Warning to All Americans That
They Are Endangering Their National Heritage*

Pennsylvania Dept. of Health

When the English pioneers settled in Jamestown and Plymouth in the early 17th century, none of them imagined that in the 20th century Americans would poison their environment. No one could then foresee a time when Americans would pollute the air, the water, and the land as if our natural resources were inexhaustible and worthless.

But that is what we are doing, and we can destroy our civilization this way. No species can exhaust its resources and endure. Nature elimi-

YEAR BOOK photo
by Wes Kemp

The author:
Brooks Atkinson,
foreground above,
*was long a foreign
correspondent and
drama critic of* The
New York Times.
*Atkinson has
written many
books and is a
Fellow of*
The American
Academy of
Arts and Sciences.

nates the species that overtax their environment. Highly developed nations like ours invite reprisals from nature.

The three and one-half centuries during which the original immigrants and their descendants have prospered in America are only a minute fragment of the life span of the continent. For millions of years, there has been organic life on the land. Between 35,000 and 40,000 years have passed since the first Asiatic tribes crossed over into what is now Alaska and made use of the rivers, forests, prairies, and minerals.

To the earliest immigrants from England and other European countries, America seemed fabulous. No one knew where this vast land ended. The early settlers took everything for granted. Everything seemed to have been waiting for centuries for the use of free men who could casually mine and plunder the land without exhausting it and who felt they could progressively consume the capital of land and stream that the centuries had so lavishly provided. Regarding trees as weeds, the pioneers destroyed them and burned them in heaps to make arable land. Suddenly released from the restraints of life in Europe, they hacked at everything that stood in their way.

By 1910, much of the forest was gone. The beavers and fur seals were nearly exterminated. Vast herds of buffalo were reduced to the few that were protected (a million buffaloes were killed every year from 1872 to 1875). The last of 5,000,000,000 passenger pigeons was in a zoo in Cincinnati. Now as we look back on those early centuries, when so much that was politically good was accomplished, we are stunned by the speed and the callousness of the destruction. But man is the Giant Predator—that "pervasive and destructive vertebrate," as William Vogt, the ecologist, once called him.

After ravaging the land and slaughtering its wildlife, the American is now going even further: he is pouring untreated sewage and industrial wastes into lakes and rivers. He is defiling the skies with smoke and exhaust gases. He is contaminating the land with pesticides. The United States Department of Health, Education, and Welfare, which is deeply involved in all these problems, has said, "We are running out of safe, clean, usable water, partly because we are dumping so much of our refuse into our main water sources—our streams. So, too, we appear to be running out of clean air in many of our more populous and industrialized areas, and for similar reasons."

Conservation Vital

Land, water, and air are limited resources. Although our population has increased from 31,000,000 to 195,000,000 in 100 years, the supply of land, water, and air has remained the same. The increase in population automatically puts increased pressure on our resources. But we use them as if they were waste products, to which we contribute the additional wastes of home and industry. Unless we change our whole concept of the environment, and unless we conserve our natural resources and use them intelligently, we cannot pass our civilization on to future generations. Only when a nation accepts responsibility for its natural resources can the momentum toward destruction be retarded.

During the 19th century, the great adventure of settling the prairies, building cities and industries, laying the transcontinental railroad tracks, and constructing beautiful ships gratified and paralyzed the American imagination. The myth of inexhaustible abundance was still the folklore of the land. Yet, even in that distant time, a Yankee named George C. Whipple made a statement that we would do well to heed now. Speaking for the first Board of Health of the state of Massachusetts, he declared: "We believe that all citizens have an inherent right to the enjoyment of pure and uncontaminated air and water and soil; that this right should be regarded as belonging to the whole community; and that no one should be allowed to trespass upon it by his carelessness or his avarice or even his ignorance." This statement is even more pertinent now than when it was made.

A Danger to Health

Pollution of the environment endangers the health of the population from a wide variety of sources. No one had thought very much about air until the last two decades. Most of us were brought up to think that if we opened the window at night, we would be invigorated by fresh air. But it is no longer fresh in most of the settled parts of the continent. It is so polluted from the combustion of coal and oil (known as "fossil fuels") that clean air has become an increasingly serious problem for about 60 per cent of the population.

Looking out of the 19th story window of my New York City apartment as I write this article, I have just counted 11 smoking chimneys. One is belching thick, black smoke that billows above a loft building. Another emits a blue haze that sweeps across the rooftops for several blocks. Two of the four soaring stacks of a power plant emit streams of brown smoke that drift into the upper atmosphere. A flake of oily ash blows through a crack below the window I have left partly open and smudges the paper on which I am writing. The 11 smoking chimneys I see are, of course, only a minute fraction of all the chimneys that are contemptuously tossing waste into the New York air. Moreover, massive and more destructive waste is coming from the exhaust pipes of automobiles—carbon monoxide, sulfur compounds, and nitrogen oxides.

Wherever there are cities, there is air pollution that affects our health. A long cloud of polluted air hangs in the sky all the way from Washington, D.C., to Boston in the eastern United States. In the West, Los Angeles, which lies in a basin surrounded by mountains, has had a long and increasingly alarming experience with smog. (Strictly speaking, the word "smog" means a combination of smoke and fog, but it is commonly used to describe the haze that air pollution creates.) The geographical location of Los Angeles prevents the "ventilation" needed to disperse the polluted air. The city has been variously referred to as a "bay of smokes" and a "gas chamber."

Since 1930, Los Angeles commissions have tried to diminish, if not eliminate, smog by prohibiting the burning of trash in household incinerators, and by compelling oil refineries and industrial plants to install devices for controlling the emission of waste products into the

*A jet airliner coming in for a landing in New York City is cloaked
in smog that shrouds the towering skyline. A cloud of polluted air
hovers in the sky all the way from Washington, D.C., to Boston.*

air. But the smog has increased. Although the smog in Los Angeles is
the most notorious in the United States, similar situations exist in many
cities. Vivid examples of air pollution can be seen in the inferno of
smoking stacks between Gary, Ind., and Chicago, Ill., or along the New
Jersey Turnpike where a complex of plants discharge smoke and gases
that blow across New York City when the wind is from the west.

Pollution of the air is estimated to cost the nation between $11,000,-
000,000 and $20,000,000,000 a year in damage to property, houses,
furnishings, and clothing. It contains caustic elements that rot building
stones and eat holes in metal roofs. Among its eccentric minor effects,
it damages the pipes of church organs. In New York City, the sheep-

YEAR BOOK photo by Don Stebbing

Exhaust fumes from motor vehicles, above, *are a major source of air pollution. Open burning of garbage and trash,* below, *also discharges pollutants into the atmosphere of many communities.*

Pennsylvania Department of Health

skin valves that let air into the pipes deteriorate rapidly. A valve that would last 20 or 30 years in a clean atmosphere lasts only above five years in New York City.

This is the air we breathe. Where the air is dirty, there is evidence which suggests that the incidence of respiratory diseases, ranging from chronic bronchitis to cancer, increases. Among older people, there is evidence that air pollution accelerates diseases that include hardening of the arteries, heart trouble, asthma, and emphysema.

The Threat of Air Pollution

Under extreme circumstances, multiple deaths have occurred during periods when temperature inversions intensified pollution. A temperature inversion occurs when a layer of warm air lies above a layer of cooler air and acts as a lid that prevents the rising and dispersion of ground pollution. There are a number of classic instances of deaths during temperature inversions. In five days in 1930, for example, 60 people died during a temperature inversion in the heavily industrialized Meuse Valley in Belgium. They had breathed excessive amounts of sulfur and hydrocarbons. In 1948, a temperature inversion in Donora, Pa., that lasted four days produced an accumulation of fumes from steel, acid, and zinc plants. Forty-three per cent of the population became ill. Twenty persons died.

In 1952, a London fog filled the ground level of the atmosphere with sulfur dioxide and additional contaminants. There were about 4,000 deaths. In 1953, between 65 and 250 New Yorkers may have died from air pollution when a stagnant weather system captured a high concentration of toxic elements that entered the lungs. In two weeks in the winter of 1963, air pollution was reported as a major factor in 647 more deaths than normal in New York City.

Air pollution poses another threat; one that is almost unbelievable.

Major Sources of Air Pollution

The three largest U.S. cities are all plagued by air pollution, but the major sources of it vary, relatively, to a marked degree. Chicago and Los Angeles use modern methods to control incineration.

YEAR BOOK diagram

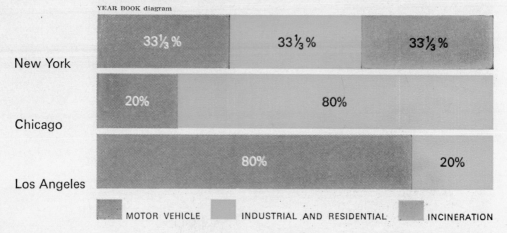

New York	33⅓%	33⅓%	33⅓%
Chicago	20%	80%	
Los Angeles		80%	20%

MOTOR VEHICLE   INDUSTRIAL AND RESIDENTIAL   INCINERATION

When A Thermal Inversion Sets In

Cool Upper Air

Warm Desert Air

Cool Sea Air

Polluted Air or Smog Is Trapped
by Warm Air Blanket

Edward J. Blood

*Smog-bound Los Angeles, above, has been called a "bay of smokes"
and a "gas chamber," as pollutants are frequently trapped by
thermal inversions. In such cases, cool air from the ocean
stagnates beneath a blanket of warm desert air, preventing
normal dispersion. When the warm air is finally blown away,
the ground air is able to escape, and the smog disperses.*

It can change the physical nature of the planet. Exhaust gases from the burning of fossil fuels increase the carbon dioxide content of the air, which, in turn, increases the temperature of the atmosphere. Unlike some other pollutants, carbon dioxide cannot be washed out of the air. The temperature increase affects life in the oceans. During the 20th century, "there has been a well documented warming of the oceans in the Northern Hemisphere," says a report by the Conservation Foundation. "The changes in marine life of the North Atlantic have been very noticeable. . . . The abundance and distribution of a number of commercial fish have shifted northward."

But this is only a minor result. If the carbon dioxide content of the atmosphere were doubled, the average temperature of the earth would rise 3.8° F. The glaciers in the north would then begin to melt, and the level of the oceans would rise and inundate coastal cities. "It is almost inevitable that as long as we continue to rely heavily on fossil fuels for our increasing power needs, the atmospheric carbon dioxide will continue to rise, and the earth will be changed, more than likely for the worse," the foundation concludes. It is also possible that high-flying jet aircraft may help to increase the atmospheric temperature by spreading a layer of haze through the atmosphere in the form of ice crystals that will not melt. In the United States, there are more than 1,000 jet planes continuously in the air. They, too, burn fossil fuels and leave residues in the atmosphere.

Those of us who remember the anxiety over fallout from nuclear fission a few years ago may have some difficulty in accepting the idea that nuclear energy used for industrial purposes is on the whole cleaner than the energy derived from burning fossil fuels and is, therefore, more desirable. Nuclear energy, as such, is not an air pollutant, but it has one tremendous disadvantage: it produces large quantities of radioactive waste—"radioactive garbage"—that cannot be carelessly flung into the air or water, or onto the land, but must be disposed of with extreme caution.

As long as we require energy to drive cars, manufacture goods, and heat houses, there is no easy solution to the problem of air pollution. The simple process of being alive creates wastes and contaminants. Nature itself contaminates the air with volcanic eruptions, forest fires, and dust storms. Absolute purity is absolutely impossible, but this does not justify massive contamination of the air over cities in the United States which are being increasingly polluted by man with toxic wastes dangerous to the health of all.

Our Natural Glory Degraded

Since rivers and lakes occupy an exalted place in the natural glory of the United States, it is depressing that we are degrading them. We treat water as if it were "a discarded piece of trash," in the angry phrase of an Alabama state conservationist. The history of America is intertwined with its rivers. This is one of the grandest facts about America. The voyages of De Soto, Marquette, Joliet, and La Salle on the Mississippi are an example of this. In 1608, a year before Henry Hudson explored the river now named for him, Captain John Smith expressed himself as astonished by the abundance and the quality of the fish in the Potomac estuary. In 1804, Lewis and Clark began their epochal penetration of the new continent by ascending the Missouri, which, like the Hudson and Potomac, is now heavily polluted. Audubon drifted down the Ohio, and Thoreau rowed up the Merrimack—both of them polluted rivers now.

Our love of America derives to an important degree from the lore of its rivers. Their names have a mystical resonance—Bitterroot, Chattahoochee, Colorado, Columbia, Green, Monongahela, Penobscot, Raccoon, Rogue, St. Johns, Snake, Susquehanna, Yellowstone. There is something almost hypnotizing about all bodies of water. People are drawn to them and gaze at them as if under some spell. As Herman Melville, the author of *Moby Dick*, put it: "They must get just as nigh the water as they can without falling into it."

People also have a less admirable trait on the shores of rivers and lakes. They use water as a dump. They throw things into it. They find rivers convenient places in which to get rid of junk. Probably the people who sail on the Potomac near Washington, D.C., love the river and find the sensation of being on it, or close to it, an idyllic experience. But some admirers who recently volunteered to help clean it picked out of it old automobile tires, mattresses, boxes, discarded automobile batteries, and a sewing machine. When the skipper of a small boat tried to retrieve a wrench he had dropped into the river, his magnet brought up nothing but beer cans. The bottom of the Potomac is lined with rubbish. Although human beings love rivers, they also use rivers contemptuously.

A Grave Water Problem

Municipalities and industries putrefy rivers on a massive scale. A century ago, when the population was small and industries were few, clean water did not seem to be a serious problem. It is one of our gravest problems now. In addition to the needs of our increasing population, the uses of water have increased with the installation of more bathrooms, washing machines, garbage disposal units, and lawn sprinklers. By the year 2000, our requirements for water will be about 1,000,000,-000,000 gallons a day. Since the available water supply is expected to be about 650,000,000,000 gallons a day, it is readily apparent that most of the water will have to be used at least twice. If it is used more than once, treatment methods will have to be more efficient than are the methods in common practice today. Sewage treatment plants that remove 80 per cent of the contaminants from water are currently regarded as good. Seventy per cent is as much as many modern plants remove.

Despite the size of the problem and the attention paid to it by government officials and responsible citizens, a lot of today's sewage is not treated at all. "It is an astonishing fact," says the United States Department of Health, Education, and Welfare, "that of the 11,420 U.S. communities with sewers, 2,139 still dump their sewage raw into local streams and watersheds."

One-third of New York City's sewage (500,000,000 gallons a day) flows raw into the Hudson and East rivers. The sewage from Detroit passes through a primary cycle of sewage treatment but not a secondary cycle. It pollutes the Detroit River so heavily that the federal government is demanding an improved treatment plant that will cost the city $100,000,000. Although Chicago treats its sewage in modern plants, the surplus effluent that is finally discharged into the Chicago Sanitary and Ship Canal contains wastes equivalent to the untreated sewage of 1,000,000 people and contains solid wastes, suspended in solution, amounting to 1,800 tons a day. Lake Michigan is an "industrial cesspool," in the phrase of U.S. Senator Gaylord Nelson of Wisconsin. Along its shoreline, it receives wastes from Illinois, Indiana, and Wisconsin cities and industrial plants. Some experts doubt that this portion of Lake Michigan can ever be cleaned. During the summer of 1965, one quarter of Lake Erie was so heavily polluted by adjacent

Discharge from a paper mill flows into Lake Erie and covers several acres of the water's surface. The lake has been described as the worst case of large-scale pollution that has ever been known. One observer has said that it is "dying."

cities and farms that its oxygen supply was virtually depleted. Lacking oxygen, fish were unable to breed and feed. "A dying lake," someone called it. Someone else has described it as the worst case of pollution on a large scale that has ever been known.

This heavy contamination is not a transient problem. At the present rate of construction, treatment plants will not keep pace with the expanding population. By 1970, the total discharge of wastes will be considerably greater than today. In 1963, it was estimated that the treatment projects then needed would cost $2,200,000,000—a sum that startles people concerned with the problem.

Water pollution consists of organic wastes from domestic sewage and industrial plants, plant nutrients that breed algae and water weeds,

U.S. Department of Health, Education, and Welfare

Municipalities and industries putrefy rivers on a massive scale, as shown by waste material flowing from a steel mill, above. The lovely Potomac, left, is so polluted even the fish die.

oil, acids, chemicals, alkalies, dyes, detergents, pesticides, and sediments. It also consists of radioactive residues from the mining of radioactive ores, nuclear testing, and intrusions of salt water. Heated water discharged from power plants is also a pollutant. Pollution kills fish on a colossal scale. Since polluted water can and does cause typhoid, dysentery, and hepatitis, clean water is not just a matter of aesthetics. It is also a matter of public health. Shellfish can transmit many diseases. The condemnation of shellfish because of contamination from sewage can also be extremely costly. When the oyster beds at the mouth of the Mobile River were condemned in 1960, the loss of income to the industry was estimated at $4,880,000 a year according to the Alabama Conservation Department.

The debasement of our rivers is an appalling sight. Take the "lordly Hudson," or the "great river of the mountains," as it has been called. Because of its romantic beauty, it has been traditionally compared to the Rhine. The comparison, unfortunately, has another aspect. The Rhine, too, is grossly polluted. Beginning as fresh water from the Alps, it picks up chemicals, potash, minerals, and oil as it flows through Germany. When it emerges in The Netherlands, visibility in the water is limited to 16 inches.

The Hudson is much the same. At Troy, it picks up sewage, pesticides, oil, and other pollutants from cities and farming areas along the Mohawk River. (One stream that empties into the Mohawk is said to be so full of oil and grease that its water cannot be used to fight fires.) From Albany south to New York City, the lordly Hudson is a long sewer. It is a little less polluted at the middle section near Poughkeepsie, but heavily polluted in the north and south sections where municipal

Home Sewage Disposal

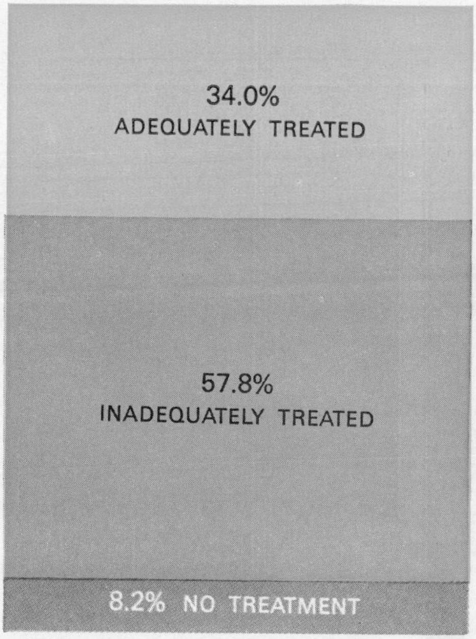

34.0%
ADEQUATELY TREATED

57.8%
INADEQUATELY TREATED

8.2% NO TREATMENT

Thousands of communities still dump raw human waste into rivers and waterways. Of all sewage discharged from American homes, only 34 per cent is adequately treated.

YEAR BOOK diagram from U.S. Public
Health Service estimates and *Chemical Week*

and industrial waste is large. Even the middle section is so contaminated that it cannot be used for drinking or for swimming without heavy chlorination. It was a joyous river a hundred years ago. Unfortunately, it is a filthy river now.

In the spring of 1965, I rode up the river from New York City to Glens Falls and back again in a helicopter with a director of the New York State Regional Development Office. From a helicopter, the configuration of the Hudson is a natural masterpiece—broad bays of open water shining in the sun, the dramatic stone wall of the Palisades, the narrow trench of the Highlands, the noble mound of Storm King across the river from the steep pitch of Breakneck Ridge, the green hills, the smooth croplands, the charming islands. No wonder Henry Hudson admired it. When he was there, the bays contained whales and bred shellfish, and the river was full of sturgeon. Sturgeon still abounded in the 19th century and were known as "Albany beef" because of their food value. It has been said that men first settled along the Hudson, not because of its navigability, but because of the abundance of fish that could be found there.

A helicopter journey today, however, discloses the negative aspects of this glorious waterway. It is a sewer and a dump. One sees oily scum, garbage dumps, sewage outlets that stain the water along the shore, long, ragged plumes of smoke from industrial plants, white and yellow waste fluids pouring out of factories and spilling into the river, decaying piers, capsized barges, abandoned buildings without roofs or windows. Each generation leaves its rubbish along the Hudson River to infect and corrupt the future. Given time, the Hudson will be a wasteland.

On the west shore across from Poughkeepsie, a large, rambling boathouse in a gay design is slowly crumbling. It is a relic of the days when boating on the river, swimming in it, and picnicking beside it were common forms of pleasure. The river is sparingly used for pleasure now. The water is green or brown and opaque in many places. It has a disagreeable odor. Much that takes place along the Hudson tends to degrade it. It has degenerated into a commercial waterway, used largely by tankers that discharge oil at the many tank colonies on the shore. The festive Hudson River Day liners with their great American flags, their streams of fluttering pennants and their holiday travelers no longer ply the upper reaches of the Hudson. Civilization has corrupted this great river.

The Plight of the Potomac

The history of the Potomac is similar. In the early 19th century, in the warm months of the year, John Quincy Adams, a gloomy Yankee, used to begin his day as President of the United States by walking from the White House to the Potomac, laying his clothes on the bank, and swimming in the water. Few things during the rest of his day seemed so clean and tonic. Modern Presidents have to swim in the White House pool which is filled with filtered and chlorinated water. The Potomac estuary in the District of Columbia is contaminated with the residue from sewage plants, sediment from upriver, sludge, trash, litter, logs, and other forms of debris from a modern city. Someday, swimming may be pleasant and safe in the Potomac if people now concerned about the river can persuade others to share their hopes. But the dirty water is far from inviting today.

In view of the history of the Potomac, and the loveliness of the parks on both shores, the filthiness of the water is particularly discouraging. George Washington, in a mood of pardonable pride, called the Potomac "the finest river in the world." When he was farming in the Mt. Vernon region, it was certainly different than today. Now 2,000,000 people

We Can Meet The Challenge

By J. I. Bregman
and
Sergei Lenormand

If no sizable effort is made to reduce and control the massive contamination of our vital resources, the nation's health, wealth, and beauty will continue to erode at an even more catastrophic rate than in the past. Although the situation is critical, it is not hopeless. Effective methods are available to deal with the problem.

The major sources of air pollution can be attacked in five basic ways:

• A relatively simple approach, already adopted in some communities, is the elimination of all open burning of garbage, leaves, trash, refuse, and junk. At a modest cost, such wastes can be collected and disposed of in modern municipal incinerators that emit far less exhaust gas than does open burning. Often garbage and trash can also be used for land fill.

• Because sulfur dioxide is one of the most noxious and damaging of the air pollutants, all heating and industrial plants can be required by municipal ordinances or state laws to burn only fuels containing a low sulfur content. If this is not possible, ways can be provided for removing or dispersing the resulting gas.

• New combustion equipment can be designed to burn fuel efficiently.

• Filtering devices can be installed to collect soot, ash, and other solid particles discharged by heating systems and industrial plants.

• Pollution caused by automobiles can be minimized by installing devices, or redesigning engines, to reduce exhaust gases. California has already passed a law requiring exhaust reduction systems on all automobiles sold in the state beginning in 1966.

Methods for eliminating the major portion of pollutants from water have been known for many years. Techniques such as filtration, aeration, settlement (in which solids are allowed to sink to the bottom of polluted water), and dilution (in which polluted water is cleansed by mixture with fresh water) can be used for primary treatment.

Chemical methods, such as chlorination, can be employed for secondary treatment. When applied to both municipal sewage and industrial wastes, a combination of these techniques can eliminate almost all objectionable materials. Most communities already have some kind of water treatment facility, but in many instances, such facilities are inadequate.

An urgent need exists for the construction of separate storm and sanitary sewerage systems. The two systems should not be combined as they so often are at present. In the first place, storm run-off does not require treatment. It can drain directly into a waterway. More important, when combined with sewage in one system, storm run-off frequently overloads treatment plant facilities. This causes much of the sewage to flow directly into nearby waterways.

To use the water available to us in the most efficient manner possible, we must conserve as much as we can. Already, in some industrial operations, water is treated in the plant and reused, cleansed, and reused many times before finally being evacuated. Hopefully, this practice will become much more widespread in years ahead.

The reduction of water and air contamination is clearly a problem that is more political and financial than technical. Some 32 states and Puerto Rico had approved some air pollution laws by 1963. Of these, however, only 15

live around the estuary. In 1985, there will be 3,000,000; in 2010, 5,000,000. Contemplating the rapid expansion of the future, Gordon E. McCallum of the United States Public Health Service says: "Our job will never end." It will be virtually impossible to keep ahead of the problem. If John Quincy Adams dipped into the Potomac every morning now, he would require medical attention. The water of the lovely river that washes our beautiful capital city is not clear, not blue, but "soupy green," as one of its custodians describes it. Although the Potomac estuary may look romantic, its contamination is real.

actually carried any enforcement authority. Among the states that now have control programs, the average expenditure is only about four cents per capita per year—less money than schoolchildren spend for candy or ice cream in a single week.

To a large extent, the problem consists of overcoming fears of federal intervention and resistance to appropriating sufficient funds for the control of the major sources of pollution.

The first federal air pollution control program of any consequence was established in 1955, with the passage of Public Law 155. This act provided for government research, as well as for grants and contracts to research organizations and universities.

In 1963, a major implementation of this act came with the enactment of Public Law 88-206, popularly known as the Clean Air Act. The act laid the foundation for interstate agreements, and the establishment of a commission with legal authority to curtail or prevent one state from polluting another. It also made substantial funds available to develop control agencies on state, county, and municipal levels. In addition, the federal government for the first time was able to take legal action when it could prove an interstate health hazard existed.

Another big step forward was the passage late in 1965 of a law giving the federal government authority to establish emission standards for motor vehicle exhausts. This means that by 1968, all new automobiles will probably be equipped with devices to control exhaust fumes.

Federal jurisdiction over water pollution advanced appreciably in 1965 when President Lyndon B. Johnson signed a bill that requires the states to establish clean water standards by 1967. Thereafter, the federal government will have the power to set standards for states that have not done so.

Residents of New York state have already given evidence that they intend to solve their own problems without pressure from the federal government. In November, they overwhelmingly approved a proposition authorizing the state to raise $1,000,000,000 through a bond issue to assist the financing of sewage treatment and other anti-pollution facilities throughout New York.

The issue of state versus federal jurisdiction—either with regard to water or air pollution—is not really the crux of the matter. The crucial issue relates to individual concern and commitment. Are we willing, for example, to spend as much to combat pollution as we spend on smoking?

The funds essential to this massive task in the coming decade may be more sizable than those needed for almost any other government program. The expense, however, may be no more than the approximately $50,000,000,000 spent for tobacco during the past 10 years, and certainly less than the roughly $100,000,000,000 expenditure for alcohol during the same period. Moreover, the longer we wait to mobilize against pollution, the more it will eventually cost. The total clean-up bill substantially increases each day we delay making a total effort to restore our environment and maintain the integrity of our natural resources.

While we may not be able to eliminate it, we have the means to control pollution. It is now imperative that we get on with the task.

General pollution of the environment will continue until the public puts a stop to it. Municipalities will economize on the treatment of sewage until the citizens assume the responsibility themselves. Industries will continue to dump their wastes into the air or the water until citizens make a public issue of it.

In this, as in all aspects of life, we need an ethic. In the legal sense, people can own land, but they do not own it in the moral sense. They are custodians of a land that each generation passes on to the next. In *A Sand County Almanac*, an inspired and pioneering book published in 1949, the late Aldo Leopold defined the land ethic: "A land ethic changes the role of *Homo sapiens* from conqueror of the land community to plain member and citizen of it. It implies respect for his fellow members and also respect for the community as such." Our natural resources are not adversaries to be conquered, nor raw products to be squandered. They are rich and wonderful parts of our inheritance. They are to be loved, respected, and wisely administered by all of us.

Since human beings have minds, they do have certain advantages over what we call dumb animals. We can reason from facts. We can

YEAR BOOK photo by Don Stebbing

"In three and one-half centuries of expansion and an increasing productivity," author Brooks Atkinson recently remarked, "Americans have had to exchange the old myth of unlimited abundance for the sobering reality of a polluted continent. We think of ourselves as intelligent beings, and in many respects we are. But we have also behaved irresponsibly, as if each generation owned the total environment and could carelessly dispose of it without any obligation whatever to the next."

save life by obeying abstract knowledge and doing some of the things that do not come easily. But in the last analysis, we are mammals. We flourish or fall, live or die, by the same natural laws that govern the wild creatures of the earth, as well as the grains in the meadow and the roses beside the house. As a nation, we acquired a beautiful land three and one-half centuries ago. We have created a civilization that is in many ways as beautiful as the land because its sovereign principle is freedom of the body, mind, and soul.

But freedom can degenerate into anarchy. Having been carelessly used, the land has lost its original grandeur and exultance. "The air we breathe, our water, our soil, and wildlife are being blighted by poisons and chemicals which are the by-products of technology and industry," President Lyndon B. Johnson said in 1965 in his "Message on the Natural Beauty of Our Country."

We are wasting and poisoning the shining green land that Americans have loved since the day they first saw it.

See also Section Two, *Water for a Thirsty World;* Section Three, WATER AND FLOOD CONTROL.

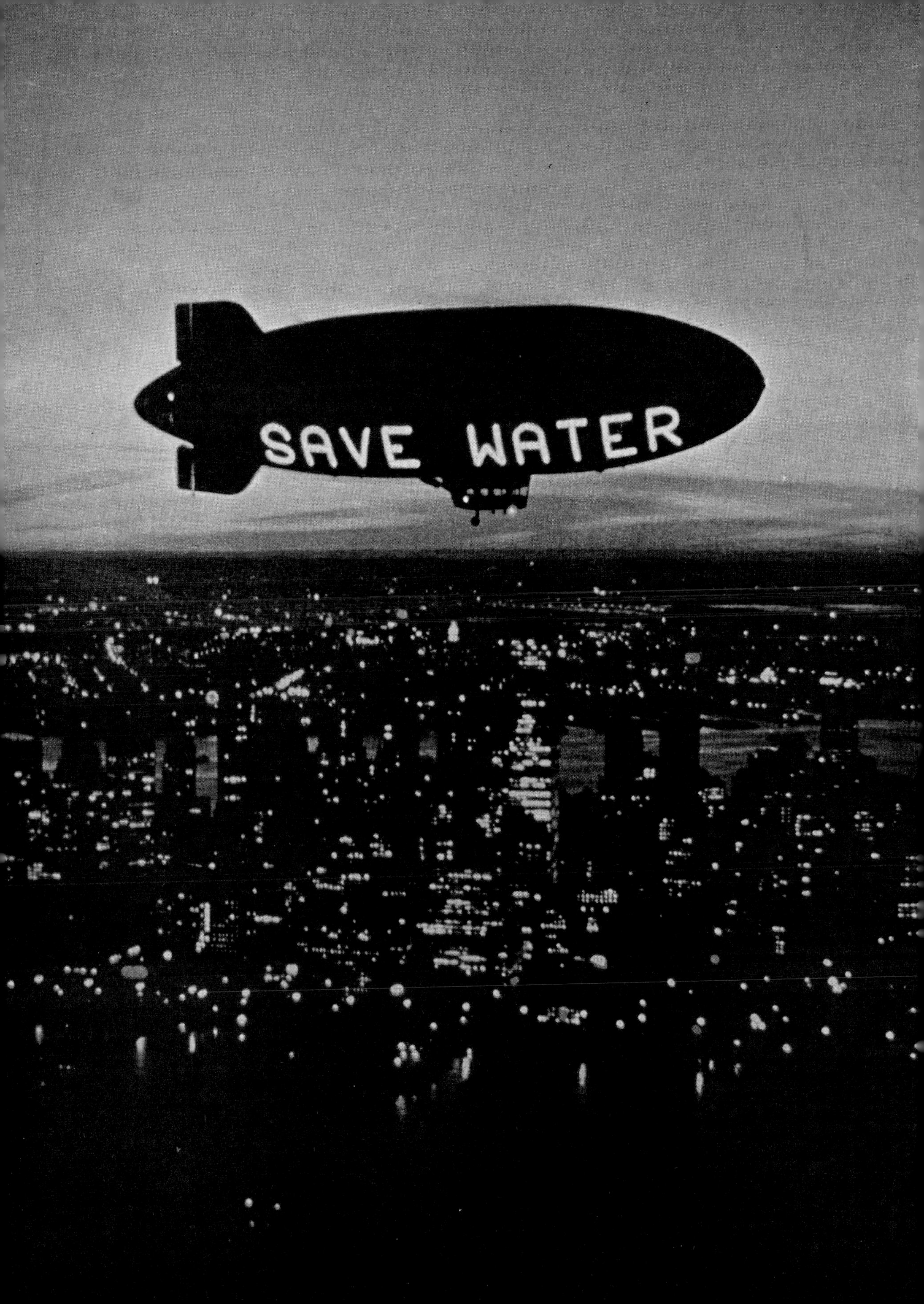
SAVE WATER

WATER
For a
Thirsty World

Though Most of the Earth Is Covered by Water, Much of Mankind Is Faced with a Shortage. Now Scientists Have Launched a World-Wide Investigation to Find Answers to One of Man's Most Basic Problems.

By Lorus and Margery Milne

A blimp hovering over New York City in the summer of 1965 conveys a clear and urgent message. Unless new water sources are found, this message will be repeated in other urban areas.

Ben Martin for Time Inc. from Pictorial Parade

When rain streaks the windows of our home in New Hampshire, we tend to take water for granted. Most people in the United States do. Yet the postman pulls a letter postmarked New York City from under his dripping raincoat, its stamp canceled with an urgent plea to "SAVE WATER."

We look through a spattered pane at storm clouds billowed and twisted by the wind from the west, realizing that only a few hundred miles south of us another west wind villainously pushes air laden with moisture out over the Atlantic Ocean. There, a heavy rainfall of fresh, pure water blends into the sea. But the parched watersheds and caking fringes of reservoirs serving New York City, Boston, and Philadelphia are left dry.

In 1965, one of the most densely populated areas on earth was in its fifth year of drought. The shrinking water reserves of New York City fell to the one-third of capacity mark. There were fears that the shortage might grow even worse. New York City's water commissioner, the mayor, the U.S. Secretary of the Interior, and even the President of the United States sought, but could not find, a quick way to satisfy the giant thirst of the city.

Each day, New York City consumes more than a billion gallons of fresh water. Even a heavy downpour replenishes its reservoirs for only a day or two. What the long-range solution to the New York water crisis will be no one can say, but this much is certain: the future of New York and of all our great cities—in fact of humanity itself— depends upon the wise use of water. For the earth's water supply is fixed; we cannot increase it. We can only find where it is, transport it to where we need it, and decontaminate it of salt and other impurities so that it is suitable for continued use and reuse.

Fortunately, the business of learning how we can best do these things has already begun. On Jan. 1, 1965, the United Nations Educational, Scientific, and Cultural Organization (UNESCO) inaugurated the International Hydrological Decade, a multinational scientific study of the world's water supply. Among the intriguing riddles to be studied is our planet's water cycle.

Some of the water pelting our windows in New Hampshire has traveled 3,000 miles. It was evaporated out of the Pacific Ocean by the sun, and for more than a week has been held as invisible water vapor in a great mass of air spinning eastward across the continent. Chilled over New Hampshire's highlands, it appeared as heavy clouds in which turbulence dashed small droplets together, making large drops heavy enough to fall. We watch in fascination as the drops slant downward, and disappear into the soft earth.

When the rain stops, much of the moisture will evaporate again, giving the gentle breeze its pleasant softness. Some of the rain will run into streams, making them gurgle. From there, the water will gush into a nearby river, its slow current emptying into a different sea—the Atlantic Ocean.

This cycle—liberation of fresh water from the sea and its return to the sea—occurs rapidly wherever a small island rises out of a tropical ocean. We discovered this on a visit to St. Lucia in the West Indies.

The dawning sun dispels the night's chill and warms the island. The air is heated, and rises. Humid air from offshore moves in to replace the dry air. As this column of moist air ascends, it expands and cools until it can no longer hold its load of water. A big white cloud forms, spreads, and thickens. By early afternoon, it grows black and heavy with vapor. Down comes the rain, drenching and cooling the island. The sun then breaks through again and evaporates most of the water from the dripping foliage and wet rocks. This evaporation cools the island, and the air column above it ceases to rise. Any remnant of cloud drifts away. The water sinks into the soil or is carried by streams to the sea. The water cycle is completed, almost like clockwork.

Fully one-fourth of the solar energy that penetrates the earth's atmosphere is used to power the cycle by lifting fresh water from the seas. This prodigious amount is over 7,000 times the energy man uses in all his machines combined. As the rotating earth brings one ocean after another into the sunshine, so much water vapor rises into the atmosphere that, if none were returned for a full year, ocean levels

The authors:
The husband-and-wife team of Drs. Lorus and Margery Milne has worked together since college days. They are now professors at the University of New Hampshire. The Milne's travels have taken them over 500,000 miles through four continents. The latest of their 17 books is "Water and Life."

This contrast between the parched desert and the vast but salty ocean symbolizes the uneven distribution of the world's water. Ironically, even if the oceans were fresh water, our water problems would not be solved. To solve them and meet the needs of the future, mankind must learn how to purify and shift more water from areas of plenty to areas of thirst.

would fall by nearly four feet. Actually, of course, most of the evaporated moisture falls back into the oceans. Only about 9 per cent falls onto the land, where it is readily useful to man. And much of this moisture, too, eventually returns to the seas.

Although Leonardo da Vinci and many others since have grasped the essentials of the water cycle, its details remain a mystery. No one really knows how much fresh water lies deep in the soil, or the complex routes it takes between a soaking rain and its return to the seas. Also, the water cycle is affected by changes in weather, such as the series of dry years that appear to follow a succession of wet years about three times each century. These changes have no known basis that

What They Cost in Water

40,000 gallons are needed to make the steel in one car.

50 gallons a day are taken from the soil by an average tree.

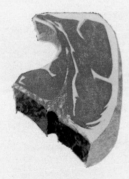

3,000 gallons in food and water are used to produce a pound of beef.

might permit either accurate prediction or attempts to control them.

If drinking water were our only requirement, there would be plenty for everybody. Each person needs only about three quarts daily in beverages and wet foods. But that is just the beginning. Fresh water is also needed to bathe, to wash clothing and dishes, to dispose of waste, to water lawns, to fight fires. How much water does all this take? The average city dweller in the United States uses about 158 gallons of fresh water daily from his community's water system.

People in highly developed countries such as the United States put additional demands on water. They want an automobile or two in the garage. They want lettuce from Arizona in the middle of winter, and corn and strawberries from California in off-seasons. They want a newspaper every day and one or two thick ones on Sunday, plus magazines and books. They want electric power so cheap that they can use it freely to open and close the garage door, to carve a turkey, to vibrate a toothbrush, or to provide music throughout the house. Every one of these has a high price in water.

Our civilization depends, for example, upon equipment made of steel. The manufacture of a ton of steel requires 65,000 gallons of water of moderate purity. When we stroll home with a thick Sunday newspaper under an arm, we are carrying the result of 180 gallons (six bathtubfuls) of fresh water used in the paper mill, plus water to grow the spruce trees to pulpwood size, plus water for the manufacture and operation of logging machinery, printing presses, and distribution equipment. About 300 gallons of fresh water are needed for the few wheat stalks that provide grain for a day's bread for one person—if bread alone is eaten. Adding up all our needs, 16,000 gallons of fresh water are actually required every day to support the accepted standard of living for each person in the United States.

Wherever we travel, we meet people striving to raise their standard of living. On a return visit to Nairobi, Kenya, after an absence of four years, we noticed that bicycles, which contain only a small amount of steel, were now outnumbered by heavy automobiles. Certainly no perspiring bicyclist consumes as much water as a refinery uses in making the gasoline to propel an automobile the same number of miles. Even the change from tribal to Western dress reflected an increase in water use, for mechanization of a clothing industry requires an added supply of water.

Industrial growth and an expanding world population seem inevitable. The Statistical Office of the United Nations expects the world population to reach 7,000,000,000 by 1999. This is double today's population—just a generation from now. If everyone then is to use 16,000 gallons of fresh water each day, from where will it come? How can disastrous water shortages be prevented?

Perhaps the desalination of sea water will be one answer. Presently several methods are being tested. One involves distillation in which salt water is boiled, and the pure water that escapes as steam is condensed and collected. Another involves freezing. Ice crystals formed from salt water are themselves pure, but they are coated with salt. This is rinsed off, and the crystals are then melted into fresh water. Still other methods make use of thin plastic semipermeable membranes through which pure water can be obtained from salt water, either by mechanical or electric power.

There are about 50 major saline water conversion plants in operation or under construction in various parts of the world, and more are being planned. For the most part, these installations supply fresh water for islands, extremely arid or desert regions, or other special locations. While the methods for producing artificially desalinated water are not now economically feasible for use on a widespread basis, they do hold some promise for regions with supplies of salt water.

But as Roger Revelle, former director of the Scripps Institution of Oceanography at the University of California at La Jolla, points out, even if all of the oceans were fresh water, our water problems would not be solved because sea water is at such a low elevation. It would cost untold sums to pump billions of gallons of sea water far inland, or to places higher than a few hundred feet above sea level. Thus, while large coastal cities may resort more and more to sea water for municipal uses, inland areas will have to learn to use their normal water resources more efficiently.

We asked Raymond L. Nace, a leading hydrologist in the U.S. Geological Survey, about the whole problem of water supply. "Thinking on a continental scale is now necessary," he responded, "involving projects that may require 10 years to plan and 20 to 40 years to build. Such planning is essential to assure rational use of our finite water supply to meet a potentially limitless water demand."

Of the 16,000 gallons per person per day used for modern civilized living, most evaporates into the air; less than half returns to rivers or sinks into the ground. This supply of used water is precious, for it can be purified and reused. Even now, the same water is used nearly four times during certain periods of the year as it passes from Pittsburgh, Pa., to Cairo, Ill., along the Ohio River. Yet, there are too many instances in which communities show little regard for water.

If arid regions are to prosper, huge amounts of water must be brought in. Already, 790 gallons of water per person per day are used for irrigation in the United States. No other single use of fresh water demands so great a volume. In this area, too, we must practice economy in the use of water, and find new means of obtaining and reusing it.

Just as communities have grown, so have local water problems. Effective action now depends upon broader views, more expensive undertakings, and a higher level of cooperative action. Feats of "continental engineering" are needed to correct the natural inequities in the distribution of fresh water. But success is possible only if people are willing to cooperate, forgetting age-old rivalries. Emotional obstacles still loom large in Southeast Asia and in the Middle East, where the fresh waters of the great Mekong River and of the River Jordan provide a major basis for a higher standard of living.

Where Precipitation Goes

RETURNED TO ATMOSPHERE BY EVAPORATION, 71%

USED BY CITIES, 0.6%
USED BY INDUSTRY, 3.4%
USED FOR IRRIGATION, 3.4%

RETURNED TO OCEAN UNUSED, 21.6%

YEAR BOOK Chart

Of all the moisture that falls on the U.S., less than 8 per cent is directed by man for his special uses. Most precipitation returns naturally to the atmosphere or the oceans.

Nature's Hidden Reservoir

There is 20 times as much water under the land's surface as in all lakes and rivers combined. This ground water continually interchanges with water on the surface. Like surface water, it is constantly in motion.

If there were no ground water, a river would be reduced to a trickle in a few rainless weeks. In actuality, water that is absorbed into the ground in rainy periods (left), empties into the river during dry periods to sustain its flow (right).

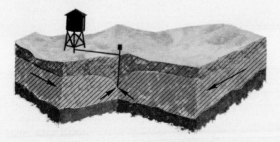

When ground water is pumped to the surface of the earth, the water table sinks near the well. If too much water is pumped from the ground, all but the deepest wells will temporarily go dry.

 SURFACE WATER

 NONPOROUS ROCK

POROUS ROCK AND SOIL

 NONSATURATED
WATER TABLE
SATURATED

YEAR BOOK Diagrams

Unfortunately, even within a country, the diversion of valuable fresh water from one region to another is likely to cause disputes. Arguments over water rights in the U.S. Southwest, for example, began during the 1930s, when a pipeline was installed to carry 1,000,000,000 gallons of Colorado River water to Los Angeles and San Diego daily. As California's cities grew, more aqueducts were added, and conflicts multiplied. In June, 1963, the Supreme Court of the United States reapportioned the water of the great river that runs through seven states and Mexico. California's share was limited to less than 3,900,000,000 gallons a day, not the 4,500,000,000 gallons actually being taken. Fortunately, Californians were by then busy laying new intrastate pipelines from the Feather River, north of Sacramento, to areas in the south.

A Los Angeles engineering firm, the Ralph M. Parsons Company, has calculated the costs and gains from diverting large amounts of water from such sources as the Fraser River and the upper reaches of the Columbia River in western Canada to dry areas in North America. This plan certainly qualifies as "continental engineering." The primary purpose of this ambitious 30-year project is to pipe water about 1,200 miles from the vast Canadian watershed. By investing $80,000,000,000 to $100,000,000,000—almost the entire U.S. federal budget for one year—in the vast project, arid states might receive daily 129,000,000,000 gallons of irrigation water, 32,000,000,000 gallons of industrial water, and, as a by-product, 100,000,000 kilowatts of hydroelectric power.

When Parsons engineers explained the details of this North American Water and Power Alliance plan to 300 officials and businessmen from both countries, many of the Canadians asked how much of the estimated income of $4,000,000,000 a year from the sale of the water would be paid to Canada. It is becoming increasingly clear that this rather common liquid, which most everyone takes for granted, has become a valuable commodity.

**In the shadow of the legendary King Solomon's Mines, at Elath, Israel, a new
plant desalts a precious 1,000,000 gallons of water from the Red Sea each day.
Though still an expensive source of fresh water, desalination pays its way
in parched areas where it is virtually the only source.**

Lloyd A. Royal, a Canadian who directs the International Pacific
Salmon Fisheries Commission, foresees a serious side effect. "Most certainly, the Parsons plan as projected would destroy a vast salmon-
producing empire," he said. Others ask whether a decrease in the flow
from these two great rivers might not alter the whole circulation pattern
of the Pacific Ocean from Oregon to Alaska.

Often the drawbacks of a giant engineering project cannot be predicted. In proposing the Unified Water Plan for the development of

189

Bradford Washburn

At any time, over 75 per cent of the earth's fresh water is frozen in icecaps and glaciers. This volume is equal to the flow of all the earth's rivers for 1,000 years. Possible effects on climate and ocean level, however, give scientists pause when schemes to melt glacial ice are proposed.

the River Jordan basin, engineers appointed by the United Nations allotted Israel 232,000,000 gallons a day. But when the Israelis began pumping water at a rate of 186,000,000 gallons a day to their croplands in the northern Negev Desert, the level of Lake Tiberias (the Sea of Galilee) fell three feet in just a few months. Saline springs in the lake bottom increased their flow, rendering the water dangerously salty. To again get water of usable quality, the yield of fresh water from this ambitious and controversial project had to be cut back to about 125,000,000 gallons a day.

The much-publicized Aswan High Dam may do little more than enhance the political popularity of Egypt's president, Gamal Abdel Nasser. When completed, the dam will hold a reservoir nearly 200 miles long, harnessing the Nile River for the first time. Below the dam, all of the water will flow through irrigation canals, allowing continuous production of rice and other crops on 3,000 square miles of now useless desert. The food produced is expected to nourish Egypt's growing population and provide commodities for export. Electric power from the great turbines is to help industrialize the country.

Some engineers wonder, however, if the dam might not produce as many problems as it solves. They are willing to accept the loss of the Nile as a navigable corridor for commerce, but they worry about the amount of water the dry air will evaporate from the huge reservoir and from the man-made ditches through which the irrigation water will travel, in boiling heat, for 1,000 miles to the Mediterranean Sea. Not only will water be lost by evaporation, but the shrinking remainder will become increasingly concentrated with salts. When it reaches Lower Egypt, where crops irrigated by the Nile are now raised, it may be too salty for use.

In addition, the health of Egyptians on the upper side of the dam is almost sure to deteriorate rapidly as soon as irrigation water flows from Aswan on a year-round basis. In any hot country that has poor sanitation, blood flukes and other agents of chronic disease penetrate the skin of people who wade in and drink irrigation water. When irrigation was introduced in Lower Egypt, the proportion of people with debilitating blood-fluke infections rose from 5 per cent to 80 per cent. Because of this, the Egyptian army finds that its rejection rate for men of the Lower Nile is now seven times as high as that of men from nonirrigated Upper Egypt. Much of the country's heavy labor force is supplied from Upper Egypt, where there is a very low incidence of blood flukes. Infections caused by this parasite are presently incurable, and even now have markedly lowered the productivity of Egypt.

President Nasser and his government are relying on the chance that a way will be found to control blood flukes and other diseases associated with continued irrigation in a warm climate. However, doctors who work in the tropics regard the Aswan High Dam

A CONTINENTAL WATER PLAN

One example of continental engineering is the Ralph M. Parsons Company plan for distributing water throughout wide areas of North America. Under this plan, rainfall in Alaska and Canada that now drains, unused, into the Pacific and Arctic oceans would be diverted to water-poor sections of the continent. This project, however, would require excavation of reservoirs and canals equivalent to more than 100 Panama Canals. And before work could begin, hydrologists would have to check for potentially harmful side effects.

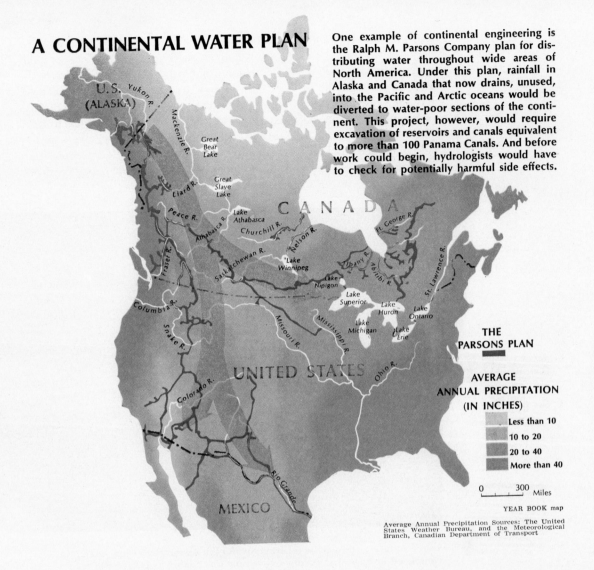

THE PARSONS PLAN

AVERAGE ANNUAL PRECIPITATION (IN INCHES)

Less than 10
10 to 20
20 to 40
More than 40

0   300   Miles

YEAR BOOK map

Average Annual Precipitation Sources: The United States Weather Bureau, and the Meteorological Branch, Canadian Department of Transport

as a desperate gamble, likely to cause far more harm than good.

Whatever the outcome of the Aswan High Dam project and other large-scale plans elsewhere, mankind must find ways of increasing the world's fresh water supply. To answer some of the most important questions raised by increasing water shortages in the United States, the Federal Council for Science and Technology, in June, 1960, invited Walter B. Langbein of the U.S. Geological Survey to head a Panel on Hydrology. Other top scientists on the panel represented the National Science Foundation, the U.S. Army Corps of Engineers, the Weather Bureau, the U.S. Public Health Service, and the Agricultural Research Service.

Because of the scope of the problem, international cooperation seemed essential. Langbein asked his colleague, Raymond L. Nace, for suggestions. Nace and Langbein produced the most far-reaching part of the panel's 37-page report, which called for a world-wide study of fresh water. Because weather dominates the water cycle and varies so

191

much from year to year, coordinated, systematic observations for a period of at least 10 years seemed necessary.

Key officials in the U.S. Department of State were keenly interested, and encouraged the project. After much further work on the plan, UNESCO formally endorsed it in November, 1964. The organization proclaimed the International Hydrological Decade (IHD), to last from Jan. 1, 1965, through Dec. 31, 1974. Financial support was voted, and a 21-member Coordinating Council was authorized to administer it.

Most activities within the program of the IHD will relate to the

United Press Int.

Scarce surface water will be hoarded behind the Aswan High Dam when it is completed in 1969. The Egyptian government is hoping its people will reap great benefits from the dam, but scientists fear possible side effects.

collection and exchange of facts and ideas. For rarely has the distinction between basic scientific knowledge and its engineering applications been so great. The hard facts are that no one really knows yet exactly where the rain goes after it sinks into the soil, or what channels the meltwater from snow follows, determining whether rivers will flood disastrously this year or not. Guesses are not good enough: new and reliable sources of information must be found. Scarcely less important to hydrologists will be the education of world leaders, whose decisions influence the supply and quality of fresh water.

During the Decade, international efforts will focus on three fronts. One group of scientists will help establish an interlocking network of observation stations on all the continents and major islands of the world. With cooperation from local governments and individual scientists, the group will strive for standardization in methods of measurement of precipitation, stream flow, sediment transport, ground water, evaporation, snow, and ice. Reliable information is now deficient or lacking for two-thirds of the land areas of the world.

The second group will assist specialists in all of the participating countries to gather their existing records into the form of "national inventories" of fresh water. From these, a reliable picture of the water balance over the entire globe will be constructed for the first time. Almost surely it will indicate the location and size of uncharted rivers and reservoirs deep in the earth. Recent discoveries prove this to be no dream. Long-abandoned wells dug by the Romans in Tunisia contain an abundance of usable water. Porous rocks beneath the Sahara are full of fresh water—perhaps the largest untapped supply in the world.

The third group will strive to assist fundamental research. Its concern will be the many factors affecting precipitation, evaporation and transpiration, and surface runoff. It will study the dynamics of reservoirs and natural lakes and rivers, the transport and deposition of sediments, movements of soil moisture, interaction between fresh water and ocean water in estuaries, river deltas, and along coasts. It will examine meltwater from snowfields, glaciers, and icecaps, and the quality and chemistry of fresh water. Perhaps most important, it will study the complex influence of man upon many of these factors.

Deliberately excluded, though, are most of the short-range problems that seem so pressing in various parts of the world: water for New York and other cities; for industry, irrigation, water power, and navigation. These, like waste disposal and pollution, await the determination of the people who must raise and spend the money necessary to solve them.

The IHD has already begun to bear fruit in some of the more advanced countries. The British government has established a Water Resources Planning Board to spur action by communities and industries to conserve water. The Congress of the United States has passed the Water Resources Research Act of 1964 which provides grants for universities and scientific foundations to tackle critical water problems. It has also passed the Water Resources Planning Act of 1965 which provides for the establishment of a water resources council and river basin commissions and encourages state participation in resolving water problems. Early in 1965, the first allotments of research funds were made to establish water research institutes in fourteen states.

The IHD is the largest international scientific program yet begun. Coming at a time when a water crisis threatens most of mankind, every one of us will gain from it. Dr. E. L. Hendricks, chief of the Surface Water Branch in the U.S. Geological Survey, repeats the point that "a science may be gauged by its ability to predict." Hydrologists want the forward strides made during the International Hydrological Decade to permit predictions that will guarantee success in providing fresh water for an increasingly thirsty world. To us, the message is clear: to manage fresh water wisely is to conserve life itself.

See also Section Two, *Polluted America;* Section Three, New York City; Water and Flood Control.

THE NEW

*An Old Region Rallies
Its Resources and People
To Enter a New Age of
Skill and Science*

By Robert A. Irwin

NEW ENGLAND

Standing in front of Boston's historic Faneuil Hall, I looked up at a bronze statue of Samuel Adams. If the statue's metallic eyes had suddenly widened in wonder, I would have been only slightly surprised. Sam Adams, garbed in a tarnished frock coat, was gazing majestically across 60 acres of rubble—and renewal. A sign nearby proclaimed this to be Boston's ambitious Government Center project.

Gone were all traces of honky-tonk Scollay Square and those steep, alleylike streets, Cornhill and Brattle, with their musty, second-hand bookstores. They had been leveled by bulldozers.

Their demise symbolized one of the greatest changes in Boston in the 162 years since Sam Adams had died. Amid the rubble, skyscrapers were going up. Gigantic cranes hovered among the rising structures. It was an impressive sight; particularly to a native who had left New England 30 years before, as I had.

The New England I had known could be characterized by one word: "old." Its factories, its institutions, its customs, its public buildings—even the attitudes of its people—were old. This gave the region a certain antique charm, but also placed it outside the mainstream of American development. Now something new, radically new, was happening. Throughout a 1,500-mile tour of the six New England states, I noticed many sights and sounds that signified change—and progress.

In Vermont, long noted for its pastoral quiet and the fact that it had more cows than people, scientists passed farmers on the way to work in a research laboratory that had, quite naturally, sprung up in a pasture. In Rhode Island, Providence had rescued its main shopping thoroughfare from the noise, fumes, and peril of auto traffic by converting Westminster Street into an attractive mall. In Connecticut, there was Hartford's Constitution Plaza; a dazzling testimonial to progress. In Maine, 75 miles north of Portland, a silvery, balloonlike radome lay in a bowl of low-lying hills; its huge horn antenna relaying television signals from the Early Bird communications satellite. In New Hampshire, in the once-depressed textile city of Keene, business leaders were busily recruiting workers from outside the community to keep pace with the demands of the city's now booming, diversified industries.

Nor was this all. Most important, New England's educational institutions were assuming a new, vital role. They were no longer regarded as cultural luxuries, but as necessities for the economic survival of the region. And they were attracting increasing numbers of dedicated researchers and teachers, as well as inquisitive students.

Quite evidently, New England had developed a new faith in the future. It seemed to be recapturing the spirit of an earlier age. From the 17th through the 19th centuries, New England and its people had played a dominant role in national life. Its swift clipper ships dominated world trade. Its shrewd Yankee traders amassed fortunes that furnished the means to build a growing nation's railroads, canals, and new industries. Its skilled craftsmen produced clocks, tools, instruments, and machines. Its fishermen harvested cod and haddock for the markets of the East. Its mills and factories clothed and shod the nation.

New England produced the literary giants of the day—Ralph Waldo Emerson, Nathaniel Hawthorne, Henry James, Henry David Thoreau, and others. New England also gave the nation its first successful ironworks, its first newspaper, its first permanent symphony orchestra.

As a result of the rapid development of the United States, it was perhaps inevitable that New England's influence would decline. Few, however, expected the decline to become as pronounced as it did. New England's share of U.S. personal income and number of factory jobs fell by more than 40 per cent from 1900 to the early 1950s. Its

YEAR BOOK photos on pages 194-195 and above by Ted Polumbaum

Foreign-born Population

■ New England

■ United States

For decades, New England's percentage of foreign born has been about twice that of the United States.

In the exclusive Boston Athenaeum, Boston's Irish mayor, John F. Collins, right, and Brahmin Charles A. Coolidge get down to work on the new Boston's problems.

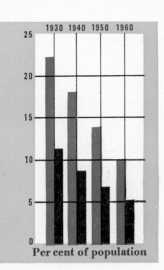

share of *value added by manufacture* (the difference between the price of a finished product and the cost of the materials that go into it), declined from about 16 per cent of the U.S. total in 1900 to a little more than 7 per cent in 1958.

But resource-poor New England had suffered other periodic setbacks in its long past. There had been one when its forests were depleted; another when the clipper ships and whalers outlived their glory. New England had experienced an economic defeat when the building of the Erie Canal and the railroads shifted the center of trade and finance to New York. Yet, Yankee ingenuity had somehow overcome those crises. The decline in the 20th century, however, involved problems seemingly even more grave than those of the past.

One was the exodus of manpower, which had begun in the 19th century but which did not become serious until the 1920s. As I stood beside the statue of Sam Adams, I thought back to the time in 1935, when I, too, had joined the exodus. In the decade 1930–1940, 43,000

197

Yankee ingenuity and water power laid the foundations of old New England's industries, such as this first successful U.S. mill for cotton spinning built by Samuel Slater in Pawtucket, R.I.

more people left New England than moved in. It was not until 1950–1960 that the net outward flow was stanched, particularly in the last five of those years. To the thousands of us who had fled in 1935, New England seemed a forgotten, dusty old corner of a country on the move. Relations among the region's various ethnic groups were far from harmonious. Politically, economically, and socially, the Irish fought the Yankees and the Italians fought the Irish. The New England I had left had an atmosphere drained of vitality.

By 1965, however, New England had experienced a dramatic turnabout in its attitudes, discarding many of the prejudices of the past and experiencing a revitalization of its inner self. In Connecticut, Rhode Island, and Massachusetts, politicians were being elected and defeated, not on the basis of their ethnic backgrounds, but because of their ability, or lack of it. Maine, New Hampshire, and Vermont, long one-party strongholds, had become two-party states.

But, of all the changes, the most striking had occurred in the area's economic development. From 1947 to the end of 1962, for example, while jobs in the textile industry were shrinking from 279,000 to 110,300, employment in the transportation equipment and electrical machinery industries rose from 167,300 to 270,000. This transition occurred without fanfare. George H. Ellis, president of the Federal Reserve Bank of Boston, told of a survey of U.S. businessmen's attitudes toward New England. The great majority, he said, were "at least a generation out of date. The great transition to science-based and skilled-service industries here had not dawned on them." They still thought of this area as "that place where all the textiles left."

How is the individual New Englander faring today? Probably the best measure of his economic health is per capita income. New

YEAR BOOK photo by Ethel M. Irwin

Typical of the new New England are these laboratories of the Scientific Engineering Institute overlooking Massachusetts Route 128 in the Waltham Research and Development Park.

England's 1950–1963 increase in absolute terms was greater than that for the nation as a whole or for any other region in the United States. Here are the figures for New England, its two leading regional contenders, and the United States:

	1950	1963	Increase
New England	$1,629	$2,766	$1,137
Pacific	1,786	2,871	1,085
Middle Atlantic	1,757	2,810	1,053
United States	1,491	2,449	958

New England obviously has shaken itself out of its slump. But how?

My quest for the answers to that question began in Greater Boston. Tom Winship, editor of the *Boston Globe*, pointed out that the first turnabout came in the early 1950s with the building of a road in the countryside surrounding Boston. "This," said Winship with typical New England understatement, "was one piece of luck; the construction of the Circumferential Highway, Route 128." (Only in Boston would a belt highway be called a circumferential road!) Eventually, "hungry" professors at Massachusetts Institute of Technology (M.I.T.) and Harvard University set up businesses along Route 128 based on some of their scientific discoveries. "Thus," said Winship, "a marriage was consummated between the academic and economic communities."

When Sputnik I was launched in 1957, the growth was intensified. As Winship put it: "The shock of the emerging Space Age caused people to take stock. They knew things had to be done—right away."

Coupled with the movement of professors into industry was an influx of new faces into politics. The election of John F. Kennedy to the presidency gave New Englanders new confidence and pride. It also helped them to overcome their long-standing distrust of the federal government.

Boston's new mayor, John F. Collins, was "another stroke of luck." His upset election in 1959 gave him a mandate for change. One of his first steps was to bring in Edward J. Logue from New Haven, Conn., to head Boston's ambitious urban renewal program. In May, 1965, the city's banking community demonstrated its faith in Collins' new Boston. The First National Bank of Boston agreed, for the first time in six years, to head a syndicate to bid on the city's bonds, which had lost their A rating on the Moody scale of municipal financial standings.

The "Circumferential Highway" Winship mentioned and the new turnpikes and other interstate highways have given New England a fresh, liberating mobility. The old, hilly, twisting, horse-and-buggy roads between thickly populated towns had discouraged meaningful communication. As a result, cities as close to one another as Providence, R.I., and Fall River, Mass. (16 miles apart), had gone their separate ways. Even an untrained ear could detect the differences in accents between the people of the two cities.

"We have been close together, but far apart," was the apt observation of Geoffrey Glendinning, vice-president of Arlington Trust Company in Lawrence, Mass. "Now the auto and the expressways have converted our congestion into an advantage. Lawrence can tap a labor pool for miles around, and our people can commute to Boston, Manchester, N.H., Route 128 plants, or wherever."

This new ease of getting from one location to another is making an interconnected urban complex of all New England, with the exception

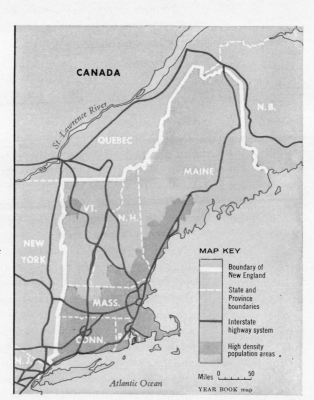

Roads That Mean Mobility

New, liberating lines of communications, such as the interstate highways, are ending the region's crippling congestion.

CANADA

St. Lawrence River

QUEBEC

MAINE

N.B.

VT.

N.H.

NEW YORK

MASS.

CONN.

N.J.

Atlantic Ocean

MAP KEY

Boundary of New England

State and Province boundaries

Interstate highway system

High density population areas

Miles 0 — 50

YEAR BOOK map

Lowry Aerial Photo

of its most out-of-the-way corners. It has widened job opportunities, choice of residence and friends, as well as the scope of recreational and cultural options. It has quickened the tempo and enriched the life of the New Englander. Bostonians think nothing of making an evening out of a Tanglewood concert in the Berkshires 125 miles away.

Even New England's remote "last stand of the Yankee" areas are coming under the influence of the interstate highways. The Dartmouth College region is one. It also epitomizes many other changes that are reshaping New England. This area's three chief towns—Hanover and Lebanon, N.H., and White River Junction, Vt.—are in a breathtaking period of transformation.

"We're sitting right in the middle of a historic crossroads in the making. We will be athwart the new interstates, one from Boston to Montreal, and the other from New York City up the Connecticut Valley and eventually to Quebec City. Industry and business know it and are buying property around here like mad," said Walter Paine, the vigorous, young publisher of the *Valley News* in West Lebanon. He pointed across the road from his neat, little publishing plant to a small, scrubby field and continued: "Eight years ago I could have bought that acre for $600. This spring I paid $6,000 for it."

Paine himself is typical of the new breed of Yankee I met. Since he

Intricate interchange of Route 128, running from upper left to lower right, with the Massachusetts Turnpike gives easy access to scores of nearby science-based industries and businesses.

201

took over the then four-year-old daily newspaper in 1956, circulation has risen 44 per cent. Paine emigrated to this area from suburban Boston "because it's an attractive, relaxing, yet exciting, place to work and live. The old disadvantages of remoteness have disappeared. The superhighway and the airplane are taking care of that."

This new mobility has not only infused fresh blood into this old Yankee area, but has also sparked some revolutionary changes in attitudes. The outlook of the people has, for one thing, become regional, rather than local. Support for the bi-state area's airport is a case in point. Funds for the Lebanon Regional Airport Authority are voted by taxpayers in both New Hampshire and Vermont.

"Those people," Paine told me, "don't care if one town is going to use the airport more than another. It's what it will do for the entire area."

This regional spirit has spread. The towns of Norwich, Vt., and Hanover, N.H., after three years of effort, an act of Congress, and the approval of the two state legislatures, set up the nation's first bi-state, regional high school district, called the Dresden School District. The Hanover high school opened to regional students in 1964.

In the same period, the area achieved another first. Its Upper Valley Development Council, founded in 1962, was the first regular interstate multicommunity, economic development council in the United States. Its director, Paul H. Guilderson, a former industrial salesman, told me how Lebanon's aldermen drafted a redevelopment plan under the Federal Housing Act only three weeks after the disastrous fire of June 19, 1964, had leveled half the city's business district. "This amounted to a revolution up here—business and city officials working on a program partly financed by federal funds," Guilderson said.

Dartmouth College has been conducting a quiet social and educational revolution right on its ivied campus in Hanover, N.H. Project ABC—"A Better Chance"—enrolled 81 bright but poor teen-age boys, mostly Negroes, in the summer of 1965. The boys who pass the intensive eight-week course are offered scholarships to one of New England's once-exclusive private preparatory schools.

George Cabot Lodge, a former U.S. Assistant Secretary of Labor and son of U.S. Ambassador Henry Cabot Lodge, is an enthusiastic supporter of ABC for his "prep" school, Groton. He commented: "The prep schools, along with New England's colleges and universities, have broadened their bases geographically, economically, and socially. It is an upgrading of education to attract the best qualified students, no matter where they come from."

Lodge and others like him are speeding a social revolution that is liberating New England even more than its expressways. Another old-line Yankee who has helped bring about this new social mobility is Boston lawyer Charles A. Coolidge. He is the son of architect Charles Coolidge and a distant relative of President Calvin Coolidge. Lawyer Coolidge was instrumental in helping to bring an end to more than a century of bitter feuding between Boston's Yankee community and its Irish population.

Historic Faneuil Hall keeps a lonely vigil as Boston builds its new Government Center.

202

Constitution Plaza has revitalized a former slum area of downtown Hartford, Conn. One of its striking showpieces is the Phoenix Mutual Life Insurance Company building, center.

I met Coolidge, a vigorous, alert 70, in his comfortable, homey office on the top floor of a substantial old stone building in Boston's financial district. He settled himself in a well-worn wooden chair behind a polished desk, which had been his grandfather's, and began: "It started six or seven years ago when a small group sat down together at Boston College. That, as you know, is the Catholic university here. The group recognized the tremendous cost to the community of the continuing lack of communication between the people who "owned" Boston (the Yankee Brahmins) and the people who "ran" it (the Irish and others). A continuing series of representative seminars was organized under Father W. Seavey Joyce, the college's dean of business. These have made a major contribution to revitalizing Boston."

That represented a revolutionary social change from the New England of deep distrust and suspicion that I had grown up in. Only after I left the region, did I realize that we old New Englanders had really been a minority. We had lived in the most foreign of all U.S. regions. As late as 1940, New Englanders who were either born abroad or had at least one foreign-born parent made up 51.5 per cent of the region's white population. The national figure was 17.8 per cent.

Despite waves of immigrants, the old stock held onto its power for decades. The late mayor James M. Curley could with truth refer to "that downtrodden majority, Boston's Irish!" In the early 1950s, a transplanted California educator remarked to Sevellon Brown, associate editor of the *Providence Journal*, that that city was "the only community I have ever lived in where the majority felt like the minority, and the minority acted as if it were the majority."

203

New England's greatest asset, brain power, is nurtured on its college campuses, such as that of the Massachusetts Institute of Technology (M.I.T.).

M.I.T., as other New England colleges, attracts talented students from many parts of the world.

Dartmouth's new Center for Mathematics rises beside the college's old Church of Christ.

YEAR BOOK photo by Ted Polumbaum

*Not only at M.I.T., but also at Harvard's new Engineering Sciences
Laboratory, students are extending scientific frontiers.*

YEAR BOOK photo by
Ethel M. Irwin

I went back to Boston University to see if a former professor of mine, sociologist Albert Morris, could explain why New England's melting pot had been so slow to heat up. "What has to be remembered," he began, "is that New England was a stable, homogeneous society for more than 200 years. Then newcomers, fleeing the Irish potato famine, arrived during the 1840s. They had been living in sod huts, suffering starvation and terrible deprivation. They were of a different religion, Roman Catholic, and many were illiterate. The old, established New Englanders reacted strongly; they weren't about to be pushed aside."

In the pioneer society of the Middle West and West, on the other hand, Morris explained, both the overseas immigrants and the U.S. natives were settlers working side by side in the building of new cities and the opening of new farmlands.

What it meant to be an immigrant in New England is told by Donald Cole in his *Immigrant City*, a historical study of Lawrence, Mass. He describes how a fire in 1875 "laid bare the shabbiness of the immigrants' living conditions. In a shack, measuring 100 x 20 feet and divided in the middle, lived a family, 77 boarders and two girl cooks. The fire started at 1:30 A.M. in a cubicle usually occupied by the two cooks but empty at the moment because they were sleeping on the floor of the main room to escape bedbugs."

Now, 90 years later, banker Geoffrey Glendinning, himself a descendant of a Yorkshire weaver, told me how far the children and grandchildren of Lawrence's immigrants had traveled. He read at random some of the names of chief executives from the city's industrial

*George Cabot Lodge
typifies the continuing
educational concern of
old Yankee families.*

205

Presque Isle, Me., refused to give up when its huge air base closed in 1961. It hired James K. Keefe, a Maine-educated Bay Stater, to head its Industrial Council. He and the council induced businesses to move into the former hangars and missile sheds, creating more than 1,000 new jobs—almost four times as many as had been lost when the base shut down.

Sheldon Dietz, Harvard (1941) and a resident of Martha's Vineyard, Mass., has brought about a revolutionary change in one of New England's oldest industries—fisheries. He has adapted the long-line method of fishing to catching swordfish, which were found to frequent New England waters at varying depths all year, not just in the summer. His two specially designed vessels carry miles of hooked and buoyed nylon rope.

directory—Batal, Forma, Giragosian, Grieco, Privitera, Rappaport, Valeska, and Vinciguerra. "Certainly," Glendinning added, "second- and third-generation Americans are as great participants in Lawrence's leadership today as the descendants of the original Yankee stock."

Wendell D. Macdonald, regional director of the U.S. Bureau of Labor Statistics in Boston, had pointed to the same general trend: "Most New Englanders are losing their old prejudices. There is a new spirit of cooperation that is making the social climate much more pleasant."

He then went into the human side of the story of New England's successful shift from textiles. New England's inventors such as Samuel Slater and Eli Whitney had simplified textile manufacturing. It was unskilled, low-paid work, and the immigrants did it. Eventually, however, as their sons and daughters became better educated, they were ready for higher paid, more skilled jobs.

As New England textile wages inched higher, the mills began to shut down and move South, where wage levels were lower. "Most of the men over 50 never got another job," Macdonald said. "The younger people found work in offices and in our growing industries. We've still got some depressed areas, and there's some suffering, but all in all the textile shut-downs have worked out to be a healthy thing for the economy of New England."

Education had helped to break down the old social barriers and get rid of the textile drag on the economy. Later it was to play a major part in leading the region into a Space Age economy. Lawyer Coolidge had

Edward W. Brooke typifies the new politics of New England. Brooke, a Republican and a Negro, defied the Democratic tide in 1964 and was re-elected attorney general of Massachusetts.

Scientist Edwin H. Land, the inventor-president of Polaroid Corporation, is an example of a successful science-industry marriage.

José Luis Sert, the world-famed Spanish architect, has been a New Englander and dean of Harvard's graduate school of design since 1953. He is standing in front of a Harvard dormitory that he designed.

noted that by the turn of the century New Englanders had become less adventurous than their enterprising forefathers. "The doldrums had set in. The people attracted to such institutions as Harvard and M.I.T. and the ideas that were generated there," he said, "tended to pull us out." George Lodge vigorously seconded Coolidge's appraisal, stressing the "extraordinary importance of Harvard and M.I.T." in the transformation of New England's economy.

Up at the University of New Hampshire, I asked economist John Hogan if this Harvard-M.I.T. influence was being felt there. He replied: "Of course it is. Its influence is permeating all of New England. Here in Durham, the federal government is putting a lot of money into scientific research. This wouldn't be going on if it weren't for the spark that came from the Harvard-M.I.T. knowledge explosion. We have some of the top people in missiles and space work right here."

The Boston-Cambridge complex—34 colleges and universities within a radius of 50 miles from downtown Boston—is perhaps New England's greatest asset. For, as Myron Tribus, Dartmouth's dean of engineering, pointed out, "Business and industry have entered a new era in which knowledge has become a prime resource. Sometime in the 1950s management began to realize this. Management also became aware that there was an actual dollar value in being close to educational facilities." This has produced some dramatic results.

Science-based industries and the educational complex that helped spawn them have served as a magnet to draw new people into the region. Thus, New England, in addition to upgrading its home-grown human resources, is recruiting outside talent.

Coolidge had observed: "In my 30 years as a Harvard fellow (five fellows, along with the president and treasurer *ex officio*, manage the university), Harvard has drawn heavily from across the nation for its

207

deans, faculty, and most of its graduate students. Talent and brains no longer are being drained away from New England. In fact, the reverse is true."

The proportion of non-New England freshmen entering M.I.T. climbed from 62 per cent in 1949 to 85 per cent in 1963. Many of them chose to make their futures in New England. A recent survey of the graduates of the 11 science and engineering colleges and universities in the Boston area disclosed that more than half remained in the region.

In a speech several years ago, M.I.T. chairman James R. Killian, Jr., cited another survey of 41,000 U.S. scientists, 14 per cent of whom had received their Ph.D. degrees in New England. He went on to say: "Because of the environment they find here, many of these outstanding men and women who came here to study elect to remain. The excellence of the region in the scientific personnel it attracts and retains is shown in its share of the total members of the nation's top scientific societies. Over 20 per cent of the members of the National Academy of Sciences work in New England."

Gerald W. Blakely, Jr., the young president of one of Boston's oldest real estate firms, Cabot, Cabot and Forbes (CCF), documented this "brain magnetism." He quickly ran down a list of seven outstanding Boston business institutions: New England Mutual Life Insurance Company, John Hancock Mutual Life Insurance Company, the Gillette Company, New England Merchants National Bank of Boston, State Street Bank and Trust Company, Polaroid Corporation, and Raytheon Company. Only the last was headed by a Bostonian, Charles F. Adams. All the others were "foreigners."

A native New Englander himself, Blakely is an "outsider" in a sense. He is the first non-Harvard man ever to head CCF. But more important, it was his vision that led to the industrial development of "the Road"—Route 128—and to providing the kind of environment Killian alluded to. Its industrial parks, Blakely said, have "proved physically attractive to research people who were already sold on the area's educational, cultural, and recreational advantages, as well as its generally relaxed atmosphere. What we are seeing in New England," he concluded, "is a solid and steady growth, a growth in quality—quality of product, skills, and way of life."

The author:

Robert A. Irwin, a WORLD BOOK YEAR BOOK senior editor, attended Newton (Mass.) public schools before he emigrated to the Middle West. He has written two other Special Reports for past YEAR BOOKS: Breakthrough in the Breadbasket (1963) and Call to the Wilderness (1965).

Too many years in the doldrums, New England is now showing that an old, urbanized region need not blindly resist change; that with brain and will, it can adapt to it instead. New England is once more making the most of its assets: its new mobility, both physical and social; the brains, mechanical ingenuity, and skills of all its people. Of overriding significance is the dramatic surge of its educational system. The vitality of its schools and colleges, with the ever-growing dependence of business and industry upon them, has given the whole region, in Tom Winship's phrase, a Space Age "leg up" on many other areas of the nation. Clearly, the old New England I left a generation ago has become a *new* New England.

See also Section One, FOCUS, LAWRENCE A. CREMIN ON EDUCATION.

CONTENTS OF SECTION THREE

YEAR BOOK contributors report on the major developments of 1965 in their respective fields.

THE YEAR ON FILE, 1965

Articles in this section are arranged alphabetically by subject matter. Titles refer directly to articles in THE WORLD BOOK ENCYCLOPEDIA.

ADEN. See SOUTH ARABIA, FEDERATION OF.

ADVERTISING in the United States and around the world exhibited strong signs of growth in 1965. Total U.S. dollar volume increased nearly 5 per cent to more than $14,500,000,000. Television led the way. Magazine advertising continued a healthy comeback (up 6 per cent). Procter & Gamble was again the top U.S. advertiser, with an advertising budget of $225,000,000.

In Canada, ad agencies billed $320,000,000, a gain of more than $23,000,000 for the year. The story was the same around the globe. As living standards increased, advertising assumed a greater importance. In terms of money spent, the major advertising countries, after the United States, were, in order, Britain, West Germany, Japan, France, Italy, and Australia.

Major U.S. developments included:
• The warning by the National Better Business Bureau that the government might crack down unless advertisers reversed the trend toward naming rivals' products and returned to the more polite practice of referring to "Brand X."
• Grey Advertising, Inc., became the fourth big agency to sell stock to the public.
• The federal Highway Beautification Act, with its restrictions on billboard advertising, became law (see ROADS AND HIGHWAYS).   EDWIN W. DARBY

See also PUBLISHING; RETAILING; TELEVISION.

AFGHANISTAN proceeded haltingly in 1965 toward its goal of a democratically based constitutional monarchy. In September, the nation elected the 216 members of the lower house and 28 of the 84 members in the upper house. Of the 56 other members in the upper house, 28 were to be named by the king; 28 elected by provincial councils.

The new government was short-lived, however. On October 24, after King Mohammed Zahir Shah asked former Prime Minister Mohammed Yousof to form a cabinet, student riots broke out. As a result, Yousof resigned, and Mohammed Hashim Maiwandwal, a former ambassador to the United States, was appointed prime minister.

Meanwhile, the East and West continued to aid Afghanistan. The Soviet Union completed an agricultural survey of thousands of acres in northern Afghanistan. The International Bank for Reconstruction and Development loaned Afghanistan $350,000 for an irrigation survey of Kunduz Valley. A consortium of U.S. universities was formed to help develop engineering education at the University of Kabul.

Population: 16,070,000. **Government:** King Mohammed Zahir Shah; Prime Minister Mohammed Hashim Maiwandwal. **Monetary Unit:** afghani (50 afghanis equal U.S. $1). **Foreign Trade:** exports, $69,000,000; imports, $126,000,000. **Principal Exports:** caracul, carpets, wool.   WILLIAM SPENCER

See also MIDDLE EAST.

AFRICA

GUINEA

Political crisis and change again characterized the African continent during 1965. Nigeria opened the year deep in the throes of its worst political crisis since independence. In the aftermath of its general elections which were held on Dec. 30, 1964, Nigeria suffered three days of political strife that was unmatched in the country's short history of independence.

Burundi, too, began the year in a sudden burst of political turmoil. Its new prime minister, Pierre Ngendandumwe, who had been asked on January 7 to form a government, was assassinated one week later. In the political maneuvering that followed, King Mwambutsa IV acted to consolidate his power. By July, he had taken personal charge

AFRICAN ANGER over Rhodesia's self-declared independence explodes as Ghana's Kwame Nkrumah, left, demands that British troops be used to prevent the move.
Wide World

GHANA

of the army, the gendarmerie, and key positions in the cabinet.

Dahomey was the scene of a political upheaval late in November when its government was ousted in a military coup. Shortly thereafter, Congo (Léopoldville) followed suit: Congolese Major General Joseph Mobutu deposed President Joseph Kasavubu and proclaimed himself head of the state. Malawi, a former member of the defunct Federation of Rhodesia and Nyasaland, and Togo, too, were embroiled in political plots and counterplots during the year. So were Angola and Mozambique, where African guerrillas continued their struggle for independence.

Turmoil in Rhodesia. It was Rhodesia, however, that managed to capture the world spotlight for 1965. On November 11, after the breakdown of a long series of dramatic exchanges with British leaders, the white minority government of Rhodesia's Prime Minister Ian Smith unilaterally declared itself independent from Britain. The British had refused to grant the country independence unless the minority government, firmly controlled by about 220,000 whites, took steps to assure eventual majority rule by Rhodesia's 4,000,000 Africans.

British Reaction. The British government denounced the Smith declaration as rebellion and treason. It expelled Rhodesia from the pound sterling monetary area and suspended its preferential tariff treatment. Controls on trade and currency were imposed, and a ban was placed on the purchase of Rhodesia's main crops, sugar and tobacco, an action that would cost Rhodesia an estimated $50,000,000 annually.

Britain's Prime Minister Harold Wilson rejected the use of British troops to bring about a change but reserved the right to send troops to maintain law and order. Legislation was immediately introduced in London to give Wilson and his cabinet far-reaching powers to legislate for Rhodesia by decree, to amend the existing Rhodesian constitution, and to wipe out any actions of Prime Minister Smith's rebellious regime. Underlying the legislation was the theme central to Britain's case, that Rhodesia remains British territory and that Smith and his government have no lawful title.

UN Condemnation. Prior to Rhodesia's unilateral seizure of independence, the United Nations (UN) General Assembly had called on Britain on October 12 to use all possible means to avert such a declaration. Following the Smith government's action, the UN Security Council condemned Rhodesia's move. The United States announced it would place a comprehensive embargo on shipments of military equipment to Rhodesia.

The Organization of African Unity (OAU) unanimously adopted a resolution threatening military intervention in Rhodesia and the breaking of diplomatic relations with Britain unless the British took decisive steps to crush Rhodesia's white minority government by December 15.

Political Life in the African nations, however, was not all ferment and upheaval. During 1965, a number of countries remained on a relatively even keel and conducted "politics as usual" through less spectacular and more conventional channels. In Cameroon, President Ahmadou Ahidjo was re-elected in peaceful balloting procedures. The Malagasy Republic likewise re-elected its President Philibert Tsiranana without political incidents. Ghana, Kenya, Senegal, and Uganda all remained relatively calm during 1965.

Inter-African Cooperation continued during the year on a number of different levels. The OAU, through its various commissions, continued to function successfully as a supranational body. Its Liberation Committee, its Social and Economic Commission, and its Educational and Cultural Commission were active throughout the year in a number of vital political and social areas.

The African Development Bank continued to serve pan-Africanism through its policy of giving special priority to projects which, by their nature or scope, concerned several members or made the economies of its members increasingly complementary. In February, the Organization for Afro-Malagasy Economic Cooperation (AMCE) was transformed into a new organization known as the Afro-Malagasy Common Organization. Operating within the context of

"Our host has been detained."

the OAU, it would seek to reinforce cooperation and solidarity between Afro-Malagasy states, as well as to speed their economic and cultural development.

In other efforts at inter-African cooperation, ministers of Guinea, Ivory Coast, Liberia, and Sierra Leone met in May to advance plans for a free trade area embracing all four countries. Representatives of nine West African states met in August and agreed in principle to establish an iron and steel authority to develop West African metallurgy.

Economic Development. Financial problems and setbacks dominated the economic climate in a number of African countries. The financial situation in Congo (Léopoldville) was reportedly worse, due in part to the cost of its continuing military operations against rebel forces. By August, however, a number of French experts were in Congo with promises of additional technical assistance. Promises of economic aid were obtained from West Germany. An agreement was also reached with Belgium under which the Congolese government's capital holdings and voting rights in the Union Miniére du Haut-Katanga were greatly increased. See BELGIUM.

Economic problems were reported in the Malagasy Republic, due largely to poor banana, rice, and sugar harvests. Malawi, whose growing budget deficit was attributable largely to the falling price of tea, was promised development aid in money or services from Australia, Denmark, Great Britain, New Zealand, Nigeria, and the United States. Ghana's economy was overshadowed by a sizable budgetary deficit, as well as a deficit in its balance of payments position abroad. Nevertheless, a variety of measures were undertaken to strengthen the country's economic position.

The Ivory Coast secured a sizable European Development Fund Loan with which to establish an 80,000-acre palm plantation and construct seven palm oil processing plants.

Other Expansion Programs. Mozambique laid plans for the construction of its first sugar refinery. It also completed and put into service a 187-mile oil pipeline. In Gabon, hopes for a deepwater port at Owende grew with receipt of a European Economic Community (EEC, or Common Market) loan of $263,000 for technical studies. In Kenya, construction began on the $103,600,000 Seven Forks hydroelectric project on the Tana River. In Nigeria, plans were made to establish a steel industry.

Liberia laid plans for the construction of an oil refinery and an iron ore washing and pelletizing plant. Cameroon, with the aid of an EEC loan negotiated late in 1964, acted to develop its second five-year development plan aimed at improving its coffee, cotton, and peanut crops. BENJAMIN E. THOMAS

See also the various African countries.

TROUBLE SPOTS IN AFRICA IN 1965

1 ALGERIA
Army ousts President Ahmed Ben Bella.

2 CONGO (Léopoldville)
General Joseph Mobutu seizes power.

3 DAHOMEY
Government toppled in bloodless coup.

4 MALAWI
Crushes army rebellion.

5 MOROCCO
Racked by antigovernment riots.

6 MOZAMBIQUE
Harassed by anti-Portuguese rebels.

7 RHODESIA
Defies Great Britain, declares independence.

8 SUDAN
Rent by violence in southern provinces.

YEAR BOOK map

AGRICULTURE

AGRICULTURE. Most nations of the world, including those under communist rule, continued to marvel at the accomplishments of U.S. farmers. But U.S. agriculture—which had long played a dominant political and economic role in American life—found itself assuming a "minority" position. That change was dramatized in the 89th Congress by the tough battles over farm subsidies and by the defeat of the so-called "bread tax"—largely at the hands of city and suburban Congressmen. At the same time the farmers' political voice was being steadily diminished in the state legislatures, as well as in Congress, by the aftereffects of the 1964 U.S. Supreme Court "one man, one vote" decisions. Thus, U.S. agriculture was accepting the change, and, in the process, it matured a bit in 1965.

Agricultural production was the most pressing communist problem. Russia again lost face as it went into world markets to trade valuable rubles for food. Shortages in Communist China were reported. Poland, with its noncollectivized agriculture embarrassed other communist-bloc agricultural planners with its continued high production.

U.S. Farmers did well in 1965. Their incomes were the highest since 1952—$14,000,000,000, up more than $1,000,000,000, or $400 per farm, over 1964. Government payments rose to about $2,400,000,000. A strong economy resulted in good demand for agricultural produce. Farm exports reached record levels.

Production expenses rose $1,000,000,000, but were more than offset by increased receipts. Feeder livestock costs went up sharply. Prices of fertilizer, repairs, taxes, interest, and depreciation also rose.

Weather was good. Spring drought in the Southwest was mostly gone by summer. The drought in the extreme Northeast cut production, but not enough to offset the fine year elsewhere. The 1965 all-crops production estimate by the U.S. Department of Agriculture (USDA) rose to a record 117 per cent of the 1957-1959 average, sharply ahead of 1964's figure of 109.

The record 161,000,000-ton production of feed grains (barley, corn, grain sorghums, and oats) was 23,000,000 tons larger than the 1964 output. It increased total supply to 217,000,000 tons. The four grains' spectacular 18 per cent increase in average yield per acre—on a 1 per cent smaller amount of land—accounted for the year's output gain. All but 5,000,000 tons of the 1965 crop was used, increasing carry-over into 1966-1967 to 60,-000,000 tons—about 25,000,000 tons below the record 1961-1962 carry-over.

Wheat *disappearance* (total use) exceeded production for the fifth consecutive year, reducing surplus stores. The cotton crop held about level with 1964 and disappearance was up slightly. But carry-over on Aug. 1, 1966, is expected to reach a new high of 16,200,000 bales. Citrus fruit production was moderately up. Fall potato output set a new high.

With larger harvests, farmers' all-crop prices in October declined an average of $5\frac{1}{2}$ per cent from the 1964 month. On specific crops the percentage

Output of Major U.S. Crops
(millions of bushels)

Crop	1965*	1964	1959-1963‡
Corn	4,171	3,584	3,817
Sorghums	666	492	550
Oats	959	882	1,044
Wheat	1,327	1,291	1,190
Soybeans	844	702	627
Rice (a)	760	731	597
Potatoes (c)	289	239	267
Sugar (b)	5,450	5,587	4,486
Cotton (d)	151	151	147
Tobacco (e)	1,913	2,227	2,092

*Preliminary; ‡average
(a) 100,000 cwt. (b) 1,000 tons; (c) 1,000,000 cwt; (d) 100,000 bales;
(e) 1,000,000 pounds

declines were: soybeans, 10; cotton, 5; corn, 4; potatoes, 22; and orange and grapefruit, 45 per cent.

Livestock and Animal Products accounted for most of the thrust in 1965's rising farm income. With per capita red meat supplies 4 per cent lower than in 1964, prices for hogs, cattle, and lambs rose 15 per cent in the year. Retail prices were up sharply. As a result, red meat consumption per person was

U.S. Production of Animal Products
(millions of pounds)

	1965*	1964	1957-1959†
Beef	18,620	18,448	13,704
Veal	1,020	1,011	1,240
Lamb and mutton	650	715	711
Pork	11,470	12,531	10,957
Eggs (a)	5,350	5,379	5,475
Chicken	6,655	6,252	4,880
Turkey	1,520	1,433	1,065
Total milk (b)	1,255	1,266	1,233
Cheese	1,755	1,726	1,396
Ice cream	3,600	3,531	3,212
Butter	1,415	1,468	1,477

*Preliminary; †average
(a) 1,000,000 dozens; (b) 100,000,000 pounds

seven pounds less than the 175 pounds in 1964. Most of the decline was in pork, with lamb and mutton down slightly and beef up slightly. Poultry consumption, however, increased two pounds, to $40\frac{1}{2}$ pounds per person.

The number of cattle on farms declined by more than 1,000,000 head, the first decrease since 1958. Cattle and calf slaughter at 40,500,000 head, rose 4 per cent from 1964. Fed-cattle prices averaged higher. Hog slaughter dropped 9 per cent, and the June-November 1965 pig crop fell about 7 per cent in the year. Hogs and pigs on farms in September numbered 12 per cent fewer than 12 months earlier. As a result, hog prices rose sharply to an 11½-year high of $30 a hundredweight in December, from $16.50 a year earlier. While slaughter of sheep fell 10 per cent, prices rose to the highest level in years.

Farm Finances. U.S. farmers' total assets rose $15,000,000,000 in the year to an estimated value of $253,200,000,000. The rise in total land value alone accounted for more than $10,000,000,000 of the asset gain. Farm debts, however, rose about $3,600,000,000, chiefly for enlargement and improvement of farms.

The Market Place. Food in 1965 was a good buy. Slightly less than 1964's record low of 18½ per cent of consumer income went for food. Per capita food consumption declined slightly, mainly in livestock products. Historically, such a decline has come only with very high prices, indicating that the well-fed, meat-consuming American will not take easily to less palatable foods (see Food).

Food expenditures, less alcoholic beverages, rose 6 per cent to $83,500,000,000 and furnished a living for over 5,000,000 people on farms and twice that many in marketing. Agriculture's interrelatedness with marketing was made evident by the more than 1,200 commodity trade associations, which spent $100,000,000 to promote food in 1965. One,

the farm-supported American Dairy Association, spent $8,200,000 to help sell dairy products.

Technology, which is constantly rewriting agricultural history, came up with many new production ideas in 1965. Among them were:
• Radio signals that operated solenoid air valves controlling irrigation water levels.
• Rolled feed grains resembling breakfast cereals to improve livestock feeding efficiency.
• Nonsouring milk that needs no refrigeration and will keep for several months, after a brief heating to 280°F. It was marketed by a British dairy early in 1965.
• Use of chemicals to accelerate defoliation and simplify harvesting of cotton, flowers, and fruits.
• Artificial insemination of quail to aid poultry genetics.

U.S. Farm Legislation. The Food and Agriculture Act of 1965 contained a number of surprises. First of all, the passage of such an important act in an off-election year may have signaled a trend away from politics in farm legislation. And for the first time since 1938, Congress enacted a farm program for a four-year period, extending into 1969.

The act was an amalgamation of general price support programs of recent years and a new set of tailored commodity plans. Direct subsidy payments to agriculture are not new, but the degree of

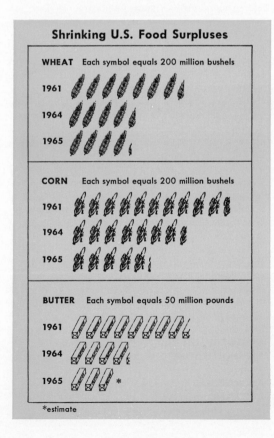

Shrinking U.S. Food Surpluses

WHEAT   Each symbol equals 200 million bushels

1961

1964

1965

CORN   Each symbol equals 200 million bushels

1961

1964

1965

BUTTER   Each symbol equals 50 million pounds

1961

1964

1965

*estimate

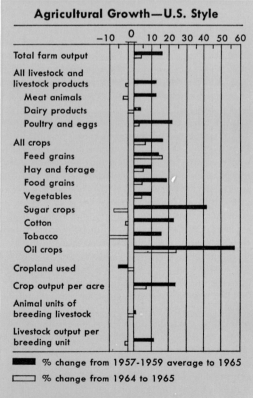

Agricultural Growth—U.S. Style

−10 0 10 20 30 40 50 60

Total farm output

All livestock and livestock products

Meat animals

Dairy products

Poultry and eggs

All crops

Feed grains

Hay and forage

Food grains

Vegetables

Sugar crops

Cotton

Tobacco

Oil crops

Cropland used

Crop output per acre

Animal units of breeding livestock

Livestock output per breeding unit

■ % change from 1957-1959 average to 1965

☐ % change from 1964 to 1965

Source: U. S. Department of Agriculture Economic Research Service

emphasis in the 1965 act was new. It supported prices not only of wheat and feed grains, but also of cotton at market levels. Under this scheme, consumers pay lower prices, so, of course, the farmers receive lower prices, which are supplemented by direct payments from the U.S. Treasury. The aim was to increase both consumption at home and sales overseas. Only peanuts, rice, and tobacco remained under the old, rigid system of high price supports.

In the words of Secretary of Agriculture Orville L. Freeman, this new legislation represented "a shift in policy away from price supports for the major commodities at levels above world market prices to a policy of using the market, both domestic and foreign, to the maximum by setting price supports as close to market levels as possible."

The main thrust of the legislation was to bring rural America into the Great Society. Secretary Freeman even suggested calling his department the Department of Food, Agriculture, and Rural Affairs.

Aside from acreage controls for specified crops, the act provided a four-year Cropland Adjustment Program to take 40,000,000 acres out of agricultural production and place it in a "scenic soil bank." The idled cropland will provide open space for recreation, wildlife protection, and other "natural beauty" purposes. Five-to-10-year land retirement contracts with individual farmers were authorized.

A Turnabout in Agriculture. Between the continued policy of crop curtailment and rising consumption, U.S. food surpluses have dwindled. By 1970, the government's surplus stocks of grain will be gone, President Lyndon B. Johnson said on signing the farm bill on November 5. The new law recognized this change. It authorized the government to go into the market and purchase food to meet needs for food assistance programs regardless of price support stock, or market prices. The Food for Peace program was shifted to the U.S. Department of State from the USDA on November 1.

A Price-Support Program for major crops through 1969 was written into the act. The major innovation was in cotton. "One-price cotton" for domestic and export sales was maintained—but at lower support levels, 21 cents a pound in 1966 versus 27.1 cents in 1965. Support would be no more than 90 per cent of the world market price after 1966. Cash subsidies of at least 9 cents a pound or more—depending on the size of and reduction in his acreage allotments— will go to the grower. The major aim was to reduce the record glut by making U.S. cotton competitive at home and in overseas markets.

The 1965 act covered revised support and subsidy programs for feed grains, rice, wheat, and wool. All entailed acreage or production curtailments, with more flexibility in cash payments. The act offered dairy farmers in milk-marketing areas a chance to vote on production quotas for fluid milk at an established premium price. Sales of milk for cheese or butter would be at lower prices.

World Agriculture. Despite adverse weather conditions in some areas, notably Australia, Communist China, and the Soviet Union, world production of most crops was at record or near-record levels. Wheat production was down slightly at 9,108,000,000 bushels from the record 1964 crop, but 14 per cent above 1955-1959. Bumper crops in Africa, Europe, and North America were offset by decreased harvests in the Soviet Union and Communist China. Both nations had to make heavy purchases (see CANADA). World corn output was also high.

WORLD CROP PRODUCTION
(000,000 omitted)

Crop	1955–59	1964	1965 (est.)	% U.S.
Barley (bu.)	3,255	4,260	4,080	10
Corn (bu.)	6,480	7,780	8,150	50
Oats (bu.)	4,085	2,920	3,075	32
Wheat (bu.)	7,969	9,300	9,180	15
Rice*	132.8	168.8	164.1	2
Sugar (tons)	49.6	72.0	70.0	8
Coffee (bags†)	58.4	51.8	76 8	0
Cotton (bales)	43.8	52.0	52.0	29

*Metric tons; excluding communist Asia. †132.276 lb.
Source: U.S. Department of Agriculture, Foreign Agricultural Service.

U.S. agriculture continued to demonstrate superiority over the Soviet system. Although the Soviet Union utilizes 75 per cent more cropland and seven times more farmworkers, it produces only half as much cotton, 10 per cent as much corn, and 5 per cent as many soybeans. It lags far behind in all meats, as well as in milk, eggs, and lard. Only butter, potato, wheat, and wool totals are above U.S. levels. See EUROPE; INTERNATIONAL TRADE AND FINANCE; RUSSIA; Section Two, INSIDE RURAL INDIA and INSIDE RURAL CHINA; and the various country articles.

U.S. Exports of agricultural goods, which have risen yearly since 1959, continued to be the largest of any nation. At a record $6,300,000,000 for all of 1964, they were double the 1955 total. One-half of all sales of U.S. rice, soybeans, and wheat were overseas. Exports accounted for $1 out of every $6 of U.S. farmers' sales. Imports of farm products slipped to $3,998,000,000. Only Great Britain's agricultural imports were higher than the U.S. total. The total volume of world trade came to about $31,000,000,000 in 1964.

The hope was real in 1965 that someday the entire world would be adequately fed. Toward this end, surplus food continued to be exported to developing nations. Over $1,500,000,000, or one-fourth of U.S. farm exports, went to the developing nations of the world under the Food for Peace program   CHARLES E. FRENCH

AIR FORCE, U.S. See NATIONAL DEFENSE.

AIR POLLUTION. See Section Two, POLLUTED AMERICA.

AIR RACES. See AVIATION.

AIRPLANE. See ARMED FORCES OF THE WORLD; AVIATION; NATIONAL DEFENSE.

ALBANIA remained a stronghold of Stalinism and a Western outlet for Communist China's views. It continued to denounce the United States as the "head of the imperialist camp." The Soviet Union, however, ran a close second for Albania's wrath, with Premier Aleksei N. Kosygin and Communist Party Secretary Leonid I. Brezhnev under attack as "the greatest splitters of the world communist movement." Both were condemned for refusing to help Pakistan in its war with India, and for appeasing the United States in Vietnam.

No significant changes occurred in domestic politics. Communist Party First Secretary Enver Hoxha remained in firm control. However, an increase of interest in the West among Albania's youth seemed to worry the regime.

Although facts about the self-isolated nation remained elusive, it was known that the regime expected to inaugurate approximately 100 industrial projects financed through $125,000,000 in credits from Communist China.

Population: 1,919,000. **Government:** Communist Party First Secretary Enver Hoxha; Premier Mehmet Shehu. **Monetary Unit:** lek (5 = U.S. $1). **Foreign Trade:** exports, $48,000,000; imports, $71,000,000. **Principal Exports:** chrome ore, foodstuffs, minerals, tobacco. TOM AND HARLE DAMMANN

See also EUROPE.

ALBERTA. See CANADA.

ALGERIA. The three-year rule of President Ahmed Ben Bella came to an abrupt end in the predawn hours of June 19, 1965. With tanks clanking in the background, Colonel Houari Boumedienne, Ben Bella's defense minister, seized power in a bloodless coup d'état.

Until then, Ben Bella had seemed to be growing in power. Moussa Hassani, the last guerrilla leader of the Socialist Forces Front (FFS), had surrendered to army troops. Hocine Aït Ahmed, the FFS commander captured in October, 1964, had been tried in secret and sentenced to death for high treason. But, in a move to reconcile all factions, Ben Bella pardoned Aït Ahmed. He also released several opposition leaders from house arrest.

Crackdown on Communists. Boumedienne's coup brought a set of new faces into the government. Most were military men or former officers. In assuming the presidency of a 26-member National Revolutionary Council, Boumedienne delegated authority to a 20-member cabinet, including 10 holdovers from the Ben Bella regime. He called for cooperation with all nations, social and economic development, and the rebuilding of the National Liberation Front (FLN) as a dynamic force in the nation. The new regime won quick recognition internationally, but was criticized by Albania and China as being "revisionist" (see CHINA).

Under Ben Bella, Algeria had a declared policy of "socialism" and was drifting toward closer relations

Pictorial Parade

TWO OLD FRIENDS, shown in 1963 photo, parted company in 1965. President Ahmed Ben Bella, left, was overthrown by Colonel Houari Boumedienne, right, in Algerian coup d'état.

with Communist China. With Boumedienne in control, Algeria began to edge toward friendlier relations with the West. In fact, the new government cracked down on communist elements.

Economic Agreements. After 20 months of hard bargaining, significant agreements were reached with France in July on oil and gas production in the Sahara. The Saharan fields will be developed jointly by France and Algeria, with additional concessions for non-French oil companies. Companies would be guaranteed against nationalization for 15 years. A revised royalty and tax schedule, based on a higher "agreed price" per barrel than any existing elsewhere in the Middle East, would boost Algerian oil revenues from $80,000,000 in 1965 to $240,000,000 in 1970. France also agreed to provide $400,000,000 for the purchase of French industrial equipment.

Another Franco-Algerian accord placed the 225,000 Algerian workers in France under the French pension and social security system. A technical cooperation pact was signed with the Soviet Union, and Communist China furnished a 13,000-ton merchant ship, doubling Algeria's merchant marine.

Population: 12,790,000. **Government:** President Houari Boumedienne. **Monetary Unit:** dinar (4.937 dinars = U.S. $1). **Foreign Trade:** exports, $625,-000,000; imports, $695,000,000. **Principal Exports:** citrus fruits, crude oil, wines. WILLIAM SPENCER

See also AFRICA; MIDDLE EAST.

AMERICAN LEGION. See VETERANS.

AMERICAN LIBRARY ASSOCIATION

AMERICAN LIBRARY ASSOCIATION (ALA).
Congressional awareness of growing library needs was reflected in the passage of legislation providing for more than $155,000,000 for training and research and for grants to public, elementary, and secondary school and college libraries.

Though this legislation, supported by the ALA, eased library needs, delegates to the 84th annual ALA conference at Detroit, Mich., in July were told that an additional $3,700,000,000 was necessary to bring libraries in the United States up to minimum national standards.

Noting that established library standards were already becoming outmoded, one ALA division, the Public Library Association, started a revision program with a $17,855 fund from the J. Morris Jones-World Book Encyclopedia-ALA Goals Award. The balance of the $25,000 fund to ALA is to be used for support of the International Relations Office of the association.

The delegates to the annual conference also considered ways of providing library service to the culturally deprived and the functionally illiterate. William T. Knox, chairman of the government's Committee on Scientific and Technical Information and a member of the President's Committee on Science and Technology, outlined a tentative plan for a network of information systems with national libraries as the heart of the complex.

Intellectual Freedom. A conference on intellectual freedom was held in Washington, D.C., during the midwinter meeting of the ALA. It brought together 65 representatives of national labor, religious, educational, civil rights, and service organizations, publishers groups, learned societies, and education associations. A legislative workshop was also held to give librarians a working knowledge of the legislative process. Both projects were supported by grants from the 1964 J. Morris Jones-World Book Encyclopedia-ALA Goals Award. An ALA conference on "Education and the Nation's Libraries" was held at Airlie House in Warrenton, Va., in the spring. The meeting attracted representatives of 54 national organizations.

Grants. ALA received a grant of $75,000 from the H. W. Wilson Foundation, Inc., to be paid over a six-year period, for the establishment of an ALA office for recruitment, education, and utilization of librarians. Grants from a number of sources were also used to initiate or continue 38 projects, of which eight were in operation overseas.

Film Award. The motion picture ". . . And Something More," prepared by the Knapp School Libraries Project, won the American Film Festival and CINE Golden Eagle awards.

The project, which is supported by the Knapp Foundation, made grants in 1965 to Farrer Junior High School in Provo, Utah; Oak Park and River Forest High School in Oak Park, Ill.; and Roosevelt High School in Portland, Ore. They will receive sufficient funds over a three-year period to bring their school libraries up to the minimum standards required by the ALA.

New Officers. Robert Vosper, librarian of the University of California Research Library (Los Angeles), was installed as president of ALA. Mary V. Gaver, professor of library service at Rutgers University, was installed as vice-president and president-elect.

Other Awards in 1965 included:

Melvil Dewey Medal for creative professional achievement, to Bertha Margaret Frick, former associate professor, Columbia University School of Library Service.

E. P. Dutton-John Macrae Award, of $1,000 for advanced study, to Mrs. Joan Allene Parmeter Nolan, librarian, Shady Grove Junior High School, Ambler, Pa.

Grolier Award of $1,000, to Sarah Lewis Jones, chief library consultant, Georgia State Department of Education, for her outstanding contributions to the reading needs of young people.

Lippincott Award of $1,000 for distinguished service to librarianship, to Mrs. Frances Clarke Sayers, former senior lecturer, School of Library Service, University of California, Los Angeles.

Melcher Scholarship of $1,500 for study in children's librarianship, to Mrs. Mary Ann Stevenson, television storytelling specialist.   CHARLES R. CARNER

See also CANADIAN LIBRARY ASSOCIATION; CANADIAN LITERATURE; EDUCATION; LIBRARY; LITERATURE FOR CHILDREN (Awards).

ANGOLA. Holden Roberto, president of the revolutionary government-in-exile of Angola, saw his influence decline in 1965. The Organization of African Unity (OAU) withdrew financial aid from Roberto's movement for independence from Portugal and offered support to the Popular Movement for the Liberation of Angola (MPLA).

Within his government-in-exile, Roberto was challenged by Armaments Minister Alexandre Taty and his supporters, who wrecked the organization's headquarters in Léopoldville, Congo. An invitation by André Martins Soma-Kassinda, leader of the newly formed Council of Angolan People, for all nationalist movements to unite and to meet with the Portuguese government was snubbed by both Roberto and the MPLA.

To counter the rebellious factions, the Portuguese government maintained an army of 48,000 in Angola. Portuguese sources claimed that rebel African forces, which once controlled 15 per cent of Angola, now had almost no territorial footholds.

Population: 4,939,000. **Government:** Governor-General Silveiro Marques. **Monetary Unit:** escudo (28.75 escudos = U.S. $1). **Foreign Trade:** exports, $148,000,000; imports, $136,000,000. **Principal Exports:** coffee, petroleum, sugar.   BENJAMIN E. THOMAS

See also AFRICA; PORTUGAL.

ANIMAL. See AGRICULTURE; LIVESTOCK; LIVESTOCK SHOW; PET; WILDLIFE; ZOOLOGY.

ANTARCTICA. See EXPLORATION.

ANTHROPOLOGY. Evidence of new types of men on the family tree gave anthropologists more areas of disagreement in 1965. The latest proposal concerning the structure of its branches came from Professor Phillip V. Tobias of the University of Witwatersrand in Johannesburg, South Africa. His suggestion is in accord with that of Louis S. B. Leakey that the branch including modern man should begin with the 2,000,000-year-old *Homo habilis* (see 1965 YEAR BOOK, MAN'S BEGINNINGS).

Tobias, however, would put Java-Peking man on the same branch rather than on a side branch, as does Leakey. Tobias puts the near-man creature *Zinjanthropus*, a skull of which Leakey discovered at the Olduvai Gorge in 1959, and *Australopithecus* from South Africa on two separate branches of the family tree, whereas Leakey considers them to be enough alike that they can be placed on the same branch.

The proposals of both Tobias and Leakey are disputed by those who agree with Professor John T. Robinson of the University of Wisconsin, who holds that the branch leading to man begins with *Australopithecus* and includes Java-Peking man. Robinson considers *Homo habilis* but a small Australopithecine.

The debate was brought into sharp conflict at a symposium on the origin of man held at the University of Chicago in April, 1965, and addressed by both Leakey and Robinson. At this symposium, Leakey announced that Mrs. Leakey had completed the restoration of a new *Homo habilis* skull. This skull from the Olduvai Gorge was found in hundreds of pieces, some smaller than the head of a match. Mrs. Leakey's painstaking reassembly of the find was praised as a monumental accomplishment.

Neanderthal Types. Dr. D. M. Badoux of the Institute of Veterinary Anatomy, Utrecht, The Netherlands, completed a study of skulls of Neanderthal men, some of whom lived during cold glacial times and others who lived during warmer (and earlier) interglacial times. He has found the skulls of those from the glacial period different in a number of ways from those of the interglacial period. Badoux suggested that these differences are due to the fact that the populations were adapted to different environments. This finding strengthened the suggestion of F. Clark Howell of the University of Chicago that the robustly built Neanderthals, with thick brow ridges, were a strictly Western European kind of man, cut off from other Neanderthal populations by the great ice sheets.

Lake Chad Man. Professor Yves Coppens, a French prehistorian and paleontologist, has assigned the name *Tchadanthropus uxori* (my wife's Chadman) to a skull fragment he found in 1961 near Lake Chad in north-central Africa. The find is of significance since it resembles the well-known Java-Peking men, but is of a much earlier period. LESLIE G. FREEMAN, JR.

ANTI-POVERTY. See POVERTY.

ARABIA. See SAUDI ARABIA.

ARCHAEOLOGY. Edward Lanning of Columbia University, who established in 1961 that men lived in Peru as early as 8500 B.C., showed in 1965 that five successive groups of hunting and gathering people occupied camps along the Peruvian coast over a period of 6,000 years. Although the region north of Lima is one of the most rainless deserts in the world, early men were able to eke out an existence there. Along the fog-nourished *loma* (broad-topped hill) meadows of the coast, they fished, gathered seeds and milled them into flour, collected snails, and hunted deer and guanaco.

Lanning has named the five successive cultures Arenal (8500-6000 B.C.), Luz (6000-5000 B.C.), Canario (5000-4200 B.C.), Corbina (4200-3600 B.C.), and Encanto (3600-2500 B.C.). Agriculture existed, he points out, at least as early as Encanto times, when cotton was cultivated. Fishermen-farmers established the first permanent villages by 2500 B.C. About this time, a large ceremonial center (one of the largest known in that area) was constructed at Chuquitanta.

In the Peruvian central highlands, another archaeologist, Rogger Ravines, discovered a workshop site where stone tools similar to those of the Canario period were made. The site, called Ambo, is thus an important link between the cultures of the coastal and highland regions.

Neanderthal Life. Though archaeologists have uncovered many Neanderthal skeletons and stone tools, only lately have they been able to piece together aspects of prehistoric man's daily life. Remains recently discovered in the Soviet Union may be of key importance. At the site of Molodova I on the banks of the Dnestr River, archaeologists found the remains of an oval hut, 23 x 33 feet in size. The remains, well over 40,000 years old, consist of many huge fragments of mammoth bone, and enclose numerous small fireplaces. Whether the structure was a dwelling, a storage area, or a ceremonial building is still unknown.

In southeastern France, Eugéne Bonifay discovered that the Neanderthal inhabitants of the Regordou Cave built numerous mounds of bones, rock, and earth. He suggested that some of the structures might have had importance in religious ceremonials.

Holy Land. Excavations by Kathleen Kenyon, director of the British School of Archaeology in Jerusalem, established the fact that the Church of the Holy Sepulchre may, indeed, stand atop Calvary and the tomb of Jesus, as tradition states. At least, the excavations establish that the church—as did Calvary—stands outside of what were the walls of Jerusalem in Herod's time. The church was built in the 4th century A.D. by the Empress Helena, who was guided by the pious tradition concerning the site of Calvary.

An early Christian manuscript, written on parchment, was found in an abandoned monastery in the

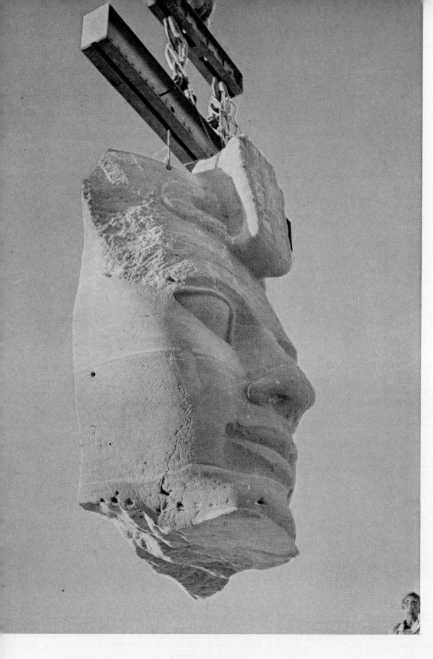

FACE-LIFTING. The 3,200-year-old great stone head of Ramses II, weighing 30 tons, was sliced from the face of the Temple of Abu Simbel and moved to higher ground to be reassembled.

Nubian Valley of Egypt. It contains a "Hymn to the Cross" and other elements of the oral tradition of early Christianity. See PROTESTANT.

Abu Simbel. After 3,200 years, the mighty Egyptian monument to Pharaoh Ramses II, Abu Simbel, standing at the edge of the Upper Nile River, was being moved by an international team of engineers. The $36,000,000 salvage operation is sponsored by the United Nations Educational, Scientific, and Cultural Organization (UNESCO). The moving process involves sawing the sandstone temple, and a smaller adjoining temple to Ramses' Queen Nefertari, into blocks weighing up to 30 tons, and then transporting them to higher ground, where they can be reassembled.

While work is going on, a lake is backing up behind the new Aswan High Dam, 175 miles downstream. By August, 1966, the rising waters are expected to spill over the temporary dam that has been built to protect the temples. The project is considered a major engineering feat.

One of the world's wonders, the temple of Abu Simbel was hewn from a sandstone cliff. Four colossal and identical stone images of the god-king, Ramses II, were carved across the 108-foot-high façade of the great temple. Each image is 67 feet high. But the statues are not the sole wonders of the temple. Abu Simbel has high-ceilinged rooms and columned halls with beautiful friezes cut 200 feet into the heart of the cliff.   LESLIE G. FREEMAN, JR.

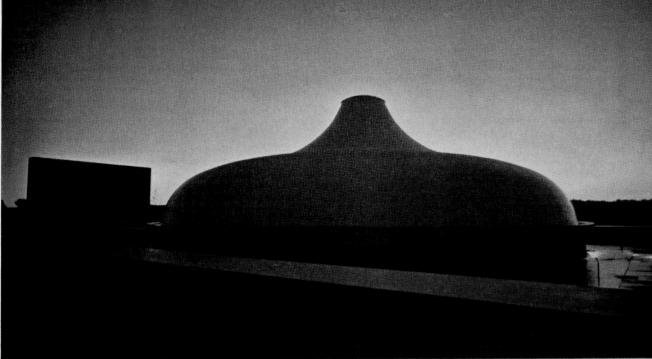

WHITE TILED DOME near Jerusalem,
designed by U.S. architects
Frederick Kiesler and Armand Bartos,
is a shrine for Dead Sea Scrolls.

ARCHITECTURE. One of the truly great architects
of the 20th century, Charles Édouard Jeanneret,
known as Le Corbusier, died on Aug. 27, 1965. His
landmark works, such as the Villa Savoye in Poissy,
France; the Swiss Pavilion at the Cité Universitaire,
Paris; Chandigarh, the capital of the Indian state
of East Punjab; and the Cathedral of Notre Dame
du Haut at Ronchamp, France, were an evident influence on the notable works produced by other
architects in 1965. Of the cathedral at Ronchamp,
Le Corbusier said, "Light is the key," and he died in
the bright sun of a Mediterranean morning while
swimming at the age of 77.

Unlike his architectural works, his city plans—
such as the ribbon of expressways surmounting long
terraces of houses and shops proposed for Algiers in
1931—remain mainly unexecuted. But they, too,
were prophecies in 1965, when the scale and scope
of architecture reached out toward total city design.

Campus Microcity. In Chicago, the University of
Illinois opened its circle campus on the southwestern edge of the Loop in September. Designed by
Walter Netsch, Jr., of Skidmore, Owings & Merrill
(designer of the Air Force Academy), the campus
spreads out from a central court of exterior assembly
spaces on a grid of esplanades that are raised over
the campus ground.

Skyscrapers. Without benefit of such substantial
ground organization, Skidmore, Owings & Merrill
prepared foundations in 1965 for a tapered steel

100-STORY TALL John Hancock
Center in Chicago will be the second
tallest building in the world and a
combination office-apartment tower.

221

shaft 100 stories high in Chicago for the John Hancock Mutual Life Insurance Company. In New York City, two structures, each 110 stories high, were slated for construction by the Port of New York Authority on a relatively small site in lower Manhattan. Designed by architect Minoru Yamasaki, the twin towers of the authority's World Trade Center will be the tallest buildings in the world, 1,350 feet high. See BUILDING AND CONSTRUCTION.

The Arch. Ascension of the 630-foot high catenary arch in St. Louis (an early design of the late Eero Saarinen) promised to be a treat for visitors to that city in 1966. When the visitors reach the keystone of the arch, placed in 1965, they will see a city rebuilding mightily, but on the familiar 18th century grid pattern. St. Louis was following other cities, where giant buildings were imposed on single-level city plans, unlike the plans of Le Corbusier.

Culture Complexes. With the completion of the Vivian Beaumont Theater in October, New York's Lincoln Center for the Performing Arts got its best building to date. And with the foundation laid for the Juilliard School of Music there, the lines of the granddaddy of U.S. cultural complexes could at last be perceived. Culture, indeed, took up architecture in thirsty gulps in 1965. The huge John F. Kennedy Center for the Performing Arts, designed by Edward Durell Stone, was begun on the banks of the Potomac in Washington, D.C. The Los Angeles County Museum of Art, by architect William Pereira, was a glittering opening success. And cities and colleges from Houston, Tex., to Smith College in Northampton, Mass., opened or began theater construction projects. See THEATER (Picture).

Civic Pride. Toronto completed its city hall. The two boomerang-shaped skyscraper office slabs, nestling a domed council chamber, were conceived as civic symbols by architect Viljo Revell of Finland. The result, like so much architecture in 1965, was grandiose, but, some thought, empty.

It was evident in a review of 1965, when many notable works of architecture were completed and more were on the drawing boards, that architecture considered by itself was not enough. In only a few places—and quite unnoticed—was architecture considered in the larger context of man and his massive problems. In Harlem, several imaginative playgrounds were opened within public housing projects. New, private planned communities developed apace in Columbia, Md.; Reston, Va.; and other areas beyond the suburban sprawl. And in Cambridge, Mass., architects Sert, Jackson & Gourley completed a married students' colony for Harvard graduate students. It was lively, economical, and contained. It demonstrated a commitment to life and indicated a model for cities in direct descent from Le Corbusier's own city plans.   RICHARD MILLER

See also CANADA; CITY PLANNING; DEATHS OF NOTABLE PERSONS; LOS ANGELES; PAINTING AND SCULPTURE; Section Two, THE NEW NEW ENGLAND.

ARGENTINA. The government of President Arturo Umberto Illia faced mounting criticism from civilian and military quarters. After two years in office, it had not been able to obtain any substantial foreign loans for the country's development. It had also failed to totally settle an oil dispute involving major foreign companies, and it was having little luck in keeping prices down.

The government's relationship with military leaders had cooled considerably during the two-year period. There was widespread disenchantment, too, with President Illia's economic and political policies. Many private banks were reluctant to renew loans to the government. The national pension fund was almost bankrupt due to the government's policy of using these funds for other purposes.

The Popular Union Party, whose members were followers of exiled dictator Juan D. Perón, was allowed to participate in congressional elections held on March 14. The party emerged as the second strongest in congress, winning better than 36 per cent of the popular vote. Observers felt, however, that the vote was not one of confidence in Perón but rather in protest of the inflationary pinch.

With foreign reserves and the trade surplus falling, Argentina's 1965 balance of payments was expected to show an unfavorable deficit of about $300,000,000, if not more. The federal budget was expected to show a $1,200,000,000 deficit. The republic had to debase its peso four times in 1965. On April 19, the peso was devaluated by 15 per cent from 149 to 173 per U.S. $1; by December 6, it had fallen to 178 per U.S. $1. These actions, however, did not help the meat and wool exporters to any notable degree, especially since the retention quotas remained in force.

Living Costs, meanwhile, rose an estimated 30 per cent. Predictions that the country was heading for a new recession proved false, however. Employment remained satisfactory. Industry generally maintained a high level of activity—an exception being the export meat packers, with several thousand workers idle. There was abundant spending power, especially in the interior, due to good harvests and high cattle prices. Industrial production was expected to rise an average 15.4 per cent; the Gross National Product by 7.5 per cent.

On June 25, Argentina formally concluded debt negotiations with 11 European nations, Japan, and the United States, for an easing of the republic's foreign indebtedness. At the close of 1964, Argentina's total public and private foreign obligations amounted to $3,355,800,000.

Population: 23,035,000. **Government:** President Arturo Umberto Illia. **Monetary Unit:** peso (178 = U.S. $1). **Gross National Product:** 1,114,-900,000,000 pesos. **Foreign Trade:** exports, $1,410,-000,000; imports, $1,077,000,000. **Principal Exports:** maize, meat, petroleum, wheat.   MARY C. WEBSTER

See also LATIN AMERICA.

ARMED FORCES OF THE WORLD. Both the United States and Russia shifted more strongly to missiles during 1965 in maintaining the nuclear balance of terror. And both had more than enough in their intercontinental ballistics missile (ICBM) force to eradicate each other. To break the grim deadlock each raced to be first to produce an anti-ICBM missile.

There was a stand-off, also, in conventional arms. The communists' greater military manpower was at least balanced by U.S. firepower, mobility, and flexibility, plus the experience gained in actual combat in Vietnam.

Missiles. The United States' ICBM lead over Russia, which was 4-to-1 in 1964, dropped to 3-to-1 during 1965, because the United States scrapped 95 Atlas and 54 Titan missiles as obsolete, and because the U.S. missile program shifted its emphasis from production to updating, improving, and refining target and guidance systems. In 1965, 800 Minuteman and 54 Titan rockets were in place in dispersed underground silos. An additional 200 Minuteman IIs, considered eight times more effective than Minuteman Is, will be deployed in 1966.

Meanwhile, the Soviets were also improving their own deadly missile system. Their ICBM force increased from 200 to 270, some in hardened silos. According to qualified observers, there were two principal advances in this field. These were the development of a solid-fueled ICBM similar to Minuteman, and a Polaris-type weapon. Formerly Russia relied upon the much bulkier liquid-fueled ICBMs. However, the Soviet Polaris-type weapon is believed to be far inferior to the new U.S. Polaris, which has a 2,500-mile range. In November, the Russians claimed to have a nuclear rocket which could be fired from a satellite in earth orbit.

The number of Soviet intermediate-range missiles remained at about 800. Most of them were fixed and zeroed in on European targets, but some were on submarines or otherwise mobile. The U.S. counterforce of 528 Polaris missiles will increase to 656 aboard 41 submarines by the end of 1966.

Air Power. The United States disclosed it will cut its strategic bomber fleet of 600 B-52s to 255 late-model B-52s by 1971. It will drop all its 80 B-58 bombers during the same period. Additionally, about 100 U.S. Navy fighter-bombers assigned strategic targets were being relieved of that responsibility. But Defense Secretary Robert McNamara hinted that a new aircraft, a variation of the F-111, the tactical fighter-bomber under development for both the navy and air force, would be introduced.

The Soviets retained their fleet of 270 bombers capable of a round-trip flight to the U.S. mainland and 1,300 medium and light jet bombers which could make it only one way.

Manpower. U.S. forces grew to support a commitment of 180,000 men in Vietnam. Meanwhile, the North Atlantic Treaty Organization (NATO) and its communist counterpoise, the nations of the Warsaw Pact, each still had about 4,500,000 men under arms.

NATO deployed 26 divisions in Europe—12 West German, five U.S., three British, two French, two Belgian, and two Dutch—plus one Canadian brigade. The Warsaw Pact nations had 212 divisions —150 Soviet and 62 eastern European—but they

COMPARATIVE MILITARY MANPOWER

	United States	Russia	Communist China
Army	1,017,000	2,000,000	2,600,000
Navy	909,000*	400,000	60,000
Air Force	834,000	900,000†	175,000
Totals	2,760,000	3,300,000	2,835,000

*Includes 204,000 marines
†Includes 230,000 Strategic Rocket Forces

were considerably under strength and only about half were combat-ready. The 150 Soviet divisions included 20 in East Germany, two in Poland, four in Hungary, and 40 in western Russia.

Communist China exploded its second nuclear device. Its continuing use of uranium-235 indicated that its goal is a hydrogen bomb. The Communist Chinese fighting force was woefully short of modern equipment. Cut off by its ideological split with the Soviet Union, the Peking regime was reported to be starting to make its own tanks, fighter aircraft, and even submarines. WARREN ROGERS

See also NATIONAL DEFENSE.

ARRUPE, PEDRO (1907-   ), a 27-year veteran of Jesuit service in Japan, was elected Father General of the Society of Jesus at a secret conclave in Rome on May 22, 1965. He serves for life, succeeding the late Father Jean Baptiste Janssens of Belgium. The new Father General came to office at a time of great change, when the Ecumenical Council and the pope were redefining the basic doctrines of the Roman Catholic Church. Father Arrupe is the 28th head of the international order for Roman Catholic men. It has given the church teachers and scholars for the past 430 years.

One of the first rescue teams in Hiroshima after the United States dropped its atomic bomb there in August, 1945, was led by Father Arrupe. He lived just outside the city at the time, and helped care for the bomb victims. Japan was made an independent Jesuit province in 1958, and Father Arrupe was elevated to Provincial, or head, of the area.

Pedro Arrupe was born at Bilbao in the Basque region of Spain. His father founded the influential Roman Catholic newspaper *La Gaceta del Norte.* Young Arrupe studied medicine at the University of Madrid before entering the Jesuit order in 1927. Four years later, after the Spanish Republic was established, Jesuits were banned in Spain. Arrupe continued his studies and training in various other European countries and in the United States. He was ordained in 1936, and sent to Japan in 1938.

ART. See PAINTING AND SCULPTURE.

ASIA

With its teeming millions, Asia remained the focus of a global struggle. It was primarily a three-way struggle for power and influence involving the anticommunist West led by the United States, the communism of the Soviet Union, and the vigorous expansionism of the Chinese communists. But a secondary struggle, no less desperate, was also being waged to achieve somehow an economic breakthrough that would enable the vast area to feed its millions. Finally, there was the struggle for political stability, with such major issues as subversion, open warfare, inefficiency, and even corruption confounding the governments of the countries in Asia.

The conflicts between the communists and anticommunists became more widespread and more intense during the year. The most active of these conflicts obviously was centered in Vietnam. The gradual disruption of the South Vietnamese government forced the administration of U.S. President Lyndon B. Johnson to make a fundamental policy decision.

Change in U.S. Policy. In April, after due consideration, President Johnson announced that the United States would do everything in its power to ensure that South Vietnam remained free of the communists.

U.S. troops poured into South Vietnam; by the end of the year, a U.S. force estimated at 200,000 men was actively engaged in the war. "Search and destroy" missions began to flush out Viet Cong regulars, as well as guerrillas, in substantial numbers. U.S. forces, consolidating their seacoast positions and bases, actively pursued the enemy into the highland areas along the Laotian and Cambodian borders. See VIETNAM.

The Escalation of the War by the United States was greeted with both relief and alarm. The Chinese communists warned that such actions would be subject to retaliation, but as 1965 ended, they had yet to make such an open move. France, too, greeted the escalation with alarm.

Australia, Britain, and New Zealand, however, backed the United States and its policies, faced as they were with Indonesia's threats and its occasional moves against Malaysia (see INDONESIA; MALAYSIA, FEDERATION OF).

Conflict over Kashmir. The war in Vietnam was only one aspect of the larger struggle. For years, India and Pakistan had engaged in a hot dispute over Kashmir. Repeated efforts by the United Nations (UN) had averted open fighting, and an uneasy truce had prevailed. But the increasing friendliness between Pakistan and Communist China, and the desire of a group of young Pakistanis to develop a more pro-Peking stance, led to an outbreak of hostilities on August 5. India charged that the

BRUTAL WAR in Asia embroils the young and the innocent as well as the combatants. These two children were orphaned by guerrilla warfare in South Vietnam.

move began with armed infiltrators disguised as passengers slipping over the Kashmir border and into Indian territory. These elements were soon followed by more obvious military units. The Indian army quickly retaliated.

Repeated efforts by the UN and the Western nations finally convinced both combatants of the need for a cease-fire. This was arranged after several weeks of intense fighting. But the issue of Kashmir remained unresolved. See INDIA; PAKISTAN.

On Other Fronts. Open violence in the power struggles of Asia was not limited to Vietnam and Kashmir. Malaysia, faced with Indonesia's "confrontation" policy, prepared its defenses for a showdown. Some Indonesian raids took place in Sarawak, where the guerrillas killed key villagers in certain areas. Similarly, Indonesian irregulars moved into Malaya proper from bases near Singapore. These were quickly disposed of, however, by Malayan troops. Again, Communist China's support for Indonesia's "crush Malaysia" policy was clearly evident, especially since some of the irregulars in Sarawak proved to be Chinese infiltrators coming directly from China via Indonesia. As if the Indonesian threats were not enough, Malaya faced a revival of communist guerrilla bands along its border with Thailand. The Federation of Malaysia, itself, lost one of its member states.

There were significant signs, however, that the Chinese use of subversion and insurgency was being effectively countered. Laos, benefiting from U.S. aid and U.S. actions in Vietnam, began to mop up Pathet Lao insurgents. Indonesia, which was closely aligning itself with Communist China, found its campaign against Malaysia sputtering. There was also a growing disaffection with the Chinese alignment on the part of Indonesia's army, which forestalled a coup by the air force and the Indonesian Communist party (PKI) late in the year.

The growing disaffection for the Chinese communists could be seen also in Thailand where resistance to the communists was stiffened along its Chinese and Laotian borders. Burma not only tightened its border restrictions against the Chinese, but it also began eliminating alien Chinese elements within the country (see BURMA).

Waning Communist Influence. The Philippines continued to be wary of Communist Chinese demands that they be permitted to work with the Chinese minority in The Philippines. Formosa maintained a strong military garrison, whose attentions were riveted on the Chinese mainland. Even Japan, while remaining meticulously neutral toward the conflicts in Asia, began to tighten up its restrictions on trade with Communist China. The Republic of Korea, ignoring the obvious communist threat from

North Korea, sent several battalions of crack troops to fight the Viet Cong in Vietnam. In effect, these moves all indicated that the threat of Communist China was being more clearly recognized by the Asian governments.

In addition, this growing sophistication was being matched by an increasing political awareness of the international dangers of the Chinese communist threat. This was most clearly seen in the splintering of the Indian Communist party. The pro-Soviet Union faction within the Indian party hotly denounced China's role in the dispute with Pakistan. By year's end, it appeared well on its way to taking over control of the Communist party in India.

Similarly, Russia's studied aloofness and disapproval was having a marked effect on leftists in Southeast Asia. A major election held in Ceylon marked the end of the procommunist government of Prime Minister Sirimavo Bandaranaike. The triumph of the middle-of-the-road conservatives over the leftist government was considered a major breakthrough in the fight against communism. These, then, were political pluses from the West's point of view.

Signs of Stability. While instability still marked many of the governments of Asia, this was not the total picture. Both Japan and the Republic of Korea managed to maintain stable governments. Korea was even able to conclude a reparations and fishing agreement with Japan despite militant student opposition. The Philippines held a national election with relatively minor bloodshed, unseating President Diosdado Macapagal and electing Ferdinand E. Marcos as its next president (see MARCOS, FERDINAND E.; PHILIPPINES, THE). Thailand survived the passing of Field Marshal Sarit Thanarat and managed to make the transition to a new prime minister very smoothly (see THAILAND).

Perhaps most important, in a general sense, was the demonstrated capacity of certain Southeast Asian governments to come together on mutual problems on economic development. This was best illustrated by the signing of an agreement in Vientiane, Laos, in August, covering the UN-sponsored Mekong River project. Cambodia, Laos, South Vietnam, and Thailand, the four countries immediately concerned, signed the agreement to harness the Mekong River system despite their pronounced differences in foreign policies and their attitudes toward Communist China.

The General Economic Picture of Asia had some bright spots but in the overall sense the picture was not encouraging. While Formosa, Japan, The Philippines, the Republic of Korea, and Thailand had relatively prosperous economies, the same was not true of other areas. India, Malaysia, and Pakistan, faced with dire threats of war, had to divert their meager surpluses to military build-ups. In some nations, such as Indonesia, the preoccupation with military adventuring threw the economies into tailspins and sent standards of living plummeting.

"I'd hide, if I knew which side of the tree is safe."

The key to much of the economic picture of Asia was, of course, Communist China. There were indications that the Chinese were relaxing some of their theoretical rigidity and allowing a small amount of private enterprise to exist in order to step-up production. Despite this, Communist China continued to depend on the international market for foodstuffs, and its promises of aid to the Asian and African countries it was wooing were meager, indeed.

Struggle for Power. Asia, then, remained an arena in which the large powers jockeyed for position. The United States, pursuing a hard-core policy against the communists, appeared to have seized the initiative in Southeast Asia for the first time. Britain, its strongest ally, provided unwavering backing via its resources in Malaysia. France alone of the Western nations appeared desirous of taking what it believed to be an accommodating position toward the Chinese. See FRANCE.

The Soviet Union, anxious over Chinese communist expansionism, continued its ideological dispute with Peking (see COMMUNISM; RUSSIA). The neutral position of India no longer held the international attraction it once had under the leadership of its late prime minister, Jawaharlal Nehru. Japan remained a question mark in Asia. Its great organizational capacities had yet to be declared on either side in any meaningful way.   JOHN N. STALKER

See also Section Two, INSIDE RURAL INDIA and INSIDE RURAL CHINA.

ASTRONAUTS. Twelve men spent a total of 1,392 weightless man-hours in space in 1965, with U.S. astronauts accounting for all but 52 man-hours. In total time aloft, the United States now had a whopping-big lead over the Russians, 1,354 to 507. And the excellent physical condition of Navy Commander James A. Lovell, Jr., and his flying companion, Air Force Lieutenant Colonel Frank Borman, after almost 14 days in space aboard Gemini VII in December was proof that man could survive lack of exercise, radiation, time disorientation, and weightlessness long enough to visit the moon and return. Another first for the United States occurred on December 16, when Navy Captain Walter M. Schirra, Jr., and Air Force Major Thomas P. Stafford were shot into space to keep a rendezvous with Lovell and Borman. See SPACE TRAVEL.

In June, the National Aeronautics and Space Administration (NASA) for the first time chose six scientists and medical doctors for astronaut training (see photos). One of the six, Duane E. Graveline, M.D., 34, resigned from the program on August 18 for personal reasons.

As of Jan. 1, 1966, NASA had 28 pilot-astronauts and five scientist-astronauts in its manned space flight program. More pilots and 10 to 20 scientists will be selected in 1966 for Project Apollo and other advanced space missions.

Wide World

NO BEATNIKS. Astronauts Charles Conrad, Jr., left, and Leroy Gordon Cooper, Jr., compare beards after their splashdown from their eight-day orbit in August.

THE NEW ASTRONAUTS

The fourth and most highly educated group of astronauts was chosen by NASA on June 29. Within the next five years or so, at least one of them might stand on the moon. These Project Apollo trainees, unlike most of the previously selected astronauts, are not experienced test pilots.

Owen K. Garriott, Ph.D., 35, was a professor of electrical engineering at Stanford University, where he specialized in ionospheric physics. He has a private pilot's license. Garriott, from Enid, Okla., is married and has three sons.

Edward G. Gibson, Ph.D., 29, was born in Buffalo, N.Y. An engineering-physicist, Gibson specialized in jet propulsion and atmospheric physics while working for his doctorate. He is married and has a son and a daughter.

Joseph P. Kerwin, M.D., 33, was a flight surgeon before becoming a qualified jet pilot in the U.S. Navy. Kerwin was born in Oak Park, Ill., and has been in the navy since 1958. Kerwin is married and has a daughter.

F. Curtis Michel, Ph.D., 31, was assistant professor of space science at Rice University, Houston. He has done research in nuclear physics and the effects of solar wind on the moon's atmosphere. He is married and has a son.

Harrison H. Schmitt, Ph.D., 30, was with the astrogeology branch of the U.S. Geological Survey at Flagstaff, Ariz. He developed lunar exploration techniques for NASA, and has trained astronauts in geology. Schmitt is unmarried.

World Book Science Service, Inc.

Gemini Crews were named for future missions. They are: *Gemini VIII* (scheduled for February or March, 1966): command pilot, Neil A. Armstrong; copilot, David R. Scott. *Gemini IX* (after July 1, 1966): command pilot, Elliot M. See, Jr.; copilot, Charles A. Bassett II.

Both Scott and Bassett are to attempt walks in space for one full orbit. Also, both Gemini craft will try to dock with an orbiting Agena rocket. This skillful "flying" by the astronauts was originally scheduled for the first Gemini VI shot.

Air Force in Orbit. Eight military pilots began training for the U.S. Air Force Manned Orbital Laboratory (MOL) project announced by President Lyndon B. Johnson on August 25. They are at the Aerospace Research Pilot School at Edwards Air Force Base in California. All the pilots have college degrees in engineering or physical science. They are:

Major Michael J. Adams, USAF, 35, Sacramento, Calif.; Major Albert H. Crews, USAF, 36, Alexandria, Va.; Lieutenant John L. Finley, USN, 29, Memphis, Tenn.; Captain Richard E. Lawyer, USAF, 33, Inglewood, Calif.; Captain Lachlan Macleay, USAF, 34, Redlands, Calif.; Captain F. Gregory Neubeck, USAF, 33, Washington, D.C.; Captain James M. Taylor, USAF, 34, Lewisville, Ark.; and Lieutenant Richard H. Truly, USN, 28, Meridian, Miss. Twelve more MOL astronauts will be picked in 1966 (see Space Travel). WADE TILLEUX

ASTRONOMY. On July 14, 1965, the Mariner IV spacecraft passed at about 5,600 miles of Mars, snapped 22 pictures, and then began beaming the first "close-up" photos of another planet back across 134,000,000 miles of space to an anxious audience on earth. The principal revelation of the photos was that the planet believed to be most like earth appears to be as barren as the moon.

The historic photos, which brought Mars 30 times closer than the best earthbound telescopes, showed a surface heavily pock-marked with craters formed by the impact of asteroids and meteoroids. About 70 craters were visible in pictures 5 through 15, indicating a probable total of more than 10,000 for the entire surface of Mars.

Some of the craters are quite deep and have sharp rims. The large number of craters also indicates that there has been little erosion of the planet's surface. Nowhere in the photographs was there any sign of water. Nor was there a sign of the "canals" some astronomers have claimed to have seen through their telescopes. Mars appears to be a very cold, dry, and lifeless planet.

Yet, the photos do not finally resolve whether there is life on Mars. Many scientists, among them Stanley L. Miller, associate professor of chemistry at the University of California, San Diego, feel there might be microenvironments on Mars able to sustain living organisms. Miller and others are working on life detecting systems that could be landed on

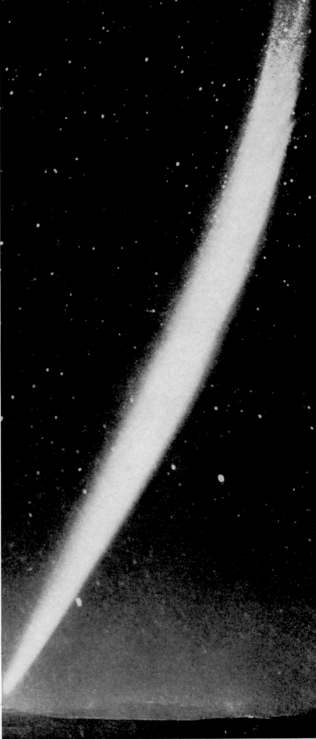

Wide World

VISITOR FROM DEEP SPACE. Comet Ikeya-Seki, with its 75,000,000-mile tail, was easily seen as it passed near the earth on its voyage around the sun.

Jet Propulsion Laboratory, California Institute of Technology

MARS CLOSE-UP. To everyone's surprise the first photographs of Mars, taken from a spacecraft, showed that the planet's surface is cratered much like the moon.

Mars by spacecraft in the Voyager series, the first of which may be launched in 1971.

Mariner IV's sensing devices were unable to detect a magnetic field around Mars. Therefore, if one exists, it is probably extremely weak and does not protect the Martian surface from high energy radiation from space as does the earth's atmosphere.

The radio signals transmitted by the spacecraft indicated that the atmospheric pressure on Mars is only about $\frac{1}{2000}$ of the earth's sea level pressure. The signals also confirmed that nitrogen is the most abundant element in the Martian atmosphere, though they also indicated that carbon dioxide is plentiful. The electron density at various levels in the atmosphere was found to be lower than theoretically predicted, and indicated that the planet's surface temperatures are probably between $-135°$ F. and $-150°$ F.

On its flight to Mars, Mariner IV collected data on particles, magnetic fields, and micrometeoroids. Additional information has been gathered since the spacecraft passed by the planet. Scientists are hopeful that the interplanetary probe will provide still more information when its looping orbit around the sun returns it to the vicinity of the earth.

Moon. Lunar experts continued their analysis and interpretation of the thousands of photographs of the moon obtained by Ranger VII, VIII, and IX spacecraft on July 31, 1964; February 20, 1965; and March 24, 1965. Even with these remarkable photos,

some showing craters only $2\frac{1}{2}$ feet across, scientists could not agree about the depth or firmness of the dust covering the moon's surface. They did agree, however, that most of the craters on the moon were formed by the impact of meteoroids. Some small craters, they also theorized, were created by the collapse of the lunar surface.

Photos of the far side of the moon, taken by the Soviet spacecraft Zond III, confirmed that it differs markedly from the side always facing the earth. The photographs taken on July 20 from a distance of about 6,000 miles, revealed a greater number of craters per square mile, and few large plainlike areas.

Solar Eclipse. The total solar eclipse of May 30 was particularly significant because of its longer than average duration—5 minutes 15.9 seconds—and because it occurred at a time of minimum sunspot activity.

As the moon passed between the earth and the sun, its shadow swept along an 8,000-mile path from New Zealand, across the Pacific, to Peru. Observations were made from a few small islands in the Cook and Society groups, and from ships, balloons, rockets, and several jet aircraft flying along the path of the eclipse.

Rotation of the Planets. Radio astronomers observing the nearby planets found that Mercury does not always show the same face to the sun. For 80 years it had been believed that the planet's period of rotation was the same as its orbital period—88 days. By bouncing radio waves off Mercury, astronomers at Cornell University's Arecibo Ionospheric Observatory in Puerto Rico established its rotation period as 59 days, plus or minus five days. The scientists also found that the planet has no detectable atmosphere and that its surface is probably similar to that of the moon.

More accurate radio observations by the Arecibo astronomers pinpointed Venus' westward rotation period at 247 days, plus or minus five days. Radio astronomers also gathered evidence that Jupiter's solid core changed its rate of rotation in 1960. Measurement of the planet's radio emission indicated that its rotational period increased by 1.2 seconds.

Comets. At Mount Wilson and Palomar Observatories, Jesse L. Greenstein and Antoni Stawikowski of the Nicolaus Copernicus University in Poland found evidence of the rare isotope carbon 13 in Comet Ikeya. Carbon 13, they found, exists in the same ratio to carbon 12 in the comet as it does on the earth. The researchers concluded that comets must have been formed in the same region of the solar system as the earth. If they had been born far from the earth, their chemical composition would probably be different from that of the earth or sun. The astronomers suggested that after the comets came into existence near the sun and earth, they were forced into very elongated, elliptical orbits by the particles and radiation released by the sun during the earliest period of the solar system.

Two Japanese amateur astronomers, K. Ikeya and T. Seki, discovered the brightest comet of the 20th century on September 18. Following its discovery, Comet Ikeya-Seki was observed by astronomers around the world. Its brightness allowed valuable observations even during daylight. After the comet passed within 300,000 miles of the sun, on October 21, its nucleus broke into several fragments.

Stars. Astronomers using the 62-inch infrared telescope at Mount Wilson Observatory found two red stars with the lowest surface temperatures known. Though both stars have about the normal 25,000,000° F. interior temperature, one star's surface temperature is only about 1200° F., and the surface temperature of the other is as low as 800° F.

Quasars and Blue Galaxies. Maarten Schmidt, working at Mount Wilson and Palomar, continued to discover more remote, fast moving quasi-stellar radio sources, or quasars. In 1965, he found five such sources farther from the earth than any other known objects. The most distant of the five, 3C-9, is many billions of light-years distant and moving away at about 149,000 miles a second, or 80 per cent of the velocity of light (186,300 miles per second).

Astronomers generally believe that a quasi-stellar source has a mass at least 100,000,000 times that of our sun, and that its energy is produced in a core that is surrounded by two layers of clouds. The innermost layer is of visible luminous gas, while the outer, invisible layer is made up of rapidly moving electrons that give off energy as radio signals as they spiral in the magnetic field surrounding the object. See 1965 YEAR BOOK, *Special Report*, THE UNFOLDING UNIVERSE.

In June, the Mount Wilson and Palomar Observatories announced that Allan Sandage had discovered an unexpected type of distant extragalactic object. According to Sandage, the nearest of the new objects is approximately 20,000,000 light-years from the earth. He named this group of objects "quasi-stellar blue galaxies." Sandage said that galaxies seem related to the quasi-stellar radio sources, but do not emit detectable radio energy even though they produce as much as 100 times more radiation than an ordinary galaxy.

One of the quasi-stellar blue galaxies, designated BSO-1, is receding at a rate of 125,000 miles per second. This speed, which also indicates its distance, makes it the second most distant object known (second to 3C-9).

The new type of quasi-stellar objects is approximately 500 times more numerous than the quasi-stellar radio sources, and at such great distances that observations of them may enable astronomers to determine the geometry of remote space and perhaps learn which of the several theories of the origin of the universe is valid.   ROBERT I. JOHNSON

See also SPACE TRAVEL.

ATLANTA. The mighty construction boom in this metropolis of the Southeast was stifled for a time by a 67-day ironworkers strike that started Sept. 1, 1965. The biggest project halted was the 41-story First National Bank, tallest and most spacious skyscraper in the Southeast. In June, the Peachtree Center Building, a 30-story office tower opened in the hub of downtown. Also under construction in the center was the 800-room Regency Hotel. The Butler Street renewal project gave strong impetus to the economy with offices, motels, and apartments under construction.

The city's new $18,000,000 Atlanta Stadium opened in April. It fulfilled local hopes when it captured major league football (Atlanta Falcons) and baseball (Atlanta Braves) franchises.

With a population doubled in 15 years and mounting traffic congestion, the metropolitan area moved ahead with plans for a 66-mile transit system. Growth also posed human problems. To fight one of the nation's highest metropolitan crime rates, 38 local law enforcement agencies created Metropol, a six-county, crime-fighting agency, in the summer of 1965.

With 40 per cent of the residents in corporate Atlanta Negroes, the city added to its stature as a stronghold of racial moderation in 1965. Mayor Ivan Allen, Jr., who testified in Washington, D.C., for the civil rights bill of 1964, was re-elected to a second term with minor opposition.   DONALD W. LIEF

ATOMIC ENERGY. For the first time since the start of the atomic age, annual federal expenditures for peaceful uses of the atom bomb began to edge up on military nuclear outlays. During the 20 years since the first man-made nuclear explosion seared the desert at Trinity Site, near Alamogordo, N.Mex., on July 16, 1945, the Atomic Energy Commission (AEC) had budgeted over $28,000,000,000 for military atomic development against $6,000,-000,000 for nonmilitary uses. The AEC in 1965, however, shut down three plutonium reactors at Hanford, Wash., leaving only 10 still in operation to produce fissionable material for bombs.

Though military requirements were largely satisfied for the time being, civilian utilization of the atom became a growing field. Sigvard Eklund, director general of the International Atomic Energy Agency, predicted that the total world nuclear power generating capacity would increase almost fivefold by 1970, an increase from the present 5,000,000 kilowatts to between 20,000,000 and 25,000,000 kilowatts. By September, 1965, U.S. firms alone had contracts for 2,500,000 kilowatts of new nuclear power capacity—equal to half the present world operating total.

Major U.S. public utility companies announced plans to expand their nuclear power plants in Illinois and New York, while the Public Service Company of Colorado ordered the West's first nuclear power station to be built 33 miles north of Denver. In Sweden, planners announced that 30 per cent of that country's power will be supplied by nuclear energy in 1980.

Reactor Development. The AEC shifted its emphasis in reactor research and development from the long-established boiling water and pressurized water reactors to advanced converters and near-breeder reactors. A converter is a reactor that uses one kind of fuel and produces another. A breeder is a converter that produces more fissionable atoms than it consumes.

A reactor pilot plant of the breeder type was placed in operation in 1965 at Oak Ridge National Laboratory in Tennessee. This reactor uses uranium dissolved in molten salt—a fuel concept which the laboratory scientists believe has potential economic advantages for electric power production. The reactor eventually will be used to test a breeder concept by transmutation of thorium to uranium.

The highest flux level ever obtained in a reactor was achieved on March 4 at the AEC Savannah River plant. A record four and two-tenths quadrillion neutrons per square centimeter per second was achieved in the production of curium 244.

Useful Explosions. Preliminary studies by two government agencies and an industrial firm indicate that nuclear blasts may unlock vast underground stores of natural gas. The El Paso Natural Gas Company in Texas has proposed a joint experiment with the AEC and the U.S. Bureau of Mines to test the technique. If accepted, it will be the first government-industry use of nuclear explosions for industrial purposes. The nuclear explosions would be used to fracture gas-bearing rock. Geologists believe that the method could recover up to seven times as much gas as is now available in the Rocky Mountain area.

The use of nuclear explosions for large-scale excavation was also studied. Among the projects considered was a new, sea-level Panama Canal. Researchers at the Lawrence Radiation Laboratory at the University of California suggested that the arid surface of the moon may be mined for water by dehydrating water-bearing deposits with nuclear explosives. They said that the method would be feasible for supplying water for lunar base operations and for direct consumption after decontamination.

Desalination of the earth's sea water by atomic power is economically feasible only for plants operating on a large scale, according to a report presented in October at the First International Desalination Symposium at Washington, D.C. Gordon F. Leitner of Aqua-Chem, Inc., Waukesha, Wis., reported that a 50,000,000 watt atomic power capability would be required to compete with fossil fuel desalination plants, even in areas where fossil fuels are relatively costly. Glenn T. Seaborg, chairman of the AEC, predicted that dual-purpose reactors designed both for desalination and the generation of electricity will be commercially available in five to 10 years. See WATER AND FLOOD CONTROL.

Neutron Trap. Scientists of the Los Alamos Scientific Laboratory have devised a method of trapping neutrons from underground atomic blasts to yield data that might require centuries to gather through the use of conventional laboratory neutron sources. The neutron trap consists of a 600-foot long vacuum pipe which channels high-energy neutrons to the ground surface and snaps shut before bomb debris or radioactive gases can escape. A wealth of data on neutron interactions is recorded in approximately 5,000th of a second. The technique also makes possible investigations of materials which are so radioactive that their own natural radiation would obliterate the effects produced by laboratory neutron sources. The new device was described to the American Physical Society, meeting in Washington, D.C., by Dr. A. W. Hemmendinger of Los Alamos.

Atomic Wood. Gamma irradiation of specially treated wood resulted in a new wood-plastic combination that is stronger and more water resistant than natural wood. The new product also resists marring, yet retains its natural wood beauty. The AEC selected 78 wood products companies in 1965 for participation in a program to develop the new material. The process, developed at West Virginia University under an AEC contract, involves impregnating wood with a liquid plastic and bombarding it with ionizing radiation.   SERGEI LENORMAND

See also ELECTRIC POWER; NUCLEAR PHYSICS.

AUSTRALIA, although visibly prosperous, was worried about its high imports and its falling international reserves. There were also misgivings in midsummer over a budget providing for expenditures that would exceed annual revenue by $286,728,000. Despite this, the government of Prime Minister Sir Robert Gordon Menzies firmly rejected industry demands for import restrictions.

A 10-year limited free-trade agreement between Australia and New Zealand was signed on August 31 (see NEW ZEALAND). The new pact was to become effective in 1966. Earlier in the year, Australia announced that its currency system would be converted to dollar-and-cent units in February, 1966.

Defense spending increased heavily in 1965 with Australia placing orders for U.S. military equipment totaling $350,000,000. Australia continued to give military aid to South Vietnam and Malaysia.

Viscount De L'Isle retired as Governor-General in May. He was succeeded by Lord Richard Gardiner Casey (see CASEY, LORD RICHARD GARDINER).

Population: 11,450,000. **Government:** Governor-General Lord Richard Gardiner Casey; Prime Minister Robert Gordon Menzies. **Monetary Unit:** Australian pound (1 = U.S. $2.23). **Gross National Product:** £7,732,000,000. **Foreign Trade:** exports, $3,038,000,000; imports, $3,313,000,000. **Principal Exports:** meat, wheat, wool.   ALASTAIR BURNET

See also ASIA; GREAT BRITAIN; VIETNAM.

AUSTRIA. The coalition government that had ruled Austria since the end of World War II was dissolved in 1965. The two-party cabinet, headed by Chancellor Josef Klaus, resigned on October 22. It had been unable to resolve differences over a forthcoming budget within the time limit set by the constitution. This meant a temporary end of the conservative People's party-Socialist party coalition which most Austrians felt had given them their best years.

President Franz Jonas reappointed the cabinet in a caretaker status until new elections could be held in the spring of 1966. Jonas had succeeded President Adolf Schaerf who had died on February 28 (see JONAS, FRANZ). Generally, it was agreed that a new coalition would be formed.

Spirit of Neutrality. During the year, the nation observed the 600th anniversary of the University of Vienna, the 150th anniversary of the Congress of Vienna, and the 150th anniversary of the founding of the Vienna Institute of Technology (see CELEBRATIONS). Also celebrated in 1965 was the 10th anniversary of the signing of the Austrian State Treaty with France, Great Britain, the United States, and the Union of Soviet Socialist Republics. The treaty had ended Allied occupation after World War II and had restored Austrian freedom on a basis of strict neutrality.

Vienna continued to serve as a meeting place for the East and the West. It facilitated cultural and business exchanges, and initiated a number of television panel shows that employed top-flight personalities from the East and the West. Austria's relations with the East had improved with the final settlement of all war claims (except with Czechoslovakia). Terrorist outbreaks continued, however, in Italian Tyrol (see ITALY).

National Economy. For the first time in years, the nation showed a $2,000,000 deficit in its balance of trade payments, as opposed to a surplus of $41,000,000 in 1964. The reason given was that Austria no longer depended on foreign loans to bolster the economy.

Bad weather, which included damaging floods and a summer drought, cut into the highly profitable tourist trade. It also affected agriculture and construction. A labor shortage still persisted.

Austria's gold reserves and foreign credits were still among the world's highest. Meanwhile, Austria's application for membership in the European Economic Community (EEC, or Common Market) continued to hang fire.

Population: 7,166,000. **Government:** President Franz Jonas; Chancellor Josef Klaus. **Monetary Unit:** schilling (25.87 schillings = U.S. $1). **Gross National Product:** 186,600,000,000 schillings. **Foreign Trade:** exports, $1,446,000,000; imports, $1,863,000,000. **Principal Exports:** iron, lumber, machinery, steel.   TOM AND HARLE DAMMANN

See also EUROPE.

AUTOMATION was viewed with considerably more optimism along the labor front in 1965 than in previous years. Continued technological advances contributed to significant increases in productivity. But, as opposed to the 1957-1962 period, unemployment decreased instead of rising.

The auto industry continued to automate assembly operations. Typically—as in the automation of the assembly of Pontiac differential gears—some operator functions were maintained, but output was increased and the volume of rejects lowered.

A new fiberglass boat factory incorporating automation ideas from the auto industry was opened by the Stanray Company in Danville, Ill. Company officials said that this one plant with its 500 workers could match the entire industry's 1964 output of small aluminum and fiberglass boats.

Numerical Control of machine tools made gains, pointing to wider use in the coming years. Only about 1,200 such units had been installed between 1954 and the end of 1961. But by 1967 there is expected to be 10 times as many such units in use. This would represent a conversion of approximately 1 per cent of the standard machine tools to automated tape controls. Unit labor cost savings from the use of numerical controls ran from 25 to 80 per cent in examples reported in a U.S. Department of Labor study.

Computers were performing more and more office tasks. In private industry, one wide survey of

233

personnel officers showed that the most common areas automated were accounting, material handling, payroll, record keeping, and sales analysis. Two-thirds of the firms reported no employment decreases despite the introduction of automation. Automation in the office seemed to be slowing down employment increases rather than causing a substantial net loss of jobs.

Government experience with computers confirmed this appraisal. Adoption of computers helped hold federal civilian employment at the 2,500,000 mark despite substantial increases in programs and operations. Computers, for example, were turning out GI insurance dividend checks at $\frac{1}{50}$ of the cost of doing it manually.

Reasons for Adopting Automation were studied by the Department of Labor. One report noted: "Cost reduction, primarily through the effect of automation on labor productivity, appears to be a major objective in decisions to automate." The case studies in the report showed substantial reduction in unit labor requirements and fewer jobs in the affected departments, but that no one was "laid off." This was accomplished by *attrition* (quitting, retirement, or death) and by transfers to expanding operations in other departments or plants.

Productivity increases reflected the widespread introduction of automation and new technology, along with the continued operation of the economy at an efficient level. A Federal Reserve Board study late in the year reported: "Output per man-hour in manufacturing has grown at a rate of about 4 per cent a year since 1960. This is a higher rate than for the postwar period as a whole or for any of the preceding cyclical upswings." Preliminary data in 1965 suggested that the trend was continuing.

Unit labor costs in manufacturing, which had been increasing in the early post-World War II period, remained almost completely stable in the previous five years. That stability stemmed from the greater-than-average productivity gains and smaller-than-average increases in employee compensation. Compensation (wages and fringe benefits) rose at an annual rate of 3.5 per cent in 1959-1964, compared with 6 per cent per year in the previous 12-year period.

Recommendations for dealing with automation problems were expected in the forthcoming reports from the National Commission on Technology, Automation, and Economic Progress and from state commissions. However, the sense of urgency had diminished as the economy continued to expand at a rate that provided jobs for all but a small percentage of the labor force.

Unemployment in September fell below 3,000,000 for the first time since October, 1957, while manufacturing employment rose more in the 12 months ended in August, 1965, than in the previous four years combined. See LABOR.   JAMES L. STERN

See also COMPUTER; MANUFACTURING.

AUTOMOBILE

The U.S. auto industry had its biggest year in 1965, with production, sales, employment, and profits soaring to all-time highs. An estimated 9,000,000 cars rolled off U.S. assembly lines during the year. This easily shattered the old industry record of 7,941,538, set in 1955. These, plus 550,000 foreign imports, ran sales a whopping million units ahead of 1964's 8,065,150 (including 486,000 imports).

There was general belief among U.S. auto industry executives that a 9,000,000 sales figure would be reached again in 1966 with an annual sale of 10,000,000 new cars likely within three years.

To pay for "wheels" in 1965, U.S. new-car buyers spent about $36,000,000,000, about $4,000,000,000 more than last year. This drove auto industry profits beyond the $3,000,000,000 mark. General Motors (GM), the industry heavyweight, broke its own record for the highest profits of any company in history.

FRONT-WHEEL DRIVE of Oldsmobile's Toronado is the most dramatic innovation of the 1966 model year. The six-passenger car has a specially modified V-8 engine.
Oldsmobile Div., G.M.C.

Porsche of America

Rolls-Royce, Inc.

Mercedes-Benz

NEW STYLING *marked three prestigious imports. The 911 model, top, gave Porsche its first new look in 16 years, while the Rolls-Royce Silver Shadow, center, had a low, sleek monocoque design, and Mercedes-Benz's luxury sedan, bottom, featured a flat roofline.*

Another all-time high was reached in 1965: traffic deaths edged above 1964's record 47,800 (see SAFETY). U.S. Secretary of Commerce John T. Conner called the death toll "intolerable." Style-conscious Detroit was forced by government action to pay more attention to the good health of the people—both inside and outside the cars it sells.

Air Pollution. All U.S.-built new cars sold in smog-sensitive California were equipped, for the first time, with a $45 device that reduced carbon monoxide and certain other gases emitted by internal combustion engines. See Section Two, POLLUTED AMERICA.

On the national scene, a U.S. Senate subcommittee on air and water pollution, headed by Senator Edmund S. Muskie (D., Me.) met to determine whether a nationwide requirement of exhaust control devices would be in the public interest. Automobile makers showed some reluctance about

nationwide application of the devices, which, they insisted, were not necessary in lightly populated areas. The automakers said, however, that they could comply with whatever conditions the Senate set up, provided they had a minimum of two years to prepare for any program adopted.

President Lyndon B. Johnson signed the Clean Air Act, containing many of the committee's proposals, on October 20. The act authorizes the Department of Health, Education, and Welfare to draw up national standards to cut down on automobile air pollution by 1968.

Crash Protection. The U.S. General Services Administration announced the 17 safety features it would demand on each of the 40,000 or so 1967 model cars it will buy. These included an exhaust-fume control device, a collapsible steering wheel, and a dual braking system.

In July, Senator Abraham Ribicoff (D., Conn.) led the Government Operations Subcommittee on Executive Reorganization to question industry leaders in a study of the government's role in highway safety. They found it difficult to get an admission from the industry that car design played a significant role in auto deaths. But they did obtain a few token concessions, and committee pressure did force some promises of future safety features.

For its 1966 cars, the industry made up a "safety package," including backup lights, multiple windshield wipers, padded dashboard, padded sun visors, rear seat belts, and windshield washers. The price of the items averaged about $50. Since the package was "standard" on all 1966 U.S. cars, the cost was passed along to the buyer.

This additional cost offset a reduction, from 10 to 7 per cent, in the federal excise tax, which went into effect May 15, 1965. An additional 1 per cent cut will occur Jan. 1, 1966, with further cuts scheduled for the future.

The combination of the tax cut and the added cost of the safety package complicated efforts to determine whether 1966 car prices were up or down in 1965. The trade publication *Automotive News* said: "When equipment changes are considered, the prices showed little change from the after tax-cut figures. GM and American Motors are down slightly, Ford held the line, and Chrysler is up."

What's New. For the U.S. industry as a whole, there were few major styling and engineering changes in the 1966 models. The four major U.S. auto companies—General Motors, Ford, Chrysler, and American Motors—offered a postwar record of 364 body styles, up 18 from a year earlier. They emphasized optional equipment designed to lure additional dollars from the buyer by allowing him to "tailor" the car of his choice. Engine and transmission options were readily available. Before options, transportation, or financing charges were added, prices ranged from $2,004 for a Rambler American to $10,456 for a Cadillac limousine.

The most unusual U.S. car among the 1966 models was Oldsmobile's Toronado. It was the first U.S. front-wheel-drive car since 1937, when the famed Cord was discontinued. The Toronado was available only as a six-passenger coupé. In simplest terms, the Toronado is pulled by its front wheels rather than by being pushed by its rear wheels.

Among the innovations on 1966 models were the Ford Motor Company's station wagon dual-action tailgate, which opened either sideways or up and down; and a stereo tape player with four speakers. Also new were Pontiac's overhead-cam, six-cylinder engine, the first such unit offered by a U.S. manufacturer; Chrysler's unique safety door handles; and American Motors' self-adjusting clutch.

Expansion Programs. Both on the domestic front and overseas, U.S. automakers allocated more than $2,000,000,000 for new plants and additions in 1965. U.S. auto firms made especially big investments abroad as they realized that production and sales of new cars in other Free World countries, estimated at over 19,000,000 cars in 1965, exceeded those in the United States. Ford Motor Company, for example, now has 124 overseas plants.

On the personnel front, the major change in the year was at General Motors, where James M. Roche succeeded John F. Gordon as head of the world's biggest manufacturing concern.   CHARLES C. CAIN III

AUTOMOBILE RACING. Jim Clark dominated the auto racing world as few men have. The 29-year-old farmer from Duns, Scotland, not only won the World Grand Prix Drivers' title for the second time, but also captured first in the Indianapolis 500.

Driving a Lotus, Clark won six of the 10 Grand Prix races, clinching the world title on August 1, the earliest in history. England's Graham Hill, 1962 champion and 1964 runner-up, was second. Newcomer Jacky Stewart, another Scot, was third. At Indianapolis, Clark's Lotus-Ford finished more than a lap ahead of Parnelli Jones of Torrance, Calif. Mario Andretti of Nazareth, Pa., was third.

Ned Jarrett of Camden, S.C., led the 1965 National Association for Stock Car Racing (NASCAR) standings. In sports car racing, two Chevrolet-powered Chaparrals, built by Jim Hall and Hap Sharp of Midland, Tex., won almost every race they entered.

Craig Breedlove of Los Angeles, Calif., and Art Arfons of Akron, Ohio, battled again for the world land speed record, driving jet-engine racers across the Bonneville Salt Flats in Utah. On November 3, Breedlove broke Arfons' one-year-old record with a 555 mph two-way average. Then Arfons, who survived a tire blowout, raised it four days later to almost 577 mph. Finally, on November 15, Breedlove made it 600.601 mph.   JAMES O. DUNAWAY

Wide World
WITH A SALUTE TO THE CROWD, Jim Clark of Duns, Scotland, won the Indianapolis 500 on Memorial Day in his Lotus-Ford racer. He later won other important events.

AVIATION

For the first time in the history of aviation, United States domestic trunk airlines topped $3,000,000,000 in annual revenues. Profits also set a record, reaching an estimated $245,000,000, about $115,000,000 more than the 1964 mark. About 49,000,000,000 revenue passenger-miles were flown, up 8,000,000,000 from 1964. Based on the historic correlation of U. S. traffic with world traffic, International Civil Aviation Organization (ICAO) members flew 120,000,000,000 passenger-miles, with estimated 1965 revenues of $9,000,000,000.

British Overseas Airways Corp.

New short-haul jet aircraft were introduced during the year. The first twin-rear-engine DC-9 was delivered to Delta Air Lines. Mohawk Airlines put the similar-appearing British BAC-III into operation, and Lake Central Airlines introduced a French-built, high-wing turboprop, the Nord 262. Orders continued for new equipment, with most manufacturers offering new configurations of present models or announcing new models, as in the case of the Boeing 737 due in 1967.

Anticipating the end of the subsidy for helicopter lines on Dec. 31, 1965, a new era of cooperation began between the airlines and the helicopter and air taxi services to and from large metropolitan airports. Airlines also featured attractive arrangements with rent-a-car operators and credit card agencies to lure more passengers.

The U.S. supersonic transport program progressed slowly. The final competitors—two airframe companies, Boeing and Lockheed, and two engine manufacturers, General Electric and Pratt and Whitney—started building their mock-ups and test engines under Federal Aviation Agency (FAA) contracts. The contracts call for a decision by the FAA on the builders of the prototype early in 1967.

Government Activities. During the year, the FAA completed the consolidation of its air traffic control centers, reducing their number from 29 to 21. The centers control all aircraft operating under Instrument Flight Rules (IFR). The new system, made possible by new developments in long-range radar, not only aided safety but also proved to be more economical.

A government task force was established to study interurban air transportation. Of special interest was the development of Vertical/Short Take-Off and Landing (V/STOL) aircraft as part of the national transportation system.

As an aid to planning, the FAA issued its predictions for the next five years. It forecast that by 1970 the airline passenger-miles will increase to 74,000,000,000 from the 54,000,000,000 flown by all U.S. airlines in 1964. General aviation (flying other than the military or commercial airlines) was expected to increase to 19,500,000 hours from

BRITISH CHALLENGER. Rear engines whining, a new BAC Super-VC-10 left London March 7 for first test flight to New York.

LANDING BY COMPUTER: AUTOFLARE

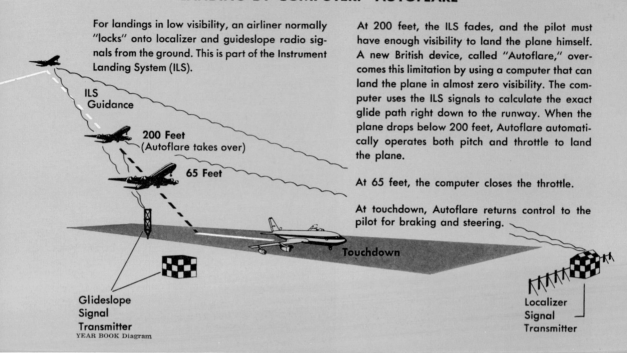

For landings in low visibility, an airliner normally "locks" onto localizer and guideslope radio signals from the ground. This is part of the Instrument Landing System (ILS).

ILS
Guidance

200 Feet
(Autoflare takes over)

65 Feet

Touchdown

Glideslope
Signal
Transmitter
YEAR BOOK Diagram

Localizer
Signal
Transmitter

At 200 feet, the ILS fades, and the pilot must have enough visibility to land the plane himself. A new British device, called "Autoflare," overcomes this limitation by using a computer that can land the plane in almost zero visibility. The computer uses the ILS signals to calculate the exact glide path right down to the runway. When the plane drops below 200 feet, Autoflare automatically operates both pitch and throttle to land the plane.

At 65 feet, the computer closes the throttle.

At touchdown, Autoflare returns control to the pilot for braking and steering.

15,500,000. The size of the air-carrier fleet was expected to remain constant at about 2,100 aircraft; of these, nearly 1,100 will be powered by jet engines. The general aviation fleet was expected to grow from about 85,000 to 105,000 aircraft. The bulk of these, the FAA predicted, will remain piston-engine powered.

Major changes in the requirements for flight engineers in transport-type aircraft were adopted by the FAA to bring the requirements in line with technical developments. Under the new regulations, the flight engineer must now be expertly qualified on a particular class of airplane rather than on aircraft in general.

Federal regulations specifically governing agricultural flying and related activities were announced by the FAA. They will be effective Jan. 1, 1966. The rules are designed to improve the safety of agricultural aviation and to protect persons and property on the ground. They established, for the first time, national standards for operator certificates, operating rules, aircraft airworthiness, pilot qualifications, and record keeping for more than 2,500 operators engaged in agricultural flying.

The first standardized-design airport tower was opened at Lawton, Okla. Each tower built under the new standards will have a functional design, tailored to air traffic control requirements, and will have a standardized working environment. They will be built entirely with FAA funds.

In a complete realignment of government agencies concerned with air transportation affairs, Charles S. Murphy became chairman of the Civil Aeronautics Board (CAB). Alan S. Boyd was appointed undersecretary of commerce for transportation, and William F. McKee FAA administrator.

Airports. In 1964, the FAA introduced a more extensive airport reporting service. This required airport operators to notify the agency before establishing or closing an airport. FAA reported 9,490 airports in operation at the beginning of 1965. This was an increase of 676 over the previous year, and compared favorably with the average annual increase of 623 over the past five years.

Texas, with 812 airports, led all other states. California, with 627 landing facilities, was second; and Alaska was third, with 549. Nearly two-thirds of the national total, 5,846, were privately owned. Lighted runways were provided at 2,773 airports, and paved runways at 2,630. At all but 29 of the nation's airports, the number of general aviation take-offs and landings exceeded those of the airlines. In 1965, the five busiest U.S. airports were Chicago-O'Hare International; Long Beach, Calif.; Van Nuys, Calif.; John F. Kennedy International (New York); and Los Angeles International.

The Spokane (Wash.) International Airport opened a new terminal building, and Dallas and Fort Worth, Tex., announced agreement on plans for a joint regional airport. See DALLAS.

Pictorial Parade

THE WORLD'S LARGEST AIRCRAFT, the Soviet AN-22, stole the show at the Paris International Air Exposition in June. It can carry 700 passengers.

International Transportation. Increased ranges of the latest aircraft enabled airlines to schedule nonstop flights between New York-Buenos Aires; Los Angeles-London; Tokyo-Seattle; and New York-Tel Aviv. Around-the-world service is now offered by at least six airlines. In July, Pan American World Airways began a weekly service of around-the-world cargo jet flights, uniting 17 of the world's major industrial centers.

The International Air Transport Association (IATA) reported a continuing rise in the number of passengers taking the North Atlantic route. During the first six months of 1965, traffic increased 18 per cent over 1964, with 1,477,850 passengers. Cargo increased 53 per cent, with 82,744 short tons. Lower passenger fares were projected for 1966, and numerous cargo fare reductions went into effect in September, 1965. Knut Hammarskjöld was named director general of IATA, effective April 1, 1966.

ICAO Assembly. The largest gathering of representatives of the 110 member states of the ICAO completed a month-long session in Montreal, Canada. The assembly, which last met in 1962, reviewed the organization's work and made decisions on future policies in the entire field of international civil aviation. The main work of the assembly was done by the executive committee and by the technical, economic, legal, and administrative commissions. These groups made recommendations on matters of general aviation, international

law, navigation equipment, regional planning, supersonic civil aircraft, and technical assistance and training.

General Aviation. The boom continued in general aviation, which includes all flying other than by the military and the airlines. General aviation aircraft output rose 20 per cent, totaling more than 12,000 aircraft. Manufacturers continued the trend toward providing a full selection of aircraft adapted to the various customer markets and announced plans to invest $20,000,000 in plant expansion. Most manufacturers were developing export businesses, and some were setting up assembly plants in foreign countries.

Noteworthy Flights. Mary Ann Noah, with her copilot, Mary Aikins, won the 19th Annual All-Women's Transcontinental Air Race (Powder Puff Derby) for the second year in a row. The race was from El Cajon, Calif., to Chattanooga, Tenn.

June Douglas, flying a Piper Cherokee 180, was the solo winner of the All-Women's International Air Race from Caldwell-Wright Airport, New Jersey, to Nassau, Bahamas.

Within a 25-hour period, Trans World Airways established three firsts in Boeing 707-320C jet aircraft. The longest of the three nonstop flights was from Oakland, Calif., to Tel Aviv, Israel, a distance of 7,998 statute miles, in 13 hours 30 minutes. The same aircraft had just returned from a flight of 5,460 miles in 10 hours 30 minutes. The third flight

241

was from Oakland, Calif., to Rio de Janeiro, Brazil, covering 6,908 miles in 13 hours 19 minutes.

The year was an active one for contests and record-breaking, with 28 international records and 40 U.S. records being established by U.S. citizens as of October 1. Of the total 722 Féderation Aéronautique Internationale aerospace recognized records, the United States holds 342 and the U.S.S.R., 135.

Aviation Trophy and Award winners in 1965:

American Institute of Astronautics and Aeronautics de Florez Training Award to Lloyd L. Kelly for his efforts in perfecting training simulators.

Barbour Air Safety Award to Arthur E. Jenks for his many contributions toward improving the techniques for flight-checking the accuracy of navigational aids.

Frank G. Brewer Trophy to Gill Robb Wilson for a lifetime of service to aviation education.

Robert J. Collier Trophy to General Curtis E. LeMay, USAF, in recognition of his accomplishments in 1964 as chief of staff of the U.S. Air Force.

Harmon International Aviation Trophies to Max Conrad for his 57-hour nonstop flight from Capetown, South Africa, to St. Petersburg, Fla., and to Joan Merriam Smith for her 27,000-mile solo flight around the world.

Wright Brothers Memorial Trophy to Jerome F. Lederer of the Flight Safety Foundation, Inc., for his contribution to aviation safety.   LESLIE A. BRYAN

See also ARMED FORCES OF THE WORLD; BALLOONS; DISASTERS; ENGINE AND ENERGY; INVENTION; NATIONAL DEFENSE; SPACE TRAVEL; TRAVEL.

AWARDS AND PRIZES presented in 1965 included the following:

General Awards

Academy of American Poets Awards. *Fellowship* to Marianne Moore, noted poet, critic, and translator. *Lamont Award* to Henri Coulette for his first book of poems *The War of the Secret Agent and Other Poems.*

American Academy of Arts and Letters and National Institute of Arts and Letters Awards. *Gold Medals* to Andrew Wyeth, painter, and Walter Lippmann, author and editor. *Marjorie Peabody Waite Award,* for "continuing integrity in his work, to Paul Burlin, painter. *Rosenthal Foundation Awards* to painter Marcia Marcus, and Thomas Berger for his novel *Little Big Man. William Dean Howells Medal,* awarded every five years for the most distinguished work of American fiction, to John Cheever for *The Wapshot Scandal. Arnold W. Bruner Award* in Architecture to Kevin Roche. *Awards in Literature* to poets Ben Belitt, Robert Bly, James V. Cunningham (also critic), and Denise Levertov; Joseph Mitchell, local historian; and novelists Pier M. Pasinetti, Henry Roth, and Harvey Swados. *Awards in Art* to graphic artists Sigmund Abeles and Joyce Reopel; painters Lee Gatch and Richard Mayhew; and sculptors David V. Hayes, Elliot Offner, and Thomas Stearns. *Awards in Music* to composers Mario Davidovsky, Gerald Humel, Earl Kim, and Harvey Sollberger. *Traveling Fellowship in Literature* to novelist Cormac McCarthy. *Award for Distinguished Service to the Arts* to Frances Steloff of The Gotham Book Mart in New York City and subject of *Wise Men Fish Here* (1965) by W. G. Rogers

American Academy of Arts and Sciences Emerson-Thoreau Medal, for distinguished achievement in literature, to Lewis Mumford for his work as a philosopher, critic, teacher, and writer.

American Institute of Architects Awards. *Honor Medal* to Hungarian-born Marcel Lajos Breuer, designer of the Whitney Museum of American Art in New York City and other notable buildings. *Allied Professions Medal* to Leonardo Zeevaert, University of Mexico professor and engineer. *Fine Arts Medal* to Mexican muralist and landscape designer Roberto Burle-Marx. *Industrial Arts Medal* to architect and industrial designer Eliot Noyes. *Edward C. Kemper Award,* for significant contributions to the institute and the architectural profession, to Joseph Watterson, editor of the journal published by the architectural institute.

American Sociological Association MacIver Award to William Goode of Columbia University for his book *World Revolution and Family Patterns* (1963).

Anisfield-Wolf Awards by the *Saturday Review,* for books that deal most creditably with race-relations problems, to Milton M. Gordon for *Assimilation in American Life;* James M. McPherson for *The Struggle for Equality: Abolitionists and the Negro in the Civil War and Reconstruction;* Abram L. Sacher for *A History of the American Jew;* and James A. Silver for *Mississippi: A Closed Society.*

Aspen Institute for Humanistic Studies Award to Martha Graham, creative dancer and choreographer, who formed her own company and established the Martha Graham School of Contemporary Dance.

Boston Medals for Distinguished Achievement, presented for the first time in 1965, to composer Richard Rodgers and Arthur Fiedler, Boston Pops Orchestra conductor for many years.

Brandeis University Creative Arts Awards to playwright Tennessee Williams, poet Stanley Kunitz, painter Mark Rothko, and composer Elliott Carter. *Notable Creative Achievement Award* to Alfred H. Barr, Jr., museum collections director at New York City's Museum of Modern Art. *Citation Awards,* for furtherance of their careers, to composer Salvatore Martirano, poet Anthony Hecht, painter Kenneth Noland, and drama critic Michael Smith.

British Royal Society of Arts Benjamin Franklin Medal to Paul Mellon, art collector and board chairman of the Mellon Institute of Industrial Research in Pittsburgh, Pa.

Columbia University Awards. *Alice M. Ditson Conductor's Award* to Jacob Avshalomov, Portland (Ore.) Junior Symphony Orchestra conductor. *Brevoort-Eickemayer Prize,* awarded every five years, to artist Edwin Dickinson, who was also honored with a retrospective exhibition at the Whitney Museum of American Art in 1965. *Frederic Bancroft Prizes,* for studies in American history, diplomacy, and international relations, to William B. Willcox, for *Portrait of a General: Sir Henry Clinton in the War of Independence;* Bradford Perkins for *Castlereagh and Adams: England and The United States, 1812–1823;* and Dorothy Borg for *The United States and the Far Eastern Crisis of 1933–1938.*

Denmark's Sonning Prize to Leonard Bernstein, composer, conductor, pianist, and New York Philharmonic musical director.

Four Freedoms Award, for service to the ideals of President Franklin D. Roosevelt, posthumously to President John F. Kennedy.

Freedom House Award to Harry S. Truman, former President of the United States (1945–1953), inscribed "Wise in policy, valiant in action, decisive in leadership, you gave a battered world new hope."

Freedoms Foundation George Washington Medal, the foundation's highest award, to Dewitt and Lila A. Wallace, editors and publishers of *Reader's Digest,* for "building under free enterprise a magazine invaluable in the continuing fight for freedom and dignity of every individual."

French Academy Novel Award to Jean Husson for *Le Cheval d'Herbeleau (Herbeleau's Horse)*. The author was cited as "a young writer of a work of imagination and superior inspiration."

German Bookseller International Nonfiction Prize, awarded every three years, to *The New York Times* science editor Walter Sullivan for *We Are Not Alone*.

Goethe Institute Goethe Medal to Richard Wolf, German author and teacher, for teaching German abroad and acting as director of the Goethe Institute in Munich; Roy Pascal, University of Birmingham (England) German professor; and Elizabeth Wilkinson, University of London German professor and chairman of the British Goethe Society.

Goncourt Academy Award for Literature to Jacques Boral for his first novel, *L'Adoration*.

Hawthornden Prize, to a British writer under 41 years of age, was awarded to William Trevor, author of *The Old Boys*.

International Publishers Prizes, awarded to Americans for the first time. *Prix International de Littérature*, awarded to a living author of world stature for a work of fiction published within the last three years that will have the most significant influence on the literature of our time, to Saul Bellow for *Herzog* (see BELLOW, SAUL). *Prix Formentor* to Stephen Schneck, also an American, for *The Night Clerk*, his first novel, not published (at award time May, 1965).

Jan Sibelius Prizes; *Annual Music Prize* to British composer Benjamin Britten. *Centennial Prizes* to Finnish composers Erik Bergman, Usko Merilainen, and Eino-Juhani Rautavaara.

National Book Committee Awards. *National Book Awards: Fiction Award* to Saul Bellow for *Herzog* (see BELLOW, SAUL); *History and Biography Award* to Louis Fischer for *The Life of Lenin; Arts and Letters Award* to Eleanor Clark for *The Oysters of Locmariaquer; Poetry Award* to the late Theodore Roethke for *The Far Field*, a posthumous publication; *Science, Philosophy, and Religion Award* to the late Norbert Wiener for *God and Golem, Inc.*, a posthumous publication. *National Medal for Literature*, presented for the first time in 1965 and at the first such White House ceremonies, to Thornton N. Wilder, novelist and playwright, for a lifetime of work.

Poetry Society of America Awards. *Alice Fay di Castagnola Award*, presented for the first time in 1965, to Paul Roche, English poet, for *Beyond All This Fiddle* (verse and prose); and Barbara Overmyer for her poetry collection and first book, not yet published. *Shelley Award* to Ruth Stone of Cambridge, Mass., as a promising poet. *Melville Cane Award* to Jean H. Hagstrum for *William Blake: Poet and Painter*.

Royal Institute of British Architects Gold Medal to Kenzo Tange, designer of the Peace Memorial Hall and Museum in Hiroshima and other buildings in Japan.

Society of American Historians Francis Parkman Prize to Willie Lee Rose for *Rehearsal for Reconstruction*.

University of Pisa International Italian History and Literature Prize to Hans Baron, University of Chicago professor and specialist on the cultural and political history and civilization of Italy.

Yale University Bollingen Prize, for American poetry, to Horace Gregory for his *Collected Poems*.

Science and Industry

Albert and Mary Lasker Foundation Awards. *Medical Journalism Awards: Newspaper Award* to Alton L. Blakeslee, The Associated Press science writer, and Jeremiah B. Stamler, Chicago Board of Health Heart Disease Control Program director, for their series "Your Heart Has Nine Lives." *Special Newspaper Citation* to Jack Nelson, *The Los Angeles Times* southeastern bureau chief in Atlanta, for his series on the care of the mentally ill in Georgia in *The Atlanta Constitution. Magazine Award* to Matt Clark, *Newsweek* medicine editor, for his story "Birth Control: The Pill and the Church." *Television Award* to Fred W. Friendly and Jay McMullen for the Columbia Broadcasting System Reports program "The Business of Heroin." *Special Television Citation* to Edgar T. Bell, manager of station KWTV (Oklahoma City), for "The Twilight World," mental retardation program written and produced by Harlan Mendenhall. *Medical Research Awards* to Albert B. Sabin, University of Cincinnati College of Medicine Distinguished Service Professor, who developed a live oral poliomyelitis vaccine; and Robert W. Holley, Cornell University Professor of Biochemistry, who isolated and analyzed a 77-subunit strand of ribonucleic acid (RNA).

American Academy of Arts and Sciences Rumford Medal, awarded every two years, to Samuel C. Collins, Massachusetts Institute of Technology Professor Emeritus of Mechanical Engineering, who pioneered in low-temperature research and invented the Collins helium cryostat to produce liquid helium; and William D. McElroy, Johns Hopkins University Biology Department chairman and director of the McCollum-Pratt Institute there, for work on the molecular basis of bioluminescence (emission of light by plants and animals).

American Chemical Society Awards. *James T. Grady Award* to Isaac Asimov, Boston University biochemist and author of many science (fact and fiction) books. *Roger Adams Award* to Arthur Clay Cope, Massachusetts Institute of Technology Chemistry Department chairman, discoverer of the Cope Rearrangement (of allylic groups in three-carbon systems) and a useful barbiturate (Delvinal).

American Physical Society Irving Langmuir Award, presented for the first time in 1965, to John H. Van Vleck, Harvard University Professor of Physics, for his studies in chemical physics.

American Society of Industry Sir William Henry Perkin Medal to Carl Shipp Marvel, University of Arizona Professor of Chemistry, a pioneer in polymer research and recently engaged in the study of high-temperature polymers.

Case Institute of Technology Albert A. Michelson Award to Luis W. Alverez, University of California (Berkeley) Professor of Physics, for discovery of significant properties of cosmic rays, neutrons, isotopes, and nuclear transformation. He is also a leading developer of quantitative tools for nuclear physics, and a pioneer in radar and aircraft landing systems.

Dickinson College Joseph Priestley Memorial Award to Joel H. Hildebrand, University of California (Berkeley) Professor Emeritus of Chemistry, for research in solubility and the structure of liquids.

Formosa Chi-Tsin Culture Foundation Achievement in Science Award to Chien-shiung Wu, Columbia University professor, for her research in nuclear forces and structure, particularly in disproving the law of parity conservation.

Franklin Institute Awards. *Frank P. Brown Medal* to William J. Levitt, for development of large-volume, high-efficiency home construction. *John Price Wetherill Medals* to John Reynolds, University of California (Berkeley) Professor of Physics, for studies of xenon isotopes; and Frederick D. Rossini, University of Notre Dame College of Science dean, for contributions to petroleum hydrocarbon chemistry and engineering. *Stuart Ballantine Medal* to Alec Harley Reeves, English scientist, for his pulse code modulation system used by Mariner IV satellite to transmit television pictures from Mars to Earth.

AWARDS AND PRIZES

Institute of Electrical and Electronics Engineers Lamme Medal to A. Uno Lamm, Swedish scientist, for developing the high-power, high-voltage mercury-arc valve and a system of control and protection for its application as a rectifier and inverter in high-voltage DC power transmission.

Lewis and Rosa Strauss Memorial Fund Albert Einstein Medal to John Archibald Wheeler, Princeton University Professor of Physics and a specialist on Einstein's theory of relativity and nuclear physics.

National Academy of Sciences Awards. *Agassiz Medal* to Sir Edward Bullard, Cambridge University (England) Geophysics Professor, for original contribution in the science of oceanography. *Carty Medal* to Alfred Henry Sturtevant, California Institute of Technology Thomas Hunt Morgan Professor Emeritus of Biology, for his analysis of hereditary patterns in the common fruit fly *Drosophila melanogaster*. *Daniel G. Elliot Medal* to George Gaylord Simpson, Harvard University Museum of Comparative Zoology Alexander Agassiz Professor of Vertebrate Paleontology, for his book *Principles of Animal Taxonomy*. *Henry Draper Medal* to Martin Ryle, Cambridge University Mullard Radio Astronomy Observatory director, for original investigation in astronomical physics. *Kimber Genetics Medal* to Alfred Day Hershey, Carnegie Institution of Washington Genetics Research Unit director, as a leader in the discovery of DNA's (deoxyribonucleic acid) role in hereditary processes and for contributions to molecular genetics. *James Craig Watson Medal* to Paul Herget, University of Cincinnati Observatory director, for contributions to celestial mechanics, particularly his application of electronic computer techniques to calculations of comets, earth satellites, and asteriods orbits. *U.S. Steel Foundation Award in Molecular Biology* to Robert S. Edgar of California Institute of Technology for his development and application of the method of "conditional lethal mutants" to determine how genes (basic units of heredity) control virus development.

National Medal of Science, presented by President Johnson, to Roger Adams, distinguished organic chemist and University of Illinois Professor Emeritus of Chemistry; Othmar Hermann Ammann, bridge designer (see DEATHS OF NOTABLE PERSONS); Theodosius Dobzhansky, Rockefeller Institute professor, noted for fundamental studies of the genetic determinants of organic evolution; Charles Stark Draper, Massachusetts Institute of Technology Aeronautics and Astronautics Department head and a leader in missile guidance developments; Solomon Lefschetz, Princeton University Professor Emeritus of Mathematics and authority on algebraic topology; Neal Elgar Miller, Yale University James Rowland Angell Professor of Psychology, known for research on principles of learning and motivation; Harold Marston Morse, Institute for Advanced Study (Princeton, N.J.) mathematician and pioneer in differential topology; Marshall Warren Nirenberg, National Heart Institute Laboratory of Clinical Biochemistry Biochemical Genetics Section head, known for studies of the genetic control of protein synthesis; Julian Seymour Schwinger (see NOBEL PRIZES [Science]; SCHWINGER, JULIAN SEYMOUR); Harold Clayton Urey, Nobel chemistry laureate (1934) and University of California (San Diego), more recently acclaimed for work on the origin of the solar system and of life on earth; and Robert Burns Woodward, Harvard University Donner Professor of Science, (see NOBEL PRIZES [Science]; WOODWARD, ROBERT BURNS).

Pacific Science Center Foundation Arches of Science Award, presented for the first time in 1965, to Warren Weaver, internationally known mathematician, educator, former research foundation executive, and author of *Lady Luck—The Theory of Probability; The Mathematical Theory of Communication; Science and Complexity; People, Energy and Food*, and other books and numerous articles. Weaver was cited "for his contributions toward public understanding of the meaning of science."

Royal Astronomical Society of London Awards. *Gold Medal* to Gerald Maurice Clemence, Yale University astronomy research associate, for his application of celestial mechanics to the motions in the solar system and for his "fundamental contributions to the study of time and the system of astronomical constants." *Eddington Medal* to Harvard Professor Robert V. Pound and Yale Assistant Professor Glen A. Rebka, Jr., for their experiments confirming Einstein's principle of equivalence (a basic assumption of the general relativity theory).

Royal Canadian Geographical Society Massey Medal to Hugh Samuel Bostock, for contributions to the Western Cordillera and the Yukon Territory. See BOSTOCK, HUGH SAMUEL.

Turin Academy of Medicine Saint-Vincent International Prize for Medical Science, awarded every four years by the Italian academy, to Michael Ellis DeBakey, Baylor University College of Medicine Surgery Department chairman, who pioneered in surgical procedures for heart and blood vessel diseases.

United Nations Educational, Scientific, and Cultural Organization Kalinga Prize, for popularization of science, to Warren Weaver, mathematician and author.

See also NOBEL PRIZES; PULITZER PRIZES; and Awards sections of articles such as ATOMIC ENERGY, AVIATION, and LITERATURE FOR CHILDREN.

BAHAMAS was temporarily stunned by a blow to its most lucrative source of trade. In June, the United States passed a law reducing American tourists' duty-free allowances for liquor and other goods purchased overseas. Bahamians feared this might discourage tourism and tourist purchases. The traffic held up, however, reaching a record 605,000 visitors.

American and other investors continued to recognize the Bahamas' value as a tax haven. Some U.S. Treasury officials hinted, however, that some funds flowing into the Western Hemisphere's "Little Switzerland" might be coming from American underworld sources.

Under the direction of Sir Stafford Sands, minister of finance and tourism, the United Bahamian party (UBP), which is dominated by Nassau merchants and professional men, helped maintain an economic boom. But growing opposition to the UBP by the Progressive Liberal party (PLP) indicated a political challenge was brewing among the islands' Negro majority.

Population: 122,000. **Government:** Governor Sir Ralph Grey. **Monetary Unit:** pound (1 = U.S. $2.80). **Foreign Trade:** imports, $79,141,820; exports, $2,687,292. **Principal Exports:** provisions, pulpwood, salt.

ALASTAIR BURNET

See also GREAT BRITAIN.

BALLET. See DANCING.

BALLOONS. See ASTRONOMY; WEATHER.

BANKS AND BANKING enjoyed a prosperous year. Bank earnings increased. The time deposits of all U.S. commercial banks rose about 15 per cent in 1965. Nevertheless, their loan-to-deposit ratio climbed to a 30-year high of 65 per cent.

Banking institutions were increasingly strapped for funds. To attract deposits, many U.S. banks were paying interest at the legal limit: 4 per cent on savings and $4\frac{1}{2}$ per cent on certificates of deposit (CDs) with maturities of 90 days or longer. Some banks were selling savings bonds, or small-denomination CDs. Later in the year, CD limits were raised to $5\frac{1}{2}$ per cent (see MONEY).

Bank Rate Hike. The Federal Reserve Board on December 5 increased the *discount rate* from 4 per cent to $4\frac{1}{2}$ per cent. (Member banks must pay the discount rate on funds they borrow from the Federal Reserve banks.) The administration had been maintaining that increased lending rates were against public policy. Immediately after the rate boost, President Lyndon B. Johnson commented: "I particularly regret that this action was taken before January, when we will have before us the full facts on next year's budget, Vietnam costs . . . and other elements in the economic outlook." See ECONOMY, THE; PRESIDENT OF THE UNITED STATES.

During the year, banks generally were mindful that the few 1964 increases in prime rates were rescinded under presidential pressure. Some banks, accordingly, only gingerly raised rates to $4\frac{3}{4}$ per cent on loans to brokers and sales finance companies. But after the discount rate change, the prime rate was increased to 5 per cent.

Overseas Loan Curbs. Banks cooperated with the administration in a voluntary program to limit the size of overseas loans to no more than 5 per cent above 1964 levels. The balance in U.S. international payments weakened during the last half of 1965, however, and measures to strengthen the voluntary program were under investigation (see INTERNATIONAL TRADE AND FINANCE).

In Britain, the Labour government's first anti-inflationary pay freeze was applied to bank workers. And in June, it ordered the Bank of England's lending rate cut to 6 per cent. It had been at a 7 per cent "crisis" level since Nov. 23, 1964. In December, the Bank of Canada raised its discount rate to $4\frac{3}{4}$ per cent, from $4\frac{1}{4}$ per cent.

Savings and Loan Associations (SLAs). Early in the year, more than 100 SLAs with dividend rates above prevailing local levels were curbed from borrowing funds from Federal Home Loan Banks. Several California SLAs that had paid 5 per cent dividends cut back to 4.85 per cent. The Federal Home Loan Banks raised their rates on loans to SLAs to $4\frac{3}{4}$ per cent. And, in August, the Federal Home Loan Bank Board issued a stringent set of guidelines—later relaxed—on loans to SLAs.

Continued squabbles among bank regulatory agencies prompted the administration to set up a panel for regular interchanges among the Federal Reserve Board, Federal Deposit Insurance Corporation (FDIC), comptroller of the currency, and Federal Home Loan Bank Board. That bickering culminated in a plan to unify federal bank regulation. The American Bankers Association opposed it, arguing that it would destroy valuable checks and balances in the banking system.

A Major Bank Failure with overtones of scandal shook the banking community on Jan. 22, 1965, when the San Francisco National Bank was declared insolvent. It had been chartered less than three years. Large depositors—including the United Automobile Workers union ($3,000,000) and several West Coast SLAs—sued for recovery of their uninsured deposits. They charged that Comptroller of the Currency James J. Saxon covered up examination reports while he tried to shore up the shaky bank for a merger with a stronger one. The suits further alleged that Federal Reserve loans to the bank gave depositors a false impression of its solvency.

Banks Diversify. The First National Bank of New York won Security and Exchange Commission approval to set up a mutual fund—first such venture since most stock market operations of banks were outlawed by the 1934 Securities Exchange Act. New

Liquid Assets Held by the Public
(billions of dollars)

	1965	Changes from Sept. 30, 1964	
Demand Deposits and Currency.	$160.7	$ 5.7	3.5%
Time Deposits:			
Commercial Banks.........	141.4	19.5	13.8%
Mutual Savings Banks......	51.6	3.7	7.2%
Postal Savings System........	.3	— .1	−33.3%
Savings and Loan Shares.....	107.7	8.6	8.0%
U.S. Government Savings Bonds	50.1	.7	1.4%
U.S. Government Securities Maturing Within One Year	49.7	2.3	4.6%
TOTAL*.................	561.6	40.6	7.2%

Note: Figures at end of September each year.
Sources: Council of Economic Advisers; *Economic Indicators*
*Detail may not add to total due to rounding.

rules governing disclosure of information to bank stockholders became effective April 30. Yet some accountants and security analysts remained critical of "misleading and inadequate" bank reports.

Merger Dispute. The nearly impossible task of breaking up already merged banks found in violation of antitrust laws led Congress to propose that six such mergers be legalized retroactively. (Two were already under court orders to unmerge.) The bill, which passed in the Senate, prohibited any lodging of antitrust charges later than 30 days after a merger. But Representative Wright Patman (D., Tex.), House Banking Committee chairman, was so opposed to the measure that he prevented a rebellious committee and the House from even considering it in 1965. WILLIAM G. DEWALD

See also Section One, SYLVIA PORTER ON THE ECONOMY.

BASEBALL

Sandy Koufax of the Los Angeles Dodgers made baseball history as he pitched outstanding games that won his team the National League pennant and the World Series. The 29-year-old left-hander, who has been called "a league unto himself," won 26 games in regular-season play and then pitched two shut-outs in the World Series.

The series matched teams that had come from sixth-place finishes in 1964 to win pennants in their respective leagues. The Minnesota Twins won the first two games of the series in Minnesota, and the Dodgers took the next three in Los Angeles. The Twins came back in the sixth game in Minnesota and then lost the clincher to Koufax, 2-0.

The National League. The Dodgers won the pennant with strong pitching, tight defense, and daring base-running (by Maury Wills, who stole an impressive 92 bases). The champions thus ended their regular season with a major league low of only 78 home runs. But they were credited with bringing a return to the old brand of baseball—tight defense and high-speed playing backed by strong pitching.

Five teams were in contention in the last month. The Dodgers then broke through with a 13-game winning streak in the last two weeks of the season, catching the San Francisco Giants, who were ahead up to the last week of play.

Koufax, whose career was threatened by an attack of bursitis in his pitching arm during the spring, came back to hurl more innings than any other pitcher. He pitched a perfect game, the fourth of his career, and he set a big league record of 382 strike-outs. Koufax, however, sat out the opening game of the World Series in observance of *Yom Kippur* (the Jewish Day of Atonement), and lost the second game before he pitched the two shutouts that won the series for the Dodgers.

Jim Maloney of Cincinnati pitched two no-hitters, one of which he lost to the New York Mets 1–0 in the 11th inning. The Mets finished last for the fourth time in as many years since joining the league. The defending champions, the St. Louis Cardinals, dropped to seventh place.

The American League. The New York Yankees finished sixth—their first time out of the first division since 1925. The first pennant came to the Twins in the fifth season of their shift to Minnesota from Washington, D.C.

The Twins' Tony Oliva repeated as batting champion of his league, as did Roberto Clemente of the Pittsburgh Pirates in the National League. Cleveland's Sam McDowell earned a reputation as the "Sandy Koufax of the American League" by striking out an impressive high of 325 batters during the season.

Satchel Paige, at 59, returned to organized baseball for the third time, and earned comeback-of-the-year mention by pitching three innings of a

Neil Leifer for *Sports Illustrated* © Time Inc.

SPORTSMANSHIP? San Francisco Giant's pitcher Juan Marichal clubbed Dodgers' catcher John Roseboro during a crucial game on August 22.

247

Business Week Magazine, Ted Rozumalski

HOUSTON'S NEW ASTRODOME, an air-conditioned sports and convention stadium, was packed by baseball fans opening day.

FINAL STANDINGS IN MAJOR LEAGUE BASEBALL

AMERICAN LEAGUE

	W.	L.	Pc.	GB.
Minnesota	102	60	.630	—
Chicago	95	67	.586	7
Baltimore	94	68	.580	8
Detroit	89	73	.549	13
Cleveland	87	75	.537	15
New York	77	85	.475	25
California	75	87	.463	27
Washington	70	92	.432	32
Boston	62	100	.383	40
Kansas City	59	103	.364	43

NATIONAL LEAGUE

	W.	L.	Pc.	GB.
Los Angeles	97	65	.599	—
San Francisco	95	67	.586	2
Pittsburgh	90	72	.556	7
Cincinnati	89	73	.549	8
Milwaukee	86	76	.531	11
Philadelphia	85	76	.528	11½
St. Louis	80	81	.497	16½
Chicago	72	90	.444	25
Houston	65	97	.401	32
New York	50	112	.309	47

Leading Batters

Batting Average—Tony Oliva, Minnesota	.321
Home Runs—Tony Conigliaro, Boston	32
Runs Batted In—Rocky Colavito, Cleveland	108
Hits—Tony Oliva, Minnesota	185
Runs—Tony Oliva, Minnesota	107

Leading Batters

Batting Average—Roberto Clemente, Pittsburgh	.329
Home Runs—Willie Mays, San Francisco	52
Runs Batted In—Deron Johnson, Cincinnati	130
Hits—Pete Rose, Cincinnati	209
Runs—Tommy Harper, Cincinnati	126

Leading Pitchers

Games Won—Jim Grant, Minnesota	21
Win Average—Jim Grant, Minnesota (21-7)	.750
Earned Run Average—Hoyt Wilhelm, Chicago	1.81
Strike-outs—Sam McDowell, Cleveland	325

Leading Pitchers

Games Won—Sandy Koufax, Los Angeles	26
Win Average—Sandy Koufax, Los Angeles (26-8)	.765
Earned Run Average—Frank Linzy, San Francisco	1.43
Strike-outs—Sandy Koufax, Los Angeles	382

one-hit, runless baseball game. The amazing veteran of almost 40 years of baseball was hired by the Kansas City Athletics late in the season, but only made this one appearance for the team.

Front Office. In a surprise move, the major league owners named William D. Eckert, retired U.S. Air Force lieutenant general, as the new commissioner of baseball to succeed Ford Frick (see ECKERT, WILLIAM D.). Earlier, the owners had established a five-man cabinet to assist the new commissioner. The National Broadcasting Company (NBC) was awarded a $30,600,000 contract to continue televising the World Series and All Star Games and to carry a "Game of the Week" for three years.

The dominance of the National League was reflected by its third straight World Series triumph; its 6-5 victory in the All Star Game; and its attendance of 13,576,521 for the season, a record for the major leagues.

The Braves, who moved from Boston in 1953, ended a 13-year stay in Milwaukee, with plans to move to Atlanta in 1966. The Los Angeles Angels paved the way during the year for their move to Anaheim, Calif., in 1966 by changing their name to the California Angels.

The controversial Leo Durocher, 59, returned to baseball after a short absence when he was named to manage the Chicago Cubs, succeeding Bob Kennedy. Durocher immediately announced he was the "manager" and not the "head coach," thereby ending the system of head coaches introduced by Cub owner Phil Wrigley.

Wes Westrum filled in for Casey Stengel after Casey broke his hip during the close of the 1965 season. He was named Mets manager for 1966. When Stengel retired, Don Heffner, a Mets coach, succeeded Dick Sisler as manager of the Reds. Sisler then took a job as coach with the St. Louis Cardinals, and Alvin Dark succeeded Heywood Sullivan as manager of the Kansas City Athletics.

Amateurs. Arizona State captured the National Collegiate Athletic Association (NCAA) title. The National Association of Intercollegiate Athletics (NAIA) crown went to Carson-Newman College of Tennessee. Windsor Locks, Conn., beat Stoney Creek, Ontario, Canada, for the Little League championship.

Award Winners in the major leagues were:
National League Most Valuable Player—Willie Mays of the San Francisco Giants.
American League Most Valuable Player—Zoilo Versalles of the Minnesota Twins.
Cy Young Award, to the "pitcher of the year"—Sandy Koufax of the Los Angeles Dodgers.
National League Rookie of the Year—Jim Lefebvre of the Los Angeles Dodgers.
American League Rookie of the Year—Curt Blefary of the Baltimore Orioles.
National League Manager of the Year—Walt Alston of the Los Angeles Dodgers.
American League Manager of the Year—Sam Mele of the Minnesota Twins.
STANLEY ISAACS

BASKETBALL. An outstanding team—the University of California at Los Angeles (UCLA)—and an outstanding player—Bill Bradley—dominated college basketball in the 1964-1965 season.

UCLA, coached by John Wooden and led by All American Gail Goodrich, became the fifth team in the tournament's history to win successive National Collegiate Athletic Association (NCAA) championships. The UCLA team won the title by whipping through Brigham Young, San Francisco, and Wichita State, before beating Michigan, 91-80, in the final game at Portland, Ore.

Bradley carried a lightly regarded Princeton team from the Ivy League championship to a third-place finish at Portland, and scored a tournament record 58 points in the consolation game against Wichita,

---

1965 College All-American Team
(Source: NCAA consensus All-American)

Players	School
Gail Goodrich	UCLA
Bill Bradley	Princeton
Fred Hetzel	Davidson
Rick Barry	Miami
Cazzie Russell	Michigan

---

which Princeton won, 118-82. Regarded by some as the best college player of all time, Bradley forsook a handsome professional basketball offer from the New York Knickerbockers to become a Rhodes scholar at Oxford University in England.

St. John's University, Jamaica, N.Y., came through with a smashing victory for retiring coach Joe Lapchick in his final season by winning the National Invitation Tournament (NIT). Lapchick thus became the first coach to win four NIT titles. Evansville went undefeated in 29 games and won its second straight NCAA small-college title with an 85-82 victory over Southern Illinois.

The Armed Forces All-Stars won the men's Amateur Athletic Union (AAU) title, and Nashville Business College won the women's title for the fourth straight year.

Professional. The Boston Celtics continued as sport's greatest dynasty by winning their seventh straight National Basketball Association (NBA) championship. The Celtics survived a last-minute scare to beat the Wilt Chamberlain-led Philadelphia 76ers, 110-109, in the seventh game of the Eastern Division play-offs, and then scored a five-game triumph over the western champions, the Los Angeles Lakers.

Bill Russell of the Celtics won the league's most valuable player award for the fourth time in five years. Chamberlain, who was traded to Philadelphia from San Francisco in midseason, won his sixth straight scoring title, and Willis Reed of the New York Knickerbockers was awarded the rookie-of-the year honors.
STANLEY ISAACS

BASUTOLAND

BASUTOLAND held its first general election on April 29, 1965, and became self-governing the following day. The country's new constitution, drawn up in London in May, 1964, provides for complete independence a year after the elections.

The general election gave the right-wing Basutoland National party 31 of the 60 contested seats in the national assembly. The Basutoland Congress party won 25 seats, and the remaining four went to the Marematlou Freedom party. Later in the year, however, two court decisions unseated several members of the National party and left it without a majority in the assembly. The National party chose Paramount Chief Sekhonyana Maseribane to serve as an interim prime minister following the defeat of its leader, Chief Leabua Jonathan, in the general election. In early July, Jonathan won a by-election and replaced Maseribane.

Chief Jonathan declared that Basutoland would continue to give refuge to political exiles from South Africa so long as they did not meddle in Basutoland's politics or use Basutoland as a base for their activities.

Population: 746,000. **Government:** Paramount Chief Motlotlehi Moshoeshoe II; Prime Minister Leabua Jonathan. **Monetary Unit:** Somali shilling (20 = U.S. $2.80). **Foreign Trade:** exports, $707,148; imports, $1,508,579. **Principal Exports:** maize, mohair, peas and beans, wool.   BENJAMIN E. THOMAS

See also AFRICA.

Wide World

CABINET CRISIS in Belgium ended in July when Pierre Harmel, who had been named prime minister, formed a coalition government.

BELGIUM changed leaders in 1965. In a general election held May 23, the coalition government of Prime Minister Théodore Lefèvre failed to capture a two-thirds majority of seats in the chamber of representatives. As a result, Lefèvre resigned and a new coalition cabinet, headed by Prime Minister Pierre Harmel, was sworn in on July 28 (see HARMEL, PIERRE). Foreign Minister Paul-Henri Spaak continued in his post. The defeat of the Lefèvre government was generally attributed to popular dissatisfaction with Belgium's linguistic law, passed in 1964, which made Flemish the official language in the northern part of the country and French the official language in the south.

Financial Differences between Belgium and its former colony, Congo (Léopoldville), were settled in talks held in Brussels early in February between Congolese Premier Moise Tshombe and Foreign Minister Spaak. Under terms of the agreement, Belgium turned over to Congo about $300,000,000 in securities that had been held by the Brussels government in private firms operating in Congo. Control of the huge Union Minière du Haut-Katanga and other mining assets was also turned over to Congo. See CONGO (LÉOPOLDVILLE).

Foreign Investments continued to play an important role in the nation's economy. In September, the U.S.-owned Caterpillar Tractor Company announced plans to build an $80,000,000 factory in southern Belgium. The General Motors Corporation went ahead with its plans to build a $100,000,000 plant near Antwerp.

Meanwhile, the Ford Motor Company announced plans for a $120,000,000 expansion program to increase its production facilities in northern Belgium. Altogether, according to an official survey, foreign holdings in Belgium totaled about $700,000,000 at the end of 1964.

With industrial output on the upswing, exports soared, particularly to the Federal Republic of Germany, where they were up 35 per cent over the first quarter of 1964. Rising retail prices and labor costs, however, neutralized the upswing.

Other Developments. The 150th anniversary of the Battle of Waterloo was the cause of some friction with neighboring France in June. French President Charles de Gaulle boycotted the celebrations, which were held near Brussels, because, it was said, he disliked being reminded of past defeats.

In November, Belgium mourned the death of dowager Queen Elisabeth. She was one of Europe's leading art patrons (see DEATHS OF NOTABLE PERSONS).

Population: 9,382,000. **Government:** King Baudouin I; Prime Minister Pierre Harmel. **Monetary Unit:** Belgian franc (49.65 = U.S. $1). **Gross National Product:** BF 672,000,000,000. **Foreign Trade:** exports, $5,590,000,000; imports, $5,901,000,000. **Principal Exports:** industrial machinery, iron and steel, textiles.   KENNETH BROWN

See also EUROPE.

BELLOW, SAUL (1915-   ), was awarded two distinguished literary prizes for his novel *Herzog*. He is, perhaps, the most outstanding American fiction writer of today. Bellow is the first American to receive the Prix International de Littérature, a $10,-000 annual prize awarded "to a living author of world stature." *Herzog* also won for its author the National Book fiction award in 1965. *The Adventures of Augie March* won the same award for him in 1954. See AWARDS AND PRIZES (General Awards).

Other fields in which Bellow is represented are short stories and essays. His play, *The Last Analysis*, about an aging comedian, had a 28-performance run at New York's Belasco Theater in 1964. *Seize the Day* (1956) is a collection of three short stories, a play, and a short novel. His first book, *Dangling Man* (1944), was followed by *The Victim* (1947). *Henderson, the Rain King* (1959), is a comic tale of a wealthy American on an African venture.

Saul Bellow comes from a Jewish family, which emigrated from Russia to Canada. He was born in Lachine, Quebec, July 10, 1915, and lived in Montreal until the family moved to Chicago in 1924. Bellow was graduated at Northwestern University (1937) with honors in anthropology and sociology. While establishing himself as a writer, Bellow taught at Pestalozzi-Froebel Teachers College, Minnesota and Princeton universities, and Bard College. He is now a University of Chicago professor.

BERRYMAN, JOHN (1914-   ), University of Minnesota Humanities Professor, was awarded the Pulitzer poetry prize in 1965 for *77 Dream Songs*. The collection of poems received enthusiastic reviews the year before. Berryman described the volume as part of a projected work, *The Dream Songs*. Fifteen "Dream Songs" appeared in *Ramparts* and won the magazine's highest award in 1963.

Over the past several years, Berryman has been a force in American poetry. He is truly original, sometimes difficult to follow, and has rare sensibility. His work is fascinating, moving, and often eloquent. Certain of his poems have been compared to Chinese paintings. Berryman is also a literary critic, has written short stories, and edited *Selected Poems of Ezra Pound*. *The Dispossessed* (1948) was his first book of poems. *Stephen Crane* (1950) is a critical biography of the author of *Red Badge of Courage*. *Homage to Mistress Bradstreet* (1956) is a long and powerful poem about Anne Dudley Bradstreet, America's first woman poet and wife of the Massachusetts Bay Colony governor.

John Berryman was born in McAlester, Okla., of Northern and Southern stock. He is a Columbia University graduate (1936), and has a degree from England's Cambridge University. He has received Rockefeller, Hodder, and Guggenheim fellowships, and taught at Harvard, Princeton, Cincinnati, Brown, and other universities.

See also PULITZER PRIZES.

BIOCHEMISTRY. For the first time, scientists worked out the exact structure of a *nucleic acid molecule*, one of the constituents of a cell that helps determine the development of its form and function. The accomplishment was hailed as a giant step in the struggle to understand the machinery of life. It was made possible through the work of Professor Robert W. Holley and his associates at Cornell University.

The nucleic acid they decoded is called "alanine transfer-RNA," and transfers an amino acid from one part of the cell to another. The team extracted and purified the nucleic acids for their study from cells of bakers' yeast. They used specific enzymes to rupture the RNA chains, which make up the nucleic acids, and then analyzed the fragments. After long and painstaking work, they found that it was possible to determine the specific sequence of nucleotide bases in this particular RNA. A similar approach had been employed 15 years ago by the Nobel laureate, Frederick Sanger, to determine the amino acid sequence in the protein insulin.

Synthesis of a Nucleic Acid. The first test tube synthesis of a substance that can replicate itself was accomplished by Professor Sol Spiegelman and his associates at the University of Illinois. The genetic molecule they synthesized was RNA, obtained originally from a virus called Q-beta.

A major obstacle to this development had been the inability to obtain a pure enzyme, free of other substances, particularly enzymes that carry out a series of related processes. Spiegelman and his co-workers succeeded in isolating such an enzyme, appropriately named *replicase*, which they obtained from cells infected with the Q-beta virus. The enzyme is not present in noninfected cells. The purified enzyme, with no additions other than the nucleotide building blocks of RNA, magnesium salts, and a bit of Q-beta replicase to act as a template, generated identical copies of Q-beta RNA.

The stage has now been set to examine details of the genetic copying process. It has been shown that the enzyme is quite specific and will not use fragmented or foreign RNA as templates.

Chemistry and Learning. It is well known that the ability of animals to learn can be altered by chemical means. One approach to understanding this process comes from the laboratory of Professor Bernard W. Agranoff at the University of Michigan. He trained goldfish to avoid an electric shock. When puromycin, an antibiotic substance which inhibits protein synthesis, was injected into the goldfish, the trained fish no longer avoided the electric shock.

Learning experiments in man indicate that there is short-term as well as long-term memory. In the studies with goldfish, puromycin interfered with the formation of long-term memory but did not affect their short-term memory.

Other laboratory observations involving rats and other animals agree that memory may be coded in the molecular structure of RNA (see PSYCHOLOGY). The experiments with puromycin, on the other hand, would suggest that the memory coding takes place by altering protein structure. It is possible that alterations in both RNA and in protein occur. Though much controversy exists in this area, it is conceivable that some of the memory and learning processes will soon be described on a chemical basis.

Growth Hormones. Little is known about the control of cell functions by large protein hormones, such as insulin or growth hormones, except that the cell is able to "recognize" the hormone. While insulin derived from cows is effective in the treatment of human diabetes, a growth hormone from the same animal is useless in the treatment of human dwarfism. The only source of growth hormone at present is human pituitary glands, and the amounts obtained from this source are inadequate relative to the needs.

The similarity of the structure of insulin from cows to that of insulin from human beings may explain its effectiveness in the treatment of human diseases. The bovine form of growth hormones, on the other hand, is a much larger molecule than the human form of growth hormones. Research at the Sloan-Kettering Institute in New York City had been directed toward the breaking of the bovine hormone into smaller fragments by using the enzyme *trypsin*. Fragments thus obtained have been used successfully to treat human dwarfism. It is plausible that one of these large fragments may have the same amino acid sequence as does the human hormone, which would explain why it has succeeded in therapy for human beings.

Origin of Life. Scientists believe that the earth's atmosphere before the advent of life consisted of hydrogen, water vapor, and ammonia. Energy from the sun, in the form of heat and ultraviolet light, and electrical energy in the form of lightning, acted on this atmosphere to produce organic chemicals which became building blocks for living matter. A number of years ago, amino acids were formed in the laboratory under conditions simulating this primordial environment. The formation of the much more complicated nucleic acid bases as well as the linking together of these molecules has been reported by Cyril Ponnamperuma, who directs the program in chemical evolution at the Exobiology Division of the National Aeronautics and Space Administration at the Ames Research Center in California. All five of the fundamental units of the nucleic acids have been produced from simpler subunits and these were demonstrated to arise from the simplest simulated primordial system.

Ponnamperuma has also shown that two subunits of nucleic acid will form and join under fairly simple conditions, and has suggested that the first nucleic acid chain originated in this manner. HAROLD FEINBERG

See also BIOLOGY; BOTANY; CHEMISTRY; MEDICINE; PSYCHOLOGY.

BIOLOGY. Clues to the origin and development of life on this planet have been found in ancient rocks that contain substances that were trapped during the early periods of the earth's history. Nobel prize winner Melvin Calvin reported in 1965 that he and a team of researchers from the University of California, Berkeley, had found phytane and pristane embedded in shale from the Soudan iron formation in Minnesota. Both substances are carbon-hydrogen compounds, and could only have been produced by living creatures.

The shale from this site is considered to be at least 2,500,000,000 years old, so that the finding pushes back previous estimates of the age of life on earth by a full 800,000,000 years. Calvin suggests that the two substances were synthesized by chlorophyll-containing plants. Since the green plant is a relatively high form of life, there must have been living things long before those that produced the phytane and pristane.

Life in Outer Space? Another source of information about life's origin, not only on earth but elsewhere in the universe, may be found through analysis of meteorites. At the Enrico Fermi Institute of the University of Chicago, Ryoichi Hayatsu and his co-workers extracted adenine and guanine from such objects. These amino acids are constituents of DNA, the genetic molecules basic to living things. Hayatsu is of the opinion, however, that such organic substances in meteorites—as well as those found in ancient rocks—reflect a random distribution of material throughout the solar system rather than the residue of living forms.

Nitrogen Fixation. Living organisms that take nitrogen from the atmosphere and use it in the production of protein, a process called nitrogen fixation, accomplish something that chemists are unable to duplicate under conditions of normal temperature and pressure. Two enzyme systems of the organisms are essential in this process. The first, hydrogenase, changes hydrogen ions into molecular hydrogen. This enzyme reaction could not take place without an electron carrier called ferrodoxin. The second enzyme system, nitrogenase, transfers molecular hydrogen to nitrogen, thus forming ammonia.

Many of these same microorganisms are also capable of photosynthesis, the process by which plants produce carbohydrates. Scientists seeking a link between photosynthesis and nitrogen fixation have noted that both make use of ferrodoxin. The findings are of important interest in that the same electron carrier participates in the two fundamental processes involving the incorporation of atmospheric gases into organic substances. They have now discovered that blue-green algae, capable of photosynthesis, also efficiently fix nitrogen. Thus it is possible that this abundant life-form may be an important source of protein.

Cell Division. The development of plants and animals from a single seed, or fertilized egg, is a subject of unceasing interest to biologists. Recently, scientists at the Rockefeller Institute studied this development in the eggs of certain snails, which are tri-lobed for a short period before they divide into two cells. The scientists found that they could remove a single lobe of these embryos without interfering with the cell nucleus. However, after the embryonic development was complete, the snails lacked certain tissues. The results were interpreted as evidence that various regions of the cell contribute genetic information to the developing organism.

Homing Salmon. The ability of spawning salmon to search out their home waters after years in the open sea has long aroused the curiosity of biologists. Experiments measuring the electrical activity of the salmon brain have provided evidence that salmon derive their homing capability from an extremely keen sense of smell.

Intense electrical activity in the olfactory lobe was recorded when adult salmon were exposed to water taken from their hatching sites. Thus it appears that salmon find their homeward migration path by their ability to sense the odor of highly diluted samples of home waters found downstream. Nonmigratory fish in the same locale were also tested, but did not respond to the odor of the waters with the same intensity.   HAROLD FEINBERG

See also BIOCHEMISTRY; BOTANY; INSECT.

BIRCH, JOHN, SOCIETY. See JOHN BIRCH SOCIETY.

BLINDNESS. The lack of accurate estimates of the world's blind population was stressed in the publications of the National Institute of Neurological Diseases and Blindness and of the American Association of Workers for the Blind during 1965. Estimates ranged from between 10,000,000 and 15,000,000, the wide variance being attributed to the fact that blindness is defined differently in various countries.

The concept of total rehabilitation of the blind adult, including independent travel, continued to gain wide acceptance. A greater number of vocations were opened to blind persons and emphasis in rehabilitation was placed on competition in open industry rather than in sheltered workshops.

Education. The process of integrated education, in which the blind child is taught in public schools alongside sighted children, continued to accelerate, especially in the underdeveloped areas of the world. It has been shown that the system can be introduced at much less cost than separate schooling programs, and it often has been shown to result in a much better social and psychological climate for the blind child.

According to the American Printing House for the Blind, 10,381 blind children in the United States attended ordinary local public schools, compared with 8,035 in special residential schools, in 1965.

International Programs. The World Health Organization (WHO), the World Council for the Welfare of the Blind, and the International Society for the Prevention of Blindness conducted co-operative programs to control the major blinding diseases and to greatly widen the availability of ophthalmic services.

The U.S. Vocational Rehabilitation Administration, in cooperation with the Indian government, conducted an experiment in industrial training in Bombay and in other cities for placement of blind persons in competitive employment. Similar work was carried on in Israel, where blind persons were trained to work in cotton mills and to operate data processing machines. Model rehabilitation centers designed to teach handicrafts and farming methods were also established by the U.S. Vocational Rehabilitation Administration in India and Syria. Similar facilities have been established in Ghana, Guatemala, Tanzania, Thailand, and Uganda by other global organizations, such as the American Foundation for Overseas Blind and the Royal Commonwealth Society for the Blind.

Braille. The availability of literature for blind people was greatly enlarged through the establishment of braille printing plants throughout the world and through the standardization by the World Braille Council of a system for adapting braille to all languages. Countries of Western Europe are now recording and duplicating books on tape, and the practice is gradually spreading to other sections of the world.   DOUGLAS C. MACFARLAND

BOATS AND BOATING enjoyed another growth year, both as an industry and as a sport. Retail sales rose an estimated 3 per cent, and sales at the New York City National Motor Boat Show hit a new record despite a decline in attendance.

By the year's end, the industry's trade associations estimated that 39,325,000 people had participated in recreational boating at least once in 1965. A total of 7,860,000 boats of all sizes and shapes were being used for recreation.

The great horsepower race in outboard motors continued. Kiekhaefer Corporation broke the 100-horsepower (hp) barrier with a new 110-hp model, the most powerful ever built. Although relatively new to the outboard field, Chrysler shortly thereafter announced a 105-hp motor, and Evinrude and Johnson each produced their most powerful engines yet, rated at 100 hp.

Kiekhaefer also took a lead in the growing inboard-outboard field by introducing a 60-hp stern drive unit, the smallest yet made.

Inventions. New ideas and products included:

A *hydrofoil kit*, suitable for installation on most conventional outboard hulls. For a cost of $450, including installation, the foils allow the boat's hull to cruise a foot out of the water, increasing speed 40 per cent while cutting fuel consumption by a similar amount.

A *one-man submarine*, made in Germany. Named the Porpoise, it is 10 feet 2 inches long; weighs

Pictorial Parade

TRIUMPH for sailor Bob Manry, who crossed the Atlantic Ocean in 79 days from Falmouth, Mass., to Falmouth, Cornwall, in his 13½-foot sailboat, the Tinkerbelle.

1,389 pounds; descends to 164 feet; and stays under water up to four hours. It costs about $3,900.

A communications system for skin divers, called the "Yack-Yack." This features a lightweight face mask with microphone and a special sound diffuser to eliminate bubble sounds. With its battery, amplifier, and speaker, the Yack-Yack amplifies the voice so that it can be heard by a diver 50 feet away.

Hydro-karting, a new form of boat racing using one-man sledlike boards propelled by tiny gasoline engines. The karts, averaging only eight feet long, reach speeds as high as 50 miles per hour. They provide the thrills of racing at a cost of $200 or less.

Legislation. The National Association of State Boating Law Administrators proposed two law revisions. They would have the effect of requiring state registration of all motorboats, including those under 10 hp, which are now exempted by the Federal Boating Act of 1958.

Sailing. William Snaith's *Figaro IV* won the Southern Ocean Racing Conference series, with victories in the Nassau Cup race and the 403-mile St. Petersburg-to-Fort Lauderdale race. The Northern Ocean Racing competition went for the second time to Sumner Long's *Ondine,* which also won the 1,300-mile Buenos Aires-to-Rio de Janeiro sail.

Ticonderoga, the 72-foot ketch skippered by Robert Johnson of Portland, Ore., beat *Ondine* by less than two hours in the 844-mile Miami-to-Montego Bay race and also finished first in the Transpacific Yacht Race, though the winner on corrected time was Don Salisbury's *Psyche.*

On the Great Lakes, Bill and Ted Schoendorf's 56-foot cutter *Blitzen* swept the Chicago-to-Mackinac race, and *Gypsy,* the 54-foot sloop skippered by Charles Kotovic of Milwaukee, won the 235-mile Port Huron-to-Mackinac race for the third time.

Donald Bever of Vermilion, Ohio, won the world star class title. The Mallory Cup for the men's national sailing championship was won by Cornelius Shields, Jr. The Adams Cup for women went to Mrs. Timothea (Schneider) Larr of Oyster Bay, N.Y. The Sears Cup for juniors was successfully defended by Robert Doyle of Marblehead, Mass., and Colin Park of Vancouver, B.C., took the O'Day Trophy for the North American single-handed title.

The University of Rhode Island beat out San Diego State for the North American collegiate championship.

Motor Racing. In unlimited hydroplane racing, the season featured nine races with prize money reaching $275,000, the highest ever. Ron Musson, driving *Miss Bardahl,* won the driving championship for the third straight year. Musson also won the prestigious Gold Cup race for the third year in a row. Then, for the first time, a "world championship" regatta was held for 180-mile-an-hour hydroplanes. The championship, and first-place money of $36,050, went to—who else?—Ron Musson in *Miss Bardahl.* James O. Dunaway

BOLIVIA found its government pitted against tin miners in a year-long battle to put the all-important mines on a paying basis. On May 17, the government declared a state of siege following an uprising by the miners over the banishment of Juan Lechin Oquendo, a major leftist union leader.

A state of siege was again declared on September 20 when the tin miners went on strike over a pay dispute. The government held fast. It exiled communist and leftist union bosses, reduced the wages of many miners, and abolished bonuses.

The government, determined to disarm the miners and end their role as a major political force, offered to increase wages in return for a pledge of normal operations. These efforts resulted in foreign loans for the rehabilitation of the mines.

General Alfred Obando Candia, commander in chief of the armed forces, was installed as co-president on May 26, assuming authority equal to that of junta chief René Barrientos Ortuño.

Population: 4,188,000. **Government:** Co-Presidents General René Barrientos Ortuño; General Alfred Obando Candia. **Monetary Unit:** peso (11.88 = U.S. $1). **Foreign Trade:** exports, $86,000,000; imports, $97,000,000. **Principal Exports:** lead, silver, tin.   MARY C. WEBSTER

See also LATIN AMERICA.

BOOKS. See CANADIAN LITERATURE; LITERATURE; LITERATURE FOR CHILDREN.

BOSTOCK, HUGH SAMUEL (1901-   ), a member of the Geological Survey of Canada for some 40 years, was awarded the Massey medal in 1965. The Royal Canadian Geographical Society cited him for contributions to the knowledge of the Western Cordillera and the Yukon Territory. Bostock's field work as head of the survey's Yukon section (1931-1949) has made him the greatest living authority on that vast, rugged country. He has been head of the Geological Survey Cordillera (British Columbia and Yukon) section since 1949. His fields of investigations include archaeology, geology, and historical geography.

During his early years with the Survey, Bostock made the first topographical maps of British Columbia's Chilcotin country. He did glaciological and physiographical studies along with geological mapping in the province. His "Physiography of the Northern Cordillera" added greatly to the geographical knowledge of the region and the headwaters of its rivers. His reports on the archaeological riches, mineral resources, and economic potential of the Yukon are invaluable. He is now preparing a glacial geology map of the Yukon.

Hugh Bostock trained as a mining engineer and geologist. He is a Royal Military College graduate (1922), and received B.Sc. (1924) and M.Sc. (1925) degrees at McGill University, and his Ph.D. in geology at the University of Wisconsin (1929). Bostock was born in Vancouver, British Columbia.

BOSTON will build an all-weather stadium as part of an $80,000,000 sports center in the city's South Station area. The stadium will have a retractable roof 720 feet in diameter that will protect 45,000 fans for baseball and 55,000 for football games. The center will also contain an 18,000-seat arena for hockey, basketball, and other entertainments.

Continuing a hectic pace in urban renewal, the city's Redevelopment Authority announced in July, 1965, a six-to-10-year plan for 31 acres adjacent to Prudential Center in the Back Bay area. Nearly half the site will become a church center for the sponsor of the $71,000,000 plan, the First Church of Christ, Scientist. The remaining 16 acres, will be leased by the church to private developers.

Government Center's first building, a 22-story state office tower, opened its doors to 3,500 employees in November. The first segment of One Center Plaza, a privately financed office building in Government Center, was to open in December.

Controversial new state legislation calling for an end to racial imbalance in public schools became a hot local issue. In November, Mrs. Louise Day Hicks won a smashing re-election as chairman of the Boston School Committee, the policy-making body. Opposed to busing students to attain racial balance, Mrs. Hicks became a strong contender for the 1967 mayoral campaign.   DONALD W. LIEF

See also Section Two, THE NEW NEW ENGLAND.

BOTANY. Scientists learned new facts about the complex process by which plants take nitrogen from the air and change it into valuable protein. In terms of man's food supply, the process is second in importance only to photosynthesis, whereby plants manufacture carbohydrates. Dr. Robert H. Burris of the University of Wisconsin reported that he and other researchers have isolated an enzyme, or chemical helper, which plays a key role in this process. The process is known as nitrogen fixation. See BIOCHEMISTRY.

Scientists believe that the enzyme binds nitrogen atoms to its surface while the nitrogen reacts to form ammonia—the first step in a long chain of reactions leading to the production of protein. Later steps in the cycle have been better understood than this first ammonia-forming step. Nearly 5,500,000 tons of nitrogen are converted each year by this nitrogen-fixation process of plants in the United States alone. The plants with this special ability are the legumes, the second largest group of flowering plants.

Fruit Ripening is known to be caused by a volatile hydrocarbon chemical called ethylene. Found in fruit tissue, the chemical acts as a hormone to stimulate ripening and make apples turn red and bananas turn yellow. Recent studies by Stanley P. Burg and Ellen A. Burg at the University of Miami (Fla.) School of Medicine have now shown that the ripening action of ethylene in fruit is greater after the fruit has been picked. According to the Burgs, this may be because a substance from the living plant inhibits ethylene's ripening action prior to harvest.

Barriers of fire-resistant plants are being seeded on the hills near Los Angeles, Calif., in an attempt to stop the brush fires that cause significant property damage each year. According to Dr. Robert Gonderman of the Los Angeles State and County Arboretum and head of the project, such fire-resistant plants do not carry a flame, but just blacken and curl up when exposed to fire.

Besides being flame-resistant, the plants must also be able to compete with natural vegetation, resist drought, and provide food for native wildlife. Included in the flameless group are Arabian scurf pea, coast saltbrush, creeping rosemary, ivy, sun rose, and yerba santa. Researchers also hope to find nonflammable plants for use in mountain areas.

Medicinal Greenhouse. A $285,000 climate-controlled greenhouse for investigating plants as potential sources of drugs was opened this year near Chicago. The new medicinal plant research station is operated by the departments of pharmacognosy and pharmacology of the University of Illinois. (Pharmacognosy is the study of the source of drugs.) Of approximately 350,000 plant species known, only about 20,000 have been screened as potential sources of drugs, according to Dr. Ralph F. Voigt, director of the station.   SERGEI LENORMAND

See also GARDEN AND LAWN.

BOUMEDIENNE, HOUARI

BOUMEDIENNE, HOUARI (1925-   ), an army colonel, seized power as Algeria's chief of state on June 19, 1965. In command of about 1,000 troops, he took over government offices in Algiers and ousted Ahmed Ben Bella, who was president of Algeria since 1962.

Boumedienne had been a trusted follower of Ben Bella for 13 years. During the Algerian struggle for independence from France, Boumedienne trained troops in Tunisia and Morocco. He returned to Algeria in 1957 to command rebel forces. The following year, he was named the new nation's defense minister and first vice-president. By early 1965, however, Boumedienne had joined the steadily growing opposition to Ben Bella's rule.

Boumedienne was born to an impoverished peasant family at Guelma in northeastern Algeria. His original name was MOHAMMED BOUKHAROUBA; the name, "Boumedienne" was adopted as an alias during the war against France. Most of his education was at Islamic schools, including Al-Azhar University at Cairo, Egypt, where he first met Ben Bella.

A slim, sharp-featured man of seemingly inexhaustible energy, Boumedienne, unlike most of his compatriots, has reddish-brown hair and green eyes. His appearance brought him the nickname: "The Swede." Boumedienne is considered more of a doer than he is a speechmaker.   WALTER F. MORSE

See also ALGERIA.

BOWLING. Dick Weber of St. Louis won his third All-Star championship, beating Jim St. John of Santa Clara, Calif., in the final three-game series. The women's championship went to Ann Slattery of Salt Lake City, who defeated Sandy Hooper of Anaheim, Calif. It was her first major title.

The American Bowling Congress (ABC) tournament at St. Paul closed after 68 days of competition among more than 28,500 men, with Tom Hathaaway of Los Angeles the all-events winner. Ken Roeth of Detroit won the singles title, and Dan Slak and Buz Bosler of Milwaukee won the doubles title.

Billy Welu of St. Louis successfully defended his ABC Masters title by beating Don Ellis of Houston in the final. The $25,000 first prize of the Firestone Tournament went to Billy Hardwick of San Mateo, Calif. In winning the tournament, Hardwick beat Weber and Joe Joseph of Lansing, Mich.

The Woman's International Bowling Congress (WIBC) tournament ended with Doris Rudell of Whittier, Calif., the singles winner. The event lasted 42 days and included more than 20,000 contestants. Donna Zimmerman of Norwalk, Conn., was the all-events titlist, and Betty Remmick and Mary Ann White, both of Denver, Colo., were the winners of the doubles championship.

Alfonso Martini of Milan, Italy, won the title in the first Round-the-World bowling tournament held in Flushing, N.Y., in July.   STANLEY ISAACS

BOXING. Controversy raged over heavyweight champion Muhammad Ali's behavior both in and out of the ring. Ali, who was born Cassius Marcellus Clay, successfully defended his title twice, even though he had been stripped of the title in 1964 by the World Boxing Association (WBA). Despite both victories, the 22-year-old champion remained unpopular with many boxing fans because of his tactics in the ring and his espousal of the Black Muslim sect. See Section Two, RED SMITH ON SPORTS.

In May, at Lewiston, Me., Ali knocked out Sonny Liston in the first round with one punch. In November, at Las Vegas, Nev., a flamboyant and taunting Ali jabbed and hooked Floyd Patterson almost at will before the fight was stopped in the 12th round.

In the Patterson fight, Ali knocked his opponent down in the sixth round, but was unwilling or unable to floor him after that. Critics accused Ali of carrying the fight in order to punish Patterson. Ali, however, contended he was unable to deliver the knockout punch because he had hurt his hand late in the fight.

Ernie Terrell of Houston, Tex., defended his WBA version of the heavyweight title in February, in New York, by beating George Chuvalo of Toronto. Terrell looked forward to a bout with Ali, whom most people recognized as the champion even though the WBA did not.

New Champions. Five championships changed hands. Jose Torres of New York won the light-

PICTURES OF THE YEAR/John Rooney, Wide World

GET UP! *Heavyweight champion Cassius Clay stands over fallen challenger Sonny Liston shouting and gesturing after he knocked him down at Lewiston, Me.*

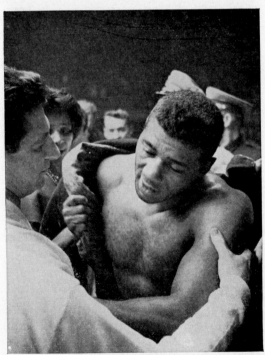

United Press Int.

BIG BACKACHE. *Trainer Al Silvani assists Floyd Patterson, suffering from a back ailment, to corner after final round of Las Vegas fight.*

heavyweight title at New York in March by scoring a nine-round technical knockout over Willie Pastrano. Dick Tiger of Nigeria and New York regained the middleweight crown he had lost to Joey Giardello in 1963 with an easy 15-round decision over Giardello at New York in October. Eder Joffre's

WORLD CHAMPION BOXERS

Division	Champion	Where Fought	Year Won
Heavyweight	Muhammad Ali	Miami	1964
Light-Heavyweight	Jose Torres	New York	1965
Middleweight	Dick Tiger	New York	1965
Welterweight	Emile Griffith	New York	1962
Lightweight	Carlos Ortiz	San Juan	1965
Featherweight	Vincente Saldivar	Mexico City	1964
Bantamweight	Masahiko Harada	Japan	1965
Flyweight	Salvatore Burruni	Rome	1965

five-year reign as bantamweight champion came to an end with a 15-round loss to Masahiko (Fighting) Harada of Japan in a match at Nagoya, Japan, in May. Salvatore Burruni of Italy, who had a victory record of 56 straight bouts, won the flyweight title at Rome in April, with a 15-round decision over Pone Kingpetch of Thailand.

Carlos Ortiz at 29, lost and regained the lightweight title. He dropped a 15-round decision to 22-year-old Panamanian Ismael Laguna at Panamá in April, then won a 15-round decision over Laguna at San Juan, Puerto Rico, in November. STANLEY ISAACS

257

BOY SCOUTS OF AMERICA began an expansion program in 1965 under the slogan "Breakthrough for Youth." Specially trained Scout leaders were sent to selected areas to work with local Scout councils in developing ways to attract more boys to Scouting. A highlight was a cooperative arrangement with the Public Housing Administration (PHA) to intensify Boy Scout programs in 3,700 public housing projects throughout the country. The expansion program also included efforts to interest corporations and labor unions in sponsoring troops.

The Farragut Wildlife Area, Idaho, was selected as the site for the 12th World Scout Jamboree to be held during the week of August 1, 1967. This will be the first of the quadrennial World Jamborees ever held in the United States. The Boy Scouts of America will be host to an expected 17,000 Scouts representing nearly 100 countries.

Silver Buffalo awards for distinguished service to boyhood were presented to Irving Ben Cooper; Austin T. Cushman; Harry J. Delaney; Royal Firman, Jr.; John H. Glenn, Jr.; Harry J. Johnson; Harry G. McGavran; David Sarnoff; Jo S. Strong; and Gustavo J. Vollmer.

Delegates to the annual meeting, held in May at Miami Beach, Fla., approved new merit badges for space exploration and communications. They also re-elected Thomas A. Watson, Jr., president of the National Council.   Joseph P. Anderson

BOYS' CLUBS OF AMERICA established the Herbert Hoover Memorial Award to honor the memory of the former President, who served as the organization's chairman of the board for 27 years. The award, a gold medallion, will be presented each year "to the man who has done the most for underprivileged youth." President Lyndon B. Johnson was the first to receive the award. The presentation was made at the White House on April 21 by Edwin Bassemier, 17, of Evansville, Ind., who had been named the 1965 "Boy of the Year."

Representatives of Boys' Clubs in Great Britain concluded plans with representatives of clubs in the United States for an exchange program to begin in the spring of 1966. Workers from England's National Association of Boys' Clubs will spend three months working with selected units of Boys' Clubs of America. An equal number of U.S. workers will spend three months in England. The program will enable the workers to share common concerns and program techniques.

Boys' Clubs in both countries were experimenting with programs designed to reach groups of boys designated as the hard-to-serve and the hard-to-reach. The first group is composed of boys who have joined a club but are then unable or unwilling to participate in program activities. The second group is made up of boys who cause concern and disturbance in the community but do not join any Boys' Club.   Joseph P. Anderson

BRAZIL was widely praised abroad for the efforts it made in 1965 to improve its economy. It was successful, for the most part, in moderating an inflationary spiral. It was also able to set its economy on a solid foundation and thus form a basis for economic growth and social progress.

At home, however, criticism of the administration of President Humberto de Alencar Castelo Branco was at times bitter. This was due largely to the government's fiscal and monetary reforms and its austerity and stabilization programs. Credit was tightened, wages frozen, and price ceilings placed on many farm and manufactured products. Brazil was thus able to hold the cost-of-living increase to 39.2 per cent for the first nine months of 1965 versus 59.6 per cent in the same period for 1964.

Economic Action. A major effort was made to keep wage increases in private enterprises below the rise in living costs. Government officials also decreed that there would be no wage increases in 1965 for 500,000 civil servants and members of the armed forces. To spur the economy, the petrochemical fields and Brazil's vast petroleum-bearing shale deposits were opened to development by private investors.

Incentives, such as improved profit remittances and guaranteed convertibility of monies entering the republic were also introduced to encourage foreign investment. Brazil re-established its international credit standing by renegotiating its heavy short-term debt and improving its monetary reserve position to about $470,000,000 by the end of September, 1965.

Political Defeat. Although the administration scored important economic successes, they were achieved via admittedly unpopular measures. This was reflected in the gubernatorial elections held on October 3, which saw parties opposed to the government sweep 10 of the 11 races. The results were a clear indication that the government had failed to establish a broad popular base.

Two antigovernment groups—the Social Democratic party of former President Juscillino Kubitschek and the Brazilian Labor party of ousted President João Goulart—scored impressive victories at the polls. The military, fearing a return to left of center political thinking, forced the government to take action. On October 27, President Castelo Branco suspended constitutional guarantees, dissolved all political parties, and gave his administration broad powers to rule by decree. On November 21, however, the president issued a decree permitting a limited revival of political organizations.

Population: 82,696,000. **Government:** President Humberto de Alencar Castelo Branco. **Monetary Unit:** cruzeiro (2,200 = U.S. $1). **Gross National Product:** 455,000,000,000 cruzeiros. **Foreign Trade:** exports, $1,433,000,000; imports, $263,000,000. **Principal Exports:** coffee, cotton, ore.   Mary   Webster
See also Latin America.

BRIDGE AND TUNNEL.

BRIDGE AND TUNNEL. Following completion of cable spinning for Portugal's great new bridge over the Tejo (Tagus) River at Lisbon, work began on the deck that will carry highway and, later, rail traffic between the northern and southern parts of the country. The bridge, when completed in 1966, will have the longest suspension span (3,323 feet) outside the United States.

Opening of Brazil's Friendship Bridge over the Paraná River, on March 27, provided the last link in a 736-mile highway between the Atlantic port of Paranaguá, Brazil, and landlocked Asunción, Paraguay's capital. The 1,812-foot cast-in-place concrete bridge includes a 952-foot clear span.

New U.S. Bridges. Work started early in the year on a new Mississippi River crossing at St. Louis. It will be the nation's first major highway bridge of orthotropic plate design when it is completed in 1967. In an orthotropic bridge, huge steel plates serve both as the roadway deck and the top flange of the main girders. A joint project of the states of Missouri and Illinois, the bridge will feature phenomenal span lengths—up to 600 feet between piers—for a bridge of this type.

Late in the year, the second Cooper River Bridge was completed at Charleston, S.C. It parallels an existing bridge built in 1929. The new $15,000,000 bridge consists of truss and steel girder spans.

New Tunnels. The long-awaited Mont Blanc Tunnel, connecting the Italian village of Entrèves and the French village of Les Pélerins, under the highest peak in the Alps, was officially opened to traffic on July 16. Its 7¼-mile length makes it the longest highway tunnel in the world. Earlier in the year, another Alpine highway tunnel was bored under southern Switzerland's San Bernardino pass. The tunnel was expected to open by 1968.

Construction started in July on the $133,000,000, six-mile underwater transit tunnel to connect San Francisco with Oakland, Calif. It will be the key link in the Bay Area Rapid Transit District's new 75-mile rail system. It will be built by a combination of sunken-tube assembly and tunnel boring.

Late in the year, first contracts were awarded for a nine-mile-long bridge-tunnel crossing the Northumberland Strait between New Brunswick and Prince Edward Island in eastern Canada. Designed for use by both rail and highway traffic, the double-deck toll crossing will include a precast trench-type tunnel and three causeways (see map, *below*).

Swiss-born Othmar H. Ammann, designer of two of the world's "longest" suspension spans, died in New York City at the age of 86. His famous bridges were the George Washington, across the Hudson River; and the Verrazano-Narrows, between Brooklyn, N.Y., and Staten Island.   M. E. JESSUP

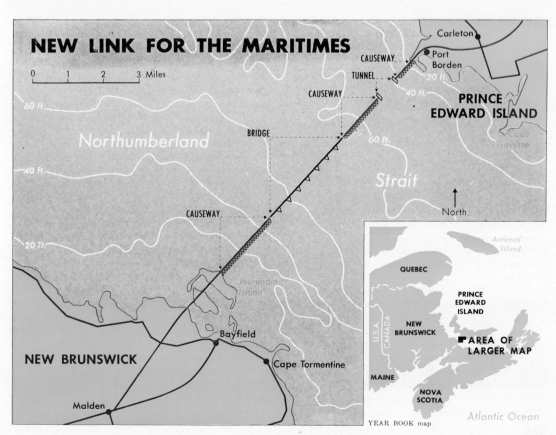

NEW LINK FOR THE MARITIMES

SCANDAL marred the world bridge match when members of the British team
were accused of using finger signals. Two fingers held closely together, left,
allegedly indicated two hearts; figure "V" signal, right, meant five hearts.

BRIDGE, CONTRACT. The international bridge world was rocked by charges of cheating leveled against two members of the British team at the world contract bridge championship at Buenos Aires, Argentina, in May. The two, Terrence Reese and Boris Schapiro, were among the world's leading players. They denied the charges, and the British Bridge League instigated an inquiry. An Italian team won the event.

In one of the most dramatic finishes in the history of the event, a team captained by Oswald Jacoby of Dallas won the Harold S. Vanderbilt Cup at the spring tournament of the American Contract Bridge League (ACBL) at Cleveland. The winning margin was four international match points. Other members of the winning team were Jacoby's son, James Jacoby, and Dr. John Fisher, both of Dallas; Ira Rubin of Fair Lawn, N.J.; Philip Feldesman of Queens Village, N.Y.; and Albert Weiss of Miami Beach, Fla.

At the ACBL summer tournament in Chicago, a team successfully defended its title in the Spingold trophy event for the first time in 30 years. The winners, all from Toronto, Canada, were Eric Murray, Sammy Kehela, Bruce Elliot, and Percy Sheardown. Entries—14,511 tables—made it the biggest in bridge history.   THEODORE M. O'LEARY

BRITISH COMMONWEALTH OF NATIONS. See GREAT BRITAIN; and articles on various countries of the Commonwealth.

BRITISH GUIANA was headed for independence after 162 years of British colonial rule. In mid-November, following 17 days of talks with Guianese leaders in London, British Colonial Secretary Anthony Greenwood announced that the colony would gain its independence on May 26, 1966.

The constitutional conference in London had succeeded largely through the efforts of the Guianese coalition government headed by Forbes Burnham, leader of the Negro-dominated People's National Congress party. Burnham had worked hard to end the internal strife that had erupted all too frequently in the past between Negroes and East Indians. Burnham, working with Peter D'Aguiar, leader of the United Force party, had introduced a budget that would devote $65,900,000 to current spending and development. A series of tax measures promulgated by former premier Cheddi B. Jagan, was swept aside. Meanwhile, Jagan continued to denounce the Burnham regime. His People's Progressive party had boycotted the constitutional conference.

Population: 683,000. **Government:** Governor Sir Richard Luyt; Premier Forbes Burnham. **Monetary Unit:** British Guiana dollar (1.75 = U.S. $1). **Foreign Trade:** exports, $95,000,000; imports, $87,000,000. **Principal Exports:** rice, rum, sugar.   ALASTAIR BURNET
See also GREAT BRITAIN.

BRITISH HONDURAS. See GREAT BRITAIN.
BRITISH WEST INDIES. See JAMAICA; TRINIDAD AND TOBAGO.

BROWN, HAROLD (1927-   ), who had been the Pentagon's top scientist, became Secretary of the Air Force, succeeding Eugene M. Zuckert. The Senate confirmed Brown's appointment on Aug. 6, 1965, shortly after President Lyndon B. Johnson nominated him.

Brown had been director of research and engineering for the Department of Defense since May, 1961. He went to that post from the Lawrence Radiation Laboratory extension at Livermore, Calif. At Livermore, the young scientist succeeded Edward A. Teller as laboratory director.

In addition to being a major contributor to the development of modern atomic weapons, Brown has done considerable work for the Atomic Energy Commission's Project Plowshare, which seeks to apply nuclear explosives to peaceful uses. He was an adviser to the U.S. delegation at the 1958 Geneva (Switzerland) conference on the detection of nuclear weapons tests.

Brown was born in New York City. He was graduated with top scholastic honors from the Bronx (N.Y.) High School of Science at the age of 15, and then went on to Columbia University to take his B.A., M.A., and Ph.D. degrees, all by the time he was 21. He majored in physics and mathematics and was a Phi Beta Kappa as a Columbia undergraduate. He is married to the former Colene McDowell. They have two daughters.   WALTER F. MORSE

BUILDING AND CONSTRUCTION outlays in 1965 reached an estimated high of $68,500,000,000, an increase of 4 per cent above the $65,900,000,000 spent in 1964. *Engineering News-Record* (ENR) predicted a 7 per cent rise in the dollar volume of heavy construction contracts for 1966. The F. W. Dodge Company, looking at total construction contracts, predicted a 4.2 per cent gain for 1966.

Costs of labor, material, equipment, and money rose sharply in 1965, pushing construction costs to new highs. The ENR 20-city construction cost index increased 2.7 per cent in the first nine months of the year. In ENR's breakdown of 11 representative building costs, mechanical costs—including plumbing, heating, ventilating, and air conditioning—took a major share of the construction dollar, ranging from a low of 3.8 per cent on one project to a high of 29 per cent on others.

Projects in Three Cities. Boston's $150,000,000 Prudential Center was dedicated in April. The focal point of this business and civic complex is the 52-story Prudential Tower office building, the ninth tallest skyscraper in the nation. Massachusetts Turnpike traffic rolls beneath the tower, which rests on 170-foot-deep bedrock foundation. See BOSTON.

When Chicago's 100-story John Hancock Center is completed in 1968, it will be the tallest building outside Manhattan. With an area of 2,300,000 square feet, it will also be the world's largest combination office-and-apartment building. Caisson

and other preliminary construction work started during the summer. See ARCHITECTURE (photograph); CHICAGO.

First-stage construction also got underway for the $525,000,000 Port of New York Authority's World Trade Center. Its twin 110-story towers will be the tallest in the world when they open sometime in 1970 or 1971. Located on a 16-acre site near the southern tip of Manhattan, the center will be headquarters for government agencies and private firms involved in international marketing.

New Codes. In March, the American Welding Society (AWS) issued addenda to its Code for Welding in Building Construction (D1.0-63) and the Specifications for Welded Highway and Railway Bridges (D2.0-63). The general purpose of both is to allow engineers to realize the potential design improvements and economies offered by the growing family of new varieties of structural steel. The AWS structural welding committee also issued its first special ruling to cover gas metal-arc welding with carbon dioxide shielding.

A revision of the New York City Building Code, adopted late in the year, permitted a great deal more latitude in the general use of prestressed and reinforced concrete.   M. E. JESSUP

See also BRIDGE AND TUNNEL; DAM; ROADS AND HIGHWAYS; TRANSPORTATION; WATER AND FLOOD CONTROL.

BULGARIA remained firmly under the control of Communist Party First Secretary Todor Zhivkov, who proclaimed himself "bound to the Soviet Union in life and death." A plot to overthrow Zhivkov was foiled in April. Subsequently, a number of workers were purged from the party.

A flurry of contacts with Romania, and a five-day visit by Yugoslavia's President Tito, suggested that an awareness of liberal trends within the communist bloc was growing in Bulgaria. Eighty per cent of Bulgaria's foreign trade was with the East European communist bloc; half of that was with the Soviet Union. Nevertheless, and contrary to Zhivkov's outspoken mistrust of the West, Bulgaria endeavored to increase its Western trade. It improved its relations with Greece, re-establishing a direct rail link with Athens. A series of arrangements was made with Italy and The Netherlands to expand Bulgaria's exports of machinery to the two countries.

Internally, the nation, still preoccupied with converting from a predominantly agricultural economy to an agricultural-industrial economy, began experimenting with decentralization.

Population: 8,260,000. **Government:** Communist Party First Secretary Todor Zhivkov; President Georgi Traikov. **Monetary Unit:** lev (1.17 = U.S. $1). **Foreign Trade:** exports, $969,000,000; imports, $1,057,000,000. **Principal Exports:** clothing, tobacco.   TOM AND HARLE DAMMANN

See also EUROPE.

BURMA, under the military rule of General Ne Win, moved increasingly toward isolation from the rest of Asia. The Burmese army continued its fight to subdue rebellious tribal groups, but with indifferent success. Civil disorders in the northern and eastern sections of the country continued; the vast delta region around Rangoon, however, remained under tight army control.

Burma's nationalization program continued. Virtually every phase of economic life, including the import-export trade, was either subject to government control or was owned outright by the state. Scores of thousands of businessmen were affected, including an estimated 750,000 Indians who returned home when their businesses were seized. Also affected were Chinese and Pakistani communities.

Despite such moves, Burma continued to export large quantities of rice, a commodity that earns about 65 per cent of its foreign exchange. Meanwhile, the basic wealth of the country allowed the nation to overcome the economic disorganization created by the nationalization drive.

Population: 25,016,000. **Government:** Revolutionary Council Chairman Ne Win. **Monetary Unit:** kyat (4.785 = U.S. $1). **Gross National Product:** 6,747,000,000 kyats. **Foreign Trade:** exports, $239,000,000; imports, $272,000,000. **Principal Exports:** lumber, oilseed meal, rice.   JOHN N. STALKER

See also ASIA.

BURUNDI was the scene of political intrigue and violence during 1965. On January 7, Mwami (King) Mwambutsa IV dismissed the government of Premier Albin Nyamoya. He called on former Premier Pierre Ngendandumwe to form a new government. Ngendandumwe was assassinated one week later. Joseph Bamina, president of the Union du Progrès National Party (UPRONA), replaced him. The murder was first attributed to communists. But on the following day, Gonzalve Muyenzi, a young Watusi extremist, confessed.

On May 10, Burundi held its first general election since its independence in 1962. Unofficial election results gave UPRONA 21 of the contested 33 seats in the legislative assembly, with 10 going to the all-Bahutu Peoples party and the remaining two to independents. The king, faced with the prospect of an assembly that would oppose him, appointed Leopold Biha, a compromise candidate, as premier. In October a coup was attempted by army officers and political leaders. Loyalist troops put down the uprising and at least 53 of the rebels were executed.

Population: 2,890,000. **Government:** Mwami (King) Mwambutsa IV; Premier Leopold Biha. **Monetary Unit:** franc (87.50 = U.S. $1). **Foreign Trade:** no figures available. **Principal Export:** coffee.   BENJAMIN E. THOMAS

See also AFRICA.

BUS. See TRANSPORTATION.

BUSINESS. See ECONOMY, THE.

CABINET. As 1966 opened, President Lyndon B. Johnson's Cabinet had four new faces in four old posts and one new post without a face. In addition, one of the Cabinet's acting members was made a full-fledged member when the President appointed Nicholas deB. Katzenbach as Attorney General on Feb. 13, 1965. Katzenbach had been acting head of the Justice Department since September, 1964, when Robert F. Kennedy resigned to run for the U.S. Senate. See KATZENBACH, NICHOLAS deB.

Luther H. Hodges, who had resigned as Secretary of Commerce on Dec. 16, 1964, was the first to leave. Liberal "independent Democrat" John T. Connor was sworn in to replace Hodges on January 18 (see 1965 YEAR BOOK, CONNOR, JOHN T.).

The second new face belonged to Henry H. Fowler, 56, a corporate lawyer who had served as an undersecretary of the Treasury until April, 1964

U.S. Cabinet as of Dec. 31, 1965
(In order of succession to the presidency)

Secretary of State	Dean Rusk
Secretary of the Treasury	Henry H. Fowler
Secretary of Defense	Robert S. McNamara
Attorney General	Nicholas deB. Katzenbach
Postmaster General	Lawrence F. O'Brien
Secretary of the Interior	Stewart L. Udall
Secretary of Agriculture	Orville L. Freeman
Secretary of Commerce	John T. Connor
Secretary of Labor	W. Willard Wirtz
Secretary of Health, Education, and Welfare	John W. Gardner
Secretary of Housing and Urban Development	(vacant)

(see FOWLER, HENRY H.). The conservative Virginia Democrat was appointed Secretary of the Treasury on March 18 to replace Republican banker C. Douglas Dillon.

Another holdover from President John F. Kennedy's Cabinet, Anthony J. Celebrezze, the Secretary of Health, Education, and Welfare, accepted a federal judgeship. On July 27, President Johnson replaced him with Republican John W. Gardner, 52, a noted educator and president of the Carnegie Foundation since 1955 (see GARDNER, JOHN W.).

The fourth to leave the Cabinet was Postmaster General John A. Gronouski, also a Kennedy appointee. He had accepted the ambassadorship to Poland. On August 29, Lawrence F. O'Brien, 48, presidential assistant for congressional relations, was named Postmaster General (see O'BRIEN, LAWRENCE F.).

The new Cabinet post, the one without a captain, was that of the Secretary of Housing and Urban Development. The new department, authorized by Congress, came into being on November 9. President Johnson postponed naming its head until sometime in 1966. See CITY; HOUSING.

CALDECOTT MEDAL. See LITERATURE FOR CHILDREN; MONTRESOR, BENI.

COMMUNIST ARMS, representing part of a shipment sent to Cambodia by Communist China, are inspected by Cambodian Prince Sihanouk, right.

CAMBODIA. Prince Norodom Sihanouk continued his efforts to appease Communist China. His attempts, however, yielded few tangible benefits to the country. Efforts toward a reconciliation with the United States proved equally fruitless, so much so that on May 3, Sihanouk formally severed diplomatic relations.

Cambodia's repeated requests for an international conference that would assure its territorial integrity and neutrality were agreeable to Britain, France, the Soviet Union, and the United States. Such a meeting, however, was rejected by both Communist China and North Vietnam.

Cambodia's domestic situation worsened during the year. The transportation system, including rails and roads, was rapidly disintegrating. Salaries of teachers and government workers frequently went unpaid. Plans for major educational developments had to be shelved because of insufficient funds. Inflation and corruption combined to push the cost of living to an all-time high. Although Sihanouk was able to secure some economic assistance from France, even this was insufficient to halt the downward trend of the economy.

Population: 6,484,000. **Government:** Chief of State and Premier Prince Norodom Sihanouk. **Monetary Unit:** riel (35 = U.S. $1). **Foreign Trade:** exports, $88,000,000; imports, $82,000,000. **Principal Exports:** maize, rice, rubber.   JOHN N. STALKER

See also ASIA.

CAMEROON. Unopposed on the ballot, incumbent President Ahmadou Ahidjo and his running mate, Vice-President John Ngo Foncha, were elected to five-year terms in March, 1965. Later, Foncha resigned his post as premier of West Cameroon but continued as vice-president in the federal government. With full time to devote to his federal duties, Foncha took over the supervision of higher education, mining, and public health.

In June, the National Democratic party won all the seats in the elections for a new legislative assembly in West Cameroon, but later joined forces with the opposing National People's Congress in an enlarged West Cameroon government. In East Cameroon, the Union Camerounaise party gained 99 per cent of the votes in the legislative elections.

President Ahidjo reported a 25 per cent increase in exports and a 27 per cent rise in imports. A five-year plan, based originally on a 1964 loan of $2,700,000 from the European Economic Community (EEC, or Common Market), benefited from additional EEC loans totaling $8,100,000.

Population: 4,346,000. **Government:** President Ahmadou Ahidjo; Premier Augustin Ngon Jua. **Monetary Unit:** CFA franc (246.85 = U.S. $1). **Foreign Trade:** exports, $118,000,000; imports, $108,000,000. **Principal Exports:** bananas, cocoa, coffee, cotton, palm oil, timber.   BENJAMIN E. THOMAS

See also AFRICA.

CAMP FIRE GIRLS, under the slogan "Think Big —See the World," adopted a program of travel and good will as part of their 1965-1966 project. This program, which carries forward the 1964 theme of friendship, also stresses ways of becoming good-will ambassadors of the United States when traveling abroad.

Highlight of the project will be a traveling study conference in the summer of 1966 for Horizon Club members (girls 14 and over). The conference, called Horizon Club Conference Afloat, will be the first of its type and scope ever to be organized by any youth service agency. It is being arranged with the help of the Council on Student Travel.

One thousand girls representing members from all 50 states will participate in a three-week shipboard program of study and visits to three Caribbean countries. They will learn about the customs, culture, history, geography, and government of each of these countries while on shipboard. On shore, they will interview government officials and Peace Corps volunteers, and tour industrial establishments. Thus, the conference will combine the attractions of an ocean voyage with an orientation to the peoples and culture of the selected countries.

In cooperation with the Library of Congress, a storybook about the Blue Birds, the youngest program level of Camp Fire Girls, was published in braille. The volume is entitled *Blue Bird Wish Comes True.*   JOSEPH P. ANDERSON

CANADA

When Canada's new flag was raised officially on Feb. 15, 1965, the hopes of the nation rose with it—hopes for a deeper unity and a stronger sense of purpose. Prime Minister Lester B. Pearson, in saluting the red and white maple leaf flag, called its unfurling the beginning of "a new stage in Canada's forward march." The year 1965, however, showed that this advance had not got fully underway. Although relations between English- and French-speaking Canadians seemed to have improved, the political scene continued to be one of uncertainty.

Prime Minister Pearson, as leader of a minority government since April 22, 1963, called a general election for November 8. Although his Liberal party won the election, it failed to achieve its main goal— a majority in the Commons. This failure weakened his position. Many questions were calling for a decision. But the continuance of a minority government made achievement of a national consensus difficult.

Accusations of scandal, intense party strife, and the indecisive results of the general election told the Canadian political story in 1965. The election, the 27th in Canada's history and the fifth in less than nine years, returned the Pearson government to office. This and three others of Canada's last five elections—1957, 1962, and 1963—had produced governments without a majority in Parliament.

Miller Services, Ltd.

In the 1965 campaign, Prime Minister Pearson had made a special point of asking for a majority so that he could speak to the provinces with a strong voice on a wide range of important federal-provincial problems. But 60 per cent of the Canadian voters said no, and gave their support to the four parties opposing him.

The Election Results. The Liberal government went into the election with 129 seats in the 265-seat House of Commons. It emerged with 131. But its share of the popular vote dropped 2 per cent since the 1963 election. In five of the 10 provinces of Canada, the Liberal party elected a total of only three House members.

This exceedingly narrow geographic base was accentuated further by the fact that 107 of the 129 Liberals came from Ontario and Quebec. The results of the election were a bitter disappointment for a party that had always prided itself on its broad national support.

The Conservatives, who had been weakened by a cabinet revolt against former Prime Minister John G. Diefenbaker in 1963, recovered much of their unity and fought a hard-hitting campaign. The 70-year-old Diefenbaker carried his message in 30,000 miles of "whistle stopping" to communities from the Atlantic to the Pacific. He hammered at the Pearson government for sheltering scandal and for sponsoring divisive policies.

Diefenbaker's seven-week campaign yielded results few commentators had predicted. The Conser-

"EYE OF DEMOCRACY"—Toronto's spacious council chamber—gets its first workaday use after opening ceremonies on September 13.

vatives increased their strength in Parliament from 95 to 97 members. They won seats in every province but Newfoundland. Their showing generally was stronger in rural districts and in the West than in urban centers. In Canada's three largest cities—Montreal, Toronto, and Vancouver—the Conservatives captured only one of the 48 seats. However, they won all the seats in two provinces and a majority in three others. Their share of the popular vote was 32 per cent, unchanged from 1963.

The New Democratic party (socialist), under the leadership of T. C. Douglas, increased its seats from 17 to 21. Its share of the popular vote rose from 13 to 18 per cent, and was largely concentrated in Ontario and British Columbia.

The declining Social Credit party lost 10 seats. It elected only 14 members—nine from the French-speaking section and five from the English-speaking wing of the party. Two independents completed the House's roster of 265 members.

The Liberal cabinet ministers, Harry Hays (agriculture) and J. Watson MacNaught (mines), were defeated, and a former Liberal minister of public works, Robert H. Winters, won a seat. A day after the election, Walter L. Gordon, the Minister of Finance and one of Pearson's closest advisers, resigned. The Conservatives welcomed back to Parliament two former cabinet ministers—George Hees (minister of trade and commerce before 1963) and E. D. Fulton (former minister of justice).

With over 10,200,000 names on the voters' list, about 74 per cent of those eligible voted. The election, which was estimated to have cost $14,000,000, strikingly confirmed the confused state of Canadian national politics. Undoubtedly the bargaining position of the Pearson government would be weakened in the Parliament due to assemble Jan. 18, 1966.

Scandals stained Canadian federal politics during the year. The first hint of wrongdoing came late in 1964 when a Conservative member of Parliament disclosed a Royal Canadian Mounted Police report that accused two executive assistants to cabinet ministers. One assistant was alleged to have attempted to bribe a Montreal lawyer acting for the U.S. government not to oppose bail for Lucien Rivard, an accused narcotics smuggler who faced extradition to the United States. A few days later, Guy Rouleau, parliamentary secretary to Pearson, resigned his post because of suggestions that his name was mentioned in the report. After a week of heated debate and counter-charges, the government agreed to a judicial inquiry, conducted by Chief Justice Frederic Dorion of Quebec.

Another scandal broke in January when the Prime Minister asked for the resignation of Minister without Portfolio Yvon Dupuis. Dupuis was accused of having taken a $10,000 bribe in connection with efforts to obtain a race track franchise in Quebec. He was later arraigned on criminal charges.

While the Dorion inquiry was underway, Rivard

Wide World
IT WAS "V" FOR PEARSON—and for minority government—after the November 8 election that gave his Liberals 40 per cent of the vote.

escaped from Montreal's Bordeaux Jail on March 2. News of the escape was greeted with stunned disbelief in Ottawa. He was captured later, extradited to Laredo, Tex., fined $20,000, and sentenced to 20 years in a U.S. penitentiary.

The Dorion report, issued in late June, questioned Justice Minister Guy Favreau's judgment in deciding against prosecution of the bribery cases. Favreau immediately resigned. He was later named president of the Privy Council, with responsibilities in federal-provincial relations. Raymond Denis, the executive assistant to the minister of citizenship and immigration, later went on trial as the bribe offerer, and the role of Rouleau was found "reprehensible" but not criminal in having interceded on Rivard's behalf. Rouleau resigned his seat in the House of Commons.

Although those accused of corruption in the scandals were all sent to trial, the revelations of criminal influences touching the offices of government damaged the Pearson administration. Only minor reorganizations of the cabinet occurred during the year. Favreau was replaced as minister of justice by Public Works Minister Lucien Cardin in July.

New Pension Plan. Despite the Pearson administration's minority status, its legislative record was impressive. One major bill enacted was the Canada Pension Plan (CPP). It gave Canadians two separate sources of retirement income. The existing noncontributory, $75-a-month, old age pension was continued, with a provision for gradually lowering the eligible age from 70 to 65 by 1970. The new compulsory, contributory plan at the end of a 10-year transitional period will pay a maximum of an additional $104.17 a month at age 65.

On Jan. 1, 1966, employees and employers both began to pay amounts equal to 1.8 per cent of wages between $600 and $5,000 a year into the CPP fund. The average worker's pension will come to about one quarter of his pay. The CPP fund was expected to have a profound effect on the Canadian economy. It could exceed $5,000,000,000 in 10 years. Those funds will be available to finance public works and other government projects. The money will be allocated to the provinces on a per capita basis and is expected to reduce the need of private borrowing by provinces and municipalities by two-thirds.

Other Legislation by the 26th Parliament in the welfare field included:
• A new Labour Standards Act, providing a minimum wage of $1.25 an hour for about 500,000 workers in activities under federal jurisdiction.
• The creation of a special secretariat to coordinate federal and provincial programs to improve economic and social opportunities for Canadians.
• The creation of the Company of Young Canadians to recruit 1,000 volunteer workers for technical, educational, and welfare roles at home and abroad.

The National Housing Act was also amended to boost the lending ceiling of the Central Mortgage and Housing Corporation by $3,600,000,000. Its aim is to aid new housing construction, slum clearance, and urban renewal.

The Redistribution Act was passed after years of discussion. It set up 10 independent commissions to redraw federal electoral maps in each of the 10 provinces to provide a better population balance between rural and urban constituencies.

Federal-Provincial Relations. A four-day conference to deal with an extensive list of federal-provincial subjects opened in Ottawa on July 19. The provinces were offered a medical care program under which the federal government would grant tax concessions to meet half the cost of provincial health insurance plans. Such plans would have to (1) cover all residents of a province on equal terms, (2) be publicly administered, and (3) have benefits transferable from one province to another. Target date for the program's operation was set for July 1, 1967.

Ownership of offshore mineral rights touched off a verbal duel between Prime Minister Pearson and Premier Jean Lesage of Quebec. Pearson insisted that legal rights should first be defined by the Supreme Court of Canada. Lesage argued that the question was political, not legal or juridical. The provinces, he said, had owned all the natural resources—including those off their shores—when they entered the Confederation. At stake were millions of dollars in license fees and royalties if undersea oil, gas, or minerals are discovered on Canada's continental shelves.

The Two Canadas. The Royal Commission on Bilingualism and Biculturalism (established in 1963) completed public hearings in 1965 and settled down to write its final report. In a preliminary report February 25, it warned that Canada was passing through the gravest crisis in its history without being fully aware of it, but predicted that a richer, more dynamic Canada would result if steps were taken to reduce tension between the two founding races.

Foreign Affairs. Canada added 10 officers to its seven-man contingent on the United Nations (UN) observer mission in Kashmir in September, after the outbreak of the India-Pakistan fighting there. Later, at UN request, Canada dispatched 95 members of the Royal Canadian Air Force to Rawalpindi, Pakistan, to form a transport unit for the UN mission. See INDIA; PAKISTAN; UNITED NATIONS.

Canadian aid to Colombo Plan countries was doubled during the year to stand at $78,000,000. *Soft* (no interest) loans were made available to these Asian countries. The Canadian University Service Overseas, a privately administered "Peace Corps," received its first substantial government assistance—$500,000. It hopes to more than double the number of its 318 volunteers in 22 underdeveloped nations.

Canada was ranked 10th among the world's dispensers of foreign aid, according to a study released early in the year by the Organization for Economic Cooperation and Development (OECD). In 1963, Canada supplied $120,000,000 of the nearly $9,300,000,000 given to poor nations, OECD reported.

In June, Prime Minister Pearson attended a Commonwealth Conference in London at which a Canadian diplomat, Arnold Smith, was named secretary-general of the newly created Commonwealth secretariat. See GREAT BRITAIN.

Defense. The reorganization of Canada's armed forces continued, with the replacing of the 11 commands of the separate services by six integrated commands: Air Defense, Air Transport, Maritime, Materiel, Mobile, and Training. The resulting economies were to contribute to the efficacy of a new $1,500,000,000, five-year program to provide more efficient combat equipment. Included in the procurement program were 125 supersonic Northrop F-5 Freedom Fighters to be acquired by the air force for tactical ground-support work.

The Budget. On July 1 Canadians gained the largest cut—10 per cent—in personal income tax in 10 years. Finance Minister Gordon had introduced it in his third budget in Parliament on April 26. Taxpayer allowances also were changed.

Gordon's budget included a controversial proposal to disallow as deductible business expense the costs of advertising directed primarily to Canadian markets in foreign-owned magazines and newspapers. This measure was approved, effective Jan. 1, 1966. It was designed to boost the advertising revenues of Canadian periodicals; the Canadian editions of *Time* and *Reader's Digest* were exempted.

CANADA

Federal revenues for the fiscal year beginning April 1, 1965, were estimated at $7,350,000,000. Gordon put fiscal 1965-1966 expenditures at $7,650,000,000. That indicated a deficit of $300,000,-

1965–66 Budgets of Canadian Provinces
($ millions)

Province	Expenditures	% Increase from 1964-65	Surplus or (Deficit)
Alberta	493.8	19.1	(22.6)
British Columbia	446.0	12.6	1.2
Manitoba	214.7	—	0.2*
New Brunswick	187.3	15.0	(17.8)
Newfoundland	178.5	13.2	(16.9)
Nova Scotia	165.6	14.0	0.1*
Quebec	1,781.9†	27.9	(229.3)
Ontario	1,459.6	12.7	(141.1)
Prince Edward Is.	41.3	24.0	(7.4)
Saskatchewan	220.7	3.0	0.3

*Based on current account.   †Excluding federal shared costs.

000 compared with the actual deficit of $83,000,000 in the previous fiscal year.

The Domestic Economy. In his budget speech, Gordon forecast a 7 per cent increase in the Gross National Product (GNP) for 1965. By the end of the third quarter, it was apparent that the bumper wheat harvest and a high level of business activity would bring a 1965 GNP of about $51,125,000,000, almost 9 per cent above the 1964 GNP. It also changed the $300,000,000 budgetary deficit the finance minister had predicted into a treasury surplus of over $500,000,000 by the end of September. Canadian exports were expected to reach a value of $10,808,000,000 in 1965.

Prairie wheat production in 1965 was estimated at 703,900,000 bushels, of which over 600,000,000 would be sold abroad, about 44 per cent to communist customers. In August, the Soviet Union bought 214,000,000 bushels for cash. The sale was valued at $450,000,000. And in October, Communist China signed an agreement to buy Canadian wheat, ranging in sales value from a minimum of $200,000,000 in three years to $900,000,000 over a five-year period.

Capital Spending, at an estimated $12,300,000,000, continued high—15 per cent above the 1964 level of construction expenditures and 11 per cent more than the 1964 outlays for machinery. Spending for social capital needs was particularly heavy. The cost of additional university facilities, for instance, rose 60 per cent above the level for 1964. Early in August, the government in Ottawa instituted a slowdown on major building projects to head off an inflation of building costs.

Unemployment rates averaged 4 per cent throughout the year, while the labor force grew to 7,490,000. The Economic Council of Canada, issuing its first report in January, called for 1,500,000 new jobs by the end of the decade, and an unemployment rate of 3 per cent. To reach these goals productivity per worker would have to advance by 2.4 per cent a year (it was 1 per cent a year from 1956 to 1963).

Finance Disaster. The Atlantic Acceptance Corporation, Ltd., a Toronto-based finance company, defaulted on $5,010,000 of short-term notes and went into receivership on June 17, bringing severe losses to thousands of investors in Canada and the United States. Although the examination of the company's financial position was not complete by the end of the year, total losses were estimated between $50,000,000 and $100,000,000. The Ontario government appointed Mr. Justice S. H. S. Hughes, of its Supreme Court, to investigate the collapse.

The Northwest Territories will not be split into two districts for the time being, the federal government decided. Instead, it appointed a three-member commission to consider steps to develop local self-government. Plans were also drawn up for the creation of a territorial public service.

The Provinces

Alberta rode a wave of prosperity in 1965. To its booming wheat sales was added the stimulus of new oil and gas finds in its north country. The biggest recent discoveries have been in the Zama Lake-Rainbow Lake area.

After 21 years in Social Credit hands, the provincial riding of Edson was won by a Liberal, William Switzer. His victory raised the opposition strength to 4 in a house of 63.

British Columbia. A succession of snow and mud slides struck Canada's Pacific Coast province early in 1965. The worst was in February, when 26 men died in a massive snow slide that overwhelmed the Granduc mining camp in the isolated Stewart region of northwestern British Columbia. See DISASTERS.

Newsprint producers in the province cut prices $10 a ton to maintain markets for their product.

Premiers of Canadian Provinces

Province	Premier	Political Party
Alberta	Ernest C. Manning	Social Credit
British Columbia	William A. C. Bennett	Social Credit
Manitoba	Dufferin Roblin	Conservative
New Brunswick	Louis J. Robichaud	Liberal
Newfoundland	Joseph R. Smallwood	Liberal
Nova Scotia	Robert L. Stanfield	Conservative
Ontario	John P. Robarts	Conservative
Prince Edward Is.	Walter R. Shaw	Conservative
Quebec	Jean Lesage	Liberal
Saskatchewan	Ross Thatcher	Liberal

Two new mills were announced: a kraft and newsprint mill at Powell River and a pulp mill at Prince George, 300 miles north of Vancouver. A total of five new pulp mills were under construction during the year.

Manitoba. Work on a $7,000,000 Centennial concert hall was begun in downtown Winnipeg. The hall, to be completed in 1967, is part of an art center that will include two museums and a planetarium.

Manitoba joined the growing list of provinces with their own flags. It adopted the Red Ensign, with Manitoba's coat of arms against a red background.

CANADA'S PAVILION, right, for Expo '67 will center around the huge inverted-pyramid structure called Katamavik (Eskimo for "meeting place"). The world fair, known officially as the Universal and International Exhibition, will cover a pier and two St. Lawrence River islands in Montreal, shown in map-diagram below. Expo '67 will open April 28, 1967.

EXPO '67

New Brunswick also adopted a distinctive provincial flag. It depicted a ship in full sail as a reminder of the province's great sailing days.

Demands increased for the official recognition of the French language. The Royal Commission on Bilingualism and Biculturism heard pleas that French be used as well as English in government, the courts, and in schools.

Plans went ahead for a massive base metal mining, steel, and chemical complex in the Bathurst area of northern New Brunswick. One company, Brunswick Mining and Smelting Corporation, earmarked $222,000,000 for the development.

Newfoundland set a new pattern in Canadian education by providing free tuition in 1965 to all first-year students at Memorial University. For next year the government promised free tuition and maintenance grants to all undergraduates at Memorial. By this step, the government said, it recognized that "the greatest asset of a country is its educated manpower."

Nova Scotia. A new national park 150 miles west-southwest of Halifax, to be called Kejimkujik, was announced for Nova Scotia. A wilderness area of forest and lake, the new national park will cover 146 square miles.

A new plant to assemble Japanese automobiles (Toyota and Isuzu) was constucted for Canadian Motor-Industries, Ltd., near Sydney, with production to begin in 1966.

Ontario's legislature sat for 98 days in its longest session in history and passed 175 bills. Among the measures was a Medical Services Insurance Act under which the government will establish a standard, voluntary health insurance plan and will pay the full premium for persons with no taxable income. Another bill provided a new official flag—the Red Ensign with Ontario's coat of arms in the fly.

Toronto put on a festive mood with the opening of its new city hall on September 13. Two curved towers of 20 and 27 stories flank the low-lying, domed central building. The $30,000,000 concrete and steel structure is set in a 12-acre square across Bay Street from the old copper-roofed city hall.

Not to be outdone, Hamilton won provincial approval of a $100,000,000 urban renewal project for 40 downtown acres. A target date of 1975 was set.

Prince Edward Island. Construction was scheduled to begin on a nine-mile tunnel, bridge, and causeway in April, 1966. It will join the island province with the mainland in New Brunswick. See BRIDGE AND TUNNEL.

A royal commission recommended the union of the province's two institutions of higher education—Prince of Wales College and St. Dunstan's University—into a new degree-granting university.

Quebec separatist violence dwindled in 1965. There was evidence of much violence among the province's criminal elements, however. Five lye-eaten bodies were found near Quebec City in October. The victims were believed to have been killed in a gangland purge touched off by provincial investigations into fraudulent bankruptcies and arson.

Total provincial expenditures topped $2,000,000,-000 for the first time in 1965, reflecting a healthy 9.9 per cent growth in economic activity in Quebec.

Twenty-eight persons, 15 of them children, died in a gas explosion that completely demolished an apartment block in suburban Montreal on March 1 (see DISASTERS).

Saskatchewan's fast-growing potash industry was expected to show a 65 per cent increase in production for 1965, to about 1,500,000 tons. Its output by 1975 was forecast at 12,000,000 tons. The Consolidated Mining and Smelting Company of Canada announced the development of a new potash property near Saskatoon, with a scheduled output of 1,000,000 tons annually when it opens in 1969.

A provincial flag, depicting a sheaf of wheat and the Saskatchewan coat of arms on a red and green field, was authorized for the province's Diamond Jubilee celebrations in 1965.

Population: 18,238,247 (1961). **Government:** Prime Minister Lester B. Pearson. **Monetary Unit:** Canadian dollar (1.0762 = U.S. $1). **Gross National Product:** (C) $51,125,000,000. **Foreign Trade:** exports, (C) $10,808,000,000; imports, (C) $11,850,-000,000. **Principal Exports:** nonferrous metals, paper and pulp, wheat.   DAVID M. L. FARR

CANADIAN LIBRARY ASSOCIATION (CLA)

held its 20th annual conference in Toronto, Ontario, in June, with "New Directions in Library Service" as its theme. The general sessions stressed the role of libraries in national life, library education, and automation.

The Book of the Year for Children medals were presented by the Canadian Association of Children's Librarians to Claude Aubry for *Le Loup de Noël* and to Mrs. Dorothy Reid for *Tales of Nanabozho.* The Canadian Library Trustees' Association presented its Merit Award to William J. Hodder of the Ottawa Public Library Board and to Newman F. Mallon of the Toronto Public Library.

Young Canada's Book Week was celebrated November 15 to 22 under the patronage of Dr. W. Kaye Lamb, National Librarian. CLA was one of several sponsors of Canadian Library Week.

University libraries were dedicated at Acadia University, Wolfville; St. Mary's University, Halifax; and St. Francis Xavier University, Antigonish, all in Nova Scotia. Waterloo University marked the opening of its new library by presenting honorary degrees to Bertha Bassam, director emeritus of the University of Toronto School of Library Science; Jack E. Brown, chief librarian of the National Science Library, Ottawa; and Robert H. Blackburn, chief librarian at the University of Toronto. The National Library building in Ottawa neared completion.   ELIZABETH H. MORTON

CANADIAN LITERATURE. With a view toward Canada's world's fair, Expo '67, and the many expected visitors from other parts of the world that may want to learn about their country, Canadian librarians prepared a list of the outstanding books that have been written in recent years about Canada. They included three historical studies showing the why and how of Canadian history—why Canada declined to join the 13 states in 1776 and how it since then has pursued its course of nationhood. These were *Canada, A Story of Challenge* by J. M. S. Careless; *Dominion of the North* by Donald G. Creighton; and *Colony to Nation* by A. R. M. Lower. For younger readers, there was *The Story of Canada* by George W. Brown.

Picture Studies of Canada today have been produced with excellent illustrations and texts. One is *Canada,* photographed by Peter Varley, and another *The Heritage of Canada in Colour* by K. McN. Wells. Accurate reporting and poetic imagery highlight *The Unknown Country* and *Tomorrow's Giant,* both by Bruce Hutchison. For boys and girls, the studies of Canada include *O Canada* by Isabel Barclay and *Across Canada* by Clare Bice.

Indians and Eskimos have always been popular subjects for Canadian readers. Among the best books in these categories are: *The Indians of Canada* and *People of the Twilight (Eskimos)* by Diamond Jeness, and the beautifully illustrated *Eskimo* by E. S. Carpenter. Favorites with children are *The Whale People* by R. L. Haig-Brown; *Glooskap's Country and Other Indian Tales* by Cyrus MacMillan; *Tales of Nanabozho* by D. M. Reid; *Nkwala* by E. L. Sharp; and *Agaguk* by Yves Theriault.

Biographies, both of individuals and groups, include *Tonty of the Iron Hand* by Fred Swayze; *The Queen's Cowboy* by Kerry Wood; *The Scarlet Force* by T. M. Longstretch; *The Golden Trail* by Pierre Berton; *The Salt-Water Men* by Joseph Schull; and *John A. Macdonald* by Donald Creighton.

Art and Literature are represented in *Eskimo Sculpture* by George Swinton; *An Anthology of Canadian Art,* edited by R. H. Hubbard; *Looking at Architecture in Canada* by Alan Gowans; *Folk Songs of Canada* by E. Fowke and R. Johnston; and *The Oxford Book of Canadian Verse,* edited by A. J. M. Smith.

Recent interest in Quebec has been reflected in three books: *The Quebec Revolution* by H. B. Myers; *Quebec States Her Case,* edited by F. R. Scott and Michael Oliver; and *Dear Enemies* by G. Graham and S. Chaput.

Reference Books. The annual paperback volume issued by the Queen's Printer in Ottawa and entitled *Canada; Official Handbook of Present Conditions and Recent Progress* has always remained popular. But for those in search of more detailed information, there was *Canada Year Book, Canadian Almanac,* and *The Canadian Annual Review.*   ELIZABETH H. MORTON

CARNEGIE MEDAL. See LITERATURE FOR CHILDREN (Awards); PORTER, SHEENA.

CASEY, LORD RICHARD GARDINER (1890-

), the descendant of a pioneer family, was named governor-general of Australia in 1965.

Lord Casey's appointment capped an extraordinary career that began in 1931 with his election to the Australian House of Representatives. He served there until 1940 when he was named the first Australian minister to the United States. In 1942, he was transferred to Cairo, Egypt, as British minister of state for the Middle East. From 1944 to 1946, he was governor of Bengal, India.

Returning to Australia, Sir Richard served as president of the nation's Liberal party from 1947 to 1949. He was re-elected to parliament. He subsequently was appointed minister for external affairs, continuing in this post until 1960. In the same period, he was minister in charge of the Commonwealth Scientific and Industrial Research Organization. Part of his time was spent also as minister of national development, works, and housing.

Sir Richard was born August 29, 1890, in Melbourne. He attended Melbourne University, then went to England to take a B.A. degree at Trinity College, Cambridge University, in 1913. He fought in Gallipoli and France in World War I. He was married in 1926 to Ethel Marian Sumner, who, like himself, is a descendant of a pioneer Australian family. They are the parents of one son and one daughter. WALTER F. MORSE

CELEBRATIONS and anniversaries observed in 1965 included the following:

Year-Long Celebrations

Austrian Celebrations. The *Congress of Vienna Sesquicentennial* commemorated the congress of 1814-1815, when European diplomats redrew the continent's map following the defeat of France's Napoleon Bonaparte. The *University of Vienna Sexcentennial* commemorated its founding in 1365 by Rudolf IV.

Jan Sibelius Year, proclaimed by Finland, commemorated its great composer's birth on Dec. 8, 1865. Centennial highlights included the Sibelius Festival (May 15-June 4), the Sibelius International Violin Competition (November 23-December 4), and the Sibelius Centenary Concert in Helsinki on December 8. Sibelius died on Sept. 20, 1957.

Mont-Saint-Michel Abbey Millennium began in September, 1965. The Benedictine abbey atop a rocky isle off France's Normandy coast was founded in 966 by Richard I, Duke of Normandy. Two hundred years earlier, Saint Aubert, Bishop of Avranches, dedicated a chapel there to Saint Michael, one of the archangels in the Old Testament.

Patagonia Centenary commemorated the founding of the Welsh colony (now Chubut Province) in southern Argentina by 150 Welsh pioneers, who arrived at Puerto Madryn on July 28, 1865. The Welsh language and customs still prevail there.

Rio de Janeiro Quadricentennial began with the advent of 1965 and Pope Paul VI's blessing, broadcast from the Vatican. The Pope also electronically lighted the huge Christ the Redeemer statue on Corcovado Mountain, high above Rio de Janeiro. The Portuguese founded Brazil's capital (1808-1960) and second largest city on Mar. 1, 1565.

Saint Augustine Quadricentennial began on Sept. 8,

1965. Florida's historic city, founded in 1565 by Spanish Pedro Menéndez de Avilés, was the first permanent white settlement in what is now the United States.

Warren G. Harding Centennial commemorated the birth, on Nov. 2, 1865, of the 29th President of the United States. He was born near Corsica, Ohio. On Nov. 2, 1965, the Harding home in Marion was formally dedicated as a national historic landmark. President Harding died in office on Aug. 2, 1923.

Westminster Abbey 900th Anniversary began on Dec. 28, 1965. Great Britain's great national church in London, where many of its kings and queens were crowned and buried, also is the burial place of many of the nation's most renowned persons. The abbey's history goes back to Edward the Confessor, who built a church on its site between 1042 and 1065. Extensive restoration followed World War II.

World War II Anniversaries. Twenty years ago, on May 7, 1945, the Germans signed terms of unconditional surrender at Allied headquarters in Reims, France. The Free World celebrated Victory Day and the end of the war in the European theater on May 8. The United States dropped its first atomic bombs on Hiroshima and Nagasaki, Japan, on August 6 and 9, 1945. On August 14, Japan accepted surrender terms. The formal signing was aboard the U.S.S. *Missouri* in Tokyo Bay on September 2.

Year of the Alps was proclaimed in Switzerland to celebrate the centennials of St. Moritz and Davos as winter-sports centers, and the centennial of the first successful ascent of the Matterhorn. A 25-year-old Englishman, Edward Whymper, reached its summit (14,690 feet) on July 14, 1865. Four of his party fell to their deaths on the way down.

Year of Dante commemorated the septicentennial of the great Italian literary genius' birth in 1265. He was born in Florence in May or June. Dante Alighieri, perhaps the greatest poet of the Middle Ages, wrote his *Divine Comedy* while in exile. He died in 1321.

Shorter Celebrations

Jan. 8–15—Battle of New Orleans Sesquicentennial. The last battle of the War of 1812 was fought on Jan. 8, 1815. Neither the British nor the Americans knew that the war had officially ended with the signing of the Treaty of Ghent (Belgium) on Dec. 24, 1814. What is now Chalmette National Historical Park marks the site of the so-called "Needless Battle."

June 10–19—Magna Carta 750th Anniversary commemorated Great Britain's Great Charter wrested from King John I in 1215, and revised in 1216, 1217, and 1225. On June 10, 1215, John accepted the barons' demands and "caused his Great Seal to be affixed to the Heads of Agreement." All terms were agreed on, and "King John and all present at Runnymede solemnly swore to abide by them" on June 15 (date on Magna Carta). The formal document was engrossed and sealed on June 19, 1215. See GREAT BRITAIN; MEMORIALS (picture).

June 18—The Battle of Waterloo Sesquicentennial commemorated the final defeat of Napoleon Bonaparte in 1815. The exiled Napoleon escaped from Elba Island on Feb. 27, 1815. His French troops began to move in June. He nearly defeated Britain's Duke of Wellington at the June 18th battle, fought between Mont-Saint-Jean and Plancenoit, 3 to 5 miles south of Waterloo, Belgium. The arrival of Prussian Marshal Gebhard von Blücher's army brought overwhelming defeat to the French. Napoleon surrendered on July 15, and the Allies exiled him in October to Saint Helena, where he died in 1821.

June 22—English Parliament Septicentennial commemorated the assembly in London "summoned by

CELEBRATIONS

King Henry II at the instance of Simon de Montfort, Earl of Leicester and Steward of England, "which met from January 20 to the second week in March, 1265," and attended by chosen representatives of the shires, cities, towns, and boroughs. Such meetings were the beginnings of Britain's parliaments.

June 26–Sept. 19—Aachen 1,200th Anniversary. This West German city, famed for its hot springs since ancient times, was the home of Charlemagne, King of the Franks (A.D. 768–814) and Emperor of the Romans (800–814). Aachen's Town Hall was built (1300–1350) on the foundation of Charlemagne's palace, and was the coronation place of many kings and Holy Roman Emperors. Charlemagne founded Aachen's great Cathedral (796). He died in 814, and is now buried there in Michaelis Chapel. The city, also known as Aix la Chapelle, has long been noted as an art and music center.

July 3–5—Idaho Diamond Jubilee commemorated the admission of Idaho Territory as the 43rd state of the Union on July 3, 1890.

July 10—Wyoming Diamond Jubilee marked the admission of Wyoming Territory as the 44th state of the Union on July 10, 1890.

Aug. 6–8—Fiefdom of Sark Quadricentennial commemorated 400 years under the British Crown. To rid this English Channel island of pirates, Queen Elizabeth I granted Helier de Carteret a charter for the fiefdom. He divided the land among 40 farmers, armed with muskets. To this day, Sark is inhabited by 40 tenant families, the heads of which sit in the Court of Chief Pleas. The court's president is appointed by the *Seneschal*, Lord of the Manor, principal government officer and judge of the island. The Lord collects an annual tithe on various products from the farmers, and in turn pays the British Crown an annual fee of 50 shillings ($17). The present and 21st head of this hereditary fiefdom is 81-year-old Dame of Sark, Sibyl Mary Collings Beaumont Hathaway.

Aug. 14–28—William Butler Yeats Centennial was celebrated at the annual session of the International Yeats Summer School in Sligo, Ireland. The famed Irish poet, playwright, and Nobel literature laureate (1923) was born in Dublin on June 13, 1865. He spent many of his young days in County Sligo, now known as Ireland's Yeats country. Yeats died at Cap Ferrat, France, on Jan. 28, 1939, and was later buried in the Drumcliffe parish cemetery, near Sligo.

Sept. 16–18—James Smithson Bicentennial was observed at famed Smithsonian Institution, Washington, D.C. The French-born English chemist and mineralogist (1765–1829), for whom the mineral *smithsonite* was named, "by his last will and testament gave the whole of his property to the United States to found under the name of Smithsonian Institution an establishment for the increase and diffusion of knowledge among men." It was established by an act of Congress, Aug. 10, 1846.

Dec. 8—Eli Whitney Bicentennial. The American inventor of the cotton gin (1793) was born in Westboro, Mass., on Dec. 8, 1765. He made his fortune, however, manufacturing guns in New Haven, Conn. He was the first to produce uniform parts for assembly by unskilled workmen.

Dec. 30—Rudyard Kipling Centennial. The celebrated English poet and storyteller, born in Bombay, India, on Dec. 30, 1865, was the first of his countrymen honored with the Nobel literature prize (1907). His memorable works include "Gunga Din," "Mandalay," "Fuzzy-Wuzzy," (poems); *The Jungle Book* and *Just So Stories*; and "Recessional" for Queen Victoria's Diamond Jubilee in 1897.

See also CIVIL WAR CENTENNIAL; LITERATURE FOR CHILDREN; SALVATION ARMY.

CENSUS. By the last day of the calendar year 1965 the big census clock in the lobby of the U.S. Department of Commerce building in Washington, D.C., showed an estimated U.S. population of about 195,800,000, including members of the armed forces overseas. It was about 193,496,000 a year earlier. The 1.2 per cent increase marked a continuation of the slowdown in U.S. population growth, the lowest since the 1.0 per cent rate of 1945.

In its detailed midyear review, the U.S. Bureau of the Census estimated the total U.S. population at 194,583,000. The gradual decrease in the net population growth rate was attributed principally to the drop in the number of births—from an estimated 4,142,000 in the fiscal year ended June 30, 1964, to 3,948,000 in fiscal 1965.

It estimated the July 1, 1965, resident population (excluding servicemen overseas) at 193,818,000. A study of this population indicated the following percentage of distribution and changes since July 1, 1960, in various U.S. age groups:

	Under 5	5-13	14-24	25-44	45-64	Over 64
Distribution	11	19	17	24	20	9
Change	+0.3	+8.8	+25.7	−0.8	+7.7	+9

The bureau also noted that nonwhites had increased slightly in the year from 11.8 per cent to 11.9 per cent of the total population. The percentage was 11.4 on July 1, 1960.

Census-by-Mail. In April, 1965, the Bureau of the Census conducted a special test census in Cleveland, Ohio. A questionnaire was mailed to each household. It was to be filled out and mailed back on Census Day, April 1. Most questions could be answered by penciling in tiny circles, thus making it possible for the questionnaires to be processed directly by the bureau's electronic devices.

About 80 per cent of the households in Cleveland mailed back their questionnaires, and most questions were answered satisfactorily. Nonresponding households were visited by census enumerators. Omitted information on returned questionnaires was obtained either by telephone or personal visit. On the basis of tests and related experience, the Census Bureau is exploring plans to make extensive use of the mail in the 1970 Census.

Other Censuses. During 1965, the bureau continued publication of results from the 1963 censuses of manufactures, business, mineral industries, commercial fisheries, and transportation. In the fall, it began issuing reports by counties of the 1964 census of agriculture.

International Program. For 18 years, the bureau, through its International Statistical Programs Office (ISPO), has provided foreign technicians with statistical advisory services and training in data collecting and processing. During fiscal 1965, ISPO trained 268 nationals of 54 countries. A. ROSS ECKLER

See also POPULATION, WORLD; VITAL STATISTICS.

CENTRAL AMERICA. See LATIN AMERICA; and the articles on the individual countries.

CEYLON held its most important election in years on March 22. As a result, Prime Minister Sirimavo Bandaranaike, who had taken the country far down the road to socialism, was soundly defeated. Of 151 parliamentary seats at stake, Mrs. Bandaranaike's Freedom party captured only 41. The pro-Western United National party headed by Dudley Senanayake won 66. These, combined with seats won by the Tamil Federalist party and others, gave Senanayake the majority necessary to take over the government.

The hotly contested election was fought, basically, over domestic issues, especially whether the country should be more completely socialized. Although racial and religious issues also colored much of the campaigning, the underlying issue remained the steadily worsening economic situation.

On March 25, Senanayake was sworn in as prime minister. He announced that Ceylon would follow a truly nonaligned international policy and that he would halt the rapid drift toward socialism.

Population: 11,678,000. **Government:** Governor-General Willam Gopallawa; Prime Minister Dudley Senanayake. **Monetary Unit:** rupee (4.788 = U. S. $1.) **Gross National Product:** 6,782,000,000 rupees. **Foreign Trade:** exports, $394,000,000; imports, $415,000,000. **Principal Exports:** coconut oil, rubber, tea. JOHN N. STALKER

See also ASIA.

CHAD, a landlocked country in central Africa, achieved complete sovereignty in January, 1965, five years after it had obtained independence from France. The French relinquished control over three subprefectures in the northern part of the country. These are Borkou, Ennedi, and Tibesti, and together they make up what is known as the *BET* prefecture.

The government granted an amnesty to over two dozen opposition leaders imprisoned since the discovery of a plot in March, 1963, to overthrow President François Tombalbaye.

The president made a state visit to Paris, where he signed a $1,760,000 fiscal convention that confirmed French support for the Chaadian franc. Chad also signed a technical cooperation agreement with Israel. In addition, the U.S. government guaranteed private American investments in Chad. The first Soviet Ambassador to Chad took up his post.

Chad and the Sudan settled a dispute that arose when President Tombalbaye accused the Sudan of aiding an opposition "Chad government in exile." The Sudan agreed to expel the exiles and cooperate in patrolling the borders.

Population: 2,945,000. **Government:** President François Tombalbaye. **Monetary Unit:** CFA franc (246.85 = U. S. $1) **Foreign Trade:** exports $26,500,000; imports $34,600,000. **Principal Exports:** cotton, hides, meat, skins. WILLIAM SPENCER

See also AFRICA.

CHEMICAL INDUSTRY. See MANUFACTURING.

CHEMISTRY. A chemical laser was developed in 1965, a feat some experts thought impossible. It uses the energy of a chemical reaction occurring within the laser to produce the laser effect, the amplification of light waves into extremely powerful beams of one frequency. In an ordinary laser, energy (such as light or electricity) from an external source is used to "pump" the laser material into a excited state so that laser action can take place.

Professor George C. Pimentel of the University of California at Berkeley and a graduate student, Jerome Kasper, filled a two-foot-long laser tube with a mixture of hydrogen gas and chlorine gas. A bright flash of light caused the hydrogen and chlorine to react, making hydrogen chloride molecules. For a small fraction of a second, these molecules held the energy of the reaction before releasing it. This allowed laser action (stimulated emission) to take place in the tube. The coherent light, emitted as the excited HCl molecules lost their energy in phase, was in the infrared range.

These researchers have also constructed a photodissociation laser using excited iodine atoms produced in the flash *photolysis* (chemical decomposition) of methyl iodide. The light produced by this reaction is also to be found in the near infrared region of the spectrum.

Other groups of workers have also reported encouraging results in the search for feasible chemical laser systems. C. K. N. Patel of Bell Telephone Laboratories in New Providence, N. J., has reported laser action by passing an electric spark through a mixture of carbon monoxide and carbon dioxide.

The future promise of chemical lasers is twofold. They will provide information about the energy states of many types of chemicals, thus making an important contribution to pure research. It also may now be possible to make a laser that does not require external, bulky energy sources.

Hydrated Electrons result from the interaction of ionizing radiation with water, and are usually represented by the symbol $\acute{e}\ aq$. Each can be thought of as the short-term association of an electron with a water molecule. The average lifetime of the hydrated electron is a very small fraction of a second, depending on its rate of reaction with other substances in the solution.

It has now been found possible to utilize the strong reducing tendencies of hydrated electrons in applications to analytical chemistry. In many ways, the hydrated electron is an ideal analytical tool because it is easily generated, is quite reactive, and has a characteristic blue color that enables it to be determined rapidly by spectrophotometric means.

Optical Properties of materials have been of great importance in helping to determine the chemical nature of things. Recently there has been an extensive revival of interest in two types of optical measurements—optical rotatory dispersion and circular dichroism. Rotatory dispersion measurements are based on the fact that many materials are optically active; that is, their crystals or solutions can rotate a beam of polarized light. Usually the degree of rotation is dependent on the particular wave length of light that is passed through the solution. The degree of rotation, plotted against a wave length as a mathematical curve, can provide valuable insights into the structural detail of the material studied.

The measurement of circular dichroism is more subtle. In addition to optical activity, the spectral absorption of the compound under study is of importance. In this case circularly polarized light (both right- and left-handed) is used rather than plane-polarized light, as in the first method. Such light may be absorbed by an optically active compound, to various degrees at various wave lengths throughout the spectrum. The circular dichroism is defined as the difference in absorption between the right and left circularly polarized light beams passing through the material. Determination of this difference at all wave lengths yields information about the electronic energy states of the molecules of the material, as well as their configurations. A limitation of the technique is that most materials are not normally optically active. Placing any material in a magnetic field, however, will render it optically active and thus capable of being studied by this method.   ROBERT A. UPHAUS

See also BIOCHEMISTRY.

CHESS. Bobby Fischer, 22-year-old U.S. chess champion, made his plays via an overseas cable in the Capablanca Memorial Tournament held at Havana, Cuba, in August. He remained in New York because the U.S. Department of State held that Cuba was off-limits to Americans and would not endorse his passport. Fischer tied for second place in the tournament, which was won by Vassily Smyslov of Russia. While the tournament was still in progress, Fischer dismissed his referee, Frank Brady, who had just published *Profile of a Prodigy: The Life and Games of Bobby Fischer.*

Play continued throughout the year to determine who would win the right to challenge Tigran Petrosian of the Soviet Union for his world chess title. Three-time world champion Mikhail Botvinnik announced in March that he was retiring from world competition, thus becoming the first player in chess history to pass up a chance to regain the title.

Pal Benko and William Lombardy, both of New York City, tied for first place in the U.S. Open championship at the University of Puerto Rico in July and August. The U.S. Women's championship at New York was won by Mrs. Gisela Gresser of New York. San Jose State captured the National Intercollegiate Championship.

Victor Korchnoi won the U.S.S.R. championship at Kiev in January without losing a single game. Russia won the European team title at Hamburg, Germany, in August.   THEODORE M. O'LEARY

CHICAGO. The University of Illinois' Chicago Circle campus on the southwest edge of the Loop opened in 1965. The major new division of the university replaced a two-year branch that began operations in 1946 to handle the influx of veterans returning from World War II. The Space Age design of the 12 buildings on the 106-acre campus was done by Skidmore, Owings & Merrill. The buildings cost some $50,000,000. Initial enrollment was 5,415, but this is expected to rise to 20,000 by 1970.

On the South Side, the University of Chicago announced, in October, a $160,000,000 three-year expansion drive. At the outset, the Ford Foundation contributed $25,000,000 on a matching basis. The funds will be used for new construction, including an arts complex and a new science center.

In November, the U.S. Urban Renewal Administration allocated $11,700,000 for the redevelopment of 105 acres in the Woodlawn area immediately south of the University of Chicago. About 60 acres will be sold to the university for further development of its south campus. The plan includes the building of middle-income housing, and a $24,000,000 Veterans Administration hospital.

Lincoln Park Project I, comprising 271 acres of the 1,000-acre Lincoln Park renewal program, got a green light from the Department of Housing and Urban Development in December. New facilities planned include a new neighborhood park, public plazas, and a pedestrian greenway system.

100-Story Tower. New structures were completed and several were planned in 1965. The Equitable Life Assurance building opened on a large double-deck plaza, and, at year-end, the Civic Center, 647 feet high, also opened. The center was built of unsheathed and unpainted steel that officials said would weather to a uniform dark brown.

In the heart of the Loop, the largest demolition job ever undertaken, the razing of the 46-story Morrison Hotel, neared completion. A 60-story skyscraper, new home of the First National Bank of Chicago will be built in its place. The $60,000,000 building will rise in a curve from a 55,000 square-foot base to a 29,000 square-foot tower. Another major building planned was a $15,000,000 70-story apartment house in the downtown area. The tower will be built of curving walls of steel and glass. But the structure that made the most news in Chicago was the John Hancock Center (see ARCHITECTURE). To be built on Michigan Avenue, the center will be a tapered shaft of glass and steel 100 stories tall.

One of the city's favorite sons was the late Adlai E. Stevenson, former governor of Illinois, who lived in a Chicago suburb and practiced law downtown before being named U.S. ambassador to the United Nations. As a mark of its esteem, the city renamed its Southwest Expressway the Adlai E. Stevenson Expressway in September. See DEATHS OF NOTABLE PERSONS (Close-Up).   DONALD W. LIEF

See also DANCING; EDUCATION.

CHILD GUIDANCE. Two long-term studies of human development, reported in 1965, suggest that measured intelligence can be increased through changes in the family or community environment. One of these, the Berkeley Growth Studies, covers an 18-year span, and deals with children who have loving mothers and children with a hostile parent. The sons of hostile mothers, according to the report, scored high in infant intelligence, but had lower intelligence scores between the ages of 4 and 18. Sons of loving mothers, on the other hand, developed from happy inactive babies into extroverted, intelligent adolescents.

In the other study, Harold M. Skeels reported on a 25-year study of persons diagnosed as retarded in infancy. Those who had been placed for adoption and had grown up in a normal home environment compared favorably in intelligence with the general population of their state. On the other hand, those who had remained in nonstimulating orphanages tended to appear below average in adult intelligence and adjustment.

The growth of child guidance activities was reflected in the meeting of the International Union of Family Organizations. Representatives from 280 organizations in 55 countries attended the meeting held in Rome, Italy, in July. They focused their attention on problems of teen-age marriages and the need in all countries for realistic family and pre-marriage counseling.

Child Guidance Clinics began to look for ways of shifting their emphasis toward needy families and away from services exclusively for middle-class families. One of the reasons was the fact that the indigent suffer mental illness at three times the rate of persons in the middle class.

The clinics gave increasing attention to the problems of the mentally retarded as well as to the emotionally disturbed. The state of Illinois opened the Reed Zone Center in Chicago in August. It is the first of six community centers through which the state will extend its clinical services to both the mentally handicapped and the mentally ill.

California was the first of the 50 states, stimulated by federal planning grants, to publish its master plan for combating mental retardation. It, too, gave high priority to establishing regional diagnostic and counseling centers.

Preschool Training. In August, the U.S. Department of Health, Education, and Welfare (HEW) reported that only one-fourth of the children who are most in need of preschool training are now attending nursery schools or kindergartens.

HEW found that only 3,200,000 children between the ages of 3 and 5 were enrolled in such schools. The nursery schools, they said, are predominantly private and beyond the reach of low-income families, while kindergartens have not been established in many areas of the United States. FRANCES A. MULLEN

See also EDUCATION.

CHILD WELFARE. Vast new programs for the welfare of children were developed under the impetus of the Economic Opportunity Act (the Anti-Poverty Act) of 1964. The Office of Economic Opportunity (OEO), using funds allocated by Congress, had approved plans by mid-February, 1965, for nearly 400 separate War on Poverty projects, including community action projects, neighborhood youth corps, Project Head Start, and other projects directly or indirectly affecting the welfare of children. See POVERTY.

Despite reports of difficulties and scandals in the rapid establishment of new programs, the projects brought new hope to hundreds of thousands of children and youths in 13,444 areas of the United States in 1965. Amendments to the Social Security Act also made major contributions to child welfare through new health programs and increased appropriations for existing programs.

The United Nations Children's Fund (UNICEF) reported that the average infant mortality rate in developing countries is five times as high as it is in the United States. To combat this situation, it has helped 113 countries develop child welfare services. See UNITED NATIONS (Close-Up). FRANCES A. MULLEN

See also JUVENILE DELINQUENCY; NOBEL PRIZES; SOCIAL SECURITY; SOCIAL WELFARE.

CHILDREN'S BOOKS. See LITERATURE FOR CHILDREN.

CHILE was harassed by nature in 1965. On March 28, an intense earthquake shook the central area. Violent storms, floods, and avalanches struck in August. Accumulated losses from these catastrophes were estimated at a minimum of $175,000,000. About 500 persons perished. See DISASTERS.

A sweeping victory in the congressional election held in March gave President Eduardo Frei Montalva the legislative muscle he needed for pushing through broad social and economic proposals.

On September 9, the Senate approved the chamber-passed controversial bill to "Chileanize" copper. Under it, the government acquired 51 per cent interest in the El Teniente mine, 25 per cent in the La Exotica property, and 25 per cent in the new Rio Blanco mine—all owned by U.S. corporations.

In July, President Frei became the first Chilean chief of state ever to visit Europe. The purpose of his trip was to draw the European nations into closer participation in the Alliance for Progress.

Population: 8,738,000. **Government:** President Eduardo Frei Montalva. **Monetary Unit:** escudo (3.37=U.S. $1). **Gross National Product:** 6,361,000,-000 escudos. **Foreign Trade:** exports, $623,000,000; imports, $609,000,000. **Principal Exports:** cotton, hides and skins, meat. MARY C. WEBSTER

See also LATIN AMERICA.

CHRONOLOGY. See pages 10 to 14.

CHURCHES. See EASTERN ORTHODOX; JEWS AND JUDAISM; PROTESTANT; ROMAN CATHOLIC.

CHINA

The People's Republic of China, in pursuit of its international revolutionary goals, experienced a succession of major reverses. Within the communist orbit, the Chinese leaders who ruled from Peking continued to scorn any compromise with the Soviet Union, castigating the new leaders in Moscow as "worse than Khrushchev" because of their commitment to "revisionism" and their limited accommodations with the West. Political setbacks at the abortive Afro-Asian conference in Algeria, as well as in Indonesia and on the Indian-Pakistani frontier, failed to deter Peking from its policy of aggressively pushing the war in Vietnam while rejecting all offers to negotiate. The explosion of China's second nuclear bomb in May symbolized the continuing modernization of its armed forces. Although the United Nations (UN) General Assembly again excluded China from membership, Peking interpreted the increased vote favoring its admission as a victory.

YEAR BOOK photo by Marc Riboud, Magnum

The second Afro-Asian conference scheduled to convene in Algeria in June was conceived by China as an opportune occasion for cementing the new nations into a common front against the West and the Soviet Union. One immediate Chinese objective was to secure a resounding condemnation of U.S. military and economic policy in South Vietnam. Peking also hoped to supplant Moscow as a champion of the emerging nations and perhaps form an international body that would rival the UN.

On the eve of the conference, however, Algeria's President Ahmed Ben Bella, who was acting as host, was ousted from power in an army coup led by Colonel Houari Boumedienne. Caught by surprise, the Chinese pressed even more openly for convening the conference. Such overt political arm-twisting, however, offended many delegates already made uneasy by the political turmoil in Algeria (see ALGERIA; BOUMEDIENNE, HOUARI).

The Chinese seemed reluctant, too, to act upon such divisive issues facing the conference as to whether the Soviet Union should participate. Subsequently, the 15-member steering committee postponed the conference until November and the delegates dispersed. In October, Peking announced that the forthcoming conference would not be justified unless it was committed in advance to denouncing American efforts in South Vietnam. As a result of China's stand, the already loosely organized group disintegrated and the forthcoming conference was canceled.

A Peking-Djakarta political axis that China had fostered in order to mobilize the "new and emerging forces" into an international body that would rival the UN collapsed, due also, in part, to China's aggressive tactics. In Indonesia, China had supplanted both the United States and the Soviet Union as the dominant foreign influence. When an abortive coup against the army was crushed by the

SINEWS OF STEEL for Communist China's industries are processed by asbestos-suited workers in mill at Anshan, in Liaoning province.

military in October, China was implicated with the rebels. As the army and the more conservative Moslem organizations in Indonesia turned upon the Indonesian communists and their allies, China's diplomatic representatives, as well as the overseas Chinese business community in Indonesia, became targets for popular hostility. In drastic contrast to earlier praise, Peking bitterly protested to Djakarta. President Sukarno repeatedly tried to assure the Chinese ambassador that Indonesia's alignment with China was unchanged. But the continuing suppression of the Indonesian Communist party (PKI), which had shifted its allegiance from Moscow to Peking, undercut China's influence in one of the richest and most populous lands in Southeast Asia (see INDONESIA).

When China tried to intervene in the India-Pakistan conflict over Kashmir, it experienced another rebuff. At the height of the hostilities, China demanded that India dismantle its frontier posts above Sikkim. Simultaneously, it threatened to launch a military attack against India from Tibet. The attack, however, failed to materialize.

The Communist Chinese continued to verbally abuse their comrades in Moscow over ideological differences, which still centered on earlier charges that the Soviet leaders were guilty of "revisionism" (see COMMUNISM). Vietnam increasingly became the focus, however, for their rivalry. While the Soviet Union attempted to restrain the North Vietnamese communists, the Chinese urged them on. China's threat that it would not "stand idly by" while the United States enlarged its role in defending South Vietnam was not backed by outright military intervention. Yet, within the North Vietnamese communist movement, China pushed steadily for an expansion of the conflict while dismissing all discussion of a negotiated settlement. This was in keeping with China's policy of encouraging guerrilla warfare against the established governments in Asia and elsewhere. See ASIA; VIETNAM.

Domestic Events. The re-election in January of Liu Shao-chi as chairman of the People's Republic of China signified a continuing retention of power by the older generation of communist leaders. Liu, who was expected eventually to succeed Mao Tse-tung as Communist party chairman, was committed to the same essential course of action, that is, challenging the Soviet Union's leadership of the communist bloc while evolving a special brand of Marxism-Leninism at home. These and other leaders who had shared the management of the Chinese communist movement for more than three decades, however, faced a major dilemma in leadership as time closed in upon them. The average age of the central committee members was about 65 years.

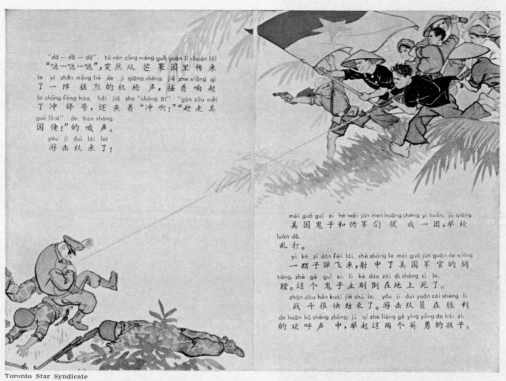

Toronto Star Syndicate

PROPAGANDA PLOY. Communist Chinese use comic book techniques to popularize ideas. Here North Vietnamese guerrillas, top right, triumph over enemy forces.

CHINESE BRASS welcome home Li Tsung-jen, third from left. Li, a former acting president of China, had fled to the West after the communist takeover in 1949.

They were troubled by the fear that the process they had observed in the Soviet Union after the death of Stalin would be duplicated in Communist China when they died, with the revolution faltering and drifting into "revisionism" under their successors. Such a trend, they believed, would betray their cause. In their view, it would inhibit the restoration of China to its "rightful" role in world affairs—the modern equivalent of its ancient imperial glory—and as the bearer of a new revolutionary mission to Africa, Asia, and Latin America.

Hero Worship. China's communists, in an attempt to ensure perpetuation of their ideas among succeeding generations, were engaged in a campaign of national indoctrination rarely equaled anywhere. Almost everyone of any consequence in China, and many ordinary citizens as well, devoted many hours each week throughout the year studying *The Thoughts of Mao Tse-tung*, a volume containing Mao's philosophic thoughts. The less ambitious contented themselves with memorizing the four volumes of Mao's *Selected Works*. Those Chinese who aspired to gain or hold positions of prominence memorized chairman Mao's writings on Chinese history, Marxism-Leninism, guerrilla warfare, economics, and poetry.

Mao's picture was to be seen almost everywhere. Schoolchildren were taught to glorify his role in China's revolution through the study of romantic stories about his exploits in the civil war. They

sang songs pledging themselves to follow his example. Thus, the communists, after wrecking the old classical Chinese body of belief associated with Confucius' teachings, were imposing a new, authoritarian orthodoxy designed to perpetuate their own values in modern China.

Incentive Farming. The still predominantly rural economy made modest gains. Eggs, fruits, pork, poultry, and vegetables were available in relative abundance. These could be purchased readily in the "free markets," where peasants were allowed to sell much of the produce from their small private plots. The subsequent improvement in both quantity and variety of diet was a tribute chiefly to the Chinese farmers' ingenuity and willingness to work when offered even modest incentives. Although their private plots constituted only a small fraction of the farmland, Chinese peasants derived more than one-half of their actual income from such "private enterprise." See Section Two, INSIDE RURAL CHINA.

Grain Shortages. Although management of the People's Communes had been decentralized, communist suspicion of "bourgeois-capitalist tendencies" blocked the granting of comparable incentives in many areas and yields were low. Because China only belatedly recognized the importance of chemical fertilizers, wheat yields remained low. China was manufacturing nearly 4,000,000 tons of fertilizer per year and importing half as much again. Yet it was less than one-fifth of what China's leaders

279

admitted was needed to increase output. Much of the winter wheat crop was hurt by the rising of alkali in the newly irrigated regions of northern China and a winter drought that extended into Manchuria. As a consequence, while China claimed a modest expansion in total harvests, it continued to import large amounts of grain. Roughly 6,500,000 tons of wheat were purchased, chiefly from Argentina, Australia, and Canada. See AGRICULTURE.

In order to pay for such imports, strike better bargains on the purchase of industrial plants, and achieve a greater independence of the Soviet Union, China increasingly shifted its trade from the communist bloc to the Western world. Although the Soviet Union remained China's largest single trading partner, full repayment of China's debt to Moscow facilitated the Western rapprochement that had brought Peking its economic contact with 125 countries and regions. The British crown colony of Hong Kong was providing more than one-half of China's free foreign exchange, or over $500,000,000 annually. Most of this was earned through the export of fruits, poultry, textiles, vegetables, and increasingly sophisticated manufactures. The Chinese communists, however, also derived income from overseas remittances as well as from the earnings of their "capitalist" enterprises in the colony. Ironically, such enterprises made China the largest single employer in Hong Kong.

China's industry continued its gradual recovery from the near disaster of the "Great Leap Forward" which had been launched in 1957 and which, through mismanagement, had caused turmoil in so many industries. Important gains were made over pre-1957 levels, particularly in sources of energy. Coal production had increased by 70 per cent and electric power output had grown by 67 per cent. Petroleum production from China's new oil wells, located chiefly in central Asia, had quadrupled. The discovery of a new oil field in Manchuria promised to further expand China's energy sources.

Steel production may well have exceeded 9,000,000 tons during the year. In showing an improvement in quality, steel reflected an increasing sophistication in China's industries, which were not only building more trucks and machine tools, but were also discovering some of the advantages of better building materials, chemicals, plastics, and synthetic fibers. Important segments of China's industry remained inefficient by Western standards. Yet the progress they had made encouraged the communist leaders to schedule a third Five-Year Plan in 1966.

Population: 700,000,000. **Government:** Communist Party Chairman Mao Tse-tung; Chairman of the Republic Liu Shao-chi; Premier Chou En-lai. **Monetary Unit:** yuan (2 = U.S. $1). **Foreign Trade:** exports, $1,600,000,000; imports, $1,100,000,000. **Principal Exports:** coal, metal ores and concentrates, soybeans, tea, textiles.   ALBERT RAVENHOLT

See also ASIA.

CITY. The Congress of the United States responded warmly to the vital urban outlook of President Lyndon B. Johnson. It enacted legislation that makes 1965 a bench-mark year for the setting of new relationships between the nation's cities and the federal government. The President's major victory in this field came with the creation of a Cabinet-level Department of Housing and Urban Development (HUD), a victory which Congress had denied John F. Kennedy. The new department, intended to represent America's city dwellers, began its life November 9, although the President deferred naming its new secretary until after the turn of the year. See HOUSING.

At first, HUD simply administered existing programs of aid for urban planning, community facilities, the Federal Housing Administration's mortgage insurance, mass transit, public housing, and urban renewal. But Congress also specified that the department be responsible for the immense task of coordinating scores of federal aid programs.

With a big Housing and Urban Development Act to administer, HUD began to add programs dealing with stronger code enforcement, rehabilitation of neighborhoods, rent supplements, and water and sewer facilities.

Congress also passed other bills aimed at upgrading urban living. It provided more aid for better law enforcement, control of air and water pollution, disposal of solid wastes, economic development, highway beautification, and public works. Funds for the War on Poverty were doubled, but its Community Action Program divided many localities into two camps. At issue was the extent to which the "poor" participated in policy making. In addition, mayors complained of being by-passed by the Office of Economic Opportunity. See CONGRESS OF THE UNITED STATES; POVERTY; Section Two, POLLUTED AMERICA.

President Johnson also expressed his interest in the life of the cities by naming Vice-President Hubert H. Humphrey, a former mayor of Minneapolis, as his liaison with the nation's mayors. Humphrey responded by inviting the mayors of every city above 30,000 population to Washington for a series of unprecedented meetings with himself and other Cabinet members. Humphrey's representatives also fanned out across the nation, inviting city halls to seek information about how they might use federal programs.

The States, too, acted in behalf of cities, although many state legislatures were not yet composed of members elected on a "one man, one vote" basis. Yet seven states (Colorado, Connecticut, Maine, Massachusetts, Nebraska, Ohio, and Rhode Island) acted on fair housing. Broader authorization for local urban renewal and redevelopment was provided in Alaska, California, Idaho, Nebraska, New Jersey, New York, Utah, and Wyoming. See STATE GOVERNMENT.

In at least 14 states, courts were called on to rule whether "one man, one vote" also affects such local governing bodies as city councils. No clear picture emerged from early lower court decisions.

Central Business Districts seemed to have turned a corner in consumer confidence, as major retail chains reported rising sales. New and remodeled department stores brightened downtown areas in Chicago, Dallas, New Haven, Pittsburgh, Sacramento, and Syracuse. Pedestrian malls and bridges over busy streets appeared. Improved mass transportation, retailers said, would add to downtown's vitality. See Section Two, THE NEW NEW ENGLAND.

White House Conference. World-wide growth of cities brought a warning of "deep trouble" from a citizens' Committee on Urban Development in December. Its views were presented at the White House Conference on International Cooperation. The committee recommended the creation of an international agency to study building technology, housing, land use, sanitation, and water supply.

In September, *Scientific American* devoted its entire issue to cities, their origin and evolution, their progress and problems. Yet, despite the concern of the experts, a Gallup Poll released in the same week that the Committee on Urban Development made its report showed that not one American in 100 regarded urbanization as the country's most important problem. DONALD W. LIEF

CITY PLANNING.
With the passage of the Department of Housing and Development Act in 1965, the Congress of the United States formally declared, "... that the general welfare and security of the nation and the health and living standards of the people require, as a matter of national purpose, sound development of the nation's communities and metropolitan areas in which the vast majority of its people live and work."

The act meant that the urban areas of the country will henceforth be represented in the President's Cabinet. Thus it was anticipated that federally assisted programs for planning orderly development and redevelopment within metropolitan areas will benefit by being better coordinated at the national level. Previously, planning assistance programs were administered by several different departments within the federal Housing and Home Finance Agency, which is not a Cabinet-level agency. It can also be expected that Congress will now lend a more sympathetic ear to administration proposals for more far-reaching forms of planning assistance and for experimentation with new concepts of urban development. See CONGRESS OF THE U.S.; HOUSING.

New Towns. The administration, in 1964 and 1965, recommended that Congress authorize the Federal Housing Administration to insure loans to builders for land acquisition and for the planning of "new towns," that is, extensive new developments with large residential, commercial, and industrial

areas, located in the countryside between large cities. But the measure failed for lack of support from industry organizations.

Nevertheless, the "new towns" concept, successfully applied in Scandinavia and in England, is currently being tried in the United States—without the benefit of specific federal assistance.

Three principal new towns were in the making in 1965. Columbia, Maryland, midway between Washington, D.C., and Baltimore, was the largest new town underway. Developer of the 15,000-acre site that will eventually house 100,000 people is Community Research and Development, Inc.

Reston, Virginia, is the first new town to complete a sizable portion of its plan. Some 300 residents were living in the first of its seven villages in 1965. Located 18 miles outside of Washington, D.C., Reston is designed to provide homes for 75,000 by 1970 in high-rise apartments and single-family units, as well as shops and employment opportunities.

Plans were nearing completion in 1965 for another such community, San Simeon, to be located near San Francisco. The 1,275-acre site near famed Hearst Castle will be built in three five-year stages by the Hearst Corporation. According to the June, 1965, issue of *California Builder*, 180 such self-contained communities have been announced in the United States. J. ROBERT DUMOUCHEL

See also ARCHITECTURE.

CIVIL DEFENSE
in the United States took on a deeper military hue in 1965 with the creation of an army liaison headquarters in each of the 48 continental states. Set up in March with the blessings of all the governors, these units will channel military help to the 5,300 state and local civil defense workers in any disaster, nuclear or natural.

William P. Durkee, director of civil defense under the Secretary of the Army, declared that the program "in no way assigns civil defense to the military." He added: "The role of the military in civil defense is to support civil authority." The state adjutant general, serving under the governor, heads the headquarters in his state. But, in a nuclear attack, he and his headquarters would be federalized under the Continental Army Command.

President Lyndon B. Johnson requested $193,900,000 for civil defense. Congress appropriated $106,780,000, most of it to continue the nationwide shelter program, and the rest for research, training, communications, and matching funds to states.

Ever since the 1961 Berlin crisis, the Department of Defense has been surveying the nation's buildings, mines, caves, and tunnels to locate potential public fallout shelters. By the end of 1965, it had found 158,203 such areas with spaces for 139,131,000 persons. It actually marked 90,374 with 76,681,000 spaces, and put 14-day supplies of food, water, medicine, and other necessities in 66,299 with 36,232,000 spaces. WARREN ROGERS

CIVIL RIGHTS

In the United States, the protection of human rights, in 1965, was closely allied with the building of the Great Society, the War on Poverty, and the improvement of the criminal law. At the same time, despite crimes of violence in the South, there was further safeguarding of the civil rights of the nation's Negro citizens. See NEGRO.

Western Europe. In France, the national cabinet finally approved a bill granting women equal legal rights with their husbands. In the past, under the Code Napoléon, husbands had the power to administer all family property, determine the education of their children, and even to forbid their wives to open a bank account or take a job.

In Great Britain, the problem of segregation of immigrants from India, Pakistan, and the West Indies continued to agitate many areas.

PICTURES OF THE YEAR / James H. Karales © LOOK Magazine

Hence, the Labour government introduced a bill prohibiting discrimination in housing and public accommodations. In addition, Parliament voted to abolish the death penalty for five years. At the end of this trial period, Parliament would vote on a new law based on its findings during the period. See GREAT BRITAIN.

Communist Countries. In criminal prosecutions in the Soviet Union, progress was made in the abandonment of the Stalinist rule that the accused is considered guilty unless he proves his innocence. But the Soviet attitude toward freedom of the press remained unchanged. Leonid S. Sobolov, chairman of the Writers' Union of the Russian Republic, declared that "absolute freedom of speech" is a "false concept." He insisted that Soviet writers always maintain a "Soviet political viewpoint."

Africa. In the emerging nations, civil rights suffered largely because the people of the new states aspired to constitutionalism, but too frequently were unprepared for modern democracy. In Algeria, in July, Colonel Houari Boumedienne overthrew the regime of President Ahmed Ben Bella, promising a modern constitution permitting the "free expression of the people's will." Meanwhile, however, a "one-party" system continued to rule. One-party government also ruled in Togo (although its record was good in protecting civil liberties) and in Ghana. See ALGERIA; GHANA; TOGO.

The Federal Republic of Nigeria, often called a model African republic, underwent a national election on Dec. 30, 1964, in an atmosphere of violence and bloodshed. Nevertheless, in 1965, the traditional British "two-party" system in Parliament was allowed to prevail, and even during the political crisis, the government imposed no censorship on foreign newsmen. See NIGERIA.

In Rhodesia, the government of Ian Smith declared its independence of Great Britain when Britain refused to sanction a new Rhodesian consti-

THE GREAT MARCH of 54 miles from Selma, Ala., to the state capital, in March, was a turning point for the rights movement in the South.

Pictorial Parade

GUARDSMEN, right, patrol the streets of the Watts
section of Los Angeles, a Negro district
that was torn by the worst race riots in the
nation in 20 years. The riots exploded after
the arrest of a Negro for reckless driving.
The lives of 34 people were lost; damage
exceeded $40,000,000. Negro leaders
Martin Luther King and Bayard Rustin, above,
flew to city in a vain attempt to end the turmoil.

tution limiting the franchise of its Negroes, who
outnumber the whites six to one. On November 11,
the United Nations General Assembly adopted a
resolution, offered by 36 African states, calling upon
Great Britain to "take all necessary steps to put an
end to the rebellion" in Rhodesia. See RHODESIA.

Latin America. In Brazil, President Humberto
de Alencar Castelo Branco dissolved the 13 political
parties. An "institutional act" authorized him to
declare a state of siege, and to cancel for 10 years
the political rights of any citizen who resisted
the government.

In Communist Cuba, Fidel Castro's government
announced, in June, a "second revolution" to purge
the schools of "intellectualism."

In the Dominican Republic, in April, the quarrel
between the rebels and the junta partly concerned
the question of the restoration of the 1963 constitution which barred political deportations. The
junta contended that the antideportation clause
of the constitution prevented the ouster of communists from the country. See DOMINICAN REPUB-
LIC; NATIONAL DEFENSE.

In Colombia, after student riots in Bogotá and
other cities, President Guillermo Léon Valencia
declared a nationwide state of siege. In Bolivia,
the government was forced to employ the army to
squelch a revolt of workers in the tin mines.

Vatican Council. On December 8, Pope Paul
VI closed Vatican Council II, which had opened in

1962. The council adopted several historic measures that bear on civil liberties. The pastoral constitution, "The Church in the Modern World," restated some of the fundamental principles of liberty and human rights. The Declaration on Religious Liberty called for "freedom or immunity from coercion in matters religious." The Declaration on the Relation of the Church to Non-Christian Religions, among other things, disassociated the Jews collectively from blame for the death of Christ, and pleaded for the elimination of anti-Semitism everywhere. See ROMAN CATHOLIC; Section Two, THE SACRED LAND.

United States. A growing public opinion held that legislation to guarantee the civic and political rights of Negroes was not sufficient to promote the "good life" of Negro citizens. Renewed efforts for education, employment, and housing were imperative. Indeed, considerations of this kind were one of the motives behind the War on Poverty. In his annual message to Congress, on January 4, President Lyndon B. Johnson emphasized that the Great Society must be "open for all Americans." See EDUCATION; POVERTY.

Voting Rights Act. On August 6, President Johnson signed the Voting Rights Act of 1965 in a solemn ceremony in the rotunda of the Capitol. In the President's words, the act is intended "to strike down restrictions to voting in all elections . . . which have been used to deny Negroes the right to vote."

The bill establishes "a simple uniform standard which cannot be used—however ingenious the effort —to flout our Constitution." It provides for citizens to be registered by U.S. government officials, if state officials refuse to register them.

The March. Perhaps the biggest single impetus in 1965 for the passage of the act was the 54-mile Freedom March of 25,000 Negroes and whites along U.S. Highway 80 from Selma to Montgomery, Ala., the state capital. See NEGRO.

Civil Disobedience. The advocacy of civil disobedience by many civil rights agitators began to awaken objections to the defiance of local laws forbidding demonstrations likely to disturb the peace. Many held that individuals possessed no right to transgress local ordinances. In a case involving the arrest of 167 demonstrators who had defied a local ordinance, Federal District Judge Frank M. Johnson in Alabama said: "The philosophy that a person may—if his cause is labeled 'civil rights' or 'state rights'—determine for himself what laws and court decisions are morally right or wrong and either obey or refuse to obey them according to his own determination, is a philosophy that is foreign to our 'rule of law' theory of government." On the other hand, the Supreme Court of the United States continued to give a very broad interpretation to the constitutional "right of the people peaceably to assemble." See LOS ANGELES.   KENNETH COLEGROVE

CIVIL WAR CENTENNIAL observance, officially begun in 1961 by an act of the Congress of the United States, came to a close in 1965. To mark the 156th anniversary of President Abraham Lincoln's birth, President Lyndon B. Johnson entertained 110 guests at the White House on February 12. On March 4, a crowd of 20,000 gathered in front of the U.S. Capitol to observe a re-enactment of Lincoln's second inauguration.

The city of Danville, Va., staged a week-long ceremony in April to commemorate its role as the last capital of the Confederacy. Highlight was a re-enactment of the arrival from Richmond of President Jefferson Davis. On April 9, national attention focused on Appomattox Court House near Appomattox, Va., where thousands gathered to recall the surrender of the Army of Northern Virginia, led by General Robert E. Lee, to the Union's Army of the Potomac, led by General Ulysses S. Grant. Principal speaker was Bruce Catton, Pulitzer prize-winning author and historian.   V. C. JONES

CLOTHING. See FASHION; TEXTILE.

CLUBS, BOYS' AND GIRLS'. See BOY SCOUTS OF AMERICA; BOYS' CLUBS OF AMERICA; CAMP FIRE GIRLS; FOUR-H CLUBS; FUTURE FARMERS OF AMERICA; FUTURE HOMEMAKERS OF AMERICA; GIRL SCOUTS; GIRLS CLUBS OF AMERICA; JUNIOR ACHIEVEMENT; SCIENCE CLUBS OF AMERICA.

COAL. See MINES AND MINING.

COIN COLLECTING. See HOBBIES.

COLOMBIA edged close to bankruptcy in 1965. Its economy was in grave straits; efforts by President Guillermo Léon Valencia to relieve the situation were thwarted by a congress that was reluctant to pass unpopular austerity measures.

In June, the International Bank for Reconstruction and Development and the International Monetary Fund refused to advance new loans until the government moved to institute needed reforms. As a result, factories were forced either to curtail operations or close down due to the lack of foreign funds to import needed raw materials.

A state of siege was invoked on May 21 following widespread riots. The riots stemmed from student protests against U.S. landings in the Dominican Republic (see DOMINICAN REPUBLIC). In July, the situation grew so tense between the administration and congress that military leaders issued a manifesto affirming their support of the government. On September 3, the administration invoked its authority under state-of-siege regulations and decreed measures to break the deadlock on economic reforms.

Population: 18,059,000. **Government:** President Guillermo Léon Valencia. **Monetary Unit:** peso, (9 = U.S. $1). **Gross National Product:** 33,090,000,-000 pesos. **Foreign Trade:** exports, $537,000,000; imports, $586,000,000. **Principal Exports:** coffee, cotton, petroleum.   MARY C. WEBSTER

See also LATIN AMERICA.

COMMUNICATIONS. The first commercial transmission of live television between continents via satellite took place on June 28, 1965. The transmission was a landmark in communications progress. Signals were relayed from the Early Bird satellite hovering 22,300 miles above the Atlantic Ocean.

Early Bird is owned by an international consortium of 47 nations of which the Communications Satellite Corporation (Comsat) is the U.S. entry. Early Bird will be used primarily to relay telephone conversations and other types of audio and visual data. It added 240 two-way voice channels between North America and Europe. Comsat's future plans include an advanced system of satellites that will create an additional 1,000 two-way voice circuits.

The continents were also joined on Sept. 15, 1965, by a fourth transatlantic telephone cable, the first to connect the U.S. mainland directly with continental Europe. It is the longest single cable span in the world, stretching 4,150 miles from Tuckerton, N.J., to St. Hilaire-de-Riez, France. By the end of the year, undersea cables, high-frequency radio, and space satellites provided some 1,500 circuits that carried millions upon millions of calls to many points around the world.

In the United States, the Bell System put a $200,-000,000 blast-resistant coaxial cable into service. It added 9,000 transcontinental telephone circuits to the existing 15,000 in the nation's long-distance network. Work was started on another blast-resistant

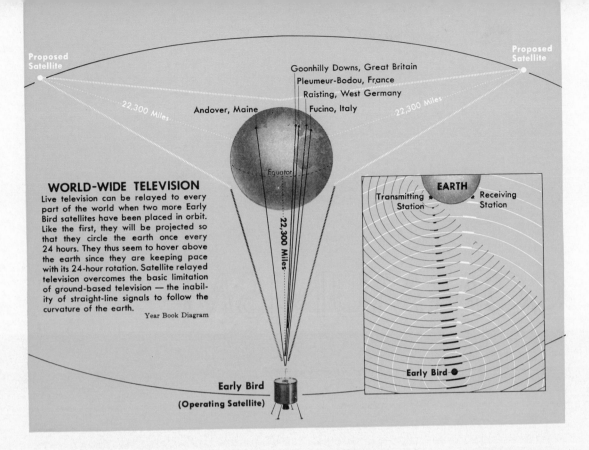

Proposed Satellite

Goonhilly Downs, Great Britain
Pleumeur-Bodou, France
Raisting, West Germany
Fucino, Italy

Andover, Maine

Proposed Satellite

22,300 Miles

22,300 Miles

Equator

22,300 Miles

EARTH

Transmitting Station

Receiving Station

WORLD-WIDE TELEVISION
Live television can be relayed to every part of the world when two more Early Bird satellites have been placed in orbit. Like the first, they will be projected so that they circle the earth once every 24 hours. They thus seem to hover above the earth since they are keeping pace with its 24-hour rotation. Satellite relayed television overcomes the basic limitation of ground-based television — the inability of straight-line signals to follow the curvature of the earth.

Year Book Diagram

Early Bird

Early Bird
(Operating Satellite)

cable between western Massachusetts and Chicago. When completed in 1966, it will carry 18,740 voice-grade channels. Plans were also announced for a similar cable from Boston to Miami, which will add 32,400 circuits to the network serving the East Coast. The vast continental network of microwave radio and coaxial cables in the United States and Canada was the equivalent of 400,000 voice-grade circuits totaling more than 140,000,000 miles. In 1965, more than 130,000,000,000 conversations traveled over these communications highways.

Electronic Switching. Another historic landmark was the May 30 opening of the Bell System's first electronic central office at Succasunna, N.J. This is a large step forward in an industry program to bring customers additional services from their telephones. By dialing simple coded instructions, users in the Succasunna area can automatically transfer all incoming calls to another number, dial frequently called numbers using only a few digits, or set up conferences using more than two telephones. The Succasunna office climaxed the largest single research and development project in Bell System history. The cost was more than $100,000,000. American Telephone & Telegraph Company board chairman Frederick R. Kappel said the Electronic Switching System (ESS), which will require about 35 years to complete, "will open up an era of communications service that is more personalized, more human, than ever before."

FCC Concern. Late in the year, the Federal Communications Commission (FCC) launched the most ambitious regulatory investigation undertaken in the 31 years of the agency's existence. The commission directed a full-fledged investigation into the rates and earnings of the Bell System. It was expected that the inquiry would take at least several years to complete. Earlier in the year, a reduction in interstate telephone rates lowered costs to users by $100,000,000. It was the largest reduction of its kind in history.

At the end of 1965, the Bell System was serving more than 75,000,000 telephones in the United States, and the nation's 2,400 independents some 15,165,000 more. Together, they accounted for about half of the world's total. The Western Union Telegraph Company, with 6,864,326 miles of telegraph channels forming another communications web across the country, handled more than 1,910,-626,000 messages.

History of another sort was almost made in September when Hurricane Betsy became the most costly storm in telephone history. Damages totaled almost $16,000,000 in Louisiana, Mississippi, and Florida as the storm knocked out a half-million telephones, downed or otherwise damaged some 5,500 poles, and interrupted 2,200 long-distance circuits.   THOMAS M. MALIA

See also ELECTRONICS; RADIO; SPACE TRAVEL; TELEVISION; WEATHER.

COMMUNISM

The international communist movement, founded in 1919 as a tightly organized system under Soviet leadership, reached the parting of the ways at the conference of Communist parties in Moscow in March. The decisions of this "consultative meeting" documented the profound disunity of the communist camp and its apparently irrevocable split into hostile factions led by the Soviet Union and Communist China.

The meeting originally had been scheduled by Soviet Premier Nikita S. Khrushchev for December, 1964. It was to be the final showdown in the verbal conflict between the giants of the communist world. But Khrushchev was deposed in October, 1964, and the new Soviet leaders, Leonid I. Brezhnev and Aleksei N. Kosygin, postponed the conference in the vain hope of a Sino-Soviet reconciliation. Finally, they convened the meeting, which turned out to be a rump session attended by only 19 of the 26 invited parties. The Chinese and their allies—from Albania, Indonesia, Japan, North Korea, and North Vietnam—refused to attend. Also absent was Romania, a member of the Soviet bloc in Europe.

Eastfoto

As expected, the gathering condemned U.S. aggression in Vietnam and called for unity against American "imperialism." But it also appealed for the cessation of open disputes among communists and proposed measures that would prepare the ground for a unifying conference of all parties. Nothing could have testified more clearly than these concessions to the decline of Soviet influence upon world communism, and to the failure of Khrushchev's successors to patch up the quarrel.

Chinese Criticism of Soviet policy, which had been resumed immediately after the failure of the initial Soviet effort at reconciliation, increased in intensity after the March conference. The antagonism was more than a product merely of Khrushchev's personality and actions. Brezhnev and Kosygin themselves became targets of the new attacks. They were charged with continuing Khrushchev's policy of "revisionism." The Chinese also continued to rule out the possibility of peaceful coexistence with the United States, a keystone in Soviet policy.

The controversy was further aggravated by the escalation of U.S. action in the Vietnam conflict (see VIETNAM). In its bid for communist leadership, the Soviet Union adopted a much more radical stance. It issued strong statements in support of North Vietnam and the communist National Liberation Front in South Vietnam, and promised increased aid to both. Kosygin made an urgent visit to Hanoi, the North Vietnamese capital, in February, 1965, and indicated his government's desire not to be outbid by the Chinese in support of a "war of liberation." A Soviet promise of increased military aid was followed by a return visit of a North Vietnamese delegation to the Soviet Union in April,

A ZEALOUS ARMY of actors charges on enemy position in a 1965 spectacular, The East Is Red, produced in Peking.

1965. This suggested that North Vietnam, formerly a warm ally of the Chinese had, at least to some degree, shifted its allegiance.

Conflict Grows. The Chinese, of course, did not moderate their condemnation of the Soviet Union. They asserted that Moscow was failing to give adequate aid to North Vietnam and the Viet Cong, and was, in fact, collaborating with the United States to stifle the "revolutionary" movement.

Repeated demands by the Soviet Union for communist unity against U.S. aggression met only with rebuffs from the Chinese. Although no concrete action was taken, the Soviet Union hinted at a desire to see the conflict ended by negotiations.

The outbreak of the war between India and Pakistan in September further magnified the differences between Moscow and Peking, with China giving strong verbal support to Pakistan, and the Soviet Union indicating its sincere hope for a peaceful solution (see INDIA; PAKISTAN). In the same month, the failure of the apparent communist effort to take over by force in Indonesia strengthened the Soviet position, which favored a political evolution to communism rather than the assumption of power through a coup (see INDONESIA).

A Strained Façade. World communism continued to preserve an outward appearance of formal unity. The Chinese were not formally expelled and did not themselves create a separate "International."

Behind the scenes, however, the chasm between the rival wings widened and deepened. Of the approximately 90 communist parties (with over 40,000,000 members), between 60 and 70 supported the Soviet Union on essential questions. The Chinese had the backing of about a dozen parties, mostly Asian. Apart from Albania, which was already in the Chinese camp, the parties of eastern Europe, Yugoslavia included, continued to side with Moscow, but on an increasingly voluntary basis.

European Satellites. As a result, the communist system no longer possessed a single center for making decisions and had no adequate institutions for settling problems of common interest. Coordination of economic policy between Soviet Russia and the East European satellite countries through the Council for Mutual Economic Assistance (COMECON) was more and more replaced by negotiations on specific issues by two or more interested states, with Yugoslavia sometimes present as an observer and Albania always absent.

The case of Romania was unique. It gradually adopted a position of nonalignment, insisting on its independence within the bloc, reducing its commitments to the Warsaw alliance, and rejecting the multilateral arrangements of COMECON. Romania continued to develop commercial exchanges with Western countries. Romania's refusal to attend the Moscow conference dramatically signalized its new role.   H. GORDON SKILLING

See also AFRICA; ASIA; CHINA; RUSSIA.

COMPUTERS were becoming more familiar to more Americans with the growing use of giant computer centers designed to serve thousands of customers. Sixteen of these time-sharing, on-line systems, which allow "multiple access" by many users simultaneously, were being experimentally developed in 1965. Foremost, perhaps, was the Massachusetts Institute of Technology's Multiple Access Computation (MAC). In this project, 110 computer teleprinters were installed about the campus—in classrooms, laboratories, and homes of key faculty members. At any time, dozens of professors and students could use a central computer's logic to get instant answers to their research questions.

Information Processing, as distinguished from data processing, was forcing the replacement of data-in/data-out systems with data-in/information-out systems. This was expected to have an enormous significance on future uses of electronic equipment, not only in business, but also throughout the social and political environment.

One example is the computer system at the Lockheed Aircraft Corporation in Marietta, Ga. There, two Sperry Rand Univac 490s, coupled with a dynamic software package of computer programs, immediately answer managerial questions about what is currently happening in the plant, enabling administrators to "truly manage their business, not just account for it."

Electronic Police. During the year, experimental police computer systems produced suspects in a Detroit holdup, tallied crime reports in Chicago, and instantly identified stolen cars in New York City. In New York's Operation CORRAL (Computer Oriented Retrieval of Auto Larcenists), an observer patrol car on Grand Central Parkway could radio the license number of a suspected car to a Univac 490. Five seconds later, waiting police were informed whether it was one of the 30,000 cars reported stolen. Computer systems have also helped apprehend felons, larcenists, forgers, and robbers, as well as car thieves. In Chicago, Operation Crime Stop, a computerized program, was credited with 3,800 arrests between April, 1964, and August, 1965.

Governor Edmund G. Brown of California announced in August the results of a six-month study in which "a miniature world of crime" had been simulated mathematically by computer experts at the Space-General Corporation at El Monte, Calif. Working with data collected from the courts, California Youth and Adult Corrections Agency, police departments, regional planning commissions, school districts, and sheriffs, a computer pinpointed areas, categories, and causes of crime.

To supply manpower for the ever-widening use of data and information processing, one institution, the Illinois Institute of Technology, in 1965 alone, trained 200 teachers and 1,800 students from high schools in the Chicago area to translate problems into various computer languages.   SERGEI LENORMAND

CONGO (BRAZZAVILLE). The bodies of Attorney General Lazare Matsokota and Anselme Massoueme, director of the government's information agency, were found beside the Congo River on Feb. 15, 1965. Government sources claimed that the two government officials were victims of kidnapers. But a conflicting report said that the two men, along with many others, had, in fact, been arrested by their own security police. The murders were interpreted as evidence of a deepening split between Premier Pascal Lissouba and President Alphonse Massemba-Débat.

Early in 1965, Congo (Brazzaville) and Congo (Léopoldville) frequently charged the other had violated their common border. By November, however, tempers had cooled enough for the two Congos to resume diplomatic relations.

The Brazzaville government made economic agreements with Algeria, Communist China, the Soviet Union, and West Germany. These provide for a cement factory, model cotton farm, palm oil refinery, and mineral exploration.

Population: 861,000. **Government:** President Alphonse Massemba-Débat; Premier Pascal Lissouba. **Monetary Unit:** CFA franc (246.85 = U.S. $1). **Foreign Trade:** exports, $20,000,000; imports, $79,000,000. **Principal Exports:** lumber, palm oil, petroleum.   BENJAMIN E. THOMAS

See also AFRICA.

PIX

"I AM THE PRESIDENT," announced General Joseph Mobutu when he overthrew Joseph Kasavubu to seize Congo government.

CONGO (LÉOPOLDVILLE). Major-General Joseph Mobutu deposed President Joseph Kasavubu in a bloodless coup d'état on Nov. 25, 1965, canceled the forthcoming presidential elections, and proclaimed himself head of the government for a five-year term. Mobutu's actions abruptly ended a behind-the-scenes struggle for the presidency between Kasavubu, the incumbent, and former Premier Moise Tshombe, who had been dismissed from office.

The coup had its origins, to a great extent, in the nationwide parliamentary elections held in March and April. These elections, at first scheduled for February, had been postponed several times because of the disorganization caused by fighting against Congolese rebels in the northern and eastern provinces. Final election results showed that Tshombe had emerged as one of the most powerful political figures in Congo.

On October 13, Tshombe was dismissed by Kasavubu on the grounds that his term had expired. Evariste Kimba was designated the new premier. Tshombe, resentful of his deposition, obtained a vote of confidence from the newly elected national assembly. To end the ensuing political turmoil Mobutu took control and appointed Leonard Mulamba as premier.

Rebel Activities. The central government managed to exercise control over most of the country during 1965, despite the operation of rebel bands and the shifts of power within the government. In January and February, the government defeated major rebel forces in northeastern Congo. Late in March, the government began clearing the area, thus preventing the rebels from gaining aid through neighboring Uganda and Sudan.

The rebels not only suffered military defeats, but they were also unable to cooperate in opposing the government. In January, rebel leaders meeting in Tanzania, announced that they intended to unify the eastern and western areas of the rebel movement under one supreme revolutionary council. But when some of the leaders met in Cairo, Egypt, in April, to work out the plan for unity, the conference collapsed. One reason was that Christophe Gbenye, a leader in the east, did not attend. A Supreme Revolutionary Council was later formed by Gaston Soumialot, but it was refused recognition by Gbenye and some of the other leaders.

Meanwhile, financial differences between Congo and Belgium were settled in talks held in Brussels in February. The Belgians turned over to the Congolese control of the huge Union Minière du Haut-Katanga, as well as Belgian assets in various Congolese firms. See BELGIUM.

Population: 15,428,000. **Government:** President Joseph Mobutu; Premier Leonard Mulamba. **Monetary Unit:** franc (50 = U.S. $1). **Foreign Trade:** exports, $117,000,000; imports, $130,000,000. **Principal Exports:** coffee, copper.   BENJAMIN E. THOMAS

See also AFRICA.

291

CONGRESS OF THE UNITED STATES

CONGRESS OF THE UNITED STATES

The lengthy first session of the 89th Congress, which convened January 4, and adjourned shortly before 1 A.M. October 23, set a record for action unsurpassed since the early days of President Franklin D. Roosevelt's New Deal. Passing some 90 major bills, Congress vastly expanded the role of the government in the Great Society. President Lyndon B. Johnson boasted that the first session of the 89th Congress compiled "a record of major accomplishment without equal or close parallel in the present era." Some observers credited Congress with increased prestige; others felt the legislative record was a presidential victory and a further decline in congressional authority.

There were several reasons for the close cooperation between the President and Congress:

● The Democratic victory in the 1964 election gave President Johnson a sweeping mandate from American voters.

● The President had two-to-one Democratic majorities in both houses. When the session opened, Democrats outnumbered Republicans 295 to 140 in the House and 68 to 32 in the Senate.

● The power of the House Rules Committee had been reduced when the Speaker of the House was authorized to by-pass the committee if it refused to bring bills to the floor.

● Senate Republican Leader Everett M. Dirksen supported critical measures such as the Voting Rights Act, Medicare, and federal aid for education.

● Seventy-one freshmen House Democrats gave Mr. Johnson 89 per cent support in crucial votes.

● The President drew on his 23 years of experience in Congress to press his program forward.

The President's "Must List" contained 88 bills when the session began, and to most of these Congress said "yes." Among the most important were the Voting Rights Act of 1965, Medicare, federal aid to education, the War on Poverty program, foreign aid, immigration, and the $4,700,000,000 excise tax cut (as of Jan. 1, 1969).

Among the bills that failed to pass—all late in the session—were repeal of Section 14(b) of the Taft-Hartley Act (after an eight-day filibuster in the Senate), home rule for the District of Columbia, and funds for a national teacher corps and low-rent housing subsidies. See WASHINGTON, D.C.

Expenditures. The 89th Congress voted record peacetime appropriations totaling $119,337,566,896. Budget totals rose accordingly. The fiscal 1966 administrative budget, estimated in January, 1965, at $99,700,000,000, was estimated at the close of the session at $107,000,000,000 with the 1967 budget estimated at somewhere near $110,000,000,000. Congress also raised the temporary federal debt ceiling to $328,000,000,000, reflecting the rising costs of the Great Society.

AN ELATED PRESIDENT tosses away a pen after signing his first Great Society bill, aid to Appalachia, passed by the 89th Congress.

CONGRESS OF THE UNITED STATES

Defense appropriations totaled $46,887,163,000, including some $1,700,000,000 for the build-up of American forces in Vietnam. A revised military construction bill was finally passed in September. The President had vetoed the original bill because he considered its requirement of congressional approval for closing military bases an encroachment on executive power. One billion dollars in pay increases for the armed forces was also provided.

Foreign aid provided by Congress in 1965 was 7 per cent less than the total asked by the President—the smallest congressional cut in a foreign aid request since the beginning of the Marshall Plan. Congress authorized $3,360,000,000 in foreign aid, but appropriated only $3,218,000,000.

Before it adjourned, Congress voted a 3.6 per cent pay increase for 1,700,000 federal employees.

Medicare. For 20 years, a plan for medical insurance under Social Security—first proposed by President Harry S. Truman—had been bitterly opposed by the powerful American Medical Association (AMA), which fought against any form of "socialized medicine." Finally, in July, Congress not only passed the Medicare legislation—officially called the Social Security Amendments of 1965— that President Johnson had demanded, but also went further by offering voluntary medical insurance that helps pay doctors' fees and expenses of some other services to those over 65 who want the coverage. The act also provided an average increase in Social Security cash benefits of 7 per cent, raising maximum family benefits from $254 to $309.20. See MEDICARE; SOCIAL SECURITY.

Other Social Legislation included the Older Americans Act of 1965, signed into law July 14. It authorized matching grants to states and funds to public and private nonprofit organizations to provide programs for the aged and to train personnel to teach them new skills (see OLD AGE). On August 4, the President signed a mental health bill providing funds to staff mental health centers and to train teachers to work with handicapped children (see HANDICAPPED, THE; MENTAL HEALTH). Five days later, another health bill became law. It called for coordinated research on and treatment of heart disease, cancer, stroke, and related diseases in regional centers. Congress also strengthened controls on the sale of barbiturates and amphetamines. Federal immunization programs for children were augmented. Cigarette packages were required to carry a warning that cigarette smoking might endanger health. See CHILD WELFARE; HEALTH; MEDICINE.

Housing. An omnibus $7,500,000,000 housing bill was passed in July. Congress refused, however, to appropriate the funds for subsidies for low-income families. Also, a new Cabinet-level Department of Housing and Urban Development was voted into existence in September to consolidate the operations of the various federal agencies in those fields. See CITY; CITY PLANNING; HOUSING.

The Voting Rights Act of 1965 became law in August. It was another step in the Negro's march toward full citizenship. The act reasserted the 15th Amendment's guarantee of Negro voting rights and set up machinery to enforce those rights. The federal government thus moved into an area previously under state domination. That state's rights issue stirred Southern opposition—by amendments, not by filibuster. But for the second time since 1938, the Senate invoked cloture on a civil rights issue. Its 70-to-30 vote on May 25 ended 24 days of debate and cleared the way for its lopsided 77-to-19 approval of the bill the following day. More than 100,000 Negroes were registered in the first three months after final passage of the act. As the Southern Democrats became aware of the new Negro voters, they might well have begun to find some disadvantages in their old alliance with Northern Republican conservatives. In any event, their influence in Congress continued to wane. See CIVIL RIGHTS; NEGRO.

The Immigration and Nationality Act amendments, enacted on October 3, abolished the quotas based on national origin and established criteria of skills and training, with relatives of U.S. citizens getting preference. Under the old 1924 law, quotas were weighted in favor of immigrants from northern Europe. See IMMIGRATION AND EMIGRATION.

Education—elementary, secondary, and higher— for the first time received substantial general aid from Congress. In April, President Johnson signed a bill providing $1,300,000,000 in federal aid for elementary and secondary schools. Because the new law provided specified services to the children rather than to the schools, it side-stepped the 20-year-old controversy over the role of the federal government toward public and private (mostly parochial) schools. School aid was tied to the $1,785,000,000 War on Poverty program—the Economic Opportunity Amendments of 1965 signed October 9— with the bulk of the funds allocated to schools in poverty-stricken areas (see POVERTY).

Higher education, a less controversial issue, had received some support in earlier sessions of Congress. In October, the Higher Education Act was passed. It authorized a three-year, $2,300,000,000 program, including federal scholarships of up to $1,000 yearly for needy college students. See EDUCATION; Section One, LAWRENCE A. CREMIN ON EDUCATION.

Appalachia Aid. In March, Congress approved a bill for $1,100,000,000 to aid economically depressed areas in 11 Appalachian states. The bulk of the funds was earmarked for highway construction. Congressmen from other states with depressed areas moved to get similar legislation. In August, their efforts came to fruition when the President signed the $3,250,000,000 Public Works and Economic Development Act to aid depressed areas with grants and loans to create new jobs over a five-year period. The money will be used for airports, parks, sewers, waterworks, and similar projects.

"O. K., Trigger—you can head for the barn now."

Farm Legislation for the first time since 1938 provided a long-term (four-year) program of price supports and subsidies. The Food and Agriculture Act of 1965 extended the low-support, high-cash subsidy program of grains to cotton.

Cotton growers will be able to sell their cotton at competitive (low) world prices and receive cash subsidies from the Treasury to maintain 1965 levels of income. The "bread tax"—a plan to shift part of the cost of wheat price supports from the Treasury to the consumer—did not pass. See AGRICULTURE.

Excise Tax Reduction was another example of Congress's going the President one better. Mr. Johnson had asked for a cut of $3,500,000,000. Congress slashed deeper. The reductions are expected to total $4,700,000,000 by Jan. 1, 1969. Most manufacturers' and retail excise taxes were reduced or repealed outright. More than 1,000 consumer goods and services were affected. See RETAILING; TAXATION.

This prodigious production of new laws kept on without letup until late in the session, when the attraction of their home districts outweighed the urgencies of the President's Great Society. Among the other measures enacted were:

The Coinage Act of 1965. It provided for silverless quarters and dimes and cut the amount of silver in half dollars from 90 to 40 per cent. See HOBBIES.

Gold Cover Repeal, ending the requirement that 25 per cent of all deposits in Federal Reserve Banks be backed by gold reserves. See BANKS and BANKING.

Water Quality Act, providing $1,320,000,000 for a federal-and-state attack on water pollution. See WATER AND FLOOD CONTROL; Section Two, POLLUTED AMERICA.

Clean Air Act, requiring exhaust controls on all new cars, possibly by Sept. 1, 1967. See AUTOMOBILE.

Highway Beautification Act, with a Jan. 1, 1968, deadline for states to control billboards and auto junkyards on interstate and primary highways or lose 20 per cent of federal road aid. See ROADS AND HIGHWAYS.

Rivers and Harbors authorizations, which totaled $2,000,000,000 and which carried a congressional veto power over water projects costing less than $10,000,000. The President said he would ignore the limitations as "repugnant to the Constitution."

High Speed Ground Transportation Act, authorizing a three-year, $90,000,000 study under which the Pennsylvania Railroad will test a 125 mph train between New York City and Washington, D.C. See TRANSPORTATION.

Presidential Succession resolution, proposing a constitutional amendment. It was cleared for submission to the 50 states in July. See PRESIDENT OF THE UNITED STATES (Close-Up).

In addition, Congress made it a federal offense to mutilate or destroy a draft card; reduced the amount of duty-free goods American tourists could bring back into the United States to $100 retail value instead of the previous $100 wholesale value; set up a National Foundation on the Arts and Humanities authorizing about $21,000,000 annually in federal subsidies for three years; provided $1,500,000 to finance federal and district commissions on law enforcement and aid to state, local, and private agencies to improve court administration, law enforcement, and prison operation; and authorized an addition to the National Park System, Assateague Island National Seashore. See PARKS; Section One, ALISTAIR COOKE ON THE ARTS.

Leaders of the first session of the 89th Congress included:

In the Senate, Carl Hayden of Arizona, president *pro tempore;* Mike Mansfield of Montana, majority leader; Russell B. Long of Louisiana, majority whip; Everett M. Dirksen of Illinois, minority leader; Thomas H. Kuchel of California, minority whip.

In the House, John W. McCormack of Massachusetts, Speaker; Carl Albert of Oklahoma, majority leader; T. Hale Boggs of Louisiana, majority whip; Gerald R. Ford of Michigan, minority leader (see FORD, GERALD R.); and Leslie C. Arends of Illinois, minority whip.　　　CAROL L. THOMPSON

See also DEMOCRATIC PARTY; JOHNSON, LYNDON B.; PRESIDENT OF THE UNITED STATES; REPUBLICAN PARTY; Section One, JAMES B. RESTON ON THE NATION.

CONSERVATION. See FORESTRY AND FOREST PRODUCTS; OUTDOOR RECREATION; PARKS; WATER AND FLOOD CONTROL; WILDLIFE; ZOOLOGY.

COSTA RICA

COSTA RICA was financially troubled in 1965. By the end of June, the nation's international reserves had dropped to $19,200,000, some $9,000,000 below the 1964 figure. These monetary difficulties were partly due to a significant trade deficit, which had been caused by a substantial drop in coffee earnings. The financial problem was somewhat alleviated, however, by a $10,000,000 International Monetary Fund (IMF) standby credit granted Costa Rica to support the republic's reserve position.

In August, the Inter-American Development Bank granted Costa Rica a loan of $5,200,000 to help rehabilitate zones affected by the eruption of the Irazu volcano. Part of the loan would be used to resettle 500 farm families whose property had been destroyed by volcanic ash and lava.

Late in the year, campaigning began for general elections scheduled to be held early in 1966. At stake were the presidency, two vice-presidencies, and 57 congressional seats. Meanwhile, work continued on the huge hydroelectric plant at Cachi, on the Reventazón River. When completed, the $12,500,000 plant will have a capacity of 64,000 kilowatts.

Population: 1,453,000. **Government:** President Francisco José Orlich Bolmarcich. **Monetary Unit:** colon (6.65 = U.S. $1). **Gross National Product:** 3,135,000,000 colons. **Foreign Trade:** exports, $113,000,000; imports, $139,000,000. **Principal Exports:** bananas, coffee, sugar.   MARY C. WEBSTER

COULSON, SIR JOHN ELTRINGHAM (1909-), a British career diplomat, was appointed secretary-general of the European Free Trade Association (EFTA) on July 27, 1965. Sir John succeeded Frank Figgures, also a Briton, who retired in 1964.

The new secretary-general was born at Bickley, Kent, Sept. 13, 1909. After attending Rugby and Corpus Christi College, Cambridge University, he entered diplomatic service in 1932. He served in his nation's embassies at Bucharest, Romania, and Paris, France, until World War II. During the war, he served in the ministry of economic warfare and, later, in the war cabinet office.

In the early years of the United Nations, Sir John was a deputy representative of the United Kingdom. He was assistant undersecretary in the foreign office from 1952 to 1955. From 1955 to 1957, Sir John was minister in the British embassy in Washington, D.C. He served three years as assistant to the British paymaster-general before being named ambassador to Sweden in 1960. After a three-year tour of duty, he returned to London as deputy undersecretary of state in the British foreign office.

As deputy undersecretary, he played a major role in carrying through the amalgamation of the foreign service, commonwealth service, and trade commission posts into a single diplomatic service.

Sir John's favorite hobbies are fishing and golf. He married Mavis Ninette Beazley in 1944. They have two sons.   WALTER F. MORSE

COURTS AND LAWS. President Lyndon B. Johnson appointed U.S. Attorney General Nicholas deB. Katzenbach to lead a National Crime Commission in a search for significant solutions to the nation's crime problems (see KATZENBACH, NICHOLAS DEB.). The commission met in September and charted an 18-month study of law enforcement and corrections.

The federal government became directly involved in a program aimed at local law enforcement by the enactment of the Law Enforcement Assistance Act. The new law authorized $10,000,000 for grants to law enforcement and corrections agencies throughout the country.

Key Decisions. State and federal courts entered new areas of decision in 1965, determining:

• Mexican domicile of the individual was not essential to New York state's recognition of a Mexican divorce.

• A federal appellate court can, under some circumstances, modify an erroneous sentence. In the past, such cases were remanded to the lower court.

• Courts may not order a blood transfusion for an adult who objects on religious grounds.

• A new trial should be granted a Virginia litigant in a civil action on the ground that pretrial newspaper accounts may have prejudiced the jury's decision.

Trial by Jury came under fire as leading jurists blamed it for delays in the courts. The chief judge of the New York Court of Appeals was joined by other leaders of the bench and bar in suggesting that arbitration, a workmen's compensation type commission, or other device should replace the jury in personal injury trials, which are clogging court dockets. The bar was almost unanimous in opposing any inroad into the right of trial by jury.

The state of Maryland was facing "the gravest crisis in the administration of criminal justice," after an October 11 decision invalidating convictions by juries from which nonbelievers in God were excluded under a provision of the state's constitution. The state's Attorney General Thomas B. Finan went on to say the decision applied to perhaps thousands of cases still before the courts, and placed in doubt all other Maryland convictions.

World Law. Judges and lawyers from more than 100 nations met in Washington, D.C., September 13 to 18 and pledged to work for a world governed by law. Making recommendations on methods to implement their pledge, the delegates to the World Peace Through Law Conference favored the creation of regional international courts. The present International Court of Justice would become an appellate court to review the decisions of the regional courts. Charles S. Rhyne, a Washington (D.C.) lawyer and former president of the American Bar Association, was elected president of the World Law Center at the meeting.

Aid for the Indigent in civil cases received great impetus in the program of the U.S. Office of

Economic Opportunity (OEO). In June, a National Conference on Law and Poverty was held in Washington, D.C. It emphasized the need to create new and bigger legal aid agencies in major cities. The OEO made specific grants during the year for neighborhood legal centers to serve impoverished areas. By summer, OEO programs had been set up in 14 communities and planned for 25 more.

Though cries of socialized law were heard from some lawyers, the American Bar Association at its February meeting endorsed the efforts to provide free legal services for the poor. See POVERTY.

Selection of Judges. In a rare action, the U.S. Senate returned a federal judgeship nomination to committee. Boston Municipal Judge Francis X. Morrissey had been nominated to be a U.S. district judge in Massachusetts. Senator Edward M. Kennedy (D., Mass.) requested the reconsideration move after strong opposition developed, chiefly on Judge Morrissey's qualifications. Earlier, the Senate Judiciary Committee had reported favorably on the nomination. After the Senate adjourned, Judge Morrissey withdrew his name from consideration.

President Johnson nominated 30 federal judges during the year, elevating four district judges to courts of appeals and appointing 11 state judges to federal judgeships. ERNEST C. FRIESEN, JR.

See also CIVIL RIGHTS; CONGRESS OF THE U.S.; STATE GOVERNMENT; SUPREME COURT OF THE U.S.

CRIME. President Lyndon B. Johnson established a 19-member national crime commission on July 26 to study the causes and prevention of crime and delinquency. Known as the President's Commission on Law Enforcement and Administration of Justice and headed by U.S. Attorney General Nicholas deB. Katzenbach, the commission was directed to develop standards and make recommendations for actions which can be taken by federal, state, and local governments to prevent, reduce, and control crime. The members were also asked to study the adequacy of law enforcement and administration of justice, and the factors encouraging respect or disrespect for law at national and local levels.

Statistics released in July by the Federal Bureau of Investigation (FBI) revealed a 13 per cent increase in serious crimes in the United States in 1964 over 1963. The sharpest increase continued to be reported in the suburbs where there was a rise of 17 per cent. Persons under the age of 18 comprised 48.4 per cent of those arrested for serious crimes.

The Supreme Court of the United States gave new constitutional protection to criminal defendants by ruling, under Amendments 6 and 14, that state courts must give defendants the right to confront and cross-examine their accusers. The precedent was set on April 5, after the Court's review of the Texas conviction of Bob G. Pointer for robbery and the Alabama conviction of Jesse E. Douglas for assault with intent to murder.

Major Crimes. Murder, kidnaping, robbery, and bombings continued to make lurid headlines in the nation's press. Malcolm X, militant 39-year-old leader of the black nationalist movement, was shot and killed on February 21 as he addressed a group of 400 Negroes in New York City. Four persons were later indicted in the slaying.

Walter A. Bowie, Robert S. Collier, Michelle Duclos, and Khaleel Sayyed, arrested in Montreal on February 27, were sentenced to long prison terms on charges of conspiring to dynamite the Statue of Liberty, the Liberty Bell, and the Washington Monument. The sentences were later reduced.

On July 8, California State Finance Director Hale Champion, his wife, and 19-month-old daughter were kidnaped by Carl Bowles and Wilbur Gray, who had been on a week-long crime spree. The kidnapers, after releasing their hostages relatively unharmed, were sentenced to life terms.

Crimes Abroad. On November 22, thieves burglarized one of London's most fashionable shops and fled with gems valued at over $1,000,000.

Two priceless manuscripts by the Italian poets Petrarch and Tasso and a valuable replica of the crown of St. Stephen, stolen from the Vatican on November 26, were found the next day in a field outside Rome. The jewels had been removed from the crown. JOSEPH D. LOHMAN

See also JUVENILE DELINQUENCY.

CUBA launched one of the strangest, most dramatic airlifts of modern times in 1965. On December 1, 75 Cuban émigrés landed in Miami, Fla. They were the vanguard of an estimated 300,000 who were leaving their homeland and the dictatorship of Cuban Premier Fidel Castro to seek asylum in the United States. The emigration had been arranged by the Swiss ambassador to Cuba, Emil Stadelhofer, with the consent of the United States and Castro. It ended a sea shuttle between Cuba and Florida in which a number of Cuban refugees had lost their lives earlier in the year. The only restrictions laid down by Castro were that neither males of conscription age nor skilled workers whose trades were necessary to the island's economy would be permitted to leave.

Government Motives. Cuban and foreign diplomats suggested, as an explanation for the exodus, that the departure of a large number of consumers would provide some relief from incessant demands for goods during a period of serious shortages. Also cited as advantageous to the Cuban government was the removal of a large segment of opposition to the regime's shortcomings.

These shortcomings had reached serious proportions in 1965. During the year, discontent had grown widespread due to the Castro regime's failure to improve standards of living after six years in power. Food shortages, rationing, and a flourishing high-priced black market continued. Rumors spoke of

PICTURES OF THE YEAR/Johnnie Evans, *St. Petersburg Times*   Lee Lockwood © 1965 Time Inc.

CUBAN DICTATOR Fidel Castro and Swiss Ambassador Emil Stadelhofer, far left, arranged, with U.S. consent, exodus of Cuban refugees, right, to the United States.

conspiratorial activity in the army. The government demonstrated its concern over rumors of an uprising by ordering all civilians—including the million-strong paramilitary vigilante committees—to hand in their arms. Rumors were widespread, too, over the possible fate of former war minister Che Guevarra who had dropped from the public view.

Cash Shortage. Tumbling world sugar prices made 1965 the bleakest year Cuba's communist leaders had ever faced. With sugar prices down, Cuba was left with a substantial part—perhaps half —of its total 6,200,000-ton sugar harvest. Until it was sold, the island had no foreign currency available to finance capital projects such as port modernization and the maintenance of expropriated oil refineries. The other half of the crop, which had risen 60 per cent over the 1964 yield and represented a return to the size of harvests produced before the communists seized power, was earmarked for Cuba's communist partners. Payment, however, was largely in terms of goods rather than cash, a policy set by the Havana-Moscow trade pact that was signed in 1965.

Population: 7,598,000. **Government:** President Osvaldo Dorticós Torrado; Premier Fidel Castro. **Monetary Unit:** peso, no exchange rate quoted. **Foreign Trade:** exports, $714,000,000; imports, $1,015,000,000. **Principal Exports:** beet and cane sugar, inorganic materials, tobacco.   MARY C. WEBSTER

See also LATIN AMERICA.

CYPRUS endured another year of unresolved hostility between its Greek and Turkish communities. Clashes continued between armed partisans in districts where the Turks were still sufficiently strong to protect themselves, but the presence of United Nations (UN) troops prevented a resumption of 1964's all-out civil war. No progress was made, however, in reconciling the two ethnic groups to an agreed future for the island. Greece and Turkey, made the more inflexible because of domestic political upheavals of their own, continued to square up to each other as the external protectors of the two embittered communities. See GREECE; TURKEY.

A report made on March 30 by the UN mediator, Señor Galo Plaza, failed to provide a hoped-for basis for a speedy settlement. Its recommendations that Cyprus continue as an independent nation pleased Cypriot President Archbishop Makarios and the Greeks generally, as did the report's refusal to accept the Turkish demand for a federation of two distinct ethnic regions. However, the report's insistence on specific minority safeguards within the unified state was a concession that the Greek Cypriots were unwilling to make.

All the interested parties were thus dissatisfied, including the supporters of General George Grivas, an advocate of *enosis* (union) with Greece. He rejected the report out of hand, as did the Turkish government. Even the British government was taken aback by the report's contention that the future of the British bases on the island "could . . . be constructively discussed among the parties to the treaty (of 1960)."

Precarious Peace. Fighting broke out in March and again in November. The most serious clash of the year took place at Famagusta, where the Greek Cypriot national guard, professing fears of a Turkish invasion, began to strengthen the fortifications of the port. This aroused the suspicions of Turkish Cypriots. Fighting broke out in which the Greek Cypriots, backed by tanks and mortar fire, demonstrated their overwhelming superiority.

UN Efforts. Despite these disturbances, the UN peacekeeping force in Cyprus succeeded in preventing wider hostilities. The force's mandate from the Security Council was renewed twice in the year. Funds for its upkeep were provided chiefly by the United States and Great Britain.

Economic Prosperity. Throughout 1965, Cyprus enjoyed visible prosperity despite the inner turmoil. Indeed, in the three years of growing communal hostility, Cyprus' foreign exchange reserves rose from $84,000,000 to $123,000,000.

Population: 595,000. **Government:** President Archbishop Makarios. **Monetary Unit:** pound (1 = U.S. $2.80). **Foreign Trade:** exports, $58,000,000; imports, $109,000,000. **Principal Exports:** fuels, machinery, textiles. ALASTAIR BURNET

See also EUROPE.

CZECHOSLOVAKIA

CZECHOSLOVAKIA made major efforts to free its economy from the stagnation that had strangled it for several years. In January, the government approved a series of reforms that would go into effect on Jan. 1, 1966. These innovations, as in other Central European communist-ruled countries, were based less on command and more on demand, less on quantity and more on quality. They emphasized skills, true cost accounting, plant profits, and wage incentives. President Antonín Novotný stressed, however, that the reform goals were to correct old deficiencies rather than to set up a whole new path for the nation.

Under the new setup, prices of such basics as bread, coal, and milk were to be fixed by the state. However, for another group of industries whose products comprised about 35 per cent of all commodities, the state would set only minimum and maximum levels. The remaining 6 per cent, whose products consisted mostly of luxury items, would allow supply and demand to establish their price range.

A New Labor Code, passed in June, confirmed the employee's right to quit; but it also made possible the discharge of an employee for inefficiency. In an attempt to restore a degree of private enterprise and improve consumer services, national committees were authorized to license carpenters, hairdressers, laundrymen, shoemakers, tailors and similar tradesmen.

Counter-attacking growing complaints that party hacks rather than qualified experts held managerial positions, the government abolished some 27,000 administrative posts. Younger men, more appropriately trained, were placed in key economic posts.

Foreign Relations. New contacts with the West were highlighted by the temporary extension of landing privileges in Prague to Pan American World Airways. There was a relaxation of tourist regulations and an end to the jamming of Voice of America radiobroadcasts.

Czechoslovakia joined the Soviet Union in heatedly criticizing U.S. policy in Vietnam and the Dominican Republic but it stimulated cultural exchanges with the United States. It also supported the Soviet Union in its war of polemics against Communist China. See COMMUNISM; VIETNAM.

Early in the year, the government relaxed its anti-Roman Catholic stand by releasing Czech Archbishop Josef Beran from house arrest so that he could attend Vatican Council II in Rome. See ROMAN CATHOLIC (Close-Up).

Population: 14,180,000. **Government:** President Antonín Novotný; Premier Josef Lenart. **Monetary Unit:** koruna (7.20 = U.S. $1). **Foreign Trade:** exports $2,668,000,000; imports, $2,249,000,000. **Principal Exports:** fuels, livestock, machinery, textiles, timber. TOM AND HARLE DAMMANN

See also EUROPE.

DAHOMEY

DAHOMEY. General Christophe Soglo, army chief of staff, ousted Dahomey's quarreling president and vice-president on Nov. 29, 1965. Tihiro Congacou, president of the national assembly, was appointed temporary president until new elections could be held and the constitution changed to avoid the overlapping powers that had embittered relations between former President Sourou Migan Apithy and Vice-President Justin Ahomadegbé.

In May, an organization urging the overthrow of the government was uncovered. This led to the removal and arrest of Supreme Court President Valetin Djibode Aplogan. A few days later, the country's only opposition party, the Rassemblement des Impératifs Nationaux, was banned on the grounds that it was involved in the plot.

President Sourou Apithy launched a government austerity program in June. Two days later, an alliance of labor unions called a 48-hour strike protesting wage cuts. The government held firm and broke the strike.

After settling a border dispute, Dahomey and Niger pledged closer economic cooperation.

Population: 2,122,000. **Government:** Acting President Tihiro Congacou. **Monetary Unit:** CFA franc (246.85 = U.S. $1). **Foreign Trade:** exports, $14,000,000; imports, $25,000,000. **Principal Exports:** coffee, palm oil, peanuts. BENJAMIN E. THOMAS

See also AFRICA.

DAIRYING. See AGRICULTURE.

DALLAS

DALLAS and Fort Worth, Tex., long friendly rivals, took important steps toward cooperation. The governing council of each city agreed to joint development of a regional airport. Voters of Fort Worth overwhelmingly approved a $7,500,000 bond issue for initial financing of the giant jet-age facility. Engineers have proposed a site roughly midway between the two thriving cities.

With the entire area enjoying flourishing economic health, unplanned growth added problems. In December, local government groups called for the formation of a 10-county planning commission.

Growth meant more government activity. In November, Dallas County moved some employees into a new 12-story structure housing mostly courts and a jail. The city chose the surrounding site for a 10-acre municipal center.

In May, Dallas voted for a new junior college, chose the first board of trustees, and approved a $41,500,000 bond issue for construction. Its first stage will open to 12,000 students in 1970; eventually, four separate campuses will be built. Also in the educational realm, the first unit of the $8,000,-000 Owen Fine Arts Center at Southern Methodist University opened in the spring. Meanwhile, in the downtown area, excavation was well advanced for the first section of Main Place, a privately financed multilevel $120,000,000 project. See 1963 YEAR BOOK, Rx FOR SICK CITIES.   DONALD W. LIEF

DAM. Mexico completed work on El Infiernillo Dam, a $100,000,000 irrigation and power project on the Balsas River, southwest of Mexico City near the Pacific Coast. The 487-foot-high dam irrigates a large area and produces 600,000 kilowatts (kw) of power. In January, joint U.S.-Mexican construction started on Amistad Dam on the Rio Grande. It was the second major international storage dam provided for by the Water Treaty of 1944.

North of the U.S. Border, work got underway in the spring on Arrow Dam on the Columbia River in southeastern British Columbia. The $555,000,000 concrete structure will impound a reservoir 145 miles long. It is one of the three big dams to be built on the Canadian part of the Columbia River under terms of the treaty signed by the United States and Canada in September, 1964.

U.S. Projects. Yellowtail Dam, the main project in a multipurpose Bureau of Reclamation program for the Bighorn River in southeastern Montana, was topped out in early October, almost a year ahead of schedule. More than 1,453,000 cubic yards of concrete went into the massive 525-foot-high-dam, the highest in the 10-state Missouri River Basin Project.

Keystone Dam, on the Arkansas River near Tulsa, Okla., was completed in May, except for its navigation lock. It is one of the 17 dams in the Army Corps of Engineers' $1,200,000,000 program to make the Arkansas River navigable for a distance of 450 miles. On the Ohio River, the Corps of Engineers

completed Pike Island Dam, in September. The new dam—from locks near Wheeling, W. Va., to the Ohio shore—is one of 19 locks and dams the corps plans for modernizing navigation on the Ohio.

Another river-improvement project was begun during the year by the Tennessee Valley Authority, when construction started on Nickajack Dam on the Tennessee River just below the 51-year-old Hales Bar Dam, which it will replace. The $66,000,000 project will include two earth-embankment sections, two parallel navigation locks, and a 10-bay spillway.

In southwestern Washington, construction of Cowlitz (River) Dam, primarily for power, was started in March by the City of Tacoma's department of public utilities. The $102,000,000 dam will be a 595-foot-high concrete-arch structure.

Overseas Projects. In January, Prime Minister Lal Bahadur Shastri of India dedicated Linganamakki Dam and the smaller Talakalale Dam, principal components of the Sharavati River hydroelectric project near the Arabian seacoast at Jog in Mysore state. Linganamakki Dam is an earth-fill masonry structure, 1.7 miles long and 203 feet high.

In New South Wales, Australia, work started in April on Blowering Dam, another unit in the long-range Snowy Mountains hydroelectric and irrigation project. It will be a rockfill dam 370 feet high with a crest length of 2,400 feet.   MARY E. JESSUP

See also DISASTERS; WATER AND FLOOD CONTROL.

DANCING. As the year opened, the New York City Ballet of New York City Center officially became part of Lincoln Center for the Performing Arts. In November, it was announced that the ballet company's school (The School of American Ballet) would follow suit after it becomes part of the dance department at the Juilliard School of Music. This will occur when Juilliard moves to Lincoln Center (probably by 1967).

The New York City Ballet made other news during 1965. In May, George Balanchine's *Don Quixote* became the first all-American, evening-length ballet (score by Nicolas Nabokov; decor by Esteban Francés). At a special preview-benefit on May 27, Balanchine assumed the title role, regularly performed by Richard Rapp. The company toured Europe during the summer, having a particular triumph in London.

In October, the resignation of Maria Tallchief from the New York City Ballet caused considerable stir. The resignation of America's most internationally famous ballerina focused sharp public criticism on Balanchine's policy of showing interest in only the very youthful and still immature, though enormously talented, female dancers.

American Ballet Theatre celebrated its 25th anniversary with a triumphant season (March 16-April 11) at the New York State Theater. Jerome Robbins' *Les Noces* (score by Stravinsky) proved a sensation. Also outstanding was Harald Lander's

Hunter College in New York City in cooperation with the New York State Council on the Arts, presented a subscription series of modern dance at the beginning of the year. José Limón, Merce Cunningham, Norman Walker, Paul Taylor, and Pearl Lang appeared with their companies. Late in the year, Alvin Ailey's Dance Theater gave two performances at Hunter College after two years of world touring.

Two-Note Score. American Dance Theatre, a repertory modern dance group directed by Limón and also sponsored by the New York State Council, danced in March at the New York State Theater. It presented works by Doris Humphrey, Pearl Lang, Donald McKayle, Alwin Nikolais, Merce Cunningham, and others. Cunningham's *Winter Branch*, performed in almost pitch darkness to a score consisting of two notes amplified into roars, created a near riot.

Beyond New York. Chicago's enterprising Harper Theatre brought the city a rich season of modern dance and ballet. It mounted a series that included Cunningham (with musicians John Cage and David Tudor), Robert Joffrey Ballet, Paul Taylor, and the Alvin Ailey Dance Theater.

Foreign companies that toured the United States included England's Royal Ballet, which brought Kenneth MacMillan's great *Romeo and Juliet*, danced to Prokofiev's score. The biggest names in ballet, Margot Fonteyn and Rudolf Nureyev, danced the leading roles.   P. W. MANCHESTER

DEAN, SIR PATRICK HENRY (1909-   ), an authority on international legal problems, succeeded Lord Harlech as British ambassador to the United States, on Jan. 5, 1965. Sir Patrick took over his new duties on April 6. Since 1960, he had been the permanent delegate to the United Nations.

Sir Patrick, the son of a Cambridge University professor, was educated there in the classics and law. He also taught law at Cambridge from 1932 to 1939. When Britain entered World War II, he joined the foreign office in London as an assistant legal adviser. He took a leading role in negotiations involving the exchange of prisoners of war.

In 1945, Sir Patrick acted as a legal adviser at the Yalta and Potsdam conferences. He served as minister at the British embassy in Rome in 1950 and 1951. During the next two years, he was senior civilian instructor at the Imperial Defense College in England. He subsequently returned to the foreign office as an assistant undersecretary in 1953, and deputy undersecretary from 1956 to 1960.

Tall and sandy-haired, Sir Patrick is devoted to fishing, hiking, and shooting. He was born in Berlin, Germany, March 16, 1909. In 1947, he married Patricia Wallace Jackson. Lady Dean was born in Argentina, where her father was manager of the British Light and Power Companies. Lord and Lady Dean are the parents of two teen-age sons, James Patrick and Peter Henry. Both youths are attending Rugby School in Rugby, England.   WALTER F. MORSE

The New York Times

MARTHA GRAHAM, an originator of modern dance, received the $30,000 Aspen Humanities Award to the delight of the entire dance world.

staging of the famous romantic ballet, *Les Sylphides* (1836), by August Bournonville.

Metropolitan Opera Ballet made modest history with an evening of ballet on April 11. The program included a striking production of Béla Bartók's *Miraculous Mandarin*. The performance was staged by Joseph Lazzini, ballet director of the Marseille Opera, in a superb setting by Bernard Daydé.

The Harkness Ballet went on its first European tour in the spring, and toured the United States for the first time in the fall. Meanwhile, the Rebekah Harkness Foundation presented a special portable stage to the White House and inaugurated it with a performance on September 29.

The reactivated Robert Joffrey Ballet made its debut during the Jacob's Pillow Dance Festival, which was also distinguished by the U.S. debut of The Netherlands Dance Theatre under its American director, Benjamin Harkarvy.

Aspen Award. To the delight of the entire dance world, Martha Graham received the $30,000 Aspen Award in the Humanities, on July 30. She and her company had a three-week season at the 54th Street Theater in November, when she presented premiéres of *The Witch of Endor*, with herself in the title role; and *Part Real-Part Dream*, a group work. *Appalachian Spring* with Ethel Winter, *Cave of the Heart* with Helen McGehee, and *Primitive Mysteries* with Yuriko were revivals of great early works in which the dancers named assumed Graham's original roles.

DEATHS OF NOTABLE PERSONS

DEATHS OF NOTABLE PERSONS

The Year 1965 will be remembered for the passing of Sir Winston Churchill, one of history's greatest statesmen, and Adlai E. Stevenson, known for his eloquence, patience, and statesmanship. Among the other notables were Martin Buber, Jewish religious philosopher; Paul Tillich, Protestant theologian; Albert Schweitzer, jungle doctor of Africa; T. S. Eliot, the poet; Dame Myra Hess, famed British pianist; Le Corbusier, the architect; Bernard M. Baruch, unofficial adviser to U.S. Presidents for 40 years; and Amos Alonzo Stagg, America's Grand Old Man of Football, who surpassed the century mark by two years.

The persons listed below were Americans unless it is otherwise indicated. An asterisk (*) means that the person has a biography in THE WORLD BOOK ENCYCLOPEDIA.

Albarda, Horatius (1904-May 17), a Netherlands lawyer and president of KLM Royal Dutch Airlines, had served as a vice-chairman (1956-1963).

Allison, Samuel King (1900-Sept. 15), University of Chicago Enrico Fermi Institute of Nuclear Studies director since 1963 (also 1946-1957), made the final countdown on the first atomic bomb explosion in New Mexico on July 16, 1945.

Ammann, Othmar Hermann (1879-Sept. 22), Swiss-born designer of New York's George Washington and Verrazano-Narrows bridges and the Delaware Memorial Bridge in Wilmington, also was among the designers of San Francisco's Golden Gate and Michigan's Mackinac Straits bridges.

*__Appleton, Sir Edward Victor__ (1892-Apr. 21), English scientist, was awarded the Nobel physics prize in 1947 for ionospheric research. He also served as vice-chancellor of the University of Edinburgh, in Scotland.

*__Artzybasheff, Boris__ (1899-July 16), Russian-born artist was known for his magazine covers and his novel methods for illustrating charts and maps. He wrote and illustrated *Poor Shaydullah* (1931), *Seven Simeons* (1937), *Axis in Agony* (1944), and *As I See* (1954), and illustrated other books.

Auslander, Joseph (1897-June 22), anthologist and translator, was Library of Congress poetry consultant (1937-1943). His books of verse include *Sunrise Trumpets* and *No Traveler Returns*. *The Winged Horse Anthology* (1929, compiled with Frank Ernest Hill) is a well-known classroom book of verse.

Avery, Milton Clark (1893-Jan. 3), pioneer abstract artist and excellent colorist and draftsman, worked from nature, and was mostly self-taught. Examples of his paintings include *Cutting Fish, The Desert, The Seine,* and *Green Sea.*

Avshalomov, Aaron (1894-Apr. 26), Siberian-born composer-conductor, lived in China for years. His work includes the operas *Kuan Yin* and *The Great Wall; Peiping Hutungs,* tonal poem; *The Soul of the Ch'in,* ballet; and *Budda and the Five Planetary Deities,* choreographic tableau.

Balokovic, Zlatko (1895-Mar. 29), Yugoslav violinist, appeared as soloist with major world orchestras for years.

Barker, Shirley Frances (1911-Nov. 18), historical novelist, wrote *Peace, My Daughters* (1949), *Fire and the Hammer* (1953), *Corner of the Moon* (1961), *The Road to Bunker Hill* (1962), and other books.

Pictorial Parade

HERO'S BIER. Body of Winston Churchill rests in St. Paul's Cathedral, London, before interment in family plot in Bladon village, near his birthplace.

United Press Int.

EDWARD R. MURROW, famed radio and television commentator, died at 57 after a long illness.

Wide World

CONSTANCE BENNETT, noted movie star and sister of actress Joan Bennett, died at age 59.

Fenno Jacobs, Black Star

LE CORBUSIER, the greatest of French architects, died while swimming on the French Riviera.

Barraquer y Barraquer, Ignacio (1884-May 13), Spanish ophthalmologist and international lecturer, invented the Barraquer suction device, *erisophake*, for intracapsular cataract extraction.

*****Baruch, Bernard Mannes** (1870-June 20), financier, philanthropist, and statesman, served as unofficial adviser to United States Presidents (1912-1952). He also served on government commissions, and represented his country at the Versailles conference (economic section, 1919) and at the United Nations Atomic Energy Commission (1946).

Beatty, Clyde Raymond (1904?-July 19), during his nearly 40 years with circuses was mauled many times by lions and tigers.

Beemer, Brace Bell (1903?-Mar. 1), played the Lone Ranger role on radio beginning in 1941 until its last live episode on Sept. 3, 1954.

Bennett, Constance (1905-July 24), screen star, played in *The Goose Hangs High, Tailspin, Three Faces East, Madame Spy* and other films.

Bevilacqua, Giulio Cardinal (1881?-May 6), lifelong friend, confessor, and former teacher of Pope Paul VI, remained parish priest at Saint Anthony's Church, Brescia, Italy, after his elevation to the Sacred College of Cardinals in February, 1965.

Billner, Karl P. (1882?-June 6), Swedish-born engineer, originated such concrete construction techniques and devices as the vacuum pump method of extracting excess water from newly poured concrete; a rock excavation by artificial freezing; the electric prestressing of reinforcing steel; and also a cancer virus microfilter. Billner developed the lightweight concrete *aerocrete*.

Bissier, Julius (1893-June 18), German artist, was famous for his abstracts, and for his ink drawings, water colors, woodcuts, and color monoprints.

Blackmur, Richard Palmer (1904-Feb. 2), Princeton University English professor, who had no formal university training, was a poet and critic (1928-1940). His many books include *Language as Gesture* and *The Lion and the Honeycomb*. See LITERATURE (Poetry).

Blackstone, Harry (1885-Nov. 16), began his career in 1904 (with his brother Peter), and for half a century did magic acts on stage.

Boland, Mary (1885-June 23), made her New York stage debut in 1905 and later played in London. She appeared in Tarkington's *Clarence* (1919). By then she was recognized as talent for either dramatic or comedy roles. Her star role in *Ruggles of Red Gap* (with Charles Ruggles and Charles Laughton, 1935) was followed by many other film successes.

Bonner, Charles (1896-Mar. 21), author of many stories, wrote the script for *Adam Had Four Sons*, a film based on his novel *Legacy*. His other novels include *The Fanatics* (1932), *Bull by the Horns* (1937), *Angel Casey* (1941), and *The Last Romantic* (1949).

Bonner, Herbert C. (1891-Nov. 7), was a Democratic U.S. Representative from North Carolina (1940).

Bossom, Lord Alfred Charles (1881-Sept. 4), British architect and pioneer builder of American skyscrapers, served in the House of Commons (1926-1955) and in 1960 was made a life peer.

Bow, Clara (1905-Sept. 26), star of *It*, a film written for her by British novelist Elinor Glyn, had leading roles in many silent and early sound pictures. She retired in 1931.

Breen, Joseph I. (1890-Dec. 5), the first director (1934-1954) of the Production Code Administration of the Motion Picture Association of America, edited films, and was known as the industry's "Czar."

Bristow, James J. R. (1891?-Jan. 28), chemical engineer, developed a low temperature-high vacuum process for concentrating juices (1937).

Brokenshire, Norman Ernest (1898-May 4), Canadian-born pioneer radio announcer, began his career in 1924, and soon won national fame.

Brophy, John (1899-Nov. 13), British author and father of novelist-critic Brigid Brophy, wrote *Waterfront* (1934), *Immortal Sergeant* (1942), *Turn the Key Softly* (1951), and *The Day They Robbed the Bank of England* (1959), all filmed.

Brown, Clarence J. (1893-Aug. 23), had been a Republican U.S. Representative from Ohio since 1939.

Browne, Irene (1896?-July 24), English actress, played in such Noel Coward productions as *Conversation Piece* (1934), *The Girl Who Came to Supper* (1963, her last Broadway appearance), and the films *Cavalcade* (1932) and *Berkeley Square* (1933).

*****Buber, Martin** (1878-June 13), Austrian-born Jewish religious philosopher, was one of the great thinkers of the century. See PROTESTANT (Close-up).

Wide World

CLYDE BEATTY, *famed wild animal trainer and circus performer, died in California.*

Wide World

FRANCES PERKINS *was the first woman to hold a Cabinet post as Secretary of Labor.*

United Press Int.

NAT KING COLE, *popular recording star for more than a generation, died of cancer at 47.*

Bucher, Walter Herman (1888-Feb. 17), Columbia University Newberry Professor Emeritus of Geology, won world renown for *The Deformation of the Earth's Crust* (1933) still considered a landmark in geology.

Bunce, Alan (1904?-Apr. 27), costar of the "Ethel and Albert" radio and television show, was radio's original Young Doctor Malone. His many stage appearances included *Valley Forge, A Perfect Alibi, Sunrise at Campobello,* and *Mary, Mary.*

Burco, Ferruccio (1939?-Apr. 26), Italian conductor of symphony orchestras in the world's major music centers, directed his first major concert in Fiume at the age of 4.

Burdick, Eugene Leonard (1918-July 26), wrote *The Ugly American* (with William J. Lederer, 1958), *Fail-Safe* (with Harvey Wheeler, 1962), both of which were filmed, *Blue of Capricorn* (1961), and other books.

***Burgess, Thornton Waldo** (1874-June 5), children's author, published his first original stories as *Mother West Wind Books* (1910-1917), followed by *Bedtime Story Book Series* (1913-1919) and *The Burgess Bird, Animal, Flower, and Seashore Books for Children* (1919-1929).

Carrillo, Julián (1875-Sept. 9), Mexican, experimented with fractional tones, developed a "Sound 13" system, and constructed special instruments (harp with 97 strings to the octave) for his music.

Carroll, Nancy (1906-Aug. 6), popular actress (1920s-1930s) starred in such films as *Abie's Irish Rose, Shopworn Angel, The Dance of Life,* and *There Goes My Heart,* appeared on Broadway, and was the mother in television's "The Aldrich Family."

Cecil, Russell LaFayette (1881-June 1), rheumatic diseases pioneer, also won prominence as editor of *Textbook of Medicine* (1927).

Chaplin, Sydney (1885-Apr. 15), English actor, appeared with his younger half brother Charles in Keystone Cops comedies, starred in the silent version of *Charley's Aunt* (1925) and other comedy films.

***Churchill, Sir Winston Leonard Spencer** (1874-Jan. 24), great statesman of world history and a legend in his lifetime, was Prime Minister of Great Britain (1940-1945) during the nation's "finest hour," and also from 1951 to 1955. He was knighted and awarded the Nobel literature prize in 1953.

Cochran, Robert Alexander "Steve" (1917-June 15), film star, played in such pictures as *I, Mobster, The Damned Don't Cry,* and *Of Love and Desire.*

Cole, Nat King (1919-Feb. 15), popular Negro entertainer and singer was born Nathaniel Adams Coles. A church organist at the age of 12, he first performed professionally as a jazz pianist, and organized the King Cole Trio in 1937. He wrote the hit song "Straighten Up and Fly Right," and made many popular recordings.

Coles, Cyril Henry (1898?-Oct. 9), for years with the British Intelligence Service, as Manning Coles wrote (with the late Adelaide Frances Oke Manning) *Drink to Yesterday* (1940), *Dangerous by Nature* (1950), and other books about espionage.

Collins, Ray (1889-July 11), who played in *Citizen Kane; See Here, Private Hargrove; Command Decision;* and other films, was Detective Lieutenant Tragg in the "Perry Mason" television series for eight years.

Collip, James Bertram (1892-June 19), Canadian biochemist and hormone research pioneer, assisted Sir Frederick G. Banting and John J. R. Macleod (discoverers of insulin and 1923 Nobel medicine laureates), in developing insulin for diabetes.

Connell, John (1909-Oct. 5), English journalist, wrote (as J. H. Robertson) *Winston Churchill, the Writer* (1956), *Auchinleck: Biography of Field-Marshal Sir Claude Auchinleck* (1959), *Wavell: Scholar and Soldier* (1965), and many earlier books.

Conover, Harry S. (1911-July 21), remembered for his New York agency (1939-1959) and natural-type, well-groomed models of magazine fame, is credited with originating the term "cover girl."

Cooper, Kent (1880-Jan. 31), The Associated Press executive director, joined the organization in 1910 and was general manager (1925-1948).

***Cosgrave, William Thomas** (1880-Nov. 16), who fought in Ireland's Easter Revolution of 1916, served as the Irish Free State executive council president (1922-1932).

***Costain, Thomas Bertram** (1885-Oct. 8), Canadian-born journalist-editor and author of many historical novels and histories, wrote *For My Great Folly* (1942), *The Black Rose* (1945), filmed, *The Silver Chalice* (1952), *The White and the Gold* (1954), and four-volume "Pageant of England" series (1949-1962).

Reverence For Life

Albert Schweitzer
(1875-1965)

The old man with the stooped shoulders, bushy hair, and ill-fitting clothes was hardly a heroic figure. Nor would it seem that he, living humbly in an obscure African jungle for more than 50 years, could have much influence on a world often motivated by selfishness and materialism. Yet, Dr. Albert Schweitzer, many believed, was one of the greatest men of the century.

In the hospital that he founded at Lambaréné, Gabon, Dr. Schweitzer died on Sept. 4, 1965, at age 90. The next day, the coffin of "le grand docteur," was raised above the heads of mourners and carried to the banks of the Ogooué River, where he was buried beside the grave of his wife.

In his lifetime, Dr. Schweitzer was renowned as physician, philosopher, theologian, historian, musicologist, and organist. But he also was a humanitarian, selflessly devoted to the welfare of all human beings.

Albert Schweitzer was born on Jan. 14, 1875, at Kaysersberg, Alsace. As a youth, he was an indifferent student, but displayed a prodigy's talent for music. By the time he was 18 and a student at the University of Strasbourg, he was an accomplished organist. His university studies were interrupted, however, by compulsory military service in 1894. During his year as a soldier, Schweitzer was deeply influenced by Jesus' injunction: *Heal the sick, cleanse the lepers, raise the dead, cast out devils: freely ye have received, freely give.*

When he reached 21 in 1896, Schweitzer vowed that he would give nine years to science and art, and then devote the rest of his life to the service of humanity.

In those nine years, Schweitzer completed his doctoral thesis in philosophy, obtained a doctorate in theology, was ordained a curate, and became principal of St. Thomas Theological College at Strasbourg. His writings profoundly influenced theological thought. He also studied the organ, and completed a review of the life and art of Johann Sebastian Bach.

True to his pledge, Schweitzer gave up his academic career in 1905. "For years," he said, "I have been giving myself out in words." Now, he said, was the time for him to put "the

religion of love . . . into practice." He entered medical school at the University of Strasbourg, where he obtained his M.D. degree. On June 18, 1912, he married Helene Bresslau, who trained as a nurse in order to share her husband's life. The next year, the Schweitzers sailed for French Equatorial Africa (now Gabon) and established a medical mission at Lambaréné.

Dr. Schweitzer helped make a clearing in the jungle himself. His first consulting room was in a refurbished chicken coop. During World War I, the Schweitzers' work was twice interrupted when the French interned them as German aliens. Dr. Schweitzer, however, continued to practice his music on dummy organ keys that he had fashioned on a table. He also began work on his classical *The Philosophy of Civilization.*

This evolved from an experience he had one day, while observing four hippopotamuses and their young on a riverbank. Suddenly, he was struck with the idea of "Reverence for Life." In an article that he wrote for the 1964 WORLD BOOK YEAR BOOK, Dr. Schweitzer explained:

"Ethics up to now had been incomplete because it had held that its chief concern was merely with the relationship of man to man. In reality, however, ethics must also be concerned with the way man behaves toward all life . . . As ethical human beings, we must constantly strive to escape from a need to destroy as much as we possibly can . . . Through reverence for life, we come into a spiritual relationship with the universe."

Armed with his concept of "Reverence for Life," Dr. Schweitzer returned to his jungle hospital in 1924 and put the ethical concept into practice for more than 41 years. His hope was to modestly demonstrate the applicability of the concept in a world beset by the miseries of disease, famine, political turmoil, and war. Said his biographer, George Seaver, an Anglican priest: "If the ethic of 'Reverence for Life,' is heard and heeded in its gentle undertones, it would prove a remedy for the world's pain. . . . Hard is the task indeed, but great is the hope." E. KENNETH FROSLID

Culver Pictures

CLARA BOW, favorite celluloid love goddess and It girl of the 1920s, died in Los Angeles.

Wide World

AMOS ALONZO STAGG, once a football coach at the University of Chicago, died at 102.

Wide World

HENRY A. WALLACE was Secretary of Agriculture and Vice-President under Roosevelt.

*Cowell, Henry (1897-Dec. 10), pianist and composer, was known for his "tone clusters," produced by striking large numbers of notes together.

*Crerar, Henry Duncan Graham (1888-Apr. 1), Chief of the Canadian General Staff (1940-1941), commanded the First Canadian Corps in Great Britain and Italy (1942-1944) and the First Canadian Army in the Rhineland and western Netherlands invasions.

Croy, Homer (1883-May 24), author of *They Had to See Paris* (1926, filmed as Will Rogers' first sound picture), *Jesse James Was My Neighbor* (1949), *Our Will Rogers* (1953), *Family Honeymoon* (1942, staged and filmed), and *Wheels West* (1955).

Dandridge, Dorothy (1924?-Sept. 8), Negro actress and singer, appeared in such pictures as *Carmen Jones*, *Island in the Sun*, and *Porgy and Bess*.

Dane, Clemence (1888-Mar. 28), English author of novels and plays, was born Winifred Ashton. *Legend* (1919) was staged and filmed as *A Bill of Divorcement*. She wrote the films *Anna Karenina* (for Greta Garbo) and *St. Martin's Lane* (for Charles Laughton).

Darnell, Linda (1921-Apr. 10), star of *Forever Amber*, played in *No Way Out*, *Letter to Three Wives*, *The Song of Bernadette*, and many other pictures.

Davidson, George (1889-June 15), Polish-born portraitist, was noted for his murals and ceiling decorations in public buildings.

De Havilland, Sir Geoffrey (1882-May 27), founder of the De Havilland Aircraft Company (1920), designed Britain's World War I fighter planes, the *Moth* (1924), the World War II *Mosquito*, and the jetliner *Comet* (1952).

Divine, Father (1877?-Sept. 10), founder and leader of the Peace Mission Cult, with headquarters near Philadelphia, Pa., is thought to have been born George Baker in Georgia.

Dixon, Sir Pierson John (1904-Apr. 22), British Foreign Service veteran, was British Permanent Representative to the United Nations (1954-1960).

Dresser, Louise (1882-Apr. 24), famed costar of such Will Rogers films as *State Fair*, *Lightnin'*, and *David Harum*, also played in *Cradle Song*, *The Girl of the Limberlost*, *The Country Chairman*, *Song of the Eagle* and many other motion pictures.

*Eliot, Thomas Stearns (1888-Jan. 4), American-born British poet and critic, was Nobel literature laureate (1948). See LITERATURE (Close-Up).

Elisabeth, Dowager Queen of Belgium (1876-Nov. 23), widow of King Albert I (1875-1934), was the mother of former King Leopold III and grandmother of King Baudouin, and a noted fine arts patron.

Erlanger, Joseph (1874-Dec. 5), and Herbert Gasser shared the Nobel medicine prize (1944) for their work on single nerve fibers.

Evatt, Herbert Vere (1894-Nov. 2), Australian Minister of Foreign Affairs (1941-1949) and champion of small nations, was UN General Assembly President (1948-1949).

*Farjeon, Eleanor (1881-June 5), English author famed for *Martin Pippin in the Apple Orchard* and other children's books, was awarded the Carnegie (1955), and the first Hans Christian Andersen (1956) and Regina (1959) medals.

*Faruk, or Farouk, I (1920-Mar. 18), the last king of Egypt, succeeded his father Fuad I in 1936 and was deposed in July, 1952.

*Field, Marshall (IV) (1916-Sept. 18), chairman of Field Enterprises, Inc. See PUBLISHING.

Fiene, Ernest (1894-Aug. 10), German-born artist, did landscapes, portraits, lithographs, and etchings. Four Fiene murals are in the new Department of the Interior Building, Washington, D.C.

Fossati, Maurilio, Cardinal (1876-Mar. 30), Archbishop of Turin, Italy, since 1930, was elevated to the Sacred College of Cardinals in 1933.

Frank, Albert Rudolf (1873-Mar. 18), German-born chemist, in 1901 proposed (with others) a method of obtaining calcium cyanamid from nitrogen, which was the beginning of the chemical fertilizer industry.

*Frankfurter, Felix (1882-Feb. 22), Austrian-born Associate Justice of the Supreme Court of the United States (1939-1962), was a Harvard University law professor (1914-1939).

Funk, Wilfred John (1883-June 1), founder (1940) and president of Wilfred Funk, Inc., and president of Funk & Wagnalls (1925-1940) Standard Dictionary concern, wrote the Reader's Digest feature, "It Pays to Increase Your Word Power," and books on word power.

*The life and career
of Adlai E. Stevenson
as interpreted by a
leading U.S. historian,
Henry Steele Commager.*

Measure Of a Man's Greatness

Adlai E. Stevenson
(1900–1965)

A

YEAR

BOOK

CLOSE-UP

308

Adlai E. Stevenson presents us with a spectacle rare in American, and probably in modern, history—a man whose public career was crowded into a few short years, whose every foray into large politics was marked by defeat, and who exercised immense authority wholly without power, an authority whose sanctions were entirely intellectual and moral. . . .

Two defeats as presidential candidate, no office, no power, yet no other American born in the 20th century had such a hold on the imagination or the affection of the American people until the triumph of John F. Kennedy.

With victory well-nigh impossible in 1952, and certainly impossible in 1956, Mr. Stevenson did well to set his sights and his standards high. He refused to compromise his principles in order to win stray votes. He addressed himself to the large task of educating the American public to the realities of domestic and, particularly, of world power.

His greatest contribution was, perhaps, that at a time when Americans were inclined to think power irresistible he reminded them of the limitations on power, that at a time when they were inclined to turn from moral responsibilities to the enjoyment of their well-earned prosperity he insisted on the primacy of moral consideration . . .

What else was it that Mr. Stevenson contributed to American public life? First, he reasserted faith in reason, and confidence in the ability of the average man to understand the great issues of politics.

This was in the tradition of the Founding Fathers who conducted the debate on the U.S. Constitution on the highest level; it was in the tradition of Lincoln—and Mr. Stevenson was a lifelong student of Lincoln's works; it was in the tradition of Woodrow Wilson who scorned talking down to the American electorate.

Mr. Stevenson brought dignity and weight to public discussion; he insisted on addressing himself not to men but to issues; he trusted the people to understand these issues. In this he was perhaps oversanguine.

Alone of his generation of politicians, Mr. Stevenson had something of Wilson's literary elegance, and without the Victorian rhetoric; he added—what John F. Kennedy was to share—wit and charm, a lightness of touch more rare in American than in British politics.

His wit, like Kennedy's, was irrepressible; it bubbled up at the most unlikely moments; it was never malicious but sophisticated, and wry, directed more often than not to his own predicament.

Secondly, Mr. Stevenson was very conscious of the intricacy and complexity of the great problems which glared upon the American people from every quarter of the globe, and he refused to delude the people with simple formulas or to deceive them with simple solutions. A trip to Korea, for example, or a "throw the rascals out" formula for corruption . . . or a program of hatred for communism.

This was an essential part of his elementary honesty—an honesty which would not stoop to deception to win votes or friends; it was part of his faith in reason, too. More than this, it was a form of pride—a pride that would not let him stoop to intellectual trickery and would not permit his country to assume that power was a substitute for justice . . .

In a curious way Mr. Stevenson seemed marked for failure, and he seemed to carry within himself a realization that fate would deny him its ultimate rewards. He had, in the fine words of Stephen Vincent Benét, "all things except success," yet knew "such glamor as shall wear sheer triumph out."

To the end he kept the promise of his Chicago acceptance speech: "In the task you have assigned me I shall always try to do justly, to love mercy, and to walk humbly with my God."

Harvard University

ARTHUR M. SCHLESINGER, SR., retired Harvard University history professor, died at 77.

United Press Int.

FARUK, exiled king of Egypt and a noted playboy, died at 45 while feasting in Rome.

Wide World

H. V. KALTENBORN, 86, the dean of the radio commentators, died of heart failure in New York.

Furman, N. Howell (1892-Aug. 2), chemist, was responsible for many such developments as the analytical separation of uranium.

Gerlier, Pierre Cardinal (1880-Jan. 17), Archbishop of Lyon (France) since 1937, was elevated to the Sacred College of Cardinals the same year.

Gildersleeve, Virginia C. (1877-July 7), internationally known educator, was dean of Columbia University's Barnard College for women (1910-1947).

Gilliard, Ernest Thomas (1912-Jan. 26), American Museum of Natural History Ornithology Department Curator and authority on New Guinea birds, contributed to the discovery and naming of 55 subspecies, six species, and one genus of birds.

Glenny, Alexander T. (1882-Oct. 5), English immunization pioneer, suggested (1923), diphtheria toxoid for man, and introduced (1938, with Sir John Boyd) tetanus toxoid for human use.

Goodenough, Erwin R. (1893-Mar. 20), Yale University Professor Emeritus of Religion, wrote the 10-volume *Jewish Symbols in the Greco-Roman Period* (1953-1962), and many other such works.

*Grew, Joseph C. (1880-May 25), U.S. Ambassador to Japan (1931-1941) when Pearl Harbor was attacked, related his years there in *Turbulent Era* (1952).

Gribanovsky, Anastassy Metropolitan (1874?-May 22), Primate and President of the Synod of Bishops of the Russian Orthodox Church Outside Russia (1936-1964), established his headquarters in New York City in 1950. See EASTERN ORTHODOX.

Hale, Creighton (1882?-Aug. 9), Irish-born actor and star of such silent films as *The Iron Claw*, *The Clutching Hand* (with Pearl White), and *Annie Laurie* (with Lillian Gish), had also appeared on stage.

*Hammond, John Hays, Jr. (1888-Feb. 12), inventor whose pioneer work includes radio control, radiodynamic torpedoes, frequency modulation, single-dial tuning for radio, and a light incendiary bomb.

Hansberry, Lorraine V. (1930-Jan. 12), author of *A Raisin in the Sun*, was the first Negro to receive the New York Drama Critics Circle award (1959) and the first to have a play on Broadway. *Sign in Sidney Brustein's Window*, opened there in late 1964.

Hanson, Lars (1887?-Apr. 8), Swedish actor known for his Eugene O'Neill roles, played the lead in his *Long Day's Journey into Night* (1956) and *A Touch of the Poet* (1953) in Sweden, and last played in New York in August Strindberg's *The Father* (1962).

Harrington, Daniel Patrick "Pat," (1900?-Sept. 2), Canadian comedian, appeared in such Broadway productions as *Ladies and Gentlemen* (1939), *Panama Hattie* (1940), *Front Page* (1946), and *Call Me Madam* (1950).

Hayward, John Davy (1905-Sept. 17), British anthologist, critic, and editor, is remembered for his *Penguin Book of English Verse* (1956), *Oxford Book of Nineteenth Century Verse* (1964), and many earlier publications.

*Hench, Philip Showalter (1896-Mar. 30), Mayo Clinic rheumatic diseases department head (1926-1957), was (with others) awarded the Nobel medicine prize (1950) for hormone research.

*Hess, Dame Myra (1890-Nov. 25), great English pianist known for her playing of Scarlatti, Bach, and Mozart, made her debut in 1907 with the London Philharmonic Orchestra.

Hives, Lord Ernest Walter (1886-Apr. 24), noted Rolls-Royce engineer and retired chairman (1957), produced such works as Merlin engines for Britain's World War II *Hurricane* and *Spitfire* planes.

Holcomb, Thomas (1879-May 24), U.S. Marine Corps commandant (1936-1944), was the first marine officer to serve as commandant and the corps' first four-star general.

Holland, Sir Henry Tristram (1875-Sept. 19), noted British medical missionary, eye surgeon, and author of *Frontier Doctor* (1958), won acclaim for work against blindness in India (1900-1948) and Pakistan.

Holliday, Judy (1923-June 7), highly talented star of *Born Yesterday* (Broadway, 1946-1949), received the Motion Picture Academy best actress award for the same role in the film (1951). She made her Broadway debut in *Kiss Them for Me* (1945).

Hoogstraaten, Willem van (1884-Sept. 11), Netherlands-born conductor of the New York Philharmonic summer concerts (1922-1938) and conductor of the Portland (Ore.) Symphony Orchestra (1925-1937), was conductor of the Salzburg Mozarteum Orchestra (1939-1945) and later conducted in Vienna, Austria.

Howard, Eugene (1881?-Aug. 1), was straight man for his brother Willie. The German-born comedy team appeared in vaudeville, Broadway productions, and on radio.

United Press Int.

BRANCH RICKEY, 84, collapsed during his induction ceremony into baseball's Hall of Fame.

Wide World

OTHMAR AMMANN, designer of some of the nation's most notable bridges, died at the age of 86.

Wide World

RED NICHOLS, bandleader and trumpet player, died during an engagement at a Nevada casino.

Huddleson, I. Forest (1893-May 26), Michigan State University Microbiology and Public Health Professor Emeritus, was widely recognized as an authority on brucellosis in man and animals.

Hylton-Foster, Sir Harry Braustyn (1905-Sept. 2), Speaker of the House of Commons since 1959, had been a member of the British Parliament since 1950.

Hylton, Jack (1892-Jan. 29), British impresario who presented *High Button Shoes* and many other productions in London (some in New York), toured Europe and America with his band (founded, 1922).

Ikeda, Hayato (1899-Aug. 13), Premier of Japan (1960-1964) was credited with establishing his country's economic recovery after World War II.

Jackson, Shirley (1919-Aug. 8), author of the horror tale "The Lottery" (1948), wrote *Life Among the Savages* (1953) and *Raising Demon* (1957) on her family life; and *Hangsaman* and other books.

Janssen, Herbert (1895-June 3), German-born opera and concert baritone known for his Wagnerian roles, appeared with the Berlin State Opera before coming to the Metropolitan Opera (1939).

Jarrell, Randall (1914-Oct. 14), University of North Carolina English Professor, poet, and critic, was Library of Congress poetry consultant (1956-1958). He received the National Book poetry award (1961) for collection *The Woman at the Washington Zoo*.

Johnston, Olin Dewitt (1896-Apr. 18), the Democratic U.S. Senator from South Carolina since 1945, was governor of his state (1935-1939, 1943-1945).

Jones, Lindley Armstrong "Spike" (1911-May 1) was famed for his City Slickers band.

Jung, Paul (1900?-Apr. 21), star clown of the Ringling Brothers and Barnum & Bailey Circus since 1934, began as an acrobat and toured vaudeville.

*__Kaltenborn, "H. V.," Hans Von__ (1878-June 14), author of *Fifty Fabulous Years* (1950), known as the "father" of his profession, made his first radio broadcast in 1922. The news analyst retired in 1955.

Kemeny, Zoltan (1908?-June 14), Hungarian-born Swiss abstract metal sculptor and painter, won the Venice Biennale sculpture grand prize (1964).

Kennedy, Tom (1885?-Oct. 6), an early Keystone Cop actor, last appeared in *It's A Mad, Mad, Mad, Mad World* (1962 film). He played such character roles as policeman, bartender, and taxi driver.

*__Kerr, Sophie__ (1880-Feb. 6), short-story writer and *Woman's Home Companion* managing editor for years, wrote *The Golden Block*, *Painted Meadows*, *As Tall As Pride*, and other novels.

Kiesler, Frederick J. (1890-Dec. 27), Austrian-born architect, sculptor, and painter, won fame in the 1920s as a European *avant-garde*. He originated the endless (free-form circular) house, designed the first theater-in-the-round in Vienna and also the "floating city" (1925) for the Paris Exhibition. His more recent work includes the Dead Sea Scrolls Sanctuary in Jerusalem (1959) and the Universal Theater for the Ford Foundation (1961).

Kilgallen, Dorothy Mae (1913-Nov. 8), newspaper columnist and radio and television personality, began her career in 1931. She appeared on "What's My Line" television show.

*__Kilpatrick, William Heard__ (1871-Feb. 13), Columbia University Teachers College Professor Emeritus of Education, originated the "project method" and "purposeful activities program" of progressive education fame.

Knappertsbusch, Hans (1888-Oct. 25), German conductor and noted interpreter of Wagnerian opera, in recent years conducted at Bayreuth Wagner festivals.

*__Kozlov, Frol Romanovich__ (1908-Jan. 30), First Deputy Premier of Russia (1958-1963), met with President Dwight D. Eisenhower in the summer of 1959, before Premier Nikita Khrushchev's visit to the United States in the fall.

*__La Follette, Philip Fox__ (1897-Aug. 18), member of the politically famous Wisconsin family, served as governor of his state (1931-1933, 1935-1939).

Lambeau, Earl "Curly" Louis (1898?-June 1), a founder, quarterback, coach, and general manager of the Green Bay Packers, was with the professional football team 31 years.

Laurel, Arthur Stanley "Stan" Jefferson (1890-Feb. 23), English-born sad-faced comedian, who with Oliver Hardy (1892-1957), made some 200 slapstick films (1926-1949).

*__Le Corbusier__ (1887-Aug. 27), an architectural giant of the century, born Charles Édouard Jeanneret in Switzerland, was noted for his world-wide influence in modern building and city planning. He also was

Wide World

BERNARD M. BARUCH, 94-year-old financier and statesman, died of a heart attack in New York.

Wide World

QUEEN ELISABETH of Belgium, at 89, died of a heart attack at Stuyvenberg Palace.

Wide World

GORDON SEAGRAVE, better known as the "Burma Surgeon," died in his jungle hospital at 68.

a painter, sculptor, and poet. See ARCHITECTURE; CITY PLANNING.

Leonty, Metropolitan (1876-May 14), Primate of the Russian Orthodox Church in America since 1950 was born Leonid Turkevich in Russia. He came to the United States in 1906. See EASTERN ORTHODOX.

Liberte, Jean (1896-Aug. 23), Italian-born artist noted for seascapes and landscapes, was an authority on casein painting.

Lind, Samuel C. (1879-Feb. 12), pioneer in radium chemistry, invented the interchangeable electroscope for radium measurements and originated the ionization theory of the chemical effects of radium rays.

Lothrop, Samuel K. (1892-Jan. 10), anthropologist, archaeologist, and authority on Central and South American cultures, wrote *Treasures of Ancient America* (1964) and other such earlier works.

Louise Alexandra Marie Irene, Queen of Sweden (1889-Mar. 7), was the wife of King Gustaf VI Adolf. The German-born, English-bred Queen was the sister of Lord Mountbatten of Burma and aunt of Prince Philip, husband of Queen Elizabeth II of Britain.

MacDonald, Jeanette Anna (1907-Jan. 14), noted soprano and wife of film star Gene Raymond, was a Broadway (*Tip Toes; Yes, Yes Yvette; Angela*), screen (*One Hour with You, Love Me Tonight, The Merry Widow*), and concert success before she and baritone Nelson Eddy made such films as *Naughty Marietta* and *Rose Marie*. She later sang in grand opera.

Mantz, Albert Paul (1901?-July 8), the only man to win the Bendix Speed trophy three times, had been a motion picture stunt aviator for 35 years.

***Maugham, William Somerset** (1874-Dec. 16), English author of *Of Human Bondage* (1915, later filmed), *The Moon and Sixpence* (1919, later an opera), and *The Razor's Edge* (1944), also wrote plays. See LITERATURE.

McKechnie, William Boyd (1887-Oct. 29), National Baseball Hall of Fame member since 1962, is the only National League manager to lead three different teams to the World Series (Pittsburgh in 1925, St. Louis in 1928, and Cincinnati in 1939).

Melachrino, George (1909?-June 18), English leader of a 40-piece string orchestra, was noted for his sweet and sentimental music. The recording artist also composed for films, stage, and radio.

***Meyer, Albert Gregory Cardinal** (1903-Apr. 9), Roman Catholic Archbishop of Chicago (1958), was elevated to the Sacred College of Cardinals in 1959.

Micara, Clemente Cardinal (1879-Mar. 11), Papal Vicar of Rome, was elevated to the Sacred College of Cardinals in 1946.

Minton, Sherman (1890-Apr. 9), Associate Justice of the Supreme Court of the United States (1949-1956), was a Democratic U.S. Senator from Indiana (1935-1941).

Monckton, Walter Turner (1891-Jan. 9), VISCOUNT OF BRENCHLEY, Minister of Labour and National Service (1951-1955) and Minister of Defense (1955-1956), was attorney-general to the Prince of Wales (1932-1936) when he became Edward VIII, and advised him during his abdication in 1936.

***Morrison, Herbert Stanley** (1888-Mar. 6), BARON OF LAMBETH, House of Commons member for years, served as Home Secretary and Minister of Home Security (1940-1945), Commons Labour party leader (1945-1951) and Foreign Secretary (1951).

Motley, Willard (1912-Mar. 4), author of *Knock on Any Door* and *Let No Man Write My Epitaph*, both filmed, also wrote *We Fished All Night*.

***Mueller, Paul** (1899-Oct. 12), Swiss chemist, was awarded the Nobel medicine prize in 1948 for discovering insect-killing properties of DDT.

Murray, Mae (1889-Mar. 23), one-time Ziegfeld *Follies* girl, played in such silent films as *The Merry Widow*, *On with the Dance*, and *Gilded Lily*.

***Murrow, Edward Roscoe** (1908-Apr. 27), remembered for his World War II eyewitness accounts of the London blitz, did radio's "Hear It Now," television's "See It Now" and "Person to Person," and was U.S. Information Agency director (1961-1964). See TELEVISION.

Muzzey, David Saville (1870-Apr. 14), educator, wrote the American history textbook first published (1911) as *An American History* and later as *A History of Our Country*, and other books.

Nichols, Ernst Loring "Red" (1905-June 28), jazz musician and recording artist, was known for the Red Nichols and His Five Pennies group.

Norden, Carl Lukas (1880-June 14) a Netherlands native, invented the Norden bombsight for World War II bomber planes.

O'Neil, Nance (1874-Feb. 7), internationally fa-

311

DAME MYRA HESS, one of the world's great pianists, died in London at 75. She retired in 1961.

HELENA RUBINSTEIN, 94, cosmetics executive, died after becoming ill at work.

SYNGMAN RHEE, former president of South Korea, died in exile at the age of 90 in Hawaii.

mous tragedienne, was noted for her ancient Greek, Spanish, Shakespearian, and Hedda Gabler portrayals. *Cimarron* was one of her better known pictures.

Onions, Charles Talbut (1873-Jan. 8), English philologist, joined the Oxford English Dictionary staff in 1894, and spent nearly 70 years preparing dictionaries and English usage textbooks.

Owen, Catherine Dale (1903?-Sept. 7), widely acclaimed beauty, acted in such plays as *Trelawney of the Wells* (1925) and Molnar's *The Play's the Thing* (1926). Her screen opposites included John Gilbert in *His Glorious Night*, Lawrence Tibbett in *The Rogue Song*, and Edmund Lowe in *Born Reckless*.

Paige, Raymond (1900-Aug. 7), music director of Radio City Music Hall in New York and conductor of its symphony orchestra for years, also was known as a conductor of radio, screen, and symphonic music.

Pate, Maurice (1894-Jan. 19), executive director of the United Nations Children's Fund since its founding as the UN International Children's Emergency Fund in 1946, had done this type of work since during World War I. See NOBEL PRIZES (Peace Prize).

*****Patri, Angelo** (1877-Sept. 12), Italian-born educator and child guidance authority, lecturer, and author of such books as *How to Help Your Child Grow Up*, also wrote the syndicated column "Our Children."

Peabody, Ernest H. (1870?-Mar. 6), mechanical engineer, developed equipment for the combustion of fuel oil, such as a steam atomizing oil burner.

*****Perkins, Frances** (1882-May 14), the first woman Cabinet member in the United States, served as Secretary of Labor (1933-1945).

Pickett, Clarence Evan (1884-Mar. 17), clergyman, was executive secretary of the American Friends Service Committee (1929-1950), a joint winner of the Nobel peace prize in 1947.

Polasek, Albin (1879-May 19), Chicago Art Institute Sculpture Department director (1916-1943) known for his small bronzes, also did a Woodrow Wilson monument for his native Czechoslovakia (1928).

Pousette-Dart, Nathaniel (1886-Oct. 17), artist, teacher, consultant, and editor, wrote *The Fundamental Principles of Creative Art* and other books.

Powell, Dawn (1897-Nov. 14), author of short stories and plays, wrote such novels as *A Time to Be Born*, *The Locusts Have No King*, and *The Golden Spur*.

Raynolds, Robert (1902-Oct. 24), wrote *The Sinner of St. Ambrose*, *The Obscure Enemy*, *Thomas Wolfe and Robert Raynolds*, and other books.

Redfield, Edward Willis (1869-Oct. 19), noted for his Bucks County (Pa.) snow scenes and Maine shore scenes, was awarded 30 or more national and international honors and prizes during his career as an artist.

Reicher, Frank (1876?-Jan. 19), one-time stage director and actor, played in numerous films, including *The Secret Life of Walter Mitty* and *Kiss Tomorrow Goodbye*.

Rennie, James (1890-July 31), Canadian-born actor, played lead roles in *Moonlight and Honeysuckle*, *The Great Gatsby*, *Alien Corn*, and many other Broadway successes, and appeared in many films.

Reynolds, Quentin (1902-Mar. 17), *Collier's* star World War II correspondent, did the commentary for the British documentary film *London Can Take It*, and also wrote several books.

*****Rhee, Syngman** (1875-July 19), was the first President of the Republic of Korea (1948-1960).

Rickey, Branch (1881-Dec. 9), noted baseball figure, founded its farm training system (1919) while manager of the Saint Louis Cardinals (1919-1942), and broke the major leagues' color line (1947) by placing Negro Jackie Robinson with the Brooklyn Dodgers.

Riiser-Larsen, Hjalmar (1890-June 3), Norwegian aviator and leader of Antarctica expeditions (1929, 1930, 1933), discovered Queen Maud Land, Princess Martha Land, and Princess Ragnhild Coast. A Scott Range peak, Mount Riiser-Larsen, was named for him.

Ruark, Robert Chester (1915-July 1), columnist, wrote *Horn of the Hunter*, *Something of Value*, *The Old Man and the Boy*, and other books.

Rubinstein, Helena (1871?-Apr. 1), famed Polish-born beauty expert and cosmetic manufacturer, began her business in Australia, went to London, and opened a Maison de Beauté in New York City in 1915.

Salote, Queen of Tonga (1900-Dec. 15), monarch of the South Sea kingdom since 1918, was noted for her dignity and charm. She delighted Londoners when she attended the coronation of Queen Elizabeth II dressed in a Tonga costume.

Santee, Ross (1889-June 28), wrote and illustrated *Apache Land* and other books, and did Southwest sketches and paintings for the *Arizona Highway* and other magazines.

*****Schipa, Tito** (1890-Dec. 16), Italian tenor, appeared with the Chicago Opera (1919-1932) and then the New York Metropolitan Opera companies.

*****Schlesinger, Arthur Meier** (1888-Oct. 30), Harvard University Professor Emeritus of History since 1954, wrote *The Colonial Merchants and the American Revolution* and many other volumes.

*****Schweitzer, Albert** (1875-Sept. 4), Nobel peace prize laureate (1952), was noted for his African jungle hospital at Lambaréné, Gabon. See CLOSE-UP.

Scott, Zachary (1914-Oct. 3), internationally known stage and screen star, played in *The Southerner*, *Mildred Pierce*, and other films, and such stage plays as *The King and I* and *Requiem for a Nun*.

Seagrave, Gordon Stifler (1897-Mar. 28), who told his story in *Burma Surgeon* (1943) and *Burma Surgeon Returns* (1946), began his life's work at Namkham in 1922. He was born in Rangoon, the son of a missionary family, which came to the United States in 1909.

Selznick, David O. (1902-June 22), motion-picture producer, is remembered for *Gone With the Wind*, *Intermezzo*, *David Copperfield*, *Dinner at Eight*, *A Star Is Born*, *Duel in the Sun*, and other great films.

Shafer, Burr (1900?-June 15), California piano merchant for the past 20 years, did drawings for the *Saturday Review* under the title "Through History with J. Wesley Smith," and had collections published.

Sharett, Moshe (1894-July 7), the first foreign minister of Israel (1948-1956), also was prime minister (1953-1955). As head of the Jewish Agency for Palestine political department, Russian-born Sharett presented his people's case before international bodies and governments throughout the world.

*****Sheeler, Charles** (1883-May 7), noted for his realistic style of painting, did American landscapes and industrial scenes. His photography specialties included Chinese jades and French cathedrals.

Shotwell, James Thomas (1874-July 15), Canadian-born Columbia University historian, was the author and editor of some 500 books. He wrote the Versailles Treaty social security article, and helped plan the United Nations.

Smith, David (1906-May 23), sculptor, pioneered in welded iron and steel constructions. He did 15 bronze *Medals of Dishonor*, *Cello Player*, and *Sacrifice*.

Sokoloff, Nikolai (1886-Sept. 24), Russian-born violinist, was the first conductor of the Cleveland Orchestra (1918-1933), and later conducted the Seattle (Wash.) Symphony Orchestra.

Spaeth, Sigmund (1885-Nov. 11), musicologist and author of many books on music, appeared on radio as "The Tune Detective."

Spring, Howard (1889-May 3), Welsh author and critic, wrote *My Son! My Son! Fame Is the Spur*, (both filmed), and other novels.

*****Stagg, Amos Alonzo** (1862-Mar. 17), Grand Old Man of Football, pioneered the forward pass and the T formation as played today. He coached college teams at Springfield, Mass. (1890-1892), the University of Chicago (1892-1933), at the College of the Pacific (Calif.) (1933-1947), Susquehanna University (1947-1953), and at Stockton (Calif.) Junior College (1953-1960).

*****Staudinger, Hermann** (1881-Sept. 9), German chemist, was awarded the Nobel chemistry prize (1953) for his study of "giant molecules."

*****Stevenson, Adlai Ewing** (1900-July 14), had been U.S. Permanent Representative to the United Nations since January, 1961. See Close-Up.

Stribling, Thomas S. (1881-July 8), was awarded the Pulitzer fiction prize (1933) for *The Store*, the second volume of his triology consisting of *The Forge* and *Unfinished Cathedral*.

*****Tillich, Paul** (1886-Oct. 22), Protestant theologian, see PROTESTANT (Close-Up).

Vance, Marguerite (1889-May 22), wrote *The Jacksons of Tennessee*, *While Shepherds Watched*, *Willie Joe and His Small Change*, and other children's books.

Varèse, Edgard (1883-Nov. 6), French-born pioneer avant-garde composer, was known as "the father of electronic music."

Victoria Alexandra Alice Mary, Princess Royal of Great Britain (1897-Mar. 28), was the only daughter of the late King George V and Queen Mary.

*****Wallace, Henry Agard** (1888-Nov. 18), Vice-President of the United States (1941-1945), was Secretary of Agriculture (1933-1940) and Secretary of Commerce (1945-1946).

Waner, Paul Glee (1903-Aug. 29), a National Baseball Hall of Fame member since 1952, played with the Pittsburgh Pirates, Boston Braves, the Brooklyn Dodgers, and New York Yankees.

Watson, Minor (1890?-July 28), character actor, played in such films as *The Jackie Robinson Story* and *Guadalcanal Diary*. His Broadway successes included *Reunion in Vienna* and *State of the Union*.

*****Weygand, Maxime** (1867-Jan. 28), in supreme command as Hitler advanced in France, he advised surrender. After World War II, Weygand was charged with collaboration, but was cleared (1948).

Wilhelm, Prince of Sweden (1884-June 5), was the younger brother of King Gustaf VI Adolf.

DEMOCRACY.

Supporters of government by the people had serious problems to worry about in all the major Western democracies. In the non-Western world—embracing the majority of mankind—the democratic cause suffered a number of setbacks, while making no distinct gains. It still seems a long way from shaping up as the wave of the future. Yet the communist countries scored no distinct gains either.

Free societies have never had a year without headaches. But the worry itself is healthy, inasmuch as it freely expresses and stimulates efforts to overcome alarming problems. What is often overlooked and seldom makes headlines is the most important achievement of the established democracies—their maintenance of free elections, civil liberties and respect for public opinion.

United States. The most troublesome problem in the United States remained the rebellion of Negroes against their treatment as second-class citizens. In the South, there were continued demonstrations against the slow progress in securing civil rights. The summer riots in the Watts area of Los Angeles, Calif., dramatized a basic grievance everywhere in the Negro community—the inequality in economic opportunity, aggravated by inferior schooling and slum housing. While the fierce resentment of Negroes enlisted the support of many white people, it also tended to stiffen opposition to the demands for social equality. See LOS ANGELES.

DEMOCRACY

Great Britain, too, faced a racial problem, in this case due to the growing prejudice against its nonwhite immigrants from many regions of its former empire. The Labour government felt obliged to make a concession to this attitude by introducing a bill to drastically limit immigration. The government firmly resisted other racial pressure, however, when the self-governing territory of Rhodesia forced the issue by declaring independence and its intention of setting up a racist state. See AFRICA; GREAT BRITAIN; RHODESIA.

Western Europe. On the Continent, General Charles de Gaulle sought re-election by announcing that he alone could save France. Opposition parties vindicated his apparent contempt of them by continuing to squabble among themselves (see FRANCE). In Germany, the less dictatorial Chancellor Ludwig Erhard won re-election, but with the aid of an ugly whispering campaign against his opponent Willy Brandt, mayor of West Berlin.

Emerging Nations. India, considered the most democratic of the "emerging nations," became embroiled in a war with Pakistan. The conflict set back the economic development of both nations. Nigeria and the Philippines were disrupted by elections that left dozens of dead, and widespread complaints of fraud.

Other Asian and African nations were generally united in opposition to the U.S. military campaign in South Vietnam, still ruled by an undemocratic, unpopular government. Latin-American countries were generally unhappy over U.S. intervention in the Dominican Republic (see DOMINICAN REPUBLIC; LATIN AMERICA). At the same time, many citizens of the United States also questioned the wisdom of a foreign policy that appeared to be antagonizing most of the world despite its stated purpose of helping to liberate peoples or protect them against the menace of communism.

Freedom to Dissent. To the credit of the democratic process, such criticisms were getting ample publicity, as were the grievances of Negroes. Similarly, dissent remained active and open in all European democracies. The French would still decide whom they wanted as president. And both major parties in the German elections stood for full democracy. In the other defeated countries of World War II—Austria, Italy, and Japan—democracy appeared to be stronger than ever before.

The nondemocratic world paid tribute to democracy by using its language. Even the communists continued to speak of their countries as "people's democracies." And the rulers of almost all the new nations at least professed a devotion to the ideals of social justice and political freedom. The basic problem of these nations remained their poor, largely illiterate populations, hardly prepared for responsible self-government. HERBERT J. MULLER

See also CIVIL RIGHTS; NEGRO; SUPREME COURT OF THE U.S.; and articles on various countries.

314

DEMOCRATIC PARTY

DEMOCRATIC PARTY

Democratic party leadership centered on one man and his program —President Lyndon B. Johnson and his call to the "Great Society." With a Democratic majority of 155 seats in the House and 36 seats in the Senate, the President pushed hard and persistently for passage of his extensive program. By the end of the first session of the Congress, he was able to call it the "fabulous 89th." See PRESIDENT OF THE UNITED STATES.

The Democrats had passed most major pledges of the party's 1964 platform, with the conspicuous exceptions of home rule for the District

JOVIAL DEMOCRATS *meet the press. They are, from left, Senators Russell B. Long, Mike Mansfield, George A. Smathers, and Vice-President Hubert Humphrey.*

United Press Int.

of Columbia and repeal of the "right to work" Section 14(b) of the Taft-Hartley Act. It had appealed to broad segments of the electorate, with its Voting Rights Act, anti-poverty proposals, education acts, and Medicare bill. See CONGRESS OF THE UNITED STATES; CIVIL RIGHTS; EDUCATION; MEDICARE; POVERTY; Section One, JAMES B. RESTON ON THE NATION.

Party Politics for the Democrats was congressional politics. The Democratic National Committee, under the continuing chairmanship of John M. Bailey, became a service bureau, more or less. It concentrated on plans to re-elect Democratic Congressmen, especially those from traditionally Republican districts who had been swept into office in the Johnson landslide of 1964. At meetings with these freshman lawmakers, their district's needs were discussed, and advice and counsel dispensed.

Vice-President Hubert H. Humphrey played an active role in these efforts. He pursued a regular program of posing for pictures with Congressmen and appearing with them on radio and television— all calculated to improve their electoral prospects. Humphrey also traveled widely, appearing before party fund-raising dinners and attending meetings of the President's Clubs, an organization to which contributors of $1,000 or more are entitled to special privileges when party bigwigs visit their cities. See HUMPHREY, HUBERT H.

State and Local Politics. Preoccupation with his legislative program limited the President's political role. He steered clear of those states in which the Democrats were almost as badly divided as the Republicans—particularly California and New York. Late in the New York City mayoral campaign— through the voice of his news secretary—he managed to endorse the Democratic candidate, Abraham D. Beame, who had won a bruising primary battle but was saddled with the support of the city's political bosses. But Johnson's mild, last-minute support was of no avail. Republican Congressman John V. Lindsay won, ending 20 years of Democratic rule. The New York state senate, which had gone Democratic for the first time in 30 years in the Johnson sweep of 1964, was restored to the Republicans in the state-wide election. The assembly remained in Democratic hands.

The New York City election produced a powerful vote-getter in Frank D. O'Connor, district attorney of Queens, who was elected president of the city council by 400,000 votes—almost 300,000 votes above Lindsay's winning margin. It made O'Connor an outstanding contender for the 1966 Democratic nomination for governor, the office held by Republican Nelson A. Rockefeller. O'Connor's rise also enhanced Senator Robert F. Kennedy's leadership claims on the state's Democratic party. Kennedy and O'Connor have been political allies. See ELECTIONS; NEW YORK CITY; REPUBLICAN PARTY; STATE GOVERNMENT.

"Aw, be a sport and move over."

In New Jersey and Virginia, the Democrats showed vigor in holding onto the governorships. Incumbent Governor Richard J. Hughes won handily in New Jersey. Lieutenant Governor Mills E. Godwin, Jr., moved up in Virginia, where the Democratic machine headed by former Senator Harry F. Byrd showed an ability to adapt to the strides being made by Negro voters and the growing strength of moderate political opinion in the state's urban areas.

The End of an Era in Democratic politics was marked by Byrd's resignation as a U.S. Senator after 32 years. Throughout all those years, Byrd never wavered from his orthodox fiscal conservatism and his defense of the balanced budget. In November, Governor Albertis S. Harrison, Jr., appointed the Senator's son, Harry F. Byrd, Jr., to the seat. The son also was a conservative but without the seniority that had made his father a powerful Senate figure. Offsetting the departure of Byrd was the announcement by liberal Senator Maurine Neuberger of Oregon that because of her health she would not seek re-election in 1966.

Public support for President Johnson's programs encouraged party leaders to expect little if any off-year slippage of the party's power in 1966. The major unknown was admittedly the war in Vietnam, the depth of the U.S. commitment there, and the trend in the fighting when Americans would be going to the polls. PETER LISAGOR

DENMARK was forced to introduce a policy of tight credit early in 1965 in order to relieve pressures on its economy. Banks were asked to deposit 20 per cent of any increases in their deposits in the Central Bank, and new funds could be invested abroad only under conditions approved by it. The spring budget included cuts in government spending as well as higher taxes on most goods except food. A ban was imposed on public building between April 1 and October 15. All these moves were designed to reduce a growing trade deficit.

Denmark remained dependent on agriculture for 40 per cent of its export earnings. It continued to make every effort, however, to encourage industrial production. As a result, a 17 per cent rise in industrial exports was recorded for 1965. A heavy balance of payments deficit and a tight employment situation had forced the issue. The need for more industrialization, however, plus the fact that home demand—despite deflationary measures—was still exceeding output, was causing a continuing imbalance in the economy.

Population: 4,746,000. **Government:** King Frederik IX; Prime Minister Jens Otto Krag. **Monetary Unit:** krone (6.902 = U.S. $1). **Gross National Product:** 58,675,000,000 kroner. **Foreign Trade:** exports, $1,897,000,000; imports, $2,015,000,000. **Principal Exports:** butter, cheese, machinery.   KENNETH BROWN
See also EUROPE.

DENTISTRY. Dental research scientists became increasingly hopeful of achieving a "breakthrough" in *periodontal* (gum and parts of the jaw that support the teeth) diseases, which cause more loss of teeth in adults than dental decay.

Dr. David F. Mitchell of Indiana University School of Dentistry told delegates to the July meeting of the International Association for Dental Research, in Toronto, Canada, that tests involving daily applications of a new antibiotic resulted in a marked reduction in the amount of dental plaque. This is a soft, sticky substance considered to be a leading cause of periodontal diseases.

Dr. Mitchell reported that the new antibiotic, when mixed with an ointment and painted on the teeth and gums of patients, revealed "some unique characteristics which make its use for a variety of oral diseases appear very favorable."

Dr. Anthony A. Rizzo of the National Institute of Dental Research told the same gathering that chronic gingivitis, the initial state of periodontal disease, may be a type of allergic reaction. Another scientist described a unique discovery of antibodies in human blood, which indicates that the human body may have a "built-in" defense mechanism against certain bacteria associated with oral disease. Another investigation with germ-free animals showed that bacteria may not be the leading cause of plaque, but that a substance found in saliva may play a major role.

Oral Cancer. While U.S. dentists continued to warn their patients about a possible relationship between smoking and oral cancer, a Danish scientist reported that world-wide studies have revealed significant geographic variations in the incidence of the disease, ranging from 5 per cent or less of all types of cancer in the United States and Europe to 45 per cent in Asian countries.

Fluoridation. Water fluoridation marked its 20th anniversary in the United States, with some 65,000,000 Americans reported to be receiving the benefits of this program. New York City began fluoridation of its water supply late in September, 1965, while Connecticut became the first state to pass a law requiring fluoridation in all communities over 20,000 persons.

Meanwhile, dental research scientists were studying topical fluoride gel applications to provide protection against tooth decay for residents of unfluoridated areas.

International Dentistry. In a speech before the annual session of the Féderation Dentaire Internationale in Vienna, Austria, in July, Dr. Erich Müller of Germany, the outgoing president, called on the world's dentists to increase preventive dental health measures, including fluoridation and educational programs for the public. Substantial fluoridation gains were reported from Australia, Canada, Ireland, and New Zealand.   LOU JOSEPH

DETROIT voters overwhelmingly supported Jerome P. Cavanagh's bid for a second four-year term as mayor. The 37-year-old mayor-elect captured a stunning 68 per cent of the vote, adding to his reputation as a bright political prospect.

Water resources were important to the Motor City in 1965. By a slim margin, citizens voted to put fluoride into the city's water supply. Also, on August 2, officials signaled the start of a four-year $98,000,000 construction project to tap Lake Huron as a second water source.

Detroit's economic foundation, the automotive industry, flourished. Confidence in the economy led to huge investments in new and expanded plants. See AUTOMOBILE; ECONOMY, THE.

Downtown, the 450-room Pontchartrain Hotel was dedicated August 2. Its handsome 25-story tower was the first major luxury hotel to open in Detroit in 37 years. Under construction was the $10,000,000 Detroit Trade Center.

In planning, a new approach to public housing—scattering it on small sites throughout the city—was emphasized. Plans call for 1,500 dwelling units to be built for $22,000,000 including land costs.

Details of a vast cultural center were presented to the public November 17. To occupy 200 acres near Wayne State University, it will take 20 years and $250,000,000 to complete.   DONALD W. LIEF

DICTIONARY. See WORDS AND PHRASES, NEW; Section Five, DICTIONARY SUPPLEMENT.

DIPLOMAT

DIPLOMAT. United States ambassadors and ministers in January, 1966, included the following:

Country	U.S. Ambassador
Afghanistan	John M. Steeves
Algeria	John D. Jernegan
Argentina	Edwin M. Martin
Australia	Edward Clark
Austria	James W. Riddleberger
Belgium	Ridgway B. Knight
Bolivia	Douglas Henderson
Brazil	Lincoln Gordon
Bulgaria	*Nathaniel Davis
Burma	Henry A. Byroade
Cambodia	Relations severed
Cameroon	Leland Barrows
Canada	W. Walton Butterworth
Central African Rep.	Claude G. Ross
Ceylon	Cecil B. Lyon
Chad	Brewster H. Morris
Chile	Ralph A. Dungan
Colombia	Covey T. Oliver
Congo (Léopoldville)	G. McMurtrie Godley
Costa Rica	Raymond L. Telles, Jr.
Czechoslovakia	Outerbridge Horsey
Dahomey	Clinton Everett Knox
Denmark	Katharine Elkus White
Dominican Republic	W. Tapley Bennett, Jr.
Ecuador	Wymberley De R. Coerr
El Salvador	Raul H. Castro
Ethiopia	Edward M. Korry
Finland	Tyler Thompson
Formosa	Jerauld Wright
France	Charles E. Bohlen
Gabon	David M. Bane
Gambia	Mercer Cook
Germany, West	George C. McGhee
Ghana	Franklin H. Williams
Great Britain	David K. E. Bruce
Greece	Phillips Talbot
Guatemala	John Gordon Mein
Guinea	James I. Loeb
Haiti	Benson E. L. Timmons III
Honduras	Joseph J. Jova
Iceland	James K. Penfield
India	Chester Bowles
Indonesia	Marshall Green
Iran	Armin H. Meyer
Iraq	Robert C. Strong
Ireland	Raymond R. Guest
Israel	Walworth Barbour
Italy	G. F. Reinhardt
Ivory Coast	George A. Morgan
Jamaica	Wilson T. M. Beale, Jr.
Japan	Edwin O. Reischauer
Jordan	Robert G. Barnes
Kenya	William Attwood
Korea, South	Winthrop G. Brown
Laos	William H. Sullivan
Lebanon	Dwight J. Porter
Liberia	Ben H. Brown, Jr.
Libya	David D. Newsom
Luxembourg	Patricia R. Harris
Malagasy Republic	C. Vaughan Ferguson, Jr.
Malaysia	James D. Bell
Mali	C. Robert Moore
Malta	George J. Feldman
Mauritania	Geoffrey W. Lewis
Mexico	Fulton Freeman
Morocco	Henry J. Tasca
Nepal	Henry E. Stebbins
Netherlands, The	William R. Tyler
New Zealand	Herbert B. Powell
Nicaragua	Aaron S. Brown
Niger	Robert Joseph Ryan

Country	U.S. Ambassador
Nigeria	Elbert G. Mathews
Norway	Margaret Joy Tibbetts
Pakistan	Walter P. McConaughy
Panama	Charles W. Adair, Jr.
Paraguay	William P. Snow
Peru	J. Wesley Jones
Philippines	William McC. Blair, Jr.
Poland	*John A. Gronouski, Jr.
Portugal	George W. Anderson, Jr.
Romania	William A. Crawford
Russia	Foy D. Kohler
Saudi Arabia	Hermann F. Eilts
Senegal	Mercer Cook
Sierra Leone	Andrew V. Corry
Somalia	Raymond L. Thurston
South Africa, Rep. of	William M. Rountree
Spain	Angier Biddle Duke
Sudan	William H. Weathersby
Sweden	J. Graham Parsons
Switzerland	W. True Davis, Jr.
Syria	Hugh H. Smythe
Tanzania	William K. Leonhart
Thailand	Graham A. Martin
Tunisia	Francis H. Russell
Turkey	Parker T. Hart
Uganda	Olcott H. Deming
United Arab Republic	John H. Burns
Upper Volta, Rep. of	Thomas S. Estes
Uruguay	Henry A. Hoyt
Venezuela	Maurice M. Bernbaum
Vietnam, South	Henry Cabot Lodge, Jr.
Yugoslavia	C. Burke Elbrick
Zambia	Robert C. Good

*Indicates minister

DISARMAMENT. In a historic foreign policy reversal, the United States agreed to participate in a nuclear test-ban meeting that would welcome representatives from Communist China. On Nov. 23, 1965, the United Nations (UN) Political Committee unanimously adopted a resolution urging a world disarmament conference.

The United States cautiously agreed, before the vote, to participate in a preliminary meeting that might lead toward the conference, but insisted upon a constructive attitude on the part of the other participants before it would attend a world conference. The resolution, an endorsement of a proposal by the 1964 conference of nonaligned nations in Cairo, Egypt, said the conference was to be held "not later than 1967." It was ratified, 112 to 0, by the UN General Assembly on November 29.

It was uncertain whether Communist China would attend either the preliminary meeting or the world conference, but Albania's favorable votes in both the Political Committee and the General Assembly were hopeful indications that it would. France, which has refused to sign the nuclear test-ban treaty, abstained.

A Stumbling Block remained, however, in the United States' desire to form a multilateral nuclear force (MLF) within the North Atlantic Treaty Organization (NATO), which many countries, especially the Soviet Union and its allies, fear will permit West Germany to get its hands on nuclear weapons. The United States argued that it alone would control the weapons, and that unless some form of participation is allowed them, the Germans will produce nuclear armaments of their own.

As methods of seismic inspection improved, some of the Latin-American and Scandinavian nations and Iran agreed to join a world-wide network to detect underground testing, hopefully making the U.S. policy on inspections more flexible. The UN Political Committee supported an appeal for the suspension of all testing, 86 to 0. Because there was no suggestion of immediate suspension or a moratorium, the United States supported the appeal, while the Soviet bloc, with the exception of Romania, abstained.

Another significant move was the adoption by the UN General Assembly on December 3 of a resolution to make Africa a "nuclear free zone."

A New Specter arose at year's end when a high-level panel of U.S. citizens suggested that the United States and the U.S.S.R. were moving rapidly toward a dangerous nuclear arms spiral with the development of effective antiballistic missile systems. The panel, headed by Dean Jerome B. Wiesner of the Massachusetts Institute of Technology, urged the United States to press for a three-year Soviet-U.S. moratorium on the production and deployment of these systems.   TOM AND HARLE DAMMANN

See also ATOMIC ENERGY.

DISASTERS. Floods, many brought by powerful cyclonic winds, were among the worst natural disasters of 1965. East Pakistan suffered two such disasters. The United States' Midwest had a difficult year. More than 35 tornadoes struck on Palm Sunday. The Mississippi River overflowed its banks in Minnesota, and rushed southward. Hurricane *Betsy* wrought havoc in wide areas north of the Gulf of Mexico.

Tragedy in the Atlantic occurred aboard the *Yarmouth Castle*. The cruise ship, supposedly in excellent condition, suddenly burned and sank while sailing from Miami, Fla., to Nassau.

Major disasters included the following:

Aircraft Crashes

Jan. 16—Wichita, Kans. A U.S. Air Force KC-135 jet tanker crashed into a residential area; 23 persons on the ground and the tanker's 7 crewmen were killed.

Feb. 6—Chile. A Chilean DC-6B crashed in the El Volcán Pass region of the Andes Mountains, killing 87 persons aboard.

Feb. 8—New York, N.Y. An Eastern Air Lines DC-7B plunged into the Atlantic Ocean off Jones Beach. All 84 persons aboard were killed.

Mar. 22—Near Bucaramanga, Colombia. An Avianca Airlines plane crashed on the Pandeazucar range in the Andes, killing 29 persons.

Mar. 26—North-West Frontier, West Pakistan. A Pakistan International Airlines DC-3 crashed near the Lowari Pass, killing 22 persons.

Mar. 31—Strait of Gibraltar. An Iberia Airlines Convair crashed into the sea and killed 50 persons.

HURRICANE BETSY hurled homes across the road that runs through Delacroix Island, southeast of New Orleans (see NEW ORLEANS*).*

DISASTERS

Apr. 10—Syria. A Jordanian Airlines plane burst into flames and crashed on the Kanisa Mountain; 54 persons were killed.

Apr. 14—Jersey, Channel Islands. A Jersey Airlines DC-3 crashed, killing 26 persons.

May 5—Santa Cruz de Tenerife, Canary Islands. An Iberia Airlines Super-Constellation ran off the runway, broke in two, and burned; 23 of the 49 persons aboard were killed.

May 20—United Arab Republic. A Pakistan International Airlines Boeing 720-B crashed near the Cairo Airport, killing 121 of the 127 persons aboard.

June 25—Near El Toro, Calif. A U.S. Air Force C-135 transport struck a Santa Ana Mountains ridge and burned; 12 crewmen and 72 marines were killed.

July 6—Near Oxford, England. A Royal British Air Force transport exploded and plunged to the ground, killing all 41 men aboard.

July 7—Near Cairo, United Arab Republic. A Russian-manned AN-12 crashed, killing 29 persons.

July 8—British Columbia. A Canadian Pacific Airlines DC-6B exploded and crashed in the Cariboo mountains, killing 52 persons.

July 25—Panay Island, Philippines. A Philippine Airlines plane crashed, killing 36 persons.

Aug. 16—Near Chicago, Ill. A United Air Lines Boeing 727 crashed in Lake Michigan, killing 30.

Aug. 24—Hong Kong. A U.S. Air Force transport plane crashed into the bay, killing 58 servicemen.

Sept. 17—Montserrat, Leeward Islands. A Pan American Boeing 707 crashed into a mountain peak; all 30 persons aboard were killed.

Oct. 27—London, England. A British European Airways Vanguard hit the airport runway in a fog and burned, killing 36 persons.

Nov. 2—French Somaliland. A plane crashed on landing at the Obock airport, killing 30 French soldiers.

Nov. 3—Costa Rica. An Argentine Air Force C-54 crashed and killed all 68 persons aboard.

Nov. 8—Near Greater Cincinnati Airport. An American Airlines Boeing 727 crashed during a storm; 58 persons were killed.

Nov. 11—Salt Lake City, Utah. A United Air Lines Boeing 727 jet crashed and burned at the city's municipal airport; 42 persons were killed.

Dec. 7—Santa Cruz de Tenerife, Canary Islands. A Spanish DC-3 charter plane struck a house, injuring 2 occupants and killing 32 on the plane.

Dec. 11—South Vietnam. A U.S. Air Force C-123 transport crashed on a mountainside, killing the 85 persons aboard.

Blizzards and Storms

Feb. 24-27—United States. A snowstorm swept the Midwest and South, and moved on to New England and the Atlantic Ocean, killing an estimated 90 persons.

Sept. 18—Western United States. Early cold and snow killed 9 persons, 3 each in Montana, Wyoming, and Colorado.

Bus and Truck Accidents

Jan. 1—Peru. A bus, on a run between Huancayo and Ayacucho, dropped down a ravine into the Mantaro River; 28 persons were killed.

Feb. 3—Zacatecas, Mexico. A bus ran off a highway over a cliff, killing 25 persons.

Feb. 13—Mexico. In a bus accident between Cocula and Tecolotlan 19 persons were killed.

June 17—Iran. A bus, on its way from Bandar 'Abbās to Yazd, plunged into a ravine, killing 21 persons.

June 29—Near Chinchallote, Honduras. A bus accident, on the Pan American Highway, killed 25 persons. Some were members of a children's ballet from Costa Rica.

Aug. 11—Istanbul, Turkey. A bus collided with a truck carrying acid. Acid burns killed 23 passengers.

Aug. 27—Near Vinton, La. A Greyhound bus collided with a lumber truck. At least 13 persons died.

Sept. 2—Northeast of Jammu, Kashmir. A bus plunged down a mountain road bank, killing 27 persons.

Nov. 1—Cairo, United Arab Republic. A trolley bus out of control plunged down a 20-foot bank into the Nile River, drowning 74 persons.

Nov. 1—Near Teotihuean Pyramid, Mexico. A bus at a crossing was cut in two by a train; 26 persons died.

Dec. 5—Sotouboua, Togo. A truck ran into a carnival crowd, killing 100 or more persons.

Dec. 8—Koru, Kenya. A bus plunged into a river, killing 28 persons.

Dec. 23—New Medford, Ore. A Greyhound bus on Interstate Highway 5 skidded on ice and swerved off the road, killing 13 passengers.

—Kransport Mountains, South Africa. A truck, loaded with workers, went out of control, and killed 37 young Africans.

Earthquakes

Feb. 18-24—Sanana Island, Indonesia. A series of earthquakes killed 71 persons.

Mar. 28—Central Chile. An earthquake shook an area from Antofagasto to Concepción, killing 420 persons. This included 170 deaths at El Cobre, where the El Soldado Tailings Dam broke.

Apr. 5—Southern Greece. An earthquake shook a 760-square-mile area of the Peloponnesus, and killed 19 persons.

Apr. 29—Pacific Northwest. An earthquake shook 4 states and British Columbia in Canada, killing 6 persons. Seattle and Tacoma, Wash., were the worst-hit areas.

May 3—El Salvador. An earthquake in San Salvador killed about 100 persons.

Explosions and Fires

Mar. 1—Montreal, Quebec. Explosion and fire destroyed an apartment building in suburban Lasalle; 15 of the 28 persons killed were children.

Mar. 4—Near Natchitoches, La. A natural gas pipeline exploded, killing 17 persons.

Aug. 9—Near Searcy, Ark. Explosion and fire in a Titan II missile silo killed 53 civilian workers.

Aug. 14—Uusikyla, Finland. An explosion at a military arsenal killed at least 5 persons.

Aug. 25—Near Louisville, Ky. A series of explosions and fire at an E. I. du Pont de Nemours & Company synthetic rubber plant killed 12 persons.

Sept. 24—Kamiseya, Japan. A U.S. Naval communications building was destroyed by fire and 12 navy personnel killed.

Oct. 16—North of Seoul, South Korea. A 105-mm howitzer shell exploded while being dismantled at a village blacksmith shop, killing 14 persons.

Oct. 22—Tila Bund, Pakistan. An explosion wrecked a canal bridge and buried 80 workers.

Oct. 30—Cartagena, Colombia. An explosion in a market building killed at least 47 persons.

Nov. 24—Keokuk, Iowa. Fire and explosion destroyed the National Guard armory crowded with square dancers; 21 persons were killed and many injured.

Dec. 20—Yonkers, N.Y. Fire in a Jewish community center building, decorated for Hanukkah (Jewish Feast of Lights), killed 9 children and 3 adults.

Floods

Apr. 5-May 8—Midwestern United States. The Upper Mississippi River, swelled by rain and melting snow, overflowed its banks in Minnesota, Wisconsin, Illinois, Iowa, and Missouri; 15 persons lost their lives during the month-long crisis.

June 11—Sanderson, Tex. A flash flood destroyed homes and killed 16 persons.

June 18—Western United States. Floods in Wyoming, Colorado, Montana, and New Mexico killed at least 13 persons.

July 16—South Korea. Floods in the central part of the country killed at least 74 persons.

July 23—Japan. Rain, floods, and landslides in the southwestern part of the country killed 28 persons.

Aug. 22—Mexico. Floods in the west and central states of Jalisco and Nayarit killed 27 persons.

Sept. 2-5—Italy. Heavy rain and floods from the Alps to Sicily took the lives of 55 persons.

Sept. 29—Honduras. Floods, set off by rains, killed at least 22 persons.

Nov. 23—Southern California. Flash floods, set off by heavy rain, caused 5 deaths.

Cyclones, Hurricanes, and Typhoons

May 12—East Pakistan. A cyclone spread destruction in 8 districts, killing about 15,000 persons.

June 19—Formosa. Typhoon *Dinah* killed 31 persons.

Aug. 7—Japan. A typhoon killed 26 persons in Kyushu and southern Honshu.

Sept. 8-10—Southern Florida and Gulf of Mexico. Hurricane *Betsy* killed 7 persons in Florida, 1 in Mississippi, and 4 in Arkansas. Louisiana, with a death toll of 75, was the worst-hit area.

Sept. 10—Japan. Typhoon *Shirley* struck Hokkaido, Shikoku, and southern Honshu islands, killing at least 39 persons.

Sept. 18—Western Japan. Typhoon *Trix* left at least 50 persons dead, and 34 missing.

Dec. 15—East Pakistan. A cyclone and high waves in the Bay of Bengal area swept fishermen and others to their deaths, with a toll of 12,000.

Mine Disasters

Feb. 2—Near Lens, France. A gas explosion in a government-owned mine killed 21 men.

Feb. 18—North of Stewart, British Columbia. An avalanche at the Granduc Mining Company copper mine, in Le Duc Glacier, killed 26 men.

Mar. 19—Near Amasya, Turkey. Gas explosions and fire at a lignite mine killed 68 men.

Apr. 9—Off Nagasaki, Japan. A cave-in, caused by an explosion, at the Nitetsu Mining Company mine on Iwo Island killed 30 or more men.

May 8—Real Del Monte, Mexico. An elevator cage fell to the bottom of a mine shaft, killing 27 men.

May 17—Near Tonypandy, Wales. An explosion in the Cambrian Colliery killed 31 men.

May 28—Near Dhanbad, Bihar, India. An explosion in the Bhori Coal Mine killed about 400 men, some of whom were working above ground.

June 1—Kyushu Island, Japan. A gas explosion at the Yamano Coal Mine killed at least 237 men.

June 7—Kakanj, Yugoslavia. A gas explosion in a coal mine killed 125 men.

Oct. 16—Sardis, W.Va. A coal-digging machine cut an electrical cable in the Clinchfield Coal Company Mars No. 2 mine. Resulting fire killed 7 men.

Dec. 28—Near Redstone, Colo. A gas explosion in No. 1 Dutch Creek Mine killed 9 workmen.

Shipwrecks

Mar. 5—Near Kurnool, India. A ferryboat capsized on the Tungabhdhra River, drowning 21 persons.

Apr. 15—Vijayavada, Andhra, India. Eight boats (tied together) capsized on the Kistna River, and drowned 40 persons.

May 23—Liwonde, Malawi. A ferryboat capsized on the Shire River, and drowned 150 persons.

Wide World

GIANT THUNDERSTORM was formed after a volcano erupted on the shores of Lake Taal, 40 miles south of Manila in The Philippines. It capsized many boats.

DISASTERS

May 27—Near Port Harcourt, Nigeria. A motorized canoe overturned in Soku Creek, drowning about 40 persons.

Aug. 4—Off Esposende, Portugal. The German freighter *Apollo* rammed into a trawler, which split in two and sank; 28 fishermen drowned.

Aug. 15—Near San Vincente, Chile. The naval cutter *Janequeo*, driven against rocks during a storm, sank with 60 men aboard.

Aug. 23—Off Samar Island, Philippines. A motor launch overturned and sank with 65 persons aboard.

Nov. 13—Off the Great Stirrup Cay in the Atlantic. The cruise ship *Yarmouth Castle*, on its way from Miami, Fla., to Nassau, Bahamas, sank after fire broke out aboard past midnight; 89 persons were lost, and 459 saved.

Tornadoes

Apr. 11—Midwestern United States. A number of tornadoes struck in Illinois, Indiana, Iowa, Michigan, Ohio, and Wisconsin, and killed 243 persons.

May 6—Minneapolis, Minn. Tornadoes swept through the city's suburbs, killing 13 persons.

May 8—Nebraska. Tornadoes in the northeast and central parts of the state killed 4 persons.

June 3—Texas. A tornado killed 3 persons in the Hale Center farming area.

July 4—Northern Italy. Tornadoes and windstorms killed 25 persons.

Aug. 27—Midwestern United States. High winds killed 3 persons in Illinois, Iowa, and Minnesota.

Train Wrecks

Feb. 10—Zaragoza, Spain. Three wooden coaches of the Madrid-Barcelona mail train caught fire and burned; 25 to 30 persons perished.

Apr. 5—Near Paraiba do Sul, Rio de Janeiro, Brazil. A passenger and a freight train crashed, killing 40 persons.

Oct. 4—Durban, South Africa. A rush-hour commuter train was derailed at a suburban station, killing 100 persons.

Dec. 9—Near Toungoo, Burma. A head-on train collision killed 76 persons.

Dec. 18—Villar De Los Alamos, Spain. The Paris-to-Lisbon Sud express and a local train hit head-on, killing at least 24 persons.

Dec. 20—Near Algueiro, Portugal. A head-on crash of a passenger train and a freight, which was on the wrong track, killed at least 22 persons.

Other Disasters

Jan. 3—Rijo, Mexico. The roof of a new village church caved in during the dedication mass; 58 persons were killed.

Jan. 31—Guadalajara, Mexico. Some 7,000 persons leaving a music festival (in a bull ring) collided with 5,000 rushing in for the next show. About 20 persons were trampled to death.

June 26—Kawasaki City, Japan. A mudslide engulfed 13 houses, and killed 24 persons.

Aug. 20—Las Cuevas, Argentina. This upper Andes village was hit by an avalanche; 37 persons were killed.

Aug. 30—Near Saas-Fee, Switzerland. An avalanche from the Allalin glacier crashed down on workers at a dam construction site, burying 40 to 100 of them.

Sept. 5—Lincoln, Nebr. Two 40-foot steel towers, supporting a cable ride, collapsed and killed 2 persons.

Nov. 27—Manizales, Colombia. Heavy rains caused a landslide, killing 32 persons.

Dec. 16—Montreal, Canada. Tons of wet concrete collapsed at a railway tunnel under construction, and killed 7 workmen.

Dec. 27—Off Yorkshire Coast, England. A drilling rig in the North Sea sank with 32 men aboard; at least 13 were drowned.

DOMINICAN REPUBLIC

DOMINICAN REPUBLIC

Tensions in the Western Hemisphere centered in the Dominican Republic in 1965. On April 25, the U.S.-supported government of President Donald Reid Cabral Huberto was toppled by a military-civilian revolt—the eighth such overthrow of government since the assassination of Rafael Leonidas Trujillo y Molina in 1961. For three days, the rebel regime demanded the return of former President Juan D. Bosch. Bosch's return, however, was opposed by Air Force General Elias Wessin y Wessin who had ousted Bosch 19 months earlier. On April 28, Wessin's forces installed their own three-man military junta. It was not acknowledged, however, by the "rebel" forces.

EMBATTLED AMERICAN GI zeroes in with his rifle on a rebel sniper post in building overlooking street in war-torn Santo Domingo. His buddies hug the wall.

PICTURES OF THE YEAR / Douglas Jones, © Look Magazine

Wide World

OUTSTRETCHED ARM of an admirer greets former President Juan Bosch on his return to Dominican Republic after two years in exile.

In the meantime, the government of the United States had been reliably informed that U.S. citizens living in the Dominican Republic were in danger and that local authorities were no longer able to guarantee their safety. To protect them, U.S. President Lyndon B. Johnson ordered 400 U.S. Marines into the republic.

On May 5, a formal cease-fire agreement was negotiated by a special commission of the Organization of American States (OAU). It was signed by the junta and the rebels. Fighting, however, continued in much of Santo Domingo and a further contingent of U.S. troops was landed to set up an international security zone in the capital. President Johnson charged that communist conspirators had gained control of the rebel movement (which rebel leaders vigorously denied); the Dominican ambassador to the OAS charged that the revolt was part of a plan to make his nation a "second Cuba."

The rebels, still demanding the return of ex-president Bosch, named Colonel Francisco Caamaño Deno as provisional president. The anti-Bosch counter-revolutionaries, led by General Wessin y Wessin, then named General Antonio Imbert Barreras as their chief. By May 10, the U.S.-backed Barreras junta, which had been led by Pedro B. Benoit, had gained control of all the country except 500 rebel-held acres in the capital.

Throughout the following months, OAS mediators met with both warring factions to find a so-

lution, but to no avail. Pertinent to the problem was the fact that the country had known nothing but military dictatorship for nearly 40 years and had had virtually no experience with democracy in the true and practical sense of the word.

In order to allay Latin-American fears that the United States was returning to "gunboat diplomacy," President Johnson asked the OAS to share the responsibility of restoring peace and political stability on the island. The OAS voted 14 to 5 to set up an inter-American military force in the Dominican Republic; the United States announced it would begin pulling out some of its troops as soon as the Latin-American soldiers began arriving to replace them. President Johnson's decision to send troops into the Dominican Republic without waiting for an OAS blessing, however, had roiled political sensibilities throughout much of Latin America (see LATIN AMERICA).

On May 19, the Barreras-headed junta claimed absolute control of the country and called for unconditional surrender by the rebels. Its demand went unheeded. Meanwhile, 1,200 Brazilian troops had arrived under the command of Lieutenant General Hugo Penasco Alvim who had served as an artillery commander under U.S. General Mark Clark in Italy during World War II. General Penasco Alvim, under an OAS mandate, was placed in command of an estimated 21,000 U.S. Marines and paratroopers and other hemispheric forces.

On August 31, the rebels who had originally touched off the uprising signed an OAS-prepared "act of reconciliation." A provisional government was set up under former Foreign Minister Héctor Garcia-Godoy, who would rule until elections could be held. This move had been made possible by the resignation, on August 30, of the Barreras military-civilian junta, reportedly following strong pressures from Washington, D.C. On September 3, Garcia-Godoy was installed as provisional president, thus ending four months of off-and-on civil warfare in which an estimated 3,000 Dominicans died and millions of dollars in property damage had been sustained. The transitional regime was charged with preparing for general elections by June, 1966.

On September 4, the United States formally recognized the Garcia-Godoy government and promised $20,000,000 in aid as a down payment on future support. The new regime faced a number of formidable tasks such as the recovery of large numbers of weapons in the hands of civilians, the issuing of bank credits to coffee growers, payments of pensions to disgruntled army officers, and dozens of other issues, including the withdrawal of the inter-American peace force. It also faced further political dissensions. Wessin y Wessin had been sent to Miami, Fla., as the republic's consul general but on arrival he rejected the post and announced that he would organize the Dominican exiles into a force that would work for the re-establishment of democracy in his country. Former President Bosch returned to Santo Domingo in September and immediately demanded that the United States pay a $1,000,000,000 indemnity for intervening in the April revolt.

With the extremists still retaining their arms, about 2,000 OAS-sponsored troops, backed by U.S. tanks, moved into the rebel-held area of Santo Domingo in mid-October. Unrest continued, however, not only in the capital but throughout the country. In November, troops loyal to President Garcia-Godoy blocked a rightist civilian attempt at a *coup d'état* in Santiago de los Caballeros, the nation's second largest city. On December 19, disturbances again erupted in Santiago, leaving at least 12 dead. The fighting had been touched off by reports that an attempt had been made to kill Colonel Francisco Caamaño Deno, who had gone to Santiago to place a wreath on the grave of a former rebel leader.

On December 20, rioting broke out in Santo Domingo, but the rioters, mostly students, were dispersed by troops of the Inter-American peace force.

Population: 3,657,000. **Government:** Provisional President Héctor Garcia-Godoy. **Monetary Unit:** peso (1 = U.S. $1). **Gross National Product:** 773,-000,000 pesos. **Foreign Trade:** exports, $180,000,000; imports, $220,000,000. **Principal Exports:** bauxite, cane sugar, coffee.   MARY C. WEBSTER

DRUG. See HEALTH; MANUFACTURING; MEDICINE.

EARTHQUAKES. See DISASTERS; GEOLOGY.

EASTERN ORTHODOX Archbishop Leonty (Turkevich), Metropolitan and Primate of the Russian Orthodox Church in America, died in New York, on May 17, at the age of 89. He was one of the last survivors of the "pioneer" generation of Orthodox missionaries in the United States. He was primate of the church since 1950.

Ireney (Bekish), the 73-year-old archbishop of Boston and New England, was elected on September 23 to succeed Leonty. He was chosen by an extraordinary church council of bishops, clergy, and laity. The new primate was born in Russia and had served as a parish priest in Poland prior to his arrival in the United States in 1952. In 1954, he was made bishop of Tokyo, Japan, and became archbishop of Boston in 1960.

Another leader of world Orthodoxy, Metropolitan Anastassy (Gribanovsky), head of the Russian Church Outside Russia, died in New York City on May 20 at the age of 91.

Interchurch Meetings. On September 9, Orthodox and Roman Catholic theologians, officially appointed by their respective hierarchies, held their first meeting at Worcester, Mass. Similar meetings with Protestant Episcopal theologians had been initiated four years before.

On December 7, Pope Paul VI of the Roman Catholic Church and Patriarch Athenagoras I voided the anathemas that had marked the schism of 1054 (see ROMAN CATHOLIC).

Internal Conflicts. Internal schisms, which began in 1963 and resulted in several court cases, continued to trouble the Serbian American Diocese. The difficulties arose between parishes loyal to the patriarch of Belgrade and those that proclaimed their independence from Yugoslavia. A similar conflict within the Bulgarian American Diocese also developed in 1965. Several Bulgarian parishes rejected the jurisdiction of Metropolitan Andrey, who was appointed from Sofia, and elected their own leader, Bishop Kirill Jonchev of Toledo, Ohio.

Outside the United States. Leaders of the Turkish government and press exerted increasing pressure on the patriarchate in Constantinople (Istanbul) as a direct result of the tensions between Greece and Turkey over Cyprus. Various branches of the Turkish government were instructed to "control" the patriarchate and to examine its affairs. Several bishops were expelled, all publications in Greek were discontinued, and a faction made up of members calling themselves "Turkish Orthodox" seized control of some of the patriarchal churches.

In the Soviet Union, the Russian Orthodox Church also faced difficulties that included the closing of some of its churches and the reduction of seminaries to only three. Official delegates from the patriarchate of Constantinople (Istanbul), for the first time, attended sessions of the Vatican Council II in Rome.   ALEXANDER SCHMEMANN

ECKERT, WILLIAM D. (1909-   ), retired U.S. Air Force lieutenant general, was elected the new commissioner of baseball, succeeding Ford Frick, who retired at 71. Though known as a much-decorated flier, the appointment came as a surprise because he was little known in big league baseball circles. His only experience in the competitive sport was on his Madison (Ind.) high school team.

Eckert was born in Freeport, Ill., Jan. 20, 1909, but was reared in Madison. He was graduated from West Point Military Academy in 1930, after having enlisted in the Indiana National Guard at the age of 15. As a young man, he was a pilot with both the 29th and the 36th Pursuit Squadrons, and, in World War II, commanded the 452nd Bomber Group stationed in England.

In 1938, the air corps sent him to Harvard's Graduate School of Business Administration where he received his master's degree two years later. After World War II, he moved into the business side of the air force. He retired in 1961 and moved to Washington, D.C., where he became director of Aeroflex Corporation's Logistics Management Institute, which advises the Pentagon. He was also an executive of several real estate and electronics companies. He married Catharine Douglas Givens on June 15, 1940. They have a daughter and a son.

Eckert was chosen for the job of baseball commissioner from among 150 nominees.

See also BASEBALL.

ECONOMY, THE

WHAT'S AHEAD FOR U.S. BUSINESS

CORPORATE PROFITS

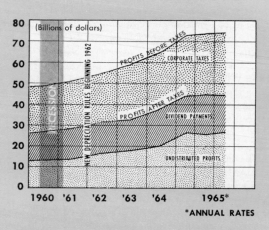

STOCK MARKET PRICES
(500 Common Stocks)

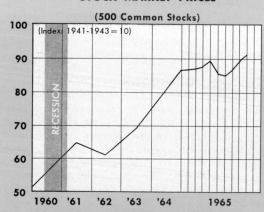

MANUFACTURING

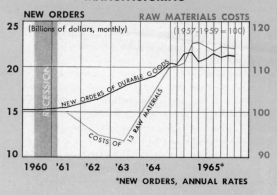

CONSTRUCTION

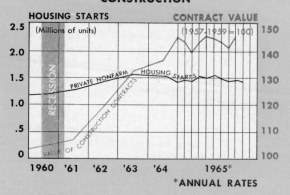

By any test, 1965 was another superb year for the U.S. economy. Performance substantially outstripped even the most optimistic forecasts that were made as the year began. And when the final figures were added up, the Gross National Product (GNP) had reached a record $675,000,000,000 of total spending on goods and services—up $7\frac{1}{2}$ per cent from 1964. A substantial revision of the statistical measurement of the GNP in midyear made comparisons with beginning-of-the-year forecasts difficult. But the margin between those estimates and the final results ranged from $10,000,000,000 to $15,000,000,000. The year-to-year GNP increase of $46,300,000,000 was achieved, with only about a 2 per cent rise in prices. The net gain, therefore, turned out to be nearly $5\frac{1}{2}$ per cent.

The U.S. rate of rise in GNP, in terms of 1964 prices, exceeded the 4 per cent average in Western Europe. Only in Western Germany (4.8 per cent) and in Italy, which had experienced a bad 1964 (3.1 per cent), were the year-to-year gains near the U.S. level. Even Japan, which was recovering from a recession in 1965, could show no better than a 2.5- to 3-per cent growth rate. Only Canada, with a booming economy, was able to outdo the United States (see CANADA).

In the less developed nations, accurate information was difficult to come by. But it seemed unlikely that any of those in the Free World managed to make any such significant gains in rate of growth. Brazil reduced the rate of its inflation to 2 or 3 per cent a month, but, in so doing, slowed the economy. See BRAZIL; MONEY.

On the other side of the Iron Curtain, the Soviet Union continued to suffer difficulties in its agricultural sector. Soviet overall growth barely equaled that of the United States. To liberate its tightly controlled economy, the Soviet Union made substantial moves during the year. It gave more decision-making to local managers and measured their performance by the profits they earned. Other Eastern European countries were taking similar steps, but their growth rates roughly paralleled the Soviet Union's—with Romania and Bulgaria in the lead and Czechoslovakia lagging, its economy almost static since 1962. A United Nations (UN) study, *Economic Planning in Europe*, told of the oppressive weight of red tape in a Soviet automobile plant. To get ball bearings it had to file application forms weighing 400 pounds and submit them to 14 different agencies.

In the United States, major changes in the measurement of GNP were made in August by the Department of Commerce, which revised all its estimates of GNP and personal income all the way back to 1929. The revisions were of two basic kinds. The first was statistical: a refinement of figures and new data—especially from the new input-output tables, which show in detail what each industry sells to and buys from others.

The second type of revision was derived from redefinitions of various categories, such as the re-

SIX KEY INDICATORS

NEW BUSINESSES AND FAILURES

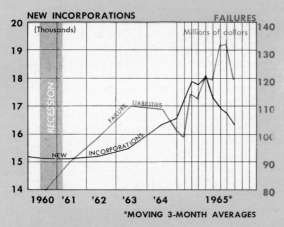

*MOVING 3-MONTH AVERAGES

EMPLOYMENT

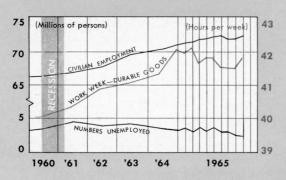

NOTE: All 1965 data adjusted for seasonal variations except for stocks, new businesses and failures, and raw materials costs.

327

moval from GNP of interest paid by consumers. Consumer interest now would be treated the same as interest on U.S. government obligations; it had never been included in the GNP. The first type of revision added $17,300,000,000 to and the second deducted $11,200,000,000 from the old 1964 GNP of $622,600,000,000. The net gain of $6,100,000,000 brought the corrected total to $628,700,000,000 for 1964.

The Booming U.S. Economy raced ahead of the forecasts to finish 1965 with a GNP of $675,000,-000,000. It ignored the economists' cautious words on a possible slowdown or flattening out of expansion after midyear. By almost every measure—employment, corporate profits, production, stock prices, retail sales, personal savings, to name a few—the U.S. economy showed continued vigor. The two

GROSS NATIONAL PRODUCT BY SECTORS OF THE ECONOMY

Sector	Calendar Years 1961 ($ billions)	1964	Percent Change	3d Quarter Annual Rate 1964 ($ billions)	1965	Percent Change
Consumer	335.2	398.9	19.0	404.6	432.2	6.8
Durables	44.2	58.7	32.8	60.5	65.4	8.1
Nondurables	155.9	177.5	13.9	179.8	191.0	6.2
Services	135.1	162.6	20.4	164.3	175.9	7.1
Business	71.7	92.9	29.6	92.6	102.0	10.2
Fixed Investments	69.7	88.1	26.4	88.8	95.7	7.8
Housing	22.6	27.5	21.7	27.2	27.6	1.5
Other bldg.	18.4	21.1	14.7	21.1	23.2	10.0
Equipment	28.6	39.4	37.8	40.5	44.9	10.9
Inventory change	2.0	4.8	*	3.8	6.1	*
Net Exports	5.6	8.6	53.6	8.8	8.1	−8.0
Government	107.6	128.4	19.3	128.7	135.2	5.1
Federal	57.4	65.3	13.8	64.9	67.1	3.4
State, local	50.2	63.1	29.7	63.8	68.1	6.7
TOTAL	520.1	628.7	20.9	634.8	677.9	6.8
Total in 1958 prices	497.3	577.5	16.1	582.6	609.7	4.7

*Not applicable.   Source: U.S. Department of Commerce.

principal business indicators that created some concern were housing starts—more than 100,000 units below the 1964 total—and the continuing deficit of the U.S. balance of payments (see HOUSING; INTERNATIONAL TRADE AND FINANCE).

Increased purchases by consumers, businessmen, and all branches of government fed the expansion, which had reached 19 quarters of consecutive gains at year's end.

Real output (GNP corrected for price increases) since the first quarter of 1961 grew 26 per cent. The major underlying factors in the 1965 expansion were somewhat increased defense expenditures—a $1,400,000,000 rise from the second to third quarter of 1965—and a high level of consumer confidence. The latter, as measured by the Survey Research

Center of the University of Michigan's Institute for Social Research, reached the highest point since 1955 in August. Its index of 103.2 was well above the level shown in the surveys of February and those taken in late spring.

The Consumer Sector. Leading the parade of consumer goods demonstrating this confidence were automobiles. Total output of more than 9,300,000 cars in 1965 was a whopping 20 per cent higher than in 1964 and 18 per cent above the previous high of 1955 (see AUTOMOBILE). Also, indicative of consumer affluence was the more than 10 per cent increase in sales of television sets. The major maker of color television tubes was forced to ration sales late in the year because manufacturing facilities were not adequate to keep up with the demand.

Total spending by consumers at the end of the third quarter was at the annual rate of $432,200,-000,000. This was up 6.8 per cent from a year earlier, but below the gain of 7.4 per cent for the similar 1963-1964 period. The increases for the private investment (business) and government sectors were 10.2 per cent and 5.1 per cent, respectively. And each of those were well above the year earlier gains (see GNP table). Despite the various stimuli to consumer spending—the continuing effects of the 1964 income tax cuts; the June, 1965, reduction in federal excise taxes; and rising consumer credit—somewhat of a leveling off in individuals' spending became apparent.

Americans still showed themselves to be thrifty as a whole, with better than 5.4 per cent of their disposable income going into savings (see BANKS AND BANKING, table). Personal income itself rose from $495,000,000,000 in 1964 to something over $530,000,000,000 in 1965. Personal taxes rose by approximately $6,000,000,000, leaving a net disposable income of approximately $465,000,000,000, up from $435,800,000,000 in 1964. See Consumer Income table.

Too Much Credit? Consumers also went deeper into debt. Installment credit rose $7,000,000,000 from $59,000,000,000 at the end of 1964. Total consumer credit increased from $76,810,000,000 in 1964 to slightly more than $84,000,000,000. If mortgage debt, totaling about $210,000,000,000 at the end of 1965, is added, the total consumer debt load comes to $294,000,000,000, or an average of $6,125 per family.

These increases were looked upon in some quarters as cause for alarm. Some analysts pointed out that the people who held most of the savings were the least likely to be in debt. Most economists, however, felt that the level of debt was well within the limits for an increasingly affluent population.

Some of the increase was, of course, a result of a rise in debt per family. While the number of borrowers increased, the number of families that went heavily into debt declined.

A whole new look at just what constitutes debt

has been taken by economists. A considerable portion of debt repayment has gone for dishwashers, refrigerators, stoves, and other equipment in family-owned homes. These payments would be considered part of rent for a non-homeowner. Furthermore, such durable goods also are assets, the payments for which might also be classified as enforced savings. Compared with business or corporate debt of $5.60 to each dollar of disposable income in 1964, consumers' debts and mortgages amounted to only 64 cents of each dollar of after-tax income.

In assessing the current dangers in consumer debt, perhaps the high rate of employment was most significant. The year's high level of economic activity brought unemployment to the lowest point since mid-1957 (see LABOR). Only 4.2 per cent of the work force was unemployed in mid-November. And with only 2 per cent of married men unable to find work, most consumers found little difficulty in taking on new debts and meeting payments on time.

Portents of Inflation. With unemployment among adult males below 4 per cent (3.7 per cent in November), the economy was believed to be approaching its capacity output from a labor point of view. Use of plant capacity, too, had risen to 90 per cent by October—only two points below the optimum or most efficient production rate (see MANUFACTURING).

Under such conditions, there is always more than a hint of inflation—pressure for wages to exceed productivity and prices of goods in short supply to rise with heightened demand. Thus, 1965 saw an almost 2 per cent rise in the consumer price index

U.S. CONSUMER INCOME AND OUTGO

	Calendar Year 1961 (in billions)	1964	% Change	3rd Quarter Rate 1964 (in billions)	1965	% Change
Personal Income...	$416.8	$495.0	18.76	$499.1	$535.9	7.37
Less Taxes......	52.4	59.2	12.98	58.8	64.6	9.86
Disposable Income.	364.4	435.8	19.59	440.3	471.3	7.04
In 1958 dollars .	350.7	406.5	15.91	410.7	432.4	5.28
Personal Outlays..	343.2	409.5	19.32	415.3	444.1	6.93
Savings..........	21.2	26.3	24.06	25.0	26.2	4.8
Nonmortgage Debt	57.7	76.8	33.10	73.5	81.9	11.43

PRICES AND JOBS

Price Index (1957–59=100)	104.2	108.1	3.74	108.4	110.2	1.66
Employed (millions)	66.8	70.4	5.39	70.5	72.2	2.41
Unemployed (millions)......	4.8	3.9	18.75	3.8	3.3	13.16

and slightly more than that for wholesale prices. Both increases were considered moderate in the face of the booming economy. But the persistent creep-up in industrial commodity prices was disquieting.

Administration concern with the possibility of the snowballing increase in prices of basic products was demonstrated on two occasions late in the year. It intervened vigorously to effect a rollback of the

THE UNITED STATES PERSONAL INCOME PIE

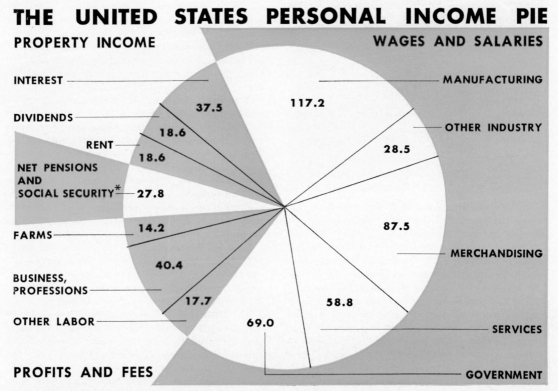

PROPERTY INCOME

WAGES AND SALARIES

INTEREST ——— 37.5

DIVIDENDS ——— 18.6

RENT ——— 18.6

NET PENSIONS AND SOCIAL SECURITY* ——— 27.8

FARMS ——— 14.2

BUSINESS, PROFESSIONS ——— 40.4

OTHER LABOR ——— 17.7

69.0

117.2 ——— MANUFACTURING

28.5 ——— OTHER INDUSTRY

87.5 ——— MERCHANDISING

58.8 ——— SERVICES

——— GOVERNMENT

PROFITS AND FEES

NOTE: Shares of income based on 1965 3rd quarter annual rate of $535,900,000,000. Figures in billions of dollars.
*Total payments of $41,200,000,000 less payroll and other deductions of $13,400,000,000 for Social Security and pensions.

THE PULSE OF BUSINESS

	Bottom of 1961 Recession (Feb., 1961, or 1st quarter)	1964 (October or 3d quarter)	1965 (October or 3d quarter)
Total output (gross national product, billion, annual rate)	$503.6	$634.8	$677.5
Outputs of industry (1957=100)	102.1	131.6	143.6*
Autos, other hard goods	94.3	129.9	148.4*
Clothing, other soft goods	110.8	134.4	140.7*
Unemployment (per cent of civilian labor force)	6.8	5.2	4.3
Farm net income (billions, annual rate)	$ 12.8	$ 12.1	$ 14.3
Retail trade (billions, monthly)	$ 17.8	$ 22.3	$ 24.0*
New construction (billions, annual rate)	$ 54.6	$ 64.9	$ 68.2*
Housing starts, private (millions, annual rate)	1.2	1.5	1.4*
Business inventories (billions)	$ 93.4	$108.5	$116.7*
Factories' new orders (billions, monthly)	$ 29.1	$ 37.5	$ 41.2*
Unfilled orders, hard goods (billions, end of month)	$ 42.8	$ 52.1	59.2
Factory workweek (avg. hrs.)	39.3	40.7	41.2
Corporation profits (billions, annual rate)			
Before taxes	$ 45.0	$ 65.3	$ 74.4
After taxes	$ 24.0	$ 37.5	$ 44.8
Spending for plant and equipment (billions, annual rate, December)	$ 33.8	$ 47.75	$ 52.95*
Exports of goods (billions, monthly)	$ 1.7	$ 2.2	$ 2.3
Imports of goods (billions, monthly)	$ 1.1	$ 1.5	$ 1.8

*Preliminary

price of ingot aluminum in November. After the major producers had announced price boosts, the government said it would sell aluminum from its stockpile. The producers soon withdrew the increases. Shortly thereafter a similar, but less vigorous, intervention brought an abortive end to increases in copper prices. See MINES AND MINING.

The Business Sector of the economy, by expanding its plant to meet the rising demands of prospering consumers, helped to hold the price line on many products. The consumer price index on durable goods actually went down, from 103.6 in January to 101.7 in September, 1965.

Expenditures for new plant and equipment totaled about $51,000,000,000 in 1965, up more than $6,000,000,000 from 1964. This continuing investment—as well as the tax cut—contributed to the ability of corporations to increase their profits despite rising wage rates. After-tax profits rose from $37,000,000,000 in 1964 to nearly $45,000,000,000 in 1965. Dividend payments also reached a new high of almost $20,000,000,000. Much of the balance of the $25,000,000,000 in retained earnings plus nearly $7,000,000,000 in new security issues were used to finance the expansion.

The Demand for Money—for plant expansion, for consumer credit, for inventories, for operating expenses of booming business—grew stronger. From September through November, interest rates on U.S. government securities began a sharp rise. It carried 91-day Treasury bills above the 4 per cent level and long-term bonds well above $4\frac{1}{4}$ per cent. Both rates were above the basic 4 per cent *discount rate*, the interest member banks must pay for funds they borrow from Federal Reserve banks.

Late in November, President Lyndon B. Johnson said he saw no reason for increases in interest rates. That, plus the metal price rollbacks, led some to fear the economy might be in for a period of direct price controls.

Throughout the year the Federal Reserve System had pursued a generally expansionary policy. Its outstanding loans to member banks rose by more than $2,000,000,000. The total money supply grew $4\frac{1}{2}$ per cent. Net borrowed reserves had reached about $1,500,000,000 in mid-October. This, together with a continuing decline in the gold stock from $15,388,000,000 on Dec. 1, 1964, to $13,809,-000,000 a year later, led the Federal Reserve Board to consider it was time to apply the brakes. On December 5, it raised the discount rate to $4\frac{1}{2}$ per cent. See BANKS AND BANKING; MONEY.

A Shift in Emphasis. This use of monetary policy reflected a growing belief by many economists that *fiscal policy* (a manipulation of government revenues and expenditures) was not sufficient to keep the economy on an even keel. So long as there was widespread unused capacity, a policy of "easy money" accompanied by appropriate fiscal action could maintain steady expansion. But as the labor situation tightened and resources were more fully used, there was increasing doubt that inflation could be contained without some monetary dampers.

Business Reaction to the rate increase was favorable. Stocks sold off at a dizzy pace in early trade on December 6, then recovered smartly. Later, stocks pushed higher, apparently putting aside any fears of deflation (see STOCKS AND BONDS).

The faith of those who believed that stock prices forecast the future course of the economy was badly shaken during the nearly five-year expansion. Stock prices fell precipitously in the spring of 1962—but without a downturn in business. Similarly, in 1965 when prices sank in June and July, there were predictions of a business decline. Rather, it would appear, the stock market more nearly reflects the expectations of investors and speculators than it serves as a predictor of future economic activity.

Industrial Production ignored the Wall Street doings and kept rolling up records. The Federal Reserve Board's index hit a high of 144.4 (1957-1959 = 100) in August. It then dropped slightly in Septem-

---

THE BIG TENS OF INDUSTRY
(Ranked in Order of Sales)

U.S. CORPORATIONS	SALES (in billions)	ASSETS	EMPLOYEES (actual)
General Motors.....	$16,997	$11,245	660,997
Standard Oil (N.J.) ..	10,814	12,489	147,000
Ford Motor.........	9,670	6,459	336,841
General Electric......	4,941	3,120	262,056
Socony Mobil Oil....	4,499	4,879	80,000
Chrysler...........	4,287	2,420	142,410
U.S. Steel...........	4,077	5,330	199,979
Texaco............	3,573	4,966	56,045
Int'l Business Machines	3,239	3,309	149,834
Gulf Oil...........	3,174	4,667	54,200

FOREIGN COMPANIES	NATION	SALES (in billions)	ASSETS
Royal Dutch/Shell.....	Neth.-Brit.	$6,824	$11,248
Unilever.............	Brit.-Neth.	4,727	2,931
National Coal Board...	Britain	2,486	2,896
British Petroleum......	Britain	2,298	3,474
Imperial Chemical.....	Britain	2,016	3,263
Volkswagenwerk......	Germany	1,999	732
Philips Lamp..........	Netherlands	1,934	2,432
Siemens.............	Germany	1,633	1,348
August Thyssen-Huette..	Germany	1,513	1,476
Fiat.................	Italy	1,452	1,299

Note: All figures for 1964.   Source: *Fortune* Magazine

---

ber and October as steel inventories that had been piled up to protect against a threatened September 1 strike were worked off (see STEEL INDUSTRY). By December, the index had exceeded its August high and stood at 148.3.

Total business sales (retail, wholesale, and factory) rose about 9 per cent. And despite the steel inventory build-up, the boom kept the important sales-to-inventory ratio at approximately the same level as the 1964 average. This was true of manufacturing as a whole as well as for retail and wholesale trade. Wage rates in manufacturing continued to rise. Nevertheless, labor costs per unit of output remained steady or even dropped a bit. The feared wage-price profits squeeze did not develop.

The Government Sector. One of the elements in the Federal Reserve decision to boost the discount rate doubtlessly was the increasingly important role that federal expenditures have come to play in the economy. For the fiscal year ending June 30, 1966, federal purchases alone will total more than 10 per cent of the GNP. A great part of this will be spent on national defense and the expanding commitment to the war in Vietnam.

Furthermore, the Great Society legislation of the 89th Congress—especially the War on Poverty, Ap-

palachia, and aid to education—added considerably to probable federal outlays (see CONGRESS OF THE UNITED STATES). To these federal totals, state and local governments have added another 10 per cent—all together accounting for about 20 per cent of the GNP (see CITY; STATE GOVERNMENT).

Government has become recognized as America's fastest growing industry. From 1955 to 1965, private payrolls increased 11 per cent. State, local, and federal civilian employment, however, rose 45 per cent in the same decade. Every sixth American worker held a government job in 1965. Wages and salaries for these payrolls, as well as purchases of other services and goods, have proved increasingly difficult to reduce. Governmental demands for goods and services could be checked by increasing taxes to cut consumer spending. But taxes are notoriously difficult to impose. Therefore, the most effective place to curb prices, so the monetary theorists argue, is on the private sector of the economy. Higher interest rates would reduce spending—and the pressure on prices.

What government spends for goods and services (see GNP table) is somewhat less than its total budget. The additional amounts are spent on such payments as farm or business subsidies, grants-in-aid, Social Security benefits, and interest on debt. These are not counted in the GNP. Of the three types of federal budgets—*administrative*, *cash*, and

Tiger in the tank.

national income—the latter best measures the impact of U.S. fiscal policies on GNP. It excludes all receipts or payments that have no bearing on current output or income earned in production. At the end of the third quarter of 1965, total *national income* federal receipts came to an adjusted annual rate of $122,100,000,000. Of the $126,200,000,000 expenditures, $67,100,000,000 was for goods and services (GNP). The rest consisted of transfers of funds to other sectors of the economy.

Net Export Sector. U.S. foreign trade contributed approximately $8,000,000,000 to the GNP, about $500,000,000 below the 1964 net balance of exports over imports. During 1965, imports increased more rapidly than exports. Imports rose 12 per cent in October to an adjusted monthly high of $2,002,-000,000; exports were up 2 per cent to $2,348,600,-000. Expectations were that the net export favorable balance would decline to about $5,500,000,000 in 1966. See INTERNATIONAL TRADE AND FINANCE.

All in all—despite the concern over housing and international trade and payments, 1965 was another "super" year. If 1966 can improve on 1965, there may be good reason to believe the U.S. economy has overcome its old habit of alternating between prosperity and recession every two or three years. WARREN W. SHEARER

See also Section One, SYLVIA PORTER ON THE ECONOMY, and its Related Articles.

ECUADOR faced mounting economic difficulties in 1965. Falling banana prices and a drop in exports, coupled with a resulting trade deficit and higher taxes, aggravated a growing restlessness over the failure of the ruling military junta to return the country to constitutional government. The value of the currency remained strong, however. A $12,000,000 stand-by arrangement with the International Monetary Fund (IMF) over a 12-month period helped tide Ecuador over any serious financial crises.

The government tightened its fiscal policies during the year. It placed a limit on credit, ordered price controls, and increased customs duties. The latter step, however, caused a merchants' strike. A compromise solution was sought, and in September, the government modified its stand.

During the year, the junta encountered opposition from nearly all of Ecuador's political leaders as well as students, most unions, and important business groups. All were demanding a prompt return to civilian rule.

Population: 5,094,000. **Government:** Military junta. **Monetary Unit:** sucre (18.18 = U.S. $1). **Gross National Product:** 15,390,000,000 sucres. **Foreign Trade:** exports, $148,000,000; imports, $169,000,000. **Principal Exports:** bananas and plantains, cocoa, coffee. MARY C. WEBSTER

See also LATIN AMERICA.

ECUMENICAL COUNCIL. See ROMAN CATHOLIC; Section Two, THE SACRED LAND.

EDUCATION

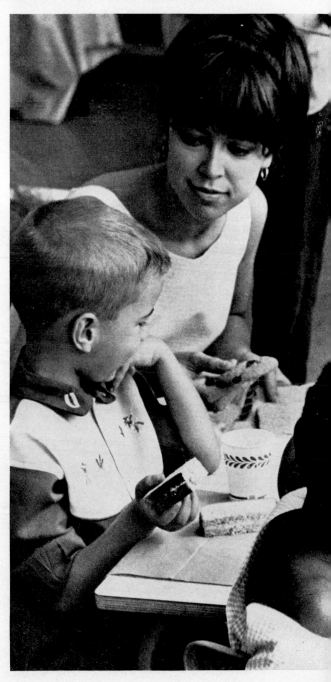

The most significant expansion of federal participation in the nation's educational plant, an important move by the states to compete with this trend, and the first broad-scale experiment offering preschool compensatory instruction to children from deprived homes occurred in 1965. At the same time, higher education witnessed the beginnings of a

PROJECT HEAD START reached 500,000 preschoolers in its first year, 1965. Its purpose is to give children from culturally deprived homes learning experiences.
The New York Times

significant reappraisal that was set in motion by widespread revolts of undergraduates in large universities against what they charged was a severe neglect of the teaching function.

Meanwhile, a White House Conference on Education served as a kind of summit meeting for the assessment of the total educational picture. Federal appropriations to the U.S. Office of Education had reached $3,800,000,000 for the 1964-1965 fiscal year. But even this plentiful amount did not include vast additional expenditures authorized by anti-poverty legislation. Total education appropriations on all levels were estimated at $39,000,000,000.

School Improvement Act. The Congress of the United States passed the pioneering Elementary and Secondary School Improvement Act of 1965. Its cost for the fiscal year that began July 1: $1,300,000,000. The act's most important provision, estimated to cost something more than $1,000,000,000, was aimed at helping the states finance the education of children from the poorest homes in urban slums and in distressed rural areas. The funds were allocated for distribution to districts according to the number of pupils from 5 to 17 years, from families with incomes of $2,000 a year or less, or families who were on relief. The remainder of the funds (about $300,000,000) are earmarked for the purchase of textbooks and other instructional materials, and for the establishment of supplementary education centers. In the centers, children from surrounding

Highlights of the Education Acts of 1965

Here are the major provisions dealing with higher education.

Title I (Community Service)

Authorizes a three-year program to enable colleges and universities to participate in the solution of rural or urban community problems in areas such as employment, health, housing, land use, poverty, transportation, youth opportunities.

Title II (Library Assistance)

Aids colleges and universities in acquiring library materials and in undertaking research aimed at improving libraries and the training of librarians.

Title III (Developing Institutions)

Endeavors to raise the academic quality of developing institutions by paying part of the cost of planning and implementing cooperative projects with established institutions, such as exchange of faculty and students, introduction of new programs, joint use of libraries and laboratories; sets up National Teaching Fellowships to encourage junior faculty members and graduate students to teach at developing institutions.

Title IV (Financial Aid to Students)

Establishes a program of federal scholarships for needy undergraduate students; recognizes the squeeze produced by spiraling cost of higher education on middle-income families and, hence, aids in the payment of interest on loans to students from families earning up to $15,000 yearly.

Title V (Teacher Corps)

Establishes a National Teacher Corps to provide a pool of experienced teachers for service in schools in low-income areas; provides fellowships for teachers and other experienced personnel who desire to enter or re-enter elementary or secondary education. Fellows will be enabled to undertake two years of graduate study leading to a master's degree or its equivalent.

Title VI (Undergraduate Facilities)

Provides financial aid for the purchase of laboratory and other special equipment and materials for undergraduate education.

schools would be able to get special instruction in subjects ranging from the arts to vocational training, and from science to foreign languages.

Perhaps the most remarkable achievement of the act, which ended 20 years of deadlock over general aid to the schools, was that it managed to overcome the opposition of those who traditionally had blocked federal aid, unless it included church-related schools. Constitutional experts have always held such aid would violate the separation of church and state. The compromise was achieved by permitting the textbook and center benefits to be shared by children of parochial schools. Thus, funds and programs remain under the control of the public schools, but materials and facilities may also be utilized by the children from parochial schools.

Said President Lyndon B. Johnson as he signed the bill on April 11: "I deeply believe that no law I have signed, or ever will sign, means more to the future of our nation."

The Higher Education Act of 1965, passed by Congress on October 20, was another pioneering measure. It provided, for the first time, federal scholarships for undergraduates. A total of 140,000 such grants, to a maximum of $1,000 (including a $200 bonus to students in the top half of their class) per student annually, would go to talented but needy candidates. At the same time, the law recognized that middle-income families have found increasing difficulties in paying for their children's

Title VIII (Federal Control)

Forbids the federal control of education under any and all provisions of this act.

Here are the major provisions dealing with elementary and secondary education.

Title I (Impoverished School Districts)

Authorizes a three-year program of grants to school districts with large numbers of families on relief, or with annual incomes under $2,000. Grants to be used for programs deemed necessary by local school boards, subject to approval of state and federal educational agencies.

Title II (Library and Textbook Materials)

Authorizes a five-year program of grants to the states for the purchase of books for elementary and secondary school libraries, and other library materials and textbooks for children in public and private schools. Materials purchased with federal funds will be owned by a public agency and must not be used for sectarian instruction or worship.

Title III (Supplementary Centers)

Sets up a five-year program of grants for community education centers to offer services that some schools in the area could not provide. Centers can be shared with parochial school children, but funds and programs remain in public school hands.

Title IV (Research Centers)

Authorizes a five-year program of grants for improving existing educational research centers, for constructing new centers, and for training research personnel.

Title V (State Education Departments)

Authorizes a five-year program of grants to strengthen state education departments, with state matching funds.

college education, without at least some loans which permit the phasing of payments. The National Defense Education Act (NDEA) of 1958 has been offering loan money to the colleges, but only for students of demonstrated financial need. Under the new law, families with incomes of up to $15,000 may go directly to commercial banks or loan agencies and apply for loans. The federal government will pay the difference between 3 per cent and the authorized interest rate of approximately 6 per cent. Thus, the middle-income family will be able to get a long-term college loan on terms equal to those which have prevailed under the NDEA. Repayments may be made within 10 years after graduation.

The Higher Education Act also offered funds over a five-year period, starting with $25,000,000 for the first year, to help the universities mobilize concerted attacks on community problems. This would be higher education's enlistment in the anti-poverty effort. It would involve the institutions in needy areas at home, in much the same way that many U.S. universities are involved in educational aid in underdeveloped countries abroad. In addition, Congress authorized—but refused to vote funds for—a 6,000-member National Teacher Corps. Trainees would have been made available in teams, under expert supervision, to schools in disadvantaged areas.

Another breakthrough provision ensured the availability of money to permit strong institutions to aid weaker ones, primarily through faculty exchanges. This was considered to have special importance in the upgrading of many hard-pressed Negro colleges in the South.

The Chicago Aid Fight. Charges of federal control of local school autonomy erupted when the U.S. Office of Education announced that it would withhold $30,000,000 in federal funds from Chicago schools. The action was taken in response to charges that the city's educational authorities were lagging in integrating *de facto* segregated schools. Although funds have been withheld from Southern school districts for noncompliance with the requirement in the Civil Rights Act of 1964 to end *de jure* segregation, no similar sanctions had ever been invoked against a Northern community. However, a combination of political pressures on the White House and promises by Chicago school spokesmen to investigate the charges led to an unfreezing of the funds within a few days.

Project Head Start. More than 500,000 children in the nation's slums and in rural poverty pockets were offered special preparation during the summer months, just prior to their first year in kindergarten or first grade under Project Head Start. The bulk of Head Start's cost of $112,000,000 was borne by the Office of Economic Opportunity, but the details were worked out by schools and education agencies in 2,500 communities across the country. By autumn, the experiment was considered so successful that President Johnson ordered it continued on an all-year basis, with communities invited to submit proposals that would be federally funded. A number of cities had already begun to make preschool education part of the effort to give disadvantaged children compensatory schooling. In New York City, where the preschool classes for 3- and 4-year-olds had begun for 1,500 youngsters the year before, the total enrollment was upped to 7,000 in 1965, and school officials were aiming at an eventual program involving 30,000 to 40,000 preschoolers.

Conant Proposal. Following publication in 1964 of his controversial book, *Shaping Educational Policy*, Dr. James B. Conant, former president of Harvard University, took steps toward implementing his proposals to strengthen education authority at the state level, thus making it possible for states to cooperate in the formulation of nationwide education policies.

Undoubtedly spurred by the belief of some of the advocates of states' rights, who sensed in the move an opportunity to compete with federal participation in education, the governors of many states responded quickly. A conference at Kansas City led to preliminary agreement to establish an interstate compact, such as Dr. Conant had proposed. The project was actively advanced by former North Carolina Governor Terry Sanford.

School Enrollment. When the 1965-1966 academic year opened, 54,200,000 students were enrolled in all institutions, public and private, from kindergarten through university, according to estimates by the U.S. Office of Education and the National Catholic Welfare Conference.

The elementary grades, from kindergarten through grade eight, accounted for about 35,900,000 pupils, compared with 35,500,000 the year before. About 30,500,000 were in public schools, and some 5,400,000 in all private schools, mostly in Roman Catholic parochial schools.

In the high schools (grades 9 through 12), the total was estimated at 12,900,000, the same as the previous year. Public high schools accounted for 11,500,-000, with private schools adding another 1,400,000.

On the college scene, the U.S. Office of Education reported 5,400,000 enrolled for credit in 2,175 institutions, an increase of 400,000 over the previous academic year. This included a junior college enrollment of over 800,000.

White House Conference. President Johnson called a White House Conference on Education, the first since 1954. The conference was held in July, in Washington. In contrast to the meeting of 11 years ago, the issue had shifted from the debate over the need for federal aid to finding new ways in which the now plentiful federal funds might be made more effective by more far-sighted leadership on the local level. The conferees agreed that the integration efforts, especially in the big cities, would have to be speeded and that schools, communities, and social welfare services must work in closer cooperation.

Does the comprehensive, public high school, such as one finds in Japan, Sweden, and the United States, enable its students to master subject matter as adequately as do the selective high schools of England, France, West Germany, and other West European countries? Is the graduate of a selective system better prepared for the rigors of the university classroom of the 1960s than the top student of the comprehensive system?

These questions have long disturbed parents and educators, nowhere more than in the United States, which finds itself engaged in intense Cold War competition.

Most European educators believe that their selective system turns out the better student. But it is difficult to make comparisons. To be fair, one would have to compare more than the competency of two graduating classes of the two systems. One would have to compare the top 15 per cent of the average U.S. senior class with the *entire* graduating class of the selective system. This is because the selective high school admits only the top 20 to 25 per cent of the students from elementary schools and then flunks out between a third and a half of them.

But even this comparison would not be fair, because it would not take into account the high price (emotional and economic) paid for a very high standard achieved by a few students in a selective system, where the youthful academic sheep are separated from the vocational school goats primarily by parental decision. Such a decision is influenced by the parents' economic status, social attitudes, and aspirations, and is made in many European countries when the child is from 10 to 12 years of age. Nor would it take into account the very high attrition rate of the selective system. For example, of 100 students admitted to a German *gymnasium*, less than 20 graduate on schedule. The majority drop out altogether; the rest of the students are grade repeaters.

But the question remained: Does more mean less, that is, can the comprehensive public school system produce the élite scholar?

To find an answer, experts from 12 research centers met regularly in the late 1950s in Hamburg, West Germany, at the Institute for Education of the United Nations Educational, Scientific, and Cultural Organization (UNESCO). In the course of their meetings, they decided to determine the feasibility of working out and giving achievement tests on an international scale.

After an encouraging pilot study, the experts organized the Council for the International Project for the Evaluation of Educational Attainment, and chose mathematics for the first test. The participating countries were Australia, Belgium, England, Finland, France, the Federal Republic of Germany, Israel, Japan, the Netherlands, Scotland, Sweden, and the United States.

About 180,000 children (ages: 13, 15–16, and 17–19) were given a newly devised test in 1964. An attitude test was also given to evaluate their interest in, and attitude toward, the instruction they were receiving. In grading, the researchers attempted to assess, among other things, the "total yield," that is, not only how well the students scored, but how many students continued to study mathematics in the later grades.

The results are still tentative, yet by late 1965 they pointed toward interesting conclusions. They showed that the selective system *does* produce a small élite with achievement high above the mass in spite of the fact that the performance of the student in the comprehensive system, in some instances, is far above that of the student in the selective system.

The early results indicated that the comprehensive system can also produce an élite of at least the same size as the European system, and that a sizable group of students in comprehensive high schools can be brought to a level of mathematical competence far exceeding the majority of students in the selective European system.

Final report on this first study is expected in 1966, after which other subject areas will be tested. But the early results of this first international test indicate, at least as far as mathematics is concerned, that more means *more*—not less. Torsten Husén

Does More Mean Less?

EDUCATION

New Appointments. But the most important aspect of the conference was less tangible. Within a few days after its conclusion, President Johnson named John W. Gardner, who had been the conference chairman, to the Cabinet post of Secretary of Health, Education, and Welfare. Gardner had been president of the influential Carnegie Corporation of New York. See GARDNER, JOHN W.

Soon afterwards, Gardner gave Francis Keppel, U.S. commissioner of education, the additional post of Assistant Secretary of Education, thus upgrading the concerns of education on the federal level. Then, in December, he named Harold Howe II to succeed Keppel in the post of education commissioner, thus making Keppel a full-time Secretary of Education. Howe, formerly director of the Learning Institute of North Carolina, was considered to be a strong administrator who believes that change is needed in U.S. education. Thus, it seemed at year-end that the interests of education were in unusually strong hands in Washington. See HOWE, HAROLD II.

Teachers. The two rival teacher organizations, the giant 905,000-member National Education Association (NEA) and the rapidly growing 110,000-member AFL-CIO-affiliated American Federation of Teachers (AFT), both chalked up victories. In New York City, the United Federation of Teachers, the AFT's flagship local, won what it called the best contract ever achieved by any teachers' local, with $900 gains in raises and benefits for most of the city's 50,000 teachers. The NEA reported victories in Utah and Oklahoma. Faced by NEA sanctions, these states appropriated additional funds to raise teachers' salaries and generally upgrade the quality of their schools.

Campus Revolt. Following the uprising at the University of California at Berkeley, and the creation of the teach-in as a form of protest at the University of Michigan, student leadership opposing administration policy in Vietnam gained wide attention. Less publicized, but more significant for education, however, were gains made by student rebels in making the undergraduate voice more influential in helping to run both the campus and the classroom. A number of other institutions, including Yale, Cornell, and the City College of New York, took steps to invite students or recent graduates to "rate" faculty members and to press for greater consideration of their teaching ability in their winning promotion and tenure.

Integration. In New York City, where strife and boycotts gave way to apparent efforts toward cooperation, the board of education announced that it would build the first of two experimental educational parks—campus-type schools for up to 15,000 pupils—as a fuller measure toward better racial integration. FRED HECHINGER

See also AMERICAN LIBRARY ASSOCIATION (ALA); LIBRARY; Section One, LAWRENCE A. CREMIN ON EDUCATION.

EDUCATIONAL FOUNDATIONS. Major educational foundations reporting on their activities in 1965 included the following:

Alfred P. Sloan Foundation, New York City, reported assets of $309,629,295 as of Sept. 30, 1965. Grants made during the year included $1,400,000 to young scientists in 52 universities and colleges for basic research. Other grants included $250,000 to National Educational Television, and $5,000,000 to California Institute of Technology. Grants to Negro education included $80,000 to National Medical Fellowships, Inc., and $56,000 to the Robert R. Moton Memorial Foundation, Inc. Dillard University in New Orleans, La., received $131,347 to strengthen opportunities for Negro students in higher education.

Carnegie Corporation of New York announced grants totaling more than $1,100,000. Radcliffe Institute for Independent Study received $100,000; Overseas Educational Service, $300,000; Massachusetts Institute of Technology, $500,000; the University of California at Irvine, $36,500; and Princeton University, $100,000.

The Commonwealth Fund, New York City, reported assets of $88,376,239 as of June 30, 1965. Income totaled $5,570,145, and appropriations, $7,067,448. Medical education and community health received $3,283,022; medical research, $108,926; fellowships and awards in the health field, $550,000; and the Division of International Fellowships, $808,000.

Ford Foundation, New York City, reported assets of $2,882,212,063 as of Sept. 30, 1964, and an income of $146,943,393. New appropriations came to $105,524,358. Grants included $67,816,510 for Special Programs; $24,146,483 for education in the United States; $5,937,785 for economic development and administration; $13,593,604 for public affairs; $15,344,260 for humanities and the arts; $17,675,977 for international training and research; $9,949,177 for international affairs; $12,482,144 for science and engineering; $8,950,972 for population; and $46,188,272 for overseas development.

John A. Hartford Foundation, New York City, reported assets of $182,830,769 as of Dec. 31, 1964. Income totaled $13,948,090. Appropriations for support of medical research and other programs came to $13,871,420.

John and Mary R. Markle Foundation, New York City, reported assets of $32,131,008 as of June 30, 1965. Income totaled $1,568,111, and appropriations $1,991,770. Grants for programs in medical education came to $451,500 and scholars in academic medicine to $771,850.

John Simon Guggenheim Memorial Foundation made fellowship awards of $2,115,700 to 313 scholars, scientists, and artists to further their careers. This is the largest total of grants made by the foundation since its founding in 1925.

Rockefeller Foundation, New York City, reported an income of $27,300,000 on investments in 1964. More than $40,000,000 was spent on world-wide programs. The foundation's chief areas of interest, with grants in each, included the following: conquest of hunger, $7,000,000; stabilization of population increases, $2,800,000; aid to major universities in developing countries, $5,900,000; and in the United States, programs in equal opportunities for Negroes and other needy persons, $5,700,000; and furtherance of the arts and humanities, $1,500,000. Other projects, including fellowships and grants-in-aid, received $13,800,000.

EGYPT. See UNITED ARAB REPUBLIC (UAR).

EIRE. See IRELAND

EISENHOWER, DWIGHT D. (1890-   ) suffered two mild heart attacks late in 1965. Chest pains awakened him the night of November 9 while he was on a golf holiday at the Augusta (Ga.) National Golf Club. At nearby Fort Gordon Army Hospital, the heart attack diagnosis was made by Dr. Thomas Mattingly, who had treated the then President for a heart attack in 1955. On November 22, Eisenhower was transferred to the Walter Reed Army Medical Center at Bethesda, Md. By year's end, he was well on his way to recovery.

General Eisenhower celebrated his 75th birthday October 14 with his wife and son John and his family at Phoenixville, Pa. Twenty-eight Republican party fund-raising dinners marked the occasion.

The 741-page second volume of his memoirs, *The White House Years: Waging Peace, 1956-1961*, was published the week of his birthday. Twenty-three newspapers bought serial rights to the manuscript, and a spate of interviews marked its appearance.

During 1965, he was in close touch with President Lyndon B. Johnson, pledging support of the administration's foreign policies. He also advised the President—before the announcement of Johnson's gall bladder operation—to be candid as soon as possible about his condition. It was advice the President heeded. Still a force in his party, Eisenhower helped in the fall campaign.   CAROL L. THOMPSON

See also REPUBLICAN PARTY.

ELECTIONS for two state governorships, five state legislatures, and many large city mayoralties were held in November, 1965. Local issues overshadowed national politics, and many voters ignored party labels in electing local candidates. The Goldwater conservative brand of Republicanism proved no more attractive than it had in 1964. However, moderate, reform-conscious Republicans won in several large cities.

Democrats won the governorships in New Jersey and Virginia. In Virginia, winning Democratic candidate Mills E. Godwin, Jr., was supported by an odd coalition of Byrd-machine Democrats, urban Negroes, and organized labor. Republican candidate A. Linwood Holton, Jr., lost the traditionally Republican Negro vote. In New Jersey, Democratic Governor Richard J. Hughes won a second term by a landslide. The Republican candidate, Wayne Dumont, Jr., campaigned almost exclusively on the "soft on communism" issue.

State Legislatures. In New Jersey, the Hughes landslide also gave Democrats control of both houses of the state legislature for the first time since 1913. Democrats retained control of the Kentucky and Virginia legislatures.

In New York, the Democrats held their majority in the assembly, but the Republicans regained their control of the senate, which they had lost in the 1964 election for the first time in 30 years. In a special Vermont election, after legislative reapportionment late in November, the Republicans retained their control of both houses of the legislature.

Urban Politics. In New York City, Republican Congressman John V. Lindsay defeated the city's incumbent Democratic controller, Abraham D. Beame, for mayor, polling 1,155,915 votes to Beame's 1,030,771. The pro-Goldwater Conservative candidate, William F. Buckley, polled only 339,127 votes (see LINDSAY, JOHN VLIET). In Philadelphia, Arlen Specter, a Democrat who ran as a Republican, was elected district attorney.

Akron, Ohio, chose John S. Ballard, its first Republican mayor in 12 years. In Louisville, Ky., Republican Alderman Kenneth Schmied was elected mayor, and Republican Marlow Cook was re-elected Jefferson County judge, with strong Negro support.

The growing importance of the Negro vote was evident in Cleveland, where state representative Carl B. Stokes, a Negro, ran for mayor as an independent Democrat and lost by only 2,143 votes to Democratic incumbent Mayor Ralph S. Locher.

In Boston, Louise Day Hicks, opponent of school integration, won 64 per cent of the vote in her re-election as chairman of the Boston School Committee. That victory put her in the running for the 1967 mayoral race.   CAROL L. THOMPSON

See also CITY; DEMOCRATIC PARTY; NEW YORK CITY; REPUBLICAN PARTY; STATE GOVERNMENT.

ELECTRIC POWER AND EQUIPMENT. A single piece of electrical equipment the size of a loaf of bread triggered the greatest power failure in history early in the evening of Nov. 9, 1965, blacking out 80,000 square miles of northeastern United States and southern Canada and throwing 30,000,000 people into darkness (see map on following page).

New York City, the most electrified city in the world, was hit hardest and longest. Its people got a harsh lesson in the versatility of electric power. About 800,000 commuters were stranded in subways. Elevators stopped in their shafts. Apartment dwellers on upper floors found themselves without water—supplied from roof tanks, which had to be filled by electric pumps.

Airports disappeared as pilots prepared to land; babies were born and surgery performed by candlelight; and one man asked a subway conductor, whom he likened to a ship's captain, to perform a marriage. Through it all, there was no panic, no widespread violence, and no lack of good humor and cooperation. See RADIO.

By 10 P.M., service throughout most of the Northeast had been restored. But not in New York City, with its huge requirements. Brooklyn waited until 2 A.M., Queens until 4:20, Manhattan until 6:58, and the Bronx until 7 A.M. Staten Island, supplied through New Jersey, had escaped the blackout.

The Cause of It All was that bread-loaf-sized device called a *relay*, or electromagnetic switch. Relays monitor the flow of current in transmission lines and regulate huge circuit breakers accordingly. The Federal Power Commission (FPC), in its December 6 report to President Lyndon B. Johnson, said a relay at the Ontario Hydroelectric Commission's Sir Adam Beck plant No. 2 near Niagara Falls had been set too low—at 375,000 kilowatts (kw).

Since 1963, when the setting was made, the average power flow had gone up to 356,000 kw. Thus, on Nov. 9, 1965, at exactly 5:16:11 P.M. E.S.T., it took only a "normal fluctuation" to activate the relay. That fluctuation was a request from Syracuse, N.Y., for 200,000 kw of power. The six-cable line was already sending 1,100,000 kw from the Beck plant and 500,000 kw from New York state to Hamilton and Toronto, Ontario. That plus the additional 200,000 kw was a load well below the six cables' capacity. But for some yet-to-be-unraveled reason, when the relay opened the circuit breaker on one cable, that cable's current jumped to the other five cables, knocking them out as well.

The Power Surged east and south into the United States, since it was blocked to the west and north. It then sought outlets in the rest of the northeast grid, called the Canada-U.S. Eastern Interconnection (CANUSE). That grid, extending from Quebec to New Jersey and from Maine into Michigan, makes possible operating economies. With their demand peaking in different periods, the 42 member utilities can swap power as they need it.

But the November 9 "tremendous thrust" of power into the United States unplugged the grid. It threw plants and lines in northern New York out of commission. Other systems in CANUSE either cut themselves out or sent reserve power into the sudden electrical vacuum. A rapid chain reaction set in, one system after another collapsing, until Consolidated Edison Company and New York City blacked out at 5:28 P.M.

The FPC Concluded that "the cascading of failure was not inevitable and should not recur," and that it would not have occurred if there had been (1) more automatic controls ready for immediate activation and (2) "sufficient spinning reserves in the New England and New York City areas." Total capacity was adequate, but not the "responsive capability to meet the drain imposed on (the reserves)."

The FPC said that more, not fewer, power system interties were needed. "It is possible that the very mixture of strong and weak interties within the CANUSE area . . . may have contributed to the inability of the affected companies to ride out the initial occurrence and hang together."

In addition to highly technical recommendations to improve the grid system and its equipment, the report suggested ways to minimize the impact of

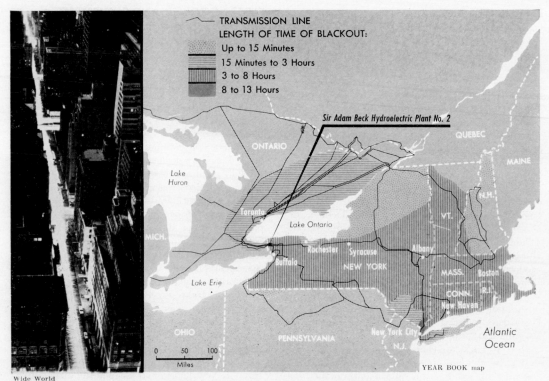

TRANSMISSION LINE
LENGTH OF TIME OF BLACKOUT:
Up to 15 Minutes
15 Minutes to 3 Hours
3 to 8 Hours
8 to 13 Hours

Sir Adam Beck Hydroelectric Plant No. 2

QUEBEC
ONTARIO
MAINE
Lake Huron
N.H.
Toronto
VT.
Lake Ontario
MICH.
Rochester Syracuse Albany
Buffalo NEW YORK
MASS. Boston
Lake Erie
CONN. R.I.
New Haven
OHIO
New York City
PENNSYLVANIA
N.J.
Atlantic Ocean

0   50   100
Miles

Wide World

YEAR BOOK map

IN THE BLACKOUT GLOOM of New York City, left, auto headlights trace the course of 49th St. The extent and duration of the power failure are shown on map.

future failures. It urged auxiliary generators for all communications, transportation, and public health facilities, as well as for restarting public utility plants. It proposed alternative manual means of operating gasoline pumps and stalled elevators. The report, signed by all five members, said that "the prime lesson of the blackout is that the utility industry must strive not merely for good, but for virtually perfect, service."

The Power Industry generally did well. Production, sales, capacity, and profits all rose. Here are the U.S. figures for the fiscal years ended June 30:

	1965	1964	% Gain
	(in millions)		
Total production (kwh)	1,116,243	1,048,261	6.5
Utilities' output (kwh)	1,015,487	950,649	6.8
Utilities' revenues	$13,030	$12,303	5.9
Utilities' net income	$2,492	$2,253	10.6

Expansion plans went ahead. As of June 30, 1965, U.S. utilities' capacity totaled 222,727,675 kw, and by year's end an additional 6,635,380 kw of capacity had been installed. Among specific projects in all this expansion was the planned $225,000,000 minemouth plant near Johnstown, Pa. It was to deliver its 1,800,000 kw to the five utilities in the Pennsylvania-New Jersey-Maryland (PJM) Interconnection by 1972. A number of utilities also were pushing into nuclear-fueled power (see ATOMIC ENERGY).

More conventionally, in June, Consolidated Edison started up the world's largest steam-turbine generator at its Ravenswood plant in New York City. The generator's nearly 1,000,000-kw rating brought the plant's total capacity to 1,800,000 kw.

Electrical Equipment manufacturers were benefiting from all this expansive activity, as well as from the blackout-induced interest in auxiliary generating equipment. For 1965, they were expecting the value of their shipments to increase $1,800,-000,000 to a total of $30,500,000,000.

The two major builders of atomic power plants, the Westinghouse Electric Corporation and the General Electric Company, between them had contracts for 19 new plants and were negotiating on several others for a total capacity of 10,000,000 kw. The biggest project in the works was a 873,000-kw generating unit for Consolidated Edison's Indian Point station in Westchester County, New York. Another major one was a 714,000-kw unit planned for the Commonwealth Edison Company's Dresden station southwest of Chicago.

Commonwealth Edison announced a grand-scale application of "heating with light" in May. The 60-story First National Bank building in Chicago will use such a heating and cooling system when it opens in 1969. Fans will draw off and recirculate the heat from fluorescent light tubes. Savings of $200,-000 a year are expected.   ROBERT E. BEDINGFIELD

See also DAM; ENGINE AND ENERGY.

ELECTRICAL EQUIPMENT. See ELECTRIC POWER; MANUFACTURING.

ELECTRONICS. Government aerospace programs continued to spur production of smaller circuit packages and more versatile solid state components. A matchbook-size television camera, for example, may handle photo assignments on the first U.S. moon landing. The tiny system, being developed for the National Aeronautics and Space Administration (NASA) by the Westinghouse Electric Corporation, replaces the conventional TV camera tube with a one-square-inch silicon wafer. Its 2,500 light-sensitive phototransistors transmit a mosaic picture. Westinghouse engineers report that this prototype will be succeeded by a similar wafer bearing 40,000 sensing elements, which will yield resolution approaching that of conventional television. Instead of electron beam scanning, digital logic circuits will scan the wafer 30 times per second—the same rate as commercial TV. The fully developed camera will weigh only $\frac{1}{3}$ pound.

The General Electric Company announced during 1965 that the cost of silicon-controlled rectifiers (SCRs) had been cut to a point where they can now be used in home lighting systems, auto ignitions, and home appliances. Basically high-speed electronic switches capable of controlling kilowatts of power, present SCRs are about the size of transistors and have the highest power amplification capacities of any semiconductor device.

Transistors Mature. The trend to replace vacuum tubes with transistors has been slowed by the inability of transistors to provide high power at high frequencies. New transistor designs, known as "overlay," "interdigitated," and "stripline," are overcoming this limitation. These new transistors were generally available for the first time in 1965. They will find wide application in military and commercial high-frequency transmitters formerly out of the range of transistors.

Despite the inroads being made by semiconductors, the future of the electron tube is still bright, according to Professor Glen Wade of Cornell University. Speaking at the 1965 International Conference of the Institute of Electrical and Electronics Engineers, he cited microwave freeze-drying of foods, high radio-frequency power for radar, and ion propulsion engines for space travel as applications where electron tubes are not likely to be replaced by solid state devices.

Lasers. The procession of new uses for lasers continued in 1965. On December 11, the Gemini VII spacecraft communicated with a ground station in Hawaii via a laser beam. Astronaut James A. Lovell, Jr., spotted the green light of a powerful ground-based argon gas laser, and then aimed his cigar-box-sized infrared emitting laser at it. By talking into a tiny microphone on the laser box, he caused its beam to pulsate. The ground station picked up the pulsing beam and converted it into an electric current which vibrated to partially reproduce Lovell's voice. Lasers are being studied by NASA as a means of communicating between vehicles in outer space.

During the year, the most powerful laser yet built for medical use was installed at the National Cancer Institute in Bethesda, Md. The surgical laser, which looks much like a dentist's drill, is being used principally for the destruction of small tumors in animals, and will be used on some human cancer patients who have not responded well to standard chemical, X-ray, and radioactive isotope treatment.

The first commercial radiobroadcast via laser beam was transmitted 10 miles, on July 13, through relatively turbulent atmosphere. In another experiment by the U.S. Army, a single laser beam simultaneously relayed the signals of all seven television channels broadcast from New York's Empire State Building. The achievement is viewed by scientists as a demonstration of the potential of lasers to relieve overcrowded portions of the radio bands.

The intense, straight-line beam of the gas laser is replacing the transit as a measuring device on some heavy construction sites. In one case, a laser beam was used to guide pipeline laying. In a similar manner, laser beams are being used in laying ship keels, building aircraft, constructing tunnels and large buildings, and aligning nuclear particle accelerators.   SERGEI LENORMAND

ELIZABETH II, QUEEN. See GREAT BRITAIN.

ELIOT, T. S. See LITERATURE (Close-Up).

EL SALVADOR remained preoccupied with the price of coffee, its principal source of income. On July 1, President Julio Adalberto Rivera began the fourth year of his five-year term by telling the legislative assembly that the nation faced grave economic prospects unless its coffee export of 1,430,000 bags annually was increased substantially under the World Coffee Agreement. International reserves reached a record $68,400,000 at the end of July, up from $53,400,000 at the outset of the year.

In order to diversify its economy, El Salvador made plans to promote, organize, develop, and finance a number of industrial enterprises. A private development company, Financiera de Desarrollo e Inversión, was formed by Salvadoran capitalists to carry out the programs.

In May, about 50,000 Salvadorans were made homeless by an earthquake in San Salvador. About 150 people died and approximately 1,000 were injured (see DISASTERS).

Population: 2,908,000. **Government:** President Julio Adalberto Rivera. **Monetary Unit:** colon (2.50 = U.S. $1). **Gross National Product:** 1,795,000,000 colons. **Foreign Trade:** exports, $178,000,000; imports, $191,000,000. **Principal Exports:** coffee, cotton, textiles.   MARY C. WEBSTER

See also LATIN AMERICA.

EMPLOYMENT. See AUTOMATION; ECONOMY, THE; EDUCATION; LABOR; Section One, JAMES RESTON ON THE NATION; SYLVIA PORTER ON THE ECONOMY; SOCIAL SECURITY; SOCIAL WELFARE.

ENGINE AND ENERGY. Fuel cells are today at the point in their development where internal combustion engines were around 1900, according to a Swedish engineering firm. The firm, which is presently constructing multikilowatt fuel cell units to power Swedish submarines, predicts a bright future for this emerging power source.

Most present fuel cells produce electrical energy through a reaction between hydrogen and oxygen. Prototype cells were developed during 1965, however, that operate on air rather than on pure oxygen, or on hydrocarbon fuels rather than on hydrogen. Other advances included improved fuel cell electrodes and electrolytes, which contribute to greater cell efficiency and longer life.

Lightweight fuel cells provided electricity for both the Gemini V mission of 191 earth orbits in August and the Gemini VII mission of 14 days in December. Trouble with the fuel cell system, however, was experienced in both flights.

MHD Generator. The generation of the first significant amount of alternating current by magnetohydrodynamics (MHD) was announced during 1965. MHD generators, another recently developed and highly efficient power source, do not have the moving parts found in conventional dynamos. Current is generated by moving a stream of conductive fluid, either a hot gas or a molten metal, through a strong magnetic field. A generator using molten metal has produced 1,840 watts of power at 215 volts. Engineers predict MHD generators can achieve efficiencies of over 70 per cent when used in tandem with conventional dynamos in commercial power stations.

Muscle Power. The process by which living muscle tissue expands and contracts has been harnessed in the design of a "mechanochemical engine" demonstrated by the U.S. Air Force in 1965. The engine's "muscle" consists of collagen, the main protein constituent of skin and leather. Rotary motion is produced by the engine when collagen fibers expand and contract in reaction to a lithium bromide solution. The device converts chemical energy directly into mechanical energy without any intermediate step such as heat or electricity. Though the power of present models is low, the air force says such engines could be used to operate delicate instruments in isolated research stations.

Ion Engines, possible sources of propulsion for future deep space missions, gained stature in 1965 when one experimental model successfully underwent a 2,600-hour test. The model develops thrust by using an electric field to accelerate charged ions produced during electron bombardment of cesium vapor. In the test, the model was turned off only for three refuelings. About 2.3 grams of cesium were consumed per hour, according to the builders, Electro-Optical Systems, Inc., of Pasadena, Calif. The 10-pound test model achieved an engine efficiency of over 55 per cent.   SERGEI LENORMAND

ENGINEERING. The American Society of Engineering Education recommended that a master's degree in engineering, awarded after five years of college study, replace the four-year bachelor's degree as the prerequisite for entering the engineering profession. The recommendation was part of a preliminary report on the goals of engineering education, released in September, 1965. The report also asked for the continuance of the four-year program leading to a bachelor's degree, but suggested that it be rated only as an "introductory" engineering degree. The report proposed an increase in liberal education requirements to better prepare engineers for new and varied reponsibilities in modern society.

The recommendations resulted from demands on practicing engineers for a higher level of professional competence. Taking part in the four-year study were 180 committees representing engineering schools and industrial firms. The survey included results of an exhaustive questionnaire submitted to 4,000 practicing engineers, visits to 169 schools of engineering, and an intensive study of five selected schools. Financial support was provided by a grant of $307,000 from the National Science Foundation.

The Starting Salary of engineering graduates climbed by 3.1 per cent in 1965. Chemical engineering became the highest paying field to enter, taking over from aeronautical and electrical engineering, which commanded top positions on the pay ladder in the past. Beginning salaries offered chemical engineers averaged $639 a month, up 5.1 per cent over 1964. For the first time, some chemical engineering graduates with a doctor's degree earned over $1,000 a month. Changes in the national defense policy accounted for a low gain in starting pay for aeronautical engineers—an average of only $4 a month.

Salaries of experienced engineers also rose, according to the Engineering Manpower Commission of the Engineers' Joint Council. The commission found that the average engineer's salary went up from $10,375 in 1963 to $11,325 in 1965. The average is based on a survey of more than 231,000 degree-holding engineers in 1,000 organizations in all sectors of the economy. The report also revealed that engineering salaries paid by the U.S. government have apparently caught up with those paid by private industry.

The Engineers' Joint Council also made a study of the nation's engineering manpower for the National Science Foundation's National Register of Scientific and Technical Personnel. On the basis of returns from 57,779 members of engineering societies, the nation's average engineer is a man, median age 41, who leans toward electronics and work management among the 115 areas of technology reported. In addition, he and his fellow engineers tend to concentrate in large numbers in New York and California. MARY E. JESSUP

ENGLAND. See GREAT BRITAIN.

ENTOMOLOGY. See INSECT.

ESPIONAGE. The murky world of espionage was illumined with the publication in November by Doubleday & Co. of a book called *The Penkovskiy Papers*, a combination of reflections, gossip, and detailed information on the Soviet spy apparatus. It was purportedly written by the late Colonel Oleg V. Penkovskiy, considered the most valuable spy to have worked for the West for years. The book named Soviet agents at work in embassies around the world and claimed the chief business of Soviet embassies is espionage in all its forms.

There were some who cast doubt on the book's authorship. They surmised that at least part of its contents may have been put together orginally by agents who worked with Penkovskiy and who wanted the material the book contained made public. Oleg Penkovskiy was a colonel in the intelligence directorate of the Soviet army with contacts leading all the way to the Supreme Military Council. He was also a trusted friend of General Ivan Serov, head of Russian military intelligence.

From the spring of 1961 to the autumn of 1962, he passed along thousands of top secret messages to the West. When he was arrested in 1962 there was a wholesale shift of Soviet agents, as well as important defections. Penkovskiy died before a firing squad in May, 1963, after supplying vital information to the United States during the Cuban missile crisis, according to *Newsweek* magazine.

ETHIOPIA reached a milestone in its 1961-1966 five-year plan as record coffee exports gave the northeast African nation its first favorable trade balance in six years. In addition, economic aid from the East and the West was helping Ethiopia to establish a better base for expansion.

Emperor Haile Selassié I, ruler of Ethiopia since 1930, laid the cornerstone for a Soviet-financed oil refinery at Assab on the Red Sea. A cement factory built with Yugoslav assistance went into production. The United States granted $39,200,000 for economic development and provided funds for a John F. Kennedy Memorial Library at Haile Selassié I University.

In June, Ethiopia's 5,000,000 registered voters elected a new 250-member chamber of deputies. But there was some impatience with the slow pace of economic and social reforms. During debate on the land reform bill, student riots in Addis Ababa caused the emperor to suspend the bill which had been criticized as being inadequate. Ethiopia and the Sudan agreed to close their borders to rebels. But little progress was made in the Somali-Ethiopian border dispute.

Population: 21,950,000. **Government:** Emperor Haile Selassié I; Premier Akilou Abde Wold. **Monetary Unit:** dollar (2.484 = U.S. $1). **Foreign Trade:** exports, $102,929,000; imports, $93,700,000. **Principal Exports:** coffee, hides, oilseeds. WILLIAM SPENCER

See also AFRICA; GREAT BRITAIN (Close-Up).

EUROPE

For the first six months of 1965, Europe was preoccupied with the problem of "bridge building." Optimism was the key word at the Western European Union (WEU) plenary sessions, held in Rome and Paris, as well as at the Council of Europe meetings in Strasbourg, France, where ways and means were discussed not only of bridging the gap between members of the European Free Trade Association (EFTA) and those of the European Economic Community (EEC, or Common Market), but also of negotiating Britain's membership in the latter. This, it was felt, would be the first supranationalist step toward an integrated Europe. Dedicated European parliamentarians even looked further ahead to a true federation—a United States of Europe.

In June, however, French Foreign Minister Maurice Couve de Murville walked out of negotiations over EEC policies on agriculture—and most hopes in Europe were dashed. No longer was there talk of "building bridges." Instead, all efforts were turned to saving the EEC from complete collapse.

This grave, and seemingly insurmountable, setback to European hopes of integration was brought about by one man, President Charles de Gaulle of France. De Gaulle's self-declared mission was to safeguard French national independence. He refused to stand for decisions affecting the superior interests of the state, such as those that might be imposed either by a "stateless technocracy"—the heads of the coal and steel pool, Euratom, and the Common Market—or by governments taking majority decisions under U.S. pressure, or by a common parliament. And it was for this basic reason that De Gaulle thwarted the supranational moves in Europe, slowed down the Common Market's progress, boycotted the Kennedy Round of tariff cut negotiations, and threatened the future of the North Atlantic Treaty Organization (NATO). Basically, De Gaulle's conception of Europe was one in which Europe's future should be a *Europe des Patries*, a Europe of nations that would defend their independence against any imposed decisions.

It was against this background that General De Gaulle ordered the French ambassador to withdraw from the Common Market negotiations. The French had demanded a Common Market responsibility for financing agricultural policy. But they had set themselves against any strengthening of the EEC institutions. Common Market financing would involve price support, export subsidies, and assistance in the disposal of agricultural surpluses at the expense of the group's consumer countries. But the Executive Commission—the EEC's, policy-making body—put forward proposals which fell into three categories:

● Agricultural levies were to be paid by member states beginning July 1, 1967.

Renault Inc.

INDUSTRIAL BOOM in Europe finds automakers racing for world markets. Here, a barge load of cars for export moves down the Seine.

Wide World

FRENCH OPPOSITION to British role in Europe was unchanged despite talks between Britain's Harold Wilson, right, and France's De Gaulle.

• Customs duties from industrial imports were to be paid by the same date.

• The European Parliament was to be strengthened to provide a measure of democratic control. It was this last condition that De Gaulle could not accept.

French Foreign Minister Couve de Murville tried to isolate the agricultural issue from the other two. He might have succeeded but for the insistence of Italy's Foreign Minister Amintore Fanfani that the commission's proposals be considered as a whole. The French plea that the agricultural regulations be completed then and there was supported by Europe's elder statesman, Belgian Foreign Minister Paul-Henri Spaak (see Section One, PAUL-HENRI SPAAK ON THE WORLD). But the issue was not solvable by compromise.

On orders from Paris, the French representative was withdrawn from the talks, and the French government announced that its representatives would not attend any further meetings. At the same time, President De Gaulle also stopped French officials from attending the Kennedy Round negotiations on tariff cuts in Geneva.

The Common Market was, in effect, in a state of suspension. In September, at a press conference, President De Gaulle underlined his greatest objection to the EEC—the system of majority voting which would come into force automatically for a wide number of decisions on Jan. 1, 1966. But annulment of this system could be done only by a com-

plete revision of the Treaty of Rome, on which the Common Market is based. General De Gaulle gave no indication when the Common Market could be "unblocked," but he said he was ready to listen to any proposals. EFTA ministers agreed in their October meeting in Copenhagen to approach the EEC with "bridge building" proposals.

The five members of the Common Market were thus left with the choice of either reshaping the Common Market in the De Gaullist mold, or holding firm to the initial concept of the union as embodied in the Treaty of Rome until such time as the aging general left the political scene. A third course —one of compromise—was an obvious one. Its possibilities were being explored at year's end by President Walter Hallstein of the EEC Executive Commission, and Spaak.

Meanwhile, the crisis had effectively ended for the time being any talk of "bridge building" between EFTA and the Common Market. But in December, there were hints from De Gaulle that France might be considering a return to the EEC.

European Defense. In the sphere of defense, General De Gaulle was again a key figure. He announced that France would withdraw from NATO by the treaty renewal date of 1969. He also indicated that NATO'S joint command structure on French soil would be dismantled. Further difficulties were made by Britain, indicating that it might be preparing to abandon proposals for an Atlantic Nuclear Force (ANF) in favor of an agreement with the Soviet Union for a ban on the spread of nuclear weapons. Another tough problem for the NATO countries was the situation in Greece and Turkey. Both countries were still tense over the continuing hostilities in Cyprus. See CYPRUS; GREECE; TURKEY.

Britain gave categorical assurances in the spring that it would not cut its army of the Rhine below those numbers agreed on in the original treaty. But, in return, it demanded that the foreign exchange drain that these troops represented be eased. Prime Minister Harold Wilson visited Bonn to discuss the question, and left with assurances that Britain's burden would be eased. See GERMANY.

International Economy centered on Britain's monetary difficulties. Several times the pound sterling was under pressure from speculative attack, and the Labour government looked across the seas for help. In late summer, there were indications that the difficulty had been solved through a stand-by credit provided by the central banks of 10 countries in the International Monetary Fund (IMF) and the Bank for International Settlements. Again, General De Gaulle upset his European partners by refusing to subscribe to the fund. See ECONOMY, THE; INTERNATIONAL TRADE AND FINANCE; MONEY; Section One, SYLVIA PORTER ON THE ECONOMY.

The EFTA reported a "remarkable record of economic growth." Austria, Denmark, Finland (an associate member), Great Britain, Norway, Sweden, and Switzerland all increased their national product by between 5 per cent and 7 per cent for 1964-1965, according to the EFTA report. Portugal was the only member whose growth rate declined—from 4.7 per cent to 4 per cent. Trade among the EFTA countries for the year was up by 17.5 per cent.

The Common Market countries, with a total population of 180,000,000, also reported an upsurge in exports, not only among themselves but also to EFTA countries and the rest of the world. Common Market exports to EFTA countries alone increased by 13.2 per cent. But there were signs that strains had developed in Europe's boom. Growth rates slowed, and some Ruhr steel mills shut down to "bring output into balance with orders."

Center Opened. Early in April, the European Atomic Energy Community (Euratom) opened a $23,000,000 plutonium research institute near Karlsruhe, West Germany. West Germany paid $6,000,000 of the building costs in addition to its usual 30 per cent share of the six-nation Euratom's joint projects. The center, named the European Institute for Transuraniums, took four years to build under a pact between Euratom and the Karlsruhe Nuclear Research Center, a joint project of the West German government and the state of Baden-Württemberg.

A move to merge Euratom with the European Coal and Steel Community and the European Economic Community was made in April. A treaty calling for the merger was signed in Brussels by Belgium, France, West Germany, Italy, Luxembourg, and The Netherlands. If ratified by the national parliaments of the six member nations, it was to have become effective Jan. 1, 1966. In the fall, however, France withdrew, thus ending hopes of such a merger in the immediate future.

Eastern Europe. Most Western European countries increased their trade with the Iron Curtain nations. Britain and France both reported a resurgence of trade with Communist China. Trade between Western Europe and the Soviet bloc again topped $3,000,000,000, despite the ban on strategic materials. Because of rigid trade pact quotas, however, much of these exports had to be balanced by imports from the East.

Despite this trading trend, the countries of Eastern Europe failed to achieve standards of living comparable to those of the Western nations. The shops still lacked both the utility and luxury goods that the workers sought.

Technological Developments. Many European statesmen advocated the pooling of European technological knowledge and technologists during the year. Typical of such cooperative ventures was the Franco-British aviation project to build the Concorde, a supersonic airliner designed to fly before 1970. Another exercise in two-country cooperation culminated in the opening of the Mont Blanc Tunnel through the Alps, linking Italy and France. See Bridge and Tunnel. Kenneth Brown

EXPLORATION. The Arctic and Antarctic continued to be focal points for exploration. A three-month expedition of the U.S. Coast Guard icebreaker *Northwind*, manned by teams from the U.S. Naval Oceanographic Office and the University of Wisconsin Polar Research Center, gathered basic oceanographic data and charted the magnetic and gravitational fields of the Kara Sea, north of Siberia. A continuous bottom profile of the sea between the Siberian coast and the Russian island territory of Novaya Zemlya was also recorded, and bottom cores were taken wherever international treaty permitted.

Eighteen residents of a U.S. Navy research station were evacuated from their Arctic island base in May because the island was melting. Known as Arlis 2, the floating, rock-strewn ice island had supported the research station since 1961 while it drifted from a point north of Alaska across the North Pole to the vicinity of Iceland, a distance of some 1,500 miles. The station was operated by the University of Alaska for the Office of Naval Research.

Antarctica. At the opposite end of the earth, the first phase of a four-year expedition into unexplored regions of Antarctica was completed in February. A nine-man team journeyed 1,200 miles across the polar icecap from the Amundsen-Scott South Pole Station to a point near the "pole of inaccessibility" (the point most remote from the Antarctic coastline). When they arrived at the site, the American team found that the Russians had been there in 1964 and had left a little hut topped by a bust of Lenin.

The National Science Foundation (NSF) announced plans to locate an eight-man Antarctic research station on the 13,000-foot East Antarctic plateau. The new outpost will be situated in the most remote and inhospitable region of the continent.

Indian Ocean. Scientists from 13 nations completed an expedition that was organized in 1959 to gather oceanographic and meteorological data on the Indian Ocean and surrounding countries. Data gathered during the expedition is expected to provide knowledge of the physical conditions which favor abundant sea life and thus improve fishing methods. Among the nations participating were Australia, Great Britain, the Federal Republic of Germany, France, India, Japan, the Union of South Africa, and the United States.

Discovery of America. An exciting cartographic discovery, which shed new light on the question of which European explorers came to the New World first, was displayed at Yale University in October. A Norse map, believed to be based on discoveries of Leif Ericson in the 11th century, shows Greenland and a large island called Vineland, which scholars have identified as a part of the North American continent. Sergei Lenormand

See also Astronomy; Space Travel.

EXPLOSION. See Disasters.

FAIRS AND EXHIBITIONS.

The New York World's Fair, which had started with a bang in 1964, ended with a whimper in 1965—at least when judged by financial results.

Despite cascades of promotional ballyhoo, the expected attendance of 70,000,000 did not develop. When the gates swung closed on October 17, the official attendance totaled only 51,607,037; with 24,458,757 in 1965 and 27,148,280 in 1964.

As a result, the World's Fair Corporation was able to repay only $11,500,000 to the holders of more than $29,000,000 worth of notes. In addition, the corporation had to abandon plans to spend $30,000,000 of expected profits to build a chain of parks in Flushing Meadow, the site of the fair.

Despite the financial outcome, however, many persons regarded the fair as a great success. It was the best-attended exposition in history. Many of the businesses that sponsored pavilions did not expect to make a profit and were elated by the heavy crowds they attracted.

General Motors' "Ride into the Future" was the most popular exhibit, attracting 29,000,000 fairgoers. In second place was the Vatican City pavilion, followed by the New York State exhibit.

As Wrecking Crews moved in on the fairgrounds, only a small handful of the buildings were tagged for survival. The Spanish pavilion, widely acclaimed for its aesthetic value and the most successful of the foreign exhibits, was being moved to St. Louis, and will stand on the banks of the Mississippi River.

Several other pavilions, including the Austrian and Danish pavilions and the General Electric and Johnson's Wax exhibits, will be moved to other sites for commercial use.

New York City intends to keep the United States and New York State pavilions where they stand for use as educational centers and tourist attractions. Two restaurants, the Top of the Fair and the Terrace Club at the Heliport Building, are also staying in business.

Expo '67. Even as the wrecking ball brought building after building tumbling down in New York, construction crews were already at work on another major exposition. Montreal, Quebec, will be host in 1967 to more than 60 nations, the Canadian provinces, more than 50 private exhibitors, and a number of religious and social organizations at its Canadian Universal and International Exhibition of 1967, popularly known as Expo '67. The fair will be built on two man-made islands on the St. Lawrence River. See CANADA (picture and map).

This fair will have a much larger number of official national exhibits than did the New York fair, since it carries the imprimatur of the Bureau of International Expositions of Paris, France.

The international bureau announced that the first official World's Fair in Asia will be held in Osaka, Japan, in 1970.   ROBERT E. BEDINGFIELD

FANFANI, AMINTORE (1908-   ), Italian minister of foreign affairs, was elected president of the United Nations General Assembly's 20th regular session on Sept. 21, 1965. An Italian president seemed especially appropriate when Pope Paul VI addressed the General Assembly on October 4.

A fall on the night of October 9 kept President Fanfani in the hospital the rest of the month. He asked to resign as foreign minister late in 1965, because of repercussions about a Vietnam "peace feeler" involving one of his friends and Mrs. Fanfani.

The Italian statesman has been an international figure since he served as premier and foreign minister of Italy (1958-1959). He was also premier during 1960-1963, and for 11 days in January, 1954. As minister of labor and social welfare (1947-1950), minister of agriculture and forestry (1951-1953), and minister of the interior (1953-1954), Fanfani instituted various national social and economic reform programs. He served as secretary general of the Christian Democratic party (1954-1959). The former university professor has a Ph. D. (political economy, 1932) from the Catholic University of the Sacred Heart (Milan), and is author of the three-volume *History of Economic Doctrine: Catholicism, Capitalism, and Protestantism;* and other works. He was born near Arezzo, the son of a country doctor.

See also UNITED NATIONS.

FARM EQUIPMENT. See MANUFACTURING.

FASHION. The mood of fashion was young in 1965. Andre Courrèges, the young French designer of the bare knee, the square cut white dress, and flat white boots, offered the freshest and boldest look. He borrowed the cowboy hat—chin strap and all—to top the geometric looks of his clothes. White textured stockings epitomized the trend. His ideas influenced every facet of fashion.

A fashion revolution broke out in London, and for the first time a British fashion invasion stormed New York City to entice millions of dollars from U.S. store buyers. Four fashion shows of 17 British ready-to-wear manufacturers presented young girls in short hairdos and even shorter skirts, adding to the young look of fashion in 1965.

In the United States, Pop Art popped into style. Then along came Op Art, which opened up a whole new area. Women dressed to match Op Art paintings, with their stripes, checks, and wavy line prints. Designs were also based on the work of the famed Dutch painter Mondrian. Dresses were divided geometrically by intersecting bands and brightened by contrasting blocks of color. They came out of Paris couture and off the drawing board of Yves St. Laurent. The Mondrian look was a success. It was adapted at all price levels, appearing even on a Mondrian boot of four bright colors.

The youth of today is a $15,000,000,000 fashion market. Hence designers watched every move they made with hawklike attention.

United Press Int.

OBSERVE! The Courrèges look that captured fashion in 1965 is modeled by French actress Claudine Auger before the Arc de Triomphe.

The great white wave took over the evening scene, lending more status if the evening gown bared one shoulder. Cristobal Balenciaga introduced such a gown in 1964, with Jacqueline Kennedy adding her stamp of approval. From then on it caught on like wildfire. White was worn everywhere, both at home and in the evening. The smartest evening wrap for the young was Mary Quant's Kalgan lamb with shaggy collar.

Hairpieces for ladies came into their own for evening in 1965. Short haircuts could be altered from a sleek look to a curly look. The pierced ear was revived by the young set, scarf hats were important additions in millinery, and makeup was brushed on.

Inaugural Gown. John Moore, a U.S. designer originally from Alice, Tex., received the coveted job of designing Mrs. Lyndon B. Johnson's sable-trimmed "Yellow Rose of Texas" inaugural ensemble. Thus his name and his contribution became fashion history. According to tradition, the First Lady's original was given to Smithsonian Institution in Washington, D.C. For the first time, a President's wife allowed a designer to make a doll size replica of her inaugural costume. Thus, the miniature First Lady gown of yellow satin carries a John Moore label and is on tour by the courtesy of Evyan Perfumes so that first ladies of many American cities can view the historic ball gown.   Peg Zwecker

The twist and its hundreds of variations and the go-go girls with leggy little black dresses gave new importance to the shoe. The rounded toe, a trend to watch, became prominent. Straps were much in evidence, heels were open, sides were pared down to add to the look of leggy young elegance. Heels continued in the medium height to lowered range category for the girl on the move.

Poor Boy Look. Women continued to wear trousers in combination with the "poor boy" sweater—a heavy ribbed sweater. This outfit was snatched up by chic girls all over the world to wear with low hipster pants. On the Riviera the girls in the know turned up in such striking color combinations as pink and currant.

The most interesting pants and jackets were designed by Courrèges. But everyone got into the act; even cover girl Jean Shrimpton designed a trouser suit. Tuffin & Foale made a hacking jacket suit in melton—the hit fabric. Charlie Chaplin's 21-year-old daughter, Geraldine, arrived in New York on her first trip to the United States, wearing a pants suit. She wore a black and white houndstooth check with matching "knack" cap, white turtle-neck sweater, and the much-touted white vinyl boots. As the year ended, fickle fashion sent out the word that pants were OUT for daytime but IN for evening. After-Seven Sportswear or Party Pants, they were called. They ran the gamut from ostrich-trimmed crepe to bell-bottom "trousers."

FEYNMAN, RICHARD PHILLIPS (1918-   ), California Institute of Technology professor of theoretical physics, was one of three Nobel physics laureates of 1965. He, Julian S. Schwinger, and Sin-itiro Tomonaga were awarded the prize for their creation of the modern theory of quantum electrodynamics. The three worked independently of each other on their prize-winning work in the 1940s.

In his approach to the difficulties in determining quantitative calculations about the interaction of a charged particle (electron) with radiation fields, Feynman set about to find simple rules, and applied them to concrete problems. He devised the *Feynman graphs* and *Feynman integrals*, calculation rules now widely used for theoretical analysis in quantum electrodynamics and also in high-energy physics. Feynman also provided a mathematical explanation for the behavior of liquid helium, for which he received the Albert Einstein Award in 1954.

Richard Feynman was born in New York City. He is a Massachusetts Institute of Technology graduate (1939). Feynman took his Ph.D. degree at Princeton (1942), and worked there (1943) on the atomic bomb project. He was a group leader at Los Alamos, N.Mex., for two years. While a Cornell University associate professor of theoretical physics, he did his work on the quantum theory of electrodynamics (1945-1950).

See also Nobel Prizes (Science Prizes); Schwinger, Julian S.; Tomonaga, Sin-itiro.

FINLAND

FINLAND made rapid strides toward its goal of full industrialization. Its associate membership in the European Free Trade Association (EFTA) had helped the economy considerably. Its policy of neutrality toward East and West resulted in a trade build-up with both Great Britain and West Germany as well as with the Soviet Union.

The four-party coalition government headed by Premier Johannes Virolainen succeeded in eliminating the deep divisions that had appeared over means of checking inflation. The risk of inflation remained, however, because of Finland's great need for imported raw materials.

Work continued during the year on the 34-mile Saimaa Canal, which, when completed, will connect Finland's southeastern industrial lake region to the Gulf of Finland and the Baltic Sea. Much of the cost is being paid for with funds from the World War II indemnity paid by the Soviet Union in 1962.

Population: 4,650,000. **Government:** President Urho K. Kekkonen; Premier Johannes Virolainen. **Monetary Unit:** markka (3.22 = U.S. $1). **Gross National Product:** 17,021,000,000 markka. **Foreign Trade:** exports, $1,332,000,000; imports, $1,550,-000,000. **Principal Exports:** agricultural products, metal products, paper, timber. KENNETH BROWN

See also EUROPE.

FIRE. See DISASTERS; FORESTRY; SAFETY.

FISHERY.

FISHERY. The U.S. catch of fish and shellfish climbed 3 per cent in 1965, not quite making up for the 1964 decline to 4,500,000,000 pounds. The value of the 1965 catch exceeded the $390,000,000 recorded in 1964. The United States continued to import about two-thirds of its edible and industrial fishery requirements, however, and continued to rank fifth in the world volume of catch. Peru, Japan, China, and the Soviet Union led the United States in total production.

Russian and Japanese fishing operations off U.S. coasts were intensified. In April, some U.S. fisheries industry spokesmen urged a boycott of all Japanese products to "halt depletion of American fishery resources by foreign fleets." Conciliatory moves by the Japanese and the near-record catch of red salmon off Alaska ended the campaign, however.

O. V. Wells, the deputy director-general of the United Nations Food and Agriculture Organization (FAO), urged action in July to halt a "catastrophic decline" in Atlantic tuna. In 1966, an international conference will be held to draft a tuna agreement.

The success of the battle against the lamprey, which destroyed lake trout in Lake Superior, led the Great Lakes Fishery Commission to consider resumption of fishery there. A. L. NEWMAN

FISHING. See HUNTING AND FISHING.

FLOOD. See DISASTERS; WATER AND FLOOD CONTROL.

FLOWER. See GARDEN AND LAWN.

FOOD.

FOOD. The chemical development of new high-quality dietary protein from vegetable sources made progress in 1965. Discovery of new and inexpensive supplies of protein for human consumption has been made imperative by the constant increase in the world's population. Producing proteins from soybeans and other vegetable sources was demonstrated to be much more efficient than the old method of converting vegetable matter to protein by first feeding it to animals to produce meat—10 times more efficient in the case of steers.

One such product, Incaparina, was shown at the Western Hemisphere Nutrition Conference in Chicago in November. Incaparina, 25 per cent protein, is a cheap vegetable mixture largely made up of enriched corn flour. Six commercial firms produce and market it under license.

Synthetic protein foods could revolutionize dietary habits. Through fiber technology, almost any natural texture can be reproduced. Flavor and color can be supplied by the addition of natural products, synthetic flavors, and flavor enhancers.

Beverages were getting away from the old-line favorites. Diet colas stabilized themselves at about half the market, while exotic flavors from the tropics—mango, passionfruit, and others—were being sold as straight, carbonated, and blended drinks (see MANUFACTURING).

Coffee purveyors made a determined counterattack by encouraging the growth of teen-age coffee houses and the proliferation of coffee-flavored drinks. They based their appeal on the coffee drinks' low calorie content and refreshingly different taste—good cold as well as hot.

Senior Citizens, who make up 9 per cent of the U.S. population, were interviewed on their food preferences. Most asked for special services rather than special products, which have won only a limited acceptance. In a few localities, hot meals delivered by volunteers working for welfare agencies helped to solve the eating problem of shut-ins and of those unable to prepare meals for themselves.

Diet Foods continued in great demand, and even the old-line companies felt forced to get into the act. The market for freeze-dried foods, which has doubled each year since 1962, expanded further. Mushrooms, peas, and shrimp preserved by the freeze-dry process were regularly added to new packaged convenience meals. Especially noteworthy were breakfast cereals that added freeze-dried fruits to their packages.

The Negro Market was developing as the fastest growing segment of food merchandising in the urban North. Foods acceptable to whites had long set the pattern for neighborhood groceries. As the Negro emerged as an increasingly important consumer, it became essential to provide the products he most desired. ALMA LACH

See also AGRICULTURE; Section Two, INSIDE RURAL CHINA; INSIDE RURAL INDIA.

PICTURES OF THE YEAR/Ernest Anheuser, *The Milwaukee Journal*

SQUEEZE PLAY by five Green Bay Packers stops Chicago Bears fullback Joe Marconi in the first quarter of an exhibition game played at County Stadium, Milwaukee.

FOOTBALL. Michigan State, which had been picked to finish as low as seventh in the Big Ten Conference, achieved its first perfect record since 1952, and was acclaimed the outstanding college football team in the country. The team, however, was defeated by UCLA in the Rose Bowl.

Arkansas, which went through its second successive perfect season for 22 straight victories to win the Southwest Conference title, was picked as the top team in an Associated Press poll. Nebraska also chalked up a perfect season, its first since 1915. The Ivy League championship was decided in a battle of unbeatens in which Dartmouth emerged with a 28 to 14 victory over defending champion Princeton.

Top Players. Mike Garrett, Southern California's 185-pound bundle of power, was awarded the Heisman Trophy as the best college football player in the country. Other top backs were Rick Norton of Kentucky, Steve Juday of Michigan State, Don Anderson of Texas Tech, and Jim Grabowski of Illinois. Top linemen included Tom Nobis of Texas, Carl McAdams of Oklahoma, Bill Yearby of Michigan, and Francis Peay of Missouri.

1965 Conference Champions

Conference	School
Big Ten	Michigan State
Southeastern	Alabama
Southwest	Arkansas
Big Eight	Nebraska
Atlantic Coast	Duke, South Carolina (tie)
Ivy League	Dartmouth
Middle Atlantic	Bucknell
Southern	West Virginia
Missouri Valley	Tulsa
Western Athletic	Brigham Young
Yankee	Maine
Pacific Athletic	U.C.L.A.

The Bowl Games

Bowl	Winner	Loser
Rose	U.C.L.A. 14	Michigan State 12
Orange	Alabama 39	Nebraska 28
Cotton	Louisiana State 14	Arkansas 7
Sugar	Missouri 20	Florida 18
Gator	Georgia Tech 31	Texas Tech 21
Sun	Texas Western 13	Texas Christian 12

Standings in National Football League

Eastern Conference

	W.	L.	T.	Pc.
Cleveland	11	3	0	.786
Dallas	7	7	0	.500
New York	7	7	0	.500
Washington	6	8	0	.429
Philadelphia	5	9	0	.357
St. Louis	5	9	0	.357
Pittsburgh	2	12	0	.143

Western Conference

	W.	L.	T.	Pc.
Baltimore	10	3	1	.769
Green Bay	10	3	1	.769
Chicago	9	5	0	.643
San Francisco	7	6	1	.538
Minnesota	7	7	0	.500
Detroit	6	7	1	.462
Los Angeles	4	10	0	.286

FORD, GERALD RUDOLPH

Professional. The Green Bay Packers and Baltimore Colts, who tied for the western division title in the regular season of the National Football League (NFL), were tied 10 to 10 at the end of their play-off game. The Packers then won 13 to 10, after 13 minutes and 39 seconds of sudden-death overtime play. The Packers went on to win the NFL championship by defeating the defending champion Cleveland Browns, 23 to 12, at Green Bay. Cleveland's Jimmy Brown was voted the league's outstanding player.

In a rematch of the previous American Football League (AFL) title game, the Buffalo Bills retained

Standings in American Football League

Eastern Division	W.	L.	T.	Pc.
Buffalo	10	3	1	.769
New York	5	8	1	.385
Boston	4	8	2	.333
Houston	4	10	0	.286
Western Division				
San Diego	9	2	3	.818
Oakland	8	5	1	.615
Kansas City	7	5	2	.583
Denver	4	10	0	.286

their championship with a 23 to 0 victory over the San Diego Chargers at San Diego. The Chargers' Lance Alworth was named the league's outstanding player.   STANLEY ISAACS

See also Section One, RED SMITH ON SPORTS.

FORD, GERALD RUDOLPH (1913-   ), a Representative in Congress from Michigan since 1948, was elected House minority leader on January 4. He was named by a 73-to-67 vote at a caucus of House Republicans, displacing 64-year-old Representative Charles A. Halleck of Indiana.

Republican Ford attracted wide public attention during the year by sharp criticism of President Lyndon B. Johnson's policies. On August 24, Ford issued a House Republican white paper accusing the Johnson administration of "an uncertain policy" on Vietnam and of misleading statements about the conflict. President Johnson asserted that Ford had violated a confidence and had distorted what the President had said at a private meeting.

Ford long has been an active party worker. As a Congressman, he followed the high middle road of moderation. He was born in Omaha, Nebr. He played center on the undefeated University of Michigan teams of 1932 and 1934, and earned his way through Yale University Law School as Yale's assistant football coach. He got his LL.B. degree at Yale in 1941. He practiced law at Grand Rapids, Mich., until World War II, when he joined the navy, and rose to the rank of lieutenant commander. The Congressman was married in 1948 to Elizabeth Bloomer of Grand Rapids. They have three sons and a daughter.   WALTER F. MORSE

See also CONGRESS OF THE UNITED STATES; REPUBLICAN PARTY.

FORESTRY AND FOREST PRODUCTS. With the demand for timber products projected to increase about 80 per cent by the year 2000, the U.S. timber industry and conservation forces were in sharp conflict in 1965 over future control of valuable stands of redwoods in California and Douglas fir and ponderosa pine in the Northern Cascades region of Washington. In California, the Save-the-Redwoods League and others battled pressures from the lumber industry and highway planners in an effort to set aside substantial acreages of virgin redwood groves as national or state parks. The North Cascades Study Team from the U.S. Departments of the Interior and Agriculture completed a comprehensive study of 7,000,000 acres of National Forest land, some of it rich in timber. It recommended establishing a National Park in part of the area. See PARKS; 1965 YEAR BOOK *Special Report*, CALL TO THE WILDERNESS.

Timber Harvesting continued at a record pace. In National Forests, a cut of 11,240,000,000 board feet, valued at $161,000,000, set a new high in fiscal 1965. This was enough timber to house the entire population of metropolitan Philadelphia. Total U.S. lumber production rose slightly to about 36,200,000,000 board feet, and imports dipped about the same amount, to 5,000,000,000 board feet. Consumption thus remained at about the same level as in 1964.

Forecast for Timber. While U.S. forests have made a comeback in recent years with timber growth exceeding cut, the supply of larger trees and quality timber was declining. A comprehensive 1965 Forest Service report, "Timber Trends in the United States," predicted major increases in demand for pulpwood and veneer logs and more moderate increases for lumber. It found timber supplies adequate to meet those demands until 1990, but warned that thereafter intensified forest management would be required.

The report also predicted that imports of pulp and related products—about 19 per cent of U.S. needs—would increase somewhat, mainly from Canada. Small tropical timber import increases also were expected for lumber and hardwood veneer and plywood. Domestic forests, however, were expected to supply most of the forecast demand. The report concluded that the timber supply outlook was relatively favorable for the pulp and paper industry but not as encouraging for the lumber and plywood industries.

Forest Fires showed a two-way trend in 1965. On National Forest lands, the number of forest fires continued to dwindle, after the 30 per cent reduction in 1964. There was an increase in fires on state and private lands, however, mostly as the result of the drought. In mid-September, about 195,000 acres in 21 counties were ravaged by what was described as the most disastrous fire in northern California's history.   A. L. NEWMAN

FORMOSA, or **TAIWAN,** which enjoyed the highest agricultural production per land unit in Asia, was shifting increasingly to manufacturing to employ its growing population. The increasing number of American, European, and Japanese enterprises on the island was indicative of the trend. The efficient and relatively low-cost Formosan labor force was being used to assemble electronic instruments, television sets, and transistor radios largely for exports.

The prospering economy permitted the United States to terminate its programs of aid on June 30. U.S. military assistance, however, continued to flow to the Nationalist Chinese forces, which numbered about 500,000.

Authorities continued to encourage birth control programs during the year; the island's population growth rate of about 3 per cent annually was creating problems of unemployment and overcrowding in the schools.

Population: 12,223,000. **Government:** President Chiang Kai-shek; Premier C. K. Yen. **Monetary Unit:** NT dollar (40.10 = U.S. $1). **Gross National Product:** 72,380,000,000 NT dollars. **Foreign Trade:** exports, $485,000,000; imports (including U.S. commodity aid) $500,000,000. **Principal Exports:** chemical products, electrical goods, fruits, sugar, textiles.   ALBERT RAVENHOLT

See also ASIA.

FORTAS, ABE (1910-   ), a Washington lawyer, was named a justice of the Supreme Court of the United States on July 28, 1965. He took the seat vacated by Justice Arthur J. Goldberg, who had resigned to become U.S. ambassador to the United Nations (see SUPREME COURT OF THE U.S.).

Fortas had long been a personal friend and confidant of President Lyndon B. Johnson and had advised him on matters that ranged from personal finances to the design of the Warren Commission that investigated the assassination of President John F. Kennedy. Fortas' clients included Robert "Bobby" Baker, a key figure in a congressional investigation into "influence peddling," and many large corporations. Fortas appeared before the Supreme Court in many landmark cases. Among them was the *Gideon v. Wainwright* case in which the Court decided that states must provide the indigent with legal counsel (see COURTS AND LAWS).

Justice Fortas was born in Memphis, Tenn., June 19, 1910, and received his B.A. degree from Southwestern College in 1930, and his law degree from Yale University in 1933.

His law career began in government service during the 1930s. He served as attorney for numerous federal agencies. In 1942, at the age of 32, he was Undersecretary of the Interior. In 1946, he entered private practice in Washington, D.C. Fortas married Carolyn Eugenia Agger in 1935.   WALTER F. MORSE

FOUNDATIONS. See EDUCATIONAL FOUNDATIONS.

FOUR-H CLUBS continued to make membership gains despite the decrease in the total nationwide farm population. This was possible because the once exclusively rural youth organization was now growing rapidly in urban communities where its emphasis was placed on preparing youths for citizenship responsibilities. By 1965, only 46 per cent of the 2,221,119 members lived on farms.

Eleven representative club members made the 1965 "Report to the Nation" to national leaders in government, business, agriculture, and education. They were: Gayle Stubbs, 17, Morris, Ala.; Sherry Lynn Smith, 17, Prescott, Ariz.; Morton Lee Johnson, 17, Fowler, Calif.; Mary Jo Smith, 18, Coolidge, Ga.; Linda Chun, 18, Honolulu, Hawaii; Joe Day, 19, Nebo, Ky.; Jack Bossard, 18, Canisteo, N.Y.; Phil McIntyre, 19, Harwood, N.Dak.; Jeffrey Muchow, 19, Sioux Falls, S.Dak.; Martha Lee Poland, 19, Morgantown, W.Va.; and Nadine Meier, 19, Kenosha, Wis.

At the 44th National 4-H Club Congress in Chicago, November 27 through December 2, national scholarships totaling $125,600 were awarded to 225 delegates. The highest honors went to: Janet Erickson, 19, Ogden, Utah; Dwight Smith, 18, Jefferson, Md.; Jerry Patton, 18, Thaxton, Miss.; Faye Perry, 18, Springfield, Tenn.; Philip Brechbill, 18, Auburn, Ind.; and Mary Jo Smith, 18, Coolidge, Ga.   FRANK B. HARPER

FOWLER, HENRY HAMILL (1908-   ), Undersecretary of the Treasury from Feb. 3, 1961, to April 10, 1964, was sworn in on April 1, 1965, as Secretary of the Treasury. He succeeded C. Douglas Dillon.

In August and September, Fowler visited nine European financial centers on behalf of an improved system of international credit and improvement in the handling of various currencies under the International Monetary Fund. See INTERNATIONAL TRADE AND FINANCE (Close-Up).

Fowler was born at Roanoke, Va., on Sept. 5, 1908. He holds a B.A. degree from Roanoke College (1929) and the LL.B. (1932) and J.S.D. (1933) degrees from Yale University Law School. From Yale, Fowler went to the legal staff of the Tennessee Valley Authority, and eventually became its assistant general counsel.

In 1938, he married Trudye Pamela Hathcote of Knoxville, Tenn. Moving to Washington the following year, Fowler served as chief counsel of the Senate Education and Labor subcommittee, and as special counsel for the Federal Power Commission (1941). In World War II, he served as assistant general counsel of the War Production Board (1942 to 1944).

In 1952 and 1953, Fowler was administrator of the Defense Production Administration and a member of the National Security Council. He also has had wide legal experience, practicing corporation law in Washington.   WALTER F. MORSE

FRANCE

France departed from tradition in 1965 and chose a president by popular vote. In previous years, its chief executive had been elected by an electoral college consisting of members of the national assembly and senate. Under an amendment initiated by President Charles de Gaulle in 1962, however, a new procedure calling for election by popular vote had been adopted as part of the constitution.

The campaign officially began on November 4 when De Gaulle

Pictorial Parade

announced his candidacy for another seven-year presidential term. His opponents, who were highly critical of his foreign as well as his domestic policies, included François Mitterand, a candidate of the left; Senator Jean Lecanuet, who, as a candidate of the Popular Republican movement, represented the middle-of-the-road Catholic party and other center groups; Senator Pierre Marcilhacy, a conservative; Paul Antier, a former minister of agriculture; and Jean-Louis Tixier-Vignancour, who represented the extreme right.

Unexpected Results. On December 5, the French voters trooped to the polls. Despite De Gaulle's hopes for an overwhelming victory, election results gave De Gaulle an unexpectedly low 44 per cent of the vote. Mitterand polled 32 per cent and Lecanuet 16 per cent. The others garnered a total of 8 per cent. Having failed to receive a 51 per cent majority as required by law, De Gaulle was thus forced into a run-off election with Mitterand.

The run-off was held on December 19. The voter turnout was the third largest in any French election. Final results showed that De Gaulle had captured 13,085,407 votes, or 55.2 per cent. His opponent, Mitterand, polled 10,623,247 votes, or 44.8 per cent. De Gaulle was thus assured of a second term as president.

De Gaulle's Policies. It was widely believed that De Gaulle, as a result of the election, would soften his stand on matters pertaining to the European Economic Community (EEC, or Common Market). France had been in open diplomatic conflict with the five other members of the Common Market ever since De Gaulle had blocked Great Britain's membership in the organization in 1963. In 1965, he had also created frictions by insisting that the Common Market countries avoid steps toward greater political integration and limit themselves, instead, to close economic cooperation. In June, he had seriously endangered the organization's existence by ordering his representatives to withdraw from meetings involving agricultural policy.

Despite international hopes, however, there was no concrete evidence by year's end that De Gaulle had materially changed his viewpoint on these issues. Nor had he revised his views regarding the North Atlantic Treaty Organization (NATO) in

UNIFORMED PRESIDENT Charles de Gaulle strides down Paris' Champs Élysées during anniversary ceremonies marking end of World War II.

FEDNEWS Photo

CHIEF COMPETITOR for Charles de Gaulle's job as president of France in 1965 campaign was François Mitterand, a noncommunist leftist.

the government disclosed that an improved atomic bomb had gone into production for France's fledgling nuclear force. The government also announced that research was continuing on nuclear warheads for 25 strategic ballistic missiles. These missiles were to be reinforced eventually by a French version of the submarine-borne Polaris missile. See ATOMIC ENERGY.

Joint Ventures. Following a visit by British Prime Minister Harold Wilson to Paris, talks were continued in London on the future of Franco-British cooperation in aeronautics. Construction of the Concorde, a supersonic airliner that was to be built jointly by France and Great Britain before 1970, got a go-ahead during the year. It was also decided that the two countries would explore the possibility of producing a short-range subsonic aerobus.

Mont Blanc Tunnel. On July 16, General de Gaulle and Italy's President Giuseppe Saragat formally inaugurated the Franco-Italian Mont Blanc Tunnel. The motor vehicle tunnel linked Chamonix, France, and Courmayeur, Italy. See BRIDGE AND TUNNEL.

Tourist Trade. Efforts were made during the year to give a boost to the ailing tourist industry through various publicity stunts, including one of giving prizes to French workers in cafes, hotels, and other public gathering places who received the most votes on cards given to visitors at ports and airports.

which French membership was to cease in 1969. International circles were still rankling, too, over De Gaulle's decision in 1965 to cut back France's dollar reserves in favor of gold and by his refusal to join other nations in moves to save the British pound sterling. See GREAT BRITAIN; INTERNATIONAL TRADE AND FINANCE; NORTH ATLANTIC TREATY ORGANIZATION (NATO); Section One, PAUL-HENRI SPAAK on THE WORLD.

Domestic Economy. In October, the national assembly approved France's fifth five-year plan. Covering the years 1966-1970, the plan provided for an annual GNP increase of 5 per cent. It would raise total French output by about 28 per cent by 1970. Per capita domestic consumption was scheduled to go up 3.5 per cent a year, resulting in a total consumption rise of about 24 per cent in five years.

The national assembly approved a balanced budget for 1966. For the second year in a row, the budget was calculated to show a small surplus. Planned outlay for 1966 would run 6.99 per cent over the 1965 budget of $18,500,000,000. Civilian capital outlays were to increase by 9.7 per cent, notably for schools, roads, and telecommunications, over 1965's $1,900,000,000 total. Expenses for civil administration were to go up 7.14 per cent from $12,200,000,000.

Nuclear Force Plans. The overall military budget of about $4,160,000,000 for 1965 was centered on the development of a nuclear strike force. In July,

"I will need another seven years at least."

These schemes, however, did not help tourism to any great extent; most visitors complained that prices for goods and services in France were too expensive, and that service help was rude. The situation was not helped when fishermen in Boulogne blockaded the port against incoming ferries laden with holiday visitors. The blockade was an outgrowth of a ban that had been placed on their use of traditional fishing grounds by the European Fisheries Convention.

Women's Rights. In March, the cabinet approved a bill that was described as the "veritable emancipation of the French wife." Under the new measure, which was designed to nullify most of the principles of the Code Napoléon, any property a woman brought into marriage would remain hers instead of becoming joint property. The same was applicable to any inheritance. The new bill additionally provided that a wife could take a job without her husband's consent and conduct her own business (see CIVIL RIGHTS).

Population: 42,920,000. **Government:** President Charles de Gaulle; Premier Georges Pompidou. **Monetary Unit:** franc (4.905 = U.S. $1). **Gross National Product:** 353,600,000,000 francs. **Foreign Trade:** exports, $8,472,000,000; imports, $10,245,-000,000. **Principal Exports:** agricultural products, iron and steel, machinery, wines.   KENNETH BROWN

See also EUROPE.

FUTURE FARMERS OF AMERICA (FFA)

merged with the 52,000-member companion organization, New Farmers of America, on July 1. The union with this Negro organization, which had chapters in 12 southern states, brought the FFA membership to a record of nearly 455,000 members in 8,130 chapters. FFA has had Negro members in other states since both organizations began, but under the 1964 Civil Rights Acts the New Farmers of America could no longer continue as a segregated group.

Floyd S. Dubben, Jr., 21, of Middlefield, N.Y., was named 1965 Star Farmer of America and awarded $1,000 at the FFA's annual convention in Kansas City, Mo., in mid-October. Dubben, also the North Atlantic regional winner, had attained a more than $50,000 net worth by 1965. He achieved this by assuming responsibility in his early teens for a herd of cows and the management of a farm.

Three other regional Star Farmers were selected, each receiving $500. They were: R. Keith James, 21, Pond Creek, Okla. (Southern); Marvin Hobbs, Walnut Grove, Ill. (Central); and Emmett S. Jobe, Jr., 21, Queen Creek, Ariz. (Pacific).

Howard L. Williams, 19, Olin, N.C., was elected national FFA president for 1965-1966, with four regional vice-presidents: William M. Kelly, Jr., 20, Winchester, N.H. (North Atlantic); Norman Gay, 19, Sumner, Ga. (Southern); James Stitzlein, 19, Ashland, Ohio (Central); and Larry E. Craig, 20, Midvale, Idaho (Pacific).   FRANK B. HARPER

FUTURE HOMEMAKERS OF AMERICA (FHA)

adopted a new four-year program at its 1965 national convention in Philadelphia, in July. The program set out two broad objectives for the FHA: (1) to help each family member recognize her abilities and strive for full family development, and (2) to participate actively in projects for family, community, and world improvement. The program provided members with suggestions for approximately 225 individual and chapter activities. It was based on the results of a nationwide interview of 1,000 youths and adults to determine the problems uppermost in the minds of today's youth.

Mary Lou Driscoll, Buckingham, Va., was elected president for 1965-1966. New vice-presidents were: Lynn Cohen, Longview, Tex. (Southern); Louette Whitbeck, Scappoose, Ore. (Pacific); Susan Weiman, Lewes, Del. (North Atlantic); Sharon Swan, Onalaska, Wis. (Central); Su Rita Coursey, Chinle, Ariz. (public relations); Jane Lynott, Duluth, Ga. (recreation); and Beverly Smith, Willimantic, Conn. (national projects). Patricia Anderson, Butler, Ala., was elected co-chairman of national projects; Joyce Lyons, Rayville, La., co-chairman of membership; Betty Johnston, Denver, Colo., treasurer; Barbara Kirlin, Houlton, Me., secretary; Chloe Ann Westfall, Hillsdale, Mich., reporter; and Jill Solander, Garnett, Kans., historian.   FRANK B. HARPER

GABON, a former French colony, took steps in 1965 to exploit the resources that exist deep in its equatorial forests. Plans were underway to build a 340-mile railroad to carry timber and minerals to a deepwater port that will be built at Owendo.

During a two-month European visit, President Léon Mba met with President Charles de Gaulle and other French officials and discussed French aid for construction of the railroad and port, as well as an electric power station and an oil refinery. In 1965, Gabonese gold production increased with the opening of new mines near Lastoursville. French sources reported a significant increase in Gabon's production of crude oil and manganese in 1965.

After the death of Dr. Albert Schweitzer, President Mba cited Dr. Schweitzer as "the oldest and greatest adopted Gabonese." Dr. Schweitzer had operated a jungle hospital at Lambaréné in Gabon since 1913. See DEATHS OF NOTABLE PERSONS (Close-Up).

President Mba also granted amnesty to three persons involved in a February (1964) plot to overthrow his government.

Population: 457,000. **Government:** President Léon Mba. **Monetary Unit:** CFA Franc (246.85 = U.S. $1). **Foreign Trade:** exports, $73,000,000; imports, $48,000,000. **Principal Exports:** iron ore, manganese, petroleum, plywood, timber.

BENJAMIN E. THOMAS

See also AFRICA.

GAMBIA

GAMBIA gained independence from Britain on Feb. 18, 1965, and became the 36th independent country in Africa. In June, parliament voted unanimously to place Gambia within the British Commonwealth on the new republic's first anniversary in 1966. Meanwhile, the British government agreed to subsidize the cost of administration until mid-1967 and to assist the country's development plan at the rate of $2,240,000 annually.

David Jawara became prime minister and formed a loose alliance with neighboring Senegal. Each state will retain its sovereignty but treaties of cooperation will unite the two countries on matters of foreign policy, defense, and development of the Gambia River. Senegal is to provide Gambia with technical assistance on military training and employ Gambians at Senegal's foreign diplomatic and consular posts to represent Gambia.

A coalition government organized in March included the United party leader, Pièrre S. N'Jie, as minister of health. But in June, the governing People's Progressive party removed him from office on the grounds that he and the United party were unwilling to work with the government.

Population: 340,000. **Government:** Prime Minister David Jawara. **Monetary Unit:** pound (1 = U.S. $2.7950). **Foreign Trade:** no statistics available. **Principal Export:** peanuts.   BENJAMIN E. THOMAS

See also AFRICA.

GAMES, MODELS, AND TOYS.

The popularity of skate boards continued upward in 1965 with sales nearing $100,000,000, triple the 1964 figure. Hospital records, however, noted the hazards of the new sport. In New Rochelle, N.Y., the city hospital reported that it treated 22 fractures resulting from skate board mishaps in 22 days. The California Medical Association called the boards "a new medical menace," and some towns and cities passed ordinances regulating use of the boards.

Miniature, electrically powered racing cars, known to enthusiasts as slot cars, were also attracting increased attention. An estimated 6,000,000 persons, the majority adults, were reportedly spending more than $150,000,000 for car kits and other slot car equipment. By mid-1965, some 2,000 slot car centers were open, and the number was expected to more than double by the end of the year. Just two years before, there had been no more than 20 such centers throughout the United States.

The centers provided tracks on which the plastic cars could be raced, and occasionally staged races at which customers competed for prizes. Control of the racers, built to $\frac{1}{24}$ and $\frac{1}{32}$ scale, requires great skill that can be acquired only through practice and experience.

Doll makers were happy over the growing popularity of G.I. Joe, a full-jointed 11-inch-high doll, made in four versions—soldier, sailor, pilot, and marine. It was the first doll to catch on with boys since the days of Raggedy Andy and represented a breakthrough for which manufacturers had long been striving. Some 8,000,000 of the dolls have been sold since it was introduced in late 1964. Bicycle sales also were high, reaching $6,000,000 in 1965.

Model Making. Dr. Ralph Brooke of Seattle, Wash., won the world individual championship at the radio-controlled model airplane championships at Ljungbyhed, Sweden, in August. The United States also captured the team championship.

At the National Model Airplane contest at Willow Grove, Pa., in July and August, Reid Simpson of Mather (Calif.) Air Force Base won both the Open National and the Grand National championships. Dubby Jett of Seagoville, Tex., repeated as senior champion, and Geoffrey M. Sauter of Orange, Mass., won the junior title. The Baltimore Aero Craftsmen won the club championship and the U.S. Air Force again won the team championship.

Other Awards in 1965 included:
Craftsman's Guild Winners. In the annual Fisher Body Craftsman's model car building championships, university scholarships went to: *Senior Division*—Geza A Loczi, Scottsdale, Ariz., $5,000; Paul H. Peterson, Pittsburgh, Pa., $4,000; Tommy L. Strine, Mansfield, Ohio, $3,000; and Jeffrey B. Wehking, Ypsilanti, Mich., $2,000. *Junior Division*—Dwight Conger, Detroit, $5,000; James E. Cotter, Mansfield, Ohio, and Michael Pietruska, Stamford, Conn., $4,000; Kenneth Wehrman, St. Louis, $3,000, and Randy Tribo, Vallejo, Calif., $2,000.   THEODORE M. O'LEARY

GARDEN AND LAWN.

Space-age plant growers and users, from home gardeners to farmers to highway builders, came into 1966 with their own share of exciting advancements and prospects. These ranged from significant research and breakthroughs in safer and more economical pest controls to official recognition of the role of flowers, trees and shrubs, and other plants in beautifying America's homes, parks, and miles of roadside.

"Pesticides" appeared not to be quite the dirty word it had been, thanks to crash research and testing programs. For example, the U.S. Department of Agriculture (USDA) in 1965 developed low-volume mist and aerosol sprayers for use on the ground. These applied small but effective quantities of insecticide and reduced the need for massive spraying from airplanes. The USDA's first year's analysis showed that pesticides applied to crops had not resulted in significant amounts in measured residue in Mississippi River silt. See Section Two, POLLUTED AMERICA.

Insects themselves and insect diseases were being used as effective biological control agents (see INSECT). A major advance was announced in the search for low-cost biological control of the Japanese beetle, which causes an estimated $25,-000,000 damage yearly to crops, ornamental plants, and turf in the eastern United States and is moving westward. Beetle-destroying bacteria were induced to form milky disease (*Bacillus popilliae*) spores in mass quantities. These, when added to the soil, were eaten by beetle grubs feeding on plant roots. These spores are now available to homeowners.

Beautifying America. Mrs. Lyndon B. Johnson personally took part in the special planting of azaleas and other flowering plants on the White House grounds and in the capital's parks (see JOHNSON, LYNDON B., picture). Jackson, Miss., took its place in the 1965 beautification sun by winning first place among cities of 100,000 to 500,000 population in the national "Cleanest Town" contest.

Flowering and ornamental plants have proved useful for beautifying and controlling costly erosion on highway embankments. The more than 35 species of annuals and perennials recommended by the USDA for this use included broom sedge, crown vetch, day lily, English ivy, honeysuckle, iris, periwinkle, yellow jasmine, and other native plants. In a search for new plants to speed beautification, two USDA scientists brought back some unusual species of ornamentals from a two-month exploration trip into the Himalaya Mountains. Included were 10 species of wild rhododendrons, five species of a flowering evergreen shrub (*Gaultheria*) related to blueberries, and jack-in-the-pulpit plants up to four feet tall.

New Flowers announced in 1965 will be found in 1966's gardens. For example, the National Chrysanthemum Society listed its regional firsts in the single and anemone types of mums, respectively: *North*—white "North Star," yellow "Premiere"; *South*—yellow "Happiness," white "Alaska"; *East*—white "Ginny Lee," white "Cloudbank"; and *West*—white "Bonnie Jean," yellow "Powder Puff." Recipient of the American Dahlia Society's Certificate of Merit was "Frontispiece."

All-America Rose Selections for 1966 were: "American Heritage," an ivory-and-salmon blended hybrid tea with long, urn-shaped buds, 50 to 60 petals, and long stems; "Apricot Nectar," a floribunda that produces five-bloom clusters of "gentle" apricot color with old-fashioned rose fragrance from June until frost, and "Matterhorn," a free-blooming white hybrid tea rose with five-inch blossoms on sturdy, straight single stems. The "John F. Kennedy" white hybrid tea rose was offered to the public. It went on display in the John F. Kennedy memorial rose garden at the World's Fair in New York City in June.

Fruits and Vegetables won All-America honors as well. Included were the hybrid cantaloupe, "Samson," and three vegetables: "Chefini" summer squash, "Triumph" cucumber, and "Savoy King" cabbage. A new hardy and consistently productive blueberry variety, "Darrow," originated by USDA's Agricultural Research Service and the New Jersey Agricultural Experiment Station, was made available for restricted planting by nurserymen and growers in 1965.   FRANK B. HARPER

See also AGRICULTURE; BOTANY.

GARDNER, JOHN WILLIAM (1912-   ), was sworn in on Aug. 18, 1965, as Secretary of Health, Education, and Welfare (HEW). He succeeded Anthony J. Celebrezze, who had been appointed a judge of the U.S. Court of Appeals. Gardner, a Republican, had joined the Carnegie Corporation of New York, a philanthropic foundation, in 1946, and became its president in 1955. At the same time, he was president of the Carnegie Foundation for the Advancement of Teaching. In these posts, he was a gadfly to public educators, prodding them to reject outmoded procedures. See EDUCATION.

Gardner set up the commission on mathematics of the College Entrance Examination Board in 1955. The commission set in motion many curriculum revisions and introduced new teaching methods. A week before his nomination for Secretary, he headed a White House Conference on Education.

Gardner was born Oct. 8, 1912, in Los Angeles, Calif. He has B.A. and M.A. degrees from Stanford University, and a Ph.D. from the University of California at Berkeley. He taught psychology at Connecticut College and was assistant professor of psychology at Mount Holyoke College. In World War II, Gardner served in the marine corps and rose to the rank of captain. He married Aida Marroquin of Guatemala, a fellow student at Stanford, in 1934. They have two daughters.   WALTER F. MORSE

GASOLINE. See PETROLEUM.

GEOLOGY. Project Mohole, the ambitious U.S. scheme to drill through the earth's crust to the underlying mantle, passed the experimental phase in 1965 after three years of fiscal and managerial difficulties. Early in the year, a site 100 miles northeast of the Hawaiian island of Maui was selected for the primary hole. Sites for six shallower probes were also chosen by the National Science Foundation, the agency responsible for the project's administration. Plans were approved for a seaborne drilling platform that will be the size of a football field.

Named for the Mohorovicic discontinuity, the layer between the earth's crust and mantle, Project Mohole will attempt to sink a drill six miles through 14,000 feet of water and 17,000 feet of the earth's crust and reach the mantle. Recovery of fossil-bearing sediments, meteorite debris, and rare mineral composites are among the objectives of the probe. Preliminary drilling tests are planned for 1967 with work on the deep hole scheduled to begin in 1968. It is expected to take three years to reach the mantle.

Meanwhile, the Soviet embassy in Washington, D.C., reported that Russia will attempt to sink a drill nine miles to the earth's mantle in 1966. The site chosen is in the Murmansk region.

Paleontology. Discovery of fossils from Pre-Cambrian times established the fact that life existed on earth much earlier than had previously been believed. One of the finds was made by a team headed by Harvard University paleontologist Elso S. Barg-

DRILLING PLATFORM to be used in Project Mohole, the attempt to drill a hole through the crust of the earth, was constructed in model form.

hoorn. By means of electron microscopy, they discovered well-preserved remains of bacteria, in samples of 3,000,000,000-year-old rock from South Africa. Barghoorn had earlier reported finding 2,000,000,000-year-old organisms in rocks from the northwest shore of Lake Superior. Another important discovery was of 720,000,000-year-old fossils of clamlike creatures called brachiopods. They were found by Andrew H. McNair of Dartmouth College in rocks of the Canadian Arctic. See BIOLOGY.

American Profile. A task force of scientists began defining the geologic profile of North America during 1965, along a belt spanning the continent and extending 500 miles into both oceans. Known as the Transcontinental Geophysical Survey, the study will chart the subsurface structure of North America from seismic data obtained by chemical and nuclear underground explosions.

Earthquakes. At the request of President Lyndon B. Johnson, plans were developed for a 10-year program of research into the nature of earthquakes. The plans call for the installation of complex instrumentation at 15 places along the San Andreas fault in California, an area of violent earthquake activity. Since the earthquakes in this part of the world originate at a depth of about 15,000 feet, instruments at four sites would be placed 10,000 feet below ground. The instruments will also be placed above ground along the fault to record very slight movements of the surface rocks. SERGEI LENORMAND

GERMANY

Germany continued to resent bitterly its status as a divided country. Although several authoritative statements were made reaffirming the Federal Republic of West Germany's determination to continue seeking reunification, no real progress was made to achieve it. Though West Germany's economy was slowing down, it still enjoyed a high degree of prosperity; the German Democratic Republic of East Germany was encountering economic trouble, largely because of difficulties in selling its coal, oil, and textiles.

The Wall. The Berlin wall, which on other occasions had been opened at Christmas and other holidays, was again sealed off in September, 1965. East Germany refused to grant any further travel passes, but there was a let-up over Christmas when half a million West Germans visited relatives in East Berlin. The communists had earlier closed a "mercy" loophole by which West Berliners had been permitted to visit sick or dying relatives in East Germany.

European Relations. With the future of Europe's political integration made questionable by the actions of President Charles de Gaulle of France, Germany steered what its leaders described as a course "between De Gaullism and Atlanticism." There was, however, no way of disguising the grave disquiet France had aroused by its blocking of the European Economic Community (EEC, or Common Market). Disappointment was all the more keen because Britain's Prime Minister Harold Wilson and Foreign Secretary Michael Stewart had offered some degree of hope on their visit to Bonn in the spring. They had agreed with the republic's leaders that the two governments should not only work toward strengthening the links between EEC and the European Free Trade Association (EFTA) but should also work to prevent further division of Europe. It was agreed, too, that the common aim was to work for the reunification of Germany. See FRANCE; GREAT BRITAIN.

GRAY-HAIRED West German Chancellor Ludwig Erhard, campaigning hard for re-election, addresses a rally in Frankfurt. He won.

United Press Int.

WEEPING GERMAN NURSE collapses at trial. She and 14 others were charged with murdering hospitalized mental patients during Nazi regime.

Economic Prosperity. International events and national elections were strong influences on the Federal Republic's economic trends. The country was enjoying its highest postwar prosperity, but business and the government were not in agreement on how it could be maintained.

There was criticism of the Central Bank's restrictive credit policy which reduced the freely available liquidity of the banks by $750,000,000. Critics of the government complained of a lack of a decisive economic policy and overlavish expenditure. An acute shortage of manpower, coupled with uncertainty over the future of the EEC accentuated the feeling of uncertainty.

Victory for Erhard. Out of 38,100,000 people entitled to vote in the October national elections,

33,100,000 went to the polls. The result was a victory for Chancellor Ludwig Erhard's Christian Democratic Union (CDU). The CDU polled 47.5 per cent of the vote, with the Social Democratic party (SDP) winning 39.3 per cent. The Liberal Free Democrats (FDP) gained only 9.5 per cent of the vote. Lacking an overall majority, 68-year-old Erhard, who was nominated to remain chancellor, immediately began efforts to achieve a CDU/FDP coalition.

These efforts ran into trouble, however, when former Chancellor Konrad Adenauer and Herr Franz-Josef Strauss, leader of the Bavarian wing of the CDU, campaigned to oust Dr. Gerhard Schröder as foreign minister. Both blamed him for a political line that encouraged an "encirclement" of Germany by France and the Soviet Union. Despite their efforts, Schröder was renamed to the post of foreign minister.

Middle East Relations were disturbed during 1965. Early in the year, a dispute broke out between the Bonn government and the United Arab Republic (UAR) following an announcement by the UAR that it had invited East Germany's chief of state Walter Ulbricht to visit Cairo in February. Bonn feared that Ulbricht's state visit would be the prelude to the UAR's eventual recognition of the East German government.

On February 24, Ulbricht arrived in Cairo, Egypt, for a seven-day visit. The Bonn government immediately halted all economic aid to the UAR. In subsequent developments, the Arab nations of the Middle East, including the UAR, severed diplomatic relations with West Germany. The rupture was prompted in part by the establishment of formal diplomatic relations between West Germany and Israel. See ISRAEL.

War Trials. A national controversy was aroused during the year by a decision of the German parliament to extend the time limit for instituting proceedings against war criminals to five years. Six former Storm Troopers from the Auschwitz concentration camp received life sentences for murder in the first of three war crimes trials in 1965.

Germany (East). Population: 17,260,000. **Government:** Communist Party First Secretary Walter Ulbricht; Prime Minister Willi Stoph. **Monetary Unit:** ostmark (2.22 = U.S. $1). **Foreign Trade:** exports (estimated) $248,000,000; imports (estimated) $2,148,830,000. **Principal Exports:** coal, machinery, potash.

Germany (West). Population: 57,845,000. **Government:** President Heinrich Luebke; Chancellor Ludwig Erhard. **Monetary Unit:** deutschmark (4.011 = U.S. $1). **Gross National Product:** 376,-800,000,000 deutschmarks. **Foreign Trade:** exports, $16,228,250,000; imports, $14,709,750,000. **Principal Exports:** chemicals, electrical goods, machinery, textiles.   KENNETH BROWN

See also EUROPE.

GHANA came more firmly under the control of President Kwame Nkrumah and his Convention People's Party (CPP). In April, 1965, the constitution was amended to allow only members of the CPP to run for the presidency. General elections, originally scheduled for June, were not held because all 198 candidates nominated by the CPP were unopposed. On June 10, the new national assembly unanimously endorsed President Nkrumah for a second five-year term. Ghana's new "corporate parliament" was enlarged to give representation to the CPP bureaucracy and party affiliates.

President Nkrumah declared the 1963 treason trials of five former officials void, and had the men, including three who were previously acquitted, brought to trial again and convicted. Nkrumah later commuted some of the death sentences to prison terms and also released 100 persons held under the country's Preventive Detention Act.

To meet its foreign exchange deficits, restrictions were placed on unnecessary imports. President Nkrumah reorganized his cabinet in April to strengthen economic planning.

Population: 7,933,000. **Government:** President Kwame Nkrumah. **Monetary Unit:** sedi (1 = U.S. $1.18). **Foreign Trade:** exports, $291,000,000; imports, $333,000,000. **Principal Exports:** cocoa, diamonds, gold, timber.　　　BENJAMIN E. THOMAS

See also AFRICA.

GILROY, FRANK DANIEL (1925-　), playwright and author of television and screen scripts, was awarded the Pulitzer drama prize in 1965 for *The Subject Was Roses*. His first Broadway play also received the New York Drama Critics Circle, the Antoinette Perry, the New York Theater Club, and the New York Outer Circle awards. The three-character play about a soldier's return to his family opened in New York in May, 1964. Gilroy's first stage success, *Who'll Save the Plowboy?* (1962), received New York's Obie (Off-Broadway) award as the season's best American play.

Beginning in 1952, Gilroy concentrated on television and screen scripts. He wrote for such television programs as the United States Steel Hour, Kraft and Lux Video theaters, and the Dick Powell Show. He also wrote "The Rifleman"; "Have Gun, Will Travel"; and other Western televison series. "The Last Notch" (1954) won high acclaim, and was filmed as *Fastest Gun Alive* (1956). He wrote (with Bernie Lay, Jr.) *The Gallant Hours*, the film (1960) story of the late Admiral William F. Halsey.

Frank Gilroy was born and lived in New York City until drafted into the army in 1943. He served three years with the Third and First armies in Europe. Gilroy received his B.A. degree (*magna cum laude*) at Dartmouth in 1950. The college produced the plays he wrote there, and gave him two Frost Playwriting awards.

See also PULITZER PRIZES; THEATER.

GIRL SCOUTS of the United States of America joined with Girl Guides from 45 other countries to sponsor the Fourth Triennial Senior Girl Scout Roundup. It was held, July 15 to 28, at the Farragut Wildlife Area, Idaho. The Roundup was designed to give those attending—9,000 girls (15 to 17 years of age) and 2,000 adult leaders—a chance to live and work with girls of different backgrounds from many parts of the world. It also provided practical experiences in self-direction and resourcefulness.

An outstanding feature of the program was the series of demonstrations dealing with the history and culture of the Northwest. These included performances by Nez Percé Indian Dancers, the Idaho Basque Dancers, and the Idaho Appaloosa horses; displays of Indian villages and fur trappers' cabins; and a replica of a Lewis and Clark expedition camp.

In appreciation for the hospitality extended them by the state of Idaho, the girls contributed 9,000 seedling trees to the area—to become a state park.

The Rural Special Areas project, designed to increase Girl Scout membership in low-income rural areas, was started in 1965. The program is in many ways similar to the two-year Urban Special Areas project that was set up in 1964 for increasing Girl Scout activity in low-income or depressed city areas. A grant of $100,000 was allocated for the purpose of training staff members to handle the new rural program.　　　JOSEPH P. ANDERSON

GIRLS CLUBS OF AMERICA (GCA), INC., established the first of 10 regional headquarters as a step to strengthen and expand the Girls Club movement. The new office, located in Los Angeles, Calif., will provide services for clubs in Arizona, California, New Mexico, and Texas. Martha May Newsom was appointed to the newly created post of Western regional field service director.

The main speaker at the GCA's 20th national conference, held in New York City in May, was Dona Mavy A. A. Harmon, an official of the Brazil Women's Council for Democracy. The delegates also welcomed another guest from Brazil, Rita de Cassia, 19, Brazil's "1965 Girl of the Year." Ruby Jo Couch, 17, of Wichita Falls, Tex., was named "1965 Girl of the Year" for outstanding accomplishments in homemaking skills. The Career Key scholarship award of $750 went to Carol Gigliotti, 17, of Niagara Falls, N.Y.

The winners of other national contests were: Lucile M. Wright Citizenship Award, Jeanie Crowley, 14, of Wichita Falls, Tex.; GCA poster contest, Alice Bimler, 12, of Allentown, Pa.; senior sewing contest, Judith Yacknick, 17, of Bristol, Conn.; junior sewing contest, Martha Beaudoin, 13, of Manchester, N.H.; senior cooking contest, Theresa Isbell, 15, of Birmingham, Ala.; and junior cooking contest, Betty Ann Florence, 13, of Niagara Falls, New York.　　　JOSEPH P. ANDERSON

GLASS. See MANUFACTURING.

James Drake, *Sports Illustrated* © Time Inc.

JACK NICKLAUS who won the Masters Golf Tournament at Augusta, Ga., had become the sport's biggest money winner by the end of the year.

GOLF. Big Jack Nicklaus won the most money; little Gary Player won the most honors.

Nicklaus surpassed Arnold Palmer's old mark for earnings in a year by accumulating $152,246, the most ever gained in the history of golf. In April, he appeared to be on his way to complete domination of the sport when he won his second Masters title with a record-breaking 17-under-par score, nine strokes ahead of Player and Palmer. He also won the Memphis, Portland, Thunderbird, and Whitemarsh competitions.

Player, the South African health faddist, became the only current player to win all four of the world's top tournaments when he captured the U.S. Open. In earlier years, he won the Masters, Professional Golfers Association (PGA), and British Open. Player won the 1965 Open by three strokes over Australia's Kel Nagle in an 18-hole play-off, after both had finished regulation play in St. Louis in a 282 tie. Player donated his purse to charity and went on to win the individual title at the Canada Cup, the World Series of Golf, the Piccadilly Match Play tournament, and the Australian Open.

The PGA championship was won by Dave Marr, who had finished last in 1964. The competition was marked by the failure of Arnold Palmer to become a serious challenger on his home course, the Laurel Valley Country Club in Ligonier, Pa. Palmer won only one tournament. The British Open went to Peter Thomson of Australia.

Cup Play. Great Britain and the United States tied for the first time in the Walker Cup competition, which began in 1922. The U.S. team then won in the Ryder Cup play, but came in third in the competition for the Canada Cup. South Africa was first and Spain second.

Women's Play. Carol Mann of Towson, Md., won the U.S. Women's Open at Atlantic City by two strokes over Mrs. Kathy Cornelius of Rancho Santa Fe, San Diego, Calif. The Ladies PGA, in Las Vegas, Nev., was won by Sandra Haynie of Alexandria, La., over Clifford Ann Creed of Fort Worth, Tex. Jean Ashley of Colorado Springs, Colo., defeated three-time amateur champion Anne Quast Welts for the U.S. Women's Amateur crown in Denver.

Amateur Golf. Bob Murphy, a Florida University senior, won the National Amateur championship at Tulsa, Okla. The Public Links title play at Pittsburgh, Pa., went to Arne Dokka of Studio City, Calif. The University of Houston won the National Collegiate Athletic Association (NCAA) championship for the eighth time in 10 years. The tournament took place at the Holston Hills Country Club in Knoxville, Tenn.

Rule Change. The controversial flagstick rule, involving a penalty for hitting an unattended flagstick, has been changed by the U.S. Golf Association (USGA) to conform with the code of the Canadian Golf Association. The new rule goes into effect in

1966. Prior to this decision by the USGA, the penalty had been determined by four contrasting rules, two in the United States, another in Britain, and the fourth, the code of the Royal Canadian Golf Association. The new rule calls for a two-stroke penalty if the flagstick is struck by a ball played from anywhere on the putting green.

Two other new rules were suggested for local adoption by the USGA, both for the purpose of achieving faster play on the greens. The first calls for a golfer to play continuously on the green until he holes out. The other permits lifting of the ball only once on the green for the purpose of cleaning it. This last rule, the USGA pointed out, is necessary because some players clean a ball so incessantly that it is a bore to spectators.

Awards. Gene Sarazen, who won the U.S. Open and the PGA title in 1922, was the 1965 winner of the Walter Hagen trophy. The trophy is annually given to the golfer or golf executive who does the most to further good relations in the sport between the United States and Britain. It is named after the first winner, Hagen, who was the 1961 recipient of the award.

Sarazen, who began golf as an eight-year-old caddie and went on to become the winner of a dozen major championships, received the trophy in August during the PGA championship at Ligonier, Pa., an event he won three times.   STANLEY ISAACS

GOVERNORS OF THE STATES holding office in

1966 are listed below, with their political affiliations and their years in office. Only two states elected governors on Nov. 2, 1965. New Jersey elected Richard J. Hughes, a Democrat, to a second four-year term. Lieutenant Governor Mills E. Godwin, Jr., also a Democrat, was elected to a four-year term in Virginia. There are now 33 Democratic and 17 Republican governors, the same as in 1965.

GOVERNORS OF THE 50 STATES

State	Governor	Terms
Ala.	George C. Wallace, D.	1963–1967
Alaska	William A. Egan, D.	1959–1967
Ariz.	Samuel P. Goddard, Jr., D.	1965–1967
Ark.	Orval E. Faubus, D.	1955–1967
Calif.	Edmund G. Brown, D.	1959–1967
Colo.	John A. Love, R.	1963–1967
Conn.	John N. Dempsey, D.	1961–1967
Del.	Charles L. Terry, Jr., D.	1965–1969
Fla.	Haydon Burns, D.	1965–1967
Ga.	Carl E. Sanders, D.	1963–1967
Hawaii	John A. Burns, D.	1963–1967
Idaho	Robert E. Smylie, R.	1955–1967
Ill.	Otto J. Kerner, Jr., D.	1961–1969
Ind.	Roger D. Branigin, D.	1965–1969
Iowa	Harold E. Hughes, D.	1963–1967
Kans.	William H. Avery, R.	1965–1967
Ky.	Edward T. Breathitt, D.	1963–1967
La.	John J. McKeithen, D.	1964–1968
Me.	John H. Reed, R.	1960–1967
Md.	J. Millard Tawes, D.	1959–1967
Mass.	John A. Volpe, R.	*1965–1967

State	Governor	Terms
Mich.	George W. Romney, R.	1963–1967
Minn.	Karl F. Rolvaag, D.	1963–1967
Miss.	Paul B. Johnson, Jr., D.	1964–1968
Mo.	Warren E. Hearnes, D.	1965–1969
Mont.	Tim M. Babcock, R.	1962–1969
Nebr.	Frank B. Morrison, D.	1961–1967
Nev.	Grant Sawyer, D.	1959–1967
N.H.	John W. King, D.	1963–1967
N.J.	Richard J. Hughes, D.	1962–1970
N.Mex.	Jack M. Campbell, D.	1963–1967
N.Y.	Nelson A. Rockefeller, R.	1959–1967
N.C.	Daniel K. Moore, D.	1965–1969
N.Dak.	William L. Guy, D.	1961–1969
Ohio	James A. Rhodes, R.	1963–1967
Okla.	Henry Bellmon, R.	1963–1967
Ore.	Mark O. Hatfield, R.	1959–1967
Pa.	William W. Scranton, R.	1963–1967
R.I.	John H. Chafee, R.	1963–1967
S.C.	Donald S. Russell, D.	1963–1967
S.Dak.	Nils Boe, R.	1965–1967
Tenn.	Frank G. Clement, D.	†1963–1967
Tex.	John B. Connally, Jr., D.	1963–1967
Utah	Calvin L. Rampton, D.	1965–1969
Vt.	Philip H. Hoff, D.	1963–1967
Va.	Mills E. Godwin, Jr., D.	1966–1970
Wash.	Daniel J. Evans, R.	1965–1969
W.Va.	Hulett C. Smith, D.	1965–1969
Wis.	Warren P. Knowles, R.	1965–1967
Wyo.	Clifford P. Hansen, R.	1963–1967

*Served previous term (1961–1963).
†Served previous term (1955–1959).

See also ELECTIONS.

GRAU, SHIRLEY ANN (1929–   ), was awarded the Pulitzer fiction prize in 1965 for *The Keepers of the House*. It is a dramatic story of racial conflict in her native Louisiana. *The Hard Blue Sky* (1958), the author's first novel, is about life of an isolated, primitive people on the Isle aux Chiens, near New Orleans. Some critics found it "not to be quite a novel." Others thought it good reading and an achievement. *The House on Coliseum Street* (1961), set in New Orleans, was not considered one of her better books.

When the author made her literary debut with *The Black Prince and Other Stories* (1955), she was widely praised as a gifted storyteller. Her collection was later published in England and in Germany. Although Miss Grau's first novels received uneven reviews, she has been highly praised for her craftsmanship.

In private life Shirley Ann Grau is the wife of Tulane philosophy professor James Kern Feibleman, himself the author of many and varied books. They are both natives of New Orleans, and live in the suburb of Metairie with their two small children. Dark-haired Shirley Ann has a varied ancestry of Louisiana Creole (Spanish and French), German, and Scottish stock. She is a graduate of Tulane's Newcomb College for women (1950), and did graduate work at the university in Renaissance and 17th century English literature.

See also PULITZER PRIZES.

GREAT BRITAIN

Great Britain spent much of the year on the brink of an economic crisis. Prime Minister Harold Wilson and his Labour party government had repeatedly to assuage international fears that the pound sterling would be devalued from the rate at which it had been fixed in 1949. Frequent recourse had to be made to foreign loans. Between November, 1964, and May, 1965, the pound was underpinned by stand-by credits of $3,000,000,000 from foreign central banks (later converted into a $1,440,000,000 withdrawal from the International Monetary Fund [IMF] and Swiss credits).

Between June and August new credits were received from the Federal Reserve Bank of New York ($750,000,000) and the Export-Import Bank ($250,000,000). In September, a further credit of $1,000,000,000 had to be secured from the central banks. Not until then did the pound sterling rally and the damaging drain of money from London cease. See INTERNATIONAL TRADE AND FINANCE; MONEY.

Chancellor of the Exchequer James Callaghan twice had to impose restrictive measures on the economy: in his April budget (when the income tax went up for the first time since 1951 and 164,000,000 pounds were drawn off in new indirect taxes); and in a cutback in government spending in July. This helped to restore foreign confidence, but Britain's weakness continued to be underscored by a persistent trade gap between rising imports and sluggish exports.

Despite the government's squeeze, industrial investment remained high and unemployment low. Wages and prices rose faster than production. A mild recession seemed likely in 1966 while the pound sterling continued on the road to recovery.

Prime Minister Wilson, meanwhile, had staked his political future on overcoming this crisis without calling a general election, although the Labour party's parliamentary majority was cut from five seats to a perilous three (a margin that, in the past, had been thought unworkable). Wilson attributed the country's difficulties to the earlier policies of the Conservative party. Labour's economic management, however, was subjected to severe criticism, too, particularly in the City of London.

Austerity Budget. On April 6, Chancellor Callaghan presented a new budget designed to trim sharply rising domestic consumption, narrow a serious balance-of-payments deficit, and shore up the ailing pound sterling. Its measures included a tax increase on beer, cigarettes, liquor, and wine; increased automobile license fees; and a stiff tax on capital gains. It also tightened British exchange controls, imposed restraints on the export of long-term capital, and outlawed most tax-free expense accounts. Despite a prolonged political battle in the

Marvin Lichtner, PIX

ROYAL HOSTESS, Queen Elizabeth II, dedicates memorial to the late U.S. President John F. Kennedy at Runnymede. Mrs. Kennedy sits at her right. See MEMORIALS (picture).

GREAT BRITAIN

House of Commons over some of the budget's provisions, the budget was subsequently adopted.

Another controversial bill, to nationalize the 14 biggest companies in the steel industry, ran into even stiffer parliamentary resistance. After the government's majority fell to two in a tense debate May 6, the bill was relegated to a low priority in Labour's program.

Economic Plan. The key to Labour's long-term economic hopes was the national plan published by First Secretary of State George Brown on September 16. It aimed at a 25 per cent rise in output between 1964 and 1970, implying an average annual growth of 3.8 per cent. Industry's expectations, however, suggested that productivity would fall short of Brown's wishes. Even so, only two industries—coal mining, and fur and leather goods—admitted to the prospect of an actual decline. The best bets for growth were considered to be chemicals, electricity supply, man-made fibers, oil refining, and telecommunications. The most serious bottleneck was likely to prove a manpower gap—despite automation—of at least 200,000 in the 1970 labor force.

Churchill Dies. Sir Winston Churchill, in his 91st year, succumbed to a cerebral thrombosis shortly after 8 A.M. on a cold Sunday morning in January. He was given a state funeral and buried at Bladon, Oxfordshire. See DEATHS OF NOTABLE PERSONS.

Conservative Leadership. Sir Alec Douglas-Home, after months of internal party grumbling by Conservatives, surrendered his leadership on July 22. Three former Conservative ministers, Edward Heath, Reginald Maudling, and Enoch Powell, stood for election to the vacant post by the party's members of Parliament; it was the first such balloting for leadership in Conservative history. The result gave Heath 150 votes, Maudling 133, and Powell 15. The victor, Edward Heath, came from a lower middle-class family. He represented a new kind of Conservative, and was expected to widen the party's electoral appeal. As leader, he issued a new policy document on October 7, with emphasis on a competitive society, a social policy of self-help, and a continuing determination to integrate Britain with Europe.

Political Upsets. Labour suffered its severest blow on January 22 with the defeat of Foreign Secretary Patrick Gordon-Walker in a parliamentary by-election held at Leyton, East London. This disaster, in a supposedly safe Labour seat, forced Gordon-Walker (who had lost his seat in the Commons in the general election of 1964) to resign from the government. Michael Stewart, a former schoolmaster who had been minister of education, was appointed in his place. The defeat cut Wilson's majority over the combined Conservatives and Liberals to

BEARDED EMPEROR Haile Selassié I of Ethiopia snaps to salute during ceremonies held in Addis Ababa for state visit of Great Britain's Queen Elizabeth II.
United Press Int.

During 1965, Queen Elizabeth II added three names—Ethiopia, Germany, and Sudan—to the long list of countries she has visited since acceding to the throne in 1953.

The royal tours of Sudan and Germany had harsh political undercurrents, but the tour of Ethiopia was pure enchantment. There, Emperor Haile Selassié I took the queen camping in the fairy-tale mountains overlooking the Blue Nile. There she slept in a silk-lined, carpeted tent, lit by electric candelabra and supplied with hot running water from a nearby spring. Her neighbors were prowling hyenas and baboons that were kept at bay by a protective thornbush fence.

The emperor took the queen to the 4,000-year-old legendary capital of the Biblical Queen of Sheba. He broke an ancient rule by escorting her into the old Coptic cathedral, hitherto barred to women, and showed her its holy relics. A medieval-like joust was held in the queen's honor, at which vividly costumed tribesmen carrying lances and shields and seated in scarlet and silver saddles, galloped to and fro in mock battle. The palace lions were shampooed and powdered for her and induced to roar a welcome. At parting, the emperor presented Elizabeth with ornaments of gold; she gave him a valuable stallion and an airplane.

The queen then flew on to Sudan, where, despite political unrest and fears for her safety, she was given a warm welcome marred only by a few displays of political slogans.

The queen was housed in the palace built by Lord Kitchener on the site where General Charles George Gordon had been assassinated 80 years before. She was entertained with camel races, tribal dancing, and processions of camels carrying Bedouin wives in howdahs.

Some 20,000 tribesmen galloped past her on camels, shouting their welcome and brandishing swords, rifles, and spears. Later, Elizabeth was shown Sudan's modern pride and joy—the new hydroelectric project on the Blue Nile, and then taken for a moonlit river cruise.

Queen Elizabeth's visit to Germany was the first one made by a reigning British monarch since before World War I. The highlight was a drive to the Berlin wall with Chancellor Ludwig Erhard and Mayor Willy Brandt. The queen also toured West Germany, visiting Bonn, Cologne, and Hamburg. The loudest and most spectacular moments of the queen's day in Hamburg came when she rode a barge through the city's harbor. Luxury liners, freighters, tankers, tugs, and ferryboats all sounded their whistles and horns while fireboats sprayed their hoses.

Royal tours seldom have tangible results, and it is hard to assess their value. Unofficially, they are costly public relations operations and, as such, they provide a useful stepping stone which others may subsequently use to try to forge stronger political, economic, and social links.

Officially, they are purely social. The queen travels with a large planeload of equerries, ladies-in-waiting, and palace staff, but no politicians. Wherever possible she also takes the royal yacht *Britannia*, using it as a floating hotel in which she can enjoy home-away-from-home privacy. This added comfort is doubly welcome, for she is often on duty—in steamy tropical heat—from after breakfast till past midnight, paying exhausting visits to dams, factories, hospitals, and schools.

It is obvious, from the amount of travel required of the queen, that the British government regards these journeys as of key political importance, particularly in the Commonwealth. Her father, George VI, spent only four months of his 15-year reign visiting overseas territories. Her grandfather, George V, was abroad officially only three months in 26 years. Elizabeth II, in less than 13 years, has spent 14 months on official travels. She has now journeyed more than 150,000 miles on five continents, visiting 21 Commonwealth and 16 foreign countries, many of them more than once. No British monarch has ever traveled so far or worked so hard to wave the Union Jack in other lands.   RHONA CHURCHILL

Elizabeth II: The Most Traveled Queen

A
YEAR
BOOK
CLOSE-UP

Thompson Newspapers, Ltd.

EVER ACTIVE British Prime Minister Harold Wilson works on state papers in hotel room between appearances at political rally in Liverpool, England.

three. But the Conservatives suffered a humiliation on March 24 in a by-election held at Roxburgh in Scotland, losing heavily to the Liberals.

Labour's majority in the Commons was again periled by the death of the speaker, Sir Harry Hylton-Foster, on September 2. Although a Labour member of Parliament—Dr. Horace King—took over the position, other nonvoting posts were held by a Conservative and a Liberal, thus restoring the party balance. But the threat of illness, absence, or individual revolt still hung over Wilson's shaky hold on power.

Commonwealth Mission. Wilson's biggest problem within his own party came as a result of his support of U.S. military policy in Vietnam. Labour left-wingers, notably the Viet Cong apologist William Warbey, grew restless at U.S. bombing attacks on North Vietnamese targets and accused Wilson of subservience to U.S. money. In a bold stroke, Wilson persuaded the Commonwealth prime ministers, at their conference held in London on June 17, to mount a peace mission to Vietnam. The refusal of Communist China and North Vietnam to accept the mission, as contrasted with U.S. approval of it, did much to consolidate Wilson's political stand. To further demonstrate communist intractability, Wilson dispatched a left-wing junior minister, Harold Davies, to Hanoi on July 8; as expected, Davies failed to contact any North Vietnamese leaders. See VIETNAM.

Rhodesian Independence. Wilson struggled hard at successive meetings in London and Salisbury to persuade Prime Minister Ian Smith of Rhodesia (a self-governing colony since 1923) against a unilateral declaration of independence. While Smith argued for independence under Rhodesia's 1961 constitution, Wilson insisted on the principle of African consent to an electoral system by which the country's 4,000,000-strong black population would have its fair say against the enfranchised white community of about 250,000.

When Smith took the plunge and declared independence on November 11, Wilson retaliated with economic sanctions, principally directed against Rhodesia's tobacco market in Britain. At the United Nations, Britain agreed to an oil embargo. British opinion was not prepared to use military force in the territory, however, despite pressures to do so from the African Commonwealth Nations. See AFRICA; RHODESIA; UNITED NATIONS.

Malaysia Erupts. Great Britain recognized Singapore as an independent state on August 9 after Malaysian Prime Minister Lee Kuan Yew suddenly declared his nation's secession from the Federation of Malaysia. The recognition agreement set up a joint defense council for Singapore and Britain continued to use the base as headquarters for its aeronaval forces as well as 50,000 troops committed to defend Malaysia against Indonesia. See ASIA; INDONESIA; MALAYSIA.

Defense Rethinking. Defense Secretary Denis Healey announced plans for a major overhaul of Britain's defense program during the year. Under a national economic plan, he pledged that the government would restrain its military spending to 2,000,000,000 pounds per annum between 1965 and 1970. This would mean a reduction of 400,000,000 pounds from the original estimates.

Aviation Minister Roy Jenkins focused a critical eye on the nation's military aircraft projects and drew loud protests in April when he canceled the TSR-2, a supersonic tactical strike and reconnaissance plane designed to duck under radar screens.

Colored Immigration. During the year, resistance built up among both Labour and Conservative politicians to further immigration from the West Indies, India, and Pakistan (see IMMIGRATION AND EMIGRATION). The parties backed social and educational spending aimed at integrating the 800,000 black immigrants already in the country; a law introduced in the Commons on April 7 prohibited racial discrimination in public places (though not in boarding houses, shops, and workingmen's clubs) and incitement to race hatred. But liberals protested a government decision on August 2 to restrict entry permits for Commonwealth citizens to 7,500 a year for professional and skilled workers only, plus 1,000 a year for Maltese immigrants.

SEE also EUROPE.

United Press Int.

SMILING NEW HEAD of Britain's Conservative party is Edward Heath, a 49-year-old bachelor shown here en route to the House of Commons.

Unions Inquiry. Trade union unpopularity, revealed in public opinion polls, pushed the government to set up a royal commission on February 2 to inquire into the conduct of unions and employers' associations. On April 8, First Secretary of State Brown, in an attempt to keep wage increases in line with production, set a national norm of $3\frac{1}{2}$ per cent. But the move was opposed by Britain's largest union, the Transport and General Workers, whose leader, Frank Cousins, sat in the Wilson cabinet as technology minister. A majority of unions agreed in September to carefully study wage claims, in a last attempt to prevent Brown from taking his own legal measures.

Royal Family. In November, Princess Margaret and her husband, the Earl of Snowdon, paid a visit to the United States. During their tour, they were guests of President Lyndon B. Johnson at the White House.

In June, Britons reacted with laughter, resentment, and some anger over the inclusion of the Beatles in Queen Elizabeth's honors list.

Population: 54,108,000. **Government:** Queen Elizabeth II; Prime Minister Harold Wilson. **Monetary Unit:** pound sterling (1 = U.S. $2.80). **Gross National Product:** 28,910,000,000 pounds. **Foreign Trade:** exports, $12,341,000,000; imports, $15,438,-000,000. **Principal Exports:** machinery, motor vehicles, textiles. ALASTAIR BURNET

GREECE was shaken by a number of parliamentary crises in 1965. They began on July 15 when King Constantine XIII ousted Premier George Papandreou after the two had clashed over the question of political influences in the army. They did not end until October, after the king appointed Stephanos Christos Stephenopoulos to the premiership. In the interim, two attempts to form governments had failed.

The new government faced serious problems. A leftist youth movement, some 40,000 members strong, continued to conduct what government officials called "sidewalk guerrilla warfare," or protest picketing. The economic outlook, too, was disturbing, with a balance of payments deficit expected to reach $54,000,000 for the year.

Foreign affairs were in no better state. The Cyprus question was still a fiery issue, with Greece committed to the principle of self-determination for the island. The nation's long-standing differences with Turkey had not been helped by the lack of a stable government. See CYPRUS; TURKEY.

Population: 8,650,000. **Government:** King Constantine XIII; Premier Stephanos Christos Stephenopoulos. **Monetary Unit:** drachma (30 = U.S. $1). **Gross National Product:** 117,640,000,000 drachmas. **Foreign Trade:** exports, $290,000,000; imports, $644,000,000. **Principal Exports:** cotton, currants, fruits, olives, tobacco. KENNETH BROWN

See also EUROPE.

GUATEMALA made plans to return to constitutional government after more than two years of government by decree. On September 15, a new constitution was promulgated. It provided for the holding of nationwide elections in March, 1966. At that time, voters would choose a president, a vice-president, a congress, and municipal officers.

The nation, meanwhile, remained under the military rule of Colonel Enrique Peralta Azurdia. In February, the Peralta government imposed a state of siege after a series of guerrilla actions in the interior. By July, however, the situation had been stabilized and the state of siege was lifted. Civil liberties were restored throughout the country.

During the year, Guatemala reached an agreement with the International Nickel Company under which a $50,000,000 mining and processing facility would be built in the northeastern area of the country. Its initial capacity would be 25,000,000 pounds of nickel annually. The Matias de Galvez Port Authority signed a $5,700,000 contract with a U.S. engineering firm and a local construction company for the expansion of port facilities.

Population: 4,412,000. **Government:** Chief of State Colonel Enrique Peralta Azurdia. **Monetary Unit:** quetzal (1 = U.S. $1). **Foreign Trade:** exports, $158,000,000; imports, $202,000,000. **Principal Exports:** bananas, coffee, cotton.   MARY C. WEBSTER

See also LATIN AMERICA.

GUINEA complained of "constant provocations" by troops operating along its border with Portuguese Guinea and threatened to report the incidents to the United Nations Security Council. During 1965, President Sékou Touré also denied reports that his country would abandon its monetary ties with the French franc.

President Touré made visits to Liberia and Sierra Leone during which he was reported to have discussed the possibility of creating a monetary zone with those countries. In an address to the Sierra Leone national assembly, President Touré affirmed Guinea's readiness to sacrifice its sovereignty for the sake of a closer association with the other African nations.

Pan American World Airways will provide technical assistance to the airways of Guinea under a $1,800,000 grant from the United States.

President Touré made state visits to the Soviet Union, Hungary, Yugoslavia, and the United Arab Republic. He later announced that the Soviet Union would help finance the Konkouré Dam, develop industry in the north, and build a dam and hydroelectric plant in the south.

Population: 3,470,000. **Government:** President Sékou Touré. **Monetary Unit:** franc (246.85 = U.S. $1). **Foreign Trade:** exports, $55,000,000; imports, $46,000,000. **Principal Exports:** bananas, bauxite, iron ore, palm oil products.   BENJAMIN E. THOMAS

See also AFRICA.

HAIDER, MICHAEL LAWRENCE (1904-   ), was elected February 15 to take over on March 1 as chairman and chief executive officer of Standard Oil Company (New Jersey), the largest petroleum firm in the world. Its earnings exceed $1,000,000,-000 a year. He succeeded M. J. Rathbone, who retired. Haider (pronounced Hide-er) had been president since 1963. He has spent his working life in the industry.

Immediately after obtaining a B.S. degree from Stanford University in 1927, he joined the Richfield Oil Company at Los Angeles as a chemical engineer. Two years later he went to the Carter Oil Company in Tulsa, Okla. In 1938, he was made manager of production engineering and research for Standard Oil Development Company.

In 1945, he went to Jersey Standard as deputy coordinator of producing activities. He was made a vice-president in 1952. He also has been manager of exploration and production for Imperial Oil, Ltd., Toronto, Ontario.

He told a newspaper interviewer that the greatest thrill of his 37-year career came in 1947 when he had charge of bringing in Leduc Well No. 1. That strike launched a Canadian oil boom.

He was born at Mandan, N.Dak., the son of a well-to-do hardware merchant and wheat grower. He enjoys sailing his 38-foot twin-engine power boat on summer weekends.   WALTER F. MORSE

HAITI remained the poorest of the Western Hemisphere countries. Its per capita income was $70 per annum or less. The illiteracy rate was about 90 per cent of a population numbering approximately 4,700,000 people. Coffee shipments, Haiti's main source of income on the export market, were down to an estimated 300,000 to 325,000 bags. This compared to 364,000 bags in 1964 and 500,000 to 550,000 in other years.

Gross reserves, which stood at $4,100,000 in mid-1965, were down from the $4,900,000 of a year earlier and were only up seasonally from the $2,900,000 at the start of 1965.

The nation's financial difficulties were eased somewhat when the International Monetary Fund gave it a stand-by authority to borrow up to $4,000,000 in foreign currencies during the year starting Oct. 1, 1965.

Congress ended its six-month session in September by giving President François Duvalier full power—as it had every year in the past—to adopt any economic and political measures needed to "preserve the sovereignty and integrity of the nation." Rebel groups, meanwhile, remained active in the Jérémie area of southwest Haiti.

Population: 4,706,000. **Government:** President François Duvalier. **Monetary Unit:** gourde (5 = U.S. $1). **Foreign Trade:** exports, $40,000,000; imports, $41,000,000. **Principal Exports:** bananas, coffee, cotton, sisal, sugar.   MARY C. WEBSTER

HANDICAPPED, THE.

HANDICAPPED, THE. A total of 136,859 disabled persons were returned to useful employment during the year ended June 30, 1965. Of these, Pennsylvania led all the states with the employment of 12,794 persons. New York was second with 9,067, and North Carolina third with 8,545.

The first Inter-American Workshop on Mental Retardation was held in Puerto Rico, October 17 to 22. Delegates from 17 countries attended.

Ralph R. Serafinn of Garden City Park, N.Y., developed a telephone device to aid deaf persons by converting long and short sounds into flashes of light. A caller can tap or hum his message into the mouthpiece in Morse code and the deaf person will receive the message as dots and dashes of light.

Awards in 1965 included:

The Public Personnel Award for 1964 of the President's Committee on Employment of the Handicapped to Courtland C. Riddle of Toledo, Ohio.

Handicapped American of the Year for 1964 to Roger Warren Irving of St. Petersburg, Fla.

Employer of the Year for 1964 to Charles F. Adams, President of Raytheon Co., Lexington, Mass.

Physician of the Year for 1964 to Dr. William A. Spencer of Houston, Tex.

Miss Handicapped America for 1964 to Linda Shoemaker of Gray, Iowa.

National Essay Contest, first prize to Marilyn Dautrich, 17, of Salt Lake City.   JOSEPH P. ANDERSON

See also BLINDNESS; HEALTH; MEDICINE; MENTAL HEALTH; OLD AGE; SOCIAL WELFARE.

HARMEL, PIERRE CHARLES JOSÉ MARIE

HARMEL, PIERRE CHARLES JOSÉ MARIE (1911–   ), a former tax law professor who helped form Belgium's Social Christian party in 1946, was named prime minister by King Baudouin I on June 18. He replaced Théodore Lefèvre, also a Social Christian party member. Harmel was sworn in on July 28. See BELGIUM.

The new prime minister was born on March 16, 1911, in Brussels, where his father was a prosperous industrialist. During the 1930s, he was president of his nation's Christian Youth Movement, a Roman Catholic organization. He became a reserve lieutenant in 1940, when Germany invaded Belgium.

Since 1946, Prime Minister Harmel has represented Liège in the Belgian chamber of representatives. In 1949, however, he served as a delegate to the United Nations (UN). He was appointed president of the Belgian delegation to the UN Educational, Scientific, and Cultural Organization (UNESCO) in 1952. From 1950 to 1961, Harmel held four cabinet posts: minister of public instruction, public offices, cultural affairs, and justice.

An expert on the tensions between French- and Flemish-speaking communities of Belgium, Harmel understands Flemish perfectly and speaks it with facility. He is about six feet tall, blue-eyed, and almost entirely bald. He is a man of quiet personality, patient, methodical, and courteous. He and Mme. Harmel and their six children live in the Mont-St. Martin section of Liège.   WALTER F. MORSE

HARNESS RACING.

HARNESS RACING. Bret Hanover, a three-year-old pacer, won horse-of-the-year honors for the second successive season. His unbeaten streak reached 35 races before he was defeated by Adios Vic. Bret's victories included the triple crown races of pacing, the Cane Futurity at Yonkers Raceway, Little Brown Jug at Delaware, Ohio; and Messenger Stakes at Roosevelt Raceway. He set world records on both mile and half-mile tracks, and won a record $340,798 for the year.

The Hambletonian, at DuQuoin, Ill., was won by Egyptian Candor, and Noble Victory won the Yonkers Futurity. Armbro Flite took the Kentucky Futurity, and then beat Egyptian Candor and Noble Victory in the Dexter Cup trot at Roosevelt Raceway to win the championship in the three-year-old trotters' division.

Despite a big financial bid for the Hambletonian, it was decided to keep the 39-year-old trotting classic at DuQuoin, Ill., rather than move it to the Liberty Belle Raceway of Pennsylvania.

Romeo Hanover was voted the outstanding two-year-old pacer; Kerry Way, the top juvenile trotter; and Cardigan Bay, leading pacer among older horses. Speedy Scot won top honors among the older trotters. Billy Haughton of Oyster Bay Cove, N.Y., led the harness drivers in earnings, and Bob Farrington of Richwood, Ohio, drove the most winners.   STANLEY ISAACS

HARPER, JOHN DICKSON

HARPER, JOHN DICKSON (1910–   ), whose work with the Aluminum Company of America began while he was in high school, was named chief executive officer of the nation's largest producer of aluminum on April 19. Harper had been president since 1963. He succeeded Lawrence Litchfield, Jr., who continued as board chairman.

During vacations at Friendsville (Tenn.) High School, Harper worked at one of Alcoa's plants in that state. He continued to do so while he attended the University of Tennessee. On graduation in 1933 he took his first full-time job with the company, handling a powerhouse switchboard. Rising steadily in the organization, he spent 18 years in its Tennessee plants. In 1951 the top management at Pittsburgh chose him to put in operation and manage a new $100,000,000 smelter plant at Rockdale, Tex.

In 1955 he was called to Pittsburgh to become assistant general manager of Alcoa's smelting division. In the next half-dozen years he advanced to executive vice-president of the entire company, whose sales exceed $1,000,000,000 a year.

With that background, Harper is understandably a man of impressive technical skill in addition to his administrative abilities. He has been described as "tough, warm, human, and instantly perceptive." He was married in 1937 to Samma Lucille McCrary of Fall Branch, Tenn. They have three sons.   WALTER F. MORSE

HARRIS, PATRICIA ROBERTS (1924-   ), attorney and educator, was appointed U.S. ambassador to the grand duchy of Luxembourg by President Lyndon B. Johnson in May, 1965. She is the first American Negro woman to serve as an ambassador. The attractive former Department of Justice attorney served in the Criminal Division's appeals and research section (1960-1961). President John F. Kennedy appointed her cochairman of the National Women's Committee on Civil Rights in 1963. When President Johnson created the Commission on the Status of Puerto Rico in 1964, Mrs. Harris was among its 13 members.

While at Howard University, Mrs. Harris served as dean of students and lecturer in law (1961-1963), and was advanced to assistant (1963) and associate (1965) professor of law. She won her J.D. degree at George Washington University Law School (1960), where she was a research assistant.

Patricia Roberts was born in Mattoon, Ill. She was elected to Phi Beta Kappa and graduated *summa cum laude* at Howard University in 1945. She did graduate work in industrial relations at the University of Chicago, and was Young Women's Christian Association program director in Chicago (1946-1949). She also served as assistant director (1949-1953) of the American Council for Human Rights. Patricia Roberts and Washington (D.C.) attorney William Beasley Harris were married in 1955.

HEALTH. Four major health bills were signed by President Lyndon B. Johnson in 1965. They provided for medical care for the aged, disease immunization programs, health research, and new controls on the sale of drugs.

The Medicare bill, signed into law on July 30, provides hospital insurance and health care for the elderly through a federalized system (see MEDICARE). A few days later, the President signed a bill extending federal grants to carry out immunization plans against contagious diseases. The bill provides $33,000,000 over a three-year period for mass immunization programs against diphtheria, measles, polio, tetanus, and whooping cough. It also provides $24,000,000 for health services for migratory farmworkers, and $50,000,000 for Public Health Service grants in the fields of general health services, mental health, and services for the chronically ill and aged.

On August 9, President Johnson signed a $280,-000,000 health research bill and announced that he was setting up a White House study group to define U.S. goals in health, education, and "happiness."

A drug abuse control act became law on July 15 when the President signed a bill to keep amphetamines (goof balls) and barbiturates from being used for antisocial, illegal, or nonmedical purposes.

VD Campaign. A counter attack against venereal disease (VD) was started by medical and public health organizations. The disease has been on the increase in the United States, especially among youth. The U.S. Communicable Disease Center reported that syphilis has risen 230 per cent among teen-agers since 1956. Part of the reason for this was attributable to the increasing resistance on the part of certain VD organisms to penicillin. The high rate among teen-agers was also due to the fact that they tend not to seek treatment, either out of ignorance or because they fear exposure.

Rabies. The incidence of rabies among wild animals caused concern in some parts of the United States. In one county in Tennessee, more than 100 persons were bitten by rabid foxes. Some public health officials called this the worst rabies epidemic among animals in recent history.

Diet and Heart Disease. Controversy continued over possible relationships between diet and heart disease. A number of studies were underway to determine what correlation exists between the two. The American Heart Association stated, however, that a sufficient correlation had been established to warrant the recommendation of a dietary program for all citizens. They suggested a diet of less animal (saturated) fat, and less foods rich in cholesterol. Many scientists and physicians believe that no such recommendations should be made until investigations of diet-heart disease relationships are completed.   HUGH H. HUSSEY

See also DENTISTRY; HOSPITAL; MEDICINE; MENTAL HEALTH.

HEATH, EDWARD RICHARD GEORGE (1916-   ), was elected leader of Great Britain's Conservative party on July 27, succeeding Sir Alec Douglas-Home (see GREAT BRITAIN).

The new party leader is regarded as an aggressive political campaigner. He was elected to parliament in 1950. In 1955, at the age of 39, he was made whip of the Conservative party in the House of Commons. Under Conservative party governments, he has served as minister of labor, president of the board of trade, and lord privy seal.

Heath was born July 9, 1916, at Broadstairs, Kent, a resort town on the English Channel, where his father, William G. Heath, was a building contractor. He attended Balliol College, Oxford University, on a music scholarship, playing the organ for church services.

Although he entered the royal artillery in World War II as a private in 1940, he advanced to the rank of lieutenant colonel in 1945 as a result of his brilliant combat record. After the war, he worked briefly in the ministry of civil service, then went to Brown, Shipley, one of London's oldest merchant banks, as a junior executive. He entered politics while working there.

Heath is one of the few men who have achieved power in the Conservative party without the advantage of being from one of Britain's leading families. He is a bachelor.   WALTER F. MORSE

HIGHWAY. See ROADS AND HIGHWAYS.

HINES, JOHN ELBRIDGE (1910-   ), Bishop of the Episcopal Diocese of Texas for the past 10 years, was installed as Presiding Bishop of the Episcopal Church in the United States in January. He is the 22nd Bishop to head the nation's fourth largest (3,500,000 members) Protestant denomination. The National Cathedral (Church of Saint Peter and Saint Paul) in Washington, D.C., is his official church now, while his working office is at the Episcopal Church Center in New York City. The Bishop's residence is in Greenwich, Conn., the Episcopal Church's national conference center.

The new Presiding Bishop is considered a liberal and is an advocate of integration. He was born in Seneca, S.C. His physican father was a Presbyterian, and his mother an Episcopalian. Four of their children grew up in their father's church, and five, including John, followed their mother's faith.

John Hines is a graduate of the University of the South (1930) and Virginia Theological Seminary (1933, D.D., 1946). Ordained in 1933, he served at the Church of Saint Michael and Saint George in Saint Louis (Mo.). He was rector of the Trinity Episcopal Church (1935-1937) in Hannibal, Mo., and of the Augustana (Ga.) Saint Paul's Episcopal Church (1937-1941), and of Houston's Christ Episcopal Church (1941-1945). He was elected Bishop Coadjutor of the Texas Diocese in 1945.

HOBBIES. A major change was made in the minting of United States coins, an action that provoked wide discussion among coin collectors. Stamp collectors were cheered by the issuance of a completely new series of regular U.S. stamps, the first such change in more than 10 years.

Coins. Opinion was divided on the probable reaction of coin collectors to the silver-saving coinage bill which President Lyndon B. Johnson signed in August. The act, which ended a silver tradition going back to 1792, cut the silver content of half dollars from 90 to 40 per cent and called for the production of new silverless quarters and dimes consisting of a sandwich of cupronickel over a pure copper core. See MONEY.

The need for the new coinage act resulted from a rapid growth in the world consumption of silver while production remained essentially stagnant. The first of the new coins, quarters, began appearing in November. The President said 3,500,000,000 would be produced in the next 12 months and twice that many, if necessary, in the 12 months after that. The coinage bill also prohibited the minting of new silver dollars for five years.

The phenomenon of the Kennedy half dollar continued. The 1965 figures were not in, but a record-breaking 202,000,000 of the Kennedy halves were minted in 1964, breaking the previous one-year

Wide World

SLOT-CAR RACING was the hobby that drew most interest and excitement in 1965. At this Detroit track, six of the tiny electric-powered cars vied for honors.

record of 92,300,000 halves produced in 1963. Yet all but a tiny percentage of the Kennedy halves have been swallowed up by collectors, hoarders, speculators, coin dealers, and novelty manufacturers.

Shortly after Winston Churchill's death, the British government announced plans to break precedent and issue a Churchill crown (a five shilling coin worth 70 cents in U.S. money). In more than 2,000 years, no British coin had ever borne the portrait of a commoner.

Stamps. Stamp collectors showed that they, too, could get excited over their hobby. In June, sheets of United Nations (UN) souvenir stamps, commemorating the International Cooperation Year, went on sale at the UN building in New York City and a near riot resulted. Because of a limit of five sheets to a customer, whole families stood in line. Apparently the collectors were aware of the fact that a 1955 UN issue, commemorating the 10th anniversary of the signing of the UN Charter and originally issued at 15 cents, is now selling at around $40. But only 300,000 of those stamps had been printed, while 2,000,000 of the 1965 issue were available.

For the first time since 1954 a new series of 18 regular (as opposed to commemorative) stamps was announced by the U.S. Post Office Department. It will be known as the Prominent American series. The first of the series to be issued was a Lincoln 4-cent stamp which came out in November. The remaining ones will be issued over the next three or four years. Among those in the series to appear for the first time on regular stamps will be Franklin D. Roosevelt, John F. Kennedy, and Frederick Douglass, a runaway slave who later became U.S. minister to Haiti.

The Post Office Department announced in September that it would close the 44-year old Philatelic Sales Agency in Washington on October 9 and that its successor, the Philatelic Sales Unit, would accept only orders of $25 or more. The American Philatelic Society condemned the change and accused the department of "catering to big money." Postmaster John A. Gronouski, Jr., relented and established a system of fees ranging from 50 cents on orders of one to 500 stamps up to $22.50 for 100,000 or more.

Commemoratives. Among those honored on the U.S. commemorative stamps were Winston Churchill, who was also honored by most of the stamp-issuing countries in the Free World, Adlai Stevenson, Robert Fulton, the poet Dante, and Herbert Hoover. An innovation in U.S. stamp design was a Salvation Army commemorative which made its impact entirely by lettering and coloring.

Great Britain, usually one of the most conservative of nations in stamp issuing policy, issued a stamp commemorating the 700th anniversary of Parliament, which was three times the width of ordinary general issues. Also for the first time Great Britain issued a block of six stamps in one unit. It commemorated the Battle of Britain.   THEODORE M. O'LEARY

HODGES, C. WALTER (1909-   ), English artist-author, was awarded the Kate Greenaway medal in 1965 for *Shakespeare's Theatre*. Its lively, informative illustrations complement in every way the authoritative and superbly written text. *The Namesake*, his second historical novel for children, was a runner-up in 1965 for the Carnegie medal.

The theater has long fascinated Walter Hodges. He designed scenery and costumes at London's Everyman Theatre early in his career (1928-1930). He was one of the designers of the Mermaid Theatre (1951) in London, and has worked on productions there. The Elizabethan (Shakespearian) theater, however, is his specialty. *Shakespeare and the Players* (1948) was especially recommended for school libraries. *The Globe Restored* (1954), an illustrated study of the Elizabethan theater for adults, also was recommended for libraries. Hodges has illustrated many books by Rosemary Sutcliff, William Mayne, E. Nesbit Bland, and other authors.

C. Walter Hodges was born in Kent, England, and studied at Goldsmith's Art College. His World War II service included the Normandy Beach landings. He is married, has two sons, and lives in Sussex.

See also LITERATURE FOR CHILDREN (Awards).

HOME ECONOMICS. See FASHION; FOOD; FUTURE HOMEMAKERS OF AMERICA; INTERIOR DESIGN.

HOME FURNISHINGS. See INTERIOR DESIGN.

HONDURAS. Air Force Colonel Osvaldo López Arellano was inaugurated constitutional president on June 6. He had been elected March 23 by the new constituent assembly in which his party earlier had captured 35 of the 64 seats. López had held power since 1963 after a military junta ousted the government of José Ramón Villeda Morales.

The nation's economic growth rate for 1965 was expected to exceed the 6.5 per cent Gross National Product (GNP) increase registered in 1964. At the end of June, international reserves had reached a seasonal peak of $27,900,000, up $13,700,000 over December, and $6,600,000 more than the seasonal peak of June, 1964. An inflow of investments and loan capital, plus heavy banana exports, were major factors in the improved position.

During the year, Honduras received sizable loans from various international agencies for the construction of its 125-mile Tegucigalpa-San Pedro Sula highway. Its ultimate cost was estimated at $24,500,000. An additional $5,200,000 loan was made by the Agency for International Development toward the construction of 600 kilometers of farm-to-market roads.

Population: 2,223,000. **Government:** President Osvaldo López Arellano. **Monetary Unit:** lempira (2 = U.S. $1). **Foreign Trade:** exports, $95,000,000; imports, $102,000,000. **Principal Exports:** bananas and plantains, coffee, lumber.   MARY C. WEBSTER

See also LATIN AMERICA.

Ray Wolfe, Jr., *Sports Illustrated* © Time Inc.

WINNING JUMP by Maryland-bred Jay Trump and jockey Tommy Smith, left, assured first U.S. victory in British Grand National Steeplechase.

MAJOR U.S. RACES OF 1965

Race	Winner	Value to Winner
Arlington Classic	Tom Rolfe	$62,500
Arlington-Washington Futurity	Buckpasser	190,475
Belmont Stakes	Hail to All	104,150
Brooklyn Handicap	Pia Star	69,680
Champagne Stakes	Buckpasser	163,875
Delaware Handicap	Steeple Jill	80,122
Flamingo Stakes	Native Charger	93,340
Garden State Stakes	Prince Saim	187,167
Gardenia Stakes	Moccasin	110,214
Gulfstream Handicap	Ampose	71,900
Hollywood Derby	Terry's Secret	80,200
Hollywood Gold Cup	Native Diver	102,100
Jockey Club Gold Cup	Roman Brother	71,500
Kentucky Derby	Lucky Debonair	112,000
Metropolitan Handicap	Gun Bow	72,540
New Hampshire Sweepstakes	Pass the Word	182,143
Preakness	Tom Rolfe	128,100
Santa Anita Derby	Lucky Debonair	89,300
Santa Anita Handicap	Hill Rise	100,000
Suburban Handicap	Pia Star	70,720
Widener Handicap	Primordial II	88,140
Woodward Stakes	Roman Brother	71,240

MAJOR FOREIGN RACES OF 1965

Epsom Derby	Sea Bird	182,824
Grand National Steeplechase	Jay Trump	62,975
Grand Prix de Paris	Hyeres III	150,000
Irish Derby	Meadow Court	155,820
Prix de l'Arc de Triomphe	Sea Bird	217,000

HORSE RACING. The unprecedented five-year-reign of Mrs. Richard C. duPont's Kelso as horse-of-the-year was ended when an eye injury took the horse out of competition. At year's end the honors were split between Louis Wolfson's four-year-old gelding, Roman Brother, which won five races in 14 starts, and Moccasin, a two-year-old filly owned by the Claiborne Farm. This filly won all of its eight races by huge margins, and earned $319,731.

Buckpasser was the outstanding two-year-old colt, with nine victories in 11 starts for a one-year earnings record by a juvenile of $568,096. The horse is owned by Ogden Phipps.

The triple crown for three-year-olds was divided among three colts. Lucky Debonair, owned by Mrs. Ada L. Rice, won the Kentucky Derby, but then broke down in the Preakness. Tom Rolfe, owned by Raymond Guest, which was third in the Derby, took the Preakness, and was second to Mrs. Ben Cohen's Hail to All in the Belmont Stakes. Tom Rolfe then captured three-year-old honors by winning four big races at Chicago, though it failed to place in the Prix de l'Arc de Triomphe at Paris.

What a Treat was voted the top three-year-old filly. Old Hat won honors among handicap fillies and mares, while Bon Nouvel was the top steeplechase horse for the second straight year.

Braulio Baeza led the jockeys in earnings, though Jesse Davidson, who rode the Ohio and West Virginia circuit, rode the most winners. STANLEY ISAACS

HOSPITAL. The American Medical Association (AMA) and the American Hospital Association (AHA) agreed on a single program for accreditation of nursing homes, and requested the Joint Commission on Accreditation of Hospitals to surpervise this activity. The commission includes representatives of AMA, AHA, American College of Surgeons, and American College of Physicians. Nursing home accreditations had previously been carried out separately by the AMA and the AHA.

The Joint Commission pointed out in its annual report that, while accredited hospitals in the United States represent only 64 per cent of all hospital beds, they account for 85 per cent of all admissions and 88 per cent of all births.

Accord between the AMA and AHA was not reached, however, in regard to the services of anesthesiologists, pathologists, psychiatrists, and radiologists under the Social Security-financed Medicare program. The AHA had sought to have such services paid for as hospital services under the Medicare program. The AMA, on the other hand, sought successfully to exclude these services. They are included only under a supplementary insurance program.

The U.S. Department of Health, Education, and Welfare announced in September that it was stepping up enforcement of the law against racial discrimination in more than 19,000 hospitals and other health facilities. HUGH H. HUSSEY

See also HEALTH; MEDICARE.

HOTEL operators and owners failed to participate in the booming U.S. economy. Revenues edged up only slightly from the $4,800,000,000 in 1964. Overseas, both American- and foreign-owned hotels prospered in the foreign travel boom. Despite the construction of some new hotels, such as the Pontchartrain in Detroit and the Sheraton-Boston, profits from real estate deals involving demolition created most of the profits at home. In fact, U.S. occupancy averaged only 64 per cent, while abroad, the average soared to 90 per cent or higher.

With the closing of the New York World's Fair, which lured $150,000,000 to the city's hotels, the anticipated closing of many well-known hotels began. The Chatham, Madison, Park Lane, Savoy-Plaza, and Sheraton East were among the first gone or scheduled to go.

Construction abroad failed to match the growth of tourist traffic overseas, where hotels enjoyed lower costs and favorable foreign exchange and tax benefits. By the end of the year, however, more than 100 American-operated hotels were located in some 100 cities abroad. Intercontinental Hotel Corporation opened hotels in New Delhi, India; Pago Pago, Western Samoa; and Hanover, Germany, for a total of 31 with over 10,000 rooms. The Hilton chain opened its 29th overseas hotel, the Tel Aviv-Hilton in Israel. Sheraton now operates 15 units abroad.   WILLIAM D. PATTERSON

HOUSING. President Lyndon B. Johnson signed the landmark Department of Housing and Urban Development Act on Sept. 9, 1965. In so doing, he established the 11th department of the federal government. The new law transferred to the department secretary "all of the functions, powers, and duties" of the Federal Housing Administration, the Housing and Home Finance Agency, and several other government bureaus. They included the Community Facilities Administration, the Federal National Mortgage Association, the Public Housing Administration, and the Urban Renewal Administration. These are the federal agencies that have evolved since the 1930s to administer the provisions of the nation's federal housing laws.

The bill was sent up to the President by a Congress that adopted the measure in both its houses by voice vote. Passage of such legislation had been a major goal of President John F. Kennedy. He first proposed the setting up of a department of urban affairs in 1962. (Despite the victory, however, President Johnson had not appointed a secretary to head the department by year-end.)

Expanded Housing Law. As significant as the creation of the new department was the enactment, on August 10, of the Housing and Urban Development Act of 1965. The act extends the provisions of earlier federal housing laws and introduces new programs of financial assistance for coping with housing problems and urban development needs.

After more than three months of congressional deliberation over the contents of the complex law, the Senate adopted the bill by a voice vote and the House of Representatives voted 251 to 168 for passage. The Congress thus authorized the expenditure over a four-year period of about $8,243,000,000 for the continuation of programs of mortgage guaranty, college housing, housing for the elderly, public and rural housing, and urban planning and renewal.

The Rent Supplement. The key new provision of the act—one that caused considerable controversy—was its so-called "rent supplement" section. Under this provision, the federal government will pay for a portion of the rent of low-income families accepted as tenants in new nonprofit housing, built by private groups, such as church organizations or labor unions. The family will pay about 25 per cent of its income for rent. The government will make up the difference. It thus hopes to stimulate construction of housing units. However, the House Appropriations Committee blocked implementation of the rent supplement provision by refusing to appropriate funds.

Other features of the housing law include:

• A program whereby existing *private* housing may be leased by local public housing agencies for use as *public* housing.

• Grants of up to $1,500 to property owners in officially designated urban renewal and code enforcement areas to cover the cost of repairs and improvements necessary to make the structures conform to urban renewal requirements.

• Matching grants to assist localities in programs of urban beautification and improvement of open-space and other public lands.

Housing Starts. The 1965 housing construction record indicated continued stabilization of the market. Total starts at year-end numbered slightly over 1,400,000—about 100,000 fewer than in 1964. New housing construction value was $21,225,000,-000 in 1965, as compared to $21,275,000,000 in 1964. Thus, the upward spiral, which reached its peak in 1963, has been leveling off since.

But the factors that make up a continuing healthy housing economy continued. They included: an ample supply of mortgage funds; rising personal income; the highly mobile U.S. population; the new rent supplement program, which can be revived if Congress appropriates funds in 1966; and the demolishing of approximately 400,000 dwelling units by urban renewal because of highway construction.

"One Fight." Secretary of the Interior Stewart L. Udall spoke in Chicago in December at the annual convention of the National Association of Home Builders. He urged conservationists and developers to work together. "It's all one fight," he said, "the fight against water and air pollution, the fight . . . to provide open space for recreation, and to build adequate housing . . ."   J. ROBERT DUMOUCHEL

See also ARCHITECTURE; CITY PLANNING; ECONOMY, THE (chart).

HOUSTON gained world attention in 1965 as the Manned Spacecraft Center directed the historic voyages of the Gemini astronauts. Throughout the flights, the complex facility flawlessly performed the role set for it by the National Aeronautics and Space Administration four years earlier.

The sports world, too, looked to Houston. Harris County Dome Stadium, the first in the United States, seemed to start a fashion in such structures in other cities around the country.

The area grew in size, population, and wealth. On March 24, Houston officially became a five-county metropolitan area. Its estimated population of 1,700,000 made it the largest metropolitan area in the South and Southwest. The city of Houston annexed 80 square miles on November 16, and planned to annex another 10.

Two culturally significant facilities were begun: July, the $12,000,000 National Space Hall of Fame Convention and Exhibit Center, and in October the Jesse H. Jones Hall for the Performing Arts, to cost $6,500,000. In addition, a distinguished design for the new $2,000,000 Alley Theater was approved.

On November 2, incumbent Mayor Louie Welch defeated former mayor Lewis Cutrer to win another two-year term. Previously, on May 19, the voters turned out in unusually large numbers to back a $59,800,000 school bond issue, the largest in Houston's history.   DONALD W. LIEF

HOWE, HAROLD II (1918-   ), was named U.S. Commissioner of Education late in 1965. The former commissioner, Francis Keppel, was given the additional assignment of Assistant Secretary for Education in September, 1965, pending Howe's assumption of office in January, 1966. This newly established post is to be a full-time position designed to cope with the growing responsibilities of federal agencies dealing with recent education, civil rights, rights, and war-on-poverty legislation.

Yale-Columbia educated Harold Howe has experience with both private and public schools. He was director the past year of the newly founded Learning Institute of North Carolina, a nonprofit organization concerned with education as related to poverty and to gifted children. Howe was superintendent of schools in Scarsdale, N.Y. (1960-1964), and principal of high schools in Andover (1950-1953) and Newton (1957-1960) in Massachusetts, and of Walnut Hills (1953-1957) in Cincinnati, Ohio. Earlier in his career, Howe taught at the Darrow School in New Lebanon, N.Y., and at Phillips Academy in Andover, Mass.

Harold Howe was born in Hartford, Conn., the son of a Presbyterian minister and former Dartmouth College professor and Hampton Institute president. His grandfather, Union Army General Samuel Chapman Armstrong, was a founder of Hampton (1868), the Virginia college for Negroes.

See also EDUCATION.

HUMPHREY, HUBERT HORATIO (1911-   ) was inaugurated as 38th Vice-President of the United States on Jan. 20, 1965. Putting in a 14-to-16-hour day, he met with President Lyndon B. Johnson four or five times a week, represented him in meetings with congressional leaders, attended sessions of the Cabinet and the National Security Council, and was charged by the President with responsibility for federal programs on civil rights, space, urban affairs, and matters of economic policy. He seemed to be the busiest Vice-President ever, and actually took charge of the government for a few hours in October when the President underwent surgery (see PRESIDENT OF THE U.S.).

Humphrey helped the President in many capacities. He successfully mediated the civil rights dispute in Bogalusa, La., in April. He was tireless in addressing conventions and civil rights groups. In June, he had conferred with French President Charles de Gaulle in Paris.

As a leading Democrat, Humphrey took an active part in the campaigns for local Democratic candidates, particularly in New York, Philadelphia, and Ohio (see DEMOCRATIC PARTY). To avoid any possible conflict of interest, Humphrey, before his inauguration, had put more than $90,000 of $171,396 total of net assets in trust. Throughout 1965, the Vice-President and his family lived in their $28,000 home in Chevy Chase.   CAROL L. THOMPSON

HUNGARY. The trend toward liberalization continued during 1965 but at a somewhat slower pace. An estimated 1,500,000 Hungarians traveled abroad as compared to 942,000 the previous year. A large percentage visited the West and there were indications that the regime was concerned by the growing numbers who had failed to return.

The economy remained stagnant, suffering from Europe's "green winter," which caused disastrous floods along the Danube River. The János Kádár regime, like those of other Central European communist nations, stepped-up economic reforms. It emphasized the need to encourage individual enterprises to experiment, to stress quality, and to train executives. But the dismissal of some 14,000 workers in 1965 failed to yield the desired reduction of bureaucracy.

On June 28, János Kádár resigned the premiership and named his close adviser and former deputy premier Gyula Kállai to succeed him. Kádár, however, retained his post as first secretary of the Hungarian Communist party. See KÁLLAI, GYULA.

Population: 10,135,000. **Government:** Communist Party First Secretary János Kádár; Premier Gyula Kállai; President István Dobi. **Monetary Unit:** forint (11.74=U.S. $1). **Foreign Trade:** exports, $1,352,000,000; imports, $1,461,000,000. **Principal Exports:** animal products, metals, motor vehicles, quarry products.   TOM AND HARLE DAMMANN

See also EUROPE.

HUNTING AND FISHING. The biggest hunting news, surprisingly, had nothing to do with actual hunting. In Washington, D.C., lawmakers studied the controversial bill S.1592, commonly called the antigun bill, proposed by Senator Thomas J. Dodd of Connecticut. Originally drawn up as an attempt at crime control, the Dodd bill became the rallying point of all antigun groups following the death of President John F. Kennedy. S.1592 did not come to a congressional vote in 1965, nor was it killed. The National Rifle Association and many hunters saw the congressional move as the first step in a campaign that would slowly choke off all use of guns.

According to the U.S. Bureau of Sport Fisheries and Wildlife report on the big game inventory for 1964 (released in August, 1965), hunting continued to increase in the United States. In spite of a larger game harvest, states reported the same or larger game populations on all species, with only a few isolated exceptions.

For Fishermen the biggest news in 1965 was that the largest fresh-water bodies of water in North America, the Great Lakes, showed signs of regaining their once huge fishing potential. Formerly a stronghold of big lake trout, commercial fishing had reduced the population of the "lakers" to a serious level. Then, the parasitic sea lamprey moved in, nearly eliminating lake trout in Lakes Huron and Michigan and making them very scarce in Lake Superior. See FISHERY.

In an effort to save fishing in Lake Superior, the United States and Canada restricted commercial fishing and began a rush program to wipe out the lamprey with a specific poison added to lamprey spawning streams. When the lamprey population began to wane, thousands of hatchery lake trout were introduced into the lake.

The Problems in Lakes Michigan and Huron somewhat differed from those in Lake Superior. At about the time the lamprey had reduced lakers there, the Saint Lawrence Seaway was completed, allowing the *alewife*, a small baitfish, to enter the lakes. With the ideal conditions they found, the fish reproduced in such large numbers that they crowded other fish. They periodically had huge die-offs, and beaches were littered with dead fish. State of Michigan biologists hoped they had found the solution in the *coho*, or silver salmon, a West Coast fish. The coho not only feeds on the alewife, but also spawns in streams where the eggs are safe from the alewife. In 1966, 800,000 cohos will be released into streams that flow into Lakes Michigan and Superior.

Even in polluted Lake Erie, which has been called a biological desert, some progress was made. But by the end of the year, it was obvious that any improvement in fishing conditions would come slowly. See Section Two, POLLUTED AMERICA.

During 1965, no fresh-water world records were broken by anglers, according to *Field & Stream* magazine, the official record keeper. CLARE CONLEY

ICE HOCKEY. The Detroit Red Wings won their first regular season championship in eight years, and the second-place Montreal Canadiens won the Stanley Cup play-offs, ending a three-year monopoly by the Toronto Maple Leafs. On June 25, the National Hockey League voted to expand to two six-team divisions no later than the 1967-1968 season. St. Louis and Los Angeles were awarded the first two franchises.

The Rochester Americans won the Calder Cup play-offs of the American Hockey League. Michigan Tech captured the National Collegiate Athletic Association (NCAA) title, defeating Boston College in the finals at Brown University. Russia took first place in the International Tournament title at Colorado Springs, Colo., and the world ice hockey championships at Tampere, Finland, with a perfect record in seven games. The United States finished sixth in the eight-team field.

Awards in the National Hockey League:
Calder Trophy (top rookie), Roger Crozier, Detroit.
Hart Trophy (most valuable player), Bobby Hull, Chicago.
Lady Byng Trophy (sportsmanship), Hull, Chicago.
Norris Trophy (best defenseman), Pierre Pilote, Chicago.
Ross Trophy (leading scorer), Stan Mikita, Chicago.
Smythe Trophy (most valuable in Stanley Cup competition), Jean Beliveau, Montreal.
Vezina Trophy (leading goalie), Terry Sawchuck and Johnny Bower, Toronto. STANLEY ISAACS

ICE SKATING. The post-Olympic year was a big one for Petra Burka of Canada and Alain Calmat of France. At the World Figure Skating Championships in Colorado Springs, Colo., in March, 18-year-old Miss Burka won the women's title by defeating European champion Regine Heitzer of Austria and U.S. champion Peggy Fleming. Calmat, 24, won the men's crown. He was followed by Scott Allen of the United States and Donald Knight of Canada. Olympic champions Ludmilla Belousova and Oleg Protopopov of Russia captured the pairs competition, while Eva Romanova and her brother, Pavel, of Czechoslovakia won the ice dance title.

In the North American championships, held at Rochester, N.Y., the U.S. team captured its first major titles since the 1961 plane crash that killed 18 of the best U.S. skaters. The men's title was taken by Gary Visconti of Detroit, who defeated Scott Allen, as he had done the week before in competition for the U.S. title. The pairs championship was taken by Vivian and Ronald Joseph of the United States and the dance competition was won by another U.S. couple, Lorna Dyer and John Carrell. The women's title went to Miss Burka.

Speed Skating had Per Ivar Moe, an 18-year-old Norwegian, as the winner of the men's world championship at Oslo, Norway. At the same meet, a Soviet team dominated the women's events. Inga Vronina, three-time Russian titleholder, took top place for a record fourth time. JAMES O. DUNAWAY

ICELAND. Prime Minister Bjarni Benediktsson visited Norway in May for preliminary talks on joining the European Free Trade Association (EFTA). Iceland had steered clear of EFTA membership in previous years, mainly because its prime industry was fishery and it felt there would be little advantage in joining the association. Import duties levied by EFTA countries on Icelandic products, however, had caused some rethinking. Fishing results were disappointing in 1965. But fish exports were up, however, and the prices favorable.

A bill introduced in the *Althing* (parliament) in May provided for the harnessing of the Thjörsá River to generate electricity. Much of this power would be used to operate a projected aluminum factory which was expected to start producing about 30,000 tons annually in 1969.

The Icelanders, meanwhile, were looking forward to the opening of their first television station in 1966. It had been established with the assistance of other Scandinavian countries.

Population: 192,000. **Government:** President Ásgeir Ásgeirsson; Prime Minister Bjarni Benediktsson. **Monetary Unit:** krona (43.06 = U.S. $1). **Gross National Product:** 11,258,000,000 kronur. **Foreign Trade:** exports, $111,070,000; imports, $131,400,000. **Principal Exports:** fish products. KENNETH BROWN

See also EUROPE.

IMMIGRATION AND EMIGRATION. An immigration reform bill was passed by the Congress of the United States in 1965 and signed into law by President Lyndon B. Johnson in a ceremony at the Statue of Liberty on October 3. Under the new law, the national origins quota system, which for 40 years had favored immigrants from the British Isles and northern Europe was abolished.

The law, as President Johnson noted, "says simply that, from this day forth, those wishing to emigrate to America shall be admitted on the basis of their skills and their close relationship to those already here." No longer will race or nationality decree which immigrants shall enter the United States. Rather, priorities will go to relatives of U.S. citizens to reunite families; to specialists with needed skills; and to refugees from political, racial, or religious persecution.

After June 30, 1968, immigration from countries outside the Western Hemisphere will be limited to 170,000 persons each year. Children, spouses, and parents of U.S. citizens, however, will be admitted without counting against this figure. Under the new law, up to 20,000 from a single nation may come to the United States. Under the old law, for instance, only 308 Greeks and 5,666 Italians could enter the United States each year.

The law was widely hailed by ethnic groups, labor unions, and religious organizations, many of whom had worked for years to repeal the national origins quota system. However, opponents of a liberal immigration law, pressured Congress to add an amendment to the administration bill as a safeguard against a rapid increase in immigrants from the Western Hemisphere.

As a result, a ceiling was set on immigration from Canada and Latin America. A limit of 120,000 immigrants a year will be accepted from the countries of the Western Hemisphere. Previously, citizens of these countries enjoyed entry into the United States without restrictions.

The new law also established a Select Commission on Western Hemisphere Immigration. The commis-

Where They Came From

Since the U.S. began counting arrivals in 1820, some 43,000,000 immigrants have come to stay. The chief sources:

Germany	6,822,807
Italy	5,030,394
Ireland	4,699,064
Austria-Hungary	4,282,823
Canada	3,748,763
Russia	3,345,161
England	2,978,901
Scandinavia	2,458,805
Mexico	1,326,370
Scotland	797,808
France	703,786
Greece	503,463
Latin America*	494,072
Poland	458,107
China	415,084
Turkey	369,122
Japan	341,861
Africa (nonslave)	55,201

*Excluding Mexico   Time Inc. © 1965

sion will study immigration from Western Hemisphere countries, and its relation to and effects on U.S. population and employment. It will make its first report to Congress by June 1, 1967, and present its final report by Jan. 15, 1968.

Statistics for the fiscal year ended June 30, 1965: 296,697 aliens were admitted, against 292,248 in fiscal 1964. Also 104,299 persons became U.S. citizens. Of the 296,697 aliens admitted, 99,381 were quota and 197,316 nonquota.

Incoming visiting aliens totaled 2,075,967, a sharp increase over the 1,744,808 of fiscal 1964. In this category, 1,323,479 came on vacation, 175,500 on business, and 50,435 as students. The United States deported 10,143 aliens, an increase over the 8,746 deported in fiscal 1964. WILLIAM McGAFFIN

INCOME TAX. See TAXATION.

INDIA

For a country that has preached and practiced nonviolence, India was beset by violence on almost every front in 1965. It was at war with Pakistan over Kashmir and the Rann of Kutch. Its frontiers were threatened from Ladakh to Sikkim by Communist China. Even on the home front, the government was faced by rioting and violence over the language issue and optional food shortages. India emerged from those ordeals militarily crippled and economically groggy. But it also emerged with a new spirit of hope and confidence. Along with this confidence, however, there was a sense of isolation. During the Kashmir crisis, India felt that its Afro-Asian friendships had faded, that Britain was hostile, and that the United States was at best neutral. Feeling thus isolated, India turned inward for strength. Characteristic of this mood was the demand that India develop its own atomic bomb independent of either the United States' nuclear umbrella or uncertain United Nations (UN) protection.

The warfare in Kashmir, however, had handed India not so much a military triumph as a political bonanza—unification of the nation. All factions buried their differences in a wave of patriotism. The image of Prime Minister Lal Bahadur Shastri was transformed from that of a man representing merely the consensus of his political party to the status of a national hero.

Food Crisis. Shastri capitalized on his sudden strength to hammer away at self-sufficiency, especially in food. India had made striking food production gains in 1964-1965, with a crop totaling 89,000,000 tons, an increase of 11 per cent in one year. But one of the driest monsoon seasons in 30 years had struck the nation, and crop expectations for 1965-1966 were not expected to reach more than 76,000,000 tons. Food rationing was introduced for the first time since the 1940s in all the major cities. Each person was limited to 12 ounces of rice or wheat per day.

In the meantime, U.S. shipments of about 500,000 tons of wheat per month helped feed one out of every 15 Indians. The United States, however, wanted assurances of self-help. India, in turn, was apprehensive that U.S. food pressure was designed to force concessions in Kashmir. See Section Two, INSIDE RURAL INDIA.

Industrial Growth. In industry, results were spectacular in the first half of the year. Gross National Product (GNP) rose 7.3 per cent, and per capita income was up 4.9 per cent. Both figures were the highest in the nation's history. But economic dislocation caused by the Kashmir war, coupled with top priorities for food and armaments, slowed down this promising industrial boom.

Marvin Lichtner, *Life* Magazine © Time Inc.

GRIM-EYED INDIAN SOLDIER, his rifle ready, mans post in a mud-and-stone bunker near Srinagar, Kashmir, scene of an earlier attack.

BRUSH-WIELDING DEMONSTRATORS who favored Indian government's plan to replace English with Hindi as official language paint out English signs in New Delhi.

HANDS CLASPED in traditional greeting, India's Prime Minister Lal Bahadur Shastri reviews a guard of honor during a state visit to Nepal.

The Language Uproar. Old antagonisms were stirred anew in February when the government attempted to make Hindi the sole official language of the nation. The south was up in arms. To them, Hindi, a northern language, was more alien than English. In widespread riots that ensued, 50 people were killed. To re-establish order, the Shastri government was forced to restore English as the national language.

The Rann of Kutch. In April, India and Pakistan clashed again over yet another border dispute—a 13,000-square-mile swampland called the Rann of Kutch. Oil was the suspected prize. Pakistan claimed the boundary ran along the 24th parallel. India was equally adamant in maintaining that it lay along a ridge north of the parallel. After some fighting, which was wilder in its claims than in actual combat, British Prime Minister Harold Wilson succeeded in persuading the antagonists to sign a truce. See PAKISTAN.

Ultimatum in Sikkim. At the height of the war in Kashmir, Communist China delivered a crude ultimatum to India to dismantle its fortifications built on Chinese territory at the Sikkim border, or face invasion. Chinese motives were open to interpretation: perhaps one objective was to help Pakistan; it was also possible the move was made to disrupt UN efforts to effect a cease-fire in Kashmir. Too, Sikkim was particularly vulnerable as the key to the Chumbi valley and gateway to oil-rich Assam. But

Marvin Lichtner, *Life* Magazine © Time Inc.

DEADLY TRAP. Two turbaned Indian soldiers, part of a dawn patrol, lie in ambush for enemy infiltrators on roadside near Srinagar, summer capital of Kashmir.

India, holding firm, offered international inspection of its fortifications. Communist China lamely withdrew its ultimatum. Chinese troops massed all along India's Himalayan frontier, however, continued to fray Indian nerves.

Foreign Relations. India attempted to win back its leadership of the Afro-Asian world during the year. It fought hard to seat the Soviet Union in an abortive Afro-Asian conference scheduled in Algiers, Algeria. Its efforts, however, came to naught when the conference was eventually canceled.

The Indians also criticized the United States for bombing North Vietnam and it urged the resumption of the 14-nation Geneva conference to settle the Vietnamese war. But U.S. President Lyndon B. Johnson rebuffed Shastri for the criticism by abruptly postponing the latter's scheduled first visit to the United States. This, plus continuing Communist Chinese hostility on the diplomatic front and preoccupation with the Kashmiri problem, prevented the government of India from taking an active role in international affairs.

Population: 489,254,000. **Government:** President Sarvepalli Radhakrishnan; Prime Minister Lal Bahadur Shastri. **Monetary Unit:** rupee (4.78 = U.S. $1). **Gross National Product:** $46,000,000,000. **Foreign Trade:** exports, $1,800,000,000; imports, $2,900,000,000. **Principal Exports:** jute, tea, textiles. KEKI R. BHOTE

See also ASIA.

INDIAN, AMERICAN. Efforts to help a half million American Indians win their way to self-sufficiency were focused on education in 1965. Indian citizens were given new and better opportunities for making the transition from a reservation-oriented culture. About 140,000 Indians from age 6 through 18, a record number, were attending public schools or those operated by the Bureau of Indian Affairs.

More than 30,000 Indian adults attended basic education classes. In April, Congress authorized $15,000,000 annually for U.S. Indian adult vocational training. More than 4,500 Indians were training in about 600 job categories during the year. New schools were opened in 17 Indian communities.

One of the nation's most underprivileged groups with an average family income of $1,500 a year, Indians participated broadly in anti-poverty programs. Job Corps centers were operating in San Carlos and Winslow, Ariz.; Mexican Springs, N. Mex.; and Neah Bay, Wash., in 1965, with seven more expected to open in other Indian areas in 1966. More than 18,000 Indians took part in the Neighborhood Youth Corps and about 10,000 were enrolled in Project Head Start. See POVERTY.

Congress appropriated $20,800,000 for payment to 12 tribal groups for judgments awarded by the Indian Claims Commission. In a September intermediate order, the commission recognized the claim of the Sioux Nation to about 17,000,000 acres of western South Dakota land. A. L. NEWMAN

INDONESIA entered 1965 to the sound of a rooster crowing over Radio Malaysia. It was an ironic reminder that the nation had yet to "crush" the neighboring Federation of Malaysia, as President Sukarno had threatened to do. Before the year ended, an even greater irony was in store for Sukarno when he himself was nearly crushed by a military coup.

In the months that intervened, Sukarno continued to move his nation in the direction of Communist China. He sent delegations to Peking and he talked constantly in terms of the "New Emerging Forces," which largely meant Communist China, Indonesia, and the less developed nations. He canceled Indonesia's membership in the United Nations (UN) and flirted with the idea of a new international organization that would form an Asian rival to the UN. See UNITED NATIONS.

The "crush Malaysia" campaign continued, with major efforts being directed toward Sabah and Sarawak. Results, however, were dubious. Although guerrilla fighters slipped across the borders from Borneo with a fair amount of ease, they found stubborn and effective opposition facing them. Occasional Indonesian incursions from bases near Singapore were quickly mopped up by Malaysian forces. The whole campaign was basically one of saber rattling with few military moves of large-scale commitment. See MALAYSIA, FEDERATION OF.

Domestic Problems assumed far greater significance as the year moved on. Basically, Indonesia was a potentially wealthy country. Its economy, however, continued to decline steadily. Sukarno continued his national policies of seizing foreign-owned properties and assets. Rice, previously a major export, was now being imported on a large scale, and rubber and oil production dropped to new lows. The underlying economic decline accounted in part for the nation's political instability.

In a large measure, much of this instability was directly related to Sukarno's placatory attitude toward the Indonesian Communist Party (PKI). The PKI, claiming some 3,000,000 members, was becoming increasingly powerful, especially in Java. Backed whole-heartedly by the Chinese, they asked for weapons to arm some 10,000,000 peasants and workers. Sukarno refused, but he increasingly favored the communists with a new policy known as "Nationalism, Religion, and Communism" (NASAKOM). The army, however, under General Nasution, was opposed to this leftward drift. It became increasingly uneasy over signs that Indonesia's air force was being infiltrated by the communists. It was disturbed, too, over the PKI's increasing restiveness that manifested itself in street rioting and in the pillaging of U.S. libraries, the U.S. embassy, and other official Western residences.

Wide World

ANTICOMMUNIST STUDENTS in Djakarta put torch to university sponsored by pro-Communist Chinese following an unsuccessful attempt to oust President Sukarno.

Wide World

UNSMILING PRESIDENT Sukarno entertains U.S. diplomats Howard P. Jones, left, and William McCormick Blair. They met to discuss strained U.S.-Indonesian relations.

On October 1, Lieutenant Colonel Untung of the palace guard kidnaped several senior military officers. His adherents seized Radio Djakarta and announced that a 45-man cabinet had been formed to run the country. Sukarno, the regime announced, was under its protection. Known communists had been included in the cabinet as well as leftist air force officers.

The army, however, quickly subduing the rebel elements in Djakarta, moved against not only the air force dissidents, but against the PKI as well. Sukarno's leftist-leaning foreign minister was given an extended leave of absence abroad, and other ministers were given assignments abroad.

At year's end, Sukarno's position as president seemed safe but it appeared he had lost some of his power. The PKI, although it had not been destroyed, showed little inclination to contest the army openly. But the knowledge that an estimated 18,000 weapons were unaccounted for, plus known smuggling of arms into Indonesia by the Communist Chinese indicated that a showdown might still come. The year ended with both sides observing an uneasy truce.

Population: 106,777,000. **Government:** President and Premier Sukarno. **Monetary Unit:** rupiah (315 = U.S. $1). **Foreign Trade:** exports, $696,000,-000; imports, $502,000,000. **Principal Exports:** palm oil, petroleum, rubber.   JOHN N. STALKER

See also ASIA.

INSECT. Ever since Rachel Carson warned against the indiscriminate use of poisonous insecticides in her *Silent Spring* in 1962, scientists have stepped-up their search for other means of insect control. By 1965, the U.S. government was supporting a wide variety of research aimed at curbing insect populations safely.

Scientists were evaluating various chemical baits or lures that entice insects into traps. They were subjecting insects to radiation and rendering them sterile. In some areas of the world, the natural enemies of insect pests were being introduced and encouraged. In others, new insecticides which attack the nervous system, called organophosphates and carbamates, were being tested and used.

Chemicals have also been developed at the University of California (Los Angeles) to prevent insects' digestive systems from getting nourishment from food. When the chemicals, called antimetabolites, are consumed by an insect they cause it to starve to death no matter how much more food is eaten. The chemicals are nontoxic to human beings and are especially suited for protecting fibers, such as woolens and rugs, from insects.

Chemical Communication. Chemical signals emitted by an insect's glandular secretions now are believed to play a central role in the organization of insect societies. Edward O. Wilson, professor of zoology at Harvard University, found that chemical signals play some part in all nine currently recognized categories of communication and response exhibited by such social insects as ants and bees.

These chemicals, called pheromones, apparently stimulate or assist in such activities as giving alarm, laying trails to food sources, grooming, sexual attraction, and maintaining the caste system of insect societies. Rate of emission, rate of diffusion, concentration of the pheromones, and emission of more than one pheromone simultaneously or in sequence are factors which give added meaning to a message and prompt various responses.

Beetle's Secret. Members of New York University's School of Engineering and Science have built a fully instrumented mechanical beetle wing that operates just like its real counterpart. The mechanical wing, modeled after the wing of the English beetle (*Melolontha vulgaris*), will be used to study the aerodynamic riddle of beetle flight. Though the wing of the English beetle appears ineffective, it produces nearly twice the lift obtainable by one of the most effective man-made aircraft wings, according to Leon Bennet, senior research scientist at New York University.

Antarctic Insect. A tiny pink insect has been found living closer to the South Pole than any other known creature. The mite, $\frac{1}{100}$ of an inch long, was found among lichens 309 miles from the pole by Keith A. J. Wise, an entomologist from Hawaii's Bishop Museum. SERGEI LENORMAND

INSURANCE. Hurricane Betsy's rampage through the Gulf states swept away what could have been an encouraging comeback year for the fire and casualty insurance companies. Betsy may have cost the world's insurance industry $750,000,000, the largest insured loss in recorded history. See DISASTERS.

Until the hurricane and the Palm Sunday tornadoes in the Midwest, the fire and casualty industry had been strengthening its position. Two years of rate increases, as well as cost-cutting, were helping the companies. As it was, 1965 turned out to be the 10th of the last 16 years when loss ratios increased. The basic reason was that the industry was selling its product—protection against loss—below cost.

Increasingly, a remedy has been administered—somewhat to the dismay of automobile and home owners, and businessmen—namely, "the most massive round of rate increases in the history of the industry." On auto coverage alone, the indicated underwriting loss may have totaled $400,000,000, topping the previous record of about $335,000,000 in 1964. In more than 40 states, automobile rates rose during 1965. Most of the increases, averaging about 10 per cent, affected drivers in 1966.

For Life Insurance, all the major trends were favorable. About 125,000,000 Americans were covered by life policies of varying amounts. Sales to the public were up about 9 per cent for the year, to more than $114,500,000,000. The total amount of life insurance in force in the United States ap-

proached $890,000,000,000—equal to nearly $15,000 of protection per U.S. family—for a 12 per cent gain from 1964. In relation to national income, France and Germany have only about 20 per cent as much life insurance in force as the United States.

According to the Institute of Life Insurance, the U.S. total should approach $1,000,000,000,000 by the end of 1966. More than 73 per cent of life insurance is purchased by persons between the ages of 20 and 39; and that bracket is increasing rapidly—46,800,000 in 1950; 48,000,000 in 1965; and 52,000,000 projected for 1970.

Servicemen's Policy. In October, a pool of life companies wrote an extraordinary group policy, offering $28,000,000,000 worth of protection to members of the armed services under the new Servicemen's Group Life Insurance program enacted by Congress. That policy brought the industry's total life sales to $142,500,000,000.

Other congressional actions brought to the fore one important question: Would the 1966 expansion of Social Security benefits and legislation providing hospital and medical care for the elderly reduce sales of private life insurance and health insurance policies? Thoughtful men in the industry felt the two developments would ultimately stimulate sales by making families more aware of the need for adequate financial protection. EDWIN W. DARBY

See also MEDICARE; SOCIAL SECURITY.

INTERIOR DESIGN. The important innovation at the furniture shows held in the manufacturing centers of North Carolina and Virginia in October, was a return to a variety of Old English styles. Some 20 U.S. manufacturers showed products based on English furniture of the 17th through the 19th centuries. One manufacturer brought out bookcase and table units with Queen Anne and Chippendale overtones. Another showed furniture with Sheraton and Hepplewhite characteristics. Ribbon motifs appeared on chair backs and headboards. Georgian-style bookcases and oval dropleaf cocktail tables were shown.

"Breakthrough Design." In England, meanwhile, a group of young designers were showing furniture as up-to-date as the latest Beatles' record.

A group called the "Breakthrough Designers" was featured in a show put on by a department store and the *Sunday Times Magazine*. The show was divided into three sections. One section featured "throw-away" furniture and furnishings designed to satisfy the so-called changing taste of young people. The most interesting item in this section was a cardboard chair. It is made of a gaily decorated rolled up, cut-out sheet that weighs two pounds but is engineered to hold 300 pounds. The sheet sells for about $6, and is folded into shape at home.

Other knockdown items that can be thrown away when the user tires of them, or when they become worn, included a tea set made of colored paper coated with nylon; a folded polypropylene table; and fiberglass tables and stools that can be grouped together in a variety of ways.

Section three featured a visionary glimpse into the future of the "Plug 'n' Clip" house, in which internal space can be pushed into different shapes by changing the positions of plastic panels that can be clipped onto walls. According to the designers, chairs in the Plug 'n' Clip house will be replaced by pneumatic seating devices that will form to the body. Floors will be warmed and soft enough for comfortable sitting, and wall decoration will be projected by colored slides.

The Op Art Craze. On a less impersonal, if more visionary note, rugs, draperies, and other fabric furnishings featured in large stores in the United States in 1965 wore designs that sometimes seemed to ripple, move, and wiggle. This was because they were based on Op Art, in which painters experiment with the puzzle of vision and illusion in art.

Education in Design. To educate young people in the United States, who will be the consumers of tomorrow, several manufacturers marketed training aids for home economics classes. Outstanding was the Kroehler Home Furnishings Classroom Kit, which included fabric cards with details of type of weave, furniture cutouts, and color photographs showing style categories. FLORENCE BYERLY COVELL

INTERNATIONAL TRADE AND FINANCE. From the American point of view, 1965 could be looked upon as an improvement over 1964. Its balance of payments gap narrowed from a deficit of slightly more than $3,000,000,000 in 1964 to an estimated $1,700,000,000 in 1965. A significant curtailment of the outflow of U.S. capital was responsible. On Feb. 10, 1965, President Lyndon B. Johnson had asked for voluntary restraints on bank loans abroad and on direct investments overseas by U.S. companies. Although the U.S. merchandise trade surplus remained sizable—about $5,000,000,000—it was almost $2,000,000,000 below 1964.

World-wide, the growth of trade slowed down in 1965. Free World imports expanded only $7\frac{1}{2}$ per cent in the first six months; for all of 1964, the growth had been 12 per cent. Their 1965 total was estimated at $163,000,000,000. But most attention was focused on the difficulties in the European Economic Community (EEC, or Common Market) and on the fluctuating fortunes of the British pound sterling.

France Began a Boycott of EEC activities in June in a dispute over the future shape of the Common Market and the adoption of a common agricultural policy and a means of financing it. This was basically interpreted as President Charles de Gaulle's drive to block both the political power of

Wide World
AUTO TARIFF BARRIERS GO DOWN as U.S. President Lyndon B. Johnson, right, and Canadian Prime Minister Lester B. Pearson sign agreement at the LBJ Ranch.

The Need For World Monetary Reform

On Sept. 27, 1965, about 2,000 men from 103 countries met in Washington, D.C. They were monetary experts who had gathered in the capital of the world's most powerful nation to ponder one of the world's most intriguing subjects—money.

Perhaps more than ever before in history, money—the muscles of commerce, the ancient symbol of wealth and power—had become a topic of international concern. Why? Because many economists believed that the Free World faced the alarming possibility of a shortage of money, or foreign exchange, with which to finance its international trade and investment, and settle its debts.

Basically, the world had no truly international currency with which to bankroll its expanding trade. Most of its trade and investment depended on gold and two so-called reserve currencies: the U.S. dollar and the British pound sterling.

At the Bretton Woods (N.H.) conference in 1944, political and economic leaders of the Allied powers had agreed that postwar commerce would be financed by gold, dollars, and pounds. In addition, they created the International Monetary Fund (IMF) to act as the agent and supervise the system.

Each member of the IMF agreed to a price (or par value) for its currency in terms of a specific quantity of gold, dollars, or pounds. The newly created IMF was to play an important part in setting these par values. It also would act as a type of bank to provide resources to countries needing help to maintain the par value of their currencies.

In the years that followed, the system worked remarkably well. It gave the world's nations enough capital and confidence to prevent the kind of runaway inflations that had plagued the world after other great wars. It helped vastly to encourage and expand world trade. Because of it, the free economies of the West were intermeshed and the wealth of nations greatly enhanced.

But by 1965, something had happened to the system. Free World reserves, capitalized at $8,000,000,000 in 1947—the year IMF began operating—had grown to $57,000,000,000 by 1957. And by 1965, they totaled $68,000,000,000. Exports, however, had risen even faster—from $101,000,000,000 in 1957 to $156,000,000,000, or a sum more than double the reserves on hand, by 1965.

Clearly, world trade was growing so fast that the reserves could not keep up with it. The world was facing a monetary drought. Unless something was done, it was feared there would not be enough foreign exchange (gold, dollars, pounds) to finance all the needed transactions among the countries of the world.

The economists were nearly all agreed that something had to be done; the world's monetary system had become outdated and in need of reform. But because the mechanics of monetary reform are abstruse, the economists were sharply divided on the specific steps to be taken.

Some experts felt that what the system needed was "more *liquidity*," or more available cash or other easily transferable assets. Those who advocated such a plan favored one of three steps to achieve it: (1) increase the price of gold, (2) modify or amend the present system without changing its structure, (3) drastically overhaul the structure of the present system.

One group urged a rise in the price of gold to increase the monetary value of a government's holdings of gold. Therefore, a given stock of gold would go further in covering international payments deficits.

The second faction wished to preserve the system's basic structure but would patch it up. They argued that the system could provide all the liquidity the world needs by continuing the trend toward more cooperation and mutual assistance among central banks.

The third group of reformers would alter the system's structure by converting the IMF into an international central bank. World liquidity—money acceptable for settling all international accounts—would be increased by authorizing this world central bank to issue claims on itself. Similar to the way the U.S. Federal Reserve district banks issue dollar bills (Federal Reserve notes) to its member banks in need of funds, so would the world central bank issue claims, or currency, to countries in need.

Presumably such money, or claims on the world central bank, would be accepted by other countries with international payments surpluses.

One of the most widely discussed reform plans would carry the idea of an "international" money even further. The industrial powers would contribute their own francs, kroner, marks, and yen to some kind of international agency that would then print, issue, and regulate the new money for use in international trade and finance. Its role would be more that of the U.S. Treasury than of the Federal Reserve System.

Each of the world's nations had its own ideas for tinkering with the international system and they were as varied as their currencies. They ranged from advocacy of a return to the gold system, to suggestions that the IMF itself be dissolved or, short of that, that it at least be made to stop all forms of automatic, easy-to-get credit.

To study the problem in depth, a number of working groups had been set up by such organizations as the European Economic Community (EEC, or Common Market), the IMF, the 21-nation Organization for Economic Cooperation and Development, and the U.S. Treasury. This was, indeed, concern at the highest possible levels.

But perhaps for the first time in history, interest in the world's monetary system—and its reform—had trickled down from the paneled offices of financial institutions and the cluttered studies of economists into the domain of the average man in the street.

If proof was needed, none better could be found than that for a period of weeks in 1965 Al Capp's popular daily comic strip character, Li'l Abner, had been hard at work with plans to solve the U.S. balance of payments problem. Thus, the captains of industry and the creation of a cartoonist were meeting on common ground—the need for monetary reform.   LEONARD OPPENHEIM

the EEC's Executive Commission and the introduction of majority voting set for Jan. 1, 1966. De Gaulle has been firmly opposed to any development that would threaten French freedom of action.

Toward year-end, however, there was a hint that France would not boycott the mid-January meeting of the foreign ministers of the six member nations: Belgium, France, Italy, Luxembourg, The Netherlands, and West Germany. Also, plans were still being laid for a further reduction in tariffs among the six nations, to a level 20 per cent below that prevailing in 1958 when the EEC was established.

President De Gaulle's suprisingly poor showing in the December 5 national elections undoubtedly reflected a widespread dissatisfaction with his attitude toward the Common Market. French businessmen have benefited greatly from the EEC, and French agriculture stands to gain a much wider market for its products when and if the new common agricultural policy is adopted. See EUROPE; FRANCE; Section One, PAUL-HENRI SPAAK ON THE WORLD.

Great Britain, meanwhile, was waging an apparently successful battle to keep from being forced to devalue the pound. During the first half of the year a significant "flight from sterling" developed. By May 12, the Bank of England had received credit totaling more than $2,400,000,000 from the International Monetary Fund (IMF) and Switzerland. By August, it got credits of $750,000,000 and $250,000,000 from the Federal Reserve Bank of New York and the Export-Import Bank, respectively.

Early in September, a new line of credit was extended to the British by the United States, Canada, Japan, and seven European nations—with the conspicuous exception of France. That rescue operation, combined with Britain's improving balance of payments, stilled fears of any near-term devaluation. British reserves began to rise again—to $2,987,-600,000 on November 30, the highest level since June, 1962. See GREAT BRITAIN.

World Money Woes. The sterling problem and the continuing U.S. gold drain intensified the search for some means of increasing monetary reserves to settle international accounts. Such reserves have been gold and the U.S. dollar—as good as gold, because of widespread confidence in its convertibility. But the decline in the U.S. gold stock from $15,388,-000,000 in December, 1964, to $13,805,000,000 in November, 1965, showed that other countries were tending to convert their dollar holdings into gold. Such a trend if carried to the extreme suggested by the French could curtail world liquidity sharply.

Late in November, a number of speakers at the White House Conference on International Cooperation urged an end to the "tyranny" of gold. Later, the conference's committee on finance and monetary affairs recommended "concerted action to devise supplementary assets to be held in official reserves" of the IMF. It did not spell out the exact form of these assets, or new type of world money.

During the first three quarters of 1965, no gain had been made in the total monetary reserves of the noncommunist world, according to an early-1966 report of the IMF. Instead, the reserves slipped a bit. They totaled $68,880,000,000 on Sept. 30, 1965, or $20,000,000 below their Dec. 31, 1964, level. The report also noted that, because of hoarding and speculation, gold equal to the entire 1965 world output had found its way into private hands. See Section One, SYLVIA PORTER ON THE ECONOMY.

In the Communist Bloc, China continued its drive to obtain foreign exchange by placing cheap goods on the Hong Kong market. From this source alone, China was adding almost $500,000,000 a year to its foreign exchange—or about half of what it earns in its entire foreign trade.

In Eastern Europe, apart from the Soviet Union, new trade relations with the West were springing up. The first U.S. commercial trade mission to Poland and Romania left Washington, D.C., in September. The seven-man team explored sales to the civilian sectors of the two nations' economies. About three quarters of Eastern Europe's trade has been among its own nations. Earlier, in May, a presidential commission on East-West trade urged that the United States relax its restrictions on commerce with the Soviet Union and Eastern Europe.

U.S. Exports of goods barely managed to exceed the $25,288,000,000 total of 1964. For the first nine months of 1965, exports were only 3 per cent ahead of the 1964 pace. A prolonged dock strike early in the year contributed to this lag. U.S. exporters also cited increasing overseas competition and trade barriers, such as Britain's 10 per cent surcharge on selected imports.

Continuing U.S. prosperity brought higher imports—about $21,000,000,000, versus $18,619,000,-000 in 1964. The September-to-October, 1965, gain was 12 per cent; for exports, it was 2 per cent. There were few noticeable changes in the pattern of trade. Agricultural exports generally slowed (see AGRICULTURE). Canada continued, by far, to be the largest purchaser of U.S. goods, followed by Japan, West Germany, and Britain. Canada remained the largest single seller to the United States, followed by Japan, Britain, West Germany, and Venezuela.

The Kennedy Round of world tariff negotiations dragged along in Geneva, Switzerland, awaiting a solution of the Common Market's difficulties. The French boycott cast a disquieting doubt on whether world-wide tariff reductions can be effected before U.S. negotiating powers expire on June 30, 1967, under terms of the 1962 Trade Expansion Act.

The eyes of those seeking to free international trade from its tariff bonds will be focused on those Geneva talks during 1966. No less a concern will be the finding of a workable method of providing adequate international monetary reserves to assure future expansion in world trade. WARREN W. SHEARER

See also articles on the individual nations.

INVENTION. President Lyndon B. Johnson appointed a commission to study the U.S. patent system, essentially unchanged since it began in 1790, and to submit recommendations for improvements by the end of 1966. Under present operations, there is a backlog of 218,000 patent applications, and the Senate judiciary subcommittee on patents, trademarks, and copyrights reported in March that the average delay between patent requests and awards was more than three years. The subcommittee said that the Patent Office was not at fault, but that the backlog was the result of steadily mounting workloads and an increasing complexity of operations.

Critics of the present patent laws asked for international agreements to reduce the necessity for filing separately in each country where protection is desired. Solutions to this problem were also sought by international agencies.

The International Patent Institute in The Hague, The Netherlands, was attempting to centralize patent searches, and proposals for a unified patent system among the six European Economic Community (EEC, or Common Market) nations were being negotiated. Denmark, Finland, Norway, and Sweden hoped to put into effect, in 1966, an international patent law which will grant one patent for all four countries.

The U.S. government, meanwhile, increased fees for patent filing and issuance from $60 to $165 during 1965, in the first major overhaul of patent fee schedules since 1932. The increased rates are expected to recover about 75 per cent of Patent Office operating costs.

During 1965 the Soviet Union became the 68th country to join the Paris Convention for the Protection of Industrial Property. The 82-year-old Paris Convention requires each member nation to treat citizens of other member nations the same as its own nationals in matters of patents, trademarks, and other industrial property rights.

From Spacecraft to Twist. In a single week, separate patents were granted for a spacecraft electrical propulsion unit and a ball bearing-mounted platform to be strapped to the feet when dancing the twist. The inventor of the dancing swivels says they also may be used for the purpose of exercising and reducing the waistline.

A New York inventor substituted balloons for gunpowder in an artificial firecracker which he patented. A delayed-action plunger, simulating the burning time of a fuse, punctures balloons to produce safe but satisfying explosions.

Flap-Light Box. Gentlemen may no longer have to light women's cigarettes if an invention by two New Yorkers finds acceptance. The men patented a self-lighting cigarette which ignites when it is touched to a chemical-bearing pad in the cigarette box top. The tips of the cigarettes contain an oxidizing agent which reacts with a reducing agent in the pads. SERGEI LENORMAND

IRAN opened 1965 with an ambitious plan—and a tragic assassination. Premier Hassan Ali Mansur launched a 30-year industrial expansion program that Shah Mohammed Riza Pahlevi called "a national progress crusade." To use the $450,000,000 anticipated oil revenues to the best advantage, the plan included austerity measures, increased taxes, and a 15 per cent cut in government spending.

Premier Mansur, architect of the plan, was shot to death in January by a high school student while on the way to Parliament with the text of a new oil agreement that had been made with five Western oil companies. The assassination did not change Iran's direction or policies. The shah named Amir Abbas Hoveida premier, and the oil agreement was duly ratified. The shah—himself the object of an unsuccessful attack by a palace guardsman—toured the provinces and distributed plots to 14,000 farmers under Phase 2 of the land reform program.

The International Bank for Reconstruction and Development approved $40,500,000 in loans to improve Iranian highways.

Population: 22,857,000. **Government:** Shah Mohammed Riza Pahlevi; Premier Amir Abbas Hoveida. **Monetary Unit:** rial (75.75 = U.S. $1). **Foreign Trade:** exports, $1,256,000,000; imports, $675,000,-000. **Principal Exports:** carpets, dried fruits and nuts, petroleum, raw cotton.   WILLIAM SPENCER
See also MIDDLE EAST.

IRAQ resumed its war with the rebellious Kurds in April despite opposition from Arab and Western leaders and even its own civilian ministers. General Mullah Mustafa al-Barzani, leader of the Kurds, accused the government of reneging on its 1964 cease-fire agreements.

The Kurdish struggle and internal political rivalries kept Iraq's economic development at a standstill. In September, the premier, Taher Yahya, and half his cabinet resigned to protest anti-Nasser influences in the government. His successor was air force chief Arif Abdel Razzak. A Communist plot was blocked, and subsequently Razzak himself tried to seize power while President Abdul Salam Muhammad Arif was absent in Casablanca. But Razzak was thwarted by Arif's brother. Razzak, a Nasserite, fled to Cairo and Foreign Minister Abdul Rahman al-Bazzaz became premier on Sept. 21, 1965.

During 1965, Iraq reached an accord with the Iraq Petroleum Company (IPC). Iraq agreed to restore 5 per cent of IPC's concessionary area. It also agreed to exploit this area on a 50-50 basis.

Population: 8,350,000. **Government:** President Abdul Salam Muhammad Arif; Premier Abdul Rahman al-Bazzaz. **Monetary Unit:** dinar (1 = U.S. $2.80). **Foreign Trade:** exports, $772,000,000; imports, $319,200,000. **Principal Exports:** cement, dates, petroleum, raw wool.   WILLIAM SPENCER
See also MIDDLE EAST.

IRELAND returned Prime Minister Seán F. Lemass and his *Fianna Fáil* (Republican) party to power in a general election held April 7. Lemass, with 72 seats, secured a two-seat majority in the *Gail* (house of representatives) over all other parties. The leader of the opposing *Fine Gael* (United Ireland) party, James M. Dillion, resigned when his party failed to improve on the 47 seats it already held.

In January, Lemass made an attempt to improve relations with Northern Ireland. He called on Northern Ireland's prime minister, Captain Terence M. O'Neill, in Belfast, and O'Neill, in turn, traveled to Dublin for a further meeting on February 9. No positive measures followed these exchanges.

Lemass and a ministerial team visited British Prime Minister Harold Wilson in London on July 26 to discuss the establishment of a free trade area between the two countries. The imposition of a tariff surcharge by Great Britain on imports had dealt the Irish economy a severe blow inasmuch as 75 per cent of Ireland's exports go to Great Britain.

Population: 2,832,000. **Government:** President Éamon de Valéra; Prime Minister Seán F. Lemass. **Monetary Unit:** pound (1 = U.S. $2.80). **Gross National Product:** £774,000,000. **Foreign Trade:** exports, $623,000,000; imports, $974,000,000. **Principal Exports:** alcoholic beverages, cattle, meat, textiles.   ALASTAIR BURNET

IRON. See STEEL INDUSTRY.

ISRAEL avoided a serious confrontation with its Arab neighbors even though 1965 marked the start of Israel's long-planned diversion of River Jordan waters to irrigate the Negev desert. The Israelis began in January by channeling water from the Sea of Galilee into a new artificial lake. The Palestine Arab underground organization El-Fatah countered with sabotage and hit-run raids.

West Germany paid Israel $75,000,000 as the final installment in war reparations to the Jews. In March, Israel's one-house parliament, the Knesset, approved the opening of formal diplomatic relations with Bonn.

Great political excitement was generated by the hostility between former Prime Minister David Ben-Gurion and Prime Minister Levi Eshkol. In July, Ben-Gurion broke with the Mapai party and registered as an independent, taking his followers with him. In the November elections, Eshkol's Mapai, in coalition with the left-wing, Achdut Haavoda labor party, won 45 of 120 seats in the Knesset. The right-wing Gahal party won 27 seats, and Ben-Gurion's Rafi party ran a poor last.

Population: 2,386,000. **Government:** President Schneor Zalman Shazar; Prime Minister Levi Eshkol. **Monetary Unit:** pound (3 = U.S. $1). **Foreign Trade:** exports, $349,000,000; imports, $826,000,-000. **Principal Exports:** citrus fruits, metal products, textiles.   WILLIAM SPENCER
See also ARCHITECTURE; MIDDLE EAST; TUNISIA.

ITALY

Italy began to emerge slowly from the economic crisis that had begun in 1962. Progress, however, was more marked in some sectors of the economy than in others. The balance of payments gains made in 1964 held steady, and anti-inflationary measures paid dividends. Italy enjoyed a booming export trade. In the first six months of 1965, exports were up 23.8 per cent over the same period in 1964. But a slackening in home demand led to overseas selling at marginal profits, and thus reduced imports of raw materials on which Italy depended for manufactured goods. Unemployment was a cause for concern. In July, 1,126,000 men were out of work. This represented a 15.15 per cent increase over the same month in 1964.

Industrial Crisis. Industrial output increased by only 0.4 per cent during the year. Although steel production was up by 28.3 per cent, and iron by 54 per cent, the important textile industry suffered a drop in output of 20.5 per cent for silk and cotton, and 3.1 per cent for man-made fibers.

The most serious area of concern, however, was the low rate of investment—despite the creation of special funds by the government for financing industry. In August, a bill was introduced to provide incentives for modernizing the textile industry. State housing subsidies were also inaugurated. The unions, however, refused to accept any kind of income policy, and wages rose 13.2 per cent.

International Relations. Premier Aldo Moro and Foreign Minister Amintore Fanfani visited the United States in April and reaffirmed Italy's confidence in the North Atlantic Treaty Organization (NATO). See NORTH ATLANTIC TREATY ORGANIZATION (NATO). In December, Fanfani submitted his resignation as foreign minister after being criticized for his role in a purported North Vietnam peace feeler. Moro, however, rejected it.

New Liners. In midyear, the twin, 46,000-ton transatlantic liners *Michelangelo* and *Raffaelo* made their maiden voyages (see TRANSPORTATION).

Tourism, meanwhile, remained a lucrative source of income. Receipts from foreign tourists for the first seven months of 1965 were up 32 per cent over the same 1964 period. The tourist industry was in turn geared to a massive road-building program, as well as such projects as the Franco-Italian Mont Blanc road tunnel, which was officially opened in July. See BRIDGE AND TUNNEL.

Population: 51,369,000. **Government:** President Giuseppe Saragat; Premier Aldo Moro. **Monetary Unit:** lira (624.83 = U.S. $1.). **Gross National Product:** 24,693,000,000,000 lire. **Foreign Trade:** exports, $5,578,000,000; imports, $7,065,000,000. **Principal Exports:** agricultural produce, chemicals, machinery, textiles.   KENNETH BROWN

See also EUROPE.

United Press Int.

ITALY'S PRIDE, the new superliner Michelangelo, receives traditional welcome in New York harbor after its maiden transatlantic voyage.

IVORY COAST. President Félix Houphouet-Boigny took a firm stand against Communist Chinese activities in Africa. He warned both government officials and students of the danger of Communist Chinese subversion which, he contended, was gradually spreading over the African continent.

Sixty persons who were accused of a plot against the government in August, 1963, were given closed-door trials in 1964, and sentenced at the end of 1964 and in early 1965. The sentences brought death for six persons, life imprisonment for two, shorter prison terms for 21.

In May, the Ivory Coast signed a $32,000,000 loan agreement with the European Development Fund for the establishment of an 80,000-acre palm oil plantation and the construction of seven palm oil processing plants. In the same month, it approved an agreement expanding Nationalist China's rice cultivation assistance program. The Ivory Coast also negotiated loans from the United States and the United Nations Economic and Social Council. These will finance the purchase of rice and the cost of mineral prospecting.

Population: 3,592,000. **Government:** President Félix Houphouet-Boigny. **Monetary Unit:** CFA franc (246.85 = U.S. $1). **Foreign Trade:** exports, $230,000,000; imports, $170,000,000. **Principal Exports:** cocoa, coffee, timber. BENJAMIN E. THOMAS

See also AFRICA.

JACOB, FRANÇOIS (1920-), Collège de France Professor of Cellular Genetics and head of the Pasteur Institute Microbic Genetics Department, was one of three French scientists awarded the Nobel medicine prize in 1965. He and his two Pasteur Institute colleagues, André Lwoff and Jacques Monod, were honored for the discovery of a new class of genes (basic units of heredity), which regulates the activity of the structural genes.

The field of research in which Jacob worked was the genetics of bacteria. His work with Monod included research on the bacterial enzyme beta-galactosidase. They discovered a type of ribonucleic acid (RNA), produced by the structural genes. They described it as a "messenger molecule," since it transmits instructions (by means of genes) from the cell nucleus to the sites of protein synthesis (ribosomes) in the other areas of the cell. Cell chemicals, or enzymes, perform the actual synthesis. Jacob and Monod determined how this chemical action is controlled.

François Jacob has worked at the Pasteur Institute since 1950, and advanced to his present position there in 1960. The Collège de France professorship was created for him in 1964. He has a medical degree (1947), a degree in science (1951), and a doctorate in science (1954). Jacob was born in Nancy, France.

See also LWOFF, ANDRÉ; MONOD, JACQUES; NOBEL PRIZES (Science).

JAMAICA found its vigorous economic efforts thwarted by trade setbacks in its principal exports. Banana prices touched their lowest in the British market since 1945. This was due in part to increased competition from the Windward Islands, but there was also a drop in British demand.

Acting Prime Minister Donald Sangstar, who was temporarily replacing ailing Sir William Alexander Bustamente, levied new taxes on automobiles, cigarettes, and whiskey in the budget he proposed on April 30. He reported rising output in mining and manufacturing, and a recovery in the tourist trade after a period of decline. He also indicated that the government planned to spend $50,000,000 on economic development in 1965-1966.

Jamaica's chief problem remained the growing gap between an annual population increase of 40,-000 and job vacancies growing at the rate of only 11,000. The cutting off of immigration into Britain (under the new rules only 1,250 Jamaicans could hope to get there each year) was bitterly resented.

Population: 1,736,000. **Government:** Governor-General Sir Clifford C. Campbell; Prime Minister Sir William Alexander Bustamente. **Monetary Unit:** pound (1 = U.S. $2.80). **Gross National Product:** 267,400,000 pounds. **Foreign Trade:** exports, $218,-000,000; imports, $282,000,000. **Principal Exports:** aluminum, bauxite, sugar. ALASTAIR BURNET

See also GREAT BRITAIN.

JAPAN was worried by signs that the unprecedented economic prosperity it had enjoyed since 1955 might be declining. Rising consumer prices, a depressed stock market, and a tightening of the job supply caused part of the concern. But a rising number of failures in small and medium businesses, declining corporate profits, and a general trend toward retrenchment were also signs of growing economic difficulties.

By contrast, wages continued to increase, the rate of unemployment remained under 1 per cent, and exports set a new record. The prevailing mood was pessimistic, however, because the unfavorable factors seemed to outweigh the favorable ones.

It was estimated that the rate of economic growth in 1965 would be 2.5 to 3 per cent in real terms as compared with 11 per cent for 1964. The 1964 Gross National Product (GNP) totaled $71,200,000,000, with national income reaching $56,100,000,000, or $580 per capita, an increase of 11.6 per cent over 1963. With exports totaling a record-breaking $7,-000,000,000 in 1964, the government set a goal of $8,000,000,000 in exports for 1965.

Political Interest during the year centered on an election—held in July—for the upper house of the *diet* (parliament), which elects half of its 250 members every three years. There were 127 seats at stake—two of these being vacancies. At issue were the administration's pro-Western policy, including its strong endorsement of the U.S. position in

Wide World

STUDENT PRINCE HIRO, whose father is heir to
the Japanese throne, roots for his school
team during an annual athletic meet in Tokyo.

South Vietnam and its handling of Japan's current business recession.

In the final count, Prime Minister Eisaku Sato's ruling Liberal-Democratic party retained its substantial majority. But the number of seats it held dropped from 144 to 141. The Socialists on the other hand gained eight seats, and Kōmeitō—a new party of the Soka Gakkai religious sect—gained seven.

A special municipal election for the Tokyo Metropolitan Assembly was held in July and marked a second setback for the Liberal-Democratic party. The assembly had been dissolved in May, two years before the term ended, following disclosures of widespread bribery and vote-buying among the Liberal-Democratic members.

Of the 120 seats at stake, the Socialists captured 45, the Liberal-Democrats 38, Kōmeitō 23, the Communists nine, and others five. What effect the two elections would have on the Liberal-Democratic position would remain unclear until the next general election, which must be held by 1968.

Japan's most significant diplomatic move of 1965 was the conclusion of a treaty establishing formal diplomatic relations with the Republic of Korea (see KOREA). The national diet ratified the treaty on Dec. 11, 1965.

Prime Minister Sato made an official visit to the United States in January. He stated that Japan's policy was to continue to maintain formal relations with Formosa (Nationalist China), but also to "con-

tinue to promote private contact" with the Chinese Communist government. He also requested that administrative control over the Ryukyu and Bonin islands, vested in the United States under the 1951 treaty of peace, be returned to Japan.

In August, Sato visited Okinawa, the first such visit by a Japanese prime minister since World War II. He reaffirmed Japan's close ties and reiterated the wish that the island be returned to Japan.

Royal Birth. On November 30, the nation rejoiced over the birth of a new son to Crown Prince Akihito and his wife, Crown Princess Michiko. The child, who was named Fumihito Aya-No-Miya, is third in line to the world's oldest throne.

A Japanese scientist, Sin-itiro Tomonaga, shared the Nobel prize in physics with two Americans in 1965 (see NOBEL PRIZES; TOMANAGA, SIN-ITIRO).

On October 9, the Japan Association for the 1970 World Exposition was officially inaugurated in ceremonies held in Tokyo. The association will be responsible for planning an official world's fair to be held in Osaka in 1970.

Population: 97,913,000. **Government:** Emperor Hirohito; Prime Minister Eisaku Sato. **Monetary Unit:** yen (362 = U.S. $1). **Gross National Product:** $71,200,000,000. **Foreign Trade:** exports, $7,036,-000,000; imports, $6,501,000,000. **Principal Exports:** light goods, machinery, steel, textiles.   JOHN M. MAKI

See also ASIA.

JEWS AND JUDAISM. Many leaders of world Jewry hailed the October 29 Vatican Council Declaration on the "Relation of the Church to Non-Christian Religions." The declaration "deplored hatred, persecutions, and displays of anti-Semitism directed against the Jews at any time and by any one." The main thrust of the document as it related to Jews was to call upon Roman Catholics to cooperate with Jews in an atmosphere of mutual respect.

Jewish communities in such Roman Catholic countries as Argentina, Poland, Portugal, and Spain were likely to benefit most by the declaration of tolerance. Pope Paul VI's visit to New York City in October, 1965, coincided with the eve of the Day of Atonement. Forty Jewish leaders (and clergymen of other faiths) met with the pope at Holy Family Roman Catholic Church in an atmosphere of cordiality. See ROMAN CATHOLIC.

Soviet Jewry. Jews in the Free World conducted a vigorous campaign to condemn the suppression of rights for their fellow Jews in Russia. Early in March, Jewish students in the New York area participated in a "Jericho March," whose theme was "Let My People Go." It was a call to the Soviet Union to permit emigration. In June, close to 20,000 New Yorkers gathered in two mass rallies to protest Soviet anti-Semitism. In September, thousands of U.S. Jews gathered in Washington, D.C., to conduct a day-long vigil for the same purpose. The Soviet government reacted sharply, denying the charges of religious persecution, but as a result of such protests there was some evidence of improvement in the lot of Jews in Russia. The presence of a large number of young worshipers at High Holy Day services at Moscow and Leningrad was a sign that oppression had not succeeded in alienating all of the younger generation of Jews in Russia.

Orthodox Life in America. A special study made for the 1965 edition of the *American Jewish Year Book* revealed that there were 1,607 Orthodox synagogues in the United States. Orthodox seminaries numbered 31, compared to only three before World War II. In New York City alone, more than $25,000,000 was spent in 1964 for Jewish all-day schools. There are no such comparative statistics for the Conservative and Reform synagogue schools.

On the national scene, Jewish leaders played an active role. More than 100 rabbis from every part of the country joined other clergymen in the historic civil rights pilgrimage from Selma to Montgomery, Ala. See CIVIL RIGHTS; NEGRO.

Martin Buber, the foremost Jewish philosopher of the 20th century, died in June in Jerusalem. His poetic essay, *I and Thou*, is regarded as one of the seminal religious books of our time. One of the spiritual leaders of the state of Israel, he preached understanding for Arabs as well as Jews. Jews and Christians throughout the world mourned his passing. See PROTESTANT (CLOSE-UP). MORRIS N. KERTZER

JOHN BIRCH SOCIETY. Throughout 1965, the John Birch Society continued as the object of considerable controversy. Governor Robert E. Smylie (R., Idaho) headed a movement among Republican leaders to persuade the Republican party to publicly denounce the society. Nevertheless, the society's intense anticommunist campaign and its ultraconservatism continued to find a wide, although scattered, support in many states. The society continued to emphasize the origin of its name, derived from a young Baptist missionary, John M. Birch, who joined the Flying Tigers in Chungking in 1941, and was killed by Chinese Communists in 1945.

Robert Welch, who founded the society in 1958, remained its president. The headquarters of the society was in Belmont, Mass., and included an editorial office, a research staff, and a speakers' bureau. This office published the monthly *American Opinion*, the *Weekly Review of the News*, and numerous pamphlets and bulletins. The society also maintained an office in Washington, D.C., as well as regional offices and reading centers in San Marino, Calif.; Glenview, Ill.; and White Plains, N.Y. There were 340 bookstore units throughout the United States. The claimed membership was over 70,000 in 1965, but the membership list was not published. Paid employees numbered 255, with a payroll of over $40,000 per week. Public meetings, often addressed by Robert Welch, were large and received wide press coverage. PAUL C. TULLIER

JOHNSON, LYNDON B.

JOHNSON, LYNDON B.

Lyndon Baines Johnson used his overwhelming mandate from the American people, the vast prestige of his office, and all his political experience in 1965 to launch his "Great Society." His success in persuading Congress to pass far-reaching social and political reforms won wide admiration. His tireless energy became legendary. He assembled a White House staff that could adapt to his high-pressure demands. See CONGRESS OF THE U.S.; PRESIDENT OF THE U.S.

HOME ON THE PEDERNALES. President and Mrs. Johnson leave the cares of his office behind as they go arm in arm into the house he has known since childhood. They bought the house, owned by his aunt, in 1951.

PICTURES OF THE YEAR/Stan Wayman, *Life* Magazine © Time Inc.

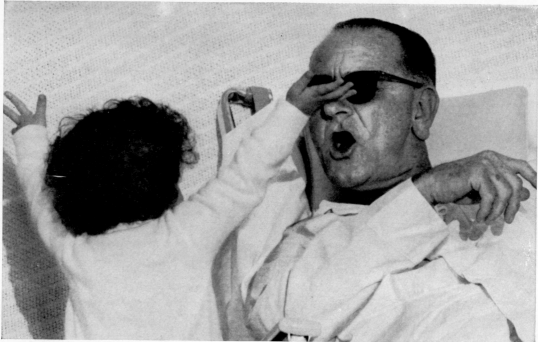

PICTURES OF THE YEAR/Roddy Mims, United Press Int.

C'MON AND PLAY WITH ME, little Courtenay Lynda Valenti seems to be urging the President as he basks on the hospital terrace after his gall bladder surgery.

Wide World

THE SCAR SEEN 'ROUND THE WORLD.
Convalescing President Johnson displays the exact location of his gall bladder operation incision.

There were critics, of course. As the war in Vietnam intensified, opposition to the war included opposition to the President. And as pressure built up, the President's irritation with his opponents sharpened. By midsummer, complaints were voiced that the President drove his staff too hard, lost his temper too often, acted too impulsively, and was too sensitive to unfavorable comment. But on balance, 1965 was the year that Lyndon Johnson proved himself to be a forceful President with an extraordinary feeling for consensus and an unusual ability to evaluate the mood of Congress.

"Y'All Come" was President Johnson's casual pre-election invitation. And his "y'all" was transformed into 200,000 formal engraved invitations to his inauguration on January 20. He chose to take the oath of office in a business suit, but evening found the First Lady, her daughters, and much of Washington in lavish floor-length gowns.

The President began his working day at 7 A.M., and, with a nap in the early afternoon, he was able to work well into the evening. In effect, he put in a two-shift day. On August 27, the President's 57th birthday, his personal physician, Vice-Admiral George Buckley, pronounced him "as fit as any man of his age (and) more active than most of them."

Health. A short hospital stay for a cold, sore throat, and cough right after the inauguration did not slow the President down. But in the fall, he was faced with a more serious condition. Early in

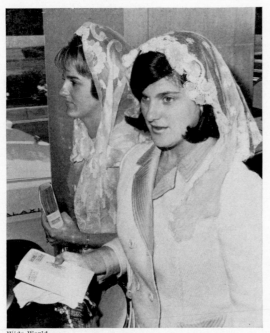

Wide World

NEW CATHOLIC CONVERT Luci Johnson,
right, goes to Holy Communion
with her friend, Warrie Smith.

Wide World

CAPITAL BEAUTIFIER, Mrs. Lyndon B. Johnson,
plants pansies on Washington's Mall during a
tour of the area near the Lincoln Memorial.

September, he suffered a gall bladder attack at his Texas ranch. Surgery was recommended. The announcement was deferred until the day after President Johnson's visit with Pope Paul VI in New York City on October 4.

The President maintained his busy schedule up to the minute he was due at the hospital. The evening he revealed his plans for surgery, he entertained 100 business, labor, and professional leaders at a White House dinner. A few hours before entering the hospital, he attended a Salute to Congress celebration, which most Congressmen missed because they were wrestling with the highway beautification bill.

His early-morning operation October 8 at Walter Reed Memorial Hospital in Bethesda, Md., was efficient and successful. His gall bladder was removed, along with a kidney stone.

The surgery tired him more than he had anticipated. After a two-week stay at the hospital, and a brief White House stay, the President went to the LBJ Ranch in Texas. He stayed at the ranch for most of the rest of the year. He returned to Washington at times to receive foreign visitors.

Social Life. The President's social calendar was crowded. He entertained 42 state governors in March. He was the host at a 13-hour Festival of the Arts at the White House in June. Two other White House conferences were held in 1965—on Natural Beauty, in May, and on Education, in July. A

third meeting—in November on civil rights—was in preparation for a full conference in 1966.

He conferred with former President Dwight D. Eisenhower several times (see EISENHOWER, DWIGHT D.). Throughout the year, he gave breakfasts, luncheons, and dinners for national leaders and members of Congress.

The Johnson Family. On his 57th birthday party at the ranch, the President received a volume of poems written by his younger daughter, Luci, and a leather-bound portfolio of family mementos prepared by his wife.

Mrs. Johnson devoted much of her time in 1965 to programs aimed at restoring and preserving the nation's natural beauty. The Washington (D.C.) Beautifying Committee was formed in February. Mrs. Johnson met with its chairman, Secretary of the Interior Stewart L. Udall, and city planners to work on the beautification of the nation's capital (see WASHINGTON, D.C.).

Luci Baines Johnson was baptized into the Roman Catholic Church on July 2, her 18th birthday. In October, it was rumored that she would announce her engagement to Patrick Nugent, 22, of Waukegan, Ill. It was made official on Christmas Eve.

In late summer, Mrs. Johnson and her daughter Lynda, 21, vacationed at Laurence S. Rockefeller's Wyoming ranch.   CAROL L. THOMPSON

See also DEMOCRATIC PARTY.

JONAS, FRANZ (1899-   ), was sworn in as the fourth postwar president of Austria on July 9. He succeeded Adolf Schaerf, who died in February. Jonas had narrowly defeated Alfons Gorbach, a former chancellor, by a vote of 2,260,992 to 2,324,474 (see AUSTRIA).

Viennese-born President Jonas began his career as a typesetter in the printing industry. Following army service in World War I, he returned to the printer's trade, eventually becoming an official in the Socialist youth movement. During the 1930s, he was an official in the Social Democratic party and, for a short time, was imprisoned by the Dollfuss government for his activities. In 1945, he entered the provisional municipal government of Floridsdorf, a suburb of Vienna.

In 1948, Jonas was made a city councilor of Vienna and, as such, was responsible for food. The following year, he was put in charge of housing, in which capacity he carried out a large building program. He was elected mayor of Vienna on June 22, 1951, succeeding Dr. Theodor Körner, who had been elected president of Austria.

Since 1949, President Jonas has been head of the Vienna branch of the Socialist party of Austria. He is one of the party's three deputy chairmen. Jonas is one of eight children. He and his wife Margarete, who is known for her work with nurseries and kindergartens, live modestly. They have no children.   WALTER F. MORSE

JONES, HOWARD MUMFORD (1892-   ), Harvard University Lawrence Lowell Professor Emeritus of Humanities, was awarded the Pulitzer nonfiction prize in 1965 for *O Strange New World*. It is a study of the formative years of American culture, and the first volume of a projected work of two volumes.

The noted scholar has written mostly for the serious student rather than for the general reader. His many published works include *American and French Culture, 1750-1848* (1927), *Education and World Tragedy* (1946), *The Theory of American Literature* (1948), *The Frontier in American Fiction* (1956), and *One Great Society* (1959). Jones also has written various volumes with other authors, and edited, with others, such works as *Plays of the Restoration and the Eighteenth Century* and the *Letters of Sherwood Anderson*.

Howard Mumford Jones was born in Saginaw, Mich. and graduated from the University of Wisconsin (1914). He received his M.A. degree (1915) at the University of Chicago, and his Doctor of Letters degree (1936) at Harvard. He has held professorships at the University of Texas, the University of North Carolina, and the University of Michigan. He was professor of English at Harvard (1936-1960), and then Lawrence Lowell Professor of Humanities until he retired in 1962.

See also PULITZER PRIZES.

JORDAN remained politically and economically stable throughout 1965. Good harvests and a boom in tourism encouraged optimism about the success of the seven-year development plan introduced by Premier Wasfi al-Tell.

King Hussein I ended speculation about his successor when he named a crown prince—his youngest brother, 18-year-old Hassan. Thus, the king by-passed his oldest brother, Prince Muhammad, and Hussein's own son, four-year-old Prince Abdullah, whose mother is British.

King Hussein issued an amnesty for all political prisoners and exiles from the 1957 crisis—about 1,700 persons—and invited them to live in Jordan.

Jordan and Israel continued to be hostile neighbors. Friction over Israel's efforts to divert the River Jordan for irrigation prompted the king to order a general mobilization on Oct. 28, 1965, to face any Israeli "aggression" during work on a dam.

Foreign aid kept flowing into Jordan. Other Arab countries granted 11,000,000 dinars ($30,800,000) for the Mukhaiba Dam project. The United States pledged $35,000,000 for three years.

Population: 2,035,000. **Government:** King Hussein I; Premier Wasfi al-Tell. **Monetary Unit:** dinar (1 = U.S. $2.80). **Gross National Product:** 118,000,000 dinars. **Foreign Trade:** exports, $18,-000,000; imports, $149,200,000. **Principal Exports:** cigarettes, olive oil, phosphates.   WILLIAM SPENCER

See also MIDDLE EAST.

JUNIOR ACHIEVEMENT (JA) reported on its expanding program of scholarships available to its members in the United States and Canada. Currently the organization awards 400 scholarships ranging from $100 to $3,200. Some are awarded on a local or regional basis, and others are open to JA members nationally. Most of the scholarships are granted in the form of cash stipends for use in any school of the winner's choice, but a few are awarded either by or for specific institutions. In general, the JA scholarships are for one year only, although those offered by colleges and universities may be renewed. A high level of performance in JA activities, and a good high school record are basic requirements for those applying for scholarships. Additional conditions for eligibility may be indicated by the donor.

The 22nd National Junior Achievers Conference was held August 22 to 27 on the campus of Indiana University at Bloomington. Gerry Michael, 18, Seattle, Wash., was installed as National Junior Achievement president. He received a prize of $1,500. Lyn Pearce, 17, Dallas, Tex., was awarded the title of marketing executive and received a prize of $1,000. Robyn Jansen, 17, St. Paul, Minn., was chosen Miss Junior Achievement of 1965 and received $250.

Junior Achievement, Inc., named J. J. Francomano executive vice-president.   Joseph P. Anderson

JUVENILE DELINQUENCY in the United States continued to rise. In July, the Federal Bureau of Investigation (FBI) reported an increase of 17.4 per cent in the number of arrests of persons under 18 years of age in 1964. In 1963, such arrests had increased by 11 per cent and, in 1962, by 9 per cent. Almost half of all the juvenile cases were handled by the police departments, without referral to the courts or the filing of an official petition of delinquency against the defendants.

The Children's Bureau reported an increase of 8 per cent in delinquency cases handled by juvenile courts in 1963. A total of 601,000 delinquency cases (518,000 different children), representing 1.9 per cent of all children aged 10 through 17, passed through the juvenile courts.

Education and Employment. The relation of delinquency to lack of education and unemployment was the basis for many public and private programs to aid youth. The U.S. Bureau of Labor Statistics published a study, in 1965, on employment of high school graduates and drop-outs in 1964 that showed the unemployment rate for graduates was 11 per cent, but as high as 17 per cent for drop-outs. Further, it was found that 40 per cent of all drop-outs came from families with incomes below $3,000 a year, while only 12 per cent of the graduates came from such low-income families.

Much of the anti-poverty legislation that was signed into law by President Lyndon B. Johnson was designed to decrease youth unemployment and increase education opportunities. The Job Corps, the Neighborhood Youth Corps, and the large-scale program for low-income families' preschool children, called Head Start, were typical examples.

World-Wide Problems. That the United States was not unique in having a serious juvenile delinquency problem became abundantly clear at the Third United Nations Congress on the Prevention of Crime and the Treatment of Offenders held in Stockholm, Sweden, in August, 1965. There, 15 out of 17 European countries reported increases in juvenile delinquency and, particularly, increases in violent crime. England and Wales, Finland, France, and West Germany reported increases in violent crimes committed by young persons. Denmark, Norway, Sweden, Switzerland, and The Netherlands reported increases in youthful crime, but indicated that the increases were confined, for the most part, to crimes against property and misdemeanors. Only the Soviet Union and Italy claimed that crime, including juvenile delinquency, was decreasing in their countries. However, no official crime statistics for the Soviet Union were made available. While international comparisons of delinquency statistics are rendered almost impossible because of differences in definitions, laws, and procedures, the general tendency of increasing juvenile crime in the Western world seems clear.   Hans W. Mattick

KÁLLAI, GYULA (1910-   ), was named premier of Hungary on June 28. He had served as first deputy premier since 1960 and was named to the new post by outgoing premier János Kádár, a lifelong associate with whom he had served a prison term when both fell from party favor. Kádár retained his post as first secretary of the Hungarian Communist party—the most powerful post in the nation. See Hungary.

Kállai is regarded as the chief exponent of party ideas in the Hungarian Communist party. He was educated at the University of Budapest, becoming a communist in 1931 while still a student. By 1945, he had risen to membership in the powerful central committee of the party. He also was named Hungary's secretary of state. From 1949 to 1951 Kállai served as foreign minister. Following his release from prison in 1954, and his restoration to favor in party affairs, he served as deputy minister of culture and then as minister of state.

The new premier is the author of a number of books, including *The Hungarian Movement for Independence, For Socialist Culture*, and *Socialism and Culture*. As premier, he faces the problem of making his nation's economy more productive. Western observers believe that Kádár chose Kállai as a man who could more readily and more effectively take part in trade negotiations with the nations of the West.   Walter F. Morse

KASHMIR. See India; Pakistan.

KATZENBACH, NICHOLAS deB

KATZENBACH, NICHOLAS deBELLEVILLE
(1922-   ), became U.S. Attorney General on
Feb. 13, 1965, after the Senate confirmed his
nomination, offered by President Lyndon B. Johnson on January 28. Katzenbach, who had joined the
Department of Justice in 1961, had been its acting
head since Sept. 3, 1964, when his predecessor,
Robert F. Kennedy, resigned to run for U.S. Senator from New York. Katzenbach was named deputy
Attorney General in 1962 and received his first
general public notice in the integration difficulties
of Mississippi and Alabama universities.

He has practiced law briefly. But most of his
earlier legal career was devoted to teaching—as an
associate professor of international law at Yale
University (1952-1956) and as a law professor at
the University of Chicago (1956-1960). He holds a
B.A. degree from Princeton University (1945);
took his law degree at Yale (1947), where he was
editor in chief of the *Yale Law Review;* and was a
Rhodes scholar at Oxford University (England).
He was an air force navigator during World War
II and was shot down over the Mediterranean,
spending two years as a prisoner of war.

Katzenbach helped Congressmen write the Civil
Rights Act of 1964 and the Communications Satellite Act. He was born in Philadelphia on Jan. 17,
1922. He and his wife, the former Lydia King
Phelps Stokes, have four children.   WALTER F. MORSE

PIX

*GRAND OLD MAN of Kenya is Jomo Kenyatta,
the country's first president. He is shown
here with one of his four wives, Ngina.*

KENNEDY, JOHN FITZGERALD (1917-1963),
35th President of the United States, was still
mourned by the nation two years after his assassination. Two valuable records of the period were published during the year—Theodore C. Sorensen's
783-page *Kennedy* and Arthur M. Schlesinger, Jr.'s,
detailed *A Thousand Days: John F. Kennedy in the
White House.* The late President's secretary, Evelyn
Lincoln, also published a best-selling memoir, *My
Twelve Years with John F. Kennedy.*

On May 14, a monument honoring the late Presi-
dent was dedicated by Queen Elizabeth II at
Runnymede, England, where King John signed
the Magna Carta in 1215. Three acres of land were
bequeathed to the United States in perpetuity (see
GREAT BRITAIN; MEMORIALS). Also in May, John F.
Kennedy received a posthumous Four Freedoms
Award for 1964 for service to the ideals of Franklin
Delano Roosevelt. The plaque was presented to the
late President's brother, Robert, by Franklin D.
Roosevelt, Jr.

Robert F. Kennedy joined in the first climb of a
peak more than 13,000 feet high in Canada's Yukon
on March 25. He planted a flag at the summit,
named Mount Kennedy in his brother's memory.

Jacqueline Kennedy, widow of the President, was
the first American to greet Pope Paul VI at a reception for him in the United Nations delegates' lounge
during his visit in October.   CAROL L. THOMPSON

See also Section Two, LEAVES FROM OUR LIVES.

KENYA. A strike was called by the 16,000-member
Railway African Union on March 5, 1965, tying up
the country's transportation system. A sympathy
strike of 20,000 members of the Local Government
Workers' Union followed. Other unions threatened
to follow suit. But Tom Mboya, minister of economic
planning, persuaded union leaders to call off the
strike, and submit the claims for increased salaries
and benefits to the industrial court.

In late June, President Jomo Kenyatta banned
public meetings and demonstrations by the Kenya
Federation of Labor and the Kenya African Workers' Congress to end what he termed public bickering and semipolitical activities. In September,
Kenyatta dissolved both unions and replaced them
with a Central Organization of Trade Unions
which would supervise union elections.

President Kenyatta appointed former leaders
of the defunct Kenya African Democratic Union
(KADU) to government positions in January. The
KADU had ended its role as an opposition party in
December, 1964, when Ronald Ngana joined the
government and the party was disbanded.

Population: 9,310,000. **Government:** President
Jomo Kenyatta. **Monetary Unit:** shilling (7.143 =
U.S. $1). **Foreign Trade:** exports, $124,000,000; imports, $195,000,000. **Principal Exports:** coffee, hides
and skins, sisal, tea.   BENJAMIN E. THOMAS

See also AFRICA.

KIWANIS INTERNATIONAL. See SERVICE CLUBS.

KOREA established normal diplomatic relations with Japan in June, 1965. It marked the end of 14 years of intermittent negotiations during which the two governments sought ways to settle issues created by Japan's colonial rule over Korea from August, 1910, until the end of World War II.

Korean bitterness over the treaty, which was signed in Tokyo on June 22, 1965, was shown by riots and demonstrations that began months before the treaty was signed and continued even afterward. The Korean national assembly ratified the treaty on August 14 by a vote of 110 to 0 with one abstention, but 62 members of the opposition Minjung party had resigned in protest before the vote was taken.

The treaty called for the establishment of diplomatic and consular relations. It affirmed that all treaties between Korea and Japan concluded before the annexation in 1910 were null and void.

Additional agreements signed simultaneously provided that: (1) Japan would provide Korea with products and services valued at $300,000,000 free of charge over a 10-year period; (2) Japan, over the same period, would make long-term low-interest loans to Korea amounting to $200,000,000; and (3) long-time Korean residents would be permitted to remain in Japan. The dispute over ownership of tiny Dokto (Takeshima) island, lying east of Korea and north of western Japan, was left unsettled.

President Chung Hee Park visited Washington, D.C., in May. He issued a statement supporting U.S. policy in Vietnam. On August 13, the national assembly voted 101 to 1 to send a 15,000-man combat division to Vietnam. See VIETNAM.

North Korea apparently shifted its support from Communist China to the Soviet Union in the dispute over leadership in the communist bloc. Soviet Premier Aleksei Kosygin visited North Korea in February after a visit to Peking. In June, Moscow reports said that the Soviet government had decided to provide military aid to North Korea after high-ranking military officers had visited Moscow. Later, there were signs that relations had cooled between North Korea and Communist China.

Syngman Rhee, the first president of the republic, died in Honolulu, Hawaii, on July 19 (see DEATHS OF NOTABLE PERSONS).

North Korea: Population: 11,289,000. **Government:** Chairman Choe Yong Kun; Prime Minister Kim Il-sung. **Monetary Unit:** won (1.20 = U.S. $1). **Foreign Trade:** no figures available.

South Korea. Population: 29,095,000. **Government:** President Chung Hee Park. **Monetary Unit:** won (271 = U.S. $1). **Foreign Trade:** exports, $120,000,000; imports, $336,000,000. **Principal Exports:** food products, light manufactured goods, minerals. JOHN M. MAKI

See also ASIA; JAPAN.

KUWAIT, with its enormous oil revenues, continued to play the financier's role in the Middle East. Two loans of $14,000,000 each rescued the United Arab Republic from a foreign-exchange crisis. Kuwait loaned Algeria and Morocco $28,000,000 each; Lebanon, $14,000,000; and Tunisia, $11,200,000, despite President Habib Bourguiba's anti-Arab stand in the Arab-Israeli conflict (see TUNISIA). Kuwait even paid for 20,000 tons of wheat for a former enemy, Iraq. But the national assembly turned down Kuwaiti membership in the projected Arab Common Market.

Despite its high per capita income (about $3,000), Kuwait suffered a recession—of sorts—in 1965. This was attributed to the fact that more than half of Kuwait's population is made up of noncitizens who tend to invest their money abroad. Chief complaints came from local merchants, who insisted they were not sharing in the nation's prosperity.

The ruler of Kuwait died in November. His brother, Crown Prince Sheik Sabah al-Salim al-Sabbah, succeeded him. The new ruler immediately named Sheik Jabr, his chief rival, as prime minister to forestall a power struggle.

Population: 564,000. **Government:** Sheik Sabah al-Salim al-Sabbah; Prime Minister Sheik Jabr al-Ahmad al-Jabr. **Monetary Unit:** dinar (1 = U.S. $2.80). **Foreign Trade:** exports, $605,800,000; imports, $327,600,000. **Principal Export:** crude petroleum. WILLIAM SPENCER

See also MIDDLE EAST.

Wide World

RIOTING KOREANS in Seoul battle gas-masked police. They were protesting the proposed signing of a treaty between South Korea and Japan.

IT'S A CONTRACT. R. Conrad Cooper, right, chief negotiator for the steel industry hands agreement to I. W. Abel, United Steelworkers' president.

LABOR. Because of the high level at which the economy was operating, most labor problems found solutions quickly in 1965. Full-time employment increased by more than 2,000,000,000 jobs between the third quarters of 1964 and 1965—the largest gain since 1949-1950. Civilian employment reached a high (seasonally adjusted) of 73,800,000 workers in the summer of 1965.

Unemployment rates continued to decline during the year, and in mid-November (seasonally adjusted) were down to 4.2 per cent, only slightly above the government target of 4 per cent and significantly lower than the 5 per cent rate prevailing a year earlier. Actual unemployment in September fell below 3,000,000 for the first time since 1957.

Wage Increases in 1965 were running over a penny an hour higher than in the previous year. The average (median) increase negotiated during 1965 was over 10 cents. Sizable wage increases were provided for in major contract settlements reached in the aerospace, aluminum, clothing, construction, container, longshore, maritime, oil, rubber, and steel industries. For example, the three-year steel contract gave 350,000 workers 10-to-19-cent an hour increases the first year and additional raises of 6 cents to 12 cents effective Aug. 1, 1967. Substantial improvements in fringe benefits were provided in the major contract settlements. Typically, the number of paid holidays was increased, an additional week of vacation was provided for long-service

workers, and pension benefits were almost doubled.

Average weekly wages of production workers in manufacturing increased by approximately $4 over 1964 levels to $107 per week. Wholesale and consumer prices increased slightly during the year, and some concern was evidenced about the possibility of inflation (see ECONOMY, THE). However, it was hoped that the wage-price trends of 1960-1964 would continue. In that period, unit labor costs did not rise because productivity gains exceeded average increases in employee compensation (see AUTOMATION; MANUFACTURING).

Strike Activity increased slightly in 1965 over previous years, even though a steel strike was averted by presidential intervention (see STEEL INDUSTRY). Time lost due to strikes was running about .20 of 1 per cent of estimated total man-hours of working time. The average for the previous five years was about .16 of 1 per cent.

Public concern about strikes again was fanned by walkouts in the longshore, maritime, and newspaper industries. Although strikes made headlines, most new contracts were reached peacefully.

Bargaining Innovations continued to reflect the concern of unions over restricted job opportunities despite the generally favorable economic outlook. The New York dock strike was settled by guaranteeing experienced workers 1,600 hours of work annually in return for acceptance of technological change and a reduction in sizes of work gangs.

The early retirement supplement negotiated in 1964 by the United Auto Workers and the auto industry was followed in 1965 by provisions in the steel industry for retirement with full pension after 30 years of service regardless of age. The minimum pension was $150 a month figured at $5 per month per year of service up to a total of 35 years. Similar improvements in early retirement provisions of other pension plans were found in most major settlements.

U.S. Union membership continued to grow slightly slower than the nonfarm labor force, and was unofficially estimated in 1964 at 16,800,000 members, or 28.9 per cent of all nonfarm workers, down from 29.2 per cent a year earlier. I. W. Abel defeated David J. McDonald by the narrow vote of 308,910 to 298,768 for the presidency of the large United Steelworkers union. Paul Jennings was declared the winner over James B. Carey in a precedent-setting government recount of ballots for the presidency of the International Union of Electrical Workers (IUE).

Presidents Al Hayes of the Machinists and Aerospace Workers and John P. Burke of the Pulp and Sulphite Workers unions retired because of age and were followed into office by Paul L. "Roy" Siemiller and William H. Burnell, respectively. O. A. Knight of the Oil, Chemical, and Atomic Workers union stepped down after 25 years. He was succeeded by Alvin F. G. Grospiron, who won over W. J. Forresten by the small margin of 75,633 votes to 72,910.

The leadership of the merged American Federation of Labor and Congress of Industrial Organizations (AFL-CIO) was changed substantially for the first time in its 10-year history at the December convention in San Francisco. It elected eight new members to the 29-man executive council. The eight, all active union presidents, reduced the number of inactive unionists on the council from 10 to two.

Labor Law and Legislation. In March, the Supreme Court of the United States issued three landmark decisions in the labor field. In one, it said that a company had an absolute right to go out of business completely (but not partly, as was the case before it) to avoid unionization. In the other two, it strengthened an employer's bargaining position by upholding his right to lock out employees and to hire temporary replacements under certain conditions.

In January, Indiana repealed its right-to-work law, which had prohibited unions and managements from negotiating union security agreements. The repeal reduced to 19 the number of states with such laws. In Congress, an attempt was made to repeal Section 14(b) of the Taft-Hartley Act that permits states to pass such laws. The repeal bill passed the House but was subject to a successful Senate filibuster in the closing days of the session.   JAMES L. STERN

LAOS moved increasingly toward political stability in 1965. In July, elections were held for a new 59-member national assembly. The fact that the civil war between the rightists, the neutralists, and the procommunist Pathet Lao was quiet enough to permit an election was considered proof that Laos was regaining it equilibrium.

The trend was attributable in a large measure to a split that had sundered the ranks of the rightists earlier in the year. It had resulted in self-exile for General Phoumi Nosavan. Subsequently, General Kong Le and his neutralists had joined forces with the remaining rightists to mount a joint offensive against the Pathet Lao. Together, they eliminated the Pathet Lao operating north of Vientiane. The Vang Vieng area was also cleared, and the road between Vientiane and Luang Prabang was opened to traffic for the first time in many months. In addition, the United States began supplying the Meo tribes in northern Laos with arms, thus enabling them to resist the Pathet Lao in that area.

Communists Lose Ground. As a result of these concerted efforts, the Pathet Lao lost ground. For the first time, there were defectors among their ranks. More and more tribal refugees were seeking the protection of the royal government. By year's end, control of the country had passed from the hands of the Pathet Lao, who in 1964 had controlled more than one-half of it, to the royal government of King Savang Vathana, which now controlled about two-thirds of the nation.

Premier Prince Souvanna Phouma began to emerge as a strong political figure. In a large measure this was due to the exile of the rival rightists and the support being given him by General Kong Le's neutralists. But equally important was the fact that the king, by assuming a more active role in the nation's affairs, was in effect giving royal support to Phouma.

Economic Progress. While it was true that the Laotian economy was still in a rudimentary stage and unable to support itself without considerable U.S. financial aid, significant progress was being recorded. There were encouraging signs that education was being carried to the villages on a primary level. Certain agricultural products were being produced locally for the first time. Measures to stabilize the currency were beginning to show results. Much of the nation's progress was due to the fact that the United States was taking a more active role. But there were significant stirrings among the Laotians that indicated their desire for more active participation in the modern world.

Population: 2,024,000. **Government:** King Savang Vathana; Premier Souvanna Phouma. **Monetary Unit:** kip (240 = U.S. $1). **Foreign Trade:** exports, $1,000,000; imports, $29,000,000. **Principal Exports:** gums, resins, tin ore, wood.   JOHN N. STALKER
    See also ASIA.

LASER. See ELECTRONICS.

LATIN AMERICA

Three major issues confronted Latin America in 1965. One of them—subversion by the communists and other extreme leftist groups—directly involved Bolivia, Colombia, the Dominican Republic, Guatemala, Peru, and Venezuela. The second issue—genuine popular discontent with authority—gained momentum in Argentina, Brazil, Chile, and Ecuador. The third issue, which centered around U.S. policy in Latin America, was perhaps the gravest. It not only involved Latin America and the United States but it also touched on that most cherished of Latin-American ideals—nonintervention.

Wide World

On April 28, President Lyndon B. Johnson sent U.S. troops to the Dominican Republic where a military-civilian coup had toppled the government. He acted following reports that the lives of U.S. citizens were in danger. Reaction to the U.S. move was immediate and world-wide. It was condemned by most of the Latin American countries. While they admitted that the United States had every right to protect its nationals, they nevertheless felt that the move was "damaging to the sovereignty of an independent nation." The sending of U.S. troops was also assailed abroad by the communist nations as "a blatant act of imperialist intervention" and a "return to gunboat diplomacy." Some Western-bloc nations, such as France, were equally vehement in protesting the move.

Communist Threat. Despite criticisms, however, which included some by members of the Congress of the United States, the President justified his actions by revealing that the revolutionary movement had taken a "tragic turn" after it had been taken over by communist leaders. These leaders, he said, seeing a chance to create disorder, had moved in with the eventual goal of seizing absolute control. See PRESIDENT OF THE UNITED STATES.

On May 1, the ambassadors to the Organization of American States (OAS) met in Washington, D.C., to consider the situation. One outgrowth of that meeting was a decision to form an Inter-American Peace Force to restore order in the Dominican Republic. The republic remained as troubled as ever at year's end. See DOMINICAN REPUBLIC.

Inter-American Conference. A result of the OAS meeting was a Special Inter-American Conference held by the OAS foreign ministers in Rio de Janeiro from November 17 to 30. While the ministers side-stepped as "intervention" a controversial U.S. proposal to establish a lasting Western Hemisphere peace force, they did lay the groundwork for a modernized and strengthened regional community of American republics. Guidelines were set for the preparation of major reforms in the OAS charter which were to be submitted to a third Special Inter-American Conference scheduled for July, 1966, in Buenos Aires. It was decided, too,

NEW HOUSES in Rio de Janeiro mark efforts of the Alliance for Progress program to eliminate slums in cities of Latin America.

that a foreign ministers' meeting should be held annually.

The Alliance for Progress program emerged as a permanent element of the inter-American system with the conferees declaring that the entire program should be continued "as long as necessary." The United States announced it was prepared to extend aid for the Alliance beyond 1971—the original terminal date of the program. The meeting also called for the elevation of the Inter-American Economic and Social Council and the cultural council to a level with the OAS Council, directly responsible to the annual Foreign Ministers' Conference.

U.S. Support. A U.S. proposal was adopted for the establishment of an inter-American office for export promotion, with the United States pledging capital and technical assistance. In the fiscal year ended June 30, the United States had extended an overall total of $1,064,000,000 in loans and grants to the Latin-American republics—excepting Cuba. The Latin American nations, over the same period, had devoted an estimated $12,000,000,000 plus for self-development programs.

The First Ordinary Legislature of the Latin American Parliament—an organization representing the legislative bodies of 13 republics—met in July in Lima, Peru. The parliament had been created to develop a continental consciousness necessary for the establishment of a Latin American Common Market. It was also pledged to fight for the elimination of all forms of colonialism and imperialism on the continent. The main topics of discussion at the July meeting centered on cultural, economic, and political integration of Latin American lands.

Population Problem. During the year, Latin America faced problems of external debt servicing, inflation, population growth, and widely fluctuating prices for such major exports as bananas, cacao, coffee, and sugar. In 1965, the continent's regional trade deficit reached an estimated $1,000,000,000, while its external financial needs totaled around $3,100,000,000—of which $1,900,000,000 represented debt repayments.

Despite the many schemes presented for economic development, it remained a fact that no program could begin to make a dent in the problems of living standards if the current birth rate—exceeding 3 per cent per annum—continued. At this rate, Latin America, which has an estimated 230,000,000 people, would have 303,000,000 by 1975 and 624,000,000 by the year 2000. See POPULATION, WORLD.

New Economic Plan. During the year, four of Latin America's most renowned leaders drew up a new plan to spark economic integration in Latin America in order to fulfill development needs. These experts were Raul Prebisch, secretary-general of the United Nations (UN) Trade and Development Conference; Jose Mayobre, executive director of the UN Economic Commission for Latin America (ECLA); Felipe Herrera, president of the Inter-American De-

velopment Bank (IADB); and Carlos Sanz de Santamaria, chairman of the Inter-American Committee for the Alliance for Progress.

Their presentation, which had been requested by President Eduardo Frei Montalva of Chile, reflected the general feeling that the nine-nation Latin American Free Trade Association (LAFTA) was failing to prepare its member republics adequately for expanded trade among themselves as well as abroad. The four-man team drew up a sweeping proposal to launch a Latin American Common Market patterned after the successful European Economic Community (EEC, or Common Market). They called for new efforts to accelerate the lowering of existing trade barriers. They also advocated the creation of conditions and incentives for investment from which future intraregional trade could grow—a trade that was at present a mere 9 per cent of the Latin American total.

The experts also noted the need for the formation of a supranational council of hemispheric foreign ministers and high trade officials who would meet regularly to reach overall decisions for a trade area that involved 230,000,000 people, a Gross National Product (GNP) of $75,000,000,000, foreign trade of $18,000,000,000, and gold and foreign reserves totaling about $2,500,000,000.

Proposed Alliance. Earlier in the year, U.S. Senator Jacob Javits of New York urged that consideration be given to the formation of a Latin American Common Market that could develop into a free trade area involving the United States and Canada.

Subsequently, President Eduardo Frei Montalva of Chile visited Europe where he urged those nations to join Latin America in a new "Alliance for Progress" involving more concerted Western European cooperation in the economic development of Latin America. Frei was convinced that the republics must be knit into the Atlantic community in a three-way relationship between itself, the United States, and Western Europe.

Ministers' Conference. The first conference of LAFTA foreign ministers was held in November in Montevideo. Results of the conference included a ministerial decision to establish a permanent ministerial council that would provide political leadership for an organization that, since its creation in 1960, had been essentially a technical group. The ministers also approved resolutions to speed up moves designed to abolish obstacles that still blocked interzonal trading. It was also decided that efforts would be made to coordinate investments, thus ensuring a more equitable economic development for the smaller nations. The ministers also agreed to the establishment of a common external tariff that would govern Latin American relations with other parts of the world.   MARY C. WEBSTER

See also articles on the various countries.

LAW. See COURTS AND LAWS; CIVIL RIGHTS; CRIME; SOCIAL SECURITY; SUPREME COURT OF THE U.S.

LEBANON experienced a parliamentary crisis in 1965 because of its "confessional representation" system of government. Under this system, Lebanon's one-chamber parliament is chosen by the people on the basis of religion; each Christian or Moslem sect elects representatives in proportion to its size. During a stormy debate over proposed amendments to a new judicial law, a religious minority in parliament succeeded in forcing the resignation of Premier Hussein Oweini and his cabinet.

Subsequently, President Charles Helou called upon former premier Rachid Karamí to form a new cabinet of nonparliamentary technicians. The vote of confidence given the new government supported Helou's contention that Lebanon should be administered by technicians and not by politicians subject to the winds of political change.

The Litani River Hydroelectric power project was completed on April 27, 1965. Eventually, the project will irrigate 88,000 unused acres. In May, the government inaugurated a five-year development plan which would cost approximately 3,000,-000,000 Lebanese pounds.

Population: 2,080,000. **Government:** President Charles Helou; Premier Rachid Karamí. **Monetary Unit:** pound (3.08 = U.S. $1). **Foreign Trade:** exports, $50,000,000; imports, $350,000,000. **Principal Exports:** fruits, textiles, vegetables.   WILLIAM SPENCER

See also MIDDLE EAST.

LIBERIA. President William V. S. Tubman dismissed three high ranking government officials for obstructing his policies. He also pardoned the country's former solicitor general and two others who had been sentenced to life imprisonment in 1955 for plotting to assassinate him.

The president continued his "unification" policy to put an end to long-standing differences between the country's remote, undeveloped rural provinces and the more advanced coastal sections. The policy of reserving special senatorial seats for the underdeveloped interior regions of counties was abolished.

In 1965, plans were made for the construction of an oil refinery near Monrovia with an expected daily output of 10,000 barrels and for a $51,000,000 iron ore processing plant at Buchanan. The national assembly approved a $48,000,000 budget for the country in March. Liberia also increased its 1964 loan from the International Bank for Reconstruction and Development (World Bank) for the construction and maintenance of roads. In June, the International Monetary Fund (IMF) authorized Liberia to draw up to $4,000,000 in 1966 as part of a long-term development loan.

Population: 1,046,000. **Government:** President William V. S. Tubman. **Monetary Unit:** dollar (1 = U.S. $1). **Foreign Trade:** exports, $83,000,000; imports, $69,000,000. **Principal Exports:** diamonds, iron, rubber.   BENJAMIN E. THOMAS

See also AFRICA.

LIBRARY. The Congress of the United States recognized the necessity for good library services by including provisions for libraries in every major act it passed relating to education during 1965.

• The Elementary Education Act of 1965 authorized $100,000,000 to states for school library resources.

• The Higher Education Act authorized $70,000,-000 annually for college library assistance and library training and research.

• The Medical Library Assistance Act authorized $23,000,000 for building medical libraries, training medical librarians, research in medical library science, and strengthening present national medical library service.

Under the War on Poverty and Appalachian Regional Development programs, public libraries inaugurated Project Head Start programs and assisted tutoring programs by preparing suitable bibliographies and furnishing meeting places.

Recruitment to the library profession remained a major problem for library associations, library schools, and librarians. In spite of sizable financial assistance from the federal government, there still remained a shortage of librarians. Accredited library schools had more graduates than ever in 1964, 2,500, but there were still more vacancies than applicants.

International Developments. The International Federation of Library Associations (IFLA) held its 31st annual meeting in Helsinki, Finland, in August. More than 200 delegates and observers attended. Among the topics discussed were the international and linguistic aspects of national library services.

German delegates told of a program that included visits of library leaders from other countries as the guests of the German government. The Soviet Union's delegates described their country's extensive translation and exchange of books and periodicals program. The U.S. delegates reported on U.S. assistance to developing countries through technical advice and arrangements for study by foreign librarians in the United States.

The International Federation for Documentation (IFD) held its annual conference in Washington, D.C., from October 7 to 9, and sponsored an open congress the following week that was attended by over 900 librarians and documentalists. Papers delivered at this congress included studies of systems of documentation and ways of training documentalists.

Under the guidance of the United Nations Educational, Scientific, and Cultural Organization (UNESCO), Ecuador, Ivory Coast, and Nigeria made advances in their public, school, or national library programs.   RUTH M. WHITE

See also AMERICAN LIBRARY ASSOCIATION (ALA); CANADIAN LIBRARY ASSOCIATION; EDUCATION; LITERATURE; LITERATURE FOR CHILDREN.

LIBYA

LIBYA observed King Idris I's 75th birthday in an atmosphere clouded with political uncertainty. The king dissolved the house of representatives in February, 1965, following numerous complaints of irregularities in the October (1964) elections. Premier Mahmud Muntasser resigned, and Foreign Minister Hussein Mazik took his portfolio pending new elections. On May 8, the voters elected 76 of 91 representatives, with 15 seats uncontested. The king then confirmed Mazik as Premier.

Although Libya has no political parties, feelings ran high among rival Arab factions. Four defeated candidates for the new assembly, all Pan-Arab nationalists, accused the government of rigging the elections. Libyan students in Paris staged a hunger strike to protest repressive measures taken against their comrades at home.

Britain began a phased withdrawal of troops from Libya. Libya advanced to seventh place (ahead of Canada) among oil producing countries as the industry continued to expand. Mobil Oil completed a 175-mile pipeline to Ras Lanuf. Libya also signed an export accord with Algeria, Morocco, and Tunisia as a step toward economic union.

Population: 1,340,000. **Government:** King Idris I; Premier Hussein Mazik. **Monetary Unit:** pound (1 = U.S. $2.80). **Foreign Trade:** imports, $700,500,000; exports, $292,300,000. **Principal Export:** petroleum. WILLIAM SPENCER

See also AFRICA.

LINDSAY, JOHN VLIET (1921-   ), a Republican Congressman from New York, was elected mayor of New York City on Nov. 2, 1965. It was the first time in 20 years that a non-Democrat had been elected to the office. See DEMOCRATIC PARTY; ELECTIONS; REPUBLICAN PARTY.

Lindsay was born on Nov. 24, 1921, in New York City where he attended Manhattan's Buckley School. After graduation from St. Paul's prep school in Concord, N.H., in 1940 he enrolled at Yale University, where he majored in history.

During World War II, Lindsay served aboard U.S. Navy destroyers in the Mediterranean and the Pacific. In 1946, after his discharge, Lindsay enrolled at the Yale University Law School. He subsequently joined a top Manhattan law firm and within five years had been made a full partner.

Lindsay was elected president of the city's Young Republicans Club in 1951. The following year, he became cochairman of the Youth for Eisenhower organization. In 1955, he was named executive assistant to U.S. Attorney General Herbert Brownell, a position he resigned in 1957 to campaign for election as Congressman from Manhattan's 17th district. He was re-elected in 1960, 1962, and 1964.

New York City's new Republican mayor was married June 18, 1949, to Mary Harrison. They have four children. WALTER F. MORSE

LIONS INTERNATIONAL. See SERVICE CLUBS.

412

LITERATURE

The name of still another literary giant, W. Somerset Maugham, was added to the lengthening record of major writers claimed by death in the decade of the 1960s. Just short of 92 years old, the English author of *Of Human Bondage* and other masterworks of the storyteller's art joined such fallen oaks as William Faulkner, Ernest Hemingway, T. S. Eliot, and Robert Frost, all men whose absence had left the landscape of letters noticeably bleak. As Cyril Connolly wrote of Maugham's passing in *The Sunday Times* of London, "A magician has vanished."

THE LIFE OF DYLAN THOMAS, by Constantine FitzGibbon, was one of 1965's *best biographies. The late poet is shown at a rehearsal of his play,* Under Milk Wood. Rollie McKenna

LITERATURE

While it was true that in 1965 the prospering book publishing industry was pouring out titles in an undiminishing stream, there appeared to be few, if any, magicians around who even hinted that they might turn themselves into towering oaks to fill up the gaps on the landscape. That seemed to be the general feeling, at least, among observers of the literary scene as year-end summaries appeared. In fact, it appeared that the opportunities for the young novelist with something to say and the ability to say it were never greater than they had been in 1965 and would be in the coming years.

Fiction

There were fewer first novels of promise than usual among the year's offerings. Perhaps the best novel by an American was Peter Matthiessen's *At Play in the Fields of the Lord*, an intense, dramatic story of fundamentalist missionaries among the Indians of the Amazon jungle. It was the first major novel of an author already well known for his popular books in the field of natural history and travel. Another of the better novels was the late John Stewart Carter's *Full Fathom Five*, a family chronicle of Chicago's rich Gold Coast community. Stylistically elegant, it won a Houghton Mifflin Fellowship for its author, a poet and college professor who died in his 50s a few months after the book's publication. A second first novel of more than passing interest was Marguerite Young's long (1,200-page), poetic tale of a woman's search for reality, *Miss MacIntosh, My Darling*. Some readers and critics found it too tedious to finish and condemned it as a bore, while others went the route and found in its dreamlike depths new hope for the novel as entertainment in a time of generally dull or repellent fictioneering.

Among the writers of established reputation there were disappointments. Norman Mailer's *An American Dream*, an oddly violent story of a man who murders his wife, exhibited flashes of his old writing skill but on the whole was of small moment. John Updike's *Of the Farm* confirmed the growing opinion of many critics that he had remained for some years a merely promising writer who had not delivered on the prospects of such earlier work as *The Poorhouse Fair* and *Rabbit, Run*. John O'Hara published his first novel in five years, *The Lockwood Concern*. It was another Pennsylvania tale, but to many critics it proved only that he should have stuck to writing short stories, where his real talent lay.

One veteran writer who had a good year commercially, if not artistically, was James A. Michener, whose *The Source*, a historical novel of Israel, went to the top of the best-seller list shortly after publication and stayed there. And there were flurries of praise, along with critical salvos, for several other veterans who brought out new work in 1965. Vardis Fisher's *Mountain Man: A Novel of Male and Female in the Early American West* got less attention than

W. SOMERSET MAUGHAM, one of the most widely read writers in the world, liked to refer to himself as a "Very Old Party." He died at 91.

it deserved, largely because of the tendency to classify all novels about the West as simply "Westerns." Actually it was a superior piece of historical fiction and perhaps his best work since the Harper Prize Novel of 1939, *The Children of God*.

Peter De Vries turned in another comic delight in *Let Me Count the Ways*, which dealt with the religious faith of a Midwestern family. After the triumph of his first novel, *Home from the Hill*, William Humphrey's *The Ordways*, the story of a family of Tennesseans who went to Texas in the last century, should have aroused more critical attention than it did. It was a solid, well-written story and a notable step forward in this writer's career. Still another novelist with "second novel" trouble was Romulus Linney. His *Slowly, by Thy Hand Unfurled*, a brief character study of a small-town woman as she reveals herself in her diary, failed to excite the kind of interest that had greeted his earlier *Heathen Valley*. It was, nevertheless, one of the most unusual and creative pieces of fiction to appear in 1965.

The Short Story was represented in two notable collections, both by women writers already well known for their novels and stories. *The Collected Stories of Katherine Anne Porter* offered dramatic evidence of her superior talents as a storyteller and drew a far better press than her novel *Ship of Fools*. The late Flannery O'Connor's talent was abundantly displayed in the collection, *Everything That Rises Must Converge*. James Baldwin's *Going to Meet the*

Man, a first collection of short stories, was uneven in quality and left most critics with the impression that his best work remains in the field of the essay.

Importations. A number of works of fiction from abroad engaged the attention of U.S. readers. Perhaps the best of them was John Braine's *The Jealous God*, in which the British author of *Room at the Top* and other books explored the conscience of a Roman Catholic teacher and the inner conflict of flesh and spirit. Other importations which aroused both critical and popular interest were Brian Moore's Irish novel *The Emperor of Ice-Cream;* Nikos Kazantzakis' fictional confession, *Report to Greco;* Günter Grass' *Dog Years*, about the Hitler madness; and Georges Simenon's *The Little Saint*, in which the French creator of Inspector Maigret wrote a serious tale of a painter risen from the Paris slums. There were also two notable short story collections from Africa: Nadine Gordimer's *Not for Publication and Other Stories* and Doris Lessing's *African Stories*.

Nonfiction

Biography, Autobiography, and Letters. The literary life unfailingly produces a large share of biography in any year, and 1965 was no exception. Among the year's most absorbing productions was Constantine FitzGibbon's brilliantly successful *The Life of Dylan Thomas*, in which the strange drama of the Welsh poet's tragic life was re-created with insight and compassion by a contemporary intent on objectivity despite personal affection. The American poet Edwin Arlington Robinson was the subject of a personal portrait in Chard Powers Smith's biographical study, *Where the Light Falls*. The book shed new light on the poet's love for his sister-in-law, Emma Shepherd. The German poet Goethe was the subject of another excellent study in Richard Friedenthal's *Goethe, His Life and Times*.

Two major novelists, one American and the other French, both of them filled with contradictions to challenge the ablest of interpreters, were subjects of notable biographies. W. A. Swanberg's detailed *Dreiser* was a compelling portrait that promised to spark a revival of interest in the Indianan's great naturalistic novels. George D. Painter's *Proust: The Later Years* was the second and concluding volume of a biography that seemed destined to become the standard work in the field.

Two essayists who came in for a share of attention were Thoreau and Montaigne. In *The Days of Henry Thoreau*, Walter Harding offered not so much a new arrangement of the materials of Thoreau's life as fresh insights on his relevance as a contemporary today. Donald M. Frame's *Montaigne: A Biography* was widely hailed as the best modern work on the great French essayist.

Several writers told their own stories, among them A. B. Guthrie, the novelist, whose *The Blue Hen's Chick* was an engaging work of Western Americana; the late Edith Sitwell, whose *Taken Care Of: An Autobiography* was completed just before she died, and Simone de Beauvoir, whose *Force of Circumstance* was a continuation of her chronicle that shed light on the French literary and political life of the last two decades.

There were two notable collections of letters published during the year, *Bernard Shaw: Collected Letters, 1874-1897*, edited by Dan H. Laurence, and *Letters of Ford Madox Ford*, edited by Richard M. Ludwig. The Shaw collection was the first of three projected volumes and it bristled with the sharp wit of his younger years. The Ford letters appeared at about the same time as Frank MacShane's lively work *The Life and Work of Ford Madox Ford* and aptly complemented it.

Two other biographical studies of interest in the literary field were John Mason Brown's *The Worlds of Robert E. Sherwood: Mirror to His Times, 1896-1939*, about the playwright who became a speech writer for Franklin D. Roosevelt, and Lord David Cecil's *Max: A Biography*, a revealing chronicle of Max Beerbohm's life and times.

There were several notable biographies of world leaders, among them James Thomas Flexner's *George Washington: The Forge of Experience (1732-1775);* Violet Bonham Carter's *Winston Churchill: An Intimate Portrait;* and the fourth and fifth volumes of Arthur S. Link's definitive study of Woodrow Wilson, *Wilson: Confusions and Crises, 1915-1916*, and *Wilson: Campaigns for Progressivism and Peace*.

An autobiography of significance against the background of the civil rights struggle was the posthumously published *The Autobiography of Malcolm X*.

History. The fields of history and biography are so closely related that it is sometimes difficult to pigeonhole a book. This was true in several specific instances in 1965, notably in the two studies: Theodore C. Sorensen's *Kennedy* and Arthur M. Schlesinger, Jr.'s *A Thousand Days: John F. Kennedy in the White House*. Both were ably written books by men who were close to the late President, but the historian's skill as displayed by Schlesinger clearly marked his book as superior, although both books complemented one another. There were examples of the biographer's skill also in Theodore H. White's *The Making of the President, 1964*, but it was essentially a work of contemporary history by a crack journalist that displayed both skill and depth.

There were elements of autobiography in Dwight D. Eisenhower's *Waging Peace: The White House Years 1956-1961*, which was essentially a work of history as recorded by the Chief Executive of those years. *Mission with LeMay: My Story*, by General Curtis E. LeMay and MacKinlay Kantor, was also a largely autobiographical work that incidentally added to the record of World War II. The former British foreign secretary added a third volume of reminiscences to the record of World War II with *The Reckoning*, the memoirs of Anthony Eden. Dean Acheson, former U.S. Secretary of State, on the

A Poet Who Mirrored the Modern Age

On a cold evening in November, 1959, a tall broad-shouldered old man walked onto the stage at Orchestra Hall in Chicago. Every seat in the auditorium was filled. People were standing in the gallery and seated on the stage. Some 2,800 people had come to hear a poet read his poems and about 1,000 more were turned away for lack of standing room. But no one was surprised at the size of the crowd, because the man on the stage who was reading in a slow, sad voice was T. S. Eliot, the most important poet of our time. Such crowds always appeared at Eliot's infrequent public readings or lectures. And this was one of Eliot's last visits to the United States. He had come to honor *Poetry* magazine on its 50th birthday and to journey (with his young wife) to his birthplace, St. Louis, Mo., for the last time.

T. S. ELIOT
(1888–1965)

416

What were the reasons for Eliot's world fame, for the 1948 Nobel prize, and the Order of Merit awarded by Queen Elizabeth II of Great Britain? Why the steady sale in the English-speaking world of his *Collected Poems* (1909–1962), which total only 221 pages, for his few books of essays and verse plays? Why did he dominate poetry in English for two decades?

The reason, in essence, is that about the time of World War I, Thomas Stearns Eliot, then a U.S. expatriate working days as a clerk in Lloyd's Bank in London, and nights as a poet, began a revolution in poetry that was to affect every poet writing in English to the present day.

That revolution was to strip poetry of the pseudo-"poetic"—of the stagey thee's and thou's, the nightingales, of cliches of thought and feeling—and bring back into poetry the rhythms of common speech. In short, T. S. Eliot was more fully responsible than anyone else for making poetry an instrument capable of dealing with the harsh realities of the modern world. In accomplishing this gigantic task, along with his friend Ezra Pound and a few like-minded U.S. poets, Eliot permanently enriched and extended poetry in English, and, hence, the lives of thoughtful, cultivated men everywhere.

Poetry at the turn of the 20th century characteristically dealt with minor themes in muted ways. Georgian and Edwardian poetry too frequently was a pale imitation of Keats and Milton and the great Victorians. After Eliot, poetry would once again give pleasure as poetry is supposed to do, and would once again be a vital instrument for dealing with the complexities of the modern world.

Eliot's first important poem was "The Love Song of J. Alfred Prufrock" (1917). With irony, precision, and exquisite lyricism, Prufrock meditated on the emptiness of his life, and became the symbol for many of frustration and despair:

*Shall I say, I have gone at dusk
    through narrow streets
And watched the smoke that rises
    from the pipes
Of lonely men in shirt-sleeves, leaning
    out of windows? . . .*

*I should have been a pair of ragged claws
Scuttling across the floors of silent seas.*

Eliot's most famous poem is "The Waste Land" (1922). In a series of scenes that dramatically shift and blend into one another, we are given the definitive image of the emotional, intellectual, and spiritual sterility of the postwar world. The poem begins:

*April is the cruelest month, breeding
Lilacs out of the dead land, mixing
Memory and desire, stirring
Dull roots with spring rain . . .*

In 1927, Eliot became a British subject. In 1943, having shifted from a skeptical to a deeply religious position, he published his *Four Quartets*, considered by many critics to be the finest religious verse of the 20th century. T. S. Eliot's ancestors came from the Somerset village of East Coker. There his ashes were interred. In the last line of the Quartet, "East Coker," he wrote:

*We must be still and still moving
Into another intensity
For a further union, a deeper communion
Through the dark cold and the empty
    desolation
The wave cry, the wind cry, the vast
    waters
Of the petrel and the porpoise. In my
    end is my beginning.*

MARK M. PERLBERG

other hand, devoted most of his *Morning and Noon* to a reconstruction of his boyhood and young manhood.

It was a good year for historians of the American scene. The most comprehensive work in the field was Samuel Eliot Morison's compendious but sprightly book, *The Oxford History of the American People*, written with his customary grace and skill. Daniel J. Boorstin published *The Americans: The National Experience*, a sequel to *The Americans: The Colonial Experience*. In this new book Boorstin carried his study of the intellectual background of the United States to the Civil War.

Other notable works on U.S. history were Bruce Catton's *Never Call Retreat*, the third and last volume of his centennial history of the Civil War; Christopher Lasch's *The New Radicalism in America, 1889-1963;* Richard B. Morris' *The Peacemakers*, an able diplomatic history of the American Revolution; Kenneth M. Stampp's *The Era of Reconstruction, 1865-1877*, and the late Perry Miller's *The Life of the Mind in America*. Joyce L. Kornbluh's *Rebel Voices: An I. W. W. Anthology* was an important historical contribution as well as a folklore treasury.

In other historical fields, there were important and fascinating works. R. A. Skelton and several colleagues published their controversial, *The Vinland Map and the Tartar Relation*. It contended that Norsemen discovered America before Columbus. Will and Ariel Durant published *The Age of Voltaire*, which brought the Durants' *The Story of Civilization* along the road from 1715 to 1756. Donald R. Morris told the absorbing story of the rise and fall of the Zulu nation in *The Washing of the Spears*. Larry Collins and Dominique Lapierre made it onto the bestseller lists with a stirring account of the Parisian resistance against Hitler in *Is Paris Burning?*

Vietnam. The conflict in Vietnam inspired a number of books, among them Robert Shaplen's *The Lost Revolution*, which was highly critical of U.S. diplomacy; David Halberstam's *The Making of a Quagmire*, also critical; John Mecklin's *Mission in Torment*, an account of Vietnam activities by a former U.S. information officer that supported the Halberstam thesis; Malcolm W. Browne's *The New Face of War*, and Robin Moore's *The Green Berets*, which described the fighting.

Essays and Criticism. One of the year's most unusual books was Nelson Algren's *Notes from a Sea Diary: Hemingway All the Way*, in which the iconoclastic Chicago novelist used the record of a tramp steamer trip to Far East ports to eulogize his favorite writer while dispensing critical comments on various other subjects, including some unfavored contemporaries. The dean of U.S. literary critics, Edmund Wilson, collected a new series of essays, reviews, and articles in *The Bit Between My Teeth: A Literary Chronicle of 1950-1965*. Essays of two French men of letters were collected in the late Albert Camus' *Notebooks: 1942-1951*, translated by Justin O'Brien, and Jean-Paul Sartre's *Situations*, translated by Benita Elsler. The American critic Lionel Trilling published *Beyond Culture* subtitled, "*Essays on Literature and Learning.*" VAN ALLEN BRADLEY

Poetry

Once again, poetry was overshadowed by events having little to do with current work. Chief among them was the death in London on Jan. 4, 1965, of T. S. Eliot, who had been for some decades dean of English-speaking poets. Though his position had been disputed and he had been called by some the reactionary figurehead of the Establishment, ultimately, the world of poetry united in acknowledging his leadership.

Eliot's death seemed to mark, more than any other event, the close of the "modern era," as it had been known for half a century. "Modern poetry" was now as much history as "Romantic poetry" or "Georgian poetry." Other indicators were the centennial of the birth of William Butler Yeats and the death of R. P. Blackmur, who was among the leading interpreters of the modern movement begun at about the time of World War I by Eliot and Ezra Pound. But poetry was now off in other directions. School texts of the future might well include the paradoxical heading: "Modern Poetry, 1915-1965."

Perhaps another, though more ironic, index was the all-day festival of arts at the White House on June 14. Here the "modern" spirit in art received what many participants regarded as the death knell of final, official acceptance. Moreover, the ceremonies were marred by an acute sense of disharmony. Several participants, including the chairman of poetry readings, Mark Van Doren, alluded to the strangeness of such celebrations in such a house at such a time.

Habit of Modernity. Meanwhile, the habits of "modernity" persisted ever more in institutional form. The Ford Foundation, for example, granted $750,000 to the University of Texas for a national translation center dedicated to "improving and expanding the art of literary translation in the United States." Years before, Eliot and Pound had insisted on the value of translation in rejuvenating modern literature and shaping a new critical temper. Now the new center, governed by 13 eminent scholars and poets, would thrash out in committee the translator's perennial problems, and a spate of subsidized translations could be looked for.

As for current work, little seemed noteworthy. The best books of the year were A. R. Ammons' *Tape for the Turn of the Year;* Louis Zukofsky's *All: The Collected Short Poems, 1923-1958;* and *The Lost World*, by the critic and poet Randall Jarrell, who was killed by an automobile on October 14. The liveliest productions were new magazines that contained work by leaders of the younger poets, much of it convincing. HAYDEN CARRUTH

LITERATURE, CANADIAN. See CANADIAN LIBRARY ASSOCIATION; CANADIAN LITERATURE.

In long straight lines
the seagulls and terns flew back
to their roosts on the craggy rocks.
They knew the fog was coming, too.

Now the water of the bay was gray like the sky,
and the end of the beach was gone.
Now the afternoon sun turned to a pale daytime moon,
then vanished into the bank of fog.

FROM HIDE AND SEEK FOG. *Pictures by Roger Duvoisin. Text by Alvin Tresselt. Only the children enjoy the thickest fog in 20 years. Publisher: Lothrop, Lee & Shepard.*

LITERATURE FOR CHILDREN

LITERATURE FOR CHILDREN. "Alice" is 100 years old. The world of children's literature is richer because a mathematician and a small girl watched a rabbit go down a hole over 100 years ago and started wondering. The story told to the real Alice has become one of the world's greatest classics, *Alice's Adventures in Wonderland*, now translated into many languages.

ILLUSTRATORS' ART

The illustrations in this article are a selection from the 10 best-illustrated children's books of 1965, according to a jury chosen by The New York Times Book Review.

Several years ago, David C. Davis of the University of Wisconsin conceived the idea of forming a Lewis Carroll Shelf Award Committee to determine which children's books, old and new, were worthy of being placed on a shelf next to "Alice." A few such "classics" are added each year. At this time, there are 85 titles. The list may be obtained from the University of Wisconsin School of Education, Madison.

Since young people are now concerned with the entire world, many of the newest books for children have a world outlook. There are stories and informational books about other lands and peoples, including a few classics newly translated into English.

Many books, such as *Red-Flannel Hash and Shoo-Fly Pie: American Regional Foods and Festivals*, by Lila Perl, will interest young people and adults. Since America has been described as a tapestry of customs from other lands, many will enjoy the unique cookery of these cultures and of the original Americans, the Indians.

Two exciting handicraft books are for family libraries: Erica Wilson's *Fun with Crewel Embroidery*, and Irene P. Miller and Winifred Lubell's *The Stitchery Book*. Hobbyists of all ages will share *Coins and Coin Collecting*, by Seymour Reit, illustrated by W. T. Mars.

American Heritage and *Horizon Caravel* books have proved to be valuable in arousing interest in history. They may be purchased individually, or by subscription. The illustrations are well reproduced, the text authentic, and the content suitable for family sharing of American and world history. *The Art of Africa* and *The Art of Ancient Rome*, new photographic picture books by Shirley Glubok, may precede a museum trip.

Science is more difficult for the layman to evaluate, but the American Association for the Advancement of Science now publishes *Science Books*, a quarterly review which includes many children's books, and whose editorial advisory board includes several librarians.

Adults may find help in answering children's questions about sex in the fourth edition of *Growing*

Up: How We Become Alive, Are Born, and Grow, by Karl de Schweinitz, with photographs. For older children's questions, guidance authority Evelyn Mills Duvall has written *Why Wait Till Marriage?*

Some picture books, biographies, histories, and collections of poetry are to be shared with the family. Poems and stories by authors known to adults are published for children, such as Conrad Aiken's picture book *Cats and Bats and Things with Wings*, poems with drawings by Milton Glaser; or E. E. Cummings' *Fairy Tales*, written for his daughter as a little girl, and illustrated by a young Canadian.

New titles about children's books and storytelling for adults are Joan Bodger's *How the Heather Looks*, which describes a joyous journey through Britain exploring Narnia, Camelot, and Johnny Crow's garden; *Summoned by Books*, a reprint of 15 speeches and essays by Frances Clarke Sayers, children's literature and book reviewing specialist for many years; *A Second Storyteller's Choice*, selected by Eileen Colwell, English children's librarian; and a paperback edition of *The Way of the Storyteller*, by Ruth Sawyer, current winner of the Laura Ingalls Wilder award and Regina medal.

Classics and Poetry

Aesop's Fables selected and adapted by Louis Untermeyer. Illus. by A. and M. Provensen.

15 Fables of Krylov. Trans. by Guy Daniels. Illus. by David Pascal. Families will enjoy these tales with a moral by a Russian fabulist equal to La Fontaine.

Raminagrobis and the Mice by Harold Berson. A La Fontaine fable adapted and illus. in line drawings.

The Ugly Duckling, Hans Christian Andersen's classic translated by R. P. Keigwin, is charmingly illustrated as a picture book by Adrienne Adams.

The Courtship, Merry Marriage, and Feast of Cock Robin and Jenny Wren, to which is added *The Doleful Death of Cock Robin.* Illus. by Barbara Cooney for children who play at "wedding" or burying a pet.

Limericks by Lear. Pictures by Lois Ehlert. Alliterative nonsense of Edward Lear finds a perfect counterpart in gay illustration of intriguing design.

Toad of Toad Hall by A. A. Milne. Reprint of a play from Kenneth Grahame's *The Wind in the Willows.*

Lullabies and Night Songs ed. by William Engvick. Music by Alec Wilder. Pictures by Maurice Sendak. For families who sing together, some quiet scenes, others with humor for impromptu dramatization.

The Real Mother Goose. Illus. by Blanche Fisher Wright. Golden anniversary ed. Introduction by May Hill Arbuthnot, Regina medalist of 1964.

I Saw a Rocket Walk a Mile: Nonsense Tales, Chants and Songs from Many Lands by Carl Withers. Illus. by John E. Johnson. Sharing folk tale and rhyme helps one gain more world understanding.

A Book of Love Poems ed. by William Cole. Illus. by Lars Bo. A beautifully made book for young teens includes English translations of verse from Ireland and Turkey.

This Land Is Mine: An Anthology of American Verse by Al Hine. Comic and lyric narrative verse from all eras since colonial times.

Picture Books

Noisy Nancy Norris by Lou Ann Gaeddert. Illus. by Gioia Fiammenghi. Noise builds up, then quiet can almost be heard. An only child learns a lesson.

Katie's Magic Glasses by Jane Goodsell. Illus. by Barbara Cooney. Until she got a pair of eyeglasses, everything looked blurry to five-year-old Katie.

The Rain Puddle by Adelaide Holl. Pictures by Roger Duvoisin. Each barnyard animal, in this gay folk tale variant, looks into the puddle and believes an animal is drowning.

Is It Blue as a Butterfly? by Rebecca Kalusky. Pictures by Aliki. Simple guessing book with objects, sounds, and perspective just right for the very young.

Stocking for a Kitten by Helen Kay. Illus. by Yaroslava. Decorative art helps tell of Babushka, who teaches one sister patience, and one, knitting.

3 x 3: Three by Three by James Krüss. Pictures by Eva Johanna Rubin. English text of rhyme, rhythm, and repetition by Geoffrey Strachan. Printed in West Germany.

Hector Protector and *As I Went Over the Water* by Maurice Sendak. Delightfully and dramatically extended adventures of a heroic messenger and a gallant sea captain.

Chie and the Sports Day by Masako Matsuno. Illus. by Kazue Mizumura. How a little Japanese girl helped her brother win the three-legged race.

Yankee Doodle by Richard Schackburg. Colorful, stylized woodcuts by Ed Emberley, depicting clothing and flags of the American Revolution, accompany this famous Revolutionary War song for all ages.

John Henry: An American Legend, by Caldecott medalist Ezra Jack Keats, is about a Negro folk hero who won against the steam drill.

Bible Stories and Christmas Stories

Shadrach, Meshach and Abednego: From the Book of Daniel. Illus. by Paul Galdone. Three young Jews refused to worship an image of gold, and were thrown into the fiery furnace.

·IV·
THE BEAR

FROM THE ANIMAL FAMILY. *Pictures by Maurice Sendak. Story by Randall Jarrell. A lonely boy finds an unusual family. Publisher: Pantheon.*

And on a trunk of tools was set
A plaster bust of Lafayette.
Each day they filled another space
To satisfy that "Just in case..."

19

FROM KANGAROO AND KANGAROO. *Pictures by Jim McMullan. Verse by Kathy Braun. Two kangaroos learn that it is folly to hoard. Publisher: Doubleday.*

David and Goliath by Beatrice Schenk de Regniers. Illus. by Richard M. Powers. David plays his harp, slays the lion and the bear to save his sheep, and kills the giant to save King Saul's armies.

In The Beginning: Paintings of the Creation by boys and girls around the world. From World Council of Christian Education and Sunday School Association.

Away in a Manger: A Story of the Nativity by Mares and Paul Nussbaumer, Swiss author and illustrator.

Starlight in Tourrone by Suzanne Butler. Illus. by Reta Fava Fegiz. Children revive an ancient Provençal Christmas custom and carol.

A Certain Small Shepherd by Rebecca Caudill. Illus. by William Pène Du Bois. Jamie of Hurricane Gap grew up without the gift of speech. One Christmas Eve a baby was born to wayfarers, and Jamie spoke.

Folk Tales of Many Lands

Tom Tit Tot ed. by Joseph Jacobs and illus. by Evaline Ness. An English folk tale similar to the German *Rumpelstiltskin*.

The Cock and the Ghost Cat by Betty Jean Lifton. Illus. by Fuku Akino. Once upon a time in Japan a red cock gave his life to save his master.

Seven Silly Wise Men by James C. Bowman and Margery Bianco. Illus. by John Faulkner.

The Valiant Chattee-Maker: A Folktale of India retold by Christine Price. A timid pottery maker is mistakenly thought to be brave.

Favorite Fairy Tales Told in Italy retold by Virginia Haviland. Illus. by Evaline Ness.

Always Room for One More by Sorche Nic Leodhas. Illus. by Nonny Hogrogian. Lachie MacLachlan, his good wife, and their ten "bairns" shared with all travelers.

The Earth Is on a Fish's Back: Tales of Beginnings by Natalia Belting. Illus. by Esta Nesbitt. Gathered from primitive civilizations for storytellers.

Down from the Lonely Mountain: California Indian Tales retold by Jane Louise Curry. Tales of the beginning involve Coyote, Cottontail, Fox, and Mole.

Jambo, Sungura: Tales from East Africa by Eleanor B. Heady. Sungura, the hare, is related to Br'er Rabbit.

The Tiger and the Rabbit, and Other Tales told by Pura Belpré. New enl. ed. of Puerto Rican folk tales.

Cricket and the Emperor's Son by Elizabeth Coatsworth. Illus. by Juliette Palmer. A Japanese tale.

Tales and Legends of Morocco by Elisa Chimenti. Trans. by Arnon Benamy. Oriental tales.

The Sea of Gold and Other Tales from Japan adapted by Yoshiki Uchida. Illus. by Marianna Yamaguchi.

Adventure and Fantasy

Coll and His White Pig by Lloyd Alexander. Illus. by Evaline Ness. A magic kingdom of talking animals with alliterative names is introduced to the youngest.

The Alligator Case by William Pène Du Bois. Another gay, fast-moving detective story with a young hero.

The Wonderful Flying-Go-Round by Dana Faralla. Illus. by Harold Berson. Fantasy as light as Mrs. Mirabella's ostrich plumes helps transform an ugly dump yard for two boys.

Tal and the Magic Barruget by Eva-Lis Wuorio. Illus. by Bettina. A lonely Welsh boy on a Mediterranean island finds a bottle imp, and the two have a wonderful summer.

The Shoe Shop Bears by Margaret J. Baker. Illus. by C. Walter Hodges. Three stuffed bears become Christmas gifts for needy children in an English town.

The Smartest Man in Ireland by Mollie Hunter. Tales of the fairy folk country centered around the bragging Patrick.

Soldier and Me by David Line. A whodunit, with English and Hungarian boy heroes.

The Ghost in the Noonday Sun by Sid Fleischman. Twelve-year-old Oliver was destined to meet exciting new adventures after he was shanghaied by Captain Scratch.

Other Lands

Musical Instruments of Africa: Their Nature, Use, and Place in the Life of a Deeply Musical People by Betty W. Dietz and Michael B. Olatunji.

A World of Doll Houses by Flora Gill Jacobs. With photos. France, Italy, Japan, The Netherlands, Sweden, and the United States are represented.

Little Monk and the Tiger: A Tale of Thailand by Arnold Dobrin. The villagers feared Mrs. Crooked, who carried off their best animals.

Shaun and the Boat: An Irish Story by Anne Molloy. Pictures by Barbara Cooney. A boatbuilder's son helps his father with the currach that wins the race.

A Letter to Anywhere by Al Hine. Gay humorous pictures by John Alcorn tell the story of postal service around the world.

Kristy's Courage by Babbis Friis. Trans. from the Norwegian by Lise Somme McKinnon. Kristy, who has been disfigured by an accident, faced her first day at school.

The Sea Wall by Eilís Dillon. Periodic floods came to the island of Inisharcain, until the young ones took a hand. Another of the author's Irish island stories is a *Family of Foxes*. People of Inishownan thought foxes were bad luck.

The Thursday Kidnapping by Antonia Forest. This runner-up for the English Carnegie medal is a whodunit.

Megan by Iris Noble. A teen-age orphan from Wales comes to western Canada in 1902, and becomes part of the family for whom she works.

I, Juan de Pareja by Elizabeth Borton de Treviño. A Negro slave in the Spanish court was honest, loyal, and became a noted artist, a different kind of hero.

The Sundowners by Jon Cleary. A story of growing up in Australia in the 1920s, long out of print, is revised for teens whose tastes grow continually more mature.

The Bushbabies by William Stevenson. Terrain and wildlife of Kenya are pictured as young Jackie and a faithful African friend try to return the bushbaby to its home.

Animal Books

The Wildlife of Africa by Jocelyn Arundel. Illus. by Wesley Dennis. From prehistoric times.

Our Wild Animals by John Bailey. Photos. by Leonard Lee Rue III, some in color. Also drawings of animal tracks.

Flying Free by Reidar Brodtkorb. Because eagles destroy profitable eider ducks and salmon, Norway has a bounty. The author freed several in Scotland.

The Gull's Way by Louis Darling. Pictures, taken as the author watched a pair of gulls, accompany this tale of courtship, nesting, and hatching.

Mississippi Possum by Miska Miles. Illus. by John Schoenherr. Instincts are unheeded in time of flood as this possum joins a Negro family in their tent.

Ice King by Ernestine N. Byrd. Illus. by Marilyn Miller. The story of an orphan ice bear, raised by an Eskimo, is told up to the death of the bear's mate.

People Are Important

Mr. Chu by Norma Keating. Illus. by Bernarda Bryson. Poetic prose tells of an American orphan at Chinese New Year in New York. Exquisite wash and line pictures.

My Little Cabbage by Susan Purdy. Humorous illustrations by author make this a fun book to arouse interest in many countries and languages.

The Fish in the Castle by Dale Fife. Illus. by Marilyn Miller. Eric finds the grunion fish, which comes on the midnight tide to lay its eggs.

The Bus Trip by Eleanor Frances Lattimore. Nine-year-old Bettina is given responsibility of taking her small brother by bus from Florida to Pennsylvania.

Robert Rows the River by Carolyn Haywood. Along the River Thames, Robert meets a Gypsy boy. Their friendship destroys a false concept many people have about gypsies.

The Empty Schoolhouse by Natalie Savage Carlson. Pictures by John Kaufmann. St. Joseph's School opens its doors to all, but an outsider stirs up racial trouble.

The Indians at Carlisle by William Heuman. An off-reservation school is founded to aid assimilation of Indians into the "white civilization."

Berries Goodman by Emily Cheney Neville. A Newbery laureate shows how prejudices of Jewish and non-Jewish adults almost brings disaster to one boy.

FROM SVEN'S BRIDGE. *Pictures and text by Anita Lobel. In a terrible temper, the king blows up the bridge, but the tale ends happily. Publisher: Harper & Row.*

LITERATURE FOR CHILDREN
Scene 1

"*My* peanut," says the Caballero. "No, *mine*," says the Señorita.

FROM PLEASE SHARE THAT PEANUT! *Pictures by Simms Taback. The text by Sesyle Joslin encourages children to share. Publisher: Harcourt, Brace & World.*

FROM ALBERIC THE WISE AND OTHER JOURNEYS. *Pictures by Domenico Gnoli. Three tales of quests by Norton Juster turn up unexpected things. Publisher: Pantheon.*

The Spider Plant by Yetta Speevack. Puerto Rican Carmen missed her little kitchen garden until her teacher gave her a spider plant.

The Velvet Room by Zilpha Keatley Snyder. A migrant story with a mystery, real people, and a happy ending.

Liza by Hope Campbell. The theater, a five-year-old boy, and a romance occupy a 16-year-old girl one summer.

Fast Green Car by W. E. Butterworth. Because of his interest in art and tire designing, Tony gets into sports-car racing.

A Sense of Where You Are: A Profile of William Warren Bradley by John A. McPhee. Evaluation of the game (basketball) and the plays make this sports biography outstanding.

History and Biography

Crete: Island of Mystery by Leonard Cottrell. King Minos, Knossos, and excavations of Sir Arthur Evans.

People in Palestine by Olivia Coolidge. From the prophecy of the Messiah through the hiding of the Dead Sea Scrolls. *Quest for the Dead Sea Scrolls*, by Geoffrey Palmer, concerns their discovery in 1947 by a Bedouin goatherd.

The Mark of the Horse Lord by Rosemary Sutcliff. Phaedrus, the gladiator, by killing, wins his freedom in 2nd century Roman Britain.

A Slave's Tale by Erik Christian Haugaard. A girl of Viking days travels far and discovers that "Gods of peace will matter little so long as men worship the sword."

Socrates by Robert Silverberg. Golden age of Greece and Socrates' contribution to philosophy.

The Crusades, by Franklin Hamilton, shows how the Middle East was influenced by religious wars.

The World of Columbus and Sons by Genevieve Foster. Was an international outlook born when Columbus discovered unknown lands and peoples? Illustrations make times live.

Jules Verne: Portrait of a Prophet by Russell Freedman. This geographer, dramatist, and scientific researcher inspired inventors, deep-sea divers, and astronauts.

The Franco-Prussian War: Germany's Rise as a World Power by Irving Werstein. Both sides presented vividly.

The Dreyfus Affair: A National Scandal by Betty Schecter. French struggle to resolve the problem of democratic or authoritarian government.

Man of Steel: Joseph Stalin by Jules Archer. An important view of 20th century European history.

Odyssey of Courage: The Story of Álvar Núñez Cabeza de Vaca by Newbery medalist Maia Wojciechowska. Exploration in the New World pictures the man and his philosophy.

Walk the World's Rim by Betty Baker. The Indian boy Chakoh admired "the dark one" in Cabeza de Vaca's party until he learned he was a slave, but it was from Esteban that he learned honor and loyalty.

Dark Pilgrim: The Story of Squanto by Feenie Ziner. His adventures as a slave in England and Spain and his contributions to the well-being of the Pilgrims.

John Quincy Adams: Son of the American Revolution by Milton Lomask. A distinguished statesman.

Andrew Jackson by Margaret L. Coit. Pulitzer prize author pictures war hero and leader of "Jacksonian Democracy."

Frontier President: James K. Polk by Bill Severn. A shy, sickly young man, who displays courage.

But worst of all, one tree branch was two. More times than not, Saru swung from the branch that wasn't there. Saru fell so many times she grew disheartened.

Now she stayed in her house in the Momo tree admiring the other monkeys, all clear-eyed and clever, as they skimble-skambled from tree to tree. Never did Saru see one fall.

FROM A DOUBLE DISCOVERY. *Woodcuts and story by Evaline Ness. A boy who shares his eyeglasses with a monkey that sees double is rewarded. Publisher: Scribner's.*

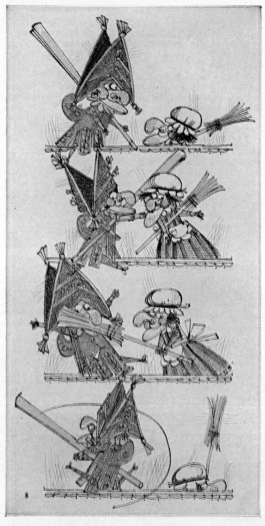

PUNCH & JUDY, A PLAY FOR PUPPETS.
Pictures and dialogue by Ed Emberley. Publisher of this version of the play is Little, Brown.

The Big Road by Tom E. Clarke. A story of youth without jobs.

Awards in 1965

Newbery Medal, for the most distinguished contribution to American literature for children in 1964, to Maia Wojciechowska for *Shadow of a Bull.* See WOJCIECHOWSKA, MAIA.

Caldecott Medal, for the most distinguished American picture book in 1964, to Beni Montresor, illustrator of *May I Bring a Friend?*, by Beatrice Schenk de Regniers. See MONTRESOR, BENI.

The New York Herald Tribune Awards were presented at its annual Spring Festival of Children's Books.
Picture Books: Harve Zemach, editor of *Salt: A Russian Tale,* illus. by Margot Zemach.
For Children 8 to 12: Julia Cunningham for *Dorp Dead,* illus. by James Spanfeller.
For Older Boys and Girls: Nat Hentoff for *Jazz Country.*

Aurianne Children's Book Award by the American Library Association Children's Services Division, for an outstanding book on animal life which develops humane attitudes toward animal life, to Sterling North for *Rascal: A Memoir of a Better Era.*

Canadian Library Association Book of the Year for Children Awards. See CANADIAN LIBRARY ASSOCIATION.

Carnegie Medal by the British Library Association, for an outstanding book for children, to Sheena Porter for *Nordy Bank.* See PORTER, SHEENA.

The Child Study Association of America Children's Book Award to Ruth Harnden for *The High Pasture.*

Kate Greenaway Medal by the British Library Association, for the most distinguished illustrated book for children, to C. Walter Hodges for *Shakespeare's Theatre.* See HODGES, C. WALTER.

Laura Ingalls Wilder Award, by the American Library Association Children's Services Division, for substantial and lasting contributions to literature for children, to Ruth Sawyer. See SAWYER, RUTH.

Regina Medal by the Catholic Library Association, awarded for lifetime dedication to the highest standards of literature for children, to Ruth Sawyer. See SAWYER, RUTH.

Thomas Alva Edison Foundation National Mass Media Awards: *For the Best Children's Book on Natural Science* to William Bixby for *The Universe of Galileo and Newton. For the Best Science Book for Youth* to Kirtley F. Mather for *The Earth Beneath Us. For Special Excellence in Contributing to the Character Development of Children* to Aimeé Sommerfelt for *The White Bungalow. For Excellence in Portraying America's Past* to George F. Scheer, editor of *Yankee Doodle Boy: A Young Soldier's Adventures in the American Revolution Told by Himself* (Joseph Plumb Martin, 1760-1850). ELOISE RUE

LIVESTOCK. See AGRICULTURE.

LIVESTOCK SHOW. A 17-year-old Illinois farm boy, John Reel of Congerville, could gasp only, "Just great—great—great," when his Aberdeen-Angus steer won the most coveted U.S. livestock honor. His 1,050-pound animal, Someday, won the grand championship at the 66th International Live Stock Exposition in Chicago, November 26 to December 4. The show's judge, Professor Herman Purdy of Pennsylvania State University, called it "the best steer I have ever judged." But three days later, Someday was sold for only $10 a pound, far below the record $30 a pound paid in 1957.

The grand champion market pig was a 220-pound black and white, shown by Roy B. Keppy of Davenport, Iowa. The market lamb grand championship went to a 95-pound Southdown entered by Purdue University, West Lafayette, Ind.

At Canada's big livestock show, the Royal Agricultural Winter Fair, held November 12 to 20, in Toronto, Ontario, Dominion Stores, Ltd., paid $13 a pound for the grand champion steer, Old Crow, matching the record bid of 1946. The champion 960-pound Angus was exhibited by Boyd P. Brown of King, Ontario, and North Salem, N.Y.

At the 67th American Royal Live Stock Show and Horse Show in Kansas City, Mo., in October, a 1,070-pound summer yearling Angus won the grand championship. It was shown by Lyle Miller, a 35-year-old farmer from Osceola, Iowa.

See also AGRICULTURE; FAIRS AND EXHIBITIONS.

LOS ANGELES. The Dodgers won the World Series, a $12,000,000 County Museum of Art opened, and a glittering new Music Center Pavilion was dedicated in Los Angeles in 1965. But it was also a year in which a bloody riot in August sent shock waves through Los Angeles neighborhoods, and city halls and state capitals throughout the United States. Even the federal government felt the tremors of the shock.

The riot began in the early evening of Wednesday, August 11. State highway policemen had made a routine arrest of a reckless driver. But the 21-year-old youth was a Negro, and he was apprehended in the Negro Watts district of Los Angeles. This is the neighborhood with the area's highest population density—nearly four times the county's average of 7.4 persons per acre. It is also the arrival point for most of the 1,000 Negroes who migrate to Los Angeles each month. News of the arrest spread through the community like wildfire and triggered a violent reaction.

The Watts Riots. By Friday night, an estimated 10,000 persons took to the streets, tossing fire bombs, breaking shop windows, and looting stores. Disorder spread throughout a 46.5-square-mile area and panic overtook adjacent neighborhoods. With the dispatch of 13,900 National Guardsmen, order was generally restored by Saturday night. But the city's skies were gray with the pall of smoke from the burning buildings in Watts.

In all, the riots took 34 lives, injured 1,032 persons, resulted in 3,952 arrests, more than $40,000,000 in property damage, and the total loss of more than 200 buildings.

The savagery of the mobs shocked the nation. On August 24, California's Governor Edmund G. Brown named a blue-ribbon commission headed by John A. McCone, former head of the Central Intelligence Agency, to investigate the riots. President Lyndon B. Johnson deplored the violence and called upon all groups to work amicably toward racial justice.

Only a Curtain-Raiser? The McCone commission report, issued December 6, saw the Watts explosion as a "curtain-raiser" for future violence unless a "revolutionary attitude" prevailed in dealing with racial problems. Its recommendations included a massive "emergency literacy program," large-scale job training and placement efforts, improved ways of processing complaints against the city's police, and greatly increased mass transit facilities to enable Negroes to commute to their jobs.

But the commission's report warned: "No amount of effort, no amount of training will raise the disadvantaged Negro to the position he seeks unless he himself shoulders a full share of the responsibility for his own welfare."   DONALD W. LIEF

See also CIVIL RIGHTS (picture); NEGRO; Section One, JAMES RESTON ON THE NATION.

LUMBER. See FORESTRY AND FOREST PRODUCTS.

LUXEMBOURG maintained its unique post-World War II record. It had no political or social crises, no strikes, and full employment. Legislation enacted during the year improved pensions and health services and raised wages, in effect, by cutting taxes. The economy remained prosperous.

The national budget for 1965 showed a total revenue of $132,000,000; expenditures were about $2,000,000 above that figure. Iron ore output was between 5,000,000 and 6,000,000 tons, the highest in years. Meanwhile, farmers were encouraged to make greater efforts to increase output.

Luxembourg shared in the prosperity based on its economic union with the Belgians and its customs union with Belgium and The Netherlands (Benelux). In addition, Luxembourg continued to participate in such international organizations as the North Atlantic Treaty Organization (NATO), the United Nations (UN), the Western European Union (WEU), and the General Agreement on Tariffs and Trade (GATT).

Population: 326,000. **Government:** Grand Duke Jean; Premier Pierre Werner. **Monetary Unit:** franc (50 = U.S. $1). **Gross National Product:** 25,-300,000,000 francs. **Foreign Trade:** exports, $236,-000,000; imports, $200,420,000. **Principal Exports:** agricultural produce, ceramics, steel products, textile articles.   KENNETH BROWN

See also EUROPE.

LWOFF, ANDRÉ (1902-   ), University of Paris Professor of Microbiology and Pasteur Institute Microbic Physiology Department head, and two other Pasteur scientists, were awarded the Nobel medicine prize in 1965. Their discoveries concern the "genetic control of enzyme and virus synthesis." Lwoff's work included proof that the genetic material of a virus which infects a bacterium (called a *phage*) can become part of its bacterial host. This host then can reproduce itself and the virus that infected it for many generations.

The two younger members of the Nobel trio, François Jacob and Jacques Monod, at one time worked in Lwoff's department at the Pasteur Institute. Lwoff began his study of the morphogenesis of protozoa (phylum, or division, of one-celled animals which reproduce by fission of the body) in the 1920s. He later worked on protozoa nutrition, and identified vitamins as microbial growth factors. Lwoff also found, with his wife Marguerite, that vitamins function as coenzymes.

André Lwoff has worked at the Pasteur Institute throughout his career. Since 1959, he also has been a University of Paris professor. He has natural science (1921), medical (1927), and doctor of natural science (1932) degrees. Lwoff was born in central France, of Russian and Polish stock.

See also JACOB, FRANÇOIS; MONOD, JACQUES; NOBEL PRIZES (Science).

MAGAZINE. See PUBLISHING.

MALAGASY REPUBLIC. President Philibert Tsiranana won by an overwhelming majority in the presidential election for a new seven-year term. In the voting on March 30, 1965, he received 2,451,441 votes out of the 2,507,067 cast. The opposition candidate, Dr. Joseph Raseta, received only 54,814 votes. President Tsiranana's party, the Social Democrat party, also won 92 of the 94 contested seats for local government councils.

In August, some 2,000,000 voters went to the polls again, this time to choose a new national assembly. President Tsiranana's party, which previously held 98 of the assembly's 107 seats, took 104 seats. The president then created two additional cabinet posts—one for agriculture, water resources, and forests; and the other for industry and mines. This reflected the president's concern with economic problems.

Economic problems were caused by poor harvests of bananas, rice, and sugar, and depressed world prices for Malagasy coffee and vanilla. A vanilla marketing conference attended by Malagasy and other producers resulted in a move to bolster prices.

Population: 5,821,000. **Government:** President Philibert Tsiranana. **Monetary Unit:** M.G. franc (246.8 = U.S. $1). **Foreign Trade:** exports, $94,000,-000; imports, $122,000,000. **Principal Exports:** cloves, coffee, rice, sugar.   BENJAMIN E. THOMAS

See also AFRICA.

MALAWI. Prime Minister Hastings Kamuzu Banda continued a search for the remaining rebels involved in the revolt of October, 1964. The revolt, led by Henry Masauko Chipembere, former minister of education, and five other cabinet ministers, had threatened to remove the prime minister from office. In January, new elections were held to fill the seats left vacant by the 1964 revolt. All of the Malawi Congress party candidates obtained offices without opposition.

In order to stamp out subversion, Dr. Banda obtained laws to give extended powers to troops and police. Later in the year, an amendment to the penal code was put before the national assembly. It made the death penalty mandatory for an act of treason.

Malawi had a growing deficit because of the falling prices of tea on world markets. But the country was assured development aid in money or services from Australia, Britain, Denmark, New Zealand, Nigeria, and the United States. Plans were made for the processing and marketing of sugar and also for the construction of cotton and textile mills.

Population: 4,060,000. **Government:** Prime Minister Hastings Kamuzu Banda. **Monetary Unit:** pound (1 = U.S. $2.80). **Gross National Product:** 50,800,000 pounds. **Foreign Trade:** no figures available. **Principal Export:** livestock.   BENJAMIN E. THOMAS

See also AFRICA.

MALAYSIA, FEDERATION OF, began the year with guarded optimism regarding its ability to withstand Indonesia's "crush Malaysia" policy. Sorties by Indonesian irregulars operating against Malaya proper were easily blocked. The determination of the British to defend Malaysia also accounted for some of the optimism.

Indeed, Great Britain bolstered its forces in Malaysia considerably during the year. Its land forces were estimated to be about 60,000. They were based mostly in Singapore but some contingents were also in Sabah and Sarawak. British naval forces in the area included a considerable number of minesweepers and patrol boats as well as a British aircraft carrier.

Despite this strong British commitment, the federation was inwardly insecure. This insecurity reached a climax when Singapore seceded from the federation and became an independent, sovereign nation under an agreement signed August 7 by Singapore's Prime Minister Lee Kuan Yew and the federation's Prime Minister Tunku Abdul Rahman. The secession left Malaya, Sarawak, and Sabah as the remaining states in the two-year-old federation.

Racial Issue. In a televised news conference, Prime Minister Lee said that in talks held earlier in Kuala Lumpur, Rahman had indicated that if Singapore insisted on continuing its federation membership it would set off communal strife between the country's ethnic Chinese and Malays.

Racial antagonism between the two groups had persisted after the formation of the federation in 1963. Each group comprised about 40 per cent of the country's total population, but the Chinese numbered nearly 75 per cent of the population in Singapore proper. Under the leadership of Lee Kuan Yew, Singapore's Chinese controlled the state's economic and private life. They also dominated the economy of the rest of the federation.

There were fears among the ultraconservative Malay leaders that the Chinese would eventually dominate Malaysia politically as well. It was these conservatives who apparently forced Prime Minister Rahman to request Singapore's withdrawal from the federation.

Commonwealth Status. Singaporeans, rallying behind Lee Kuan Yew after the secession, began to envision Singapore as playing a role in Asia similar to that of Hong Kong. To that end, Lee Kuan Yew rescinded an order previously issued by Prime Minister Rahman closing Peking's Bank of China in Singapore.

Meanwhile, the new nation announced it hoped to maintain a neutral, nonaligned status. It also hoped it could continue its defense arrangements with Great Britain, and it remained opposed to Indonesia's "crush Malaysia" policy. On October 16, Singapore became a member of the British Commonwealth of Nations.

FEDERATION DISSOLVED. Prime Minister Lee Kuan Yew of Singapore announces that his nation has seceded from the Federation of Malaysia to become an independent state.

The Singapore withdrawal raised some sharp questions about the underlying assumptions behind the creation of Malaysia as a federation. In point of fact, however, ministers of both Malaysia and Singapore immediately began a series of meetings to discuss economic as well as military cooperation between the two states. In September, Singapore was admitted to membership in the United Nations by unanimous vote of the General Assembly.

General Economy of Malaysia continued sound. The groundwork was being laid for a long-range capital development program to increase the nation's already considerable productivity. Revenue from rubber, tin, and agricultural produce was good and, with Commonwealth support, the necessary capital for development projects was available.

In August, a new paramount ruler of Malaysia was elected for a five-year term by a council of the hereditary rulers of Malaysia's nine Malayan states. The new ruler was 58-year-old Prince Ismail Nasiruddin Shah, sultan of the state of Trengannau. He was sworn in on September 21.

Population: 11,561,000. **Government:** Supreme Head of State Sultan Ismail Nasiruddin Shah; Prime Minister Tunku Abdul Rahman. **Monetary Unit:** dollar (3.06 = U.S. $1). **Gross National Product:** $4,801,000,000. **Foreign Trade:** exports, $2,028,000,000; imports, $2,203,000,000. **Principal Exports:** iron ore, lumber, rubber. JOHN N. STALKER

See also ASIA.

MALI, breadbasket of Africa during the colonial era, boldly and ambitiously moved toward industrialization during 1965. The landlocked country in west Africa placed particular emphasis on the construction of food processing plants. But one of the consequences of rapid industrial development was a balance of trade deficit caused chiefly by the imports of machinery and equipment.

Mali signed an economic aid agreement with the Soviet Union calling for the delivery of a 50,000-ton capacity cement factory. Mali received a gift of two 75-kilowatt (kw) generating plants from Communist China.

Mali also turned to the West for aid, accepting French help in developing the upper Niger region. Regionally, Mali combined with Guinea, Mauritania, and Senegal in the Sénégal River Basin Development Project that was built under the sponsorship of the United Nations.

In an attempt to curb profiteering and shortages, the Mali assembly passed legislation to regulate all food sales through regional and consumer cooperatives.

Population: 4,563,000. **Government:** President Modibo Keita. **Monetary Unit:** franc (246.85 = U.S. $1). **Foreign Trade:** exports, $33,000,000; imports, $49,000,000. **Principal Exports:** fresh-water fish, livestock, peanuts. WILLIAM SPENCER

See also AFRICA.

MANITOBA. See CANADA.

MANUFACTURING

MANUFACTURING plants in the United States and in virtually all of the industrialized nations of the world pushed their output to near-capacity to meet the demands of their booming economies. By November, U.S. personal income had reached a record annual level of more than $545,000,000,000, a major contributing factor in the boom. It gave people the wherewithal to buy more goods. Another factor was the reduction in excise taxes, which, in effect, cut prices of many manufactured items.

U.S. manufacturing in 1965 accounted for 30 per cent of all nonfarm jobs and 22 per cent of all personal income. Despite the recent growth of the government and service sectors of the economy, manufacturing continued to be, by far, the most important (see ECONOMY, THE). And its more than 18,000,000 employees were also consumers.

As one industry roared along—automobiles, for example—its suppliers of parts and materials, in turn, saw their manufacturing operations pick up. In short, as manufacturers sold to one another and to their employee-consumers, the boom gained speed, feeding on itself.

Bulging Order Books were taxing plant capacity. Government economists estimated it at about 91 per cent in the third quarter, the highest operating rate in years. Overtime pay and the use of inefficient machines gave impetus to expansion in almost every industry. Manufacturers' outlays for new plant and equipment rose to a record $21,880,000,000, up almost 18 per cent from 1964.

In some industries expansion plans were so ambitious that there were predictions of oversupply within a year or two. For instance, when ammonia plants whose capacity will be doubled or trebled come into full production in 1967, it is feared there will be a surfeit of ammonia. But the industry says that ammonia, a major building block for fertilizers, will be in greater demand as the world-wide need for food grows more intense.

The Machine Tool Industry—which makes the machines that make the machines that make the finished products in factories—thrived on the general drive to expand. It wrote $50,000,000 worth of orders at its 10-day show in Chicago in September. Total new orders for metal-cutting tools stood at $103,800,000 for September, against $83,600,000 a year earlier. It was the best year for the industry since the Korean War.

Productivity in Manufacturing has risen steadily with the introduction of new machinery, automation, computerization, and new technology (see AUTOMATION). The new efficiencies in production combined with a feverish sales pace brought manufacturers their best profit year in history. Yet prices were stable. The consumer price index for durable goods actually declined, from 103.6 in January to 101.7 in September, the lowest since early 1963.

In a *New York Times* survey of the first 500 industrial companies to report their nine-month figures,

earnings rose 18.2 per cent from the 1964 period, to a record $11,691,801,138. The world's largest manufacturer, General Motors Corporation, turned in the largest net profit of any company anywhere at any time—$1,539,000,000 for the nine months.

In a new trend, factories were mass-producing goods tailored to the customer's individual needs and tastes. That undoubtedly helped expand profits. Professor Martin K. Starr of Columbia University noted this basic change in industry. Writing in the *Harvard Business Review*, he called it *modular production*. It uses, but goes beyond, automation and computers. Its essence, he said, is to "design, develop, and produce those parts which can be combined in the maximum number of ways."

The Urge to Merge continued apace in 1965. It was confirmed during spring hearings before the U.S. Senate Subcommittee on Antitrust and Monopoly. In a sampling of 611 acquisitions between 1948 and 1964, the assets of the absorbed companies totaled $21,000,000,000. The economics director of the Federal Trade Commission said that within 10 years 200 companies might be in control of two-thirds of the nation's manufacturing assets. Further cautions were raised at a March conference on "antitrust in an expanding economy," sponsored by the National Industrial Conference Board.

Textile Companies have become noticeably merger-conscious. A wave of mergers and acquisitions has eliminated many of the small, marginal producers. Now, the industry, led by larger, more sophisticated producers, has become stronger than it has been in years. In March, two of the industry's oldest companies, West Point Manufacturing and Pepperell Manufacturing, merged.

In addition to merging, the industry has been making heavy capital expenditures—for new plant and equipment and for research and development. Such investment has resulted in new fibers, new combinations of fibers, and many new uses for textile products. Burlington Industries was developing a $2,000,000 R & D center in North Carolina, just part of its $13,000,000-a-year R & D budget.

Several external factors have helped as well. Pressure from low-cost imports has eased with farm legislation that eliminated the premium U.S. mills had to pay above the world cotton price (see AGRICULTURE). Further pluses were the general growth of population and rising personal incomes. As a result, order backlogs were at record levels, and those for cotton goods double the 1964 total. Earnings, at $205,000,000, were 35 per cent ahead of the 1964 figure on the basis of an 8 per cent increase in sales to $19,200,000,000.

Drugmakers also got important help from legislation. Medicare enhanced sales prospects in future years. In 1965, sales rose 10 per cent to $4,100,000,000. And, according to a *Forbes* magazine year-end survey of 30 industries, the drug group (10 companies) was the most profitable of all.

The introduction of new drugs increased to a total of 24 in 1965. Offerings of new drugs had fallen off sharply—from 63 in 1959 to 17 in 1964—chiefly because of a slowing of research advances and the stiff new federal regulations requiring proof of effectiveness, as well as safety, of any new drugs introduced. The U.S. Food and Drug Administration (FDA), however, took steps in 1965 to speed procedures for approval of new drugs.

The Chemical Industry set new highs in production, sales ($35,800,000,000), and profits ($3,160,-000,000). Nylon continued to show good growth. Domestic shipments of nylon yarn and monofilament were estimated at 770,000,000 pounds, 12 per cent above 1964.

Chemical firms perhaps were the most active in overseas spending on plant and equipment. Their total outlays came to $2,570,000,000; their overseas investments to $870,000,000, or up 40 per cent from 1964. From July, 1964, to June, 1965, the industry set up 78 new chemical plants abroad and expanded 33 others, established 20 nonmanufacturing units, and sold 17 licenses, according to a study by Booz, Allen & Hamilton.

Plastic and resin output rose to 11,400,000,000 pounds, 14 per cent above 1964. Man-made fiber production increased 15.6 per cent to 3,500,000 pounds. One of the fastest growing plastics has been acrylonitrile-butadiene-styrene (ABS), its output expanding about 19 per cent a year. Its leading markets: automobiles and appliances, followed by shoe heels, plastic pipe, telephones, and luggage.

Aerospace and Defense business rose with the increasing U.S. involvement in Vietnam. After three successive years of reduced Pentagon spending, the military budget was rising. About $2,500,000,000 was added to the $49,000,000,000 for the fiscal year ending June 30, 1966. Of all these funds, the aerospace industry took in $21,000,000,000 in 1965.

The risks involved in defense contracts in recent years had been so great that most manufacturers were driven to diversify into civilian lines. The revival of military orders became so much additional profit in 1965. See AVIATION; NATIONAL DEFENSE.

Beverage Makers succeeded in slaking the thirst of millions of prosperous Americans and making millions of dollars in 1965. The total U.S. drinking tab came to about $17,000,000,000—hard liquor and beer, $7,000,000,000 each; and soft drinks, $3,000,000,000. Despite their lower sales, soft-drink makers showed the best growth in profits. They did well in catering to changing public tastes by introducing new drinks and repackaging old ones.

The two dominant companies, which together accounted for more than half of soft-drink sales, the Coca-Cola Company and PepsiCo, Inc., were exploring the snack-food business to complement their liquid line. Pepsi had already acquired Frito-Lay, and Coca-Cola was still shopping after its talks with National Biscuit Company collapsed.

Electrical Equipment producers were pressed in 1965 to do just that—produce. Prosperous consumers seemed unable to buy enough electric carving knives, power toothbrushes, and color-television sets. Sales of consumer products rose 3.5 per cent, to about $7,700,000,000 in the year. The total for all electrical goods came to $30,000,000,000, or some 5 per cent above 1964 (see ELECTRIC POWER).

But it was color-TV that caused the big scramble in the industry. Its pioneer, Radio Corporation of America (RCA), did well but was meeting competition. Zenith Radio Corporation was selling possibly 25 per cent of the color sets, against RCA's estimated 36 per cent. Other major contenders were General Telephone and Electronics' Sylvania division, Magnavox Company, and Motorola, Inc. RCA's grip on the color-tube business was loosened as Motorola, Sylvania, and Zenith developed independent suppliers. See TELEVISION.

Farm Equipment proliferated and became more specialized, as the industry strived to meet the demands of prospering and more sophisticated farmers (see AGRICULTURE). Powerful, four-wheel-drive tractors and complicated tomato-harvesting machines, which do the work of 100 men with a crew of 20, were selling extremely well. As a matter of fact, sales of all equipment and farm supplies were booming. The estimated 1965 total was $30,000,000,000.

The industry was rolling at record levels in all departments but profits. Heavy start-up costs for expansion and bringing out new equipment ate into earnings. In the fiscal year ended Oct. 31, 1965, J. I. Case Company's profits were off 19 per cent; Deere & Company's, 16 per cent; and those of Massey-Ferguson, Ltd., 11 per cent below the year earlier.

The Glass Industry took exception to a U.S. Tariff Commission report in June that favored restoration of the lower 1962 duties on imported glass. To meet foreign competition, the major U.S. flat glass makers cut their prices by 2 per cent to 7 per cent in June. Their sales, for the first time, exceeded $1,000,000,000, up about 4 per cent from 1964's $975,912,000 total. Earlier in the year, Pittsburgh Plate Glass Company announced a new heat-and-glare-reducing window glass with a slightly amber-tinted reflective coating that still permits good visibility.

Paper Industry sales, production, and profits advanced in step with other industries. Paperboard output, a popular measure of general economic activity, was pushing to 94 per cent of plant capacity at year's end. With industry sales totaling about $17,000,000,000, consumption was expected to exceed the 46,000,000 tons of 1964 by 5 per cent—a use of 485 pounds of paper products a person.

While generally the papermakers' profits were higher than they had been in 10 years, a number of the big companies failed to match their performances of the 1950s. It was in those years when capacity was stepped-up and newcomers entered the field. According to a *Forbes* survey, two of the fastest growing firms in the paper business were the once exclusively timber companies: Boise Cascade Corporation and Georgia-Pacific Corporation.

The Rubber Industry rode the crest of an unprecedented automotive boom, doing nearly a $12,000,000,000 business in 1965. Tire sales increased 11.5 per cent, to some 177,000,000 casings—original equipment up 20 per cent to 59,000,000 tires, and replacement sales up 6.5 per cent from 1964.

In the United States, total use of rubber by the industry rose 5.5 per cent in the year, to 2,030,000 tons. Natural rubber had 517,000 tons (or 25.5 per cent) of that total, compared with 483,000 tons (or 25 per cent) in 1964. The rest was synthetic. Free World consumption totaled 4,680,000 tons (1,830,000 of it natural), compared with 4,390,000 tons (1,780,000 natural) in 1964.

In 1965, Goodyear Tire & Rubber Company researchers developed a new production technique that slashed processing time. The raw rubber is cut into small pieces, then carefully washed and forced through an extruder-dryer. It takes minutes, compared with as long as a month under the old curing methods. ROBERT E. BEDINGFIELD

See also AUTOMOBILE; AVIATION; FOOD; FORESTRY AND FOREST PRODUCTS; PETROLEUM AND GAS; Section One, SYLVIA PORTER ON THE ECONOMY; STEEL INDUSTRY; TRANSPORTATION.

MARCOS, FERDINAND EDRALIN (1917-   ), was inaugurated President of The Philippines on December 30. He defeated incumbent President Diosdado Macapagal in the November 9 election. Marcos, formerly a member of the ruling Liberal party, switched to the Nacionalistas, when President Macapagal ran for an unprecedented second term.

Defeat at the polls is unknown to Ferdinand Marcos. The brilliant lawyer was elected to the House of Representatives in 1949, to the Senate in 1959, and had served as Senate President since April 6, 1963. Marcos grew up a politican, trained by his father, also a well-to-do lawyer and politician.

Young Ferdinand joined the United States Army and fought on Bataan. He was captured, tortured, and survived the infamous Death March. He later escaped and fought as a guerrilla. He was wounded five times, and received several American medals and some 20 Philippine decorations.

Ferdinand Marcos was born at Sarrat, in the Luzon province of Ilocos Norte. He is a University of The Philippines graduate (1939), and passed the bar examination with the highest grade in his country's history. He married Imelda Romauldez in 1954, the year she was Miss Manila. Mrs. Marcos, the daughter of a prominent family, campaigned with her husband. They have three children.

See also PHILIPPINES, THE.

MARINE CORPS, U.S. See ARMED FORCES OF THE WORLD; NATIONAL DEFENSE.

MARKS, LEONARD HAROLD (1916-   ), a Washington lawyer, took office on Sept. 1, 1965, as director of the U.S. Information Agency, which employs 11,000 persons in information and propaganda work around the globe. Marks succeeded Carl T. Rowan, who returned to newspaper work.

Leonard Marks had been a partner in a law firm whose regular clients are major newspapers and broadcasting stations. He also had been attorney for the Austin (Tex.) television station owned by the family of President Lyndon B. Johnson. A close friend of the Johnsons, Leonard Marks was the personal representative of the President in plans for the inauguration, and his wife, Dorothy, was asked by Mrs. Johnson to help move the Johnson family from Texas into the White House in 1963.

Marks was born March 5, 1916, in Pittsburgh, Pa. He won his law degree at the University of Pittsburgh and taught law there until 1942, when he was named assistant general counsel of the Federal Communications Commission (FCC). During most of his service in this post, which continued to 1946, he headed the foreign broadcasting intelligence service. It kept watch on World War II propaganda broadcasts from other nations.

Marks is described as a cheerful, bustling man. His wife, Dorothy Ames, is a former newspaper reporter. They have two sons. WALTER F. MORSE

MASER. See ELECTRONICS.

MAURITANIA, under the leadership of President Moktar Ould Daddah, helped form the Common Organization of African and Malagasy States (COAM) on Feb. 15, 1965. Holding its first conference at Nouakchott, the capital of Mauritania, the COAM promised aid to the Congolese government at Léopoldville, condemned alleged Ghanian subversion, and issued a warning against Communist Chinese penetration of Africa.

By May, however, President Daddah became disenchanted with the COAM, and, the following month, he withdrew his country from membership. The official reason given was that Mauritania did not want to be a member of an organization that would harm the authority of the Organization of African Unity (OAU). Unofficially, Mauritania objected to the membership of Congo (Léopoldville) in the COAM.

During 1965, Mauritania recognized Communist China and established diplomatic relations with Romania and North Vietnam. President Daddah shuffled his cabinet but he remained prime minister. In May, the Mauritanian Peoples party won 95 per cent of the votes for a new national assembly.

Population: 718,000. **Government:** President Moktar Ould Daddah (also Prime Minister). **Monetary Unit:** franc (246.85 = U.S. $1). **Foreign Trade:** exports, $15,000,000; imports, $32,000,000. **Principal Exports:** dates, iron ore, livestock. WILLIAM SPENCER

See also AFRICA.

McCONNELL, JOHN PAUL (1908-   ), was advanced from U.S. Air Force Deputy Chief of Staff to Chief of Staff on January 31, succeeding General Curtis Emerson LeMay, 58, who retired. McConnell had been in Washington as deputy chief about two years, having been brought there after serving in the U.S. European Command.

McConnell holds two bachelor of science degrees, one from Henderson State College, Arkadelphia, Ark., and the other from the U.S. Military Academy at West Point. He began his military career as a second lieutenant in the U.S. Army Air Corps, advanced to colonel in 10 years, and was made a major general in 1950. During World War II, he was deputy chief of staff of the Army Air Force Training Command for Southeast Asia, then senior and air staff officer and chief of staff of the U.S. Air Force in the China theater.

From 1947 to 1950 McConnell was special assistant to the air force chief of staff. His other postwar assignments included commanding the 7th Air Division in London, England; being director of plans at Strategic Air Command headquarters at Offutt Air Force Base, Nebraska; and commander of the 2nd Air Force. Among the honors he holds are the Distinguished Service Medal and the Legion of Merit Award. He was born Feb. 7, 1908, at Booneville, Ark. He married Sally Dean in 1946. They have a son and a daughter.   WALTER F. MORSE

McKEE, WILLIAM FULTON (1906-   ), retired vice-chief of staff of the U.S. Air Force, was sworn in on July 1, 1965, as administrator of the Federal Aviation Agency (FAA). He succeeded Najeeb E. Halaby, who later became a vice-president of Pan American World Airways.

General McKee was nominated by President Lyndon B. Johnson on June 22 shortly after President Johnson signed a bill that exempted McKee from the requirement that only a civilian may head the FAA. The agency's principal function has been to work for air safety, but McKee was given the additional task of enlarging the FAA's role in developing a 2,000-mile-an-hour airliner.

McKee retired from military service in 1963 after a 35-year career. He then served about a year as a management expert for the National Aeronautics and Space Administration.

Born Oct. 17, 1906, at Chilhowie, Va., McKee is a graduate of the U.S. Military Academy at West Point and of the Coast Artillery School. McKee's posts since World War II included assistant vice-chief of staff of the air force, vice-commander of the Air Material Command at Wright-Patterson Air Base in Ohio, and commander of the Air Force Logistics Command. Although he was No. 2 in command of the U.S. Air Force and now supervises all flying in the United States, General McKee has never held a pilot's license. He and his wife Gertrude have two sons.   WALTER F. MORSE

MEDICARE. Legislation providing for a national comprehensive program of health care for the aged was passed by the Congress of the United States and signed into law on July 30. It was hailed by its supporters as a vast new resource to improve the health and welfare of all the people. Opponents viewed it as a serious threat to the foundations on which our nation was built.

The question of whether the federal government should provide some kind of health protection for Americans had been a concern of Congress for 30 years. In principle, compulsory health insurance was supported as early as 1935 by President Franklin D. Roosevelt, but he did not urge the inclusion of such a program in the original Social Security Act.

In 1945, President Harry S. Truman sent a special message to Congress proposing a federal program of health insurance under Social Security. Though hearings were held on the Truman proposal, no action was taken. There was no further action until 1961, when a federal matching grant program for medical assistance for the aged was approved. Medicare bills were approved in 1964 by both the House and the Senate, but the measures then went to a committee, where they were deadlocked until Congress adjourned. The overwhelming majority of supporters for President Lyndon B. Johnson's legislative program in the 89th Congress assured passage of Medicare.

"Perhaps if you didn't struggle, doctor, it wouldn't hurt so."

Opponents sponsored an "Eldercare" bill, which had the support of the American Medical Association. This placed responsibility for the administration of the program on the states, though funds were to be provided through federal grants-in-aid. After considering a variety of proposals, the powerful House Ways and Means Committee, on March 29, reported out of committee its recommendations for Medicare in the form of a new Social Security bill, H.R. 6675. This was passed and enacted into law with only minor changes.

Provisions of the Law. The new law establishes two coordinated health insurance programs, one designated as "basic" and the other as "supplementary," with both to go into operation July 1, 1966. The basic plan provides protection against the cost of hospital and related care, and automatically covers everyone who is 65 years of age, except aliens with less than five years of residence in the United States, aliens without status as permanent residents, and federal employees eligible for government health insurance under another law. This insurance will be financed by increases in the Social Security payroll tax. For those aged persons who are not covered by Social Security or the Railroad Retirement Insurance program the cost will be met by appropriations from general tax revenues.

The supplementary plan provides for doctors' bills and other medical and health services. Participation is voluntary, but subject to the same eligibility requirements. It will be financed by monthly premiums of $3 paid by the participants, and an equal contribution from federal government general revenues.

Basic Plan. The basic plan, covering hospital insurance, includes the following benefits:

Hospitalization up to 90 days in each spell of illness. The patient pays the first $40 of hospital costs. If he stays more than 60 days, he pays $10 for each additional day up to the 90-day limit. In-patient psychiatric hospital services are covered with a lifetime limit of 190 days.

Nursing Home Care up to 100 days in a qualified nursing home or other facility for each duration of illness after a stay of three or more days in a hospital. There is no charge to the patient for the first 20 days. The patient pays $5 for each day above 20, up to the 100-day limit.

Health Services up to 100 home visits by nurses or technicians in a cne-year period following discharge from a hospital (after at least a three-day stay) or an extended care facility. The insurance covers the full cost of such visits. The services furnished must be in accordance with a plan set up and periodically reviewed by a physician.

Out-Patient Diagnostic Services including tests and related diagnostic services, other than those performed by physicians, that are normally provided by hospitals to out-patients. The patient pays $20 of the charge for each diagnostic study made by the same hospital in a 20 day-period. The patient also pays 20 per cent of the charges above $20. The insurance covers the remaining 80 per cent.

Supplementary Plan. This medical insurance supplements the basic plan by covering most of the other major medical expenses except those for dental services, medicines, and drugs. A participant in the supplementary plan pays $50 of his annual costs for the services and supplies covered. He also pays 20 per cent of the annual costs above $50, while the insurance pays 80 per cent. The benefits include:

• Physicians' services, including surgery, whether performed in a hospital, clinic, office, or home.

• Up to 100 home nursing visits each year in addition to those allowed in the basic plan, and without any requirement for prior hospitalization.

• Various services and supplies whether provided in or out of a medical institution such as X-ray and other diagnostic tests, radiological treatments, surgical dressings, splints, casts, iron lungs, and other specified prosthetic devices.

In preparation for beginning the supplementary program, application forms were sent to 15,200,000 Social Security and Railroad Retirement beneficiaries in September. By December, 9,000,000 persons had returned the forms. Of this group 88 per cent asked to be enrolled in the optional supplementary plan. JOSEPH P. ANDERSON

MEDICINE. British scientists were able to determine the three-dimensional structure of an enzyme for the first time in 1965. A enzyme is a complex molecule that produces a chemical action in the body while the enzyme itself remains unchanged. The particular enzyme that a team of London scientists studied was *lysozyme*, one of the most potent bacteria killers in the human body. It was first discovered more than 40 years ago in teardrops by Sir Alexander Fleming, who later discovered penicillin. Though Sir Alexander paid his assistants to produce the tears he needed for his experiment, he was unable to put the substance to practical use.

The enzyme appears to be the body's own antibiotic, functioning in much the same way as penicillin. It is found in teardrops, white cells, mucus secretions, egg white, and other animal fluids. Scientists at the Royal Institution in London were able to map the structure of the enzyme by using an X-ray technique that permitted them to visualize the order and positions of the atoms in crystallized molecules of lysosome. The enzyme has a molecular weight of 14,600 and somewhat resembles coiled intestines. Mapping the structure of this enzyme could well be an important first step toward "tailoring" enzymes for specific purposes such as the destruction of bacteria.

Leprosy Control. A major step toward the control of leprosy appeared to have been found by Dr. Elizabeth Garbutt of the National Institute of

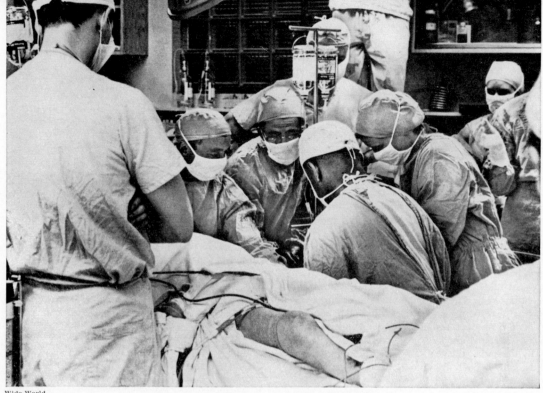

Wide World

A MEDICAL RECORD was established at the Boston City Hospital when a pig's liver was substituted for a 34-year-old woman's diseased liver. She lived 18 days.

Medical Research in London, who announced she had grown leprosy bacilli in tissue culture for the first time. The control of this disease has been slowed by the inability of investigators to grow the bacillus experimentally, though it was discovered as early as 1874. Dr. Garbutt grew the organism in human lung cells and rat fibroblasts for 224 and 452 days, respectively. Methods of eradicating and controlling the bacilli can now be found through laboratory studies. Leprosy is estimated to afflict about 10,000,000 people in the world.

Sonar, the technique by which sound waves are used to detect submarines underwater, was turned to the service of medicine by doctors at the Walter Reed Army Medical Center in Washington, D.C. Using an ultrasound device, they located a chip from a brass cartridge buried in the eye of an 11-year-old boy. The small ultrasound source projected waves that were read as blips on a phosphorescent screen. After the chip was located, it was successfully removed with forceps to which another ultrasound source was attached.

Use for Gold. A new medical use was found for gold. Dr. John P. Gallagher and Dr. Charles F. Geschickter of Washington, D.C., used gold leaf as a material to seal hemorrhaging blood vessels and openings in membranes. The malleable gold leaf was applied to the bleeding surface after first building an electrostatic charge on the metal by rubbing it with a camel's-hair brush that had been stroked along a rubber comb. The electrostatic charge made the metal adhere to the tissue. It was found that the gold leaf could be left in place indefinitely, plugging the leak without causing a blood clot.

Cancer Studies. Two reports were presented in October that related to the effects of smoking and air pollution on the development of lung cancer. Though both were held responsible for the alarming increase in lung ailments, particularly emphysema, the surveys found that cigarette smoking, rather than air pollution, was the major source of a rise in lung cancer in the United States.

One report was given at a conference on smoking and health held by the American Cancer Society in New York City. The study concurred with the conclusions of earlier studies that smoking is the chief villain in producing lung cancer. But this study also found that people who stop smoking at any stage in their life increase their life expectancy. The lungs of light smokers who give up the habit return virtually to normal in about five years, those of heavy smokers do so in about 15 years. According to Dr. E. Cuyler Hammond of the society's research bureau, the earlier studies that indicated little or no benefit from a halt in smoking had been misleading. This was because many of those who stopped did so after becoming ill, or following a heart attack. This study covered a sample of the population that stopped smoking without immediate medical reasons for doing so.

MEDICINE

The other report was presented at a meeting of the New York Academy of Sciences by Dr. Warren Winkelstein, Jr., professor of preventive medicine at the State University of New York in Buffalo. He found, after studying 77,811 men, that for all economic levels the death rate from chronic respiratory diseases was higher in areas of high air pollution, but that cancer of the lung and air passages was actually lower in these same polluted areas.

Legislation. The President's Commission on Heart Disease, Cancer, and Stroke, a panel of 28 persons named by President Lyndon B. Johnson early in 1964, issued its report recommending a nationwide program to combat the three diseases. The recommendations of the report covered medical research, education, and practice, and contemplated spending $3,000,000,000 over a five-year period, plus an undetermined amount in state and other spending. The key recommendation of the commission was for the creation of a national network of centers for patient care, research, and teaching in the three disease areas.

By the end of the year, a number of major health bills had become law, one of which provided $280,000,000 for research. Another was the highly controversial Medicare bill. See HEALTH; MEDICARE; POVERTY.   HUGH H. HUSSEY

See also BIOCHEMISTRY; DENTISTRY; HOSPITAL.

MEMORIALS dedicated or announced in 1965 included the following:

Abraham Lincoln: On the Prairie was presented to Salzburg, Austria, on July 28, a gift of sculptress Anna Hyatt Huntington. The 18-foot equestrian bronze portrays a young Lincoln reading a law book.

Atomic Age Memorial at the University of Chicago is to commemorate the first sustained nuclear chain reaction at its Stagg Field on Dec. 2, 1942. British sculptor Henry Moore unveiled there in September a model of his proposed *Nuclear Energy.* The 12-foot bronze was described as a mushroom (an atomic cloud) on a tripod of variegated legs, a skull (man's mind), and a cathedral or church, indicating hope.

Bryce Park in Washington, D.C., was dedicated by Britain's Princess Margaret on November 17, as a memorial to Lord James Bryce. The British Ambassador to the United States (1907-1913) wrote the classic history, *The American Commonwealth.*

Dag Hammarskjöld Memorial, an arched stairway at the United Nations headquarters building was dedicated on October 25. It leads to the north side gardens, and was suggested by the United Nations Secretary-General who died in an African plane crash in 1961. The stairway and an 88-foot stainless steel flagstaff were gifts of the state of New York.

Edward R. Murrow Center of Public Diplomacy was dedicated at Tufts University Fletcher School of Law and Diplomacy, Medford, Mass., on December 6. See DEATHS OF NOTABLE PERSONS.

Franklin Delano Roosevelt Memorial in Washington, D.C., was dedicated on April 12, the 20th anniversary of the late President's death. It is in front of the National Archives building, facing Pennsylvania Ave-

IN MEMORY OF JOHN F. KENNEDY, Great Britain dedicated land at Runnymede, Surrey, scene of the signing of the Magna Carta, as a memorial to the martyred President.

nue. The simple white Vermont marble block, inscribed "In Memory of Franklin Delano Roosevelt, 1882-1945," and the site were designated by the President in 1941. Sealed inside the base are the names (not made public) of his living associates responsible for the memorial.

Freedoms Foundation American Credo Monument was unveiled by former President Dwight D. Eisenhower on May 31, at the foundation's headquarters in Valley Forge, Pa.

General of the Army Douglas MacArthur Plaza in New York City was dedicated on January 27. The block-long street, between 48th and 49th streets, parallels the East River Drive, and is in front of the United Nations Plaza building.

José Martí Statue in New York City was dedicated on May 18. Anna Hyatt Huntington's bronze equestrian shows the Cuban hero toppling from his saddle. He was killed in Cuba's war for independence at the Battle of Dos Ríos, May 19, 1895.

Sam Rayburn Statue was dedicated on January 6, the 83rd anniversary of the famed Texan's birth. The life-size bronze is in the main stairs hallway of the Rayburn House Office Building, Washington, D.C.

Sir Winston Churchill Memorials. A memorial stone was unveiled in the west nave of Westminster Abbey by Queen Elizabeth on September 19, after the Battle-of-Britain Thanksgiving service there.

Switzerland unveiled a Churchill Monument on the northern shore of its Lake Thun on September 18. The granite block, with a Churchill likeness, is inscribed "In War Resolution, in Defeat Defiance, in Victory Magnanimity, in Peace Good Will."

U.S.S. Massachusetts began its role as a memorial to Massachusetts' 13,000 World War II dead on July 4, at Fall River.

MENTAL HEALTH.

President Lyndon B. Johnson, calling attention to the fact that one out of 10 Americans is in need of mental health care and about half the hospital beds are filled with mental patients, signed a bill to help staff community mental health centers and to train teachers for handicapped children. The bill, signed on August 4, provided authorization for the appropriation of $360,000,000 over a three-year period, $224,000,000 of this for staffing mental health centers. Under the new law, 6,000 teachers were to start training in 1965 and twice that number were to be in school by 1967.

Addiction. The American Medical Association (AMA) called the attention of the medical profession to the growing problem of addiction to barbiturates and other nonnarcotic sedatives. The AMA Committee on Alcoholism and Addiction issued a statement urging physicians to prescribe such drugs wisely. Many people try to relieve anxiety, tension states, insomnia, and other manifestations of stress by self-medication with alcohol and over-the-counter or prescription sedatives, the committee of AMA authorities noted.

A synthetic narcotic, *methadone hydrochloride*, appeared to offer hope as a treatment for heroin addiction. The first clinical trials with 22 heroin addicts indicated that methadone effectively blocks the addict's craving for heroin, restores normal physical and mental functions, and permits return to work. Investigators at Rockefeller Institute and Beth Israel Hospital in New York City reported that the addicts apparently were unable to get a "kick" from heroin while they were getting methadone.

The methadone treatment was combined with extensive social counseling in stages extending over several months. The patients were gradually permitted to work their way back to normal society. The 22 heroin-using volunteer patients were 19 to 37 years old. At the end of 15 months, two patients were near complete rehabilitation and the others were in various stages of progress.

Schizophrenia. A foundation to study the most common mental disease, schizophrenia, was formed in 1965. It is known as the American Schizophrenia Foundation, and it plans to study the disease along biological rather than purely psychological lines. It will focus on the mounting evidence that this mental disease is a metabolic disorder (as arteriosclerosis and diabetes are thought to be), not just a manifestation of psychological and sociological disorders.

Tests conducted at the University of Liverpool, England, on 808 individuals gave support to this theory that schizophrenia is a metabolic disorder. The researchers found "pink spots" in the urine of those with the mental disease. The spots, which are considered to be a chemical compound that is called 3,4-DMPE, are an abnormal product of the individuals' metabolism.   HUGH H. HUSSEY

See also HANDICAPPED, THE; PSYCHOLOGY.

METALLURGY.

Titanium became a prime candidate as the material for airframe construction in supersonic transports following the discovery by the Lockheed Aircraft Corporation of Burbank, Calif., that a titanium alloy exhibits greater fracture toughness than the best aluminum alloys. The cost, however, is said to be about twice the cost of an aluminum airframe.

High-strength fabrics woven from metal yarn were developed for use in paragliders, parachutes, and other spacecraft re-entry decelerators. The process involves drawing high-temperature alloys into fine wires which are then spun into metal yarn for weaving. The resultant cloth has high strength and is heat resistant.

Dr. F. N. Rhines of the University of Florida found that a gold film as thin as 50,000,000ths of an inch could be applied to steel to increase its toughness. The process prevents hydrogen embrittlement, caused by hydrogen atoms in chemicals of the surrounding environment.

Researchers at the Bell Telephone Laboratories and the Western Electric Engineering Research Center, both in New York City, discovered a new form of tantalum in 1965. They call it beta tantalum. The metal has higher electrical resistance than previously known tantalum and becomes a superconductor at a much lower temperature.   SERGEI LENORMAND

See also MINES AND MINING; STEEL INDUSTRY.

METEOROLOGY. See WEATHER.

MEXICO

MEXICO received international recognition of its healthy economy and wise fiscal policies in 1965. Early in the year—for the first time in Mexico's history—its peso was recognized as "hard" by the International Monetary Fund (IMF). The IMF qualified the currency as "acceptable without limitation in international operations because of its solid parity to exchange." This remained true even though its total foreign debt, excluding obligations of less than a year, had reached $1,825,000,000 at the end of August, and despite the fact that its 1965 trade deficit might reach a possible $500,000,000.

During the first half of 1965, the economy was in a state of adjustment, and full of stress and strain as the government deliberately held back public spending while it cleaned up part of the fiscal "mess" inherited from the previous regime.

On September 1, President Gustavo Días Ordaz, who had taken office in December, 1964, delivered his "State of the Union" address. He promised that various development programs would continue, but with financial and economic rigor that would maintain monetary stability and ward off inflation.

He noted that the Gross National Product (GNP) during the first half of the year had climbed by 6 per cent over the same period in 1964. This had been accomplished despite the channeling of heavy sums meant for public works into paying off debts instead. He added that public investment would reach $1,280,000,000 in 1965, thus implying a big spurt in the latter part of the year.

In July, the government launched a new industrialization drive. It appealed to private Mexican and foreign investors to help it open a planned 370 new industrial units which called for the investment of an estimated $1,500,000,000. The new units would satisfy internal demand, reduce the need to import, create new jobs, and contribute to Mexico's export program. The government offered tax and land concessions to spur action.

Mexico was concerned over the depletion of its sulfur reserves during the year. To remedy this, it limited sulfur exports to the equivalent of only 10 per cent of new reserves discovered the previous year. The new ruling was to become effective Jan. 1, 1966. Although this directly affected the U.S.-owned Pan American Sulphur Company, the firm showed its faith in Mexico by announcing plans to build a $44,000,000 fertilizer facility in Coatzacoalcos in partnership with local interests.

Torrential rains wrought havoc on crops in the summer, leaving hundreds homeless and ruining millions of dollars worth of foodstuffs.

Population: 42,244,000. **Government:** President Gustavo Díaz Ordaz. **Monetary Unit:** peso (12.59 = U.S. $1). **Gross National Product:** 192,300,000,000 pesos. **Foreign Trade:** exports, $1,054,000,000; imports, $1,493,000,000. **Principal Exports:** cotton, fish, sugar.   Mary C. Webster

See also Latin America.

MIDDLE EAST

A sequence of diplomatic storms swirled across the Middle East during 1965, resulting in many vocal battles but little military action. In fact, warfare in the region was limited to the Kurdish mountains of Iraq and the highlands of Yemen. The Arabs talked of strong military countermeasures against Israel's diversion of the River Jordan waters for irrigation of the Negev desert but, when Israel actually began the diversionary work, Arab responses were limited to short bursts of gunfire and isolated acts of sabotage. The United Arab Republic (UAR),

AN ANCIENT WAY of life still exists in oil-rich Iran. Here, a shepherd drives his sheep across pipelines that transport crude oil 175 miles to the Persian Gulf.
Rene Burri, Magnum

probably the only Arab state capable of large-scale war, was too heavily committed in Yemen and too shaky economically to make the effort.

UAR President Gamal Abdel Nasser got considerable diplomatic mileage out of a new element in Middle Eastern relationships—the rivalry of East and West Germany. He reacted to the announcement of West Germany's $80,000,000 arms agreement with Israel with an invitation to East German leader Walter Ulbricht to visit Cairo. Nasser also hinted that the UAR would recognize East German sovereignty. West Germany, torn between commitments of aid to the Arabs and a 10-year policy of not dealing with states that recognize East Germany, temporized. Ulbricht received red-carpet treatment on his visit, with East Germany granting $78,000,-000 in credits to the UAR, even though there was no diplomatic recognition. In May, West Germany established diplomatic relations with Israel. As a consequence, all the Arab states except Libya, Morocco, and Tunisia severed relations with Bonn, while Arab rioters damaged the West German embassy in Baghdad.

President Nasser's behavior had an effect on United States policy in the Middle East. U.S. relations with the UAR deteriorated to a new low in January when Nasser described the surplus food program as "wheat, meat, and leftovers." An angry

U.S. House of Representatives voted to suspend all food shipments to the UAR. The U.S. Senate lifted the suspension later, and, in the final vote on the foreign aid bill, Congress agreed to leave to the President's discretion the question of aid to uncooperative nations. Wheat shipments worth $38,000,-000 rescued the UAR at the last moment, but even with shipments of Soviet grain, the UAR was down to a month's food reserves. Despite harsh words, relations improved during the year as the UAR met its obligations to U.S. firms and stopped aiding the rebels in Congo (Léopoldville).

A Moderate Note. Tunisia's President Habib Bourguiba broke Arab unity, urging rapprochement in the Arab-Israeli conflict. In a speech to students at Tunis, he pointed out that any Arab attack on Israel would fail, and suggested that both sides hold talks leading to a permanent settlement, with Palestine refugees being given the right to return to a special area in Israel. Official reaction in most Arab capitals was to denounce Bourguiba as a deviationist, but, in several Arab summit conferences, there were signs of lukewarm support for Bourguiba's suggestion.

Arab leaders also took no overt action in support of the "Palestine Liberation Organization," ostensibly created by the Arab League to recover Palestine from the Jews. At the Casablanca summit meeting

Wide World

IRAN MOURNS the death of Premier Hassan Ali Mansur, who was assassinated by a 20-year-old student. Later, the assassin was executed by a firing squad.

in September (which Tunisia boycotted), the moderate note of "Bourguibism" was clearly evident. The Arab states agreed to respect each other's independence, to refrain from automatic aid to all rebel movements, to improve standards of journalism, and to seek realistic press laws.

Political Progress. In the Middle East, there were many trivial acts stemming from chauvinism. The Iranian parliament, for example, adopted a motion renaming the Suez Canal the "Canal of Darius" in retaliation for Arab insistence on "Arab" for Persian Gulf. But, overriding such notes of disunity, there was some achievement, including political progress.

Afghanistan elected its first legislature, with 300 seats in two houses. Among the successful candidates were four women. Turkey returned to government by a single dominant party, reversing a practice that began in 1960 when a coup resulted in a coalition of several parties. Although the victorious Justice party was the heir-apparent of the Democratic party of Adnan Mendéres, discredited and overthrown by the Turkish army for seeking a dictatorship, there was no question of the Justice party's right to lead, and Turkey's policy remained essentially the same.

The Kurdish Problem haunted Iraqi President Abdul Salam Muhammad Arif. Under pressure from his army commanders, Arif resumed the war against Mullah Mustafa al-Barzani. Their commanders feared that Barzani's forces were becoming so strong in northern Iraq as to strike for independence instead of internal autonomy. By October, the Kurds had established their own radio station and were driving back invading government forces. Hemmed in by Kurds and pro-Nasserist Ba'athists, President Arif miraculously clung to his job.

Social Justice. In the Arab world, the Ba'ath party kept power only in Syria. The party nationalized nearly everything and issued a new platform calling for the liberation of Palestine, a new constitution, and a public democracy founded on social justice and equality among citizens.

The University of Al-Azhar in Cairo issued a *futwa* (edict) forbidding Muslim women to marry communists. Women in Yemen went to the movies for the first time.

A United Nations (UN) subcommittee of 24 urged Britain to end the state of emergency in Aden. A special committee on Oman recommended that Britain and the sultan of Oman meet with the imam to establish standards for meeting the "legitimate aspirations of the people of Oman."

An old generation receded further with the deaths of former Premier Moshe Sharett of Israel, Syrian strongman Khalid al-Azm, and former King Faruk, who died of overeating in Rome.   WILLIAM SPENCER

See also Section One, PAUL-HENRI SPAAK ON THE WORLD; and Middle East country articles.

MINERALOGY. See GEOLOGY; METALLURGY; MINES AND MINING.

Manchete, *Life Magazine* © Time Inc.

GREAT QUARTZ CRYSTAL RUSH brought out thousands to dig for the semiprecious mineral on farmland in the interior of Brazil.

MINES AND MINING. U.S. aluminum and copper producers found themselves in the center of an economic-political power struggle late in 1965. As demand for both metals grew, the federal government—with a President determined to prevent any inflationary price rises—watched apprehensively.

On October 29, Olin Mathieson Chemical Corporation raised its ingot price $\frac{1}{2}$ cent, to 25 cents a pound. Other producers followed suit. Two days later, President Lyndon B. Johnson began a broad-scale counter-attack. One of his weapons was the 1,400,000-ton U.S. stockpile of surplus aluminum. He authorized release of 100,000 tons, and within two weeks he raised it to 300,000 tons. Hints of anti-trust actions, tax investigations, and reviews of federal power rates to the industry were among the administration's pressures. By November 10, the Aluminum Company of America had rolled back its price to $24\frac{1}{2}$ cents. The war was over.

The Copper Crisis came to a head a week later, when Secretary of Defense Robert S. McNamara announced plans to sell 200,000 tons of surplus copper, to put curbs on exports, and to seek to suspend duties on copper imports. Producers' prices of copper had risen from 31 cents to 38 cents a pound since Jan. 1, 1964, the latest in October, when Chile ordered U.S. producers there to charge 38 cents. Most foreign and U.S. firms fell into line. Two days after McNamara's move, on November 19, the Anaconda Company rolled its price back to 36 cents.

MODEL BUILDING

Metal Production. Both battles reflected the tremendous increase in the use of metals. Free World output of copper, for instance, rose from 3,900,000 tons in 1959 to 5,300,000 tons in 1964. Here is the U.S. performance for various metals:

	Average Monthly Output (thousands of tons)		Price Per Pound (October)	
	1964	1965	1964	1965
Aluminum	212.7	226.2	$ .24	$ .245
Copper	138.0	143.2	.3361	.3568
Lead	66.6	69.7	.136	.16
Zinc	47.9	51.1	.1357	.145

Expansion Plans, to increase mine and refinery capacity—as well as new facilities themselves—were announced frequently during the year. The Kennecott Copper Corporation was developing a major lead mine in southeastern Missouri. American Metal Climax, Inc., and Homestake Mining Company announced a joint venture in the same area.

Coal Production of all types reached 515,000,000 tons, up 4 per cent from 1964's 494,000,000 tons. Public utilities, coal's biggest customers, increased their use of coal $8\frac{1}{2}$ per cent to about 242,000,000 tons. Coal has made notable gains on oil and natural gas. And coal-derived gasoline threatened the oil companies in another quarter (see PETROLEUM AND GAS). High steel production raised that industry's use of coal to 109,000,000 tons from 1964's 96,000,000 (see STEEL INDUSTRY). ROBERT E. BEDINGFIELD

MODEL BUILDING. See GAMES, MODELS, AND TOYS.

MONACO, a tiny 512-acre principality perched on the edge of the Mediterranean, suffered crisis after crisis in 1965. They were caused in part by ruling Prince Rainier III and his wife, former film star Grace Kelly, who were trying to sweep away what the prince called "the faded glamor of the past" and introduce a popular, middle-class tourist industry. Rainier took the view that Monaco should be developed as a tourist resort, and not just as a center for yacht owners and high-stake gamblers.

Prince Rainier's plans were resisted by Greek shipping magnate Aristotle Onassis, head of the Societé des Bains de Mer, the company that runs the casino at Monte Carlo and other enterprises. When the prince talked of nationalizing the country's industries, Onassis threatened to move his multimillion dollar shipping interests to London, England, or Athens, Greece.

Rainier received some support from President Charles de Gaulle of neighboring France. Following a visit by Prince Rainier with De Gaulle, observers believed that a trial of strength between Rainier and Onassis was imminent. In the fall, Rainier made a further bid to wrest control of the Societé des Bains from Onassis by increasing the company's capital, thus making himself the principal shareholder.

Population: 30,000. **Government:** Prince Rainier III. **Monetary Unit:** Monégasque franc (4 = U.S. $1). **Principal Sources of Income:** shipping and tourism. KENNETH BROWN

MONEY. Inflationary tendencies threatened most Free World countries in 1965 despite restrictive policies and high interest rates. A slowdown in economic growth became a concern in Europe. An unprecedented fifth year of expansion pushed output close to effective capacity in the United States, and for the first time in years inflation became a danger.

Installment credit advanced over 10 per cent, to about $65,000,000,000. Yet interest rates increased little until September. Federal Reserve operations had permitted one of the largest peacetime monetary expansions ever—from $141,000,000,000 in currency and demand deposits in December, 1960, to $167,400,000,000. The 1965 increase of 4.8 per cent was over twice the average annual gain since 1951. Time deposits rose 16 per cent.

The U.S. Money Supply increased deceptively little during the first half of the year. But unexpectedly large tax receipts increased commercial banks' Treasury deposits (which are not counted as money but do permit banks to extend credit). When the government spent those funds, they became checking account credits, or new money, and contributed to rapid monetary growth.

Until September, Treasury bill rates held at less than 4 per cent and Treasury bond rates, at less than the new-issue $4\frac{1}{4}$ per cent legal limit. Both rates then rose sharply. The monetary expansion and growing expectations of inflation prompted the Federal Reserve Board (FRB) to increase the *discount rate* (the interest rate charged on loans to member banks) from 4 per cent to $4\frac{1}{2}$ per cent in early December (see BANKS AND BANKING). The FRB also raised the maximum rate on certificates of deposits from $4\frac{1}{2}$ per cent to $5\frac{1}{2}$ per cent. Market interest rates increased correspondingly, with prime rates advancing from $4\frac{1}{2}$ per cent to 5 per cent and government security yields going to cyclical highs.

The U.S. Balance of Payments deficit was reduced in 1965. However, close to another $2,000,000,000 of the accumulated dollar holdings of foreign governments, principally France, were cashed for Treasury-held gold.

To take into account that foreigners often willingly hold dollars, a new method of measuring the balance of payments was introduced. It counts only a foreign *government's* purchases of U.S. gold and its accumulated dollar holdings but not the holdings of foreign *individuals* or *private firms*, as before. The new yardstick reduced the 1964 deficit from $3,100,000,000 to $2,800,000,000 and the deficit for the last three quarters of 1965 from an annual rate of $1,700,000,000 to $1,300,000,000. There was discussion in 1965 of reform to take pressure off the dollar and the pound by creating a new internationally controlled monetary unit. See INTERNATIONAL TRADE AND FINANCE (Close-Up).

Foreign Exchange Rates generally held firm in 1965. Britain's pound strengthened from $2.7848 in November, 1964, to $2.8037 a year later. All other sterling area currencies rose with it. Brazil, whose cruzeiro sank from \$.00065 to \$.00055 in the same period, planned a severe devaluation in 1966 to 2.2 "strong" cruzeiros to the dollar. Other significant November-to-November changes in rates of foreign currencies were:

Nation (and unit)	1964	1965
Albania (lek)*	\$.02	\$.20
Chile (escudo)	.40	.2950
Colombia (peso)*	.09	.057
Ghana†	2.81 (pound)	1.18 (cedi)
Macau or Macao (pataca)	.21	.1785
Sierra Leone†	2.80 (pound)	1.4127 (leone)
Uruguay (peso)*	.0475	.0170
Yugoslavia (dinar)*	.0013	.0008

* Revalued † New currency unit
Note: See individual country articles for other rates

The Coinage Act of 1965. Congress made the first major revision of the U.S. coinage system in 173 years. It was necessary because the value of the silver in the coins was approaching the coins' face value. The act eliminated silver in dimes and quarters and substituted a nickel alloy with a copper core. Silver in the half dollar was reduced from 90 per cent to 40 per cent. *Seigniorage* (the difference between face value and minting costs) of the new coins increased nearly tenfold. See HOBBIES.   WILLIAM G. DEWALD

See also ECONOMY, THE; Section One, SYLVIA PORTER ON THE ECONOMY.

MONGOLIAN PEOPLE'S REPUBLIC. See OUTER MONGOLIA.

MONOD, JACQUES (1910-   ), University of Paris Professor of Metabolic Chemistry and Pasteur Institute Cellular Biochemistry Department head, shared the 1965 Nobel prize in medicine with two of his Pasteur colleagues. He, François Jacob, and André Lwoff, long noted for their research in genetics, were honored for discoveries concerning "genetic control of enzyme and virus synthesis."

Discovery of a type of ribonucleic acid (RNA) and the regulatory genes was the work of Monod and Jacob. They also collaborated in further research on the bacterial enzyme *beta-galactosidase*, after Monod had proved that the cell produces this enzyme as a totally new protein molecule.

The first research that Monod did, after receiving his science degree (1931), was on the evolution of organic life. He went to the University of Paris as an assistant zoology professor in 1934, and, in 1936, studied in the United States on a Rockefeller scholarship. He won wide acclaim for research on the growth of bacterial cultures, and was awarded his doctorate (1941). At the Pasteur Institute, Monod served as laboratory head, and in 1953 was advanced to his present position there. He also has been a University of Paris professor since 1959. Jacques Monod was born in Paris. He is an excellent cellist, and at one time considered playing professionally.

See also JACOB, FRANÇOIS; LWOFF, ANDRÉ; NOBEL PRIZES (Science).

MONTRESOR, BENI (1926-   ), internationally known stage and costume designer, was awarded the Caldecott medal in 1965 as illustrator of *May I Bring a Friend?* Beatrice Schenk de Regniers wrote the fantasy in verse about a boy and his animal friends. Book designing was new to Montresor when he came to New York in 1960. Since then he has designed 10 or more books. He is author and illustrator of *House of Flowers, House of Stars* (1962), and *The Witches of Venice* (1963).

The Italian artist did sets and costumes for the Glyndebourne Festival production of Debussy's opera *Pelléas et Mélisande* (1962) and Menotti's *The Last Savage*, premièred by the New York Metropolitan Opera (1963). More recent productions include Richard Rodgers' Broadway musical *Do I Hear a Waltz?* and Rossini's *Cinderella* performed by the Metropolitan Opera National Company.

Beni Montresor was born in Verona, Italy. He studied at the art school there, the Academy of Fine Arts in Venice, and at the Centro Sperimentale di Cinematographia in Rome. He says, "I was born liking the theater," and concerning the church altars in his country, "They were the most beautiful stages of my childhood." Montresor was well known in Europe as a theater and cinema designer before he came to the United States. He designed for Paddy Chayefsky's *Middle of the Night*, and other plays.

See also LITERATURE FOR CHILDREN (Awards).

MOROCCO. King Hassan II moved dramatically to assert his authority and alleviate the political and economic chaos that had paralyzed his country for six months. On June 8, 1965, the king dismissed the cabinet and suspended the assembly. He appointed a temporary cabinet of 25 members—all "king's men"—and named himself premier. Invoking a state of emergency, he pledged radical changes in the government and fiscal reforms.

The king's bold action had been prompted by a series of crises. Trouble began in January, when 600 persons, mainly students, were arrested for refusing to observe the obligatory daily fast during the Islamic observance of Ramadan. This was followed by student unrest over inadequate scholarships, poor instruction, and other grievances. Eventually, the students rioted and were joined in violence by unemployed workers. Before the army restored order, at least 25 were killed and hundreds injured.

Meanwhile, parliamentary action had been all but stymied. Premier Ahmed Bahnini's 1965-1966 budget was defeated, and a walkout blocked assembly action on a new three-year plan.

Population: 13,840,000. **Government:** King Hassan II; Premier Ahmed Bahnini. **Monetary Unit:** dirham (5.06 = U.S. \$1). **Gross National Product:** no figure available. **Foreign Trade:** exports, \$389,000,000; imports, \$449,000,000. **Principal Exports:** citrus fruit, iron ore, phosphate rock.   WILLIAM SPENCER

See also AFRICA.

MOTION PICTURES

If there was an optimistic look to the American motion picture industry in 1965, it was not without good reason. Domestic production, which had been gradually inching forward from a 1961 low of only 131 feature films, suddenly surged to about 250, a rise of 25 per cent over the previous year. Movie attendance was up also to an estimated 45,000,000 a week, as against 43,600,000 in 1964. And, despite rising ticket prices, certain pictures seemed headed for record grosses. Far in the lead was *My Fair Lady*. In a single year of limited engagements it had racked up an astonishing $46,000,000. No less impressive was the $20,000,000 earned by *Goldfinger*, the third of the James Bond thrillers. Produced in England for less than $3,000,000, it is expected to earn at least 15 times its cost from the world market.

Censorship, a recurrent problem for the motion picture industry, seemed definitely on the wane in 1965. State and local censor boards, already operating on shaky legal grounds, were further weakened by a March 1 decision of the Supreme Court of the United States in which, for the first time, the narrow constitutional basis for censorship was spelled out. Because of this ruling, censor boards in Maryland and New York were wiped out. By the end of 1965, official censorship remained only in Kansas and Virginia, and in perhaps 30 U.S. communities.

Significant, too, was an announcement late in November changing the name of the Legion of Decency to the National Catholic Office of Motion Pictures. The significance lay less in the change of name than in the change of approach that accompanied it. Instead of merely condemning—or in some instances, boycotting—films which the church disapproved, emphasis now would be upon building support for the pictures it endorsed.

Fully in keeping with this growing liberalization of the screen was the announcement made in October by the Motion Picture Association of America of a proposed overhaul of the industry's own self-regulatory Production Code Administration and the code itself. The code was to be both simplified and made more flexible to adjust to present and future changes.

A fitting climax to all this economic and political well-being was the official recognition of motion pictures as an art form in 1965. Signed into law by President Lyndon B. Johnson on September 29, the National Foundation on the Arts and Humanities Act included grants for the formation of an American Film Institute.

Film Trends. Pacesetter for the year was the late Ian Fleming's indestructible *bon vivant*, Agent 007—better known as James Bond. The Bond film *Thunderball*, a Christmas release, promised to match the popularity of the earlier *Goldfinger*, and reissues of *Dr. No* and *From Russia with Love* outgrossed the

Warner Brothers

SPLAP! Four thousand cream pies were used to shoot the messiest pie-throwing scene of them all in Warner Brothers' The Great Race.

20th Century Fox Film Corp.

THE VILLAIN of Those Magnificent Men in Their Flying Machines was played by Terry-Thomas. In the film, he competes in a London-to-Paris air race.

newer pictures. Inevitably, every studio put its own variation of the Bond character into production.

Augmenting the tongue-in-cheek heroics of this national Bond drive were a number of films that put the accent completely on humor. Significantly, these included some of the year's most expensive and lavish productions, such as *Those Magnificent Men in Their Flying Machines* and *The Great Race*. Others, like *What's New Pussycat?*, *The Loved One*, and two British-made imports, *Help!* and *The Knack*, liberally laced their humor with sex. Supplementing this essentially adult fare were better than two dozen comedy musicals beamed at the teen-age market—films with titles like *How to Stuff a Wild Bikini* and *Winter A-Go-Go*. What makes this so remarkable is that less than five years ago, comedy had all but disappeared from the U.S. screen.

No less remarkable was the increasingly candid treatment of sex in U.S. films. Pictures like *The Sandpiper*, *Harlow*, *Sylvia*, and *The Cincinnati Kid* involved story elements specifically barred by the Production Code. Indicative of the coming change in code standards was the approval of *The Pawnbroker*, despite scenes of complete nudity, on grounds that they were germane to the theme of a basically moral film: the compassionate story of a man brutalized by Nazi concentration camp horrors.

But apart from *The Pawnbroker*, the number of films of serious intent could be counted on the fingers of one hand. Stanley Kramer's star-laden *Ship of Fools* made meaningful comment on the self-interest and moral passivity that paved the way for the Nazis in 1933. *The Bedford Incident* pointed an alarmed finger at the militarist mentality in an era of nuclear warfare. *King Rat* and the English-made *Darling* portrayed the inner emptiness of individuals who advance themselves at the expense of others. And George Stevens' *The Greatest Story Ever Told* proffered a ponderous recapitulation of the New Testament, but with no particular relevance to our times. Even the best of the foreign imports—Olivier's *Othello*, Fellini's *Juliet of the Spirits*, Antonioni's experimental *Red Desert*—seemed curiously remote and uninvolved. Fittingly, the year ended with the release of David Lean's sumptuous *Doctor Zhivago*—a U.S. picture based on a Russian book, filmed in Spain by an English director, with an Egyptian star, Omar Sharif. Nothing could have been more indicative of the present tendency in films to entertain everybody while offending no one.

Awards in 1965 included:

Academy of Motion Picture Arts and Sciences Award for 1964 to: *My Fair Lady*, best film; Julie Andrews in *Mary Poppins*, best actress; Rex Harrison in *My Fair Lady*, best actor; George Cukor, *My Fair Lady*, best director; Lila Kedrova in *Zorba the Greek* and Peter Ustinov in *Topkapi*, best supporting actress and actor; *Yesterday, Today and Tomorrow*, best foreign film.   ARTHUR KNIGHT

MOTORBOAT RACING. See BOATS AND BOATING.

MOZAMBIQUE. African nationalists continued to struggle for independence from Portugal. Dr. Eduardo Mondlane, head of the Mozambique Liberation Front (MLF), claimed that his guerrilla forces had inflicted casualties on Portuguese troops in many parts of the country. Portugal, however, maintained that such activity amounted to a few acts of banditry rather than a war for liberation.

Early in 1965, leaders of the MLF and the followers of Paul Gumane met at Dar es Salaam, Tanzania, to coordinate their activities against Portugal. Several other nationalist groups joined forces in a new organization called the Mozambique Revolutionary Committee. By the end of May, however, Portuguese police reportedly had broken up the underground operations of Mondlane's rebels.

In Mozambique, plans were laid for the construction of the country's first sugar refinery, to be built near Lourenço Marques. A 187-mile oil pipeline, said to be the longest in sub-Saharan Africa, was completed and put into service. It links the port of Beira in Mozambique with Umtali in Rhodesia.

Population: 7,058,000. **Government:** Governor General Rear Admiral Manuel Maria Sarmento. **Monetary Unit:** escudo (28.75 = U.S. $1). **Foreign Trade:** exports, $91,000,000; imports, $136,000,000. **Principal Exports:** cotton, sugar.   BENJAMIN E. THOMAS
See also AFRICA.

MUNICIPAL GOVERNMENT. See CITY.

MURPHY, CHARLES SPRINGS (1909-   ), once an administrative assistant and special counsel to former President Harry S. Truman, was named chairman of the Civil Aeronautics Board (CAB) by President Lyndon B. Johnson on April 28, 1965. Murphy succeeded Alan S. Boyd, who became Undersecretary of Commerce for Transportation.

Murphy has resided in Washington, D.C., since 1934. His first government post was as a law assistant in the office of the U.S. Senate's legislative counsel. Later, he spent 11 years as an assistant to the legislative counsel, ending his Senate career in 1946. Among the many laws he helped write was the landmark Agricultural Adjustment Act of 1938. Under the act, the federal government supported prices, encouraging farmers not to grow certain crops and paying them for the storage of crops.

Truman called Murphy to the White House staff as an administrative assistant in 1947. Murphy was designated the President's special counsel in 1950 and became the principal White House expert on drawing up legislation. He entered private law practice in Washington with the firm of Morison, Murphy, Clapp & Abrams after President Dwight D. Eisenhower took office in 1953. In 1960, Murphy was appointed Undersecretary of Agriculture.

The head of CAB was born at Wallace, N.C. He received B.A. (1931) and LL.B. (1934) degrees from Duke University. Residing in Annapolis, Md., he is married and has three children.   WALTER F. MORSE

MUSEUMS in the United States, which served more than 200,000,000 visitors during the year, made special studies of their exhibits in an effort to better meet the needs and interests of the public. At the Milwaukee Public Museum, experiments were made with the arrangement of exhibits, and the reactions of the visitors to each were recorded and analyzed. The Atomic Energy Commission sponsored tests of the effectiveness of its displays, and Harvard University made a nationwide study for the U.S. Office of Education of the value of art exhibitions and related programs for children.

Educational Projects. The Boston Children's Museum selected objects from its collection to be loaned to teachers for their use in elementary school classes. The objects were packaged by the museum in portable boxes. Old Sturbridge Village, Mass., collaborated in another school-related program by providing a historically accurate setting for a telecast depicting boyhood on an 1812 farm. The National Broadcasting Company distributed 250,000 kits to teachers for use with this telecast.

Installations. The National Cowboy Hall of Fame and Western Heritage Center was dedicated at Oklahoma City. The Pennsylvania state museum, the William Penn Memorial, occupied its new circular building in Harrisburg. A courtyard of a 16th century Spanish castle was installed at the Metropolitan Museum of Art in New York City as the impressive entrance to its new library wing. The Smithsonian Institution in Washington, D.C., opened a physical anthropology hall in the Natural History Museum and a military history hall in the Museum of History and Technology. The Institution also commemorated the 200th anniversary of the birth of its founder, James Smithson, in the fall.

The National Park Service opened new museums at Cape Cod National Seashore, Rocky Mountain National Park, and Wupatki National Monument. Homes designed by two important U.S. architects, Andrew Jackson Davis and Frank Lloyd Wright, were made historic house museums by the National Trust for Historic Preservation.

Exhibitions. The Baltimore Museum of Art, the Walters Art Gallery, and the Peabody Institute Library collaborated in an exhibition tracing the art of penmanship in Western culture. Among the important traveling exhibitions were the Dead Sea Scrolls and ancient sculpture from India.

Museums Abroad. The new Israel Museum in Jerusalem, which houses the Dead Sea Scrolls, opened in May. Special exhibitions commemorating the 700th anniversary of Dante's birth and the 750th anniversary of the signing of the Magna Carta were organized by the British Museum in London. Museums throughout Canada engaged in expansion programs in preparation for the Centennial of Confederation in 1967.   RALPH H. LEWIS

See also ARCHITECTURE; FAIRS AND EXHIBITIONS; PAINTING AND SCULPTURE.

MUSIC

With the "Big Five" orchestras (in order of seniority, New York, Boston, Chicago, Philadelphia, and Cleveland) committed to contracts that call for 48 to 52 weeks of employment in the near future, the dream of the unending music season became reality in many U.S. cities. The pattern was completed when the Chicago Symphony signed a precedent-breaking contract in September, 1965. Thus the days when summer music filled a midyear gap, set off by blank spaces in the calendar in late spring and early fall, were gone for good in these cities.

The extension of the services of the major orchestras seemed to impose no strain on the ability of the public to enjoy the music provided. The New York Philharmonic ended its first 11-month season in the summer of 1965 with a series of 12 outdoor concerts in the city's parks. In a concert in August in Manhattan's Central Park, the orchestra drew as many as 70,000 for works as uncompromising as the *Ninth Symphony* of Beethoven. The full dozen programs attracted 462,500 listeners—nearly 25 per cent more than the total attendance for eight months of subscription concerts.

With the lengthened schedules came increased financial needs, but, increased financial resources were available, or would be soon, for many orchestras. The National Foundation on the Arts and the Humanities Act of 1965, signed into law in September, authorized an appropriation of $63,000,000 over a three-year period for federal assistance to the arts. And the Ford Foundation announced an $85,-000,000 program for symphony orchestras that should have particular significance for the smaller ensembles with limited endowments.

As if to stress the financial strain, both the Chicago and St. Louis symphonies (two of the oldest in the nation) began their concerts in the autumn after prolonged labor negotiations. But Chicago signed a five-year contract, as did the Minneapolis Symphony. St. Louis got a three-year pact.

Touring Orchestras. Though traveling orchestras were commonplace, a few tours still made news. The major overseas junket by a U.S. orchestra went to the Cleveland ensemble and its conductor George Szell. The Chicago Symphony was the first group to make an extended trip to the 49th state, Alaska. The British Broadcasting Corporation (BBC) Symphony on its first visit to the United States played a memorable New York series, concentrating on contemporary music. The Moscow Philharmonic and Czech Philharmonic (of Prague) were visitors in the autumn.

Ives and Stravinsky. New music, first heard in 1965, included the *Variations for Orchestra* by Stravinsky, which Robert Craft directed with the Chi-

The New York Times

IN CENTRAL PARK in Manhattan, some 70,000 heard Beethoven's Ninth Symphony in the first of a series of outdoor concerts.

447

cago Symphony in April, and the *Fourth Symphony* of Charles Ives. The Ives work was begun in 1896 and completed 20 years later. It was heard, in part, in 1927, but at Ives death in 1954, the manuscript was in such a poor state that years of work were required for the preparation of a critical edition suitable for performance. Leopold Stokowski and the American Symphony Orchestra gave the belated world première in April, with two associate conductors assisting him in passages of tricky, cross-rhythms. For many critics, it was the discovery of a major American composition.

Moses and Aaron. The operatic event of the year, unquestionably, was the Covent Garden production in late June of Arnold Schönberg's *Moses and Aaron.* Georg Solti conducted, and there was general agreement that, although it had been heard previously in Zurich and Berlin, it was this London production that fully demonstrated the significance of the work for the theater. Peter Hall of the Royal Shakespearian Company was stage director. The United States was scheduled to hear *Moses and Aaron* in a production by the Boston Opera in May, 1966.

National Opera Company. In the United States, the focus of operatic interest was the new Metropolitan Opera National Company, which took to the road in September after an initial series of performances in Indianapolis. Destined to wander until mid-June, 1966, it would visit some 70 cities with its four productions, stressing the talents of its bright young American singers and the skill of some of the best directors and stage designers in the business.

Fresh Repertory was everywhere in evidence. Shostakovich's *Katerina Ismailova* was back in a New York City Opera Company production. An earlier Shostakovich opera, *The Nose*, based on a satiric fantasy by Gogol, received its U.S. première at Santa Fe, N.Mex., in August. Russian opera continued to flourish in New York in the autumn with Prokofiev's *The Flaming Angel*, produced by the New York City Company, and Tchaikovsky's *The Queen of Spades* at the Metropolitan.

New Operas included Jack Beeson's *Lizzie Borden*, and Ned Rorem's *Miss Julie*, based on Strindberg's drama. Both works were given their premières by the New York City Opera. Santa Fe saw *The Stag King*, by the young West German composer, Hans Werner Henze. Handel's *Julius Caesar* was performed in Kansas City, Mo., and in Dallas, Tex. Alban Berg was widely acclaimed as one of the masters of 20th century opera. His *Lulu* was a hit of the San Francisco Opera season, and his bleakly powerful *Wozzeck* was a major triumph of the Lyric Opera of Chicago.

Milestones. The year brought its share of milestones, including the death of Edgar Varèse shortly after his 80th birthday. Marian Anderson, a great lady, retired after a career that already belonged to history. But the greatest attention went to the return to the public stage of Vladimir Horowitz, after a dozen years in which he played exclusively for the recording microphone and for himself. At Carnegie Hall in May he proved to most critics that his extended sabbatical had brought him even greater depth as an artist. Already a figure of legend, he was capable of creating legend anew.

Again No Pulitzer. Controversy of the year was the decision of the Pulitzer Prize advisory board to skip the award in music for the second consecutive year. The controversy was intensified when the New York Music Critics Circle determined that it could not decide on the best new work by a U.S. composer —from the 269 which had been heard in New York City during 1965. Instead, it gave a special citation to the *Fourth Symphony* of Charles Ives.

The New Recordings. Columbia Records made two of their issues seem like spot news coverage of historic events. The Horowitz recital at Carnegie Hall was available complete on disks shortly after the event, and a major autumn release was the Charles Ives *Fourth*, as performed by Leopold Stokowski. The four operas of Wagner's *Ring of the Nibelung* were finally available in stereo with the release of *Götterdämmerung* on London Records. Other exceptional releases were Berg's *Wozzeck* and Mozart's *The Magic Flute*, both under Karl Boehm, and the *Gurrelieder* of Schönberg as directed by Rafael Kubelik.　　　　　ROBERT C. MARSH

Wide World

VLADIMIR HOROWITZ performed in Carnegie Hall in May, ending a 12-year absence from the concert stage.

MUSIC, JAZZ. Jazz musicians suffered setbacks in 1965. A few top artists achieved artistic and commercial success, but opportunities to perform were fewer. Many jazz night clubs closed, even the world-famous Birdland in New York City.

The most popular jazz artist of the year was Ramsey Lewis, a Chicago pianist with a style strongly linked to the blues. Lewis appealed to teen-agers and to older fans with his recording, "The In Crowd," which sold more than 1,000,000 copies.

Avant-garde jazz musicians had difficulty finding audiences. Hence, many moved to Europe where they found listeners more receptive to their musical experiments. Prominent among them was saxophonist Ornette Coleman.

Because of the difficulty in obtaining work, very few new jazz groups were formed. An exception was Charles Lloyd, a saxophonist and flutist who left Cannonball Adderley's group to start an *avant-garde* quartet of his own.

Big band jazz found itself in great economic difficulties. Maynard Ferguson and Lionel Hampton gave up their orchestras and formed combos (small groups) that were more easily booked. Count Basie was able to keep his orchestra going, partly through the help offered by such artists as Frank Sinatra and Tony Bennett, with whom his band was teamed in concert tours. Leonard G. Feather

See also Deaths of Notable Persons.

Robert W. Young, Globe

BIG BEAT SINGERS Sonny & Cher, a husband and wife team, were among the most popular acts in show business during 1965.

MUSIC, POPULAR. While the Beatles maintained their position as the kings of pop in 1965, there was an upsurge in the acceptance of many U.S. and British vocal groups. The screams of teen-agers and the jingle of cash registers resounded across the land for the colorfully attired, long-haired Salvatore Phillip Bono, 25, professionally known as Sonny, and for his attractive (longer-haired), 19-year-old wife, Cher.

Somewhat more sophisticated in style were the Beach Boys, exponents of the so-called "surfing sound." Their big hit of the year was "Help Me, Rhonda." Female favorites included the Supremes. This trio of young Negro girls from Detroit rose high on the charts with "Stop! In the Name of Love." The girl vocalist most popular with young record buyers was Petula Clark of "Downtown" fame.

Several British groups continued to enjoy tumultuous success in England and in the United States. Among them were Gary and the Pacemakers, Herman's Hermits, and the Dave Clark Five.

Folk Rock. A trend away from trivial song subjects was indicated by the success of "Eve of Destruction," written by a 20-year-old composer, P. F. Sloane. Recorded by Barry McGuire, a former member of the New Christy Minstrels, it dealt with such matters as war, integration, and the draft. The success of "Eve of Destruction" led to a style called folk rock. The rash of "protest songs" led to a reaction in the form of songs representing a more posi-

tive attitude. Typical of these was "The Dawn of Correction," composed and sung by a trio known as The Spokesmen.

Leading folk singers and composers soon became a part of the folk rock movement. Some, including an American rock group called the Byrds, used socially provocative lyrics and added unusual electronic sound effects. After they had scored a hit with a Bob Dylan song, "Hey Mr. Tambourine Man," Dylan himself was soon heard in a folk rock performance of his own, a pounding song with an apparently symbolic lyric, "Like a Rolling Stone."

For the Adults. In the more sophisticated popular music field, the most successful performers, both commercially and artistically, included Barbra Streisand; Frank Sinatra, who at 50 scored with a nostalgic song, "September of My Years"; and Andy Williams. New popular songs aimed at adult audiences comprised material chiefly from Broadway musicals, notably from Miss Streisand's starring vehicle *Funny Girl*. Songs from *The Sound of Music* enjoyed renewed attention with the release of a recording from the motion picture version of that popular stage success. In the world of country music, Johnny Cash, George Jones, Buck Owens, and Jim Reeves headed popularity lists.

The deaths of two long-prominent singers, Nat King Cole and Sam Cooke, led to the posthumous reissue of albums, indicating that their fame is unlikely to fade for years. Leonard G. Feather

NATIONAL
DEFENSE

NATIONAL DEFENSE

The war in Vietnam took a sudden, bitter turn that locked massive U.S. land, sea, and air forces in direct combat with communist regulars as well as guerrillas. By the end of 1965, the 22,000 Americans in Vietnam with orders only to "advise and assist" had become more than 180,000 and they were fighting in all-U.S. combat units. Another 50,000 served aboard aircraft carriers and other U.S. naval vessels in the South China Sea.

The grave new chapter opened February 7, when President Lyndon B. Johnson sent 49 aircraft from the carriers U.S.S. *Hancock* and *Coral Sea* against the military base of Dong Hoi in North Vietnam. The

Cornell Capa, Magnum

raid, with South Vietnamese also participating, was in retaliation for a Viet Cong guerrilla attack on Pleiku which killed eight Americans.

Three days later, the guerrillas blew up a barracks at Qui Nhon, killing 22 Americans, and again a retaliatory air raid struck military targets in the north—this time 160 U.S. and South Vietnamese planes on February 11. One week later, U.S. jets, unaccompanied by South Vietnamese, attacked a guerrilla concentration in Binh Dinh province in the south, marking the first departure from the U.S. advise and assist role. The first nonretaliatory air raid against the north came March 2. Soon, U.S. strikes were about on a daily basis, against targets in both north and south.

The first American combat troops were 3,500 of the 3rd Marine Division, that landed at Da Nang on March 8 and 9. Their mission was to guard the big U.S. air base at Da Nang against marauding guerrillas. They pushed a perimeter 10 miles out and promptly clashed with enemy patrols, the first time on March 12. As the fighting flared, the rest of the 3rd Marine Division shifted from Okinawa to the Da Nang area. Other elements joined it, forming the 3rd Marine Amphibious Force.

The U.S. Army sent in the newly formed airmobile 1st Cavalry Division, the 1st Infantry Division, and the equivalent of a third division—the independent 173rd Airborne Brigade, and one brigade each from the 101st Airborne Division and the 25th Infantry Division.

American officials said the massive introduction of U.S. ground troops prevented communist forces from "mauling" the weary South Vietnamese army. Intelligence officers reported the enemy intended to cut the country in two where it narrows in the central highlands. Secretary of Defense Robert S. McNamara said on June 16 that it was "probable that more than 10,000 men infiltrated from the north into the south during the past year." He said they included one regular North Vietnamese army battalion—the 2nd of the 325th Division spotted in Kontum province—and perhaps eight others.

THE BOSS. Robert S. McNamara, U.S. Defense Secretary, prepares to testify on Capitol Hill on his controversial cost-cutting measures.

UP AND AT 'EM! *Sprint antimissile missile,
under development in 1965, roars up at target
from White Sands Missile Range launch site.*

Funds and Manpower. President Johnson asked Congress on August 4 for an extra $1,700,000,000 for the build-up. The same day, Secretary McNamara disclosed the armed forces would be increased by 340,000 men to a total of 2,980,000. The additional money was appropriated as part of the fiscal 1966 budget. The increased manpower, to come mostly from stepped-up draft calls, would make possible another division for the army, its 17th, and three new separate brigades.

Viet Cong Strength was estimated by McNamara at 200,000, including 70,000 full-time, hard-core regulars, 100,000 part-time irregulars, and 80,000 propagandists and others in "political cadres." He said South Vietnamese forces totaled 545,000, counting regional and local defense troops as well as regular army, but excluding the national police.

It was the administration's second trip to Capitol Hill during the year for special war funds. On May 4, the President requested $700,000,000 more for the war. The request, couched as part of a congressional expression of support for his policies, was approved May 6. But a number who voted for it warned against escalating the fighting or more deeply involving U.S. forces.

Bombing Lulls. Twice during the year, President Johnson halted the bombing of North Vietnam in a bid for peace. The first suspension began May 13, when, in a Washington speech, he repeated his call for "unconditional discussions," first made April 7, and blamed Communist China for prolonging the fighting against North Vietnam's best interests. North Vietnam denounced the speech as a "contemptible trick" aimed at splitting allies, and the bombing was resumed May 18. The second lull began Christmas Eve. The President accompanied it with a much-publicized diplomatic offensive. He dispatched distinguished envoys and appealed to virtually every head of state to help him start peace talks. See PRESIDENT OF THE U.S.

Dominican Crisis. Fierce fighting broke out in Santo Domingo on April 24, when army and civilian rebels staged a bloody coup to restore exiled former President Juan D. Bosch to power in the Dominican Republic. They succeeded in ousting the regime headed by Dr. Daniel Reid Cabral Huberto, but anti-Bosch elements of the air force and navy opposed them in bitter fighting that deeply and controversially involved the United States.

On April 28, 405 U.S. Marines moved by helicopter from the amphibious assault ship U.S.S. *Boxer* and landed in a polo field three miles from the U.S. embassy in downtown Santo Domingo. Their orders were to protect Americans and any other foreigners. By May 5, there were 19,363 U.S. troops in the city: 6,924 marines and 12,439 soldiers, mostly from the 82nd Airborne Division. They helped evacuate 2,694 Americans and 1,373 nationals of other countries. But, by then, their mission had changed to include thwarting communists who, the

JOINT CHIEFS, from left, are General John P. McConnell, air force; Admiral D. L. McDonald, navy; General Earle G. Wheeler of the army, chairman; General H. K. Johnson, army; General Wallace M. Greene, Jr., marine corps commandant.

United States charged, had infiltrated the rebel movement to take it over.

The rebels hotly denied any communist danger and accused the U.S. forces of siding with the rightist junta fighting the rebels. They said they would have won but for American intervention.

As a measure of stability returned under a provisional government, the United States withdrew all the marines and most of the soldiers. By year's end, the 8,060-man Inter-American Force (created by the Organization of American States in the crisis) included 6,000 troops of the 82nd Airborne and 300 U.S. Air Force men, plus 1,130 soldiers from Brazil, 20 from Costa Rica, 250 from Honduras, 150 from Nicaragua, and 210 from Paraguay.

Casualties. The toll of dead and wounded rose quickly in Vietnam. American battle deaths for the year reached 1,365 for a total of 1,620 over the five years of fighting. The wounded came to 7,634, of whom 6,110 fell in 1965. A total of 149 were missing and another 25 were known to be prisoners. Nonbattle deaths amounted to 463 at year's end, including 359 in 1965 alone.

In the Dominican Republic, 25 Americans died in fighting and 151 suffered wounds. Another 16 were killed in nonhostile activity. See DOMINICAN REPUBLIC; VIETNAM.

Defense Budget. The Congress of the United States provided $46,887,163,000 in defense funds for fiscal 1966. The appropriation included $1,700,000,000 in emergency funds for military operations in Vietnam. The total, which was $85,681,000 less than President Johnson requested, gave the army $10,973,094,000, the navy and marines $13,957,200,000, the air force $17,519,600,000, and other Department of Defense activities the sum of $4,437,269,000.

Pay Raise. Congress also approved a $1,000,000,000 military pay increase, effective September 1. Commissioned and warrant officers with more than two years of service received a flat 6 per cent raise; those with less service received an average of 22 per cent. Enlisted men with more than two years of service drew a flat 11 per cent increase; those with less, an average of 17.3 per cent. It was the first pay increase in the last category since 1952.

On April 24, President Johnson issued an executive order designating Vietnam and adjacent waters a combat zone. It made military pay for service in the area exempt from U.S. income taxes, retroactive to Jan. 1, 1964.

United States Army

Secretary McNamara authorized the army on June 16 to organize the "1st Air Cav." It was created at Fort Benning, Ga., drawing men and equipment from the 2nd Infantry Division and the experimental 11th Air Assault Division there. But it took its name from the renowned old 1st Cavalry Division in Korea, adding the "airmobile" to signify how it goes into battle.

U.S.S. AMERICA, new conventionally fueled attack carrier, has a flight deck of more than 4½ acres. It is second in size only to the nuclear carrier Enterprise.

The 1st Air Cav. arrived in Vietnam September 12 and 13, boasting 15,787 officers and men, 434 aircraft, and 1,600 light ground vehicles. By comparison, a regular infantry division has about 15,900 personnel, 101 aircraft, and 3,200 ground vehicles. Lacking both the big guns and logistical staying power of standard units, it depended upon speed and mobility. A few months of bitter fighting proved its worth. Upon leaving Saigon November 29 following his seventh visit, McNamara said, "I am sure that . . . we will wish to add another air cavalry division to the forces of the U.S. Army."

Expansion. To man its new division and three new brigades, the army set up new training centers at Fort Benning, Ga., and Fort Bliss, Tex. It expected to produce 408,000 soldiers in fiscal 1966, a 213,000 increase over the year before.

United States Navy

The navy was also caught up in two concurrent crises of 1965, Vietnam and the Dominican Republic. The strain was eased by lifting manpower ceilings to 943,000 (including 223,000 marines) and activating 23 ships and 16 landing craft from the reserve fleet, adding them to the 868 total, and assigning all 39 to Pacific stations.

The navy also broke up nuclear-powered Task Force One. The carrier U.S.S. *Enterprise*, biggest and fastest ship in history, and the missile-carrying frigate, U.S.S. *Bainbridge*, left the Atlantic Fleet October 25 for the Pacific. The missile cruiser

"He says he must have burned his credit card by mistake."

U.S.S. *Long Beach* stayed behind with the missile frigate *Truxton*. The *Enterprise* and the *Bainbridge* took up battle stations off the Vietnamese coast, the first nuclear vessels ever to engage in combat.

The Marines, boosted in numbers to 223,000, practiced what they preached in furious and successful encounters with the communists in Vietnam. On August 18 and 19, some 5,000 of them surprised and eliminated a crack Viet Cong regiment on Van Luoung peninsula in a classic air-sea-ground assault closely supported by aircraft, naval gunfire, and artillery. From September 7 to 9, they repeated the operation on nearby Batangan peninsula, but this time joining forces with South Vietnamese units. When not fighting, the 40,000 marines in Vietnam were busy trying to make friends with the peasants through medical care and other "civic action" projects. The marines maintained three divisions and three air wings, plus the nucleus of a fourth of each, in the Atlantic and Pacific Fleet Marine Forces.

The Coast Guard, a Department of the Treasury agency in what technically is peacetime, operated seventeen 82-foot cutters and nine smaller vessels off Vietnam. The boats' mission, under navy control, was to choke off infiltration of supplies by coastal junks. At home, the service saved more than 15,000 lives and rescued property valued at $1,873,673,600, more than four times its $452,856,736 budget for the year. Patrols off Florida picked up more than 3,000 Cuban refugees during 1965, for a total of 9,000 since 1959.

United States Air Force

The air force, although primarily cast in a strategic role, found itself deeply enmeshed in the tactical struggle in Vietnam. It struck in hundreds of sorties daily, north and south, with propeller planes, jets, and even Strategic Air Command (SAC) B-52 jet bombers. The B-52s, based on Guam, had been converted to drop conventional "iron bombs" instead of nuclear ones.

Air force pilots, like their navy and marine colleagues, braved heavy antiaircraft fire on trips north. They developed evasive skill, however, and had amazing success avoiding Soviet-built surface-to-air missiles (SAM-2) similar to those that knocked down high-flying U-2 spy planes over Russia and Cuba. North Vietnamese MIG-17 jet fighters steered clear after two of them were downed July 10 by Sidewinder air-to-air missiles near Hanoi.

Department of Defense

Secretary McNamara, ever a lightning rod for critical bolts from Capitol Hill, did it again. Aside from reviving the bomber-missile tussle with plans for a reduction in SAC aircraft, he stirred old outcries with new base closings and his third "realignment" of the reserves. McNamara announced on December 6 he was merging, reducing, or shutting down 149 military installations as "surplus to our needs." Included were 126 in 39 states and the District of Columbia as well as 23 in 10 foreign

countries. He said military effectiveness would not suffer in eliminating 53,000 military and civilian jobs, and saving $410,000,000 a year. It brought to 852 the number of facilities so curbed since 1961.

Reserves. On September 30, McNamara ordered the army to abolish its 751 reserve units, a total of 55,000 men, some of them in the six remaining reserve divisions. The 55,000 men could go into a pool of unassigned reservists. Or they could join a "selected force" drawn from 18 states—three divisions and six brigades to be trained to the "highest possible state of combat readiness." The 145,000-man "selective force" would include 130,000 National Guardsmen from 822 companies and detachments and 15,000 reservists from 160 companies.

Draft Quotas moved to a post-Korean high during the year, from 17,000 in August to 27,400 in September, 33,600 in October, 36,450 in November, and 45,224 in December. The December quota, cut to 40,200 when the marine corps canceled its call for 5,024 due to increased enlistments, was still the largest since the Korean War's 53,000 in May, 1953.

Personnel Changes. Stanley R. Resor succeeded Stephen Ailes as secretary of the army. Harold Brown replaced Eugene M. Zuckert as secretary of the air force. General John P. McConnell took over from General Curtis E. LeMay as air force chief of staff.   WARREN ROGERS

See also ARMED FORCES OF THE WORLD.

NEGRO. If the passage of the Civil Rights Act of 1964 was the most significant event of the civil rights revolution, the deed that ratified that revolution was the signing, on August 6, of the administration's Voting Rights Act of 1965.

The purpose of the act was to remove barriers raised in Southern states against Negroes' voting. The act's key provisions were:

• The suspension of literacy and other qualification tests in any state or county where they were in force on Nov. 1, 1964, and where less than half the voting age population was registered or voted in the 1964 presidential election.

• The Attorney General was empowered to send federal examiners when he receives 20 or more complaints in writing, or where he has other reason to believe an examiner is needed to prevent voting discrimination.

• The Attorney General was empowered to file suit to challenge poll taxes as requirements for voting, both in state and in local elections.

Enforcement. Federal examiners were sent by the Department of Justice into 32 counties in Alabama, Louisiana, Mississippi, and South Carolina between August 10 and October 29. They registered more than 76,000 Negroes. The department estimated an additional 144,000 were registered by voluntary compliance with the act, for a total of 55,000 a month. But this fell far short of the 80,000 a month predicted by civil rights leaders. According to the

*THURGOOD MARSHALL, 57, is the new
Solicitor General, the man who argues the
government's case before the Supreme Court.*

U.S. Civil Rights Commission, the principal reasons for the lower total, which slackened at year-end, was a lack of federal registrars and insufficient publicity given the drive in some Southern counties.

Other Legislation passed in 1965 to aid Negroes, as well as other Americans, included the doubling of the President's War on Poverty (see POVERTY) and the appropriation of funds for Operation Head Start. See EDUCATION.

The Great March. The major force that led to the passage of the Voting Rights Act was the Selma-to-Montgomery Freedom March. It took place in the spring. The events leading up to the march began in January, when the Reverend Martin Luther King announced that he would call for street demonstrations in Selma, Ala., if Negroes were not permitted to register to vote in large numbers in that state. King chose Selma because it had become a symbol of intransigence in the rights movement.

The demonstrations began on January 18, when King was punched and kicked as he and other Negroes registered at Selma's formerly all-white Hotel Albert. On February 1, King and some 770 Negroes were arrested for picketing against voting requirements. On February 3, 1,000 Negro schoolchildren in nearby Marion were arrested as they attempted to march to the county courthouse. Two days later, Dr. King, who was released on bail, flew to Washington to confer with the President on a new voting rights law. But the arrests mounted, as did

pressure for a march to the state capital to confront Governor George Wallace with a protest against the denial of Negro voting rights.

Acts of Violence focused the attention of the nation and caused the President to describe the situation in Selma an "American Tragedy." On February 10, Sheriff James G. Clark and his deputies drove 165 Negro children and teen-age demonstrators on a forced march, using clubs and cattle prods. On March 7, police charged into a line of demonstrators using night sticks, tear gas, and whips. Seventeen Negroes were hospitalized. On March 11, a white Unitarian minister from Boston, the Reverend James J. Reeb, a civil rights volunteer, died of wounds received in a beating.

A 26-year-old Negro, Jimmy Lee Jackson, died of gunshot wounds received earlier in a clash between state troopers and rights demonstrators. But the march to Montgomery, which Wallace had attempted to block, received a go-ahead from the Federal District Court on March 17. It began March 21. To protect the participants, President Johnson federalized the Alabama National Guard and ordered regular forces into the state. The nation's conscience was aroused. Clergymen from every denomination, as well as hundreds of private citizens, flew to Selma to participate in the 54-mile, four-day demonstration. At its end, 25,000 marchers entered the state capital.

Under the protection of government troops, the march went off without incident, but one white woman, Viola Gregg Liuzzo, 39, a Detroit housewife and civil rights volunteer, was shot to death on March 25 as she was driving to Montgomery to pick up marchers. In December—after an earlier acquittal of her three Klansman attackers on a murder charge—a white jury convicted them, under an 1870 law, of conspiring to deprive a citizen of his civil rights. To nearly everyone's surprise, the men were sentenced to the maximum penalty of 10 years in prison.

Watts Riots. Smoldering Negro resentment against lack of jobs, poor living conditions, and discrimination in the North erupted in Los Angeles in the worst U.S. riots in 20 years. See LOS ANGELES.

Negro Firsts. Despite the riots and the violence, it was a year of progress for the U.S. Negro. In Georgia, for example, because of redistricting in Fulton County (Atlanta), 10 Negroes were elected to the state legislature. U.S. Court of Appeals Judge Thurgood Marshall became the nation's 33rd Solicitor General, the chief lawyer who represents the U.S. government in cases tried before the Supreme Court. Mayor-elect John Lindsay of New York City appointed Robert O. Lowery, 49, fire commissioner. The United Church of Christ elected Dr. Hollis F. Price, head of Le Moyne College in Memphis, as moderator; and a Negro actor, Bill Cosby, 27, became a costar of a popular weekly television series.   MARK M. PERLBERG

NEPAL changed leaders in 1965. On January 26, King Mahendra named Surya Bahadur Thapa as chairman of the Council of Ministers (prime minister). Thapa, who had been vice-chairman before his promotion, succeeded Tulsi Gin.

In June, former Prime Minister K. I. Singh was released from prison after having served 14 months of a two-year sentence on charges of sedition. He had been imprisoned after an unsuccessful attempt at a coup d'état.

Communist China agreed in August to grant Nepal a $28,000,000 loan for highway construction. The highway would link Katmandu, Nepal's capital, with Pokhara in the central region of the kingdom. China also promised to provide technicians. In another pact signed in September, Yugoslavia agreed to sell Nepal machinery and petroleum products. In return, Yugoslavia agreed to buy semi-finished goods and raw materials. Earlier, the first consignment of British military aid to Nepal had arrived in Katmandu. The aid was part of a U.S.-British program to help modernize the Nepalese army's equipment.

Population: 10,210,000. **Government:** King Mahendra; Prime Minister Surya Bahadur Thapa. **Monetary Unit:** rupee (7.143 = U.S. $1). **Foreign Trade:** exports, $106,000,000; imports, $156,000,000. **Principal Exports:** jute, oilseeds, rice.

See also ASIA.

NETHERLANDS, THE, faced a crisis in the royal House of Orange for the second year in succession. In 1964, Princess Irene had married Prince Carlos de Bourbon y Parma and changed her religious faith to Roman Catholicism. In 1965, her sister, Crown Princess Beatrix, shocked the nation by announcing on June 28 that she planned to marry German diplomat Claus von Amsberg, a former member of a Nazi youth organization.

With bitter memories of the German occupation in The Netherlands, the news outraged most of the nation. But pleas for tolerance and restraint from the government, coupled with Beatrix's obvious happiness, eased the crisis. In August, Queen Juliana presented parliament with a bill to ratify the union, which it did, 132 to 9, on November 10.

The economy in 1965 failed to offset a 1964 deficit of $276,200,000 caused by increases in wages and spending, and a considerable trade gap. The government talked of applying more rigorous price policies. Exports had increased by 11 per cent, but there was concern over the mounting outflow of liquid funds.

Population: 12,220,000. **Government:** Queen Juliana; Prime Minister Victor G. M. Marijnen. **Monetary Unit:** guilder (3.598 = U.S. $1). **Foreign Trade:** exports, $5,856,400,000; imports, $7,044,200,000. **Principal Exports:** iron and steel, machinery, petroleum products.   KENNETH BROWN

See also EUROPE.

NEW BRUNSWICK. See CANADA.

NEW GUINEA, a tropical island in the Pacific Ocean, continued under the joint control of Indonesia and Australia. One portion, West Irian, belonged to Indonesia. Australia administered the eastern portion—one section as a United Nations (UN) trusteeship and the other (Papua-New Guinea) as a colony with limited self-government.

Papua-New Guinea continued its push toward independence in 1965. A select committee of its newly elected house of assembly began drafting a constitution which it hoped to have ready by 1968. Indigenous personnel were being incorporated into government positions and plans were being laid to establish a university for the education of the territory's future leaders.

In April, a UN Trusteeship group visited New Guinea and put its seal of approval on what Australia was doing and planned to do in the territory. The group also recommended that the territory should have a name other than Papua-New Guinea. Papuans were already suggesting Paradisea as the appropriate name for the state-to-be. Australia, meanwhile, continued to finance Papua-New Guinea's budget. The Australian government also indicated that it was prepared to give the people of the area whatever status they wanted for their future country. This could mean absolute independence, or a self-governing status combined with some continuing political dependence on Australia.

NEW ORLEANS suffered a staggering billion dollar damage when Hurricane Betsy slammed through the city on September 9, followed by a 26-foot tide on the Mississippi that surged over levees and dikes. The city called for federal help in the massive tasks of physical salvage and financial restoration.

Damage was severe, partly because New Orleans is largely below sea level. Special teams of army engineers tirelessly pumped streets and basements free of muddy, polluted, snake-infested waters. Medical teams inoculated hundreds against typhoid and diphtheria and an epidemic was thus averted. Some 70 deaths were attributed to the storm.

The city's basic vitality helped it bounce back swiftly, partly with the help of federal disaster assistance. Although debris remained, the great wharves were bustling with cargo within a month.

Undamaged by Betsy was the steel framework of the 45-story Plaza Tower, which was topped out in 1965. Also to be part of the city's new skyline are the 33-story International Trade Mart and 47-story Louisiana House, both underway. These and even higher skyscrapers are possible with the use of prestressed concrete pilings which overcome New Orleans' soft subsoil.

Presiding over the city's economic revival—marked by a 27 per cent increase in construction in 1965—was Mayor Victor H. Schiro, who was elected to a second term in November.   DONALD W. LIEF

See also DISASTERS (picture).

ROBERT F. WAGNER, mayor of New York since 1954, brushed a tear from his eye when he announced he would not seek re-election.

JOHN V. LINDSAY fought a spirited campaign to become the first non-Democratic mayor of New York City since 1945.

NEW YORK CITY residents, reputed to be the least concerned of any U.S. urbanites about civic problems, were roused by a spirited mayoral campaign in which underdog John V. Lindsay, 43, a Congressman from the city's "silk-stocking" district, scored an upset victory. Lindsay became the first non-Democrat since Fiorello LaGuardia to win the post of mayor of the nation's largest city. His triumph was interpreted as a sign of rising Republican fortunes, but Lindsay had campaigned in behalf of "independent, nonpartisan government."

In a three-man race, Lindsay polled 1,155,915 votes to Democrat Abraham D. Beame's 1,030,771. Conservative party candidate William F. Buckley, Jr., ran a poor third, although voting patterns indicated that he drew crucial support from Beame.

On the day Lindsay was to be sworn into office, Jan. 1, 1966, the city was in the throes of a paralyzing transit workers strike. This, like other key issues, was rooted in New York's shaky financial posture. Regardless of the eventual wage settlement, the new mayor was pledged to maintain the subsidized 15-cent subway fare—although some called it uneconomic. In higher education, too, he would have to resolve the issue of whether the City University of New York should remain tuition-free.

The Pope's Visit. For 14 hours in October, Pope Paul VI toured New York in the first New World trip by a reigning pontiff. He addressed the United Nations, calling on its members to strive for peace.

He passed before 4,000,000 spectators lining the streets and climaxed the visit by celebrating Mass before 90,000 at Yankee Stadium. See ROMAN CATHOLIC.

Blackout. For a dozen hours beginning on November 9, New York City and a vast area of the Northeast were hit by a sudden electric power failure. Incredibly, New Yorkers took total blackout calmly. Even among 800,000 stranded subway patrons there was little panic. There was negligible looting, few serious accidents, and most essential hospital services were maintained. See ELECTRIC POWER.

Water Shortage. If the power failure gave sudden evidence of the great city's dependence upon outside forces, the long-continuing drought in the East provided another nagging reminder. New York's reservoirs dipped to 36 per cent of capacity despite efforts by the city to reduce water consumption.

Culture. The outstanding architectural achievement of the year was CBS/51 W 52, corporate headquarters of the Columbia Broadcasting System. The gray granite and dark glass tower was the only skyscraper designed by the late Eero Saarinen. In Lincoln Center, the handsome Vivian Beaumont Theater opened, but its first offering was roundly rapped by the critics. A remodeled and modernized landmark opened in Times Square: the 23-story Allied Chemical Building. It replaced the old *New York Times* structure. DONALD W. LIEF

See also MUSIC; PUBLISHING; THEATER.

NEW ZEALAND faced economic uncertainty as its wool prices fell, its imports rose, and its balance of payments slipped to a deficit. There were even whispers of devaluating the pound. These, however, were quickly silenced by the authorities. Although a domestic boom persisted for most of the year, the cumulative effect of restraining measures began to build a real credit squeeze.

Although New Zealanders had fewer fears of an early British entry into the European Economic Community (EEC, or Common Market), they recognized their vulnerability as an exporter of four primary products—butter, cheese, meat, and wool—to one main and distant customer, Great Britain. However, new hopes mixed with caution greeted the signing of a limited free trade area agreement with Australia on August 31 (see AUSTRALIA).

Population: 2,687,000. **Government:** Governor-General Sir Bernard Fergusson; Prime Minister Keith J. Holyoake. **Monetary Unit:** pound (1 = U.S. $2.80). **Gross National Product:** 444,000,000 pounds. **Foreign Trade:** exports, $1,074,000,000; imports, $961,000,000. **Principal Exports:** butter, cheese, meat and meat preparations, wool.   ALASTAIR BURNET

See also GREAT BRITAIN.

NEWBERY MEDAL. See LITERATURE FOR CHILDREN (Awards); WOJCIECHOWSKA, MAIA.

NEWFOUNDLAND. See CANADA.

NEWSPAPER. See PUBLISHING.

NICARAGUA pushed its industrial development programs during the year. Under the government's industrial incentive law, several factories were being built in and around Managua. To help maintain this industrial expansion, the Agency for International Development (AID) granted Nicaragua $3,000,000 toward the development of private industries. An additional $3,500,000 was received from the Inter-American Development Bank (IADB) to help develop medium- and small-scale industry.

The national budget for 1965 was about $65,100,000—the largest in Nicaragua's history. About $16,000,000 of this sum was allotted to the Ministry of Public Works, which was engaged in a large-scale road-building program. A second loan from the IADB, totaling $12,000,000, was made to help finance the construction of over 377 miles of secondary roads. Other loans, totaling $15,800,000, were made to help the nation diversify its economy.

During the year, a serious drought threatened the nation's corn crop. An estimated 10,000 acres of cotton were burned off as a result of the drought, but the total crop was up 29 per cent.

Population: 1,697,000. **Government:** President René Schick Gutierrez. **Monetary Unit:** cordoba (7.05 = U.S. $1). **Gross National Product:** 2,936,-000,000 cordobas. **Foreign Trade:** exports, $118,-000,000; imports, $137,000,000. **Principal Exports:** coffee, cotton, meat.   MARY C. WEBSTER

See also LATIN AMERICA.

NIGER reached an accord with Dahomey over ownership of Lete Island, a disputed territory that lies midstream in the Niger River. The island would be shared jointly by each country. Their citizens would enjoy equal rights. Dahomey also granted landlocked Niger a free port zone in Cotonou.

President Hamani Diori escaped assassination on April 13. The attack occurred in Niamey, where the president was attending a service to mark the Feast of the Sacrifice, a Muslim observance. Eniste Amadou Diop, the would-be assassin, proved to be a member of the outlawed Sawaba party. He had entered Niger secretly from Ghana, where he had reportedly been trained in subversion by agents of Communist China. Bitter exchanges between Niger and Ghana ensued. President Diori said: "In spite of his (Ghana President Kwame Nkrumah) denials, we are convinced of his guilt."

Niger inaugurated direct telephone service with Nigeria, cutting two days in the delivery time of telegrams formerly routed via London or Paris. The last French army contingents left Niger, and France gave the Niger army $2,600,000 in equipment.

Population: 3,154,000. **Government:** President Hamani Diori. **Monetary Unit:** CFA franc (246.85 = U.S. $1). **Foreign Trade:** exports, $21,600,000; imports, $24,200,000. **Principal Exports:** livestock, peanuts.   WILLIAM SPENCER

See also AFRICA.

NIGERIA began 1965 in the midst of a political crisis that threatened to tear the five-year-old nation apart. The crisis stemmed from charges of illegal nominating procedures and violence in the election for parliament on Dec. 30, 1964. As a result, the country was split between northern and southern political factions. In the north, there was the Nigerian National Alliance, composed primarily of the Nigerian National Democratic party (NNDP) and the Northern People's Congress (NPC). The south was dominated by the United Progressive Grand Alliance (UPGA), formed by the National Convention of Nigerian Citizens and the Action Group.

Before the election, the UPGA called for a boycott of the polls, and many candidates withdrew. The voting was followed by a political crisis, but a compromise was found. Plans were made for amending the constitution, and new elections held.

On Oct. 12, 1965, however, violence broke out anew in Western Nigeria, following reports of a rigged election. By year's end, the violence had subsided and an uneasy peace had been restored.

Population: 57,300,000. **Government:** President Nnamdi Azikiwe; Prime Minister Alhaii Sir Abubakar Tafawa Balewa. **Monetary Unit:** pound (1 = U.S. $2.80). **Gross National Product:** $3,870,-000. **Foreign Trade:** exports, $608,000,000; imports, $633,000,000. **Principal Exports:** cocoa, peanuts, petroleum.   BENJAMIN E. THOMAS

See also AFRICA.

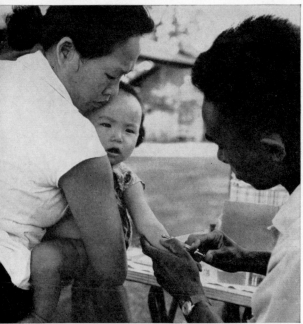

UNICEF

DISEASE CONTROL is just one of many activities of the United Nations Children's Fund (UNICEF), the winner of the 1965 Nobel peace prize.

NOBEL PRIZES in literature and science were presented at ceremonies in Stockholm, Sweden, on Dec. 10, 1965. The peace laureate, selected by the Norwegian Parliament's Nobel Committee, was presented in Oslo, Norway.

Literature Prize was presented to Mikhail A. Sholokhov, the third Russian to be awarded this honor since the prizes were first presented in 1901.

Peace Prize was presented to the United Nations Children's Fund, and accepted by its executive director, Henry Labouisse. Founded in 1946 and renowned as the United Nations International Children's Emergency Fund, the agency retains the acronym UNICEF. It was made a permanent United Nations agency in 1953, and given its present name. The prize honorarium is to be used to create a Maurice Pate Memorial Fund, commemorating its first and late executive director. See DEATHS OF NOTABLE PERSONS.

Science Prizes were presented to a Japanese, three French, and three American scientists. *Chemistry Prize* was awarded to Robert B. Woodward, Harvard University Donner Professor of Science. *Medicine Prize* was shared by François Jacob, André Lwoff, and Jacques Monod, all Pasteur Institute department heads in Paris, France. *Physics Prize* was shared by Richard P. Feynman, California Institute of Technology Professor of Theoretical Physics; Julian S. Schwinger, Harvard University Professor of Physics; and Sin-itiro Tomonaga, Tokyo University of Education Professor of Physics.

See also FEYNMAN, RICHARD P.; JACOB, FRANÇOIS; LWOFF, ANDRÉ; MONOD, JACQUES; SCHWINGER, JULIAN S.; SHOLOKHOV, MIKHAIL A.; TOMONAGA, SIN-ITIRO; UNITED NATIONS; WOODWARD, ROBERT B.

NORTH ATLANTIC TREATY ORGANIZATION

(NATO) faced the most serious crisis of its 16 years of existence when, in September, 1965, French President Charles de Gaulle threatened to dismantle it. He served notice that France would withdraw from NATO by the treaty renewal date of 1969, ending joint command of military forces in France. It was not clear whether NATO committees there, with their adjuncts, would be obliged to leave.

In Washington, behind-the-scenes consultations to counter these threats began. Several leading American ambassadors, including David Bruce (Great Britain) and Charles Bohlen (France), conferred with U.S. Department of State officials.

Another split among member nations was threatened a month later, in October, when Michael Stewart, British foreign secretary, indicated that Great Britain might abandon its own proposals for an Atlantic Nuclear Force (ANF). This force was originally proposed as a body to which Britain could assign her four Polaris submarines. The reason for this apparent about-face was that Britain wished to seek agreement with Russia for a treaty banning the spread of nuclear weapons.

In talks with Stewart, Dean Rusk, U.S. Secretary of State, made it clear that the United States still supported the original concept of a NATO nuclear force (Multilateral Force, MLF) in which Germany could take part. In Bonn, West Germany, the Federal Republic of Germany continued to regard MLF as the best solution for allowing German participation. See DISARMAMENT.

The North Atlantic Council had met earlier, in May, at London. The ministers noted that little had been done toward removing tensions in Europe. They also expressed regret that so little progress had been made toward disarmament, and declared: "So long as the threat of aggression, direct or indirect, persists, the prime task of the Atlantic alliance will be to maintain a defensive posture adequate to deter attack and meet it effectively should the need arise."

The Ministers of Defense of NATO member countries met in Paris in June and decided to pay special attention to the defense problems of Greece and Turkey. Then, in December, the foreign and defense ministers held their year-end meeting in Paris. They agreed to consider further the threat of Communist China's nuclear strength. U.S. Secretary of Defense Robert McNamara warned the group that future Chinese development of long-range missiles will be of great concern.

NATO: Headquarters: Paris. Secretary-General: Manlio Brosio (Italy). Supreme Allied Commander in Europe: General Lyman L. Lemnitzer (U.S.). **Total Strengths:** Land Forces, 3,121,000; Naval Forces, 35 carriers, 33 cruisers, 181 submarines, 54 nuclear submarines; Air Forces, 925 ICBMs, 480 fleet ballistic missiles, 630 long-range heavy bombers, 580 medium-range bombers. *(KENNETH BROWN*

NORWAY ended the 30-year-old rule of its Labor party in the fall elections. A coalition cabinet was formed in which the Conservatives held six of the 15 seats. The new government was pledged to work for "enlightened capitalism." The previous government's policy of nationalization had fallen into disrepute following an impartial inquiry that reported "waste, mismanagement, and corruption." The new cabinet's chief concern was the adverse balance of trade due to rising imports. There was further anxiety about export prospects in view of the protectionist attitude of the European Economic Community (EEC, or Common Market). See INTERNATIONAL TRADE AND FINANCE.

In May, the nation's Institute of Atomic Energy agreed to participate in research and development with the U.S. Atomic Energy Commission in a project at Halden, in southern Norway. During the year, a comprehensive agreement with all the trade unions gave wage increases of between $4\frac{1}{2}$ per cent and 5 per cent to about 230,000 Norwegian workers.

Population: 3,751,000. **Government:** King Olav V; Prime Minister Per Borten. **Monetary Unit:** krone (7.15 = U.S. $1). **Gross National Product:** 37,771,000,000 kroner. **Foreign Trade:** exports, $1,355,100,000; imports, $1,858,100,000. **Principal Exports:** fish, iron and steel, nonferrous metals, paper and paper board.   KENNETH BROWN

NOVA SCOTIA. See CANADA.

NUCLEAR PHYSICS. Nine years after the detection of the first artificially produced neutrinos, scientists working in a South African gold mine found the first naturally produced ones. The neutrino has perplexed scientists for many years. No other elementary particle—of which more than 100 different kinds are recognized today—is remotely like the neutrino. It apparently has no mass and possesses no electrical charge. It travels near the speed of light and can shoot through 600,000,000,000 miles of liquid hydrogen or 1,000,000 miles of solid lead without hitting anything.

The laboratory in which the first naturally produced neutrinos were discovered, on February 23, was 10,492 feet below ground in a mine near Johannesburg. It was constructed under the direction of Frederick Reines of the Case Institute of Technology in Cleveland, Ohio, and J. P. F. Sellschop of the University of Witwatersrand in Johannesburg. Reines had collaborated with Clyde L. Cowan in the earlier discovery of artificially produced neutrinos. In this underground laboratory he devised a way to detect the occurrence of mu-mesons derived from cosmic-ray neutrinos. The neutrinos registered their presence in the mine shaft when a mu-meson shot through parallel banks of detectors filled with mineral oil, which emitted brief flashes of light at each occurrence. In all, seven such natural neutrino events were recorded. A joint Indian-Japanese-British team, working in the Kolar gold fields in southern India reported observing one such neutrino about a month after the announcement from Johannesburg.

Time Reversal. Study of the breakdown of time-reversal-invariance, discovered last year, continued in 1965. The effect was first seen by James H. Christenson and his collaborators when they observed that a K_2° meson was able to decay into a pi-minus and a pi-plus meson pair. The results of this experiment threw doubt on the crucial principle, built into almost every physical theory, that the laws of the universe remain unchanged even when the direction of time is reversed. Physicists call this the time-reversal-invariance principle, or T-invariance.

During the year it was suggested that a possible explanation for the decay that Christenson observed, other than a breakdown of the T-invariance principle, might be the operation of a previously undetected fifth fundamental force. The four known fundamental forces, or interactions, are the gravitational, the weak (responsible for nuclear beta-decay), the electromagnetic, and the strong (responsible for nuclear binding forces). If, in addition, there were a fifth force that acted differently on antimatter than on matter, its presence would explain Christenson's results without involving a violation of the T-invariance principle. Such a force would be expected to be very weak, weaker even than the gravitational force. To date, however, a search for this force has yielded negative results. The search is being conducted by teams at the Centre Européan pour Recherches Nucléaires (CERN) synchrotron in Geneva, Switzerland, and at the British Nimrod Accelerator at Harwell, England.

A Huge Explosion, followed by an intense and devastating fire, completely demolished the experimental area of the Cambridge (Mass.) Electron Accelerator in the early morning hours of July 5. Eight persons were injured, one of whom died later. As a result of this accident, the electron accelerator, one of the largest, will remain unusable for at least a year. Damage was estimated at $1,000,000. The blast occurred during the filling, for the first time, of a newly constructed 40-inch liquid hydrogen bubble chamber. At the time of the blast, almost 95 per cent of the bubble chamber's capacity of 500 liters had been filled with the highly inflammable liquid hydrogen. The exact cause of the explosion remains unknown. The bubble chamber did not itself explode; instead, it dumped its contents into a safety container, from which the evaporating hydrogen was vented up an exhaust stack where it burned safely at the top.

The accelerator, built under federal grants totaling $12,000,000, is operated jointly by Harvard University and the Massachusetts Institute of Technology.   S. MATTHEW PRASTEIN

See also ATOMIC ENERGY; PHYSICS.

NYASALAND. See MALAWI.

O'BRIEN, LAWRENCE FRANCIS (1917-   ), was sworn in as Postmaster General of the United States on November 3. The ceremony took place on the front steps of the post office in tiny Hye, Tex. O'Brien succeeded John A. Gronouski, Jr., who had been sworn in as ambassador to Poland a half hour earlier by President Lyndon B. Johnson.

The new Postmaster General was born in Springfield, Mass., on July 7, 1917. He attended Northeastern University, where he obtained his LL.B. degree in 1942. After graduation, O'Brien did real estate and public relations work in Springfield, but he had been active in politics since 1938, while still in school. He was the key organizer of John F. Kennedy's senatorial and presidential campaigns. After Kennedy became President, O'Brien was made his liaison man to handle relations with Congress.

Following the death of President Kennedy, O'Brien served as director of campaign organization for Lyndon Johnson. On Jan. 20, 1965, President Johnson made him his special assistant in charge of congressional relations.

O'Brien is regarded as a skilled politician who did a superb job of shepherding the Johnson program through the 1965 session of Congress. He married Elva Brassard on May 30, 1944. They have a son, Lawrence Francis O'Brien III.   WALTER B. MORSE

See also POST OFFICE.

OCEAN. The murky world under the sea lost some of its mystery as teams of men explored the depths off California's coast from a 12-by-58-foot steel cylinder, resting at a depth of 205 feet below the ocean surface. The aquanauts studied fish and other marine life and mapped sections of the ocean floor. Their program, which began on August 28 and lasted for 45 days, also tested the ability of men to live, work, and do appropriate research for long periods at such depths. Among the participants was Astronaut Lieutenant Commander M. Scott Carpenter, who acted as team leader for one of the three groups of 10 aquanauts.

The steel cylinder, named *Sealab II*, was anchored to the ocean shelf 1,000 yards offshore at La Jolla, Calif. It represented the second phase of the navy's "Man-in-the-Sea" program. The first phase, conducted in 1964 off Bermuda in *Sealab I*, did not go to as great a depth nor did it encompass as ambitious a research program.

A Practical Gain from oceanographic research came from undersea drilling where great success was made in mining diamonds from the continental shelf off the coast of South Africa. Attempts to map new diamond deposits in the same area during the year led to the drilling of more than 3,000 holes in the bed of the Atlantic Ocean. Studies were also made of the waters around Alaska to determine

U.S. Navy

SEALAB II was a home for aquanauts for 45 days after August 28. The vessel was lowered to the ocean bottom, 205 feet below the surface, off La Jolla, Calif.

if gold could be mined there in a similar way, and scientists on a research vessel in the Pacific sought to evaluate the feasibility of mining manganese nodules from the sea down to a depth of 15,000 feet.

Ocean drilling in the deep-sea was carried out in the spring of 1965 by the Joint Oceanographic Institutes' Deep-Earth Sampling (JOIDES) program. JOIDES was formed by the four leading oceanographic institutions—Woods Hole (Mass.) Oceanographic Institution; Scripps Institution of Oceanography of the University of California; Lamont Geological Observatory of Columbia University; and the Institute of Marine Sciences of the University of Miami. The drilling was executed aboard *Caldrill I*, and resulted in six holes in the Blake plateau off Jacksonville, Fla. Samples of sediment 40,000,000 years old were recovered.

Economic Benefits. A report by the National Academy of Sciences' Committee on Oceanography, "The Economic Benefits from Oceanic Research," was published in January. It estimated the extent to which basic and applied research could contribute to the living standards of man and the extent to which savings could be realized. The conclusion was that a yearly investment of $166,-000,000 for research may result in a yearly return of $536,000,000 over a 10-year period.   F. F. KOCZY

See also EXPLORATION; GEOLOGY.

OIL. See PETROLEUM and GAS.

OLD AGE. The year 1965 will go down in U.S. history as the "Year of Medicare." After extended debate, and in spite of determined opposition from the American Medical Association, Congress passed the bill which provides hospital care benefits for persons over 65, financed by compulsory payments under the Social Security system, and supplementary medical insurance for the partial payment of doctor bills. The medical insurance section is voluntary, and about nine out of 10 elderly people are expected to participate in it. The program becomes effective July 1, 1966. See MEDICARE.

Older Americans Act. Another act of Congress, known as the Older Americans Act of 1965, sets up an Administration on Aging within the Department of Health, Education, and Welfare. Through this act, signed by President Lyndon B. Johnson on July 14, Congress recognized a special responsibility of the national government to look after the welfare of older people. The Administration on Aging is directed by a commissioner appointed by the President. The first commissioner is William D. Bechill, formerly executive secretary of the California Citizens' Advisory Committee on Aging.

The Administration on Aging will serve as a clearing house and coordinating agency for government activities in areas such as Social Security, health, housing, employment, and public assistance. It will also administer grants for these purposes.

The major grant program will provide money to states for community planning, services for older people, and training personnel to work with older persons. For this purpose, $5,000,000 was authorized for fiscal 1966, and $8,000,000 for 1967. The money will be assigned to the states in relation to their population of persons over 65. New York will get about $286,000 for 1966, California $249,000, and Alaska $51,000. Grants for research and development projects were also provided in the amount of $1,500,000 for 1966, and $3,000,000 for 1967.

VISTA. During the year a number of older people enlisted in Volunteers in Service to America (VISTA), which was established under the Economic Opportunity Act of 1964. These VISTA volunteers work and live in areas of poverty in the United States. They receive allowances for living expenses, and, at the end of their period of service, up to two years, a lump sum of $50 for each month they have worked. See POVERTY.

International Meeting. Specialists in the study of aging (gerontology) will hold their 1966 Triennial International Congress of Gerontology in Vienna, Austria, during the last week of June. Participants include scientists who study the biology of aging, others who study the behavior and social adjustment of older people, and specialists on living standards, housing, and social welfare.   ROBERT J. HAVIGHURST

ONTARIO. See CANADA.

OPERA. See MUSIC.

OUTDOOR RECREATION. The demand for more—and better—opportunities for outdoor recreation continued to grow in 1965, with visits to parks and other areas setting records. But new programs to help finance acquisition of new state and federal outdoor recreation areas by sale of a $7 federal Land and Water Conservation Fund automobile sticker proved disappointing.

Sale of the sticker, admitting purchasers to most federal recreation areas for a year, began in March. But instead of the expected 5,000,000, only 285,000 stickers were sold by year's end. The sticker sales were but one source of money for the fund. Other sources include sale of surplus federal property, motorboat fuel taxes, and various special user fees.

By year's end, at least 18 states had submitted outdoor recreation development plans. The states were Alaska, Arizona, California, Connecticut, Idaho, Indiana, Louisiana, Missouri, Montana, Nebraska, New Hampshire, New Jersey, New York, Ohio, Oregon, Pennsylvania, Rhode Island, and Wisconsin. Some had already received matching grants out of the allocations totaling almost $76,000,000 for the purchase of recreation lands.

The federal Water Project Recreation Act was signed into law in July. It called for enhancing recreation opportunities and protecting fish and wildlife at multipurpose water projects.   A. L. NEWMAN

See also BOATS AND BOATING; HUNTING AND FISHING; PARKS; WILDLIFE.

OUTER MONGOLIA, PEOPLE'S REPUBLIC OF,
disclosed in June that it had been promised Soviet
economic aid that would total $733,333,333, be-
tween 1966 and 1970. It was nearly $200,000,000
more than the aid extended from 1961 through 1965.

Earlier in the year, Mongolian Premier Yumzhagin Tsedenbal had visited the Soviet Union. At
the end of week-long talks held in Moscow, both
nations issued a joint communiqué assailing the
United States for its role in Vietnam. See VIETNAM.

Despite Mongolia's request to Peking that it withdraw all Communist Chinese working in Mongolia,
approximately 4,500 such workers remained to
complete construction projects in the country. Communist China, however, continued to block the landlocked nation's trade through the nearest ports in
north China. In addition, it withheld new aid, and
reduced trade with Mongolia.

Meanwhile, about 5,000 Soviet construction
troops continued to work in Mongolia. They were
mostly in Darkhan, a new industrial city for 60,000
people being built 120 miles north of Ulan Bator.

Population: 1,091,000. **Government:** Chairman
of the Presidium of the Great People's Khural
Zhamsarangin Sambu; First Secretary of the People's
Revolutionary Party and Premier Yumzhagin
Tsedenbal. **Monetary Unit:** tughrik (4 = U.S. $1).
Foreign Trade: exports, $76,000,000; imports,
$114,000,000. **Principal Exports:** cattle, hides, wool.

PACIFIC ISLANDS and the vast ocean reaches surrounding them received increased attention during
1965. Some of the islands enjoyed independent
status; others remained under the control of Australia, France, Great Britain, New Zealand, and the
United States. The total population in the area was
approximately 2,500,000 people. The most pressing
question regarding the Pacific Islands centered
around their eventual disposition, as a world-wide
movement against "dependencies" grew.

The United States Trust Territories began to receive increased economic and educational aid from
the United States in a move to prepare them for
some form of autonomy. The U.S. territories of
Guam and Samoa in particular received additional
support for educational and agricultural programs
that would eventually contribute to their ability in
self-government. In all these efforts, the state of
Hawaii played a leading role.

The United States also sponsored the area's first
Micronesian Congress, which was designed to bring
together the representatives of people inhabiting
islands thousands of miles apart. Only France
seemed hesitant to lay the groundwork for some independence in its Society Islands and New Cale-
donia. Britain, however, prepared plans for the
eventual independence of Fiji. Australia and New
Zealand also worked to stimulate educational institutions and thus prepare the peoples of their man-
dated areas for independence.   JOHN N. STALKER

PAINTING AND SCULPTURE

Perhaps the most impressive accomplishment of the art world in 1965 was the opening
of the Los Angeles County Museum of Art, an
imposing complex that cost some $12,000,000
and represented the culmination of years
of endeavor. If some sensitive viewers were
not completely taken with the design of the
building, everyone admitted that the undertaking was a major achievement.

Major Acquisitions were made by important institutions the world over. The most awe-inspiring
was the purchase late in 1964 by the National Gallery of London of the *Bathers*, a large, late Cézanne.
The picture was obtained at a record price for a
Cézanne: $1,330,000. This purchase aroused contro-
versy that frequently attends the sale or purchase of
major works in Great Britain, but the consensus remained, when the picture was displayed early in
1965, that it was eminently suited for the great company it joined.

In the United States, the major acquisition was
the remainder of the Chester Dale collection, which
went by the donor's bequest to the National Gallery
in Washington, D.C. Seen as a whole, the collection
appeared to be the choice of a highly individual collector who knew his mind and was not a slave of the
merely fashionable. In New York City, meanwhile,
the Metropolitan Museum of Art acquired the last
major portrait by Jacques Louis David, as well as
capital works in other fields.

Private Purchases. The salesroom continued its
surprising and expensive way. Prices for minor

YEAR BOOK Photo by Don Stebbing
*ALONE TOGETHER. The haunted sculptures of
Alberto Giacometti seemed symbolic of modern
man. The Italian artist died at 64 early in 1966.*

REMBRANDT'S winsome portrait of his son
Titus in a fur cap brought the second highest
sum ever achieved in an open sale: $2,234,000.

of John Singleton Copley opened in Washington, D.C. It was to travel to Boston and New York City. The exhibition was distinguished, and it occasionally provoked a minority opinion that Copley's English work was, as he himself felt, of more importance than his work done in America before the Revolution. The enterprising Munson-Williams-Proctor Institute in Utica, N.Y., examined another famous American, John J. Audubon, who proved to have a much broader range than had ever been thought. The Metropolitan Museum of Art mounted a show that examined "Three Centuries of American Painting."

The major display of old European art in the United States was that devoted to the Italian baroque. It was mounted by the Detroit Institute of Arts. If, to a specialist it may have had unsatisfactory aspects, it nonetheless gave a new view to the American public of this crucial century in European art. A major examination of Mannerism was put on in Manchester, England, and a major study of the School of Fontainebleau was presented in Fort Worth, Tex. An exotic culture was evoked by an exhibition of bronzes of ancient India organized by the Art Institute of Chicago, the Nelson-Atkins Museum in Kansas City, and the Cleveland Art Museum.

Zurbarán was examined in Madrid, and the feeling again was noted that one-man displays, even of the dead and very great, are risky business. More rewarding was the exhibition devoted to the Guardis in Venice, and if it asked more questions than it answered, it still was a show of high distinction. The loveliest of exhibitions of ancient works was that in Paris devoted to the "Treasures from French Churches." The museum in Prague uncovered long-forgotten and "lost" Hapsburg treasures, including major works by Titian, Veronese, and Tintoretto. The paintings had gone dirty and unnoticed in storerooms in Hradčany Castle in Prague.

The late works of Paul Klee were shown extensively in Basel, Switzerland, and a major examination of Giacometti was mounted in New York for an extensive U.S. tour. Klee stood up better than Giacometti, who seemed more nearly the elegiac, minor figure many have always thought him to be.

And contemporary work continued to emerge. For example, an enormous Henry Moore sculpture, *Reclining Figure*, was set in place at Lincoln Center in New York. Yet, Picasso, at 84, who was represented in an exhibition of new work in Manhattan was as usual, still the best young artist of the year.

Awards. Albert Burri of Italy and Victor Vasarely of France won gold medals at the 8th annual São Paulo Biennial. Robert Rauschenberg of New York won first prize in the Corcoran Gallery's 1965 Biennial of Contemporary U.S. Painting, held in Washington, D.C.   JOHN MAXON

See also ARCHITECTURE; Section One, ALISTAIR COOKE ON THE ARTS.

works no longer reached the stratosphere, but prices for major works continued to set records. For example, in late spring, a ballet scene established a new record for a Degas of just under $500,000, and in mid-October, a Cézanne landscape sold for $800,000. Both purchases took place in New York City. Also, a small Rembrandt portrait ($24\frac{1}{2}$ by $20\frac{1}{2}$ inches) fetched the next highest sum, $2,234,000, ever achieved in an open sale. The picture was a winsome rendering of the artist's son, Titus, as a child in a fur cap (see above). Its purchase in London by the Norton Simon Foundation of Los Angeles caused a furor, but the picture's exportation was ultimately permitted.

Major European collections disposed of in London included the Wenner-Gren collection from Stockholm, the Stoclet collection from Brussels, and, of most interest before the sales, that of Captain George Spencer-Churchill, with works by Pieter Bruegel the Elder (the famed *Peasant Wedding*) and Rubens. The feeling generated by these and other sales was that there is a scarcity of first-rate material, and for the little available there is extraordinary competition.

Major Exhibitions. A number of major exhibitions were held all over the world. The feeling—long held in many quarters—grew that there are too many such shows with too many priceless treasures (the *Mona Lisa*, for example) being shipped about.

In the United States, a major display of the work

Wide World

WHITE-CAPPED *Prime Minister Lal Bahadur Shastri of India, left, and Pakistan's President Ayub Khan were adversaries in Kashmir dispute.*

PAKISTAN and India clashed over Kashmir in a tragic war that left no victors except perhaps Communist China. For years Pakistan had urged that a United Nations (UN) plebiscite be held in predominantly Moslem Kashmir to decide its status. India, after originally agreeing to this, felt that the UN preconditions for a plebiscite had not been fulfilled and that Kashmir, which legally acceded to India, had become a nonnegotiable internal matter. It was India's move to assimilate Kashmir even more by treating it as just another of its 16 states that precipitated an outbreak of hostilities in 1965.

In August, Pakistani guerrillas crossed a previously established cease-fire line into Indian-held Kashmir in hopes of igniting a popular uprising against India. The Kashmiris, however, did not take the hint. An estimated 6,000 guerrillas were rounded up. India, alarmed over the danger of a Vietnam type of war in Kashmir, decided to wipe out the bases from which such infiltrations were being staged. Its troops crossed the cease-fire line and captured strategic Haji Pir Pass. Pakistan hit back with tanks.

By September 1, it was all-out war. India opened up a second front on the plains of the Punjab with Lahore, the principal city of West Pakistan, a prime target. Pakistan's U.S.-built F-86 jets locked with India's French-built Mystères. Even Communist China threatened to enter the war in order to lend the Pakistani a helping hand (see CHINA, PEOPLE'S REPUBLIC OF).

Under the pressures of logistics realities, United Nations (UN) Secretary-General U Thant's patient mediation, and a resolute UN, whose role was strengthened by the rare phenomenon of a U.S.-Soviet Union accord, India and Pakistan reluctantly agreed to a cease-fire. At year's end, however, neither side had pulled back to even the old 1948 cease-fire line. Meanwhile, a dispute over the Rann of Kutch, which had precipitated sporadic fighting earlier in the year, still simmered despite a cease-fire signed on June 29. See INDIA.

Economy in High Gear. Until the Kashmir crisis, Pakistan had been enjoying an economic boom. Its Gross National Product had risen 4.1 per cent, industrial production 11 per cent, and agriculture 5 per cent in the first eight months, compared with the same 1964 period. This steady growth was the result of enlightened government policies, a vigorous private sector, high domestic savings, and wise usage of foreign aid resources. In fact, Pakistan enjoyed an international reputation as the nation that had made the most judicious use of foreign aid among the developing countries. But the war in Kashmir, plus a U.S. decision to withhold aid temporarily, forced Pakistan to trim its investment down to basic industries and defense.

U.S. Aid Withdrawn. A major crisis arose when the United States, as the dominant member of the nine-nation "Aid Pakistan" club, succeeded in having aid meetings postponed, ostensibly to wait until its foreign aid bill cleared Congress. But in Pakistan, this move along with U.S. President Lyndon B. Johnson's abrupt postponement of President Ayub Khan's visit to the U.S. in April was widely interpreted as a disciplinary measure following Pakistan's flirtation with Communist China. President Ayub's response, however, was that "Pakistan seeks friends, not masters." His countrymen demanded a boycott of U.S. goods.

Foreign Policy. Pakistan was busy disengaging itself from old commitments and alliances, especially the Southeast Asia Treaty Organization (SEATO) and the Central Treaty Organization (CENTO). President Ayub Khan, realizing that snubbing the Soviet Union had not resulted in increased Western aid, visited the Soviet Union to normalize relations. He returned to Pakistan with a pledge of $100,000,000 in aid. In Pakistan's relations with Communist China, there were almost the makings of a Peking-Rawalpindi axis. China gave Pakistan a $60,000,000 interest-free loan, and its "moral" support of Pakistan in the Kashmir crisis kept the military equation in the area in constant suspense.

Population: 107,009,000. **Government:** President Mohammed Ayub Khan. **Monetary Unit:** rupee (4.788 = U.S. $1). **Gross National Product:** $9,800,000,000. **Foreign Trade:** exports, $467,000,000; imports, $1,050,000,000. **Principal Exports:** cotton, jute, textiles.   KEKI R. BHOTE

See also ASIA.

PANAMA. President Marco Aurelio Robles set a middle-of-the-road course for his administration, both at home and abroad, during 1965. He prevented nationalist elements from taking the Canal Zone issue into the streets and worked with the United States in negotiation of Canal Zone problems. The president's position was strengthened by a U.S. decision to negotiate a new treaty that would "effectively recognize" the republic's sovereignty over the Canal Zone.

The new agreement, however, was expected to go far in meeting all Panamanian demands for a revision of the status of the Panama Canal. The two nations also agreed to negotiate another accord whereby a new sea-level canal might be built across the republic.

The International Monetary Fund (IMF) granted its first stand-by agreement to the republic during the year. It was a $7,000,000 credit, available over a 12-month period, which would help Panama achieve a balanced budget while avoiding any increase in its floating debt. In turn, Panama held back on expenditures and introduced new tax measures.

Population: 1,270,000. **Government:** President Marco Aurelio Robles. **Monetary Unit:** balboa (1 = U.S. $1). **Gross National Product:** 491,400,000 balboas. **Foreign Trade:** exports, $68,000,000; imports, $198,000,000. **Principal Exports:** cotton, jute, textiles. MARY C. WEBSTER

See also LATIN AMERICA.

PARAGUAY continued to enjoy relative economic well-being in 1965. Its gross holdings of convertible foreign exchange stood at $6,200,000 at the end of June, up 250.6 per cent above the level of a year earlier. Exports, although affected by the worst floods in 50 years, were still able to rise to $24,600,-000 in the first six months as compared to the 1964 figure of $23,700,000. Imports climbed to $20,100,-000 from $15,400,000 of the previous year, with foreign purchases of machinery and apparatus accounting for a good proportion of the import increase. Meat exports for the year were expected to total $20,000,000 versus $15,000,000 in 1964.

The internal economy also improved, and the country's infant industries were running full tilt. Much of the credit for Paraguay's well-being was due to its strong-man president, Alfredo Stroessner, who had brought stability to the country.

Paraguay ran into difficulties with Argentina during the year in connection with the shipping and importing of its products via the river system. An agreement was signed, eventually, whereby all ships of the Paraguayan merchant fleet would use Montevideo port (Uruguay) for the transshipment of goods.

Population: 1,980,000. **Government:** President Alfredo Stroessner. **Monetary Unit:** guaraní (126 = U.S. $1). **Foreign Trade:** exports, $41,724,000; imports, $31,517,000. **Principal Exports:** coffee, meat, lumber. MARY C. WEBSTER

See also BRIDGE AND TUNNEL; LATIN AMERICA.

PARENTS AND TEACHERS, NATIONAL CONGRESS OF (PTA), conducted a nationwide drive to collect books for schoolchildren in the isolated mountain regions of Appalachia. The project, "Books for Appalachia's Children," was undertaken at the request of the Office of Economic Opportunity as a part of the anti-poverty program. Local PTA's in all sections of the country collected 1,100,000 new and used children's books.

In addition to books, the project provided book shelves that could be assembled from the specially designed wooden crates in which the books were shipped. The crates were built by PTA fathers and members of high school shop classes. After the books arrived in Louisville, Ky., they were transported by the Louisville and Nashville Railroad without charge throughout the region. College students, known as Appalachian Volunteers, played a big part in distributing the books.

A new "Guide to a School Pedestrian Safety Program," prepared by the PTA in cooperation with the Automotive Safety Foundation, was distributed to PTA units throughout the country.

Delegates to the 69th annual convention in Albuquerque, N.Mex., in May elected Mrs. J. M. Herndon of Columbia, S.C.; Mrs. James A. King of Sherwood, Ore.; Mrs. R. W. Scoville of Kansas City, Kans.; and Mrs. James W. Ure of Salt Lake City as regional vice-presidents. JOSEPH P. ANDERSON

PARKS. President Lyndon B. Johnson stimulated national interest in preserving scenic beauty with his January 4 State of the Union message and his special Message on Natural Beauty, which he sent to Congress on February 8. He followed up by calling a White House Conference on Natural Beauty, held May 24 and 25 in Washington, D.C. It was the third such conference held this century. (Theodore Roosevelt held the first in 1908, John F. Kennedy the second in 1962.) The First Lady also took a leading role in the President's drive for beautification of the countryside (see ROADS AND HIGHWAYS).

New Park Areas. Congress moved rapidly to approve two important new park and recreation areas in the East, both within reach of 40,000,000 people, or about 20 per cent of the U.S. population. On September 1, President Johnson signed legislation authorizing the creation of a 72,000-acre Delaware Water Gap National Recreation Area. It will extend along both the New Jersey and Pennsylvania shores of the Delaware River, from Stroudsburg, Pa., to Port Jervis, N.Y. A new dam will create a 37-mile-long lake.

On September 21, the President signed legislation establishing the Assateague Island National Seashore, preserving some 9,000 acres of dunes and beach off the Maryland and Virginia coasts—the last undeveloped seashore between Massachusetts and North Carolina. As did the Delaware recreation area and the Fire Island National Seashore in New

York, Assateague Island was also following the new conservation idea of locating recreation areas within an easy day's drive for millions of people.

Congress also established the Spruce Knob-Seneca Rocks National Recreation Area in West Virginia and set aside 100,000 scenic acres famed for trout fishing, along the upper Potomac Valley.

National Monuments established in the year were the Agate Fossil Beds, Harrison, Nebr.; Alibates Flint Quarries, Borger, Tex.; Golden Spike, Brigham City, Utah; and the Pecos, Pecos, N.Mex.

New historic sites established included the Herbert Hoover birthplace in West Branch, Iowa, and the Hubbell Trading Post in Ganado, Ariz. Funds were authorized for full development of historic Ellis Island as an addition to the Statue of Liberty National Monument. The Nez Percé National Historic Park was established near Spalding, Idaho.

The long-awaited federal North Cascades Study Team's report was issued in early January, 1966. It recommended establishing a 698,000-acre National Park in northern Washington. See 1965 YEAR BOOK Special Report, CALL TO THE WILDERNESS.

The National Park Service (NPS) reported in May that 1964 total visits to NPS areas had surpassed its earlier estimate of nearly 100,000,000 by 2,475,100.   A. L. NEWMAN

See also FORESTRY AND FOREST PRODUCTS; HUNTING AND FISHING; OUTDOOR RECREATION.

PEACE CORPS. Volunteers of the Peace Corps functioned as ambassadors of peace and good will for the United States during the crisis that erupted in the Dominican Republic in the spring of 1965.

There were 102 corpsmen on duty when the sudden outbreak of revolution produced a situation judged so dangerous by President Lyndon B. Johnson that he sent in thousands of soldiers and marines. The Peace Corps volunteers maintained contact with both sides of the brushfire war from the very start. Unarmed, but protected by their identification as Peace Corpsmen, they were the only Americans who were able to come and go freely, even during the peak of the fighting.

The welcome afforded the volunteers by both the rebels and the military junta was a testament to the image they had created as skilled technicians who had come to the Dominican Republic with no other mission than to help the people of the republic to help themselves.

A Vote of Confidence. At one point during the crisis, Peace Corps officials in Washington gave serious thought to discontinuing Peace Corps work in the country and bringing the volunteers home. They decided to keep the programs going, however, after a secret ballot was taken of the 40 Dominicans who were working in the Office of Community Development, the Dominican counterpart of the Peace Corps. The Dominicans voted, 40 to 0, for the Americans to stay.

As the year ended, there were over 100 volunteers helping the Dominicans with agriculture, community action, and health problems.

The 30-member contingent to Indonesia was withdrawn in April, 1965. The move, made by mutual agreement between the United States and Indonesia, was not considered a reflection on the volunteers' work but was a result of tension between Indonesia and Malaysia.

Culture Shock. Marking the fourth anniversary of the Peace Corps, 850 former volunteers met for three days in March in the nation's capital. The affluence and frenetic pace of U.S. life jarred the sensibilities of many of the returning young people. One commented: "Until you have seen poverty in a foreign country, you have not seen real poverty." Another complained of the difficulty to "really communicate what you have seen and done and felt."

The Corps' postservice employment director, Dr. Robert Calvert, Jr., pointed to another cause of "culture shock" to the returning volunteers:

"For most, their service has been the most exciting experience of their life.... Having worked in responsible positions with the mayor of an Andean village or with the ministry of education in a newly emerging African nation, (he) finds it difficult to adjust down to the role assigned in the United States to the 25-year-old."

Number in Service. The volunteers in the Dominican Republic were part of a total overseas force of 9,912 serving in 46 countries. Another 2,297 were in training in the United States, giving the Peace Corps a total strength of 12,209. Of this figure, 7,182 were men and 5,027 women.

Latin America had the largest number, 4,185 assigned to 18 countries. Africa was next with 3,811 serving in 17 countries. There were 2,532 in eight countries of North Africa, the Middle East, and South Asia, and 1,681 in three Far Eastern nations.

Of the $104,100,000 that Congress provided for Peace Corps expenses in fiscal 1965, $85,449,000 was spent or obligated. For fiscal 1966, Congress approved an appropriation of $114,100,000.

Deaths. Since 1962, 18 volunteers have died during their service with the Peace Corps. Eight of these deaths occurred in 1965: Joy Darling, 22, of Jamestown, N.Y., was killed in a motorcycle accident in Bolivia. Donald Humphrey, 25, of Moses Lake, Wash., who had served in Chile, died from a brain tumor in a Washington (D.C.) hospital.

Joseph R. Rupley, 24, of Orinda, Calif., was shot to death by police in Venezuela in a case of mistaken identity. Stanley Edward Kowalczyk, 20, of Gilman, Wis., died after a motorcycle accident in Nigeria. Francis L. Kirking, 22, of Cashton, Wis., was drowned in Iran. Robert Zech, 24, of Ponce, Puerto Rico, and Garrith Simons, 22, of St. Louis, Mo., died in a traffic accident in the Dominican Republic. James Driscoll, 20, of New York City, was killed by a truck in Togo.   WILLIAM McGAFFIN

PERSONALITIES

PERSONALITIES OF 1965.

Americans chose President Lyndon B. Johnson as the man they admired most for the third consecutive year. Second on their list, for the fourth time in five years, was former President Dwight D. Eisenhower. Senator Robert F. Kennedy of New York was third, up from fifth place a year ago. Pope Paul VI, the first reigning Roman Catholic pope to visit the United States or the Western Hemisphere, ranked fifth among the world's most admired men. He was 10th in 1964.

General William Childs Westmoreland was the *Time* Man of the Year, described in the magazine's cover article as "the sinewy personification of the American fighting man in 1965."

Mrs. Jacqueline Kennedy was the Americans' choice as most admired woman for the fourth consecutive year. She far outranked any other woman for the honor, George Gallup's Institute of Public Opinion reported. For the third straight year, First Lady Mrs. Lyndon B. Johnson was second on the list. Newcomer Princess Margaret of Great Britain, who visited the United States for the first time in November, 1965, was 10th on the list.

Entries marked * indicate that the persons have biographies in THE WORLD BOOK ENCYCLOPEDIA.

Aitken, Virginia, of New York City, is the first foreigner to become a Buddhist nun in Formosa. Aged 22, she joined the nunnery at Hsinchu as Ming Chueh on January 10, after about six months in Formosa.

Bond, Janet M., of Princeton, N.J., was elected Mercer County coroner as a write-in candidate in November. She has no duties and gets no salary, but the 21-year-old Mount Holyoke College student said that it was one way to get into politics.

THINK POSITIVE

Melissa "Missy" Baron of Lakewood, Calif., and her parents attended all the inaugural events in Washington, D.C. When writing President Johnson, she conceded that it would be difficult for him to get them tickets, but "I would rather think positive, not negative. Please try your hardest."

Boone, Pat (Charles Eugene), the singer, actor, and a Protestant, was praised in the Vatican's *L'Osservatore Della Domenica* by the newspaper's often critical Adrianna Zarri. She wrote, "We have no complaint about you. No exhibitionism, no scandals, no love affairs. Just one love: a serious marriage." About his singing: "No screaming, no grimaces, no contortions. A deep, velvet, measured voice—in fact, a gentleman's voice."

Boswell, Charles A., a Birmingham (Ala.) insurance man, was named Blind Father of the Year by the American Foundation for the Blind. The father of three children, he was blinded in action during World War II in Europe. He took up golf, and won the National Blind Golf championship 13 times and the International title seven times.

*Byrd, Harry Flood, retired from the U.S. Senate in November because of ill health. He had served since 1933, was chairman of its Finance Committee for 11 years, and bitterly opposed deficit spending.

Pictorial Parade

UNEXPECTED VISITOR. Deposed Soviet Premier Nikita S. Khrushchev visited a Moscow art exhibition in April, his second public appearance since falling from grace.

Wide World

BEATLE DRUMMER Ringo Starr married hairdresser Maureen Cox, thus becoming the second member of the group to marry.

Harvey, a research scientist, have five sons and a daughter. The daughter is a housewife, and the sons are in professional fields. Mrs. Fletcher said, "What a child really needs is to be held down to certain ideals."

Galloway, Robert E., a Memphis (Tenn.) businessman, was decorated with the U.S. Army's fourth highest medal for bravery, the Silver Star. His commander cited the second lieutenant for courage in action during the World War I battle at Nantillois, France, but someone forgot to follow through. Galloway said, "I wasn't really much. I was leading some troops against the enemy. I couldn't get back so I had to get forward. I was more afraid of the general than the Germans."

Guess, Fred, an 83-year-old English farmhand, retired after working on the same farm for 69 years without missing one day of work or taking a vacation. Now he plans to wander about the fields he loves. "I'll take my sheepdog and my gun and I may get a few rabbits."

SEE HERE, PRIVATE HARGROVE

Pfc. Christopher P. Hargrove is the 20-year-old son of the World War II Marion Lawton Hargrove, author of *See Here, Private Hargrove*. Christopher had no difficulty adjusting to army life. He is the oldest of six children, and entered the service in August, 1964, after two years at Stanford University.

Hennessey, Luella, for 25 years a private nurse for the Kennedy family, received a B. S. degree at Boston University in June. The late John F. Kennedy per-

The former Virginia governor (1926-1930) had long been a leading Democrat in his state. He served in the Virginia senate (1915-1925).

Celucci, Mary Grace, of Delanco, N.J., was elected labor secretary of her fourth grade class. She had to clean the blackboard, put the chalk in place, and, on Fridays, clean the room and take care of anything out of place. She wrote to U.S. Secretary of Labor W. Willard Wirtz: "Please write and tell me what your duties are." He wrote back, "Same here."

Cole, Thomas, a New York grocery boy, attended a midnight buffet party given for visiting Princess Margaret of Great Britain. He was the escort of actress Elaine Stritch, who had written her shopping list on the back of her invitation, and had left it by mistake with Cole. Aware of its importance, Cole returned it to Miss Stritch, and was thusly rewarded.

CORONATION IN SIKKIM

Maharajah Palden Thondup Namgyal and his American-born Maharani, the former Hope Cooke of New York, were enthroned as chogyal (king) and gyalmo (queen) of the tiny Himalayan kingdom on April 4, in Oriental ceremonies in Gangtok. The Maharajah succeeded to the Sikkim throne on the death of his father in December, 1963.

Evans, Patsy, of Miami, Fla., and now 119 years old, is the oldest woman (person, perhaps), as of early December, to enroll in the federal program of health care (Medicare). She was born of slave parents in McCaysville, Ga.

Fletcher, Lorena Chipman, of Provo, Utah, was chosen American Mother of the Year by the American Mothers Committee, Inc. She and her husband,

United Press Int.

TOURIST Astronaut John Glenn stood among the Monument of Discovery figures in Lisbon, Portugal.

UP TO HIM. *While the nation watched, Gemini flight director Chris Kraft tensely considered bringing Gemini V down early because of a faulty fuel cell.*

suaded her to get a college degree and work with retarded children. "The President said he would come to my graduation . . .," she said. "I guess he'll know I'm getting it."

*Hodgkin, Dorothy Crowfoot,** the first English woman awarded the Nobel chemistry prize (1964), was named to the Order of Merit by Queen Elizabeth II. A woman had not been named to the order since famed Florence Nightingale was so honored.

*Hutchins, Robert M.,** one-time president and chancellor of the University of Chicago and now president of the Fund for the Republic, Inc., was named Father of the Year by the National Father's Day Committee. He has four children.

Klinck, Richard E., 37-year-old sixth-grade teacher at the Reed Street Elementary School in Wheat Ridge, Colo., was chosen Teacher of the Year. He began his professional career in the Denver suburb 13 years ago. Klinck is a conservationist, likes outdoor life, and sixth-graders. He, Mrs. Klinck, and their 9-year-old daughter Jeannine spend their vacations visiting National Park Service areas.

*Lausche, Frank J.,** Democratic U.S. Senator from Ohio, received a salary increase (from $22,500 to $30,000) on January 1, as did the other members of Congress. He voted against the increase in 1964, and now gives this extra money to a scholarship fund at Muskingum College, New Concord, Ohio.

Lawson, Mr. and Mrs. Samuel, of Auckland, New Zealand, became the parents of quintuplets on July 27. They were named Samuel Christian Clayton, Lisa Gay, Deborah Ann, Shirlene Jan, and Selina Joy. Mrs. Lawson said, "I expected four, but five! Oh, dear me, no." Five-year-old Lee Ann, when told about the new brother and sisters, said, "I don't want no brothers." The quintuplets are New Zealand's first.

HONORED. *Former President Dwight D. Eisenhower was given an honorary degree by Ohio University President Vernon R. Alden, right.*

Maher, Mrs. Gay, of Medford, N.J., is the first woman to make a solo trans-U.S. helicopter flight (February 6-16, Culver City, Calif., to Atlantic City, N.J.). She spent about 40 hours in the air, and said it is a great way to see the country.

The Voyage of the *Tinkerbelle*

Robert Neal Manry, the 47-year-old copy editor of *The Cleveland Plain Dealer,* crossed the Atlantic alone in the *Tinkerbelle.* His 13½-foot sailboat is the smallest known craft yet to make a nonstop, eastern voyage of the ocean. He embarked on June 1, from Falmouth, Mass., and landed at Falmouth, England, on August 17. Manry and *Tinkerbelle* were immaculate for the landing. They were towed the last three miles for safety reasons. Ashore, Manry embraced his family, shook hands with dignitaries, and then knelt to kiss the concrete at the Customs House quay. Overhead, a Royal Air Force plane dipped in salute. Small boats swarmed Falmouth Bay and tumultuous cheers filled the air. Manry and his family returned to the United States on the luxury liner *Queen Mary.* Back in Cleveland, Ohio, on September 1, they were given a great homecoming.

*Marx, Groucho (Julius), the only surviving member of the three famous comedian brothers, was asked to give his personal papers to the Library of Congress, because ''Mr. Marx is part of the American scene.''

McBride, Lester, an Australian, talked nonstop for 113 hrs. 1 min., set a new world record, and stopped 60 seconds after midnight of New Year's Eve (Jan. 1, 1966). Clive Jorgensen, an American, held the previous record of 112 hours.

Outram, Harry, of Perth, Australia, who traded a three-month-old camel in on an automobile, was allowed $173 on a new car. He got the camel from his brother, who got it from hinterland tribesmen.

Palmeri, Robert J., staged a two-day hunger strike to get to South Vietnam. The 6-foot, 22-year-old soldier, a September arrival in Worms, West Germany, left there on November 19. After a three-week leave, the New York man was to report in San Francisco to join a unit to South Vietnam.

Peale, John S., was ordained by his famous father on June 27 in New York City. The Reverend Dr. Norman Vincent Peale told his son ''to stand up for your convictions and avoid fads of the time, whether in religion or politics.''

AMERICA'S SWEETHEART

Mary Pickford was honored with a month-long retrospective showing of her films at the Paris *Cinematèque* (national motion-picture museum) in the fall, sponsored by the French government. *Little Annie Rooney* and *Coquette* (Academy best actress award, 1928-1929) were among her many films. She also starred in *Coquette* on Broadway (1935).

Senanayake, Senaka, a Ceylonese artist and veteran of 25 one-man exhibitions on five continents at the age of 13, presented one of his paintings to President Johnson in February during an exhibit in Washington, D.C. Senaka began painting at the age of 6, and also is an accomplished sculptor.

Sites, Sharon, a 34-year-old widow and dental secretary, sailed alone from Los Angeles, Calif., to Hawaii. With only five months' experience, she left June 12 on the *Sea Sharp.* Her pet turtle died 12 days out. She broke her right wrist four days before landing, was picked up, and towed to shore at Honolulu on July 21. Mrs. Sites sailed 2,300 miles in 40 days.

*Smith, Margaret Chase, Republican U.S. Senator

Pictorial Parade

LIKE THE GUARDSMEN, John marches for his mother, Jacqueline Kennedy, and cousins during Buckingham Palace Guard change.

from Maine, cast her 2,000th straight vote on June 14, a record dating back to June 1, 1955. A resolution honoring her was immediately introduced and passed. Tributes and three standing ovations brought tears. She has been a Senator since 1948.

MERRY CHRISTMAS TREES

Merry Christmas Trees is the daughter of Mr. and Mrs. Jack Trees of Columbus, Ohio. She has two brothers named Douglas Fir and Jack Pine.

*Untermeyer, Louis, the poet, literary critic, and editor, now 80, went back to New York City's DeWitt Clinton High School to get his diploma 65 years late. He left when 15, joined the family jewelry business, quit when a vice-president, and then gave full time to his profession. ''It was not defiance, merely defeat.'' Geometry was his problem.

Wagner, Robert F., who did not choose to seek another term as mayor of New York City, revealed a 1953 campaign story about a taxicab driver who confused him with the German composer Richard Wagner. The driver said to a passenger (a friend of Wagner) ''I'm going to vote for Wagner because my daughter got married two weeks ago and they played some of his music at the wedding.''

Wyszynski, Mrs. Bernice, bought a 1962 Pontiac Tempest automobile for 1,395 bananas. This price was quoted in a *Bristol* (Conn.) *Press* advertisement. She rushed to the used-car company with 25 bananas as a down payment, and was told that ''bananas'' meant ''bucks.'' The $ sign before *bananas* had been dropped from the ad. But she filed a false advertising complaint with the State Consumer Protection Department, the commissioner agreed with her, and she got the car for the quoted price.

PERU. Constitutional guarantees were repeatedly suspended during the year due to unrest and "vest-pocket" guerrilla warfare. They were first suspended on April 6 for a 30-day period following two days of street rioting in Lima over a bus fare increase. On July 5, after the police had arrested over 250 known extremists and communists in a crackdown aimed at wiping out procommunist terrorists, guarantees were again suspended for 30 days. They were repeatedly suspended thereafter through October 2 as a necessary security measure.

On August 13, Peruvian air force planes bombed a large jungle area of the central Andes. It was part of a step-up in the government's offensive against small bands of guerrillas.

On September 13, the opposition-dominated congress forced the resignation of the cabinet, after heavily criticizing it for being over-tolerant of communist elements. President Fernando Belaúnde Terry, however, repeatedly said during the year that the armed forces had the situation under control and that the communist issue was being exaggerated by the opposition for political reasons.

Population: 11,770,000. **Government:** President Fernando Belaúnde Terry. **Monetary Unit:** sol (26.82 = U.S. $1). **Foreign Trade:** exports, $666,-000,000; imports, $571,000,000. **Principal Exports:** copper, cotton, fertilizer.　　MARY C. WEBSTER

See also LATIN AMERICA.

PET. A Scottish terrier, Champion Carmichael's Fanfare, owned by Mr. and Mrs. Charles Stalter of Woodcliff Lake, N.J., captured the best-in-show honors at the Westminster Kennel Club dog show in New York City in February. The victory was the 32nd best-in-show award for the female terrier, an American record. The champion was handled by John Murphy of Allendale, N.J., whose recommendation that Carmichael's Fanfare be retired after her crowning triumph was accepted by Mr. and Mrs. Stalter. The Westminster show attracted 2,573 dogs.

At the International Kennel Club show in Chicago in April, the best-in-show honors went to Champion Ru-Mar's Tsushima, C.D., a female Doberman pinscher owned by Margaret Carveth of Portola Valley, Calif. The Chicago show drew a record 2,982 entries. More than 40,000 spectators attended, a record for the International.

American Kennel Club registration figures showed the poodle once more ranking as the most popular breed of dog in the United States. Next in order, as in both 1964 and 1963, were German shepherds, beagles, dachshunds, and chihuahuas. But the German shepherds gave the poodles a closer run for top place than in 1964, reflecting the fact that many persons were possibly acquiring the larger dogs because of their growing apprehension over increasing crime rates in cities and in suburban communities.

On the Human Side. Pennsylvania set a precedent when it decided that the state needed an official state dog and passed legislation designating the Great Dane as such.

The nation's foremost beagle fancier, President Lyndon B. Johnson, granted a "presidential pardon" to Lord Geoffrey of Rock Valley, a beagle owned by Mr. and Mrs. Rocco Ruggiero of Rockville Centre, N.Y. The dog had chewed up a $10 bill, and the Ruggieros sought the pardon on the facetious ground that their dog had destroyed government property.

The winner of the 12th annual Ken-L-Ration Dog Hero medal was Patches, a powerful, 85-pound collie-malamute owned by Marvin H. Scott of Spanaway, Wash. Patches saved his master's life by pulling him out of the freezing waters of a lake after Scott had injured both legs falling from an ice-covered pier. Other finalists included two German shepherds. One captured a holdup man, though it was severely wounded, and the other attacked a copperhead snake to save the lives of two small children. Also a finalist was a collie-shepherd that attacked an angry bull and thus saved a farmer's life.

Cats. Triple Grand Champion Shawnee Trademark, a silver domestic male tabby owned by Bill and Nikki Shuttleworth of Jeffersontown, Ky., was named *Cat of the Year*. *Opposite Sex Cat of the Year*, also owned by the Shuttleworths, was Triple Grand Champion Shawnee Whitewash, a copper-eyed white Persian female. Named *Kitten of the Year* was Larks-Purr Precious of Castilia, a blue cream Persian female, owned by Marcena Myers of Aliquippa, Pa. *Opposite Sex Shorthair of the Year* was Triple and International Grand Champion Shan Ling Whisper, a blue point Siamese female owned by Marjorie Elliott of Toronto, Canada. *Opposite Sex Longhair of the Year* was Grand Champion Sharmin' Fella, owned by Mrs. Merald Hoag of Rockville, Md.

Tropical Fish. An increasing number of institutions encouraged the tending of tropical fish by inmates and patients. Wardens of several prisons reported improved morale among the prisoners after they had been permitted to have aquariums. Tropical fish periodicals reported that they had received a number of well written articles about fish from prisoners. Various local aquarium societies sponsored fish tanks in children's hospitals and mental institutions.

Old aquarium favorites in the United States were augmented by the importation of a variety of tropical fish, including newly discovered types of cichlids from Africa.

A variety of new aquarium equipment also appeared on the market. The emphasis was on new kinds of filtering equipment for aquariums and on various methods for deterring the development of algae in the tanks. One of the most promising algae deterrents that has yet been found involved the use of ultraviolet rays.　　THEODORE M. O'LEARY

PETROLEUM AND GAS. It was an exceptional year for the oil industry, with total U.S. consumption of petroleum products up nearly 4 per cent from the more than 4,000,000,000 barrels in 1964. It was the next to largest increase in a decade.

The increased demand meant higher prices. At year-end, average gasoline prices were their highest since 1961 after four years of decline. Thus, the gasoline-refining companies enjoyed improved financial health; industry profits were estimated at about 10 per cent over 1964.

Factors behind the rising demand included: record auto sales, the trend to larger cars with bigger motors, the boom in aviation, and a generally cold spring that boosted the use of heating oil.

Despite the 4 per cent rise in use, refinery runs and domestic crude oil production increased by less than 2 per cent. Thus, excess stocks of refined products and crude oil were reduced. The increasingly stepped-up extraction of liquid hydrocarbons from natural gas has cut into crude oil output.

Oil Import Changes for the first quarter of 1966 were announced by the U.S. Department of the Interior in December. For the first time, petrochemical companies that did not refine crude oil were allocated a share of the quota of heavy oil from overseas. Also allowable imports of *residual oil* (a cheap, heavy fuel oil) were increased more than 50 per cent. Overall, however, the petroleum import quotas were virtually unchanged.

The petrochemical allocation cleared the way for a $600,000,000 Phillips Petroleum-Commonwealth Oil venture in Puerto Rico (see PUERTO RICO). The residual oil increase had been sought by East Coast industrial and utility consumers and fought by competing coal producers and eastern railroads. Residual oil, mostly from Venezuela, has been cutting into U.S. coal markets in recent years.

Natural Gas use, however, failed to show the spectacular growth of previous years, gaining less than 4 per cent. Despite the industry's concern about declining reserves, there was a marked slowdown in natural gas exploration. For instance, 909 exploratory wells were drilled in 1959, but only 575 in 1964. The industry blamed increasing regulation by the Federal Power Commission (FPC) for the slowdown.

In August, the FPC established a pattern for setting uniform prices to be charged by natural gas producers in various areas of the nation. Industry reaction was unfavorable to the unanimous FPC decision, which applied specifically to the Permian Basin area of southeast New Mexico and southwest Texas. It provided a higher price ceiling (16.5 cents a thousand cubic feet) for gas from new gas wells and a lower ceiling (14.5 cents) for all other gas, including by-product gas from oil wells. The industry felt the ceilings would discourage exploration and production. But the FPC said the higher prices allowed on gas from new wells would spur exploration.

Overseas, rising living standards and booming economies increased the consumption of petroleum products in 1965 by a healthy 10 per cent. As recently as 1961, U.S. use of liquid petroleum exceeded that of all the rest of the Free World; now U.S. consumption is 4,500,000 barrels a day less.

Exploration was also booming, with activity as usual highest in Canada—particularly in the Rainbow Lake field of northern Alberta. A "significant" gas well was brought in near Anchorage, Alaska, in November by Pan American Petroleum Corporation. And it was announced December 21 that British Petroleum, Ltd., had found gas in commercial quantities under the North Sea, near Hull, England. A week later, however, British Petroleum's drilling rig, the *Sea Gem*, sank (see DISASTERS).

Gasoline from Coal. Earlier, Continental Oil Company abandoned its North Sea well because the flow of gas was "not sufficient . . . to warrant completion of the well as a commercial producer." Continental, however, was pushing ahead with its plans for making gasoline out of coal. In October, it agreed in principle to a $620,000,000 take-over of all the productive assets of Consolidation Coal Company, second largest U.S. coal producer and a leader in coal-to-gasoline research. Consolidation Coal was reported to have found a method of extracting gasoline from coal at a cost of 11 cents a gallon—about half that of earlier methods. EDWIN W. DARBY

PHILADELPHIA elected its first Republican official since 1953. Arlen Specter, a 35-year-old Democrat running on the GOP ticket for the post of District Attorney, defeated the incumbent James C. Crumlish, Jr. Calling for "a return to reform," Specter—for three years an assistant district attorney under Crumlish—won by 36,221 votes. His victory was a stinging rebuke to the Democratic organization.

Also in the November election, voters approved bond issues totaling $82,500,000 for various municipal improvements. In this total, $25,000,000 was earmarked for the port. This meant that the Philadelphia Port Corporation could move ahead with its program to rebuild piers and other facilities.

The downtown area and the historic Independence Hall area were in the midst of building booms. In the city hall's shadow, a 20-story Municipal Services Building was dedicated October 27 by Vice-President Hubert H. Humphrey. Nearby, the Penn Center renewal continued with completion of 4 Penn Center and with the start of demolition for Continental Square, a major, privately financed office structure. Along the mall leading to Independence Hall, the Rohm and Haas Building was finished. It was followed by groundbreaking for a new federal mint.

In the education field, Temple University, the nation's second largest private university, became publicly supported on December 1. Tuition for its 21,000 students will drop sharply. DONALD W. LIEF

PRESIDENTIAL CANDIDATE Ferdinand Marcos gives victory sign to crowd at a political rally in The Philippines. Marcos was the winner by a large majority.

PHILIPPINES, THE. Filipinos were preoccupied with politics during 1965. On November 9, the nation ended the longest, most vigorous, and expensive presidential election in its history. President Diosdado Macapagal sought re-election to another four-year term, leading the Liberal party ticket. His vice-presidential running mate was Senator Gerardo Roxas. The opposition Nacionalistas championed Senator Ferdinand Marcos as their presidential candidate and Senator Fernando Lopez for vice-president. Early in the summer, a new political "third force" emerged, the Party for Philippine Progress. Senator Raul Manglapus became its candidate for president, teamed with Senator Manuel Manahan for vice-president. Also at stake were eight seats in the 24-man Senate, and 104 seats in the House of Representatives.

When the votes from 43,000 precincts were finally tallied, Marcos had won the presidency by a decisive majority. In December, he was proclaimed president by Congress, together with his running mate Lopez as vice-president. A majority of Liberals were elected to the House of Representatives. The Nacionalistas won most of the Senate seats, but not enough to give them firm control.

Growing Lawlessness crippled the productive efforts of many Filipino farmers, who feared that accumulating goods would make them targets for gangsters. Cattle rustling, fishing with explosives, and widespread smuggling were symptoms of deteriorating law and order which congress failed to curb with remedial action. Joined with an archaic land tenure system and less than effective government credit and technical services, these trends thwarted achievement of self-sufficiency in basic food production.

Economic Growth was evident chiefly among larger enterprises engaged in manufacturing, banking, insurance, mining, timber, and sugar. Disparities in wealth between the few very rich and the many who had little continued. A new law raising the industrial minimum wage from the equivalent of roughly one U.S. dollar per day to one and one-half dollars had yet to be fully enforced.

Staging Area. The Philippines became an increasingly vital staging area for American men and supplies moving to Vietnam. Although the Congress hesitated to sanction sending a proposed contingent of 2,000 Philippine army engineers and soldiers to Vietnam, military medical units and hundreds of Filipino civilian technicians continued helping the South Vietnamese while others worked in Laos and Thailand.

Population: 32,926,000. **Government:** President Ferdinand Marcos. **Monetary Unit:** peso (3.91 = U.S. $1). **Gross National Product:** 16,941,000,000 pesos. **Foreign Trade:** exports, $735,000,000; imports, $770,000,000. **Principal Exports:** coconut products, minerals, pineapple, sugar, timber. ALBERT RAVENHOLT

PHONOGRAPH RECORD. See RECORDINGS.

PHOTOGRAPHY

PHOTOGRAPHY. Competitive battles were waged by manufacturers both in the United States and abroad to get their share of the $2,000,000,000 photo equipment business. A large number of new and improved cameras and accessories appeared in 1965. These included new types of film and new flash bulb units.

Polaroid Corporation produced two Color Pack cameras at reduced prices by replacing metal bodies with plastic ones. These were later followed by the Polaroid Land Swinger, a simple, fixed-focus, single-shutter-speed version with built-in flash unit that required only setting the aperture to get a correct exposure. Also new was the Polaroid Land 180, a lightweight, nonautomated, versatile filmpack model for professionals.

The long-rumored Leicaflex, a 35mm single-lens reflex, made its debut early in the year. Built to Leica standards, it features automatic-reopen diaphragm, instant-return mirror, battery-powered exposure meter, focal-plane shutter with speeds up to 1/2,000 second, and interchangeable lenses. Zeiss Ikon announced a new 35mm Contaflex Super that has aperture and shutter speed coupled to a built-in light meter. The new Ikomatics, models F and A, marked Zeiss Ikon's entry into the "Kodapak" cartridge instant-load field. Model F was priced at $26.98, and model A at $52.98. Several other new models, geared to Europe's 35mm "Rapid System" of simplified loading, also made their first appearance in the United States.

New in 1965 was the Graflex XL, which has a standard camera body with or without rangefinder/viewfinder; an optional body for 47mm extreme wide angle; a variety of backs to accommodate roll, sheet, and Polaroid pack film; and eight high-resolution lenses. Accessories include lens spacers for copy and macrophoto, sports viewfinder, and Stroboflash.

Kodak introduced new versions of two 35mm cameras and six Instamatic cameras, all of which were redesigned to accommodate the unique "flash-cube." Kodak also unveiled its new Super 8 movie system, requiring a new camera and projector, that produces a film frame and projection picture 50 per cent larger than the conventional 8mm system.

The maker of the popular Rolleiflex line announced a subminiature model called the Rollei 16. This first departure from the twin-lens reflex principle is $4\frac{1}{2}$ inches long and yields 18 12x17mm negatives to the roll.

Film News. In 1965, an improved Panatomic-X was announced by Kodak. The film offers greater image sharpness for extreme enlargement and protects against image flare. It is available only in the 135 size. An improved Kodachrome II, Type A, became available in Super 8 cartridges for the new Instamatic movie cameras. The 50 feet of 8mm film do not have to be turned over, and are run without interruption.

AN IDYLLIC SUMMER DAY and two boys in a boat helped Bill Strode of the Louisville Courier-Journal become the Newspaper Photographer of the Year in Annual NPPA contest.

PHOTOGRAPHY

Flash. Two exciting innovations in photo lighting reached the camera fan in 1965. One was the new Flashcube introduced by Sylvania, to be used with Kodak's new 35mm and Instamatic cameras. The tiny cube contains four blue flashbulbs. After one is fired, the cube rotates by itself to a new bulb.

Introduction of Honeywell's Auto/Strobonar/600 marked the first completely automatic electronic flash. A built-in sensor reads the amount of light reflected from the subject and turns the flash off at the proper light level.

Awards in 1965 in various categories of photography included the following:

27th Annual Newspaper National Snapshot Awards. Grand Prize Winners ($1,000): *Color*—Wray Langston, Akron, Ohio; *Black-and-white*—Robert L. Meyers, Cincinnati, Ohio. Second Prize ($500): *Color*—Edward A. Sargeant, San Diego, Calif.; *Black-and-white*—Donald A. Kearns, Andover, Mass. Third Prize ($250): *Color*—Mrs. Irma B. Vitalis, Kenmore, N.Y.; *Black-and-white*—Mrs. Marvalee D. Feikert, Honolulu, Hawaii.

20th Annual Collegiate Competition, sponsored by Kappa Alpha Mu (KAM), National Press Photographers Association (NPPA), University of Missouri School of Journalism, and World Book Science Service, Inc. **NPPA's Colonel William Lookadoo $500 Scholarship** to Ken Heinen, University of Missouri. First place winners from the University of Maryland: *College Life*, Ken Firestone; *News*, William Clark; *Pictorial* and *Best Print of Show*, Nancy Ringgold; from Southern Illinois University: *Sports*, George Cassidy; *Category X*, Frank Salmo; from the University of Missouri: *Portfolio* and *Feature*, Ken Heinen; *Portrait/Personality*, Al Satterwhite; *Picture Story*, John Millaire.

1965 High School Competition, sponsored by KAM and NPPA. Honeywell Academic Grant ($500 scholarship) to Tom Houghton of Shasta High School, Redding, Calif.

Photographic Society of America 1965 Progress Medal Award to Beaumont Newhall, FPSA, director of George Eastman House, Rochester, N.Y.

White House News Photographers Association. 1965 Grand Award to Carl Kramer of United Press International Photos.

Joseph A. Sprague Memorial Award by NPPA, to Don Swenson, *Evansville* (Ind.) *Sunday Courier & Press*, and Hugh B. Terry, president and general manager of Time-Life Broadcast, Inc.; and KLZ-TV, Denver.

Fifth Annual Anscochrome of the Year Photographic Contest, sponsored by Ansco. $1,000 Grand Prize to Arthur Olson, Heart O'Lakes Camera Club, Fergus Falls, Minn.

23rd Annual Pictures of the Year Competition, sponsored by NPPA, University of Missouri School of Journalism, and World Book Science Service, Inc. **Newspaper Photographer of the Year**—Bill Strode, *Louisville Courier-Journal* and *Times*. **Magazine Photographer of the Year**—John Dominis, *Life*. **Two Special Merit Awards—Newspaper Portfolio**—Strode; **Magazine Portfolio**—Dominis.

Awards in other categories in order of first, second, and third place were as follows:

Spot News—James Pickerell, *Black Star*; Rod Hanna, *Topeka Capital-Journal*; Charles O'Rear, *Kansas City Star*. **General News**—Roddey Mims, United Press International (UPI); Ken Heinen, *Columbia Missourian*; Tom Colburn, *Houston Chronicle*. **Newspaper Picture Story (News)**—James Bourdier, Associated Press (AP); Dave Mathias, *Denver Post*;

Tom Colburn, *Houston Chronicle*. **Newspaper Picture Story (Feature)**—Heinen; Paul Shane, *La Crosse* (Wis.) *Tribune;* Jim Vestal, San Luis Obispo (Calif.) *Telegram-Tribune;* (Honorable Mention) Heinen; **Feature**—Gary Settle, *Topeka Capital-Journal;* Hank Daniel, *Charlotte Observer;* A. C. Reed, *Wichita Eagle and Beacon*.

Sports—Morrie Berman, *Pittsburgh Post-Gazette;* Don Hunter, *Charlotte News;* Settle, *Topeka Capital-Journal*. **Sports Picture Story**—Settle; J. Bruce Baumann, *Evansville* (Ind.) *Courier & Press*.

Pictorial—G. M. Converse, *Christian Science Monitor;* Philip Morgan, *Charlotte Observer;* David Cupp, *Charlotte Observer*. **Portrait and Personality**—Frank Wurzel, UPI; Bill Stapleton, WBSS; Bob Miller, *Milwaukee Journal-Sentinel*. **Category X—Magazine and Newspaper**—O'Rear.

Magazine Portfolio—Dominis; William Allard, *National Geographic;* Bruce Dale, *National Geographic*. **Magazine News**—James H. Karales, *Look;* Larry Burrowes, *Life;* Burrowes (2nd place also). **Magazine Picture Story**—Lennart Nilsson, *Life;* Albert Modvay, *National Geographic;* Bill Garrett, *National Geographic*. **Magazine Sports**—Garrett; Arthur Rickerby, *Life;* Neil Leifer, *Sports Illustrated*. **Magazine Pictorial**—Bruce Dale, *National Geographic;* Howard Sochurek, *Life,* and Allard. **Magazine Feature**—Allard and Dominis; Stan Wayman, *Life;* Dale. **Magazine Portrait and Personality**—Flip Schulke, *Black Star;* Allard; David J. Boyer, *National Geographic*.

Best Newspaper Use of Photographs—*The Miami News; Louisville Courier-Journal; Louisville Times*. **Best Magazine Use of Photographs**—*National Geographic*.

Picture Editor's Award—Tom Smith, *National Geographic Magazine;* George Gill, *Louisville Courier-Journal;* Bill Latham, *Louisville Times*. FRANK E. FENNER

PHYSICS. The effects that occur in superconducting systems were of great interest to physicists during 1965. Considered a rare oddity 10 years ago, superconductivity is now known to be a common phenomenon that occurs in many substances, most of which are metals, at temperatures near absolute zero. Superconductivity represents the frictionless flow of an electric charge.

In 1962, Brian D. Josephson, a graduate student at Cambridge University, predicted the possibility of superconductive "tunneling," or the ability of supercurrents to pass through a thin sandwich of normally insulating material contained between two superconducting sheets. He said that this process should generate some light. The effect, called "Josephson tunneling," has now been observed by I. K. Yanson, V. M. Svitstunov, and I. M. Dmitrenko of the Ukrainian Academy of Sciences in the Soviet Union, and independently by B. N. Taylor, D. N. Langenberg, D. J. Scalapino, and R. E. Eck of the University of Pennsylvania.

In addition to predicting the possibility of supercurrents in insulators, Josephson showed by his calculations that applying a direct current voltage across the sandwich of insulator between superconducting sheets should produce an alternating supercurrent with a frequency proportional to the applied voltage. Furthermore, he predicted that the alternating supercurrent would be accompanied by the emission of *photons* (electromagnetic radiation) of the same frequency. Lastly, he showed that an alternating current voltage across the sandwich would produce a direct supercurrent. All these effects have now been verified in detail.

The list of materials that are superconductive was extended by the discovery that compounds of graphite and alkali metals can become superconductors, the first such discovery for graphite compounds.

Superfluid Helium. A basic similarity between the effects of superconductivity and those of the superfluidity that occurs in liquid helium below 2.19° K. (*Kelvin* scale, degrees centigrade above absolute zero) has been long suspected. Superfluidity represents the frictionless flow of matter. Paul L. Richards and Philip W. Anderson of the Bell Telephone Laboratories in New York constructed an experiment to show an analogue of the Josephson effect occurring in superfluid helium.

They constructed a device to permit the flow of liquid helium from a high-level reservoir into a low-level reservoir through a pinhole orifice. By theory it could be shown that the matter waves in the two reservoirs would oscillate at different frequencies proportional to the level of liquid helium in each reservoir.

In analogy with the Josephson effect, it could further be predicted that the flow through the orifice would contain an alternating component related to the difference in reservoir levels. Richards and Anderson placed an ultrasonic vibrator below the orifice, which generated another alternating flow of liquid helium through the orifice. As predicted, the flow through the orifice halted at regularly spaced intervals. The two physicists concluded that this showed that the matter-wave fields in the two reservoirs were coupled in phase.

Super Magnets. The greatest continuous magnetic fields ever generated in a laboratory were produced at the National Magnet Laboratory, operated by the Massachusetts Institute of Technology in Boston. Physicists there constructed a magnet that creates a continuous field of 255,000 gauss. Previously, the highest continuous field that could be sustained for at least a minute had been about 152,000 gauss produced at the Naval Research Laboratory in Washington, D. C. A field of 255,000 gauss is 500,000 times the strength of the earth's magnetic field. The magnet can hold this intense field for about a minute.

The National Magnet Laboratory's device is a three-coil solenoid that draws its power from direct current generators. These generators supply a current up to 40,000 amperes at 250 volts. The magnet produces pressures up to 60,000 pounds per square inch, a pressure higher than that found in the deepest part of the ocean.

Light. Physicists at the Columbia Radiation Laboratory in New York have discovered a new factor in the process by which light is produced in a gas under the influence of electricity. Their findings may have an important bearing on the light displays of the aurora borealis, the light from a comet's tail, or even the light produced by a gas laser. The new finding was reported in November by physicists Martin Lipeles, Robert Novick, and Norman H. Tolk. They showed that low-energy ions can excite the electrons of a gas to such a state that they will emit light. Ions are atoms or groups of atoms that have become electrically charged.

In the past it had always been thought that only high-energy ions could produce this effect. The new experiments were done with helium ions having energies as low as five volts. These were injected into chambers filled with a number of different types of gases. According to Novick, the role of low-energy ions must, from now on, be considered in any explanation of light produced by a gas laser.

New Facilities. The Lincoln Laboratories of the Massachusetts Institute of Technology dedicated their new Haystack Microwave Research Facility. It will serve as a radio telescope, as a ground terminal for space communications, and as a tracking and measurements radar station.   S. MATTHEW PRASTEIN

See also ELECTRONICS; ENGINE AND ENERGY; NUCLEAR PHYSICS.

PLASTICS. See MANUFACTURING.
POETRY. See LITERATURE.

POLAND set the stage in 1965 for anniversary celebrations to be held in 1966. The communist regime said it would observe the 50th anniversary of the formation of Poland as an independent state. Roman Catholics, who comprise 90 per cent of the population, declared they would celebrate the millennium of the introduction of Christianity into Poland.

Persistent reports in Rome and the Polish-American press suggested that Pope Paul VI would like to be invited to the celebration. Stefan Cardinal Wyszynski, the Roman Catholic primate of Poland, let it be known that he would visit the United States and Canada in August of 1966 to participate in Polish-American commemorative festivities.

An uneasy truce developed between church and state. One such indication was the church convocation in Wrocław commemorating the 20th anniversary of the church's administration of the western territories ceded to Poland by Germany after World War II. There, Polish prelates gave full support to the regime on maintaining the borders at the Oder and Neisse rivers. But the atmosphere clouded in December when Cardinal Wyszynski and the Polish bishops wrote West German bishops inviting them to join the millennium celebrations and work toward Polish-German reconciliation. The government reacted angrily, accusing the churchmen of meddling in foreign affairs.

In Foreign Affairs, the Poles indicated they would like to attempt the double role of intermediary between Moscow and the Atlantic powers, and Moscow and West Germany. Numerous visits occurred in and outside Poland between Western and Polish and Soviet leaders. In November, President Lyndon B. Johnson's Vietnam peace overtures cropped up in Warsaw, where newly appointed U. S. Ambassador John A. Gronouski, Jr., held a three and a half hour conference with the Chinese ambassador to Poland. See VIETNAM.

In July, the government announced that Poland would reform its economy to provide greater incentives. By year's end, however, the changes were far more conservative than those being adopted in other communist countries. This was probably a reflection of the growing influence of the hard-line "partisan" faction of the party. Trade agreements, meanwhile, were concluded with firms in Austria, Great Britain, Italy, Sweden, and West Germany.

In May, Communist party leader Wladyslaw Gomulka was re-elected to office.

Population: 31,711,000. **Government:** Communist Party First Secretary Wladyslaw Gomulka; Premier Jósef Cyrankiewicz; President (Chairman of the Polish Council) Edward Ochab. **Monetary Unit:** zloty (4 = U.S. $1). **Foreign Trade:** exports, $2,096,000,000; imports, $2,072,000,000. **Principal Exports:** coal, meat, metals.   TOM AND HARLE DAMMANN

See also EUROPE.

POLLUTION. See Section Two, POLLUTED AMERICA.

POPULATION, WORLD.

Every hour during 1965, the population of the world increased by about 7,000 people. The net gain for the year was about 65,000,000; the total world population was an estimated 3,300,000,000. The vital statistics underlying this increase revealed a two-to-one ratio in favor of births over deaths.

A tragic paradox of world population growth in 1965 was that over four-fifths of the babies born during the year would be to mothers living in those areas of the world where food was scarce and living conditions marginal. Over 2,000,000,000 of the world's people were in the so-called "developing" countries of Africa, Asia, and Latin America. Many of them, however, were on the verge of famine; living standards were extremely low; illiteracy was high. Yet the birth rates in these areas continued to range between 40 to 50 births per 1,000 population per year.

The demographic situation in the "have" countries of Europe and North America remained very different. Birth rates were under fairly effective control and were in reasonable balance with modern low-death rates. The results, therefore, were a much slower rate of population growth. In the developed countries, food was abundant, the standard of living was high, and literacy was virtually universal.

The Imbalance between birth rates and death rates in the "have-not" countries was resulting in annual rates of population increase ranging from 2 per cent to 3.5 per cent and over. This meant that population in these countries would double in 20 to 30 years, and that most of the "have" industrialized countries of Europe would double their populations in from 75 to 150 years. See CENSUS; VITAL STATISTICS.

A recently published survey made by the United Nations covered world population trends and projections of future population growth. At the present time, according to the report, world population stood at 3,300,000,000. If the current trends continued, it said, this population would more than double by the year 2,000 to as much as 7,400,000,-000. If birth rates could be reduced in the high fertility "have-not" countries, however, population might be held to about 5,200,000,000.

Latin America, Asia, and Africa had birth rates of around 40 to 50 per 1,000 population. In Japan and most northern and western European countries, rates were below 20 (Ireland, Iceland, and The Netherlands were exceptions). In southern Europe, except Italy and Greece, they were rather higher; in North America, Oceania, and Russia they were 20 to 25. In Eastern Europe, rates varied from Hungary's 13 to Yugoslavia's 21. The lowest birth rate in Western Europe was Sweden's 14.

Population growth rates around the globe largely reflected variations in birth rates. The fastest growing region was Latin America. Brazil and Mexico, at present gaining 3 per cent a year, would double their population in 23 years. The slowest growing continent was Europe, with four of its countries—Austria, Belgium, Hungary, and Sweden—expanding 0.5 per cent or less. Their populations were expected to double in 140 years. In Asia, Japan had the lowest rate of 0.9 per cent, about the same as Great Britain's. The growth rate in the United States was 1.4 per cent.

Population Control was becoming of increasing importance to many nations. During the year, India began manufacturing a birth control device known as the Lippes loop (see Section Two, INSIDE RURAL INDIA). At a meeting held in Geneva, Switzerland, in May, the World Health Organization (WHO) announced it would include birth control research and advice in its international programs.

On June 7, the Supreme Court of the United States held, 7 to 2, that Connecticut's 1879 law forbidding the use of birth control devices was unconstitutional. In a historic decision, the Court ruled that the law violated Amendments 1, 3, 4, 5, 9, and 14 to the United States Constitution.

Earlier, in January, the first grant of federal funds to aid a community birth-control program was made to Corpus Christi, Tex., by the Office of Economic Opportunity under the War on Poverty program (see POVERTY). Later in the year, the U.S. Food and Drug Administration approved the marketing of the first "sequential" oral contraceptive in the United States.   ROBERT C. COOK

PORTER, SHEENA (-   ), a great-grand niece of the famous English novelist George Eliot, was awarded the Carnegie medal in 1965. *Nordy Bank* is the story of half Welsh Bronwen and her family, set along the Welsh border. *The Knockers* (1965) has the same geographical background. Local legends play an important part in this story.

Country ways, small towns, and family life characterize Miss Porter's novels. In *The Bronze Chrysanthemum* (1961) strange happenings and good fun follow the purchase of a mother's birthday present. *Hills and Hollows* (1962) is a story of country life, disturbed by proposed urban development. *Jacob's Ladder* (1963) is a lovely book about two schoolgirls and a desolate old mansion.

Sheena Porter is a children's librarian by profession, trained at Loughborough School. She was born in the small market town of Melton Mowbray, in Leicestershire. A childhood in the country, which included haymaking, herding cows, and the like, is reflected in her books. She loves animals, is interested in archaeology and, like some of her book characters, delights in exploring the countryside. Miss Porter was an editorial assistant in a publishing house for a time, but found life in London not to her liking. She has lived in six counties, now resides in Shrewsbury, Shropshire, and devotes much of her time to writing.

See also LITERATURE FOR CHILDREN (Awards).

PORTUGAL remained adamantly opposed to independence for Angola and Mozambique, its overseas provinces in Africa. It was reportedly spending 40 per cent of its annual budget, or about $122,500,-000, to suppress the guerrillas who were fighting for freedom there. See ANGOLA; MOZAMBIQUE.

In July, Américo Deus Rodrigues Tomaz was reelected as Portugal's president by more than 95 per cent of the National Electoral College. Later, in November, parliamentary elections were held. The National Union party of Premier António de Oliveira Salazar provided the only candidates and 74.1 per cent of the electorate voted. The results of both elections indicated that despite criticism the Portuguese were not ready to change regimes.

A massive drive to make the southern coastal region of Portugal a European holiday resort gained momentum and a good deal of foreign investment during the year. At year's end, reports indicated that tourism had played a major role in the nation's economy. About 1,500,000 had visited the country. Total income from tourism reached $237,500,000.

Population: 9,140,000. **Government:** President Américo Deus Rodrigues Tomaz; Premier António de Oliveira Salazar. **Monetary Unit:** escudo (28.85 = U.S. $1). **Gross National Product:** 78,300,000,000 escudos. **Foreign Trade:** exports, $429,430,000; imports, $673,790,000. **Principal Exports:** cork, fish, timber, wines.   KENNETH BROWN

See also EUROPE.

POST OFFICE. President Lyndon B. Johnson poked a little fun at the world's largest and least profitable business establishment in February, 1965. He noted that a speed record had been set in 1861 when copies of Lincoln's first inaugural address were sent from Washington, D.C., to California. It took seven days 17 hours, used the railroad and 75 ponies, and cost $10 per ounce. "Today," he said, "for only five cents we can send three ounces of presidential addresses across the country—at about the same rate of speed."

The U.S. Post Office Department, even before the presidential twit, was trying hard to cope with the increasing bulge in its mailbags. Over 71,600,000,000 pieces of mail were carried in fiscal 1965—one a day for every person in the United States.

The use of the ZIP code was increased. And a new system, called Vertical Improved Mail (VIM), promised rapid delivery throughout large, new office buildings which have built-in conveyor system equipment. In June, the Philco Corporation was awarded $1,800,000 to build optical scanners that could mechanically sort machine-printed or typewritten ZIP-coded mail at the rate of 36,000 pieces an hour directly to the postmen's delivery stations.

A New Postmaster General. Lawrence F. O'Brien was sworn in as Postmaster General on November 3, replacing John A. Gronouski, Jr., who had been appointed U.S. ambassador to Poland (see O'BRIEN, LAWRENCE F.).

It was believed that one of O'Brien's first moves in 1966 would be to ask Congress to merge airmail and first-class mail into a new "priority mail" category. Priority mail would cost a penny or two more per ounce than the current 5 cent first-class rate, and would be delivered in the fastest possible way, whether by truck, train, or plane.

Under U.S. Law, the addressee of a piece of mail that was deemed communist propaganda by the Post Office had been required to specifically request delivery of such mail. In February, however, officials of the Post Office Department, testifying before a congressional committee investigating invasion of citizens' privacy, announced that it was destroying the lists of those receiving mail from communist countries. Then, in support of this move, the Supreme Court of the United States struck down the law on May 24. It ruled that the law was a limitation on the exercise of the addressee's rights under Amendment 1 of the U.S. Constitution. Citizens can now receive mail from communist countries without fear of harassment.

The department received a $5,300,000,000 appropriation from Congress for fiscal 1966, an increase of $1,400,000,000 over fiscal 1965. The number of Post Office employees totaled 610,146, an increase of four per cent over the 1964 figure. They were being used mainly to handle the 1,200,000 city, 300,000 rural, and 90,000 business addresses added to the delivery system in 1965.   LAWRENCE F. O'BRIEN

POULTRY. See AGRICULTURE.

POVERTY

President Lyndon B. Johnson's War on Poverty in the United States was rapidly gathering momentum. On October 21, Congress appropriated $1,500,000,000 to finance it in fiscal 1966. This was nearly twice the amount—$793,300,000—appropriated for the program in the fiscal year ended June 30, 1965.

The anti-poverty campaign, begun by Congress on Aug. 20, 1964, was designed to help the 35,000,000 Americans who exist in conditions of poverty. The program has encountered various growing-pain problems and run into heavy criticism. But R. Sargent Shriver, Jr., the 50-year-old director of the Office of Economic Opportunity (OEO), which runs the program, gave Congress a reassuring report at the end of 1965. He said the first nine months' results reinforced his confidence that poverty in the United States "shall be abolished in our time."

The war opened on several major fronts:

Community Action Programs (CAP) in 415 communities received nearly $233,000,000 from the OEO. In keeping with the OEO statute, some 3,000 of the poor themselves were sitting on the governing boards of local CAP agencies. In addition, more than 70,000 of the poor were employed in local programs. CAP projects included education, homemaker services, health clinics, training and guidance for the aged, job training, day-care centers, credit unions, and legal services.

Project Head Start, an $85,000,000 CAP program staffed by 40,000 teachers and half a million volunteers, was carried out in the summer of 1965 to prepare 561,359 disadvantaged preschool children for entry into the public schools in September. The program, conducted in all 50 states, was considered so successful that it has been made a year-round project. See EDUCATION.

The Job Corps was launched in October, 1964, with a congressional appropriation of $183,000,000 to give job training to high school drop-outs, aged 16 to 21. By Nov. 25, 1965, more than 16,000 young men and women were enrolled in 74 Job Corps centers. The men were learning such occupational skills as automotive and small boat repair, retail sales, welding, food preparation and service, and landscaping. The women were being taught such skills as hairdressing, child care, industrial sewing, and business and clerical techniques.

The Neighborhood Youth Corps provided summer and part-time jobs for underprivileged youths of 16 to 21. Toward the total of 278,426 jobs in 642 projects in fiscal 1965, the federal government contributed $132,500,000 of the total $146,000,000 cost. Two-thirds of the jobs were for students who worked up to 15 hours a week. Out-of-school youths filled the remaining third. They worked as many as 32 hours a week, and received up to eight hours

Paul E. Glines, Office of Economic Opportunity

LEARNING A SKILL, maintenance of office machines, this young Job Corpsman works on an adding machine in an urban Job Corps center.

PATTERN OF POVERTY IN THE U.S.A.

The darker the shading the deeper the poverty—based on figures from the 1960 census. Shadings show the percentage of families in each U.S. county with incomes under $3,000 a year, which is the statistical watershed of poverty. The nationwide average of 21.4 per cent falls within the lightest, or "wealthiest," areas.

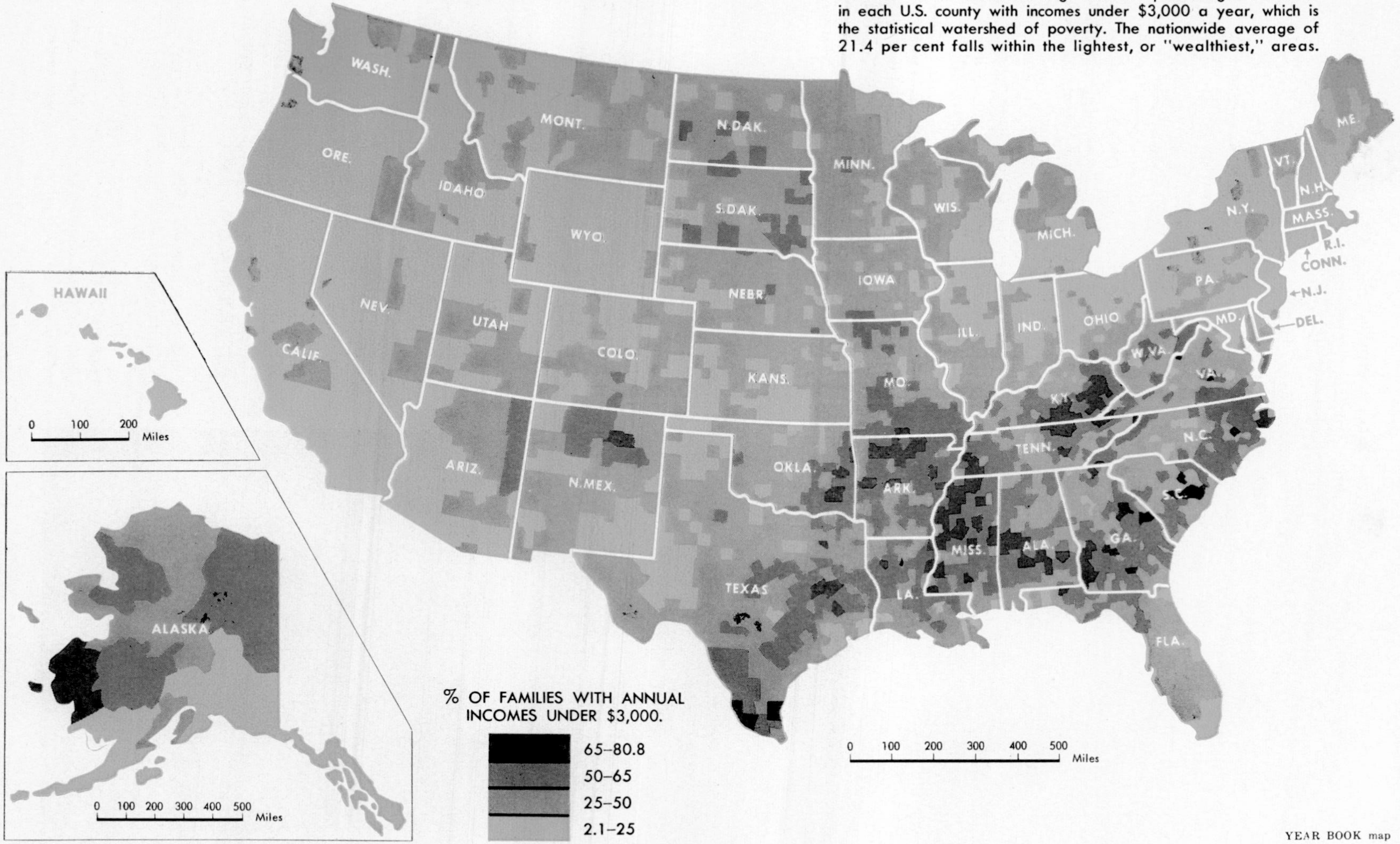

% OF FAMILIES WITH ANNUAL INCOMES UNDER $3,000.

65–80.8
50–65
25–50
2.1–25

484

POVERTY FIGHTER LYNDON B. JOHNSON *finishes a meal with youthful workers in a new Job Corps camp at Catoctin Mountain Park, Maryland.*

of counseling and remedial education. The youths were paid $1.25 an hour.

VISTA, or the Volunteers in Service to America, also known as the domestic Peace Corps, supplied the front-line fighters in the War on Poverty. On Nov. 25, 1965, there were 1,370 VISTA volunteers at work on 191 projects in the field and 371 in training. Serving in city and rural slums, they were training people for jobs, inducing drop-outs to return to school, counseling juvenile delinquents, and working in settlement houses.

A College Work Study project was providing federally subsidized part-time jobs for needy college students. More than 100,000 are expected to be enrolled by June, 1966. Over the next few years, the program will seek to make it possible for 50,000 young people to graduate from college every year.

Operation Upward Bound offered further help to precollege young people for the first time in the summer of 1965. This intensive "catch-up" study program was created for students from poor families who had mediocre school records but who were considered to have talents worth developing at college. Of 2,061 who participated in 1965, more than 1,500 continued in the fall semester as college freshmen or as special students combining college and remedial work. In fiscal 1966, some $25,000,000 of Community Action funds will be used to help 25,000 youths enroll in precollege centers at 200 to 250 colleges and universities.

The nation's 5,500,000 elderly poor were not neglected. The OEO set up programs to train them to work with neglected infants, serve as home health aides, take care of children from broken homes in rural and urban slums, and to care for mentally retarded children. See OLD AGE.

Small Business. Economic Opportunity loans of up to $25,000 were provided to small business proprietors unable to tap other credit sources. By late November, 31 Small Business Development Centers had opened in 23 states and the District of Columbia. The centers granted 632 loans totaling $8,200,000.

A rural loan program helped 14,000 poor people buy small farms or finance small rural businesses. A work-experience program had provided job training for 104,000 adults, mostly unemployed heads of families, at a cost of $132,400,000 by November 25. These were just some of the opening actions in the administration's War on Poverty.

Counter-attacks by both Republicans and Democrats were made against the anti-poverty program. Senate Republican Leader Everett M. Dirksen of Illinois called the program a "boondoggle" and a "colossal disgrace." Representative Adam Clayton Powell, Jr., powerful Negro New York Democrat and head of the House Education and Labor Committee, threatened at one point to hold up action on a renewal of the program. He charged that it had spawned "giant fiestas of political patronage."

POVERTY

Later, Powell said he would cooperate on Director Shriver's assurance that independent agencies would have access to anti-poverty funds and that the poor would be represented on local governing boards. That prospect so alarmed the nation's mayors that they accused the OEO of "fostering class struggle." Their fears were quieted after a conference with Vice-President Hubert H. Humphrey.

Charges of Scandal and mismanagement of funds arose as the War on Poverty progressed. In December, the OEO cut off funds to Boston's entire anti-poverty program pending an investigation into "wrongdoing and mismanagement." There had been earlier temporary delays or holdups in initial grants to other cities, until certain OEO conditions were met.

In October, the OEO had held back $2,200,000 in funds from New York City's Haryou-Act project in Harlem—Congressman Powell's district. Public accountants had found chaotic bookkeeping practices—records missing, checking accounts overdrawn, and vouchers unpaid. Haryou's director, Livingston L. Wingate, relinquished his post under fire until Feb. 1, 1966. Until that date, Haryou's board of directors said, he was to "concentrate all of his time to clarifying Haryou-Act's fiscal matters from Jan. 1, 1965, to Oct. 31, 1965."

Job Corps Centers were the focus of much criticism, particularly at St. Petersburg, Fla.; Camp Kilmer in Edison, N.J.; and Camp Breckinridge, near Morganfield, Ky.—where rioting broke out August 20. In the Kentucky disturbance, 13 persons were injured before Federal Bureau of Investigation agents and U.S. marshals quelled the riot. Some of the 650 students at the camp complained of being

War on Poverty Appropriations
(in millions for fiscal years ending June 30)

Program	1965	1966
Job Corps	$183.0	$ 235.0
Work Training	132.5	255.0
Work Study	56.0	60.0
Community Action	240.1	685.0
Migrant Workers	15.0	20.0
Rural Areas	25.7	35.0
Work Experience	112.0	150.0
Adult Basic Education	19.0	30.0
VISTA	3.2	17.5
Administration	6.5	12.5
Total	$793.0	$1,500.0

fed "slop," of restrictions on passes to Morganfield, of overcrowding, of alleged mistreatment by security guards, and of general misinformation given to them before they entered the Job Corps.

In his report to Congress, Shriver conceded "there have been problems in the first Job Corps year—some of which have been exaggerated. . . . Some center operations have taken longer than others to become efficient and meaningful—but great progress overall is undeniable." WILLIAM McGAFFIN

PRESIDENT OF THE UNITED STATES

PRESIDENT OF THE UNITED STATES

Lyndon Baines Johnson began his first full term in office on Jan. 20, 1965, with a sweeping mandate from the American people for the policies that he termed the "Great Society." Despite the almost unbelievable accomplishments of the Congress under the President's leadership, the attention of the nation in 1965 was on President Johnson as commander in chief of the U.S. forces fighting in Vietnam. In 1965, as the war there intensified, it became the main concern of the President and of the American people.

HIS 57th BIRTHDAY A WEEK AWAY, the President takes time out from the cares of office to have this official photograph taken in the White House.

Wide World

THE PRESIDENT *gets close staff work from his two fellow Texans, speech writer Jack Valenti, left, and press secretary Bill D. Moyers, right.*

By the end of the year, the United States had more than 180,000 men fighting in Vietnam although the nation was not officially at war. In July, the President told the nation that the situation in Vietnam would "get worse before it gets better." After days of consultation, he announced that 50,000 additional troops were being sent to Vietnam (raising the total there to 125,000) and that monthly draft calls were to be increased from 17,000 to 35,000. In April, the President had classified Vietnam and its adjacent waters as a combat area retroactive to Jan. 1, 1964. In doing so, the President gave $25,000,000 in income-tax exemptions to U.S. servicemen there.

Although the President left the door open for "unconditional negotiations" with the North Vietnamese to end the war, he insisted that the United States was pledged to help South Vietnam "remain independent and free of aggression." However, at home, the President was dismayed by widespread demonstrations against the war in Vietnam and by the academic community's strong opposition to it. Yet he had the majority of the people behind him on his policy. See VIETNAM.

By year's end, increased U.S. commitment to the war seemed to be turning the tide. At least, in the words of U.S. Secretary of Defense Robert S. McNamara, "We have stopped losing." A concerted "peace offensive" seemed to be underway. After the expiration of a 30-hour Christmas truce, the United States continued the lull in its bombing attacks on North Vietnam. See NATIONAL DEFENSE.

As 1966 opened, four U.S. "peace envoys" had visited the leaders of nine nations—Algeria, Britain, Canada, France, India, Italy, Poland, Tunisia, and Yugoslavia. The four were: Ambassador to the United Nations Arthur J. Goldberg, Ambassador at Large W. Averell Harriman, Special Presidential Assistant McGeorge Bundy, and Assistant Secretary of State G. Mennen Williams.

The Dominican Republic revolution in late April prompted the President to send U.S. marines into that country. On a telecast from the White House on May 2, he said he had acted to prevent take-over by a "band of Communist conspirators" (see DOMINICAN REPUBLIC). Later, after U.S. forces on land and in ships offshore had built up to more than 30,500 men, the Dominican problem was turned over to the Organization of American States (see LATIN AMERICA).

There was, however, a great deal of criticism of the action at home and abroad, but the President maintained that the United States could not permit the spread of communist governments anywhere in the Western Hemisphere.

A positive step in hemispheric relations was the announcement by the President in September, of a general agreement on a new treaty with Panama that would "effectively recognize" Panama's sovereignty in the Canal Zone (see PANAMA).

Soviet-U.S. Relations also improved, but the high-level visits that the President hoped to schedule did not materialize. In April, President Johnson named a 12-member committee to study ways of increasing trade with the Soviet Union and the nations of East Europe. In September, he revealed that a commercial mission would visit Poland and Romania (see INTERNATIONAL TRADE AND FINANCE).

Other Foreign Affairs actions included his:

• Refusal to intervene in the Indian-Pakistani dispute and his support of United Nations (UN) efforts to stop the fighting in Kashmir.

• Justification of U.S. military action in Laos.

• Appointment of a nine-man advisory council to make a country-by-country check of the foreign aid program.

• End-of-the-year White House visits with the heads of three governments—Pakistan's President Ayub Khan, British Prime Minister Harold Wilson, and West German Chancellor Ludwig Erhard.

The Great Society. On Jan. 4, 1965, the President delivered his State of the Union message to Congress. For the first time since Franklin D. Roosevelt's message of 1936, it was given in the evening. A television audience of more than 31,000,000 heard his discussion of foreign policy and the goals of the Great Society. Fourteen task forces had prepared reports for him on the nation's needs.

On January 25, he sent a budget to Congress calling for total federal cash spending for the 1966 fiscal year of $127,400,000,000—much of it tabbed for Great Society legislation. Increased Social Security benefits, including Medicare, were to be financed out of increased Social Security taxes. He estimated a deficit of $6,300,000,000; but in June he noted it would be $2,500,000,000 less than his January estimate.

Congressional Action on a presidential succession amendment was high on Mr. Johnson's "must legislation" list. Early in the year, he and Vice-President Hubert H. Humphrey had reached agreement on the procedure to be followed if the President were disabled (see accompanying Close-Up). As the session moved into high gear, he kept up pressure for his wide-ranging program—aid to Appalachia, Medicare, foreign aid, excise tax cuts, aid to education, legislation to preserve the nation's natural beauty, and a host of other measures.

To most of these requests Congress said "yes." But his requests for home rule for the District of Columbia, repeal of the controversial section 14(b) of the Taft-Hartley Act, and funds for rent subsidies for low-income families were denied (see CONGRESS OF THE UNITED STATES).

Civil Rights was a major concern for President Johnson. After the violent dispersion of civil rights

NEW U.S. INTELLIGENCE CHIEF. Retired Admiral William F. Raborn took over as head of the Central Intelligence Agency.

AN OLD NEW DEAL FRIEND of the President, Washington (D.C.) lawyer Abe Fortas, was named a Justice of the U.S. Supreme Court.

U.S. INFORMATION AGENCY got a new chief in July. Leonard H. Marks replaced Carl T. Rowan, who returned to writing.

TROUBLESHOOTER Joseph A. Califano, Jr., 34, was taken from the Department of Defense to become a special assistant to the President.

protesters in Selma, Ala., on March 7, and the murder of a white Unitarian minister who had joined the marchers, the President talked at the White House for three hours with Alabama's Governor George C. Wallace on March 13. He said, "I told the Governor that the brutality in Selma . . . just must not be repeated."

On March 16, the President sent a voting rights bill to Congress (which passed it on August 4, despite Southern opposition). Four days later, on March 20, the President mobilized selected units of the Alabama National Guard to help patrol a protest march the next day from Selma to the state capitol in Montgomery. Wallace had wired the President that the state of Alabama was too poor to protect the marchers. After the march, a white civil rights worker, Mrs. Viola Liuzzo, was slain—allegedly by the Ku Klux Klan—on the highway between the two cities. President Johnson, in a television address, urged Klan members to resign and Congress to investigate this "hooded society of bigots."

Labor. The President intervened in the 27-day East Coast longshoreman strike in February. He asked Secretary of Labor W. Willard Wirtz to request the dockmen to return to work in ports where settlements had been reached. Again, in August, he asked Secretary Wirtz to make recommendations in a two-month-old maritime strike. The strike soon ended when negotiators accepted his suggestions for mediating the automation issue (see LABOR; TRANSPORTATION).

When a steel strike threatened in August, the President used all his political acumen and the powers of his office to bring about a settlement. He persuaded union and industry leaders to cooperate. After a new contract was signed, fears were voiced that White House intervention was making collective bargaining obsolete. See STEEL INDUSTRY.

Administrative Efficiency in the executive branch of the government was high on the President's agenda. An executive order, in February, established a Council on Equal Opportunity under the chairmanship of the Vice-President. The council, with Cabinet-level status, was asked to coordinate the civil rights activities of all federal agencies.

In May, the President set up an Environmental Science Services Administration, merging the Weather Bureau, the Coast and Geodetic Survey, and the Central Radio Propagation Laboratory of the National Bureau of Standards (see WEATHER).

In an executive order, on May 9, he issued new regulations providing a code of ethical conduct for all employees in the executive branch and all in military service. The new regulations required all heads of federal agencies responsible to the President to file reports on their personal finances.

In August, in an economy move, President Johnson asked all nondefense agencies to reduce their spending for fiscal 1966 by almost $9,000,000,000. He also announced a new "revolutionary" cost-control system for year-round planning and budgeting of government programs.

Education was another major concern. He convened a White House Conference on Education in July. He told the 700 delegates that he planned to create a series of fellowships in honor of the late Adlai E. Stevenson, enabling young people from around the world to intern in UN agencies.

Presidential Appointments. Several Cabinet appointments were made by President Johnson in 1965 (see CABINET). In January, he named Ramsey Clark as Deputy Attorney General, succeeding Nicholas deB. Katzenbach, who became the new Attorney General (see KATZENBACH, NICHOLAS deB.).

Other administrative appointments included: *January*, Lloyd Nelson Hand as protocol chief, replacing Angier Biddle Duke. *February*, William Driver as Veterans Administration administrator; Thomas C. Mann as Undersecretary of State for Economic Affairs; Jack Hood Vaughn, as assistant secretary for Inter-American Affairs. *March*, Carl E. Bagge and Charles R. Ross, a reappointment, as members of the Federal Power Commission; John L. Sweeney as chairman of the Appalachian Regional Commission and James J. Wadsworth as a member of the Federal Communications Commission. *April*, William F. Raborn as director of the Central Intelligence Agency; Joseph W. Barr as Undersecretary of the Treasury; Charles L. Schultze

BACK FROM VIETNAM, the President's special assistant for national security affairs, McGeorge Bundy, parries questions on Asian war.

as the new director of the Bureau of the Budget.

May, Franklin D. Roosevelt, Jr., Undersecretary of Commerce, as chairman of the Equal Employment Opportunity Commission. *June*, Stanley Resor as Secretary of the Army.

July, Bill D. Moyers as press secretary; Harold Brown as Air Force Secretary; Major James U. Cross as a presidential military aide; Judge Thurgood Marshall as Solicitor General (see MARSHALL, THURGOOD); Leonard H. Marks as director of the U.S. Information Agency; Joseph A. Califano, Jr., as a special presidential assistant; National Broadcasting Company's correspondent, John W. Chancellor, as director of the Voice of America; Abe Fortas as a Justice of the Supreme Court (see FORTAS, ABE). *September*, Maxwell D. Taylor as special presidential consultant on diplomatic and military affairs; William H. Stewart as Surgeon General.

November, Kermit Gordon as chairman of the Medicare program's 16-member Health Insurance Benefits Advisory Council, Barnaby C. Keeney as chairman of the National Endowment for the Humanities, S. Dillon Ripley as chairman of the Federal Council on the Arts and Humanities.

December, Harold Howe II as U.S. Commissioner of Education (see HOWE, HAROLD, II).

Overseas Appointments. The President won praise for the caliber of his diplomatic appointments. Of the 116 U.S. ambassadors, 85 were career Foreign Service officers. Of Johnson's 50 diplomatic

"Lyndon's doing what I'd have done, but I'd have enjoyed it more."

The Bayh Amendment —What It Would Do

A constitutional amendment on presidential disability and succession was adopted by Congress on July 6, 1965, and sent to the states for ratification. Its two major provisions seek to correct what many regard as serious deficiencies in the structure of the presidency. The first would empower the President, whenever the office of Vice-President is vacant, to "nominate a Vice-President," who would take office when confirmed "by a majority vote" of each house of Congress.

Without this amendment, the Constitution provides no means for filling the office of Vice-President between elections. It merely empowers Congress to provide for the succession to the presidency only when both the offices of President and Vice-President are vacant. The line of succession, as set forth in the Presidential Succession Act of 1886, as amended in 1947, goes from the Vice-President to the Speaker of the House, the President *pro tempore* of the Senate, the Secretary of State, and then to the other department heads in order of rank (see CABINET).

The second provision establishes two procedures by which the Vice-President could become Acting President when the President was disabled.

First, if the President himself concluded that he was unable to perform the duties of his office, he could so advise the President *pro tempore* of the Senate and the Speaker of the House, in writing. The Vice-President would then immediately assume the powers and duties of the office as Acting President and would continue to do so until the President advised the congressional officers that he was able to resume his responsibilities.

If a disabled President could not, or did not, initiate a transfer of his powers and duties to the Vice-President, a second part of the provision would come into operation. The Vice-President, acting in concert with a majority of the Cabinet "or of such other body as Congress may by law provide," could advise the President *pro tempore* of the Senate and the Speaker of the House that the President was disabled and take over as Acting President.

The President could reclaim his office by informing the congressional officers in writing that he had overcome his disability. But if, within four days, the Vice-President and a majority of the Cabinet "or of such other body" did not agree that he had recovered, then Congress would resolve the issue. If it decided, by at least a two-thirds vote of each house, that the President was still unable to discharge his duties, the Vice-President would continue as Acting President. Otherwise, the President would resume his office.

Congress would be subject to two deadlines: If in session, it would be required to make its decision within 21 days after receiving the duly written declaration. If not in session, it would be required to assemble within 48 hours and make its decision within 21 days thereafter.

While the Constitution was silent on how a President's disability was to be determined, it was ambiguous on whether the Vice-President succeeded temporarily to the "powers and duties" of the office, or to the office itself.

The chief impetus for the proposed amendment springs from recent history. After President Dwight D. Eisenhower's heart attack in 1955, he arranged a written understanding with his Vice-President, Richard M. Nixon, on disability. The plan was continued in its essentials by Presidents John F. Kennedy and Lyndon B. Johnson.

But its inadequacy became apparent with President Kennedy's assassination. The resulting vacancy in the vice-presidency put two aged congressional leaders next in line to the presidency. Also, if President Kennedy had clung to life in a coma indefinitely, he could neither have governed nor certified his inability. An awareness spread through Congress that more than a private understanding was required to preserve the nation from a headless government in the Nuclear Age. It gave overwhelming approval to SJ Res 1, known as the "Bayh Amendment," after its chief congressional manager, Senator Birch Bayh (D., Ind.). If it is ratified by 38 states within seven years, it will become an amendment to the Constitution.

LOUIS W. KOENIG

AN UTTERLY RELAXED VIEW of foreign affairs was given by President Lyndon B. Johnson at this impromptu press conference in the White House.

appointments, only three could be labeled "political." His 1965 appointments included:

February, W. Averell Harriman as Ambassador at Large. *July*, Harlan Cleveland, as U.S. Ambassador to the North Atlantic Treaty Organization (NATO); Livingston T. Merchant, as U.S. executive director of the International Bank for Reconstruction and Development (the World Bank); Henry Cabot Lodge as Ambassador to South Vietnam; Associate Supreme Court Justice Arthur J. Goldberg as U.S. Representative to the UN, succeeding the late Adlai Stevenson. *August*, John A. Gronouski, Jr. as Ambassador to Poland. *October*, William M. Rountree as Ambassador to the Republic of South Africa; William H. Weathersby as Ambassador to Sudan. *November*, M. P. Jones as U.S. Ambassador to Malawi.

State Visitors from Abroad who conferred with President Johnson included:

January, Japanese Premier Eisaku Sato, Canadian Prime Minister Lester B. Pearson. *March*, British Foreign Secretary Michael Stewart. *April*, Canadian Prime Minister Pearson, British Prime Minister Wilson, Italy's Premier Aldo Moro.

May, President Chung Hee Park of South Korea. *June*, West German Chancellor Ludwig Erhard, Australian Prime Minister Robert G. Menzies. *August*, Ghana's Foreign Minister Alex Quaison-Sackey. *October*, Pope Paul VI, who met the President in New York City.   CAROL L. THOMPSON

See also DEMOCRATIC PARTY; JOHNSON, LYNDON B.

PRICE, HOLLIS FREEMAN (1904-   ), President of LeMoyne College, was elected Moderator of the United Church of Christ during its biennial convention in July, 1965. He is the first Negro elected to this high position of the 2,000,000-member Protestant denomination. Dr. Price serves for two years, and will preside at the denomination's next biennial convention in 1967. In the meantime, he will visit congregations across the country as representative of the church organization. Dr. Price succeeded the Reverend Dr. Gerhard W. Grauer of Chicago.

A churchman and educator for many years, Dr. Price is known nationally and internationally. He taught economics at Tuskegee Institute in Alabama for 10 years before going to Memphis as dean of LeMoyne in 1941. He has been president of the college since 1943. Dr. Price is a member of the Memphis Committee on Community Relations, composed of 10 Negroes and 10 white persons. It has been credited with furthering integration there without much of the racial disorder common today.

Hollis Freeman Price was born in Capahosic, Va., where his father served as principal of the Gloucester Normal School. After high school, Hollis attended Williston Academy in Easthampton, Mass. He is a graduate of Amherst College (1927) in Massachusetts, and took his M.A. degree at Columbia University (1931). Brandeis University (1958) and Amherst (1962) have both honored him with Doctor of Laws degrees.

493

PRICE, (MARY) LEONTYNE (1927-   ), opera and concert soprano, was awarded the Spingarn medal in 1965 by the National Association for the Advancement of Colored People (NAACP). Honored as an American Negro of distinguished achievement, the citation read, in part, "in recognition of her divinely inspired talent. . . ." The famous prima donna was in Europe when selected for this honor in June. The presentation, made by the Metropolitan's general manager Rudolf Bing, was delayed until Jan. 2, 1966.

Since her first Broadway role as Saint Cecilia in Virgil Thomson's *Four Saints in Three Acts* (April, 1952), Leontyne Price has had many triumphs. As the co-star of *Porgy and Bess* (1952-1954), she toured the United States and Europe. She has sung in the world's major music centers, and is now a leading prima donna of the great opera houses. In May, 1960, Miss Price appeared for the first time at Milan's Teatro alla Scala, and in January, 1961, made her Metropolitan Opera debut as Countess Leonora in *Il Trovatore*. On Oct. 23, 1961, she opened the Metropolitan's 1961-1962 season as Minnie in Puccini's *Girl of the Golden West*.

Mary Leontine Price was born in Laurel, Miss., but came to fame as Leontyne Price. She was educated at Central State College, Wilberforce, Ohio, and Juilliard School of Music in New York City.

PRINCE EDWARD ISLAND. See CANADA.

PRISON. The critical shortage of qualified manpower in the field of prisons and correctional institutions was considered by the Congress of the United States, which passed legislation providing for a three-year nationwide study of the problem. The measure was signed into law on September 10 by President Lyndon B. Johnson. Written by Representative Edith Green of Oregon, it provided for a study of current and anticipated needs for all levels of personnel in correctional work, problems of recruitment and retention, and changes needed in professional school curricula.

Myrl E. Alexander, director of the U.S. Bureau of Prisons, reported in January that the population of federal prisons had dropped more than 6 per cent in 1964, the second consecutive year in which the number of prisoners was reduced. The drop from 23,000 to 21,500 followed a 4 per cent decline in 1963.

Capital Punishment. The world-wide trend toward the abolition of capital punishment was highlighted in England, in October, by an act of Parliament establishing a moratorium on the death penalty for at least five years. This culminated a 15-year campaign by a Labour member of Parliament, Sydney Silverman.

Earlier, on June 5, New York joined 12 other states which have abandoned the death penalty in whole or in part, when Governor Nelson A. Rockefeller signed a bill abolishing the death penalty for all except two classes of murder: killing of police,

or slaying of prison guards and inmates by prisoners attempting to escape.

Freedom of Worship. On April 11, six Black Muslim inmates at San Quentin filed suits, totaling $39,000,000, in Federal Court in San Francisco against California prison authorities who, they alleged, denied them an approved place of worship.

Escapes and Releases. On July 8, Ronald A. Biggs, sentenced to prison for participating in the $7,000,000 British mail train robbery in 1964, escaped from prison. Biggs was the second of the robbers to escape. Charles Winslow escaped in 1964.

A 62-year-old Negro, Charles Kemp, who escaped from a Georgia prison 26 years ago and had led an exemplary life since, was arrested in Florida on traffic charges and faced return to prison. Governors Carl Sanders of Georgia and Haydon Burns of Florida agreed to hold proceedings in abeyance as long as Kemp continued to be a good citizen.

On May 20, 86-year-old William A. Hightower left a California prison after nearly 44 years, for the murder of a Roman Catholic priest in 1921.

Also released, on April 20, was Theodore Jordan, Jr., who spent 27 years in an Oregon prison for murder and was cleared after it was established that his 1932 confession had been forced.   JOSEPH D. LOHMAN

See also CRIME.

PRIZE. See AWARDS AND PRIZES; NOBEL PRIZES; PULITZER PRIZES.

PROTESTANT. Reports issued during 1965 indicated that U.S. Protestants were continuing to assure their churches a secure place in national life. Membership kept pace with population and financial support increased. Members of 41 denominations, reporting in 1965 to the National Council of Churches (NCC), gave a record $3,000,000,-000, $115,000,000 more than NCC announced in its 1964 report. (As always, most of this money—over $81 out of every $100—was used for local congregational purposes.) Gifts for new church construction among all religious groups topped $1,000,000,000, the second highest figure in history.

But despite the impressive statistics, a number of public opinion surveys revealed that not all was well. A Louis Harris poll in August revealed that far fewer Protestants than Roman Catholics were represented in that half of the U.S. population which claimed to attend church weekly.

Meanwhile, a survey conducted by the American Institute of Public Opinion reported a decline of regular weekly church attendance from 49 per cent in 1958 to 45 per cent in 1965. The same survey revealed that in 1957, 69 per cent of the sample polled expressed belief that the influence of religion was growing, while in 1965 only 33 per cent expressed a similar belief, and 45 per cent felt that it was declining. Protestantism shared in the destiny of all religions in such surveys, for it remains by far the largest religious family in North America.

Modern Explorers of Religion

Two of the modern world's foremost religious thinkers died during 1965. Martin Buber, an exemplar of Jewish thought, died on June 13; and Paul Johannes Tillich, a Protestant Christian theologian, died on October 22. The urgency and profundity of contemporary religious inquiry was made clear through the half-century careers of these men in an age that is often called nonreligious or secular.

Parallels between the lives of these religious philosophers are obvious. Buber, born in 1878 in Vienna, Austria, and Tillich, born in Prussia in 1886, pursued teaching careers in German universities. Their opposition to Adolf Hitler forced them to leave Germany; Buber went to Jerusalem, and Tillich to New York City. They were friends, generous in acknowledging mutual influences. Few modern Jews had impact on Christian thought as did Buber, and Tillich was read by Jews and other non-Christians.

Martin Buber drew deeply on the Hebrew Bible, which he translated into incomparable German. In 1904, he discovered Hasidic thought, a form of 18th century Judaism that arose in Poland. It bypassed religious formalism and stressed joyful communion with the Divine. From his grandfather, he had learned to appreciate the disciplined reasoning of the Talmud. He transformed ideas from these divergent sources into a highly personal vision that was at first mystical and later prophetic. Yet, he was not acceptable to Jerusalem's rabbis, who did not permit him to teach religion at Hebrew University. He did not practice Judaism in the ritual sense and was not expressly devoted to internal concerns of Jewish communal life.

As a Christian, Paul Tillich often commented on the New Testament and was attracted to idealist thought of the kinds that influenced early Christians and many 19th century German Protestants. He created the first really original theological system in America in 200 years, and spent his American years in seminaries and divinity schools before enthusiastic students. Yet, intensely interested as he was in all forms of contemporary thought he, too, was often regarded as a heretic in his tradition and he had little interest in the ordinary practices of the churches.

At first glance or first hearing both men seemed to be misfits in the modern world. But people sensed a *charism*, a gift of personal presence and power in each, so they were often patient to learn from both. Buber, who looked like an ancient prophet or a bearded medieval mystic, seemed too imprecise for today's philosophers. Tillich's "philosophy of being" seemed jarring and out of date to American thinkers, just as he himself looked like an old-style German professor. Neither man was facile or clever. Yet both addressed the human condition and commented on modern existence so profoundly that they succeeded in shaping a new religious language for many.

Buber's language concerned a "philosophy of dialogue." He believed that man can come into his fulfillment and can find meaning only through deeply personal and complete "encounters"—"I-Thou" relationships—with "others," and with "the Other," who is God. Tillich and Buber both recognized that the reality of God was a problem for people in the Space Age. Tillich advocated speaking of God as "the Ground of Being, the source of all that is" and he spoke of religion as "ultimate concern."

Buber spent little time discussing the character of "the eternal Thou" (or *du*, the intimate form of "you" in German) and Tillich chose to speak of God symbolically. Thus, both men concentrated on man and were often regarded as humanists because of their understanding of man's problems and his possibilities.

Jerusalem was Buber's home in his later years. There he devoted himself to his family, his students, his friends. Tillich taught at New York's Union Theological Seminary and after retirement gave himself tirelessly as a teacher and writer at Harvard University and the University of Chicago.

Buber's best-known works are *I and Thou* (1923), *Between Man and Man* (1947), and *Eclipse of God* (1952); Tillich's are *The Prostestant Era* (1948), *The Courage to Be* (1952), and *Systematic Theology*. MARTIN E. MARTY

*Martin Buber
(1878-1965)*

*Paul Tillich
(1886-1965)*

A
YEAR
BOOK
CLOSE-UP

Criticism in Canada. In Canada, debates on the role and destiny of religion paralleled those in the United States. Pierre Berton's book *The Comfortable Pew*, which criticized the church for following, not leading, in modern society, became one of Canada's all-time best sellers. Berton, a newspaper columnist and a television celebrity, had written the book at the invitation of the Anglican Church. The United Church of Canada also invited criticism and received it in a published symposium, *Why the Sea Is Boiling Hot*. The United Church also undertook surveys which revealed that it shared with U.S. Protestantism the problem of a growing cleavage between clergymen and laymen on social issues. In the Canadian survey, the clergy were far more liberal on the social and on some of the doctrinal issues than were the laymen.

Clergy-Laity Debates. The year saw an intensification of debate in the United States between clergy and laity. The most controversial issue was the growing U.S. involvement in South Vietnam. When a Quaker pacifist burned himself to death outside the Pentagon as a sign of protest, the general public saw how deep had become the concern of some believers. Protestants were also involved in a "Clergymen's Emergency Committee for Vietnam" which visited the battle areas and voiced pleas for immediate peace negotiations.

Evidence of the clergy's heightened concern for social issues appeared at the Sixth World Order Study Conference, convoked by the NCC at St. Louis, Mo., in October. The conference advocated admission of the People's Republic of China (Communist China) to the United Nations. It urged that the United States confine bombing to military targets in South Vietnam; that it not bomb North Vietnam; and that it work toward immediate peace negotiations. In July, two prominent independent religious journals chided the NCC for not engaging more strenuously in antiwar activities. The general board of NCC did call for reappraisals of governmental policies. But, after his tour of the Far East, Council President Bishop Reuben H. Mueller issued a statement generally approving U.S. policies there. And, in a controversial tour sponsored by the U.S. Department of Defense, Ben R. Hartley, editor of *Presbyterian Survey*, published by the Presbyterian Church in the United States (Southern), emphatically endorsed U.S. policies in Vietnam.

Civil Rights formed the second principal area of public controversy involving U.S. Protestantism. The single most publicized event was the Selma-to-Montgomery march in Alabama in March. Many Protestants took part in this demonstration. Among them, it was pointed out, was a significant number of "conservative evangelicals" representing a religious tradition which had been less active on the civil rights front in the past. Also, the conservative Southern Baptist Convention at its 108th annual meeting went on record as supporting a program of positive leadership in racial change. And, in Mississippi, a Committee of Concern was organized so that white Protestants could join others in rebuilding Negro churches burned in explosions of racial violence.

The increasing involvement of Protestants in the racial revolution met some resistance. The disastrous riots in Los Angeles led many who opposed integration and the clergy's advocacy of demonstrations to rally their forces. Some Protestant clergymen were accused of contributing to violence through their support of "civil disobedience."

Such accusations were not without effect. Presbyterian Robert H. Heinze reported that the official magazine of the United Presbyterian Church in the U.S.A., *Presbyterian Life*, experienced a decline in circulation because many laymen protested its encouragement of civil rights activity. "*Presbyterian Life* is in trouble, and I'm glad," he said, noting that the trouble indicated that the journal wanted to deal in matters of consequence and that its points were being heard. Meanwhile, the bishop of the Episcopal diocese in New York, the Rev. Horace W. B. Donegan, announced that several substantial gifts to the as yet uncompleted Cathedral of St. John the Divine had been withdrawn because of his advocacy of racial integration. See CIVIL RIGHTS; LOS ANGELES; NEGRO.

Church-State Controversy. Protestants were also embroiled over relationships of church and state. This issue was occasioned principally by dramatic legislative changes which were a part of President Lyndon B. Johnson's "Great Society" program. Key to the problem was the increasing involvement of the federal government in aid to higher education and extension of its work in the field of public welfare. Because many federal programs were administered in part through Protestant church agencies, some Protestant leaders showed renewed concern over programs that threatened old practices and doctrines on separation of church and state. The Southern Baptist Convention, for instance, was most divided over the acceptance by Protestant colleges of federal grants or loans. See EDUCATION; Section One, LAWRENCE A. CREMIN ON EDUCATION.

Ecumenical Activity. On the positive side, Protestants increasingly involved themselves with the ecumenical movement in efforts to increase Christian cooperation, unity, and eventual reunion. Vatican Council II continued to attract Protestant attention. At Geneva, Switzerland, on May 23, a committee of Roman Catholics and members of the World Council of Churches, in which Protestants play a substantial part, met for the first time to discuss areas of cooperation. In the United States, Lutherans met with Roman Catholics to discuss the ancient Nicene Creed, at Baltimore, in July. Also, Reformation Day observances across the nation in October involved Protestants and Roman Catholics and frequently saw Protestants discussing Catholicism with sympathetic insight.

The ecumenical record saw setbacks as well as advances. In a forward step, the World Council of Churches dedicated a new $3,000,000 headquarters at Geneva, in July. And in Canada, Anglicans approved in principle the activities that could lead to eventual merger with the United Church of Canada. In the United States, conservative evangelical editor Carl F. H. Henry called for stepped-up efforts by the evangelicals who are not in the ecumenical movements to find each other and to work together. And the long aloof Lutheran Church-Missouri Synod voted in June to participate in forming a "Lutheran Council in the U.S.A.," thus ending a century-long policy of ecumenical isolation. But efforts leading to a possible 22,000,000 member merger of six denominations in the United States made haste slowly at a Consultation for Church Union at Lexington, Ky., in April. Leading Methodist layman Charles C. Parlin, for example, was quoted as saying that Methodists were generally disinterested in union of the churches.

Theological Debate was intense during 1965. American Protestants joined a debate which was widely publicized in England after the appearance, in 1963, of Anglican Bishop John A. T. Robinson's *Honest To God*. The debate revolved around efforts of some Christians to deal with themes of faith without reference to "beyondness," to a God "out there," to transcendence or metaphysics. In the United States, a number of younger theologians were featured in the public press as "Christian atheists" who wanted to talk about Jesus Christ and the Church, but who spoke in dramatic terms about the cultural reality of "the death of God." The attention of the press came late in the year and the debates, long confined to seminaries and theological journals, broke into the public view.

Deploring such trends, Bishop Otto Dibelius of Germany's Evangelical Church spoke for many Protestants on his own 85th birthday when he scorned the "spiritual climate of the world (which) has shown an increasing trend toward pure intellectualism. The image of the church to modern man should be that of a power that overcomes the world and offers the joy of faith and victory," he said.

Liberal Protestantism saw the passing of some of its most eloquent spokesmen in the death of Unitarian layman Adlai E. Stevenson, often regarded as a model representative of one religious viewpoint; of Dr. Albert Schweitzer; and of theologian Paul Tillich. See DEATHS OF NOTABLE PERSONS.

Statistics. *The 1966 Year Book of American Churches* noted that 203 Protestant bodies reported a total clergy of 333,562, with 231,587 pastors with active charges. Two hundred twenty-one Protestant bodies reported 293,830 churches, with a membership of 68,299,478. Twenty Eastern bodies reported 1,524 churches with 3,166,715 members and 1,974 clergy, with 1,507 with active charges.   MARTIN E. MARTY

PSYCHIATRY. See MENTAL HEALTH; PSYCHOLOGY.

PSYCHOLOGY. A chemical basis for learning and memory was discovered by researchers in both the United States and Denmark. This involves ribonucleic acid (RNA), which is present and produced in every living cell.

A few years ago experiments with flatworms (planarians) linked RNA with the memory process. It was found that the trained habits of one flatworm could be chemically transferred to an untrained worm, and that this was possible only when the transfer procedures did not damage the RNA.

The new studies have provided similar evidence that the RNA in brain cells is likely the basis for memory even in higher mammals. Two independent teams of scientists working with rats, one in the United States consisting of F. R. Babich, A. L. Jacobson, S. Bubash, and Ann Jacobson, of the University of California in Los Angeles, and one in Denmark consisting of E. J. Fjerdingstad, T. Nissen, and H. H. Røigaard-Peterson of the University of Copenhagen, reported the new experiments.

The U.S. team trained a group of rats to approach a food cup at the sound of a click. After five days of training, when the habit was well established, RNA was extracted from the brains of the trained rats and injected into the abdominal cavities of an equal number of untrained rats. The untrained rats were tested at intervals during the next 24 hours for their responses to the click. Compared with a third group of control rats, which had received similar brain extracts but from untrained rats, the second group of rats approached the food cup more often than could be accounted for by chance.

The Danish team of scientists used slightly different procedures. They substituted light for sound as the stimulus, and water for food as the reward. In addition, the procedure for injecting the RNA from the trained rats into the untrained ones differed slightly. In spite of these differences, however, the results were essentially the same.

PKU. Studies of the relationship between proteins and brain functions were not limited to RNA synthesis. At the Regional Primate Research Center of the University of Wisconsin, carefully controlled experiments were carried out to learn more about the mechanism by which the disease called phenylketonuria (PKU) produces permanent intellectual impairment. The disease is caused by a genetically determined inability to metabolize a protein (phenylalanine) in the normal way. The Wisconsin scientists succeeded in demonstrating that abnormalities, which simulate those associated with PKU in man, could be induced in rhesus monkeys by feeding them a diet high in phenylalanine, more than could possibly be metabolized in the normal way. It now seems likely that critical experiments can be performed on the mechanism of intellectual damage so that eventually a means can be found of counteracting the effects of PKU in humans. ROBERT W. GOY

See also MENTAL HEALTH.

Arthur Siegel

MARSHALL FIELD, editor and publisher of two Chicago newspapers and publisher of Field Enterprises Educational Corporation, died at 49.

PUBLISHING. Books, magazines, and newspapers rolled off the press in record numbers. *Publisher's Weekly* estimated that some 30,000 new books appeared in 1965. The Magazine Publishers Association reported that magazine circulation exceeded 210,000,000 copies per issue, and daily newspaper circulation (per day) reached an estimated 60,640,000, according to the Audit Bureau of Circulation.

The circulation figures accurately reflected the state of health of magazine and book publishers. But for metropolitan newspapers, 1965 was a rocky year. Rising costs and strikes or the threat of strikes afflicted large-city dailies.

In the past 20 years, newspaper circulation in suburban areas has increased almost 9,000,000, whereas circulation in metropolitan areas increased only some 300,000. The largest growth during this period occurred in cities and towns with a population of less than 100,000. This trend of two decades continued in 1965.

Newspaper Mergers. In San Francisco, the Hearst newspapers, the *Examiner* and the *News-Call Bulletin*, and the locally owned *Chronicle* agreed to consolidate their production plants. Also, the *Examiner* left the morning field to the *Chronicle* and merged with its sister newspaper to form the *Examiner and News-Call Bulletin*. The two Sunday newspapers, the *Examiner* and the *Chronicle*, also merged. The arrangement leaves San Francisco, which is the 12th largest city in the U.S. in population, with one morning, one

evening, and one newspaper published on Sundays.

In New York City, publishers confirmed what had been rumored for many months: talks have been going on for two years about consolidating publishing operations. New York City publishers also confirmed reports that stated they have discussed mergers that might bring the number of morning and afternoon newspapers to two each. There are now three morning and three afternoon newspapers in the nation's largest city.

Newspaper Closures. A new U.S. metropolitan paper shut down after losing several million dollars attempting to compete with existing dailies. In Atlanta, Ga., the *Times* collapsed in August after 14 months of publication. The *Times*, which described itself as the voice of conservatism in the state, raised some $3,000,000 with a public stock sale and had anticipated losses for two years while it was establishing itself. But lack of anticipated advertising revenue put the *Times* more than $1,000,000 in the red within a year, and the circulation declined from 125,000 to 60,000. Left in Atlanta were the *Journal* and the Sunday *Journal Constitution*, both under the same ownership.

Even the venerable newspapers were subject to the tightening economics of metropolitan journalism. In Indianapolis, the 78-year-old *Times* ended publication. That Scripps-Howard evening newspaper had a circulation of more than 90,000 and a payroll of 420 persons. The newspaper reported its revenues "had fallen increasingly short of more rapidly expanding payroll and production expense." The remaining newspapers are owned by Eugene C. Pulliam.

Automation. The newspaper, whose major function is to report change, has been one of the few industries to isolate itself from the great change in industry, automation. But rising costs and the inability of employer and employee to work out satisfactory contracts have plunged the newspaper industry into the new industrial revolution. Plants all over the country began to install machinery or to initiate plans for drastic changes in their news and mechanical departments. One expert stated that fully automated newspapers will be in operation in two cities by 1967. Cost of the changeover: $2,000,000 each.

The first fully automated newspaper plant was constructed during 1965 in Reading, England, by Lord Thomson, the owner of more than 100 newspapers. He said he would gradually install computers in all his other newspaper plants. He forecast that eventually "one big computer will set type for the whole of England."

The computer is the specter that newspaper employees fear. It was one of the causes of the 25-day newspaper strike and shut-down in New York City in September and October.

Employees want protection from automation. In New York City, the American Newspaper Guild sought a job-security clause in its contract with *The*

New York Times. When the *Times* refused to meet this and other Guild requests, the union struck. All other city newspapers but the *Post* shut down. In the middle of the strike/shut-down, the *Herald Tribune* resumed publication. A complicating factor in the negotiations was the unwillingness of publishers to grant to the Guild what they had given the craft unions that operate machinery: a veto power over the installation of new machinery. (Before the strike, the *Post* installed a computer but removed it when the typographical union objected.)

The strike was settled when the *Times* agreed to grant job protection to all employees at work at the time the contract was signed.

Face-Lifting. Newspapers paid attention to their looks during the year. The standard column width, about two inches, was increased by the *Christian Science Monitor*, the *Dallas News*, the *Louisville Courier-Journal*, and others. This was accomplished by reducing the number of columns on a page from the usual eight to five or six. The use of color in advertisements leaped so fast that more than one-third of the newspapers were equipped to serve advertisers who want color reproduction.

Marshall Field, 49, editor and publisher of the Chicago *Sun-Times* and the *Chicago Daily News* and publisher of Field Enterprises Educational Corporation, which publishes THE WORLD BOOK ENCYCLOPEDIA, died in September of a heart attack. Marshall Field, Jr., became assistant to the general manager of both newspapers and a director of the Educational Corporation. Roy M. Fisher, formerly executive editor of THE WORLD BOOK YEAR BOOK and SCIENCE YEAR, which are published by the Educational Corporation, became editor of the *Daily News*.

Robert C. Ruark, also 49, died in London in 1965. He was a nationally syndicated columnist and best-selling author.

Books. A distinguished U.S. firm, Alfred A. Knopf, celebrated its 50th anniversary. Knopf is famous for the high quality of its list, the visual excellence of its books, and the introduction into the United States of many top-flight European writers. Two mergers occurred. Dell Publishing Company bought Barnes & Noble, and Crowell-Collier purchased The Macmillan Company.

Magazines. *The New Yorker* was 40 years old in February. *The Nation* celebrated its 100th birthday. *The Journal of the History of Ideas* celebrated its 25th, and the *National Review* was 10 years of age in 1965. One major magazine, *Show*, went out of business, despite a circulation of 200,000.

The Minneapolis *Star & Tribune* purchased a 50 per cent interest in the 114-year-old *Harper's Magazine*. The book house, Harper & Row, retained the other half interest in the magazine.

In sum, the concern among magazine publishers that marked the past few years was gone in 1965, buried beneath an estimated $1,000,000,000 in advertising revenue.

MELVIN MENCHER

PUERTO RICO saw its economy grow by approximately 10 per cent in the fiscal year ended June 30. The only sector that continued to decline was agriculture. It had been plagued by drought. Investments in machinery and equipment and in new businesses, however, reached $57,499,550. This was more than quadruple the $13,301,000 figure for 1963-1964. Tourism swelled the economy by $110,000,000. The purchasing power of the wage earner's dollar, however, dropped from 88 cents to 86 cents due to a 2.4 per cent rise in the consumer price index.

The Commonwealth Oil Refining Company opened an aromatics plant at its $41,000,000 petrochemical complex in Penallas during the year. It also announced plans for a $4,500,000 ethylbenzene facility, a $10,000,000 to $12,000,000 paraxylene plant (in partnership with Hercules Powder Company), and a $4,000,000 cyclohexane facility (with a member of the Royal Dutch Shell Oil group). Phillips Petroleum Corporation worked on plans for a potential $600,000,000 petrochemical program, but actual production was deferred until December, when the oil imports and quota system was clarified in Washington, D.C. (see PETROLEUM AND GAS).

Population: 2,349,544. **Government:** Governor Roberto Sanchez Vilella. **Monetary Unit:** U.S. $1. **Foreign Trade:** exports, $830,000,000; imports, $1,146,000,000. **Principal Exports:** food products, textiles, vegetables.

MARY C. WEBSTER

PULITZER PRIZES in journalism, literature, and art were announced on May 3, 1965, following recommendations by the Advisory Board of the Pulitzer School of Journalism at Columbia University.

The music prize was withheld for the second consecutive year (see MUSIC). No prize was awarded for an editorial cartoon. The other prizes were conferred as follows:

For the Most Disinterested and Meritorious Public Service Rendered by a U.S. Newspaper: a gold medal to *The Hutchinson News* for its crusade and successful suit in state courts that forced the Kansas senate to be reapportioned on a population basis.

For a Distinguished Example of Reporting on International Affairs: $1,000 to Joseph A. Livingston, *The Philadelphia Bulletin* financial editor, for his articles on the economic independence of Russia's East Europe satellite countries.

For a Distinguished Example of Reporting on National Affairs: $1,000 to Louis M. Kohlmeier of *The Wall Street Journal's* Washington (D.C.) bureau for his articles on the growth of the fortune of President Lyndon B. Johnson and his family.

For a Distinguished Example of Local Reporting: *General Reporting*, $1,000 to Melvin H. Ruder, founder (1946), publisher, editor, and reporter of *The Hungry Horse News*, Columbia Falls, Mont., for his coverage of the floods in the northwestern part of the state in 1964. *Special Reporting*, $1,000 to Gene Goltz of *The Houston Post* for his exposure of government corruption in Pasadena, Tex., which resulted in reforms there.

For a Distinguished Example of Editorial Writing: $1,000 to John R. Harrison of *The Gainesville* (Fla.) *Sun* for his editorials on housing conditions, which

QUEBEC

helped win municipal approval of a minimum housing code.

For an Outstanding Example of News Photography: $1,000 to German-born Horst Faas, a combat photographer of The Associated Press, for his pictures of the war in South Vietnam.

For the Best Nonfiction by an American Author: $500 to Howard Mumford Jones for *O Strange New World.* See JONES, HOWARD MUMFORD.

For the Best Fiction by an American Author: $500 to Shirley Ann Grau for *The Keepers of the House.* See GRAU, SHIRLEY ANN.

For a Distinguished Book of the Year on U.S. History: $500 to Irwin Unger for *The Greenback Era.* See UNGER, IRWIN.

For a Distinguished Biography or Autobiography Preferably on an American Subject: $500 to Ernest Samuels for his three-volume *Henry Adams.* See SAMUELS, ERNEST.

For the Best Original American Play: $500 to Frank D. Gilroy for *The Subject Was Roses.* See GILROY, FRANK D.; THEATER.

For a Distinguished Volume of Verse by an American Author: $500 to John Berryman for *77 Dream Songs.* See BERRYMAN, JOHN.

Traveling Fellowships to the highest ranking graduates of the Columbia University Graduate School of Journalism for a year of travel and study abroad, $2,000 each to: David E. Rosenbaum of Tampa, Fla.; Richard J. Pothier of Quincy, Mass.; and Robert D. Lee of Estherville, Iowa.

Fellowship in Critical Writing, $1,500 to Richard C. Kostelanetz, who planned a year's study of such arts as music and painting at Columbia University in New York City.

QUEBEC. See CANADA.

RABORN, WILLIAM FRANCIS, JR. (1905-   ),

retired U.S. Navy vice-admiral who directed the development of the Polaris missile, became director of the Central Intelligence Agency (CIA) on April 22. He succeeded John A. McCone, 63, a former industrialist, who retired.

Raborn had been deputy chief of naval operations, directing research, when he retired from the navy in September, 1963. He then became vice-president of program management for Aerojet-General Corporation of Azusa, Calif., a large electronics and missile manufacturing firm. He had worked on guided missile development since 1949 and was regarded as a skillful administrator.

The new director of the CIA was born June 8, 1905, in Decatur, Tex., one of eight children, and grew up in Marlow, Okla. He was graduated from the U.S. Naval Academy in 1928. He became a naval aviator in 1934. After varied peacetime service, he established the Aviation Gunnery School at Pearl Harbor. During World War II, he served as executive officer on the carrier *Hancock* in the Pacific.

Raborn was decorated for conspicuous gallantry as the executive officer of the *Hancock.* He was advanced to vice-admiral in 1960. He and Mrs. Raborn, the former Mildred T. Terrell, have two children, a daughter and a son.   WALTER F. MORSE

RACING. See AUTOMOBILE RACING; BOATS AND BOATING; HARNESS RACING; HORSE RACING; TRACK AND FIELD.

RADIO. It was dramatically demonstrated on Nov. 9, 1965, that radio is the Number 1 communications lifeline for the public in a national emergency.

When the Northeast blacked out, its citizens relied almost entirely on transistor radios for news and guidance throughout the emergency.

During the blackout, the stations were run on auxiliary power. Many of them, once they got back on the air, suspended commercials. Manhattan's WNYC called off-duty firemen and policemen to service. The stations helped keep an atmosphere of calm by recounting little acts of heroism performed during the night. And they dispensed a good deal of practical advice. They told families what to do with their oil burners and their refrigerators. They asked the citizenry to stay off the telephones and warned listeners to beware of thawed frozen foods.

Wrote *New York Times* TV critic Jack Gould: "The tireless commentators of the major stations injected...relaxed humor and...comraderie that undoubtedly contributed to the city's calmness."

A week after the big power failure, Radio Corporation of America (RCA) announced its new lowest priced transistor radio ($9.95). RCA forecast that the sale of portable transistor radios of all makes would reach an all-time high of over 5,500,000 units in 1965. At the same time, the Electronic Industries Association reported 1965 radio sales in all categories (home, FM, and auto) were up over 1964.

In Programing, networks continued to emphasize news coverage while local stations discovered talk shows. Disk jockeys received strong competition from a flock of hot-line, call-in shows around the nation. The programs spotlighted phone inquiries from listeners on a wide variety of subjects.

There were more new applications for AM radio stations than ever, and station sales were strong.

Crosley Broadcasting purchased WWDC-AM-FM in Washington, D.C., for more than $4,000,000, and KEWB (Oakland, Calif.) was sold by Crowell-Collier to Metromedia for $2,500,000.

One 1965 station sale was of deep concern to many in the radio industry. It was the sale of pro-civil rights outlet WBOX, Bogalusa, La., after monthly revenues fell from $4,000 to $400 as the result of an advertisers' boycott allegedly inspired by the Ku Klux Klan. Prior to its sale, WBOX received financial assistance from many broadcasters around the country for several months.

According to official Federal Communications Commission figures, radio time sales (network, local, and national spot) for 1964 were up 7.3 per cent (to $763,768,000) over the previous all-time high of 1963. A *Broadcasting Magazine* survey of top local and network representatives revealed that 1965 would be an even better year for radio, with predictions of billing increases ranging from 12 to 15 per cent.   JUNE BUNDY CSIDA

See also ELECTRIC POWER; TELEVISION.

RAILROAD. See TRANSPORTATION.

RECORDINGS. A technological development in 1965 seemed on its way to becoming the most important innovation in the recording field since the introduction of the long-playing record. It was the appearance on the mass market of slow-motion tapes, both in cartridge and open-reel forms. With slow-motion tapes, playing at $1\frac{7}{8}$ to $3\frac{3}{4}$ inches per second, the economic gap between the less expensive disk recordings and tapes was almost closed. This was primarily because more music could be put on less tape. For example, the new (open reel) Maria Callas version of *Tosca* was available on one compact reel, and 12 Haydn symphonies, conducted by Sir Thomas Beecham, became a two-reel set.

Auto Stereo. Public reaction was strong and intense. Open-reel tapes were sold principally for home use. Cartridge tapes were sold for use in automobiles. Many listeners felt that the enveloping sound of four-speaker stereo, as heard in a car, was even more exciting than conventional two-speaker home stereo. By installing four loudspeakers, two on either side of the car, and by feeding a sealed cartridge into a small transistorized player, the driver could hear music, theoretically forever, because one end of the tape was looped to the other.

Automobile stereo was soon engaged in the battle of the systems, a battle similar to the one that took place in 1950, when one company's introduction of the 45 rpm record upset plans for a single-speed $33\frac{1}{3}$ rpm industry. Since 1962, most cartridges had been equipped to play four-channel stereo. During 1965, eight-track tape cartridges, carrying twice the amount of recorded material, were introduced.

The two systems were not compatible, and some 1966 automobiles were equipped (optionally) with eight-track players, which were useless for the more common four-track tapes. Confusion reigned among the buying public, for in 1965 there were more than 5,000 four-track cartridges on sale, plus a few hundred eight-track tapes.

Two Historic Recordings of classical music were released. One was an album of the return of pianist Vladimir Horowitz to Carnegie Hall. The other was the recording of the *Fourth Symphony* of the late U.S. composer Charles Ives. See MUSIC.

Broadway and Hollywood were again the sources of popular recordings. The original cast album of the Broadway musical, *The Roar of the Greasepaint, the Smell of the Crowd*, was well received. One song from the show "Who Can I Turn To?" showed signs of becoming a standard favorite. Among the many albums of Hollywood origin were those featuring music from the motion pictures *Goldfinger*, *The Sandpiper*, and *Mary Poppins*.

Total sales of albums and single records reached close to the $500,000,000 mark during the year. According to industry estimates, 68 per cent of single record buyers were 19 years old or younger, while 66 per cent of the purchasers of sets of long-playing records were 20 or older.   LEONARD G. FEATHER

RECORDINGS FOR CHILDREN. An outstandingly successful motion picture, Walt Disney's *Mary Poppins*, dominated children's records throughout 1965. Numerous versions of the score, available in editions ranging in price from 99-cent budget disks to $3.98 packages, helped make 1965 one of Disneyland Records biggest years.

Television also played a major role in the field. Successful shows, such as "The Munsters" and "The Addams Family," were enough to inspire Golden Records to put out its own "Famous Monsters" LP.

Each year the best recordings for children are rated by a poll sponsored by the National Academy of Recording Arts and Sciences. The ratings are based on artistic excellence, not on sales results. The best record of the year, according to the poll, was the "Young Person's Guide to the Orchestra," by Benjamin Britten. On this disk, produced by RCA Victor, Arthur Fiedler conducts his Boston Pops Orchestra, and Hugh Downs narrates.

In second place was "Chim Chim Cheree and other Children's Favorites," by Burl Ives and the Children's Choir. Next in order of merit were "Daniel Boone," with Fess Parker; the *Mary Poppins* soundtrack album; and "A Spoonful of Sugar" (also from "Poppins"), recorded by Mary Martin and the Do Re Mi Children's Chorus.   REN GREVATT

RECREATION. See FAIRS AND EXHIBITIONS; HUNTING AND FISHING; OUTDOOR RECREATION; PARKS.

RED CROSS offices and chapters were directed to adhere to policies of nondiscrimination by the National Board of Governors. All units were advised of the action by Chairman E. Roland Harriman and President James F. Collins.

The policy statement which cited the organization's traditional ideal of humanitarian service, read as follows:

"In the performance of its manifold humanitarian services the policy and practice of the American Red Cross have been and will continue to be based on the fundamental concepts that no person shall be deprived of Red Cross service because of his race, religious beliefs, or national origin.

"That no person shall in receiving Red Cross service be segregated on the basis of such criteria in facilities controlled by the Red Cross.

"With respect to both volunteer and paid staff of the Red Cross there shall be no discrimination based on such criteria in regard to recruitment, assignment or promotion, or other conditions of employment."

The board of governors also decided to list any student who takes part in or contributes to a Red Cross service program as a youth member of the American Red Cross.

World Red Cross Day was observed on May 8, with the theme highlighting what young people are doing through the organization.   JOSEPH P. ANDERSON

RELIGION. See EASTERN ORTHODOX; JEWS AND JUDAISM; PROTESTANT; ROMAN CATHOLIC.

REPUBLICAN PARTY

Leaders of the Republican party struggled to build a façade of unity after the disastrous national elections of 1964. Their first major move was to replace a symbol of the defeat, Dean Burch of Arizona, as chairman of the Republican National Committee, with Ray C. Bliss, Ohio state party chairman. But even this change was accomplished in an atmosphere of tension and discord. It revealed a deep philosophical split, which had first manifested itself with the nomination of Senator Barry M. Goldwater of Arizona as the party's presidential nominee in 1964.

As Goldwater's hand-picked national party chairman, Burch repre-

Pictorial Parade

sented the ultraconservative elements. To most moderate and liberal Republicans, he took a narrow view of all other elements in the party and thus was regarded as a divisive influence. Bliss, on the other hand, spurned all labels of ideology and looked upon himself simply as a political technician and administrator, or in his own words, as a "nuts and bolts man." But almost before he could firmly assume control of the party machinery, he was embroiled in the dispute between conservatives and the moderate-liberals.

Associates of Goldwater had formed the Free Society Association, with the former Senator as its honorary chairman. They described it as a conservative "political education" group, denying that it was a "splinter" group that would frustrate efforts to reunite all factions of the party. Other party leaders, however, felt it would seek to perpetuate the Goldwater philosophy and divert badly needed funds from the party treasury.

Party elders also were disturbed by the activity of the militantly conservative John Birch Society. Senate Minority Leader Everett M. Dirksen, Senator Thruston B. Morton of Kentucky and a former national chairman, as well as former Vice-President Richard M. Nixon, condemned the views and actions of the far right wing group. See JOHN BIRCH SOCIETY.

New Unity Group. Under Bliss' chairmanship, the party hoped to pull together the diverse strands of acceptable philosophy in a group known as the Republican Coordinating Committee. It consisted of party congressional leaders, governors, and such eminent leaders as former President Dwight D. Eisenhower and former presidential candidates Thomas E. Dewey and Nixon. Its aim was to plan party strategy and develop a coherent and effective political opposition to the party in power. But with Goldwater a member, it found itself bickering over party doctrine and the insistence of the splinter groups to stay in business.

Bliss managed to make wholesale changes in the national committee staff and to attract General Lucius D. Clay, a close adviser to former President

REPUBLICANS' GLAMOR CANDIDATE John V. Lindsay mingles with the crowd on his way to winning New York City's 1965 mayoral election.

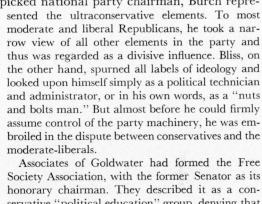

Wide World

FORMER PRESIDENTIAL NOMINEES meet to update the Republican platform. They are, from left, Barry Goldwater, Dwight Eisenhower, Richard Nixon, Thomas Dewey.

Eisenhower, as national finance chairman. Aware of the importance of state party organizations, Bliss recognized that the Republicans had a powerful nucleus in the governorships of a third of the states, especially in the populous states of Michigan, New York, Ohio, Pennsylvania, and Wisconsin.

In the Congress, although in the minority by lopsided margins, Republicans sought to find alternatives to President Lyndon B. Johnson's "Great Society" proposals. They either attempted to modify the proposals by amendments, or opposed them outright when they ran counter to traditional Republican positions.

An example of determined opposition was the successful fight led by Senator Dirksen of Illinois against the repeal of Section 14(b) of the Taft-Hartley Act. That section permits individual states to pass so-called "right to work" laws, which forbid the union shop (see CONGRESS OF THE UNITED STATES). In the House, Minority Leader Gerald R. Ford of Michigan directed most of his criticism at the President's conduct of the war in Vietnam (see FORD, GERALD R.).

But generally, the Republicans made little headway against the overwhelming Democratic majorities in both House and Senate. Republican spokesmen warned against the intrusion of the federal government into areas of state and local responsibility—notably in education, urban affairs, and social welfare. Predictions were freely made that many of the new programs would be difficult to administer and therefore susceptible to mismanagement and ineffectiveness.

The most notable Republican endeavor in the foreign field was a critique of the government's policy toward the North Atlantic Treaty Organization (NATO) and the Western alliance by a committee led by Representative Paul Findley of Illinois. Its findings were critical of U.S. efforts to monopolize the alliance and urged a greater dissemination of Allied officers in the NATO command structure. In the main, however, Republicans supported administration policies in Vietnam and the Dominican Republic to a far greater extent than many Democrats.

The 1965 Elections gave the party little cause to be heartened, particularly in the gubernatorial races in New Jersey and Virginia. Many were confident that New Jersey's incumbent Democratic Governor Richard J. Hughes could be unseated by state Senator Wayne Dumont, Jr. Dumont chose to devote most of his campaign to the case of a Rutgers University professor who had expressed a hope that the Communist Viet Cong would win in the war against South Vietnamese and American forces. Hughes defended the state university professor on the grounds of academic freedom, and apparently the people of New Jersey agreed. Dumont lost by 350,000 votes, the largest margin in state history, despite the support he got from Nixon.

In Virginia, a Roanoke attorney, A. Linwood Holton, Jr., was thought to have an excellent chance to defeat the Democratic candidate, Lieutenant Governor Mills E. Godwin, Jr. Both men campaigned as moderates and made strong bids for labor, Negro, and urban votes. The outcome, however, painfully showed the results of the doctrinal division within the Republican party. Because of Holton's moderate approach, the Virginia Conservative party entered a candidate, William J. Story, Jr., whose vote total added to Holton's might have elected the Republican. However, political observers concluded that Story probably drained off some conservative Democratic votes from Godwin as well.

Scattered Successes were scored by Republicans in municipal elections. An erstwhile Democrat, Arlen Specter, won the district attorney's race in Philadelphia under the Republican banner. Specter had the support of Governor William W. Scranton and U.S. Senator Hugh Scott. His victory represented the party's first triumph in 12 years in that Democratic-controlled city.

Far and away the most dramatic election was the contest for mayor of New York City. In John V. Lindsay—who won impressively as a "fusion" candidate under the broad banner of the Republican, Liberal, and Independent Citizens labels—the Republicans may have found a potentially glamor-

ous national candidate for the future. Lindsay—at 44, a graduate of Yale, a Congressman from Manhattan's 17th District since 1959, tall, handsome, and articulate—was being hailed as "a Republican Kennedy" almost before the returns were in. Although he shunned the Republican label in predominantly Democratic New York, Lindsay gave the moderate-liberal elements in his party a great boost in morale by his clear-cut victory over Democrat Abraham Beame. See ELECTIONS; LINDSAY, JOHN V.; NEW YORK CITY.

Lindsay ruled out any national aspirations during his four years as mayor. While political experts tended to take such declarations with a grain of salt, they believed Lindsay must move considerably toward the center. With his liberal record in Congress, the party's conservatives would find it hard to endorse him as a national candidate.

Republican leaders realized that much will depend upon the forces that ultimately gain control of the party. Assumptions were made that Lindsay's victory in New York and moderate-liberal candidates' strong showings in other industrial urban areas would convince the party that a more moderate course than that of the 1964 campaign was the Republicans' best chance for repairing their national fortunes.   PETER LISAGOR

See also CITY; DEMOCRATIC PARTY; STATE GOVERNMENT.

RESOR, STANLEY R. (1917-   ), a Republican, was sworn in on July 7, 1965, as Secretary of the U.S. Army. For three months preceding the swearing-in ceremonies, he had served as undersecretary of the department of the army. Resor's nomination as secretary had been submitted by President Lyndon B. Johnson on June 18. It was confirmed by the Senate on June 30. Resor succeeded Stephen Ailes, who had resigned to return to private law practice in Washington, D. C.

The new secretary of the army was born on Dec. 5, 1917. He attended Yale University, from which he graduated in 1939 with a B.A. degree. In 1946, he graduated from Yale Law School with his LL.B. degree. During World War II, Resor served with the U.S. Army in Belgium, France, and Germany. He was awarded the coveted Silver Star for heroism. Entering the service as a second lieutenant, Resor rose to the rank of major.

In 1947, Resor began the practice of law in New York City. A member of the firm of Debevoise, Plimpton, Lyons and Gates, he was noted for forensic skills and a cool detachment of mind that made him a formidable legal opponent.

Before coming to Washington, D.C., the new secretary of the army made his home in New Canaan, Conn. His wife, the former Jane Lawler Pillsbury, is the daughter of John Pillsbury, a former chairman of the board of directors of the Pillsbury Flour Mill Company.   WALTER F. MORSE

"It followed me home. Can I keep it?"

RETAILING. At Tiffany's Manhattan store a sterling silver service for eight, including gold-finished plates, sold for $9,000 in 1965; prices on a single place setting of sterling silver flatware ranged from $45 to $90. Tiffany's total silverware sales were a booming 20 per cent ahead of 1964.

It was a measure of the spending mood of affluent Americans in 1965. Another reading was provided by a report from the retailers of tuxedos, tail coats, and formal wear accessories. Their sales topped $55,000,000, a record.

The nation's number-one retailer, Austin T. Cushman, chairman of the board of Sears, Roebuck and Co., summed up the situation. He repeated his 1964 observation that Christmas season sales would be limited only by the physical ability to move people through the stores in the hours available— with this difference for 1965: The retailers had built themselves more stores.

Retail Sales increased, all told, a whopping 8 per cent in 1965, to about $282,700,000,000, an increase of $21,100,000,000 over the 1964 total. The general merchandise sector—department, discount, variety, and mail order stores—ran about 13 per cent ahead of the 1964 pace. And wholesalers' total sales rose more than 6 per cent above the 1964 volume of $164,580,000,000. Merchandising—retail and wholesale—by September, 1965, was providing more than a fifth of all U.S. nonfarm jobs.

Disposable personal income, the amount people had to spend after such things as taxes, was at an all-time high (see ECONOMY, THE). With Americans typically spending a good 93 per cent of disposable income, it was not hard to understand the boom.

Two Other Sales-Boosting Factors during 1965 were tax cuts and increases in Social Security benefits. At midyear, many federal excise taxes were abolished or reduced, eliminating a total of $1,750,000,000 in levies on such things as jewelry and luggage. In effect, it cut the consumer price.

Social Security benefits to those over age 62 were increased, retroactive to Jan. 1, 1965, adding to the money available for spending. (But Congress also voted to increase Social Security paycheck deductions to the tune of $2,500,000,000 effective Jan. 1, 1966.) See SOCIAL SECURITY; TAXATION.

Americans were spending smaller and smaller shares of their incomes on food and more on durable goods, such as TV sets and cars. See FOOD.

Another noticeable trend in 1965 retailing was the comeback of the downtown stores. Two factors were apparent: the tremendous rebuilding in the central cities and the comparative slowdown in the growth of the suburbs (see CITY). Underscoring this trend was the announcement late in the year that Bergdorf Goodman will open its first branch store—not in a suburb, but in the 100-story John Hancock Center, abuilding in Chicago. New York City's specialty store hoped to open its Chicago branch in July, 1968 (see ARCHITECTURE).   EDWIN W. DARBY

RHODESIA attracted world-wide attention on Nov. 11, 1965, when Prime Minister Ian D. Smith, the leader of the white minority government, unilaterally declared Rhodesia independent from Great Britain. The declaration followed Britain's refusal to grant the colony independence unless the minority government, firmly in the hands of some 224,000 whites, took steps to assure eventual majority rule for the country's 4,126,000 blacks. Britain had demanded eventual rule for the African majority and immediate improvement in their political and social status.

Britain denounced the Smith declaration as treasonable, expelled Rhodesia from the pound sterling area, and suspended its preferential tariff treatment. Controls on trade and currency were imposed, and a ban was placed on the purchase of Rhodesia's main crops, tobacco and sugar. Britain's Prime Minister Harold Wilson rejected the use of force to bring about change but reserved the right to send troops to maintain law and order. See UNITED NATIONS (UN).

Throughout the weeks leading up to the unilateral declaration of independence, there had been considerable unrest, including an attempt at a general strike and a certain amount of civil disturbance. Most of the antigovernment agitation had been promoted by the black nationalists who had hoped to weaken the government and force the British to put troops in Rhodesia to restore order. Their activities, however, had been rendered ineffective by strong police action.

The day following Rhodesia's declaration, Prime Minister Smith ordered Sir Humphrey Gibbs to step down as Governor-General. Gibbs, however, refused, declaring: "I hold office by pleasure of Her Majesty . . . I remain your lawful Governor and the lawfully constituted authority in Rhodesia."

To prevent Britain's claim as Rhodesia's lawful ruler from being published, Smith imposed tight press censorship. He also issued an emergency regulation making it a crime for a radio to be turned on in a public place if a broadcast might "endanger public safety."

The strongest reaction to Rhodesia's declaration of independence came from other African countries. On their urging, the United Nations Security Council condemned Rhodesia and called on all states to deny Rhodesia recognition or assistance of any kind. The Organization of African Unity (OAU) threatened military intervention in Rhodesia and the breaking off of diplomatic relations with Britain unless Britain took immediate steps to crush the "illegal" Rhodesian government. The United States responded by announcing a comprehensive embargo on shipments of military equipment to Rhodesia.

Neighboring Zambia (formerly Northern Rhodesia), fearful that Rhodesia would cut off power from the Kariba Dam, called on British troops to protect its border and the dam which is shared by

Wide World

A FATEFUL ACT was performed by Rhodesian Prime Minister Ian Smith, who
signed a document that unilaterally declared his country independent of Britain.

both Zambia and Rhodesia. The British reacted by
sending an air force squadron to Zambia.

At year's end, the trade embargo imposed on
Rhodesia was taxing the country's resources, and
the government imposed austerity measures, including gasoline rationing. Under the gas-rationing
plan, however, doctors, diplomats, and disabled
persons, as well as such government departments as
the railroads, the Central African Airways, and the
Central African Power Corporation were exempt.

On December 31, the government of Prime
Minister Smith announced changes in the cabinet.
The Duke of Montrose, who had held the ministry
of agriculture, became minister of external affairs
and defense. He succeeded Clifford Du Pont, who
was named officer administering the government.
George W. Rudland, minister of transport and
power, also took the agriculture portfolio. His responsibility for traffic and roads went to Basil T.
Musset, minister of local government and housing.

Population: 4,350,000. **Government:** Prime Minister Ian D. Smith. **Monetary Unit:** pound (1 =
U.S. $2.80). **Gross National Product:** $878,000,000.
Foreign Trade: exports, $627,000,000; imports,
$377,000,000. **Principal Exports:** asbestos, chrome
ore, gold, tobacco.   BENJAMIN E. THOMAS

See also AFRICA.

RHODESIA AND NYASALAND, FEDERATION OF.
See MALAWI; RHODESIA; ZAMBIA.

ROADS AND HIGHWAYS. Road construction
was being used as the chief means of aiding the
depressed 11-state Appalachian region under a new
federal program enacted in March, 1965. The Appalachian Regional Development Act of 1965 provided up to 70 per cent of the cost for a 2,350-mile
network of developmental highways in Appalachia
and of 1,000 miles of access roads. The expected
federal cost for the six-year period from July, 1965,
to July, 1971, was about $840,000,000. It was the
first federal highway program since the early days
of U.S. road construction to be focused primarily
on economic growth.

The Highway Beautification Act became law on
October 22. President Lyndon B. Johnson said the
bill "does not represent all we want, or all we need
. . . but it is a first step." He had referred to the
measure as "Lady Bird's Bill," because of the First
Lady's energetic campaigning for it after suggesting
the legislation to him.

The law authorized the use of federal funds to
compensate owners for the removal by July, 1970,
of billboards and junkyards within 660 feet and
1,000 feet, respectively, of rural highways, both
interstate and primary. States would pay one-fourth
and the federal government three-fourths of the
costs. Federal limits of $20,000,000 a year were
placed on each program for fiscal 1966 and 1967.

The act also allocated 3 per cent of each state's
federal highway aid fund for landscaping and beau-

tifying roadsides. No matching was necessary. A top limit of $120,000,000 was put on this use in each of fiscal years 1966 and 1967.

Interstate Progress. Nearly half of the 41,000-mile National System of Interstate and Defense Highways was open to traffic at year's end. Almost 2,500 miles were completed during 1965. Construction was underway on an additional 6,200 miles. The program, begun in 1956, was to be completed by 1972, with the federal government bearing 90 per cent of the cost. Total federal expenditures and authorizations under the program stood at over $21,000,000,000. In August, Congress authorized the apportionment of some $3,000,000,000 from the federal Highway Trust Fund for fiscal year 1967. Total cost of the program was expected to reach $46,800,000,000 by 1972.

Among those 2,500 new miles of 1965 highway was an 11-mile stretch of Interstate 91 in Connecticut—from Meriden to a few miles south of Hartford. That last link in no-traffic-light driving from New York City to Boston opened on October 28.

Across the country a month earlier, U.S. Secretary of Commerce John T. Connor dedicated a 245-mile length of Interstate 70—St. Louis to Kansas City, Mo. Driving time was $3\frac{3}{4}$ hours.

Work also went ahead on the federal aid primary and secondary highway systems. Edwin T. Haefele

See also Automobile; Safety; Transportation.

ROCHE, JAMES MICHAEL

ROCHE, JAMES MICHAEL (1906-), who started in the automobile industry in 1927, was elected president and chief operating officer of General Motors Corporation on June 1, 1965. He succeeded John F. Gordon, 65, who retired. The position, in the world's largest manufacturing concern, pays $700,000 a year and up. Since 1962, Roche had been executive vice-president responsible for foreign operations, for the household appliance and engine group, and for the Allison division. Before that, he had been vice-president for distribution, directing the marketing of all GM cars.

Most of his career was with GM's Cadillac division, directing sales of the most expensive auto in the corporation's line. He was born in Elgin, Ill., on Dec. 16, 1906. Roche was graduated from Elgin High School in 1923. He was briefly a co-operator of a service station in that Chicago suburb, then became a statistician for a utility in nearby Aurora.

His GM career began in 1927 as a statistician for a Cadillac sales and service branch in Chicago. In 1935 Roche was moved to Detroit as head of the Cadillac business management department. He became the division's personnel director in 1943 and general sales manager from 1950 to 1957. He is credited with producing large sales of GM products in Canada and in other nations. His wife, his high school sweetheart, is the former Louise C. McMillan. They have two sons and a daughter, and four grandchildren. Walter F. Morse

ROMAN CATHOLIC. The fourth and final session of Vatican Council II opened on September 14, with Pope Paul VI concelebrating Mass with 26 council fathers. In his opening address, the Holy Father characterized the entire Vatican Council II as the spirit of love for God, the church, and all mankind. Regretting the enforced absence of some members of the church from communist countries, he nevertheless extended his love to all, including the very ones who prevented their attendance. He also announced the setting up of an Episcopal Synod of bishops for collaboration and consultation.

Council Documents. Eleven new documents were added to the five promulgated by the end of the third session, which were: Constitution of the Sacred Liturgy, Decree on the Media of Social Communication, Constitution on the Nature of the Church, Decree on the Eastern Rite Church, and Decree on Ecumenism. The ones promulgated on October 28 were: Decree on the Pastoral Office of Bishops in the Church; Decree on the Adaptation and Renewal of the Religious Life, with greater emphasis on direct apostolic action and modification of dress; Decree on Priestly Training; Declaration on Christian Education, including parental obligations; and Declaration on the Church's Relations with non-Christian Religions, including the condemnation of displays of anti-Semitism and a denouncing of all prejudice and discrimination on the basis of race, religion, nationality, or tribe.

After promulgating a Decree of the Constitution on Divine Revelation and a Decree of the Lay Apostolate on November 18, Pope Paul VI announced plans for the convocation of the aforementioned Episcopal Synod in 1967, the reorganization of the Roman Curia, the imminent publication of new Statutes for the Sacred Congregation of the Holy Office now to be known as the Congregation for the Doctrine of the Faith, the beginning of processes for the beatification of Pope Pius XII and Pope John XXIII, the building of a church in Rome in memory of the council, and a special Jubilee of the Church beginning on January 1, 1966, and lasting until Pentecost (May 29, 1966).

Four final texts were promulgated December 7. These were a Declaration on Religious Liberty, a Decree on Priestly Life and Ministry, a Decree on Pastoral Constitution of the Church in the Modern World, and a Decree on the Church's Missionary Activity. The mission schema establishes an international commission for the unification of mission activity and to bring aid from clergy and laity to the poor in body and soul of the entire world.

On the same day, joint declarations were read in

POPE PAUL addressed the UN General Assembly on October 4. Behind him are, left to right, U Thant, Amintore Fanfani, and C. V. Narasimhan.

Vatican Council II, Church in Transition

"*Ite in Pace!*" (Go in peace!) With these words Pope Paul VI dismissed the bishops and fathers of Vatican Council II on Dec. 8, 1965, thus concluding the most important religious event of this decade, perhaps of this century.

What did Vatican Council II actually accomplish? Final answers to this question will have to await the verdict of history, for some of the most revolutionary decisions of the council fathers must be carried out at national and local levels before their true implications can be measured.

Nevertheless, the main outlines of the renewal brought about by the council seem to most observers, both inside and outside Roman Catholicism, to be these:

• It seems fairly safe to assert that the decisions of the council on religious liberty represent the most dramatic change in official policy. The decree affirming the right of individual worship clearly represents a step that promises far-reaching changes in the relations among the various faiths and between Church and state throughout the world.

• The trend toward the centralization of administrative authority in the Roman Catholic church, which began even before the Middle Ages, seems to have been reversed by the reaffirmation of the "collegiality" of bishops. This means that in the exercise of his office as ruler and teacher of the church, the pope is not a solitary master, nor even a benevolent despot, but the principal member of a community of authority that he shares with other bishops.

• The people do not *belong* to the church, they *are* the church. Vatican Council II, therefore, devoted a large part of its deliberations to the priestly ministry of the laity in the church and in the world. So marked was this trend that "a theology of the laity" threatened to become a cliché—a danger faced by very few earlier councils. Part of this rediscovery was embodied in the decrees restricting the use of Latin in worship and approving the vernacular languages.

• Throughout the council, accredited observers from other Christian groups

The Spirit of Ecumenism.

were the guests of the church. This symbolized the concern of the church for a new relation among all Christians. Not only the observers, however, but the entire Christian world, had a real sense of participation. Unlike previous "ecumenical councils," Vatican Council II was ecumenical in spirit, as well as in form.

• Nor was the horizon of the council restricted to the Christian world. Jewish-Christian relations entered a new phase with the decree condemning anti-Semitism, and the affirmation of the values of other religions opened the door for fruitful dialogue on a world scale.

But, there were, of course, certain disappointments. Some questions were postponed or sidetracked. Some documents seemed watered-down in the interests of compromise.

The teaching of the church about birth control received a great deal of unofficial attention, but the pope reserved further decisions for a later time. The relation between the Bible and tradition is the subject for further study. Nevertheless, almost everyone would agree that the bishops and theologians who had worked at the council through its four sessions had the right to heed the farewell of Pope Paul and to "go in peace" after a job well done.   JAROSLAV PELIKAN

See also Section Two, PATHS TO DIALOGUE.

A
YEAR
BOOK
CLOSE-UP

Rome and Istanbul bringing mutual excommunications between the representatives of the Roman Catholic and the Eastern Orthodox churches to an end. This annulment represents the greatest reconciliation of the two bodies since their schism in 1054. Its announcement resulted in the greatest applause of the entire council by the delegates.

Adjournment. Pope Paul called Vatican Council II, which adjourned December 8, the greatest in the history of the church. Two ideas may sum it up—the first and the last words that Jesus spoke to His Apostles. His first word was "Come." His last words, spoken after the Resurrection and just before He ascended into heaven, were, "Go therefore and make disciples of all nations." The council opened with Pope John XXIII extending his arms to the bishops who are the successors of the Apostles and to the whole world saying "Come, come to Rome." Very fittingly, the last schema to be passed and proclaimed was the one on missions—a beautiful parallel to the final words about making disciples of all nations. The delegates began with liturgy or the "Come into the sanctuary"; they finished with the decree to "Go into the world."

Pope Paul and Peace. The Holy Father asked all to pray for peace in 1965, and peace was his constant concern. The pope sent special appeals toward this end to the hierarchy of Vietnam, to the clergy and people of the Dominican Republic, to the presidents of France and Italy on the occasion of the opening of the Mont Blanc Tunnel, and to the Sudanese premier. He further begged for prayers for peace between India and Pakistan.

An autographed copy of his Bombay address, pleading for peace, was sent to Secretary-General U Thant of the United Nations in January. The Holy Father later suggested that the observances of the 20th anniversary of the signing of the United Nations Charter in San Francisco end with a prayer, warning that "war would be the end not of difficulties, but of civilization."

UN Visit. On October 4, Pope Paul VI brought his message of peace in person to the United Nations in response to the invitation of the Secretary-General. Arriving in New York after the longest nonstop flight ever taken by a pontiff, he was greeted by officials of the United Nations and of the United States. Nearly 4,000,000 New Yorkers cheered him as his car toured many sections of the city on the way to St. Patrick's Cathedral. His visit included a 46-minute meeting with President Lyndon B. Johnson. The pope's principal address was made in the General Assembly Hall of the United Nations. Millions who followed it on radio and television heard his now famous words "No more war, war never again."

Following a meeting with religious leaders of various faiths at the Holy Family Church, he proceeded to the Yankee Stadium to celebrate a papal Mass for peace before 90,000 people. During the Mass, five lectors recited petitions in the official languages of the United Nations: Chinese, English, French, Russian, and Spanish, and 12 children representing the six continents of the world symbolically received Holy Communion for the vast congregation. Stopping briefly at the Vatican Pavilion of the World's Fair, he returned to the airport, closing an unprecedented 14-hour pilgrimage for peace.

Whereas Pope Paul's pilgrimage to the Holy Land, in 1964, was to a civilization that is not Christian, but Jewish and Islamic, and his visit to India the same year brought him closer to Buddhists and Hindus; his United Nations visit signified an involvement with all men of all religions and all races in their common striving for unity and peace. Pope Paul had proclaimed once again, "Blessed are the peacemakers."

Encyclicals. Pope Paul's second encyclical, entitled *Mense Maio* (in the Month of May), appeared May 1, and is another prayer for peace and an appeal for prayers for the council. A third encyclical, *Mysterium Fidei* (The Mystery of the Faith) September 3, defends the doctrine on the Eucharist as established by the Council of Trent in the 16th century. It came in response to recently spread opinions held inconsistent with the meaning of transubstantiation, or the change occurring in the bread and wine at the moment of consecration of the Mass. The encyclical also defends the private celebration of the Mass, when it is not possible to celebrate publicly, and the preservation and adoration of the Eucharist outside of Mass.

New Cardinals. The appointment of 27 cardinals by Pope Paul brought the Sacred College of Cardinals to 103 members, the largest number in history. Representing four continents and 20 countries, the new cardinals include three Eastern Rite Patriarchs, a second Negro African prelate, and three from communist countries, two of whom have been imprisoned. Other new cardinals are from Belgium, Brazil, Ceylon (the first), France, Germany, Italy, Spain, Switzerland (the first in four centuries), and the United States.

World-Wide Ministry. The Catholic population throughout the world increased by more than an estimated 5,500,000 in the past year. In The Philippines, the 400th anniversary of the establishment of Christianity there was celebrated, while the millennium of the founding by St. Aubert of the historic Abbey of Mont St. Michel in France was observed in Europe.

Beatification. Blessed Jacques Berthieu, a missionary killed in Madagascar (1896), was beatified in ceremonies at St. Peter's Church on October 17. On December 5, Blessed Charbel Makholouf, who lived many years as a hermit in the mountains of his native Lebanon, was also beatified at St. Peter's.

U.S. Roman Catholics took an active part in the liturgy. Their population increased by 766,248, reaching 45,640,619. FULTON J. SHEEN

ROMANIA

ROMANIA shifted leadership in March, 1965, following the death of Gheorghe Gheorghiu-Dej, First Secretary of the Romanian Communist party and President of the Council of State. Nicolae Ceausescu succeeded him as first secretary; Chivu Stoica became chairman of the council of state, and Ion Gheorghe Maurer became president of the council of ministers.

The ninth party congress held in July changed its name from the Romanian Workers party to Romanian Communist party and formalized the new name of the nation as the Socialist Republic of Romania. It also approved a new constitution which defined more clearly the rights of citizens.

The regime continued to steer an independent course between Peking and Moscow in their dispute over dogma. In accordance with its "defiance of Moscow" policy, Romania was the only member of the Soviet bloc to vote in the United Nations Political Committee for a resolution calling for an end to all nuclear bomb testing.

Population: 19,422,000. **Government:** Communist Party First Secretary Nicolae Ceausescu; President of the Council of Ministers Ion Gheorghe Maurer. **Monetary Unit:** leu (6=U.S. $1). **Foreign Trade:** exports, $915,000,000; imports, $1,220,000,-000. **Principal Exports:** machinery, petroleum and petroleum products, timber. TOM AND HARLE DAMMANN

See also EUROPE.

ROOSEVELT, FRANKLIN DELANO, JR.,

(1914-   ), was named to a two-year term as chairman of the Equal Employment Opportunity Commission (EEOC) which came into existence on July 2, 1965. The Senate confirmed his nomination, which had been submitted by President Lyndon B. Johnson, on May 26. On that day, Roosevelt resigned as undersecretary of commerce, a position he had held since 1963.

Roosevelt was elected to the U.S. House of Representatives from New York in 1949 to fill the unexpired term of Sol Bloom, following which he was twice re-elected for two-year terms.

Roosevelt is the son of Franklin D. Roosevelt, the 32nd President of the United States. He was born on Campobello Island, New Brunswick, Canada, on Aug. 17, 1914. The new EEOC chairman holds an A.B. degree from Harvard University (1937) and the LL.B. degree from the University of Virginia (1940). He has been married twice and has two sons and two daughters. Aside from his public life, he has been in the automobile business. He served in the navy in World War II, and was decorated for heroism. WALTER F. MORSE.

ROTARY INTERNATIONAL. See SERVICE CLUBS.

ROWING. See SPORTS.

RUANDA-URUNDI. See BURUNDI; RWANDA.

RUBBER. See MANUFACTURING.

RULERS OF THE WORLD. See fact tabs under various country articles.

RUSSIA

While Nikita S. Khrushchev spent 1965 in quiet retirement in a country house near Moscow, his successors were running the Soviet Union in a businesslike manner, quite unlike that of their predecessor. As the supreme ruler of the U.S.S.R., Khrushchev had been impulsive, unpredictable, and dynamic. In contrast, his two successors— Leonid I. Brezhnev, a veteran party functionary, and Aleksei N. Kosygin, an economics specialist—were staid and serious. They were not unduly exalted or publicized, and "the cult of personality," which had begun to surround Khrushchev, was not renewed.

During his years of rule, Khrushchev had uprooted much of the

HOLD IT, TOVARISHCH! A Russian soldier snaps photographs of his comrades assembling in Red Square for the Moscow parade on May Day, 1965.
PICTURES OF THE YEAR / Dean Conger © National Geographic Magazine

Stalinist system and introduced many major re-forms. But in 1965, his earlier achievements were covered by a cloak of silence, and his name was not mentioned in public discussions. The new leaders re-examined Khrushchev's policies and repeatedly charged him of taking harebrained and reckless measures without adequate analysis.

Brezhnev and Kosygin gave the impression of wishing to avoid Khrushchev's errors. They made decisions only after thorough study by specialists and with due regard for orderly procedures. Great emphasis was placed on the role of the social sciences in policy formation. They introduced con-crete sociological studies and revived political sci-ence activities.

This concentration on cautious, piecemeal reform suggested a pragmatic rather than a doctrinaire approach. Yet, one action was swift, and indicated political rather than economic motives. Khrushchev had radically divided the party into two parallel hierarchies at the regional level, one for agriculture and one for industry, abolishing the district com-mittees that had formerly controlled them. His move, which seemed to stress practical operating functions, was reversed by the new leadership. The party was reorganized with 85 unified regional com-mittees and about 2,400 district committees.

Following Khrushchev's ouster, First Secretary Brezhnev assumed the additional post as head of the party's Bureau for the Russian Republic and also gained membership in the Presidium of the Supreme Soviet. In December, 70-year-old Anastas I. Mi-koyan retired with honor from the chairmanship of of Presidium of the Supreme Soviet, though he re-mained a member of the Communist Party Presidi-um. Succeeding Mikoyan was Nikolai V. Podgorny, a member of the party Secretariat. More puzzling, perhaps, was the simultaneous removal of the dynamic and ambitious Aleksander N. Shelepin from his post as deputy premier, although he re-tained his membership in the party Presidium and the Secretariat of the Central Committee.

Earlier, Vitali S. Titov and Leonid F. Ilyichev were removed as party secretaries, and the appoint-ments of Kirill T. Mazurov to full membership in the party Presidium and Dmitri F. Ustinov to the Secretariat and to the Presidium as an alternate were announced. Mazurov and, later, Dmitri S. Polyansky became first deputy premiers. At lower levels, some officials who had been close to Khrush-chev were replaced, and others, fired by him, were reappointed.

Party Membership. The Soviet Communist party had grown to over 10,000,000 full members, and almost 1,000,000 candidates—a grand total of 11,158,169 by Jan. 1, 1965. It was becoming an educated group: 15 per cent of its members had a higher education; 33 per cent a secondary or in-complete higher education; and 28 per cent an incomplete secondary education. More than a

third of the members were said to be "specialists" —agronomists, economists, engineers, technicians, etc. Moreover, it was a relatively young party, 54 per cent were under 40 years old, and 79 per cent were 50 or less.

There was evidence of greater freedom for writers and scholars, and of vigorous discussion of alternative policies among experts and specialists. The removal of Ilyichev, Khrushchev's chief spokesman on ideological questions, suggested somewhat looser doctrinal controls. So did an article by Aleksei M. Rumyantsev, editor of *Pravda*, on Feb. 21, 1965. Stressing the important place occupied by the intellectuals, Rumyantsev urged the need for "different schools," "different styles," and freer individual expression. He re-iterated, however, the necessity for writers and artists to accept party direction, socialist realism, and dialectical materialism.

Others followed Rumyantsev's lead. After a debate in the press on trial procedures, a strong statement by a lawyer, in favor of the "presumption of innocence," was published. Economists of un-orthodox viewpoint pressed their views on economic reform, and some of the most prominent received Lenin prizes. Among historians, there was contro-versy over Stalinist interpretations of history and demands for greater scholarly objectivity. In

TAPE RECORDS pupils' answers to an English lesson in Baku, on the Caspian Sea. All classes in the school are being conducted in English.

science, Trofim D. Lysenko, who had dominated biological theory under Stalin and Khrushchev, lost his commanding position.

The memoirs of Ilya Ehrenburg, which sharply censured the Stalinist era, continued to appear, and his earlier works were published, although subjected to critical reviews. In March, there was a surprising criticism by *Pravda* of the conservative literary journal *Oktyabr* and, in September, an unprecedented censure of *Izvestia* by Rumyantsev himself. His removal as editor of *Pravda* 10 days later, however, raised anew the question of how far the party was willing to relax its control over the arts and sciences.

The new leaders did not reverse the trend toward de-Stalinization for which Khrushchev had been personally responsible. Although Kosygin had been a close associate of Stalin, and Brezhnev was a product of the Stalinist school, neither showed a desire to restore the old order.

Agricultural Reforms. Khrushchev left behind many unsolved economic problems. The rate of development had slowed, agriculture had stagnated, and planned improvements in welfare had not fully materialized. Reforms in agriculture came first. After a session of the Central Committee in March, Brezhnev condemned the previous leadership for administration by fiat, petty tutelage of farms, ill-conceived reorganizations, ostentation, and ballyhoo. He specifically criticized the amalgamation of collective farms, the conversion of others to state farms, the abolition of the machine tractor stations, and, in addition, the discouragement of proper crop rotation.

Although a revised collective farm statute was forecast, no basic changes were planned for the agricultural system. Nor would the enlarged farms be divided immediately. Specific measures, however, were taken to improve productivity and to raise the farmers' income. Farmers were promised greater freedom to plan crops according to local conditions. The state also agreed to double its investment in agriculture by producing more tractors, improving pastures and repair facilities, and increasing the supply of electric power.

Industry's Turn came at a meeting of the Central Committee in October. Major reforms were announced and ratified shortly after at a session of the Supreme Soviet. The changes were based on 11 months of study and discussion. The direction had been indicated by the restoration of the Council of Ministers (cabinet) in the defense industry in March, and by experiments in greater plant autonomy in selected industries.

In their speeches before the plenum, both Kosygin and Brezhnev sharply criticized industrial planning and organization. The entire administrative structure established by Khrushchev was then reorganized. The regional economic councils were abolished, and the "branch principle" of industrial administration was re-established under the control of nine centralized All-Union ministries.

This reconstruction represented, however, not a return to the Stalinist system of bureaucratic control from Moscow, but a compromise between centralized planning and broadened autonomy for industrial enterprises.

Foreign Policy. The post-Khrushchev regime found itself at an impasse created by its wish to continue peaceful coexistence, including cultural and economic relations with the United States, while restoring its badly damaged friendship with Communist China. The increased U.S. intervention in the Vietnamese war aggravated the problem, leading Russia to adopt an increasingly critical attitude toward U.S. actions. See CHINA, PEOPLE'S REPUBLIC OF; VIETNAM.

A visit by Kosygin to Hanoi, North Vietnam, in February paved the way for more military aid to North Vietnam, including the offer of Soviet volunteers in case of need. This action in a Chinese sphere of influence aroused suspicions in Peking and led to accusations of inadequate assistance and even of Soviet-American collusion to weaken the cause of the "revolution." Although agreeing publicly with North Vietnam on the conditions necessary for peace negotiations, Russia seemed more anxious to seek a peaceful settlement than China. Thus, the Soviet Union found itself accused of giving insufficient support to the communist cause of national and colonial revolution.

Throughout the year, a constant stream of Asian visitors to Moscow, including Prime Minister Lal Bahadur Shastri of India, testified to Russia's concern over the Chinese threat to its dominant position within the communist movement. No success, however, was attained in papering over the cracks in the communist bloc. See COMMUNISM.

The Bitter Dispute over Soviet payments to the United Nations (UN) ceased when the United States dropped the issue, thus permitting the organization to resume its normal voting procedures. The outbreak of the Indian-Pakistani war in September created an extraordinary unity between Moscow and Washington over the urgency of settling the issue peacefully. It was clear that both countries were alarmed by the prospect of a war in which they might ultimately be involved with Communist China. See UNITED NATIONS (UN).

Population: 232,500,000. **Government:** First Secretary of the Communist Party Leonid I. Brezhnev; Premier Aleksei N. Kosygin; Chairman of the Presidium of the Supreme Soviet Nikolai Podgorny. **Monetary Unit:** ruble (.90 = U.S. $1). **Gross National Product:** 187,888,000,000 rubles. **Foreign Trade** (1964): exports, $7,605,000,000; imports, $7,670,000,000. **Principal Exports:** fuels, iron and steel, machinery and heavy equipment, metals, vegetable products. H. GORDON SKILLING

See also EUROPE.

RWANDA. The housing and feeding of refugees, who had fled from Rwanda to neighboring African countries to escape tribal war, proved to be an international challenge in 1965. The flight of the refugees was the result of a conflict between the Inyenzi terrorist organization, which wanted to restore the Watusi monarchy, and the Bahutu people, who supported the government in power. In February, the government of Congo (Léopoldville) agreed to grant permanent asylum in its Kivu province to some 60,000 Watusi refugees from Rwanda. The United Nations established an airlift in June to take another 3,000 Rwanda refugees from crowded areas in Léopoldville to Tanzania.

Rwanda President Grégoire Kayibanda did not attend the February conference of French-speaking African states at Nouakchott, Mauritania, because of the press of other duties. But he later had his country join the newly formed Organisation Commune Africaine et Malgache. Economic assistance came from many sources, including France and West Germany. In August, Nationalist China offered technicians to assist in agricultural development.

Population: 2,868,000. **Government:** President and Premier Grégoire Kayibanda. **Monetary Unit:** franc (50 = U.S. $1). **Foreign Trade:** no statistics available. **Principal Exports:** coffee, cotton, minerals.   BENJAMIN E. THOMAS

See also AFRICA.

SAFETY organizations in 1965 moved strongly in particular areas toward the long-term reduction of accidents. But the statistics for the first 10 months indicated clearly that the upward trend in total accidents had not yet been reversed: the probable number of accidental deaths for the year was up 1 per cent, to 106,000. Public accidents, chiefly in transportation and recreation, increased the death toll the most. Automobile accidents were responsible for about 46 per cent. Occupational and home accidental deaths did decrease, however, in 1965.

The projected rate of 54.7 accidental deaths for each 100,000 of population was lower than in 1964, but higher than in any other year since 1957. Accidents (of all types) remained the leading cause of death among persons aged 1 to 37, and ranked fourth as a killer of persons of all ages.

More than 10,000,000 people suffered disabling injuries in all classes of accidents, with home injuries leading, and injuries while at work next.

Motor Vehicle Accident Tolls were seemingly headed for another all-time high—49,000 fatalities for the year. In spite of the continually increasing number of automobiles, drivers, and travel-miles, however, the traffic death rate, based on population, has generally moved downward since the peak in 1937. The final 1965 figures, however, should show a slight increase in the rate over the previous year.

Based on the 10-month statistics, the cost of all accidents for the whole year was at least $17,000,000,000. This sum includes medical and hospital expenses, wage losses, insurance costs, and lost production time in industrial accidents.

Safety Programs. Among the auto accident prevention programs launched or intensified by safety groups in 1965, the success of the National Safety Council's program for driver improvement through classroom re-education was considered outstanding. A new approach to safety education, the CBS News audience-participation television documentary, "The National Drivers Test," set a record for the size of the audience viewing a public service program.

Federal government hearings in Washington, D.C., were aimed at safer vehicles, and the new model cars appeared with more automotive safety features. Other hearings investigated the safety of automobile tires. See AUTOMOBILE.

A major question remained unanswered: Are automobile buyers willing to pay for new safety equipment not currently available on factory-equipped cars? This would include shoulder harnesses and collapsible steering columns. The auto industry, though, felt the best way to reduce auto deaths is to make drivers more safety conscious.

Baltimore, Md., and Hamilton, Ohio, won the National Safety Council's Trustees Award for the best overall safety programs in 1964.   HOWARD PYLE

SAILING. See BOATS AND BOATING.

SAINT LOUIS recalled its golden era as a major port as it witnessed continued rejuvenation of its Mississippi riverfront. Climaxing a 30-year civic dream, the final eight-foot steel section of the graceful Gateway Arch was carefully fitted into place in late October.

The soaring 630-foot-high arch symbolizes the city's role in America's westward movement. In its shadow, workmen rushed completion of the 55,000-seat Busch Memorial Stadium, being built with $16,000,000 in private funds. Nearby, another privately financed project, $45,000,000 Mansion House, thrust three 28-story apartment towers skyward.

In the city's western section, St. Louis University planned a $70,000,000 expansion after completing 14 new dormitories in the past six years. And the West End urban renewal project was the nation's first to get federal aid for rehabilitation grants to poor homeowners, as authorized by the 1965 Housing and Urban Development Act (see HOUSING). Additional building in Mill Creek Valley, formerly 465 acres of notorious slums, was turning the area into a favored in-town neighborhood.

A new mayor took over the leadership of St. Louis' renaissance on April 20. He is Alphonso J. Cervantes, who defeated three-term Mayor Raymond R. Tucker in the March Democratic primary. Mayor Cervantes' policies appeared likely to be as dedicated to continued community progress as those of his predecessor.   DONALD W. LIEF

SALVATION ARMY representatives from 71 countries gathered in London, England, on June 24, for a 10-day observance of the Salvation Army's 100th anniversary. The celebration included a meeting of an international congress, the fourth in the history of the world-wide organization.

Founded in the slums of East London on July 2, 1865, the organization has grown into a world-wide movement consisting of 25,000 officers and 30,000 employees who carry out the Army's spiritual and social ministry through 20,000 centers.

The celebration opened with an inaugural session of the congress in Royal Albert Hall, at which Queen Elizabeth II extended greetings. It was the first time a reigning British monarch had attended a Salvation Army meeting. Also on hand were British leaders and London-based diplomats. Church leaders who attended included Dr. Arthur Michael Ramsey, Archbishop of Canterbury, and John Cardinal Heenan of the Roman Catholic Church.

The centennial program was climaxed with an observance of Founder's Day on July 2. The event, held in Westminster Abbey, was attended by 3,500 persons, including 50 descendants of the founder and first Salvation Army General, William Booth. A white stone bust of the General, who died in 1912, was unveiled and presented to the Dean of Westminster Abbey by Wycliffe Booth, General Booth's grandson.   JOSEPH P. ANDERSON

SAMUELS, ERNEST (1903-   ), Northwestern University Professor of English, was awarded the Pulitzer biography prize in 1965. The third volume of his Adams biography, *Henry Adams: The Major Phase*, was highly praised in 1964. *Henry Adams: The Middle Years* (1958) won Samuels the Frederic Bancroft and Francis Parkman prizes in 1959. *The Young Henry Adams* was published in 1948. Samuels is continuing his study of the great American historian and philosopher.

"As a student of literature," Samuels said, "I was hypnotized by the brilliance of his (Adams) style. No American has written history like he did." Adams was awarded the Pulitzer prize posthumously (1919) for *The Education of Henry Adams*. The autobiography was published after the author's death in 1918, and was a best-seller of that year.

Ernest Samuels was born and educated in Chicago. He is a University of Chicago graduate (1923), and received his law (1926), M.A. (1931), and Ph.D. (1942) degrees there. He practiced law in El Paso, Tex. (1928-1930), and in Chicago (1933-1937) with his brother. Samuels taught business English at the Bryant & Stratton College in Chicago (1931-1936), and English at Washington State College (1937-1939). Samuels joined the Northwestern University faculty in 1942. He was made a full professor in 1954, and chairman of its English Department in 1964.

See also PULITZER PRIZES.

SAN FRANCISCO observed the 20th anniversary of the United Nations Charter with ceremonies in the Opera House, June 25 to 26. Addresses by world statesmen including President Lyndon B. Johnson and Adlai E. Stevenson recalled the hopes that led to the drafting of the Charter in 1945.

Two transportation superlatives in the city involved parking and rapid transit. The first phase of the San Francisco International Airport garage, accommodating 2,700 autos, was dedicated in October. Believed to be the world's largest parking structure, it will handle 8,000 cars when finished in 1975. At year's end, work began on the even more massive San Francisco Bay rail transit tunnel. The tube will carry commuters four miles across and 130 feet beneath the bay, connecting downtown Oakland and San Francisco. See BRIDGE AND TUNNEL; TRANSPORTATION.

On Market Street, Fox Plaza—a 29-story, $20,000,000 complex—was topped out. The skyline was also enhanced by the 33-story Hartford Insurance Group's building, dedicated in April. Also underway were the 43-story Wells Fargo Building and the 56-story Bank of America tower.

Voters approved a bond issue of some $33,600,000 in November to build a new Medical Center, but vetoed proposals to modernize the Opera House and Veterans Building.   DONALD W. LIEF

SASKATCHEWAN. See CANADA.

SAUDI ARABIA formally completed the transfer of power, announced in November, 1964, as former King Saud recognized his half brother Faisal's royal prerogatives and left the country. He went to Vienna for medical treatment, then settled in Athens with six sons, a host of servants, and a personal fortune of $600,000,000. In Riyadh, the Saudi government renamed all public buildings and confiscated the former royal palaces.

King Faisal met with President Gamal Abdel Nasser of the United Arab Republic at Juddah and reached an agreement for a cease-fire in the Yemen civil war (see YEMEN). Saudi Arabia also signed a border agreement with Jordan. This defined a desert area between the two states that had been in dispute since the end of World War I.

Saudi Arabia's first five-year plan, to become effective in 1966, was introduced. A first priority was given to development of agriculture. The United States agreed to pay the cost of setting up a desalination plant. Saudi Arabia also formed a fertilizer corporation to exploit phosphate deposits, and signed an oil concession pact with a French consortium to exploit Red Sea oil deposits.

Population: 6,820,000. **Government:** King Faisal. **Monetary Unit:** riyal (4.50 = U.S. $1). **Foreign Trade:** exports, $1,043,900,000; imports, $319,400,000. **Principal Exports:** dates, hides and skins, petroleum.   WILLIAM SPENCER

See also MIDDLE EAST.

SAWYER, RUTH (1880-), storyteller and author of many children's stories and books, was accorded several high honors in 1965. She was awarded the Regina medal for a lifetime of contributions to children's literature, and the Laura Ingalls Wilder award, presented every five years, for lasting contributions to children's literature. Miss Sawyer also was honored with a storytelling festival that was held in Provincetown, Mass., on May 21.

Among the storyteller's specialties are Irish folk tales. Many were told to her by the family's Irish nurse, Johanna. Miss Sawyer gathered firsthand material in such countries as Ireland, England, France, and Spain. Being a linguist, she came to know the people of these lands. *This Way to Christmas* (1924), *Picture Tales from Spain* (1936), *The Enchanted Schoolhouse* (1956), *The Year of the Christmas Dragon* (1960), and *Roller Skates*, which won the Newbery medal in 1937, are a few of her popular books.

Ruth Sawyer's father was a widely traveled importer. She is a graduate of Columbia University (1904). She and Albert C. Durand, a physician, live in Back Bay Boston. They were married in 1911 and have a son and a daughter.

See also LITERATURE FOR CHILDREN (Awards).

SCHOOL. See CIVIL RIGHTS; EDUCATION; Section One, LAWRENCE A. CREMIN ON EDUCATION.

SCHWINGER, JULIAN SEYMOUR (1918-), Harvard University Professor of Physics, was one of three scientists awarded the Nobel physics prize in 1965. The others were Richard P. Feynman and Sin-itiro Tomonaga. They created the modern theory of quantum electrodynamics, described as having "deep-ploughing consequences for the physics of elementary particles."

Each scientist worked independently of the other two, using his own method to encounter the difficulties involved in calculations of the interaction between a charged particle (electron) and the radiation fields around it. Schwinger devised a complex and highly mathematical formulation. He and Feynman completed their work in the late 1940s.

Julian Schwinger and Richard Feynman were born in New York City the same year. Schwinger was 14 when he enrolled at the College of the City of New York. He went to Columbia University two years later, where he received his B.A. (1936) and Ph.D. (1939) degrees. He was a University of California (at Berkeley) research associate (1940-1941), taught physics at Purdue University (1941-1943), and did research at the Massachusetts Institute of Technology Radiation Laboratory (1943-1946). He joined the Harvard faculty in 1945, and was made a full professor in 1947. Schwinger was a co-winner of the first Albert Einstein award (1951).

See also FEYNMAN, RICHARD P.; NOBEL PRIZES (Science); TOMONAGA, SIN-ITIRO.

SCIENCE AND RESEARCH. Congress maintained a close scrutiny of federal funds for research and development, but, also, for the first time, gave major attention to the related subject of how funds for science are distributed to educational institutions.

A penetrating study issued in October by the Research and Technical Programs Subcommittee of the House Committee on Government Operations assailed the premise that federal expenditures for basic research have improved science education in the U.S. The report was entitled "Conflicts Between the Federal Research Programs and the Nation's Goals for Higher Education."

New Policy. By summer's end President Lyndon B. Johnson had issued a major policy directive on federal support of university-based research, and his science adviser, Donald F. Hornig, predicted the new policy would bring important changes.

As the President stated to his Cabinet and heads of federal departments and agencies, "More support will be provided under terms which give the university and the investigator wider scope for inquiry, as contrasted with highly specific, narrowly defined projects." Hornig later told a press conference that university administrators would be given more responsibility for overseeing the use of such funds.

Geographical Distribution. The President also associated himself with the have-not institutions

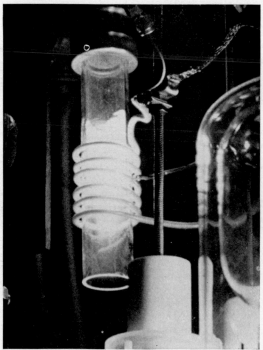

Air Force Office of Scientific Research

PLASMA TORCH, *capable of producing temperatures up to 100,000°F., is a new research tool for study of high-temperature chemical reactions.*

that advocate geographical distribution of federal research funds. In his statement, President Johnson declared, "At present, one-half of the federal expenditures for research go to 20 major institutions, most of which were strong before the advent of federal research funds. During the period of increasing federal support during World War II, the number of institutions carrying out research and providing advanced education has grown impressively. Strong centers have developed in areas which were previously not well served. It is a particular purpose of this policy to accelerate this beneficial trend since the funds are still concentrated in too few institutions in too few areas of the country."

All this seemed rather mild when contrasted with the remarks of *Science* editor Philip Abelson in an article he wrote at the end of the year questioning America's ability to maintain technical leadership in the world because too much is being spent on socially and economically unprofitable research programs. Commenting on nuclear research, he remarked, "Never, in the history of science, have so many fine minds been supported on such a grand scale, and worked so diligently, and returned so little to society for its patronage." He further raised this provocative consideration: "Who will make the decisions? Will it be a broadly informed electorate? Or will it be a narrow oligarchy at the seat of highly centralized power?" SERGEI LENORMAND

SCIENCE CLUBS OF AMERICA showed continued vitality in 1965 as students exhibited 1,160,000 science projects in fairs across the nation.

Top Winners from among the 418 finalists at the 16th National Science Fair-International, held at St. Louis, Mo., in May, were:

Toshiko Fujitsu, 18, of Kyoto, Japan, for her project, *Studies on Insect Galls in Structure and Formation.*

Robert J. Sanders, 16, of Lamesa, Tex., for *Effect of High Frequency on Plant Functions.*

Beverly A. Shoenberger, 17, of Atlanta, Ga., for *An Analysis of the Rapid Growth of Kudzu.*

Kennon R. Strauss, 18, of Shreveport, La., for *Low Frequency Electron Paramagnetic Resonance Spectroscopy.*

Carin C. Clamann, 16, of San Antonio, Tex., for *A Closed Ecological System.*

Curtis Bryant, 15, of Le Mars, Iowa, for *Studying the Solar Atmosphere.*

Letantia B. Jankowski, 17, of Lodi, N.J., for *Chorioallantoic Studies.*

Frank B. Lutz, Jr., 17, of Athens, Ala., for *Determination of Susceptibility to a Transplanted Tumor.*

David E. Lunsford, Jr., 17, of Lubbock, Tex., for *Scientific Applications for Egg Candling.*

Randy B. Wright, 17, of Salt Lake City, Utah, for *Effect of Radiation on the Growth and Structure of Crystals and X-Ray Diffractions.*

John R. Gott III, 18, of Louisville, Ky., for *Pseudopolyhedrons—A New Class of Geometric Figures.*

Virginia L. Delaney, 17, of Framingham, Mass., for *Abnormal Pregnancies in the Lebistes reticulatus.*

John M. Graham, Jr., 18, of Wilmington, Del., for *Origin of Melanophores from the Neural Crest in the Chicken Embryo.*

Health Awards were given by the following organizations: *American Dental Association*—Kathlene A. Zimmerman of Mount Joy, Pa., and John S. Sabol of Lafayette, Ind. *American Medical Association*—Johnna Lou Russel of Albuquerque, N.Mex., and Ronald G. Owens of Sylacauga, Ala. *American Pharmaceutical Association*—Michael J. Telepchak of Tamaqua, Pa. *American Veterinary Medical Association*—D. T. Crowe of Clintonville, Wis.

Special Awards were given by the following organizations: *American Chemical Society*—Susan Delphine Delaney of Bladensburg, Md., and Alfred Arthur Hagedorn of Colorado Springs, Colo. *American Institute of Mining, Metallurgical, and Petroleum Engineers, Inc.*—Noel Dunivant, Jr., of Whiteville, N.C.; Alan Correll Hull of Oneonta, Ala.; and Larry Willard Loveridge of Provo, Utah. *American Patent Law Association*—William Andrew Voelkle of Houston, Tex. *American Psychological Association*—Cynthia Bess Miller of Indianapolis, Ind. *American Society for Metals*—Larry Willard Loveridge of Provo, Utah. *American Society for Microbiology*—Carolina Mederos of Winter Park, Fla. *Entomological Society of America*—Gary E. Hatch of Provo, Utah. *National Committee for Careers in Medical Technology*—Margaret Janssen of Henrietta, Tex. *National Pest Control Association*—Daniel Charles Kurtak of Bishop, Calif. *Optical Society of America*—Victor Michael Martin of Jacksonville, Ala. *Society of Women Engineers*—Mary Doris Ruggere of Kingston, Pa.

The National Aeronautics and Space Administration (NASA) awarded two-day visits to NASA facilities to: Dale Fritz of Arnett, Okla.; Bryan Grummon of Glendive, Mont.; Alan Hull of Oneonta, Ala.; Ronald Polinsky of Reading, Pa.; John Rollins of Lawton, Okla.; and William Voelkle of Houston, Tex.

The Atomic Energy Commission awarded trips to the Argonne National Laboratory to: Patricia Anderson of Los Alamos, N.Mex.; Frederick R. Aronson of Hillsdale, N.J.; George Stuart Beal of Burlington, Ontario, Canada; Alan Curtis Huber of Evansville, Ind.; John Forbes Hutchinson of Philadelphia, Pa.; Charles William Jernigan of Tallahassee, Fla.; Frederick Otto Nietzel of Dyer, Ind.; Kennon Strauss of Shreveport, La.; Herbert Terry of San Diego, Calif.; and Randy B. Wright of Salt Lake City, Utah.

The U.S. Air Force (USAF) honored finalists in 10 special categories with plaques, expense-paid trips to USAF research facilities, and salaried summer jobs at research laboratories in the fields of their individual interests. The 10 and their categories were: *Aerospace Biological Sciences*—David F. Hayes of Vernon, Conn. *Aerospace Chemistry*—Jeff B. Bentley of Temple, Tex. *Aerospace Dynamics*—Robert Stephens of Brookfield, Wis. *Aerospace Electronics and Communications*—Raymond C. Kurzweil of Queens Village, N.Y. *Aerospace Environmental Sciences*—Robert I. Smith-Johannsen of Glens Falls, N.Y. *Aerospace Medicine*—Felice R. Tillman of Metairie, La. *Aerospace Physics*—Alan Curtis Huber of Evansville, Ind. *Aerospace Physiological and Social Sciences*—John C. Hawkins of Salt Lake City, Utah. *Aerospace Propulsion*—William A. Voelkle of Houston, Tex. *Mathematical and Computational Sciences*—Thomas J. Hysong of Washington, D.C. The Aerospace Education Foundation of the Air Force Association also awarded slide rules to winners.

Westinghouse 24th Annual Science Talent Search scholarships went to: Larry D. Howard, 17, of Canoga Park, Calif., $7,500; John R. Gott, 17, of Louisville, Ky., $6,000; Louis H. Rowen, 16, of New York City, $5,000; James A. Strauchen, 16, of Forest Hills, N.Y., $4,000; and Helen A. Greer, 16, of Brooklyn, N.Y., $3,000. FOSTER P. STOCKWELL

SCULPTURE. See PAINTING AND SCULPTURE.

SENEGAL. Early in 1965 Senegal held trials for political leaders who had opposed the government the previous year. They were charged with inciting troops to disobedience, spreading false news, and committing acts that endangered public safety. The trials resulted in the sentencing of several former leaders of the opposition Parti du Régroupement Africain-Sénégal. In June, 29 men were sentenced on charges of subversion and attempting to revive the Parti Africain d'Indépendance, a communist-oriented group which had been prohibited in Senegal since 1960.

The country faced several economic problems. The withdrawal of French troops resulted in a loss of revenue to people in Senegal who had supplied them with food and services. The removal of a French subsidy on Senegalese peanuts also contributed to a budget deficit of over $20,000,000.

President Léopold Sédar Senghor met with Mali President Modibo Keita in May. They agreed to cooperate with Mauritania and Guinea on development of the Sénégal River Basin.

Population: 3,358,000. **Government:** President Léopold Sédar Senghor. **Monetary Unit:** CFA franc (246.85 = U.S. $1). **Gross National Product:** $674,000,000. **Foreign Trade:** exports, $124,000,000; imports, $155,000,000. **Principal Exports:** peanuts and peanut oil.   BENJAMIN E. THOMAS

See also AFRICA.

SERVICE CLUBS and organizations reached important milestones in their numerical growth and program development. They also took action to strengthen organizational structure and to stimulate new areas of service.

Kiwanis International observed its Golden Anniversary with a year-long program of special projects designed to highlight the community services provided by the organization during the past 50 years. The activities included planting of trees and shrubs, pledges to initiate or complete much needed local community projects, and financial contributions to institutions providing health, welfare, and recreation services.

The organization continued to grow outside of the United States and Canada, as well as within. Clubs have been chartered in 30 countries under the international extension policy since the first one was established in Mexico in 1962. Representatives of the 11 European clubs, at a meeting held in June, urged the establishment of a European federation to encourage the formation of additional clubs and to unify and coordinate their activities.

The Board of Trustees of the Kiwanis Foundation authorized a new program designed to bring the story of America's heritage to citizens of the U.S. and Canada. The program will include the distribution of brochures to individual members, Kiwanis clubs, and other organizations.

Delegates to the 50th annual convention, held July 4 to 8 in New York City, elected Edward C. Keefe, of Oklahoma City, president, and R. Glenn Reed, Jr., of Marietta, Ga., president-elect.

Lions International delegates, attending the 48th annual convention at Los Angeles, July 7 to 10, learned that more members were enrolled during the 12-month period from July 1, 1964, to June 30, 1965, than in any previous year of the organization's history. Total membership at the end of this period was 760,178. There were 19,455 clubs in 132 countries and geographical areas. Lions International became the first service organization to charter a club in Spain. It was organized in Madrid.

Walter H. Campbell, of Miami Beach, Fla., was installed as president. He called for a reaffirmation of the goals of international understanding and cooperation, and an appraisal of the means by which these goals can be achieved.

Clubs in Maryland launched a program of sending law books and periodicals to libraries in 22 underdeveloped countries. The purpose of this program was to help the people to understand the workings of our democracy and help them design free governments of their own.

Clubs in Florida sent magazines to 73 recipient Lions Clubs in 23 countries in an attempt to advance international cooperation and good will.

Rotary International sponsored a special awards program to mark its 60th anniversary. The awards honored one club in each of the 278 Rotary districts and two non-districted clubs for outstanding projects of service. Since the first club was organized on Feb. 23, 1905, in Chicago, Rotary has grown to be an international organization with 580,000 members in 12,166 clubs, in 129 countries and geographical regions.

The Rotary Foundation began a new program to advance international understanding. The Group Study Exchange enables teams of young business and professional men to spend two months as guests of the organization in another country. In return, the clubs of the host country will send similar study groups to the United States. The teams will have an unusual opportunity to gain extensive knowledge of the host country and the ways of its people through visits to schools, churches, governmental and voluntary agencies, and through widespread interviews and lectures.

Interact, the club for young men of high school age, started by Rotary in 1962, continued its spectacular growth. By November, 1965, there were 950 clubs in 46 countries with 22,000 members.

The 56th annual convention of Rotary International was held May 30 to June 3 in Atlantic City. C. P. H. Teenstra of Hilversum, The Netherlands, was installed as president. Richard L. Evans, a resident of Salt Lake City, Utah, was elected president-nominee.   JOSEPH P. ANDERSON

SHIPS AND SHIPPING. See TRANSPORTATION.

SHIPWRECK. See DISASTERS.

SHOLOKHOV, MIKHAIL ALEKSANDROVICH

(1905-   ), Russian author of epic novels, was awarded the Nobel literature prize in 1965. He was cited for "the artistic power and integrity with which in his epic of the Don he has given creative expression to a historic phase in the history of the Russian people." *And Quiet Flows the Don* (*The Quiet Don* in Russia) is his greatest success. The four-volume narrative is the story of all agricultural Russia, and has been translated into many languages.

The author was only 21 when he began writing the Don epic, published between 1928 and 1940. It and *Virgin Soil Upturned* (1932, 1955-1959), about the collectivization of farms in his Don region, encompass the author's life. His second novel, published in two parts, also has national appeal. Sholokhov writes only about agricultural Russia. He worked for a time in Moscow, but found big city life distasteful and returned to his native village of Kruzhilin. A third novel, *They Fought for Their Country*, appeared in 1943 and 1944. Short-story collections include *The Azure Steppe* (1924-1927) and *Stories of the Don* (1927-1928).

The formal education of Mikhail Sholokhov ended when he was 13. He fought in the civil war, turned communist in 1920, and became a party member in 1932.

See also NOBEL PRIZES (Literature).

SHOOTING. See SPORTS.

SIERRA LEONE.

Prime Minister Albert M. Margai declared in April, 1965, that his government's aim during Sierra Leone's fifth year of independence would be to increase the level of employment and double the national output in all fields.

In order to raise funds for its development program, Sierra Leone increased import duties on alcoholic beverages, motor cars, radios, and other items. A campaign also was launched to raise $35,000,000 in local loans.

In May, Sierra Leone took part in a conference in Freetown to form plans for a free trade area including Guinea, Ivory Coast, Liberia, and Sierra Leone. Also the first stage of an electric power station was opened, financed by the International Bank for Reconstruction and Development.

Dr. John Karefa-Smart, former Minister of External Affairs, announced his resignation from the governing Sierra Leone People's party in favor of the opposition All-People's Congress, but he retained his seat in the House of Representatives.

Population: 2,739,000. **Government:** Governor-General Henry L. Boston; Prime Minister Albert M. Margai. **Monetary Unit:** leone (1 = U.S. $1.40). **Gross National Product:** $219,000,000. **Foreign Trade:** exports, $81,000,000; imports, $84,000,000. **Principal Exports:** cassava, chrome, diamonds, iron ore, palm oil.   BENJAMIN E. THOMAS

See also AFRICA.

SKATING. See ICE HOCKEY; ICE SKATING.

SKIING.

The aspirations of the U.S. skiing team to gain a top place in Alpine competition were shaken in March at the American International Ski Races in Vail, Colo. There, French women and Austrian men skiers scored decisive victories.

Marielle Goitshel of France took first place in both the slalom and the giant slalom and a fourth place in the downhill. In all, the French women scored a total of 62 points to 38 for Austria and 28 for the United States. Jean-Claude Killy of France won the men's combined with victories in the slalom and giant slalom, but Austria's depth of talent showed in the team standings. Austria scored 194 points, France, 92, and the United States, 55. The best Austrian skier was Heini Messner, who won the downhill and came in second in the slalom.

Another visitor from Europe, Toralf Engan of Norway, set a North American ski jump record on February 7 with a leap of 324 feet at Leavenworth, Wash. A month later, John Balfanz regained the record for the United States with a 325-foot leap at Iron Mountain, Mich. The world ski-flying record was raised to 475.7 feet by Peter Lesser of East Germany in a meet at Mitterndorf, Austria.

The U.S. Ski Educational Foundation signed Bob Beattie, the U.S. 1964 Olympic ski coach, to a three-year contract.   JAMES O. DUNAWAY

SOAP BOX DERBY. See SPORTS.

SOCCER.

St. Louis University won its fifth National Collegiate Athletic Association (NCAA) championship. St. Louis eliminated defending champion Navy with a 3 to 1 victory in a semifinal match, and then bested Michigan State 1 to 0 on a penalty kick by Carl Gentile. The National Association of Intercollegiate Athletics (NAIA) title was won for the second straight year by Trenton State, with a 6 to 2 victory over Earlham College. Brown University won the Ivy League championship.

The National Open Challenge Cup, representative of supremacy in amateur soccer in the United States, was won by the New York Ukrainian Nationals. After tying the Hansa Club of Chicago 1 to 1 in their first game, the Ukrainians won, 2 to 1, to regain the title they lost last year.

Poland won the International Soccer League Championship, and then took the American Challenge Cup by upending the perennial winner, Dukla of Czechoslovakia. Internazionale of Milan won its second straight world's championship by beating Independiente of Buenos Aires.

Liverpool won the English Soccer Cup, defeating Leeds United, 2 to 1. Manchester United won the English Soccer League's First Division championship, and thus returns to European championship soccer for the first time since 1958, when a plane crash killed eight members of the team. The European Cup winner was West Ham United of England.   STANLEY ISAACS

SOCIAL SECURITY underwent its most important change since the original Social Security Act was passed in 1935. In addition to the provisions for payment of hospital and other major medical expenses, popularly called Medicare, the new law includes a number of far-reaching and comprehensive changes (see MEDICARE). The new amendments provide for:

• An across-the-board increase of 7 per cent in all cash benefits under the present Social Security program.

• Additional benefit increases for workers retiring in the future and their dependents or survivors.

• An increase from $1,200 to $1,500 as the amount that a retired worker may earn in a year without losing a part of his Social Security payment.

• An option for widows to draw benefits at age 60 on a reduced scale. Full benefits will still be payable at the age of 62.

• Payment of benefits to widows aged 60 or over and to widowers aged 62 or over who remarry.

• Payment of benefits to children of retired, disabled, or deceased workers, if children attend school or college, until they reach the age of 22.

• An extension of coverage to self-employed physicians and internes, additional state and local government employees, and employees of certain nonprofit organizations.

• Exemptions of coverage to members of religious sects, such as the Amish, who are conscientiously opposed to the acceptance of the benefits of any public or private insurance.

• Changed eligibility requirements so that any person with a disability lasting 12 months or expected to result in death can get disability benefits.

• Traditional insured status for persons aged 72 and over so that three, four, or five quarters of coverage will qualify them for monthly Social Security benefits.

• A revised tax schedule that provides for a tax rate of 4.2 per cent each for employer and employee (and 5.4 per cent for self-employed) on earnings up to $6,600 effective Jan. 1, 1966.

• Establishment of an Advisory Council on Social Security in 1968 and every fifth year thereafter to review the entire Social Security and Health Insurance system and report to Congress.

The Social Security program reached an important milestone when it completed the first quarter of a century of payments in 1965. The first monthly Social Security check was paid to Miss Ida Fuller of Ludlow, Vt., in January, 1940. In May, 1965, William Kappel, a retired utility worker from Fort Wayne, Ind., became the 20,000,000th beneficiary. Kappel received his first Social Security check and warm congratulations from President Lyndon B. Johnson in a special ceremony at the White House.   JOSEPH P. ANDERSON

See also CHILD WELFARE; OLD AGE; SOCIAL WELFARE.

SOCIAL WELFARE provisions of the 1965 amendments to the Social Security Act will enable states to extend hospital and medical care benefits for needy persons under 65 and for dependent children under 21. The amendments also expand public assistance benefits and provide for increased grants to assist states in making major improvements in their welfare and child health programs.

The War on Poverty program, despite serious criticism from many quarters, including that of professional social workers, continued to make significant inroads in disadvantaged urban and rural areas. See POVERTY.

A new governmental agency, the Administration on Aging, was established by the Older Americans Act, which was signed into law on July 14. It became the seventh operating agency in the Department of Health, Education, and Welfare. The administration supersedes and will expand the work of the Office of Aging. Its major responsibilities include informational, consultative, and research activities; administration of grants, and stimulation of states and communities to use more effectively their resources and services for older people. William D. Bechill was named commissioner of the agency. See OLD AGE.

Project ENABLE. A nationwide program of parent counseling aimed at strengthening the family life of the poor was launched by three social welfare organizations, the Child Study Association, the Family Service Association of America, and the National Urban League. The new project, named ENABLE, will utilize the technique of group discussion with parents on such problems as child rearing, discipline, education, and unemployment. It will draw on the resources of the poor by involving them in solving their own problems.

Appointments. John W. Gardner was appointed Secretary of the Department of Health, Education, and Welfare to succeed Anthony J. Celebrezze, who was appointed Judge of the Sixth Federal Circuit Court of Appeals (see GARDNER, JOHN W.). C. F. McNeil was named director of the National Social Welfare Assembly to succeed Robert M. Bondy. McNeil was formerly executive director of the Health and Welfare Council of Philadelphia.

Awards in 1965 included:
National Association of Social Workers Tenth Anniversary Award to Wilbur J. Cohen, Undersecretary of the Department of Health, Education, and Welfare, for "outstanding public service in the application of social work knowledge to the solution of social problems."
National Conference on Social Welfare 1965 Distinguished Service Awards to James V. Bennett, retired director of the Federal Bureau of Prisons; Sidney Hollander, volunteer leader in social welfare; and Cora Kasius, retired director of publications service and editor for the Family Service Association of America.   JOSEPH P. ANDERSON

See also CHILD WELFARE; MEDICARE; SOCIAL SECURITY.

SOMALIA, hard-hit by drought in early 1965, still managed to make economic gains, particularly in communications and transportation.

A big assist came from West Germany and Italy which agreed to cover the budgetary deficit caused by food purchased to offset the drought. In March, Somalia began building a $13,445,000 all-weather network of roads in dry-farming areas. The project was sponsored by the United Nations Special Fund, the International Development Association, and the European Economic Community (EEC, or Common Market).

Premier Abdirizak Haji Hussein reorganized the country's civil service and formed two new ministries, works and communications. He also granted 23 amnesties to officers who had led a coup in northern Somalia in 1961.

Somalia was host to the Sixth World Muslim Congress in January, 1965. Delegates from 33 countries met to discuss means of promoting Islamism, establishing a common Moslem language, and reducing Israeli influence in Africa.

Population: 2,211,000. **Government:** President Aden Abdullah Osman; Premier Abdirizak Haji Hussein. **Monetary Unit:** somalo (7.143 = U.S. $1). **Foreign Trade:** exports, $31,800,000; imports, $44,700,000. **Principal Exports:** bananas, hides, leopard pelts, livestock.   WILLIAM SPENCER

See also AFRICA.

SOUTH AFRICA, REPUBLIC OF,

SOUTH AFRICA, REPUBLIC OF, strengthened the Nationalist government's control over the African majority, and continued to resist foreign opposition to its policies of racial segregation.

In February, the government announced the suspension of its controversial 90-day detention law under which persons could be detained without trial. But other new laws strengthened police powers. An Emergency Planning Bill was passed in April giving the government sweeping powers to marshal men and materials in times of sabotage or revolt. Also in April, a new Police Amendment Bill empowered police to search without warrant any persons, places, or vehicles within a mile of the country's borders. The new police powers were required, it was contended, to counter the infiltration of saboteurs.

The Nationalist party gained additional strength over the United party in March elections. In August, the formation of two new ultranationalist parties was reported. The parties, the Conservative and the Republican, criticized the Nationalist government for, as they put it, "favoring the blacks at the expense of the white population."

South Africa continued to deal harshly with those attempting to alter its apartheid policy. In March, four Africans were sentenced to a total of 21 years imprisonment on charges of being members and furthering the aims of the banned Pan Africanist Congress. Later, 12 white South Africans were found guilty under the country's Suppression of Communism Act. Also, five trade union officials were restricted under terms of the same act.

In April, the United Nations (UN) Security Council committee that had studied the feasibility of an economic boycott of South Africa reported that many of South Africa's trading partners indicated that a boycott of South Africa would cause severe dislocations in their own economies. Despite this report, the UN Special Committee on Apartheid called on the Security Council to urge UN member states to sever economic, military, and diplomatic relations with South Africa.

South Africa adopted a defense budget of $322,000,000, an amount five times greater than that for 1959-1960. The country also experienced a $7\frac{1}{2}$ per cent increase in Gross National Product (GNP) during 1965, and employment reached its highest level since 1951.

Population: 17,700,000. **Government:** President Charles R. Swart; Prime Minister Hendrik F. Verwoerd. **Monetary Unit:** rand (1 = U.S. $1.40). **Gross National Product:** $24,431,000,000. **Foreign Trade:** exports, $1,586,000,000; imports, $2,282,000,000. **Principal Exports:** asbestos, citrus fruits, diamonds, gold, uranium.   BENJAMIN E. THOMAS

See also AFRICA.

SOUTH AMERICA. See LATIN AMERICA; and articles on the various countries.

SOUTH ARABIA, FEDERATION OF, developed into a sizable headache for both Great Britain and the Middle East during 1965. The British, committed to grant independence to the federation by 1968, made abortive efforts to organize conferences with federation and Aden colony leaders and establish the ground rules for a transfer of power. A conference was called in March, but postponed when 16 member states said they would not send representatives. British proposals to send a constitutional commission to South Arabia in May and July were rebuffed. Chief Minister Abd al-Qawi Maqawi said the federation's terms were a provisional government, an interim constitution, free elections under United Nations (UN) supervision, and a central parliament responsible only to the UN.

Terrorists, based in Yemen, allegedly were responsible for the murders of two British officials in Aden, numerous bombings, sabotage of military installations, and labor strikes. In September, British High Commissioner Sir Richard Turnbull suspended the Aden constitution and dismissed the Council of Ministers, including Chief Minister Maqawi. Aden's Arabs responded with new strikes.

Population: 750,000. **Government:** British High Commissioner Sir Richard Turnbull. **Monetary Unit:** dinar (1 = U.S. $2.80). **Foreign Trade:** figures not available.   BENJAMIN E. THOMAS

See also MIDDLE EAST.

SPACE TRAVEL

In almost all important aspects of space achievement, U.S. leadership became increasingly evident in 1965, although the Soviet Union still held a slight advantage in booster power.

Space was populated by 10 American astronauts during the year, including four who achieved the first rendezvous of spacecraft in orbit, demonstrating a maneuver vital to the success of U.S. lunar flight plans and other important future activities.

NASA

Other Important Events in 1965 included:

• Obtaining the first close-up views of another planet, Mars, in the most significant space exploration achievement of the year. See ASTRONOMY.

• The initiation of regular service in three major applications of space flight—television via the first commercial communications satellite, weather study via the first operational weather satellite, and the first all-weather ocean navigation system.

• Progress in the development of major space systems, including Apollo for the manned exploration of the moon, and in unmanned systems such as Surveyor, the Lunar Orbiter, and the highly complex Orbiting Astronomical Observatory.

Major milestones in space technology were achieved in the development of nuclear rockets, the demonstration of the feasibility of giant solid-propellant rockets, and the use of fuel cells for electrical power in spacecraft.

Manned Operations. The first manned Gemini flight, Gemini III, was a three-orbit mission successfully flown by Project Mercury veteran Virgil I. Grissom and John W. Young on March 23 in the *Molly Brown*. During the flight, which proved the merit of the craft, Gus Grissom performed the first orbital maneuvers of a U.S. space vehicle.

Earlier, on March 18 and 19, the Soviets orbited the two man Voskhod II. On this flight, Cosmonaut Aleksei A. Leonov left the craft and took man's first walk in space.

Gemini IV carried James A. McDivitt and Edward H. White II into space for four days, June 3 to 7. White left the craft and maneuvered about in space for about 20 minutes with the aid of a space gun that ejected jets of oxygen. Both he and Leonov were anchored to their spacecraft, orbiting at 17,500 mph, by tether lines.

Astronauts L. Gordon Cooper, Jr., and Charles Conrad Jr., were aloft in Gemini V from August 21 to 29. This flight proved that man can withstand the eight days in space required for a round trip to the moon.

Thus, the duration of Gemini flights proceeded from four-and-a-half hours to four days to eight days, and finally to the 14-day mission in December flown by astronauts Frank Borman and James A. Lovell, Jr. in Gemini VII.

RENDEZVOUS of the Gemini spacecraft is seen in this photo of Gemini VII taken from Gemini VI's window by Astronaut Thomas Stafford.

NASA

Novosti, Pix

FIRST SPACE WALK was performed in March by Soviet Cosmonaut Aleksei A. Leonov, at right. In June, U.S. Astronaut Edward H. White II, left, ventured outside Gemini IV for 20 minutes.

This was preceded by the first attempt at rendezvous, which was planned for October 25 when an unmanned Agena (an upper stage rocket) was launched as the target vehicle for a later rendezvous with Gemini VI. But the Agena exploded. It was decided under revised plans that the Gemini VI spacecraft, piloted by Walter M. Schirra, Jr. (42-year-old veteran of a six-orbit Mercury flight) and Thomas P. Stafford, would rendezvous with Borman and Lovell's Gemini VII craft, which was orbited on December 4.

Launch teams worked around the clock at Cape Kennedy to clean up Complex 19 after the Gemini VII launch and to make ready Gemini VI's Titan II launch vehicle. After an aborted attempt on December 12, Gemini VI lifted off at 8:37:26 (EST) on December 15, exactly at the planned moment. It soared into an orbit 20 to 85 miles lower than Gemini VII and was 1,200 miles behind. Then, Navy Captain Schirra, with seven precisely timed bursts of thruster rockets based on computer computations, maneuvered Gemini VI into higher and wider orbits until the two ships were within one foot of each other. For about six hours both craft flew history's first "formation" space flight. During this rendezvous the four astronauts came close enough to see one another and to snap breathtaking photos through the windows of their spacecraft. Gemini VI splashed down on December 16; Gemini VII two days later.

Unmanned Exploration. The Ranger flights of February 17 and March 21, concluding the series, supplied thousands of exceedingly sharp photos of the moon's surface, showing craters and other fine details. During the closing moments of the March flight, photos were flashed directly back to TV screens across the nation as the craft rushed toward its impact point in the crater Alphonsus. Details a few feet in length were visible.

The Space Environment. Analysis of information obtained by satellites led to the conclusion that there are solar streams—steady, intense localized streams of particles flowing from the sun—as well as the general solar wind and the periodic solar flares. And observations made with devices on sounding rockets discovered sources of intense X rays in widely separated portions of the universe, for which no satisfactory explanation could be given.

Three Pegasus Satellites provided data on micrometeoroids, or space dust. With panels that unfolded to 96 feet in length, they measured the frequency and strength of impacts and confirmed assumptions regarding the Apollo spacecraft design.

Space Applications. The Communications Satellite Corporation (COMSAT) orbited the first commercial communications satellite, Early Bird, on April 6. It flew in a "stationary" position 22,000 miles above the equator, midway in the Atlantic, to provide telephone, telegraph, television, and other links between Europe and the United States. In

October, Early Bird enabled Europe to see Pope Paul's visit to the United Nations on television.

The Soviet Union launched a communications satellite of its own in April. It was Molniya I (Lightning), which transmitted color television from Moscow to eastern Siberia.

The launching on July 2 of Tiros X, first of the weather satellites funded by the Weather Bureau, marked the beginning of a fully operational weather satellite system. With the aid of a photo taken by Tiros IX, launched earlier in the year, Hurricane Betsy was located precisely in the Atlantic and the Gemini V spacecraft was returned to earth one orbit early, safely clear of the danger area.

The U.S. Navy announced in January that the Transit navigation satellite system was in operation. Computers in navy ships were able to obtain automatic fixes on one of the three satellites in the system, providing all-weather, world-wide coverage.

Apollo Progress. Peak effort was achieved in Apollo as the program passed its halfway mark. Work proceeded on schedule toward a major program milestone, the launching early in 1966 of the unmanned Apollo/Saturn IB space vehicle on an "all-up" flight test in a suborbital trajectory.

All systems of the vehicle were delivered to Cape Kennedy and, at year-end, preparations were well advanced for the launch. The Saturn IB is an improved version of the Saturn I, which completed on July 30 an unprecedented record of 10 successes in as many flights. Saturn I, which will no longer be flown, was used in developing such systems as liquid-hydrogen technology, and the clustering of high-thrust engines that are being used in the larger Saturn vehicles of the Apollo program.

Development testing proceeded for all systems of the Apollo/Saturn V space vehicle, the 36-story behemoth to be employed in the manned lunar missions. Work continued on schedule toward the beginning in 1967 of unmanned flights of this vehicle.

The test stand for the Saturn V second stage at the Mississippi Test Facility, east of New Orleans, was being readied for use in early 1966. Work on a stand for testing the giant first stage was proceeding on a schedule calling for completion in the second half of the year.

At the Merritt Island launch area in Florida, structural work was completed on the Vertical Assembly Building, a nearly cubical structure 52 stories high, believed to be the largest building in the world in total volume.

Surveyor, designed for soft landings on the moon, passed a major milestone when the Centaur launch vehicle, fueled with liquid hydrogen, was fired toward an imaginary moon late in 1964 and then was declared ready to carry Surveyor.

The Lunar Orbiter, which will orbit the moon and photograph large portions of its surface for mapping purposes, proceeded on schedule toward a first flight in the latter part of 1966.

The Orbiting Astronomical Observatory (OAO), perhaps the most difficult unmanned spacecraft project ever undertaken by the United States, passed its design review and was scheduled for launching early in 1966.

Rocket Technology. Nuclear rocket propulsion passed an important milestone in May when the NERVA rocket was fired successfully for 43 minutes at Jackass Flats, Nev.

In September, the world's largest known rocket engine, a cylinder 22 feet in diameter and 80 feet long, burned 840 tons of solid fuel to produce a tongue of flame as tall as New York's Empire State Building in a test firing at Homestead, Fla. The test proved the feasibility of very large-scale solid-propellant rockets.

Meanwhile, the Soviets conducted two flights of their new Proton spacecraft, powered by a new booster vehicle. The 26,900-pound Proton I was somewhat heavier than the largest U.S. payload, which had been orbited earlier on June 18 by an Air Force Titan III-C.

In December, France became the third nation with the ability to place satellites in orbit when a French satellite was launched in the Sahara.

Future Planning. With approval of President Lyndon B. Johnson, the Department of Defense began the development of a Manned Orbiting Laboratory (MOL) to investigate whether man can perform tasks of military value in space, to develop technology and equipment, and to perform related experiments.

A Titan III launch vehicle will propel the MOL, consisting of a space laboratory about the size of a house trailer and a modified Gemini spacecraft, to be used to return the two astronauts to earth. The Air Force is managing the MOL program.

The National Aeronautics and Space Administration (NASA) began definition of the Voyager program, in which unmanned spacecraft are to fly by later land on planets beginning with Mars.

Definition was also begun on a program of Apollo applications, in which the capabilities of the Apollo flight hardware and ground systems were to be made available for the next steps in space science and after the lunar landing.

Space Budget. For the fiscal year that began July 1, 1965, the national space budget totaled slightly over $7,000,000,000, including an appropriation of $5,175,000,000 to NASA. Most of the remainder was spent by the Department of Defense.

Personnel. Dr. Robert C. Seamans, Jr., 47, succeeded Dr. Hugh L. Dryden in the post of deputy administrator of NASA. One of the pioneers of astronautics, Dr. Dryden died on December 2. Dr. Mac C. Adams, formerly of the Avco Corporation, was appointed NASA's associate administrator for advanced research and technology.   JAY HOLMES

See also ASTRONAUTS; Section One, JOHN H. GLENN, JR., ON SPACE.

SPAIN

SPAIN carried out a threat it had made in 1964 and imposed severe border restrictions on Gibraltar, the British fortress on its southernmost tip. Spain argued that the base which had been ceded to Great Britain in 1713 under the Treaty of Utrecht, rightly belonged to it. Britain refused to discuss the issue until Spain ceased its harassments, which included a roadblock through which only four cars an hour were allowed to pass.

The nation was enjoying an unprecedented period of prosperity. Its revenues from tourism for the first six months of 1965 were 19 per cent higher than in the corresponding period of 1964. An estimated 10,640,000 tourists had taken advantage of Spain's favorable rate of exchange. The economy was bolstered further during the year by an inflow of foreign investment capital—$100,342,138 from the United States and $1,628,490 from Canada. First-year results of the nation's four-year development plan were encouraging, too; 641 firms were setting up plants at a cost of $750,000,000.

Population: 31,839,000. **Government:** Chief of State and Premier Francisco Franco; Vice-Premier Agustin Muñoz Grandes. **Monetary Unit:** peseta (60 = U.S. $1). **Foreign Trade:** exports $954,000,000; imports, $2,259,000,000. **Principal Exports:** cork, olives and olive oil, wine.   Kenneth Brown

See also Europe.

SPINGARN MEDAL. See Price, (Mary) Leontyne.

SPORTS. Adolfo López Mateos, a former president of Mexico, was appointed head of the Olympic Organizing Committee for the 19th Olympics, to be held in Mexico City October, 1968. He later became ill, and his place was taken by General Jose de Jesus Clark Flores.

During October, athletes from 20 countries gathered in the Mexican capital for a week-long "Little Olympics" to test the effects of the city's 7,400-foot altitude on their performances. Results varied, but most sports physicians and athletes agreed that distance runners and swimmers would certainly be adversely affected. Some doctors, however, felt an even greater menace would be diarrhea (known to tourists as "Montezuma's Revenge") caused by the change in altitude, water, and food.

The International Olympic Committee (IOC) voted to allow separate East and West German teams in the 1968 Games. Germany, divided in almost everything else, had fielded unified teams in the last four Olympics.

Arthur Lentz of New York was elected executive director of the U.S. Olympic Committee (USOC), replacing J. Lyman Bingham. In other action, the USOC gave working control of its Olympic Track and Field Committee to the Amateur Athletic Union (AAU) by awarding the AAU 23 of the 45 votes on the committee.

Awards. Bill Bradley of Princeton won the AAU's James E. Sullivan Award for his outstanding performances in basketball. Sandy Koufax of the Los Angeles Dodgers was named Sportsman of the Year by *Sports Illustrated* magazine.

Among the 1965 Sports Results were:

Curling. The Scotch Cup, emblematic of the world championship, was won by the Superior, Wis., rink, skipped by Raymond Somerville. Superior also took the U.S. men's championship, while the women's crown was won by the Indian Hill Country Club of Winnetka, Ill.

Handball. Jim Jacobs of New York won his second straight U.S. Handball Association four-wall singles title, and shared the doubles crown with Marty Decatur. The Obert family of New York dominated three-wall play, with Carl Obert winning the singles and Oscar and Ruby Obert the doubles. Oscar Obert also won his fifth one-wall singles championship, while Ken Holmes of Brooklyn and Walt Ulbrich of New York took the doubles. In AAU play, Pat Kirby of New York won the four-wall singles and Ruby and Oscar Obert the doubles. Ken Davidoff of New York won the one-wall singles, and Howie Eisenberg and Dave Norvid of Brooklyn captured the doubles title.

Rowing. Navy won the Intercollegiate Rowing Association regatta, but undefeated Harvard beat Navy by five lengths and was considered the fastest college crew in history. At the Royal Henley regatta in England, however, Harvard ran into its nemesis, the Vesper Boat Club of Philadelphia. Vesper had beaten Harvard in the 1964 U.S. Olympic trials, and now the team did it again at Henley, as both crews broke the course record. Then Vesper, which won the 1964 Olympics for the United States, was in turn beaten in the Henley finals by the revenge-minded Ratzeburg Rowing Club of West Germany, the 1964 Olympic runner-up. In singles, the Henley Diamond Sculls were won by Don Spero of New York.

Shooting. James Bellows of Encino, Calif., won the National Skeet Shooting Association all-around championship for men, and Evelyn Jones of Dallas won the women's title. In trapshooting, the men's Grand American was won by D. C. Poutier of Alden, N.Y., and the women's by Nancy Krebs of Ripon, Wis. The national service-rifle championship was taken by David H. Meredith of the Army, while perennial pistol champion Army Sergeant W. B. Blankenship again won the National Trophy match.

Weight Lifting. Three Olympic champions dominated their divisions in the 1965 world championships at Tehran, Iran. They were featherweight Yoshinobu Miyake of Japan, lightweight Waldemar Baszanowski of Poland, and heavyweight Leonid Zhabotinsky of Russia. Russia and Poland led the scoring with two winners each.

Other Champions. *Archery*, world championships: men, Matti Haikenen, Finland; women, Marie Lindheim, Finland; men's team, U.S.; women's team, U.S. *Bicycling*, Tour de France winner: Felice Gimondi, Italy. *Billiards*, world professional pocket title: Cicero Murphy, Brooklyn. *Bobsledding*, two-man: Britain; four-man: Canada. *Fencing*, world championships: foil, Russia; épée, France; saber, Russia. National Collegiate Athletic Association (NCAA) champion: Columbia. *Gymnastics*, AAU champion: Southern Connecticut Club. NCAA champion: Penn State. *Lacrosse*, intercollegiate: Navy. *Polo*, open: Santa Barbara-Oakbrook. *Volleyball*, intercollegiate: University of California. *Water Skiing*, men's national champion: Chuck Stearns, Bellflower, California; women's national champion: Dicksie Ann Hoyt of Fair Haven, New Jersey.   James O. Dunaway

See also the articles on various sports.

STAMP COLLECTING. See Hobbies.

STATE GOVERNMENT At least 20 legislatures reapportioned one or both of their houses in 1965. Some were temporary arrangements and some remained subject to court approval. Reapportionments were recorded as final in at least nine states, in view of acceptance by courts or absence of litigation. For three of these, courts did the redistricting by remapping one or both of the houses. In another case, a court did so for one house but upheld the legislature's plan for the second chamber.

These developments continued a historic surge of reapportionment action taken since the 1964 decisions of the U.S. Supreme Court requiring all state legislative districts to be as nearly equal in population as feasible. Since then, 34 states had taken reapportionment actions, which were either final or under court review as 1965 ended. Reapportionment action was pending in 11 others.

Finance. State budgets were at record highs because of population growth and increased demands for services. New tax legislation produced a total of new revenue unprecedented for a single year. Of the 47 states with regular legislative sessions in 1965, a large majority raised rates of one or more taxes. Frequently these were broad-based taxes.

Idaho and New York enacted their first sales taxes—3 per cent and 2 per cent, respectively. Sales taxes were increased in Colorado, Hawaii, Kansas, Rhode Island, South Dakota, Washington, and Wyoming. Two of those states and seven others applied the sales tax to additional transactions.

Both individual and corporate income taxes were raised in Arizona, Hawaii, Kansas, Montana, and Utah. Individual income taxes were increased in Iowa, Minnesota, and Wisconsin; and corporation income taxes, in Connecticut. Nine legislatures voted to increase taxes on motor fuel, six on alcoholic beverages, and an impressive 22 on cigarettes.

Figures reported in 1965 set state revenue from all sources at $45,200,000,000 in 1964, up more than 10 per cent from the year before, and total expenditures at $42,600,000,000, up 7.6 per cent.

Education continued to receive a larger share of the budgets and budget increases than any other function. All levels of schooling shared in the rise.

To combat school drop-outs, the age for compulsory school attendance was raised in Hawaii, Maine, Vermont, and Wisconsin. Action to launch or expand community and junior colleges was particularly widespread; measures for those purposes were voted in at least 15 legislatures. See EDUCATION; Section One, LAWRENCE A. CREMIN ON EDUCATION.

Health and Welfare. Enactments to strengthen mental health services and combat mental retardation were common, including expansion of community clinics. In 26 states, legislatures passed laws seeking to protect babies and children from physical abuse. Most of the laws required official medical reports. In the last three years 47 states have adopted laws of this type.

Connecticut in 1965 became the first state to require fluoridation of its water. Legislatures of six states authorized public provision of birth control information or devices, or both. See CHILD WELFARE; HEALTH; SOCIAL WELFARE.

Highway Safety. Georgia and North Carolina legislatures adopted vehicle-inspection laws. Iowa, Minnesota, and New Hampshire raised the driver license age requirement from 16 to 18 for applicants without stipulated driver-training; Utah raised it similarly from 16 to 17. Michigan authorized cancellation of under-18 driver licenses on the request of parents. In West Virginia, 16- and 17-year-olds—with parental consent—got junior licenses.

Civil Rights commissions were set up in Arizona and Iowa, and strengthened in Alaska, Colorado, Missouri, and New York. California legislation provided for suspending licenses of real estate brokers for "blockbusting." Several states—including Colorado, Connecticut, Maine, Ohio, and Rhode Island—enacted laws against discrimination in housing. See CIVIL RIGHTS; NEGRO.

Consumer Protection. Laws regulating installment selling were adopted in California, Nebraska, Nevada, and New Mexico; and laws to combat deceptive advertising in Delaware, Nevada, and New Mexico. FRANK SMOTHERS

See also CRIME; COURTS AND LAWS; ELECTIONS; GOVERNORS OF THE STATES.

STEEL INDUSTRY in 1965 surmounted three crises and went on to pour nearly 130,000,000 tons of ingots and castings. Shipments of finished steel were about 5,000,000 tons above the 1964 total of 84,900,000 tons.

These happy results were facilitated by the failure of two of the feared crises to come to a head, and by the relatively weak impact of the third. First came the May 1 strike deadline. Trouble was averted by an interim wage agreement and by a truce until September 1. As that date approached fresh fears arose. Five days before the deadline, President Lyndon B. Johnson entered into the dispute with telephone appeals to both sides to reach a "responsible and decent settlement." Before the contract was signed on September 6, he had to bring the negotiators to the White House, win an eight-day extension of the strike deadline, and make deadlock-breaking proposals to both sides. See LABOR.

The Third Crisis immediately confronted the industry: The expected collapse of demand while customers used up the steel they had stockpiled against a possible strike. But the seemingly insatiable demand for automobiles and the gradually increasing military orders quickly ate into the stockpiles. From the first week in November to the first week in December, the industry's operating rate rose from 62.7 to 67.4 per cent of capacity.

A profit squeeze was expected by the steel companies despite record sales of about $22,500,000,000 for 1965. They felt that the costs of the new contract outran the rise in productivity. Although the President did not exact any industry pledge on prices during negotiations, he had praised the new contract as noninflationary and later warned generally on price rises. A number of people in the steel industry, in fact, thought that the President's all-out attack on the aluminum industry for seeking a small price increase two months later was really aimed at steel (see MINES AND MINING).

World Capacity for making steel grew in 1965 to more than was needed in hot-rolled products such as wire rod and reinforcing bars. It was beginning to be true of more sophisticated products like sheet and strip. U.S. imports of steel rose from 6,400,000 tons in 1964 to about 10,000,000 tons.

Late in the year, two British and three West German steel mills reduced operations to bring output into line with demand. Total world output of crude steel, excluding China, was estimated to have doubled since 1953. U.S. production was more than a quarter of the total; and Russia's, about a fifth.

Inter-Industry, as well as overseas, competition inhibited U.S. price rises. One executive calculated that in 1964 alone rival packaging materials had cut back the market for tinplate by 350,000 tons. The industry, meanwhile, has rolled tinplate thinner than ever, bonded steel to cheaper materials, and made tinless steel for cans. ROBERT E. BEDINGFIELD

STOCKS AND BONDS.

Stock prices and the volume of trading advanced to all-time high ground in 1965. In the second week of December over 48,000,000 shares changed hands, the largest weekly volume in the 173-year history of the New York Stock Exchange (NYSE). A surge of sales beginning in September kept brokers hopping until year-end.

Several automation steps, including computerized transfers of stock certificates and a talking computer that quoted prices on request, helped the exchange handle its welter of business. Modernization was not limited to the United States. In October, the Montreal and Canadian stock exchanges moved into the new automated 47-story Stock Exchange Tower in Montreal.

Investor exuberance reflected unparalleled U.S. corporate profits and a deluge of dividends, including a record $1,495,000,000 payout by General Motors Corporation. During the third quarter, profits before taxes totaled $74,600,000,000 at an annual rate, while after-tax profits were $44,900,-000,000, up more than $8,000,000,000 from the 1964 national total. See ECONOMY, THE (charts).

Small Investors lent strong support to the 1965 bull market. Low-priced and unlisted stocks gained popularity after midyear. Mutual fund sales in the first 10 months of 1965 surpassed 1964's record full-year sales. And a new survey revealed a population of 20,120,000 stockholders, three times the 1952 shareowner total.

All investors did not share the general optimism. Some were *selling short*, or selling stock they did not own hoping to deliver it later when prices declined. During each of the last six months of 1965 the NYSE short interest position increased, posting a record gain of almost 2,000,000 shares in December to a high of 12,000,000 shares. Stock prices sagged 7 per cent in May and June, but then rebounded. The Dow-Jones industrial average ended 1965 at a historic closing high of 969.26, an overall gain of about 11 per cent. On Dec. 31, 1964, it had been 874.13.

More New Securities to finance the capital boom were issued by corporations than in 1964. Bonds continued relatively attractive. Interest paid is deductible from taxable income, while dividend payouts are not. Only 15 per cent of new issues in 1965 were stocks in comparison with 20 per cent in 1964.

Europe's Economic Doldrums infected overseas stock prices and trading. Anti-inflationary economic policies damped spending and industrial growth. The major European stock indexes closed 1965 well below their highs for the year. However, Italy's, as well as Japan's, markets seemed to be recovering.

There was increased foreign interest in U.S. securities. The boom, as well as instant price quotation service for U.S. stocks in Europe, helped. A record of more than 5 per cent of U.S. mutual fund sales went to foreign buyers in 1965.

Security Regulatory Steps in 1965 included:
• Action by the NYSE to reduce the influence of floor traders in running the exchange and to increase the role of members who deal directly with the public.
• Support by the Securities and Exchange Commission (SEC) of the National Association of Security Dealers' quotations of over-the-counter stock prices at wholesale, rather than retail, as before.
• A new SEC rule requiring that the type of data included with proxy statements be given to stockholders, even when proxies are not solicited.
• Moves by the SEC for added disclosure of the finances of securities firms themselves and of foreign firms whose shares were traded in the United States.

Corporate Insiders' short-term trading profits came under fire in 1965. The SEC sued the Texas Gulf Sulphur Company and 13 of its officials in April to recover profits from stock and options they had acquired before the public had assimilated news of the company's rich Canadian ore discovery in 1964. The suit sought to reimburse those who sold their stock to insiders. The SEC, for the first time, suspended top officials of a Wall Street brokerage firm—Shearson, Hammill & Co., Inc.—for Securities Act violations by subordinates in a West Coast branch of the company.

Anthony De Angelis, found guilty in the $150,-000,000 salad oil swindle of 1963, was sentenced to 20 years in prison. The scandal had caused the bankruptcy of a securities firm. WILLIAM G. DEWALD

See also BANKS AND BANKING; MONEY.

SUDAN returned to representative government in 1965 after weathering a series of political crises. Following the overthrow of President Ibrahim Abboud in November, 1964, Premier Sir-el Khatim el-Khalifa resigned, but was asked to continue a caretaker government until elections in 1965.

In March, representatives of the Sudan African National Union (SANU), chief political organization in the largely Negro south, met with Arab northerners at Juba to negotiate internal autonomy for the south. But the conferees could not agree. Throughout 1965, Negro rebels pushed their demands for the withdrawal of all northerners.

In April, Sudan's registered voters cast ballots for the north's 173 seats in the new Constituent Assembly. The south, entitled to 60 seats, refused to participate in the election. The returns gave the Umma party 75 seats, the National Union party (NUP) 54 seats, and the Communist party, later outlawed by the national assembly, 8 seats. Premier el-Khalifa again resigned. The assembly chose Umma leader Mohammed Ahmed Mahgoub to head a Umma-NUP coalition cabinet.

Population: 13,700,000. **Government:** Premier Mohammed Ahmed Mahgoub. **Monetary Unit:** pound (1=U.S. $2.80). **Foreign Trade:** exports, $247,000,000; imports, $282,900,000. **Principal Exports:** cotton, gum arabic, peanuts.   WILLIAM SPENCER

See also AFRICA.

SUPREME COURT OF THE UNITED STATES.

Criminal procedures dominated the work of the Supreme Court during 1965, as the U.S. Constitution was brought to bear upon both federal and state criminal actions. Due process of law cases led the list of significant decisions. The Court held that television coverage of the Billie Sol Estes swindle trial in 1962 voided a conviction. The 5-to-4 decision ruled that television coverage of *notorious* cases was prejudicial to the rights of the accused. But since only four Justices held that television coverage of *any* trial would be prejudicial and unconstitutional, no clear-cut ban on all courtroom TV could be read into the decision.

The Court voided a provision of the California constitution that had permitted a court to comment upon the silence of a defendant in a criminal case. Such a provision was held contrary to the Fifth Amendment, which was ruled applicable to state proceedings through the due process clause of Amendment 14. Reviewing a Texas conviction, the Court held, for the first time, that the guaranty in Amendment 6 of a defendant's right to be confronted with the witness against him also applies to states. The Court again based its ruling on Amendment 14's due process clause.

The Court clarified a widely debated issue that arose after its 1961 *Mapp vs. Ohio* decision that illegally seized evidence was inadmissible in a criminal trial in a state court. In *Linkletter vs. Walker*, the Court ruled that its 1961 decision would not be retroactive. Persons convicted in such trials predating the *Mapp* decision will not be entitled to a retrial on that ground.

Change in the Court's Composition accounted for the reversal of one of the Court's 1959 decisions. The late Justice Felix Frankfurter wrote for a majority of five at that time that a federal judge could punish a person for criminal contempt without a hearing or jury trial. On Dec. 6, 1965, the Court reversed this earlier position in a 5-to-4 decision, which found the new member, Associate Justice Abe Fortas, voting with the four 1959 dissenters. In the new case, a witness who had refused to testify before a grand jury was brought before a federal judge and, still refusing to testify, was sentenced on the spot. The Court ruled that such sentencing without a hearing could be done only for disruptive or threatening behavior in the courtroom.

Employers' Rights in labor disputes were more clearly defined in two decisions on March 29, 1965. The Court ruled an employer might go out of business—if he closed all, not just some, of his plants—during a labor dispute even though he was motivated by a desire to resist unionization (see LABOR).

In the second case, the Court upheld the right of employers in a multi-company bargaining unit to lay off union employees and replace them with non-union employees for the duration of a so-called "whipsaw strike." In the case before the Court, the union had tried to win its demands by striking against competing food stores one at a time.

In Other Decisions ranging across the full scope of its jurisdiction the Court ruled that:

• The Virginia poll tax as it applied to eligibility to vote in federal elections was unconstitutional.

• Connecticut's 1879 law against use of birth control devices was in violation of six amendments. Justice William O. Douglas said the decision was based on a "right of privacy older than the Bill of Rights." See POPULATION, WORLD.

• California was not entitled to minerals under the ocean beyond the three-mile limit. The 5-to-2 decision ended 20 years of litigation and congressional consideration. The majority held that the waters between the mainland and the state's offshore Channel Islands were not "inland waters."

The New Court. The vacancy created by the resignation of Associate Justice Arthur J. Goldberg to become U.S. ambassador to the United Nations was filled by the appointment of Washington (D.C.) lawyer Abe Fortas, who was sworn in October 4. The other members of the Court during 1965 were Chief Justice Earl Warren and, in order of seniority, Associate Justices Hugo Black, William O. Douglas, Tom C. Clark, John Marshall Harlan, William J. Brennan, Jr., Potter Stewart, and Byron Raymond White.   ERNEST C. FRIESEN, JR.

See also CONGRESS OF THE UNITED STATES; COURTS AND LAWS; FORTAS, ABE.

SWAZILAND continued to push for governmental reforms that could lead to future independence from Great Britain. But the 1964 constitution and elections, intended by Britain to result in a balanced legislative body of African traditionalist, African nationalist, and European forces, had unexpected results. Paramount Chief Sobhuza II and his newly formed traditionalist Imbokodvo party won a sweeping victory.

In April, Simon Nxumalo announced that his opposition Swaziland Democratic party would join forces with Chief Sobhuza's Imbokodvo movement. In June, the Joint Council of Swaziland Political Parties, representing the four nationalist political parties, objected to the present government and demanded reforms.

Chief Sobhuza requested the British Resident Commissioner to start talks leading to independence. The British government increased the number of Swaziland appointed members on the 10-man Executive Council of Swaziland from two to four and requested the appointment of a local committee to review the constitution and recommend changes.

Population: 295,000. **Government:** Resident Commissioner B. A. Marwick; Paramount Chief of the Swazi Sobhuza II. **Monetary Unit:** rand (1 = U.S. $1.40). **Foreign Trade:** No statistics available. **Principal Exports:** tin, tobacco.   BENJAMIN E. THOMAS

See also AFRICA.

SWEDEN, the largest and richest of the Scandinavian nations, saw the fiscally bright future it had enjoyed during the first half of 1965 fade somewhat during the last half of the year. Like so many Western European countries, Sweden was in the throes of near-inflation.

There were signs of discord on the labor-management front, where an acute shortage of labor had strengthened the bargaining position of the labor unions. Foreign exchange reserves had been declining. Exports, which had risen by 10 per cent over the 1964 figures, had failed to keep pace with imports, which were up by 15 per cent. Business spending on capital equipment had failed to rise largely because of tight control of bank lending.

Despite these trends, Sweden continued to maintain its international reputation as the most welfare-conscious nation in the world. Allocations for social welfare remained the largest item in the nation's operating budget. Higher old-age pensions and cash allowances for dependent children were instituted during the year.

Population: 7,722,000. **Government:** King Gustav VI Adolf; Prime Minister Tage E. Erlander. **Monetary Unit:** krona (5.172 = U.S. $1). **Gross National Product:** 77,900,000,000 kronor. **Foreign Trade:** exports, $3,801,200,000; imports, $3,988,600,000. **Principal Exports:** iron and steel, machinery, paper and pulp.   KENNETH BROWN

See also EUROPE.

SWIMMING. The University of Southern California won both the National Collegiate Athletic Association (NCAA) and Amateur Athletic Union (AAU) indoor titles, and the Santa Clara Swim Club won the men's and women's titles in the AAU outdoor championships.

In the NCAA competition, held at Iowa State, Roy Saari of Southern California again won three events—the 200-, 500-, and 1,650-yard free-style. Double winners were Fred Schmidt of Indiana (100- and 200-yard butterfly), Ken Sitzberger of Indiana (one- and three-meter diving), Gary Dilley of Michigan State (100- and 200-yard backstroke), and Steve Clark of Yale (50- and 100-yard free-style).

Five American records were set in the AAU championships at Yale by Olympic medalists Steve Clark (100-yard free-style) and Don Schollander (200-yard free-style) of Yale, Thompson Mann of North Carolina (100-yard backstroke), Greg Buckingham of Atherton, Calif. (400-yard individual medley), and Roy Saari (200-yard individual medley). Patty Caretto and Jeanne Hallock, Commerce, Calif.; Cynthia Goyette, Detroit; Cathy Ferguson, Los Angeles; and Mrs. Joel O'Connell, Santa Clara, Calif.; each set U.S. records in the AAU meet.

World records were set at the AAU outdoor championships by Patty Caretto, Martha Randall, Claudia Kolb, Kendis Moore, Steve Krause, and the Commerce women's team.   STANLEY ISAACS

SWITZERLAND continued to fight overexpansion by maintaining limits on bank interest, foreign investments, real estate, and mortgages. The embargo it had placed on nonessential building was extended through 1966 and the gasoline tax was increased.

The labor situation was a further problem. A fifth of Switzerland's labor force comes from neighboring countries; assimilation had proved difficult. By federal decree, the number of foreign workers admitted to Switzerland was to be cut by 10 per cent by the end of 1965. It was hoped that the manpower loss would be offset by automation.

In June, the government dismissed the chairman of the Federal Banking Commission for unethical conduct and replaced him with a former finance minister. The dismissal followed the chairman's arrest in connection with the closing of two Swiss banks. Both banks had granted a large number of insufficiently secured loans.

In July, mountaineers and Alpinists from all over the world converged on the picturesque village of Zermatt to celebrate the first ascent of the Matterhorn 100 years earlier. See CELEBRATIONS.

Population: 5,776,000. **Government:** President Peter Tschudi. **Monetary Unit:** franc (4.318 = U.S. $1). **Gross National Product:** 50,000,000,000 francs. **Foreign Trade:** exports, $2,647,000,000; imports, $3,610,000,000. **Principal Exports:** chemicals, machines, watches and clocks.   KENNETH BROWN

See also EUROPE.

SYRIA. The ruling Ba'ath party continued on a path toward Arab socialism as industry was nationalized and the nation's traditional pattern of individual enterprise was severely disrupted. The first to fall were nine oil companies that were declared state property in January, 1965. Next, cereal companies, pharmaceutical importers, and cotton exporters were nationalized. Then, the government took over small and medium-sized beer, glass, pottery, and textile companies. Finally, Syria's 55 ginning mills were expropriated.

The government's action caused great resentment among businessmen and farmers, prompting a rash of strikes and violence in the major cities. A plot to assassinate President Amin el-Hafez was uncovered in late January. However, el-Hafez issued an amnesty for the plotters in a conciliatory gesture to win public support for the party's program.

In December, a power struggle within the Ba'ath party resulted in the resignation of Prime Minister Youssef Zayyin. President el-Hafez selected Salah al-Din Bitar to replace him.

Population: 5,750,000. **Government:** President Amin el-Hafez; Prime Minister Salah al-Din Bitar. **Monetary Unit:** pound (3.82 = U.S. $1). **Foreign Trade:** exports, $176,100,000; imports, $235,200,000. **Principal Exports:** cotton, wheat.   WILLIAM SPENCER

See also MIDDLE EAST.

TANGANYIKA. See TANZANIA.

TANZANIA, a federal union of the former countries of the United Republic of Tanganyika and Zanzibar, worked out a knotty political problem in 1965. In May, the Zanzibar Revolutionary Council voted to support a single party in Zanzibar, the Afro-Shirazi party, and to dissolve all other political organizations. The National Assembly of Tanzania, however, passed an interim constitution bill in July establishing the Tanganyika African National Union (TANU) as the official party but recognizing the existence of the Afro-Shirazi party and the separate government institutions in Zanzibar. In August, 1965, the TANU and the Afro-Shirazi party nominated President Julius Nyerere to continue in office. He was re-elected in September.

Tanzania's industrial plan, completed in April, called for the exploitation of coal deposits in the south, the expansion of sisal processing factories, and the establishment of various industries.

Tanzania, frequently mentioned as a staging platform for subversive activity in East Africa, signed pacts with Communist China for a fivefold increase in the volume of Tanzanian-Chinese trade.

Population: 10,603,000. **Government:** President Julius Nyerere. **Monetary Unit:** shilling (7.143 = U.S. $1). **Gross National Product:** $707,000,000. **Foreign Trade:** exports, $193,000,000; imports, $128,000,000. **Principal Exports:** cloves, coffee, cotton, sisal.   BENJAMIN E. THOMAS

See also AFRICA.

TAXATION from all sources in the United States reached a record high in the fiscal year ended June 30, 1965. There were prospects of increased federal spending to pay for the expanded programs of the Great Society and the growing U.S. involvement in Vietnam. But increased tax revenue would help to bridge the gap. Federal tax receipts in fiscal 1965 totaled $114,435,000,000, which is $2,200,000,000 more than the fiscal 1964 total.

President Lyndon B. Johnson sent Congress a cash budget in January, 1965, calling for record peacetime federal spending of $127,400,000,000. He cut

Fiscal 1965 Federal Tax Collections
(millions of dollars)

Type of Tax	Amount	Change in Year
Corporation income	$ 26,131	+ 7.4%
Individual income	53,661	− 1.3%
Employment.............	17,104	− 1.7%
Estate and gift..........	2,746	+13.6%
Excise and other........	14,793	+ 6.0%
TOTAL...............	$114,435	+ 1.9%

defense spending $2,300,000,000 to some $49,000,-000,000. (This figure was later revised upward because of the war in Vietnam.) The federal budget did not include increased Social Security benefits, financed separately out of increased Social Security levies (see CONGRESS OF THE U.S.; MEDICARE; SOCIAL SECURITY).

The record tax collection reduced the estimated federal deficit for 1965. In June, the President announced that the deficit would total some $3,800,-000,000, about $2,500,000,000 less than the estimate made by the administration in January, 1965.

Excise Tax Cut. The first session of the 89th Congress reduced excise taxes at President Johnson's request. The total tax cut suggested by the President was $3,500,000,000, but Congress increased it to $4,600,000,000. Of that amount, $1,750,000,000 in excise taxes were eliminated when the legislation took effect, June 22, 1965. The rest of the cut would be applied in stages until Jan. 1, 1969.

Although President Johnson asked producers and retailers to pass the cut along to consumers, some manufacturers contended that rising costs forced them to pocket the additional funds. In general, retailers, selling some thousand items from phonograph records to garden tools, dropped their prices. Federal excise taxes on theater tickets were eliminated as of Dec. 31, 1965.

State Tax Collections rose about 7.8 per cent in the 1965 fiscal year. The total climbed to $26,100,-000,000 from the preceding year's total of $24,200,-000,000. All states except South Dakota reported some increase.

The five states showing the steepest percentage rise in revenue over the 1964 fiscal year were Delaware (20.3 per cent), Indiana (16.5), Rhode Island (13.8), Mississippi (13.2), and Alaska (12.8).

Seven states collected nearly half of all state tax revenue in fiscal 1965. They were, in order of the size of receipts: California, New York, Pennsylvania, Michigan, Illinois, Texas, and Ohio. See STATE GOVERNMENT.

Local Taxes. During the 12-month period from July 1, 1964, through June 30, 1965, collections of locally imposed taxes (municipal and county) totaled

States' Major Tax Sources in Fiscal 1965
(millions of dollars)

Type of tax*	Amount	Rise in Year
General sales (37)	$6,710	10.3%
Selective sales:		
Motor fuels (50)	4,295	5.8%
Tobacco products (48)	1,284	7.3%
Alcoholic beverages (50)	917	6.1%
Insurance (50)	743	5.0%
Individual income (36)	3,642	6.7%
Corporation income (38)	1,932	13.9%
Property (44)	765	5.9%
Death and gift (49)	731	11.2%
Severance (29)	503	2.8%

*Number of states collecting tax shown in parentheses.

$25,500,000,000, nearly as much as the total of state tax collections for approximately the same period. These pushed the total bill—exclusive of Social Security deductions—to the U.S. taxpayer above the $166,000,000,000 level.   CAROL L. THOMPSON

See also CITY; PRESIDENT OF THE U.S.

TAYLOR, PRINCE ALBERT, JR. (1907?-   ), the first Negro minister to be elected President of the Methodist Council of Bishops, took office in April, 1965. He succeeded Bishop Lloyd C. Wicke of New York City, and serves for one year. In 1964, Bishop Taylor was made head of the Methodist churches in the New Jersey area. There are 600 or more Methodist churches there, and a large majority of the congregations are made up of white persons.

Before going to New Jersey, Bishop Taylor served as Bishop of Liberia for eight years. He was head of the Christian Education Department at Gammon Theological Seminary in Atlanta, Ga., for four years. He also has held pastorates in North Carolina and in New York City.

Prince Albert Taylor, Jr., comes from a family of Methodist ministers. His father, grandfather, and an uncle were all ministers. Two of his brothers are Methodist ministers, and his five sisters married ministers. The name "Prince," the Bishop said, "is a name my grandmother gave my father," but he does not know where it originated. The Bishop was born in Hennessey, Okla., and, during most of his childhood, lived in Mississippi. He attended Huston-Tillotson College in Austin, Texas, and studied for the ministry at Gammon Theological Seminary. The Bishop and his wife have one daughter, Mrs. Joseph Butts of Atlanta, Ga.

TELEPHONE AND TELEGRAPH. See COMMUNICATIONS; SPACE TRAVEL; TELEVISION.

TELEVISION

Color television, which has been around for more than a decade, finally arrived in 1965. In September, 96 per cent of NBC's programs, 50 per cent of CBS's, and 40 per cent of ABC's were in color.

By October, there were 4,450,000 color sets in American homes, 90 per cent more than the October, 1964, total of 2,345,000. Christmas demand was so strong it seemed inevitable there would be more than 6,000,000 color sets in use by Jan. 1, 1966.

The New Offerings of the season fared poorly, however. And, in spite of a 1,200,000 increase in U.S. TV households since 1964, studies indicated that 2,800,000 fewer viewers were watching the new fall shows than in the previous year.

Among the new programs quickly axed were "The Steve Lawrence Show" and "Convoy." Also dropped were several holdovers from the previous season—"The King Family," "Shindig," "Rawhide," and "Slattery's People." Earlier casualties included "The Rogues," "Mr. Novak," and "The Defenders."

Some of the most successful of the new shows were "Get Smart!" a James Bond spoof with Don Adams as a bungling agent; "Hogan's Heroes," a comedy set in a World War II prisoner of war camp; "Green Acres," another "Beverly Hillbillies" offshoot; and two adventure dramas: "Run for Your Life" and "I Spy." In "I Spy," Bill Cosby became the first Negro actor to co-star in a network TV dramatic series.

The Specials. On the whole, the networks, as usual, did a better job on specials and news coverage than on regular programs. Specials that were well received included Barbra Streisand's Emmy-winning one-woman show "My Name Is Barbra" (CBS); the Julie Andrews-Gene Kelly musical hour (NBC); two specials celebrating Frank Sinatra's 50th birthday (CBS and NBC); Lady Bird Johnson's tour of historic U.S. landmarks (ABC); and CBS's "National Drivers' Test."

The networks were highly praised for their coverage of such historic events as Pope Paul VI's visit to New York City, the civil rights march in Alabama (see NEGRO), the Gemini flights, President Lyndon B. Johnson's inauguration, and the ceremonies in London marking the death of Sir Winston Churchill.

NBC Television

"THE MAN FROM U.N.C.L.E.," and other shows, capitalized on the James Bond mania. It starred Robert Vaughn, left, and David McCallum.

NBC Television

"GET SMART!" popular new series, starred Don Adams as a bungling secret agent. Barbara Feldon, right, co-starred. KAOS spy, left, was Barbara Bain.

Emmy Awards went to Barbra Streisand, NBC's color tour of the Louvre, Alfred Lunt and Lynn Fontanne for "The Magnificent Yankee" (NBC), and to Dick Van Dyke for "The Dick Van Dyke Show" on the CBS network.

The estimate of total TV business (network and local) for 1965 made by the Television Bureau of Advertising (TBA) was $2,475,000,000. Even if TBA's estimate proved high there was no doubt that TV's 1965 billings increases would be substantially more than 1964 revenues.

Changes Occurred at the top level of two of the networks. Robert E. Kintner became the board chairman of the National Broadcasting Company. He was replaced as president and chief executive officer by William D. Scott, who had been president of NBC-TV. James Aubrey, Jr., was removed from his post of president of CBS-TV in February. He was replaced by John A. Schneider.

Educational Television. There were 109 educational television (ETV) stations in 1965 (as compared to 88 in 1964) and the future of ETV never looked brighter. President Lyndon B. Johnson demonstrated his personal interest in ETV by sending Vice-President Hubert H. Humphrey to the 41st annual convention of the National Association of Educational Broadcasters.

During the convention both Humphrey and FCC Chairman E. William Henry advised the educators not to limit themselves to educational material only,

NBC Television

FRANK SINATRA starred in two specials within two weeks. One was on CBS, the other on NBC. They marked his 50th birthday.

CBS Television

"MY NAME IS BARBRA," was the title of a CBS special that won 23-year-old Barbra Streisand an Emmy Award and many new fans.

TENNIS. Spain rose to a top place among the tennis powers by defeating the United States in Davis Cup competition, 4 to 1, at Barcelona. It was the fourth time in six years that the U.S. team failed to reach the challenge round. Spain then defeated India, but was no match for the Australians, who retained possession of the Davis Cup with a 4 to 1 victory at Sydney's White City Stadium in December.

Except for one notable victory by Virginian Arthur Ashe of the University of California at Los Angeles, it was a poor year for the United States. Ashe scored a victory over Roy Emerson of Australia in the quarterfinals of the American championships at Forest Hills, Long Island, N.Y. He then was beaten by Manuel Santana, star of the Spanish Davis Cup team, in the semifinals. Margaret Smith of Australia won the women's title, defeating Mrs. Billie Jean (Moffitt) King of Long Beach, Calif. Emerson and Fred Stolle, another Australian, won the men's doubles title, while Carole Graebner of Santa Monica, Calif., and Nancy Richey of Dallas won the women's doubles.

Emerson retained his Wimbledon title by defeating Stolle, and Miss Smith defeated Maria Bueno of Brazil in the women's final. The Wimbledon men's doubles were won by Australians John Newcombe and Tony Roche. The women's crown went to the Bueno-King team. STANLEY ISAACS

TEXTILE. See MANUFACTURING.

but to also report on vital national issues and community problems. Otherwise, said Henry, some of their ETV licensees might be in jeopardy. Meanwhile, the U.S. Office of Education announced that federal aid in the form of matching funds to ETV stations has totaled $11,300,000 since May, 1963.

In October, it was estimated there were about 173,000,000 TV sets in use throughout the world. America led the list with 68,200,000 sets; followed by Japan (17,700,000), England (15,100,000), and Russia (12,100,000). The Congolese were last with one set for every 2,500 people.

U.S. TV shows were so popular in other countries that foreign replay rights brought American TV packagers a $75,000,000 gross in 1965—$5,000,000 more than in 1964. NBC's "Bonanza," telecast in 59 countries last year, was viewed by a weekly world audience of 350,000,000.

Early Bird, the first privately owned communications satellite, was launched with much enthusiasm last spring. Programing ranged from the first live transatlantic colorcast and the pope's visit to New York, to a heart operation in Houston, Tex. See COMMUNICATIONS; SPACE TRAVEL.

Edward R. Murrow, who had been one of the top radio and TV newscasters and who became the director of the United States Information Agency, died in April. Murrow first gained fame for his moving and incisive radio reports from London during air raids in World War II. JUNE BUNDY CSIDA

THAILAND enjoyed a relatively prosperous year under its new premier, Thanom Kittikachorn. The economy was bolstered by a considerable amount of U.S. aid. More important, perhaps, was the fact that the government was spreading this aid into the rural areas as part of an all-out effort to unify the nation, and create a strong economy.

Every effort was being made to bring the six northeastern provinces into closer relationship with the central government. This was being accomplished through a variety of programs. Special stations, manned by agriculturists, health and social welfare workers, and teachers, were established in the provinces. These stations, in turn, were supplemented by hundreds of Mobile Development Unit personnel. In the face of suspected North Vietnamese infiltration, they helped to maintain loyalty to the central government.

The effects of the unification drive could be seen, too, in the new 380-mile Friendship Highway and its 500 miles of feeder roads. The long-range economic effect of the highway was expected to result in the opening up of new markets for the corn, jute, and tobacco crops grown in the rural northeastern area.

Population: 31,647,000. **Government:** King Bhumibol Adulyadej; Premier Thanom Kittikachorn. **Monetary Unit:** baht (20.83 = U.S. $1). **Foreign Trade:** exports, $599,000,000; imports, $667,000,-000. **Principal Exports:** rubber, tin. JOHN N. STALKER

See also ASIA.

THEATER

Clyde Hare

There were no extraordinary developments in the theater in the United States or in the rest of the world in 1965. Conditions were unfavorable to the self-sustaining, or commercial theater, and the dearth of significant new plays continued everywhere.

But at the same time the noncommercial theater was receiving more support than ever from public funds, especially in countries where the stage had been, or (as in the United States) was beginning to be, subsidized by the government, by large foundations, and by public-spirited groups.

Thus, in the Western Hemisphere there was considerable support for the distinguished Minnesota Theater Company at the Tyrone Guthrie Theater in Minneapolis and the Stratford (Ontario) Shakespeare Festival in Canada. The Canadian group extended its program well beyond its original exclusive concentration on Shakespearian drama. In 1965, it produced Chekhov's *The Cherry Orchard*, as well as Shakespeare's *Henry IV*, Parts 1 and 2.

Lincoln Center's Theater. Potentially the most important new stage venture in the United States was the Repertory Theater Company of New York City's Lincoln Center for the Performing Arts. But it could not be said that its early career was free from failure and friction. After an unsatisfactory start early in 1964, the organization started its season in the fall of the same year with a catastrophic production of the lurid Elizabethan tragedy, *The Changeling*. By that time, moreover, dissatisfaction with management and poor public reception of its programs led to the withdrawal of the gifted stage director, Elia Kazan, and the resignation of Robert Whitehead, manager of the company.

Ironically, the next two presentations still under Whitehead's leadership were highly commended. One was Arthur Miller's new play, *Incident at Vichy*, a treatment of the moral issues posed by the conquest of France by the Nazis. The play was well staged by the veteran director, Harold Clurman. The other was Molière's *Tartuffe*, which was brilliantly revived by the young director, William Ball, who later established a noteworthy repertory company in Pittsburgh, Pa.

A New Administration under the young San Francisco directors, Herbert Blau and Jules Irving, took charge in July and opened Lincoln Center's newest building, the superbly designed Vivian Beaumont Theater. But the first production, Georg Büchner's early 19th century historical drama *Danton's Death*, was an overproduced and noisy affair that left everybody disappointed. However, it seemed likely that the next productions, Congreve's *The Way of the World*, Sartre's *The Prisoners of Altona*, and Brecht's modern parable, *The Caucasian Chalk Circle*, would prove far more successful.

NEW REPERTORY GROUP, the American Conservatory Theater, opened in Pittsburgh. Scene, left, is from the company's Tiny Alice.

Robert Walker, *The New York Times*

VIVIAN BEAUMONT THEATER, the newest unit of Manhattan's Lincoln Center, opened in October. In the reflecting pool is Henry Moore's Reclining Figure.

The European Stage. In the meantime, the most satisfactory recently established institutions were to be found in England. These were the Royal Shakespeare Company of London, the National Theatre under the leadership of Sir Laurence Olivier, which produced Arthur Miller's Salem witchcraft drama, *The Crucible*, and the continuing Chichester summer festival theater Olivier founded in 1962.

On the Continent, Edward Albee's *Who's Afraid of Virginia Woolf?* received more acclaim than any other American play produced at the time-honored *Comédie Française*. Also, interest continued to be aroused by the *Berliner Ensemble* of East Berlin (which visited London with great success) and by Erwin Piscator's West Berlin *Freie Volksbuehne* (Free People's Theater), which produced provocative topical dramas such as *The Deputy* and *The Oppenheimer Affair*.

Importation. New York received a number of noteworthy visits by foreign companies. Perhaps the most interest was aroused by the first appearance in 42 years of the Moscow Art Theater. Among the four works it presented were Chekhov's masterpieces, *The Three Sisters* and *The Cherry Orchard*.

Nevertheless, it cannot be said that the new plays produced in the United States, England, or Continental Europe had extraordinary merit. A good Broadway revival of Tennessee Williams' *The Glass Menagerie* and the first professional U.S. production of O'Neill's long one-act play, *Hughie*, aroused moderate interest. Also in the U.S. theater, Albee's

metaphysical drama *Tiny Alice*, won a small following, and the worthy, if severely limited, realistic family drama, *The Subject Was Roses*, by Frank Gilroy, slowly won public acclaim as well as the 1965 Pulitzer prize. In the fall, the off-Broadway theater brought forth a second poetic drama of power in the play *Hogan's Goat*.

Success on Broadway was reaped chiefly by a few light comedies, such as William Goodhart's farcical treatment of conflict between conservative middle-aged parents and their unconventional children in *Generation*. Another hit was the musical, *On a Clear Day You Can See Forever*. It brought a winsome new star to Broadway in Barbara Harris, the leading lady.

In England, where the commercial West End theater had severe financial problems, there was much disappointment in new plays by Harold Pinter (*The Homecoming*) and John Osborne (*Inadmissible Evidence*). However, there were at least two better-than-average plays—Peter Shaffer's striking historical play about the conquest of Peru by Pizzaro, *The Royal Hunt of the Sun*, and Michael Dyne's *The Right Honourable Gentleman*, a drama of political and private intrigue in Victorian England.

Awards for the 1964-1965 Season included:

New York Drama Critics Circle Award to: *The Subject Was Roses*, best play of the season; *Fiddler on the Roof*, best musical.   JOHN GASSNER

See also GILROY, FRANK; PULITZER PRIZES; Section One, ALISTAIR COOKE ON THE ARTS.

THEATER, AMATEUR. Perhaps because many national leaders emphasized the fact that cultural events ought to be part of every young person's experience, children's theater—especially for children from culturally deprived homes—was on the upswing in 1965. To youngsters gathered in New York City parks during the summer, a company called Theatre in the Street performed *Ching Ling and the Magic Peach*. The play was based on an ancient Chinese legend. The stage for the performances folded down from the side of a truck. In Harlem churches in August, the City-Wide Coordinating Committee sponsored *The Tortoise and the Magic Drum*, a play for children that was adapted from an African fairy tale. The actors were young people between 16 and 21 years of age.

Plays for older children were often topical. At Youth House in the Bronx in New York, young audiences first saw teen-age actors in *The Winner*, a play about school drop-outs. Afterward, they debated whether it was better for drop-outs to return to school or seek jobs.

Elsewhere in the nation, children's plays based on familiar stories were popular. Robert Browning's *The Pied Piper of Hamelin*, adapted by Bette Butterworth was presented at the State University of New York, at New Paltz. Schoolchildren played most of the parts. Admission was free.   Alice Griffin

See also EDUCATION.

TOGO. President Nicolas Grunitzky assumed direct command of the Togo army in January, 1965, after ousting Major Emmanuel Bodjole, the army chief of staff. Official circles in Lomé denied rumors of a military plot against the state and claimed that Bodjole's removal was part of a long-planned reorganization of the army. Major Bodjole was the acknowledged leader of the insurgent group that assassinated former President Sylvanus Olympio in January, 1963.

Elections in June for 195 municipal and 370 district council seats resulted in a sweeping victory for the Parti de l'Unité Togolaise, which captured 99 per cent of the votes cast.

An agreement was reached with West Germany in April for the construction of a $960,000 health institute. And in July, the Togo national assembly gave unanimous approval to the country's first five-year development plan. The plan runs from 1965 to 1970 and calls for the spending of $115,000,000 from public funds and private investment.

Togo reopened its frontier with Ghana in July. The border had been closed intermittently since 1963 because of disputes between the two countries.

Population: 1,598,000. **Government:** President Nicolas Grunitzky. **Monetary Unit:** franc (246.85 = U.S. $1). **Foreign Trade:** exports, $17,160,000; imports, $27,220,000. **Principal Exports:** cocoa, coffee, palm-oil products.   Benjamin E. Thomas

See also AFRICA.

TOLBERT, WILLIAM RICHARD, JR. (1913-   ), Vice-President of Liberia, was elected President of the World Baptist Alliance by acclamation on June 29, 1965. He is the first Negro to head the international association of Baptist groups from 120 or more countries. He serves until the alliance meets again in 1970. The Reverend Dr. Tolbert had been a vice-president of the alliance since 1960.

The World Baptist Alliance met in Miami, Fla., in 1965. The American delegates at the convention termed the Tolbert election a "breakthrough," and were quite elated. The Liberian was not surprised, saying, "You see, we are not really racially conscious in Liberia."

The Reverend Dr. Tolbert is pastor of the Mt. Sinai Baptist Church, which he founded in the Todee district of Liberia in 1956. He formerly served as pastor of the Zion Praise Baptist Church in his hometown of Bensonville. He is also a farmer, and board chairman of the Bank of Liberia and the Mesurado Corporation of Liberia. He has served as vice-president of Liberia and president of the Senate since 1951. He was a member of the House of Representatives (1943-1951), and before that, distribution officer (1935-1943) and head of the Liberian treasury department (1935). He was educated at the University of Liberia. The Tolberts have six daughters and two sons. Mrs. Tolbert is the daughter of a prominent Liberian jurist.

TOMONAGA, SIN-ITIRO (1906-   ), Tokyo University of Education Professor, was one of three scientists awarded the Nobel physics prize in 1965. The English translations of his work on the modern theory of quantum electrodynamics arrived in the U.S. about the time Richard P. Feynman and Julian S. Schwinger, who shared the prize with Tomonaga, completed their work on the theory in the late 1940s. Professor Tomonaga is the second Japanese awarded the Nobel physics prize. Hideki Yukawa received it in 1949 for the discovery of the meson.

International recognition first came to Professor Tomonaga for his theory on neutrons, work he did during the early 1940s. He was a professor at Tokyo University of Education then, when it was called Bunrika University. Tomonaga served as president of Tokyo University of Education from 1956 to 1962.

Sin-itiro Tomonaga was born in Kyoto. His father, Sanjuro Tomonaga was a Kyoto University professor of philosophy for many years. Young Tomonaga is a graduate of Kyoto. He received a degree in atomic physics there in 1929. He and Hideki Yukawa worked together at Kyoto. Tomonaga later joined the Scientific Research Center, where he worked for the noted physicist Yoshio Nishina. He also spent a year in Germany studying with Werner Heisenberg before World War II.

See also FEYNMAN, RICHARD P.; NOBEL PRIZES (Science); SCHWINGER, JULIAN S.

TORNADOS. See DISASTERS; WEATHER.

TRACK AND FIELD. Every major distance-running record (a total of 12) from one mile to 20,000 meters fell under a furious assault led by Ron Clarke of Australia, Michel Jazy of France, and Kipchoge Keino of Kenya.

The record battered most frequently was the one for the classic 5,000-meter distance, held since 1956 by Russia's Vladimir Kuts. It was, in fact, the oldest major world record in existence. But in 1965, Clarke, Jazy, and Keino beat this standard a total of 16 times. At the year's end, Keino held the record at 13 minutes 24.2 seconds, but all three were confident of taking it still lower.

Keino also knocked 9.4 seconds off the 3,000-meter steeplechase world record, Jazy secured world records in the mile and the two-mile, and Clarke chalked up a total of six world marks, including the first three miles ever run under 13 minutes. The 1,000-meter world record was broken by Jurgen May of East Germany. May also ran the year's fastest times for 800 meters and 1,500 meters.

While the distance men were making history *en masse,* Randy Matson of Pampa, Tex., was doing it single-handed. The 20-year-old, 260-pound Texas A & M sophomore put the 16-pound shot 70 ft. 7¼ in., breaking Dallas Long's world record by nearly a yard. Two other throwers set impressive world records. Czech discus star Ludvik Danek raised his

own mark to 213 ft. 11½ in., and Gyula Zsivotzky of Hungary added eight feet to the hammer record with a throw of 241 ft. 11 in.

The Soviet Union made a strong comeback from its Olympic failure of 1964. For the first time in seven dual meets, the Russian men's team defeated the U.S. men, 118-112, at Kiev. The Russian women won their seventh straight victory over an improving U.S. women's team, 63½-43½.

In September the Russian men won the new European Cup team competition, edging West Germany 90 to 89. And the Soviet women topped off the year by winning the distaff European Cup.

Communist Chinese athletes led the world's performers for the year in two events. Chen Chia-chuan reportedly ran 100 meters in 10 seconds, tying the world record. But since China is not a member of the International Amateur Athletic Federation, Chen's mark had no chance of being recognized. In the high jump, Ne Chih-chin cleared 7 ft. 4⅝ in., a leap bettered only by Valeri Brumel of Russia.

Feud Renewed. The four-year-old war between the Amateur Athletic Union (AAU) and the National Collegiate Athletic Association (NCAA) flared anew after an Olympic-year truce. The NCAA put pressure on its member universities and their student-athletes to boycott all AAU-sanctioned meets, including the AAU's championship meet in

New World Track and Field Records Established in 1965

Subject to recognition by the International Amateur Athletic Federation (IAAF)

MEN

Event	Holder	Country	Where Made	Date	Record
1,000 Meters	Jurgen May	E. Germany	Erfurt, Germany	July 20	2:16.2
Mile	Michel Jazy	France	Rennes, France	June 9	3:53.6
2,000 Meters	Jozsef Odlozil	Czechoslovakia	Houstaka, Czechoslovakia	Sept. 8	6:01.0
3,000 Meters	Kipchoge Keino	Kenya	Hälsingborg, Sweden	Aug. 27	7:39.5
3,000 Meter Steeplechase	Gaston Roelants	Belgium	Brussels, Belgium	Aug. 7	8:26.4
2 Miles	Michel Jazy	France	Melun, France	June 23	8:22.6
3 Miles	Ron Clarke	Australia	London, England	July 10	12:52.4
5,000 Meters	Kipchoge Keino	Kenya	Auckland, N.Z.	Nov. 30	13:24.2
6 Miles	Ron Clarke	Australia	Oslo, Norway	July 14	26:47.0
10,000 Meters	Ron Clarke	Australia	Oslo, Norway	July 14	27:39.4
10 Miles	Ron Clarke	Australia	Melbourne, Australia	March 3	47:12.8
20,000 Meters	Ron Clarke	Australia	Geelong, Australia	Oct. 27	59:22.8
1 Hour	Ron Clarke	Australia	Geelong, Australia	Oct. 27	12 mi., 1,006 yds.
440 Yard Relay	Stanford (Frische, Rubin, McIntyre, Questad)	U.S.A.	Fresno, Calif.	May 9	0:39.7
2 Mile Relay	Oklahoma State (Metcalfe, J. Perry, Von Ruden, D. Perry)	U.S.A.	Fresno, Calif.	May 9	7:18.3
6,000 Meter Relay	France (Vervoort, Nicolas, Jazy, Wadoux)	France	Paris, France	June 25	14:49.0
Broad Jump	Ralph Boston	U.S.A.	Modesto, Calif.	May 29	27 ft. 4¾ in.
Shot-Put	Randy Matson	U.S.A.	College Station, Tex.	May 8	70 ft. 7¼ in.
Discus Throw	Ludvik Danek	Czechoslovakia	Sokolov, Czechoslovakia	Oct. 7	213 ft. 11½ in.
Hammer Throw	Gyula Zsivotzky	Hungary	Vienna, Austria	Sept. 4	241 ft. 11 in.

WOMEN

Event	Holder	Country	Where Made	Date	Record
100 Meters	Ewa Klobukowska and Irena Kirszenstein	Poland	Prague, Czechoslovakia	July 9	0:11.1
200 Meters	Irena Kirszenstein	Poland	Warsaw, Poland	Aug. 8	0:22.7
440 Yards	Judy Amoore	Australia	Perth, Australia	Feb. 27	0:52.4
80 Meter Hurdles	Irina Press	Russia	Moscow, Russia	Oct. 24	0:10.3
Shot-Put	Tamara Press	Russia	Kassel, Germany	Sept. 19	61 ft.
Discus Throw	Tamara Press	Russia	Moscow, Russia	Aug. 11	195 ft. 10 in.

which a U.S. team to face Russia was chosen. Athletes were told they would lose their scholarships if they ran in AAU meets.

The AAU retaliated, albeit weakly, with threats of suspension for any athlete competing in meets sanctioned by the NCAA-backed U.S. Track and Field Federation (USTFF). The NCAA's action was more effective. Only a dozen or so NCAA collegians competed in the AAU championships, substantially weakening the national team.

As a result of the boycott and the subsequent American loss to the Soviet Union, the Senate Commerce Committee investigated the AAU-NCAA feud. A cease-fire was forced on the disputants by the Senators, and Vice-President Hubert H. Humphrey named an impartial five-man panel to arbitrate the dispute, with a report due Feb. 15, 1966.

Cross-Country. Ron Larrieu of Los Angeles, a 28-year-old truck driver, won the National AAU championship, with the Toronto Olympic Club taking the team title. Senior John Lawson of Kansas University won the NCAA individual crown, while Western Michigan repeated its 1964 team victory. Lawson also won the USTFF championship, leading his Jayhawks to the team title. JAMES O. DUNAWAY

TRADE. See ECONOMY, THE; INTERNATIONAL TRADE AND FINANCE; RETAILING; Section One, SYLVIA PORTER ON THE ECONOMY.

TRAIN WRECKS. See DISASTERS.

TRANSPORTATION.
The performance of U.S. commercial transport companies moved generally upward in 1966, reflecting continued growth of the nation's economy. Air, sea, and land transport all recorded gains in traffic and profits. Capital outlays, at $2,830,000,000, were up nearly 20 per cent from the 1964 figure of $2,380,000,000. Of the 1965 total, railroad capital spending accounted for $1,680,000,000, compared with $1,410,000,000 in 1964.

In a report released late in 1965, the Transportation Association of America put the nation's total transportation bill for 1964 at $126,600,000,000, or at about 20 per cent of the U.S. Gross National Product (GNP). Here is the itemized bill, in billions of dollars:

Passengers		Freight	
Private auto	$60.0	Trucking	$40.2
Intercity (air)	2.9	Railroad	10.3
Intercity (surface)	1.2	Water	2.8
		(Overseas, 1.5; coastal, .6; inland, .4; lakes, .3)	
Local (transit, cab)	2.9	Pipelines	1.0
International	1.1	Air freight	.6
All other	1.8	All other	1.8
Total	$69.9	Total	$56.7

U.S. Government Activities. Federal expenditures for transport accounted for some 11 per cent of the fiscal 1966 budget. Total transport expenditures of $10,900,000,000 were down slightly from fiscal 1965's $11,300,000,000.

Alan S. Boyd, former chairman of the Civil Aeronautics Board, was appointed Undersecretary of

Commerce for Transportation, and A. S. Lang, former director of data systems for the New York Central Railway, was appointed Deputy Undersecretary for Transportation Research. Those appointments were among the signs of a growing federal concern with transportation.

Also indicative was the accumulation of advisory reports on transport policy and research needs. Such data were being used to formulate a more consistent transportation policy and to produce new legislative recommendations. One such proposal was President Lyndon B. Johnson's call for a federal Department of Transportation in his State of the Union message on Jan. 12, 1966.

Among the more controversial reports was one from the Interagency Maritime Task Force, set up by the President to review merchant marine policy. Its report, released in October, argued for a more flexible subsidy system designed to increase incentives for cost reduction in ship design and operation. Shipowners and union leaders immediately attacked it, contending the program would weaken, rather than strengthen, the American merchant marine.

A December report, in sharp opposition to that of the task force, called for "a vigorous program of government support for all segments of our merchant fleet and for our shipbuilding industry." It was approved by 11 of the 15 members of the President's Maritime Advisory Committee.

The Panel on Transportation Research and Development reported to the Secretary of Commerce in May. It recommended a comprehensive R & D program for federal funding, including sponsorship of university research in transport totaling $10,000,000 annually.

Legislation. The Congress, which had failed to make major changes in transport laws in 1964, grappled with few new proposals in 1965. One bill, however, seemed highly significant as the possible forerunner of federal sponsorship of R & D. It authorized the expenditure of $90,000,000 over a three-year period. The funds were to be used by the "Secretary of Commerce to undertake research and development in high speed ground transportation."

This program was the latest outgrowth of the concern, lately voiced by Senator Claiborne deB. Pell (D., R.I.), over passenger transport in the *Northeast Corridor* (Boston to Washington, D.C.). Under the act, several eastern railroads will test experimental high speed rail systems. The Pennsylvania Railroad was to have a fleet of up to 50 experimental passenger cars by the fall of 1966 and begin operating 125-mph test trains between New York City and Washington, D.C. President Johnson, in signing the bill on September 30, added that "we will be investigating all the new and promising concepts of high speed ground travel."

Such other concepts were included in a Massachusetts Institute of Technology study submitted to the Department of Commerce late in the year. It

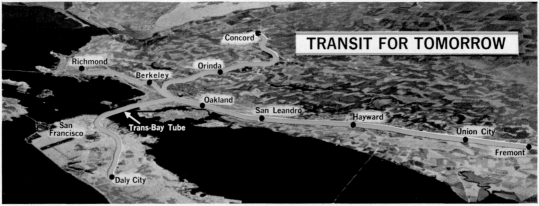

TRANSIT FOR TOMORROW

Ritter, *Newsweek*

*SAN FRANCISCO'S BILLION-DOLLAR ROUTE to freedom from traffic congestion
will open in 1971 on completion of the 75-mile Bay Area Rapid Transit system.*

listed four possible plans for 200- to 300-mph travel: grade-level guideway, elevated right-of-way, bored tunnel, and deep-rock tunnel. The first would be cheapest to build but least feasible technologically for the speeds envisaged. The last, at 500 feet below ground, would cost the most to construct but would afford the most routing flexibility and the most isolation from any physical disturbance. The report urged that a detailed $10,000,000 research program be started immediately to determine the feasibility of developing one of these systems by 1980.

Transit Aid. Under legislation previously passed, the Housing and Home Finance Agency (HHFA) awarded transit demonstration grants of $3,600,000 to the state of New Jersey and $5,100,000 to a subsidiary of the Port of New York Authority to modernize and improve rail commuter services between New Jersey and New York City.

A grant of $3,000,000 was also made to continue commuter services on the New York, New Haven & Hartford Railway. New York City's Transit Authority received a HHFA grant of $23,400,000 to purchase 200 new subway cars.

RAILROADS

The trend toward rail system consolidations continued as the directors of the Chesapeake & Ohio and the Norfolk & Western approved a merger plan. If upheld by the Interstate Commerce Commission

(ICC), a railway system of some 26,460 miles of track with assets of nearly $6,000,000,000 would be created. It would rival and compete with the proposed Pennsylvania-New York Central system.

A U.S. Supreme Court decision on November 22 gave a boost to the merger movement. It held that the public interest in efficient transportation outweighed antitrust considerations. It sent the Seaboard Air Line-Atlantic Coast Line railroad merger case back to the lower federal court for full review.

Rate Disputes. The Southern Railway's fight, begun in 1963, to obtain approval of its reduced rates on grain carried in its "Big John" 90-ton hopper cars was won in September. The ICC approved the rates after an order from the Supreme Court to reconsider its earlier denial of the lower rates. D. W. Brosnan, president of the Southern, estimated the annual savings to shippers may total $40,000,000.

In late September, 131 eastern and 44 western railroads agreed on a compromise to end their 11½-year dispute over splitting coast-to-coast freight revenues. Under the plan, railroads in the 11 Western states would lose about $13,000,000 annually—half of their loss under the ICC plan.

Modernization Programs continued. Typical was the opening of the control and coordination center of the Southern Railway in Atlanta, Ga., in July. Utilizing microwave communications, high-speed

U.S. DOMESTIC TRANSPORT—TRAFFIC, REVENUES, AND PROFIT

(in millions)

Mode	Freight Ton-Miles		Passenger-Miles		Operating Revenues		Net Income	
	1964	1965*	1964	1965*	1964	1965*	1964	1965*
RAILROADS.......	658,639	695,000	18,245	17,300	$9,857	$10,060	$698	$800
TRUCKING........	370,500	400,000	...	...	9,397	10,200	122	N.A.
INTERCITY BUS....	...	...	22,700	22,700	729	773	55	60
AIRLINES	803	960	44,238	55,000	3,043	3,500	144	220

*Estimate, Sources: Association of American Railroads, American Trucking Associations, National Association of Motor Bus Operators, Air Transport Association, Civil Aeronautics Board.

xerography, and computers in a coordinated system allowed the railroad to keep track of some 90,000 car movements each day. Instant location, rerouting and control of every freight car on the line thus was possible from the Atlanta headquarters office.

In July also, the first U.S. automobile piggyback service was offered to passengers between Chicago and Washington, D.C., on trains of the affiliated Chesapeake & Ohio and Baltimore & Ohio lines. For a charge of $60, a traveler's car rides along with him on the same train. This type of service has been available in Europe for a number of years.

OCEAN SHIPPING

The U.S. merchant fleet dropped into second place, behind Britain, in aggregate gross tonnage, according to a *Lloyd's Register of Shipping* report for the year ended June 30, 1965. The figures: for Britain, 4,437 ships and 21,530,264 tons; for the United States, 3,416 ships and 21,527,349 tons, a 12-month drop of almost 1,000,000 tons. Of the U.S. total, 9,500,000 tons were in the reserve fleet of inactive vessels. The U.S. active fleet was the world's fourth largest, after Britain, Liberia, and Norway. Japan was in fifth position; and the Soviet Union was sixth, with 8,237,847 tons—a gain of more than 1,200,000 tons in the year.

Labor Disputes disrupted shipping twice during the year. First, a 33-day dock strike halted all shipping in New York Harbor and other North Atlantic ports until it was settled in February. Then, for more than two months in the summer the same ports and those on the Gulf Coast were tied up by striking ships' officers and radiomen. See LABOR.

Passenger Travel between U.S. and overseas ports totaled 840,000 in 1964. Transatlantic ships carried 259,000 passengers in the first six months of 1965, an 11 per cent decline from the year-earlier volume. Declines were greater in tourist class than in first or cabin class traffic.

A number of new luxury liners made maiden voyages to New York in 1965 including:

• The Home Lines' 39,241-ton *Oceanic.*
• The Italian Line's 46,000-ton *Michelangelo* (see ITALY, picture), in May, and its sister ship, *Raffaello,* in August.
• The Norwegian Line's sleek, 24,000-ton *Sagafjord.*

WATERWAYS

St. Lawrence Seaway traffic for the 1965 season (April-December) was expected to reach 44,000,000 tons. Seaway cargoes via the Montreal-Lake Ontario section totaled 39,440,173 tons in 1964.

Total U.S. inland waterway transport was estimated to have risen 7 per cent in ton-miles of freight carried in 1965. It had increased from 234,172,000,-000 ton-miles in 1963 to 250,165,000,000 in 1964, or a rise of almost 7 per cent. The Great Lakes and Mississippi River Systems carried nearly four-fifths of the traffic.   EDWIN T. HAEFELE

TRANSIT

Congress appropriated the first funds for the three-year, $375,000,000 federal urban mass transportation assistance program. For the year ending June 30, 1966, it voted $60,000,000 for outright grants and another $5,000,000 for loans. An additional $187,500 was for administrative expenses.

President Johnson officially ushered in the "subway age" for the nation's capital on September 10. On that date he signed legislation authorizing construction of a 25-mile subway and rail transit system in the metropolitan Washington (D.C.) area. Its cost was put at $431,000,000 (see WASHINGTON, D.C.).

San Francisco's Bay Area Rapid Transit District (BART) unveiled a modern rapid transit car with carpeted floor, tinted windows, and wide upholstered seats. The car's comfort and luxury are designed to lure drivers out of their autos and onto the system. The first actual excavation work on the Market Street subway started on September 28. Full-scale construction was to get underway sometime late in 1966. Projects would include subways, aerial lines, and a four-mile underwater tube. See picture on opposite page; BRIDGE AND TUNNEL; SAN FRANCISCO.

Other Transit Developments. The Cleveland (Ohio) Transit System received a federal grant of $9,200,000 toward a 3.8-mile rapid transit extension to that city's Hopkins Airport.

In the Boston area, the Massachusetts Bay Transportation Authority approved an initial expenditure of $75,000,000 for two 12-mile rapid transit extensions: one to the South Shore, the other northward to suburban Reading.

The Delaware River Port Authority began work on a 10.6-mile rapid transit route in the Philadelphia area, from Camden to Lindenwold, N. J.

And in Canada, Montreal was building a completely new 16.1-mile subway at a cost of $225,000,-000. Toronto was adding 14.5 miles to its subway system, with an 8½-mile segment, the Bloor-Danforth subway, scheduled to open in February, 1966.

Voter Approval of two mass transit projects was won in the November elections. The voters of Atlanta and four of its surrounding counties approved the creation of a metropolitan transit system. Voters in a fifth county, Cobb, rejected the plan. In Philadelphia, voters endorsed a multimillion-dollar loan to extend the Broad Street subway.

Two states acted to ease the plight of the commuter. New York created a Metropolitan Commuter Transportation Authority to oversee operation of the Long Island Rail Road, which the state had purchased for $65,000,000.

Washington state authorized cities to levy excise taxes of up to $1 per month per household to subsidize city-owned or leased transit lines. One source could be a tax on utility bills.   EUGENE B. MCCAUL

See also AUTOMOBILE; AVIATION; CITY; ROADS AND HIGHWAYS.

TRAVEL, the largest single item in international trade, experienced a year of prosperity and problems. The travel boom was world-wide in 1965. Other than Americans, about 75,000,000 people spent $11,000,000,000 on their jaunts, an increase of 8 per cent in travel expenditures over 1964. Foreign travel spending by U.S. citizens—some 15,800,000 of them—was also up 8 per cent to a record total of $3,665,000,000.

The United States apparently maintained its new position, gained last year, as the number one host nation of the world. A million foreign visitors spent a record $1,360,000,000 in the United States. This was a tribute to the effective work of the U.S. Travel Service in selling trips to America abroad.

Yet the sum of this activity was the largest U.S. "travel gap" on record: an estimated $1,745,000,000 deficit between outbound expenditures and inbound receipts. This, despite efforts by the administration to discourage Americans from going abroad, contributed further to the nation's chronic balance of payments deficit, which threatened the stability of the dollar. See INTERNATIONAL TRADE AND FINANCE.

In fact, the problem posed by 1964's travel deficit inspired the White House to seriously consider a $100 exit tax on all U.S. tourists bound overseas. Arguments, both here and abroad, that the proposal would spark reprisals, disturb world trade, and violate the historic U.S. policy of freedom of travel, caused it to be shelved despite strong U.S. Treasury Department support.

"Discover America." As an alternative to the travel tax, the following two-part program was effected: (1) Congress reduced the duty-free customs allowance for returning tourists from $100 wholesale to $100 retail, and (2) a Discover America campaign was launched under the supervision of Vice-President Hubert H. Humphrey. The campaign was vigorously directed by Robert Short, a prominent Minnesota businessman. The campaign received substantial financial support from companies with a stake in domestic tourism.

Results have been inconclusive because of staffing and other problems, but the program seems to have begun selling America to Americans. Domestic travel in 1965 was up an estimated 7 per cent.

Freedom of Travel. One effect of the economic and political cross-currents was to put the freedom of two-way travel prominently on the agenda of international travel conferences. All vigorously and eloquently endorsed freedom of travel as an inalienable human right and urged the elimination or reduction of barriers and red tape to allow free movement of all citizens of the world. The United Nations (UN) was petitioned to declare 1967 the International Travel Year for observance of the cultural, political, and socioeconomic values of world travel. WILLIAM D. PATTERSON

See also AVIATION; FAIRS AND EXHIBITIONS; HOTEL; OUTDOOR RECREATION; PARKS.

TRINIDAD AND TOBAGO energetically pressed its industrial development and diversification plans. In the budget announced on January 15, the corporate tax system was reshaped to spur increases in exports and employment. A new capital gains tax was pegged at below 20 per cent of any gain. The maximum rate of income tax, which was to become effective in January, 1966, was cut from 90 to 70 per cent. Such efforts, both long-range and immediate, succeeded in attracting new foreign investments.

Violence in the sugar belt marred the economic progress. Resentment toward mechanization of the sugar industry, coupled with interunion rivalry, touched off flare-ups at major plants. On March 9, the authorities declared a state of emergency. This move was followed by the passing of an industrial stabilization act that curtailed the right to strike and imposed strict penalties for wildcat strikes.

Unemployment persisted at the rate of 14 per cent. The rapid population increase was no longer offset by hitherto easy emigration into Great Britain (see GREAT BRITAIN).

Population: 990,000. **Government:** Governor-General Sir Solomon Hochoy; Prime Minister Eric E. Williams. **Monetary Unit:** WI dollar (1.714 = U.S. $1). **Foreign Trade:** exports, $405,000,000; imports, $426,000,000. **Principal Exports:** cocoa, petroleum and petroleum products, sugar. ALASTAIR BURNET

TRUCKING. See TRANSPORTATION.

TUNISIA. President Habib Bourguiba broke with his Arab brethren over the Palestine problem. Addressing the Tunisian Students' Federation on April 21, 1965, he urged discussions between Arab and Israeli leaders toward a settlement based on the United Nations resolutions of 1948. He said that the Arabs could not win a war with Israel, and that the Palestine Arabs should win their own freedom, as Tunisia had. His views caused demonstrators to attack the Tunisian embassy in Cairo. Tunisia severed relations with the United Arab Republic and boycotted all Arab summit conferences in 1965. See MIDDLE EAST.

In May, the Tunisian national assembly approved a four-year development program designed to achieve a 6.5 per cent increase in the country's Gross National Product by 1968. To start accumulating the necessary aid, Tunisia signed loan agreements with the United States for $10,000,000. Finland agreed to send forestry experts to help Tunisia's forest service. And an Italian consortium began exploiting the al-Borma oil fields discovered in 1964. The oil production for 1965-1966 was expected to supply all local needs.

Population: 4,653,000. **Government:** President Habib Bourguiba. **Monetary Unit:** dinar (.52 = U.S. $1). **Foreign Trade:** exports, $129,700,000; imports, $248,400,000. **Principal Exports:** olive oil, phosphates, wines. WILLIAM SPENCER

See also AFRICA.

TURKEY held an election in October, 1965, that reversed the results of a coup five years earlier. The conservative Justice party, successor to the defunct Democratic party of Adnan Mendéres that was ousted by the army in 1960, won over 55.5 per cent of the vote and 240 of 450 seats in the grand national assembly. Former Premier Ismet Inönü's Republican People's party took 134 seats, and other minority parties were awarded the remaining 76 seats in the assembly. Suleyman Demirel, leader of the Justice party, was named premier.

Prior to the election, Turkey was politically unstable. Premier Inönü resigned in February when the assembly rejected his budget. Suat Hayri Urguplu led a caretaker government until the elections.

Turkey received $70,000,000 in credits from the Organization for Economic Cooperation and Development (OECD) to meet its foreign debt obligations. In March, the Middle East's largest steel mill at Eregli, built by the Koppers Corporation, a U.S. consortium, opened for business.

Population: 32,264,000. **Government:** President Cemal Gursel; Premier Suleyman Demirel. **Monetary Unit:** lira (9 = U.S. $1). **Gross National Product:** 60,738,000,000 lire. **Foreign Trade:** exports, $411,000,000; imports, $537,000,000. **Principal Exports:** cotton, fruits, nuts, tobacco.   WILLIAM SPENCER

See also MIDDLE EAST.

TYPHOONS. See DISASTERS; WEATHER.

UGANDA moved closer toward a one-party system on Jan. 1, 1965, when former opposition leader Basil Bataringaya joined forces with the ruling Uganda People's Congress (UPC) party. Soon afterward, Prime Minister Milton A. Obote refused to recognize either of the two remaining minority parties as the official opposition. In May, Bataringaya was appointed minister of internal affairs. Consolidating its power still further, the UPC planned legislation that would make the Buganda kingdom tribalist movement, Kabaka Yekka, an unlawful organization. In July and August, several members of the national assembly and other leaders left the Kabaka Yekka party to join the majority UPC.

Soviet industrial experts assisted the government in a six-month survey of Uganda's industrial potential. In an attempt to improve the nation's living standards, Uganda negotiated a $17,000,000 loan from Great Britain and the commitment of $25,000,000 in aid and loans from Communist China and Yugoslavia. The United States agreed to contribute $280,000 toward the construction of an Institute of Public Administration.

Population: 7,423,000. **Government:** Prime Minister Milton A. Obote. **Monetary Unit:** shilling (7.143 = U.S. $1). **Gross National Product:** $530,000,000. **Foreign Trade:** exports, $153,000,000; imports, $87,000,000. **Principal Exports:** coffee, copper, cotton.   BENJAMIN E. THOMAS

See also AFRICA.

UNGER, IRWIN (1927-   ), University of California Associate Professor of History, was awarded the Pulitzer history prize in 1965. *The Greenback Era: A Social and Political History of American Finance, 1865-1879* is the author's first major work yet published. He left the California campus at Davis in the summer on a year's sabbatical leave. He is now in Washington, D.C., preparing a biography of Salmon P. Chase, who served in President Abraham Lincoln's Cabinet as Secretary of the Treasury. The American Council of Learned Societies awarded Unger a grant to do the Chase biography.

Prior to going to the University of California several years ago, Professor Unger taught at Columbia University, at the University of Puerto Rico, and at Long Beach State College in California. He studied at the City College of New York (now the City University of New York), and at Columbia University, where he received his Ph.D. degree in 1958.

Irwin Unger was born and grew up in New York City. He attended the James Madison High School there. Professor Unger is married and has three sons.

See also PULITZER PRIZES.

UNION OF SOUTH AFRICA. See SOUTH AFRICA, REPUBLIC OF.

UNION OF SOVIET SOCIALIST REPUBLICS (U.S.S.R.). See RUSSIA.

UNITED ARAB REPUBLIC (UAR) renominated and then re-elected its President, Gamal Abdel Nasser, for a third six-year term in 1965. Nasser's majority was a solid 99.992 per cent of the vote. The official count listed 489 invalid ballots and 65 intrepid voters opposed to his re-election.

Nasser's near-unanimous support at the ballot box did not mean full acceptance of his program among Egyptians, however. There were rumblings of political dissension, even in the monolithic Arab Socialist Union (ASU), when the economy was hard-hit by poor harvests, a boll weevil invasion, high prices, and a foreign exchange shortage. A temporary U.S. ban imposed by Congress on shipments of wheat caused the UAR to go to the Soviet Union and Communist China for help.

Premier Ali Sabry instituted a series of austerity measures to cover the anticipated $67,000,000 deficit in the 1965-1966 budget. These included a 25 per cent reduction in certain allowances for government officials, and a forced savings plan requiring workers to contribute a half-day's pay per month. Workers also were forced to work overtime without pay for one hour daily per month.

Several Espionage Cases disturbed the UAR during the year. A group of Germans was seized in February and charged with harassing German rocket experts working on Egyptian projects, and with spying for Israel. The leader, Wolfgang Lotz, pleaded guilty. Another incident involved Mustafa

UNITED COMMUNITY FUNDS

Amin, editor of the newspaper *Akhbar el Yom*, who was charged with being a spy for the U.S. Central Intelligence Agency. The Egyptian Communist party, bowing to threats of arrests, announced that it had dissolved itself to become a part of President Nasser's ASU.

The discovery of a Muslim Brotherhood plot to assassinate President Nasser was made public in September. More than 2,000 members of the brotherhood were arrested, and 400 of the "hard core" were jailed for trial later in the year.

The UAR invited East German President Walter Ulbricht to Cairo for a state visit, causing a break in relations with West Germany. The break was not final, nor did Nasser recognize East German sovereignty. Thus, aid from both Germanys, amounting to about $78,000,000 from each, continued to flow into UAR projects.

Industrial Development. Finance Minister Kaissouny opened a paper pulp plant at Edfu built with a U.S. loan of $7,000,000, and praised the U.S. for its "no strings" assistance.

Population: 30,270,000. **Government:** President Gamal Abdel Nasser; Premier Ali Sabry. **Monetary Unit:** Egyptian pound (2.6 = U.S. $1). **Foreign Trade:** exports, $503,000,000; imports, $916,000,000. **Principal Exports:** cotton and cotton goods, petroleum products, rice. WILLIAM SPENCER

See also MIDDLE EAST; TUNISIA; YEMEN.

UNITED COMMUNITY FUNDS AND COUNCILS (UCFC)

adopted uniform nationwide accounting and reporting procedures; continued to place heavy emphasis on obtaining support for local United Funds from national corporations; and honored George Meany, president of AFL-CIO, for nearly 25 years of fostering close cooperation between UCFC and organized labor.

Over 400 leaders of Community Health and Welfare Councils met in Philadelphia at the biennial Citizens Conference on Community Planning in January. At the 15th annual Campaign Leaders Conference at Dayton, Ohio, in June, volunteers from over 200 communities discussed ways of improving local fund campaigns. The UCFC also began an extensive study of the emerging health and welfare needs of metropolitan areas.

A total of $546,729,465 was raised in the 1965 campaigns of the United Funds, Community Councils, and Community Chests throughout the nation.

Awards in 1964 included:

The UCFC United Community Service Award to Benson Ford, vice-president, Ford Motor Company, Detroit, Mich., for "Distinguished leadership in furthering the United Way."

The First Newton D. Baker II Award to Robert B. Miller, chairman, Federated Publications Inc., Battle Creek, Mich., for "his leadership of the Calhoun County Community Council's Hospital Development Committee, which initiated and completed a coordinated and comprehensive hospital expansion program." JOSEPH P. ANDERSON

UNITED NATIONS

UNITED NATIONS

Three major events marked 1965 as a memorable year in the history of the United Nations (UN). On January 21, Indonesia became the first nation ever to withdraw from the UN when its ambassador, Lambertus N. Palar, handed UN Secretary-General U Thant a formal letter of resignation (see INDONESIA). In October, Pope Paul

EMPTY SEATS in United Nations General Assembly dramatize absence of Indonesian delegation. Indonesia formally withdrew from the UN in January.
United Press Int.

VI of the Roman Catholic Church made an unprecedented transatlantic flight to New York City to address the UN General Assembly. It was the first time a reigning Roman Catholic pontiff had addressed the UN in person (see ROMAN CATHOLIC).

Between the two events, one disturbing and the other reassuring, the UN celebrated the 20th anniversary of the signing of its charter (on June 26, 1945) in ceremonies held on June 25 in San Francisco. It was a birthday that found the UN still pursuing its primary role as keeper of the world's peace in what U Thant called "various ominous conflicts" in Africa, Asia, Latin America, and the Middle East.

Asian Crisis. The war in Vietnam continued to preoccupy the UN. U Thant asserted that it was poisoning great power relations and complicating U.S.-Soviet Union negotiations on nuclear weapons controls. UN efforts to negotiate peace contacts between the warring factions in Vietnam were confined in the main to "quiet diplomacy." Formal UN action was not employed inasmuch as neither North Vietnam nor its chief protagonist, Communist China, were UN members.

In the Indian-Pakistani dispute over Kashmir, however, the UN scored a notable success when it obtained a cease-fire in September. By its actions, the UN helped avert a threatened U.S.-Communist China confrontation directly involving 550,000,000 Indians and Pakistanis. See INDIA; PAKISTAN.

Middle East Tensions. The continuing rancor within the Israeli-Arab world in the Middle East prompted an Israeli complaint to the UN about a series of raids by saboteurs allegedly operating from Jordan (see ISRAEL; JORDAN). In a dispute involving Oman, the UN called on Great Britain to remove its military forces and curtail its political influence there. In Cyprus, a UN-sponsored peace force continued to maintain an uneasy truce (see CYPRUS).

Trouble in Africa. A decision by Rhodesia to declare itself unilaterally independent on November 11 created a major crisis for the UN. The African nations, backed by the Soviet Union, blamed Great Britain for not preventing the declaration and demanded that compulsory sanctions be instituted against white minority rule in Rhodesia. On December 16, most of Africa's UN diplomats, including nearly all of the Commonwealth members, walked out on British Prime Minister Harold Wilson's address to the Assembly. On December 17, Great Britain, backed by oil-trading countries, announced an oil embargo against Rhodesia (see RHODESIA).

Latin American Coup. The United States action in sending its marines into the Dominican Republic, where a coup had toppled the government, provoked alarm among some members of the UN. The U.S. contended that its move, which had been prompted by a desire to prevent a communist takeover in the troubled republic, was under the jurisdiction of the Organization of American States

United Nations

NEWLY APPOINTED U.S. Ambassador to the United Nations Arthur J. Goldberg addresses General Assembly during debate on UN dues.

(OAS) and did not therefore require UN action. Under pressure, however, the United States permitted the UN to authorize a call for a cease-fire and to send a UN fact-finding representative to report the facts directly to it.

Soviet demands to condemn U.S. intervention, and a Uruguayan proposal to remove all outside military units failed to obtain the required seven votes. Subsequently, the United States announced that its forces in the republic had been put under an OAS-authorized Inter-American Peace Force command. See DOMINICAN REPUBLIC; LATIN AMERICA.

Financial Impasse. As 1965 began, the UN faced an unresolved financial crisis over unpaid assessments that it had carried over from 1964. At issue, primarily, was the Assembly's right to impose mandatory assessments for peace-keeping forces. The Soviet Union and France (the two largest debtors) and 11 other nations maintained that the assessments were illegal and refused to pay them. The United States insisted on the observance of Article 19, which stipulated that members more than two years in arrears on their assessments should have no vote in the Assembly. The resulting impasse, during which the UN recessed in order to avoid a showdown, left the world organization in a state of suspense for months.

In August, however, newly appointed U.S. Ambassador to the UN Arthur J. Goldberg announced that the United States would accept "the simple and inescapable" fact that a majority of the members were unready to apply Article 19. Goldberg had succeeded Adlai E. Stevenson as ambassador on the latter's death. See GOLDBERG, ARTHUR J.; DEATHS OF NOTABLE PERSONS (CLOSE-UP).

Although the U.S. decision came too late to benefit the 19th session, it made it possible for the 20th session, which convened in New York City on September 21, to observe normal voting procedures.

Assembly Opens. Following a call to order by Alex Quaison-Sackey of Ghana, president of the 19th session, the 114-member Assembly elected Italian Foreign Minister Amintore Fanfani as president of the new session (see FANFANI, AMINTORE). The following day, the Assembly elected chairmen of its seven principal committees and named the 17 nations whose chief delegates would serve as vice-presidents under Fanfani. The entire group, Fanfani included, comprised the Assembly's Steering Committee which later approved an agenda for the 20th session. Most of the 108 items on it were carry-overs from the 19th session. Included were two questions involving Communist China, as well as such major items as disarmament, international space research, Korea, the apartheid policies of the Republic of South Africa, and the Palestine refugees.

Membership Issue. The two questions involving Communist China concerned (1) its admission to the

UN and (2) its treatment of the people of Tibet. From the U.S. point of view, the Assembly's key act was the denial on November 17 of Communist China's latest bid to displace Nationalist China (Formosa) in the UN. In a 47 to 47 tie, the closest vote on record (but with two-thirds needed for approval), U.S. opposition to China's admission prevailed. In the key procedural vote establishing the two-thirds requirement, the tally was 56 to 49; a switch of only four votes would have reversed the count and allowed a decision by majority vote.

On the second issue—Tibet—the Assembly appealed to Communist China to respect the human rights of the Tibetans.

The Assembly, also with Communist China in mind, endorsed a nonaligned nations' call for a world disarmament conference for 1967. The U.S. announced it would sit down with China and the other nuclear powers in planning sessions. China, however, said it would not take part as long as the Chinese nationalists (Formosa) "usurped" its seats. In other disarmament actions, the Assembly set top priority on measures to halt the spread of nuclear weapons and to stop underground nuclear testing (see DISARMAMENT).

Other UN Actions. For the first time, the Assembly voted *not* to act on (that is, not to accept) the credentials of delegates from the Republic of South

UNICEF—MOTHER TO MILLIONS

The United Nations Children's Fund (UNICEF) received the 1965 Nobel peace prize in recognition of its contributions to the health, well-being, and education of hundreds of millions of mothers and children since its founding in 1946. On its current annual budget of $33,700,000 (less than one-fourth the cost of one nuclear powered submarine), it had 543 projects underway in 118 countries.

First launched after World War II to help save a generation of European war babies, UNICEF shifted in 1950 (as Europe recovered) to the needs of some 800,000,000 children in the underdeveloped countries. Since then, it has established 29,610 health centers in 100 countries to teach maternal care and dispense drugs, soap, and vitamins.

Working with other UN specialized agencies, UNICEF has supplied vaccine for 200,000,000 antituberculosis shots. More than 21,000,000 treatments have been given for trachoma and related eye diseases. More than 2,000,000 have been treated for leprosy. In its fight against yaws, 41,000,000 persons have been treated. Antimalaria insecticides provided by UNICEF to 28 countries helped protect 45,000,000 persons in 1964. Its nutrition proj-

ects distribute garden tools, and help workers start back yard poultry farms.

Nearly one-third of UNICEF aid goes to training—of nurses, pediatricians, village midwives, welfare workers, schoolteachers, and social development planners. Teamed with United Nations Educational, Scientific, and Cultural Organization (UNESCO), UNICEF has helped equip 2,500 schools and 400 vocational centers in 55 countries.

Close to the public heart and the only UN agency that receives funds from individuals, UNICEF obtained nearly $3,000,000 in 1965 from the worldwide sale of its greeting cards, plus about $2,500,000 from Halloween collections made by Canadian and U.S. schoolchildren. Almost 80 per cent of its budget, however, comes from 121 nations, of which the United States contributes 40 per cent.

Maurice Pate, a veteran of former U. S. President Herbert C. Hoover's World War I relief work, directed UNICEF for 18 years. Henry Labouisse, former head of U.S. foreign aid programs, was named UNICEF executive director after Pate's death in January, 1965 (see DEATHS OF NOTABLE PERSONS). Labouisse, under a 30-nation board, daily battles the appalling odds the average child faces in the underdeveloped nations. Typically, UNICEF will spend the $54,000 Nobel prize money to train more experts to help children.   MILT FREUDENHEIM

Africa. The African delegates, led by Guinea and Mali, argued that the white delegates from South Africa did not represent the country's black African majority (see SOUTH AFRICA, REPUBLIC OF).

A new Convention (treaty) on the Elimination of All Forms of Racial Discrimination was approved and sent to all member governments for ratification. If ratified by its Senate, the United States would become answerable to complaints from other countries alleging discrimination inside the United States. The U.S. Senate, however, had not ratified a UN Human Rights treaty since it pigeonholed the antigenocide convention sent it by President Harry S. Truman in 1949.

Population Control. President Lyndon B. Johnson told the UN at its birthday celebration in San Francisco that $5 spent on population control is equivalent to $100 invested in other economic aid to the developing countries. The UN Economic and Social Council approved population control "action programs" to countries requesting them. See INDIA; POPULATION, WORLD; Section Two, INSIDE RURAL CHINA; INSIDE RURAL INDIA.

Economic Measures. "The poorer two-thirds of the world become still poorer, relative to the other third," Secretary-General U Thant reported during the year, noting the declining flow of aid to the "have not" nations. UN Special Fund director Paul G. Hoffman said the U.S.-initiated UN Develop-

ment Decade (1960-1970) was falling short of its goal of devoting 1 per cent of national income of the economically advanced countries to foreign aid. The Assembly merged the Special Fund and Technical Assistance programs, and set up a new Industrial Development Board for have-not areas.

World Conference on illiteracy was held by the UN Educational, Scientific, and Cultural Organization (UNESCO) in Tehran, Iran, during the year. In Paris, UNESCO and the UN-affiliated International Telecommunication Union held a meeting on the use of satellites for direct broadcast of televised news and programs across national frontiers.

Membership. Indonesia's withdrawal from the UN in January reduced membership to 114, but the formal admission of three new members in September raised UN membership to 117. The new members were Singapore, Gambia, and the Maldive Islands in the Indian Ocean. See GAMBIA; MALAYSIA, FEDERATION OF.

Council Changes. With ratification by two-thirds of the UN member nations, the Charter was amended to enlarge the Security Council from 11 to 15 nations. The Assembly elected Argentina, Bulgaria, Japan, Mali, New Zealand, and Nigeria to fill old and new vacancies with special provisions for Africa, Asia, Communist East Europe, and white Commonwealth nations. The Economic and Social Council was enlarged to 27 nations.   MILT FREUDENHEIM

URUGUAY faced serious problems in 1965. It was plagued by bank scandals, social unrest, and a stagnant economy. Inflation had caused living costs to rise an estimated 60 per cent. There was a substantial short-term foreign debt, and gross foreign currency reserves of the central bank were practically exhausted. A continuing trade deficit that had existed for over a decade was the main source of Uruguay's external payments problems. Attempts to reduce imports had seriously affected industry.

After protracted negotiations, the republic reached a refinancing agreement with U.S. commercial banks in September. It reportedly provided for an extended debt settlement of $58,000,000—secured by nearly $60,000,000 in gold bullion—plus some $30,000,000 in new credits from U.S. banks. There also were signs that Uruguay had reached accords with its European creditor nations.

In October, the country announced its long delayed exchange and import reforms. It curbed exports and set up a single, fluctuating free rate of exchange to be determined by "supply and demand."

Population: 2,663,000. **Government:** Council Chairman and President Washington Beltran. **Monetary Unit:** peso (60 = U.S. $1). **Foreign Trade:** exports, $179,000,000; imports, $198,000,000. **Principal Exports:** beef, wool, sheepskins. MARY C. WEBSTER
    See also LATIN AMERICA.

UTILITIES. See COMMUNICATIONS; ELECTRIC POWER; PETROLEUM AND GAS.

VENEZUELA enjoyed political stability and an economic upswing during 1965. The government devoted considerable attention to the training of technicians and the fostering of industrialization—not only to provide employment but also to diversify Venezuela's petroleum-based economy. Early in the year, it was predicted that general industry's contribution to the Gross National Product (GNP) for 1965 would exceed that of petroleum for the first time. Even so, investments by foreign-owned oil firms were expected to reach about 1,000,000,000 bolívars—up 10 per cent over 1964.

In order to maintain a projected 7.2 per cent growth rate (while facing a 3.1 per cent annual population increase), Venezuela planned to hike industrial production 12 per cent a year. On April 2, President Raúl Leoni announced an industrialization program that called for the establishment of 361 new plants. Most affected by the program would be Guayana, where developing industries were to produce steel products, pulp and paper, manganese, industrial chemicals, and construction material.

Population: 8,920,000. **Government:** President Raúl Leoni. **Monetary Unit:** bolívar (4.50 = U.S. $1). **Gross National Product:** 25,930,000,000 bolívars. **Foreign Trade:** exports, $2,242,000,000; imports, $1,272,000,000. **Principal Exports:** coffee, iron ore, petroleum and petroleum products. MARY C. WEBSTER

See also LATIN AMERICA.

VETERANS from 50 countries, representing 140 veterans' organizations, participated in the 11th assembly of the World Veterans Federation at Lausanne, Switzerland, May 5 to 9. The world organization, founded in 1950, works for world peace through the United Nations (UN) and stimulates national programs of direct services to veterans.

Legislation for U.S. veterans and their dependents resulted in the following additional benefits:
• Veterans with service-connected disabilities will receive an increase in compensation averaging 10 per cent. Dependents will receive a comparable increase.
• Veterans receiving special vocational rehabilitation training will receive a 30 per cent increase in their basic subsistence allowance. The increase reflects the rise in the cost of living since 1948 when the previous allowance was established.
• Veterans having serious disabilities resulting from a service-connected disease or injury will be able to begin vocational training as long as 19 years after being discharged. Previously, the period for all but blinded veterans was nine years.
• Children of deceased or totally disabled veterans attending school under the War Orphans Educational Assistance Program will receive assistance up to a maximum of $130 per month. The previous top amount was $110 per month.
• Veterans who could not take advantage of home loan provisions of the GI Bill will now qualify for government insured mortgages under the 1965 Housing and Urban Development Act.

Facilities. Vigorous opposition by veterans organizations to President Lyndon B. Johnson's proposal that some Veterans Administration (VA) hospitals and other facilities be closed resulted in the establishment of a special advisory committee to determine whether the proposed action was desirable. The committee modified the original recommendations as follows: (1) that the VA close six of the 11 hospitals originally scheduled for closing; (2) that two old soldiers homes be closed out of the four originally designated for closing, and (3) that nine VA regional offices be merged instead of 17 originally marked for consolidation.

William J. Driver was appointed Administrator of Veterans Affairs. He succeeded John S. Gleason, a former national commander of the American Legion.

American Legion posts, working closely with the National Child Welfare Commission, urged state legislatures to adopt laws that would protect children from physical abuse; provide stricter accounting for sale of dangerous drugs; require use of eye safety devices in classrooms where eye damage is a possibility; and establish a policy of giving all newborn infants a test for mental retardation.

Delegates to the 47th national convention, meeting in Portland, Ore., approved revisions in eligibility requirements to permit veterans of the Cold War to become members. At present only veterans of World War I, World War II, and the Korean War are eligible. L. Eldon James, a Virginia attorney, was elected national commander.

American Veterans Committee (AVC), in contrast to other veterans organizations, gave conditional support to the proposed closing of VA hospitals and merging of regional offices. The AVC urged that before facilities are eliminated, there be assurance that the facilities are marginal, that employment rights of affected employees are protected, and that the closings be spread over a period of time.

Delegates to the AVC 18th annual convention in Atlantic City, June 25 to 27, elected John S. Stillman, an attorney from New York City, national chairman.

American Veterans of World War II and Korea (AMVETS) held their 21st annual convention, August 23 to 26, in Boston, Mass. They elected Ralph E. Hall, a businessman from Fort Meyers Beach, Fla., national commander.

Veterans of Foreign Wars (VFW) held their 66th annual convention in Chicago from August 13 to 20. Delegates learned that despite an annual increase in total membership, there has been a net loss of 802 posts over a 10-year period. The delegates approved a program to offset criticisms of veterans, stop erosion of veterans benefits, and deal effectively with threats from communism. Andy Borg, an attorney from Superior, Wis., was elected commander in chief. JOSEPH P. ANDERSON

VIETNAM

Vietnam, the strategic "Balcony of the Pacific," became the scene of a stepped-up war that not only increasingly involved the armed forces of the United States, but also the diplomats of nearly every large nation, East and West. See NATIONAL DEFENSE.

Early in 1965, the communist Viet Cong were winning the war. Receiving war supplies and reinforcements from the north, they occupied more than 50 per cent of South Vietnam and exercised control over another 30 per cent. Encouraged by their success, the Viet Cong moved to Phase III of their classical communist "war of liberation." No longer was this merely a war of subversion, infiltration, and terrorism (Phase I), or a war conducted by small guerrilla bands that roamed the sparsely populated countryside almost at will (Phase II). In addition, it was a war that involved whole regiments that were formed not only from the cadres of "pajama-clad" guerrillas, but also the regular khaki-garbed troops of North Vietnam.

The communists abandoned their hit-and-run tactics early in January, 1965, and stood and fought at Binh Gia, a Roman Catholic refugee town 40 miles southeast of Saigon. After six days of fighting, they scored a major victory. Then, in the weeks that followed, they began to besiege the tiny hamlets in the central highlands. Growing bolder, they ambushed relief columns, stepped-up their terror bombings in Saigon, and even threatened the major air base at Da Nang.

Search and Destroy. Noting the shift in communist tactics as well as the military build-up, President Lyndon B. Johnson decided on a course of action that increasingly involved the United States in the Vietnam war. In January, U.S. Air Force planes began to hit the "Ho Chi-minh trail," the jungle supply route that served the Viet Cong. In February, American planes launched attacks into North Vietnam, destroying barracks and troop staging areas. As the war escalated, U.S. Marines were dispatched to guard the Da Nang air base. By March, American troops were flooding into Vietnam in ever increasing numbers. By July, they began regularly to take the field with South Vietnamese troops and carry the fight to the enemy.

Search and destroy missions began major sweeps in rebel-held areas. Carrier-based planes from the U.S. Seventh Fleet raked Viet Cong and North Vietnamese troop concentrations. The air force's B-52 bombers from Guam "pattern bombed" targets. Constant use of helicopters to airlift ground troops and evacuate wounded gave the anticommunist forces a mobility never before seen in warfare. During the year, U.S. forces swelled from 22,000 advisers to more than 180,000 men actively engaged in fighting the war.

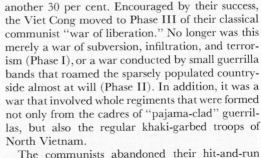

U.S. Air Force

FIGHTER BOMBER, with vapor trailing from its wingtip, dives at Viet Cong target. The U.S. plane carries one bomb, plus machine guns.

United Press Int.

FIRST OFFENSIVE OPERATION of U.S. paratroopers took place in May, when
U.S. Army helicopters ferried them into battle above a massive artillery barrage.

The Escalation of the War in Vietnam and the growing U.S. commitment to it, however, did not meet with 100 per cent approval either in the United States or in the rest of the world. In the United States, the war was protested on college campuses by students who became known as "Vietniks." A few students burned their draft cards and were arrested for violating the Selective Service Act. "Teach-ins" were held by professors.

Twice during 1965—May and December—President Lyndon B. Johnson called for a lull in the bombing in North Vietnam in the hope that the respite would create an atmosphere that would bring the communists to a conference table. The United States, he said, was willing to sit down and negotiate "unconditionally." The reply from the North Vietnamese capital of Hanoi, however, was "no"; there could be no conferences until U.S. forces had been pulled out of South Vietnam.

Except for a shaky 30-hour truce at Christmas— and one that was planned for the Vietnamese lunar holiday in January, 1966—the communists kept right on fighting the war.

During the year, Pope Paul VI appealed to Hanoi for peace, as did Prime Minister Harold Wilson of Great Britain, and many other heads of state. In the communist world, Soviet Russia and China, vying for leadership of the communist nations, tried to outdo each other in their support of North Vietnam (see COMMUNISM).

At year's end, the pace of the escalation had slowed, the efforts of diplomats to end the war had increased, and the military position of the South Vietnamese and the United States and their allies was at least better than it had been at the beginning of 1965.

Internal Turmoil. One of the factors that encouraged the communist build-up and their bolder tactics at the beginning of 1965 was the instability of the South Vietnamese government. From the time when Premier Ngo Dinh Diem was overthrown in November, 1963, until June, 1965, there had been no fewer than 12 changes in South Vietnam's top leadership. Rival political factions had left South Vietnam in a state of political turmoil. The government seemed unable to administer the war effectively. As a result, morale among Vietnamese troops sagged, enlistments dwindled, and desertions increased.

The country finally experienced stability on June 19, 1965, when Nguyen Cao Ky, an air force vice-marshal, became head of a military government that had Buddhist support. A front was formed that gave promise of ending much of the religious squabbling in South Vietnam. Premier Ky adopted a platform

Larry Burrows, *Life* © Time Inc.

ENEMY BULLETS stream by helicopter as U.S.
Marine's gun jams. On the floor are two
wounded crewmen, one of whom is dying.

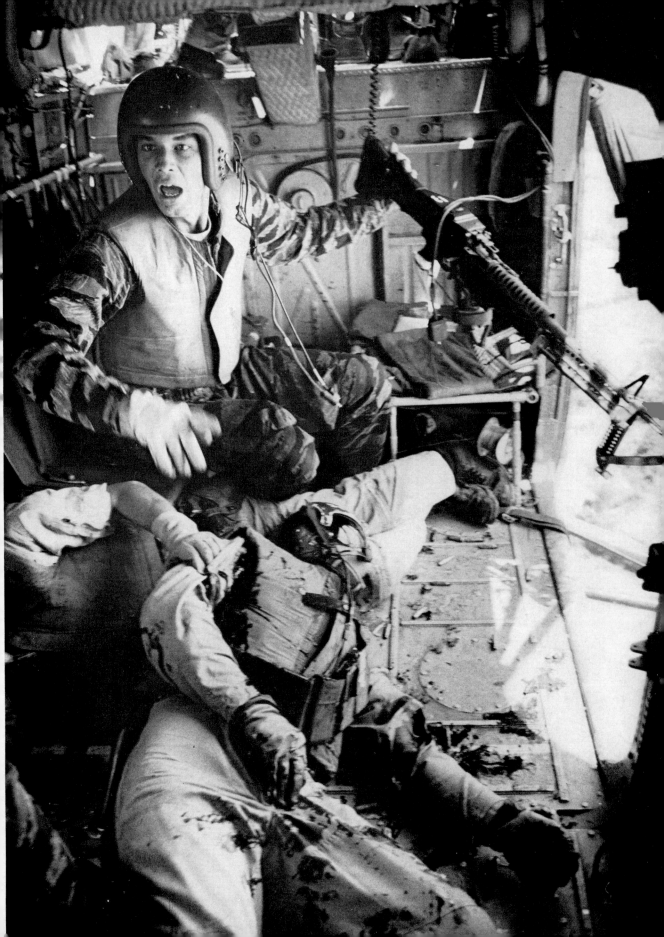

A WOUNDED MARINE is carried by his buddies to helicopter for evacuation. Wounded were often delivered to hospitals in minutes.

that promised austerity, mobilization, and reform.

With the achievement of a relatively stable government, Vietnamese civilians began to take a more active role in the war. Intelligence reports began to increase in accuracy and the flow of information expanded. The U.S. armed forces, in cooperation with the South Vietnamese, launched a massive civil affairs movement in an effort to bring villagers into support of the government. And, as further evidence of their renewed support, the South Vietnamese refused to heed a Viet Cong call for an hour-long general strike on Oct. 15, 1965.

Internally, the South Vietnamese took steps to curb the inflation that had been rampant in the economy. Military troops, according to an agreement worked out by the U.S. and South Vietnam governments, were paid in script to prevent black marketeering in currencies. More rigid control of profiteers and black marketeers was put into effect by the government of Premier Ky. The government also began a major attempt to handle Vietnamese refugees from the war areas more adequately. Students from high schools and universities began to volunteer for the rebuilding of much of their shattered country. On September 4, Premier Ky initiated a new land reform program that was designed to make peasants landowners or give them a chance to lease land at reasonably low rates.

FLAG DRAPED COFFINS of eight U.S. servicemen killed in action against the Viet Cong are placed in transport plane prior to the long journey home.

Background To the Crisis In Vietnam

According to a very old Vietnamese legend, there once was a king named Hung Vuong, who had a daughter of rare beauty. One day, two young men arrived at the king's palace to ask for the hand of his daughter, My Nuong. One was Son Tinh (God of the Mountain); the other was Thuy Tinh (God of the Water). Both were handsome, rich, and powerful, and the king had difficulty in choosing between them. Finally, the king decided that the first to return with wedding gifts would marry the princess.

The next day, the God of the Mountain arrived first with a rich treasure of gold, jade, ivory, and silver. Accordingly, Son Tinh took My Nuong to his mountain home. When the God of the Water finally arrived at the palace, he was angered to find the princess gone.

In his rage, the God of the Water created whirlwinds and monstrous floods. He also raised an army by converting the animals of the sea into warriors. But because the God of the Mountain was equally powerful, the war raged on and on—to no apparent conclusion. For the higher Thuy Tinh raised his water, the higher Son Tinh raised his mountain.

During 1965, the higher the United States raised its commitment in Vietnam, the higher became the commitment of the Vietnamese communists. As more men poured into the war on both sides, the emphasis was increasingly on military action. Yet fundamentally, the struggle is a political one.

U.S. General Walter Bedell Smith pointed out that fact to the French in 1954. "Any second-rate general should be able to win," he said, "if there were the proper political atmosphere." More than 10 years later, U.S. Ambassador Henry Cabot Lodge sounded a similar theme: "The Viet Cong campaign is, above all, a political affair."

Ambassador Lodge, of course, did not suggest that the military war has no relationship to the political war. Of course, a military victory for either side would provide a landscape in which political seeds could be sown and allegiance eventually be made to

bloom. On the other hand, military action and its by-products—terrorism, the indiscriminate killing of civilians—can also work to a disadvantage in a war for the minds of men. Thus, military action can only be a factor in the larger political war. It can conquer a people, but not necessarily win them.

The problem, some experts believed, was not merely one of winning the military war and then transplanting ideas of Western democracy in Vietnamese soil. In Vietnam, a country with a feudal social system and a rice-paddy economy, democracy and communism are *equally* alien.

The South, with its U.S.-style constitution, still has not made a success of representative government. The war, of course, has interfered, but so has the inbred corruption of the bureaucrats, rampant factionalism, and the psyche of an Oriental people, who are accustomed to a mode of life that, in some ways, is the antithesis of democracy. On the other hand, Ho Chi-minh's one attempt at a communist-style land reform in 1956 was a miserable failure, collapsing in a blood bath that the communists have been trying to explain away ever since.

In the main, the Vietnamese peasant, who comprises most of the country's population, gave his allegiance to whichever side provided him with "security" not only in terms of protection, but also in food supplies. The aim of the U.S. government, according to President Lyndon B. Johnson, is to provide that security, and create the kind of atmosphere that will allow the Vietnamese to evolve their own form of government.

This may be a noble objective, but many observers doubt U.S. willingness to go so far as to allow the Vietnamese their "free" choice, if that choice is communism. Thus, far from playing a passive role, the United States is committed to promoting what it regards as the *right* political decision. Broadly, this means that the Vietnamese adopt the general precepts of a modern and free society and then adapt them to their own ancient culture. For U.S. citizens, their military leaders, diplomats, Congressmen, and President, it

A YEAR BOOK CLOSE-UP

Background To the Crisis In Vietnam

(continued)

not only calls for a sympathetic understanding of Vietnamese nationalism, but for a comprehension of the other fundamental aspirations of the Vietnamese people.

Fortunately, history affords many insights into what can be done to understand and win the minds of the Vietnamese. The Vietnamese were an identifiable people more than 2,000 years ago. At first, they settled in the Red River delta in North Vietnam. Faced by a harshness of climate in which there were six months of near drought followed by six months of torrential monsoon rain, the Vietnamese developed a rice economy in which the family became an important unit.

For many years, the Vietnamese family units spread south along the seacoast, eventually reaching the Mekong delta, a rich rice-producing area comparable to that of the Red River. On the way, they all but by-passed the central highlands that today are inhabited by a primitive people whom the French called the *montagnards* (mountain people). The Vietnamese called these primitives *moi* (savages) and an antipathy grew up between them that lasts to this day. In fact, it is the hostility between the Vietnamese and the montagnards that largely hinders the U.S. Army Special Forces from developing counter-insurgency forces in the central highlands.

Early in their history, the Vietnamese were conquered by the Chinese, who ruled for a thousand years. In the process, the Vietnamese were introduced to Confucianism, given Chinese education, and exposed to Chinese methods of administration. The Vietnamese also acquired a Chinese invention—the mandarin. Mandarins were scholars steeped in Confucian philosophy who obtained their nonhereditary titles only after years of study. Significantly, it was their aim to absorb the accumulated wisdom of the past in order to achieve the moral perfection that qualified a man to rule.

It was not until the 10th century that Vietnamese peasants endowed with a nationalistic fervor revolted and ended Chinese rule. But the basic concepts gained during that rule remained a primary part of the Vietnamese character. On the other hand, much of North Vietnam's current history can be related in a framework of its continuing struggle against China. It is probably this latent hostility to China that keeps Ho Chi-minh from calling on Chinese manpower for greater aid. For Ho Chi-minh advertises himself as a nationalist and the presence of large numbers of Chinese might erase one of his strongest and most emotional selling points in the minds of the Vietnamese people.

The ancient mandarin system, likewise, has a direct bearing on Vietnam's current history. For it was a mandarinlike preoccupation with the past and an inability to cope with the threat of French colonialism in the 19th century that led to the subjugation of Vietnam and 50 years of French rule. This French colonial period, marked by numerous nationalist-inspired insurrections, ended in a disastrous defeat for the French at Dien Bien Phu and the Geneva agreement of 1954.

The Vietminh who defeated the French were a coalition of nationalists, not just communists. Hence, Ho Chi-minh is better recognized as a nationalist in the minds of the South Vietnamese people, most of whom have yet to discover all the realities and consequences of communism. That is why the government of South Vietnam has never consented to free elections in all of Vietnam, as agreed upon at Geneva. For it is almost a certainty that Ho Chi-minh would win such an election.

In the struggle for the minds of the Vietnamese, U.S. leaders and the citizens who elect them will have to confront the facts of history and derive important lessons. The military war may require arms, determination, and patience. But the larger political war also demands insight.

In the ancient war between the legendary gods, the God of the Water eventually withdrew to the sea. It is the expressed wish of the U.S. to do likewise—but only after the Vietnamese people have a chance to evolve their own form of democracy in peace.   E. KENNETH FROSLID

A
YEAR
BOOK
CLOSE-UP

"We just seem to be pounding his feet into the ground."

Michael Gregory, PIX

VIETNIKS, as they were called, paraded the streets of San Francisco and other cities to protest the involvement of the United States in the Vietnam war.

South Vietnam's economy, because of the war effort, was in a shaky condition. The government had a total of 32,000,000,000 piasters ($435,000,000) in circulation but the deficit for 1965 was nearly 20,-000,000,000 piasters. In the last three years, inflation had caused the price index to go up by 40 per cent. In addition, the economy was strained by the fact that one in 15 of the country's 16,012,000 population was a refugee.

North Vietnam. The economy of North Vietnam also suffered drastically because of the war. A manpower drain caused by the needs of the armed forces prompted the government to initiate forced labor drafts to maintain production. And because of a food shortage, rice rations were cut.

U.S. bombing, although aimed primarily at military installations, also had an effect on the civilian economy. In addition to striking such targets as airfields, barracks, missile sites, and oil and ammunition depots, the bombs disrupted transportation and interfered with industrial production.

North Vietnam. Population: 18,797,000. **Government:** President Ho Chi-minh; Premier Pham van Dong. **Monetary Unit:** dong (2.94 = U.S. $1). **Foreign Trade:** statistics not available.

South Vietnam. Population: 16,012,000. **Government:** Premier Nguyen Cao Ky. **Monetary Unit:** piaster (60 = U.S. $1). **Foreign Trade:** statistics not available.　　　　　JOHN N. STALKER

See also ASIA.

561

VITAL STATISTICS

VITAL STATISTICS. For the first year since 1953, U.S. births totaled fewer than 4,000,000. The 1965 estimate was 3,800,000—for a birth rate per 1,000 of population of about 19.5, the wartime 1945 rate.

While the death rate leveled off during 1965, the causes of death showed a slightly different pattern. Hypertensive heart disease was less lethal in 1965

U.S. Vital Statistics
(12 months through November)

	1964	1965
Live births....................	4,047,000	3,789,000
Birth rate*..................	21.2	19.6
Infant deaths (under age 1)....	98,000	94,300
Deaths....................	1,802,000	1,825,000
Death rate*..................	9.4	9.4
Marriages..................	1,719,000	1,771,000
Divorces (from 37 reporting areas January–November).........	287,363	306,891

*Per 1,000 of population. Source: U.S. Public Health Service.

than in 1964. But the suicide rate of 11.6 per 100,000 topped the average of any of the 10 previous years.

Marriage and divorce continued to grow in popularity. About 1,800,000 couples were joined in the year, up 5 per cent from 1964. Divorces rose about 7 per cent; most of the increase came in California, Illinois, and North Carolina.   ROBERT A. IRWIN

VOCATIONAL EDUCATION. See EDUCATION.

WAR ON POVERTY. See POVERTY.

WASHINGTON, D.C., came within a legislative whisker of gaining the right to govern itself for the first time since 1871. But, despite political support of the White House, the House of Representatives failed to approve a Senate-passed bill that would have set up a mayor-council government.

Despite this defeat, President Lyndon B. Johnson scored several legislative successes in Washington's behalf. In September, he signed a bill approving a $431,000,000, 25-mile subway-rail transit system. And a long-sought civic goal was realized in the passage of the 1965 Housing Act which granted special permission to the city to participate in urban renewal. To explore ways to restore the decaying old business district, the Redevelopment Land Agency received $900,000 in federal aid. Federal money will also finance two-thirds of the cost of reconstructing two blocks along F Street.

Among major new construction projects were the massive and controversial Sam Rayburn House Office Building, reputed to be the costliest ($89,600,000) public building ever erected, and the almost as monumental John F. Kennedy Cultural Center. Groundbreaking for the center took place in December. Also, excavation began at year-end for L'Enfant Plaza, a $63,000,000 project in the southwest renewal area. It will include three office buildings, a hotel, a garage, and a spacious plaza. DONALD W. LIEF

See also CITY PLANNING.

WATERWAYS. See TRANSPORTATION.

WATER AND FLOOD CONTROL. The fourth consecutive year of drought in the northeastern states drew down reservoirs, serving millions of people, to dangerously low levels. The driest spring and summer since 1869 forced metropolitan areas, such as New York City, to take emergency water-saving steps (see NEW YORK CITY).

On July 14, President Lyndon B. Johnson directed the Federal Water Resources Council to take steps necessary to avert a critical water shortage. On August 18, the President determined that federal disaster assistance was necessary in parts of Delaware, New Jersey, New York, and Pennsylvania.

In the northeast, where unlimited water had long been taken for granted, the fact of an enduring water shortage came as a shock. Water experts believed the 1965 water crisis would be an increasingly chronic national problem. They urged that long-range measures be taken now for the wise use of water in the future. See Section Two, WATER FOR A THIRSTY WORLD.

Water Pollution Control on the federal level was strengthened with the enactment of the Water Quality Act of 1965. The new law established a Water Pollution Control Administration under an assistant secretary of Health, Education, and Welfare. The act also called for a federal yardstick of water quality. President Johnson, in signing the measure on October 2, attacked the polluting of rivers by industries and cities. "The clear, fresh waters which were our national heritage have become dumping grounds for garbage and filth," he said. "There is no excuse for chemical companies and oil refineries using our major rivers as pipelines for toxic wastes." See Section Two, POLLUTED AMERICA.

Congress approved an accelerated saline water conversion program costing as much as $185,000,000 through 1972. Studies indicated that a 150,000,000-gallon-per-day desalination plant, fueled by nuclear power, could produce water at a competitive cost of about 30 cents a thousand gallons.

The Water Resources Planning Act, enacted in July, provided for coordinated planning of water development through establishment of a Federal Water Resources Council and river basin commissions. Congress also enacted the Federal Water Project Recreation Act (see OUTDOOR RECREATION).

U.S. Flood Losses in the first nine months of 1965, exclusive of tidal flooding, exceeded $750,000,000, compared with an annual average of $350,000,000. In addition, September's Hurricane Betsy caused damage exceeding $1,000,000,000 in Florida and Louisiana. June floods in the South Platte and Arkansas River basins in Colorado and Kansas caused losses of $575,000,000—$300,000,000 of it in metropolitan Denver. In April, run-offs from heavy winter snows resulted in record high flooding of the upper Mississippi River and damage of $200,000,000. See DISASTERS (Floods).   A. L. NEWMAN

WEATHER. Study of the atmosphere, the oceans, and the earth—and prediction of the weather problems they produce—were brought under the direction of a single federal agency. The new Environmental Science Services Administration (ESSA) was formed on July 13, 1965, by merging the U.S. Weather Bureau and the U.S. Coast and Geodetic Survey, both part of the Department of Commerce. Robert M. White, head of the Weather Bureau, was named director of the new agency. The Central Radio Propagation Laboratory at Boulder, Colo., became the third arm of ESSA in October. White said the merger would accomplish several goals, one of which is to establish an integrated warning network to alert the public to earthquakes, floods, hurricanes, seismic sea waves, and tornadoes. Another aim of the joint agency is to pool expensive scientific instruments and facilities for use by all three branches. Similar agencies have been organized by Japan and the Soviet Union.

The Weather Bureau and the Coast and Geodetic Survey will retain their names within the ESSA. George P. Cressman was appointed director of the Weather Bureau, and Rear Admiral James C. Tison became director of the Coast and Geodetic Survey, replacing Rear Admiral H. Arnold Karo.

World Weather Centers. The first of three world weather centers was opened Jan. 1, 1965, near Washington, D.C. It will be linked with similar centers in Moscow, U.S.S.R., and Melbourne, Australia, to form the World Weather Watch, a unit of the United Nations World Meteorological Organization. The network will exchange meteorological data gathered by both U.S. and Soviet weather satellites and by automated stations on land and sea.

In keeping track of the world's weather, meteorologists will make wider use of computers and unmanned monitoring stations. Computers are also being developed to produce updated world weather maps by taping data radioed from satellites and automated stations.

Satellites. Constant-level, balloon-borne weather monitors were being considered for duty as "satellites of satellites." Under the plan, weather data would be collected from the monitors by the orbiting satellites, and then telemetered to weather centers. Calculations made at the National Center for Atmospheric Research at Boulder, Colo., by Fedor Mesinger show that thousands of balloons could be released to float at constant levels. These would have a random distribution even after circling the globe for long periods. The technique will be tested in a balloon-borne weather survey of the Southern Hemisphere planned as a joint project of New Zealand and the United States.

As part of the same project, 100 free-floating balloons are scheduled to be launched over a one-year period from Christchurch, New Zealand. The balloons are designed to assume altitudes of 20,000 feet; 40,000 feet; and 80,000 feet. Weather informa-

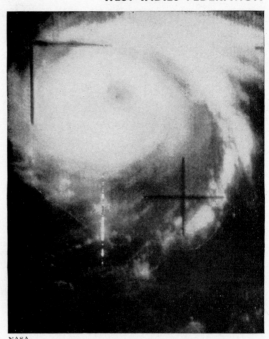

NASA

THE FURY of Hurricane Betsy was photographed from above by the satellite Tiros X, six days before the hurricane struck the Gulf Coast on September 12.

tion beamed from the balloons will be collected by ground-based meteorologists and used in testing short- and long-term forecasting methods.

Hurricane Speed Check. Maximum wind speeds of hurricanes and tropical storms have been estimated to within 25 miles per hour by analyzing photographs taken by Tiros weather satellites (see photo). Scientists at the Weather Bureau's Meteorological Satellite Laboratory developed the speed check method to serve in lieu of direct measurements now being taken by aircraft fly-throughs.

Need for Manpower. During 1965, President Lyndon B. Johnson stressed the need for even more atmospheric research. In a message to Congress, he noted that the development of methods for altering weather would mean vast economic and social gains. The most critical problem retarding increased atmospheric research is the lack of trained personnel. The National Science Foundation is placing emphasis on attracting young scientific talent to work on such programs as the control of hurricanes and tornadoes.

The need for weather control was felt around the world in 1965 as drought continued in the northeastern United States as well as in Communist China, India, Italy, Portugal, South Africa, South Korea, and Spain. SERGEI LENORMAND

WEIGHT LIFTING. See SPORTS.

WEST INDIES FEDERATION. See JAMAICA; TRINIDAD AND TOBAGO.

Patrick K. Snook

VANISHING MONARCH OF THE NORTH? Scientists know little about the polar bear—how long it lives, its range, whether it is decreasing or holding its own. The world polar bear population is estimated at between 10,000 and 12,000.

WILDLIFE. Delegates from nearly every nation in the Western Hemisphere attended the Inter-American Specialized Conference on Conservation of Renewable Resources in Mar del Plata, Argentina, in October. The conference marked the 25th anniversary of the approval of the Convention on Nature Protection and Wildlife Preservation in the Western Hemisphere. The delegates formalized a renewed international dedication to the goal of protecting rare and endangered species of wildlife.

The United States had advanced this objective in September, when President Lyndon B. Johnson set aside 300 acres at the Patuxent Wildlife Research Center in Laurel, Md., for an intensive program to rebuild 78 native stocks of birds and mammals threatened with extinction. Conservationists hailed the move, noting that in the last 150 years the United States has lost nearly 40 species—half of them since 1900. First propagation efforts are to be directed to sandhill cranes, Aleutian Canada geese, snail hawks, and tule white-front geese.

Hope for Whoopers. The center also will work with Canadian officials to obtain wild whooping crane eggs for hatching. The wild whoopers had reached a new peak of 44 when they flew south in October from Canada to their new winter home at Aransas National Wildlife Refuge in Texas. A new 90-acre area had to be prepared in the refuge; the whoopers' old feeding grounds had been taken over by wild geese and sandhill cranes.

Wildlife officials believe the upward trend in the whooping crane population offers hope that this most publicized of the endangered species now has better than an even chance for survival.

Waterfowl Restrictions. With the breeding population of mallard and pintail ducks at the lowest levels in history, waterfowl hunting regulations issued by the U.S. Department of the Interior in August reduced bag and possession limits for these species and continued relatively restricted bags on other waterfowl.

While conditions in the prairie pothole breeding grounds had improved and duck populations were generally rising, wildlife officials believed continued rebuilding of duck populations is still essential to prepare for future demands and lean years. See Hunting and Fishing.

Polar Bear Parley. Scientists from five nations—Canada, Denmark, Norway, the Soviet Union, and the United States—met in September at the University of Alaska, near Fairbanks, to assess the future of the polar bear. Their first conclusion was that they knew little about the life and habits of the huge arctic beasts.

There was concern, however, that the polar bear has been losing ground. Hunters have been using airplanes to track down and herd the bears within their gunsights. Alaska cut its 1965-1966 polar bear hunting season by 20 days.   A. L. Newman

See also Zoology; Zoos and Aquariums.

564

Patrick K. Snook

INROADS BY HUNTERS have caused worldwide concern. In Alaska alone, the 1965 kill by sportsmen exceeded 300 of the animals.

WOJCIECHOWSKA, MAIA (1927-   ), was awarded the Newbery medal in 1965 for *Shadow of a Bull*. Her novel was cited for the "spareness, tension, and grace with which it describes the young boy's search for courage and self-determination." The setting is Spain, where young Maia saw the great Manolete in the ring on "one of his finest afternoons." That memorable day in 1942 and several later sojourns in Andalusia were the beginnings of *Shadow of a Bull. Odyssey of Courage* is a deeply significant story of a Spanish conquistador. *Odyssey of Courage* and *A Kingdom in a Horse* were both published in 1965.

Writing poetry was one of the author's earliest avocations. Her first children's book, *Market Day for 'Ti André* (1952), was written in Haiti. Miss Wojciechowska's varied career, which began in New York City, includes tennis professional, magazine editor, and translator and broadcaster for Radio Free Europe. Her native language is Polish, and she also speaks French, Italian, Spanish, Portuguese, and English. She is an authority on bullfighting, and actually trained in Mexico to enter the ring.

The Wojciechowskys came from Warsaw. The father was an aide to Poland's first Field Marshal, Józef Pilsudski (1867-1935), and Chief of Staff of the Polish Air Force in England during World War II. The family lived in several European countries, and eventually settled in Los Angeles, Calif.

See also LITERATURE FOR CHILDREN (Awards).

WOODWARD, ROBERT BURNS (1917-   ), Harvard University Donner Professor of Science, was awarded the Nobel chemistry prize in 1965 for "meritorious contributions to the art of organic synthesis." During the last two decades, he has developed fundamental techniques for the synthesis of organic substances, greatly advancing the laboratory production of these materials. An early achievement was the first total synthesis of quinine in 1944.

Among Woodward's other laboratory successes are the first complete polymerization of "protein analogues," which resemble natural proteins in animals and plants (1947), and the first total synthesis of a steroid, important in human metabolism (1951). In 1960, he synthesized chlorophyll, and definitely established the structure of this life-giving, green plant pigment.

Boston-born Robert Woodward acquired much of his early knowledge in chemistry at home in his basement laboratory. The Massachusetts Institute of Technology awarded him a B.S. degree in 1936, when he was only 19. The following year he received a Ph.D. degree in chemistry there. Woodward went to Harvard University as a postdoctoral assistant. He advanced to a full professor by 1951, Morris Loeb Professor of Chemistry in 1953, and Donner Professor of Science in 1960.

See also AWARDS AND PRIZES (Science and Industry, National Medal of Science); NOBEL PRIZES.

WORDS AND PHRASES, NEW. The stepped-up conflict in Vietnam, the accelerating U.S. space program, and the vogue of surfing added new words and phrases to the language in 1965 and gave old words new meanings. Among them were:

anticryptography. The devising of easily deciphered codes.

aquanaut. One who explores *inner* space, *i.e.*, the vast depths of the ocean.

camp. In matters of taste, a person, place, or event that is extreme, yet, nevertheless, charming or otherwise enjoyable.

cold cat. A catapult launch that failed because the launching device lacked the power necessary to put an airplane into the air.

d.b. Short for "dirty book."

desk pilot. One who helps manage a space flight from the ground.

educational park. A group of play, primary, secondary, and high schools in a parklike setting, designed to serve an extensive surrounding area.

embryatics. Study and treatment of the unborn infant.

employeeistic. Descriptive of a society made up largely of employees.

EVA (extra vehicular activity). The activity of an astronaut outside an orbiting vehicle.

folk-rock. A popular music style containing elements of folk music, rock-and-roll, and social protest. See MUSIC, POPULAR.

Gemini Twins. The two astronauts in a Gemini (Lat. for "twins") capsule.

HALO. Descriptive of a parachute platoon, the members of which bail out from high altitudes (HA) and pull the release cord of the chute for a low-altitude opening (LO).

militaristocrat. A military man belonging to the aristocracy.

multiman. Descriptive of a space flight involving more than one astronaut.

outerror. To exceed someone in the number of errors made.

pop-top. A can that can be opened by detaching a small lid which pops when lifted.

rackcar. A railroad flatcar with a tiered rack for transporting automobiles.

REP. Radar Evaluation Pod.

skateboard. A board mounted on roller-skate-type wheels and used for recreation.

sloburb. A fast-growing, unplanned urban community with a standard assortment of neon-lighted filling stations, motels, used-car lots, hamburger stands, bars, supermarkets, and the like.

spacefarer. A space traveler.

spacewalk. Said of an astronaut maneuvering outside his space vehicle but attached to it by a cord.

sprawl-in. A protest made by sprawling.

superregion. A densely populated area such as the New York to Boston megalopolis.

surfer's knob. A knob that sometimes develops below the knees or on the top of the feet of surfboarders.

talking typewriter. A typewriter, programmed with a sound track, designed to teach preschool children to read and write.

teach-in. A meeting at which a speaker attempts to clarify a current issue, such as the U.S. government's Vietnam policy.

think tank. An office concerned with the designing of policy and with research.

Vietnik. Angry protestor to U.S. policy in Vietnam.

vodkatini. A martini that is made with vodka as the main ingredient.   I. WILLIS RUSSELL

WRESTLING.

Iowa State scored a stunning upset in the National Collegiate Athletic Association (NCAA) championships at Laramie, Wyo., in April. The Iowa Cyclones dethroned Oklahoma State with a one-point, 87-86, victory. Oklahoma State, winner of 24 out of 34 NCAA titles, led by 22 points going into the final round, and had five men competing against Iowa State's two. But both of the Iowa finalists won, and that, combined with six third-place points, gave the Cyclones the title. Mankato (Minn.) State edged California State Polytechnic of San Luis Obispo, 57-54, for the NCAA small-college crown.

The Multnomah Athletic Club of Portland, Ore., won the Amateur Athletic Union (AAU) championships held in San Francisco in April. Russ Camilleri of the San Francisco Olympic Club was named the meet's outstanding wrestler.

Other winners in the AAU competition were: Ray Sanchez of Cheyenne, Wyo. (114½-pound); Dick Sanders of Multnomah (125½-pound); Chikara Murano of New York City (138½-pound); Jim Burke of San Francisco (154½-pound); Wayne Baughman of the U.S. Air Force (191½-pound); Jerry Conine of Multnomah (213½-pound); and Larry Kristoff of Chicago (heavyweight).

Kristoff went on to take a third in the world amateur free-style championships at Manchester, England, and thus earned the only U.S. medal. Iran won the world title.   STANLEY ISAACS

YEMEN

YEMEN remained in the grip of a three-year-old civil war during most of 1965. Unlike preceding years, however, there was hope at year's end that a peaceful solution might be near.

Hopes for an earlier settlement had been shattered in January when a cease-fire was broken by the royalist forces. The royalists, who were supporters of deposed Imam Mohammed al-Badr, had the military support of Saudi Arabia. Their opponents, the republican forces of President Abdullah al-Salal, were backed by the United Arab Republic (UAR).

The war, however, had seemingly become a costly stalemate and, on August 24, the UAR and Saudi Arabia signed a new agreement providing for an immediate cease-fire. It also called for a plebiscite to decide whether Yemen would continue as a republic or revert to a monarchy.

By the end of October, the UAR reportedly had begun withdrawing some of its troops from Yemen. In November, Yemeni delegates representing royalists and republicans met at Harad to plan a transitional government and to provide the basis for a referendum in 1966.

Population: 5,000,000. **Government:** President Abdullah al-Salal; Premier Hassan al-Amri. **Monetary Unit:** riyal (100 = U.S. $1). **Foreign Trade:** no statistics available. **Principal Exports:** coffee, hides, salt, skins.   WILLIAM SPENCER

See also MIDDLE EAST: UNITED ARAB REPUBLIC.

YOUNG MEN'S CHRISTIAN ASSOCIATION

(YMCA) completed 75 years of World Service, a program sponsored jointly by the YMCAs of Canada and the United States. The program is administered by an international committee composed of 244 representatives from both countries.

World Service now supports 90 projects in agriculture, education, health, industry, and recreation in 40 countries. Its 1965 budget was $2,500,000. A force of 60 World Service secretaries administers these programs. The program began in 1889 with the appointment of two YMCA secretaries to serve in India and Japan. The program also has been expanded in recent years to include World Service Work Camps and an international Camper Exchange Program.

Delegates to the 39th annual meeting of the National Council of the YMCA, held in Pittsburgh, Pa., from May 7 to 10, were told that the number of associations still practicing some form of discrimination had been cut from 432 in 1964 to 135 at the beginning of 1965. The members of the council adopted a "Statement of Belief" reaffirming their 1963 policy on achieving complete racial equality.

W. Walter Williams of Seattle, Wash., was re-elected president of the National Council. Mrs. Richard W. (Elizabeth) Howe of Livingston, N.J., was elected vice-president, the first time in the history of the YMCA that a woman has held this high office.   JOSEPH P. ANDERSON

**YOUNG WOMEN'S CHRISTIAN ASSOCIA-
TION (YWCA)** workers from 34 countries took part
in an international training institute held from February to May, 1965, under the sponsorship of the
YWCAs of the United States and Canada. The institute, which began with a three-week seminar at
Buck Hill Falls, Pa., focused on the contribution of
the YWCA in a rapidly changing world. Following
the seminar, the participants, in teams of five or six,
attended one of 23 workshops held in the United
States and Canada. The concluding meeting was
held in Banff, Alberta. Many of the workers from
Africa, Asia, and Latin America stressed the concern of their members for achieving a growing
awareness of social customs in a changing world.

In addition to taking part in the institute, some
YWCA leaders joined visitors from other countries
at training and observation programs in various
parts of the United States. One of them, Dr. Una B.
Porter, O.B.E., a psychiatrist from Melbourne,
Australia, and president of the World YWCA, also
attended a Y-Teen conference in the South.

The third National Y-Teen Conference was held
in Washington, D.C., from August 8 to 14. More
than 700 teen-agers and 150 adults discussed the
conference theme, "Youth's Role in National and
International Affairs." Vice-President Hubert H.
Humphrey and Mrs. Lloyd J. Marti, YWCA president, addressed the group.   JOSEPH P. ANDERSON

YUGOSLAVIA embarked on what President Tito
labeled its "third revolution" by closing all shops,
without warning, on Saturday, July 24. (The first
revolution was the overthrow of the Nazis and
Fascists in 1941; the second, the 1948 break with
Stalin.) Only bread, milk, and meat were sold,
while behind shuttered windows and locked doors
government accountants worked out new prices. On
Monday, July 26, the government announced reforms designed to mesh the economy with the free
markets of the world. These required more decentralization of industry and less central planning. Unprofitable businesses, unless essential, would no
longer be sustained by state subsidies.

Currency was devalued from 750 dinars to 1,250
dinars per dollar, thereby establishing an exchange
rate the West could respect. Steep price rises in
consumer goods and services were called for, and an
immediate increase in the cost of living was officially
estimated at 24 per cent.

Despite the resultant confusion and unemployment, the reforms proceeded smoothly. Many
prices were freely established. Factory production
increased, although labor forces and operations
were reduced. By November, the trade deficit for
the year had been cut to about $200,000,000.

These measures were initiated with the help of the
International Monetary Fund, which gave Yugo-
slavia an $80,000,000 stand-by credit (see Section
One, SYLVIA PORTER ON THE ECONOMY). They an-

ticipated Yugoslavia's joining the General Agreement on Tariffs and Trade (GATT) and improving its association with the European Economic
Community (EEC, or Common Market). Considered the natural outgrowth of the 1964 constitution, the reforms fundamentally meant that the
economy would depend more on the profit motive
and the laws of supply and demand. Politically, they
represented victory for the "liberals" and underscored Yugoslavia's trail-blazing experimentation
and departure from dogmatic Stalinism.

For the first time in many years, the United
States became Yugoslavia's principal export market,
accounting for about 40 per cent of Yugoslavian exports. But business with the Eastern bloc also increased to 38 per cent of the total foreign trade. The
general economy suffered, however, from floods.

Yugoslavia's relations with its Balkan neighbors
were the best in years, marked by numerous high-
level visits. Although Yugoslavia remained highly
critical of U.S. policy in Vietnam, relations with the
United States were otherwise good.

Population: 19,615,000. **Government:** President
Tito; Vice-President Alexsandar Ranković. **Monetary
Unit:** dinar (1,250 = U.S. $1). **Gross National Prod-
uct:** 3,475,000,000,000 dinars. **Foreign Trade (1963):**
exports, $893,000,000; imports, $1,321,000,000. **Principal Exports:** machinery, meat, transportation
equipment.   TOM AND HARLE DAMMANN

ZAMBIA, a former member of the dissolved
Federation of Rhodesia and Nyasaland, celebrated
its first anniversary as an independent nation on
October 24. It did so in an atmosphere of crisis
caused by deteriorating relations with its former
partner in the federation, (Southern) Rhodesia.
These relations subsequently grew even more
strained when Rhodesia unilaterally declared itself
independent of Great Britain (see RHODESIA).

In January, Zambia signed an agreement with a
British firm for the building of a steel mill that would
use ore imported from Rhodesia. Later, however,
the plan was changed to use local ore and thus avoid
dependence upon Rhodesian mines. In November,
a power station was blown up, and President Kenneth Kaunda called upon Britain for protection
from Rhodesian terrorists. Zambia achieved significant economic advances over 1964, including an increase of 11 per cent in mineral output, 17 per cent
in manufacturing, and 10 per cent in employment.
There was also a 16 per cent increase in the Gross
National Product.

Population: 3,730,000. **Government:** President
Kenneth Kaunda. **Monetary Unit:** pound (1 = U.S.
$2.80). **Gross National Product:** 190,900,000 pounds.
Foreign Trade: no statistics available. **Principal
Exports:** asbestos, cobalt, copper, lead, manganese,
tobacco, zinc.   BENJAMIN E. THOMAS

See also AFRICA.

ZANZIBAR. See TANZANIA.

ZOOLOGY. Several species of whale will become extinct unless there is a strict enforcement of reduced catch quotas, marine biologists reported in 1965. The basis on which whale catches are calculated is the "blue whale unit." One such unit may consist of one blue whale, or two finback whales, or two and a half humpback whales, or six sei whales.

Despite recommendations of the International Whaling Commission that the 1964-1965 season's catch be held to 4,000 units, the 15 whaling fleets of Japan, Norway, and the U.S.S.R. set themselves a combined quota of 8,000 blue whale units. Actual catches, however, fell short of the combined quota. The combined fleets were able to sight and kill only 7,000 finback whales, compared with a take of 27,000 finbacks during the 1960-1961 season.

Scientists estimate the remaining finback whale population to be 34,000 to 35,000, and prescribe a limit of 2,500 blue whale units for coming seasons, though they doubt this limit will be observed.

Into the Sea. The polar bear is slowly evolving into a marine mammal, according to Martin W. Schein of Pennsylvania State University. Unlike most mammals, which use their hind legs when they swim, the polar bear uses its hind legs as a pusher, much as a whale uses its tail. Over millions of years of evolution, the polar bear's hind legs may well become a tail, according to Schein, who has been studying the seagoing bears on Spitsbergen archipelago, east of Greenland. Two other mammals that have gone through the process of evolving from land animals to sea animals are the whale and the walrus. See WILDLIFE.

Thirst Study. Thomas J. Cade, associate professor of zoology at Syracuse University, is studying desert birds that can survive for long periods without water. He hopes to find out how the birds are able to reduce the amount of body water normally lost through respiration and excretion. He also hopes to determine how the birds are able to continue eating dried seeds without increasing their thirst, and the way deprivation of water affects their life cycle. Scientists are also studying the same problems in relation to the pocket mouse of the United States and the African desert antelope.

Other Developments included the discovery of an Angora mouse among the hundreds of thousands of inbred mice raised at the Jackson Laboratory in Bar Harbor, Me. This animal now joins the cats, goats, and rabbits called Angora because of their unusually long hair. Margaret Dickie, who discovered the Angora rodent, said it was surprising that such a mutant had not appeared sooner among mice.

Chicken fanciers were surprised to learn that a baby chick is conditioned to its mother's call even before it breaks out of its shell. The discovery was made by Duke University zoologists, who had attached tiny microphones to unhatched eggs. The chick embryo responds to its mother's call by clapping its bill. SERGEI LENORMAND

ZOOS AND AQUARIUMS. The National Zoological Park in Rock Creek Valley in the District of Columbia began an extensive remodeling and modernizing program that is to be completed in 10 years. The zoo, a branch of the Smithsonian Institution, houses about 830 different species, including some of the most famous animals of modern times. A resident of the zoo is Smokey the Bear. Others are Ham, the chimpanzee who made space history with a 420-mile flight down the Atlantic missile range, and the rare white tiger that starred on a television program showing the birth of her three cubs.

A five-acre "Amazon rain forest," with treetop sprinklers to ensure heavy "rain," was added to Florida's well-known Monkey Jungle, south of Miami. The addition was constructed specifically as a habitat for South American monkeys, and contains plants native only to the Amazon region. One exception is the banana tree, a native of Asia. A map at the head of the trail lists the various species of monkeys to be found in the rain forest.

New Concepts. The Bronx Zoo in New York City began construction of a windowless, horseshoe-shaped building to house 100 species of nocturnal animals. It will be opened in the fall of 1966. It and other zoos have had small exhibits of such animals for several years, but this will be the first major exhibit of its kind in any zoo. Most of the nocturnal creatures, such as clouded leopards, gopher tortoises, leaping galagos, nosy aardvarks, pit vipers, and vampire bats are color blind to the red lights that will shine on them during the day. Visitors can thus view them in their active state. At night, when the public has left, brilliant white lights will be turned on so that the animals can sleep.

The Philadelphia Zoological Gardens opened its rare mammal house, with the animals exhibited behind glass to protect them from airborne diseases. A feature is a flushing system that automatically cleans the larger cages every 90 minutes. Other new additions included a 92-cage reptile house at the Atlanta (Ga.) Zoo, an ape house at the West Berlin Zoo, and an insect house at the Tama Zoo in Tokyo, Japan. New sections were also opened at the modern Milwaukee Zoo, scheduled for completion in 1967 on a 165-acre tract of land.

Births. For the first time in more than 100 years, trumpeter swans in captivity produced young. A total of 11 baby trumpeter swans were hatched—five at the Philadelphia Zoological Gardens and six at the city park in Great Bend, Kans. The trumpeter swan, nearly extinct for many years, has been protected by federal and state laws since 1918.

At the Jacksonville (Fla.) Zoo, an unusual baby, half donkey and half zebra, was born in August. Zoo officials had mated a Mexican burro and a Grant's zebra to produce the animal, which they now call a *dozeb*. Apparently the first of its kind, the baby dozeb has striped legs and ears, like its zebra mother, but a gray body, like its donkey father. R. MARLIN PERKINS

CONTENTS OF SECTION FOUR

In its function of keeping all WORLD BOOK owners up-to-date, THE WORLD BOOK YEAR BOOK herewith offers a significant new article from the 1966 edition of THE WORLD BOOK ENCYCLOPEDIA. This article, chosen because of its timeliness and lasting value, should be indexed in THE WORLD BOOK ENCYCLOPEDIA by means of THE YEAR BOOK cross-reference tabs.

THE WORLD BOOK SUPPLEMENT

An overview of world history in a concise and easy-to-read article by T. Walter Wallbank, Professor Emeritus of History at the University of Southern California.

WORLD HISTORY

The contributor of this article is T. Walter Wallbank, Professor Emeritus of History at the University of Southern California.

WORLD, HISTORY OF. The history of the world is the story of man—from the first civilization to the Space Age. The story covers a period of about 5,000 years, beginning about 3000 B.C. At that time, or even a little earlier, men developed a way to write down their experiences. Those early writings began the record of man's progress that we study today as world history.

Before the development of writing, human beings had existed for at least 500,000 years—a hundred times longer than the total span of recorded history. The long period before writing began is called *Prehistoric Times*. Scientists have pieced together the story of that period. Life during Prehistoric Times is described in the article PREHISTORIC MAN.

World history shows that civilization today is the product of many cultures. For thousands of years, various peoples have borrowed ideas and inventions from

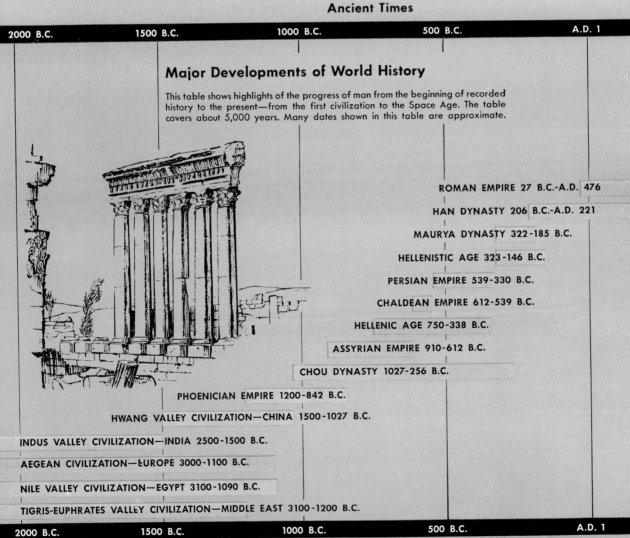

Ancient Times

2000 B.C.	1500 B.C.	1000 B.C.	500 B.C.	A.D. 1

Major Developments of World History

This table shows highlights of the progress of man from the beginning of recorded history to the present—from the first civilization to the Space Age. The table covers about 5,000 years. Many dates shown in this table are approximate.

ROMAN EMPIRE 27 B.C.-A.D. 476

HAN DYNASTY 206 B.C.-A.D. 221

MAURYA DYNASTY 322-185 B.C.

HELLENISTIC AGE 323-146 B.C.

PERSIAN EMPIRE 539-330 B.C.

CHALDEAN EMPIRE 612-539 B.C.

HELLENIC AGE 750-338 B.C.

ASSYRIAN EMPIRE 910-612 B.C.

CHOU DYNASTY 1027-256 B.C.

PHOENICIAN EMPIRE 1200-842 B.C.

HWANG VALLEY CIVILIZATION—CHINA 1500-1027 B.C.

INDUS VALLEY CIVILIZATION—INDIA 2500-1500 B.C.

AEGEAN CIVILIZATION—EUROPE 3000-1100 B.C.

NILE VALLEY CIVILIZATION—EGYPT 3100-1090 B.C.

TIGRIS-EUPHRATES VALLEY CIVILIZATION—MIDDLE EAST 3100-1200 B.C.

2000 B.C.	1500 B.C.	1000 B.C.	500 B.C.	A.D. 1

The gray bars show, approximately, the years covered by each major development. The bars with broken ends indicate continuing developments.

each other. This exchange is called *culture diffusion*. See CULTURE (How Cultures Grow and Change).

Throughout most of world history, the most important regions for new ideas and inventions were the Middle East, Egypt, India, and China. But during Modern Times—the period of the last 500 years—Western civilization has made rapid progress, while other civilizations lagged. As a result, the course of culture diffusion changed. During Modern Times, the flow of ideas and inventions has swept from West to East. The development of worldwide systems of communication and transportation conquered barriers of time and distance.

Mankind's progress through the centuries has been marked by many changes, and every generation has faced the challenge of serious problems. Great civilizations have developed, flourished for a time, and then collapsed. International disputes have brought on terrible wars. In every age, millions of persons have suffered hunger and hardship, while others enjoyed prosperity. Today, we live in the greatest civilization of all times. But war and widespread poverty still are the most important problems of mankind. Man has greater knowledge and more technological power than ever before. As a result, he probably has a better chance to meet the challenge of today than any generation of the past.

This article deals broadly with man's progress from Ancient Times to the present. It provides general information on how civilized ways of life developed and advanced in various regions of the world. It describes how these cultures mingled and made lasting contributions to later civilizations. Separate WORLD BOOK articles, especially the articles on each country, provide details about the major events of world history.

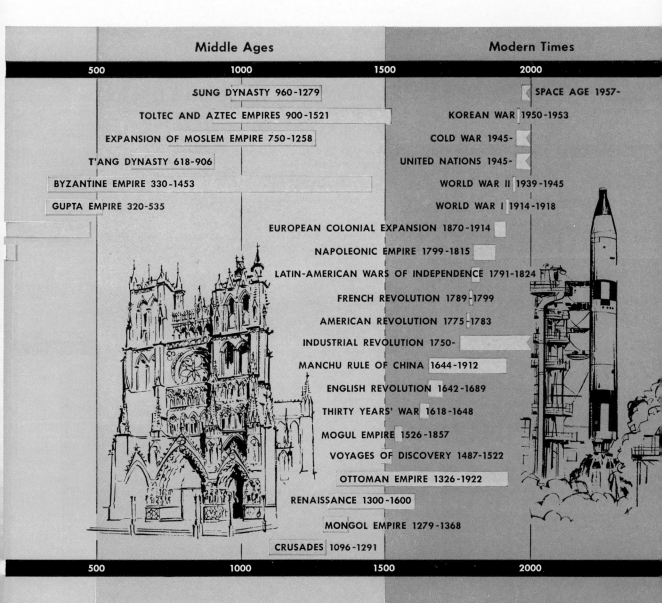

Middle Ages | Modern Times

500 | 1000 | 1500 | 2000

SUNG DYNASTY 960-1279
SPACE AGE 1957-
TOLTEC AND AZTEC EMPIRES 900-1521
KOREAN WAR 1950-1953
EXPANSION OF MOSLEM EMPIRE 750-1258
COLD WAR 1945-
T'ANG DYNASTY 618-906
UNITED NATIONS 1945-
BYZANTINE EMPIRE 330-1453
WORLD WAR II 1939-1945
GUPTA EMPIRE 320-535
WORLD WAR I 1914-1918
EUROPEAN COLONIAL EXPANSION 1870-1914
NAPOLEONIC EMPIRE 1799-1815
LATIN-AMERICAN WARS OF INDEPENDENCE 1791-1824
FRENCH REVOLUTION 1789-1799
AMERICAN REVOLUTION 1775-1783
INDUSTRIAL REVOLUTION 1750-
MANCHU RULE OF CHINA 1644-1912
ENGLISH REVOLUTION 1642-1689
THIRTY YEARS' WAR 1618-1648
MOGUL EMPIRE 1526-1857
VOYAGES OF DISCOVERY 1487-1522
OTTOMAN EMPIRE 1326-1922
RENAISSANCE 1300-1600
MONGOL EMPIRE 1279-1368
CRUSADES 1096-1291

500 | 1000 | 1500 | 2000

WORLD HISTORY / *Ancient Times*

The greatest cultural journey of all times took place when man crossed the gulf between barbarism and civilization. The development of civilization was made possible by the invention of farming. After men discovered ways to grow crops and raise animals, they no longer had to roam in search of food. They could settle down in villages. Some became farmers and herdsmen. Others became craftsmen, merchants, religious leaders, teachers, soldiers, or government officials. They developed the skills, tools, beliefs, and laws that produced the early civilizations of mankind. In these civilizations, the first cities were built and the first nations were organized. Some nations of Ancient Times expanded into empires that spread over large parts of the world.

The early civilizations made many contributions to later generations. Probably the most important of these contributions was the invention of a system of writing, about 3000 B.C. At that time, man started to write down a record of his life. The year 3000 B.C. opened the period called *Ancient Times* or *Ancient History*. According to most historians, this period ended at about A.D. 476.

The development of Western civilization was strongly influenced by many peoples of Ancient Times. Among them were the Sumerians, Babylonians, Egyptians, Hebrews, Phoenicians, Assyrians, Chaldeans, and Persians. As civilization advanced, the Greeks and the Romans originated many arts and sciences that became basic to Western ways of life. Important cultures also developed in the eastern part of the world—in India and China. Almost from the beginning of Ancient Times, many peoples of the West and the East exchanged ideas and inventions, and the cultures of the world mingled.

Ruins of a Roman Temple in Baalbek, Lebanon

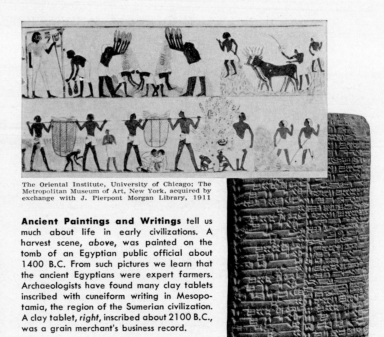

The Oriental Institute, University of Chicago; The Metropolitan Museum of Art, New York, acquired by exchange with J. Pierpont Morgan Library, 1911

Ancient Paintings and Writings tell us much about life in early civilizations. A harvest scene, *above*, was painted on the tomb of an Egyptian public official about 1400 B.C. From such pictures we learn that the ancient Egyptians were expert farmers. Archaeologists have found many clay tablets inscribed with cuneiform writing in Mesopotamia, the region of the Sumerian civilization. A clay tablet, *right*, inscribed about 2100 B.C., was a grain merchant's business record.

Cradles of Civilization

The first important civilizations of the world developed in four river valleys. These valleys were (1) the land between the Tigris and the Euphrates rivers in the Middle East, (2) along the Nile River in Egypt, (3) the vast region watered by the Indus River in India, and (4) along the Hwang Ho (Yellow River) in China.

The four valleys are generally known as the "cradles of civilization." The valley civilizations of the Middle East and Egypt formed the basis for present-day Western civilization. The Indus civilization formed the basis of the civilization of what is now India and Pakistan. The Hwang Ho civilization developed into the present-day Chinese civilization, and strongly influenced the civilization of Japan.

While civilization was developing in the four valleys, people in most other parts of the world were still following primitive ways of life. Little cultural progress was being made in such regions as northern and central Europe, central and southern Africa, northern and southeastern Asia, or most of North America. In parts of Central and South America, some civilized ways of life were developing. But they did not become advanced civilizations until hundreds of years later.

The Middle East of ancient times was made up largely of the fertile valleys of the Tigris and the Euphrates rivers. The area curved from the southeastern end of the Mediterranean Sea around the Arabian Desert to the Persian Gulf. Because of its shape, the ancient Middle East became known as the Fertile Crescent. Today, this region includes Iraq, Israel, Jordan, Lebanon, and Syria, and part of Turkey. For a description of the ancient region, see FERTILE CRESCENT.

The birthplace of the Middle East civilization was Sumer, in southern Mesopotamia (now Iraq). The Sumerians probably migrated to Mesopotamia from the highlands of what is now Iran or Turkey. By 3000 B.C. they had built an advanced civilization of independent city-states. These city-states had no central government or unified army. As a result, Sumer was unable to resist invasions by envious neighbors. About 2300 B.C., Sumer was conquered by a famous empire builder, Sargon of

The Cradles of Civilization: 1. the Tigris and Euphrates Valleys, 2. the Nile Valley, 3. the Indus Valley, 4. the Hwang Valley.

MAJOR EVENTS OF ANCIENT TIMES

c. 3100 B.C. Cuneiform writings of the Sumerians began the recorded history of the Middle East.

c. 3100 B.C. King Menes united Lower and Upper Egypt, and formed one of the world's first national governments.

c. 2500 B.C. The Indus Valley civilization of India began in the cities of Harappa and Mohenjo-daro.

c. 2300 B.C. Sargon of Akkad conquered the Sumerians and united their city-states under his rule.

c. 1750 B.C. Hammurabi established the Babylonian empire.

c. 1600-1400 B.C. The Minoan civilization flourished on the Mediterranean island of Crete.

c. 1500 B.C. The Aryans of central Asia invaded India.

c. 1500 B.C. The Shang dynasty began its 500-year rule of China.

1000's B.C. Latin tribes settled south of the Tiber River, and Etruscans settled in the northeastern region of the Italian peninsula.

750-338 B.C. Athens, Corinth, Sparta, and Thebes developed as the chief city-states of Greece during the Hellenic Age.

509 B.C. The Latins rebelled against their Etruscan rulers and established the Roman Republic.

338 B.C. Philip II of Macedonia defeated the Greeks and made Greece part of the Macedonian Empire.

331 B.C. Alexander the Great defeated the Persians at Arbela (Irbil), and opened his path of conquest to northern India.

322-185 B.C. The Maurya Empire of northern India spread over all India and part of central Asia.

221-207 B.C. The Ch'in dynasty established China's first strong central government and completed the Great Wall that protected China from invaders.

206 B.C. The Han dynasty began its 400-year rule of China.

146 B.C. The Romans destroyed Corinth and conquered Greece.

55-54 B.C. Julius Caesar led the Roman invasion of Britain.

27 B.C. Augustus became the first Roman emperor.

A.D. 70 Roman forces under Titus captured and destroyed Jerusalem.

78-200 The Kushan empire ruled Afghanistan and northwestern India.

105 The Chinese invented paper.

293 Diocletian divided the Roman Empire into four prefectures and set up two capitals—Nicomedia in Asia Minor, and Milan in Europe.

313 Constantine granted the Christians of the Roman Empire freedom of religion in the Edict of Milan.

320 India began its golden age under the rule of the Gupta dynasty.

395 The Roman Empire split into the East Roman Empire and the West Roman Empire.

476 The German chieftain Odoacer deposed Romulus, the last emperor of the West Roman Empire.

Sargon of Akkad was the first great empire builder of history. He conquered Sumer about 2300 B.C. Country after country then fell to Sargon's invading armies until he ruled most of the Middle East.

Directorate-General of Antiquities, Government of Iraq

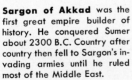

573

Akkad. Another invader, Hammurabi, conquered Sumer about 1750 B.C. Hammurabi made Babylon his capital, and the region became known as Babylonia.

Both Sargon and Hammurabi helped preserve and advance the Sumerian civilization. Sargon united the city-states under a strong central government. Hammurabi organized hundreds of laws, most of which were originated by the Sumerians, into one *code* (set) of laws. The *Code of Hammurabi* established what was probably the world's earliest social order based on the rights of the individual. The code influenced the laws of many countries for hundreds of years. See HAMMURABI; SARGON.

The Sumerians also probably invented the first system of writing, called *cuneiform* (wedgelike) writing. With this writing, men started the record of events that make up written history. Many clay tablets with cuneiform writing have been found in the Middle East. These tablets reveal the high development of early Middle East civilization. They include hundreds of financial documents, and many studies in astronomy, mathematics, and medicine. Some of the first literature of world history also was written by the Sumerians and Babylonians. This literature includes the famous *Epic of Gilgamesh*. One of the Gilgamesh stories describes a great flood, similar to the story of a worldwide flood told in the Old Testament. For descriptions of the many achievements of the Babylonians and the Sumerians, see BABYLONIA; SUMER.

For several hundred years after 1200 B.C., no single ruler controlled the Middle East. As a result, several peoples developed important cultures in various parts of the region. Of these peoples, the Hebrews and the Phoenicians had a great influence on future civilizations.

The Hebrews, also called Jews, developed and spread their idea of one God. The Jews worshiped one God during a time when most other peoples worshiped many gods. Judaism also put great emphasis on the ideals of brotherhood, charity, human dignity, and universal peace. These ideals became the chief elements of moral living for many persons of future generations. The Hebrew Bible, or Old Testament, became a basic part of Christianity, the most widespread religion of Modern Times. Islam, the religion of the Moslems, was built on Judaism and Christianity. See JEWS.

The Phoenicians became famous for two achievements—their alphabet and their great colonial empire. The Phoenician alphabet was the basis of the Greek alphabet. All other Western alphabets developed from the Greek alphabet. The colonial empire of the Phoenicians was one of the first links between civilized areas in Ancient Times. The Phoenicians were great explorers and traders. Their ships sailed throughout the Mediterranean Sea and around the west coast of Africa. The Phoenician empire consisted of many colonies and trading posts. One of the most important Phoenician colonies was Carthage. See PHOENICIA.

Three empires rose to power during the period when small nations were important in the Middle East. The first of these empires was built by the Assyrians. By 700 B.C., they had become the masters of the Fertile Crescent. The Assyrians conquered and ruled many peoples by terror. Their cruelty to captives was a form of what is now called psychological warfare. The Assyrians were

conquered by the Chaldeans about the year 612 B.C.

Nebuchadnezzar II, the famous ruler of the Chaldeans, rebuilt Babylon as a magnificent city. His royal palace was surrounded by terraced gardens. These gardens, known as the "hanging gardens of Babylon," became one of the ancient Seven Wonders of the World. The Chaldeans made important discoveries in astronomy and believed they could foretell the future by studying the stars. They probably invented astrology. Chaldean rule of the Middle East ended in 539 B.C. after the Persians captured the city of Babylon.

The Persians ruled about 200 years, and their empire spread over all the Middle East. They built excellent roads that supplied their vast empire with a communications network. Unlike the Assyrians, the Persians ruled the many peoples of their empire sternly but with justice, not by terror. The Persians became famous for developing an efficient system of government. Their theories of justice were guided by the teachings of their religion, Zoroastrianism (see ZOROASTRIANS).

Egyptian Civilization developed in the rich valley of the Nile River. The kingdoms of that region were united under a single ruler, Menes, about 3100 B.C. Egyptian pharaohs ruled Egypt until about 1090 B.C., except for a period of about 160 years. The Hyksos invaded Egypt during this period (see HYKSOS). After about 1090 B.C., a succession of conquerors ruled Ancient Egypt.

The Egyptians built one of the world's great early civilizations. The huge pyramids near the present site of Cairo show their engineering skill. The Egyptians probably invented post and lintel architecture, the basis of much present-day building (see ARCHITECTURE [table, Architectural Terms (Post and Lintel)]). The Egyptians also were among the first people to use a type of paper, instead of clay tablets, for their records. They wrote on a paper made from the fibers of a water plant called papyrus. The Egyptians were great artists, astronomers, and engineers. They were great merchants, too. Their caravans carried goods throughout the vast desert regions surrounding Egypt. Their ships sailed to the major ports of the world. Egyptian traders spread many elements of their culture among the peoples who lived along the routes of commerce, on both land and sea. See EGYPT, ANCIENT.

The Indus Valley Civilization began about 2500 B.C. in the region that is now West Pakistan. Archaeologists have found Sumerian relics in the ruins of the Indus cities of Harappa and Mohenjo-daro. These relics show that the Indus people traded with the people of the Middle East. The Indus Valley cities had buildings made of brick, and efficient sewerage systems. The Indus people also developed a system of writing that has never been translated. The Indus civilization disappeared mysteriously about 1500 B.C. At about that time, the Aryans, ancestors of the present-day Hindus, invaded the Indus Valley. They came from the plains of Asia through the Himalayan mountain passes. The light-skinned Aryans found many dark-skinned Dravidians living in northern India.

Several features of life in present-day India developed in ancient times. Perhaps the most important was the custom of dividing people into separate social classes, called *castes*. The caste system of India today probably developed from Aryan rules that forbade intermarriage with the Dravidians. See CASTE.

The Hwang Ho Civilization probably began about the same time as the civilizations of the three other cradle valleys. But the earliest Chinese records date from only about 1500 B.C. Under the rule of the Shang dynasty (1500-1027 B.C.), the Chinese had a well-organized government and a system of writing. They worshiped a supreme god and other gods, including ancestral spirits. The early Chinese developed many arts. They were especially skilled at casting beautiful bronzes. The Chou dynasty ruled China from about 1027 to 256 B.C. Many lasting features of Chinese life developed during this period. Probably the most important early Chinese idea was a belief in a "Mandate of Heaven." According to that belief, if a ruler behaved badly, he no longer had the approval of the gods, and could be overthrown. The mandate was one of the first declarations of a people's right to revolt.

 ## Civilization Advances

From the cradle lands, civilized ways of life spread to many other regions of the world. Great civilizations rose in lands where barbarism had been the way of life for thousands of years.

In Europe and Asia, many barbarians became civilized. They took over the ideas and inventions of the cradle civilizations, and also created cultural patterns of their own. In Europe, the Greeks and the Romans developed most of the arts, philosophies, and sciences that became the chief ingredients of Western civilization. In Asia, the Indians and the Chinese developed lasting forms of art, government, and religion.

As civilized cultures advanced and spread, the people of various regions often exchanged ideas or inventions. This mingling of cultures occurred through commerce, conquest, and migration. Traders carried the products of one culture to others over long routes of commerce. The soldiers of conquering armies often settled in lands far from their own. Large groups of people migrated from one region to another, and brought the customs of their homelands with them. Many adopted the ways of life of the people they joined. In this way, the developing cultures of the world often mingled.

The mingling of civilized cultures during Ancient Times was an important development in world history. Ever since, much of mankind's progress has been made by the exchange of ideas among the peoples of the world. See MIGRATION.

The Greeks developed the first advanced civilization on the European mainland, and made many contributions to Western civilization. Their most important contribution probably was the idea of democracy. The ancient Greeks glorified individual freedom. They stressed man's right to criticize, be curious, and be different. The Greeks thought deeply about such questions as: What is the good life? What is beauty? What is truth? In pondering such questions, the Greeks developed the study of philosophy.

The right to think freely was basic in the work of the artists, scientists, and writers of ancient Greece. Democratic ideas were also used in government. The Greek form of democracy in government differed from present-day democracy. But the Greeks set forth certain democratic principles that are still followed today.

Casts from The Oriental Institute, University of Chicago, original in Egyptian Museum, Cairo.

Scenes of Conquest carved on both sides of a slate tablet tell how King Menes united two warring Nile Valley states and established the Egyptian nation about 3100 B.C. Each picture is a symbol of a heroic deed of Menes. Such picture symbols formed the system of hieroglyphic writing developed in ancient Egypt.

Wide World

Ruins of Mohenjo-daro, a center of the ancient Indus Valley civilization, still stand in present-day West Pakistan. The brick buildings of the city are at least 4,500 years old.

A Shang Dynasty Bronze shows the skill of ancient Chinese artists who perfected their style of carving during the 1500's B.C. This wine vessel is only about six inches tall.

The Art Institute of Chicago, Lucy Maud Buckingham Collection

In developing their great civilization, the Greeks freed themselves from traditions of the past. As a result, the Greeks produced new and lasting forms of art, politics, and science.

Greek civilization grew out of an early civilization called the Aegean Civilization (3000-1100 B.C.). The most important center of the Aegean Civilization was the Mediterranean island of Crete. The people of Crete built their culture on the ideas and inventions of the cradle civilizations of Egypt and the Middle East.

Crete became the stepping stone of Western civilization. The island linked Europe with Egypt and the Middle East. From about 1600 to 1100 B.C., people from the European mainland often raided Crete. They intermarried with the Cretans and became the people we call Greeks. The Greeks developed their great culture on the European mainland in such city-states as Athens, Corinth, Sparta, and Thebes. See AEGEAN CIVILIZATION; CRETE.

The ancient Greeks called themselves Hellenes, and their homeland was known as Hellas. The period of Greek history from 750 to 338 B.C. is called the Hellenic Age. During this period, Greek culture reached great heights of development. Greek armies and traders colonized many areas along the Mediterranean and Black seas. As ancient Greece expanded, the leaders of the powerful Persian empire tried to take over the country and its colonies. A long war between the two nations ended with the defeat of the Persians in 479 B.C.

After the Persian defeat, Athens became the leading city of Greece. During the Golden Age of Greece (461-431 B.C.), magnificent buildings were constructed and great works of art and literature were produced. No culture has produced so many lasting achievements in such a short period. From the Golden Age of Greece came the great works of men such as Aeschylus, Euripides, Herodotus, Phidias, Socrates, and Sophocles. The period is often called the Age of Pericles, after the brilliant leader of the Athenian government. See GOLDEN AGE; PERICLES.

The progress and riches of Athens were the envy of the other city-states of Greece. Hostility between the Athenians and their fellow Hellenes led to the Peloponnesian War (431-404 B.C.). Athens was defeated in that war. The victorious city-states soon started to quarrel among themselves. However, the political quarrels did not halt the work of Greek scholars. Aristotle and Plato produced their great philosophical works during this period.

In 338 B.C., the quarreling Hellenes were conquered by invaders from Macedonia, led by Philip II. His son, Alexander the Great, became the ruler of Greece. Alexander expanded his empire throughout the Middle East and Egypt, and as far east as northern India. Under Alexander and his successors, Greek culture spread and combined with other cultures. This great period of Greek civilization became known as the Hellenistic Age. The largest city of Hellenistic Greece was Alexandria, in Egypt. Alexandria was the home of some of the great scientists of Ancient Times. There, Eratosthenes estimated the circumference of the earth, and Euclid developed the fundamentals of plane geometry. The Hellenistic Age began about 323 B.C. and ended about 146 B.C., when the Romans conquered Greece.

For a description of life in ancient Greece and the story of how Greek civilization developed, see the article GREECE, ANCIENT.

The Romans were people of the Italian peninsula whose culture had lagged far behind that of the Greeks. It took them more than a hundred years to conquer all the empire that had flourished during the Hellenistic Age. The Romans invaded Greece about 146 B.C. and completed their conquest about 30 B.C. They adopted Greek forms of art and literature, and Greek architectural methods. A culture known as the Greco-Roman culture developed. The Romans built well-planned cities, massive aqueducts and bridges, and vast systems of roads. They became famous for their civic buildings, municipal baths, hospitals, stadiums, and triumphal arches. Greco-Roman sculptors created lifelike statues and portraits in marble. Famous Roman writers included Cicero, Julius Caesar, Livy, Ovid, Tacitus, and Virgil. Latin, the language of the Romans, became the basis of the Romance languages of today.

At the height of their power, the Romans ruled a vast empire. The Roman Empire was truly a "world state." It included many countries with widely different customs. The Romans showed careful respect for these customs, and they won the good will of many of the people they governed. The Romans generally ruled with a strong sense of justice and order.

The Roman legal system became the basis of the legal codes of many present-day European and Latin-American countries. Roman laws were enforced by efficient public officials. Many political terms that are common today originated in Rome. They include such words as *plebiscite, census, consul, municipal,* and *senate.*

One of the most important contributions of the Romans to Western civilization was the preservation of Christianity. Christ was born during the reign of the Emperor Augustus, and was crucified during the rule of Tiberius. The early Christians were persecuted by the Romans. But Christianity eventually became the official religion of the Roman Empire, and spread throughout the world. It became a major ingredient of Western civilization, and the world's most widespread religion.

The development of Roman culture spanned a period

The Triumphal Arch was an outstanding feature of Roman architecture. The famous Arch of Septimius Severus, built in A.D. 203, stood in the Roman Forum, center of government of ancient Rome.

Tomczak, Pix from Publix

of about 2,500 years. This period probably began about 2000 B.C., when people related to the Greeks migrated from Northern Europe to the Italian peninsula. The period ended in A.D. 476 after a Germanic conqueror overthrew the last emperor of the West Roman Empire. The East Roman Empire continued for another thousand years as the Byzantine Empire. For the dramatic story of how Rome grew from a small village in Italy to become the capital of one of the world's greatest empires, see the article ROMAN EMPIRE.

The Indians of Ancient Times made great progress in developing their civilized culture. They did so chiefly during the years of the Mauryan and the Gupta empires. During the Mauryan period, two of the world's most important religions—Hinduism and Buddhism—developed. The Mauryan civilization reached its highest development under Emperor Asoka, who spread Buddhism throughout India. Buddhism later spread to China and other eastern countries. Hinduism became the chief religion of India after Asoka's death. The teachings of these two religions and their importance to millions of persons throughout Asia are described in the articles BUDDHISTS; HINDUS.

India's golden age developed during the empire of the Gupta dynasty (A.D. 320-535). Its center of learning was the city of Nalanda. Indian mathematicians invented the system of numerals that was later taken over by the Arabs and became known as the Arabic system. The Indians also invented the decimal system, with a symbol for the zero. Poets, dramatists, and other writers produced many masterpieces of Indian literature in Sanskrit, the classical Indian language (see SANSKRIT LANGUAGE AND LITERATURE). Indian artists of the period created fine paintings and sculptures. Some of these ancient works may still be seen in Hindu temples and caves throughout India.

The Chinese of Ancient Times, like the Indians, made important cultural progress under the rule of two dynasties. The vast country was unified and protected from invaders by the Great Wall of China during the Ch'in dynasty (221-207 B.C.). The unification of China led to the great advances made under the Han dynasty that followed the Ch'in period.

During the 400 years of the Han period, many basic ways of Chinese life developed. Most of these ways of life came from the teachings of Confucius, one of the world's great philosophers. They included ancestor worship and many rules of conduct that lasted in China until Modern Times. Confucianism became one of the most important religions of the world. See CONFUCIANISTS.

The Chinese philosophers and scholars of the Han period were among the first to organize the facts of nature into various subjects. These subjects included astronomy, botany, chemistry, and mineralogy. They also compiled one of the first dictionaries, and wrote the first scholarly history of China.

The most famous invention of the Han period was paper, made for the first time from wood. During the same era, the Chinese invented a *seismograph* (an instrument that records earthquakes). Another famous invention of the Han period was the breast-strap harness for beasts of burden. This invention allowed animals to pull heavy loads without choking. The Chinese used the breast-strap harness several hundred years before it became known in Europe or other civilized regions.

American School of Classical Studies at Athens

Ballots Made of Broken Pottery were used by the citizens of ancient Athens to get rid of any politician who began acting like a dictator. Whenever 6,000 or more ballots were cast against an Athenian official, he was sent into exile for 10 years.

Eliot Elisofon, *LIFE* © Time Inc.

A Sculptured Gateway of the Great Stupa, a famous Buddhist monument in India, was carved about 100 B.C. India was the birthplace of two great religions—Buddhism and Hinduism. Buddhism spread to China, and Hinduism became the chief religion of India.

Paper was invented by the Chinese in A.D. 105. The first paper was made from the bark of mulberry trees. This fragment of Chinese paper, a treasure of the British Museum, is about 1800 years old.

© British Museum

577

Mankind reached another important cultural landmark during the thousand-year period of the Middle Ages. The ideas and inventions of many peoples were brought together and combined. An important mixture of cultures formed a way of life in Western Europe known as medieval culture. Most historians set the beginning of the Middle Ages at about A.D. 476, the time of the fall of Rome. They end the period in the middle or late 1400's.

Medieval culture was built on the ruins of the Greek and Roman civilizations. Both these civilizations were almost destroyed during the early years of the Middle Ages. Those early years became known as the Dark Ages. During the Dark Ages, many fierce barbarian tribes roamed over the lands of the fallen West Roman Empire. Their conquests even threatened to wipe out civilization in Western Europe.

At the same time that civilization was struggling to survive in Western Europe, civilized cultures were prospering in other regions. In southeastern Europe, the Byzantine Empire enjoyed great wealth. In the Middle East, a new empire—the Moslem Empire—climbed to great power. In the East, China's civilization reached new heights of achievement and Japan enjoyed its golden age. Unlike China, India was unable to continue its earlier important advances. Internal warfare and many invasions slowed progress in India during most of the Middle Ages.

Most regions of the world that were uncivilized during Ancient Times remained uncivilized during the Middle Ages. These uncivilized regions included much of the interior of Africa, and most of North America and South America. However, important civilized cultures were developed by the Aztec, Inca, Maya, and Toltec Indians in parts of Central America and South America.

The Cathedral at Amiens, France

French Government Tourist Office

P.I.P. Photos

Carcassonne, in southwestern France, is the finest example of a medieval walled city in Europe. It stands on the site of a Roman city of the 400's.

Western Europe During The Middle Ages

Christianity was the most important civilizing force in Western Europe during the Middle Ages. After the fall of Rome, the Roman Catholic Church became much more than a religious institution. It became the most powerful political and social influence in the life of Western Europe.

At first, the church converted the Germanic invaders of Rome to Christianity. Later, its missionaries spread Christianity among the barbarians of northern Europe. At the same time, much Greek and Roman scientific knowledge was preserved in the church's monasteries. For hundreds of years, Christian monks were probably the only scholars of Western Europe.

The development of a new political system provided a crude form of law and order during the Middle Ages. This system, called *feudalism*, replaced the governmental units of the Roman Empire. Under feudalism, almost all the land of Western Europe was governed and owned by the church or by powerful nobles. From time to time, landowning nobles gave land to other nobles in return for military assistance. Almost all the people worked as farmers and lived under the protection of the nobles. The ruling nobles quarreled about land almost constantly. In most of these quarrels, the church acted as peacemaker to settle the disputes. See FEUDALISM.

During the 600's, Palestine—the birthplace of Christianity—came under Moslem rule. A desire by the

Empires of the Middle Ages: Byzantine Empire, A.D. 565 (gray); Moslem Empire, 750 (lined); Mongol Empire, 1294 (blue).

MAJOR EVENTS OF THE MIDDLE AGES

486 Clovis became king of the Franks and founded the Merovingian dynasty, rulers of the first French state.

527-565 Justinian I ruled the Byzantine Empire and developed the famous Justinian Code of law.

622 Mohammed, founder of the Islamic religion, fled from Mecca to Medina. Mohammed's flight, called the *Hegira*, marks the beginning of the Moslem calendar.

611 The Omayyad Caliphate established the capital of the Moslem Empire at Damascus.

711 The Moslems invaded Spain and began an occupation that lasted about 700 years.

732 Charles Martel led the Franks in defeating the invading Moslems at Tours. The victory prevented the Moslems from conquering Europe.

750 The Abbasid Caliphate replaced the Omayyads as rulers of the Moslem Empire, and established a new capital at Baghdad.

c. 770 The Chinese invented wood-block printing.

771 Charlemagne became ruler of the Franks.

800 Pope Leo III crowned Charlemagne Emperor of the Holy Roman Empire in the West.

843 The Treaty of Verdun divided Charlemagne's empire into three parts, and began the national development of France, Germany, and Italy.

862 Rurik, chief of the Varangians (vikings), established his rule at Novgorod and founded the Russian Empire.

878 Alfred the Great of England defeated the Danes in the Battle of Edington.

969 The Fatimids conquered Egypt and made Cairo the center of the Moslem Empire.

987 Hugh Capet became king of France and founded the Capetian dynasty that ruled until 1328.

c. 1000 Leif Ericson sailed west from Greenland to the North American mainland. He was probably the first explorer to reach North America.

1016 Canute became king of England and brought the entire country under Danish rule.

1037 The Seljuk Turks conquered most of the Iranian kingdoms.

1066 Norman forces under William the Conqueror defeated the Anglo-Saxons in the Battle of Hastings, and ended Anglo-Saxon rule of England.

1099 Christian forces captured Jerusalem, ending the First Crusade.

1187 Moslem troops under Saladin recaptured Jerusalem.

1192 Yoritomo became the first shogun of Japan.

1215 Barons of England forced King John to grant the Magna Carta.

1279 Kublai Khan led the Mongols in completing the conquest of China.

1368 Ming dynasty established its 300-year rule of China.

c. 1440 Johannes Gutenberg, a German printer, invented movable type.

1453 The Ottoman Turks captured Constantinople (Istanbul) and overthrew the Byzantine Empire.

Bettmann Archive

Medieval Monks copied many manuscripts of Greek and Roman scholars, and preserved the knowledge of Ancient Times.

Moslem Scientists and physicians were the leading scholars of the Middle Ages. They made many discoveries that advanced astronomy and medicine.

Courtesy of Smithsonian Institution

579

European nobles to free the Holy Land led to several military expeditions against the Moslems. These expeditions, called the Crusades, brought Western Europe into contact with an advanced Moslem civilization (see CRUSADES). Many ideas and inventions of the Moslems were brought back to Europe by the crusaders. The Crusades also spurred European interest in trading with China, India, and other distant lands. This interest in world commerce encouraged explorers to find new trade routes to the East. It also revived European craftsmanship and manufacturing. As a result, many towns were built in Western European countries.

A new class of people developed in the towns of Western Europe. This class consisted of craftsmen, merchants, and traders. Many people moved from the farmlands to the towns. At the same time, many feudal lands were combined and formed large political units. These became states, such as England, France, Portugal, and Spain. As these states were established, nationalism and patriotism developed among their people. Such ideas became important forces in the political development of Europe during Modern Times.

During the 1300's, a new civilization was rising in Western Europe. Its moral and spiritual basis was provided by Christianity. Its wealth and thriving cities were supported by widespread commerce. Its education and learning grew with the help of proud and nationalistic monarchies. In the new Western European civilization, the first important universities of Europe were established in Bologna, Cambridge, Heidelberg, Oxford,

Paris, and other cities. There, scholars made important scientific progress, especially in geography, mathematics, and medicine. Much of the scientific progress was based on scholarly achievements of the Moslems. From the Moslems, for example, Europe got its system of numerals and the decimal system. The Moslems had taken over those important systems from the Indian mathematicians of the Gupta dynasty.

During the gradual development of medieval culture, several important European languages came into popular use. Latin remained the language of the Roman Catholic Church and of most scholars. Popular languages such as Italian, French, and Spanish developed from Latin. English came largely from Germanic languages. Much important literature was written in the popular languages. Medieval literature included great epic poems, songs of the troubadours, and ballads about Robin Hood and other folk heroes. Two masterpieces of literature were written—Dante's Divine Comedy and Chaucer's Canterbury Tales.

The most impressive feature of medieval culture was probably Gothic architecture. Gothic cathedrals, such as Canterbury, Chartres, and Notre Dame of Paris, still stand among the finest buildings of the world. They combine many skills of medieval artists and craftsmen. Gothic cathedrals have towering spires, stained glass windows, and ornamental sculptured figures. Gothic architecture largely symbolizes the great power of medieval Christianity and the strong religious feelings in Western Europe during the Middle Ages. For a description of life in Europe during medieval times, see the article MIDDLE AGES.

 ## The Byzantine Empire

Southeastern Europe was the center of a strong empire during the Middle Ages. This empire grew out of the East Roman Empire. Its capital and military stronghold was Constantinople (now Istanbul). Constantinople stood on the site of ancient Byzantium, and the new empire became known as the Byzantine Empire.

The Byzantine Empire was the chief civilizing influence among the Slavic peoples of Eastern Europe. There, civilization was spread mostly by missionaries of the Byzantine Church. Byzantine missionaries converted most of the peoples of the Balkans and Russia to Christianity. The Byzantine Church was united with the church at Rome for many years. But rivalries developed between the two groups, and in 1054 they became separated. The Byzantine Church later became known as the Eastern Orthodox Church. Its members still form the largest Christian group of Eastern Europe, and it has members in many other parts of the world. See EASTERN ORTHODOX CHURCHES.

Byzantine culture was a mixture of several cultures. The power of the Byzantine Empire was built on the Roman traditions of justice and a strong central government. The Byzantine arts, including the famous Byzantine mosaics, combined Greek art forms with strong influences from the Orient. These influences were brought to Constantinople chiefly by Byzantine traders. Their caravans traveled far into Central Asia, and their ships crossed the Black Sea and sailed many miles into the waterways of Russia.

Brown Brothers

Thousands of Crusaders marched through medieval Europe toward Palestine, hoping to free the Holy Land from Moslem rule.

The Byzantine Empire was an important force in defending Western Europe from invasion during the Middle Ages. Many times, the Byzantine armies threw back the Moslems and several barbarian tribes that tried to conquer their empire. If the Byzantine Empire had fallen to such invaders, Western Europe undoubtedly also would have been overrun. The Byzantine civilization flourished until Constantinople fell to the Turks in 1453. See BYZANTINE EMPIRE.

 The Moslem Empire

One of the most advanced cultures of the Middle Ages had its center in the Middle East. This important culture originated with the Arabs. They established a new religion, Islam, and converted millions of persons. The Arabs built a huge empire that grew larger than the Roman Empire of Ancient Times. From about 750 to the 1200's, the Islamic empire extended from the Atlantic Ocean to the borders of India. The Islamic empire became known as the Moslem Empire. The term *Moslem* comes from the Arabic word *Muslim*, meaning *one who submits* (to God). The religious teachings of Islam are described in the article ISLAM.

The vast expanse of the Moslem Empire brought many cultures together. Moslem culture was a mixture of the ancient cultures of the Middle East, Egypt, India, and China. It also included important contributions of Greek culture that had long been forgotten in Western Europe. For example, many writings of Aristotle and other valuable philosophical works were brought to Spain and Sicily by the Moslems. Such works were then translated into Latin for European scholars.

In addition to gathering and preserving many important cultural works, Moslem scholars produced great works of their own. The Arabs made a number of contributions to the study of algebra. In fact, the word *algebra* is Arabic, and means *transposing* (see ALGEBRA [History]). A medical book written by Avicenna, an Arab scientist, was the chief text used by physicians for over 600 years. Avicenna and other Moslem scientists also wrote important textbooks on astronomy and mathematics. Moslem geographies included the most complete maps of the world during the Middle Ages. Moslem poets, including Omar Khayyám, wrote some of the world's literary masterpieces. Moslem art blended the artistic forms that had developed in Persia, the Byzantine Empire, Egypt, and Spain. This blending created a distinctive style known as Islamic art. Its chief feature was ornamental design. Islamic artists developed forms of design because their religion prohibited the creation of lifelike images of any creatures. The designs were used in painting, weaving rugs, brocading cloth, and decorating leather and fine pottery. The distinctive patterns of Moslem art also appeared in the magnificent tilework that decorated the *mosques* (Moslem houses of worship). See ISLAMIC ART.

Moslem traditions still strongly influence life in certain regions of the world. Most of the Middle East, for example, is known as the *Arab World*. In Southeast Asia, and in such countries as India and Pakistan, Moslem ways of life are followed by millions of people. The development of the Moslem Empire during the Middle Ages is described in the article MOSLEMS.

New York Public Library

Medieval Society in Europe was made up of several classes of people who were ruled by a king or a feudal lord—the central figure in the painting, *above*. At his right stand the clergymen who advised him, and at his left are the noblemen who led his armies. The lower panel shows merchants, *left*, and peasants, *right*.

Justinian I ruled the Byzantine Empire during its Golden Age. He gathered many Roman laws into one legal code. The famous *Justinian* Code became the basis of the laws of most western European countries.

Reproduction from *Byzantine Painting*, courtesy Skira Inc., New York

A Persian Miniature shows Mohammed, founder of the Islamic religion, receiving a message from the angel Gabriel. Mohammed based his teachings on those of Jesus and the Hebrew prophets.

Bettmann Archive

581

China During The Middle Ages

The civilized culture of ancient China advanced greatly during the Middle Ages. Chinese civilization progressed in spite of many invasions by fierce barbarians, among them the Mongols and the Tartars. Most of the invaders adopted Chinese ways of life. Some, especially the Mongols, spread Chinese civilization to many other lands.

The Mongols conquered all China in 1279, and their famous ruler, Kublai Khan, built a vast empire. The Mongol Empire is often called the largest land empire in all history. It extended more than 4,600 miles, from the Yellow Sea of Asia to the Danube River of Europe.

During Kublai Khan's rule, many Chinese ideas and inventions of the early Middle Ages reached Europe and the Middle East. Kublai Khan encouraged commerce and travel with other civilized peoples. The travels of Marco Polo from Venice to many Far East lands were made chiefly under Kublai Khan's sponsorship (see POLO, MARCO). Soon after the death of Kublai Khan, the Mongols lost control of most of their empire. The Chinese regained control of their own country in 1368, when the Ming dynasty began its 300-year rule of China (see MONGOL EMPIRE).

China's contributions to civilization during the Middle Ages came chiefly during the T'ang dynasty (618-906) and the Sung dynasty (960-1279). The T'ang period became known as the golden age of Chinese civilization. During this period, the Chinese invented printing. The world's oldest printed book is the *Diamond Sutra*, printed in China in 868 (see BOOK [picture]). Chinese arts and literature flourished during the same era. Lasting contributions were made by two of the greatest Chinese poets, Li Po and Tu Fu. Their poems, written in words of great beauty and simplicity, still inspire many poets in all parts of the world. During the Sung period, the Chinese invented gunpowder, the magnetic compass, and movable type for printing. Scholarly advances also were made during the T'ang and Sung dynasties. Chinese scholars produced important dictionaries, encyclopedias, and histories.

Japan During The Middle Ages

Japan developed its basic civilization and rapidly advanced to a golden age during the Middle Ages. Little is known of Japan's early days. Buddhist monks and merchants brought civilized ways of life to Japan from China and Korea. By the A.D. 550's, many Japanese were practicing Buddhism. They also were producing arts and crafts similar to those of the Chinese. The Japanese took over the Chinese system of writing, and their scholars produced many works in Chinese styles. The early Japanese also adopted basic Chinese methods of government. Unlike the Chinese, however, the Japanese thought of their emperor as godlike. They believed an emperor must never be overthrown. The Japanese also developed as important parts of their culture a belief in the superiority of soldiers, and a great respect for stern military conduct.

Civilization developed so rapidly in Japan that a golden age flourished there from the late 700's to about 1150. During Japan's golden age, Kyoto was established as the nation's capital. Kyoto became one of the largest cities of the world during the Middle Ages. At the height of Japan's golden age, the emperor lost much of his political power to the heads of noble families. These noblemen, called *shoguns*, ruled Japan for hundreds of years. But they all ruled in the name of the emperor. Deep respect for the emperors of Japan and strict obedience to military discipline lasted into Modern Times. In fact, these basic elements of Japanese culture became strong influences on the course of history during the early 1900's. See JAPAN (History).

India During The Middle Ages

India was invaded by many peoples during the Middle Ages. As a result, little progress was made in developing the civilization that had flourished in India during Ancient Times.

The most important invaders of India were the Moslems. They pushed into the plains of northern India from Afghanistan and central Asia. Unlike the Mongol invaders of China, the Moslem invaders of India did not unite with the people they conquered. Some Indians gave up their Hindu religion and became Moslems. But most Indians did not accept the Moslem customs or the Islamic religion. Largely because of their religious differences, the people of India became culturally divided. This deep cultural division has lasted for hundreds of years. It became the basis for the political partition of India into two independent countries— India and Pakistan—in 1947.

Other Civilizations During The Middle Ages

Most regions of Africa, North America, and South America remained uncivilized during the Middle Ages. But these continents did have some civilized areas. Northern Africa, of course, had been civilized since the days of ancient Egypt. Some civilizations also existed on the west and east coasts of Africa. Similarly, only a few areas of North and South America were civilized. In parts of Central and South America, some Indian groups developed highly advanced civilizations.

Africa. The Sahara separated the civilized northern area of Africa from the largely uncivilized African interior. Most Africans south of the Sahara were Negroes who had primitive tribal cultures. During the Middle Ages, Arab traders of northern Africa carried Moslem culture to western Africa. There, the Arabs established the state of Ghana. The Negroes of Ghana became converted to the Islamic religion. They also adopted many Moslem ways of life. The Negroes gradually gained control of Ghana and built a large empire. During the 1000's, the Malinke people conquered Ghana and expanded it into the Mali empire. The capital of the Mali empire, Timbuktu, became an important African center of trade and Moslem culture. In southern Africa, the Zimbabwe civilization lasted from

Chinese Printing was a well-established art hundreds of years before Europeans began using movable type in the mid-1400's. The Chinese invented printing about 770, during the T'ang dynasty.

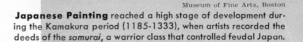

Japanese Painting reached a high stage of development during the Kamakura period (1185-1333), when artists recorded the deeds of the *samurai*, a warrior class that controlled feudal Japan.

about 900 to 1500. Ruins of fortresses of that Negro civilization still stand in southern Rhodesia.

The Arabs also established trading settlements on the east coast of Africa, including Kilwa, Mombasa, and Zanzibar. There, Arab goods were exchanged for iron, ivory, and slaves from the African interior.

The Americas. The first people who lived on the North and South American continents probably came from Asia. They were later called Indians. Most Indians of the Americas followed primitive ways of life. But during the Middle Ages, some of these tribal peoples developed civilized societies. Their societies reached about the same cultural level as the cradle civilizations of Ancient Times.

An important Indian civilization was developed by the Maya of Central America. The Maya developed a calendar, a system of writing, and a system of mathematics. They built huge temples that were much like the pyramids of ancient Egypt. The Aztec and the Toltec developed civilizations in what is now Mexico, and the Inca built a magnificent empire in what is now Peru. Most of these Indian civilizations lasted until early Modern Times. They were destroyed by European conquerors. The customs and skills of the Indians were of little interest to the Europeans. But the Europeans learned about many new foods from the Indians. These foods included cocoa, corn, peanuts, potatoes, and tomatoes. See INDIAN, AMERICAN.

Indian Temples built during the 700's were covered with sculptured religious figures. The famous Shore Temple, carved out of granite, stands on the Indian Ocean coast, 30 miles from Madras.

Pyramids of the Maya, built about A.D. 1000, are relics of an early civilization of the Americas. *El Castillo*, 75 feet tall, is at Chichén Itzá, in Yucatan.

Aztec Images of gods or goddesses were decorated with rough carvings of religious symbols. This massive stone statue of the goddess Coatlicue is over 8 feet tall.

WORLD HISTORY / *Modern Times*
Early Period: 1453-1900

Mankind made giant cultural strides during an era that many historians call the early period of Modern Times. They generally date this period from the collapse of the Byzantine Empire in 1453 through the 1800's. It was an era of scientific achievement, industrial revolution, and sweeping political and social change.

The people of Western Europe made almost all the important cultural advances during the new era. Little progress was made in the Middle East, India, or China. As a result, these ancient centers of civilization came largely under the control or influence of Western civilization.

The power of the Western European nations rose on a strong tide of scientific achievements. Some of these achievements made possible long sailing trips and voyages of discovery. Others increased food production and revolutionized manufacturing methods. The European nations sent explorers and military forces throughout the world. They sought markets for European products and raw materials for European industries.

British, French, Portuguese, and Spanish colonies were established in the newly discovered lands of the North and South American continents. Thousands of Europeans migrated to these lands, and brought the customs and ideas of Western civilization. Many colonists of the Americas also wanted to develop certain new ideas that were sweeping Europe—democracy, nationalism, and religious toleration.

By the early 1800's, most of the colonists of North and South America had freed themselves from European rule. But European nations still governed large colonial empires in Africa, Asia, and the Middle East. European rule of these regions did not meet serious challenge until the 1900's.

Ken Lambert, FPG

The Clock Tower of the Houses of Parliament, London

The Huntington Library

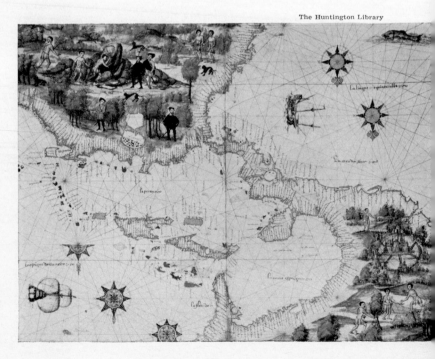

An Exploration Map of the Caribbean region appears in an atlas published in 1547. It is fairly accurate, but by today's map-making methods, the map shows the region upside down.

The Renaissance

The great advance of Western civilization during Modern Times started during a 300-year period of cultural awakening called the Renaissance. The Renaissance actually began in the early 1300's in Italy. There, artists and scholars supported the idea of individual freedom. They urged people to cast off the ancient customs and rules that governed life during the Middle Ages. The basic Renaissance idea of individual freedom became a cultural force that spread throughout most of northern Europe.

Important cultural achievements resulted from the spirit and vigor of the Renaissance idea. Many world masterpieces of architecture, literature, painting, and sculpture were created. Famous Renaissance artists and writers included Cervantes, Hans Holbein, Leonardo da Vinci, Michelangelo, Raphael, and William Shakespeare. Revolutionary discoveries in astronomy and physics were made by Nicolaus Copernicus and Galileo. Other Renaissance scholars, including Desiderius Erasmus and Saint Thomas More, developed a *humanist* philosophy. This philosophy stressed the importance of man and his enjoyment of life. It influenced many political and social movements of Modern Times. The humanist philosophy also inspired a strong religious movement called the Reformation. The Reformation led to the establishment of Protestant churches in England, Germany, and many other countries. See HUMANISM; REFORMATION.

Exploration and commerce expanded rapidly during the Renaissance. The spirit of the times called for enjoyment of the good things of life—tasty foods, elegant clothes, and elaborate homes. Merchants were en-

European nations and their colonies in the late 1800's (black).

MAJOR EVENTS OF MODERN TIMES— EARLY PERIOD: 1453-1900

1492 Christopher Columbus reached America and claimed it for Spain.

1492 The Spaniards captured Granada and ended the rule of Spain by the Moslem Moors.

1517 The Reformation began in Germany.

1519-1522 Ferdinand Magellan commanded the first voyage around the world.

1526 Babar, a Moslem ruler, conquered India and established the Mogul Empire.

1532 Francisco Pizarro invaded Peru, beginning the Spanish conquest of the Inca Empire.

1588 The Royal Navy of England defeated the Spanish Armada and established England as a great naval power.

1613 Michael Romanov became Czar of Russia and started the 300-year rule of Russia by the Romanovs.

1644 Manchus conquered China and established their rule that lasted until 1912.

1688 The "Glorious Revolution" deposed James II of England.

1763 The Treaty of Paris ended the Seven Years' War in Europe, and the French and Indian War in America.

1776 The 13 American colonies of England signed the Declaration of Independence.

1789 The French Revolution began.

1815 Napoleon Bonaparte was defeated at the Battle of Waterloo, ending his ambition to rule Europe.

1824 Armies of Simón Bolívar and Antonio José de Sucre defeated the Spaniards at Ayacucho, ending the Latin-American wars of independence.

1842 The Treaty of Nanking ended the "Opium War" and granted important trading rights in China to Great Britain.

1847 Liberia was established as the first independent Negro republic of Africa.

1853-1854 Commodore Matthew Perry visited Japan and opened two ports to U.S. trade, ending Japan's isolation.

1858 Great Britain took over rule of India from the East India Company after the Sepoy Rebellion.

1865 Union forces defeated the Confederates in the American Civil War after four years of fighting.

1867 Emperor Mutsuhito regained his traditional power from the shogun and established Japan's capital in Tokyo.

1867 The British North America Act established the Dominion of Canada.

1869 The Suez Canal opened.

1871 Germany became united under the Prussian king, who ruled the new empire as Kaiser Wilhelm I.

1882 Great Britain invaded and occupied Egypt.

1885 Leopold II of Belgium established the Congo Free State and controlled it as his personal possession.

1895 Japan took control of Formosa after the Chinese-Japanese War.

1898 The United States took control of Guam, Puerto Rico, and the Philippines following the Spanish-American War.

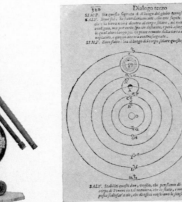

Museo di Fisica e Storia Naturale, Florence, Italy (Alinari)

The Pierpont Morgan Library

Telescopes Used by Galileo to make revolutionary discoveries in astronomy are displayed in a museum in Florence, Italy. Galileo's chart of the solar system was published in 1632. He has been called the father of modern experimental science.

couraged to bring fine goods of all kinds from distant lands to European markets.

To meet the demands of the merchants, adventurous explorers competed to find the best trade routes to the Far East. Historic voyages were made by Pedro Álvares Cabral, Christopher Columbus, Vasco da Gama, Bartolomeu Dias, Ferdinand Magellan, and others. They opened new sea routes for traders who wanted to avoid the difficult land routes across the Middle East and Asia. An important sea route to Asia was established by way of the Cape of Good Hope. Other sea routes led to the Americas. See EXPLORATION AND DISCOVERY (The Great Age of Discovery).

As goods poured into Europe from distant lands, a commercial revolution developed. Gold and silver imports created a new kind of wealth. Investment opportunities were provided by the creation of *joint-stock companies*. These companies got money to do business by selling shares of stock to a number of individuals. They formed the basis of the corporations of today. The first stock exchanges were also established.

European standards of living rose with the growth of commerce and the use of goods from other countries. European markets were supplied with luxurious chintz fabrics, porcelains, rugs, and silks. Foods from distant lands included bananas, cocoa, coffee, lemons, oranges, and tea. In the same period, a slave trade developed with Africa.

The expansion of overseas commerce led to the establishment of European colonies in many countries. Some of the colonies, chiefly those in tropical countries, were established almost entirely as trading centers. They served as temporary outposts where European manufactured goods were exchanged for raw materials. Many other colonies became permanent. They included the English colony of Virginia, the French colony of Quebec, and the Spanish colonies of New Spain (Mexico) and Peru. These colonies in North and South America formed a pattern for European colonization of many other lands in the years to come.

Life during the Renaissance, and the many cultural achievements of this period of history, are described in the article RENAISSANCE.

 ## The Age of Reason

During the 1600's and 1700's, an intellectual revolution swept over Western Europe. Traditional principles that had served scholars for hundreds of years were discarded. The leading thinkers of the era insisted that reason was the sole test of truth. The period became known as the Age of Reason.

The most important contribution of the Age of Reason was probably the development of the modern scientific method. Scientists now applied the reasoning process to their studies of basic natural laws. They organized general rules for reaching scientific conclusions that are still followed today (see SCIENCE [How Scientists Work]).

One of the steps of the scientific method was careful experimentation. To carry out such experimentation, scholars needed precise instruments. Their needs were met by inventors of the era. Many important instruments were developed, including the microscope, sextant, slide rule, chronometer, air pump, and adding machine.

With important new instruments to aid them, scientists advanced rapidly. The discoveries of Sir Isaac Newton revolutionized astronomy. Benjamin Franklin and Alessandro Volta discovered the nature of electricity. Robert Boyle, Antoine Lavoisier, and Joseph Priestley founded modern chemistry. René Descartes invented analytic geometry. William Harvey discovered how blood circulates in the human body.

The scientific method was so successful in solving problems of nature that some philosophers applied its principles to human problems. A group of French scholars used the tests of reason in dealing with problems of economics, education, government, and religion. The French scholars, known as the *philosophes*, attacked many evils of the times. These evils included religious

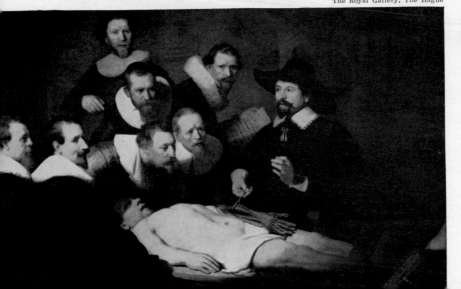

The Study of Human Anatomy opened the way to important medical discoveries in Europe during the 1600's. Rembrandt portrayed this study in his famous painting *The Anatomy Lesson.*

The Royal Gallery, The Hague

Magellan's Ship, *Victoria,* was the first to circle the earth.

Brown Bros.

intolerance, superstition, tyranny, unjust laws, and the slave trade. The most famous member of the French group was probably Voltaire. Others included Montesquieu, Denis Diderot, and Jean Jacques Rousseau. Their writings not only attacked evils, but also expressed a basic faith. That faith symbolized the spirit of the era—belief in mankind's ability to solve problems, with reason as the most important tool.

The Age of Reason was also a period of achievement in the arts. The form of the modern novel was developed by Henry Fielding. The poem took on new brilliance in famous couplets written by Alexander Pope. Great painters of the era included Thomas Gainsborough, Francisco Goya, William Hogarth, Rembrandt, Sir Joshua Reynolds, and Antoine Watteau. Many modern forms of music, such as the concerto, opera, symphony, and oratorio, were developed. Outstanding composers of the period included Johann Sebastian Bach, George Frideric Handel, Joseph Haydn, and Wolfgang Amadeus Mozart.

🌐 Democracy and Nationalism

Two powerful political forces—democracy and nationalism—took shape during the 1600's and 1700's. Democracy developed from revolutions that established the right of people to govern themselves. Such revolutions ended *despotism* (absolute control by a ruler) in England, America, and France. Nationalism developed from the strong feelings of national pride that united the people of each country as they fought for their democratic ideals.

The English Revolution of the 1600's was the first important attack in Modern Times on the absolute power of kings. The attack was stimulated by the democratic ideas that developed during the Age of Reason. The English revolution actually was a series of struggles. At one time, the fight was led by the Puritans, a religious group with strong democratic principles. A republic called a commonwealth was established in England in 1649. As a republic, England came under

German Consulate General
Page of a Prayer Book of the 1400's, found in France.

Bettmann Archive
Utopia, a mythical country, was described by St. Thomas More.

Plays of William Shakespeare were often staged in the courtyards of English inns during the late 1500's and early 1600's.
Bettmann Archive

A Bakery, shown in a French encyclopedia of the 1700's.
New York Public Library

the rule of Oliver Cromwell, a Puritan leader. Cromwell ruled as a dictator. The monarchy was restored in 1660. But the English people continued to fight for a strong voice in their government. In 1688, James II was deposed during the "Glorious Revolution," and William and Mary took the throne. The English revolutionary movement ended in 1689. That year, Parliament adopted the Bill of Rights, assuring the basic rights of the English people.

The Bill of Rights took away most powers of the English monarch and guaranteed the liberty of the English people. The document became an important rallying point of English nationalism. The Bill of Rights provided legal grounds for people to revolt against a bad government. This idea spread to many other countries, chiefly through the works of John Locke. Locke, a political scholar, was probably the most influential writer of early Modern Times. See LOCKE, JOHN.

The American Revolution was based chiefly on the right of people to revolt. This right had been established during the English revolution. The American colonists restated it in the Declaration of Independence of July 4, 1776. The Declaration was written by a committee headed by Thomas Jefferson. The committee borrowed from the works of Locke and other political writers, but the language of the Declaration had a special force. Phrases such as "all men are created equal" made the Declaration of Independence one of the most important documents in the history of human liberty. See UNITED STATES, HISTORY OF (Declaring Independence).

British rule in the colonies ended, and a new nation—the United States of America—was formed during the Revolutionary War (1775-1783). The new nation's first system of government, established by the Articles of Confederation, proved unsatisfactory. A new system of government under the United States Constitution was set up in 1789.

The Constitution established the United States as a republic. The Constitution also framed a system of federalism that divided power between the national and state governments. In 1791, the first 10 amendments to the Constitution came into force. These amendments, known as the Bill of Rights, state the basic rights of all citizens. The United States Constitution became a model for the constitutions of many other countries, including most of the Latin-American republics.

During the American revolution and the early years of the republic, strong feelings of democracy developed in the United States. Since then, democracy has become the chief rallying point of American nationalism. Many events of today are influenced by America's support of democracy throughout the world.

The French Revolution (1789-1799) was a great political and social upheaval, marked by disorder and violence. During the First French Republic (1792-1799), most symbols of despotism or privilege in France were wiped out. Titles of nobility were eliminated, and "citizen" became the only French title. The French revolutionists issued a great document of democratic principles—the Declaration of the Rights of Man (see RIGHTS OF MAN, DECLARATION OF THE).

The French revolutionary struggle was climaxed by a reign of terror under the rule of radical leaders such as Georges Jacques Danton and Maximilien Robespierre. The guillotine, a beheading instrument, became a symbol of the French revolution. Thousands of aristocrats, and many citizens who opposed the radicals, were guillotined. During this period, the French armies won many victories against foreign enemies of revolutionary France. In 1794, the period of terror ended. Soon after, the nation came under the stern rule of Napoleon Bonaparte, the great French military genius. The stirring events of the 10-year French revolutionary struggle are described in the article FRENCH REVOLUTION.

Napoleon led France to victory after victory until, in 1812, the French controlled most of Western Europe (see NAPOLEON I). The French soldiers fought to defend and spread the democratic principles in which they believed. Their battle cry of "liberty, equality, and fraternity" stirred the democratic and nationalistic feelings of many peoples. Almost all the European monarchs lost most of their powers in revolutionary movements that swept over much of Europe.

Democratic Reforms and New Nations appeared in Europe after Napoleon was defeated in the Battle of Waterloo in 1815. At the Congress of Vienna (1814-1815), Austria, Great Britain, Prussia, and Russia remade the map of Europe (see VIENNA, CONGRESS OF). For political reasons, the great powers tried to smother the democratic and nationalistic forces that were sweeping over Europe. To hold back democracy, they restored the former monarchies of France, Holland, Spain, and the Italian states. In some areas, to stop nationalism, the great powers joined people of different nationalities under a single ruler. For example, they put the Belgians under the rule of the Dutch king. They agreed to let the Swedish king rule the Norwegians. Most of these efforts failed. Democratic movements succeeded in many countries. During the 1830's, Belgium broke away from the Dutch. In 1875, France established a lasting republican government. By the 1880's, many nations of Western Europe had constitutions and some democratic institutions. At the same time, strongly nationalistic people had unified many small states and formed new nations, such as Austria-Hungary, Germany, and Italy.

Colonial wars of independence created new nations in Latin America. The colonists were inspired by the principles of democracy and nationalism that had developed in Europe and the United States. By 1824, most of the Latin-American countries had been freed from European rule. New, independent nations included Argentina, Bolivia, Brazil, Chile, Colombia, Ecuador, Peru, and Venezuela. See LATIN AMERICA (Struggle for Independence).

 The Industrial Revolution

During the late 1700's and the 1800's, an industrial revolution changed much of Western civilization. Machines replaced many hand tools that civilized man had used for thousands of years. With the new machines, vast quantities of goods could be produced rapidly. Never before had mankind been able to make such great use of the world's natural resources.

The chief ingredients of the industrial revolution were manufacturing machines. The story of their invention,

The English Revolution of the 1600's was the first important attack in Modern Times on the absolute power of kings. Charles I walked to his execution in 1649 during a Puritan rebellion led by Oliver Cromwell.

Bettmann Archive

Historical Pictures Service

The American Revolution created the nation that became the leader of the Free World. The Battle of Concord was the second clash between the Americans and the British in the Revolutionary War. The U.S. Constitution became the model of the constitutions of many nations.

The Pennfylvania Packet, _and Daily Advertifer._

WE, the People of the United States, in order to form a more perfect Union, eftablifh Juftice, infure domeftic Tranquility, provide for the common Defence, promote the General Welfare, and fecure the Bleffings of Liberty to Ourfelves and our Pofterity, do ordain and eftablifh this Conftitution for the United States of America.

Historical Society of Pennsylvania

The French Revolution began on July 14, 1789, with an attack on the Bastille. This famous prison in Paris symbolized the hated government of King Louis XVI.

New York Public Library

development, and economic significance is told in the article INDUSTRIAL REVOLUTION.

Industrialism changed the lives of millions of people. When the era began, most families lived in farm areas. Towns and villages served chiefly as market centers for the farmers. As industry developed, factories were built in many towns. These towns grew rapidly into industrial cities. People streamed into the cities to take jobs tending the machines in the factories. Railroads and waterways were built to link many cities. They also provided transportation between the cities and the farmlands, forests, and mines. The invention of the telegraph furnished instant communication between distant places.

The growth of industrialism brought social changes of great importance. A middle class of people appeared. The members of the middle class were neither nobles nor peasants. Most of them were businessmen and wealthy landowners. The middle class grew in size and influence. It owned most of the factories, hired the workers, and operated the banks, mines, railroads, and shops. Most members of the middle class believed that business should be regulated by supply and demand, without government controls. This idea formed the basis of the economic system known as *capitalism*. The principles of capitalism were set forth by the Scotch economist Adam Smith. See CAPITALISM; SMITH, ADAM.

The rapid growth of industrialism produced many problems. Most factory workers were poorly paid and suffered great hardships. They were not permitted to form labor unions, and their working conditions were not regulated by law. The situation led to widespread attacks against the evils of the capitalist system. *Socialism* became the chief rallying point for many persons who opposed the capitalist system. The socialists wanted to put all industrial production under the control of governments. From that basic principle, Karl Marx, a German writer and social philosopher, developed the theories of *communism*. Marx called for the workers to revolt against the middle class and set up state-owned economic systems.

Many reforms supported by members of various social movements were adopted generally during the 1800's. In several countries, workers won the right to form labor unions. Laws regulating working conditions in factories were passed in Great Britain and the United States during the 1830's. Later, many other countries also passed laws that improved the conditions of industrial workers. Great Britain and Germany pioneered in social legislation that provided accident, sickness, and unemployment insurance for industrial employees.

By the late 1800's, most industrial nations had laws that regulated working conditions and also raised the people's standards of living. But the followers of Marx continued to call for a class war and for the violent overthrow of capitalism. The Marxist movement developed into communism in Russia in the early 1900's.

Imperialism. The industrial nations needed large supplies of raw materials for their factories. The vast continents of Africa and Asia had these materials in abundance. Africa and Asia also had millions of people who still used ancient tools of production. These two continents provided good markets for the wide variety of manufactured goods being produced in the industrial nations of Europe.

The European nations established many colonies in Africa and Asia during the 1800's. They did so (1) to insure a flow of raw materials, and (2) to control large markets. European colonial rule extended over most of Africa. Great Britain and France were the leading colonial powers of that continent. Nearly a third of Asia came under the colonial rule of Great Britain, France, The Netherlands, Portugal, and Spain. China had closed most of its ports to Europeans. But they were opened in 1842 after Britain defeated China in the Opium War (see CHINA [The "Unequal Treaties"]).

By the late 1800's, huge European empires had spread over most of the world. The largest empires were those of Great Britain, France, and Germany. Important colonies also were established by Belgium, The Netherlands, and Portugal. This colonial expansion became known as *imperialism*. The United States acted to protect the independent countries of Latin America from European colonial expansion. The protective policy of the United States was set forth in the Monroe Doctrine in 1823. However, the influence of the United States over Latin America was often called imperialism too. See IMPERIALISM; MONROE DOCTRINE.

 ## The Close of an Era

Industrialism and imperialism climaxed an era of Modern Times that is often called Europe's "wonderful century." Most European nations had become economically wealthy and militarily strong. They ruled vast regions of the world through powerful colonial systems. Their arts, sciences, and scholarship reached high levels of development. The European way of life during the 1800's formed the most advanced civilization the world had ever known. The United States, Canada, and some other countries of the Western Hemisphere were rapidly developing along the European pattern. In contrast, most nations of Africa and Asia remained primitive or at the levels of civilization they had reached during the Middle Ages.

The Opium War with China helped the victorious British to expand their colonial empire in the Orient during the mid-1800's.

Historical Pictures Service

Smoking Factory Chimneys throughout Europe signaled the start of the Industrial Revolution during the mid-1700's. The rise of industrialism reshaped Western civilization and changed the lives of millions of persons in all parts of the world.

The superior position of the chief European nations met with little challenge during the 1800's. As a result, certain attitudes shaped the basic philosophy of the era. These were:

1. The belief that it was right for millions of colonial peoples to be ruled by European nations.

2. Acceptance of nationalism as the chief political principle of the major European nations.

3. Faith in democracy as a political system that would someday be adopted throughout the world.

4. The certainty that capitalism, although subject to reforms, would develop as the only important economic system.

5. Hopefulness based on the idea that science was a complete blessing to mankind, and that man's progress depended almost entirely on scientific developments.

These were the chief attitudes of Western civilization as a great era of history drew to a close during the early years of the 1900's. All were soon to change.

The Telephone was invented in 1876, and hastened industrial development. Its inventor, Alexander Graham Bell, opened a New York City to Chicago line in 1892.

European Wealth and power were reflected in the elegance of society life during the late 1800's, when the nations of Europe ruled most of the world.

WORLD HISTORY / *Modern Times*
The 1900's

The first half of the 1900's was a period of great change—perhaps the most rapid and widespread change in all history. Most of the attitudes of the previous era were shattered. The costliest and most destructive wars in history were fought. Political and social upheavals overturned many long-established governments. At the same time, science made giant advances. Revolutionary technological inventions altered basic ways of life and thrust mankind into the Space Age.

The 1900's opened with most of the world under the rule of European nations. But by the 1960's, the huge European empires had collapsed. Colonialism was a thing of the past. In Africa alone, more than 30 new nations established their independence. Traditional European nationalism lost much of its force. By the 1960's, most European countries were trying to solve important problems cooperatively. They were members of organizations set up for their joint defense or for pooling their economic resources. On the other hand, nationalism exploded with full force in Africa and Asia. It became the chief moving spirit of the newly independent nations.

The 1900's dawned with the idea that democracy and capitalism would spread throughout the world. By the 1960's, that idea had proved false. More than a billion persons were living under communism.

In 1900, it was generally assumed that mankind would use scientific achievements only to build better ways of life. But in 1945, the invention of the atomic bomb demonstrated that man could also use science to produce tremendous destructive power.

By the 1960's, the people of an industrialized country hardly realized how much life had changed in 50 years. They took for granted airplanes, atomic energy, automation, radio, refrigerators, color motion pictures, tele-

Blastoff at Cape Kennedy

WORLD BOOK Science Service, Inc.

592

vision, synthetic materials, and superhighways crowded with automobiles. None of these things had even existed in 1900.

The Space Age opened in 1957 when Russia launched the first artificial satellite to circle the earth. During the next few years, U.S. and Russian rockets sent many scientific instruments into space. Soon afterward, astronauts of the two countries traveled around the earth in spaceships. By the mid-1960's, American and Russian scientists had solved many problems of extended space travel. The world was wondering how soon astronauts would land on the moon. See SPACE TRAVEL.

In the 1960's, people were also accustomed to great achievements from medical science. During the first half of the century, many traditional methods of diagnosing, treating, and preventing disease had been revolutionized. The new methods were aided by drugs that previously had been unknown. The new drugs included antibiotics, sulfonamides, and certain serums and vaccines (see DRUG). Rapid medical progress was chiefly responsible for healthier and longer lives in many parts of the world. In 1900, a baby born in the United States had a life expectancy of 47.3 years. By 1965, this figure had increased to 71 years.

World Wars I and II

War—fought on a greater scale than ever before—overshadowed world developments during the early 1900's. World War I raged from 1914 to 1918, and World War II from 1939 to 1945.

Wide World

The Tragedy of a World War was mirrored in the faces of the French people watching German troops march into Paris in 1940. The French government surrendered after France's armies were defeated early in World War II.

Noncommunist countries (brown), communist countries (black) in the mid-1960's.

MAJOR EVENTS OF THE 1900'S

1901 The Australian states united to form a commonwealth.

1905 Japan defeated Russia in the Russo-Japanese War.

1912 The Republic of China was established.

1914 The assassination of Archduke Francis Ferdinand of Austria-Hungary started World War I.

1917 Revolutionists overthrew Czar Nicholas II and the Bolsheviks seized power in Russia.

1920 The Panama Canal opened.

1920 The League of Nations was established.

1922 The Fascist party seized control of Italy and Benito Mussolini became dictator.

1922 The Union of Soviet Socialist Republics was established.

1923 Mustafa Kemal (Atatürk) established the Republic of Turkey and modernized Turkish institutions.

1933 Adolf Hitler became dictator of Germany.

1935-1936 Italian troops invaded and annexed Ethiopia.

1939 Francisco Franco became dictator of Spain after 32 months of civil war.

1939 Germany invaded Poland, starting World War II.

1941 The Japanese attacked Pearl Harbor, and the United States entered World War II.

1945 The United Nations was established.

1945 The first atomic bombs used in warfare were dropped by U.S. planes on Hiroshima and Nagasaki.

1945 World War II ended in Europe on May 8 and in the Pacific on September 2.

1946 The United States granted independence to the Philippines.

1947 Great Britain granted independence to India and Pakistan.

1948 The United States established the European Recovery Program (Marshall Plan) to aid Europe's economic recovery.

1949 The North Atlantic Treaty Organization (NATO) formed by the United States, Canada, and 10 European nations.

1949 The Chinese Communists completed their conquest of China.

1950 North Korean communist troops invaded South Korea, starting the Korean War.

1957 Russia opened the Space Age by launching Sputnik I, the first artificial satellite to circle the earth.

1959 Communist guerrilla forces of North Vietnam began a campaign of terror against U.S.-supported South Vietnam.

1962 Russia agreed to U.S. demands that missiles be removed from Cuba, ending a serious Cold War crisis.

1963 Russia, the United States, and Great Britain signed an agreement banning the testing of nuclear weapons above ground. Other nations signed later.

1965 Indonesia became the first country to resign from the United Nations.

In World War I, for the first time in history, mankind came to know total war. Entire populations of the fighting nations worked in the war effort. Millions of men, women, and children were killed. Whole cities were destroyed. The fighting forces clashed on vast battlefields—on land, in the air, on the sea, and under the sea. The weapons of total war included bombs and missiles of tremendous destructive power. During World War II, the atomic bomb was developed. Its development led to a bomb a thousand times more powerful—the hydrogen bomb. Thus, mankind's most terrible war helped produce a weapon that could wipe out entire civilizations if used in another total war. The many phases of the two world wars are described in the articles WORLD WAR I and WORLD WAR II.

Out of the horror of each world war came an attempt by mankind to prevent war forever. The first attempt was made after World War I with the creation of the League of Nations (see LEAGUE OF NATIONS). But the League failed to settle many post war problems. It also was powerless to prevent a rising tide of aggression by Japan, Italy, and Germany during the 1930's. The second attempt was made toward the end of World War II with the establishment of the United Nations. Since 1945, the UN has worked for international peace and security in two chief ways. First, the UN has provided a meeting place where nations can discuss their quarrels peaceably. Second, the UN has conducted worldwide programs to help nations solve problems of health, food shortages, and social injustice. The structure, operations, and accomplishments of the UN are described in the article UNITED NATIONS.

The UN has carried on its peace-keeping tasks in an atmosphere of great tension and unrest. The most important results of World War II were the shift of world power to the United States and Russia, and the collapse of European empires. The shift of power to these two nations produced a bitter struggle that has divided most of the world. The United States and Russia became the leaders of two competing systems of government—democracy and communism. The collapse of colonial empires brought about the rise of many new nations in Africa, Asia, and the Middle East. These new nations have had many great political, economic, and social problems.

The Rise of New Nations

One by one, the vast European empires collapsed after World War II. Great Britain, France, Belgium, The Netherlands, and the other large colonial powers had been weakened by their losses during the war. They no longer could hold their colonies by force. Furthermore, many Europeans had come to believe that it was morally wrong to rule other people against their will.

The most striking and rapid independence movement took place in Africa. In 1950, there were only four independent countries on the vast African continent. By mid-1965, Africa had 37 independent countries. In Asia, independent governments were established after World War II in Burma, Cambodia, Ceylon, India, Indonesia, Korea, Laos, Malaysia, Pakistan, and Viet-

nam. The Philippines were granted independence by the United States. In the Middle East, the nations that became independent after World War II included Cyprus, Israel, Jordan, Lebanon, and Syria.

Most of the newly independent nations had been under the rule of colonial powers for many years, or even for centuries. In some cases, a colony's land and other natural resources were developed almost entirely for the benefit of the colonial power. Generally, the colonial power gave the people little training in self-government. On the other hand, imperialism brought certain benefits to many colonial peoples. In some lands, tribal wars and certain uncivilized customs were stopped. In many colonies, the ruling powers established modern educational systems and public health services. In several countries, particularly in India and the Philippines, democratic methods of government were introduced. During the course of their economic development, most of the colonies were equipped with modern communication and transportation systems.

The new nations faced many problems as a result of years of imperialism. But they had been brought in contact with the chief elements of Western progress—education, advanced technology and medicine, and new agricultural and industrial methods.

 ## The Rise of Communism

The challenge of communism has shaped much of history during the 1900's. Communism's goal is to replace all governments with communist dictatorships. The communist movement exploded with full force just after World War II ended in 1945. Ever since, the democratic nations of the world, led by the United States, have fought the spread of communism. By the 1960's, however, communist dictatorships had been established in Eastern Europe and the Balkans. Communist governments also ruled China—the largest country of Asia—and several other Asian nations.

The great struggle between communism and democracy is called the Cold War. The chief weapons of the Cold War are the power of ideas; and economic, military, political, and technological power. Using these weapons, each side tries to demonstrate its superiority. Each side also uses these weapons in competing for the support of certain nations that have remained neutral in the struggle. These *unaligned* or *uncommitted* nations include most of the new countries of Africa and Asia. Many neutral nations have accepted economic and military aid from both sides.

The United Nations has been a battleground of the Cold War almost continuously. The United States depends on the UN to settle most Cold War disputes. But Russia tries to weaken the authority of the UN.

The most important demonstration of Cold War attitudes on the UN came in 1950, when the UN acted to stop communist North Korea from invading South Korea. The Korean War (1950-1953) was the first war in which troops of a world organization acted as "police" to fight an aggressor nation. In the Korean War, strong military units of the United States and many other democratic nations formed the UN army. However, Russia declared that the UN had no right to act at all. Russia aided the North Koreans with war sup-

UN Forces prevented a communist take-over of South Korea by North Korea. The Korean War (1950-1953) was the first war fought by a world organization to stop aggression.

plies. Communist China sent large forces to fight on the side of North Korea. See KOREAN WAR.

Several incidents of the Cold War became so serious that they could have touched off another world war. Serious incidents occur from time to time in Berlin, where the communists built a wall between the two sections of the city. West Berlin is a stronghold of democracy, and East Berlin is the capital of communist-controlled East Germany. Probably the most serious Cold War incident was the Cuban crisis of 1962. The United States revealed that Russia had installed missiles in Cuba that could launch atomic attacks on U.S cities. The crisis passed after Russia removed the missiles See BERLIN; CUBA (The Cuban Crisis).

In spite of several more tense incidents, the Cold War seemed to ease during the late 1950's and early 1960's. Russian leaders talked much of "peaceful coexistence." In 1963, Great Britain, Russia, and the United States signed a treaty banning all nuclear testing except underground tests. Many other countries that did not have atomic weapons at the time signed the treaty later.

The story of the worldwide struggle between democracy and communism is told in the articles COLD WAR and COMMUNISM.

Many New African Nations were born during the 1950's and early 1960's. The flag of Burundi was raised in 1962.

Angry Germans rebelled against Russian rule of East Berlin on June 17, 1953. Unarmed Germans fought a losing battle against the tanks used by the Russians to put down the uprising.

WORLD HISTORY / *The World Today*

We live in the most highly developed civilization of all history. At the same time, we face many problems so serious that they could destroy the world as we know it. But there is also hope. Never before has mankind reached our high level of technological power and scientific knowledge. For this reason, we probably have a greater chance of solving the problems of our times than any previous generation.

The most important problem of the times is how to prevent another world war. The bitter struggle between democracy and communism that started after World War II still continues on a worldwide scale. But a new trend seems to be developing in the Cold War, with Communist China as its moving force.

Communist China—the giant of Asia—has become a dangerous storm center of international politics. China has challenged Russia for the leadership of the communist nations. The Chinese communists declare that the communist nations will some day go to war against the democracies. The Chinese accuse Russia of deserting basic communist aims by signing the nuclear test ban treaty. Russia, in turn, accuses the Chinese communists of misrepresenting the basic communist aims. Albania, a former Russian satellite, supports China, and Russia's grip on other communist nations may be weakening. Most of the satellite nations of Eastern Europe are leaning toward independent policies. These satellites are seeking increased trade and closer diplomatic relations with the Free World.

The United States is in a position somewhat like that of Russia. America is no longer the undisputed leader of the democracies. Most European nations have become economically strong and no longer depend on American financial aid. France is urging that Europe also stop depending on America's military might for defense of the continent. France has criticized U.S. policy in Vietnam, where Americans helped the South Vietnamese fight the communist forces of North Vietnam. Most of the other democracies have supported U.S. policy in Vietnam. But they have not always followed other American policies in the Far East. Some have diplomatic or trade relations with Communist China. The United States has not established such relations with Communist China.

The problem of preventing war is closely linked with the question of how to rescue millions of persons from hardship and poverty. More than half the people of the world do not have enough food to eat. Most of these people cannot even read or write. Hunger and illiteracy are widespread in the underdeveloped countries. These countries include the newly independent African and Asian nations, and many Latin-American countries.

The problem of widespread poverty is seriously complicated by a rapidly increasing world population. The increase is so rapid that it is often called the "population explosion." If the increase continues, the present world population of more than 3,000,000,000 will rise to about 4,000,000,000 by 1975, and will be about 6,000,000,000 by the year 2000. The rate of population growth is generally much higher in the underdeveloped countries than in the developed countries.

Progress in solving the great problems of our times depends chiefly on international cooperation. A large-scale war can be prevented only if the powerful nations settle their quarrels peaceably. If hunger and illiteracy are to be reduced, the developed countries must help the underdeveloped countries. The United Nations has been a forum for the peaceful settlement of several bitter international quarrels. In addition, UN agencies have helped the developed nations give aid to the underdeveloped nations. Extensive foreign aid programs are the established policies of most of the large countries, including the United States and Russia. The major nations also provide important educational opportunities for many students of the underdeveloped countries.

Future historians will judge how well we have met the challenge of our times.   T. WALTER WALLBANK

The United Nations, New York

Devaney from Publix

CONTENTS OF SECTION FIVE

This section lists important new words to be included in the 1966 edition of THE WORLD BOOK ENCYCLOPEDIA DICTIONARY. This dictionary, first published by Field Enterprises Educational Corporation in 1963, keeps abreast of our living language with a program of continuous editorial revision. The following new-word

THE DICTIONARY SUPPLEMENT

supplement has been prepared under the direction of the editors of THE WORLD BOOK and Clarence L. Barnhart, editor in chief of THE WORLD BOOK ENCYCLOPEDIA DICTIONARY. It is presented as a service to owners of the encyclopedia and as an informative feature to subscribers of THE YEAR BOOK.

A

ab·surd·ist (ab sèr′dist), *adj.* of or having to do with the Theater of the Absurd. —*n.* a playwright who uses the techniques of the Theater of the Absurd.

activation analysis, a method of identifying minute amounts of an element by analyzing the radiation given off when a substance containing the element has been bombarded with neutrons.

ad·i·po·ni·trile (ad′ə pō nī′trəl, -trēl, -tril), *n.* a chemical used as an intermediate in the manufacture of nylon. *Formula:* $NC(CH_2)_4CN$ [< *adip*(ic acid) + *nitrile*]

aer·o·dist (ār′ō dist), *n.* a tellurometer adapted to aircraft use for geographical survey. [< *aero-* + *dist*(ance)]

ag·gior·na·men·to (äd jôr′nä men′tō), *n. Italian.* (in the Roman Catholic Church) the modernization of old customs and practices.

ag·ri·busi·ness (ag′rə biz′nis), *n.* the production, processing, and distribution of agricultural products.

a·mi·nop·ter·in (am′ə nop′tər in), *n.* a yellow crystalline compound used in treating leukemia and as a poison to kill rodents. *Formula:* $C_{19}H_{20}N_8O_5·2H_2O$. [< *amino-* + Greek *pterón* wing, feather + English *-in*]

am·phi·mix·is (am′fə mik′sis), *n. Biology.* the union of two distinct gametes in fertilization. [< *amphi-* + Greek *míxis* a mingling]

an·ti·nov·el (an′ti nov′əl), *n.* a novel that avoids conventional techniques, especially by subordinating action to precise descriptions of physical and mental states.

art brut (ár brüt′), *French.* **1.** work of art, especially a painting, free of cultural influence and without any particular technique. **2.** (literally) raw art.

as·tro·bleme (as′trə blem), *n.* one of the ancient meteoritic scars on the earth's surface. [probably < *astro-* + *blem*(ish)]

a·ton·al·ist (ā tō′nə list), *n.* a composer or champion of music characterized by atonality.

Augmented Roman, a system of representing the basic unit speech sounds of English consisting of 43 letters. The Augmented Roman alphabet is used in teaching reading.

B

back·ground·er (bak′groun′dər), *n.* **1.** *U.S.* a press conference held to explain the background of some event or policy by an official who cannot be identified or quoted directly. **2.** a bulletin explaining the background of some event or policy.

bal·lute (bə lüt′), *n.* a parachute in the form of a balloon, used to descend through very thin atmosphere, especially during reëntry. [blend of *balloon* and (para)*chute*]

ban-the-bomb·er (ban′ʜʜ bom′ər), *n. Informal.* an advocate of world-wide nuclear disarmament.

Bil·dungs·ro·man (bil′dúngs rō män′), *n. German.* a novel whose theme is the growth and development of its hero.

bi·o·ce·nose (bī′ō sē′nōs), *n.* a specific geographical area studied as to the organisms that inhabit it and their relation to the environment of that area. [< New Latin *biocenosis* < Greek *bíos* life + *koínōsis* a mingling, sharing < *koinós* common]

bi·o·de·grade (bī′ō di grād′), *v.t.* **-grad·ed, -grad·ing.** to break down (a detergent, etc.) by bacterial action.

bi·o·en·gi·neer·ing (bī′ō en′jə nir′ing), *n.* the application of various principles of engineering to the study and control of biological processes, structures, and products.

bi·o·gen·ic (bī′ō jen′ik), *adj.* produced by living organisms, as certain marine sediments.

biological clock, an internal mechanism which controls the rhythm or cycle of various activities, such as photosynthesis in an organism.

bi·o·tron (bī′ə tron), *n.* a structure or laboratory apparatus in which climatic conditions can be strictly controlled for use in plant and animal studies. [< *bio-* + *-tron*, probably suggested by *cyclotron*]

birth trauma, the anxiety which a child experiences as a result of being born, considered in psychoanalytic theory as a possible source of neuroses in later life.

boa·tel (bō tel′), *n.* a motel at a marina. [blend of *boat* and *motel*]

bo·son[2] (bō′son), *n.* any of a class of particles in quantum mechanics, two or more of which may occupy the same state. Bosons include mesons and photons. [< Satyendra Nath *Bose*, born 1894, an Indian physicist + *-on*, as in *electron*]

brain drain, *British Informal.* a shortage of professional labor caused by the emigration of scientists, technicians, etc., to more favorable labor markets abroad.

bro·de·rie an·glaise (brô drē′ än glez′), *French.* open embroidery on white linen or cambric, with designs cut out of the foundation material.

bru·tal·ism (brü′tə liz əm), *n.* a style of architecture using plain, massive, structural components, usually of concrete.

burn-up (bèrn′up′), *n.* the consumption of fuel in a nuclear reactor.

bus·tee (bus′tē), *n.* (in India) a slum. [< Hindustani *bastī* village; district, quarter]

C

cab·a·let·ta (kab′ə let′ə; *Italian* kä′bä let′ä), *n.* an operatic song in rondo form with variations imitating the hoofbeats of a cantering horse. [< Italian *cabaletta*]

Ca·poid (kā′poid, kä′-), *n.* a member of a Negroid race that includes the Bushmen and Hottentots. —*adj.* of or belonging to this race. [< *Cape* (of Good Hope) + *-oid*]

cat cracker, a device to crack petroleum with a catalyst. [short for *catalytic cracker*]

cat·e·nane (kat′ə nān), *n. Chemistry.* a compound of carbon molecules interlocked like the links of a chain, but not chemically bonded together. [< Latin *catēna* chain + English *-ane*]

ce·no·te (si nō′ti), *n.* a natural underground reservoir of water; sinkhole. Cenotes typically occur in the limestone of Yucatán peninsula. [< Spanish *cenote* < Maya *conot*]

ceph·a·lo·spo·rin (sef′ə lə spôr′in, -spōr′-), *n.* any of a group of antibiotics chemically related to penicillin, derived from a mold originally found in sewage. [< New Latin *Cephalosporium*, the genus name of the mold < Greek *kephalē* head + *sporá* seed]

CFA franc, the monetary unit of various African countries in the French Community, including the republics of Cameroon, Chad, Congo (Brazzaville), Dahomey, Gabon, Niger, Senegal, Togo, and Upper Volta, worth 1/50 of a French franc. [abbreviation of *Communauté Financière Africaine* African Financial Community]

chem·i·sorp·tion (kem′ə sôrp′shən, -zôrp′-), *n.* adsorption in which a single layer of molecules is held with great strength to a surface by a chemical bond. [< *chemi*(cal) + (ad)*sorption*]

cho·ri·o·car·ci·no·ma (kôr′ē ō kär′sə nō′mə, kōr′-), *n.* cancer of the chorionic tissue, especially in the placenta during or immediately following pregnancy. [< *chorio*(nic) + *carcinoma*]

chur·chi·an·i·ty (chèr′chi an′ə ti), *n.* overemphasis on ecclesiastical and denominational matters in Christianity. [< *church* + (Christ)*ianity*]

cir·ca·di·an (sèr kā′di ən), *adj.* of or having to do with a biological or behavioral process that recurs in an innate daily rhythm, as the '24-hour cycle of sleep and wakefulness in man. [< Latin *circā* around + *diēs* day + English *-an*]

Cloud Nine, *Slang.* an unreal place; fanciful condition.

coes·ite (kō′sīt, -zīt), *n.* a very dense form of silica, occurring naturally in meteoritic or nuclear-bomb craters and produced synthetically by subjecting quartz to very high pressure. [< Loring *Coes,* Jr., born 1915, an American chemist]

collision course, 1. a course taken by an object, especially a ballistic missile, that will cause it to collide with its target. **2.** any course that will result in a clash or conflict: *Race relations are on a collision course* (James C. Tanner).

col·lu·vi·um (kə lü′vi əm), *n., pl.* **-vi·a** (-vi ə) or **-vi·ums.** loose material deposited at the base of a slope mainly by gravity, as talus.

com·sat (kom′sat′), *n.* a communications satellite: *The agreement does not preclude the use of active relay comsats at a later period* (New Scientist).

cor·ti·co·trop·in (kôr′tə kō trop′in), *n.* an adrenocorticotropic extract from animal pituitary glands, used especially in treating rheumatic conditions; ACTH.

cos·mo·drome (koz′mə drōm′), *n.* a launching site for spacecraft. [< *cosmo*(naut) + (air)*drome*]

cross-in·fec·tion (krôs′in fek′shən, kros′-), *n.* infection transmitted between hospital patients having different infectious diseases.

cry·o·bi·ol·o·gy (krī'ō bī ol'ə ji), *n.* the study of the effects of low temperatures on living things. [< Greek *krýos* cold + English *biology*]

D

dance drama, a drama in which the story is told by elaborate dance movements, formalized gestures, and chanting or dialogue. Japanese No plays are dance dramas.

did·ger·i·doo (dij'ər ə dü'), *n.* (in Australia) a native musical wind instrument consisting of a long hollow sapling or bamboo stem that makes a droning or wailing sound.

dimethyl sulf·ox·ide (sulf ok'sīd, -sid), a by-product of wood pulp manufacture, long used as a solvent and now in experimental medicine to relieve pain and prevent ice crystallization in body cells. *Formula:* C_2H_6OS

di·sul·fi·ram (dī sul'fə ram), *n.* a crystalline compound widely used in the treatment of chronic alcoholism. *Formula:* $C_{10}H_{20}N_2S_4$ [< tetraethylthiu*ram disulfi*de, the chemical name]

dol·ce vi·ta (dōl'chä vē'tä), *Italian.* 1. a way of life given over to pleasure and amusement; self-indulgent or dissolute living. 2. (literally) sweet life.

dong (dông, dong), *n.* a unit of money in North Vietnam, worth about 28 cents. The unit of South Vietnam is the piaster. [< Annamese *dong*]

do·pa (dō'pə), *n.* an amino acid found in various plants, isolated from a variety of bean or made synthetically. *Formula:* $C_9H_{11}NO_4$ [< *d*(ihydr)*o*(xy)*p*(henyl)*a*(lanine)]

Dutch hoe, a hoe which is pushed instead of pulled.

E

earth science, any science dealing with the earth, as geology, meteorology, or oceanography.

ec·crine (ek'rīn, -rin), *adj.* 1. (of or having to do with certain sweat glands) secreting a substance without a breakdown of its own cells. 2. exocrine. [< *ec-* + Greek *krīnein* to separate]

ec·dy·sone (ek'də sōn), *n.* a hormone produced in the prothoracic glands of insects that promotes growth and molting. [< *ecdys*(is) + (horm)*one*]

ec·u·mene (ek'yú mēn, e kū'mə-nē), *n.* the habitable part of the world; the part of the world inhabited by man. [< Greek *oikouménē(gē)* the inhabited (world); see ECUMENICAL]

eightfold way, 1. *Nuclear Physics.* a theory based on eight quantum numbers for classifying elementary particles into groups with the same characteristics, such as similar mass, spin, or parity. 2. *Buddhism.* the eight virtues that lead to the cessation of pain.

e·kis·tics (ē kis'tiks), *n.* the study of the ecology of human beings in settlements or communities. [< Greek *oikistikē* (< *oikistês* settler < *oîkos* house) + English *-ics*]

e·las·mo·saur (i laz'mə sôr), *n.* any of a group of large marine reptiles with very long necks, small heads, and paddlelike limbs and tail that lived during the Cretaceous period in North America.

e·las·tase (i las'tās), *n.* an enzyme occurring in the pancreatic juice that digests elastin. [< *elast*(in) + *-ase*]

e·lec·tro·sur·ger·y (i lek'trō sėr'jər i), *n.* surgical diathermy.

Eu·ro·dol·lar (yùr'ō dol'ər), *n.* a U.S. dollar held by a foreign interest and involved in a transaction outside of the United States.

explosive bolt, a bolt which can be exploded by remote control to separate two components, as one stage of a guided missile from its booster.

eye dialect, *Linguistics.* the phonetic respelling of words to represent pronunciations that suggest dialect or nonstandard speech, as *sez* for *says* or *wuz* for *was.*

F

fer·mi·on (fėr'mi on), *n.* (in quantum mechanics) any of a class of particles, including protons, neutrons, and electrons, only one of which can occupy a given state at one time. [< Enrico *Fermi* + English *-on*, as in *electron*]

five-pins (fīv'pinz'), *n.* (in Canada) a game played with five wooden pins at which a ball is bowled to knock them down.

FLQ (no periods), Front de Libération Québecois (an organization of Quebec nationalists that advocates using terrorist methods to bring about the separation of the province of Quebec from the rest of Canada).

fly-by-wire (flī'bī wīr'), *adj.* of or having to do with an electronic guidance system that adjusts the path of a space capsule automatically after it is turned on manually: *Mercury spacemen are tempted by three separate systems for controlling their capsules—manual, automatic, and fly-by-wire* (Time).

frame of reference, 1. the standards by which a person compares something to form an attitude, make a judgment or analysis, etc.: *. . . the inability of the Congressional Committee, with its domestic orientation and limited frame of reference, to read the larger questions of international reality* (Bulletin of Atomic Scientists). 2. *Mathematics.* a set of lines or planes used as a reference for describing the position of a point, line, etc.

G

gallium arsenide, a crystalline compound of gallium and arsenic, used as a semiconducting device in tunnel diodes and lasers. *Formula:* GaAs

gig·a·cy·cle (jig'ə sī'kəl), *n.* 1. a billion cycles. 2. a billion cycles per second: *The highest frequency of coherent radio-type waves yet generated is about . . . 50 gigacycles* (Wall Street Journal). [< *giga-* + *cycle*]

glove box, a plastic box or similar enclosure containing a controlled environment, with rubber gloves fastened around holes in the side of the box through which a person can manipulate things in the box without introducing outside contamination; isolator.

glue snif·fing (snif'ing), the practice of inhaling the vapors of glue containing amyl alcohol to induce a narcotic effect.

gog·gle-box (gog'əl boks'), *n. British Slang.* a television set.

gray nurse, an Australian shark about 15 feet long, with sharp teeth, thought to attack people.

Great Society, 1. the domestic policies and programs advocated by President Lyndon B. Johnson for the United States. 2. the administration of Lyndon B. Johnson, from 1965.

H

hal·o·thane (hal'ə thān), *n.* a sweetish, nonexplosive gas, widely used as a general anesthetic; Fluothane. [< *halo*(gen) + (e)*thane*]

hard detergent, a detergent that cannot be decomposed by bacteria in sewage.

hard-line (härd'līn'), *adj.* favoring strong action or rigid adherence to a policy.

heat sink, any of various devices or materials that absorb heat, such as heat exchangers or metallic elements.

helical gear, a gearwheel whose teeth run at an angle to the shaft.

Ho·a Hao (hō'ə hou'), a religious sect of Vietnam, believing in a simplified and mystical form of Buddhism.

ho·mo·trans·plant (hō'mō trans'-plant, -plänt; hom'ō-), *n.* a homograft.

ho·ra (hôr'ə, hōr'ə), *n., pl.* **-ras.** a lively Israeli folk dance performed by couples moving around to the left or right in a circle. [< Hebrew *hōrāh* < Romanian *horă*]

hul·ly gul·ly (hul'i gul'i), a dance consisting of the twist performed as a square dance.

hy·per·bar·ic chamber (hī'pər-bar'ik), an airtight compartment in which oxygen under high pressure is forced into the lungs and heart of a person undergoing open-heart surgery, treatment for poisoning, etc.

I

idiot box, *U.S. Slang.* a television set.

im·mu·no·hem·a·tol·o·gy (i-mū'nō hem'ə tol'ə ji, -hē'mə-), *n.* the study of autoantibodies and other autoimmune factors in the blood cells and tissues.

in u·te·ro (in ū'tə rō), in the uterus; before being born. [< Latin *in uterō* < *in* in; *uterus* womb]

i·on·o·gram (ī on'ə gram), *n.* a record or graph of data transmitted by an ionosonde.

i·on·o·sonde (ī on'ə sond), *n.* an instrument for studying the ionosphere. [< *iono*(sphere) + (radio)-*sonde*]

PRONUNCIATION KEY: hat, āge, cãre, fär; let, ēqual, tėrm; it, īce; hot, ōpen, ôrder; oil, out; cup, pùt, rüle, ūse; child; long; thin; ᴚHen; zh, measure; ə represents a in about, e in taken, i in pencil, o in lemon, u in circus.

ITA[2] (no periods), Initial Teaching Alphabet, a system of representing the basic unit speech sounds of English by means of 43 letters in teaching reading: *New characters in the ITA system are, in the main, combinations of ordinary letters* (Manchester Guardian).

J

jack·fruit (jak'früt'), *n.* **1.** the jack (tree), widely cultivated in tropical regions. **2.** its fruit. **3.** the durian.

ju·do·gi (jü dō'gi), *n.* a loose, white cotton jacket and trousers worn by judo wrestlers, with a sash whose color varies with the degree of the wearer's expertness. [< Japanese *jūdōgi* < *jūdō* judo + *ki* clothing]

Ju·gend·stil (yü'gənt shtēl'), *n. German.* the art nouveau of Germany and Austria.

jum·buck (jum'buk'), *n.* (in Australia) a sheep. [< a native name]

ju·ri·met·rics (jùr'i met'riks), *n.* the branch of jurisprudence that studies judicial decisions. [< *juri*(dical) + *-metrics*, as in *econometrics*]

K

ken·do (ken'dō), *n.* a Japanese form of fencing, in which bamboo or wooden sticks are used for swords. [< Japanese *kendō*]

ker·nic·ter·us (kər nik'tər əs), *n.* a form of jaundice that causes damage to the brain of infants, resulting from the accumulation of bile pigment in the central nervous system. [< New Latin *kernicterus* < German *Kernikterus* < *Kern* kernel, nucleus + *Ikterus* icterus]

ke·ryg·ma (kə rig'mə), *n. Theology.* the proclamation of God's revelation in Christ, especially as preached by the Gospels. [< Greek *kḗrygma* (literally) proclamation < *kērýssein* to proclaim]

Klein bottle (klīn), *Geometry.* a continuous, one-sided surface formed by bending the small end of a tapering tube, passing it through one side, and then joining its flared opening to the opening on the wide end. [< Felix *Klein*, 1849-1925, a German mathematician]

Krem·lin·ol·o·gy (krem'lə nol'ə ji), *n.* the study of the policies and practices of the Soviet Union.

L

Land of Lincoln, a nickname for Illinois.

Land of Opportunity, a nickname for Arkansas.

LEM (no periods), Lunar Excursion Module (a module designed to separate from a spacecraft near the lunar surface).

lin·ac (lin'ak), *n.* a linear accelerator. [< *lin*(ear) *ac*(celerator)]

li·pot·ro·pin (li pot'rə pin), *n.* a pituitary hormone that stimulates the conversion of stored solid fats into liquid form for use by the body. [< *lipotrop*(ic) + *-in*]

long·wall (lông'wôl', long'-), *adj.* of or designating a system of mining in which the whole seam of coal, ore, etc., is removed and nothing is left to support the roof except the shaft pillars.

lum·pen·pro·le·tar·i·at (lúm'pən prō'lə tär'i ət), *n.* the section of the proletariat that lacks class-consciousness: *These are not the real working class. These are the lumpenproletariat, tainted by petty-bourgeois ideology* (New Yorker). [< German *Lumpenproletariat* < *Lumpen*(volk) rabble (< *Lump* ragamuffin < *Lumpen* rag) + *Proletariat* proletariat]

M

machine translation, 1. translation from one language to another by an electronic computer. **2.** the result of this process.

mac·ro·glob·u·lin (mak'rō glob'yə lin), *n.* a globulin with an abnormally high molecular weight, found in the blood plasma of persons suffering from rheumatoid arthritis.

mag·ne·form (mag'nə fôrm), *n.* a device for shaping metal, consisting of interchangeable magnetic coils of wire whose powerful magnetic fields cause metal to compress or expand to a desired shape. [< *magne*(tic) + *form*]

magnetic bottle, *Nuclear Physics.* any arrangement of magnetic fields for confining or constricting charged particles in a controlled thermonuclear reaction. Magnetic bottles are formed in the pinch effect, in mirror machines, and in stellarators.

Mao·ism (mou'iz əm), *n.* the Communist ideology of Mao Tse-tung, Chinese Communist leader, characterized by rigid adherence to Marxian doctrine.

mer·cap·to·pu·rine (mər kap'tō pyùr'ēn, -in), *n.* a compound that inhibits the metabolism of nucleic acid, used in the treatment of acute leukemia; Purinethol. *Formula:* $C_5H_4N_4S$ [< *mercapt*(an) + *purine*]

MHD (no periods), **1.** magnetohydrodynamic. **2.** magnetohydrodynamics.

mi·cro·cir·cuit (mī'krō sėr'kit), *n.* a highly miniaturized electronic circuit, usually formed of micromodules, or of extremely thin films deposited by evaporation in a high vacuum.

mi·cro·e·lec·tron·ics (mī'krō i lek'tron'iks, -ē'lek-), *n.* the branch of electronics dealing with microminiaturization.

mirror machine, *Nuclear Physics.* a tube with magnetic mirrors at each end for confining charged particles.

Mod or **mod** (mod), *n. British Slang.* one of a group of teen-agers affecting extreme neatness of appearance and a foppish liking for very fine or stylish clothes. [< *modern*]

mog·gie or **mog·gy** (mog'i), *n., pl.* **-gies. 1.** *British Slang.* **a.** a cat. **b.** an untidy woman or girl. **2.** *British Dialect.* a calf or cow. [perhaps alteration of the name *Maggie*]

MOL (no periods) or **M.O.L.,** Manned Orbiting Laboratory.

mon·o·a·mine oxidase (mon'ō ə men', -am'in), an enzyme present in animal and plant tissue which oxidizes and destroys amines such as norepinephrine and serotonin.

mo·sa·i·cism (mō zā'ə siz əm), *n. Biology.* the presence of different or antagonistic genetic characteristics in adjacent cells of the body, chiefly due to faulty cell division.

mo·sa·i·cist (mō zā'ə sist), *n.* a maker of mosaics; dealer in mosaics.

N

na·mas·te (nä mäs'te), *n.* (in India) a way of greeting by pressing together the palms of one's hands. [< Hindi *namaste* < *namas* bow]

neph·a·nal·y·sis (nef'ə nal'ə sis), *n., pl.* **-ses** (-sēz). **1.** analysis of the cloud formations over a large area, using weather charts drawn especially from photographs taken by weather satellites. **2.** a chart of such cloud formations. [< Greek *néphos* cloud + English *analysis*]

new math or **new mathematics,** *U.S. Education.* mathematics designed to give the student an understanding of basic mathematical structures, concepts, and processes, with less emphasis on formal drills.

ni·da·tion (nī dā'shən), *n. Physiology.* the implantation of the fertilized egg in the lining (decidua) of the uterus: *Nidation ... in Man takes place about a week after fertilization* (New Scientist). [< Latin *nīdus* nest + English *-ation*]

non·art (non'ärt'), *n.* **1.** the negation of art: *He tends to look upon a good deal of Abstract Expressionism as nonart* (New Yorker). **2.** a work that rejects or parodies conventional forms and techniques of art.

non·chro·mo·so·mal (non'krō mə sō'məl), *adj.* transmitting hereditary characters without chromosomes; not chromosomal or Mendelian: *The nonchromosomal system involves genes but follows rules completely different from the chromosomal one* (N.Y. Times).

no·o·sphere (nō'əs fir), *n.* human thought and feeling conceived as a region above and surrounding the biosphere: *... the "noosphere" [is] the psychological habitat in which we live and on whose resources we must draw* (Sir Julian Huxley). [< Greek *nóos* mind + English (bio)*sphere*]

nu·cle·o·phil·ic (nü'kli ə fil'ik, nü'-), *adj.* strongly attracted to the nuclei of atoms: *nucleophilic ions or molecules.*

O

OAO (no periods), orbiting astronomical observatory.

o·cean·aut (ō'shə nôt), *n.* an explorer of an ocean or sea: *French oceanauts last summer (1963) lived in a prefabricated village 36 feet below surface in the Red Sea* (Science News Letter). [< *ocea*(n) + *-naut*, as in *astronaut*]

off-line (ôf'līn', of'-), *adj.* **1. a.** (of equipment associated with an electronic computer) operating outside of direct control by the central equipment. **b.** not operating in real-time. **2.** (of a railroad operation, service, etc.) being outside of the area served by the line. —*adv.* outside the direct control of central equipment: *These tapes have to be ... analyzed by a Mercury or Atlas computer working off-line* (New Scientist).

Ol·do·wan (ol′də wən, ōl′-), *adj.* of or having to do with a pebble culture of eastern Africa that preceded the Abbevillean and Acheulian cultures, represented by tools discovered in Oldoway (or Olduvai) Gorge, Tanganyika; Olduvai. Also, **Olduwan.**

ol·i·go·troph·ic (ol′ə gō trof′ik), *adj.* not providing nutrition, as a lake with scant vegetation.

omega minus, *Nuclear Physics.* a negatively-charged elementary particle of extremely short life, produced in a nuclear accelerator after its existence and properties were predicted by the eightfold way.

on-line (on′līn′, ôn′-), *adj.* **1. a.** (of equipment associated with an electronic computer) operating under the direct control of the central equipment. **b.** operating in real-time. **2.** (of a railroad operation, service, etc.) being or taking place on the regular line. *—adv.* under the direct control of central equipment: *[The] computer is connected "on-line" to the plant* (London Daily Telegraph).

open enrollment, *U.S.* the transfer of children from neighborhood public schools attended chiefly by one racial group into other neighborhood schools in order to attain racial balance in the enrollments.

optical art, a form of abstract painting in which unusual optical illusions and effects are produced by means of highly complex geometrical designs; op art: *What optical art loses through impersonality it gains in universality of appeal* (John Canaday).

OSO (no periods), orbiting solar observatory: *OSO was launched in March 1962* (New Scientist).

P

pa·chu·co (pə chü′kō), *n.* *U.S.* a zoot-suited young tough of Mexico or of Mexican descent. [< Mexican Spanish *pachuco*]

pan·op·tic (pan op′tik), *adj.* commanding a full view; seeing everything at once: *... his panoptic survey of the American scene called "America as a Civilization"* (Atlantic).

pan·o·rama[4] a continuously passing or changing scene: *the panorama of city life.*

par·a·in·flu·en·za (par′ə in flü en′zə), *n.* a respiratory illness similar to influenza, caused by any of various myxoviruses that are associated with the common cold and various other respiratory diseases.

par·a·med·i·cal (par′ə med′ə kəl), *adj.* having to do with medicine in an auxiliary capacity; involving services, studies, etc., that are related to but not part of the medical profession: *The complexity of health problems has given rise to many paramedical callings, from the university physiologist to the hospital aide* (Harper's).

pen·ta·quine (pen′tə kwēn, -kwin), *n.* a yellowish, crystalline, synthetic drug, used in the treatment of malaria, often in combination with quinine. *Formula:* $C_{18}H_{27}N_3O$

per·cep·tron (pər sep′tron), *n.* an electronic device that automatically recognizes and identifies shapes or patterns by means of a system of photoelectric cells and electronic-brain units. [< *percep*(tion) + (elec)*tron*]

pher·o·mone (fer′ə mōn), *n.* a substance secreted externally by certain animal species, especially insects, to affect the behavior or development of other members of the species.

pho·to·de·tec·tor (fō′tō di tek′tər), *n.* a semiconductor device that detects radiant energy, especially infrared radiation, by photoconductive or photovoltaic action, used in electronic equipment to detect changes in temperature, in solar telescopes, etc.

phys·i·o·sorp·tion (fiz′i ō sôrp′shən, -zôrp′-), *n.* adsorption in which one or more layers of molecules are held weakly to a surface by physical forces. [< Greek *phýsis* nature + English (ad)*sorption*]

phy·to·chrome (fī′tə krōm), *n.* a bluish, light-sensitive pigment in plants which absorbs red or infrared rays and acts as an enzyme in controlling growth and other photoperiodic responses.

pol·y·mer·ase (pol′i mə rās), *n.* an enzyme that polymerizes nucleotides to form nucleic acid. [< *polymer* + *-ase*]

po·lyn·ia or **po·lyn·ya** (pə lin′yə, pol′ən yä′), *n.* a space of open water in the midst of ice, especially in the arctic seas. [< Russian *polyn′ya*]

por·phyr·i·a (pôr fir′i ə), *n.* a metabolic disorder marked by the presence of porphyrin in the blood. [< New Latin *porphyria* < *porphyrin*]

PPLO (no periods), pleuropneumonia-like organism (a filterable microorganism, such as the Eaton agent, that resembles both viruses and bacteria).

pre·hom·i·nid (prē hom′ə nid), *adj.* of or having to do with a group of extinct, manlike primates regarded as immediate ancestors of the hominids. *—n.* a prehominid animal.

print·out (print′out′), *n.* **1. a.** the printed output of an electronic computer. **b.** the act of producing such an output. **2.** printing out.

progressive jazz, a jazz style closely resembling bebop, but technically more elaborate and experimental.

pro·mo (prō′mō), *n.* *U.S. Informal.* a television announcement of a forthcoming program on the same network. [short for *promotion*]

pye-dog (pī′dôg′, -dog′), *n.* an ownerless dog of low breed found in towns and villages of India and other parts of Asia. [< Hindi *pāhī* outsider + English *dog*]

Q

quantum number, one of a set of numbers assigned to an atomic system, specifying the number of quanta or units of energy, angular momentum, etc., in the system.

quark (kwôrk), *n. Nuclear Physics.* one of a hypothetical set of three elementary particles, each with an electric charge less than that of the electron, whose existence and properties were predicted by the eightfold way. [< the phrase "three quarks" in *Finnegans Wake*, a novel by James Joyce]

qua·si-stel·lar (kwā′sī stel′ər, -zī; kwä′si-, -zi-), *adj.* having to do with or designating an extragalactic object or body that appears to be larger than a star but smaller than a nebula and that is the source of powerful emissions of electromagnetic waves.

R

radio pill, a miniaturized radio transmitter enclosed in a plastic capsule that can be swallowed and used to transmit signals on gastrointestinal and other conditions as it passes through the body.

Ra·man effect (rä′mən), the scattering of incident light by the molecules of a transparent substance, in such a way that the wavelengths of the scattered light are lengthened or shortened. [< Sir Chandrasekhara V. *Raman,* born 1888, an Indian physicist, who discovered it]

ra·win·sonde (rā′win sond), *n.* **1.** the gathering of temperature, pressure, wind speed or other atmospheric information by means of a balloon-borne radiosonde tracked by radiocompass and sometimes radar. **2.** a radiosonde used for this purpose. [< *rawin* + (radio)*sonde*]

re·a·li·a (ri ä′li ə), *n.pl.* actual objects, such as types of woods or fabrics, used as tools in teaching. [< Late Latin *reālia,* neuter plural of *reālis* real; see REAL[1]]

real-time (rē′əl tīm′), *n.* equivalence in time or speed between the output of an electronic computer and a particular physical process which needs this output for its effective operation. *—adj.* having to do with or operating in real-time.

re·im·plan·ta·tion (rē′im plan tā′shən), *n.* the replacing or resetting of a part of the body that has been severed or removed.

rem·a·nence (rem′ə nəns), *n.* **1.** the state or quality of being remanent. **2.** *Physics.* the flux density remaining in a substance after the magnetizing force has ceased.

res·pi·rom·e·ter (res′pə rom′ətər), *n.* a device for measuring the degree and nature of respiration.

rhi·no·vi·rus (rī′nō vī′rəs), *n.* any of a group of viruses associated with the common cold and other respiratory diseases. [< Greek *rhís, rhīnós* nose + English *virus*]

Rich·ter scale (rik′tər), a scale for indicating the magnitude of earthquakes, ranging from 0 to 10. [< Charles Francis *Richter,* born 1900, an American seismologist]

ri·om·e·ter (rī om′ə tər), *n.* an instrument for recording the strength of radio noise and the level of its absorption by the ionosphere. [< *r*(elative)*i*(onospheric)-*o*(pacity) *meter*]

PRONUNCIATION KEY: hat, āge, cãre, fär; let, ēqual, tėrm; it, īce; hot, ōpen, ôrder; oil, out; cup, pút, rüle, ūse; child; long; thin; ᴛнen; zh, measure; ə represents a in about, e in taken, i in pencil, o in lemon, u in circus.

rocket belt, a portable, rocket-powered device equipped with controls, used experimentally to propel a person through the air.

rock·et·sonde (rok′it sond), *n.* a rocket used to gather information on that portion of the lower atmosphere which is inaccessible to balloons. [< *rocket* + (radio)*sonde*]

S

sal·chow (sal′kov), *n.* a jump in figure skating in which the skater leaps from the inside back edge of one skate, rotates in the air, and lands on the outside back edge of the other skate.

sca·lo·gram (skā′lə gram), *n.* a graded series of related questions or problems which become progressively more difficult to answer. Scalograms are used in psychological and other tests to measure the uniformity and consistency of responses. [< *scale*³ + *-gram*¹]

sec·ond-strike (sek′ənd strīk′), *adj.* **1.** (of a nuclear weapon or force) able to retaliate or strike back after a nuclear attack. **2.** of retaliation; retaliatory: *second-strike capability.*

se·dia ges·ta·to·ria (se′dyä jes′tä tô′ryä), *Italian.* the portable throne on which the Pope is borne on ceremonial occasions.

seed money, *U.S.* money used by a foundation to support or finance various causes.

set theory, a mathematical system or theory that deals with sets, their properties, and their relationships: *Set theory is widely used in teaching to demonstrate how things can be grouped and how groups are related to one another* (Scientific American).

shig·el·lo·sis (shig′ə lō′sis), *n.,* *pl.* **-ses** (-sēz). bacillary dysentery. [< New Latin *Shigella* genus name of the bacillus + *-osis*]

SINS (no periods), Ship's Inertial Navigation System (used in nuclear-powered submarines).

slant-hole drilling (slant′hōl′, slänt′-), the drilling of oil wells in a slanting instead of a vertical direction, especially with the unlawful purpose of tapping oil belonging to adjacent properties.

sloppy Joe, *U.S. Slang.* a large, loose or baggy sweater.

social insurance, insurance of a person against unemployment, illness, etc., through government action: *There are several types of social insurance, such as accident insurance or workman's compensation, sickness and old-age insurance, and unemployment insurance* (Emery S. Bogardus).

soft·ware (sôft′wăr′, soft′-), *n.* **1.** the design stage or plans of a machine or component. **2.** a program or set of standard procedures for a computer system.

soil mechanics, the study of the physical characteristics of soil and other loose materials on which buildings, highways, etc., may be erected.

sol·vate (sol′vāt), *n., v.,* **-vat·ed, -vat·ing.** a chemical substance produced by the combination of the ions or molecules of a solvent and a solute. —*v.i., v.t.* to become or cause to become a solvate.

Sprach·ge·fühl (shpraH′gə fYl′), *n. German.* feeling for language; sensitivity to what is right or proper in speech: *It doesn't take much Sprachgefühl to recognize that Mr. Wilder is ... being a mite folksy* (New Yorker).

ster·e·o·reg·u·lar (ster′i ō reg′yə-lər, stir′-), *adj.* of or having to do with a polymer that has a definite and regular spatial arrangement of the atoms in its repeating units: *stereoregular rubber.*

strange·ness (strānj′nis), *n.* **1.** the quality or state of being strange. **2.** *Nuclear Physics.* a property of certain elementary particles, used in explaining their relatively slow rate of decay.

strange particle, *Nuclear Physics.* any of the heavier, unstable elementary particles, comprising the heavy mesons and the hyperons, so called because their relatively long life appeared to be inconsistent with existing atomic theories.

T

thi·a·ben·da·zole (thī′ə ben′də-zōl), *n.* a drug used in the treatment of trichinosis and other parasitic diseases, especially of animals. [< *thia*(zolyl)*ben*(zimi)*dazole*]

think factory, *Slang.* a center of scientific or technological research: *The engine comes out of Dr. Farrington Daniels's think factory at the University of Wisconsin* (New Scientist).

thi·ram (thī′ram), *n.* a white crystalline compound used as a fungicide, seed disinfectant, and bacteriostat. *Formula:* $C_6H_{12}N_2S_4$ [< (tetramethyl)*thi*(u)*ram* disulfide]

ti·ki (tē′kē), *n.* **1.** a Polynesian deity, regarded as the creator of man. **2.** an image of wood or stone representing this deity.

ti·la·pi·a (ti lā′pi ə), *n.* any of a genus of fresh-water cichlid fishes important as a source of food in Africa and Asia.

to·ko·no·ma (tō′kə nō′mə), *n.* an alcove in a Japanese house for the decorative display of scrolls, prints, and flowers. [< Japanese *tokonoma*]

ton·do (ton′dō), *n., pl.* **-di** (-dē) or **-dos.** **1.** a painting in circular form. **2.** a carved relief in circular form. [< Italian *tondo* (literally) plate < *tondo* round, ultimately < Latin *rotundus;* see ROUND, ROTUND]

trans·fer·ase (trans′fə rās), *n.* any of various enzymes that transfer a radical from one molecule to another, as transaminase and kinase.

transfer RNA, a form of ribonucleic acid that delivers amino acids to the ribosomes during protein synthesis: *There is at least one transfer RNA for each of the 20 common amino acids* (Scientific American).

tunnel vision, a disorder of the eyes in which the range of vision is contracted, so that only objects in the direct line of sight are seen clearly.

twi-night (twī′nīt′), *adj. U.S. Baseball.* starting late in the afternoon and continuing at night under lights: *a twi-night double-header.* [< *twi*(light)-*night*]

two·fer (tü′fər), *n. U.S. Slang.* **1. a.** a pair of theater tickets sold for roughly the price of one. **b.** a coupon for obtaining such tickets. **2.** any item sold at two for the price of one: *twofer cigars.* [alteration of *two for* ...]

typh·lol·o·gy (tif lol′ə ji), *n.* the science dealing with blindness. [< Greek *typhlós* blind + English *-logy*]

U

un·der·ed·u·cat·ed (un′dər ej′ú-kā′tid), *adj.* poorly or insufficiently educated: *By overemphasizing courses in "methodology" at the expense of regular academic subjects, they've produced a generation of undereducated teachers* (Wall Street Journal).

un·free·dom (un frē′dəm), *n.* the state of being unfree; want of freedom: ... *the struggle against injustice and unfreedom* (London Times).

u·ni·fied field theory (ū′nə fīd), any theory seeking to unify different physical theories or laws, especially a theory developed by Albert Einstein in which electric, magnetic, and gravitational phenomena are treated as parts or phases of a single process.

u·til·i·dor (ū til′ə dôr), *n.* (in Canada) a system of elevated and insulated conduits carrying water, steam, etc., to communities situated on the permafrost. [< *utility;* perhaps patterned on *humidor*]

V

vo·ag (vō′ag′), *n. U.S. Informal.* **1.** vocational agriculture. **2.** a teacher or advocate of vocational agriculture.

vo·ed (vō′ed′), *n. U.S. Informal.* vocational education: *Vo-ed, as teachers call it, is dismally inadequate to meet the demands upon it* (Time).

voice·print (vois′print′), *n.* a spectrographic record of the sound patterns formed by a person's voice: *Voiceprints, just as fingerprints, appear to be unique and almost unchangeable [and] may eventually take their place with fingerprints as a positive means of identification* (New York Times).

W

walk·ie-look·ie (wô′ki lúk′i), *n.* a creepie-peepie.

wave function, (in quantum mechanics) a mathematical function describing the propagation of waves by an elementary particle.

wig·let (wig′lit), *n.* a little wig; small hairpiece: *Wiglets ... come in a variety of shapes and colors and attach to your present hair* (San Francisco Chronicle).

X-Y-Z

xer·arch (zir′ärk), *adj. Ecology.* originating in dry habitats: *a xerarch plant succession.* [< *xer-* + Greek *archē* beginning]

yab·bie (yab′i), *n.* a small fresh-water crawfish of the Australian bush. [< a native Australian name]

zirc·al·loy (zérk′al′oi, zėr′kə loi′), *n.* an alloy of zirconium and some other metal or metals: *The fuel is canned in zircalloy* (New Scientist).

HOW TO USE THE INDEX

This index covers the contents of all editions of THE WORLD BOOK YEAR BOOK from 1962 to 1966. It indexes subjects discussed in the first four sections of each edition, and lists the titles of all new or revised articles from THE WORLD BOOK ENCYCLOPEDIA appearing in the supplement section.

Each index entry is followed by the edition years (in italics) and the page numbers, as:

ADVERTISING, *66*-210, *65*-206, *64*-204, *63*-174, *62*-118

This means that information about advertising begins on the pages indicated for each of the editions.

An index entry that is the title of an article appearing in THE YEAR BOOK is printed in capital letters, as: **AUTOMOBILE.** An entry that is not an article title, but a subject discussed in an article of some other title is printed: **Tires.**

THE YEAR BOOK INDEX

The various "See" and "See also" cross references in the index list are to other entries within the index. Clue words or phrases are used when two or more references to the same subject appear in the same edition of THE YEAR BOOK. These make it easy to locate the material on the page, since they refer to an article title or article subsection in which the reference appears, as:

Human rights: civil liberties, *65*-266, *64*-274; *Special Report,* *65*-164; United Nations, *66*-551, *64*-517. See also **Civil Rights**

The indication "*il.*" means that the reference is to an illustration only. An index entry in capital letters followed by "*WBE*" refers to a new or revised WORLD BOOK ENCYCLOPEDIA article, which is printed in the supplement section, as:

WORLD, HISTORY OF: *WBE*, *66*-570

JANUARY

1-Dec. 31—American Bible Society Sesquicentennial.
1-Dec. 31—Winston-Salem Bicentennial Year. North Carolina city of Salem founded by Moravians in 1766.
1-31—March of Dimes.
  —United Cerebral Palsy Month.
1—New Year's Day.
1-8—Universal Week of Prayer.
1-May 29—World-Wide Roman Catholic Church Jubilee celebrates end of Vatican Council II.
6—Epiphany, Twelfth Day after Christmas.
10—89th Congress of U.S. Opens second session in Washington, D.C.
16—World Religion Day.
21—Chinese New Year. Yuan Don, Year of the Horse.
23-29—National Junior Achievement Week.
23-30—National YMCA Week.
30—Franklin D. Roosevelt Day (Ky., W. Va.).
30-Feb. 6—Youth Week.

FEBRUARY

1-28—American Heart Month.
  —American Music Month.
1—National Freedom Day.
2—Candlemas Day.
  —Ground-Hog Day.
6-12—National Children's Dental Health Week.
7-13—Boy Scout Week.
12—Abraham Lincoln's Birthday.
13-19—National Crime Prevention Week.
13-20—Negro History Week.
14—Saint Valentine's Day.
18-27—Date Festival and Arabian Nights Pageant, Indio, Calif.
19-26—Future Farmers of America Week.
20-26—Catholic Book Week.
20-27—Brotherhood Week.
22—George Washington's Birthday.
  —Shrove Tuesday: *Mardi Gras of the French; Pancake Day of the English;* and *Carnival of the Italians.*
23—Ash Wednesday.

MARCH

1-31—American Red Cross Fund Drive.
  —Children's Art Month.
1—National Teachers Day.
  —Saint David's Day, patron saint of Wales.
1-Apr. 10—Easter Seal Campaign.
6—Purim, Jewish Feast of Lots.
6-12—Girl Scout Week.
16—Robert H. Goddard Day, father of modern rocketry and space flight.
17—Saint Patrick's Day.
20—First Day of Spring (8:53 P.M., E.S.T.).
20-26—Camp Fire Girls Birthday Week.
  —National Wildlife Week.
25—Annunciation Day.
26-Apr. 2—International Puppet Festival, Braunschweig, West Germany.
27-Apr. 2—National Boys' Club Week.

APRIL

1-30—Cancer Control Month.
  —Freedom Shrine Month.
  —National Hobby Month.
  —Teaching Career Month.
1—April Fools' Day.
1-24—First World Festival of Negro Arts, Dakar, Senegal.
2-6—International Book Fair for Children and Youth, Bologna, Italy.
3—Palm Sunday.
5-12—Passover.
7—World Health Day.
8—Good Friday.
9—Bataan Day (Philippines).
10—Easter Sunday.
12-15—Catholic Library Association Conference, San Antonio, Texas.
13—Sieur de La Salle Tercentenary, commemorates French explorer's arrival in Canada.
  —Thomas Jefferson's Birthday.
14—Pan American Day.
17-23—National Garden Week.
  —National Library Week.
24—Daylight Saving Begins in many U.S. areas.
24-30—Canada-U.S. Goodwill Week.
  —Good Human Relations Week.
  —National YWCA Week.
  —Youth Temperance Education Week.
26—Confederate Memorial Day (Ala., Fla., Ga., and Miss.).

MAY

1-31—International May Festival, Wiesbaden, West Germany.
1—May Day.
  —Law Day.
  —Loyalty Day.
1-7—Be Kind to Animals Week.
  —Mental Health Week.
  —National Goodwill Week.
1-8—National Family Week.
  —National Music Week.
4—Penumbral Eclipse of Moon, visible from Africa, Europe, Asia, Pacific, and Antarctica.
7—Kentucky Derby, Louisville, Ky.
8—Mother's Day.
  —V.E. Day.
8-14—National Girls Club Week.
  —National Hospital Week.
8-June 19—Multiple Sclerosis Hope Chest Campaign.
10—Confederate Memorial Day (N.C., S.C.).
15—Rogation Sunday.
  —Rural Life Sunday.
16-22—Girl Guard Anniversary Week.
19—Ascension Day.
20—Annular Eclipse of Sun, visible from Atlantic, Europe, Asia, and Africa.
21—Armed Forces Day.
22-29—National Salvation Army Week.
23—Victoria Day and Queen's Birthday, official celebration in Canada.
25-26—Shabuot, Jewish Feast of Weeks.
26-June 12—International Grieg Festival, Bergen, Norway.
29—Pentecost, or Whitsunday.
30—Memorial (Decoration) Day.
  —Confederate Memorial Day (Va.).
  —500-Mile Speedway Race, Indianapolis, Ind.

JUNE

3—Confederate Memorial Day (Ky., La., Tenn.).
  —Jefferson Davis' Birthday.

A
PREVIEW
OF
1966

1966 JANUARY 1966

SUN.	MON.	TUE.	WED.	THU.	FRI.	SAT.
						1
2	3	4	5	6	7	8
9	10	11	12	13	14	15
16	17	18	19	20	21	22
23 30	24 31	25	26	27	28	29

1966 FEBRUARY 1966

SUN.	MON.	TUE.	WED.	THU.	FRI.	SAT.
		1	2	3	4	5
6	7	8	9	10	11	12
13	14	15	16	17	18	19
20	21	22	23	24	25	26
27	28					

1966 MARCH 1966

SUN.	MON.	TUE.	WED.	THU.	FRI.	SAT.
		1	2	3	4	5
6	7	8	9	10	11	12
13	14	15	16	17	18	19
20	21	22	23	24	25	26
27	28	29	30	31		

1966 APRIL 1966

SUN.	MON.	TUE.	WED.	THU.	FRI.	SAT.
					1	2
3	4	5	6	7	8	9
10	11	12	13	14	15	16
17	18	19	20	21	22	23
24	25	26	27	28	29	30

1966 MAY 1966

SUN.	MON.	TUE.	WED.	THU.	FRI.	SAT.
1	2	3	4	5	6	7
8	9	10	11	12	13	14
15	16	17	18	19	20	21
22	23	24	25	26	27	28
29	30	31				

1966 JUNE 1966

SUN.	MON.	TUE.	WED.	THU.	FRI.	SAT.
			1	2	3	4
5	6	7	8	9	10	11
12	13	14	15	16	17	18
19	20	21	22	23	24	25
26	27	28	29	30		

1966		JULY			1966	
SUN	MON	TUE	WED	THU	FRI	SAT
					1	2
3	4	5	6	7	8	9
10	11	12	13	14	15	16
17	18	19	20	21	22	23
24/31	25	26	27	28	29	30

1966		AUGUST			1966	
SUN	MON	TUE	WED	THU	FRI	SAT
	1	2	3	4	5	6
7	8	9	10	11	12	13
14	15	16	17	18	19	20
21	22	23	24	25	26	27
28	29	30	31			

1966		SEPTEMBER			1966	
SUN	MON	TUE	WED	THU	FRI	SAT
				1	2	3
4	5	6	7	8	9	10
11	12	13	14	15	16	17
18	19	20	21	22	23	24
25	26	27	28	29	30	

1966		OCTOBER			1966	
SUN	MON	TUE	WED	THU	FRI	SAT
						1
2	3	4	5	6	7	8
9	10	11	12	13	14	15
16	17	18	19	20	21	22
23/30	24/31	25	26	27	28	29

1966		NOVEMBER			1966	
SUN	MON	TUE	WED	THU	FRI	SAT
		1	2	3	4	5
6	7	8	9	10	11	12
13	14	15	16	17	18	19
20	21	22	23	24	25	26
27	28	29	30			

1966		DECEMBER			1966	
SUN	MON	TUE	WED	THU	FRI	SAT
				1	2	3
4	5	6	7	8	9	10
11	12	13	14	15	16	17
18	19	20	21	22	23	24
25	26	27	28	29	30	31

5—Trinity Sunday.
11—Queen Elizabeth II's Birthday, official celebration, London, England.
11-25—Mozart Music Festival, Würzburg, West Germany.
13-19—National Little League Baseball Week.
14—Flag Day.
19—Father's Day.
19-24—Canadian Library Association Convention, Calgary, Alberta.
20-July 22—All England Lawn Tennis Championships, Wimbledon, England.
21—First Day of Summer (3:33 P.M., E.S.T.).
27-Aug. 28—Aspen Music Festival and School, Aspen, Colo.
29—Feast of Saints Peter and Paul.

JULY

1-31—National Arts and Crafts Month.
1—Dominion Day (Canada).
2-Aug. 21—Berkshire Festival, Lenox, Mass.
4—Independence Day.
—American Philippine Friendship Day (Philippines).
4-10—National Safe Boating Week.
10-16—American Library Association Convention, New York, N.Y.
14—Bastille Day (France).
17-23—Captive Nations Week.
23-Sept. 11—Shakespeare Festival, Ashland, Ore.
24-30—National Farm Safety Week.
24-Aug. 28—Richard Wagner Festival, Bayreuth, West Germany.
26-Aug. 31—International Music and Drama Festival, Salzburg, Austria.

AUGUST

5-7—All American Indian Days, Sheridan, Wyo.
6—All-American Soapbox Derby, Akron, Ohio.
—Feast of the Transfiguration.
13-Sept. 7—International Music Festival, Lucerne, Switzerland.
14—Atlantic Charter Day.
—V-J Day (original).
15—Feast of the Assumption.
21-Sept. 10—International Festival of Music and Drama, Edinburgh, Scotland.
23-27—Little League Baseball World Series.

SEPTEMBER

1-30—Youth Month.
2—Great Fire of London Tercentenary.
5—Labor Day.
7-14—National Child Safety Week.
15-16—Rosh Hashanah, Jewish New Year.
17—Citizenship Day.
—Constitution Day.
22-Oct. 1—International Pianoforte Competition, Leeds, England.
23—First Day of Autumn (6:43 A.M., E.S.T.).
24—Yom Kippur, Jewish Day of Atonement.
24-Oct. 1—National 4-H Club Week.
25—National Gold Star Mothers Day.
25-Oct. 1—Christian Education Week.
25-Oct. 2—National Sunday School Week.
25-Oct. 9—Festival Week of Opera, Theater, and Ballet, West Berlin.
28-Dec. 25—900th Anniversary of the Norman Conquest of England and Coronation of William (I) the Conqueror.

OCTOBER

1-31—National Science Youth Month.
2-8—National Employ the Physically Handicapped Week.
3—Child Health Day.
9-15—Fire Prevention Week.
—Y-Teen Roll Call Week.
10—Thanksgiving Day (Canada).
12—Columbus Day.
15—National Newspaper Carrier Boy Day.
—World Poetry Day.
16-22—Aloha Week (Hawaii).
21—English Thanksgiving Day.
24—United Nations Day.
29—Penumbral Eclipse of Moon, visible in North and South America, western Atlantic, Pacific, New Zealand, northeast Asia, and Arctic.
30—Daylight Saving Time Ends in many U.S. areas.
—World Temperance Day.
30-Nov. 5—National Children's Book Week.
31—Halloween, or All Hallow's Eve.
—Reformation Day.

NOVEMBER

1-30—March for Muscular Dystrophy Month.
1—All Saints' Day.
2—All Souls' Day.
4—World Community Day.
4-Dec. 4—Jewish Book Month.
5—Guy Fawkes Day (England).
6-12—American Education Week.
8—General Election Day (U.S.).
11—Remembrance Day (Canada).
—Veterans Day (U.S.).
12—Total Eclipse of Sun, visible in Southern Hemisphere.
13-19—YMCA-YWCA World Fellowship Week.
14-20—National Stamp Collecting Week.
15-Dec. 25—National Christmas Seal Sale.
18-24—National Farm-City Week.
20-26—Latin America Week.
22—Feast of Saint Cecilia.
24—Thanksgiving Day (U.S.).
24-Dec. 25—World-Wide Bible Reading.
25-Dec. 3—International Live Stock Exposition, Chicago.
27—First Sunday in Advent.
27-Dec. 1—National 4-H Club Congress, Chicago.

DECEMBER

2—Pan American Health Day.
4—Second Sunday in Advent.
4-11—Universal Bible Week.
6—Feast of Saint Nicholas, patron saint of children and sailors.
7—Twenty-Fifth Anniversary of the Pearl Harbor Attack by Japanese.
8—Feast of the Immaculate Conception.
8-15—Hanukkah, Jewish Feast of Lights.
10—Nobel Prizes Presentations in Stockholm, Sweden, and Oslo, Norway.
—United Nations Human Rights Day.
11—Indiana Sesquicentennial, admitted to the Union as 19th state in 1816.
13—Santa Lucia Day (Scandinavian countries).
15—Bill of Rights Day (U.S.).
18—Third Sunday in Advent.
22—First Day of Winter (2:29 A.M., E.S.T.).
25—Christmas Day.
Feast of the Nativity.
31—New Year's Eve.